कृपासिन्धु भगवान् श्रीकृष्ण (Lord Kṛṣṇa, the ocean of mercy)

धृतराष्ट्र-संजय (Dhṛtarāṣṭra-Sañjaya)

अर्जुनको उपदेश (Prescript to Arjuna)

प्रजापतिकी शिक्षा (Teachings of Prajāpati)

सूर्यको उपदेश (Precept to Sun)

समदर्शिता (Impartiality)

अनन्यचिन्तनका फल (Undivided devotion fructified)

ध्रुवपर अनुग्रह (Shower of grace on Dhruva)

1080

|| Oṁ Śrī Paramātmane Namaḥ ||

Śrīmad Bhagavadgītā

Sādhaka-Sañjīvanī [with Appendix]-Vol. I

Commentary

By Swami Ramsukhdas

[With Sanskrit text, Transliteration and English Translation]

(Translated into English by S. C. Vaishya)

Revised by R. N. Kaul & Keshoram Aggarwal

tvameva mātā ca pitā tvameva
tvameva bandhuśca sakhā tvameva
tvameva vidyā draviṇaṁ tvameva
tvameva sarvaṁ mama devadeva

Gita Press, Gorakhpur, India

First Edition to Four Reprints		16,000 Copies
Fifth Revised Edition	2005	4,000 Copies
	Total	20,000 Copies

Price : { Vol. I & II } Both Volumes together Rs. 100 (Rs. One Hundred)

Each volume separately Rs. 50 (Rs. Fifty)

ISBN 81-293-0063-X

Printed & Published by **Gita Press, Gorakhpur—273005 (INDIA)**

(a unit of Gobind Bhavan-Karyalaya, Kolkata)

✆ (0551) 2334721; Fax 2336997

website:**www.gitapress.org** | e-mail:**booksales@gitapress.org**

Publisher's Preface

Śrīmad Bhagavadgītā holds an incomparable and unique position in world literature. It recalls the divine voice of Lord Kṛṣṇa, through which many of His mysteries and inner secrets are revealed. In communicating these for the benefit of mankind, the Lord has invoked Arjuna, as an interlocutor or questioner. The small book, full of the Lord's extraordinary thoughts and views from the very heart, was never excelled in the past, nor would ever be, in the future.

Our revered Param Shraddheya Shri Swami Ramsukhdasji has delved deep into the bottomless depths of this profound scripture and extracted invaluable gems, which in his magnanimity, he has through his commentary in Hindi, called 'Sādhaka Sañjīvanī' offered for the benefit and spiritual advancement of aspirants. It is obvious that this commentary is singularly different and distinctive, in many respects, from other publications. Though we claim no far-reaching study of other critiques and annotations, yet we are struck by new interpretations, new meanings and new revelations in this commentary, arising from many verses, such as; Chapter one–Verses: ten, nineteen, twenty and twenty-five; Chapter two—Verses: thirty-nine and forty; Chapter three–Verses: three, ten, twelve, thirteen and forty-three; Chapter four–eighteen and thirty-eight; Chapter five–Verses: thirteen and fourteen; Chapter six–Verses: twenty and thirty-eight; Chapter seven–Verses: five and nineteen: Chapter eight –Verse: six; Chapter nine–Verses: three and thirty-one: Chapter ten–Verse: forty-one; Chapter eleven–Verses: twenty-six, twenty-seven, forty-five and forty-six; Chapter twelve–Verse: twelve; Chapter thirteen–Verses: one, nineteen, twenty and twenty-one; Chapter fourteen–Verses: three, twelve, seventeen and twenty-two; Chapter fifteen–Verses: seven and eleven; Chapter sixteen—Verses: five and twenty; Chapter seventeen—Verses: seven and ten; Chapter eighteen–Verses: thirty-seven and seventy-three, etc.

We are confident that with an in-depth study of the commentary, aspirants would discover many different facets and resolutions, from these and other verses, for their better understanding and help in forging ahead with their Sādhanā.

In the present times, unfortunately, there is a dearth of books, which would in simple language and with lucidity, explain and delineate the correct path and milestones of an aspirant's progress, and this void often results in their predicament. Therefore, the publication of a detailed commentary, in plain words and simple style with clarity and offering elucidation and explanation, such as this work, is at once a most welcome and important step.

Swamiji Maharaj's commentary is apparently, neither intended to promote a new or particular philosophical viewpoint, nor in the least, a means to display learning; but that it should and would act as a life-giving boon, like the Sañjīvanī herb, for all aspirants, no matter which creed, faith, religion, or language or place, they belong to. The Buddhist, Jain, Parsi, Muslim, Christian and others etc; in studying this book, would discover in it, a basis for their advancement, in accordance with and supportive of the tenets of their individual faiths or religions and they would find enough material in this book, to help achieve their spiritual goals.

To gain spiritual bliss, we humbly urge aspirants to study the commentary deeply and sincerely, understand the writing and endeavour to put into practise the contents, for their own forward progress in the world.

Gorakhpur **Publisher**

Śrī Gītā Jayantī (1988)

Preface to the First Revised Edition

Śrīmad Bhagavadgītā-Sādhaka Sañjīvanī—with commentary by Param Shraddheya Shri Ramsukhdasji Maharaj in its English version has, on all hands, been an outstanding and much appreciated exposition of the divine and immortal work. It has been reprinted before and is now ready for another printing. Time was, therefore, opportune for a revision of this masterly analytical and exhaustive commentary, so that, if necessary, clarify and amplify comments in order to enhance its understanding and gainful usefulness.

The result may be called a revision or a mere new work. It is a revision, in as much it retains the basic concept, approach and arguments of the first edition. What is new, however, is the elucidation and precise explanation of some comments in English, in order to eliminate any possible ambiguity or loss of clarity. It is in this light that changes made must be read. The amendments are unpretentious, and are intended to make reading easy.

The book is, at the same time, somewhat new, in as much as, an opportunity has been taken, importantly, to include—with the approval of the author, Param Shraddheya Shri Ramsukhdasji Maharaj—two additional and valuable appendices at the end of the commentary on the Gītā. The first Appendix entitled, "A bird's eyeview of the Gītā", is a summarised essence of the scripture, highlighting its core and offering a capsulised version for quick comprehension and ready reference. The second Appendix, covers the traditional and other suggested "Methods of Recitation of the Gītā", to help devotees to seek and achieve spiritual benefit of worship, through the Gītā. Both these sections were authored by Param Shraddheya Shri Ramsukhdasji

Maharaj and originally included in his monumental and celebrated book, "The Gītā Darpaṇa—The Gītā A Mirror", and published by the Gita Press.

The Publishers are confident that the changes effected, would make this revised edition of the Bhagavadgītā-Sādhaka Sañjīvanī of greater interest to the English readers and would be acclaimed by them. This edition makes it still more comprehensive, more meaningful and beneficial, for aspirants of spiritual elevation, as to students of the Gītā, as well as to the perspicacious members of different creeds and faiths, idealogies and religions interested in this unique and secular publication—The words of God.

May, the publishers urge the readers to study this revised edition of the Gītā, with deep profundity and put into creative practice, the knowledge gained, with a view to their advancement in the world.

—Publisher

FOREWORD

वंशीधरं तोत्त्रधरं नमामि मनोहरं मोहहरं च कृष्णम्।
मालाधरं धर्मधुरन्धरं च पार्थस्य सारथ्यकरं च देवम्॥
कर्त्तव्यदीक्षां च समत्वशिक्षां ज्ञानस्य भिक्षां शरणागतिं च।
ददाति गीता करुणार्द्रभूता कृष्णेन गीता जगतो हिताय॥
सञ्जीवनी साधकजीवनीयं प्राप्तिं हरेर्वै सरलं ब्रवीति।
करोति दूरं पथिविघ्नबाधा ददाति शीघ्रं परमात्मसिद्धिम्॥*

vaṁśīdharaṁ tottradharaṁ namāmi
manoharaṁ mohaharaṁ ca kṛṣṇam
mālādharaṁ dharmadhurandharaṁ ca
pārthasya sārathyakaraṁ ca devam
karttavyadīkṣāṁ ca samatvaśikṣāṁ
jñānasya bhikṣāṁ śaraṇāgatiṁ ca
dadāti gītā karuṇārdrabhūtā
kṛṣṇena gītā jagato hitāya
sañjīvanī sādhakajīvanīyaṁ
prāptiṁ harervai saralaṁ bravīti
karoti dūraṁ pathivighnabādhā
dadāti śīghraṁ paramātmasiddhim

---

* I bow down to Kṛṣṇa the Divine, the flute-holder, holder of the reins, the usurper of hearts and infatuation, the wearer of garlands, the holder of the Axis of Dharma and the Charioteer of Arjuna.

Sung by Lord Kṛṣṇa, the Gītā—drenched in ambrosial compassion—is the provider of initiation into duty, lessons of equanimity, alms of enlightenment and surrender and is for the welfare of mankind.

Bestower of the gift of life, this Sādhaka Sañjīvanī tells in simple terms the art of realizing Hari. It also removes the obstacles in the path and quickly gives the supreme accomplishment of God-realization.

By meditating and contemplating on the Gītā and by preparing this commentary, I have been very much spiritually benefited; I also have a clear understanding of the subject matter of the Gītā. It is my firm conviction that if our brothers and sisters reflect on it, they will also receive spiritual benediction. I do not have even an iota of doubt about it, that by meditating and contemplating on the Gītā, great benefits would accrue to them.

कृष्णानुग्रहदायिका सकरुणा गीता समाराधिता
कर्मज्ञानविरागभक्तिरसिका मर्मार्थसन्दर्शिका।
सोत्कण्ठं किल साधकैरनुदिनं पेपीयमाना सदा
कल्याणं परदेवतेव दिशती सञ्जीवनी वर्द्धताम्॥

kṛṣṇānugrahadāyikā sakaruṇā gītā samārādhitā
karmajñānavirāgabhaktirasikāmarmārthasandarśikā
sotkaṇṭhaṁ kila sādhakairanudinaṁ pepīyamānā sadā
kalyāṇaṁ paradevateva diśatī sañjīvanī varddhatām*

Swāmī Rāmasukhadāsa

---

* May, by the Grace of Lord Kṛṣṇa, the adorer and seeker of Gītā, that is full of compassion, the knower of the truth of Karma (action), Jñāna (knowledge); virāga (renunciation) and Bhakti (devotion), reflecting the shower of subtle and deep meanings be, sought and enjoyed with enthusiasm, by seekers, and the grantor of Kalyāṇa, the Supreme Lord, may this Sādhaka Sañjīvanī continually promote and perpetuate spiritual benefits in a seeker's life.

GLORY OF GĪTĀ

Unfathomable and illimitable is the glory of Śrīmad Bhagavad Gītā. This holy book, the Bhagavad Gītā, is counted among the scriptural trio, the 'Prasthāna Traya'. The three royal ways of welfare of mankind, are known by the name of Prasthāna Traya: one is the 'Vedic Prasthāna' called the Upaniṣad; the second is metaphysical or 'Philosophical Prasthāna' called the Brahma Sūtra; and the third is, 'Smārta Prasthāna', called the Bhagavad Gītā. There are 'Mantras' (mystical rubrics), in the Upaniṣads., 'sūtras' (aphorisms) in the Brahma Sūtra and 'ślokas' (verses), in the Bhagavad Gītā. Though the Bhagavad Gītā has only Ślokas', yet these being the very voice of God, are verily mantras. Pregnant, as the ślokas are with meaning and import of great profundity, these can be called 'sutras' also. The Upaniṣads are of use and value for the deserving only, and the Brahma Sūtras, are of use and importance for men of erudition and learning, but the Bhagavad Gītā is for, one and all.

The Bhagavad Gītā is a most unusual and many facetted scripture. It contains highly useful and detailed material for a seeker, be he of any country, costume, community, disposition, creed, 'varṇa' or any 'āśrama' (station), in life. It is so, because there is in it, neither denunciation nor praise of any creed or denomination, in particular; instead it deals with the essence of pure Reality only. Pure Reality (the Supreme Lord or Paramātmā), as that which is wholly beyond change in Nature and the nature-born things and is ever-eternally immutable and uniform, in the midst of the flux in space, time, things, being, circumstance etc. Real 'Tattva', (essence), is ever-present in its perfect form, in each man, wherever and however, he is. But that is not realized because of attachment and aversion—rāga and dveṣa—born of the changeable nature of things in a person. Only on achieving complete freedom from attachment and aversion, it is automatically realized and with ease.

The teachings of Bhagavad Gītā are singularly divine. Numerous commentaries have been written on it and several more are being written, yet new and fresh ideas continue to surge, in the hearts and minds of saints, seers and sages, of wisdom. However much thought may be given to this profound Song Celestial, the meaning and deeper implications thereof, none can fathom in their entirety. The deeper they delve into it, the more profound the meanings are to be found, therein. When the range of the finer emotions of a learned person is not easily judged how can then the magnitude of emotions encased in the words of God, whose forms and names are infinite, be ever assumed?

There is such a uniqueness in this small-sized work, that a real seeker of one's salvation (kalyāṇa) irrespective of varṇa, āśrama, nationality, creed, belief etc., is at once attracted by the mere study of this treatise. If a man reads and grasps, even a little, from this sacred book, several satisfying disciplines or ways, become available to him for his life's fulfilment. Different authorities exist for the study of respective systems of philosophy, but the unique significance of the Gītā, is that all the seekers of salvation are eligible for its study.

In explaining different disciplines (sādhana), and in communicating the meanings in detail, no hesitaion was felt in repeating matters about each discipline in the Bhagavad Gītā, and yet its size has not increased unduly. No single holy book of wisdom exists, which expounds the full import of Reality with such precision and prolification. A man with intense yearning for his 'kalyāṇa' (goal) can realize Godhead, the Supreme Truth, in each and every circumstance; can achieve his salvation, even in critical circumstances like war. Thus the art of supreme fulfilment in each walk of behaviour, is taught in the Gītā. No other book of its kind or parity, has come to our notice.

Gītā is a book of grace. Most wonderous, divine and peace-giving feelings arise by its recitation, or taking its refuge. Great peace of mind is obtained by its sheer recitation. One method is, first to memorise the meanings of all the 'ślokas' of the Gītā, and then reverse recitation of the same, sitting in solitude, without the aid of the book, beginning from the last 'śloka', "Yatra Yogeśwaraḥ Kṛṣṇaḥ ...." to the very first one, "Dharma Kṣetre Kuru Kṣetre......" Then much peacefulness prevails. If the Gītā is recited in its completeness, everyday once or as many times, new special and distinctive meanings arise in the reader's mind. Even, if there is any query or doubt in one's mind, it gets resolved automatically, during the course of recitation.

In reality, no person is competent or capable enough, to fully sing the glory of this scripture. Who would dare describe the great majesty of the infinitely glorious and holy Gītā?

SPECIFIC GOAL OF GĪTĀ

The Gītā, has not originated with any specific 'ism' or belief, in view e.g., neither from Dvaita, Advaita, Viśiṣṭādvaita, Dvaitādvaita, Viśuddhādvaita, Acintya-Bhedābheda, nor any cult, creed or doctrine. The supreme objective of the Gītā is, that man's salvation must be ensured in every circumstance, to whatever, 'ism', belief or creed he might belong; so that he should in no case, be deprived of God-realization. The very birth of a being, ('jīva') in human form, is meant only for his 'kalyāṇa' i.e., salvation. There are no conditions in the world, which make man's salvation impossible. The reason, is that God is eternally present in equal measure, in every circumstance. So a seeker has just to make the right use of the circumstance facing him, whatever its nature. The implication of 'right use', is to give up the desire for favourable circumstances, in the event of painful circumstances; and to utilize the favourable circumstance in the service of others. By such 'right use', man rises above, both pain and pleasure and attains equanimity.

There arose in God, before creation, a 'saṅkalpa' (a resolve) of multiplying Himself in many forms. By this wish, the one God, became manifest in two forms; Śrī Kṛṣṇa and Śrījī, for the exchange and promotion of love. Both staged a play (Līlā), in order to mutually conduct the sport. By God's wish, endless number of beings (who were there since eternity) and objects of play (bodies etc.) came into being. The play takes place, only when the players on both the sides are free. For this, the beings were granted freedom by the Lord. Śrījī's attraction lay focussed only on God, there was never a slip on her side. Thus, there was the līlā of love between God and Śrījī. But the other 'jīvas', who were there, assumed their part, with the matter of the play (created and destructible materials) by mistake, for their coincidental joy, whereby they got into the cycle of birth and death.

The objects of a play are only meant for play, not for anyone's personal possession. But these beings forgot to play the right game, misused their freedom and began to regard the materials of the play, as personally their own. Therefore, they got entangled in matter and totally turned away from God. Now, if these beings had shunned the perishable material of forms and looked towards God, then they could be free from the great pain of births and deaths, forever. Thus withdrawing from the world, the 'jīva' would realize his eternal relationship with God 'only for the sake of this realization, the Bhagavad Gītā, has come down to us.

YOGA OF GĪTĀ

The word 'Yoga' of the Gītā is pregnant with many wondrous meaning. We can place these under three heads:

(i) Derived from the root 'Yujir Yoge' (युजिर् योगे) the word 'yoga' has the implied meaning—eternal kinship with equanimous (समरूप) God; as in 'Samatvaṁ yoga ucyate' (2.48) etc. This meaning has importance in the Gītā.

(ii) Originating from the root 'Yuj Samādhau', the word 'yoga', implies—stability of citta i.e., a state of trance during meditation; as in 'Yatroparamate cittaṁ niruddhaṁ yogasevayā' (6.20) etc.

(iii) Deduced from the root 'Yuj Saṁyamane', the word 'yoga' means—controling power, divine prowess, magnetic impact; as in 'Paśya me yogamaiśwaram' (9.5) etc.

Wherever the word 'Yoga' has appeared in the Gītā, it has in it the primacy of one of the aforesaid three meanings, the other two meanings having a secondary place only. As in the word 'yoga' derived from 'yujir yoge', there is the predominance of the meaning of equanimity, though on realization of equanimity, meditational stability and divine prowess* also accrue automatically. In the word 'yoga' from 'Yuj samādhau', there is the supermacy of transcendental stability, but on achievement of this state, equanimity and prowess follow, automatically. In the word 'yoga' from 'Yuj Saṁyamane', there is the dominance of divine prowess and majesty, but on realization of this prowess, equanimity and stability also, follow suit on their own. Thus the word 'yoga' of the Gītā has very pervasive and profound meanings.

---

* The power of creation, preservation and destruction etc., of the entire universe which belongs only to God—that power the Yogī does not acquire—Jagadvyāp āravarjam (Brahmasūtra 4.4.17). The power which a Yogī gains, enables him to conquer nature (Gītā 5.19), meaning that no amount of favourable or unfavourable circumstances, can in anyway affect him.

In the Yogadarśana of Sage Patañjali, the word 'yoga' is the name given to the control of cittavṛttis (mental tendencies and mind-stuff) from taking various forms—'Yogaścittavṛttinirodhaḥ' (1.2) and the effect of that yoga has been pointed out, as the lodgement of draṣṭā (the witness) in one's own self: 'Tadā Draṣṭuḥ svarūpe'vasthānam' (1.3). In this way, the very result of Yoga as depicted in the Yoga-Darśana of Patañjali has been given the name 'yoga' in the Gītā (2.48; 6.23). The implication is, that the self-proved natural state of equanimity totally cut off from the cittavṛttis, is called 'yoga' by the Gītā. On realizing lodgement in equanimity, (eternal unison—Nityayoga), there is never a disunion or deviation from it. There is a desireless transcendental state, (nirvikalpa avasthā) when there is control over mental tendencies. But on realization of equanimity there is 'desireless transcendental awareness 'nirvikalpāvasthā.' This 'desireless transcendental awareness— nirvikalpa bodha—is the illuminator of statelessness, as well as, of other states.

For a seeker to have experience of equanimity or eternal unison, three yoga-ways have been expounded in the Gītā—the Path of Action, the Path of Knowledge and the Path of Devotion. There is an inalienable relationship of the three bodies—the gross, the subtle and the causal,—with the world. To, employ these three, in the service of others—is the Path of Action. The realization of one's identity and lodgement within one's own self, after dissociating from these, it is the Path of Knowledge; and surrendering one's self to God—is the Path of Devotion. In order to accomplish these yogas, and attain one's salvation, man is endowed, with three powers (i) power to act (strength), (ii) power to know (knowledge), and (iii) power to believe (faith). The power to act is for rendering service to the world selflessly—that is Karmayoga; the power to know, is meant for Self realisation—that is Jñānayoga; and the power to believe, is to totally surrender to God, after regarding God as one's own and one's own self, as God's—this is Bhaktiyoga. He, in whom interest to act dominates, is qualified to adopt the Path of Action. He, in whom inquisitiveness for Self-realisation dominates, is eligible and qualified, for the Path of Knowledge. He, in whom faith and belief in God dominates, is qualified for the Path of Devotion. All these three Yoga-paths are independent means of God-realization. All other means are also implicit in these three paths.*

The main object of all the paths, is to accomplish separation from non-self. However, there does remain a difference in these disciplines in attaining separation, but after completing this breach with matter (non-self), all means lead to realization of one equanimous; supreme Godhead. This very realization of 'Paramātmatattva', the Gītā has called 'Yoga'; and verily, this is called, 'Nityayoga'—the Eternal Union.

It is not right, that there has been given only a description, in the Gītā of Karmayoga, Jñānayoga, or of Bhaktiyoga. Besides these three yogas, there is a description of yajña (sacrifice), dāna (charity), tapa (penance), dhyānayoga (yoga of meditation), prāṇāyāma (control of breat..), haṭhayoga (austere discipline of body etc.), layayoga (yoga of rhythmic unison) etc. The reason

* The Lord has said in the Śrīmad Bhāgavata:

"Yogāstrayo mayā proktā nṛṇāṁ śreyovidhitsayā; jñānam karma ca bhaktiśca nopāyo'nyosti kutracit (11.20.6)." i.e., "Three Yogas have been stated by Me for seekers eager for their welfare: those of knowledge, action and devotion. There is nowhere, any other way of total well-being."

The same thing has been observed in the Adhyātma Rāmāyaṇa and Devī Bhāgavata:

"Mārgāstrayo Mayā Proktāḥ Purā Mokṣāptisādhakāḥ; Karmayogo Jñānayogo Bhaktiyogaśca śāśvataḥ" (Adhyātma. 7.7.59).

Mārgāstrayo Me Vikhyātā Mokṣaprāptau Nagādhipa; Karmayogo Jñānayogo Bhaktiyogaśca śattama (Devi. 7. 37.3.).

for it is, that Arjuna's questions in the Gītā are not about war, but really about salvation. Lord Kṛṣṇa's purpose in discoursing this Gītā was not the conduct of war. Arjuna definitely wanted his salvation (2.7; 3.2; 5.1). Therefore, as many means of his welfare, which have been reflected in the scriptures, have been with precision, detailed in the Gītā. Keeping in view all those means, the Gītā is specially held in high esteem; the reason being, that a seeker might belong to any belief, creed, or doctrine, but one's salvation is indeed, dear and open to all.

Two Disciplines of Seeking

In a 'Jīva' (being)—there is an 'aṁśa' (element) of the Conscious God and an 'aṁśa' of the inert nature (prakṛti). By the dominance of the Conscious-part, one seeks God; and by the dominance of the inert part, he desires the world. Between these two, the yearning for God could be satisfied, but the desires of the world are never fulfilled. Some worldly desires seemingly fulfilled are never satiated, but owing to worldly attachment, ever new desires arise. In fact, the satisfaction of worldly desires or achievement of worldly objects, is not within the authority of desire, but is subject to karma. God-realization is not under the power of karma, and it is attained by the intense longing of one's own self. Its reason is, that each karma (act), has a beginning and an end; so the result too is bound to have a beginning and an end. How can then a beginningless and endless God, be realized by karmas, which are origin and end bound? But seekers have often understood, that as the worldly objects are achieved by the predominance of activities, so also the realization of God would be achievable through the dominance of activity. As the assistance of body, senses, mind and intellect, has to be taken in achieving the objects of the world, so also in God-realization, the assistance of body, senses, mind, intellect will have to be called for, they argue. Therefore, such seekers practise spiritual discipline, erroneously with the help of their inert body etc., to realize God.

By practising the Yoga of Meditation for a long time, i.e., gradually fixing one's mind on God, when the 'citta' (mind) gets controlled, having no worldly attachment and being incapable of realising God, due to inertness, it becomes unconcerned with the world. On the citta (mind) becoming unconcerned, the seeker becomes completely cut off from the mind or inertness, and he gains experience of Godhead automatically (Gītā 6.20). But a seeker, who having accepted his axiomatic and eternal unison with God, from the beginning without accepting in the least, his kinship with inert matter, traverses the course of his discipline, he experiences the Supreme Tattva (essence) early, and with ease.

Thus, for seekers who wish to realize God, there are two disciplines or ways of seeking Him. The discipline, in which there remains dominance of 'antaḥkaraṇa' (the inner faculty) i.e., wherein a seeker observes discipline with the assistance of matter which goes by the name of 'karaṇa sāpekṣa sailī'. (Discipline aided by the Inner faculty). The second discipline, in which the seeker, from the very beginning, follows the discipline by himself, without the assistance of matter, is called, 'Karaṇa Nirapekṣa Śailī' (Discipline unaided by the Inner faculty). God-realization, in both these disciplines, takes place only by Karaṇa Nirapekṣatā i.e., by one's own self (after a complete breach with matter). Realization via 'Karaṇa Sāpekṣa Śailī' comes very late, whereas it happens immediately, through 'Karaṇa Nirapekṣa Śailī'. There are four main differences, between these two disciplines of seeking God.

(i) Assistance of matter, (body-senses-mind-intellect) has to be taken in the 'Karaṇa Sāpekṣa Śailī', but no such assistance is necessary, in the 'Karaṇa Nirapekṣa Śailī', instead the assumed relationship with matter, is to be sundered or broken up.

(ii) There is, creation of a new state of mind in the 'Karaṇa Sāpekṣa Śailī', but there is realization after breach with all states of mind in the 'Karaṇa Nirapekṣa Śailī'.

(iii) There is, in the discipline aided by the instrument, ('Karaṇa Sāpekṣa Śailī') an acquisition of occult powers (siddhis), but in the discipline unaided by the instrument, (Karaṇa Nirapekṣa Śailī,) there is a direct and intuitive experience of Reality, on severance of relationship with matter.*

(iv) God-realization, in the 'discipline aided by the inner faculty' is never immediate, but in the 'discipline unaided by the Instrument' God-realization (siddhi) is immediate, as soon as a breach with matter is complete, either after surrendering to God, or on being established in the self.

In the Yogadarśana of Patañjali, importance is given to 'discipline aided by the antaḥkaraṇa' in the realization of yoga, but in the Gītā, importance is attached only to 'discipline unaided by the faculty', in the realization of yoga (योगसिद्धि). It is alright if the mind gets tuned to God, but if it is not so tuned, then

* If it were possible to have direct God-realization with the 'Discipline aided by Instrument' (Cittavṛttinirodha), then the 'Vibhūti-Pāda' (wherein 'Siddhis' are described) of Patañjali's Yogadarśana, would have been futile. Those 'siddhis' or powers, which are acquired by the 'Discipline Aided By Instrument', are hurdles in the path of God-realization. Even in the Pātañjali Yogadarśana, the 'siddhis' are regarded as obstacles—'Te samādhāvupasargā vyutthāne siddhayaḥ' (3.37) i.e., these (siddhis) are obstacles in the attainment of Samādhi and are 'powers' during 'Vyutthāna' (behavioural) world; 'Sthānyupanimantraṇe saṅgasmayākaraṇaṁ punaraniṣṭaprasaṅgāt' (3.51) i.e., on being called by the gods guarding the directions, (by offering temptations of the enjoyments of their realms); neither should one have attachment for them, nor should one take pride in them; because in doing so, there is again a possibility of the loss of realization (aniṣṭa) or a fall.

nothing happens—this is the basis of the 'discipline, aided by the inner faculty'. Whether or not, mind is attuned to God, it does not matter; but one's self should be attached to God—this reflects the 'discipline unaided by the inner faculty'. The import and implication of all this is, that, in the 'Karaṇa Nirapekṣa Śailī', there is direct relation of the self with God, with a total breach of ties, with the mind intellect complex. Therefore, realization in the 'Karaṇa Sāpekṣa Śailī' is affirmed by practice, but there is no need for any other steps, in the 'Karaṇa Nirapekṣa Śailī'. The reason is that, there is 'axiomatic eternal union' (nitya yoga) with God. Thus, there is no necessity of any practice in believing or knowing, one's unitive relation with God; just as on accomplishment of marriage, when a woman accepts a man as her husband, she needs to do nothing further, in so believing. So also, on being told by someone that 'here is Gaṅgājī' no further exercise is to be done, even to realise it.* In the 'Karaṇa Nirapekṣa Śailī', The primacy is only of knowing (viveka) and believing (bhāva). If one says, 'I have no relation with inertness (body etc.) at all'—even without such an experience, if a seeker firmly believes in this from the very outset, then also such a realization, clearly dawns upon him. As he was in bondage under the mistaken belief that, 'I am the body and the body is mine', so too, by cultivating the right belief that, 'I' am not the body and the body is not mine', a seeker becomes liberated; because,

* In fact, no worldly illustration is completely befitting, pertaining to the matter of knowing or believing in God. The reason, is that in believing or knowing, the world, there is the association of mind and intellect, but in believing and knowing there is no association of mind and intellect at all, meaning thereby that God's experience is the realization by one's own self, not by mind-intellect. Secondly, the act of believing and knowing the world has a beginning and an end, but there is no such beginning and end, in believing and knowing God. Reason being that there is no relation of our being with the world at all, whereas our relation with God is, since the very beginning, and will always be so.

as a principle, by not relying on, the accepted belief it tends to melt away. God, has clearly told us in the Gītā, that an ignorant person, accepting his link with the body, regards himself, as the doer of things that happen— 'Ahaṅkāravimūḍhātmā kartāhamiti manyate' (3.27). But an enlightened person, does not regard himself as the doer, of those activities—'Naiva kiñcit karomīti yukto manyeta tattvavit' (5.8). It means therefore, that to root out a false belief, it is necessary to stress a true belief.

'I am a Hindū', 'I am a Brāhmaṇa', 'I am a Sādhu', etc., such beliefs, become so firm that until man does not give these up by himself, no one else, can make him change his belief. Similarly, the belief that, 'I, am the body', 'I, am the doer' etc., also becomes so firm, that it is difficult for a seeker to give these up. But, these worldly beliefs being unreal and untrue, are not everlasting and are instead, changeable. As against these beliefs, such as, 'I am not the body', 'I am God's' etc., being real and true are never lost, but there is only a degree of forgetfulness, a turning of back on these. Therefore, a real belief on becoming firmly rooted, does not remain as mere belief, but is transmuted into a realized awareness (experience).

Though, 'Discipline aided by inner faculty has been described in the Gītā (as in, 4.24—30; 6.10—28; 8.8—16; 15.11 etc.) yet 'Discipline unaided by inner faculty' alone, has been described with great emphasis (as in, 2.48,55; 3.17; 4.38; 5.12 (first half); 6.5; 9.30-31; 12.12; 18.62, 66,73 etc.). The reason is, firstly that God desires that seekers should realize Him, early and easily. In the second place, Arjuna has sought from Him, the means of his own salvation, on being confronted with a situation of war. Thus, the 'Discipline unaided by the faculty' alone, could be of use, for his salvation; because by this discipline of 'Karaṇa Nirapekṣa Śailī', man can achieve his salvation, under all circumstances even while carrying out his activities, according to scriptural injunctions of karma. Only, through this discipline (without any practice) Arjuna's delusion was ended and memory of his real self revived (18.73).

The 'Discipline unaided by the inner faculty', is useful for all, in equal measure; because there is no necessity, for any special ability, condition etc. In this discipline, by developing an intense desire for God-realization, and immediate separation from matter being accomplished, the eternal God, is realized. Just as many year's darkness might be, eliminated by merely kindling a candle, so also, a very old relationship with matter (of countless births) there might be, is cut off by a strong and keen yearning, for God-realization. Therefore, this intense yearning is a much higher state, than even 'Samādhi'—a state of meditative poise—born of Karaṇa Sāpekṣatā. There is even, a deviation from the highest state of 'nirvikalpa samādhi'—into routine behaviour, as with a beginning and an end, of 'Samādhi' also. So long as there is, a beginning and an end, there exists an affinity for matter. On renunciating the tie with matter, then seeking spiritual discipline with the beginning and no end instead, there arises the realization of an eternal union with God.*

In reality, there was never a disunion (viyoga) with God, and this is not, even possible. Separation from God appears only by an assumed relationship with the world (saṁyoga). A man intensely eager for God-realization, realises God immediately, after renouncing the assumed link with the world and merges with Him.

* Till there exists a tie with inertness, two states do obtain; because changeable as it is, the inert Nature never remains uniform. Thus these two states of entry into and exit from equipoise—'Samādhi' and 'Vyutthāna'—arise out of their tie with inertness. On severance of a tie with inertness, what remains is 'Sahajāvasthā', eternal stateless state, which is called 'Sahaja Samādhi' by the saints. There is then no relapse or return from it.

Even the need to purify the inner faculty arises, only in the 'Karaṇa Sāpekṣa Śailī', and not in the 'Karaṇa Nirapekṣa Śailī'. As, when a pen is good, writing can be excellent but that does not improve the writer, so also on the inner faculty being pure, activities could be pure but not the mind of the doer. The doer becomes pure, on a breach of the tie with the inner faculty; because the very belief in one's kinship with this, is the root of impurity.

Axiomatic is 'Jīva's (the being's), eternal union (yoga) with the ever-available (nitya prāpta) God; thus there is no need for any instrument for His realization. Only the sight needs to be turned towards that side, as is observed in Śrī Rāmacaritamānasa, 'Śaṅkara Sahaja Sarūpu Saṁhārā' (1.58.4) meaning, Lord Śaṅkara contemplated on the nature of His own self, turned his looks into Himself. A thing looked at, is perceived by us, only by turning the gaze to it and it becomes known, to be there. In the same way, by simply discerning it, Nitya Yoga, is experienced. But, on account of desire, expectation and enjoyment of worldly pleasures, a great difficulty is felt in turning our sight or attention towards it, and in realizing it. Till the mind remains tied to the acquisition and enjoyment of worldly objects, there is no capacity in man to turn his gaze towards his real Self. If, by any reason, chance or perception the gaze happens to be directed toward the self, it would be extremely difficult to hold it there permanently. The reason is, that intense endearment (priyatā), for destructible materials, which resides in the heart, does not permit the understanding of one's eternal and obvious relationship with God; and even if it is well comprehended, it does not allow its stability. If intense longing prevails the Reality (tattva) is realized, then this longing has the power to destroy the very attachment, for the world.

All the three yogas—Karmayoga, Jñānayoga and Bhaktiyoga—spoken of in the Gītā are realizable through the discipline of 'Sādhana 'Karaṇa Nirapekṣa' i.e., through one's own self. As the activity and material, are neither ours nor for ourselves, instead these belong to others and are meant for the service of others. The belief or thought thus discriminately arrived at, that 'I am not the body, nor is the body mine, I am God's and God is mine', is not born of the 'discipline aided by antaḥkaraṇa and body etc., (practice), because it involves a breach of the tie with matter. Thus, in Karmayoga the seeker himself, gives up his relationship with inertness, in Jñānayoga the seeker realizes his own self; and in Bhaktiyoga, the seeker surrenders himself to God.

In this 'Sādhaka Sañjīvanī' commentary on the Gītā too, primary importance is given to the 'discipline unaided by inner faculty'; because this commentary has been written, keeping in view the way a seeker's salvation is attained, easily and without delay.

Apropos This Commentary

Since my early age, I had a special interest in the Gītā. Meditative introspection on the Gītā and association with and utterances of saints and great souls, have been of immense help to me in understanding the real import, of the Gītā. The Gītā, brims with ideas, infinite and astounding, which provide great satisfaction. The ability to understand these ideas fully, and express these with perfection, is not within my power. But when certain Gītā-loving gentle persons pressed me hard and especially urged me, then I felt like preparing a commentary on the Gītā, with the object, that its hidden heart-touching ideas—mārmika bhāva—may be revealed to me, so that others also, may in turn introspect and meditate upon these, and these ideas may become intelligible, to them too.

First, a commentary on the twelfth chapter was written which was published in Vikrama Saṁvat 2030, under the name of, 'Gītā Kā Bhaktiyoga'. A few years latter, a commentary on the thirteenth and fourteenth chapters was dictated, which was published in Vikrama Saṁvat 2035 as, 'Gītā Kā Jñānayoga'. A thought arose thereafter, that since there are three 'Yogas'—Karmayoga, Jñānayoga and Bhaktiyoga—it would be more appropriate if three books were prepared on the three yogas. With this in view, a commentary on the twelfth chapter, was recast, enlarged and combined with the commentary of the fifteenth chapter, which was published in Vikrama Saṁvat 2039, as 'Gītā Kā Bhaktiyoga', (second edition). Then, a commentary on the third, fourth and fifth chapters, was dictated, which was published in two volumes, under the title, 'Gītā Kā Karmayoga'. Its delayed publication came in Vikrama Saṁvat 2040.

A different kind of format (Śailī), was followed in the afore-mentioned three books—'Gītā Kā Bhaktiyoga', 'Gītā Kā Jñānayoga', and 'Gītā Kā Karmayoga'; the order adopted in them was, first the context (sambandha), then the verse (śloka), then the emotional import (bhāva), next the analysis of the verse (anvaya); and last, the 'pada'-wise commentary. After the publication of these three volumes, the format was again changed in the following order; first, the context, then the verse and last, the commentary. In making the change, the inspiration came from others also. The idea behind this change was, that the reading material should be reduced a little, and set out early, so that the readers would not have to spend more time in reading, and that the book was prepared speedily, to reach the readers, early. With this frame-work, the commentary on the sixteenth and the seventeenth chapters, was got ready first. This was published in Vikrama Saṁvat 2039, under the name of 'Gītā Kī Sampatti Aura Śraddhā'. A commentary on the eighteenth chapter, was prepared thereafter, which was also published in 2039, under the title: 'Gītā Kā Sāra.'

After the commentary on the sixteenth, seventeenth and eighteenth chapters was completed, someone suggested that it would be better, if the meaning of the 'ślokas' was also provided; for if the reader first grasped the meaning of the 'śloka', it would be easier for him to follow the commentary. Thus in the second edition of 'Gītā Kī Sampatti Aura Śraddhā' (Vikrama Saṁvat 2040) the meaning of 'ślokas' was also added. With the addition of the meaning of the verses, a change in the order of the commentary on the 'padas', was also introduced.

Later, a commentary on the tenth and eleventh chapters was prepared and published, under the name of, 'Gītā Kī Vibhūti Aura Viśvarūpa-Darśana'. Then followed a commentary on the seventh, eighth and ninth chapters, which was published as 'Gītā Kī Rāja-vidyā'. Thereafter, came a commentary on the sixth chapter, which was published as, 'Gītā Kā Dhyānayoga'. Last was dictated a commentary, on the first and second chapters, which was published as, 'Gītā Kā Ārambha'. All these four books, were published in Vikrama Saṁvat 2041.

It was thus that by the grace of God, a commentary on the whole of the Gītā was published by the Gita Press, in ten separate volumes. In its publication, several difficulties, of paper etc., continued to arise, but with the effort of 'Satsaṅgī' brothers, the work of publishing these went on satisfactorily. The public also accepted these books with enthusiasm and pleasure, with the result that several books, underwent two or three editions.

The present commentary has not been dictated sitting at one place, and the order of dictation has also not been systematic, from the first chapter to the eighteenth. Therefore, many variations may appear from the pre and post (pūrvāpara) view, between the first and the last chapter. But seekers will feel no difficulty in it, anywhere. At some places a difference in interpretation might also appear, but in that of Karmayoga, Jñānayoga and Bhaktiyoga—all the three are independently instrumental in God-realization, and there is no real difference. The primary feeling (bhāva), while dictating the commentary has been, as to 'how early the seekers could be benefitted'. For this reason, there has been a change in its language, diction etc., in this commentary.

In this, the interpretation of many ślokas, is contrary to other commentaries. But the intention is not, in the least, to show that other commentaries are wrong; instead, I have interpreted the verses as seemed non-controversial, apt, corresponding to the context, rational, viable, satisfying and dear to me. There has never been my intention of anyone's refutation or confirmation.

The meaning of Śrīmad Bhagavadgītā, is very profound. By its reading, its teaching, introspection, meditation, and contemplation, unique, strange and ever new ideas and emotions continue to arise, whereby the mind and intellect, being thrilled, become contented. While dictating this commentary, whenever the mood to capture these emotions arose, a strange flood of thought used to overwhelm me, as to how and which of the ideas should I relate—and I used to find myself at bay, in this regard. Yet with the help of my associates, and respectworthy friends and at their behest and persuasion, I could dictate something. They used to write down those ideas and, after a revision, these were briefly published in the form of books. Thereafter, whenever there arose occasions to scan through these books, several discrepancies seemed to have crept into them, and it appeared that all the ideas had not been included and many had been left out. So revisions and enlargements continued to be made in these, from time to time. Therefore, our readers are requested, to accept and give appropriate importance only to contents written later, instead of comments, made earlier.

The commentary, on the whole Gītā, being in several separate volumes, a difficulty was felt in their revision and publication and in obtaining all of these volumes together. Keeping this in view, the commentary on the whole Gītā has been published now, in one single volume, in the form of the present book. Before doing this, the whole commentary published earlier, has again been looked into and necessary revisions, alterations and enlargements have also been introduced. The commentary on the thirteenth and the fourteenth chapters, has been revised. Care has also been taken to maintain the uniformity of language and diction. Many things which were deemed unnecessary, have been omitted, many new matters have been inserted, and many others, have been shifted from one place to an appropriate place elsewhere. Matters which had been variously repeated, have also been omitted, as far as possible, though not completely. Repetition deserving special attention and considered useful for seekers, has not been omitted. Several shortcomings are still possible in this work, for which I seek the reader's pardon, with folded hands. Readers are also requested to kindly intimate any mistakes they may come across. This will facilitate rectification, in future editions.

A compendium of research articles, of new and novel themes, pertaining to the Gītā has been prepared separately and published under the title, 'Gītā Darpaṇa'.

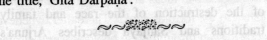

Contents

Seventh Chapter

Jñāna-Vijñāna (knowledge & realisation) Yoga

Eighth Chapter

Akṣhara-Brahma (knowledge of imperishible Brahma) Yoga

|| Shri Hari ||

First Chapter

INTRODUCTION

After the expiry of twelve years of exile and residing in an unknown place for one year, the Pāṇḍavas demanded half of their kingdom from Duryodhana, as was his promise but he refused to give even as much land as could be covered by the point of a needle, without waging war. The Pāṇḍavas sought permission from their mother Kuntī, and accepted the challenge of a war. After this decision, both the Kauravas and the Pāṇḍavas, began preparation for it.

Sage Veda Vyāsa had great affection for Dhṛtarāṣṭra, the blind king of Hastināpura. Due to his affection, he said to Dhṛtarāṣṭra, "War and massacre of the Kṣatriyas is inevitable. If you want to see the scene of the battlefield, I can endow you with divine sight so as to enable you to see scene of war, from the place you are sitting." Dhṛtarāṣṭra said, "I have been blind all my life. Now I don't want to see the slaughter of my own kith and kin. But I want to hear the details of the war." Then sage Vyāsa said," I endow Sañjaya with this divine sight by which he will know, hear and see, not only the incidents of the battlefield but also the ideas, in the minds of the warriors and will narrate these to you." Saying so, sage Vyāsa endowed Sañjaya with divine vision.

The battle started on the battlefield of Kurukṣetra at the appointed hour. Sañjaya stayed in the battlefield, for ten days. When Bhīṣma being badly wounded with arrows, fell off the chariot, Sañjaya conveyed the message to Dhṛtarāṣṭra who at that time was in Hastināpura. Hearing this news, Dhṛtarāṣṭra was filled with great sorrow and started to cry. Then he asked Sañjaya to narrate to him all the details of the war. Upto the twenty-fourth chapter of the Bhīṣma-Parva (section), Sañjaya narrated the incidents of the war.* At the beginning of the twenty-fifth chapter, Dhṛtarāṣṭra asks Sañjaya—

* In the Mahābhārata there are eighteen sections. In those sections there are several sub-sections. In the Bhīṣma section there is this Bhagavadgītā, a sub-section which begins with the thirteenth chapter of the Bhīṣma section and ends with the forty-second chapter.

धृतराष्ट्र उवाच*

धर्मक्षेत्रे कुरुक्षेत्रे समवेता युयुत्सवः।
मामकाः पाण्डवाश्चैव किमकुर्वत सञ्जय॥१॥

dhṛtarāṣṭra uvāca

dharmakṣetre kurukṣetre samavetā yuyutsavaḥ
māmakāḥ pāṇḍavāścaiva kimakurvata sañjaya

Dhṛtarāṣṭra said:

O Sañjaya†, assembled at the holy-field of Kurukṣetra, eager to fight, what did my sons and the sons of Pāṇḍu, do? 1

Comment:—

'Dharmakṣetre kurukṣetre'—In Kurukṣetra the gods performed holy sacrifice. King Kuru also performed penance there. Thus being saturated with a spiritual atmosphere, the field of Kurukṣetra has been called the field of righteousness (Dharmakṣetra).

Here by the word 'Kṣetra' in 'Dharmakṣetra' and 'Kurukṣetra' Dhṛtarāṣṭra means to say that this is the land of the Kurus. This is not merely a battlefield, but a land of pilgrimage, in which human beings by performing holy actions, can attain benediction in this life. Therefore, by consulting noble persons, this land has been chosen, for both mundane and ultra mundane benefits.

In this world generally, there are three root causes of disputes viz., land, wealth and woman. Out of these three, the kings primarily fight for land. Hence, there is the significance of the name 'Kurukṣetra' here. In the Kuru-family the sons of Dhṛtarāṣṭra, as well as, those of Pāṇḍu, are included. Therefore, both of them have an equal claim over the land of Kuru. But

---

* Within the dialogue between Vaiśampāyana and Janamejaya there is the dialogue between Dhṛtarāṣṭra and Sañjaya; and within the dialogue between Dhṛtarāṣṭra and Sañjaya there is the dialogue between Śrī Kṛṣṇa and Arjuna.

† Sañjaya was born of Gavalgaṇa. He possessed knowledge and righteousness like sages. He was Dhṛtarāṣṭra's minister (Mahābhārata Ādi. 63/97).

the Kauravas refuse to give the Pāṇḍavas their share of land, so war between them becomes inevitable.

Though the word 'Kurukṣetra' is fair and justified, because the land belongs to both the cousin groups, yet Indian culture, is so unique that righteousness is given top priority in it. Therefore, even an action such as war, is performed on the field of righteousness—a land of pilgrimage, so that the warriors may attain salvation. Therefore, the word 'Dharmakṣetra', has been used along with 'Kurukṣetra' here.

There is one more point, which needs attention. In the first verse of the first chapter of the Gītā, the first word is 'Dharma', and in the last verse of the eighteenth chapter the last word is 'Mama'. Therefore, if 'Dhar' is taken from the first word and 'Ma' from the last word, the word becomes 'Dharma' (righteousness). Therefore, the whole of the Gītā, comes within righteousness viz., by following the path of righteousness, the principles of the Gītā are followed, and by discharging one's duty according to the doctrines of the Gītā, the path of righteousness, is followed.

From these words 'dharmakṣetre kurukṣetre' all of us should know that all actions should be performed by following the path of righteousness. Every action, should be performed, not with a selfish motive, but for the welfare of all, and the scriptures should be the authority in determining what ought to be done and what ought not to be done (Gītā 16/24).

'Samavetā yuyutsavaḥ'—Duryodhana did not accept the peace negotiations despite repeated proposals from many kings. Nay, when Lord Kṛṣṇa came to intervene as a mediator, Duryodhana bluntly refused to part with, even as much land as could be covered by the point of a needle, without waging a war (Mahābhārata, Udyoga. 127/25). Thus, Pāṇḍavas had no alternative but to fight. Thus the two groups assembled to fight for their rights.

Though the two groups assembled to fight, yet Duryodhana had a keener desire for war, in order to usurp the kingdom by fair means or foul, just means or unjust viz., by hook or crook.

Thus his side was very keen to wage a war.

The Pāṇḍavas, had the virtue of righteousness on their side. For the sake of justice, they were prepared to face any hardship. Knowing the deadly consequences of a war, Yudhiṣṭhira did not want to indulge in it. But, as by obeying their mother, the five Pāṇḍavas had married Draupadī, Yudhiṣṭhira by obeying his mother, became willing to fight.* Thus, Duryodhana, and the members of his group were eager to fight for usurping the kingdom, while the Pāṇḍavas, were compelled to fight for righteousness.

'Māmakāḥ pāṇḍavāścaiva'—The Pāṇḍavas, regarded Dhṛtarāṣṭra (being the elder brother of their father) as their father, and obeyed his order, whether it was just or unjust. Therefore, here the word 'Māmakāḥ' includes both the Kauravas and the Pāṇḍavas†. But the word 'Pāṇḍava', has been mentioned separately, because Dhṛtarāṣṭra was not fair and just to the Pāṇḍavas. He was not impartial, he had partiality‡ for his sons. So the word 'Māmakāḥ', has been used for his sons, while 'Pāṇḍava' has been used for the

* Kuntī, the mother of the five Pāṇḍavas was very forbearing. She had a unique personality. She did not desire worldly pleasures and kingdom. She asked Lord Kṛṣṇa to grant her the boon of adversity. But there were two things which always pinched her. The first of them was that villains such as Duryodhana etc., wanted to make her beloved daughter-in-law naked in the assembly. This insulting, hateful and inhuman behaviour pained her very much.

Secondly when Lord Kṛṣṇa on behalf of the Pāṇḍavas went to Hastināpura with a proposal of conciliation, Duryodhana, Duḥśāsana, Karṇa and Śakunī etc., wanted to arrest Him. Hearing this incident, Kuntī thought that those villains should be killed, otherwise their increasing sins would lead them to damnation. It was because of these two factors that Kuntī ordered her sons, the Pāṇḍavas to fight.

† Though the term 'Kaurava' includes both Duryodhana etc., the sons of Dhṛtarāṣṭra as well as Yudhiṣṭhira etc., the sons of Pāṇḍu, yet in this verse Dhṛtarāṣṭra has used the term 'Pāṇḍava' for Yudhiṣṭhira etc. So the term 'Kaurava' stands for Duryodhana etc.

‡ Dhṛtarāṣṭra had a partial outlook because he thought that Duryodhana etc., were his sons while Yudhiṣṭhira etc., were Pāṇḍu's sons. So he never checked Duryodhana from committing evil deeds such as poisoning Bhīma and throwing him into the water, trying to burn the Pāṇḍavas alive in the house made of lac, gambling with Yudhiṣṭhira by foul means, sending an army to the forest to destroy

sons of Pāṇḍu. Thus, his feelings find expression in his speech. It was because of his partial attitude, that he had to suffer the torture of the destruction of his family. Therefore, every human being should learn a lesson, that he should not be partial to members of his house, street, village, province, country and sect, because partiality leads to conflict, rather than love and goodwill.

The term 'Eva' (also), with the term 'Pāṇḍavāḥ' has been used to point out the fact, that the Pāṇḍavas should not have waged war because they were righteous to the core. But they also came to the battlefield, to wage war. So what did they do there?

[**'Māmakāḥ' and 'Pāṇḍavāḥ'***—Sañjaya will explain the word 'māmakāḥ', from the second to the thirteenth verses to Dhṛtarāṣṭra. Seeing the army of the Pāṇḍavas, his son Duryodhana told Droṇācārya, the names of the chief generals of the Pāṇḍava-army, in order to cause hatred in his mind against the Pāṇḍavas. After that, Duryodhana named the principal warriors of his army, praised their skill in warfare. In order to please and cheer up Duryodhana, Bhīṣma blew his conch loudly. Hearing the sound of his conch, the conchs and trumpets etc., of the Kaurava-army blared forth. Then, from the fourteenth to the nineteenth verses, Sañjaya explains the word 'Pāṇḍavāḥ', as was asked by Dhṛtarāṣṭra. He says, Kṛṣṇa, a supporter of the Pāṇḍavas, seated in a chariot, blew his conch. After him Arjuna, Bhīma, Yudhiṣṭhira, Nakula and Sahadeva etc., also blew their conchs. The terrible sound of those conchs rent the hearts of the army of Duryodhana. After that Sañjaya, while talking about the Pāṇḍavas, starts the dialogue between Śrī Kṛṣṇa and Arjuna, from the twentieth verse.]

---

the Pāṇḍavas and so on. The reason was that Dhṛtarāṣṭra had the feeling that somehow or the other if the Pāṇḍavas were killed, his sons would rule over the whole empire.

* Describing 'Māmakāḥ' and 'Pāṇḍavāḥ' separately Sañjaya uses the words 'Duryodhana' (1/2) and 'Pāṇḍavāḥ' (1/14).

'Kimakurvata'—'Kim', has three meanings—doubt, reproach (blame) and question.

The incident of the war cannot be doubted, because after ten days of fighting when Bhīṣma fell off the chariot, Sañjaya conveyed the message to Dhṛtarāṣṭra, at Hastināpura.

There cannot be reproach (blame) also because Dhṛtarāṣṭra did not blame his sons and the Pāṇḍavas, for the war, when the war was already going on.

Therefore 'Kim' means a question here. Dhṛtarāṣṭra questions Sañjaya to relate him all the incidents in details, and in sequence so that he may understand them properly.

Appendix—'My sons' (māmakāḥ) and 'Pāṇḍu's sons' (Pāṇḍavāḥ)—this distinction caused attachment—aversion which led to war and commotion (stir). The result of Dhṛtarāṣṭra's attachment-aversion was that all the hundred Kauravas were killed while even a single Pāṇḍava was not killed.

As curd is churned, a stir is caused in it by which butter is extracted, similarly the stir caused by the distinction between 'my sons' (māmakāḥ) and 'Pāṇḍu's sons' (pāṇḍavāḥ) caused yearning for benediction in Arjuna's mind by which butter in the form of the Gītā came into light.

It means that the commotion produced in Dhṛtarāṣṭra's mind caused war while the commotion produced in Arjuna's mind revealed the Gītā.

Link:—Then Sañjaya answers his question—

सञ्जय उवाच

दृष्ट्वा तु पाण्डवानीकं व्यूढं दुर्योधनस्तदा।
आचार्यमुपसङ्गम्य राजा वचनमब्रवीत्॥२॥

sañjaya uvāca

dṛṣṭvā tu pāṇḍvānīkaṁ vyūḍhaṁ duryodhanastadā
ācāryamupasaṅgamya rājā vacanamabravīt

Sañjaya said:

At that time, seeing the army of the Pāṇḍavas drawn up in battle array, approaching Droṇācārya, prince Duryodhana, spoke the following words. 2

Comment:—

'Tadā'—'Tadā', means the time when both the armies were arrayed and Dhṛtarāṣṭra was very much anxious to hear the account of the battlefield.

'Tu'—Dhṛtarāṣṭra put the question about his sons and the sons of Pāṇḍu. So Sañjaya uses the word 'Tu', to tell Dhṛtarāṣṭra first about his sons.

'Dṛṣṭvā* pāṇḍavānīkaṁ vyūḍham'—It means that the army of the Pāṇḍavas was arrayed in good order viz., the warriors had no difference in their opinion†. Righteousness, and Lord Kṛṣṇa, were in their favour. Therefore, the Pāṇḍavas, though fewer in number, had greater impact. Seeing their army arrayed, Duryodhana was also influenced. So he, approaching Droṇācārya, spoke prudent and serious words.

'Rājā Duryodhanaḥ'—Duryodhana was called 'Rājā', the king, because Dhṛtarāṣṭra had the greatest attachment and affection for Duryodhana. Moreover, Duryodhana was the prince. He looked after the affairs of the empire, while Dhṛtarāṣṭra was only the nominal head. Duryodhana was the main cause of the warfare also. It was because of all these factors, that he was called king by Sañjaya.

---

* In this chapter the term 'Dṛṣṭvā' has been used three times—seeing the Pāṇḍava-army, Duryodhana approaches Droṇācārya (1/2); seeing the Kaurava-army, Arjuna lifts his bow (1/20); seeing his kith and kin, Arjuna is filled with extreme passion (1/28). In the first two cases the term 'Dṛṣṭvā' has been used for seeing the army while the third time it has been used for seeing the kith and kin which changes Arjuna's feeling.

† There was a difference of opinions in the Kaurava-army because Duryodhana and Duḥśāsana etc., wanted to wage the war. But Bhīṣma, Droṇa and Vikarṇa did not want. And there is a rule that where there is difference in opinions, there vigour subsides.

'Ācāryamupasaṅgamya'—It seems, that there were three reasons why Duryodhana approached Droṇācārya:—

(i) He went for his selfish interest, so that he could arouse ill-will in Droṇācārya's heart, against the Pāṇḍavas and Droṇācārya might be specially partial to his army.

(ii) It was proper on his part to go to Droṇācārya, to express his regard for him, because he was his preceptor.

(iii) It is very significant, for the chief warrior not to leave his position otherwise the whole order of the army is disturbed. So, it was proper on the part of Duryodhana, to go to Droṇācārya.

Here a question may be raised that, Duryodhana should have first of all approached Bhīṣma because Bhīṣma was the commander supreme. Then, why did he approach Droṇācārya? The answer is, that Droṇa and Bhīṣma both loved the Pāṇḍavas, and the Kauravas, but Droṇa had special kindness and love for Arjuna. Moreover, Duryodhana had a pupil-preceptor relationship with Droṇa, but he had no family relationship with him. Therefore, it was proper on his part to go to Droṇa, to please him. In practical life also it is seen that a man for his selfish interest, tries to please a person who is not closely related to him, by offering him regard.

Duryodhana thought, that Bhīṣma was his grandfather. So it was easy to please him, even if he was displeased, because of his family relationship. So Bhīṣma, also loved him very much. Bhīṣma, blew his conch loudly, to please and cheer up Duryodhana (1/12).

'Vacanamabravīt'—Here, it was sufficient to use the word 'Abravīt' (spoke), which also includes 'Vacanam' (words). So there was no need to use the word 'Vacanam'. Even then, the term 'Vacanam' has been used, which shows that Duryodhana spoke prudent and meaningful words, in order to arouse ill-will in Droṇācārya's heart, against the Pāṇḍavas and to win his favour, so that he could fight whole-heartedly, on the Kauravas side and they would gain victory. Thus the term 'Vacanam' was used with a selfish motive.

Link:—Duryodhana approaching Droṇa speaks the following words:—

पश्यैतां पाण्डुपुत्राणामाचार्य महतीं चमूम्।
व्यूढां द्रुपदपुत्रेण तव शिष्येण धीमता॥ ३॥

paśyaitāṁ pāṇḍuputrāṇāmācārya mahatīṁ camūm
vyūḍhāṁ drupadaputreṇa tava śiṣyeṇa dhīmatā

Behold, O Master, this mighty army of the sons of Pāṇḍu, arrayed for battle by your talented pupil Dhṛṣṭadyumna, the son of Drupada. 3

Comment:

'Ācārya'—By addressing Droṇa as 'Ācārya', it seems that Duryodhana means to say that he is the preceptor, who taught the Kauravas and the Pāṇḍavas, the science of warfare. So he should not be partial, to either of the groups.

'Tava śiṣyeṇa dhīmatā—By this phrase Duryodhana means, that Droṇa is so simple hearted, that he has taught the science of warfare to Dhṛṣṭadyumna, Drupada's son, who is born to kill him (Droṇa), and who is so clever, that he is determined to vanquish and kill ṇone other than, his own preceptor.

'Drupadaputreṇa'—It means that Drupada, with the motive of getting your honour killed, got a holy sacrifice performed, by the two Brāhmaṇas (men of the priest-class) named Yāja and Upayāja, and thus Dhṛṣṭadyumna, was born. The same Dhṛṣṭadyumna was standing before him, as commander of the rival army.

Though Duryodhana, could speak the word Dhṛṣṭadyumna instead of 'Drupadaputra', the son of Drupada, yet he intentionally used 'Drupadaputreṇa', to remind Droṇācārya of the enmity that Drupada, had with him. So he really meant that it was a good opportunity, to take a revenge.

'Pāṇḍuputrāṇāṁ, etāṁ vyūḍhāṁ mahatīṁ camūṁ paśya'— Behold the mighty army of the Pāṇḍavas, arrayed for battle by the son of Drupada. It means that Duryodhana wants to say, "O master, the Pāṇḍavas, whom you love, have made the son of Drupada, the general of their army so that he may kill you. Had they loved you, they would never have appointed him as a general."

Though the army of the Kauravas, was larger than that of the Pāṇḍavas, the army of the Kauravas was eleven 'Akṣauhiṇī*, while that of the Pāṇḍavas was only seven 'Akṣauhiṇī', yet the army of the Pāṇḍavas seemed to Duryodhana, larger than what it actually was. The army of the Pāṇḍavas, seemed more formidable to Duryodhana because:—

(i) It was arrayed in such a manner, that even a small army seemed larger to Duryodhana.

(ii) All the warriors of the Pāṇḍavas army, were united and of one mind. So it seemed greater in strength and enthusiasm.

Drawing Droṇa's attention to the army of the Pāṇḍavas, Duryodhana wants to say to Droṇācārya, that he should not regard the army of the rival group as ordinary (small). He should fight with all his might and it would not be difficult for him to defeat the son of Drupada, because he was his pupil.

'Etāṁ paśya', means that the army of the Pāṇḍavas is arrayed for the battle. So you should take a quick decision how to get victory over them.

Link:—After requesting Droṇācārya, to behold the army of the Pāṇḍavas, Duryodhana shows him the chariot-warriors of the army, of the Pāṇḍavas.

* One 'Akṣauhiṇī' army consists of 21,870 chariots, 21,870 elephants, 65,610 horses and 1,09,350 foot-soldiers (Mahābhārata, Ādi. 2/23—26).

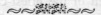

**अत्र शूरा महेष्वासा भीमार्जुनसमा युधि।
युयुधानो विराटश्च द्रुपदश्च महारथः॥४॥
धृष्टकेतुश्चेकितानः काशिराजश्च वीर्यवान्।
पुरुजित्कुन्तिभोजश्च शैब्यश्च नरपुङ्गवः॥५॥
युधामन्युश्च विक्रान्त उत्तमौजाश्च वीर्यवान्।
सौभद्रो द्रौपदेयाश्च सर्व एव महारथाः॥६॥**

**atra śūrā maheṣvāsā bhīmārjunasamā yudhi
yuyudhāno virāṭaśca drupadaśca mahārathaḥ
dhṛṣṭaketuścekitānaḥ kāśirājaśca vīryavān
purujitkuntibhojaśca śaibyaśca narapuṅgavaḥ
yudhāmanyuśca vikrānta uttamaujāśca vīryavān
saubhadro draupadeyāśca sarva eva mahārathāḥ**

There (in the army of the Pāṇḍavas) are mighty archers, peers in warfare like heroic Arjuna and Bhīma, such as Sātyaki and Virāṭa and the great chariot-warrior Drupada. Dhṛṣṭaketu, Cekitāna, the valiant king of Kāśī, Purujit, Kuntibhoja and Śaibya, the best of men, are also there. Mighty Yudhāmanyu, valiant Uttamaujā, Abhimanyu, the son of Subhadrā and the five sons of Draupadī, are also there. All of them are great chariot-warriors. 4—6

Comment:—

'Atra śūrā maheṣvāsā bhīmārjunasamā yudhi'—Those who possess large bows and shoot with bows and arrows, are called 'Maheṣvāsā (the mighty archers). They are very valiant and extraordinary warriors. In warfare, they are as strong as Bhīma, and in the use of weapons and missiles such as bows and arrows etc., as good as Arjuna.

'Yuyudhānaḥ'—Yuyudhāna (Sātyaki), learnt the science of warfare, from Arjuna. Thus he was obliged to him, that he did not go to the side of Duryodhana, even though Lord Kṛṣṇa had given Duryodhana, his Nārāyaṇī army. In order to arouse malice in the mind of Droṇācārya, Duryodhana, first of all, mentions the name of Yuyudhāna, the disciple to Arjuna. He means to say, "You have taught Arjuna archery and granted him the boon that you would try that he would be a matchless archer, in this world (Mahābhārata, Ādi. 131/27). Thus you have so much love for him. But he is so ungrateful, that he is arrayed in the army against you, while Arjuna's disciple Yuyudhāna is arrayed on his side."

[Yuyudhāna was not killed in the warfare but in a mutual fight among the Yādavas.]

'Virāṭaśca'—Duryodhana says, "It was Virāṭa, who was responsible for insulting the warrior, Suśarmā. Again, it was because of him, that you became unconscious with the Sammohana (beguiling) weapon, and we had to flee from the battlefield, leaving behind his cows. The same king Virāṭa is opposing you."

Droṇācārya had no enmity or malice against king Virāṭa. But Duryodhana thinks that if he names Drupada after Yuyudhāna, Droṇācārya may think, that Duryodhana is instigating him to fight against the Pāṇḍavas, and he is arousing feelings of enmity with them. So Duryodhana names Virāṭa before Drupada, so that Droṇācārya may not see through his trick, and may fight bravely.

[King Virāṭa and his three sons, named Uttara, Śveta, Śaṅkha were killed, in the war of Mahābhārata.]

'Drupadaśca mahārathaḥ—Duryodhana says, "You reminded Drupada of your old friendship but he insulted you in the assembly, saying that he was a king and you a beggar, and thus there was no question of any friendship between him and you, and beget a son who would kill you. The same great chariot-warrior, named Drupada is arrayed to fight against you."

[King Drupada, was killed in the warfare by Droṇācārya.]

'Dhṛṣṭaketuḥ'—How foolish this Dhṛṣṭaketu is, that he is fighting on the side of Śrī Kṛṣṇa, who killed his father Śiśupāla, with a disc, in the assembly.

[Dhṛṣṭaketu was killed by Droṇācārya.]

'Cekitānaḥ'— The entire yādava-army is ready to fight on our side, but that solitary yādava is fighting on the side of Pāṇḍavas.

[Cekitāna was killed by Duryodhana.]

'Kāśirājaśca vīryavān'—This king of Kāśī is very valiant, a great chariot-warrior and is fighting on the side of the Pāṇḍavas, so be careful, as you have a very formidable foe to deal with.

[The king of Kāśī was killed, in the battle of Mahābhārata.]

'Purujitkuntibhojaśca'—Though both Purujit and Kuntibhoja, being Kuntī's brothers, are maternal uncles to us and the Pāṇḍavas, yet being partial, they are arrayed to fight against us.

[Purujit and Kuntibhoja—both were killed at the hands of Droṇācārya.]

'Śaibyaśca narapuṅgavaḥ'—Śaibya is the father-in-law to Yudhiṣṭhira. He is noble and very powerful. He is also our relative, but he is on the side of the Pāṇḍavas.

Yudhāmanyuśca vikrānta uttamaujāśca vīryavān'—Yudhāmanyu and Uttamaujā, who are very strong and valiant warriors of Pāñcāla country, have been assigned the task of protecting the wheels of my enemy Arjuna's chariot. So keep an eye on them.

[Yudhāmanyu and Uttamaujā, were slain in their sleep, by Aśvatthāmā.]

'Saubhadraḥ'—He is Abhimanyu, the son to Kṛṣṇa's sister named Subhadrā. He is very brave. He learnt the art of piercing an array of soldiers, standing in the form of a circle, while he was in his mother's womb. So beware of him.

[Abhimanyu was killed by Duḥśāsana's son, when he unjustly hit him, with a mace on the head.]

'Draupadeyāśca'—Draupadī, gave birth to five sons named

Prativindhya, Sutasoma, Śrutakarma, Śatānīka and Śrutasena respectively, from Yudhiṣṭhira, Bhīma, Arjuna, Nakula and Sahadeva. Watch her five sons, carefully. She openly insulted me in the assembly. So avenge that insult, by killing her five sons.

[Aśvatthāmā killed the five sons, while they were asleep at night.]

'Sarva eva mahārathāḥ'—All of them are great chariot-warriors. They are well-versed in the scripture and in the use of arms (A great chariot-warrior is, one who can manage ten thousand archers). There is a large number of such great chariot-warriors, in the army of the Pāṇḍavas.

Link:—Duryodhana described valour, bravery and skill of the army of the Pāṇḍavas, in warfare so that hatred might be aroused in Droṇācārya, against the Pāṇḍavas, and he might be full of greater zeal. But, then a second thought came to his mind, that Droṇa was at heart partial to the Pāṇḍavas. So he might make a peace-treaty, with the Pāṇḍavas. As soon as, this thought came to his mind,he described the heroes of his side, who were very well trained in warfare, in the next three verses.

अस्माकं तु विशिष्टा ये तान्निबोध द्विजोत्तम।
नायका मम सैन्यस्य सञ्ज्ञार्थं तान्ब्रवीमि ते॥ ७॥

asmākaṁ tu viśiṣṭā ye tānnibodha dvijottama
nāyakā mama sainyasya sañjñārthaṁ tānbravīmi te

O best of the twice-born (Brāhmaṇa), know the principal warriors, the generals of my army also; I name them for your information. 7

Comment:—

'Asmākaṁ tu viśiṣṭā ye tānnibodha dvijottama'—Duryodhana says to Droṇācārya, "O best of the twice-born, you should know that in our army also, there are great chariot-warriors, who are in no way less valiant and less trained in warfare, rather they are more valiant and better trained."

In the third verse 'Paśya', and here 'Nibodha' verbs, are used because the army of the Pāṇḍavas is standing in front of them, therefore Duryodhana uses the verb 'Paśya' (behold). But the army of Kauravas, is not in front of Droṇācārya, it is on the side of his back. So Duryodhana, uses the verb 'Nibodha' (Know).

'Nāyakā mama sainyasya sañjñārthaṁ tānbravīmi te'—I mention the names of the chief generals, marshals and great chariot-warriors of my army, to draw your attention to them.

'Sañjñārtham' means, that there are innumerable generals, who cannot be named easily. Therefore, I am just drawing your attention, as you know all of them.

In this verse, Duryodhana probably wants to say, that his side is in no way weaker than that of the Pāṇḍavas, but is rather stronger, yet according to political prudence however weak the army of an enemy may be; it should not be regarded as weak. Therefore, one should not have in the least, a feeling of neglect and indifference, towards the enemy. So Duryodhana already described the warriors of the other side, to make Droṇa careful and now he is giving the names of the warriors of his army.

Secondly, after seeing the army of the Pāṇḍavas compact and well disciplined, Duryodhana was overawed and also somewhat afraid. The reason was, that in spite of being smaller there were several righteous persons, and as also Lord Kṛṣṇa Himself, in that army. Righteous persons and God bear their influence on all the creatures, including those having the most sinful conduct, and even on animals, birds, trees and plants. The reason is, that God and righteousness are eternal, while all the temporal powers are transient. Therefore, Duryodhana is also influenced by the army of the Pāṇḍavas. But because of the material and temporal power, he wants to assure Droṇācārya, that their army is superior to that of the Pāṇḍavas. Therefore, they can easily gain victory over the army, of the Pāṇḍavas.

भवान्भीष्मश्च कर्णश्च कृपश्च समितिञ्जयः।
अश्वत्थामा विकर्णश्च सौमदत्तिस्तथैव च ॥ ८ ॥

bhavānbhīṣmaśca karṇaśca kṛpaśca samitiñjayaḥ
aśvatthāmā vikarṇaśca saumadattistathaiva ca

Yourself, Bhīṣma, Karṇa and Kṛpa ever victorious in battle; and Aśvatthāmā, Vikarṇa and Saumadatti (Bhūriśravā), the son of Somadatta. 8

Comment:—

'Bhavānbhīṣmaśca'—You and Bhīṣma both are unique. So if you fight with your full vigour, neither the gods, genies, devils, nor men can encounter you. Both of you are famous for your valour throughout the world. Bhīṣma has been a celibate since birth and he cannot be killed, without his own will.

[In the Mahābhārata, Droṇācārya was killed by Dhṛṣṭadyumna, while Bhīṣma died during summer solstice, of his own free will.]

'Karṇaśca'—Karṇa is very brave. I believe, that he by himself can gain a victory over the army of the Pāṇḍavas. Even Arjuna, is no match for him. Such a valiant warrior is standing on our side.

[Karṇa was killed by Arjuna, in the war of Mahābhārata.]

'Kṛpaśca samitiñjayaḥ'—Kṛpa, is immortal.* He is our well-wisher and can gain victory over the whole army of the Pāṇḍavas. Though Duryodhana, after mentioning the names of Droṇācārya and Bhīṣma, should have named Kṛpācārya. Yet, Duryodhana had more faith in Karṇa, than in Kṛpācārya. So Karṇa's name was spontaneously uttered by him. But he wanted to please Droṇācārya and Bhīṣma by calling Kṛpācārya, as ever victorious in battle, lest they should regard it as an insult to Kṛpācārya.

'Aśvatthāmā'—He is also immortal. Being your son, he is

* Aśvatthāmā, Bali, Vedavyāsa, Hanumān, Vibhīṣaṇa, Kṛpa (Kṛpācārya), Paraśurāma and Mārkaṇḍeya—these eight are immortal. In the scripture it is written.

very valiant. He is well versed in the science of warfare as he has learnt it, from you.

'Vikarṇaśca saumadattistathaiva ca'—You should not think that only the Pāṇḍavas are righteous. On our side, my brother Vikarṇa is also very righteous and brave. Similarly Bhūriśravā, the grandson of our great grandfather's brother, Bāhlīka and the son of Somadatta, is also very righteous. He has also performed several holy sacrifices, by offering great gifts. He is also a very brave and great chariot-warrior.

[In the warfare, Vikarṇa was killed by Bhīma, and Bhūriśravā was killed by Sātyaki.]

Here, by mentioning these names Duryodhana means to say, "O preceptor (Ācārya), in our army, there are so many valiant warriors, such as you, Bhīṣma, Karṇa, Kṛpācārya etc., while in the army of the Pāṇḍavas, such valiant warriors are not seen. In our army, two great warriors named Kṛpācārya and Aśvatthāmā are immortal, while in the army of the Pāṇḍavas there is none. Moreover, in our army there is no scarcity of righteous persons, therefore, we need not be afraid of them.

अन्ये च बहवः शूरा मदर्थे त्यक्तजीविताः ।
नानाशस्त्रप्रहरणाः सर्वे युद्धविशारदाः ॥ ९ ॥

anye ca bahavaḥ śūrā madarthe tyaktajīvitāḥ
nānāśastrapraharaṇāḥ sarve yuddhaviśāradāḥ

And there are many other heroes well trained in warfare, who, equipped with various weapons and missiles, have staked their lives for my sake. 9

Comment:—

'Anye ca bahavaḥ śūrā madarthe tyaktajīvitāḥ'— Besides the above-mentioned heroes, there are many great chariot-warriors, such as Bāhlīka, Śalya, Bhagadatta, Jayadratha etc., in our army, who have come here to fight, by staking their lives for me. They may be killed in the war, but they will not run away from the battlefield. How should I express my hearty thankfulness, to them before you?

'Nānāśastrapraharaṇāḥ sarve yuddhaviśāradāḥ'—All these heroes are experts in the use of weapons, such as swords, maces, tridents and missiles, such as arrows and javelins etc. They are in everyway, experts in the science of warfare.'

*Link:—When Duryodhana by his cleverness could not deceive Droṇācārya, who did not say anything, he had a second thought. This thought is described by Sañjaya in the next verse.**

अपर्याप्तं तदस्माकं बलं भीष्माभिरक्षितम्।
पर्याप्तं त्विदमेतेषां बलं भीमाभिरक्षितम्॥ १०॥

aparyāptaṁ tadasmākaṁ balaṁ bhīṣmābhirakṣitam
paryāptaṁ tvidameteṣāṁ balaṁ bhīmābhirakṣitam

Our army is inadequate and is easier to be conquered, as it is protected by Bhīṣma (a well-wisher of both the armies). But their army marshalled by Bhīma, is unconquerable (because Bhīma guards it well). 10

Comment:—

'Aparyāptaṁ tadasmākaṁ balaṁ bhīṣmābhirakṣitam'—Duryodhana thinks about his army because of unrighteousness and injustice, Duryodhana is afraid that, "Our army though larger than that of the Pāṇḍavas, is easier to be conquered, because our army is unwieldy, indisciplined, disunited and faint-hearted, while the army of the Pāṇḍavas, is compact, disciplined, united and fearless. The chief protector of our army is Bhīṣma, who is friendly to both the armies. He, is a great devotee of Kṛṣṇa He, in his heart has great respect for Yudhiṣṭhira and love for

* Sañjaya by means of the divine insight he was endowed with by Sage Vyāsa, was able to know even the minds of the warriors (Mahābhārata, Bhīṣma. 2/11).

Arjuna. Therefore, though outwardly, he is on our side, yet at heart, he is a well-wisher of the Pāṇḍavas. He is the field-marshal of our army. Under these circumstances, how can our army gain victory, over the Pāṇḍavas?

'Paryāptaṁ tvidameteṣāṁ balaṁ bhīmābhirakṣitam'— But, this army of the Pāṇḍavas can be victorious over our army, very easily because all the warriors of their army are united, without having any difference of opinions. The protector of their army, is Bhīma who is brave and who has always defeated me, since childhood. He has taken a pledge to kill all the hundred brothers including me, he is bent on destroying us. His body is as strong and hard as an adamant. I poisoned him but it did not kill him. Having such a protector as Bhīma, the army of the Pāṇḍavas is certainly capable of gaining victory over our army.

Here, a doubt may arise that Duryodhana named Bhīṣma, who was their field-marshal in defence of their army, but he named Bhīma, who was not a field-marshal in defence of the army of the Pāṇḍavas. The answer is, that at that time Duryodhana was not thinking about the field-marshals, but about the strength of the two armies. Duryodhana, was very much influenced by Bhīma's power, so he named Bhīma, as the protector of the army of the Pāṇḍavas.

An Important Matter

Arjuna, beholding the army of the Kauravas raises his bow (Gītā 1/20), while Duryodhana, seeing the army of the Pāṇḍavas approaches Droṇācārya and requests him to watch the army of Pāṇḍavas, arrayed for battle. It proves that Duryodhana's mind has been by fear-struck.* Though afraid,

* When the conchs of the army of the Kauravas blared forth, their sound had no effect on the army of the Pāṇḍavas. But when the conchs of the army of the Pāṇḍavas blared forth, their sound rent the hearts of Duryodhana etc., (1/13,19).

It proves that by following the path of injustice and unrighteousness the hearts of Duryodhana etc., had become weak and horror-struck.

yet with his cleverness he wants to please Droṇācārya, and instigate him, against the Pāṇḍavas. The reason is, that in Duryodhana's heart, there are unrighteousness, injustice and sin, and it is a rule that an unrightcous, unjust and sinful person cannot live, happily and peacefully. On the other hand, in Arjuna's heart there are righteousness and justice. So he does not play any trick and have any fear to serve his self-interest. He is fearless, courageous and brave. That is why, he orders Lord Kṛṣṇa, "O Kṛṣṇa, place my chariot, between the two armies" (1/21). It means that a person, who depends on perishable riches and property, etc., and whose heart is full of unrighteousness, injustice and ill-feeling, does not possess real power. He is hollow from within, and is never fearless. On the other hand one who depends on God and follows righteousness, is never fearful. His power is real, and he always remains free from cares and fears. Therefore, strivers, who aspire for God-realization should perform their duty by depending only on God, and for His sake, renounce unrighteousness, and injustice etc. They should never follow the path of unrighteousness, by attaching importance to material prosperity and contact-born pleasures, because these two lead men to damnation, rather than to peace.

Appendix—Arjuna, instead of accepting the Lord's Nārāyaṇī army well-equipped with arms and ammunition, accepted unarmed Lord Kṛṣṇa* while Duryodhana in place of Lord Kṛṣṇa accepted His Nārāyaṇī army. It means that Arjuna had an eye on Lord Kṛṣṇa while Duryodhana had an eye on His stately power. The heart of the person, who has an eye on God, is strong because God's strength is real. But the heart of the person who

---

*evamuktastu kṛṣṇena kuntīputro dhanañjayaḥ
ayudhyamānaṁ saṅgrāme varayāmāsa keśavam (Mahā. Udyoga. 7/21)

"When Lord Kṛṣṇa said so, Arjuna, Kuntī's son in the battlefield instead of accepting the Lord's one Akṣauhiṇī army, accepted unarmed Lord Kṛṣṇa as his helper who wouldn't fight in the war."

has an eye on worldly power is weak as the strength of the world is unreal.

Link:—Now Duryodhana to please Bhīṣma instructs all the great chariot-warriors of his army, and says:—

अयनेषु च सर्वेषु यथाभागमवस्थिताः।
भीष्ममेवाभिरक्षन्तु भवन्तः सर्व एव हि॥ ११॥

ayaneṣu ca sarveṣu yathābhāgamavasthitāḥ
bhīṣmamevābhirakṣantu bhavantaḥ sarva eva hi

Now all of you, stationed in your respective positions on all fronts, guard Bhīṣma, in particular, on all sides. 11

Comment:—

'Ayaneṣu ca sarveṣu yathābhāgamavasthitāḥ bhīṣmamevābhirakṣantu bhavantaḥ sarva eva hi'—All of you (warriors), stationed in your respective position on different fronts, should guard Bhīṣma on all sides.

By saying the above words, Duryodhana wants to please Bhīṣma, so that he may be partial to his army. Secondly, he gives instruction to the warriors of his army, to see that Śikhaṇḍī should not face Bhīṣma. If Śikhaṇḍī comes in front of Bhīṣma, the latter will not use his arms and weapons against him, because he was a woman in the previous birth. In that birth also, first he was a woman and later he changed into a man. So Bhīṣma, by regarding him as a woman, has promised not to fight with Śikhaṇḍī. Śikhaṇḍī, had taken birth by Lord Śiva's boon, to kill Bhīṣma. Therefore, if Bhīṣma is protected from Śikhaṇḍī, he will kill all other warriors of the army of Pāṇḍavas, and their victory is certain. Therefore, Duryodhana gives instruction to all the great chariot-warriors of his army, to guard Bhīṣma.

Link:—Finding Duryodhana discouraged by getting no hopeful response, from Droṇācārya, Bhīṣma in order to express his affection for him, cheers him up. This is expressed by Sañjaya, in the next verse.

तस्य सञ्जनयन्हर्षं कुरुवृद्धः पितामहः।
सिंहनादं विनद्योच्चैः शङ्खं दध्मौ प्रतापवान्॥ १२॥

tasya sañjanayanharṣaṁ kuruvṛddhaḥ pitāmahaḥ
siṁhanādaṁ vinadyoccaiḥ śaṅkhaṁ dadhmau pratāpavān

The grand old man of the Kaurava race, their glorious grand-uncle Bhīṣma, cheering Duryodhana roared loudly like a lion, and blew his conch. 12

Comment:—

'Tasya sañjanayanharṣam'—Here, it should have been said, that Bhīṣma blew his conch and it cheered Duryodhana. But it is said that Bhīṣma, cheering up Duryodhana, blew his conch. Sañjaya wants to state that the very action of blowing the conch, will certainly cheer up Duryodhana. To express this influence of Bhīṣma, Sañjaya uses the adjective 'Pratāpavān' (glorious).

'Kuruvṛddhaḥ'—Though in the Kuru race Bāhlīka (the younger brother of Bhīṣma's father Śāntanu), was older than Bhīṣma, yet Bhīṣma, possessed better knowledge of righteousness and God, than all other old members, in the race. So Sañjaya, calls him 'Kuruvṛddhaḥ', (the grand old man of the Kaurava race).

'Pratāpavān'— Bhīṣma was well-known for his renunciation of wealth and woman i.e., he did not accept any kingdom nor did he marry. He was well-versed in military science and scriptures. So the warrior class were very much influenced by him.

When Bhīṣma for his brother Vicitravīrya kidnapped all by himself, the daughters of the king of Kāśī, from the place where their suitors had assembled to marry them, the Kṣatriya suitors attacked him, but he alone defeated all of them. He was so well-versed, in the science of weapons and warfare, that he did not accept his defeat even against his preceptor Paraśurāma, who had taught him the science of weapons etc. Thus he had great influence over the Kṣatriyas (warrior class), because of his skill in military science.

When Bhīṣma was lying on a bed of arrows Lord Kṛṣṇa said to Yudhiṣṭhira, "If you want to put any question on righteousness (Dharma), ask him now, because the sun of the knowledge of scriptures, is going to set, i.e., Bhīṣma, a great scholar of scriptures is going to die."* Thus, we see that he had great mastery over the scriptures and others were very much influenced by this knowledge.

'Pitāmahaḥ'—This word seems to mean that Droṇācārya did not attach any importance to the tricks played by Duryodhana. He understood that Duryodhana wanted to deceive him. So he remained silent. But Bhīṣma is the grand-uncle of Duryodhana. So he sees Duryodhana's child-like behaviour, in his tricks. Hence Bhīṣma unlike Droṇācārya, breaks his silence and blows his conch to cheer up Duryodhana, and show his affection for him.

'Siṁhanādaṁ vinadyoccaiḥ śaṅkhaṁ dadhmau'—When a lion roars ferociously, even large wild animals like elephants etc., get horror-struck. Similarly, by roaring ferociously, Bhīṣma blew his conch to cheer up Duryodhana, and terrorise the warriors, of the hostile army.

Appendix—Duryodhana's relationship with Droṇācārya was that of pupil-teacher while with Bhīṣma he had the family relationship. Where there is the pupil-teacher relationship, there is no partiality but in family relationship because of the affection for the family, partiality ensues. Therefore having heard the tricky words uttered by Duryodhana, Droṇācārya remained quiet which discouraged Duryodhana. But because of family-affection, having seen Duryodhana sad, Bhīṣma blew the conch in order to encourage Duryodhana.

---

* Mahābhārata, Śānti. 46/23

Link:—In the verse that follows, Sañjaya narrates the effect of sounding the conch by Bhīṣma.

ततः शङ्खाश्च भेर्यश्च पणवानकगोमुखाः।
सहसैवाभ्यहन्यन्त स शब्दस्तुमुलोऽभवत्॥१३॥

tataḥ śaṅkhāśca bheryaśca paṇavānakagomukhāḥ
sahasaivābhyahanyanta sa śabdastumulo'bhavat

Then conchs, kettledrums, tabors, drums and cow-horns, suddenly blared forth and the noise was tumultuous. 13

Comment:—

'Tataḥ śaṅkhāśca bheryaśca paṇavānakagomukhāḥ'—Bhīṣma had not blown his conch to declare war, his purpose was to cheer up Duryodhana, but the army of the Kauravas thought that the war was declared. So hearing the sound of the conch, all musical instruments such as conchs etc., of the Kaurava-army suddenly blared forth.

Conchs are found in the sea. These are blown in adoration of God, on auspicious occasions and for declaring a war. 'Kettle-drums' (bherī), are drums with large hollow bowls of iron, with tops made of skins of buffaloes and are beaten with a wooden stick. They are kept in temples and forts, and are beaten, specially on functions and auspicious occasions. 'Tabors' (paṇava), are small drums like a tambourine. These are made of iron or wood, with tops covered by the skin of goats, and are beaten with hand or a wooden stick. Their beating is regarded as auspicious, as adoration to Lord Gaṇeśa. 'Ānaka' (drum), is a musical instrument made of clay, with the top covered by leather and beaten with a hand. 'Gomukha' (cow-horn), is a musical wind instrument, consisting of a long metal tube usually bent like a serpent, having a cow shaped mouth and is blown with the mouth.

'Sahasaivābhyahanyanta'*—Kaurava-army was full of great

* Here instead of saying that the army of the Kauravas blared forth their musical instruments, it has been said that the instruments blared forth. This construction of the sentence shows enthusiasm and ease of the army.

enthusiasm. Therefore, as soon as Bhīṣma blew his conch, all their musical instruments suddenly blared forth, all at once without much effort.

'Sa śabdastumulo'bhavat'—The sound of the musical instruments, such as conchs etc., of the Kaurava-army, standing in divisions and sub-divisions, was tumultuous, and was echoed all over.

Link:—In the beginning of this chapter, Dhṛtarāṣṭra asked Sañjaya, "What did my sons and the sons of Pāṇḍu do, while assembled on the battlefield?" Therefore, Sañjaya explained from the second to the thirteenth verses, what Dhṛtarāṣṭra's sons did. In the next verse, Sañjaya says what Pāṇḍu's sons did.

ततः श्वेतैर्हयैर्युक्ते महति स्यन्दने स्थितौ।
माधवः पाण्डवश्चैव दिव्यौ शङ्खौ प्रदध्मतुः ॥ १४॥

tataḥ śvetairhayairyukte mahati syandane sthitau
mādhavaḥ pāṇḍavaścaiva divyau śaṅkhau pradadhmatuḥ

Then, seated in a glorious chariot drawn by white horses, Śrī Kṛṣṇa as well as Arjuna, blew their divine conchs. 14

Comment:—

'Tataḥ śvetairhayairyukte'—The Gandharva (a celestial musician) named Citraratha gave Arjuna, one hundred divine horses. It was ordained that they would always remain one hundred in number even though many of them were killed, on the battlefield. They could go to heaven or live on the earth. Out of these, one hundred horses, four beautiful and well-trained horses, were harnessed to Arjuna's chariot.

'Mahati syandane sthitau'—The Fire-god (Agni) suffered from indigestion because a lot of 'ghee' (clarified butter) was offered in a holy sacrifice to him. Therefore, though the fire-god wanted to cure his indigestion by consuming medicinal herbs of the Khāṇḍava forest, but he was unable to do it because it was protected by other gods. Whenever he tried to burn it, 'Indra', the king of the gods extinguished the fire with the rain. At last, with Arjuna's help Agni cured his indigestion, by burning the whole forest and being pleased with Arjuna, Agni gave him a very large and glorious chariot. As many weapons and missiles as could be accommodated in nine bullock carts, were held in it. It was gilded and glorious. Its wheels were strong and huge. It's flag, shone like lightning over about a 'Yojana (eight miles), in distance. In spite of being so long it was neither heavy, nor could, it stop or be entangled in trees etc., Hanumān (the monkey-god, who acted as a spy in Rāma's march against Rāvaṇa), was the emblem on the flag.

'Sthitau'—'Sthitau' means, that the beautiful and glorious chariot became more so, because Lord Kṛṣṇa Himself, and His dear devotee Arjuna, were sitting in it.

'Mādhavaḥ pāṇḍavaścaiva'—'Mā' is Lakṣmī, the goddess of wealth and prosperity, and 'Dhava,' is the husband or owner. Therefore, 'Mādhava' means the Lord of Lakṣmī, Śrī Kṛṣṇa, the incarnation of Lord Viṣṇu. Here, Pāṇḍava, has been used for Arjuna, because he is the chief among the Pāṇḍavas—'Pāṇḍavānāṁ Dhanañjayaḥ; (Gītā 10/37). [Lord Kṛṣṇa says, "Among the Pāṇḍavas, I am Dhanañjaya (Arjuna).]" (He has been called chief among the Pāṇḍavas, because he had no individuality, apart from Lord Kṛṣṇa.)

Arjuna and Śrī Kṛṣṇa were the incarnations of 'Nara' and 'Nārāyaṇa', respectively. In the beginning of every 'Parva' (section) of Mahābhārata, there is salutation to Nara (Arjuna) and Nārāyaṇa (Lord Kṛṣṇa). Thus, from this point of view also, Lord Kṛṣṇa and Arjuna both, were chiefs. Sañjaya also says in the last verse of the Gītā, "Wherever there is Śrī Kṛṣṇa, the Lord of Yoga, and wherever is Arjuna, the wielder of the bow (Gāṇḍīva bow), there are prosperity, victory, glory and righteousness; this is my conviction" (18/78).

'Divyau śaṅkhau pradadhmatuḥ'—Lord Kṛṣṇa and Arjuna, loudly blew their conchs, which were glorious and divine.

Here, it. may be stated, that it was proper on the part of Bhīṣma to blow his conch first, because he was the field-marshal of the Kaurava-army. But how far was it justified on the part of Lord Kṛṣṇa, the chariot-driver of the Pāṇḍava-army, to blow the conch, when the field-marshal, Dhṛṣṭadyumna of the Pāṇḍava-army, was there? The answer, is that Lord Kṛṣṇa is ever chief, whether He works as a chariot-driver or a great chariot-warrior. He is ever great, whatever the rank He may hold, because His rank is 'Acyuta' (fixed), He never deviates from his divine nature. In Pāṇḍava-army, Lord Kṛṣṇa was the chief and director. Even when, he was a boy, Nanda and Upananda etc., obeyed him. Therefore, they, by obeying him, started to worship Govardhana, (a mountain), instead of Indra, the king of gods, who had been worshipped for generations. It means, that the Lord, in whatever state, place and circumstance, He may live, is ever the chief. Therefore, Lord Kṛṣṇa was the first in the Pāṇḍava-army, to blow his conch.

One, who is really inferior, regards himself as superior, after getting an appointment to a high post. On the contrary, one who is really superior is superior everywhere, and he elevates the post, at which he works. Thus, Lord Kṛṣṇa, while working as a chariot-driver, elevated that post.

Link:—Sañjaya in the next four verses, in explaining the previous verse and giving some more details, describes the blowing of conchs by other warriors.

पाञ्चजन्यं हृषीकेशो देवदत्तं धनञ्जयः।
पौण्ड्रं दध्मौ महाशङ्खं भीमकर्मा वृकोदरः॥ १५॥

pāñcajanyaṁ hṛṣīkeśo devadattaṁ dhanañjayaḥ
pauṇḍraṁ dadhmau mahāśaṅkhaṁ bhīmakarmā vṛkodaraḥ

Hṛṣīkeśa (Śrī Kṛṣṇa), blew his conch named Pāñcajanya, Dhanañjaya (Arjuna), his conch called Devadatta; while Vṛkodara (Bhīma), of terrific deeds, blew his mighty conch the Pauṇḍra. 15

Comment:—

'Pāñcajanyaṁ hṛṣīkeśaḥ'—'Hṛṣīkeśa', means the master of mind and senses, Lord Kṛṣṇa who pervades the mind and intellect of all viz., who is acquainted with the hearts of all the people, arranged on the side of the Pāṇḍavas, blew his conch named Pāñcajanya. Lord Kṛṣṇa having killed demon named Pañcajana who appeared in the form of a conch, used him as a conch. So His conch was named as 'Pāñcajanya."

'Devadattaṁ dhanañjayaḥ'—The word 'Dhanañjaya means conqueror of wealth. At the time of the holy sacrifice named Rājasūya, Arjuna took over wealth of many rulers on gaining victory, over them. So Arjuna was called 'Dhanañjaya.* Indra, the king of gods, gave Arjuna the conch named Devadatta, while he was fighting with demons named Nivātakavaca etc. It produced such a loud and horrifying sound that the army of the enemies became terror-struck. This conch was blown by Arjuna.

'Pauṇḍraṁ dadhmau mahāśaṅkhaṁ bhīmakarmā vṛkodaraḥ'—Bhīma, was named 'Bhīmakarmā (doer of tremendous deeds) because he killed demons, such as Hiḍimba, Baka and Jaṭa etc., and valiant warriors, such as Kīcaka and Jarāsandha etc. In his belly, besides the heat which helps to digest food, there was a special fire, named 'Vṛka' which digested a lot of food, very easily. It was because of his great digestive power, that he was named 'Vṛkodara.' Thus, Bhīma who was the doer of terrific deeds and possessed strong digestive power, blew his mighty conch, Pauṇḍra.

अनन्तविजयं राजा कुन्तीपुत्रो युधिष्ठिरः।
नकुलः सहदेवश्च सुघोषमणिपुष्पकौ॥ १६॥

* Mahābhārata, Virāṭa. 44/13

anantavijayaṁ rājā kuntīputro yudhiṣṭhiraḥ
nakulaḥ sahadevaśca sughoṣamaṇipuṣpakau

King Yudhiṣṭhira, son of Kuntī, blew his conch Anantavijaya; while Nakula and Sahadeva, blew their conchs, the Sughoṣa and Maṇipuṣpaka, respectively. 16

Comment:—

'Anantavijayaṁ rājā kuntīputro yudhiṣṭhiraḥ nakulaḥ sahadevaśca sughoṣamaṇipuṣpakau'—Arjuna, Bhīma and Yudhiṣṭhira—the three were Kuntī's sons while Nakula and Sahadeva were Mādrī's sons. So the adjective 'Kuntīputra' (Kuntī's sons) has been used for Yudhiṣṭhira.

Yudhiṣṭhira has been called a king because he was the ruler of half of the Indraprastha kingdom before exile and according to the promise and the law, he should have been a king after living in exile for twelve years and one year's incognito residence. Moreover, by calling him a king, Sañjaya wanted to hint that he would be the king of the entire territory afterwards.

काश्यश्च परमेष्वासः शिखण्डी च महारथः।
धृष्टद्युम्नो विराटश्च सात्यकिश्चापराजितः॥ १७॥
द्रुपदो द्रौपदेयाश्च सर्वशः पृथिवीपते।
सौभद्रश्च महाबाहुः शङ्खान्दध्मुः पृथक् पृथक्॥ १८॥

kāśyaśca parameṣvāsaḥ śikhaṇḍī ca mahārathaḥ
dhṛṣṭadyumno virāṭaśca sātyakiścāparājitaḥ
drupado draupadeyāśca sarvaśaḥ pṛthivīpate
saubhadraśca mahābāhuḥ śaṅkhāndadhmuḥ pṛthak pṛthak

The king of Kāśī, the excellent archer and Śikhaṇḍī, the great chariot-warrior, Dhṛṣṭadyumna and Virāṭa, and the invincible Sātyaki, king Drupada, as well as, the five sons of Draupadī, and the mighty-armed Abhimanyu, son of Subhadrā, all of them blew their respective conchs. 17-18

Comment:—

'Kāśyaśca parameṣvāsaḥ śikhaṇḍī ca mahārathaḥ dhṛṣṭadyumno virāṭaśca sātyakiścāparājitaḥ drupado draupadeyāśca sarvaśaḥ pṛthivīpate saubhadraśca mahābāhuḥ śaṅkhāndadhmuḥ pṛthak pṛthak'—The great chariot-warrior Śikhaṇḍī, was very brave. He in his previous birth was a woman, (the daughter named Ambā of the king of Kāśī), and in this birth also, was born as a daughter to king Drupada. Afterwards, she became a man by getting manhood from a genie, named Sthūṇākarna. Bhīṣma knew all this and therefore, he regarded him as a woman, and did not shoot arrows at him. Arjuna while fighting kept Śikhaṇḍī ahead, shot arrows at Bhīṣma and overthrew him from the chariot.

Arjuna's son Abhimanyu, was very brave. In warfare, he killed many warriors, by entering the array of soldiers stationed, in the form of a circle formed by Droṇa. At last, six great chariot-warriors of the army of Kauravas, surrounding him by foul means, attacked him with weapons and missiles. He was killed, when Duḥśāsana's son, hit him on the head, with a mace.

Sañjaya, mentioned only one warrior named Bhīṣma, who blew his conch from the Kaurava-army, while he mentioned eighteen warriors, such as Lord Kṛṣṇa, Arjuna, Bhīma etc., from the Pāṇḍava-army. It seems that Sañjaya, did not want to describe the unrighteous side of the Kaurava-army, in detail. But, he had great regard for Lord Kṛṣṇa, the Pāṇḍavas and the Pāṇḍava-army, because of their righteousness. So he thought it proper, to describe the warriors of Pāṇḍava-army, in more detail and he took delight in describing them.

Link:—In the next verse is described the effect of the sound of the conchs on the Kaurava-army.

स घोषो धार्तराष्ट्राणां हृदयानि व्यदारयत्।
नभश्च पृथिवीं चैव तुमुलो व्यनुनादयन्॥ १९॥

sa ghoṣo dhārtarāṣṭrāṇāṁ hṛdayāni vyadārayat
nabhaśca pṛthivīṁ caiva tumulo vyanunādayan

The terrible din, echoing through the sky and the earth, rent the hearts of Dhṛtarāṣṭra's sons, who had usurped the kingdom by unjust means. 19

Comment:—

'Sa ghoṣo dhārtarāṣṭrāṇāṁ hṛdayāni vyadārayat nabhaśca pṛthivīṁ caiva tumulo vyanunādayan'—The sounds of the conchs of the Pāṇḍava-army, was so thunderous, roaring and horrifying, that it echoed through the sky and the earth, and rent the hearts of the Kauravas, who had usurped the empire, and also of the kings, who had come to fight on their side. It means, that, as a weapon or a missile, rends the heart and causes it pain so does, the sound of the these conchs. That sound discouraged the Kaurava-army and its warriors were horror-struck, at the formidable strength of the Pāṇḍava-army.

Sañjaya was relating the incidents to Dhṛtarāṣṭra. So it seems that it was not proper on his part to mention, 'Dhārtarāṣṭrāṇām' (Dhṛtarāṣṭra's sons). He should have mentioned 'Tāvakīnānām' (his sons and relatives), which would have been polite. But he used the word correctly, because it was justified on his part to use it as he meant to say, that his sons usurped the kingdom. Their hearts were rent, because they were unrighteous. Therefore the use of the word is justified further.

Here a question may arise why there was no effect of the sound of the war instruments, such as conchs etc., of the eleven Akṣauhiṇī army (In an Akṣauhiṇī army there are 109350 foot soldiers, 65610 horses, 21870 chariots and 21870 elephants) of the Kauravas* on the Pāṇḍava-army, but the sound of the conchs

* It was impossible for Duryodhana to have such a large eleven Akṣauhiṇī

of seven Akṣauhiṇī army of the Pāṇḍavas rent the hearts of the Kaurava-army. The answer is that the hearts of those who are righteous and just, are impregnable. Pāṇḍavas had ruled over the empire with justice and righteousness, before their exile and also demanded their empire from the Kauravas, which was a just demand. On the other hand, the hearts of those who are unrighteous, unjust and sinful, are weak, doubtful and full of fear. It is their sin or injustice, which weakens their hearts. Duryodhana and his group, tried their best to kill Pāṇḍavas, by any means—fair or foul. They usurped their empire and caused them much trouble. Thus, they stood for unrighteousness. So the sound of the conchs of seven Akṣauhiṇī army of the Pāṇḍavas, rent their hearts, with a piercing pain.

This incident, warns a striver, that he should never have unjust and unrighteous dealings, through his body, speech and mind, because these weaken the heart and create fear, in it. For example, the creatures of the world, including the gods and the demons, were afraid of Rāvaṇa, the king of Laṅkā. But when he abducted Sītā, he being terrified, looked here and there, to see if anyone was watching him (Mānasa 3/28/4-5).

Link:—In the first verse, Dhṛtarāṣṭra put a question, about his sons and sons of Pāṇḍu. Sañjaya answered the question, from the second to the nineteenth verse. Now Sañjaya starts

army. But when the Pāṇḍavas were exiled, Duryodhana adopted the policy of Yudhiṣṭhira. As Yudhiṣṭhira ruled over the subjects with justice and righteousness to give them comfort, thinking it his duty, Duryodhana also did the same to establish his influence over them. It was because of his good behaviour towards the people for thirteen years that the army which liked the Pāṇḍavas, came over to his side. Thus he could win the confidence of nine Akṣauhiṇī army because of his good behaviour. Lord Kṛṣṇa gave him one Akṣauhiṇī army. Moreover he tricked one Akṣauhiṇī army of king Śalya of Madra to his side which had been on the side of the Pāṇḍavas. Therefore on the side of the Kauravas there was an army eleven Akṣauhiṇī in number while on the Pāṇḍava side it was seven Akṣauhiṇī.

the dialogue in the next verse between Lord Kṛṣṇa and Arjuna, which is known as 'The Bhagavadgītā'.

अथ व्यवस्थितान्दृष्ट्वा धार्तराष्ट्रान् कपिध्वजः।
प्रवृत्ते शस्त्रसम्पाते धनुरुद्यम्य पाण्डवः॥ २०॥
हृषीकेशं तदा वाक्यमिदमाह महीपते।

atha vyavasthitāndṛṣṭvā dhārtarāṣṭrān kapidhvajaḥ
pravṛtte śastrasampāte dhanurudyamya pāṇḍavaḥ
hṛṣīkeśaṁ tadā vākyamidamāha mahīpate

Now, O Lord of the earth, seeing Dhṛtarāṣṭra's sons arrayed against him, and the fighting about to commence with missiles, Pāṇḍava (Arjuna) whose ensign bears the Hanumān, lifting his bow, spoke the following words, to Kṛṣṇa. 20

Comment:—

'Atha'—This word means, that now Sañjaya begins the Bhagavadgītā, in the form of a dialogue between Lord Kṛṣṇa and Arjuna. This dialogue, ends with the word 'Iti' used in the seventy-fourth verse of the eighteenth chapter. Similarly, the gospel of the Gītā begins, with the eleventh verse of the second chapter, and ends with sixty-sixth verse of the eighteenth chapter.

'Pravṛtte śastrasampāte'—Though Bhīṣma had blown his conch to cheer up Duryodhana, not to declare war, yet the Kaurava and Pāṇḍava armies thought that the war had been declared, and so they became ready with weapons and missiles in their hands. Seeing them equipped with weapons and missiles, Arjuna also lifted his bow, named Gāṇḍīva.

'Vyavasthitān dhārtarāṣṭrān dṛṣṭvā'—By these words Sañjaya means, "When your son Duryodhana saw the army of Pāṇḍavas, he fled to Droṇācārya. But when Arjuna saw the army of Kauravas, he lifted his bow." 'Dhanurudyamya' (took his bow)—it shows, that Duryodhana was filled with fear, while Arjuna was fearless, courageous and valiant.

'Kapidhvajaḥ'—By using this epithet 'Kapidhvajaḥ', Sañjaya wants to remind Dhṛtarāṣṭra of Hanumān, sitting on the banner of Arjuna's chariot. When Pāṇḍavas used to live in the forest, one day suddenly, the wind dropped a divine lotus having a thousand leaves before Draupadī. She was very much pleased to see it, and she said to Bhīma, "O excellent among the brave, bring me several lotuses of this kind." Bhīma, started to satisfy her desire. When he reached the Kadalī forest, he happened to meet Hanumān. Both of them talked about many things. At last Hanumān desired to grant him a boon. Bhīma said, "May your kindness continue to be with me!" Hanumān said, "O son of wind-god, when uneasy by being injured with arrows and weapons, enter the army of the enemy and make a roar, I'll enhance that roar by adding my own power to it. Moreover, by sitting on the banner of Arjuna's chariot I'll make such a roar, that it will be deadly terrifying to your enemy, and you will gain a victory, over them and kill them very easily."* Therefore, the victory of those, on whose banner Hanumān was sitting, was certain.

'Pāṇḍavaḥ'—Dhṛtarāṣṭra, used the word 'Pāṇḍavāḥ' in his question. Therefore, Sañjaya also used the word 'Pāṇḍavaḥ', several times (as in 1/14 and here in 1/20) to remind Dhṛtarāṣṭra of the Pāṇḍavas.

'Hṛṣīkeśaṁ tadā vākyamidamāha mahīpate'—Duryodhana, seeing the army of Pāṇḍavas, approaching his preceptor Droṇa, spoke the words cleverly; while Arjuna seeing the army of Kauravas approaching Lord Kṛṣṇa, who is a world-teacher, who is acquainted with the hearts of all, and who is the inspirer of mind and intellect etc., spoke the words full of bravery, courage, and duty.

---

* Mahābhārata, Vana. 151/17-18

अर्जुन उवाच

सेनयोरुभयोर्मध्ये रथं स्थापय मेऽच्युत ॥ २१ ॥
यावदेतान्निरीक्षेऽहं योद्धुकामानवस्थितान् ।
कैर्मया सह योद्धव्यमस्मिन्रणसमुद्यमे ॥ २२ ॥

arjuna uvāca

senayorubhayormadhye rathaṁ sthāpaya me'cyuta
yāvadetānnirīkṣe'haṁ yoddhukāmānavasthitān
kairmayā saha yoddhavyamasminraṇasamudyame

Arjuna said:

O Acyuta, (Acyuta means one who does not deviate from his divine glory) place my chariot between the two armies and hold it there, till I have carefully observed the war-minded warriors, with whom, I must wage this war. 21-22

Comment:—

'Acyuta senayorubhayormadhye rathaṁ sthāpaya'—The two armies were stationed at such a distance, from each other from where they could shoot arrows etc., at each other. Arjuna asked Lord Kṛṣṇa to place the chariot in the middle. It was middle in two ways (i) The middle of the breadth of the armies. (ii) The middle of the two armies viz., equidistant from the two armies should be the same. His purpose was to see the two armies, easily.

'Senayorubhayormadhye' has been used in the Gītā three times—here (in 1/21), in the twenty-fourth verse of this chapter and in the tenth verse of the second chapter. He uses this phrase three times, because the first time he asks Kṛṣṇa to place the chariot between the two armies (1/21), then Lord Kṛṣṇa placing the chariot between the two armies, tells Arjuna to behold the Kauravas (1/24) and afterwards, preaches the gospel to despondent Arjuna, right there (2/10). To begin with, Arjuna was valiant, but when he saw his kith and kin in battle array, he developed an attitude of disinterest being overtaken by attachment. Finally,

Lord Kṛṣṇa preached the gospel of the Gītā, which dispelled his attachment. It means, that a man in whatever circumstances he is, by making proper use of circumstances, can be free from desires and can realize God, because God (Paramātmā), always remains uniform in all circumstances.

'Yāvadetānnirīkṣe'haṁ......raṇasamudyame'—How long should the chariot be placed between the two armies? Arjuna says, "Hold the chariot there, till I have carefully observed those war-minded kings with their armies, who are stationed in the army of Kauravas and with whom I have to wage war. Let me see the heroes, I have to encounter. Let me, also see which of them are inferior, superior and equal to me, in heroism."

Here, by the phrase 'Yoddhukāmān,' Arjuna means to say, that they sent a proposal of conciliation, but the Kauravas did not accept it, as they had a keen desire to wage war. So, he wants to observe the warriors and their bravery, which makes them so confident to wage war.

योत्स्यमानानवेक्षेऽहं य एतेऽत्र समागताः ।
धार्तराष्ट्रस्य दुर्बुद्धेर्युद्धे प्रियचिकीर्षवः ॥ २३ ॥

yotsyamānānavekṣe'haṁ ya ete'tra samāgatāḥ
dhārtarāṣṭrasya durbuddheryuddhe priyacikīrṣavaḥ

I desire to watch the evil-minded Duryodhana's well-wisher rulers, who have assembled here with their armies and are ready to fight. 23

Comment:—

Dhārtarāṣṭrasya* durbuddheryuddhe priyacikīrṣavaḥ'— Here Arjuna, by calling Duryodhana evil-minded, wants to convey how Duryodhana conspired for their destruction several times and tried his best to humiliate them. Arjuna says, "We are the

* There are two meanings of the term 'Dhārtarāṣṭra'—(1) Dhṛtarāṣṭra's sons or relatives, (2) those who usurp kingdom. Here this term has been used for Dhṛtarāṣṭra's son, Duryodhana.

lawful owners of half the empire but he wants to usurp it. He is evil-minded and these kings have assembled here to try to do good to him. But the duty of a friend, is to give him such advice as may add to his welfare now and hereafter. But, these kings instead of removing his evil-mindedness, want to enhance it and are really degrading him, by instigating him to wage war. They are not thinking of his welfare here and hereafter. As friends, they should have advised him to rule over, half of the kingdom and handover the other half, to us, the Pāṇḍavas. Thus, he would have ruled over half of the empire, and his life in the next world would also have been protected."

'Yotsyamānānavekṣe'haṁ ya ete'tra samāgatāḥ'— I want to observe the warriors, who are so impatient to wage war. They have favoured unrighteousness and injustice; so they are sure to be ruined in the war, against us.

'Yotsyamānān'—it means that Arjuna wants to see those, who have a keen desire to fight.

Link:—In the next two verses, Sañjaya tells us what Lord Kṛṣṇa did after hearing Arjuna's words.

सञ्जय उवाच

एवमुक्तो हृषीकेशो गुडाकेशेन भारत।
सेनयोरुभयोर्मध्ये स्थापयित्वा रथोत्तमम्॥ २४॥
भीष्मद्रोणप्रमुखतः सर्वेषां च महीक्षिताम्।
उवाच पार्थ पश्यैतान् समवेतान्कुरूनिति॥ २५॥

sañjaya uvāca

evamukto hṛṣīkeśo guḍākeśena bhārata
senayorubhayormadhye sthāpayitvā rathottamam
bhīṣmadroṇapramukhataḥ sarveṣāṁ ca mahīkṣitām
uvāca pārtha paśyaitān samavetānkurūniti

Sañjaya said:

"O Bhārata" (born in Bharata-family), thus addressed by Guḍākeśa (one who has control over sleep viz., Arjuna), Hṛṣīkeśa (the Lord of the senses) placed the magnificent chariot between the two armies, in front of Bhīṣma, Droṇa and all the kings, and said, "O Pārtha (the son of Pṛthā, Kuntī), behold all these Kurus, assembled here." 24-25

Comment:—

'Guḍākeśena'—'Guḍākeśa' has two meanings (i) 'Guḍā' means 'curled' and 'Keśa' means 'hair.' It means one having curly hair (ii) 'Guḍākā' means 'sleep' and 'Īśa' means 'master.' It means, one who has conquered sleep. Arjuna had curly hair and he had conquered sleep. So he has been called 'Guḍākeśa'.

'Evamuktaḥ'—One, who is not a slave to sleep, idleness and worldly pleasures, but is a slave (devotee) to God; God listens to such a person and even obeys him. Having said so, in order to carry out the wish of his devotee-friend Arjuna, Lord Kṛṣṇa, placed the chariot between the two armies.

'Hṛṣīkeśaḥ'—'Hṛṣīka' means 'senses' and 'Īśa' means 'Lord.' Thus 'Hṛṣīkeśa means the Lord of the senses. In the twenty-first verse and also in this verse, this word has been used because Lord Kṛṣṇa, who is the inspirer of minds, intellects and senses and who commands the whole world, has become a chariot-driver to carry out Arjuna's wish. It shows how kind He is to Arjuna.

'Senayorubhayormadhye sthāpayitvā rathottamam'—Lord Kṛṣṇa stationed Arjuna's noble chariot in the open space, between the two armies.

'Bhīṣmadroṇapramukhataḥ sarveṣāṁ ca mahīkṣitām'— Lord Kṛṣṇa placed the chariot with His sagacity, at such a point from where his kinsmen such as Bhīṣma, his preceptor Droṇa and chief kings and warriors of Kaurava-army, could be clearly seen.

'Uvāca pārtha paśyaitān samavetānkurūniti'—In the word 'Kuru', the sons of both Dhṛtarāṣṭra and Pāṇḍu are included, because both of them belong to the Kuru family. Lord Kṛṣṇa, by saying 'Behold all these Kurus assembled here' means, that by seeing them, Arjuna may think that they are all one, whether they are on his side or on the opposite side and whether they are good or bad and thus a feeling of kinship may develop in him. This feeling of kinship may lead to attachment and make him inquisitive. Thus, by making Arjuna an instrument, Lord Kṛṣṇa wants to preach the gospel of the Gītā for the benediction of the creatures of Kali-age. Therefore, Lord Kṛṣṇa, instead of using 'Dhārtarāṣṭrān', used the words 'Kurūn'. If he had used 'Dhārtarāṣṭrān', Arjuna would have become enthusiastic and Lord Kṛṣṇa, could not have got a chance to preach the gospel of the Gītā and Arjuna's delusion, born of kinship, could not have been destroyed. But, Lord Kṛṣṇa, thought it His duty to destroy Arjuna's delusion. As a surgeon, first gives medicine, to a patient suffering from a boil so that it may suppurate and then performs an operation, to remove the diseased part, in the same way, God first arouses the hidden delusion of Arjuna and then destroys it. Here, Lord Kṛṣṇa by using the phrase 'kurūn paśya' first arouses delusion in order to destroy it, by advice later.

Arjuna in the twenty-second and twenty-third verses of this chapter wanted to behold and observe them. So Lord Kṛṣṇa says, "Behold these Kurus." Lord Kṛṣṇa could have placed the chariot without uttering any words but he intentionally used the phrase 'kurūn paśya' to arouse attachment in Arjuna.

There is a vast difference, between love for the family and love for God though there is also a little similarity. When we have love for members of our family, we overlook their faults, because we have a feeling of mineness with them. Similarly, God also does not heed the shortcomings of His devotee, because He has the feeling that he is His own. But, in domestic love, importance is attached to matters such as body etc., while in love for God, there is importance of feelings. In family love, there is importance of delusion, while in love for God, there is importance of alliance. In family-love, there is darkness, while in divine love, there is light. In family-love, a man is negligent of his duty, while in love for God, being engrossed in love, a man may forget his duty momentarily, but is never negligent of his duty. In family-love, there is pre-eminence of the family, while in love for God, there is pre-eminence of God.

Link:—In the above-mentioned verse, Lord Kṛṣṇa told Arjuna to behold the Kurus. In the next verse, Sañjaya describes what happened after that.

तत्रापश्यत्स्थितान्पार्थः पितॄनथ पितामहान्।
आचार्यान्मातुलान्भ्रातॄन्पुत्रान्पौत्रान्सखींस्तथा ॥ २६ ॥
श्वशुरान्सुहृदश्चैव सेनयोरुभयोरपि।

tatrāpaśyatsthitānpārthaḥ pitṝnatha pitāmahān
ācāryānmātulānbhrātṝnputrānpautrānsakhīṁstathā
śvaśurānsuhṛdaścaiva senayorubhayorapi

Standing there, Arjuna then saw in both the armies, his uncles, grand-uncles, teachers, maternal uncles, brothers, cousins, sons, grandsons, friends, fathers-in-law, and well-wishers, as well. 26

Comment:—

'Tatrāpaśyatsthitānpārthaḥ pitṝnatha pitāmahān ācāryānmātulānbhrātṝnputrānpautrānsakhīṁstathā śvaśurānsuhṛdaścaiva senayorubhayorapi'—When Lord Kṛṣṇa, told Arjuna to behold the Kurus on the battlefield, Arjuna saw the members of his family, assembled on both sides. He saw his father's brother, named Bhūriśravā, who was just like his father. He saw his grand-uncles—Bhīṣma and Somadatta etc., preceptors—Droṇa and Kṛpa etc., maternal uncles, such as Purujit, Kuntibhoja, Śalya and Śakuni etc., brothers and cousins—Bhīma and Duryodhana etc., sons, such as Abhimanyu, Ghaṭotkaca, Lakṣmaṇa (Duryodhana's son) etc., grandsons, such as the sons of Lakṣmaṇa; friends of Duryodhana, named Aśvatthāmā etc., and also his friends; fathers-in-law such as Drupada and Śaibya etc., and also well-wishers, such as Sātyaki and Kṛtavarmā etc.

Link:—In the next verse there is description of what Arjuna did, after seeing members of his family, in both armies.

तान्समीक्ष्य स कौन्तेयः सर्वान्बन्धूनवस्थितान् ॥ २७ ॥
कृपया परयाविष्टो विषीदन्निदमब्रवीत् ।

tānsamīkṣya sa kaunteyaḥ sarvānbandhūnavasthitān
kṛpayā parayāviṣṭo viṣīdannidamabravīt

Arjuna, the son of Kuntī, seeing all those relations present there and standing at their appointed places was filled with extreme compassion and uttered these following words, in sadness. 27

Comment:—

'Tān sarvānbandhūnavasthitān samīkṣya'—Besides the warriors mentioned in the previous verse, Arjuna saw great grandfathers, such as Bāhlīka etc., brothers-in-law, such as Dhṛṣṭadyumna, Śikhaṇḍī and Suratha etc., sister's husbands, such as Jayadratha etc., and several other relatives, who were posted in different positions in both armies.

'Sa kaunteyaḥ kṛpayā parayāviṣṭaḥ'—'Sa kaunteyaḥ' means, that Arjuna, who was ordered by mother Kuntī to wage war and who full of valour and stout-heartedness, entered the battle-field to observe the chief warriors of the Kaurava-army, was overcome by cowardice.

After seeing the warriors, who were related to him, through family and learning, on both the sides, Arjuna suddenly developed an attitude of kinship with them because he thought that on both sides there were his kinsmen and they would be killed in the war. In this way it was his family that would be destroyed on either side. Thinking thus his stout-heartedness gave place to cowardice and he gave up the idea of war. This faint-heartedness, has been called by Lord Kṛṣṇa (in 2/2-3) 'Kaśmalam' viz., dejection and 'Hṛdayadaurbalyam' viz., weakness of the heart. Arjuna (in 2/7) also accepted it as 'Kārpaṇyadoṣopahatasvabhāvaḥ' viz., nature being tainted by the weakness of faint-heartedness. 'Kṛpayāviṣṭaḥ' means, that faint-heartedness is a temporary phase in him, while stout-heartedness is a permanent virtue, of his life. Thus the temporary phase of faint-heartedness cannot last too long, while his stout-heartedness will remain, forever.

What is extreme cowardice? Extreme cowardice in Arjuna is, that he does not think and make effort to kill his cruel and unrighteous opponents, such as Duryodhana, Duḥśāsana and Śakuni etc., who, without any reason, insulted the Pāṇḍavas gave them trouble and tried to kill them, somehow or the other. On the other hand, he is taking pity on them (Gītā 1/35,46) and is thus deviating from his duty, of the warrior-class.

'Viṣīdannidamabravīt'—Arjuna, is very much dejected after thinking over the consequences of a war for the family, tribe and country, and speaks the following words.

अर्जुन उवाच

दृष्ट्वेमं स्वजनं कृष्ण युयुत्सुं समुपस्थितम् ॥ २८ ॥
सीदन्ति मम गात्राणि मुखं च परिशुष्यति ।
वेपथुश्च शरीरे मे रोमहर्षश्च जायते ॥ २९ ॥
गाण्डीवं स्रंसते हस्तात्त्वक्चैव परिदह्यते ।
न च शक्नोम्यवस्थातुं भ्रमतीव च मे मनः ॥ ३० ॥

arjuna uvāca

dṛṣṭvemaṁ svajanaṁ kṛṣṇa yuyutsuṁ samupasthitam
sīdanti mama gātrāṇi mukhaṁ ca pariśuṣyati

vepathuśca śarīre me romaharṣaśca jāyate
gāṇḍīvaṁ sraṁsate hastāttvakcaiva paridahyate
na ca śaknomyavasthātuṁ bhramatīva ca me manaḥ

Arjuna said:

O Kṛṣṇa, at the sight of these kinsmen thus arrayed here, eager to wage war, my limbs give way, my mouth is parched, my body shivers and hair stand on end. The bow, Gāṇḍīva slips from my hand, my skin burns all over. My mind is reeling as it were and I am not able even, to stand. 28—30

Comment:—

'Dṛṣṭvemaṁ svajanaṁ kṛṣṇa yuyutsuṁ samupasthitam'— Arjuna loved the name Kṛṣṇa, very much. So he has been addressed by this name in the Gītā nine time, more than any other name. Lord Kṛṣṇa, similarly loved Arjuna's name 'Pārtha' (the son of Pṛthā, Kuntī). Therefore, while talking together, both of them addressed each other by these names and this fact was well-known to other people also. Therefore, Sañjaya at the end of the Gītā in 18/78 mentions 'Kṛṣṇa', and 'Pārtha'—'Yatra yogeśvaraḥ kṛṣṇo yatra pārtho dhanurdharaḥ (viz., wherever is Kṛṣṇa, the Lord of Yoga and wherever is Pārtha (Arjuna), the wielder of the bow).

Dhṛtarāṣtra, in the first verse of this chapter, uses the phrase 'Samavetā Yuyutsavaḥ' (gathered together desirous to fight) and Arjuna here has said, 'Yuyutsuṁ Samupasthitam' (arrayed eager to fight). But there is a vast difference, in the views of the two. Dhṛtarāṣtra is partial to his sons. So, he uses the words 'Māmakāḥ' (Mine), and 'Pāṇḍavāḥ' (Pāṇḍu's). But Arjuna is impartial. So he uses the term 'Svajanam' (Kinsmen), which includes, persons of both sides. It means, that Dhṛtarāṣṭra is worried about the death of his sons in the warfare, while Arjuna is worried about the death of warriors, in both armies, because he thinks that both the warring groups, are his own kith and kin.

Till now the word 'Dṛṣṭvā' (having seen), has been used three times—'Dṛṣṭvā tu pāṇḍavānīkam' (Having seen the army of the Pāṇḍavas) (1/2), 'Vyavasthitān dṛṣṭvā dhārtarāṣṭrān' (Having seen Dhṛtarāṣṭra's party arrayed) (1/20), and here 'Dṛṣṭvemaṁ svajanam' (Having seen these kinsmen). It means, that there is no change in the attitude of Duryodhana, as far as war is concerned. But, there is a lot of change in Arjuna's attitude. First, after seeing the sons of Dhṛtarāṣṭra, Arjuna like a hero, gets ready for war. But after seeing his relatives present there, he is overwhelmed with extreme compassion, his bow slips from his hand, and he is not inclined to fight.

'Sīdanti mama gātrāṇi........bhramatīva ca me manaḥ'—Thinking of the consequences of the war, Arjuna is worried and sad. So his limbs are giving way, his mouth is getting parched, his body shakes, and his hair is standing on an end. The same Gāṇḍīva bow, the sound of whose string, terrified enemies, is dropping from his hand and his skin is burning all over.* His mind is reeling, he is in a dilemma, and he is unable even to stand at the war-front. He feels, as if he will fall unconscious, and thinks it is a sin to wage war.

Link:—After describing the eight signs of his sadness in the previous verses, now Arjuna mentions the inappropriateness of war with inauspicious omens, he sees.

निमित्तानि च पश्यामि विपरीतानि केशव।
न च श्रेयोऽनुपश्यामि हत्वा स्वजनमाहवे॥ ३१॥

nimittāni ca paśyāmi viparītāni keśava
na ca śreyo'nupaśyāmi hatvā svajanamāhave

O Keśava, I also find the omens inauspicious and I do not see any good in killing my kith and kin, in battle. 31

* Worry had been compared with pyre. There is a little difference between the two. Worry burns a living man while pyre burns a dead man.

Comment:—

'Nimittāni ca paśyāmi viparītāni keśava'—O Keśava, I find the omens* inauspicious. Enthusiasm in the beginning of an activity, leads it to success, while dilemma leads, to failure. So Arjuna says that the omens—that his limbs are giving way, his body is shaking, his mouth is getting parched—are not auspicious.† Besides, these, other omens, such as the falling of a meteor, untimely eclipse, earthquake, horrible sound of birds and animals, obliteration of a black mark in the moon, falling of blood from clouds, are inauspicious and all of these augur ill.

'Na ca śreyo'nupaśyāmi hatvā svajanamāhave'—I do not see any good, in killing my kith and kin either in this world or in the next, because only a sinner can destroy his kith and kin. Therefore, sin, alone will accrue to us by killing them, and that sin will lead us to hell.

In this verse, in both 'Nimittāni paśyāmi' (I see omens) and 'Śreyaḥ anupaśyāmi' (I see good)‡ Arjuna wants to say that, whether he goes by the omens or by this common sense, it is certain that it is futile to wage war, and there is no good in it, for them and for the entire world.

Link:—In the next verse Arjuna expresses his reluctance to get such an undesirable victory.

न काङ्क्षे विजयं कृष्ण न च राज्यं सुखानि च।
किं नो राज्येन गोविन्द किं भोगैर्जीवितेन वा॥ ३२॥

---

* The omens are not responsible for the occurrence of the incidents, they merely fortell the incidents.

† What Arjuna is regarding as omens are not omens in fact. They are the defects of senses, body, mind and intellect which Arjuna finds in him because of his sadness.

‡ Here the verb 'Paśyāmi' has been used for the omens of the past and the present and verb 'Anupaśyāmi' has been used for the consequence in future.

na kāṅkṣe vijayaṁ kṛṣṇa na ca rājyaṁ sukhāni ca
kiṁ no rājyena govinda kiṁ bhogairjīvitena vā

O Kṛṣṇa, I covet not victory, nor kingdom, nor pleasure. O Govinda, of what use to us is kingdom or luxuries or even life? 32

Comment:—

'Na kāṅkṣe vijayaṁ kṛṣṇa na ca rājyaṁ sukhānī ca'— Suppose, we get victory and then we get the kingdom of the entire earth and also pleasures. These are of no avail. I do not want either victory, kingdom or pleasure.

'Kiṁ no rājyena govinda kiṁ bhogairjīvitena vā'—When we do not desire anything (victory, kingdom and pleasure) of what use to us, is kingdom or pleasure? Victory, kingdom and pleasure, seem pleasant only, when there is desire for these. But we have no desire for these. So, how can these be pleasant to us? After killing our kith and kin, we have no desire to live, because after death, who will enjoy pleasure? The so-called pleasure, will rather lead us to worry and unhappiness.

Link:—In the next verse Arjuna gives the reason, why he has no desire for victory etc.

येषामर्थे काङ्क्षितं नो राज्यं भोगाः सुखानि च ।
त इमेऽवस्थिता युद्धे प्राणांस्त्यक्त्वा धनानि च ॥ ३३ ॥

yeṣāmarthe kāṅkṣitaṁ no rājyaṁ bhogāḥ sukhāni ca
ta ime'vasthitā yuddhe prāṇāṁstyaktvā dhanāni ca

Those, for whose sake we seek kingdom, enjoyment and pleasure, are here, arrayed on the battlefield, staking their lives and property. 33

Comment:—

'Yeṣāmarthe kāṅkṣitaṁ no rājyaṁ bhogāḥ sukhāni ca'— Whatever kingdom, pleasure and enjoyment we desire, we want these for our relatives and friends. With these, we want to please and serve our teachers, uncles, grand-uncles, and sons etc. We do not want to possess these for our personal enjoyment.

'Ta ime'vasthitā yuddhe prāṇāṁstyaktvā dhanāni ca'— But all of these are arrayed here on the battlefield, staking their lives and property. They have decided to sacrifice even their lives, on the war front. If all of them are killed, for whom should we desire kingdom, prosperity and pleasure?

'Prāṇāṁstyaktvā dhanāni ca', means that they are standing on the battlefield, staking their lives and prosperity. If they had got a desire for life and prosperity, why would they stand here, to be slain? It means, that they have renounced, every hope.

Link:—In the next two verses there is description of the people, for whom Arjuna wants kingdom, pleasure and enjoyment.

आचार्याः * पितरः पुत्रास्तथैव च पितामहाः ।
मातुलाः श्वशुराः पौत्राः श्यालाः सम्बन्धिनस्तथा ॥ ३४ ॥
एतान्न हन्तुमिच्छामि घ्नतोऽपि मधुसूदन ।
अपि त्रैलोक्यराज्यस्य हेतोः किं नु महीकृते ॥ ३५ ॥

ācāryāḥ pitaraḥ putrāstathaiva ca pitāmahāḥ
mātulāḥ śvaśurāḥ pautrāḥ śyālāḥ sambandhinastathā
etānna hantumicchāmi ghnato'pi madhusūdana
api trailokyarājyasya hetoḥ kiṁ nu mahīkṛte

Teachers, uncles, fathers, sons, as well as grand-uncles, maternal uncles, fathers-in-law, grandsons, brothers-in-law and other relatives, though they may kill me, I would not seek to slay

* In the twenty-sixth verse Arjuna by saying 'Pitṝnatha pitāmahān...' has mentioned uncles and grand-uncles first but here by saying 'Ācāryāḥ pitaraḥ....' he has mentioned teachers first. It means that because of his love for his kith and kin there he mentions uncles first, while in this context of 'not slaying' he first mentions the teachers who are great well-wishers of human beings.

them, even for the sovereignty of the three worlds; and least, for this earth? 34-35

Comment:—

[Lord Kṛṣṇa in the twenty-first verse of the sixteenth chapter, says that passion, anger and greed, these constitute the triple gates to hell. Really these three, are different forms of passion. These are born out of our attachment for worldly things and person. Passion has two sides—to get the desired thing, and to get rid of undesired one. Desired things include accumulation and enjoyment. The desire for, accumulation is known as 'greed' and, desire for enjoyments, is called 'passion.' If desire for accumulation and enjoyment is not satisfied, anger accrues. In anger, men perform actions, to destroy those who create obstacles, in the fulfilment of their desires. It proves, that men fight to get desired things and to get rid of undesired ones. But Arjuna, does not want to fight for either of the two.]

'Ācāryāḥ pitaraḥ....kiṁ nu mahīkṛte'—If our kith and kin, being prompted by greed or anger want to slay me, I do not seek to kill them, out of anger or greed, because these two are the gateways to hell.

Here the word 'Api' has been used, two times by Arjuna. It means, first why should they kill me when I do not create any obstacle to their selfish motive? Even then suppose, they slay me, by thinking that I worked as an obstacle to their selfish motive, I do not seek to slay them. Secondly, though there is no possibility for the sovereignty of the three worlds coming to me by killing them, yet, if I get it, I do not seek to slay them.

'Madhusūdana'*—It means that you killed the demons, such as Madhu etc. But these teachers, such as Droṇa etc., and grand-uncles, such as Bhīṣma etc., are not demons, they are our near and dear ones. So, why should I have a desire to kill them?

* Lord Kṛṣṇa is called Madhusūdana because he killed the demon named Madhu.

'Ācāryāḥ'—I should serve respected and benevolent teachers, such as Droṇa etc., rather than fight them. It is appropriate on our part, even to sacrifice out lives at their feet.

'Pitaraḥ'—How can we slay our uncles (fathers), out of anger or greed, when we have got this body linked with them?

'Putrāḥ'—It is our duty to bring up our sons and our brother's sons, even though they may stand against us or act badly.

'Pitāmahāḥ'—When our grand-uncles are worthy of adoration, as our father, they deserve still greater adoration, from us. Though, they may rebuke and punish us, yet we should not cause any suffering to them, we should rather serve them and give comfort to them.

'Mātulāḥ'—Our maternal uncles, being the brothers of our mothers, who rear us, deserve adoration from us.

'Śvaśurāḥ'—These fathers-in-law, are the father to my wife and my brother's wives. They are just like fathers to us. So how can I slay them?

'Pautrāḥ'—We should bring up our grandsons, in a better way, than our sons, rather than kill them.

'Śyālāḥ'—How can we slay the loving brothers of our wives?

'Sambandhinaḥ'—I should serve and bring up all the relatives, rather than kill them. It is improper on our part, to kill them, even for the sovereignty of the three worlds.

Link:—Now Arjuna justifies his intention, not to slay his kith and kin, even from a point of view of consequences.

निहत्य धार्तराष्ट्रान्नः का प्रीतिः स्याज्जनार्दन।
पापमेवाश्रयेदस्मान्हत्वैतानाततायिनः ॥ ३६ ॥

nihatya dhārtarāṣṭrānnaḥ kā prītiḥ syājjanārdana
pāpamevāśrayedasmānhatvaitānātatāyinaḥ

O Janārdana, (Janārdana, the name of Śrī Kṛṣṇa, means a person who is worshipped by people for prosperity and emancipation), what delight can we derive by slaying the sons of Dhṛtarāṣṭra? Sin alone will attach us by slaying these desperadoes. 36

Comment:—

'Nihatya dhārtarāṣṭrānnaḥ kā prītiḥ syājjanārdana pāpamevāśrayedasmānhatvaitānātatāyinaḥ—We cannot derive even the slightest joy, by slaying the sons of Dhṛtarāṣṭra and the warriors of their army. If we kill them, out of anger or greed, we shall have to repent, because the memory of those kinsmen will obsess us and the grief of their death, will torment us. We cannot get joy in this world, by killing them and sin will accrue, to us in the next world, which will torment us there.

There are six kinds of desperadoes—one who sets fire, who poisons, who murders, who seizes wealth, who usurps kingdoms and those who kidnap others' wives.*

Duryodhana and his companions have committed all these criminal offences. They secretly set fire to the residence, where Pāṇḍavas were expected to be sleeping, they poisoned Bhīma and threw him into water; they made an attempt on the life of Pāṇḍavas; while gambling, deceitfully they deprived Pāṇḍavas of their wealth and kingdom, and in the assembly, Duryodhana insulted Draupadī, by calling her his waiting-maid and persuaded Jayadratha to kidnap Draupadī, and he kidnapped her.

In the scriptures, it is mentioned that there is no sin in killing a desperado (Manusmṛti 8/351). But, it is also mentioned in the scriptures, that non-violence is of great virtue. Therefore, why should we slay our kith and kin, out of anger and greed?

Though Duryodhana etc., being desperadoes, deserve to be killed, yet sin will accrue to us as a result of such action, because they are our kith and kin. It is mentioned in the scriptures, that

* Vasiṣṭha smṛti 3/19

one who kills his kith and kin, is a great sinner. So how can we kill them? Therefore, it is better to break off our relationship with them, rather than to kill them. In the same way, as relationship could be cut off from a son, but he cannot be slain.

Link:—Having pointed out the evil consequences of war, Arjuna now dwells upon the sheer impropriety of waging war.

तस्मान्नार्हा वयं हन्तुं धार्तराष्ट्रान् स्वबान्धवान्।
स्वजनं हि कथं हत्वा सुखिनः स्याम माधव॥ ३७॥

tasmānnārhā vayaṁ hantuṁ dhārtarāṣṭrān svabāndhavān
svajanaṁ hi kathaṁ hatvā sukhinaḥ syāma mādhava

O Mādhava, therefore we should not slay the sons of Dhṛtarāṣṭra, our kinsmen; for how can we, by killing our own kinsmen, gain happiness? 37

Comment:—

'Tasmānnārhā vayaṁ hantuṁ dhārtarāṣṭrān svabāndhavān'— The arguments against the slaughter of our kith and kin, advanced so far (from 1/28 to this verse) are enough to convince us, that it is improper to indulge in a destructive activity, like war. How can we, who are regarded as virtuous persons, perform such a hideous act?

'Svajanaṁ hi kathaṁ hatvā sukhinaḥ syāma mādhava'— Mādhava, if mere thought of their slaughter, is so painful, just imagine how much more painful, it would be to slay them, after being blinded by avarice and anger. How can we feel happy after their slaughter? They are our close relations.

Delusion, which is born of a sense of mine, deprives Arjuna of his sense of duty, as a member of the warrior-class. Where there is delusion, there is no discretion. When discretion is suppressed by delusion, the sense of duty, gets blurred.

Link:—The question arises, why Duryodhana does not think along the same lines, as you are thinking, since you are also his kith and kin. Arjuna explains this, in the two verses that follow.

यद्यप्येते न पश्यन्ति लोभोपहतचेतसः।
कुलक्षयकृतं दोषं मित्रद्रोहे च पातकम्॥ ३८॥
कथं न ज्ञेयमस्माभिः पापादस्मान्निवर्तितुम्।
कुलक्षयकृतं दोषं प्रपश्यद्भिर्जनार्दन॥ ३९॥

yadyapyete na paśyanti lobhopahatacetasaḥ
kulakṣayakṛtaṁ doṣaṁ mitradrohe ca pātakam
kathaṁ na jñeyamasmābhiḥ pāpādasmānnivartitum
kulakṣayakṛtaṁ doṣam prapaśyadbhirjanārdana

Although these people, with their understanding (discrimination) clouded by greed do not perceive the evil of destruction of their own families and the sin accruing from enmity towards friends, yet O Janārdana (Kṛṣṇa), why should we, who see clearly the sin involved, in the destruction of the family, not think of turning away from such a sin? 38-39

Comment:—

'Yadyapyete na paśyanti lobhopahatacetasaḥ kulakṣayakṛtaṁ doṣaṁ mitradrohe ca pātakam'—Greed, consists in desiring to have more and more of wealth, property, praise, respect and rank. It is because of greed, that Duryodhana etc., lost discretion and so they do not think about the disastrous consequences of war and the sin, that will accrue out of it.

This extraordinary greed, had deprived them of their sense of discretion, and little do they realize, that the kingdom for which they are bent upon committing the sin of destroying their kith and kin, will not stay long, with them. The pleasure of possession, is soon followed by the pain of deprivation, which far outweighs the pleasure of possession. With minds clouded by greed for the kingdom they do not perceive the deadly sin, which will arise by destroying their own families.

A battle causes loss of time, energy, life and property, and people are assailed by worries and hardships. When there is a quarrel between two friends, they turn into enemies. Drupada and Droṇa had been friends since childhood. After getting the kingdom one day Drupada insulted Droṇa, with the result, that their friendship turned into enmity. To avenge his insult Droṇa got Drupada defeated by his pupil, Arjuna, and thus got half of his kingdom. Then Drupada, got a holy sacrifice performed to destroy Droṇa, and thus both Dhṛṣṭadyumna and Draupadī, were born. Thus, they do not perceive the evil of destruction of the race, and the sin, that will accrue from enmity towards friends.

An Important Matter

We managed life well, without things which we do not possess. The paucity of things was not so painful as it is, if we miss those things, after possessing them. But these things can be with us for a short time, only, because these can stay with us so long as our fortune favours us, and then they, slip away. Thus, we remain the same as we were, without getting these. We had to work hard to get them and are now sad, after losing them. After getting them, we felt somewhat happy, only because of our greed. If we do not have this evil of greed, we can never be happy after getting the things. Similarly, we get happiness from members of our family, because of love and delusion. Thus, we see that we derive worldly pleasure out of evil. Without evil, no worldly pleasure is possible. If there is no greed, there cannot be any pleasure, in accumulation of wealth. Greed destroys our discretion, and we cannot think in the right perspective.

'Kathaṁ na jñeyamasmābhiḥ prapaśyadbhirjanārdana'—Arjuna says—"Though Duryodhana etc., do not perceive any guilt in the extermination of their family, and sin accruing from enmity towards friends yet we should desist from such a sin. (It will be described from the 40th verse to the 44th verse), because we know it very well, that destruction of family is an evil, and enmity towards friends, is a sin. If those friends cause up pain, it will not be harmful for us, because pain will destroy our sins and purify us. But, if we have feelings of malice and enmity, those feelings remain with us, in other births also, will instigate us to commit sins and lead us to, degradation. Therefore, we should certainly forsake such a sin.

Here, Arjuna is thinking about the greed of Duryodhana etc., but he is not thinking about his own, infatuation and delusion. So he cannot understand his duty. It is a rule, that a man cannot perceive his failings as long he perceives defects, in others. He feels rather proud of his superiority, that he has no defect, while the fact is that, everyone generally, possesses one defect or the other. If we find fault with others, it is also a defect. Beings proud of one's own virtues and finding fault with others are the two defects which we do not perceive in us, though we do possess these. Thus Arjuna cannot perceive his own infatuation and delusion, because he is finding fault with Duryodhana, and is proud of his virtue (all evils persist under the cover of pride).

Link:—Now in the next five verses, Arjuna mentions the sins accruing from destruction of one's own family.

कुलक्षये प्रणश्यन्ति कुलधर्माः सनातनाः ।
धर्मे नष्टे कुलं कृत्स्नमधर्मोऽभिभवत्युत ॥ ४० ॥

kulakṣaye praṇaśyanti kuladharmāḥ sanātanāḥ
dharme naṣṭe kulaṁ kṛtsnamadharmo'bhibhavatyuta

With the destruction of a family its agelong family traditions disappear and with the absence of family traditions, impiety takes hold of the entire family. 40

Comment:—

'Kulakṣaye praṇaśyanti kuladharmāḥ sanātanāḥ'—In a war, there is destruction of family. The family has its agelong traditions and time-honoured usage. But when a family is destroyed, its pious traditions and usage, which lead the living and dead members of the family to benediction, also perish, because no one remains, to maintain these.

'Dharme naṣṭe kulaṁ kṛtsnamadharmo'bhibhavatyuta'—When pious traditions and pious conduct, perish, people lose their virtues and righteousness, and impiety takes hold of an entire family.

Now the doubt arises, how impiety takes hold of the family when it is destroyed. The answer is, that when people who wage war are killed, impiety takes hold of the children and women, who do not take part in battle, but are left behind. The reason is that when fit and experienced persons die in battle, no one is left behind to control the children and women, and to teach them good conduct and virtuous behaviour. So they do not behave decently that is supposed to mark, righteous persons. So impiety takes hold of them.

अधर्माभिभवात्कृष्ण प्रदुष्यन्ति कुलस्त्रियः ।
स्त्रीषु दुष्टासु वार्ष्णेय जायते वर्णसङ्करः ॥ ४१ ॥

adharmābhibhavātkṛṣṇa praduṣyanti kulastriyaḥ
strīṣu duṣṭāsu vārṣṇeya jāyate varṇasaṅkaraḥ

When impiety prevails, O, Kṛṣṇa, the women of a family become perverse and with their degradation, O, Vārṣṇeya (descendant of Vṛṣṇi), a hybrid mixture of castes, results. 41

Comment:—

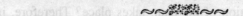

'Adharmābhibhavātkṛṣṇa praduṣyanti kulastriyaḥ'—By following righteousness, inner sense is purified. With the purification of inner sense; intellect becomes pure and pious and placid (sāttvikī). Intellect has discrimination between right and wrong. But, when there is growth of impiety, in family, the conduct of members in the family, becomes bad. Bad conduct fouls the inner sense whose inner sense, makes the intellect 'tāmasī' (the intellect which veils knowledge and binds one to carelessness is called 'tāmasī'). With this 'Tāmasī' intellect, men lose discrimination, regard the undesirable as desirable, and the desirable as undesirable and act against ordinance of scriptures. With such an intellect women become depraved viz., unchaste.

'Strīṣu duṣṭāsu vārṣṇeya jāyate varṇasaṅkaraḥ'—Depraved women give birth to hybrids.* If man and woman belong to different castes, the offspring born of the couple, is known as a hybrid, (mixture).

Here, Arjuna by addressing the Lord as 'Kṛṣṇa', means to say that He attracts everyone. He further asks him, in which direction, He will pull his family.

Arjuna addresses him as Vārṣṇeya, because He belonged to the Vṛṣṇi clan. He means to say, to what clan will his descendants belong, when destruction of his clan, takes place? Therefore, it is not proper to destroy the clan.

सङ्करो नरकायैव कुलघ्नानां कुलस्य च।
पतन्ति पितरो ह्येषां लुप्तपिण्डोदकक्रियाः ॥ ४२ ॥

saṅkaro narakāyaiva kulaghnānāṁ kulasya ca
patanti pitaro hyeṣāṁ luptapiṇḍodakakriyāḥ

A mixture of castes leads the family as also the destroyers of a family to hell. Deprived of the ritual offerings of rice-balls and

* 'Saṅkaraḥ' means the mixture of contrary things. When men do not perform duties and righteousness, intermixture of castes, races, dresses, languages and foods etc., ensues.

water, the manes of their family also have a downfall. 42

Comment:—

'Saṅkaro narakāyaiva kulaghnānāṁ kulasya ca'—The offsprings, that are born of an intermixture of castes, are not religious-minded and do not possess righteousness and rectitude, because they themselves are the product of persons, without virtue. So they behave against traditions and decorum of a race. Those who kill persons of a race war are called destroyers of the race. Such persons, lead not only themselves but also the whole race, to hell, because of destruction of traditions, of the race.

'Patanti pitaro hyeṣāṁ luptapiṇḍodakakriyāḥ'—The manes of the destroyers of a race, fall because they do not get the ritual offerings of rice-balls (Piṇḍa) and water from them. The reason is, that when they get these offerings, because of those virtuous actions, they go to higher worlds. But, when they do not get those offerings, they cannot continue to live in those worlds and they are degraded.

A descendant, who is a hybrid has no regard for his ancestors, and he has no sentiment to offer anything, to them. Moreover, even if he offers anything, such as obsequies, as a social custom, without any regard and against the ordinance of scriptures, that is not received by the manes. The reason is, that he is not eligible to perform such rites. So they have a fall.

Appendix—There are two types of manes—'ājāna' and 'martya'. The manes who live in the world of manes are 'ājāna', while the manes who go to the world of manes after dying from the human-world are 'martya'. The 'martya' manes being deprived of the ritual offerings of rice-balls and water, have a downfall. Only those 'martya' manes have a downfall who have affinity for the family and offspring and expect to receive the ritual offerings of rice-balls and water.

Colophon—In the colophon of the Gītā the three expressions 'brahmavidyāyāṁ', 'yogaśāstre' and 'śrīkṛṣṇārjunasaṁvāde' have been used in the singular number but 'Śrīmadbhagavadgītāsu' and 'upaniṣatsu'—these two expressions have been used in the plural number. It means that in all the upaniṣads, Śrīmadbhagavadgītā is also an upaniṣad in which 'brahmavidyā' (the discipline of knowledge), 'yogaśāstra' (the discipline of action) and 'Śrīkṛṣṇārjuna saṁvāda' (the discipline of devotion)—the three have been included.

In the Gītā 'Śrīkṛṣṇārjuna saṁvāda' viz., the dialogue between Lord Kṛṣṇa and Arjuna begins with devotion and ends in devotion. In the beginning Arjuna, being confused with regard to his duty, takes refuge in God—'śiṣyaste'haṁ śādhi māṁ tvāṁ prapannam' (Gītā 2/7) and in the end being inspired by the Lord for taking refuge in Him alone, by the expression 'māmekaṁ śaranaṁ vraja', Arjuna takes refuge in Him alone, when he declares—'kariṣye vacanaṁ tava' (I will do your bidding). Arjuna asked Lord Kṛṣṇa the means by which he might attain the highest good (Gītā 2/7, 3/2, 5/1). Therefore the Lord has also described 'Jñānayoga' (the discipline of knowledge) and 'Karmayoga' (the discipline of action) in the Gītā.

दोषैरेतैः कुलघ्नानां वर्णसङ्करकारकैः ।
उत्साद्यन्ते जातिधर्माः कुलधर्माश्च शाश्वताः ॥ ४३ ॥

doṣairetaiḥ kulaghnānāṁ varṇasaṅkarakārakaiḥ
utsādyante jātidharmāḥ kuladharmāśca śāśvatāḥ

Agelong caste-traditions and family-customs of the destroyers of a family get eradicated because of the intermixture created by the bad deeds of these destroyers of clans. 43

Comment:—

Doṣairetaiḥ kulaghnānāṁ.......kuladharmāśca śāśvatāḥ'— With the destruction of a race in war, family-traditions are ruined. With the ruin of family-traditions, impiety takes hold. With the growth of impiety, the women become depraved. With the vices there ensues an intermixture of castes. With the intermixture of castes caste-traditions of the clan-destroyers are ruined.

What are 'Kula Dharma' and 'Jāti Dharma'? In every caste, a family has its own traditions, customs and decorum which are known, as, 'Kula Dharma', whereas, the traditions of a caste as a whole, are known as 'Jāti Dharma' or 'Varṇa Dharma.' These traditions are general and these are approved by the scriptures. These traditions get ruined, if not followed.

उत्सन्नकुलधर्माणां मनुष्याणां जनार्दन।
नरकेऽनियतं वासो भवतीत्यनुशुश्रुम॥४४॥

utsannakuladharmāṇāṁ manuṣyāṇāṁ janārdana
narake'niyataṁ vāso bhavatītyanuśuśruma

We have heard, O Janārdana, that men, who have lost their family traditions, dwell in hell, for an indefinite period of time. 44

Comment:—

'Utsannakuladharmāṇāṁ manuṣyāṇāṁ janārdana narake'-niyataṁ vāso bhavatītyanuśuśruma'—God has endowed man, with discretion and the right to perform, new deeds. hence, he is free to perform good or bad actions. He should use discretion in performing actions. But he being captive of greed, of pleasure etc., does not use his discretion and acts against the ordinance of scriptures, and family-traditions. Consequently, he is criticised, insulted and looked down upon, in this life and suffers tortures of hell for a long time, in the life to come. This is, what we have heard from our elders and ancestors.

In the word 'Manuṣyāṇām' the clan-destroyers and all other

members of the race, including ancestors of the race-destroyers viz., manes and their descendants, have been included.

Link:—In the verse that follows, we are told how Arjuna was influenced by the description of disastrous consequences of fighting a battle.

अहो बत महत्पापं कर्तुं व्यवसिता वयम्।
यद्राज्यसुखलोभेन हन्तुं स्वजनमुद्यताः ॥ ४५ ॥

aho bata mahatpāpaṁ kartuṁ vyavasitā vayam
yadrājyasukhalobhena hantuṁ svajanamudyatāḥ

Alas! Goaded by the lust for throne and enjoyment, we seem bent on perpetrating the great sin, of killing our kinsmen. 45

Comment:—

'Aho bata mahatpāpaṁ kartuṁ vyavasitā vayaṁ yadrājya-sukhalobhena hantuṁ svajanamudyatāḥ'—Duryodhana and his companions, are villains. Being goaded by greed, they are not guided by righteousness and so they are prepared to wage a war. We have the power to discriminate between righteousness and unrighteousness, virtue and vice, but we are also prepared to wage war to kill our own kinsmen, just like ignorant people. So it is something very surprising and shocking. By doing so, we are going to commit a great sin, by turning a deaf ear to the teachings of preceptors and scriptures.

The word 'Aho' expresses surprise. It is surprising, that we have decided to commit sin by waging this war, even having known its horrifying consequences. The word 'Bata', expresses sorrow. It is a matter of sorrow, that we are prepared to slay our kith and kin, being over powered by greed, for a transient kingdom and pleasure.

Greed for kingdom and pleasure, is the only cause, for

perpetrating the great sin of killing our kinsmen. It means, that if we get victory in the battle, we shall get kingdom, wealth, honour, glory, power, pleasure and luxuries. Such greed for kingdom and enjoyment, is totally unjustified for such people as us.

In this verse, Arjuna wants to say that a man can carry out the behest of scriptures and teachers etc., only by honouring his own good ideas, and his own knowledge. But he who dishonours them, cannot adopt virtuous principles of scriptures and teachers. Thus good thoughts and ideas do not arise up in him. Then, who can check him from possessing evil thoughts and performing evil actions? Similarly, if we disregard our knowledge, who can check us from committing the great sin of killing our kinsmen?

Here, Arjuna is thinking about the disastrous consequences of war and so he is not willing to wage it. But he is not thinking that his feelings of attachment, selfishness and delusion for the family, are responsible for his behaviour which is totally wrong for a thoughtful, righteous and brave member, of the warrior-class.

[Arjuna in the thirty-eighth verse states that Duryodhana etc., with mind blinded by greed do not perceive the evil of destruction of their own clan and the sin accruing from enmity towards friends. Here, he says that goaded by the greed for throne and enjoyment, they themselves are prepared to commit a great sin. It proves that Arjuna knows that greed is the cause of sins. But, in the thirty-sixth verse of the third chapter, he asks, "Impelled by what does a man commit sin, unwillingly? And why?" The answer is, that he has a feeling of attachment and affection for the family, so he wants to turn away from war. He thinks, that greed is the root cause of the sin of destruction of one's own clan. But, by hearing the gospel of the Gītā, he wants to know the path or discipline by pursuing which, he may obtain the highest good—the supreme bliss (Gītā 3/2). So, in the third chapter he asks, which is the force that impels a man to abandon his duty viz., (in 3/36) Arjuna, asks the question as a striver, about his duty, not as a person, having attachment for his family.]

Link:—Engrossed in surprise and sorrow, Arjuna in the verse that follows relates his decision, arrived at after these arguments.

यदि मामप्रतीकारमशस्त्रं शस्त्रपाणयः।
धार्तराष्ट्रा रणे हन्युस्तन्मे क्षेमतरं भवेत्॥४६॥

yadi māmapratīkāramaśastraṁ śastrapāṇayaḥ
dhārtarāṣṭrā raṇe hanyustanme kṣemataraṁ bhavet

It would, indeed, be better for me, if the sons of Dhṛtarāṣṭra armed with weapons, killed me in battle, with me, while I will be unarmed and unresisting. 46

Comment:—

'Yadi māmapratīkāramaśastraṁ śastrapāṇayaḥ dhārtarāṣṭrā raṇe hanyustanme kṣemataraṁ bhavet'—Arjuna says, "If I turn away from the war, perhaps our opponents will also desist from it. Why will they fight, if we are determined not to fight? But even if, regarding us as their enemy, they zealously, armed with weapons kill me, that will indeed be in my own interest, as it will be a kind of repentance for the determination, which I had made, in the war to kill my preceptors, and I shall be purified of the sins. It means that if I do not wage war, I will escape sin and my race, will not be destroyed."

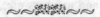

[When a man talks about a subject, it has its effect, on him also. When Arjuna, possessed by extreme passion, started to speak in sadness, in the twenty-eighth verse, he was not so much overwhelmed with grief as he was now. Then, Arjuna did not turn away from war, but went on speaking, overwhelmed with grief. But at last, he turns away from war, and sits down having laid down his bow and arrow. Lord Kṛṣṇa did not speak, to enable Arjuna to give an outlet for his feelings of sadness completely, because he knew, that his teachings would be of some avail to him, only when there was an outlet for his sorrow.]

An Important Fact

Worldly people will support the arguments adduced by Arjuna, but they will not agree with Lord Kṛṣṇa, who will justify war later. The reason is, that as Arjuna is full of attachment and love, the worldly people also belong to the same class. So they cannot understand the point of view, expressed by Lord Kṛṣṇa, who always thinks about the welfare and benediction of beings. They will say that Arjuna wanted to escape the sin, by not waging war, but it was Lord Kṛṣṇa, who inspired him to wage war. So, it was not proper on His part, to do so.

The fact is, that Lord Kṛṣṇa did not make Arjuna wage war. He reminded him of his duty only. It was Arjuna, who had invited Lord Kṛṣṇa, to the war front. But seeing his kinsmen on the hostile side, he was turning away from his duty. So Lord Kṛṣṇa reminded him not to neglect his duty, out of delusion but to wage war, because there was nothing more welcome to a member of the warrior-class than a righteous war.

For example; if a man is going to Badrīnārāyaṇa, but by mistake he starts going in the opposite direction. He then happens to meet a person, who asks him where he was going. The latter, tells him that he has taken the wrong direction, so he should turn back, in order to reach his destination. Here, the person shows the right direction (way), to the man who had lost it. Similarly, Lord Kṛṣṇa showed Arjuna the right direction, of his duty.

After seeing his kinsmen arrayed, on the war front, Arjuna said to Lord Kṛṣṇa, "I will not fight" (2/9). But after hearing the gospel of Lord Kṛṣṇa he did not say "I'll not fight" but he said, "I will carry out your bidding" (18/73) viz., "I will do my duty." It shows, that Lord Kṛṣṇa reminded him of his duty.

The fact is, that war was inevitable because Lord Kṛṣṇa Himself, while revealing his supreme divine form to Arjuna, said, "I am the mighty world-destroying time, the destroyer of the world. My purpose here is to destroy these people. Even if you do not kill them, all those warriors arrayed in the enemy's camp, will not survive" (11/32). Thus this destruction of human beings was inevitable, even if Arjuna did not fight. If Arjuna did not fight, Yudhiṣṭhira, who with his four brothers married Draupadī by obeying his mother, would certainly fight by obeying her. Similarly, Bhīma would never deviate from the war because he had already taken a pledge to kill the Kauravas. As far as Draupadī is concerned, she had even said, that if her husbands, the Pāṇḍavas did not fight, her father (Drupada), her brother (Dhṛṣṭadyumna), her five sons and Abhimanyu, would fight against the Kauravas*. All these facts, show that the war was inevitable.

A man cannot control the happenings that are pre-destined. By discharging his duty one can attain salvation, but by neglecting it, he can degrade himself. It means that man is free to attain, either desirable or undesirable results. Therefore, Lord Kṛṣṇa, by reminding Arjuna of his duty, has preached to human beings, that they should always discharge their duty, by following the ordinance of scriptures and never turn away from these.

* Mahābhārata, Udyoga. 82/37-38.

Link:—In the preceding verse, Arjuna expressed his intention based on many arguments. What he did after this, is contained, in the verse that follows.

सञ्जय उवाच

एवमुक्त्वार्जुनः सङ्ख्ये रथोपस्थ उपाविशत्।
विसृज्य सशरं चापं शोकसंविग्नमानसः ॥ ४७ ॥

sañjaya uvāca

evamuktvārjunaḥ saṅkhye rathopastha upāviśat
visṛjya saśaraṁ cāpaṁ śokasaṁvignamānasaḥ

Arjuna, grief stricken on the battlefield, having spoken thus, and having laid down his bow and arrow, slumped into the central part of the chariot. 47

Comment:—

'Evamuktvārjunaḥ saṅkhye rathopastha upāviśat visṛjya saśaraṁ cāpaṁ śokasaṁvignamānasaḥ'—War, is the root cause of all evils. It will destroy a race and will lead us to hell in the next world. By thinking so Arjuna, overwhelmed with sorrow, became firmly determined not to wage war. Arjuna, who had come to the battlefield with great zeal with Gāṇḍīva bow in his hand, put the bow and arrow down, and overwhelmed with sorrow, sat on the seat of the chariot.

The main reason of Arjuna's grief, is that when Lord Kṛṣṇa placed the chariot between the two armies and asked Arjuna, to behold the Kauravas, he saw Bhīṣma and Droṇa standing in front of him. So his attachment was aroused. Thus, he thought about the destruction of his race (which Duryodhana etc., did not perceive being goaded by greed) and the sin, accruing from it. Then he said that, even if the warriors of the hostile army killed him, while he was unarmed and unresisting, that would be for his good. Thus empowered by delusion, Arjuna perceives good in turning away from war, and even in his death and finally having abandoned his bow and arrow and overwhelmed with grief, sits on the middle seat of the chariot. Thus, we see that it is delusion, which changes a hero's (Arjuna's), great courage to consternation.

ॐ तत्सदिति श्रीमद्भगवद्गीतासूपनिषत्सु ब्रह्मविद्यायां योगशास्त्रे श्रीकृष्णार्जुन-संवादेऽर्जुनविषादयोगो नाम प्रथमोऽध्यायः ॥ १ ॥

oṁ tatsaditi śrīmadbhagavadgītāsūpaniṣatsu brahmavidyāyāṁ yogaśāstre śrīkṛṣṇārjunasaṁvāde'rjunaviṣādayogo nāma prathamo'dhyāyaḥ

Thus with the words, Oṁ, Tat, Sat—the names of the Lord as sung in the Upaniṣad of the Bhagavadgītā by the Lord, the science of Brahma, the scripture on Yoga, the dialogue between Śrī Kṛṣṇa and Arjuna, ends the first chapter entitled, 'The Yoga of Dejection of Arjuna'.

The colophon at the end of each chapter, written by sage Veda Vyāsa reveals the glory and greatness of the Gītā. 'Oṁ, Tat, Sat'*—this has been declared as the triple designation of the Absolute. These three names, lead the beings to benediction and turn us towards God and spirituality and break off our relationship with the world. These wash away the mistakes, which we might have committed in pronouncing the verses, words and letters, in the chapter. So these three are pronounced at the end of each chapter.

By 'Oṁ' sage Veda Vyāsa means, that this may wash away the mistakes of the verses, 'Tat' may turn his verses towards God, and 'Sat' means, that these verses may give an imperishable fruit. 'Iti', means that he has no other personal motive besides this one.

The Gītā has been called 'Śrīmad' because it possesses paramount beauty, and it is called 'Śrīmadbhagavad', because

* Vide—Gītā 17/23—27

it has been uttered by Lord Kṛṣṇa, who possesses six 'Bhagas' i.e., divine traits—wealth, virtue, glory, greatness, knowledge and dispassion.

It has been called the Gītā, because it has been sung by the Lord Himself. According to the rules of Saṁskṛta grammar, it should have been called 'Gītam', yet it being the essence of Upaniṣads, in feminine gender, it has been called the 'Gītā.'

The essence of all Upaniṣads, is contained in it and it has emanated from the tongue of the Lord Himself, so it is called 'Upaniṣad.'

It is called 'Brahmavidyā (Supreme Knowledge), because it leads the living being, to benediction without any distinction of caste, creed and colour. It is called 'Yogaśāstra' because different Yogas (Disciplines), such as Karmayoga (the Discipline of Disinterested Action), Jñānayoga (the Discipline of Knowledge), Dhyānayoga (the Discipline of Meditation) and Bhaktiyoga (the Discipline of Devotion), are contained in it. By following anyone of these disciplines a striver, can realize his identity with God (Paramātmā).

It is a dialogue, between Lord Kṛṣṇa and the devotee Arjuna. Arjuna has asked questions without hesitation, and Lord Kṛṣṇa has answered them with generosity. So it is called a dialogue between Śrī Kṛṣṇa and Arjuna.

In the first chapter, there is description of Arjuna's dejection. By the company of God and saints, this dejection may create dispassion and thus may lead to benediction. Though Duryodhana, also possessed dejection, yet having disinclination for God, his dejection is not called 'Yoga'. But it is called Yoga, in the case of Arjuna as he could realize his identity with God, by means of this 'Yoga.' So this chapter is entitled 'The Yoga of Dejection of Arjuna.'

The purpose of the concluding words, which are given at the end of each chapter, is that even a single chapter well meditated upon may lead a striver to benediction.

Words, letters and the Uvāca (said) in the first chapter

(1) In this chapter in **'Atha Prathamo'dhyāyaḥ'** there are three words, in **'Dhṛtarāṣṭra Uvāca'** and **'Sañjaya Uvāca'** etc., there are twelve words, in verses, there are five hundred and fifty-eight words and there are thirteen concluding words. Thus the total number of words, is five hundred and eighty-six.

(ii) In this chapter in **'Atha Prathamo'dhyāyaḥ'** there are seven letters, in **'Dhṛtarāṣṭra Uvāca', 'Sañjaya Uvāca'** etc., there are thirty-seven letters, in verses there are one thousand, five hundred and four letters and the concluding letters are forty-eight. In this way the total number of letters in this chapter is one thousand, five hundred and ninty-six. Each verse, in this chapter consists of thirty-two letters.

(iii) In this chapter **'Uvāca'** (said) has been used six times, **'Dhṛtarāṣṭra Uvāca'** once, **'Sañjaya Uvāca'** thrice and **'Arjuna Uvāca'** twice.

Metres Used in the first Chapter—

Out of the forty-seven verses, of this chapter, in the first quarter of the fifth verse, as well as the thirty-third verse, and in the third quarter of the forty-third verse 'ra-gaṇa' being used there is **'ra-vipulā'** metre; while in the first quarter of the twenty-fifth verse and the third quarter of the ninth verse 'na-gaṇa' being used, there is **'na-vipulā'** metre. The remaining forty-two verses have the characteristics of right **'pathyāvaktra'** Anuṣṭup metre.

Second Chapter

INTRODUCTION

Duryodhana mentioned the great warriors of the two armies, but Droṇācārya did not utter a word. So Duryodhana became sad. Then, Bhīṣma blew his conch loudly to cheer Duryodhana. Hearing the sound of his conch, the conchs, drums and cow-horns etc., of the Kaurava and the Pāṇḍava armies blared forth. After this (from the twentieth verse) the dialogue between Lord Kṛṣṇa and Arjuna began.

Arjuna asked Lord Kṛṣṇa, to place his chariot in the midst of the two armies. The Lord, having placed the chariot between the two armies, in front of Bhīṣma and Droṇa etc., asked Arjuna to behold the Kurus. Having seen his kinsmen, he was filled with compassion and sadness, that he cast away his bow and arrows, and slumped into the seat of the chariot.

The second chapter starts with Sañjaya telling Dhṛtarāṣṭra, what Lord Kṛṣṇa had said to Arjuna, when he was overwhelmed with grief.

सञ्जय उवाच

तं तथा कृपयाविष्टमश्रुपूर्णाकुलेक्षणम्।
विषीदन्तमिदं वाक्यमुवाच मधुसूदनः ॥ १ ॥

sañjaya uvāca

taṁ tathā kṛpayāviṣṭamaśrupūrṇākulekṣaṇam
viṣīdantamidaṁ vākyamuvāca madhusūdanaḥ

Sañjaya said:

Madhusūdana (He who destroyed the demon named Madhu), addressed the following words to Arjuna, who was overwhelmed with compassion and in deep distress and whose eyes were flooded with tears of despondence. 1

Comment:—

'Taṁ tathā kṛpayāviṣṭam'—Arjuna advises Lord Kṛṣṇa to place his chariot in between the two armies, so that he may behold the war-minded warriors who dared to risk their lives, by fighting against such a valiant warrior, as he. But the same heroic and zealous Arjuna, at the sight of his kinsmen, becomes overwhelmed with grief, his limbs give way, his mouth is parched, his body shivers, his hairs stand on end, his bow slips, from his hand, his skin burns all over and his mind reels. His bravery turns into faint-heartedness and he slips into the seat of the chariot. Sañjaya, conveys the same feelings of Arjuna, who was drowned in distress and despondency.

'Aśrupūrṇākulekṣaṇam'—Such a valiant warrior, Arjuna was full of familial attachment and his eyes were full of tears, that he could not even see, clearly.

'Viṣīdantamidaṁ vākyamuvāca madhusūdanaḥ'—Lord Kṛṣṇa (Madhusūdana), said the following words (the words which will be repeated in the second and third verses) to Arjuna, who was overwhelmed with grief because of his loss of courage.

Here, 'Viṣīdantamuvāca' was enough, because the word 'Vākyam' is also included in the verb 'Uvāca'. But the word 'Vākyam' has a special meaning. These words of Lord Kṛṣṇa, are very profound and uncommon. These attack Arjuna's faint-heartedness and despondency, which overpowered Arjuna, in the discharge of his duty. They make him aware of his weakness and arouse in him a desire for benediction. It is because of these profound words of Lord Kṛṣṇa, that Arjuna by becoming His disciple and seeks refuge in Him (2 /7).

Sañjaya by using the word 'Madhusūdana', means to say that Lord Kṛṣṇa is the killer of demon, Madhu i.e., He is the destroyer of people having a villainous nature, and so He will certainly destroy wicked natured Duryodhana, and his group.

Link:—The next two verses, contain what Lord Kṛṣṇa told Arjuna:—

श्रीभगवानुवाच

कुतस्त्वा कश्मलमिदं विषमे समुपस्थितम्।
अनार्यजुष्टमस्वर्ग्यमकीर्तिकरमर्जुन ॥ २ ॥

śrībhagavān uvāca*

kutastvā kaśmalamidaṁ viṣame samupasthitam
anāryajuṣṭamasvargyamakīrtikaramarjuna

The Blessed Lord said:

Arjuna, how has this affliction overtaken you at this odd hour? It is shunned by noble souls; neither could it bring heaven nor fame to you. 2

Comment:—

['Arjuna'—Lord Kṛṣṇa, addresses him as 'Arjuna' which means, pure in heart. The Lord means to say, how he has become faint-hearted, when it is quite unbecoming of him.]

'Kutastvā kaśmalamidaṁ viṣame samupasthitam'—Lord Kṛṣṇa, being surprised asks Arjuna, why he has developed faint-heartedness, instead of valour and zeal, at this juncture. A man is surprised in two ways—out of his own ignorance, and as a warning to others. Lord Kṛṣṇa's surprise here is, a warning to Arjuna, so that he may be aware of his duty.

'Kutaḥ' means that this faint-heartedness is not permanent in him, it is only a temporary phase, which will go away.

'Samupasthitam' means, you are faint-hearted, not only in words and feelings, but also in actions, you are overcome by this faint-heartedness and therefore you sat in the middle of the chariot, after abandoning your bow and arrows.

* The Lord is called 'Bhagavān' because he possesses six 'Bhagas' (divine traits). They are wealth, virtue, glory, greatness, knowledge and dispassion.

'Anāryajuṣṭam'— Great people do not become faint-hearted, they shun the feeling because, it does not lead them, to any good.

Great men who want to achieve success do so with fixed objectives, during activity as well as non-activity. They do not shirk their duty. According to prevailing circumstances, they perform their duty thoroughly, with zeal and readiness, in order to achieve emancipation. So, it is not proper on his part to refrain from the duty of fighting, because of cowardice.

'Asvargyam'—If we leave aside the goal of success and consider the matter from a worldly point of view, the attainment of heaven, is the highest achievement. With this timidity you cannot even attain the heaven.

'Akīrtikaram'—Even without having the aim of attainment of heaven, a noble person performs those deeds which bring him name and fame in the world. But this cowardice would defame you. So it does not befit you at all, to be faint-hearted.

Here, the Lord by giving these three expressions 'Anāryajuṣṭam', 'Asvargyam' and 'Akīrtikaram', in a sequence has explained that there are three types of persons (i) Thoughtful—whose aim is to attain benediction, (ii) Virtuous—who by doing virtuous actions want to attain heaven, (iii) and Ordinary—who want name and fame in the world. So, by giving the above-mentioned three kind, Lord Kṛṣṇa wants to warn Arjuna that, his affliction would bring him neither benediction, nor heaven nor fame, but would degrade and defame him, and lead him to hell.

Link:—In the verse that follows, Lord Kṛṣṇa points out what to do, when a person is in the grip of cowardice.

क्लैब्यं मा स्म गमः पार्थ नैतत्त्वय्युपपद्यते ।
क्षुद्रं हृदयदौर्बल्यं त्यक्त्वोत्तिष्ठ परन्तप ॥ ३ ॥

klaibyaṁ mā sma gamaḥ pārtha naitattvayyupapadyate
kṣudraṁ hṛdayadaurbalyaṁ tyaktvottiṣṭha parantapa

O Pārtha (son of Pṛthā viz., Kuntī), yield not to cowardice. It does not befit you. Cast off this petty faint-heartedness and wake up, O vanquisher of foes. 3

Comment:—

'Pārtha'*—Lord Kṛṣṇa addresses Arjuna as 'Pārtha', to remind him of Mother Kuntī's message† and arouse in him feelings of bravery which befits the members of a warrior-class. It means, that he should not disobey his mother by showing cowardice.

'Klaibyaṁ mā sma gamaḥ'—It is because of faint-heartedness that Arjuna perceives it, righteous not to wage war and unrighteous to wage war. Therefore to warn him, Lord Kṛṣṇa says that it is impotence rather than righteousness, not to wage war. So he should abandon this weakness.

'Naitattvayyupapadyate'—You should not have developed this timidity in you, because you are, the son of a brave mother of warrior-class, and you yourself are also brave. Therefore, this weakness does not befit you at all.

'Parantapa'—You are the scorcher and vanquisher of foes. So, will you gladden your enemies by showing your disinclination for war?

'Kṣudraṁ hṛdayadaurbalyaṁ tyaktvottiṣṭha'—Here, 'Kṣudram', has two meanings—(i) This faint-heartedness will make you lowly viz., it will deprive you of salvation, heaven or fame and if you

---

* Being the son of Pṛthā Arjuna is called 'Pārtha'. This word manifests intimacy between Lord Kṛṣṇa and Arjuna. In the Gītā Lord Kṛṣṇa has used this address thirty-eight times, more than any other address. The second place goes to 'Kaunteya' which has been used twenty-four times.

When Lord Kṛṣṇa wants to say something special or give assurance to Arjuna or there is an overflow of love for him, He calls him 'Pārtha.' By addressing him thus, he wants to remind him that besides being the son of his father's sister, he is his loving devotee and friend (Gītā 4/3). Therefore He tells him something very secret and true for his welfare.

† Kuntī's message to Arjuna and to Bhīma who were ever eager to fight—

It is the time for which the mother of the warrior-class gives birth to her sons.

do not abandon it, you will become insignificant. (ii) This faint-heartedness, is petty. So it is not difficult for a brave person like you to abandon.

You are thinking that being virtuous, you do not want to commit a sin by waging war, but it is your cowardice. So by abandoning it, you should discharge your duty, by arraying yourself to wage war.

Lord Kṛṣṇa knows for certain, that it is Arjuna's first and foremost duty to wage war. So, He, without caring for Arjuna's lame excuses, orders him quickly to wage war, with full preparations.

Appendix—This fact has been described in detail by the Lord ahead from the thirty-first verse to the thirty-eighth verse of this chapters.

Link:—In the first chapter, Arjuna gave several arguments against the war. But without attaching importance to his arguments, Lord Kṛṣṇa suddenly scolded Arjuna for his faint-heartedness, and ordered him to array himself to wage war. So Arjuna without getting any satisfactory reply to his arguments, got excited and spoke abruptly.

अर्जुन उवाच

कथं भीष्ममहं सङ्ख्ये द्रोणं च मधुसूदन।
इषुभिः प्रतियोत्स्यामि पूजार्हावरिसूदन॥४॥

arjuna uvāca

kathaṁ bhīṣmamahaṁ saṅkhye droṇaṁ ca madhusūdana
iṣubhiḥ pratiyotsyāmi pūjārhāvarisūdana

Arjuna said:

O slayer of Madhu, and slayer of foes, how shall I fight Bhīṣma and Droṇa, with arrows, on the battlefield? Both of them are worthy of our worship. 4

Comment:—

[Arjuna addresses the Lord as 'Madhusūdana' and 'Arisūdana', because he had killed unrighteous, villainous and cruel demons, such as Madhu etc., and foes also who always are jealous of others, without rhyme or reason. But how can he kill his great well-wisher, the respected grandfather Bhīṣma, and adorable preceptor Droṇa, who have great affection for him?]

'Kathaṁ bhīṣmamahaṁ saṅkhye droṇaṁ ca'—I am not turning away from war because of faint-heartedness, but because it is unrighteous for me to fight, with the revered grandsire Bhīṣma and venerable teacher Droṇa. I would be called unmanly if I were afraid of death. I am not afraid of dying but I do not want to kill my venerable elders, who have always been very affectionate to me.

Grandfather Bhīṣma, has loved me since my childhood. When I addressed him as father, he very affectionately used to say, that he was my father's father. Similarly, my adorable preceptor Droṇa, has been so kind to me that he imparted to me better training, than he imparted even to his son. He taught the use of Brahma-weapon, (a kind of weapon which caused infallible destruction and set in motion by incantation) to both of us, but as far as its control or end is concerned, he taught that only to me, not to his son. He also granted me a boon that no one would excel me, in military science. So it is a mortal sin, to wage war against them.

'Iṣubhiḥ pratiyotsyāmi pūjārhau'—Both Bhīṣma and Droṇa being elderly are venerable and adorable. They have a right to attack me. But it is a deadly sin for me to fight against them with my arrows.

Link:—In the preceding verse, Arjuna, being excited, revealed his decision to Lord Kṛṣṇa. Now being influenced by Lord Kṛṣṇa's words and balancing his decision, with that of Lord Kṛṣṇa, he says.

गुरूनहत्वा हि महानुभावान्
श्रेयो भोक्तुं भैक्ष्यमपीह लोके।
हत्वार्थकामांस्तु गुरूनिहैव
भुञ्जीय भोगान् रुधिरप्रदिग्धान्॥ ५॥

gurūnahatvā hi mahānubhāvān
śreyo bhoktuṁ bhaikṣyamapīha loke
hatvārthakāmāṁstu gurūnihaiva
bhuñjīya bhogān rudhirapradigdhān

Better to live on alms in this world, than to slay these noble elders, because after killing them we could enjoy only blood-stained pleasure, in the form of wealth and sense-objects. 5

Comment:—

[It seems after reading this verse, that the words of Lord Kṛṣṇa, uttered in the second and third verses, had some effect on Arjuna. He is thinking, that though Lord Krsna knows that it is not justified for him to kill his venerable elders, yet he is unable to understand why He is ordering him to wage war. So Arjuna, does not speak with excitement, but speaks, somewhat, politely.]

'Gurūnahatvā hi mahānubhāvān śreyo bhoktuṁ bhaikṣyamapīha loke'—Arjuna, first presents his point of view, saying that if he did not fight with reverend Bhīṣma and Droṇa etc., Duryodhana by himself, would not fight with him either. Thus he would lose his kingdom and suffer. Then he would be leading a life of misery and could even depend on alms. But he thinks it better to live on alms, than to slay his reverend elders.

'Iha loke' means—if I live on alms, people in the world will dishonour, reproach and insult me, but I think accepting alms is better than killing my reverend preceptors.

'Api' (Even) means—for me slaying the noble preceptors and living on alms—both are forbidden. But, I think it is more sinful to kill the preceptors, than to live on alms.

'Hatvārthakāmāṁstu gurūnihaiva bhuñjīya bhogān rudhirapradigdhān'—If I carry out your command to wage war, I would enjoy blood-stained pleasure, which will not give me peace and salvation.

Here, a question might arise, that Bhīṣma and Droṇa etc., preceptors were attached to Kauravas, because of pecuniary motives. Therefore, what is the objection if 'Arthakāmān' is taken as an adjective qualifying 'Gurūn'. The answer is, that it is not proper, because they had no desire for money. It was incumbent upon them to fight on Duryodhana's side, because they had eaten his salt.

Secondly, Arjuna has used the term 'Mahānubhāvān (most noble). So, how can the most noble souls desire money? Those who desire money could not be most noble. Therefore, here 'Arthakāmān', is the adjective which qualifies 'Bhogān'.

An Exceptional Fact

Lord Kṛṣṇa, in the second and the third verses, orders Arjuna to array himself by casting off, petty faint-heartedness and fight. But Arjuna gets him wrong, because he thinks that Lord Kṛṣṇa had ordered him to wage war, so that he might enjoy the pleasure of kingship.* Arjuna however perceived only evil, in waging the war. He said that it would be better for him, if his opponents killed him in the war. So with his mind affected by grief he sat slumped on the seat of the chariot (1/47). He had also said, that Duryodhana and his companions being goaded by greed, were prepared to wage war. Now Arjuna says, for himself that if he

* The worldly people having a materialistic outlook cannot even think of spiritualism. Here Arjuna also being overtaken by family attachment and infatuation is thinking only of materialism rather than spiritualism. So he is thinking that Lord Kṛṣṇa wants him to wage the war so that he may obtain kingdom but Lord Kṛṣṇa wants him to attain salvation.

carries out his order and wages war, he will enjoy only blood-stained pleasure in the form of wealth and sensual enjoyment. Thus, he perceives nothing but evil, in waging war.

When an evil comes to us, in the form of an evil, it is easier to do away with it, than when it comes in the garb of something good. Rāvaṇa and devil Kālanemi, could not be recognized by Sītā, and Hanumān respectively, because both of them disguised themselves, as sages. Similarly, Arjuna perceives that it is virtuous not to wage war and it is an evil to wage the war, but he is completely mistaken. Hence, even Lord Kṛṣṇa, finds it difficult and time consuming, to bring Arjuna round, to the realization of this fact.

Today in the name of unity in society, people are determined to abolish caste, stage of life system (Varṇa Āśrama) thinking of their action, as virtuous. But they are not thinking about the disastrous consequences, that this abolition would force the people, to lead a degraded and demoniacal life. In the same way, in the accumulation of wealth, people do not perceive falsehood, fraud, dishonesty, knavery and treachery etc., as evils. Thus, here for Arjuna also, an evil of unmanliness has disguised itself, as righteousness and thus he says how he can slay his noble elders. It means, that whatever Arjuna considers a virtue, is in fact, an evil. But, it does not appear to him, to be an evil, as in the abandonment of his duty, has crept in the guise of virtue of nonviolence, because of his attachment for his relatives.

Appendix—The feelings of elders and preceptors such as Bhīṣma and Droṇa etc., are noble and pure because even while waging the war, they have no partiality.

Link:—The holy words of God had a singular effect and exerted a deep and far reaching influence, on Arjuna, as a result of which, he starts doubting the correctness of his decision, not to wage war. In such a state of mind, Arjuna says.

न चैतद्विद्मः कतरन्नो गरीयो
यद्वा जयेम यदि वा नो जयेयुः।
यानेव हत्वा न जिजीविषाम-
स्तेऽवस्थिताः प्रमुखे धार्तराष्ट्राः ॥ ६ ॥

na caitadvidmaḥ kataranno garīyo
yadvā jayema yadi vā no jayeyuḥ
yāneva hatvā na jijīviṣāma-
ste'vasthitāḥ pramukhe dhārtarāṣṭrāḥ

We don't know which is meritorious for us, to fight or not to fight, nor do we know, whether we shall win or they will conquer us. The sons of Dhṛtarāṣṭra, by killing whom we do not even wish to live, are arrayed against us. 6

Comment:—

'Na caitadvidmaḥ kataranno garīyaḥ'— I cannot decide whether I should wage war or not, because you consider it better to wage war but I do not do so, as it is a sin to kill noble elders and preceptors.

'Yadvā jayema yadi vā no jayeyuḥ'—If I carry out your order and wage war, we do not know, whether we shall win or lose.

Here, it does not mean that Arjuna has no confidence in his own power, but he is uncertain about the future, because no one knows, what may happen in future.

'Yāneva hatvā na jijīviṣāmaḥ'—Not to speak of pleasures and kingdom, we do not even wish to live by killing our kinsmen because by killing them we shall be bereaved of them and thus shall suffer pangs of bereavement.

'Te'vasthitāḥ pramukhe dhārtarāṣṭrāḥ'—Dhṛtarāṣṭra's sons, are our kinsmen and they are arrayed against us. So, how can we kill them? We are damned, if we wish to live, by killing them.

Link:—Finding himself at the crossroads Arjuna, being restless, prays to Lord Kṛṣṇa.

कार्पण्यदोषोपहतस्वभावः
पृच्छामि त्वां धर्मसम्मूढचेताः।
यच्छ्रेयः स्यान्निश्चितं ब्रूहि तन्मे
शिष्यस्तेऽहं शाधि मां त्वां प्रपन्नम्॥ ७॥

kārpaṇyadoṣopahatasvabhāvaḥ
pṛcchāmi tvāṁ dharmasammūḍhacetāḥ
yacchreyaḥ syānniścitaṁ brūhi tanme
śiṣyaste'haṁ śādhi māṁ tvāṁ prapannam

My nature is overwhelmed with the vice of faint-heartedness and my mind is confused with regard to my duty. I entreat you, tell me what is decidedly good for me. I am your disciple. Do instruct me, who have taken refuge, in you. 7

Comment:—

'Kārpaṇyadoṣopahatasvabhāvaḥ pṛcchāmi tvāṁ dharmasammūḍhacetāḥ'—Arjuna did not think it desirable to turn away totally, from the war, but to escape the sin, he did not find any other alternative. So he wanted to turn away from war and he thought of such action, as a virtue, rather than a vice of faint-heartedness. But, when Lord Kṛṣṇa called his action faint-hearted and unmanly, Arjuna was reminded of his duty, as a member of the warrior-class for whom it was not befitting to run. So Arjuna by conceding his faint-heartedness, says that first his nature even as a member of the warrior-class, was weighed down with the weakness of faint-heartedness and secondly, his mind was confused with regard to his duty. Being overpowered by delusion, he could not take the right decision, about its righteousness.

In the third verse Lord Kṛṣṇa advised Arjuna, "Cast off your petty faint-heartedness and stand up, for war." So his doubt should have been removed. But he still had some doubt, because, on the one hand he thought that it was a sin to kill the kinsmen and the adorable elders, but on the other hand, being a member of the warrior-class it was his duty to wage war. So he was confused with regard to his duty, and he entreats Lord Kṛṣṇa to tell him, what his real duty is.

'Yacchreyaḥ syānniścitaṁ brūhi tanme'—In the second verse of this chapter, Lord Kṛṣṇa told him that his dejection was a shame and it should be shunned by noble souls. So Arjuna thought, that he should also follow the path, adopted by noble souls. Therefore, he prays to Lord Kṛṣṇa, to tell him what is decidedly good for him.

First Arjuna was agitated and distressed, and he asks what was good for him. It shows that, an awakening for salvation as a goal is not aroused in a man, so long as he is satisfied with his present situation. But when he is dissatisfied and he wants to rise above it, he becomes aware of his real aim i.e., salvation.

'Śiṣyaste'ham'—When Arjuna entreated Lord Kṛṣṇa, to tell him what was decidedly good for him, he thought that such a question could be put to a teacher, not to a chariot-driver. Arjuna's conviction, that he was a chriot-warrior, while Kṛṣṇa was his charioteer, whom he ordered to place the chariot between the two armies, had gone. So he becomes His disciple and declares, "I am your disciple, so tell me what is decidely, good for me."

'Śādhi māṁ tvāṁ prapannam'—Arjuna thinks, that the preceptor can guide the disciple and a disciple will have to shoulder the responsibility to translate his teachings into practice, and then make effort to attain salvation. But he wants to hand over this responsibility, to his preceptor. As the mother of a breast-sucking child, not the child who falls sick, takes medicine for his recovery, the teacher take over responsibility of the disciple, who takes refuge in him. So Arjuna, by depending on the teacher and surrendering to Him says, "I have taken refuge in You, instruct me."

Here, Arjuna by using the phrase 'Tvāṁ prapannam' says,

that he has taken refuge in Him. But actually he had not taken completely refuge in Him. Had he done this, he would not have uttered the words 'Instruct me', because a disciple has no responsibility of his own, the full responsibility lies with the teacher. Secondly, in the ninth verse he says, "I shall not fight." It also shows that he had not really taken refuge in Him, otherwise he might have not uttered these words. A disciple, who takes refuge in his teacher has no say, no responsibility of his own, he becomes merely an instrument, in the hands of his preceptor and does whatever his teacher wants him, to do. Therefore, Lord Kṛṣṇa in the sixty-sixth verse of the eighteenth chapter says, "Seek refuge in Me, alone" (18/66). Then Arjuna, in the seventy-third verse of the eighteenth chapter says, "I shall act according to Your word." It is here, that Arjuna really takes refuge, in Him.

In this verse, there are four points spoken by Arjuna, which need attention—

(i) My nature is weighed down, with the vice of faint-heartedness and I entreat you because my mind is confused with regard to my duty. (ii) Tell me he entreats, what is decidedly good for me. (iii) I am Your disciple. (iv) Instruct me who has taken refuge in You. If we think over these four points, one by one, we realise that as far as the first point is concerned, the person to whom the question is asked, is free, whether he answers the question or not. The second point, shows that it is his duty to answer. In the third, the responsibility to guide the disciple, so that he may attain salvation is that of the teacher. In the fourth, the full responsibility for salvation of the disciple, is the teacher's.

Link:— In the previous verse, Arjuna takes refuge in Lord Kṛṣṇa, but he thinks that Lord Kṛṣṇa wants him to wage the war, which he regards as unrighteous and so He will again order him to wage war. Secondly, he thinks that perhaps he has not been able to convey his feelings to Him. So in the next verse, Arjuna clearly expresses his feelings to Him, against the war.

न हि प्रपश्यामि ममापनुद्याद्
यच्छोकमुच्छोषणमिन्द्रियाणाम् ।
अवाप्य भूमावसपत्नमृद्धं
राज्यं सुराणामपि चाधिपत्यम् ॥ ८ ॥

na hi prapaśyāmi mamāpanudyād
yacchokamucchoṣaṇamindriyāṇām
avāpya bhūmāvasapatnamṛddhaṁ
rājyaṁ surāṇāmapi cādhipatyam

Even on obtaining undisputed sovereignty and an affluent kingdom on this earth as well as lordship over the gods in heaven, I do not see any remedy that can remove my grief, which withers my senses. 8

Comment:—

[Arjuna thinks Lord Kṛṣṇa, wants him to wage war, so that he may gain victory and kingdom, and thus his grief may be removed. But he is so grief stricken, that even the joy of victory, is not likely to remove his grief.]

'Avāpya bhūmāvasapatnamṛddhaṁ rājyam'—Even if I obtain an undisputed sovereignty and affluent kingdom, on this earth, and my subjects become happy and prosperous, and I may have no enemy on the face of earth, it will fail to remove my grief.

'Surāṇāmapi cādhipatyam'—Not to talk of worldly pleasure, even lordship of Indra (the king of the gods) over the gods, cannot remove my worry and grief. In verses, thirty-two and thirty-three of the first chapter, Arjuna wanted to turn away from war, because of his attachment for his kinsmen. But here, he wants to turn away from war because he thinks that it is an obstacle, to salvation. So there is a lot of difference, between the two situations.

'Na hi prapaśyāmi mamāpanudyād yacchokamucchoṣaṇa-mindriyāṇām'—How sad I shall become, after the death of my kinsmen, when I am so much grieved after thinking of it! If I grieved over the loss of a kingdom, it might be overcome by gaining it. But I am grieved at thinking of the massacre of my kinsmen. If I gain a kingdom, it will rather enhance my grief, because who could enjoy the kingdom, after the death of my kinsmen? Therefore, undisputed sovereignty and an affluent kingdom on this earth and lordship over the gods cannot remove the grief, that is parching my senses.

Link:—What Arjuna did after saying that, even possession of material objects would not relieve him of his grief, is contained, in the verse that follows—

सञ्जय उवाच

एवमुक्त्वा हृषीकेशं गुडाकेशः परन्तप।
न योत्स्य इति गोविन्दमुक्त्वा तूष्णीं बभूव ह ॥ ९ ॥

sañjaya uvāca

evamuktvā hṛṣīkeśaṁ guḍākeśaḥ parantapa
na yotsya iti govindamuktvā tūṣṇīṁ babhūva ha

Sañjaya said:

O scorcher of enemies, after addressing the indwelling lord thus, Arjuna, the conqueror of sleep, said to Him, "I'll not fight", and became silent. 9

Comment:—

'Evamuktvā hṛṣīkeśaṁ guḍākeśaḥ parantapa na yotsya iti govindamuktvā tūṣṇīṁ babhūva ha'—Arjuna honoured the Lord's word and wanted to obey it. But after thinking seriously, over what Lord Kṛṣṇa had said and applying his own mind to his thoughts, came to the conclusion, that war could result in providing him with an affluent kingdom, honour and fame. But it would not wipe out his grief, worry and misery. Therefore, it was not befitting for him to wage war. So Arjuna speaks his mind in clear words "I'll not fight."

Having declared his decision not to fight, and having nothing more to say, Arjuna became quiet.

Link:— In the next verse, Sañjaya describes what happened, when Arjuna flatly refused to fight.

तमुवाच हृषीकेशः प्रहसन्निव भारत।
सेनयोरुभयोर्मध्ये विषीदन्तमिदं वचः॥१०॥

tamuvāca hṛṣīkeśaḥ prahasanniva bhārata
senayorubhayormadhye viṣīdantamidaṁ vacaḥ

O Bhārata (Dhṛtarāṣṭra, born in Bharata dynasty), Śrī Kṛṣṇa, as if smiling, addressed the following words to the despondent Arjuna while in the midst of the two armies. 10

Comment:—

'Tamuvāca hṛṣīkeśaḥ prahasanniva bhārata senayorubhayormadhye viṣīdantamidaṁ vacaḥ'—Arjuna filled with valour and enthusiasm, had entreated Lord Kṛṣṇa to place his chariot between the two armies, so that he could behold the warriors. It was befitting for Arjuna, to get ready for fighting which was his objective. But there, instead of waging war, he felt grieved. So Lord Kṛṣṇa, started the gospel of the Gītā.

'Prahasanniva'—(Smiling, as it were) means, that when Lord Kṛṣṇa perceived that Arjuna's enthusiasm for the war, had changed into grief, he smiled. Secondly, in the seventh verse he said, "Do instruct me who have, taken refuge in You". But in the ninth verse he says, "I"ll not fight". So Lord Kṛṣṇa smiled, because the devotee who takes refuge in his preceptor, just becomes an instrument in the hands of his preceptor and a preceptor is fully responsible for the duty of the disciple. The disciple, has no option but to obey his preceptor and do, as his teacher wishes. Arjuna's declaration, 'not to fight' is practically a withdrawal from his refuge, in the Lord. 'Iva', means that Lord Kṛṣṇa must have burst into laughter, after hearing Arjuna's decision of not fighting, but He spoke smilingly.

When Arjuna said, "I'll not fight", Lord Kṛṣṇa, should have told him to do, as he wished (18/63). But He thought that Arjuna, was unable to take the right decision, because he was overwhelmed with grief and worry. So, there was an overflow of Lord Kṛṣṇa's love, for him. God instead of paying attention to the words of his devotees, judges them by their feelings. So Lord Kṛṣṇa, instead of paying attention to Arjuna's words, "I'll not fight," started the gospel, from the next verse.

Moreover, He accepts those devotees who take refuge in Him, even by words as his own, because of His boundless grace.

'Hṛṣīkeśaḥ'—'Hṛṣīkeśa', means that the Lord is the indweller viz., He knows feelings of beings, Lord Kṛṣṇa knows, that Arjuna is turning away from war, because he is overpowered by the urge of attachment for his kinsmen, and he does not see his grief melting away, by merely acquiring a kingdom. So he says "I'll not fight." But, he also knows that as soon as his delusion is destroyed, he will act upon His instruction.

In 'Idaṁ vacaḥ' uvāca, the use of the word 'Uvāca' (spoke), was sufficient, there was no need to use the word 'Vacaḥ' (word), because 'Vacaḥ' is also included in 'Uvāca.' It seems a repetition, but actually it is not so. The word, 'Vacaḥ' has been used to point out, the secret wisdom, contained in the next verse uttered by Lord Kṛṣṇa, in simple and easily understandable language.

Appendix—On the sacred (righteous) soil of Kurukṣetra on one side the Kaurava-army is arrayed while on the other side the Pāṇḍava-army is arrayed. In the middle of the two armies a glorious chariot drawn by white horses is placed. In one part of that chariot Lord Kṛṣṇa is seated while in another part Arjuna is seated. The Lord starts preaching the divine gospel for the benediction of mankind by making Arjuna, an instrument and first of all He describes the discrimination between the body and (the embodied soul) its possessor.

Link:—Lord Kṛṣṇa preaches the gospel of freedom, from grief to grieved Arjuna and says—

श्रीभगवानुवाच

अशोच्यानन्वशोचस्त्वं प्रज्ञावादांश्च भाषसे।
गतासूनगतासूंश्च नानुशोचन्ति पण्डिताः ॥ ११ ॥

śrībhagavānuvāca

aśocyānanvaśocastvaṁ prajñāvādāṁśca bhāṣase
gatāsūnagatāsūṁśca nānuśocanti paṇḍitāḥ

The Blessed Lord said:

Arjuna, you grieve for those who should not be grieved at, yet speak as if a man of wisdom. The wise grieve, neither for the living, nor for the dead. 11

Comment:—

[A man is grieved when he classifies objects and persons, into two divisions—One's own, and not one's own, such as, our kinsmen and not our kinsmen, of our caste and not of our caste, of our stage of life and not of our stage of life, our followers and not our followers. We have a sense of mine, attachment, love and desire for those, who we regard as ours. Through these—a sense of mine and desire etc., faults such as grief, worry, fear, perturbation, commotion and strain etc., arise. The root of all faults, is a sense of mine and desire etc., this is a rule.

At the beginning of the Gītā, Dhṛtarāṣṭra asked, "What did my sons and the sons of Pāṇḍu do?" It shows his partiality towards his own sons and attachment for them, though the Pāṇḍavas, regarded him more than their father.

Arjuna also developed the same attachment, but he had no partiality, he was impartial and so he uses the terms 'Seeing all these relations' (1/28) and 'How can we, by killing our own kinsmen, be happy' (1/37). It means that, Arjuna had attachment for the Kuru family, and because of possibility of destruction of the family, he was grieved. To remove this grief, Lord Kṛṣṇa preaches the gospel of the Gītā, which begins with this eleventh verse. In the end, Lord Kṛṣṇa declares that there is no justification for Him, to grieve and he should take refuge in Him, alone, and not grieve—'Grieve not' (18/66). The reason is, that dependence on the world leads to grief, while supreme or exclusive devotion to the Lord, leads to the state which is free from faults such as grief and worry etc.]

'Aśocyānanvaśocastvam'—There are two things in the world—real and unreal, the soul and the body. Both of these are not to be grieved at as the real is imperishable, and therefore, should not be grieved for and the unreal, is bound to perish, as it is perishing every moment, so it should not be grieved at. It means that these are grieved at, only because of ignorance or lack of discrimination. Whatever circumstances, in the form of birth-death, profit-loss etc., a man finds himself in, are result of his fate viz., his previous actions. It is sheer ignorance to feel happy or sad, in those, favourable or unfavourable circumstances, because these are transient.

'Prajñāvādāṁśca bhāṣase'— On the one hand, you speak words of wisdom, but on the other hand, you grieve. It shows that you are merely talking tall, actually you are not wise, because the wise do not grieve, for anyone.

You also say that with the destruction of a family, its age old traditions disappear, women become depraved and there ensues an intermixture of castes, which leads to hell and deprived of the ritual offerings of rice-balls (Piṇḍa) and water, their manes also fall—these words, as of the wise, also prove that a body is perishable, while the soul is imperishable. Had the soul not been imperishable, how could you have feared the fall of the killers and members of the family? Further, you would not have worried about the fall of manes. Your worry and fear prove, that a body is perishable while its master, the soul is eternal. So it is not right to grieve for them.

'Gatāsūnagatāsūṁśca'—It is out of ignorance, that you grieve for the bodies because these will all perish. You should not lament for them. Such grief is a mistake.

It is also a great mistake to grieve for those who are dead because they suffer torture, if their people, grieve for them. The departing soul has to drink and eat the tears and phlegm* shed by people here. Similarly, we should not grieve or worry for those who are living, because grief (worry) does not help them, in anyway. We should rather care for and help them.

Arjuna's limbs were giving way and his mouth was getting parched. The root of such feelings, is his identity with the body. Such identity creates affinity for those who nurse this body. That affinity gives birth to grief and worry in thinking of their death. So one is grieved (worried) and sad after thinking of those, who are living as well as those who are dead. One is grieved (worried) about the dead because deprived of the ritual offerings of rice-balls and water, the manes, have a downfall (1/42), and he is worried about the living ones, because they are arrayed on the battlefield, staking their lives and property (1/33). Both types of worries relate to their bodies. So they are of the same character.

---

* The departing soul has to eat and drink the phlegm and tears shed by the relatives. So we should not lament the death of a relative but should perform obsequies (Pañcatantra, Mitrabheda 365).

The departing soul hereafter drinks the tears shed by the relatives here (Skanda Purāṇa, Brāhma. Setu. 48/42).

Instead of grieving, for those who are dead, we should offer ritual water and rice-balls etc., because it is our duty. Similarly, we should make arrangement to care for those who are living. So we should give a serious thought to it which enables us to understand our duty, while worry (grief), destroys the power of thinking.

'Nānuśocanti paṇḍitāḥ'—Discrimination between the real and the unreal, is called 'Paṇḍā' (wisdom), and one who has developed discrimination, is known as 'Paṇḍita' (wise). Such wise men do not grieve, because they can discriminate between the real and the unreal—the imperishable self (soul) and the perishable body. Grief arises, only when the unreal is accepted as real i.e., when there is a desire to maintain the body forever. For the real, there is no grief or worry, at all.

Appendix—There is one division of the body (Śarīra) while another division is of the self (Śarīrī). Both have no relationship at all with each other. Both are quite different in nature. One is insentient while the other is sentient. One is perishable while the other is imperishable. One is mutable while the other is immutable. One is kaleidoscopic while the other remains the same for time immemorial—'bhūtagrāmaḥ sa evāyaṁ' (Gītā 8/19), 'Sarge'pi nopajāyante pralaye na vyathanti ca' (Gītā 14/2).

The body and the self—both are not to be grieved. The body ever perishes, therefore it is not to be grieved, while the self never perishes, therefore it is also not to be grieved. One is grieved only because of one's own folly. The body is continuously separating automatically while the self is ever attained to all. The wise men who know this distinction between the body and the self, never grieve for any being whether dead or alive. In their view the division of the changing body is different from that of the never changing self i.e., the ever existent entity.

The gospel of the Gītā begins with the discrimination between the body and the self. Other philosophical classics describe the 'self' and the 'non-self' in an objective manner and it becomes a matter of study but the Gītā instead of describing the self and non-self objectively, describes 'deha-dehī', 'Śarīra-śarīrī' (body and its owner) on the basis of the personal experience of all persons. This is uniqueness of the Gītā. The striver who wants to attain salvation first of all must know 'Who I am'. Arjuna has also asked Lord Kṛṣṇa to tell him the highest good for him (Gītā 2/7). Salvation can only be attained by discriminating the self from the body. So long as a man holds 'I am body', he may listen to gospels, may preach gospels to others, may practise spiritual discipline but salvation is not possible.

It is a blunder to accept (assume) a thing, which is not one's own, as one's own and to disown a thing which is one's own. Only the thing, which may ever live with us and with which we may ever live can be our own. The body in the same state doesn't stay with us even for a moment while God ever lives with us. The reason is that the body belongs to the class of the world, while the self belongs to the class of God. Therefore it is the greatest blunder to assume the body as one's own and not to assume God as one's own. In order to rectify this blunder, the Lord in the Gītā first of all describes the discrimination between the body and the self and awakens the striver to the fact, "You (self) are not the entity which dies viz., you are not the body. You are the knower while the body is 'the known' (the Gītā 13/1). You are eternal and pervade everywhere 'nityaḥ sarvagataḥ' (Gītā 2/24), 'yena sarvamidaṁ tatam' (Gītā 2/17) while the body is unipresent. You are a resident of the divine world while the body is a resident of the matter (mortal) world. You are a fragment of God—'mamaivāṁśo jīvaloke' (Gītā 15/7) while the body is a fragment of 'Prakṛti' (Nature)—'manaḥ ṣaṣṭhānindriyāṇi prakṛtisthāni' (Gītā 15/7). You ever live in immortality while the body ever lives in mortality. By the decay and death of the body you don't decay and die in the least. Therefore, you shouldn't be obsessed by grief, worry and fear etc.

The self is not attached and limited to anybody, therefore it is said to be pervading everywhere—'sarvagataḥ' (Gītā 2/24), 'yena sarvamidaṁ tatam' (Gītā 2/17). Therefore the true nature of a striver is merely an ever existent entity, not śarīrī (one having a body) rather it is 'aśarīrī' (having no relation with the body). Therefore the Lord has also designated it as 'अव्यक्त'—unmanifest (Gītā 2/25), 'अव्यक्तादीनिभूतानि' unmanifest beings (2/28), the body is decaying every moment and it is 'Asat'. 'Asat' has no existence 'नासतो विद्यते भाव:' (2/16). How a striver having relationship with the body even whose existence is not there can be termed 'śarīrī? A striver is neither 'Śarīra' (body) nor 'Śarīrī' (dehī). In this section the Lord has used the term 'Śarīrī' (dehī) for the ever existent entity in order to explain it to the strivers. By calling it as 'Śarīrī' He means to say that a striver is not body.

When we reflect upon the nature of the body and the self, we perceive that the body and the self have their own identity and when we don't reflect upon them, then they have also their own identity. On reflection there is no difference in the reality of their true nature but by reflecting upon them the striver's delusion is destroyed and the human life becomes successful by attaining its aim.

In human life there is predominance of discrimination. Therefore 'I am not body'—this discrimination is possible only in the human body. The sense of 'I' and 'mine' in the body is not the work of human intellect but that of beastly intellect. Therefore Śrī Śukadevajī Mahārāja says to king Parīkṣit—

tvaṁ tu rājan mariṣyeti paśubuddhimimāṁ jahi
na jātaḥ prāgabhūto'dya dehavattvaṁ na naṅkṣyasi

(Śrīmadbhā. 12/5/2)

'O King! Now give up this beastly intellect that you will die. As the body was non-existent in the past, it was born afterwards and will die in future, it is not the case with you (the self) that you were non-existent in the past, were born afterwards and will die in future.'

Link:—In the next two verses, the Lord explains why it is unwise to grieve for what is imperishable.

न त्वेवाहं जातु नासं न त्वं नेमे जनाधिपाः ।
न चैव न भविष्यामः सर्वे वयमतः परम् ॥ १२ ॥

na tvevāhaṁ jātu nāsaṁ na tvaṁ neme janādhipāḥ
na caiva na bhaviṣyāmaḥ sarve vayamataḥ param

In fact, there was never a time when I or you or these kings, were non-existent. Nor is it, right that we shall cease to be in future. 12

Comment:—

[There are two things in the world, the soul (the real) and the body (the unreal) and both of these are not to be grieved for, because the soul never ceases to be and the body is ever perishable. So here it is explained that the soul is immortal, while the body is mortal.]

'Na tvevāhaṁ jātu nāsaṁ na tvaṁ neme janādhipāḥ'—People think that I did not exist before My incarnation and you and these kings were also non-existent before our birth. But it is not so. All of us certainly existed, because the real is always existent, unaffectedly time, place and circumstances etc.

'I, you and these kings, had their previous existence'—this declaration could suffice. But contrarily it is said—'I, you and these kings had no such pre-existence—this is not true'. The reason is, that by the latter expression 'that there was no such pre-existence—is not true', the fact of their pre-existence is emphasized.

It means, that the real is eternal. It was never a naught. By the term 'Jātu', the Lord means to say that in all times—past, present and future and in all climes, circumstances, states, incidents and things etc., this real never ceases to be ever.

Here, by using the word 'Aham' Lord Kṛṣṇa identifies Himself with other people, in order to explain that the real never ceases to be, while in the fifth verse of the fourth chapter Lord Kṛṣṇa says, "You and I have taken many births. I know them all, while you don't know", which shows that He as the Lord, is different from other. In the fifth verse of the fourth chapter, the Lord expresses His excellence, eminence and glory as compared to ordinary mortals, while in this verse He expresses His unity, with the soul of common men.

'Na caiva na bhaviṣyāmaḥ sarve vayamataḥ param'—In future, the bodies will not continue to be the same and one day they will perish, but the (soul) will never cease to be, because the real is eternal. It was, neither non-existent in the past, nor will be in, future.

Lord Kṛṣṇa has talked about the past and the future, by saying that there was never a time, when they were non-existent, nor they will cease to be. But, He has not talked about the present, because they are clearly seen at present through the bodies. In their present existence, there is no trace of doubt. But if we think seriously, we come to know that we (the soul) exist at present, but the bodies are kaleidoscopic. Therefore we should realize that the soul is different from the bodies, because we have our existence, at present as we had in the past and we will have, in future, while the bodies are perishable.

A man realises his existence, before sleep and after sleep, but he has his existence during sleep also ever while his body is undergoing changes every moment, and it will perish one day. Similarly, the bodies of all of us—I, you and these kings—did not exist in the past, nor will exist in future and presently also perishing, every moment, but our self existed in the past, will exist in future, and exist now.

Our entity is transcendental as we living subject know time—present, past and future objectively. Subject is always distinct from object. Thus the Lord has spoken this verse to explain this transcendental entity of the Self.

An Exceptional Fact

Lord Kṛṣṇa, in this verse says that the bodies are perishable while the self is imperishable. It is a rule, that what exists in the beginning and the end, also exists in the middle, and what does not exist in the beginning and the end, does not exist in the middle, either.

But the question arises that how, in the middle these bodies are visible? The answer is that senses, mind and intellect, with which we see and worldly objects, which are seen—both are perishable and change every moment. Man (self) identifies himself, with the seen. Then, he is called a seer. When the instruments of perception and the objects of perception, are all perishable and transient, then how can the apparent onlooker, be permanent? The apparent entity of a seer (onlooker) is there, because of affinity between the seer, the senses and the seen. In case, there is no such affinity, then this apparent entity of the seer fades away. But, the base of the apparent entity which is truth, persists. That truth, is called the base of creation, preservation, destruction and illuminator of all seeming entities. These names—base and illuminator are only in relation to objects which they base and illumine. In the absence of those objects, the truth ever remains, as it is. He who has an eye for that truth, can never grieve. This way, 'I', 'you' and 'these kings', are not to be grieved at all.

Appendix—In this verse there is the description that God and the self both are endowed with the same characteristics. The Lord declares, "I as Kṛṣṇa, you as Arjuna and all these people as kings neither existed in the past nor will exist in future. But all of us as ever existent entity existed in the past and will also exist in future. It means that I, you and these kings—these three are different as far as the bodies are concerned but they are the same as far as the self is concerned. The bodies neither existed in the past nor will exist in future but the entity of the soul (self) did exist in the past, shall exist in future and does exist at present. When these bodies didn't exist, the entity of the self was there and when these bodies will cease to exist, that entity will still remain. There is nothing else except one ever existent entity.

I, you and these kings—by saying so the lord means that the entity of God and entity of the embodied self are one and the same viz., in 'Is' and 'Am' there is only one pure consciousness. It is because of 'I' (ego) that 'am' is used. If there is no affinity for 'I' (ego), then 'am' will not remain but only 'Is' will remain. That 'Is' viz., pure consciousness rather than the body is our true identity. Therefore one should not grieve for the body.

As an incident of the past and the future is perceived far away, so also is an incident of the present. The reason is that as we (the self) have no connection with the past and the future, similarly we have no connection with the present. When we (the self) have no connection at all with them, then what is the difference between the past, the future and the present for us? These three are within limits of time but the self transcends the limits of time. Time has divisions while the self is eternal and indivisible. It is only by regarding the body as self that there appears difference between the past, the future and the present. In fact the past, the future and the present don't exist for the self, it being eternal.

Many ages may change yet 'Śarīrī' (the self) doesn't undergo any change, it remains the same because it is a fragment of God. But the body does ever change, it doesn't remain the same even for a moment.

देहिनोऽस्मिन्यथा देहे कौमारं यौवनं जरा।
तथा देहान्तरप्राप्तिर्धीरस्तत्र न मुह्यति॥ १३॥

dehino'sminyathā dehe kaumāraṁ yauvanaṁ jarā
tathā dehāntaraprāptirdhīrastatra na muhyati

Just as boyhood, youth and old age, changes in this physical body do not affect the soul likewise is the change to another body. Wise man never gets disturbed about this. 13

Comment:—

'Dehino'sminyathā dehe* kaumāraṁ yauvanaṁ jarā'—The body, does not remain the same, but it always changes. It passes by stages, through babyhood, youth and old age. The statement 'Dehino'sminyathā dehe', proves that soul is separate and the body is separate. The soul is the 'Seer', and the body is the 'Seen'. Hence the changes of babyhood and youth etc., in the body, are not in the soul. The soul is changeless.

'Tathā dehāntaraprāptiḥ'—As, one does not grieve for the body when it passes through babyhood, youth and old age; similarly one should not grieve, when the soul passes on, to another body. As babyhood, youth and old age are different stages of physical body, so (attaining) another body after death, is a stage, for the subtle and causal body.

If we perceive in the right perspective, we come to know, that the body does not pass through babyhood, youth and old age only, but it changes every moment. Similarly, subtle and causal bodies, also change, every moment†.

Now, the question arises, that we can perceive our physical body, but we do not perceive our subtle and causal body and

---

* The born one passes through babyhood, youth and old age; but here 'Deha' has been used for the human body.

† The physical body is left by a man (soul) when he attains another body. But subtle and causal bodies are not left until he attains salvation. He has affinity for them so long as he does not attain salvation.

their change. Wakefulness, sleep and sound sleep respectively, are regarded, as states of physical, subtle and causal bodies. In sleep, (dream) a baby sees itself as a baby, a youth sees himself as a youth and an old man sees himself, as an old man. It proves that a subtle body, also changes. Similarly, in childhood one gets more soundsleep than in youth, and in old age, it further decreases. It shows, that there is a change in causal bodies also. Secondly, a man is more refreshed in his childhood and youth after sleeping, than he is in his old age. It also proves, the change in causal bodies.

When one acquires the body of a god, a bird or an animal etc., (because of identification of the self with the body), one thinks oneself as the same, it is a change in subtle body. Similarly, the nature (habit) of a god is different from that of a bird or an animal. It shows change, in causal body.

A man passes through babyhood, youth and old age and thus there is a change in his body but he experiences, that he is the same.* It proves, that there is no change, in his 'self' (soul).

Here a doubt comes to our mind, that we experience a change in the physical body, but we have no knowledge about our previous bodies, after getting new bodies. The answer is, that there is so much of pain at the time of death and rebirth, that one forgets one's previous birth. When a man suffers from paralysis or old age, his memory becomes weak. Similarly, by the pangs of death and birth, one becomes oblivious of his previous birth†. But, one who dies suddenly without any pain, can have a memory of his previous birth‡.

---

* In the sacred books this knowledge is called 'Pratyabhijñā'.

† A man dies by becoming unconscious because of much pain amidst his lamenting kinsmen (Śrīmadbhā. 3/30/18). At the time of death his breath stops and memory is lost (Śrīmadbhā. 3/31/23).

‡ The impression of the previous birth of those who die suddenly and then are reborn suddenly, continues for sometime but as they grow up, their dream like old memory is lost (Mahābhārata, Anuśāsana. 145).

When a man rises, after a sound sleep, he says, that he slept soundly and he was not aware of anything. It means, that he knows that he was not aware of anything, during sound sleep. This knowledge of nothingness by the self, proves that the self existed, even during sound sleep. Thus, his own self existed before his sleep, during his sleep and also, after his sleep i.e., the self (soul) exists continuously. None, feels its non-existence at any time, rather he feels his existence, incessantly. He who feels himself separate from the body, realizes that he is liberated and in that liberated state he ever remains so. In that liberated state, he may not know what bodies he possessed in the past, but his realization that he is separate from the body, remains intact.

'Dhīrastatra na muhyati'—The wise man (enlightened one), is he, who can discriminate between the real and unreal. Such a man, is never deluded and he is not reborn, because attachment for the guṇas (qualities, modes), is the cause of birth in good and evil wombs, and he breaks off his attachment with the qualities (modes).

Here 'tatra', has been used, for the difference between the soul (spirit) and the body, the real and the unreal, the permanent and the transient. It means, that these are totally different and one is never deluded about this, because he knows, that he is different from the body.

Appendix—The body never remains uniform while the self never becomes multiform. The body neither existed before birth nor will exist after death and at present also it is dying every moment. In fact the process of its death begins as soon as it comes to the womb. At the death of boyhood, youth ensues, at the death of youth, old age ensues and at the death of the old age, the embodied self passes on to another body. The body undergoes all these states. Boyhood, youth and old age—these three states are of the physical body and passing on of the embodied self to another body is the state of the subtle body and the causal body. But the entity of pure consciousness transcends all these states. The states change while the self remains the same. Thus the enlightened one, who discriminates the distinctiveness of the body from that of the self, is never deluded.

The embodied soul in order to reap the fruit of its actions goes to numberless wombs, to hell and heaven. This utterance proves that eighty-four lac forms of life are left, heaven and hell are left but the self ever remains the same. Womb (bodies) change but the self (Śarīrī) doesn't change. The self remains one, so it goes to several wombs and several worlds. The entity which goes to several wombs does not get tainted with anyone, doesn't get entangled anywhere. If it gets tainted and entangled anywhere, then who will reap the fruit in eighty-four lac forms of life? Who will go to heaven and hell? Who will attain salvation?

Birth and death are not our (of the self) traits but are the traits of the body. Our age viz., age of the self is beginningless and endless within which several bodies are born and they die. As we change several clothes but by changing clothes we ourselves don't change, we remain the same (Gītā 2/22); similarly the entity of the self even by transmigrating to several bodies ever remains the same. It means that our freedom and detachment are axiomatic. Our life doesn't depend on a particular body. Because of being detached, we even by transmigrating to several bodies, remain the same, but by assuming our attachment to the body, we have to take birth in several wombs. The assumed attachment doesn't stay but we go on getting attached to other things and persons etc. If we don't get attached to them, salvation (detachment) or independence is self-evident or spontaneous.

Link:—Now, Lord Kṛṣṇa urges us that we should be indifferent to sorrow and suffering, arising from transitory and perishable things, like the body etc.

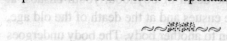

मात्रास्पर्शास्तु कौन्तेय शीतोष्णसुखदुःखदाः ।
आगमापायिनोऽनित्यास्तांस्तितिक्षस्व भारत ॥ १४ ॥

mātrāsparśāstu kaunteya śītoṣṇasukhaduḥkhadāḥ
āgamāpāyino'nityāstāṁstitikṣasva bhārata

O son of Kuntī, bodily sense-objects, which give rise to the feelings of heat and cold, pleasure and pain etc., are transitory and fleeting, therefore, Arjuna bear these patiently viz., remain unaffected by them or ignore them. 14

Comment:—

[Here a doubt arises that in the verses from the eleventh to the thirteenth and then again from the sixteenth to the thirtieth there is a context of the spirit and the body, why are then these two verses about contacts of 'senses with objects' inserted in between? The explanation is that in the twelfth verse as the Lord placed Himself also in the category of the other people, here He wants to say that the body is equally transient as other worldly objects are and therefore these two verses fit in the context.]

'Tu'—'Tu' (indeed), has been used to explain, that transitory things, such as bodies etc., are different, from the permanent soul.

'Mātrāsparśāḥ'—Senses, including the inner sense, are called 'Mātrā' and 'Sparśāḥ, means 'Contact'. Therefore, all objects which are perceived by senses, are called 'Mātrāsparśāḥ (bodily senses).' Can affinity with objects, also be included in 'Mātrāsparśāḥ'? No. The reason is, that it is not 'inner sense', but the 'self', which accepts this affinity and that affinity remains, even when the objects are lost.* A woman bereaved of her husband fifty years ago, and if anyone called her as the wife of her husband Mr. A, she becomes alert, even today. It shows that the assumed

* The affinity with the unreal can perish only if we deny it. Actually the self has no affinity with the unreal. But it has accepted this affinity. So it can't be rooted out by any other means such as penances etc. It will be rooted out only when we cease to accept it.

affinity, has not yet broken off. It means that though objects are lost, yet the assumed affinity persists.

'Śītoṣṇasukhaduḥkhadāḥ'—Here, 'Śīta' (cold) and 'Uṣṇa' (hot), stand for favourable and unfavourable circumstances. Favourable circumstances, give us pleasure while unfavourable ones give pain. If the terms 'Śīta' and 'Uṣṇa mean cold and heat, then these will represent only objects of touch and their meanings will be limited. These will not represent all sense-objects, and circumstances. Therefore, it is proper to take their meanings, as 'favourable' and 'unfavourable' circumstances. The fact is, that the favourable (desirable) or unfavourable (undesirable) circumstances and things cannot give pleasure or pain, but it is the affinity with them, which is the cause of pleasure and pain. So the Lord has called the objects 'Sukhaduḥkhadāḥ' (producers of pleasure and pain).

'Āgamāpāyinaḥ'—All objects, have a beginning and an end, they are born and disappear. So they are 'Āgamāpāyī', i.e., they appear and disappear.

'Anityāḥ'—It may be said, that objects may not have pre-existence or post-existence, but in between, they do exist. The Lord declares, that as they are 'Anitya' (transient) they do not exist even, in the interim. They change, every moment. They change, so swiftly, that no one can see them, again in the same form, because they do not maintain the same shape, the next moment. Therefore, the Lord has called all objects, as 'anitya.'

It means, that all worldly objects are transitory and fleeting, and they change every moment. Not only objects, but the senses, including the inner sense with which we perceive objects, are also transitory. There is always a change, in them. For example, the senses get tired by the evening, while working throughout a day and get refreshed in the morning, after a night's sleep.

Here, all objects in a gross sense are called 'āgamāpāyinaḥ' (appearing and disappearing). In a finer sense, these are called, 'anityāḥ' (changing every moment). In a more fine way, they will be described in the sixteenth verse of this chapter, as 'asat' (non-existent), while the soul described earlier, as eternal will be called as 'sat', (ever-existent), in the sixteenth verse of this chapter.

Mere knowledge, of agreeable and disagreeable senses is not at all defective. But attachment with and aversion to them or pleasure and pain, in relation to them is a fault. Not to be affected by such an evil, is expressed by the expression 'tāṁstitikṣasva'.

Secondly, the body and senses and their actions, have a beginning and an end, while you as a spectator, are different from them. They always change, but you never change. Therefore, you should remain unaffected by them i.e., you should ignore them. To remain unaffected (untainted) is called here, 'titikṣā'.

Appendix—As the body never remains uniform but changes every moment, similarly all the worldly objects (Prakṛti viz., Nature and its evolutes) which are perceived by senses-mind-intellect, never remain uniform, they undergo union and disunion. We feel happy with the union of those objects which we like and their disunion makes us sad. We feel happy with the disunion of those objects which we don't like and their union makes us sad. Objects are also fleeting and transient. Similarly the senses and the inner faculty are also fleeting and transient and the pleasure or pain caused by the union or disunion of these objects is also fleeting and transient. But the self ever remains the same, it is immutable and eternal. Therefore one should bear them (pleasure and pain) patiently viz., one shouldn't feel happy and sad by their union and disunion but remain unaffected by them. Pleasure and pain—both are different but their seer is one and he is separate (unaffected) from both of them. By seeing the changeable, the immutability of the self (soul) is naturally perceived as the unchangeable only can see the changeable.

Hence the term 'Śīta' stands for favourableness while 'uṣṇa' stands for unfavourableness. It means that when it is very much cold, a tree dries up and when it is very hot, then also a tree dries up; therefore the result of both 'hot' and 'cold' is only one. Therefore the Lord orders to bear them viz., to rise above them.

Pleasure-pain, joy-grief, attachment-aversion, desire-anger etc., are fleeting and kaleidoscopic while the self (soul) remains the same. A seeker commits a blunder that he sees the changing condition but doesn't perceive the self. He accepts the condition but doesn't accept the self. The condition neither existed in the past nor will exist in future; therefore it doesn't exist at present also though it appears to exist. But in the self there is neither beginning nor end nor middle at all. A condition never remains uniform and the self never becomes multiform. Whatever is seen is a 'condition' and the intellect which sees it is also a 'condition'. The thing which is to be known is a 'condition' and the thing which knows it is also a 'condition'. In the self there is neither anything to be seen nor there is one who sees it; there is nothing to be known nor one who knows it. The object to be seen and he who sees it etc., are subject to conditions. The object to be seen and the seer who sees it—will not remain but the self will remain, because the condition will perish but the self will remain. It means that by having connection with the object to be seen (scene), the self becomes the spectator. If it has no connection with the object to be seen, the self will remain but it will not be named as the spectator. In the same way the self (pure consciousness) by having affinity for 'Śarīra' (body) is called 'Śarīrī'. If it has no relationship with the body, the self will remain but it will not be named 'Śarīrī' (Gītā 13/1). Therefore the Lord has used the term 'Śarīrī' for the self or pure consciousness in order to merely explain it to human beings.

Link:—In the next verse, Lord Kṛṣṇa talks of the result of remaining unaffected with objects.

यं हि न व्यथयन्त्येते पुरुषं पुरुषर्षभ।
समदुःखसुखं धीरं सोऽमृतत्वाय कल्पते॥ १५॥

yaṁ hi na vyathayantyete puruṣaṁ puruṣarṣabha
samaduḥkhasukhaṁ dhīraṁ so'mṛtatvāya kalpate

O the best of men, a person to whom pain and pleasure are alike, and who is not tormented by these sense-objects, becomes eligible, for immortality. 15

Comment:—

'Puruṣarṣabha'—Men, generally try to change inevitable circumstances. But, Arjuna instead of trying to change these, has thought of attaining benediction, which shows, that he is the best of men.

'Samaduḥkhasukhaṁ dhīram'—A resolute person remains alike in pleasure and pain. He experiences pleasure and pain, only when he is attached to three guṇas (qualities, modes) born of matter (nature) (Gītā 13/20-21). But when he gets immersed in the self, he does not experience pleasure and pain, and becomes unruffled.

'Yaṁ hi na vyathayantyete puruṣam'—To a man of steady wisdom, the sense-objects do not give pain. Pleasure, ensuing from the contact of sense-objects, is perturbing (Vyathā). Similarly, pain arising from their separation is also disconcerting. He who has an eye for equanimity cannot be happy or sad by these objects. Such a person knows what are favourable and unfavourable circumstances, but he remains unaffected by them. They do not leave any impression, on his mind.

'So'mṛtatvāya kalpate'—Such a man of steady wisdom, becomes eligible for immortality viz., he acquires the capability of realizing immortality. Being capable, he realizes immortality instantly, because his immortality is axiomatic. It was only because of ones affinity with objects (body etc.,) that it was obscure.

A special word

This human life, has not been bestowed upon man to experience pleasure and pain, but to attain the supreme bliss having obtained which, he has nothing else to seek (Gītā 6/22). If we remain greedy and desirous of acquiring favourable circumstances, we shall not be able to make use of those circumstances, because our energy will be wasted in the enjoyment of those circumstances, rather than in making proper use of these. Similarly, if we grieve over unfavourable circumstances or in their possibility, we will not be able to make use of them, rather we will be brooding over these. To get pleased over favourable circumstances is their enjoyment. The use of favourable circumstances, for mere maintenance of a body, and for the welfare of poverty-stricken people, is their proper use. Thus, riches in the form of favourable circumstances, should be considered, as property of the poor. We should neither be pleased with desirable circumstances, nor displeased with undesirable ones, but we should make the best possible use of these. Otherwise, we shall have to suffer pain.

It is a proper use of desirable circumstances, if having satisfied our needs, we use these to serve the needy and the destitute, instead of enjoying these ourselves. Actually, our riches are for the needy and the poor. So we should utilize these for their welfare. These are, the poor and the destitute, who have enabled the rich to be proud of, their riches. Had all others been multimillionaires could these millionaires have had pleasure and pride out of their being millionaires? No. The poor and destitute people, are the cause, of their pleasure and pride. Therefore, the rich people should serve the desolate and the destitute, as it is their duty to do so. But if they don't do so and enjoy the riches themselves they only are thankless.

Now, the question arises, how to make use of undesirable circumstances. The answer is that undesirable circumstances are painful, when there is desire for pleasure. If that desire is renounced, then undesirable circumstances cannot be painful. If a patient is given bitter medicines and painful injections, he is not upset, rather he is pleased, because he knows that bitter medicines and painful injections, are cures for his disease. Thus, it is the proper use of undesirable circumstances, to bear pain, without having any grudge, against it. If one gets displeased with bitter medicines etc., then that is brooding over unfavourable circumstances. It will result in great misery.

If we enjoy pleasure and are tormented by pain, we may get heaven or hell but cannot be eligible for salvation, because salvation, is attained by those, who remain alike in pleasure and pain.

The Lord, in the fourteenth verse, has said that objects give rise to feelings of pleasure and pain, but these are transitory and fleeting. The moment we acquire them, their decay and parting starts. These were neither with us in the past, nor will remain in future and present, also they are going to be naught. But by enjoying these we are spoiling our nature, and are depriving ourselves of attainment of salvation. Therefore, if we make proper use of the available circumstances, we shall rise above pleasure and pain, and attain a state of the highest bliss.

Appendix—The self is in the form of an entity. In that entity there is no perturbation. When the self identifies itself with the body, then perturbation ensues. Therefore a person who assumes himself to be seated in the body can't be free from torment. Freedom from torment means—not to rejoice on obtaining what is pleasant and not to grieve on receiving what is unpleasant (Gītā 5/20). By being free from torment a man's intellect (understanding) becomes firm—'sthirbuddhirasammūḍhaḥ' (Gītā 5/20).

To rejoice and to grieve in favourable and unfavourable circumstances means to be tormented. To rejoice and to grieve is 'bhoga' of pleasure and pain. The seeker of pleasure and sufferer in pain can never be happy. A striver should not rejoice and grieve in favourable and unfavourable circumstances but should utilize these circumstances. The favourable and the unfavourable circumstances are determined by fate; and to utilize those circumstances by regarding them as material for spiritual progress, is the real valour. This valour results in immortality. Utilization of favourable circumstances is to provide happiness to others and to render service to them; while the utilization of unfavourable circumstances is to renounce the desire for pleasure or favourable circumstances. By utilizing the unfavourable circumstances a striver discovers the reason for pain. The reason for pain is the desire for pleasure—'ye hi saṁsparśajā bhogā duḥkhayonaya eva te' (Gītā 5/22). The person (bhogī) who enjoys pleasure and suffers pain has a downfall while he (yogī) who utilizes pleasure and pain, by rising above pleasure and pain, attains immortality.

Link:—In the next three verses also, the nature of the real (spirit), and the unreal (matter, body), is dwelt.

नासतो विद्यते भावो नाभावो विद्यते सतः।
उभयोरपि दृष्टोऽन्तस्त्वनयोस्तत्त्वदर्शिभिः ॥ १६ ॥

nāsato vidyate bhāvo nābhāvo vidyate sataḥ
ubhayorapi dṛṣṭo'ntastvanayostattvadarśibhiḥ

The unreal has no existence and the real, never ceases to be; the truth of both these, has been perceived by seers of truth. 16

Comment:—

'Nāsato vidyate bhāvo'—This body, neither existed in the past, before birth, nor will exist in the future after death, and is also perishing, at present. Thus, actually it is non-existent. This body is the world in miniature. The change in the body signifies the change, in the world. Similarly, the non-existence of a body signifies the non-existence of the world, in all the times.

The entire world is burning like wood continuously in the

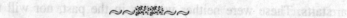

fire, of time. On firewood being burnt, ash remains. But this time-fire consumes the world, in such a way that no remains, are left. There is total annihilation of the world. Therefore, it has been said, that the unreal has no existence.

'Nābhāvo vidyate sataḥ'—The real never ceases to be. The Ātmā (spirit or soul) remains constant. It existed, before the birth of the body, exists now, when the body is undergoing change and will exist, after the death of the body. Similarly, God also ever remains the same, while the world undergoes a change, every moment.

A Vital Fact

The world is kaleidoscopic, it changes every moment. So it cannot be seen in the same state, the very next moment. Bodies are taking birth, and dying every moment, but the process is not perceived, with these dull physical eyes.* Similarly, the world is also perishing, all the time. But it is not perceived, because the senses, mind and intellect etc., also belong to the same class, to which the world belongs. So, how can the perishable perceive, the perishable? Only the imperishable (self), (spirit) can perceive it.

Secondly the self cannot perform any activity, without assistance of the world (body, senses, mind and intellect). It proves, that all activities take place in the world rather than, in the self. The self has no affinity with activities, and objects. It proves, that the world, with body, mind, senses and intellect etc., is non-existent. Only the super soul (God), is ever existent, who ever remains untainted and is the basis and illuminator, of the entire world.

'Ubhayorapi dṛṣṭo'ntastvanayostattvadarśibhiḥ'—Seers of truth, have perceived the truth, about the real, and the unreal, or the

* Though there is a continuous process of birth and death of bodies, yet the process is not perceived because of the subtle speed of time.

soul and the body. The fact is, that the real is ever-existent, the unreal has no existence, but it seems to exist because of the light of the real. Therefore the essence of the real (Sat), and the unreal (asat) is 'sat', (ever-existent). The real has been called as 'Parā Prakṛti' (higher or sentient nature) (Gītā 7/5), 'Kṣetrajña (self, soul) (Gītā 13/1-2), 'Puruṣa' (spirit) (Gītā 13/19) and 'akṣara' (the imperishable) (Gītā 15/16), while the unreal has been called 'aparā prakṛti' (lower or insentient nature), Kṣetra (non-self), prakṛti (matter) and 'Kṣara' (the perishable).

Arjuna is grieved by thinking, that the warriors will die. So, the Lord explains that the real never dies, and the unreal never exists as it is continuously dying. Therefore, it is not wise, to grieve.

In the eleventh verse, it has been said, that 'paṇḍita' (the wise) grieve neither for the living, nor for the dead. In the twelfth and thirteenth verses the word 'dhīra' (wise or enlightened) has been used for the person, who realizes the distinction, between the soul and the body; in the fifteenth verse also 'dhīra', has been used for a person who does not grieve over, the decay of the body and the world, In the sixteenth verse 'tattvadarśī' (the seers of truth), has been used for a discerning person, who distinguishes between the real and unreal. All these words dhīra etc., show that the wise do not grieve and if they grieve, it means, that they are not wise.

Appendix—The ever-existent entity (self) is real and except that entity whatever Prakṛti (Nature) and its evolutes (actions and objects) are, they are all unreal and kaleidoscopic. Those great souls who have perceived the truth about both the real and the unreal viz., those, who have realized the self, hold that the unreal has no existence and the real never ceases to be viz., there is nothing except that entity (the real).

The Lord in the fourteenth and fifteenth verses described the transitory nature of the body; here the same has been described by the expression—'nāsato vidyate bhāvaḥ' (the unreal has no existence); and in the twelfth and thirteenth verses the eternal nature of the 'Śarīrī' (self) was described, that has been mentioned here by the expression—'nābhāvo vidyate sataḥ' (the real never ceases to be).

'Nāsato vidyate bhāvo nābhāvo vidyate sataḥ'—In these sixteen letters there is the gist of all the Vedas, Purāṇas and scriptures. 'Asat' and 'Sat'—these two have been called by several names such as 'Prakṛti' (Nature) and 'Puruṣa' (self), 'Kṣara' (perishable) and 'Akṣara' (imperishable), 'Śarīra' (body) and 'Śarīrī' (self), transitory and eternal, perishable and imperishable etc. Whatever is seen, heard, understood, thought of and determined etc., is 'unreal' and the organs of senses, by which the actions of seeing, hearing and thinking etc., are done, are also 'unreal' and whatever seen is also 'unreal'.

In the half verse (sixteen letters) three roots have been used—

(1) 'bhū sattāyām'—as 'abhāvaḥ' and 'bhāvaḥ'

(2) 'as'bhuvi'—as 'asataḥ' and 'sataḥ'

(3) 'vid sattāyām'—as 'vidyate' and 'na vidyate'

Although these three roots mean only an 'entity' yet in their subtle form they have also their independent meanings—as the meaning of 'bhū' root is 'utpatti' (origin), the meaning of 'as' root is 'sattā' (entity) existence and the meaning of 'vid' root is 'vidyamānatā' (existence of the present).

The meaning of the expression 'nāsato vidyate bhāvaḥ' means 'asataḥ bhāvaḥ na vidyate' viz., the unreal has no existence or the unreal is non-existent because it is continuously perishing (changing). The unreal is not present. The unreal is not acquired. The unreal is not constant. The thing which is born, certainly dies—this is the rule. As soon as it is born, it starts perishing at once. It perishes so quickly that no one can see it two times viz., having seen it once, it can't be seen in the same condition the second time. This is the principle that the thing which has no existence at any time is always non-existent. Therefore the world is always non-existent. However existence we may give to the world, however importance (value) we may attach to it, but it doesn't exist at all. The unreal is neither acquired, nor was acquired nor will ever be acquired. It is not possible to acquire the unreal.

'Nābhāvo vidyate sataḥ'—This expression means—'sataḥ abhāvaḥ na vidyate' viz., the real never ceases to be rather the real is existent, it is never non-existent (changeable). The entity which ceases to be is not called the real. The entity of the real is ever-existent. The real is ever present. The real is ever attained. The real is ever constant.

The real never ceases to be in any place, thing, person, action, incident, circumstance, state and time etc. The reason is that the place, time and thing etc., are unreal (kaleidoscopic) but the real ever exists the same, in it there is never any change, it never ceases to be. Therefore the real is ever-existent. To whatever extent we may deny the existence of the Supreme Soul, to whatever extent we may neglect Him, to whatever extent we may have disinclination for Him, to whatever extent we may disregard Him, to whatever extent we may contradict His existence by giving arguments but He never ceases to be. The non-existence of the real is not possible. No one can destroy the imperishable entity (Gītā 2/17).

'ubhayorapi dṛṣṭaḥ'—Seers of truth have not created (produced) the real entity but they have seen it viz., perceived the truth about it. It means that non-existence of the unreal and existence of the real—the truth of both of these have been perceived by the liberated enlightened souls who perceive only the real entity viz., realize the self-evident 'Is'. The base of the unreal is also real and the truth about the real is also real—by knowing this, in the view of the exalted souls no other entity except the real entity 'Is' remains.

The non-existence of the unreal and the existence of the

real prove that only the real exists. In that real entity there is no such duality as 'deha' (body) and 'dehī' (self).

So long as the unreal's existence is assumed, there is discrimination. But when the unreal ceases to exist, then discrimination changes into Self-realization. 'Ubhayorapi dṛṣṭo'-ntastvanayostattvadarśibhiḥ'—in this expression in 'Ubhayorapi' there is discrimination; in 'antaḥ' there is Self-realization and in 'dṛṣṭaḥ' there is perception of the real viz., discrimination changed into Self-realization and only the entity remained. There is nothing except that entity—this is the most important fact of the Discipline of Knowledge.

The unreal has no existence—this is true and the real never ceases to be—this is also true. It is the duty of a striver to accept this truth. A striver may have this realization or not, he has to accept this fact. One has to accept the entity 'Is' and to deny 'No'—this is Vedānta, this is the main gist of the Vedas.

In the world in spite of the appearance of both—existence and non-existence there is predominance of 'non-existence'. In God also both of them appear, but there is predominance of 'existence.' In the world within 'non-existence' there are existence and non-existence and in God within 'existence' there are existence and non-existence. In other words in the world within 'eternal disunion' there are union and disunion while in God within 'eternal union' there are union and disunion (meeting-separation). Therefore in the world only non-existence persists while in God only existence persists.

Link:—In the next two verses, there is description, of the real and the unreal.

अविनाशि तु तद्विद्धि येन सर्वमिदं ततम्।
विनाशमव्ययस्यास्य न कश्चित्कर्तुमर्हति॥ १७॥

avināśi tu tadviddhi yena sarvamidaṁ tatam
vināśamavyayasyāsya na kaścitkartumarhati

Know that to be imperishable, by which all this world is pervaded; for none can bring about the destruction, of the indestructible. 17

Comment:—

'Avināśi tu tadviddhi'—Here 'tu' (indeed), has been used to explain 'Sat' the real out the two 'sat' (real) and 'asat' (unreal), described in the preceding verse.

The Lord advises Arjuna, to realise that imperishable entity. He explains that this entity is abstract. By calling it abstract, (parokṣa), the Lord means to say, that this abstract imperishable entity, is pervading the whole world, which appears as separate, from that entity. In reality, only this all-pervading entity exists, while the world which appears to exist, does not exist really.

By the term 'tat' (that), it is not meant to say that 'sat tattva' (the real), stands afar, but it means, that it is not a subject of senses and inner sense.

'Yena sarvamidaṁ tatam'*—The abstract-entity is described here. This whole world, is pervaded by that imperishable entity. As ornaments made of gold have nothing but gold, weapons made of iron, have nothing but iron, pots of clay have nothing but clay, and in ice, there is nothing but water, similarly, this world is pervaded by 'sat' (real) (imperishable). So, in the world, there is nothing to be realised except the real.

'Vināśamavyayasyāsya na kaścitkartumarhati'—The spirit

* Yena sarvamidaṁ tatam' has been used in the Gītā three times. Here it has been used for the imperishable by which the whole world is pervaded. It is described with the view of 'Sāṅkhyayoga' (the Discipline of Knowledge). In the twenty-second verse of the eighth chapter it has been used for God (Supreme Puruṣa) Who can be attained by exclusive devotion. Again in the forty-sixth verse of the eighteenth chapter there is the description, 'By whom all this is pervaded' which also is with the point of view of devotion.

(Soul), is imperishable,* while the body is perishable, and is perishing every moment. No one, can check its process of destruction. But whether you wage war or withdraw from it, the imperishable cannot be destroyed and the perishable cannot be saved.

Here the word 'asya' means, that whatever reality appears in the kaleidoscopic body, is because of real entity (self), and that self (spirit), is different from the body.

Appendix—In practical life we say, 'This is a man, this is an animal, this is a tree, this is a house' etc. In these expressions 'man, animal, tree, house' etc., neither existed in the past nor will exist in future and at present also they are perishing every moment. But in them the eternal reality 'Is' ever remains the same. It means that 'man, animal, tree, house' etc., are the world (unreal) and 'Is' is the imperishable Self (the real). Therefore 'man, animal, tree, house' etc., are different but in all of them 'Is' (Eternal reality) remains the same. Similarly in 'I am a man, I am an animal, I am a god' etc., bodies are different but 'am' or 'is' remains the same.

'Yena sarvamidaṁ tatam'—This expression here has been used for the embodied soul while in the twenty-second verse of the eighth chapter and in the forty-sixth verse of the eighteenth chapter, this expression has been used for God. It means that the self has the same characteristics as all-pervading God has. Therefore as God is detached from the world, so is the self naturally detached from the body and the world—'asaṅgo hyayaṁ puruṣaḥ' (Bṛhadā. 4/3/15), 'dehe'sminpuruṣaḥ paraḥ' (Gītā 13/22). The self is not seated in a particular body. It is not attached to any body. But without realizing this detachment, it is following the cycle of birth and death.

---

* In the Gītā the Lord has called the spirit as well as Himself imperishable. But the difference is that the Lord incarnates and conceals Himself by His free-will while the spirit seated in Matter takes birth and dies because it identifies itself with the body.

अन्तवन्त इमे देहा नित्यस्योक्ताः शरीरिणः ।
अनाशिनोऽप्रमेयस्य तस्माद्युध्यस्व भारत ॥ १८ ॥

antavanta ime dehā nityasyoktāḥ śarīriṇaḥ
anāśino'prameyasya tasmādyudhyasva bhārata

These bodies acquired by the imperishable, indefinable and eternal soul, are spoken of, as perishable. Therefore, O Arjuna, fight. 18

Comment:—

'Anāśinaḥ'—A thing, which never changes, never decays and never gets extinct, in the least, by any cause, under any circumstances, is called 'anāśī'. The soul (spirit), is not exposed to, destruction or change. So, it is indestructible or imperishable.

'Aprameyasya'—The soul, is beyond the domain of senses, speech and mind, so it is indefinable. It can be experienced, only by having faith in scriptures, and saints and their gospels.

The scriptures and saints, do not compel anyone to have faith in them. One, is free to have such faith or not to have it. In case one reposes faith in them, that 'tattva' (reality), is the object of his faith, otherwise it is not the object of, his faith.

'Nityasya'—The soul, does not undergo any change, it never ceases to be, it exists all the time.

'Antavanta ime dehā uktāḥ śarīriṇaḥ'—These bodies, of imperishable, indefinable and eternal soul, are spoken of as perishable i.e., they have an end. It means that these are perishing, every moment. They are nothing but, a mass of decay.

In the above sentence, a singular number, has been used for the soul, while plural for the bodies. Firstly it is so because the bodies of every embodied soul are of three kinds—physical, subtle and causal and secondly because a single soul, pervades all worldly bodies. Further in the twenty-fourth verse, the Lord calls it all-pervading viz., omnipresent. It means, that all the bodies are perishable, while soul is imperishable.

An Exceptional Fact

All the bodies which, are perceptible, are perishable, while the soul is imperishable and eternal. But this immortal soul, though different from body, identifies itself with the body and develops 'an ego' or 'I'ness with it, and thus regards its death, as self's (soul's) death. He who identifies himself, with wealth and learning etc., calls himself as wealthy and learned etc. Similarly, when one accepts a body, as one's own, one develops the feeling of attachment or mineness for it, and this attachment, extends to wealth and family etc., because he accepts these as his own, by having affinity with these. By this affinity of 'I'ness and 'Mineness', all evils are born, one cannot discriminate, between the real and the unreal, and is thus grieved, while the wise are not grieved, because they realize that the real cannot perish and the unreal cannot exist.

'Tasmāt* yudhyasva'—Lord Kṛṣṇa directs Arjuna, to fight i.e., discharge his duty, by discriminating between the real and unreal. He means to say, that he should not grieve but wage war, because the soul is imperishable, while bodies are perishable.

An Exceptional Fact

In the seventeenth and eighteenth verses, there is a notable explanation of the real and the unreal, because the Lord wants Arjuna, to realize the real. By realizing the essence, one gets rid of the unreal, spontaneously. Thus by realizing this fact, he would discharge his duty. It shows, that every human being, without any distinction of caste, creed, colour or stage of life, can freely follow either the Discipline of Action, or Discipline of Knowledge, for his salvation. But, in practical life, a duty should be discharged,

* Here the word 'Tasmāt', has been used for drawing a conclusion after reasoning. In the Gītā 'Tasmāt' has been used either for drawing the conclusion after reasoning or at the end of a context. In 2/30, 3/19, 8/7 and 8/27 verses it has been used at the end of a context while in 2/25, 2/27, 2/37, 2/68, and 11/33 it has been used to conclude reasoning.

according to one's varṇa (caste) and āśrama (stage of life), by following the ordinance of scriptures. Therefore, here while discussing the real and the unreal according to the discipline of knowledge Lord Kṛṣṇa, orders Arjuna to fight or in other words he advises Arjuna to discharge his duty even if he follows discipline of knowledge.

Further, in the thirteenth chapter, where there is a description of virtues of knowledge Lord Kṛṣṇa in 13/9, also lays emphasis on non-attachment, and non-identification of the self, with a son, wife, home etc. If only hermits, had deserved the Discipline of knowledge (Sāṅkhyayoga), the Lord would not have mentioned, the need for non-attachment and non-identification of the self, with a son, wife, home etc., because hermits, have no sons, wives and homes etc.

Thus, by meditating on the Gītā, both the Disciplines of Knowledge, as well as Action (Karma), have proved to be independent means, for God-realization for all human beings, without distinction of any varṇa or stage of life.

Appendix—The Lord at the outset of His gospel explained that both 'gatāsūn' (dead) and 'agatāsūn' (living) are not to be grieved for. Then in the twelfth and thirteenth verses in order to explain that 'gatāsūn' is not to be grieved, He explained the real (the eternal) and in the fourteenth and fifteenth verses in order to explain that 'agatāsūn' is not to be grieved, He described the unreal (the transitory). Then He explained both 'Sat' (the real) and 'Asat' (the unreal) in the sixteenth verse. After that by discussing the existence of the real and non-existence of the unreal specially in the seventeenth and eighteenth verses, He completes this sub-topic.

Though there is existence only of the soul, not of the body, yet a man commits an error that he first sees the body and then perceives the soul in it; first sees the form (appearance), then perceives the existence. How long will this outward polish stay?

A striver should reflect upon whether the soul (self) existed first or the body existed first. On reflection it is proved that first there is the self and then there is the body, the existence is first and the appearance is afterwards. Therefore a striver first should perceive the self as existent, not the body.

Link:— Upto the previous verse, there is description of seers who know the soul, as imperishable. In the next verse, Lord Kṛṣṇa to emphasize the same fact, speaks of those, who do not regard the soul as indestructible, by a negative inference.

य एनं वेत्ति हन्तारं यश्चैनं मन्यते हतम्।
उभौ तौ न विजानीतो नायं हन्ति न हन्यते॥ १९॥

ya enaṁ vetti hantāraṁ yaścainaṁ manyate hatam
ubhau tau na vijānīto nāyaṁ hanti na hanyate

Both of them are ignorant, one who holds the soul as, the slayer and the other who considers it, as slain; for the soul, neither slays, nor is slain. 19

Comment:—

'Ya enaṁ vetti hantāram'— One who considers the soul as slayer is ignorant because the soul does not act. But by identifying with the body, it accepts itself as a doer. As an artisan, however clever he may be, cannot work without tools, similarly, the soul without body cannot do anything. Therefore, the Lord, in the thirteenth chapter, declares, that he who sees that all actions are performed by prakṛti (nature) alone, realizes the self, as non-doer (13/29). It means, that the self is not a doer. But, by identifying Itself with body it assumes Itself to be the doer of actions, performed by the body. If a man, does not identify himself with the body, he is not at all, a doer, of any activity.

'Yaścainaṁ manyate hatam'—One who holds the soul as slain, is also ignorant. As the soul is never the slayer, so it is never killed, because the soul, always remains unaffected and unchanged. Only the perishable and changeable, can be slain. How could the imperishable and unchangeable, be slain?

'Ubhau tau na vijānīto nāyaṁ hanti na hanyate'—Both of these, who holds the soul as slayer, and he, who considers it as slain, are ignorant. A question arises, whether he, who holds the soul as slayer, as well as slain, is not ignorant. The answer is, that he is also ignorant, because the soul is neither a destroyer, nor can it be destroyed. It is always the same, without any change. Therefore, one should not grieve.

The soul, has been described, neither as a slayer nor as slain, because it was in the context of war, before Arjuna. But, actually the soul, is free from all acitons and modifications.

Appendix—This Śarīrī (the possessor of the body) neither slays anyone nor is slain by anyone—it means that it is neither a doer of an action nor is an object of action nor is affected in anyway. Those, who, like the body, hold the Śarīrī as the slayer and as the slain, indeed don't attach importance to the discrimination between the body and the self but attach importance to indiscrimination.

Link:—In the next verse the Lord explains how this soul is immortal.

न जायते म्रियते वा कदाचि-
न्नायं भूत्वा भविता वा न भूयः।
अजो नित्यः शाश्वतोऽयं पुराणो
न हन्यते हन्यमाने शरीरे॥ २०॥

na jāyate mriyate vā kadāci-
nnāyaṁ bhūtvā bhavitā vā na bhūyaḥ
ajo nityaḥ śāśvato'yaṁ purāṇo
na hanyate hanyamāne śarīre

For the soul there is neither birth nor death; nor does it come into existence after having been born. It is unborn, eternal, constant and primeval. It is not killed, even when the body, is slain. 20

Comment:—

[The body constituted of elements, undergoes six kinds of modifications—to be born, to exist, to change, to grow, to decay and to perish. But, the soul remains unaffected by, these changes. The Lord explains this fact, in this verse.]

'Na jāyate mriyate vā kadācinna'—The soul, unlike a body is never born, it is eternal. So the Lord in 15/7, has declared, 'This soul in the body, is an eternal portion of Myself.'

The soul never dies. Only that, which is born, dies. The soul remains unaffected by all kinds of changes. Of all these changes, birth and death, are the most important ones. Therefore, the Lord has used 'Na jāyate' and 'Ajaḥ', for the unborn and also 'Na mriyate, and 'Na hanyate hanyamāne śarīre, for the unslain, twice.

'Ayaṁ bhūtvā bhavitā vā na bhūyaḥ'—This imperishable element, does not exist, on coming into being, unlike a child, that exists after birth and has a beginning and an end, it is free from different kinds of changes and is without beginning and end.

'Ajaḥ'—This soul is never born, so it is called 'Ajaḥ' viz., unborn.

'Nityaḥ'—The soul is eternal. It does never decay in the least while the bodies and senses decay and lose their strength.

'Śāśvataḥ'—The soul is constant and changeless.

'Purāṇaḥ'—It is ancient and primeval. Generally a thing which becomes old does not grow, it rather perishes. But the soul neither grows nor perishes.

'Na hanyate hanyamāne śarīre'—The soul is not slain even when the body is slain. Lord Kṛṣṇa means to say that the body undergoes six modifications because it is perishable while the soul is imperishable.

Here in these verses Lord Kṛṣṇa has made such a distinction between the body and the soul, as is rarely found anywhere else in the Gītā.

Arjuna was grieved after thinking about the death of his kinsmen in the war. So Lord Kṛṣṇa wants to explain to him that the soul is not killed even when the body is slain, so he should not grieve.

Appendix—Our (of the self) nature and the nature of the body are quite different. We (the self) are not attached to the body, are not mingled with the body. The body is not attached to us, it is not mixed with us. Therefore at the death of the body we are not affected at all. By now we have passed through innumerable bodies, but what difference did it make in our entity (existence)? What loss did we sustain? We remained the same—'bhūtagrāmaḥ sa evāyaṁ bhūtvā bhūtvā pralīyate' (Gītā 8/19). Similarly at the death of the body we'll remain the same.

As hands, feet and nose etc., are organs of the body, likewise the body is not an organ of the self. That which flows and varies is not an organ* (of the imperishable) as phlegm and urine etc., flow and an ulcer (boil) varies, so they are not organs of the body. Similarly the body which flows and varies is not an organ of the self.

Link:—In the nineteenth verse, Lord Kṛṣṇa told Arjuna that soul neither slays, nor is slain. In the twentieth verse, He explained how it is not slain. Now, in the next verse, He explains how it does not slay.

वेदाविनाशिनं नित्यं य एनमजमव्ययम्।
कथं स पुरुषः पार्थ कं घातयति हन्ति कम्॥ २१॥

* adravaṁ mūrttimat svāṅgaṁ prāṇisthamavikārajam
atatsthaṁ tatra dṛṣṭaṁ ca tena cettattathāyutam

vedāvināśinaṁ nityaṁ ya enamajamavyayam
kathaṁ sa puruṣaḥ pārtha kaṁ ghātayati hanti kam

O Pārtha, How can, a man who realises this soul to be imperishable, eternal and free from birth and decay, slay, anyone or cause anyone to be slain? 21

Comment:—

'Vedāvināśinaṁ nityaṁ ya enamajamavyayam kathaṁ sa puruṣaḥ pārtha kaṁ ghātayati hanti kam'—The man, who realizes this soul to be imperishable, eternal and free from birth and decay, can have no inclination to slay, anyone or cause anyone, to be slain. He is free from egoism i.e., he has no feeling of an agent in him, and so actions do not taint him.

Here, Lord Kṛṣṇa has explained that the soul is free from six kinds of modifications (i.e.) to be born, to exist, by the term 'Aja', to change, to grow by the term 'nitya', to decay by the term "avyayam' and to perish by the term 'avināśī'.

Now, a question arises, If the Lord by the terms 'na hanyate hanyamāne śarīre' and 'kaṁ ghātayati hanti kam' had merely to tell Arjuna that the soul is neither a doer nor an object of action then why he used words 'not a slayer' or 'not a slain' for the soul. The answer is that the theme is of a war, so it is necessary to say so. But He means, that the soul, is neither the agent (doer), nor the object of action. Therefore, one while discharging duty, should not grieve, while slaying anyone or causing anyone to be slain, but should discharge one's duty, in accordance with the ordinance of scriptures.

Appendix—A thing which is produced (born) certainly perishes, it has not to be perished (destroyed). But the thing which is not born, never perishes. We passed through eighty four lac forms of bodies but no body stayed with us and we didn't stay with any body; but we remained the same and apart. Those bodies didn't possess this power of discrimination but only this human body has been endowed with it. If we don't realize it, we disregard the discrimination bestowed upon us by God.

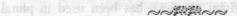

Link:—In the next verse, Lord Kṛṣṇa explains that the soul is free from change by giving an illustration.

वासांसि जीर्णानि यथा विहाय
नवानि गृह्णाति नरोऽपराणि।
तथा शरीराणि विहाय जीर्णा-
न्यन्यानि संयाति नवानि देही॥ २२॥

vāsāṁsi jīrṇāni yathā vihāya
navāni gṛhṇāti naro'parāṇi
tathā śarīrāṇi vihāya jīrṇā-
nyanyāni saṁyāti navāni dehī

As a person discarding worn-out clothes, puts on new ones, so an embodied soul, casting off old bodies, enters into others, which are new. 22

Comment:—

'Vāsāṁsi jīrṇāni yathā vihāya navāni gṛhṇāti naro'parāṇi tathā śarīrāṇi vihāya jīrṇānyanyāni saṁyāti navāni dehī'—In the thirteenth verse of this chapter, it has been mentioned in brief that a wiseman does not get deluded, when the soul, transmigrates from one body to another. Now, Lord Kṛṣṇa by giving an illustration explains, that as a man by casting off old clothes is not grieved, so a man casting off worn-out bodies, should not grieve.

Here the word nara' (man), has been used for a human being, including men-women, boys-girls, young-old etc., all.

As a man discarding old clothes, puts on new ones, so does an embodied soul, casting off worn-out bodies, enter into new bodies. The casting off, of worn-out bodies is called death, while its acquiring new bodies, is called birth. So long as, this embodied soul has connection with prakṛti, it goes on acquiring new bodies, according to actions of the past, or according to thoughts at the moment of death.

Here the term 'śarīrāṇi' (bodies), has been used in plural

form. It means, that so long as an embodied soul, does not get emancipated, it goes on acquiring new bodies, upto eternity. The bodies, it has acquired are countless. The term 'dehī' has been used, to indicate, all embodied souls.

In the first half of this verse, there is mention of discarding of worn-out clothes, while in the second half, there is reference to casting off worn-out bodies.* So, how can the illustration of old clothes befit bodies, when bodies of even children and young men, die? The answer is, that end of age, means the worn-out bodies, whether they are of children, youngmen or old men.

In this verse, the Lord by using the terms, 'yathā' (as) and 'tathā' (so), has explained that as a man, discarding worn-out clothes, puts on new ones, so does an embodied soul, casting off worn-out bodies, acquire other bodies, which are new.

Here, a doubt arises, that a man is free in casting off old clothes and putting on new ones, but he is not free to cast off an old body and enter into a new one. The answer is, that Lord Kṛṣṇa does not mean to talk about freedom and dependence. His aim is to dispel the grief, arising from the separation of a body. One should not grieve, over the death of a body, because the soul remains unattached and unchanged. From this angle, this example is appropriate.

Another question that arises is, that a man is happy by discarding old clothes and putting on new ones, whereas he feels grieved, while casting off an old body and getting into a new one. The reason is, that a man by identifying himself with a body, wants to live long and thinks of the death of the body, as his own death. Thus, he gets sad. The grief (sadness), is the result of the desire to live, not because of death. 'I may

* If we perceive by applying our discrimination we come to know that the body is wearing out every moment and it reaches a stage when it completely dies. But we don't realize this fact because we don't pay attention to it. This is darkness or ignorance (lack of discrimination).

live'—this desire is latent, and he has to die, and that causes grief. But if he were to discriminate between the real and the unreal, he need not be sad, he rather rejoices. Thus, it is because of his ignorance, that he weeps. In his ignorance, he is like a child, who weeps, while his old clothes are taken away and he is made to put on new ones. To remove this ignorance, the Lord has used 'yathā' (as) and 'tathā' (so) words, by giving an illustration of clothes.

Lord Kṛṣṇa, has used the verb 'gṛhṇāti' for putting on clothes and 'saṁyāti' (enter), for embodied soul, because people generally think out of ignorance, that man changes clothes, living at his own place while an embodied soul has to go and enter new bodies. So Lord Kṛṣṇa, has used these two verbs, keeping the worldly point of view in mind.

Something Noteworthy

In the Gītā in 'Yena sarvamidaṁ tatam' (2/17), in 'Nityaḥ sarvagataḥ sthāṇuḥ' (2/24) phrases, the soul has been described as all-pervading, eternal, omnipresent and constant, while in phrases such as 'Saṁyāti navāni dehī' (2/22) and 'Śarīraṁ yadavāpnoti' (15/8), it is said that the soul migrates (enters) into another body. So, there seems to be a contrast, but in fact, there is none. For example, when a person grows from his babyhood to youth, he says that he has grown young. But the fact is, that he is the same, it is the body which has grown young. By identifying himself with the body, he grafts the change of his body upon himself. Therefore, in fact the soul does not migrate. But, because of Its identification with bodies, It seems to migrate.

Now, a question arises, why this cycle of birth and death, has been going on from times, immemorial. From the view-point of the Discipline of Action, to reap the fruit of virtuous and evil actions, and from the view-point of the Discipline of Knowledge due to ignorance, and from the view-point of the Discipline of Devotion, due to disinclination for God, this cycle of birth and death goes on. The basic factor behind these three is, that God has granted liberty to living beings, to make proper use of their lives, but they misuse it and so they have to go through a cycle of birth and death. They can be free from this cycle, by making proper use of this liberty. It means, that if they start working for the welfare of others, by renouncing their selfishness, they will be free from this cycle. Moreover negligence in discrimination* is the root cause of birth and death. If we attach importance to discrimination, we can be free from the shackles of birth and death. Similarly, disinclination for God, is the cause of birth and death, which can be eliminated by having an inclination for Him.

Appendix—A man wants new articles, so the Lord also gives him new articles (body etc., material). When the body grows old, God bestows upon him the new body. Therefore 'having new desires' is the cause of his birth and death. Those who have new desires, will get new things times without number. In a man there is one power of the will and another of the life-breath. If he has power of the will and his life-breath ends, he has to be re-born. If he has no will (desire), he has not to take re-birth when his life-breath ends.

An illustration is applicable only to a certain extent, not to the full extent. Here the illustration of casting off old clothes and putting on new ones is applicable to the extent that as a man, by changing several clothes, remains the same, similarly the self, by casting off worn-out bodies and by acquiring several new bodies, remains the same. As by casting off old clothes we don't die and by putting on new clothes we are not born,

* Negligence in discrimination means that we don't act according to what we know. We know that it is wrong to tell a lie. But still we do so in order to achieve selfish ends. We know that it is wrong to give pain to others. But we derive sadistic pleasure in torturing others. Similarly we know that bodies are perishable but we have attachment and infatuation for them. This is known as an affront to our knowledge.

similarly by casting off worn-out bodies, we don't die and by acquiring new bodies, we are not born. It means that the body dies, we (the self) don't die. If we die, who will reap the fruit of virtuous and sinful actions? Who will acquire new bodies? Who will be in bondage? Who will attain salvation?

Link:—In the next three verses, there is the description that the soul is super-mundane.

नैनं छिन्दन्ति शस्त्राणि नैनं दहति पावकः।
न चैनं क्लेदयन्त्यापो न शोषयति मारुतः ॥ २३ ॥

nainaṁ chindanti śastrāṇi nainaṁ dahati pāvakaḥ
na cainaṁ kledayantyāpo na śoṣayati mārutaḥ

Weapons cannot cut the soul, nor can fire burn it, water cannot drench it, nor can wind make it dry. 23

Comment:—

'Nainaṁ chindanti śastrāṇi'—Weapons cannot cut the soul because they are made of the earth-element which cannot even reach the soul. So how can they hurt the soul?

'Nainaṁ dahati pāvakaḥ'—Fire cannot burn the soul, because the soul is beyond the reach of fire. It means that fire can never bring any change ever in it.

'Na cainaṁ kledayantyāpaḥ'—Water cannot drench the soul because water cannot wet it. Water can never bring any change in it.

'Na śoṣayati mārutaḥ'—Wind cannot dry the soul because it is beyond the reach of wind. It can never bring any change in the least in it.

Thus out of the five gross elements four cannot hurt the soul. Now, the question arises—why has Lord Kṛṣṇa not mentioned the fifth element—ether? The answer is, that Ākāśa (ether) is actionless. Earth, water, fire, wind are born of ether and these are incapable of acting on ether. Therefore, when they cannot even hurt ether, how can they hurt the soul, which is beyond the reach of even Matter or nature (prakṛti)? These elements with attributes cannot reach the soul, which is without any attributes (Gītā 13/31).

The soul is eternal. All the four elements such as the earth etc., are activated by the power of the soul. So, how can they impair the soul, the source of their power? The soul is all-pervading, while the four elements, such as the earth etc., are the pervaded ones. How can the pervaded ones, hurt the all-pervading one?

Here, the context is of war. Arjuna is grieved at the thought of the imminent death, of his kinsmen. Therefore, Lord Kṛṣṇa explains to Arjuna that the soul cannot be hurt by any weapons. A weapon can cut the body, not the soul, a fire-emitting missile can burn the body, but not the soul, the Neptune noose (Varuṇa weapon), can drench a body but not the soul, and the wind-missile can dry the body but not the soul. It means that the soul is not hurt by any weapons and missiles, it remains the same, while it is the body alone which decays and dies. So, it is sheer ignorance to lament for it.

Appendix—We say, 'This is a body'—there is a change in the body, but in 'Is' (Śarīrī) there is no change. Similarly when we say, 'There is wood or timber', then there is variation in wood, not in 'Is'. Wood is cut, 'Is' is not cut. Wood burns, 'Is' does not burn. Wood becomes wet, 'Is' doesn't get wet. Wood dries, 'Is' does not get dry. Wood never remains uniform while 'Is' never becomes multiform.

अच्छेद्योऽयमदाह्योऽयमक्लेद्योऽशोष्य एव च।
नित्यः सर्वगतः स्थाणुरचलोऽयं सनातनः ॥ २४॥

acchedyo'yamadāhyo'yamakledyo'śoṣya eva ca
nityaḥ sarvagataḥ sthāṇuracalo'yaṁ sanātanaḥ

This soul is uncleavable, incombustible and neither can be wetted nor dried. It is eternal, all-pervading, stable, constant and everlasting. 24

Comment:—

[In this verse it is described why weapons etc., cannot hurt this soul.]

'Acchedyo'yam'—This soul is incapable of being cut. Even incantation and curse cannot cut this soul, while they can cut the body, as Śākalya was beheaded by Yājñavalkya's curse, because the former could not answer the latter's questions.

'Adāhyo'yam'—This soul cannot be burnt by fire, because it is impervious to fire. It cannot be burnt even by incantation and curses, as the hunter was burnt to ashes, by Damayantī's curse. Only that can be burnt by fire, which is prone to fire. The soul is beyond burning.

'Akledyaḥ'—The soul is impervious to water. Water, incantation, curse and medicines etc., cannot drench it. As it is said, that the tune of 'Mālakośa song wets a stone, and moon-light wets the moon-gem. But the soul cannot be wetted by them.

'Aśoṣyaḥ'—The soul cannot be dried by wind, incantation, curse and medicines etc., as sage Agastya dried the sea.

'Eva ca'—By using these two words, Lord Kṛṣṇa means to say, that the soul is beyond the reach of any action. So it should not be grieved for.

'Nitya'—The soul is eternal, it remains the same all the time.

'Sarvagataḥ'—The soul pervades all men, things and bodies etc., equally.

'Acalaḥ'—It is immovable, there is no movement in it.

'Sthāṇuḥ'—It is stable. It does not even shake or vibrate.

'Sanātanaḥ'—It is everlasting and beginningless.

Something Noteworthy

The world is transitory, while the soul is eternal. Matter is kaleidoscopic, while the soul is stable. All things and persons etc., of the world are movable, while the soul is immovable and all worldly objects, are subject to birth and decay, while the soul is everlasting.

Lord Kṛṣṇa says that men identify themselves with bodies and material things, and so they do not realize, that they are different from worldly things, but even then, the soul remains uniform and constant, all the time.

Appendix—'Sarvagataḥ' (All-pervading)—the self does not mere pervade a body but it is all-pervading—realization of this fact is salvation (liberation from worldly bondage). As the body is seated in the world, we are not seated in the body. We (the self) have never had our union with the body, we have no union, won't have any union and it is not possible to have a union with the body. The body is quite afar from us. But because of desire, the sense of mine and identification with the body it appears as if we have union with the body.

In fact the Śarīrī doesn't need the body at all. The Śarīrī without the body, also remains in bliss.

अव्यक्तोऽयमचिन्त्योऽयमविकार्योऽयमुच्यते।
तस्मादेवं विदित्वैनं नानुशोचितुमर्हसि ॥ २५ ॥

avykto'yamacintyo'yamavikāryo'yamucyate
tasmādevaṁ viditvainaṁ nānuśocitumarhasi

This soul is unmanifest, inscrutable and immutable. Therefore, knowing it as such, you should not grieve. 25

Comment:—

'Avyakto'yam'—The soul unlike a body is unmanifest, because it cannot be perceived by any one of the senses.

'Acintyo'yam'—Mind and intellect etc., cannot be perceived by senses but they are thinkable. But this soul is inscrutable.

'Avikāryo'yamucyate'—The soul is immutable i.e., it does not undergo any change while matter is changing, all the time. The cause of the entire creation is matter. That causative nature (matter) is subject to change. The soul is beyond any change, as it is transcendental.

In the twenty-fourth and twenty-fifth verses, Lord Kṛṣṇa has described the soul, by giving eight adjectives of negation and four adjectives of affirmation. But the fact is that it cannot be described in words, because how can tongue illumine the soul, which is an illuminator of the tongue etc.? Therefore, this realization about the soul is, its real description.

'Tasmādevaṁ viditvainaṁ nānuśocitumarhasi'—Thus, by knowing (realizing), the soul as uncleavable, incombustible, unmanifest, everlasting and immutable etc., one cannot grieve.

Link:—In the next two verses, Lord Kṛṣṇa says, that even if one thinks of the soul as changeable, (which is against the basic (principle), one should not grieve.

अथ चैनं नित्यजातं नित्यं वा मन्यसे मृतम्।
तथापि त्वं महाबाहो नैवं शोचितुमर्हसि॥ २६॥

atha cainaṁ nityajātaṁ nityaṁ vā manyase mṛtam
tathāpi tvaṁ mahābāho naivaṁ śocitumarhasi

O mighty-armed, even if you suppose this soul as constantly undergoing birth and death, even then, you should not grieve over it. 26

Comment:—

'Atha cainaṁ nityajātaṁ nityaṁ vā manyase mṛtaṁ tathāpi tvaṁ mahābāho naivaṁ śocitumarhasi'—Lord Kṛṣṇa, by using the terms, such as 'atha ca' and 'manyase' means that it is a fact that the soul is unborn (Gītā 2/20), yet if you accept the contrary, you should not grieve, because one who is born is bound to die, and one who dies, is bound to be reborn. None can escape this eternal rule.

A seed sown in the earth, assumes different shapes—sprout, plant, tree and then it dries up and decays. The fact is, that the seed undergoes change, every moment. If this seed had remained the same, even for a moment; how had it passed different stages upto the last one of its drying up, as a tree? It gave up its prior form—it is its death; and it assumes a new shape—it is its birth. Thus it passes, through birth and death, every moment. Similarly, this body also undergoes a change, every moment. Sperm gets mixed with ovum and the mixture, grows into a baby which is born. With its birth, the process of death sets in, which culminates in death. Thus, this body undergoes a continuous change i.e., it is born, it decays and dies.

Therefore Lord Kṛṣṇa says to Arjuna that even if he holds the view that the soul undergoes birth and death like a body, there is still no ground for grieving.

जातस्य हि ध्रुवो मृत्युर्ध्रुवं जन्म मृतस्य च।
तस्मादपरिहार्येऽर्थे न त्वं शोचितुमर्हसि॥ २७॥

jātasya hi dhruvo mṛtyurdhruvaṁ janma mṛtasya ca
tasmādaparihārye'rthe na tvaṁ śocitumarhasi

Death is sure of him who is born, and rebirth is assured of him who is dead. You should not, therefore, grieve over the inevitable. 27

Comment:—

'Jātasya hi dhruvo mṛtyurdhruvaṁ janma mṛtasya ca'— According to the previous verse, if the soul is regarded as constantly taking birth and constantly dying, one should not grieve, because death is sure of him who is born, and rebirth is assured of him who is dead.

'Tasmādaparihārye'rthe na tvaṁ śocitumarhasi'—This cycle of birth and death has been going on from time immemorial and will continue upto eternity. Therefore, you should not lament over the inevitable. These Dhṛtarāṣṭra's sons and Bhīṣma, Droṇa etc., who are born will surely die, you cannot save them and after death, they will certainly take rebirth, you cannot stop it. So why should you grieve?

As the sun has risen, it will certainly set, and if it is set, it will definitely arise. This is an inevitable fact, which is known to all. Therefore, none grieves over the setting of the sun. It implies that one should not grieve over the death of anybody.

Whatever the Lord has stated in these two verses (26th and 27th) is not God's real theory. By the expression 'Atha ca' the Lord has put forth the argument of the people, who identify, themselves with the body. This is not a correct principle. In no case Arjuna should grieve. To bring home this point to him, Lord Kṛṣṇa has explained from that angle also.

In these two verses, Lord Kṛṣṇa says that all the worldly things, including the bodies, undergo change from one form to another. Abandoning the first form is called death and change to the second form is called birth. One should not grieve over this cycle because it inevitably goes on.

Appendix—A man is grieved if a dear one dies or there is loss of money. Similarly we are grieved when we think about the future—if the wife dies, what will happen? If the son dies, what will happen? etc. We are grieved and worried because we don't attach importance to discrimination. Changes in the world and in circumstances are inevitable. If circumstances don't change, how will the cycle of the world continue? How will a person pass from boyhood to youth? How will a fool become learned? How will a patient become healthy? How will a seed turn into a tree? Without change the world will become like a static thing. In fact only a mortal dies, an immortal never dies. It is everyone's obvious experience that after death the body remains lying, but the self, the owner of the body transmigrates. If importance is attached to this experience, there can't be any worry or grief. At the death of Bāli, Lord Rāma draws Tārā's attention towards this experience—

Tārā bikala dekhi Raghurāyā, dīnha jñāna hari līnhī māyā.
Chiti jala pāvaka gagana samīrā, pañca racita ati adhama śarīrā.
pragaṭa so tanu tava āgeṁ sovā, jīva nitya kehi lagi tumha rovā.
upajā jñāna carana taba lāgī, līnhesi parama bhagati bara māgī.

(Mānasa, Kiṣkindhā 11/2-3)

We should think over when no body remained in eighty-four lac forms of life, how will this body remain intact? When eighty-four lac bodies didn't remain as 'I' and 'mine', how will this body remain as 'I' and 'mine'? This discrimination is possible only in human body, not in other bodies.

Link:—In the next verse Lord Kṛṣṇa mentions the simple law of nature about birth and death.

अव्यक्तादीनि भूतानि व्यक्तमध्यानि भारत।
अव्यक्तनिधनान्येव तत्र का परिदेवना॥ २८॥

avyaktādīni bhūtāni vyaktamadhyāni bhārata
avyaktanidhanānyeva tatra kā paridevanā

O Bhārata (Arjuna), all beings were imperceptible before they were born and will become so again when they are dead; they are perceptible only in the intermediate stage. Why then the lamentation? 28

Comment:—

'Avyaktādīni bhūtāni'—All the beings seen now, were not perceived before birth.

'Avyaktanidhanānyeva'—These beings will also not be perceived after death.

'Vyaktamadhyāni'—All these beings are manifest in the interim (after birth and before death). Their bodies were non-existent before birth and will remain non-existent after death, just like in a dream. During life they seem to exist but actually they are going into non-existence every moment.

'Tatra kā paridevanā'—It is the principle that the thing which does not exist either before or after has no real existence in its midstate also. Therefore, these bodies which were unmanifest in their origin and will be unmanifest in their end, are unmanifest even now, though they seem visible. But the soul existed in the past, exists now and will also exist in future. So there is no point in lamenting for both these situation.

Appendix—A thing, which does not exist at the beginning and at the end, has never any existence, while a thing, which exists at the beginning and at the end, ever exists.* That which never exists, is 'asat'—unreal (body) and the entity which ever exists, is 'sat'—the reality. We have our eternal disunion with the unreal while with the real we have our eternal union.

---

* (1) 'yastu yasyādirantaśca sa vai madhyaṁ ca tasya san'

(Śrīmadbhā. 11/24/17)

'The thing which exists at the beginning and at the end, also exists in the midstate and that is true.'

(2) 'ādyantayorasya yadeva kevalaṁ kālaśca hetuśca tadeva madhye'

(Śrīmadbhā. 11/28/18)

'The entity which existed at the beginning of this world and which will remain in the end and which is the root cause and illuminator of this world, the same Super Soul (God) also exists in the midstate.'

(3) 'na yat purastāduta yanna paścānmadhye ca tanna vyapadeśamātram'

(Śrīmadbhā. 11/28/21)

'The thing which didn't exist before origin and will not remain after annihilation (end), doesn't exist in the middle also, it is merely an imagination, merely a name.'

Link:—Now, the Lord dwells upon the marvellous nature of the soul.

आश्चर्यवत्पश्यति कश्चिदेन-
माश्चर्यवद्वदति तथैव चान्यः ।
आश्चर्यवच्चैनमन्यः शृणोति
श्रुत्वाप्येनं वेद न चैव कश्चित् ॥ २९ ॥

āścaryavatpaśyati kaścidena-
māścaryavadvadati tathaiva cānyaḥ
āścaryavaccainamanyaḥ śṛṇoti
śrutvāpyenaṁ veda na caiva kaścit

One perceives the soul as a wonder, some speak of it an amazement while others hear of it in wonderment; while none knows it even after hearing of it. 29

Comment:—

'Āścaryavatpaśyati kaścidenam'—The knowledge of the wondrous self is not achieved through the senses. The self can be known by the self itself, it is beyond the realm of senses. As 'I am'— this knowledge requires no proof, no instrument, it is self-evident. Its consciousness cannot be experienced as separate from 'I'. This is intuited by the person himself. This is not a subject of senses and intellect. Therefore, the knowledge of self is said to be a marvel.

The term 'paśyati' has two meanings—to see with eyes and to know the self by one's own self. Here it has been used in the sense of knowing the self by one's own self (Gītā 2/55; 6/20 etc.,).

When one sees with one's eyes, there are three things necessary—the onlooker, the object to be seen and sight i.e., the power to see. But while knowing the self these three are not necessary. 'I am'— this cannot be perceived by senses, mind and intellect, but by one's own self.

When we want to search for a thing in a dark room, we need

eye-sight as well as light. But if there is light-lamp, there is no need for another lamp to see the lamp which is lit. Similarly, there is no need for other means to perceive the self. The self has its own light by which it can be lit and known.

A body is of three kinds—physical (gross), subtle and causal. The body which is nourished by food and water for its growth, is physical (gross) body. This gross body is the object of senses. The subtle body consists of seventeen elements—five senses, five organs of action, five vital airs, mind and intellect. The subtle body can be perceived by intellect and not by senses. The latencies (vāsanās) form the causal body. If we reflect, on the three kinds of bodies, it is evident that the gross body is not the self, as it changes every moment and it is an object of knowledge. Similar, is the case with the subtle body. The causal body, is an evolute of nature. But the self is beyond nature, therefore the causal body, is also not the self. As far as, the knowledge of the self, is concerned, it is beyond them and this knowledge is marvellous. This is 'āścaryavatpaśyati.' When the soul ceases its identification with the body, it knows itself and therefore, it has been said that one perceives the soul as a wonder.

Here in this verse, as well as, in the third verse of the seventh chapter, Lord Kṛṣṇa has used the term 'Kaścit' i.e., 'Someone knows Me in reality.' It means, that it is very difficult to know the imperishable, but actually it is not so. The fact is, that it seems difficult, only because there are a few aspirants, who sincerely want to know the soul.

'Āścaryavadvadati tathaiva cānyaḥ'—Other persons speak of it as marvellous, because it is beyond the reach of words. Speech is illumined, by the self, then, how can it describe the illuminator? The great souls who speak of it, can just give a kind of hint to draw the attention of the listeners.

Here, the term 'Anyaḥ' has been used to emphasize the

fact, that only a few liberated souls who possess metaphysical knowledge, can explain it fully to an aspirant and enable him, to attain the imperishable. All do not possess the ability to remove his doubts and give satisfactory answers, to his arguments.

'Āścaryavaccainamanyaḥ śṛṇoti'—Other persons hear of it, as marvellous. Listening to scriptures and advice of other worlds, is quite different from voice of the soul. It means, that this soul is something marvellous and uncommon and is beyond the reach of senses, mind and intellect etc. It illuminates these.

Here, the term 'Anyaḥ' has been used to explain the fact, that the person who hears is different, from the one who knows, and from other who is capable of explaining it to an aspirant in such a manner, that its full nature, is revealed to him.

'Śrutvāpyenaṁ veda na caiva kaścit'—There are some who do not know it, even on hearing. It means that, merely hearing, will not help one to know it. On hearing, when one gets established in one's own self, one will know one's own self* by oneself.

Now a question arises, that an aspirant on hearing the words of scriptures and a preceptor, gets knowledge, why has it been said then, that there are some who do not know it, even on hearing of it? The answer is, that it is the aspirant himself, who by having faith in the words of scriptures and preceptor, gains knowledge. Otherwise there have been several incarnations of God, and there also have been liberated souls, who held discourses on metaphysics, and by hearing their discourses the people should have gained metaphysical knowledge. But, actually it has not happened. Their discourses, can be helpful to a striver having faith, but he, will also have to get himself established in his own self. This expression does not mean to convey, that knowledge of the self is impossible; it rather conveys that it is beyond the senses. However hard efforts by a man may make him to know

* This fact has been pointed out in the Gītā several times—(2/55; 3/17; 6/20; 15/11).

it, ultimately he will have to know himself, by his own self.

What is knowing of the self, by the self? There is a difference between doing, perceiving and knowing. Doing involves organs of action, perceiving involves senses, while knowing is done by the self Itself.

The senses actually do not know; rather they only perceive which is useful in daily activity.

This knowledge, of knowing oneself by one's ownself, is of two kinds—'I am different from the body and the world;' and secondly, 'I have identity with God.' In other words, it can be said, 'I have no affinity with the kaleidoscopic, perishable world, while I have constant affinity with unchangeable, imperishable God.' After possessing this kind of knowledge, one can know the soul in reality. This knowledge, is beyond the reach of speech and intellect.

Appendix—The self cannot be known merely by hearing viz., by practice but can be known by having inquisition, by hearing from enlightened and experienced exalted souls—'yatatāmapi siddhānāṁ kaścinmāṁ vetti tattvataḥ' (Gītā 7/3). 'Āścaryavadvadati tathaiva cānyaḥ'—it means that out of the enlightened exalted souls, only someone can explain its true nature to others. All the enlightened souls can't explain it.

As in the world a couple doesn't get married merely by hearing but the man and the woman accept each other as wife and husband and then they are married. Similarly no one can know God merely by hearing but after hearing, when he accepts Him himself and gets established in Him, then he will know Him by his own self. Therefore by hearing a man can learn the facts pertaining to knowledge, can narrate them to others, can write them, can lecture on them, can discuss them but can't realize the self or God.

One can't know God merely by hearing but can know Him by worshipping Him after hearing from others—'śrutvānyebhya upāsate' (Gītā 13/25). If the person, who describes the Supreme Soul, is a God-realized soul and the listener (striver) has esteemed faith and inquisition, there can be immediate Self-realization.

Link:—The next, is the concluding verse, about discrimination between the body and the soul.

देही नित्यमवध्योऽयं देहे सर्वस्य भारत।
तस्मात्सर्वाणि भूतानि न त्वं शोचितुमर्हसि ॥ ३० ॥

dehī nityamavadhyo'yaṁ dehe sarvasya bhārata
tasmātsarvāṇi bhūtāni na tvaṁ śocitumarhasi

O Bhārata, this soul residing in the bodies of all, can never be slain. Therefore, you should not grieve, for any being. 30

Comment:—

'Dehī nityamavadhyo'yaṁ dehe sarvasya bhārata'—The soul, residing in bodies of men, gods, animals, birds, insects etc., cannot be slain i.e., it is imperishable.

The term 'Avadhyaḥ', has two meanings—(i) It should not be slain, (ii) It cannot be slain. For example, a cow should not be killed, because it is a deadly sin to kill a cow. But in case of the soul, it does not mean that it should not be slain, but it means that the soul cannot be slain in anyway by anyone. It has also been mentioned in 2/17, that none can bring about the destruction of the indestructible substance.

'Tasmātsarvāṇi bhūtāni na tvaṁ śocitumarhasi'—Therefore, you should not grieve for all beings because the soul is indestructible, while the perishable body cannot remain the same even for a moment.

Here, 'Sarvāṇi bhūtāni', plural number has been used to emphasize the fact that, one should not grieve, for any living being.

The body is perishable, because its nature is such. It is

perishing every moment. But, the self is imperishable. If this reality is realized, then no grief is, possible.

Related and Noteworthy

In this section from the eleventh to the thirtieth verses, it is explained that the soul, which is imperishable and real, is different from a body which is perishable and unreal. Unless, one can discriminate between the soul and the body, one cannot follow anyone of the disciplines, either of Disinterested Action, Knowledge or Devotion. Not only this, but also one who wants to go to heaven should know, the distinction between the two. After the death of a body, who will go to heaven? Therefore, all the philosophers who are believers, in spite of having different opinions about philosophy, agree with the fact, that the soul is different from the body. Here the Lord wants to explain this distinction clearly.

This is everyone's own experience also, that a body changes from babyhood to youth and then to old age. But, there is an unchangeable one that knows this change. That one, is the soul. Therefore, the changeable and the unchangeable, can never be identified. In this section, Lord Kṛṣṇa, has not used a philosophical terminology, because people think that philosophy is a subject for study only. So he has used such words as, the real and the unreal, the perishable and the imperishable etc. One, who can discriminate between the two, is not grieved in the least, while, one who merely studies philosophy, is grieved.

A man may study the six systems of philosophy and may possess knowledge about the Absolute, the soul, the Nature and the world. But, his knowledge is purely theoritical. On the other hand, a striver or a devotee may be concerned who wants to realize his identity with God or who wants to surrender himself to God, by renouncing his assumed affinity for prakṛti, and the world, his knowledge is practical. There is a vast difference in these two sorts of knowledge.

Appendix—The Lord has described the discrimination between the 'deha' (body) and 'dehī' (possessor of the body) from the eleventh to the thirtieth verses. While describing this topic Lord Kṛṣṇa has not used a philosophical terminology such as brahma-jīva, prakṛti-puruṣa, jaḍa-cetana, māyā-avidyā, ātmā-anātmā etc. The reason is that the Lord, instead of making it a subject for study, wants to make it a subject of everyone's experience and wants to prove that every man can discriminate the body from the self. It needs no study, no eligibility.

If a man applies the discrimination between the real and the unreal on his body, he is a striver (seeker) and if he applies it on the world, he is learned. By keeping himself aloof, if a person discriminates between the real and the unreal, he may become learned by possessing bookish knowledge (not learning) but he can't attain Self-realization. But he who discriminates between the real and the unreal in his own body, can attain Self-realization. It means that discrimination between the real and the unreal in the world is for pedantry while the Gītā is not for pedantry. Therefore the Lord, instead of using the philosophical terminology, has used simple words such as 'deha-dehī', 'Śarīra-Śarīrī' viz., the body and its possessor. Those who discriminate between the real and the unreal in the world, they keeping themselves aloof, make themselves the authority on the knowledge of the Gītā. But any person, who discriminates the body from the self in him, is eligible for Self-realization. For Self-realization the discussion on discrimination between the body and the self, is useful and in order to gain learning, the discussion on 'tattva' the Divinity is useful. Therefore the striver who wants to realize the self, first of all should discriminate his own self from the body that the body has no connection with the self and the self has no connection with the body viz., 'I am not body'. He, who has assumed the existence and greatness (value) of the body with as much truth, firmness, belief and doubtlessness, should assume (accept) the existence and value of the Self (Soul) with the same truth, firmness, belief and doubtlessness and should realize the self.

The body is the means only for performing an action and an action is performed only for the world. As a writer uses a pen only for writing and when he stops writing, he puts the pen at its proper place, similarly a striver should use the body while doing an action and should leave the body in its original position when the work is finished—he should be detached from it. The reason is that if we do nothing, what is the need of the body?

An important fact for a striver is to renounce the known unreal. If a striver renounces what he knows as unreal, his spiritual discipline will become natural and easy and his aim will be attained. The lovability of a striver for the end (aim) is called his spiritual discipline. That lovability is not acquired by anything, person, power etc., or by practice but that is acquired by having the sense of 'mine' for the end (Lord). The person in whom a striver has the sense of 'mine', naturally becomes lovable (dear) to him. But the real sense of mine is with that object (or person) in which (or in whom) there are the following four traits—

1. With whom we have identity (oneness) of the self.
2. With whom our relationship is eternal.
3. From whom we never want anything.
4. To whom we may surrender all what we have.

These four conditions are applicable only in God. The reason is that our relationship with the body and the world is not eternal and the category of the self is quite different from that of the world and body. How can there be identity of the kaleidoscopic world with the never changing self? The identity of the self with the body, which is perceived, is not real but is assumed. This assumed identity is only to perform duty. It means that we can serve the person with whom we have assumed our identity but we can't have the sense of 'mine' with him.

In order to renounce the known unreal, it is necessary that a striver should renounce the relationship which our discrimination does not support. Assuming a person, with whom we have neither eternal relationship nor identity of the self, our own and for us, is anti-discrimination relationship. So long as there is anti-discrimination relationship, no spiritual discipline will lead to Self-realization. By having affinity with the body, a person may undergo austere penance, may have trance, may go round the world, his delusion can't be destroyed and the Supreme Truth can't be attained. Having renounced the anti-discrimination relationship delusion is destroyed and the Supreme Truth is realized. Therefore a striver shouldn't be at ease without renouncing the anti-discrimination relationship. If we don't renounce our assumed anti-discrimination relationship with the body, the body will leave us certainly. Then what is the difficulty in renouncing our kinship with the body? Therefore a seeker may follow any discipline, he will have to accept the truth, "I am not body and the body is not mine and it is not for me because I am 'aśarīrī' (self) and the self is unmanifest."

So long as a striver has the kinship of 'I' and 'mineness' with the body there is no realization of the Supreme Truth and he remains bound by virtuous actions, useful reflection and attachment to Trance. He may perform virtuous actions such as performance of sacrifice, undergoing penances, offering charity, may reflect upon the soul or the Supreme Soul or be established in trance, he is not totally free from bondage. The reason is that assumption of the kinship of the self with the body is the root of bondage and also of the flaw which causes all flaws. If the assumed affinity of a striver with the body is totally wiped out, sinful actions will not at all be performed by him and he will not be attached to virtuous actions. There will not be any meaningless reflection by him at all, and he will not be attached to meaningful reflection. He will not be fickle in the least and will neither be attached to trance, constancy or absence of all thoughts. Thus at the destruction of attachment of the gross (physical) body to actions, of the subtle body to reflection and of causal body to constancy, his aim will be attained viz., his delusion will be destroyed and the Supreme Truth will be realized. Therefore the Lord at the outset of His gospel has described the discrimination between the body and the self in order to wipe out a striver's (self's) relationship with the body.

Link:—Arjuna was grieved, by apprehending the death of his kinsmen and preceptors. Moreover he was afraid that sin would accrue to him, by killing them and that sin would lead him to hell. Therefore Lord Kṛṣṇa preached this gospel in the eleventh to the thirtieth verses. Now, He starts the worldly standpoint and reminds Arjuna of his duty, as a member of the warrior class.

स्वधर्ममपि चावेक्ष्य न विकम्पितुमर्हसि।
धर्म्याद्धि युद्धाच्छ्रेयोऽन्यत्क्षत्रियस्य न विद्यते॥ ३१॥

svadharmamapi cāvekṣya na vikampitumarhasi
dharmyāddhi yuddhācchreyo'nyatkṣatriyasya na vidyate

Looking at your own duty as well, you should not falter for there is, nothing more meritorious to a person of the warrior class (Kṣatriya) than a righteous war. 31

Comment:—

[In the first two verses, He describes the benefit of war.]

'Svadharmamapi cāvekṣya na vikampitumarhasi'—Man (soul) is a fragment of God. But by identifying himself with the body, noting himself as a Brāhmaṇa (of the priest class) or a Kṣatriya (of the warrior class) etc., he has to discharge his duty as a member of that class. Similarly one who acknowledging himself as a teacher or a father, has to discharge the duty of a teacher or a father.

Here, the duty of a Kṣatriya has been called 'Dharma' (righteousness)*. It is the foremost duty of a Kṣatriya not to

* In the eighteenth chapter (18/42— 48) the Lord has described the innate

flee from war front. For a Kṣatriya, righteousness is upheld by waging war. So, Lord Kṛṣṇa asks Arjuna to discharge his duty, by waging war. He should never shirk that duty.

'Dharmyāddhi yuddhācchreyo'nyatkṣatriyasya na vidyate'— There is nothing more welcome to a man of the warrior class than a righteous war viz., which is his main duty (Gītā 18/43). Similar, is the case with, the people of other classes—the priest, the business and the labour classes.

Arjuna, in the seventh verse of the second chapter, requested Lord Kṛṣṇa to tell him what is good for him. In response to his request, Lord Kṛṣṇa tells him, that he would attain salvation by performing his duty of waging a righteous war. So, he should not retreat from it.

Appendix—Having described the discrimination between 'deha' (body) and 'dehī' (self) the Lord from this verse to the thirty-eighth verse describes the performance of one's duty. The reason is that the Supreme Truth which is realized by the discrimination between 'deha' and 'dehī', the same Supreme Truth can be realized by the proper use of the body, by performing one's duty. In discrimination 'knowing' is important and in performance of one's duty 'doing' is important. Though discrimination is important for a man, as it is useful for him in practical and spiritual life and also in this world as well as the other world, yet the Lord mentions performance of one's duty for the person, who doesn't understand the discrimination between the body and the self, so that instead of becoming a scholar by possessing bookish knowledge or rot learning, he may realize the Truth.

It means that a person who wants to know Godhead but without having a keen intellect and a keen self-denial (detachment), couldn't know Him by the Discipline of

---

duties of the people of four castes. There the term 'Dharma' (18/47) stands for one's duty. Thus the terms 'Karma' and 'Dharma' are synonymous.

Knowledge, he can know the Supreme Soul by the Discipline of Action (Gītā, 5/4-5).

Arjuna was a Kṣatriya (member of the warrior class). Therefore the Lord has mentioned the duty of a Kṣatriya. In fact here 'the duty of a Kṣatriya' is the denotation for the duties of the four 'Varṇas'. Therefore it means that the members of other 'Varṇas' (castes) such as Brāhmaṇa (member of the priest class) etc., should also discharge their duties (Gītā, 18/42—44). ['Svadharma' (one's own duty) has been mentioned as 'Svabhāvaja karma', 'Sahaja karma' and 'Svakarma' etc., (Gītā 18/42—48). Discharge of one's duty for the welfare of others, by renouncing selfishness, pride and the desire for fruit, is performing 'svadharma'. Discharge of 'Svadharma' (one's duty) is 'Karmayoga' (the Discipline of Action).]

यदृच्छया चोपपन्नं स्वर्गद्वारमपावृतम्।
सुखिनः क्षत्रियाः पार्थ लभन्ते युद्धमीदृशम्॥ ३२॥

yadṛcchayā copapannaṁ svargadvāramapāvṛtam
sukhinaḥ kṣatriyāḥ pārtha labhante yuddhamīdṛśam

Fortunate are the Kṣatriyas, O Pārtha, who get such an unsolicited opportunity for war, which offers an open gateway, to heaven. 32

Comment:—

'Yadṛcchayā copapannaṁ svargadvāramapāvṛtam'— Duryodhana imposed a condition on the Pāṇḍavas, "If you lose while gambling, you will be exiled for twelve years and will reside in an unknown place for one year. Then after thirteen years you will regain your empire. But, if you are identified during that one year period, you will again be exiled for twelve years." The Pāṇḍavas, accepted the condition and suffered twelve years in exile, and one year's incognito existence. After expiration of the period, when the Pāṇḍavas demanded their empire, Duryodhana refused to give them, even as much land as could be covered by the point of a needle, without waging war. The Pāṇḍavas made several efforts for a compromise, but Duryodhana bluntly refused. Therefore, Lord Kṛṣṇa says to Arjuna, "You have got this unsought and unsolicited opportunity, for waging a war. Such a righteous war, is an open gateway to heaven."

'Sukhinaḥ kṣatriyāḥ pārtha labhante yuddhamīdṛśam'—Those Kṣatriyas, who get such an opportunity are really lucky. He means to say, that the happiness which is derived by discharging one's duty, is far superior to worldly pleasures which could be enjoyed, even by animals and birds.

Link:—In the next four verses, Lord Kṛṣṇa explains the evil consequences of not waging a war.

अथ चेत्त्वमिमं धर्म्यं सङ्ग्रामं न करिष्यसि ।
ततः स्वधर्मं कीर्तिं च हित्वा पापमवाप्स्यसि ॥ ३३ ॥

atha cettvamimaṁ dharmyaṁ saṅgrāmaṁ na kariṣyasi
tataḥ svadharmaṁ kīrtiṁ ca hitvā pāpamavāpsyasi

If you do not wage such a righteous war, then in abandoning your duty and forfeiting your honour, you shall incur sin. 33

Comment:—

'Atha cettvamimaṁ dharmyaṁ saṅgrāmaṁ na kariṣyasi tataḥ svadharmaṁ kīrtiṁ ca hitvā pāpamavāpsyasi'—Even if you do not want to discharge your duty, by waging war, bound by your own action born of your nature, you will have to engage in it against your will (18/60). If you do not wage war, you will neglect your duty and you will not only lose your reputation, but incur sin, also. Moreover, by abandoning your duty, you will have to accept the duty of others, and so you will incur sin and by abandoning war, you will be regarded as an unmanly warrior, and thus you will lose your honour and reputation.

अकीर्तिं चापि भूतानि
कथयिष्यन्ति तेऽव्ययाम्।
सम्भावितस्य चाकीर्ति-
र्मरणादतिरिच्यते ॥ ३४ ॥

akīrtiṁ cāpi bhūtāni
kathayiṣyanti te'vyayām
sambhāvitasya cākīrti-
rmaraṇādatiricyate

All beings will ever recount your undying infamy and that is surely, worse than death for a man, enjoying popular esteem. 34

Comment:—

'Akīrtiṁ cāpi bhūtāni kathayiṣyanti te'vyayām'— Men, gods, genies, and demons etc., and all, who do not have even the least friendship or enmity with you, such simple beings will recount your infamy and dishonour and will call you a coward, if you do not wage war. They will disparage your chivalry, and will say that you proved to be a coward, which could not even be imagined.

By using the word 'te' (thy) Lord Kṛṣṇa means to say, that Arjuna who is renowned in heaven, in this world, as well as, in the infernal world, for his courage, will be called a coward. By using the term 'avyayām' (everlasting) He means that as he is famous for his excellence and bravery, he will be unpopular for his weakness and timidity forever.

'Sambhāvitasya ākīrtirmaraṇādatiricyate'—In the first half of this verse, the Lord discussed Arjuna's disparagement by common people. Now He is talking in general terms.

In the world, if any man, who is regarded superior to others and enjoys popular esteem, loses his honour and fame, his infamy is more painful to him, than even death. Because in natural death he does not lose his name and fame while he loses these by shunning his duty. In case of natural death, no crime or sin is committed, but shirking duty is a sin, which brings much discredit.

भयाद्रणादुपरतं मंस्यन्ते त्वां महारथाः ।
येषां च त्वं बहुमतो भूत्वा यास्यसि लाघवम् ॥ ३५ ॥

bhayādraṇāduparataṁ maṁsyante tvāṁ mahārathāḥ
yeṣāṁ ca tvaṁ bahumato bhūtvā yāsyasi lāghavam

The great chariot-warriors, who held you in high esteem, will consider you as lowly, thinking that you have desisted from war, out of fear. 35

Comment:—

'Bhayādraṇāduparataṁ maṁsyante tvāṁ mahārathāḥ'—If you think that you have desisted from war, in order to attain salvation by avoiding sin, it is not true. If you had thought of it as a sin to wage the war, you might have spent sometime in devotion and meditation in solitude, and would not have invited Me to wage this war. Therefore, if you desist from the war, all the living beings will think that you have done so out of fear, not out of a sense of duty and righteousness, as it is the first and foremost duty of a Kṣatriya to fight.

'Yeṣāṁ ca tvaṁ bahumato bhūtvā yāsyasi lāghavam'—The great chariot-warriors such as Bhīṣma, Droṇa, Kṛpa and Śalya etc., who hold you in high esteem for your mighty valour, (because you have defeated several demons, gods and demigods etc.,) you will fall in their esteem as one who has fled from the war-front out of fear, of death.

अवाच्यवादांश्च बहून्वदिष्यन्ति तवाहिताः ।
निन्दन्तस्तव सामर्थ्यं ततो दुःखतरं नु किम् ॥ ३६ ॥

avācyavādāṁśca bahūnvadiṣyanti tavāhitāḥ
nindantastava sāmarthyaṁ tato duḥkhataraṁ nu kim

Your enemies, disparaging your strength, will speak in unbecoming terms. What could be more distressing than this? 36

Comment:—

'Avācyavādāṁśca bahūnvadiṣyanti tavāhitāḥ nindantastava sāmarthyam'—Your sworn enemies, such as Duryodhana, Duḥśāsana and Karṇa etc., in spite of knowing your deeds of valour, will be little your strength and will laugh at you and call you a coward and impotent. How will you bear those insolent jokes and irrepairable ignominy?

'Tato duḥkhataraṁ nu kim'—What can be more painful than this? It is generally seen that a person of respectable and high standing, cannot tolerate insults from persons of low standing and he performs deeds of mighty valour, beyond expectation. Similarly, you will not be able to tolerate ignominy and slander and so there will be no alternative for you, but to wage the war that has been declared. So, how could you bear that ignominy?

Link:—After explaining the adverse consequences of not waging the war, in the preceding four verses, in the next two verses Lord Kṛṣṇa, explains the favourable consequences of war.

हतो वा प्राप्स्यसि स्वर्गं जित्वा वा भोक्ष्यसे महीम्।
तस्मादुत्तिष्ठ कौन्तेय युद्धाय कृतनिश्चयः॥ ३७॥

hato vā prāpsyasi svargaṁ jitvā vā bhokṣyase mahīm
tasmāduttiṣṭha kaunteya yuddhāya kṛtaniścayaḥ

Slain in battle you will gain heaven, victorious you will enjoy the sovereignty of earth; therefore, arise, O son of Kuntī, determined to fight. 37

Comment:—

'Hato vā prāpsyasi svargaṁ jitvā vā bhokṣyase mahīm'—In

the sixth verse of this chapter, Arjuna raised a question that they did not know whether they would conquer the sons of Dhṛtarāṣṭra or Dhṛtarāṣṭra's sons, would conquer them. So Lord Kṛṣṇa answers the question and says, "If you are killed by Karṇa etc., you will attain heaven and if you gain victory, you will gain the kingdom. Thus righteous warfare would result in good, both here and hereafter. So you should be prepared to wage war, otherwise you risk to lose both." Kṛṣṇa by addressing Arjuna as Kaunteya wants to remind him of the message to wage the war, sent by his mother when He went to the Kauravas, with a proposal for a treaty. Therefore, he should rise to the occasion with full determination.

Arjuna was determined not to fight and Lord Kṛṣṇa, in the third verse of this chapter, ordered him to rise to the occasion. Here, Arjuna is in a dilemma, whether to wage war or not. So Lord Kṛṣṇa exhorts him to be determined to fight, without having any doubts.

Here, Lord Kṛṣṇa wants to say that everyone should discharge his duty very sincerely and enthusiastically, to the best of his power and ability, in whatever circumstances, he is placed. Humanity demands it.

Appendix—By discharging one's duty, one makes advancement in this world and other world. It means that by discharging one's duty and by abstaining from what ought not to be done, one attains perfection here as well as hereafter.

सुखदुःखे समे कृत्वा लाभालाभौ जयाजयौ।
ततो युद्धाय युज्यस्व नैवं पापमवाप्स्यसि॥ ३८॥

sukhaduḥkhe same kṛtvā lābhālābhau jayājayau
tato yuddhāya yujyasva naivaṁ pāpamavāpsyasi

Treating alike victory and defeat, gain and loss, pleasure

and pain and engage yourself in battle. Fighting thus you will incur no sin. 38

Comment:—

[Arjuna was thinking that by killing his kinsmen he would incur sin. So Lord Kṛṣṇa clarifies that it is not the war but desire, which induces a man to incur sin. So by renouncing desire, he should be engaged in war.]

'Sukhaduḥkhe same kṛtvā lābhālābhau jayājayau tato yuddhāya yujyasva'—In a war a man either gains victory or suffers defeat. Victory results in gain, while defeat results in loss. Worldly people, view gain with pleasure and loss with pain. But your aim is not to think of victory and defeat, gain and loss, and pleasure and pain, but your goal is to discharge your duty by treating the agreeable and the disagreeable, alike. By doing so you will incur no sin viz., you will be free from bondage.

Everyone should discharge his duty earnestly and efficiently, whether he has a desire or not for its fruit. By refusing to be affected by favourable and unfavourable circumstances, the mind becomes steady. So treating the two equally, one should discharge one's duty. Moreover, one should not perform an action for the sake of pleasure, and refrain from another, for fear of its pain. Scriptures should be the authority in determining what ought to be done and what ought not to be done (Gītā 16/24).

'Naivaṁ pāpamavāpsyasi'—Here, the word, sin, has been used both for sin and virtue. The former, leads to the bondage of hell and the latter to the constraints of heaven. Both of these deprive a man of salvation and binds him to follow the cycle of birth and death. So, Lord Kṛṣṇa exhorts Arjuna, to discharge his duty of waging war, by being even-minded. This will help him to escape the bondage of both sin and virtue.

Something Noteworthy Regarding This Section

In this section of eight verses from the thirty-first to the thirty-eighth Lord Kṛṣṇa has disclosed several variegated feelings.

(i) While delivering a discourse or explaining a subject, the beginning should deal with positive aspects, the middle with negative aspects and the conclusion should again deal with positive aspects. In this context also, Lord Kṛṣṇa in the thirty-first and thirty-second verses, explains the favourable consequences of discharging one's duty; in the middle from the thirty-third to the thirty-sixth verses, He explains the adverse consequences of not performing one's duty; and again concludes, in the thirty-seventh and thirty-eighth verses, by explaining the favourable consequences of discharging the duty and orders Arjuna to act accordingly.

(ii) In these verses, Lord Kṛṣṇa has also clarified the doubts arising in the mind of Arjuna. For example Arjuna says, "I don't foresee any good, ensuing from the slaughter of kinsmen" (1/31). Lord Kṛṣṇa replies in 2/31, "There is nothing more welcome to a man of the warrior class, than a righteous war." In 1/37 Arjuna says,"How can we, by killing our kinsmen, be happy?" Lord Kṛṣṇa replies in 2/32, "Happy are the Kṣatriyas who get the opportunity of waging such an, unsolicited warfare." In 1/44 Arjuna says, "The consequence of the war will lead to hell." In 2/32,37 Lord Kṛṣṇa says, "The war is an open gateway to heaven." In 1/36 Arjuna says, "Sin alone will accrue to us by waging the war and by slaying them." Lord Kṛṣṇa replies in 2/33, "If you do not wage such a righteous war and abandon your duty, you will incur sin." In 1/40 Arjuna says, "The result of the war will be that impiety will take hold of the entire family." Lord Kṛṣṇa in 2/33 says, "If you do not wage such a righteous war, you will abandon your duty viz., righteousness."

(iii) In 2/5 Arjuna insists and says, "It is better to live on alms, than to wage war." Therefore, Lord Kṛṣṇa in 2/38, orders him to wage war. Uddhava had a desire to live with Lord Kṛṣṇa. So Lord Kṛṣṇa directed him to go to the northern mountains and do penance there (Śrīmadbhāgavata 11/29/41). It means that, desire of any type is an obstacle to salvation.

(iv) In these verses Lord Kṛṣṇa has explained in details some of the things which were referred to in brief, in the second and third verses of this chapter. For example earlier the expression 'anāryajuṣṭam' (it is shunned by noble souls) was used, here the expression 'dharmyāddhi yuddhācchreyo'nyat' (any other thing more welcome than a righteous war) has been used. There the term 'asvargyam' (not leading to heaven), was used here the expression 'svargadvāramapāvṛtam, (an open gateway to heaven), has been used. There the term 'akīrtikaram' not bringing fame was used, here the expression 'akīrtim cāpi bhūtāni kathayiṣyanti te'vyayām' (all creatures will even recount your undying infamy) has been used. There, Lord Kṛṣṇa ordered Arjuna to fight by using the expression 'tyaktvottiṣṭha parantapa' here, also, He orders him the fight by using the expression 'tato yuddhāya yujyasva'.

Appendix—The Gītā teaches the remarkable art of spiritual upliftment through one's own dealings so that a person, under all circumstances, having all kinds of dealings sanctioned by the scriptures, may attain salvation. Generally other scriptures mention that if you want to attain salvation, become a recluse by renouncing mundane materials and live in solitude because the mundane affairs and spiritual upliftment can't go together. But the Gītā declares that at whatever place you are, whatever sect you follow, whatever principle you live up to, whatever religion, school of thought, 'Varṇa' (caste), 'Āśrama' (stage of life) you follow, by following them if you act according to the gospel of the Gītā, it will lead you to salvation. The Supreme Truth, which recluses and saints attained in solitude by practising spiritual discipline for years together, will be attained in practical worldly life by following the teachings of the Gītā. By becoming even-minded in success and failure, performance of one's duty without the desire for fruit, is to act according to the gospel of the Gītā.

What can be more terrible circumstance and activity (action) than a war? When a man can attain salvation under such a terrible circumstance and activity as a war, then what other more terribe circumstance and activity will be there in which he may not attain salvation? According to the Gītā sitting on a seat in loneliness and meditating on God can lead to salvation (Gītā 6/10—13) and waging a war can also lead to salvation.

Arjuna wanted neither heaven nor kingdom (Gītā 1/32, 35, 2/8). He wanted to turn away from the sin which would accrue by killing his kith and kin (Gītā 1/36, 39, 45). Therefore the Lord appears to say, "If you don't covet heaven and kingdom and want to turn away from the sin, discharge your duty of fighting in the war treating the agreeable and the disagreeable alike, thus you will incur no sin—'naivaṁ pāpamavāpsyasi'. The reason is that sin is not incurred by waging war; but uneven-mindedness (partiality), desire, selfishness and ego are the causes of sin. It is your duty (dharma) to wage war. Sin is incurred by not performing one's duty and by doing which should not be done."

In the preceding verse the Lord seemed to say to Arjuna, "If you want to gain kingdom and heaven, it is proper for you to perform your duty," while in this verse He seems to say, "If you don't want to gain kingdom and heaven, it is proper for you to discharge your duty by being even-minded." It means that it is improper not to discharge one's duty under any circumstances.

Link:— The Lord, in the next two verses, authorizes Arjuna to be guided by even-mindedness, already mentioned in the preceding verse and he describes its glory.

एषा तेऽभिहिता साङ्ख्ये बुद्धिर्योगे त्विमां शृणु।
बुद्ध्या युक्तो यया पार्थ कर्मबन्धं प्रहास्यसि ॥ ३९ ॥

eṣā te'bhihitā sāṅkhye buddhiryoge tvimāṁ śṛṇu
buddhyā yukto yayā pārtha karmabandhaṁ prahāsyasi

O Pārtha (Arjuna), this attitude of mind has been presented to you from the point of view of Jñānayoga (Discipline of Knowledge); now hear of the same, from the point of view of Karmayoga (the Discipline of Selfless-Action). Equipped with this state of mind, you will be able to completely shake off the shackles of Karma (Action). 39

Comment:—

'Eṣā te'bhihitā sāṅkhye buddhiryoge tvimāṁ śṛṇu'—Here the word 'Tu' (indeed) has been used to show that the description of the Discipline of Action, is different from the Discipline of Knowledge.

The term 'Eṣā' has been used for equanimity, which has been described in the preceding verse and which has already been explained in the Discipline of Knowledge, (from the eleventh to the thirtieth verses). When a man discriminates between the body and the soul, he gets established in equanimity automatically because it is attachment to the body which is an obstacle in the way of equanimity. So this ideal of equanimity has already been presented from the point of view of 'Sāṅkhyayoga' (Discipline of Knowledge); now listen to a discourse on equanimity in the context of 'Karmayoga' (Discipline of Action).

'Imām' (this) term has been used to explain how this equanimity is attained by the Discipline of Action and what its importance is?

'Buddhyā yukto yayā pārtha karmabandhaṁ prahāsyasi'—Arjuna was afraid of the sin that would accrue by waging the war (1/36, 45). But Lord Kṛṣṇa says that sin does not accrue by waging the war as it is your duty, but it accrues by having attachment and aversion. So if you attain equanimity, no sin will accrue and your duty of waging the war, will not lead you to bondage.

In the seventh verse of this chapter Arjuna asked Lord Kṛṣṇa to advise him what was good for him. Hence, Lord Kṛṣṇa answers his query. First, He mentioned the means of Sāṅkhyayoga (Discipline of Knowledge), and then laid great stress on performance of duty, and told him that there was nothing more welcome to a Kṣatriya, than a righteous war (2/31). Then, He told him that no sin would accrue, if he had equanimity (2/38). Now, He explains the same equanimity, in the context of 'Karmayoga' (Discipline of Action).

A Karmayogī performs action to set an example, to the masses (Gītā 3/20) without any selfish motive. By doing so, he attains equanimity, easily. Having attained equanimity, he is easily liberated, from the bondage of actions.

This (Thirty-ninth) verse, should have been placed after the thirtieth verse, as it rightly belonged there, because from the eleventh verse to the thirtieth verse, the Lord explained even-mindedness, from the view-point of the Discipline of Knowledge, and now He describes it from the view of Discipline of Action. So it seems improper, to insert these eight verses, from the thirty-first to the thirty-eighth, here. But really it is not so. The reason is, that before describing equanimity in the Discipline of Action, it is necessary to describe, what one ought to do and what one ought not to do. It was Arjuna's duty, to wage a righteous war. It was not his duty to abandon war, because by doing so, he would incur sin. So Lord Kṛṣṇa, in these eight verses, described what Arjuna ought to do and what he ought not to do (2/31—38). Then, he explained equanimity. It means, that first from the eleventh verse to the thirtieth verse, he explained equanimity, through as elucidation of the real and the unreal, by mentioning that the real is real and the unreal is unreal and none can change these. Then, from the thirty-first verse to the thirty-eighth verse, having explained what one ought to do, and what one ought not, from the thirty-ninth verse, He exhorts Arjuna never to desist from his duty, but to always perform duty with even-mindedness, in success and failure.

Appendix—'Karmayoga' (Discipline of Action) is divided into two parts—'kartavya vijñāna' (the science of duty) and 'Yoga vijñāna' (the science of equanimity). The Lord from the thirty-first verse to the thirty-seventh verse mentioned the science of duty in which He described the favourable consequences of discharging the duty and adverse consequences of not discharging the duty. Now from this verse to the fifty-third verse He mentions the science of equanimity.

The equanimity which the Lord mentioned in the preceding verse, can be attained both by 'the Discipline of Knowledge' and 'the Discipline of Action'. By knowing the discrimination between the body-division and the self-division and renouncing affinity with the body-division, is 'The Discipline of Knowledge' while by knowing the duty-division and the non-duty-division and by renouncing what ought not to be done and discharging one's duty, is 'the Discipline of Action'. A man by following one of the two disciplines should attain equanimity. The reason is by attaining equanimity a man is freed from the bondage of action.

One is 'Dharma Śāstra' (Pūrva mīmāṁsā) [The scripture for duty] and one is 'mokṣa śāstra' (Uttara mīmāṁsā) [The scripture for salvation). Here from the thirty-first verse to the thirty-seventh verse, there is description of 'Dharma Śāstra', while from the thirty-ninth verse to the fifty-third verse there is description of 'Mokṣa śāstra'. By 'Dharma śāstra' (discharging one's duty) there is both kinds of progress*—mundane and spiritual. In 'Dharma śāstra' the discharge of one's duty is important. Either call it 'Dharma' or duty—it is one and the same.

Not to do what ought to be done is 'non-discharge of duty'

* 'yato'bhyudayaniḥśreyasasiddhiḥ sa dharmaḥ' (Vaiśeṣika 1/3, 2/39).

and to do what ought not to be done is also 'non-discharge of duty'. Duty is that in which a person having renounced his desire for pleasure, pleases others and which involves his own welfare as well as the welfare of others. By discharging one's duty, 'Yoga' (equanimity) is naturally attained. Without discharging one's duty a man can't attain equanimity (Gītā 6/3). Having attained equanimity, knowledge of Truth is naturally attained—which is the result of both—'Karmayoga' (the Discipline of Action) and 'Jñānayoga' (the Discipline of Knowledge).

नेहाभिक्रमनाशोऽस्ति प्रत्यवायो न विद्यते।
स्वल्पमप्यस्य धर्मस्य त्रायते महतो भयात्॥ ४०॥

nehābhikramanāśo'sti pratyavāyo na vidyate
svalpamapyasya dharmasya trāyate mahato bhayāt

In this path (of selfless action), there is neither loss of effort, nor any adverse result. Even a little practice of this discipline (dharma) protects one from great danger (of birth and death). 40

Comment:—

[Lord Kṛṣṇa has explained the importance of disinterested action in the latter part of the thirty-ninth and this fortieth verse in four ways:—(i) By it, one becomes free from shackles of actions. (ii) There is no loss in effort. (iii) There is no adverse result. (iv) Even a little practice of it (dharma) protects, one from great fear.]

'Nehābhikramanāśo'sti'—In this path of disinterested action, there is no loss of attempt viz., the partial practice of this Yoga (Discipline of Disinterested Action) has its corresponding benefit. The desire to attain equanimity is the beginning of equanimity. Such a beginning never gets wasted because desire for attaining the real is also real.

'Iha' (in this) means that in this world human beings are

authorized to attain equanimity. All other bodies (births) are to enjoy worldly pains and pleasures, there is no opportunity for them to do away with attachment and aversion because pleasures can be enjoyed only by having attachment and aversion. If there are no attachment and aversion, no pleasure can be enjoyed and such actions will lead to spiritual discipline.

'Pratyavāyo na vidyate'—Actions which are performed with a desire for fruits, can give adverse result, if there is any error in the pronunciation of incantations, or in performing sacrifice, etc. Suppose, a man performs sacrifice, for the birth of a son, but if it is not performed according to scriptures, it might result in the death, of a member of the family, instead of blessing him with a son. Sometime, if the result is not quite contrary, it may be less harmful, as the son may be born crippled. But, one who performs actions, without having any desire for fruits, becomes equanimous and so there is no adverse result from his effort.

What is adverse result? Unevenness of mind, is an adverse result. Attachment and aversion, is unevenmindedness. This uneven-mindedness leads to a cycle of birth and death. But, when a man becomes equanimous, attachment and aversion, are rooted out and on annihilation of attachment and aversion, there is no unevenness of mind, and therefore any adverse result, is out of the question.

'Svalpamapyasya dharmasya trāyate mahato bhayāt'—Even a little practice, of this discipline of disinterested action, which brings about equanimity, protects one from the great fear of birth and death. So unlike action for fruits, which ends after its fruits, it does not perish viz., its fruit is not wealth or property, which are perishable. Equanimity, which a striver attains, by facing favourable and unfavourable circumstances, gets fixed in him and becomes permanent. A devotee (striver), deviating from the path of Yoga, having enjoyed heavenly pleasures for many years and having taken birth in the houses of righteous persons, does not lose knowledge or even-mindedness gained, in his previous birth (Gītā 6/40—45) because this knowledge or even-mindedness, is real.

'Dharma' (Duty) is used in two senses—(i) Charity viz., kindness, in giving help (money, food, clothes etc.,) to the poor, and suffering people (ii) Discharging one's duty, according to the ordinance of scriptures. By performing one's duty, without desiring its fruit, one develops equanimity automatically, because it is axiomatic. Therefore, here, equanimity has been called 'Dharma' (duty).

Something Noteworthy about Equanimity

Some people opine constant remembrance of God is not useful unless there is concentration of mind. But the gospel of the Gītā, does not attach much importance to this opinion, it attaches more importance to equanimity. According to the Gītā, a striver who has attained equanimity, is an exalted soul. Even when, a man is imbued with all qualities, if he does not gain equanimity, according to the Gītā, he cannot be called, a perfect soul.

This equanimity, is of two kinds—of the mind and of the self. The Lord, pervades everywhere equally. One who gets oneself established, in Him, gains victory over the world, and is liberated.

But this equanimity of self, can be known by equanimity of the mind (Gītā 5/19). Equanimity of the mind, consists in remaining even-minded, in success and failure (Gītā 2/48). Such a person, remains even-minded in praise and reproach, success and failure, profit and loss, pleasure and pain etc., (Gītā 5/20). This sort of equanimity, never perishes and it results in nothing, but salvation.

Whatever, virtuous actions, such as penance, charity and pilgrimage etc., are performed by a man, these perish after giving fruit, but equanimity, does not perish and it leads man to salvation or God-realization (Gītā 5/3), while concentration of mind, may lead him to accomplishments (siddhis) but not to salvation.

Appendix—The Lord has mentioned the glory of equanimity in four ways in the thirty-ninth and fortieth verses—

(i) 'karmabandhaṁ prahāsyasi'—By equanimity a man shakes off the shackles of Karma (action).

(ii) 'nehābhikramanāśo'sti'—There is no loss of effort.

(iii) 'pratyavāyo na vidyate'—There is no adverse result of this effort.

(iv) 'svalpamapyasya dharmasya trāyate mahato bhayāt'—Even a little practice of this discipline (dharma) protects one from the great danger of birth and death.

Though in the first point the three remaining points are included, yet there is a little difference in them; as—

(i) The Lord first in the normal way declares that by equanimity a man shakes off the shackles of Karma (action). The reason of bondage is the attachment to the modes viz., it is his assumed affinity with Prakṛti (Matter) and its evolutes (Gītā 13/21). In equanimity there is no affinity with Prakṛti and its evolutes; therefore the man is freed from the shackles (bondage) of action. As in the world many virtuous and sinful actions are done, but those actions don't bind us because we have no relationship with them, similarly the even-minded person has no relationship with the actions done by his body.

(ii) If equanimity merely begins viz., there is an aim of attaining equanimity, there is inquisitiveness to attain it, then this beginning is not destroyed. The reason is that the aim to attain the imperishable is also imperishable while the aim to gain the perishable, is also perishable. The aim to gain the perishable leads to destruction (fall) while the aim to attain equanimity leads to salvation—'jijñāsurapi yogasya śabdabrahmātivartate' (Gītā 6/44).

(iii) There is no adverse result of this equanimity. If there is any error in pronouncing the sacred text in the performance of actions which are done with a desire for fruits, the result of those actions can be adverse.* But if there is equanimity in life, and an error is committed, and if there is slip in carefulness, the action does not give adverse result (bondage). For example if a paid servant while lighting a lantern in the dark drops it and breaks it, we are angry with him. But if our friend who never wants anything from us, drops the lantern and it is broken, we don't get angry but ask him not to mind it as it matters little. Therefore he who performs actions with the desire for fruit, may have adverse result of his actions but how can the result of the actions of the person, who doesn't covet any fruit, he adverse? It can't be.

(iv) Even a little equanimity protects one from the great danger of birth and death viz., it results in salvation. As actions done with an interested motive perish after bearing fruit, in that way even a little equanimity does not perish after bearing fruit but it only leads to salvation. If virtuous actions such as religious sacrifice, charity and penance etc., are performed with a desire for fruit, their result is perishable (gain of money, wealth and heaven

* There is a mythological story that Tvaṣṭā performed a religious sacrifice in order to get a son who would kill Indra. In that sacrifice the sages performed the sacrifice with the sacred text 'indraśatruṁ vivardhasva'. In the word 'indraśatru' if there is 'ṣaṣṭhītatpuruṣa' compound-word, it means 'Indra's enemy' and if there is 'bahuvrīhi' compound-word, it means 'he whose enemy is Indra.' By the difference of 'samāsa' (compound-word), there is difference in sound. Therefore in 'ṣaṣṭhītatpuruṣa' compound word, the word 'indraśatru's' last letter 'tru' will be pronounced with 'udātta' sound while in 'bahuvrīhi' compound-word, the word 'indraśatru's' first letter 'i' will be pronounced with 'udātta' sound. The aim of the sages was to do the 'antyodātta' pronunciation of the word 'indraśatru' but they did 'ādyodātta' pronunciation. So because of the difference in sound in the pronunciation of the sacred text there was adverse result and thus Indra became the killer of Vṛtrāsura, Tvaṣṭā's son. Therefore it is said:

mantro hīnaḥ svarato varṇato vā mithyāprayukto na tamarthamāha
sa vāgvajro yajamānaṁ hinasti yathendraśatruḥ svarato'parādhāt

(Pāṇinīya Śikṣā)

etc.,) and if they are performed without the desire for fruit, their result is imperishable (salvation). Thus virtuous actions such as sacrifice, charity and penance etc., can bear two types of fruit but the fruit of equanimity is only salvation. As a traveller, while travelling stops on the way or sleeps, he has not to go back to the place from where he started his journey but he has covered the distance upto the place where he stops or sleeps. Similarly as much equanimity is attained in life, that never perishes.

'svalpamapyasya dharmasya trāyate mahato bhayāt'—Even a little feeling of disinterest is true while fear even being great is untrue. As for a bundle of cotton, a lot of fire is not required, the cotton may be one bundle or a hundred bundles, a match stick is enough to burn it. When one match stick is applied to the cotton, the cotton itself becomes fire and helps in burning the remaining cotton. In the same way detachment is fire and the world is cotton. Being detached from the world, the world itself perishes because the world in fact has no existence at the root, so one can't be attached to it.

The least renunciation is real and the biggest action is unreal. An action ends while renunciation is endless. Therefore actions such as sacrifice, charity and penance etc., perish after giving fruit (Gītā 8/28) but renunciation (renunciation of the fruit of action) never perishes—'tyāgācchāntiranantaram' (Gītā 12/12). By renouncing the egoistic notion only, infinite universes are renounced because this sense of ego has sustained the entire universe (Gītā 7/5).

There may be a big heap of grass, can it face fire? It may be very dark, can it face light? If there is a fight between darkness and light, will darkness win? Similarly if there is a fight between ignorance and knowledge, will ignorance win? Can the greatest fear face fearlessness? Equanimity even if it is a little is complete and fear even if great is incomplete. A little equanimity is great because it is true and the great fear is little (without existence) because it is untrue.

What is the import of calling equanimity or the feeling of disinterestedness 'a little.' The feeling of disinterestedness is great, but we understand and experience it a little, so it has been called a little. In fact our understanding is a little, equanimity is not a little. Our view has not grasped it fully, so there is defect in our view, not in equanimity. Similarly we have valued the unreal more, it does not mean that the unreal is great but value accorded by us is great. Therefore if we value the real more, the real will become great viz., its value will be realized and if we don't value the unreal, the unreal will become a little. In fact the unreal may be great or a little; it has no existence 'nāsato vidyate bhāvaḥ' and the real may be great or a little, its existence is ever present—'nā bhāvo vidyate sataḥ'. Therefore in Upaniṣads the Supreme Soul has been called smaller than a molecule and the biggest of all—'aṇoraṇīyān mahato mahīyān' (Kaṭha. 1/2/20, Śvetāśvatara 3/20).

Link:—In the next verse Lord Kṛṣṇa explains to Arjuna, how to attain equanimity.

व्यवसायात्मिका बुद्धिरेकेह कुरुनन्दन।
बहुशाखा ह्यनन्ताश्च बुद्धयोऽव्यवसायिनाम्॥ ४१॥

vyavasāyātmikā buddhirekeha kurunandana
bahuśākhā hyanantāśca buddhayo'vyavasāyinām

O Joy of the Kurus, in this blessed path, the intellect is determinate and concentrated, whereas the intellect of the undecided (infirm), is scattered in many directions, and is endlessly diverse. 41

Comment:—

'Vyavasāyātmikā buddhirekeha kurunandana'—To a seeker of God-realization, the intellect is determinate and single-pointed viz., he has only one decision and that is to attain equanimity, in the form of God-realization. Attachment to the world, is the main obstacle to this attainment of equanimity, and that can be removed, through determinate intellect.

Why is determinate intellect one? The reason is, that in it there is renunciation of desire, for worldly objects etc. This renunciation of desire is singular, whether it pertains to wealth and riches or honour and praise. But, there are objects of different types and a person wants to acquire these. Just as, there are different kinds of objects, such as different kinds of sweets, in the same way, there are endless desires for acquiring numerous objects of various types in various ways. Therefore, a desirous person cannot have one intellect.

In the Discipline of Action (in this verse), and in the Discipline of Devotion (in 9/30), there is mention of intellect, which is determinate and single-pointed, but it is not so, in the Discipline of Knowledge. The reason is, that in the Discipline of Knowledge, one comes to know the self first, and then his intellect becomes determinate and pointed, while in the Discipline of Action, as well as Devotion, it is the determinate intellect which comes first and then it is followed by self-realization. Therefore, in the Discipline of Knowledge there is importance of knowledge, while in the Disciplines of Devotion and Action, there is importance of a single-minded pursuit.

'Bahuśākhā hyanantāśca buddhayo'vyavasāyinām—The infirm in mind being desire-ridden, clings to pleasure and prosperity, and so the intellect of such persons, grow endlessly. For example, they may have a desire to get a son, the means adopted for the fulfilment of other desire, such as medicine, incantation, oblation and blessings of a saint etc., are branches of the same desire. Similarly, a man wants to get money of this is one desire (intellect) and to get it through business, service, theft, robbery, cheating etc., are many branches, of that intellect. Such a man, with endless desires, having many branches cannot even take decision about God-realization.

Appendix—The real aim is only one. Unless a man has a singular aim, he has endless aims and there are numerous branches of each aim. He has endless desires and the means for the fulfilment of each desire are also many.

Link:—The ways of the infirm-in-mind (worldly people) have been described in the next three verses.

यामिमां पुष्पितां वाचं प्रवदन्त्यविपश्चितः।
वेदवादरताः पार्थ नान्यदस्तीति वादिनः॥ ४२॥
कामात्मानः स्वर्गपरा जन्मकर्मफलप्रदाम्।
क्रियाविशेषबहुलां भोगैश्वर्यगतिं प्रति॥ ४३॥

yāmimāṁ puṣpitāṁ vācaṁ pravadantyavipaścitaḥ
vedavādaratāḥ pārtha nānyadastīti vādinaḥ
kāmātmānaḥ svargaparā janmakarmaphalapradām
kriyāviśeṣabahulāṁ bhogaiśvaryagatiṁ prati

Arjuna, those who are obsessed by desires, who look upon heaven as the supreme goal and argue that there is nothing beyond heaven and pleasures and who are devoted to the letter of the Vedas, are unwise. They make this type of flowery speeches recommending many acts of various kinds, for the attainment of pleasure and prosperity, and with rebirth as their fruit. 42-43

Comment:—

'Kāmātmānaḥ'—Desire-ridden are those, whose sole aim in life is to hunt after enjoyment. They think that it is nothing but desire, which inspires a man to action and without it, a man is stone-dead. Moreover, they identify themselves with desires.

But the fact is, that a man himself is a fragment of God and thus, is eternal while desires are fleeting and these increase and decrease. The self and desire, are totally distinct. But desire-ridden people, never realize this distinction and it is only out of delusion that they identify themselves with desire.

'Svargaparā'—They look upon heaven and its pleasure, as their supreme goal and all their efforts are directed towards that base end. Here the term 'Svargaparā', refers to such men, who have faith and belief in heaven etc., as described, in the Vedas and scriptures.

'Vedavādaratāḥ pārtha nānyadastīti vādinaḥ'—They are interested in the Vedas, only for the sake of the ritualistic contents, which deal with earthly and heavenly pleasure. The aim of their life, is to enjoy celestial pleasure here, and hereafter, rather than to attain God-realization, or emancipation.

'Yāmimāṁ puṣpitāṁ vācaṁ pravadantyavipaścitaḥ—They cannot discriminate between, the real and the unreal, the perishable and the imperishable. Such unwise persons utter flowery words of the Vedas, which describe and recommend various acts, for the attainment of pleasure and prosperity.

Here, the word 'puṣpitām' has been used to show that such speech is just flowery with an attractive appearance, without bearing any permanent fruit. Satisfaction, comes out of fruit only, not from flowers and leaves.

'Janmakarmaphalapradām'—That flowery way instead of giving any permanent and eternal fruit, gives fruit which prolongs the wheel of birth. In language flowery importance is attached to pleasure, and attachment to pleasure is the cause of birth (Gītā 13/21).

'Kriyāviśeṣabahulāṁ bhogaiśvaryagatiṁ prati'—That, flowery utterance deals with a number of rituals for the attainment of pleasure and prosperity. In these rituals there is abundance of different kinds of rites, involving various methods, actions, objects and much strenuous physical labour (Gītā 13/21).

भोगैश्वर्यप्रसक्तानां तयापहृतचेतसाम्।
व्यवसायात्मिका बुद्धिः समाधौ न विधीयते ॥ ४४ ॥

bhogaiśvaryaprasaktānāṁ tayāpahṛtacetasām
vyavasāyātmikā buddhiḥ samādhau na vidhīyate

Those, whose minds are carried away by such flowery words (who are attracted towards pleasures and who are deeply attached to pleasure and prosperity), cannot attain the determinate intellect, concentrated in God. 44

Comment:—

'Tayāpahṛtacetasām'—Their minds are carried away by such flowery language, that there is great pleasure in heaven—there are celestial damsels, a blissful garden and there is nectar etc.

'Bhogaiśvaryaprasaktānām'—Pleasures of five senses—sound, touch, colour, taste, smell, comfort to the body, and desire for respect and praise are 'bhoga', (the worldly enjoyments). Accumulation of money and material to enjoy those worldly pleasure, is called 'aiśvarya' (prosperity). Those who cling to pleasure and prosperity, are called 'Bhogaiśvaryaprasaktānām.' Such people are called demoniacal* (asura). In saṁskṛta 'asu' stands for life-breath and he who wants to maintain life-breath is an 'asura'.

'Vyavasāyātmikā buddhiḥ samādhau na vidhīyate'—Such people, who instinctively cling to pleasure and prosperity cannot attain the determinate intellect to realize God, because their intellect has become impure. Similarly, the people who have pride for their being learned, by acquiring the worldly arts or science or knowledge etc., cannot attain the determinate intellect, (decision), to realize God.

Something Noteworthy

All-gracious God, by His grace has bestowed discrimination

* The people possessing the mode of passion who are being described here have been called people possessing demoniacal traits in the sixteenth chapter by the Lord (16/11, 16/16).

upon human beings, so that they may attain God or salvation. But human beings giving a cold shoulder to this discrimination cling to pleasure like birds and animals. They forget that enjoyment of pleasure is not the goal of human life, but its supreme object is the attainment of perfection, and all the circumstances, whether favourable or unfavourable, they are placed in, are means to attain perfection (God-realization). So they cannot have the sole desire for God-realization.

The fact is that worldly pleasures and objects are not a real obstacles to God-realization, but attachment to these, is the main hindrance. So long as, this attachment continues, not to talk of God-realization the people cannot even make up their minds to attain God, because their minds are drawn away, by worldly pleasure and prosperity etc.

Appendix—If there is any obstacle to the attainment of salvation, it is the desire for pleasures and prosperity (accumulation of wealth). As an ensnared fish can't move ahead, similarly a man, entangled in pleasures and prosperity, can't move ahead towards God. Not only this but the man attached to pleasures and prosperity, can't even have the determinate intellect to realize God.

He who regards the world as true, to him Karmayoga will quickly lead to Self-realization. A Karmayogī serves the world by discharging his duty viz., he does every action for the welfare of others in a disinterested manner. He feels happy with the happiness of others and is sad (moved) with the sadness of others. By feeling happy seeing others happy, his desire for pleasure is wiped out and by being moved at the sufferings of others, his desire for prosperity (accumulation) is wiped out.*

* In fact the real service is rendered by the person who has totally renounced the desire for pleasure and prosperity otherwise the service is fake. But if the aim is real (for the welfare of others) the fake service also turns into real service.

Link:—To confirm something, it is necessary that one should view the pros and cons of a matter. In the previous three verses, there is the description of the infirm-in-mind who are obsessed by desires. Now, Lord Kṛṣṇa inspires Arjuna, to attain the ideal by being established in the Eternal Existence (God), transcending the three guṇas (attributes), and being free from all desires.

त्रैगुण्यविषया वेदा निस्त्रैगुण्यो भवार्जुन।
निर्द्वन्द्वो नित्यसत्त्वस्थो निर्योगक्षेम आत्मवान्॥ ४५॥

traiguṇyaviṣayā vedā nistraiguṇyo bhavārjuna
nirdvandvo nityasattvastho niryogakṣema ātmavān

O Arjuna, the Vedas deal with the three Guṇas (attributes) and their evolutes. Be free from those attributes, rise above the polarity of opposites, remain balanced, be unconcerned about the meeting of wants and preservation, of what has been already attained and get established in the self. 45

Comment:—

'Traiguṇyaviṣayā vedā—Here, the reference, is to the ritualistic portions of the Vedas, which deal with the three guṇas (attributes) and their evolutes, in the form of worldly and heavenly enjoyment. The purpose is not to censure the Vedas, but to glorify the selfless spirit. In reference to a diamond a piece of glass is compared the aim is to eulogize the diamond, rather than to censure glass. The Vedas do not only deal with means to satisfy desires of the worldly minded people, but they also contain sublime and elevating ideas on God and the means to realize Him.

'Nistraiguṇyo bhavārjuna'—O Arjuna, be free from the evolutes of these attributes viz., be free from worldly enjoyment, as well as, means of attaining such enjoyment.

'Nirdvandvaḥ'—For a striver to transcend the worldly enjoyment, it is inevitable to be free from the pairs of opposites such as attachment and aversion etc., because these are his real enemies and are the stumbling block, in his spiritual progress (Gītā 3/34).*

Here, Lord Kṛṣṇa orders Arjuna to rise above the pairs of opposites, because through their deluding nature, human beings are enveloped in utter ignorance (Gītā 7/27). When a striver gets rid of this delusion, he can worship Him with a firm resolve (Gītā 7/28). By transcending these pairs of opposites, he is easily freed from bondage (5/3), one becomes undeluded (15/5) and he is not bound (4/22). So the Lord, wants him to be free from the pairs of opposites.

Another aspect is that if a person develops attachment for one person or a thing, he is sure to develop aversion to other persons or things. By having such attachment to the world, an aspirant turns indifferent to God. This indifference is a sort of aversion to God. But if one develops true devotion to God, without having any attachment or aversion to the world, he develops total disinclination for it.

This total disinclination has three stages. In the first stage, the aspirant has no hatred for unfavourable circumstances but there is 'Upekṣā (neglect), in the second stage, there is 'Udāsīnatā' (unconcernedness), while in the third stage, there is total disinclination. In the last stage, (total disinclination), attachment and aversion, are totally wiped out. If this process is considered minutely, we find that in 'Upekṣā' there remain impressions of attachment and aversion, in 'Udāsīnatā' the feelings of attachment and aversion remain, while in total disinclination there are neither impressions nor feelings of attachment and aversion. In this state, attachment and aversion are totally wiped out.

'Nityasattvasthaḥ'—The advice is to rise above the pairs of opposites and to get established in the omnipresent and everlasting God.

* 'Dvandva' means having opposite feelings for something as the feelings of attachment and aversion, pleasure and pain etc., for the world. This misleads an aspirant to bondage.

'Niryogakṣema*'—Do not have the desire even for the provision of the means required (Yoga) and the preservation of what has already been attained, because I provide for and preserve all for those who have exclusive devotion for me† (Gītā 9/22).

'Ātmavān'—Having the aim of God-realization, get established in the self (Eternal existence or God).

Appendix—'Nirdvandvaḥ'—In fact the discrimination between the insentient-sentient, real-unreal, eternal-transitory, perishable-imperishable etc., is also a pair of opposites. The desire for gain and security is also a duality. Because of duality 'All is God'—this reality is not realized. The reason is when all is God, then how can duality between the sentient (self) and the insentient (Matter) subsist? Therefore the Lord has declared Himself both immortality as well as death, and 'Sat' as well as 'Asat' (unreal)—'amṛtaṁ caiva mṛtyuśca sadasaccāhamarjuna' (Gītā 9/19).

Link:—In the next verse, Lord Kṛṣṇa explains what one achieves by transcending the three guṇas (attributes).

यावानर्थ उदपाने सर्वतः सम्प्लुतोदके।
तावान्सर्वेषु वेदेषु ब्राह्मणस्य विजानतः॥ ४६॥

yāvānartha udapāne sarvataḥ samplutodake
tāvānsarveṣu vedeṣu brāhmaṇasya vijānataḥ

As on obtaining a reservoir of water flooded on all sides there is no use for a small reservoir of water. So A Brāhmaṇa, who obtains enlightenment, has the same use for all the Vedas, or say no use at all. 46

* 'Yoga' means providing unacquired things and 'Kṣema' means preservation of the things procured.

† Though here it is the context of the Discipline of Disinterested Action, yet it seems proper to take it as the Discipline of Devotion because Lord Kṛṣṇa, time and again, orders Arjuna to be His devotee and He also accepts him as His devotee in 4/3. He also takes the responsibility of provision and protection (9/22).

Comment:—

'Yāvānartha udapāne sarvataḥ samplutodake'—A small reservoir of water is useful, in a place where there is no other source of water. But nobody ever, pays any attention to such a reservoir of water where there is a big reservoir of pure water. Moreover that such a small reservoir of water becomes dirty and impure and cannot be used for drinking purpose, after washing and bathing in it. But water from a large stream remains clean and pure, even after washing and bathing in it.

'Tāvānsarveṣu vedeṣu brāhmaṇasya vijānataḥ'—Likewise oblations, charities, penances and pilgrimages etc., mentioned in the Vedas, are of use to those who are ignorant. But these become meaningless to the illumined souls who have realized God. The same kind of comparison has been made, in the seventieth verse, that the emancipated souls are like sea, as several rivers fall into it but its magnitude remains the same, similarly the illumined souls remain undisturbed though several kinds of pleasure and enjoyment merge into them.

A great soul who possesses knowledge of the Lord, the Vedas and the scriptures is called 'Brāhmaṇasya vijānataḥ.'

By using the term 'tāvān', Lord Kṛṣṇa means to say that the great soul after realizing God transcends the three attributes (modes), rises above the pairs of opposites viz., becomes free from attachment and aversion, gets established in the self and remains unconcerned about provision and preservation. He always remains devoted to God.

Appendix—There is no end of worldly pleasures. There are endless universes and there are endless pleasures in them. But if they are renounced and one becomes detached from them, they come to an end. Similarly there are endless desires. But if they are renounced, they come to an end and the man becomes desireless.

Link:—In the thirty-ninth verse, Lord Kṛṣṇa asks Arjuna to listen to the discourse on an even mind. In the next verse He orders him to perform his duty in order to attain that equanimity (evenness of mind).

कर्मण्येवाधिकारस्ते मा फलेषु कदाचन।
मा कर्मफलहेतुर्भूर्मा ते सङ्गोऽस्त्वकर्मणि॥ ४७॥

karmaṇyevādhikāraste mā phaleṣu kadācana
mā karmaphalaheturbhūrmā te saṅgo'stvakarmaṇi

Your right is only to perform your duty, but never to claim its fruit. Do not be the cause of the fruit of action nor let your attachment be for inaction. 47

Comment:—

'Karmaṇyevādhikāraste'—Your right is to perform your duty, you are free in it, because no other bodies as those of animals and birds etc., are free to perform new actions. Only human beings are eligible to perform new actions. The gods can perform new actions and can bestow money and material upon human beings, according to the ordinance of the Lord but they are so steeped in enjoyment, that it is not possible for them to perform new actions. They are destined only to reap the fruit of their meritorious deeds. The creatures in hell also cannot perform new actions as they suffer the fruits of their actions. God has bestowed this human birth, the very last of all births so that by performing new actions in the form of selfless service to others, a person may achieve salvation and be freed from the bondage of the cycle of birth and death. If he remains engaged in selfish actions, these will result in bondage. In case he is given to indolence and heedlessness, he will follow a cycle of birth and death. Therefore, the Lord advises human beings, to render selfless services for common good.

The term 'Karmaṇi' has been used in singular number, to emphasize the fact that though man has to perform several duties in his life, he can perform only one at a particular time. Arjuna, belonging to the warrior class, has several duties, such as fighting, generosity and bravery etc., but presently he could perform only one of these—to wage the war.

A Vital Fact

In the births of others i.e., those of birds, animals, insects and even gods, the creatures can reap the fruits of their actions but cannot perform new actions. However there are two things about human life viz., reaping the fruits of deeds of earlier lives, and secondly performing new ones. God has bestowed upon man this human body, so that by performing new virtuous actions without having a desire for their fruits, he may attain God-realization or salvation. As far as the fruit of his previous actions is concerned, it may come in the form of favourable and unfavourable circumstances. He cannot change those circumstances, but can make proper use of these and these can lead him to salvation, if he uses these properly.

An important fact, which needs attention, is that favourable or unfavourable circumstances cannot make a man happy or sad. It is merely his ignorance, which makes him happy or sad as he identifies himself with those circumstances and becomes the experiencer of happiness or sadness. If he gives a serious thought, he will come to know that the external circumstances cannot make his internal self, either happy or sad. He should make proper use of the favourable circumstances by serving others and of the undesirable ones, by renouncing the desire to enjoy pleasure.

In unfavourable circumstances, a man should not be perturbed but should think that the sins committed to get pleasure, are perishing in the form of unfavourable circumstances and this thought is a kind of repentance for the sins committed. Secondly, it is a fore-warning to us that we shall have to face adverse consequences if we commit sins again. So, we should perform actions for the welfare of all creatures, rather than for our own pleasure.

For insects, birds and animals etc., the fruit of past actions and also the present actions are only to work out their destinies. But in case of human beings the fruit of past actions as also the present activities, are the means for their salvation.

'Mā phaleṣu kadācana'—You cannot claim the fruit of action, because you are not free in getting it, which is dispensed by the Lord. If you perform actions with a desire for fruits, you will get into bondage (Gītā 5/12). It is the desire for fruit which makes a person an agent for actions. With the passing away of desire, a sense of doership is gone. Obliteration of the sense of doership, does not lead a man to bondage. It means that a man is much more entangled in desires.*

Secondly, all actions are performed with the help of worldly objects and persons. So it is dishonest, to desire the fruit of those actions, for only one's own self.

The desire for fruit of actions is not beneficial for human beings. 'Never lay claim to its fruit'—this expression proves that it is upto a man whether he lays claim to the fruit of an action or not. He is free in this respect. The term 'Phaleṣu' has been used in the plural, because a man by performing an action desires several fruits such as riches, respect and reputation etc.

The means to be free, from the desire for fruits of actions are as follows—(i) Desire causes a feeling of lacking something. Its fulfilment makes one a slave. Its non-fulfilment causes suffering. The pleasure derived out of fulfilment of desire, gives birth to new desires and a man goes on getting interested in performing new actions, in order to reap their fruit. By understanding this fact in the right perspective, a man becomes free from the desire for the fruit of action.

* Actually God-realization does not depend on actions but on feelings and knowledge because He is ever attained. It is the desire for fruits which is an obstacle to God-realization.

(ii) Actions have a beginning and an end, these are not eternal. So, how can their fruits be eternal? But the self is eternal. How can the eternal get any benefit from the perishable? By understanding this fact, one becomes detached from the world and attains God-realization.

In order to be free from the desire for fruits of actions, an aspirant should have discrimination as well as feelings to serve others. Discrimination will be helpful to an aspirant in renouncing his comforts, while the feelings of service to others, will enable him to do good to others. By doing so a striver can follow the Discipline of Disinterested Action, in the right sense.

'Mā karmaphalaheturbhūḥ'—Let you not be responsible for the fruits of action. It means, that you should not have the least attachment for the body, senses, mind and intellect etc., because attachment for these will make you responsible for the fruit of action. In the eleventh verse of the fifth chapter also, Lord Kṛṣṇa by using the term 'Kevalaiḥ' (only) wants to say that the follower of the Discipline of Disinterested Action, should abandon feeling of mineness for the body, mind, intellect and senses.

If a striver becomes the agent (doer) of a virtuous action, even without having a desire for its fruit, he is held responsible for the fruit of the action, because by doing so he has accepted his affinity for the mind, intellect and senses etc., which are unreal. Actually, we have no affinity with them, they have their affinity with the world. When anybody else performs action for the good of others, we do not accept our affinity for the action and its fruit and so are not held responsible. We should adopt the same attitude in the case of our own actions also, so that we may not be held responsible for the fruit of actions.

'Mā te saṅgo'stvakarmaṇi'—Let your attachment not be to inaction, because by leaning towards inaction, you will become lazy and idle, and like the desire for fruit it will also mislead you to bondage. The reason is that, indolence and prolonged sleep etc., also give pleasure viz., Tāmasika joy, (Gītā18/39) which misleads either to the lower births of insects, birds and beasts etc., or to infernal regions (Gītā 14/18). It means that, attachment misleads to bondage and is the cause of birth in good and evil wombs (Gītā 13/21).

You should not be attached to inaction by thinking that it will lead you to progress, here and hereafter, because the real essence is beyond action or inaction.

In this verse, the Lord means to say that a striver should remain detached from objects, men, action, incidents, circumstances and physical, subtle, causal bodies etc., without having the least affinity for them.

In this verse there are four points which need attention—(i) Your right is to perform your duty (action) only. (ii) Never lay claim to its fruit. (iii) Do not be the cause of the fruit of action. (iv) Let your attachment be not to inaction. Out of these four points, the first and the fourth, have the same theme as both of these lay emphasis on the performance of duty or action. Similarly, the second and the third points have the same theme, as in both of these it is mentioned, that you should not desire or be the cause of the fruit of action.

It means that, by leaning towards inaction you will have affinity to tāmasika temperament, such as idleness and laziness. By having attachment for action and its fruit you will have affinity for rājasika temperament. But when a striver is free from laziness, idleness, actions, fruit of actions, etc., he gets the joy born of knowledge and light and having attachment for it, he has affinity to sāttvika temperament. Affinity with these is the cause of birth and death. Therefore, a striver should not have attachment for either of them. Doing one's duty without having any attachment to them, is called the Discipline of Disinterested Action.

Appendix—One is the division of actions and one is the division of fruit (result). A man's right is in the division of actions (performance of duty), not in the division of fruit. The reason is that performance of duty is under the control of a man while awarding the result of past actions is ordained by destiny viz., 'Prārabdha'. If we perceive from the view-point of Karmayoga whatever material (thing, ability and power) we have obtained, that is 'Prārabdha' and their proper use viz., by assuming them not as ours or for us, but by assuming them as others' and for them, and rendering service with them to others is 'Puruṣārtha'.

The important fact about Karmayoga is—protection of the rights of others by performing one's duty and renouncing the fruit of action viz., renouncing one's right. By protecting the right of others, old attachment is wiped out and by renouncing one's own right, new attachment is not born. Thus when old attachment is wiped out and new attachment is not born, a man becomes 'vītarāga' (free from attachment). By becoming 'vītarāga' one realizes the self. The reason is in attaining Self-realization, attachment to the unreal things is the only obstacle—

rāgo liṅgamabodhasya cittavyāyāma bhūmiṣu
kutaḥ śādvalatā tasya yasyāgniḥ koṭare taraḥ

It means that attachment (attraction) of the mind to objects, persons and actions is the main sign (mark) of ignorance. As when the hollow of a tree catches fire, it does not remain green any more but it is dried up, similarly he who has caught fire in the form of attachment, can't attain peace.

Link:—After asking Arjuna to perform his duty, in the preceding verse, the Lord describes how he should remain even-minded, while performing actions.

योगस्थः कुरु कर्माणि सङ्गं त्यक्त्वा धनञ्जय।
सिद्ध्यसिद्ध्योः समो भूत्वा समत्वं योग उच्यते ॥ ४८ ॥

yogasthaḥ kuru karmāṇi saṅgaṁ tyaktvā dhanañjaya
siddhyasiddhyoḥ samo bhūtvā samatvaṁ yoga ucyate

O Dhanañjaya (the conqueror of wealth), perform actions (duties) being steadfast in the path of Yoga, renouncing attachment, having become even-minded in success and failure; and that equanimity (equilibrium) is called Yoga. 48

Comment:—

'Saṅgaṁ tyaktvā'—You can become indifferent, only if you have no attachment for actions, their fruits; place, time, incidents, circumstances, bodies and minds etc., which belong to matter, because without being indifferent to actions, these cannot lead you to salvation.

'Siddhyasiddhyoḥ samo bhūtvā'—Renunciation of attachment will result in evenness of mind. A man should be even-minded, in favourable and unfavourable circumstances, in honour and dishonour, and in praise and reproach.*

A follower of the Discipline of Disinterested Action, should be so even-minded while performing actions, that he should not bother about their accomplishment or non-accomplishment, for getting the fruit or not, for getting salvation or not. He should remain devoted to his duty. If an aspirant has not realized detachment and equanimity, he should aim at evenness of mind. By having this approach, a striver will attain equanimity finally, which will lead to God-realization or Self-realization (2/53).

'Yogasthaḥ kuru karmāṇi'—Lord Kṛṣṇa says, that the essence of true Yoga lies in even-mindedness, in success, as well as, failure. The person who keeps the mind ever in the poised state

* While explaining this verse Śrī Śaṅkarācārya writes—O Dhanañjaya, being established in Yoga perform actions only for God without even having the desire to please Him. Knowledge gained by purification of mind as a result of the desireless (without the desire for fruits) actions is called 'Siddhi' (Success) and whatever is contrary to it (lack of knowledge) is 'Asiddhi' (Failure). Perform actions being even-minded amidst success or failure. This evenness of mind or equanimity is called 'Yoga'.

is called steadfast in Yoga. The sameness of mind should remain intact from the beginning of an action, to its end. It should not be a temporary phase, otherwise the propensities of attraction and repulsion, will go on coming up. We should never allow such propensities to develop.

'Samatvaṁ yoga ucyate'—Yoga is, nothing but equanimity i.e., equanimity is the embodiment of Lord Himself. Further, in the nineteenth verse of the fifth chapter, Lord Kṛṣṇa says, "Those whose mind is established in equanimity, have conquered the mortal plane, because Brahma (the Absolute) is flawless and equanimous, hence they are established in the Eternal."

Here, Yoga has been defined as equanimity, while in the twenty-third verse of the sixth chapter, it will be defined as, the state which is free from the contact of pain. Actually, both the definitions are the same. When a man suffers from ring-worm or itching eczema, he gets satisfaction by scratching it. The pleasure of itching, is followed by the painful sensation of burning. Being the result of a disease both these sensations are really painful. Similarly, the pleasure and pain received from attachment to the world, are equally painful. Therefore, Yoga can either be defined as the state, free from the contact of pain viz., free from pleasure and pain or equanimity in pleasure and pain; both are the same.

It means that through all actions performed by physical, subtle and causal bodies should render service to the world, without having any selfish motive. This alone will lead to equanimity.

Something Noteworthy about Intellect and Equanimity

Intellect is of two kinds—indeterminate and determinate. The intellect of those whose aim is to enjoy worldly pleasure and prosperity, is indeterminate (Gītā 2/44) while the intellect of those whose aim is equanimity and salvation is determinate. Indeterminate intellects are endlessly diverse, while the determinate one, is single. Those whose intellects are endlessly diverse, are themselves undecided (Gītā 2/41) and are worldly. But those whose intellect is single, have rightly resolved (Gītā 9/30) and they are strivers.

Equanimity is of two kinds—of the mind and of the self. To remain even, in favourable or unfavourable circumstances, without having any attachment or aversion, is equanimity of the mind, while equanimity of the self is union with God (2/53).

There is a distinction between the worldly people and strivers. The goal of the worldly people, is to enjoy pleasure and prosperity and their intellects are not determinate but are scattered in many directions and are endlessly diverse. On the other hand, the striver's intellects are determinate and the strivers in their practical life maintain equanimity in success and failure, profit and loss, and favourable and unfavourable circumstances, without having attachment and aversion. Such strivers conquer the mortal plane and are established in the Eternal (Gītā 5/19).

Appendix—In Pātañjala Yogadarśana the control of the mind has been called 'yoga'—'yogaścittavṛtti nirodhaḥ' (1/2). As a result of this yoga the seer rests in the self—'tadā draṣṭuḥ svarūpe'vasthānam' (1/3). Thus in Pātañjala Yogadarśana what has been called the result of yoga, the Gītā declares the same as 'yoga'—'samatvaṁ yoga ucyate'; 'taṁ vidyād duḥkhasaṁyogaviyogaṁ yogasaṁjñitam' (Gītā 6/23). It means that the Gītā declares that when a man (self) is totally detached from the mind and naturally rests in the self, that state is called 'yoga'. By getting established in this yoga (equanimity), there is no deviation from it; therefore it is also called 'Nityayoga' (eternal union). When the mind is controlled 'Nirvikalpa avasthā' (state of cessation of thoughts) ensues. But when by equanimity a man rests in the Self that is 'Nirvikalpa bodha' (knowledge of Truth) or 'sahajāvasthā' (Self-realization). 'Nirvikalpa bodha' is not a state but it transcends all states, it is their illuminator and is the result of all yoga-disciplines. The states are both 'nirvikalpa' (without distraction) and 'savikalpa' (with distraction) but 'bodha' is only 'nirvikalpa'. Thus the yoga of the Gītā is more remarkable than that of Pātañjala yogadarśana.

The person who is not of 'mūḍha' (deluded) and 'kṣipta' (volatile) inclination but is of 'vikṣipta' (sometimes constant, sometimes volatile) inclination is eligible (qualified) for yoga of Pātañjala Yogadarśana. But all the persons who want to attain God are eligible for the yoga of the Gītā (God-realization). Not only this but the person who, instead of attaching importance to pleasure and prosperity, attaches importance to this yoga—such a seeker of the yoga (equanimity) also transcends the fruit of Vedic rituals performed with some motive—'jijñāsurapi yogasya śabdabrahmātivartate' (Gītā 6/44).

Link:— In the next verse, Lord Kṛṣṇa explains the superiority of equanimity (which has been described from the thirty-ninth verse to the forty-eighth verse) to a motivated action viz., action with a selfish motive.

दूरेण ह्यवरं कर्म बुद्धियोगाद्धनञ्जय।
बुद्धौ शरणमन्विच्छ कृपणाः फलहेतवः ॥४९॥

dūreṇa hyavaraṁ karma buddhiyogāddhanañjaya
buddhau śaraṇamanviccha kṛpaṇāḥ phalahetavaḥ

O Dhanañjaya, action with a selfish motive is far inferior to that performed with equanimity of mind. Seek refuge in this evenness of mind, for low are those, who crave for fruit of action. 49

Comment:—

'Dūreṇa hyavaraṁ karma buddhiyogāt—Action with a selfish motive is, far inferior to that performed with equanimity of mind. Actions have a beginning and an end and connection with their fruits, is also temporary. We get associated and dissociated with them. But Yoga (equanimity) is eternal, it never deserts us, it suffers no change. Therefore, selfish action is much inferior to equanimity.

Action without equanimity, mislead to pain, as well as to the cycle of birth and death, because they have no power to lead one to salvation. Equanimity is the ability to neutralize actions. If there is no equanimity, one will develop one's egoism and attachment, to the body. This egoism and attachment are beastly. In the Bhāgavata sage Śukadeva says to king Parīkṣit, 'O king, renounce this beastly nature which is causing fear of death in you' (12/5/2).

'Dūreṇa'—As light is the contrary of darkness, an action performed with equanimity of mind, is contrary to the action performed with a selfish motive. An action performed with equanimity leads to God-realization, while motivated actions mislead to the wheel of birth and death.

'Buddhau śaraṇamanviccha'— Seek refuge in this evenness of mind viz., remain established in this evenness of mind, which will enable you to realize yourself.

'Kṛpaṇāḥ phalahetavaḥ'—It is very lowly to crave for fruit of action. To accept one's affinity for actions, fruits of actions and bodies etc., means, to crave for fruit of action. Therefore, Lord Kṛṣṇa, in the forty-seventh verse, exhorts Arjuna not to have the fruit of action, as his object.

The eternal truth is different from perishable action and the fruit of action. What can be more ignoble than this, that the eternal should be subservient to the perishable fruit of action?

Appendix—An action with a selfish motive is far inferior to yoga (equanimity) viz., it does not lead to salvation. As a molecule is far smaller than a mountain viz., a molecule can't be compared with a mountain, similarly an action with a selfish motive is far inferior to yoga viz., an action can't be compared with yoga. Yoga (equanimity) is skill in action—'yogaḥ karmasu kauśalam' (Gītā 2/50). Therefore without yoga, an action is of a very low order, is worthless and is an obstacle—'karmaṇā badhyate jantuḥ'.

In Karmayoga 'Karma' is Karaṇa Sāpekṣa (dependent on external and internal organs) but 'yoga' is Karaṇa Nirapekṣa (independent of external and internal organs). Yoga is not attained by actions but is attained by service and renunciation. Therefore Karmayoga is not Karma (action). Karmayoga is Karaṇa Nirapekṣa viz., discrimination predominating discipline. If there is no predominance of service and renunciation, it will be Karma, not Karmayoga (Discipline of Action) at all.

Equanimity leads to God-realization, but actions done with an interested motive lead to the cycle of birth and death. Therefore a striver should depend on equanimity, should remain established in equanimity. By being established in equanimity, he will not remain destitute and nothing will remain to be done, to be known and to be attained by him. But he, who works with an interested motive (for him), ever remains destitute and bound.

In the Gītā three terms have been used for Karmayoga—Buddhi, yoga and Buddhiyoga. In Karmayoga, there is no predominance of action (Karma) but there is predominance of 'yoga'. Yoga, Buddhi and Buddhiyoga—the three are synonyms. In Karmayoga because of the predominance of determinate intellect, it is called 'Buddhi' and because of the predominance of renunciation by discrimination, it is called 'yoga' or 'buddhiyoga'.

In 'Dhyānayoga' (Discipline of Meditation) there is predominance of concentration of 'mind', while in Karmayoga there is predominance of 'intellect'. While tryng to control the mind, serenity and fickleness linger for a long time because in it a striver wants to withdraw the mind from the world and wants to concentrate it on God. While withdrawing the mind from the world, in its conception the existence of the world persists. This is a rule that so long as there is assumption of any other entity except God, the mind can't be fully controlled. Therefore upto the stage of trance also there are two states—trance and deviation from trance (relapse). But in Karmayoga because of the predominance of intellect, there is prominence of discrimination. While applying discrimination both the real and the unreal remain. A karmayogī applies the unreal things for the service of others by regarding those things as the material for the service. By such conception the attachment for the unreal is quickly and easily renounced.

The mind is not continuously concentrated but it is concentrated at times and in loneliness. But determinate intellect viz., a single pointed determination of the intellect always remains steadfast.

Link:— In the next verse, Lord Kṛṣṇa explains the result of equanimity of mind.

बुद्धियुक्तो जहातीह उभे सुकृतदुष्कृते।
तस्माद्योगाय युज्यस्व योगः कर्मसु कौशलम्॥५०॥

buddhiyukto jahātīha ubhe sukṛtaduṣkṛte
tasmādyogāya yujyasva yogaḥ karmasu kauśalam

Endowed with equanimity, one frees the self in this life from good (virtue) and evil (vice) alike; therefore, devote yourself to this Yoga of equanimity; skill in action lies in (the practice of this) Yoga. 50

Comment:—

'Buddhiyukto jahātīha ubhe sukṛtaduṣkṛte'—A person, endowed with equanimity, becomes free from virtue and vice like omnipresent God (Gītā 2/38).

In the state of equanimity, a man while living in the world detaches himself from the world, and remains untouched by virtues and sins, as a lotus leaf by water.

Man himself is sentient and is free from virtue and sin,

but by identifying himself with the unreal body etc., sins and virtues accrue. If he does not identify himself with the unreal, he will remain untouched by virtues and sins, and unconnected with them like the sky.

'Tasmādyogāya yujyasva'—Therefore, devote yourself to the Yoga of equanimity, viz., remain established continuously in equanimity. You cannot attain that equanimity, so long as you have attachment and aversion. You are the knower of pleasure and pain. It means, that you are different from them and you are as a onlooker, who remains equanimous. So realize that equanimity.

'Yogaḥ karmasu kauśalam'—Skill in action lies in the practice of this Yoga. Equanimity, in success and failure, is skill in action.

In this verse, Lord Kṛṣṇa has not defined Yoga, but He has explained the importance of Yoga (equanimity). If we interpret it as, 'skill in action is Yoga', it means, that the action of a thief carried out skilfully, will also be called Yoga. Therefore, this interpretation does not seem proper. Some people may define Yoga 'skill in action approved by the scriptures.' But, by doing so the people will be bound by the fruits of action and will not be able to attain equanimity. Therefore, it is proper to interpret, equanimity in action as skill or wisdom. The reason is, that he who remains even-minded while performing actions, is not bound by such actions and their fruit.

Secondly, in the first part of this verse, as well as in the previous two verses there is the reference of Yoga (Equanimity) rather than skill. So this interpretation seems to be reasonable.

Appendix—If we reflect upon the expression 'yogaḥ karmasu kauśalam', it may have two meanings—

(i) 'karmasu kauśalam yogaḥ'—skill in actions is yoga.

(ii) 'karmasu yogaḥ kauśalam'—In action yoga is skill.

If we interpret it in the first way that skill in actions is yoga, then the actions of a thief or a swindler carried out very skilfully, will be called 'Yoga'. This interpretation is not proper and moreover here is not the topic of forbidden actions. If we regard only virtuous actions to be carried out skilfully as 'Yoga', then the man will be bound being attached to the fruit of those virtuous actions—'phale sakto nibadhyate' (Gītā 5/12). Therefore he will not attain equanimity and his sufferings will not perish.

In the scriptures it is mentioned—'karmaṇā badhyate jantuḥ' viz., a man is bound by actions. Therefore the actions which naturally lead him to bondage, may lead him to salvation—this is indeed skill in actions. Salvation is attained by 'yoga' (equanimity), rather than by skill in actions. Yoga (equanimity) has neither its beginning nor end. But even the most virtuous actions begin and end and there is union and disunion of their fruit also. How will a person attain salvation by what begins and ends and of which there is union and disunion? How will the imperishable be attained by the perishable? Equanimity is the form of God—'nirdoṣaṁ hi samaṁ brahma' (Gītā 5/19). Therefore 'yoga' is important, not actions.

If the first interpretation is regarded as correct, even then within 'skill', equanimity or feeling of disinterest will have to be accepted. If skill in actions is yoga, then what is skill? While answering this question we'll have to say that only 'Yoga' (equanimity) is skill. In such a situation why should we not accept the direct meaning that yoga (equanimity) in actions is skill. When in the expression 'yogaḥ karmasu kauśalam' the term 'yoga' has certainly been used, then there is no need of interpreting the word 'Kuśalatā' (skill) as yoga.

If we reflect upon this topic, there is the reference of 'Yoga' (equanimity) rather than 'skill in actions'. The Lord by declaring 'samatvaṁ yoga ucyate' has also defined 'yoga'. Therefore in this reference 'yoga' is 'vidheya' (predicate), 'skill in actions' is not predicate. 'Yoga' (equanimity) is skill in action viz., while doing actions there should be even-mindedness, there should not be any attachment or aversion—this is skill in actions. Therefore 'yogaḥ karmasu kauśalaṁ'—this is not the definition of Yoga, but it is the glory of 'Yoga'.

In the first half of this verse (fiftieth) the Lord has declared that a person endowed with equanimity becomes free from virtue and vice (sin). If he is freed from virtue and sin, then which action will be done with skill? Therefore freedom from virtue and sin does not mean that he does not do any action because no one under any circumstances can remain even for a moment without undertaking action (Gītā 3/5). So here freedom from virtue and sin means—freedom from their fruit. In the fifty-first verse also the Lord has mentioned the renunciation of the fruit of action by the expression 'phalaṁ tyaktvā'.

In the Gītā the term 'Kuśala' has also been used in the tenth verse of the eighteenth chapter. There within 'akuśala karma' all the actions performed with an interested motive and actions forbidden by the scriptures, have been included while within 'kuśala karma' all the actions done with disinterested motive and actions sanctioned by the scriptures, have been included. There is a beginning and there is an end of 'Akuśala' and 'Kuśala' actions but there is no beginning or end of 'Yoga'. Attachment and aversion bind a man; agreeable and disagreeable actions don't bind him. Therefore the actions, which are performed by being attached to them, may be very virtuous, will lead to bondage because by those actions even if the abode of Brahmā is attained, one has to return (Gītā 8/16). Therefore the man, who does not shun the disagreeable actions with aversion and does not perform the virtuous actions with attachment, is indeed a man of true renunciation, is intelligent, is free from doubts and is established in the self (Gītā 18/10).

The above description proves that the expression 'yogaḥ karmasu kauśalam' means 'Yoga (equanimity) in actions is skill'—this should be accepted. The Lord also orders to perform actions being steadfast in Yoga—'yogasthaḥ kuru karmāṇi' (Gītā 2/48). It means that actions are not significant but 'Yoga' (equanimity) is significant. Therefore only 'Yoga' (equanimity) in actions is skill.

Link:—The Lord now gives examples to substantiate what has been said in the preceding verse.

कर्मजं बुद्धियुक्ता हि फलं त्यक्त्वा मनीषिणः।
जन्मबन्धविनिर्मुक्ताः पदं गच्छन्त्यनामयम्॥ ५१॥

karmajaṁ buddhiyuktā hi phalaṁ tyaktvā manīṣiṇaḥ
janmabandhavinirmuktāḥ padaṁ gacchantyanāmayam

As wise men endowed with equanimity, renounce the fruits of actions, they also freed from the shackles of births and attain the blissful supreme state. 51

Comment:—

'Karmajaṁ buddhiyuktā hi phalaṁ tyaktvā manīṣiṇaḥ'—Those endowed with equanimity, are really wise. In the tenth verse of the eighteenth chapter also, it is explained that, the man who does not hate disagreeable action nor is attached to an agreeable one, is wise.

An action even without the desire for its fruit will bring about fruit. No one can dispense with its fruit. Suppose a farmer sows seed without a selfish motive, will he not get corn? He will definitely get corn. In the same way if a person works in a detached spirit, he will get its fruit. Therefore, renunciation of fruit means, renunciation of manifest and latent desires for fruit and attachment for fruit. All people are free and capable of renouncing such desires.

'Janmabandhavinirmuktāḥ'—The wise aspirants, endowed with equanimity of mind are freed from the wheel of birth and death. As in the state of equanimity, they do not in the least, possess evils, such as attachment and aversion etc., which are the root cause of rebirth. Thus they become free from the shackles of birth and death, forever.

'Padaṁ gacchantyanāmayam'—'Āmaya' means ailment. An ailment is a blemish. A thing which is free from all sorts of blemishes is called 'Anāmaya (spotless). Wise people endowed with equanimity attain the state, which is free from any kind of blemish. This state has been called eternal state, in the fifth verse of the fifteenth chapter and 'everlasting imperishable state', in the fifty-sixth verse of the eighteenth chapter.

Though in the Gītā (in 14/6) sattva quality (the mode of goodness) has also been called flawless, yet in fact, the self or God is flawless because by attaining Him one has not to follow the wheel of birth and death. Lord Kṛṣṇa has called Sattva quality also flawless, because that also helps a man in attaining God-realization.

Self (soul) is immutable while the evolutes of matter (nature)—body and the world are mutable. When this self (soul) identifies itself with the mutable body, it itself assumes taint with mutable nature. But, when it renounces this assumed identification, it realizes its pure self. This is a blissful supreme state, free from evil.

In this verse the terms 'buddhiyuktā' and 'manīṣiṇaḥ' have been used in the plural, to express the idea that all those who get established in equanimity undoubtedly attain the blissful supreme state, without any exception. It proves that when a striver has no affinity to the perishable body and the world, he attains that state automatically. No effort is required for such a state to be created, as it always is there.

Appendix—Why Yoga (equanimity) in actions is skill—the Lord explains its reason in this verse by the term 'hi' (reason).

The fruit of 'Sāttvika' (good) actions is pure, the fruit of 'Rājasa' action is pain and the fruit of 'Tāmasa' action is ignorance (Gītā 14/16)—a man with equanimity transcends these three kinds of fruit. The renunciation of the fruit of actions has two meanings—renouncing the desire for fruit; and not to feel happy and sad in favourable and unfavourable circumstances which are the fruits of actions.

In fact the entire world which is born and perishes is nothing but the fruit of actions. If the fruit of actions is renounced, no bondage remains.

The term 'manīṣī' means wise men. According to the preceding verse performance of actions with equanimity is wisdom—'sa buddhimānmanuṣyeṣu' (Gītā 4/18).

'Padaṁ gacchantyanāmayam'—The term 'gacchanti' has three meanings—(1) To have knowledge, (2) to go, (3) to attain. Here attainment of the blissful supreme state means—to have knowledge of being free from the shackles of birth and death and of the attainment of the natural state, free from all sorts of blemishes. The reason is that only that is renounced which is in fact ever renounced and only that is attained who is in fact ever attained.

This verse proves that 'Karmayoga' (Discipline of Action) is an independent means for salvation or benediction. By 'Karmayoga' the renunciation of the world and attainment of God—both ensue.

Link:— In the next two verses, Lord Kṛṣṇa explains the steps to atain the blissful supreme state, which is free from blemish.

यदा ते मोहकलिलं बुद्धिर्व्यतितरिष्यति।
तदा गन्तासि निर्वेदं श्रोतव्यस्य श्रुतस्य च॥५२॥

yadā te mohakalilaṁ buddhirvyatitariṣyati
tadā gantāsi nirvedaṁ śrotavyasya śrutasya ca

When your intellect crosses the mire of delusion, you will then

acquire indifference, to what has been heard and what is yet to be heard, (about enjoyments of this world and the next). 52

Comment:—

'Yadā te mohakalilaṁ buddhirvyatitariṣyati'—The state which favours, egoism in this body and attachment for the body, family, kinsmen and objects, is called delusion. Actually, there is no egoism and attachment, for the body etc. They are merely assumed. Pleasure and displeasure, in favourable and unfavourable circumstances and evils, such as partiality, hatred, envy and jealousy etc., are a quagmire. When the intellect of a man gets entangled in this mire of delusion, he is perplexed and cannot think properly.

He, himself is sentient, but by accepting his affinity for the insentient body and things etc., he identifies himself with them. Thus by closing his eyes to the real goal, he gets engrossed in worldly pleasure and prosperity. This is called, entanglement in the mire of delusion. But the intellect which takes the firm decision to be free from the worldly pleasures and prosperity and to attain salvation, is called the 'Intellect' transcending the mire of delusion.

There are two means to cross the swamp of delusion—discrimination (2/11—30) and selfless service. Acute discrimination between the real and the unreal, makes one indifferent to the unreal world, and a keen desire for selfless service for the welfare of others, enables one to renounce the desire for one's own pleasures. In the same way as when a disciple for his preceptor, a son for parents, a servant for his master develop a wish for providing all sorts of comforts to them, then their desire for comfort goes away automatically.

The Discipline of Knowledge, is somewhat difficult to practise, because the desire for pleasure may linger on in it. When a striver comes across pleasures, he deviates from his spiritual path and inclines towards them. But a striver who has the feeling for service to others, utilizes the material for the service of others, and thus his desire for pleasures perishes easily. Therefore, Lord Kṛṣṇa has mentioned the Discipline of Disinterested Action, as superior to and easier than the Discipline of Knowledge (5/2-3) and by it a striver quickly reaches Brahma—the Absolute (5/6).

'Tadā gantāsi nirvedaṁ śrotavyasya śrutasya ca'—The pleasure which men have enjoyed and heard* of and also the pleasures of heaven etc., which are yet to be heard of, are transient. So, how can they give peace and joy to the man's self which is permanent? Thus men become dispassionate. When intellect gets out of the mire of delusion, then acute discrimination is developed that the world is ephemeral while he (the self) is eternal and therefore, how could the kaleidoscopic world provide peace to him? With this attitude of mind, he automatically develops detachment, from the whole world.

Lord Kṛṣṇa has used the term 'hear' instead of 'enjoy' because there is attraction for pleasure after hearing about it. Thus 'hearing' is an important factor for the attraction of pleasures. Hearing as a means occupies an important place in the Disciplines of Knowledge and Devotion for spiritual progress also.

The terms 'yadā' (when) and 'tadā' (then) have been used to emphasize the fact, that there is no rule that it will take so many years or months or days, to develop this acute dispassion. As soon as, your intellect crosses the mire of delusion, you will become dispassionate. It involves no much delay.

श्रुतिविप्रतिपन्ना ते यदा स्थास्यति निश्चला।
समाधावचला बुद्धिस्तदा योगमवाप्स्यसि ॥ ५३ ॥

śrutivipratipannā te yadā sthāsyati niścalā
samādhāvacalā buddhistadā yogamavāpsyasi

* Here the term 'Hear' denotes the sense of sound, touch, colour, taste and smell.

After your intellect, confused by hearing conflicting doctrines, has become stable and firm (steady) on God, you will then attain Self-realization or union, with God. 53

Comment:—

[After crossing the mire of delusion also, there may be confusion of mind by hearing conflicting spiritual doctrines. So Lord Kṛṣṇa induces Arjuna to get rid of that confusion.]

'Śrutivipratipannā te yadā sthāsyati niścalā samādhāvacalā buddhistadā yogamavāpsyasi'—Arjuna was in a fix, whether he should perform his duty as a Kṣatriya or he should avoid the slaughter of his kith and kin. If he protected his family, he would shirk his duty. If he performed his duty of fighting, then the family would not be protected. So he was bewildered.* Therefore Lord Kṛṣṇa persuades Arjuna to keep the intellect firm in case of scriptural opinions and steady in regarding God-realization.

First of all, a striver is unable to make up his mind whether to have honest and sincere dealings with the worldly people, or to attain God. Then he decides that he has to render selfless service to the world. Having taken this decision, he starts showing indifference and dispassion to the worldly pleasures. Then in the spiritual path he comes across different opinions of the scriptures. So it becomes difficult for him to decide, which opinion he should follow. In that case by good company or faith etc., he is either able to take the decision or he surrenders himself to God. Then by God's grace his intellect becomes firm. Secondly, in all the scriptures and religions, God, soul and the world, have been described in different forms and ways. But all of them agree, "I am soul, not body," "The world is to be ignored", "God is to

* A person may be in a dilemma in two ways—in worldly affairs and in scriptural ordinances or sects such as dualism and non-dualism etc. It is more difficult to be free from the dilemma of the scriptural ordinances than from that of the worldly affairs. So Lord Kṛṣṇa explains that a striver should have a determinate intellect that he has to realize only God whatsoever may happen.

be realized." By taking this decision the intellect of the striver becomes steady. Then he realized God easily. So the only obstacle to God-realization is lack of firmness of intellect.

The greater the deficiency in reaching at a decision regarding the contrary spiritual doctrines and in his own emancipation, the greater the delay there is. But in both cases as soon as the intellect becomes steady and determinate, eternal union with God is realized.

The intellect should be unshakable in order to renounce affinity for the world, as mentioned by the expression 'state of severance from union with pain,' in the twenty-third verse of the sixth chapter; while it should be steady in order to have affinity for God as expressed by the expression 'evenness of mind is called Yoga', in the forty-eighth verse of the second chapter.

Here in 'tadā yogamavāpsyasi' Yoga, means to become established in union with God, from whom there is no disunion. Only the striver has to abandon his affinity with the unreal. This union can be realized either by selfless service viz., Discipline of Disinterested Action, or discrimination viz., Discipline of Knowledge, or love for God viz., Discipline of Devotion, or meditation or annihilation of the world viz., Discipline of Annihilation (Layayoga) or by the process of restraining breath viz., Discipline of Austerity (Haṭhayoga) etc.

Appendix—There are two divisions of delusion—'mohakalila' viz., the worldly delusion and 'śrutivipratipatti'—scriptural (philosophical) delusion. Attachment to the body, wife, sons, wealth, property etc., is 'worldly delusion' and 'Dvaita' (dualism), 'Advaita' (non-dualism), 'Viśiṣṭādvaita' (qualified dualism) and 'dvaitādvaita' (dualism-non-dualism)—to get entangled in these 'isms' is 'scriptural delusion'. By renouncing these two types of delusion, a man gets detached from pleasures and his intellect becomes stable. When the intellect becomes stable, 'Yoga' is attained viz., the distance from God comes to an end and you come near to God. By 'Karmayoga' you come near God, by 'Jñānayoga' difference is wiped out and there is 'Abheda' and by 'Bhaktiyoga' there is 'abhinnatā' viz., the devotee becomes God's own self. By attaining perfection in either Karmayoga or Jñānayoga, a striver gets the fruit of both (Gītā 5/4-5).

If a person has the only aim of salvation and has no selfish motive by having affinity for wealth-property and family-relatives etc., then he crosses the worldly delusion. If he does not want to gain bookish knowledge (rot-learning) by studying the scriptures but has the only aim to realize the self, he crosses the scriptural delusion. It means that a striver, should neither be enamoured by the worldly delusion nor by the scriptural (philosophical) differences of opinions viz., he should not insist on any sect or religion. Thus he becomes eligible for 'Yoga', salvation or devotion. Besides this there is no need of any special eligibility (qualification).

Link:—Arjuna then puts the question about the illumined one whose intellect has crossed the mire of delusion and who has become steadfast and firm on God.

अर्जुन उवाच

स्थितप्रज्ञस्य का भाषा समाधिस्थस्य केशव।
स्थितधीः किं प्रभाषेत किमासीत व्रजेत किम्॥५४॥

arjuna uvāca

sthitaprajñasya kā bhāṣā samādhisthasya keśava
sthitadhīḥ kiṁ prabhāṣeta kimāsīta vrajeta kim

Arjuna said:

O Keśava, what is the mark of a person of steadfast wisdom, who realises (sthitaprajña) God? How does such a man of firm

wisdom, speak, sit and how does he walk? 54

Comment:—

[Here Arjuna asks about the marks of a man of steadfast wisdom. Before he puts this question he had some doubt about the superiority of intellect or actions (2/47—50). Lord Kṛṣṇa, in fifty-second and fifty-third verses said, "After crossing the mire of delusion when your intellect has become steadfast and firm on God, you will attain Self-realization or union with God." Hearing this, Arjuna wants to know the mark of one who attains Self-realization viz., who becomes a man of steadfast wisdom. He had doubt about action and knowledge, which he will ask further (in 3/1-2). Had Arjuna put a question regarding his doubts about action and knowledge, in the fifty-fourth verse here, then his question regarding the mark of the man of steadfast wisdom, would have been much delayed.]

'Samādhisthasya'*— Here, this term has been used for the person who has attained God-realization.

'Sthitaprajñasya'—This term has been used both for the enlightened (God-realized) soul, as well as the striver. The striver who is of a firm resolve and who never budges from his spiritual path, is also called a man of steadfast wisdom. The realized soul whose intellect is already steadfast, is also a man of steadfast wisdom.

Now, the question arises, while Arjuna put the question about the enlightened soul only, why Lord Kṛṣṇa included the striver too. The answer is that, in the Discipline of Knowledge aspirants generally develop disinclination for activities. The perfect soul gets total disinclination. An aspirant of the Discipline of Devotion, has an inclination to the recitation of Divine name, meditation, association with holy men and study of the scriptures etc. These activities pervade in abundance, in him. In the perfect state, only

* Here the word 'Samādhi' has been used for God as it was also used in the forty-fourth verse of this chapter.

activities pertaining to God are performed. Thus there is a clear difference in the degree of activities, of aspirants and realized souls in both the Disciplines of Knowledge and Devotion. But in the Discipline of Action, the flow of activities goes on as usual, without any change, in both the stages—as a striver and a perfected soul. So, there is a description of strivers, from the forty-first verse to the forty-fifth verse, and also from the forty-seventh verse to the fifty-third verse. Thus, in the context, the means by which strivers, can be perfect souls´ have been enunciated and the marks of the perfect soul, have also been described.

'Kā bhāṣā'—What is the description or mark of an enlightened soul? (Lord Kṛṣṇa answers this question in the next verse).

'Sthitadhīḥ kiṁ prabhāṣeta'—How does the enlightened soul speak? (Lord Kṛṣṇa will answer this question in fifty-sixth and fifty-seventh verses.)

'Kimāsīta'—How does he sit viz., how does he become dispassionate? (Lord Kṛṣṇa has answered these in verses from fifty-eighth to sixty-third.)

'Vrajeta kim'—How does he walk viz., how does he behave? (Lord Kṛṣṇa has answered this question in the verses sixty-fourth to seventy-first.)

Link:—Lord Kṛṣṇa, in the next verse, answers Arjuna's first question.

श्रीभगवानुवाच

प्रजहाति यदा कामान्सर्वान्पार्थ मनोगतान्।
आत्मन्येवात्मना तुष्टः स्थितप्रज्ञस्तदोच्यते॥५५॥

śrībhagavānuvāca

prajahāti yadā kāmānsarvānpārtha manogatān
ātmanyevātmanā tuṣṭaḥ sthitaprajñastadocyate

The Blessed Lord said:

O Pārtha (Arjuna), when a man discards all his desires visiting the mind, and is self-satisfied in own self, he is said to be stable, in wisdom. 55

Comment:—

[According to the gospel of the Gītā, a striver, can attain perfection, (God-realization), by any discipline (that of Disinterested Action or Devotion etc.,) which he follows according to his interest and liking and his perfection is described by that means only. Example—A striver following the Discipline of Devotion worships God constantly, meditating on Him with exclusive devotion (12/6). Therefore, in the enlightened state, he becomes free from malice towards all beings (12/13). In the Discipline of Knowledge the striver perceives himself detached from these guṇas (attributes) (modes) and is above them (14/19) and in the enlightened state, he sits like a witness firmly established in God, beyond all the guṇas, having risen above them (14/22—25). Similarly, in Karmayoga it is the abandoning of all desires that is important. Hence the enlightened soul abandons all desires. In this verse Lord Kṛṣṇa dwells upon this point.]

'Prajahāti yadā kāmānsarvānpārtha manogatān'—It means that desire does not exist in the self, because the self is everlasting while desire is transient. Moreover it does not stay permanently in the mind but comes into it—'manogatān'. But the man by identifying himself with body, senses, mind and intellect, accepts the desire visiting the mind as resting in his own self.

'Jahāti'—Use of the prefix 'Pra' before the verb 'jahāti', indicates that there is no trace of any desire left in him. A man can neither renounce his own self nor the things which are not his own, but he can renounce only the things which actually are not his own, but he has mistaken them as his own. Similarly, desires do not exist in one's own self, but one accepts them as existing in one's own self, so he has to cast them off.

The term 'kāmān' (desires) also includes the term 'sarvān' (all), yet 'sarvān' has been added to emphasize the fact that, every fragment of all the desires should be cast off.

'Ātmanyevātmanā tuṣṭaḥ'—After abandoning all the desire completely, a man is satisfied in himself and with himself i.e., he is spontaneously contented in his own self.

Contentment is of two kinds—one is said to be a virtue as it relates to inner sense. It is there as a result of no desire in the inner sense. But the other kind is the self itself. As the self never has any trace of discontentment so it is called contentment incarnate the Self itself). The latter contentment is eternal. It knows no change. It is spontaneous. It is not the result of any practice or thought. The intellect of such a contented men always remains steadfast automatically.

'Sthitaprajñastadocyate'—Actually a man is always steady in wisdom, but when he accepts his desires, because of unsteady mind, he does not realize his stableness in wisdom. When he abandons his desires viz., accepts the non-existence of desires, he realizes his stability in wisdom.

A striver has to make effort to concentrate his mind, but by renouncing desires he does not have to do so, instead he attains this stage, in a spontaneous manner.

In the discipline of action, the striver is concerned with actions more than anything else. Action without selfish motive, is said to be the means for a sage to attain Yoga (Gītā 6/3). Therefore such a striver is concerned with actions relating to the stage when he is a striver, as well as when he is an enlightened soul. Whatever standard an enlightened soul sets, people in general, follow the same (Gītā 3/21). The Lord has explained, in the fourth chapter also, that the striver following the Discipline of Disinterested Action while performing actions remains detached and while remaining detached he performs actions (4/18).

In the fifty-third verse Lord Kṛṣṇa had advised two things

to Arjuna, to keep his intellect immovable regarding scriptural doctrine and steady in God. So He has used the term 'yadā' (when) and 'tadā' (then) which explain, that a striver is called stable in wisdom when he is completely free from desires, and is satisfied in the self. It also means that he is called a striver so long as he has even a fragment of desire left and an enlightened soul when desires are totally renounced. Therefore, two important factors have been explained in the verse—to renounce the desire and to get established in God.

The same two factors have been explained, in verses fifty-six; fifty-seven; fifty-eight; fifty-nine; sixty and sixty-one; sixty-two to sixty-five; sixty-six to sixty-eight; sixty-nine; seventy and seventy-one and seventy-two.

Appendix—One division is of those who are of unsteady intellect while the other division is of those of steady intellect. The Lord has described the men of unsteady intellect from the forty-first verse to the forty-fourth verse; now He describes the men of steady wisdom from the fifty-fifth verse to the seventy-first verse. When a striver having renounced the worldly inclination is established in the self, he is said to be stable in wisdom.

He, who has the aim of God-realization, has a determinate and single pointed intellect because God is also only one. But he who has the worldly aim, his intellect is full of numberless desires because worldly objects are numberless (Gītā 2/41).

In order to attain equanimity, steadiness of intellect is very necessary. In Pātañjala Yogadarśana importance has been attached to stability of mind (concentration of the mind). But the Gītā attaches importance to the stability of intellect (steadfastness of aim). The reason is that in God-realization the steadiness of the mind is not so important as is the steadiness of intellect. By the steadiness of mind worldly 'siddhis' (accomplishments or occult powers) are gained but by the steadiness of intellect, spiritual perfection (salvation) is attained. In Karmayoga steadiness of intellect is important. If the mind becomes concentrated, how will a Karmayogī discharge his duty? The reason is that when the mind becomes steady, the outward activities stop. The Lord also orders Arjuna to discharge his duties being steadfast in Yoga (equanimity)—'yogastha kuru karmāṇi' (Gītā 2/48).

The Lord by using the terms 'prajahāti' and 'kāmānsarvān' means that there shouldn't be even a trace of desire, but it should be renounced totally. The reason is that this desire is the main stumbling block to God-realization.

Link:—The next two verses deal with the manner in which a realised soul speaks.

दुःखेष्वनुद्विग्नमनाः सुखेषु विगतस्पृहः।
वीतरागभयक्रोधः स्थितधीर्मुनिरुच्यते ॥ ५६ ॥

duḥkheṣvanudvignamanāḥ sukheṣu vigataspṛhaḥ
vītarāgabhayakrodhaḥ sthitadhīrmunirucyate

He, whose mind remains unperturbed in sorrow, who does not crave for pleasure, and who is free from passion, fear and anger is called a sage with stable wisdom. 56

Comment:—

[Arjuna puts a question, attaching importance to action, while Lord Kṛṣṇa answers, attaching importance to feelings, because a change in feeling brings about a corresponding change in action.* The Lord is discussing here, the feeling or the motive which change the character of action throughout outwardly, it may seem quite different.]

* Whenever in the Gītā Arjuna puts a question attaching importance to action, Lord Kṛṣṇa answers it attaching importance to feelings and understanding because an action is performed according to the feelings and understanding. For example Arjuna in the fourteenth chapter asked, "What are the marks of him who has transcended the three modes?" Lord Kṛṣṇa attaching importance to feelings replies, "He remains even-minded."

'Duḥkheṣvanudvignamanāḥ'—There is no end to sorrow, calumny, dishonour and unfavourable circumstances, in this world. But a man of wisdom, remains unperturbed, because the aim of his life is to discharge his duty to the best of his ability and capacity, for the welfare to others, without having any desire for its fruit. So, he always remains happy and unperturbed even in the most unfavourable circumstances.

'Sukheṣu vigataspṛhaḥ'—He does not crave for any kind of pleasure such as praise, honour and favourable circumstances etc., nor does he have a desire to prolong, such a state. He remains unruffled in the midst of favourable or hostile circumstances.

'Vītarāgabhayakrodhaḥ'—Our entanglement with worldly things, is known as attachment (rāga). If a stronger person tries to deprive us of worldly possessions, it arouses fear in us, whereas if a weaker person does so, it arouses anger in us. But a person who is keen to do good to others, automatically gets rid of attachment. This freedom from attachment, leads him to fearlessness and calmness. Thus he becomes free from attachment, fear and anger.

So long as there are perturbations, cravings, attachment, fear and anger, even in a small measure, a man is called a striver. But when he is totally free from them, he becomes an enlightened soul.

[Lust, desire, craving and greed etc., are forms of attachment. In attachment there is an attraction, for the perishable worldly objects.]

'Sthitadhīrmunirucyate'—The mind of such a follower of the Discipline of Selfless Action, becomes stable. Here, the term 'muni' has not been used, for a person who keeps silent. The Lord has also not used the term 'mauna' for penance of speech, but He has used it for mental penance (Gītā 17/16). So here, 'muni' has been used for a contemplative person, free from desire and attachment. He contemplates to remain unattached, like an enlightened soul. Throughout his practice he is very cautious to remain unattached. Such cautiousness automatically persists in an enlightened soul. That awareness leads him to attainment of beatitude (Gītā 3/19). It is because of this virtue of awareness, that he has been described by the term 'muni.'

यः सर्वत्रानभिस्नेहस्तत्तत्प्राप्य शुभाशुभम्।
नाभिनन्दति न द्वेष्टि तस्य प्रज्ञा प्रतिष्ठिता॥५७॥

yaḥ sarvatrānabhisnehastattatprāpya śubhāśubham
nābhinandati na dveṣṭi tasya prajñā pratiṣṭhitā

He, who remains unattached under all conditions, he who is neither delighted at good, nor dejected with evil, is stable in wisdom. 57

Comment:—

[In the previous verse, Lord Kṛṣṇa explained that a man of stable wisdom remains unperturbed, while discharging his duty. In this verse, he explains, that such a man remains stable in favourable and unfavourable circumstances, which he comes across as a result of the deeds he performs.]

'Yaḥ sarvatrānabhisnehaḥ'—He remains unattached everywhere viz., he is not attached to his body, senses, mind, intellect, family and possessions. He never identifies himself with them, but always remains untainted by them. Despite his physical association with senses, objects, circumstances and individuals etc., he remains quite unattached with them, through the self.

'Tattatprāpya śubhāśubhaṁ nābhinandati na dveṣṭi—He remains untainted and unaffected by good and bad, favourable and unfavourable circumstances. Experiencing good or pleasant, he is not delighted. This delight means mental joy and expression of joy through words. By encountering evil or unpleasant, he is not dejected. This dejection means mental suffering and despair, and the thought why and how this situation has occurred, and how to get rid of the unpleasant situation. He remains untainted in favourable and unfavourable circumstances, which we got as a result of destiny.

The expression, 'tat, tat', signifies that meeting with all agreeable and disagreeable persons, incidents, objects and circumstances that can possibly cause mental perturbations; he neither rejoices in them nor hates them whenever, wherever, and however, he may meet with them.

'Tasya prajñā pratiṣṭhitā'—His determinate intellect, now becomes stable in God. He understands that he is entirely unconcerned with the good and evil of the world, because these always change, while he (soul) always remains the same. There is no modification in the self, while in the evolutes of matter, there is always modification. Man identifies himself with the body and regards the modification of the body as modification in his own self. But when he realizes the two as separate, his intellect becomes stable.

The second interpretation is, that limitless and endless God cannot be perceived by the intellect, which is limited. So the intellect merges in God and then there remains nothing besides God. This is fixation of intellect in God or stability in wisdom.

A Karmayogī is ever active. Therefore, the Lord, in the fifty-sixth verse, mentions that he neither craves for success (pleasure) nor is he perturbed in failure (sorrow), while in this verse He declares that he neither delighted at receiving the agreeable nor dejected at the disagreeable.

Link:—Now, Lord Kṛṣṇa answers the third question, "How does an equanimous person sit?"

यदा संहरते चायं कूर्मोऽङ्गानीव सर्वशः।
इन्द्रियाणीन्द्रियार्थेभ्यस्तस्य प्रज्ञा प्रतिष्ठिता॥५८॥

yadā saṁharate cāyaṁ kūrmo'ṅgānīva sarvaśaḥ
indriyāṇīndriyārthebhyastasya prajñā pratiṣṭhitā

When, like a tortoise, withdrawing its limbs from all sides, he detaches completely his senses from sense-objects, his wisdom is stable. 58

Comment:—

'Yadā saṁharate cāyaṁ kūrmo'ṅgānīva sarvaśaḥ indriyāṇīndriyārthebhyastasya prajñā pratiṣṭhitā'—Here, the purpose of the illustration of the tortoise is, that as a tortoise withdraws its six limbs—four legs, a tail and a head—into the shell to protect itself against possible dangers, so does an enlightened one also withdraw his five senses and one mind from sense-objects. If he has the least affinity with senses, he cannot be a man of stable wisdom.

Here the verb 'saṁharate', has been used, to emphasize the fact, that he does not even think of worldly pleasures.

In this verse the term 'yadā' has been used but 'tadā' is not used. The reason is, that when the senses are withdrawn from their sense-objects, the self which is axiomatic, is realized, because that is beyond the limit of time. So the word 'tadā' which denotes time, has not been applied. Self-realization or God-realization is axiomatic, and is beyond the reach of senses, but we are veiled by the curtain of pleasures and thus cannot realize Him. He still exists. But as soon as that veil is removed viz., we renounce our affinity to the worldly pleasures, and He is revealed.

Link:—Lord Kṛṣṇa explains in the next verse, that mere withdrawal of the senses from sense-objects, is not the mark of a man of steadfast wisdom.

विषया विनिवर्तन्ते निराहारस्य देहिनः।
रसवर्जं रसोऽप्यस्य परं दृष्ट्वा निवर्तते॥५९॥

viṣayā vinivartante nirāhārasya dehinaḥ
rasavarjaṁ raso'pyasya paraṁ dṛṣṭvā nivartate

Sense-objects cease to exist for him, who does not enjoy them with his senses, but the taste for them may persist. This relish, also disappears from a man of stable mind, when he, realises the Supreme. 59

Comment:—

'Viṣayā vinivartante nirāhārasya dehinaḥ rasavarjam'— A man becomes an abstainer in two ways (i) Fasting by one's own will or owing to sickness. (ii) Abstaining from sense enjoyments. Here, the term has been used, to refer to a striver, who withdraws his senses from sense-objects.

The senses of a sick man become unfit for indulgence, but craving in them, for sense enjoyment persists. He hopes to enjoy these after recovery. Similarly, sense-objects cease for the abstinent striver, but the taste persists. It means that his body and senses come under restraint, but his mind wanders.

The dispassionate strivers who have instinctively no attachment for pleasure, become free from this taste. The striver who wants to follow the spiritual path but is not dispassionate, can restrain his body and senses by thinking of the adverse consequences of sense enjoyments, though his taste persists.

'Raso'pyasya paraṁ dṛṣṭvā nivartate'—The relish of the man of steadfast wisdom, who realises the Supreme, disappears. It is a rule. But the contrary that with the disappearance (cessation) of relish, a striver attains steadfast wisdom, is not true.

'Raso'pyasya' means that a striver has feeling in his egoism viz., 'I ness'. This taste changes itself into attachment. Therefore, a striver should have determination that he as a striver has no attachment, no desire. This sort of determination (aim) frees him from relish, and after realizing God this relish disappears altogether.

Appendix—By accepting the existence and attaching value to pleasures, in the mind there ensues a subtle attraction, lovability and sweetness for pleasures, it is named 'Rasa' (relish). As a greedy man rejoices at heart by receiving money and a voluptuary is rejoiced at heart by coming in contact with a woman, it is called 'Rasa'. After enjoying pleasure a man declares, "Oh! how much I relished!'' This is recollection of that 'Rasa' (relish). This relish abides in the assumed ego (I'ness) (cijjaḍagranthi). The gross form of this relish is attachment to pleasures.

So long as a man has relish for sense enjoyments, he has to depend on Prakṛti (Matter) and its evolutes (actions, objects and persons). When he is free from this relish, his dependence totally perishes, his dependence on sense enjoyments stops and he is no longer a slave to them.

So long as a person accepts the existence of pleasures, attaches importance to them and has relish for them, the spiritual (unworldly) relish for God is not revealed. Not to speak of unworldly relish, he can't have the determinate intellect to attain Him (Gītā 2/44). After merely withdrawing outwardly the senses from sense objects, the relish (taste) persists. By attaining Self-realization this taste disappears, this relish disappears—'paraṁ dṛṣṭvā nivartate'. It means that when a striver realizes that he is different from the world and realizes his identity with God, then the perishable taste disappears. With the disappearance (cessation) of the perishable taste, imperishable (non-stop) relish is aroused.

After Self-realization this relish for pleasures certainly disappears but even before Self-realization by being indifferent to it, by reflection, by good company and by the grace of saints, a striver can be free from this relish. The company of the enlightened exalted souls can also free a striver from this taste (relish).

The three disciplines—Karmayoga, Jñānayoga and Bhaktiyoga can free a striver from the perishable relish. When a striver starts relishing the taste of service in Karmayoga, the taste of Self-realization in Jñānayoga and the taste of devotion (love) in Bhaktiyoga, his relish for the perishable pleasures starts disappearing. As a child in childhood relishes toys but when he grows up, he starts relishing wealth, then his relish for toys naturally disappears. Similarly when a striver relishes the spiritual discipline, the relish for mundane pleasures naturally disappears.

When relish persists and pleasures are enjoyed, then a man's heart melts and he is overpowered by pleasures. But when he is freed from relish, he may come across worldly pleasures but they don't cause the least agitation in his mind (Gītā 2/70). He has no such inclination that pleasure may attract him. As you put a bag of money before an animal, it does not covet for it and after seeing a beautiful woman it is not lustful. An animal doesn't know the value of money and a woman but an enlightened exalted soul knows money as well the woman (Gītā 2/69), yet he is free from greed and lust. When we have an itching sensation in any organ of the body, we scratch it with our fingers, and when this sensation ends, it does not make any difference in fingers, there is no alteration in them. Similarly an enlightened soul uses the sense-objects but his mind remains the same unperturbed and free from agitation. The reason is that being free from relish, he has no inclination for enjoying pleasures. Whatever he does, he does it for the welfare of others and to comfort them. Contemplation on the sense-objects for one's own pleasure leads one to ruin or fall (Gītā 2/62-63). But even the use of the sense-objects not for one's own pleasure, does not lead to bondage (Gītā 2/64-65).

The perishable relish (taste) is instantaneous, it does not last long. The relish which we have for a woman or money at the beginning does not persist in the same degree afterwards. We relish the food at the beginning but after each morsel the relish decreases and finally ends and then we have a dislike for that food. But the imperishable relish never lessens but always remains the same. Enjoyment of the perishable relish results in inertness, shortage, grief, diseases, fear, commotion and other evils.

A voluptuous person can't escape these evils because pleasures certainly lead to these evils. Therefore the Lord has mentioned the perception of misery and evil in them—duḥkhadoṣānudarśanam (Gītā 13/8). The man freed from evils such as desire etc., pursues his salvation (Gītā 16/21-22).

Link:—What is the harm if this relish does not cease, is explained in the next verse.

यततो ह्यपि कौन्तेय पुरुषस्य विपश्चितः।
इन्द्रियाणि प्रमाथीनि हरन्ति प्रसभं मनः॥ ६०॥

yatato hyapi kaunteya puruṣasya vipaścitaḥ
indriyāṇi pramāthīni haranti prasabhaṁ manaḥ

The turbulent senses, O son of Kuntī, forcibly sway the mind of even a wise man, who practises self-control. 60

Comment:—

'Yatato hyapi kaunteya puruṣasya vipaścitaḥ indriyāṇi pramāthīni haranti prasabhaṁ manaḥ'*—The term, 'wise man' has been used, for the man who practises self-control, who performs his duty without attachment and desire for its fruit, one who discriminates between the real and the unreal and who thinks of the welfare of all creatures. The turbulent senses of even such a wise man carry away his mind towards pleasures. The reason is, that so long as mind is not permanently established in God, the past influences of enjoyment of pleasures, attract the senses and mind towards pleasures, forcibly. Even, some sages could

* Here Lord Kṛṣṇa has called the senses turbulent and in the thirty-fourth verse of the sixth chapter Arjuna has called the mind turbulent. It means that both the senses and the mind are turbulent. Similarly here it is explained that senses carry away the mind, while in the sixty-seventh verse of this chapter it is explained that the mind carries away discrimination. It means that both senses and mind are impetuous. So a striver should control both of them.

not control this temptation. Therefore, a striver should never trust his senses and should be always on his guard.* Moreover, he should never feel proud of sense-control.

Link:— In the next verse, Lord Kṛṣṇa explains, how to control the turbulent senses, which forcibly carry away the mind of even a wise man, in whom the taste for sense-objects still persists.

तानि सर्वाणि संयम्य युक्त आसीत मत्परः ।
वशे हि यस्येन्द्रियाणि तस्य प्रज्ञा प्रतिष्ठिता ॥ ६१ ॥

tāni sarvāṇi saṁyamya yukta āsīta matparaḥ
vaśe hi yasyendriyāṇi tasya prajñā pratiṣṭhitā

Having controlled all the senses, a striver should engage in meditation, devoting himself heart and soul to Me. His wisdom (mind) is stable, (constant) whose senses are under control. 61

Comment:—

'Tāni sarvāṇi saṁyamya yukta āsīta matparaḥ'—By controlling the senses, a striver should devote himself, heart and soul to Me. Moreover, he should not feel proud of his sense-control, because pride goes before a fall. He should, rather, feel that it was only God's grace, which enabled him to control his senses. Generally, in a striver following the Discipline of Action, there is predominance of action. Therefore, he develops egoism. Due to this egoistic feeling, he pays little attention to the divine grace, though the endowment of human body, inclination, practice and success of this discipline, are all the result of divine grace. By His special divine grace, the Lord is exhorting the striver to be devoted to Him. Thus, he should devote himself heart and soul to Him, thinking that he is God's and God is his, while he is

* A man should not live in loneliness with a woman even though she is his mother, sister or daughter because the impetuous senses enslave even a wise man (Manu. 2/215).

neither of the world nor is the world his. He should infuse a sense of 'I' in only God, not in the world, at all.

This section deals with the Discipline of Disinterested Action. So, Lord Kṛṣṇa should have told Arjuna some method of that discipline. But Lord Kṛṣṇa time and again has laid great emphasis on devotion to Him, and has glorified it very much. So He declares— "Among all Yogīs, he who worships Me with faith, his innermost self merged in Me, is considered by Me, to be the best Yogī—most devout (Gītā 6/47)."

'Vaśe hi yasyendriyāṇi tasya prajñā pratiṣṭhitā'—In the fifty-ninth verse, Lord Kṛṣṇa said, that even with the cessation of sense-objects, a striver does not become a man of steadfast wisdom. But, here he says that the wisdom of the striver who has controlled his senses, is stable. Why? The clarification is that, in 2/59 even at the cessation of the sense-objects the taste (relish) for sense enjoyments persists. But here in this verse, the senses of the striver are controlled and his taste has also disappeared. Thus the striver becomes stable in wisdom, (mind) at the cessation of taste.

Appendix—The Lord exhorts the striver following Karmayoga to devote himself heart and soul to Him by using the term 'matparaḥ'—this is a special feature of devotion because without being devoted to Him, total control over senses is difficult.

In Karmayoga there is renunciation and renunciation leads to peace and happiness. This happiness follows cessation of miseries. This is with a result of attaining something. A Bhaktiyogī attains eternal bliss. Therefore without the bliss attained by devotion (love), senses are not totally controlled. Secondly in Karmayoga only by intense dispassion (detachment), senses are controlled but in devotion (being devoted to God) even by a little dispassion, senses are easily controlled. Therefore the Lord has used the term 'matparaḥ'.

Link:—When a striver devotes himself heart and soul to God, his senses are controlled and his relish (taste) for sense enjoyments disappears. But what about those who do not devote themselves to God? The answer is provided in the next two verses.

ध्यायतो विषयान्पुंसः सङ्गस्तेषूपजायते।
सङ्गात्सञ्जायते कामः कामात्क्रोधोऽभिजायते॥ ६२॥
क्रोधाद्भवति सम्मोहः सम्मोहात्स्मृतिविभ्रमः।
स्मृतिभ्रंशाद् बुद्धिनाशो बुद्धिनाशात्प्रणश्यति॥ ६३॥

dhyāyato viṣayānpuṁsaḥ saṅgasteṣūpajāyate
saṅgātsañjāyate kāmaḥ kāmātkrodho'bhijāyate
krodhādbhavati sammohaḥ sammohātsmṛtivibhramaḥ
smṛtibhraṁśād buddhināśo buddhināśātpraṇaśyati

Contemplating constantly on the objects of senses, a man develops attachment for them; from attachment springs desire and from desire (unfulfilled) originates anger. From anger arises delusion; from delusion, confusion of memory; from which grows loss of reason; and with loss of reason (discrimination), he goes to complete ruin. 62-63

Comment:—

'Dhyāyato viṣayānpuṁsaḥ saṅgasteṣūpajāyate'—When a man does not devote himself to God viz., he does not meditate on God, he broods on objects of senses, because in that case there is nothing else to contemplate on, except the world. Thus, by brooding over them, he develops attachment for them. Due to this attachment he enjoys sense-objects. This enjoyment may be mental or physical. The pleasure resulting from enjoyment, enhances attachment. Due to this enhanced attachment, he repeatedly dwells on sense-objects. It is a rule that the enhanced attachment persists, whether he enjoys the sense-objects or not.

'Saṅgātsañjāyate kāmaḥ'—By developing attachment for

sense enjoyments, one has a desire to acquire and enjoy those sense-objects.

'Kāmātkrodho'bhijāyate'— Gratification of desire misleads to greed and one who creates an obstacle in the possibility of its gratification, becomes a victim of anger. The desire for respect and honour on the ground of caste, stage of life and virtues etc., also causes anger, if some obstacles are put in its gratification.

Desire is a rājasika trait; delusion a tāmasika one, and anger lies between the two. If you are angry with either, it means that you have attachment for something or the other. If you are angry with a man who defames you, it means that you are attached to fame. If you are enraged with a person who censures you, it proves your pride of innocence and so on.

'Krodhādbhavati sammohaḥ'—From anger, ensues delusion. In fact, delusion ensues not only from anger, but also from desire, greed and attachment.

(i) Delusion born of desire, veils discrimination and so a man goaded by desire performs undesirable actions.

(ii) Out of anger, a deluded person utters harsh and pinching words, to even friends and adorable ones, and performs wrong and cruel deeds.

(iii) Delusion born of greed makes a man blind and he cannot distinguish between the real and the unreal, the right and the wrong and he cheats others by using fraudulent methods.

(iv) Delusion born of attachment, creates partiality.

Now the question arises, why Lord Kṛṣṇa has said that delusion ensues from anger while it ensues from desire, greed and attachment, as well. If we give a serious thought, we come to know that goaded by desire, greed and attachment, a man thinks of his own selfish motive and pleasure, while in anger he thinks of doing evil to others. Thus, delusion born of anger is more disastrous, than that born of the other three. Therefore

Lord Kṛṣṇa has said that delusion ensues from anger.

'Sammohātsmṛtivibhramaḥ'—From delusion arises confusion of memory. It means that a man forgets his aim to attain salvation, or to follow the spiritual path, in accordance with the ordinance of the scriptures etc.

'Smṛtibhraṁśād buddhināśaḥ'—From confusion of memory arises loss of reason viz., a man cannot discriminate between right and wrong.

'Buddhināśātpraṇaśyati'—Loss of discrimination paves the way to self-destruction.

Therefore, it is obligatory for all strivers to devote themselves heart and soul to God, in order to escape self-destruction.

Brooding on the objects of senses, leads to attachment; attachment leads to desire; desire to anger; anger to delusion; delusion to loss of memory; loss of memory to loss of reason and finally, loss of reason leads to utter ruin. Though, it takes time to describe this order yet the rise of these propensities leading to the destruction of man is, as fast as death caused by an electric shock.

Link:—Lord Kṛṣṇa, in the next verse, answers the fourth question—How does a man of steadfast wisdom walk?

रागद्वेषवियुक्तैस्तु विषयानिन्द्रियैश्चरन्।
आत्मवश्यैर्विधेयात्मा प्रसादमधिगच्छति॥ ६४॥
प्रसादे सर्वदुःखानां हानिरस्योपजायते।
प्रसन्नचेतसो ह्याशु बुद्धिः पर्यवतिष्ठते॥ ६५॥

rāgadveṣaviyuktaistu viṣayānindriyaiścaran
ātmavaśyairvidheyātmā prasādamadhigacchati
prasāde sarvaduḥkhānāṁ hānirasyopajāyate
prasannacetaso hyāśu buddhiḥ paryavatiṣṭhate

But a self-controlled Yogī in practice or a striver, while using objects with the senses, which are controlled and freed from attraction and aversion he attains placidity of mind. With the attainment of such placidity, all his sorrows come to an end; and the intellect of such a person of tranquil mind, soon becomes, firmly established in God. 64-65

Comment:—

'Tu'—In the previous verse, Lord Kṛṣṇa said, that by contemplating on the objects of senses a man goes to complete ruin, while here He says that the striver, free from attachment while using the sense-objects with the senses, becomes firmly established in God. So the Lord has used the term 'tu' (but), to differentiate between the two.

'Vidheyātmā'—To achieve his aim it is very necessary for a striver, specially for a Karmayogī, to control his mind, otherwise he may have attachment for pleasure and thus may go to ruin.

'Ātmavaśyaiḥ rāgadveṣaviyuktaiḥ indriyaiḥ'—As the term 'vidheyātmā' has been used for controlling the mind, so the word 'ātmavaśyaiḥ' is used, for sense-control. In worldly dealings, senses should be kept under control, and for sense-control they should be free from attachment and aversion. Therefore, Lord Kṛṣṇa, in the thirty-fourth verse of the third chapter, has warned strivers and said, "attachment and aversion are rooted, in all sense-objects. A striver should not come under their sway, because they are verily his enemies." Similarly He has said in the third verse of the fifth chapter, "The striver who is free from the pairs of opposites, such as attachment and aversion etc., is easily set free from bondage."

'Viṣayān caran'—A striver, who has controlled his mind and whose senses are controlled and free from attachment and aversion, uses the sense-objects, but does not enjoy them viz., he does not derive pleasure from them. And it is enjoyment, rather than use, which leads him to ruin.

'Prasādamadhigacchati'—A striver who utilizes the sense-objects being free from attachment and aversion attains placidity (purity) of mind. This placidity (serenity) of mind, is called mental austerity (Gītā 17/16) which is superior to the austerity of body and austerity of speech. So a striver should neither enjoy the sense-objects with attachment, nor should renounce them with aversion, because both attachment and aversion lead him to affinity for the world. Such a striver attains placidity of mind and if that placidity of mind, is not enjoyed, that leads to God-realization.

'Prasāde sarvaduḥkhānāṁ hānirasyopajāyate'—With the attainment of such placidity of mind, all his sorrows come to an end, because it is attachment only, which causes sorrows. These sorrows give birth to desire which again causes sorrow. When attachment goes away, the mind becomes serene and that serenity destroys all sorrows. Actually all the sorrows are born because of affinity for matter and its evolutes—the world and the body. A striver has affinity for the world, with the desire to enjoy pleasures. This desire is born of despair or the feeling of something lacking in himself. When there is placidity of mind, despair disappears. When despair is lost, there is no desire for pleasures, and when there is no desire for pleasures, affinity for the world automatically breaks off, and then sorrows disappear. It means that placidity of the mind, results in breaking off affinity for the world and establishment of the self in God.

Here 'Sarvaduḥkhānāṁ hāniḥ' does not mean that a striver will not come across unfavourable and sorrowful circumstances; but it means that those circumstances cannot create commotion and agitation in his mind.

'Prasannacetaso hyāśu buddhiḥ paryavatiṣṭhate'—The intellect of such a person of tranquil mind, soon becomes firmly established in God viz., the striver himself becomes established in God and his intellect has no doubts, in the least.

Something Remarkable

Enhancement of either placidity or uneasiness for God, enables a striver to realize God. The Gopīs were locked up by their husbands, brothers and parents and prevented from meeting Lord Kṛṣṇa. The uneasiness to meet the Lord, destroyed their sins and the placidity of mind by meditation on God, destroyed their virtues. Thus, being free from sins and virtues, and leaving their bodies, they were the first to meet God. But in the worldly affairs, placidity and uneasiness of mind, lead a man to bondage and strengthen the bondage, because his aim is to enjoy the worldly pleasures. The living examples are common worldly people who are entangled in the worldly snare, because of placidity and uneasiness, in mundane affairs.

The inner self, is overwhelmed in placidity and uneasiness. Just as the colour which is added to liquid wax becomes a permanent part of it, in the same way, whatever thoughts are put into the overwhelmed inner self these become a permanent part of it and lead the striver to salvation or to damnation. Therefore a striver should neither be pleased nor displeased, while gaining or losing the most charming objects of the world.

Appendix—There are two divisions—one of 'Bhoga' (pleasures) and one of 'Yoga'. If a 'Bhogī' (voluptuary) having attachment and aversion dwells upon the objects of senses, he goes to ruin (fall) (Gītā 2/62-63). But if a 'Yogī' freed from attachment and aversion utilizes sense-objects, he does not go to ruin, rather he attains God.

A person freed from likes and dislikes does not enjoy and relish pleasures because it is not his aim. He utilizes the sense-objects without coming under the sway of attachment, having the sense of detachment (Gītā 3/34). Therefore he attains placidity (purity) of mind. The use of sense-objects with the sense of renunciation, is indeed not 'Bhoga'. From the view-point of people it appears that he is using sense-objects; therefore here the expression 'viṣayān caran' has been used.

By being free from attachment and aversion, placidity of mind is attained. There should be cheerfulness every time, there should not be any distress, there should not be monotony—this is 'Prasāda' (placidity of mind). If a striver is not satiated with this placidity and he does not enjoy it, it will very quickly lead him to God-realization.

Link:—Lord Kṛṣṇa clarifies the point of view expressed in the previous two verses by negative inference.

नास्ति बुद्धिरयुक्तस्य न चायुक्तस्य भावना।
न चाभावयतः शान्तिरशान्तस्य कुतः सुखम्॥ ६६॥

nāsti buddhirayuktasya na cāyuktasya bhāvanā
na cābhāvayataḥ śāntiraśāntasya kutaḥ sukham

He, who has not controlled his mind and senses, can have no determinate intellect; nor can such an undisciplined man have a sense of duty. A man without having a sense of duty, can have no peace; and how can there be happiness, for one lacking peace? 66

Comment:—

[In the Discipline of Disinterested Action, control over the mind and senses is important, because without control, desire persists and with the persistence of desire, the mind does not get fixed. Therefore, it is obligatory for a striver following the Discipline of Action to control his mind and senses. What happens to the man who has not controlled his mind and senses, is explained in this verse.]

'Nāsti buddhirayuktasya'—He who has not controlled his mind and senses cannot have determinate intellect* that he has

* Without change of the sense of I (egotism), senses are not controlled

only to realize God, because he indulges in worldly pleasures and seeks prosperity. He develops desire for riches, honour and bodily comforts etc. These numerous desires, keep his intellect obsessed and do not allow him to have a stable intellect.

'Na cāyuktasya bhāvanā'—He whose intellect is not determinate, cannot have the feeling, that he has to discharge his duty by renouncing attachment and desire etc., because he has not fixed the aim of his life.

'Na cābhāvayataḥ śāntiḥ'—The man, who does not discharge his duty efficiently and sincerely, can have no peace, whosoever he may be.

'Aśāntasya kutaḥ sukham'—How can he who lacks peace be happy? He cannot be happy, because his heart is filled with agitation and commotion. Despite acquiring all agreeable sense-objects, his mental perturbation cannot be wiped out. In other words he cannot be happy.

Link:—In the next verse, Lord Kṛṣṇa explains why the intellect of a person who had not controlled his mind and senses, cannot be determinate.

इन्द्रियाणां हि चरतां यन्मनोऽनु विधीयते।
तदस्य हरति प्रज्ञां वायुर्नावमिवाम्भसि॥ ६७॥

indriyāṇāṁ hi caratāṁ yanmano'nu vidhīyate
tadasya harati prajñāṁ vāyurnāvamivāmbhasi

Just as the wind sails a ship on water, the mind that yields to one of the wandering senses, takes away the discrimination of man. 67

---

and without sense-control there cannot be determinate intellect. But if a striver changes his egotism and accepts that he is a striver whose aim is nothing but God-realization, his mind and senses are instinctively controlled.

Comment:—

[God has bestowed upon man a human body to attain Him. So a man should firmly resolve to attain God-realization. This resolve, removes his attachment for pleasures and makes his intellect determinate. But what happens if the intellect does not become determinate, has been described here.]

'Indriyāṇāṁ hi caratāṁ yanmano'nu vidhīyate'—Senses are involuntarily drawn to the sense-objects. Mind that follows anyone of the senses, is naturally led astray by it. For example, while relishing a tasteful dish, the sense of taste gets attached to it, and then it attracts the mind, and thus the misdirected mind gets entangled in this taste.

'Tadasya harati prajñām'—When the mind gets entangled in pleasures, man immediately loses his determinate intellect that he has to realize God only.

'Vāyurnāvamivāmbhasi'—A ship without a rudder is at the mercy of a strong wind. As a rudderless ship does not reach its destination, a misdirected mind takes away man's discrimination.

A strong wind either pushes away the ship in the wrong direction or sinks it. But a skilful sailor, manages the ship in such a way, that the wind instead of pushing it away from its course, helps it in sailing and reaching its destination. Similarly, the misdirected mind misguides discrimination, in two ways—It leads it astray from the path of God-realization and engages it in sense-pleasures or it ruins him by entangling it, in prohibited pleasures. But a controlled mind and senses do not take the intellect away ward, they rather help one in realizing God (2/64-65).

Appendix—Here a doubt may arise, why have the meanings of the terms 'yat' and 'tat' been taken 'mind' rather than 'senses' viz., why has it been said that the mind rather than senses takes away reason? The clarification is that in the sixtieth verse of this chapter it has been said that senses sway the mind and in the forty-second verse of the third chapter it is mentioned that mind is superior to the senses and intellect is greater (subtle, higher and more powerful) than the mind. It proves that senses sway the mind and the mind sways the intellect. Secondly in swaying the intellect; the mind is important, senses are not important. The reason is that unless the mind accompanies senses, senses don't know sense-objects—'adhiṣṭhāya manaścāyaṁ viṣayānupasevate' (Gītā 15/9). In Śrīmadbhāgavata Dattātreyajī Mahārāja declares—

tadaivamātmanyavaruddhacitto na veda kiñcid bahirantaraṁ vā
yatheṣukāro nṛpatiṁ vrajantamiṣau gatātmā na dadarśa pārśve
(Śrīmadbhā. 11/9/13)

''He, whose mind is tied up in the soul, has no knowledge of anything outward or inward. I saw that an arrow-maker was so much engrossed in arrow-making that he did not notice the king's cavalcade in procession passing by him.''

The arrow-maker had the sense of hearing and its sense-object was sound also, but he could not hear because his mind was not diverted towards the procession. When without the mind, the senses can't even know their sense-objects, then how can they sway the intellect? They can't.

Link:— In the next verse, Lord Kṛṣṇa describes the condition of the striver, who has controlled his senses.

तस्माद्यस्य महाबाहो निगृहीतानि सर्वशः।
इन्द्रियाणीन्द्रियार्थेभ्यस्तस्य प्रज्ञा प्रतिष्ठिता ॥ ६८ ॥

tasmādyasya mahābāho nigṛhītāni sarvaśaḥ
indriyāṇīndriyārthebhyastasya prajñā pratiṣṭhitā

Therefore, O mighty-armed, his intellect is stable, whose senses are completely controlled against sense-objects. 68

Comment:—

'Tasmādyasya mahābāho nigṛhītāni sarvaśaḥ indriyāṇīndriyārthebhyastasya prajñā pratiṣṭhitā'—Lord Kṛṣṇa concludes the topic of the mind and the senses, by using the word 'tasmād' (therefore) and says, that the intellect of a person whose mind and senses are completely free from the worldly attractions, is stable.

By giving the term 'sarvaśaḥ' (completely), He means to explain that his senses are not inclined towards pleasures, whether he lives in the world or in seclusion and even if his mind and senses are directed to the sense-objects, they do not lead his intellect, astray.

'Nigṛhītāni' (restrained) means that the senses have no attachment for the sense-objects. As a snake, without teeth has no poison, senses without attachment and aversion, have no poison to degrade a man from a spiritual path; these become sublimated and lead a striver, to divinity.

This verse means, that if a striver has determination that his aim is to realize God, rather than to enjoy worldly pleasures and prosperity, his intellect will become stable.

Link:—What is the difference between a striver whose senses are completely restrained from their objects, and an ordinary man? Here is the answer.

या निशा सर्वभूतानां तस्यां जागर्ति संयमी।
यस्यां जाग्रति भूतानि सा निशा पश्यतो मुनेः ॥ ६९ ॥

yā niśā sarvabhūtānāṁ tasyāṁ jāgarti saṁyamī
yasyāṁ jāgrati bhūtāni sā niśā paśyato muneḥ

That, which is night to all beings, in that state (of Divine

Knowledge and Supreme Bliss) an emancipated person keeps awake. And that (the everchanging worldly happiness), in which all beings keep awake, is night, to the enlightened seer. 69

Comment:—

'Yā niśā sarvabhūtānām'—Those worldly people whose senses and mind are uncontrolled and who are immersed in pleasure are, asleep in the dark, because they never think that the aim of human life, is emancipation or salvation. Further, they never think 'What is God?' 'What is Self-realization?' 'Why are we suffering?' 'Why are there all these burning sensations?' Where will our misdeeds take us?' Turning away from these thoughts, is complete darkness, for the worldly people.

Here the term, 'bhūtānām', has been used to explain the fact that human beings who hanker after pleasures and prosperity, and are immersed in them, are like other beings, such as birds and beasts etc., because both have no inclination for God-realization. If there is any difference between the two, it is that discrimination, human beings is much more developed than beasts' and birds, and therefore, by using discrimination, they can serve others and attain salvation or God-realization, while birds and beasts cannot. On the other hand, if they misuse this discrimination in hankering after pleasures and prosperity, they can be more harmful to the society, than even wild beasts. Animals and birds eat food, only to sustain their life, they never hoard. But human beings are given to hoarding, whatever they get. Therefore, they create obstacles to the utilization of those things by others.

'Tasyāṁ jāgarti saṁyamī'—When the worldly people remain asleep in the dark, having no inclination for God-realization, the seer who has controlled his senses and mind and who has no attachment for pleasures and prosperity and whose aim of life is only God-realization, remains wakeful because his intuition, his concepts and precepts, are all filled with Divinity.

'Yasyāṁ jāgrati bhūtāni'—The worldly people who want to accumulate wealth, by means fair or foul, and who hanker after transient sensual pleasures, honour and praise etc., are wakeful of mundane affairs.

'Sā niśā paśyato muneḥ'—The worldly people, feel very happy and deem themselves very wise, in enjoying and hoarding worldly pleasures. These, a seer, in the state of Divine Knowledge and Supreme Bliss, perceives as dark.

As children, while playing marbles attach great importance to small balls, of glass or clay, so people attach importance to worldly prosperity and pleasure and for gaining these they employ all sorts of means, fair or foul. But a self-controlled seer, knows that all mundane pleasures, prosperity and praise etc., are transient, illusory and changing, while God and his own self, are eternal, real and permanent. He also knows, how the best use of mundane objects can be made, and how far they can be utilized, for the welfare of others. He uses them in the service of others.

In spite of the manifest appearance of the world to the mind and senses, he has a firm conviction that the world is a mere illusion, and has no real existence at all. So wakefulness of the worldly people, is just like a dark night for him.

Appendix—The worldly people remain busy in hoarding wealth and enjoying pleasures and value them. They are very clever and expert in worldly affairs. They learn different types of arts and crafts, make several inventions, regard the worldly achievements as their progress, glorify worldly things, perform austere penance in order to enjoy pleasures by living forever, worship gods, and recite (sacred text) incantation etc. But an enlightened liberated exalted soul and strivers perceive all this as dark, they don't attach the least importance to such a progress, because from their view-point the entire world upto the abode of Brahmā has no existence at all—'nāsato vidyate bhāvaḥ' (Gītā 2/16), 'ābrahma bhuvanāllokāḥ punarāvartino'rjuna' (Gītā 8/16).

The worldly people remain engrossed in worldly affairs and think that there is nothing besides these pleasures—nānyadastīti vādinaḥ' (Gītā 2/42), 'kāmopabhogaparamā etāvaditi niścitāḥ' (Gītā 16/11). Spirituality is beyond the access of their intellect. But a striver following the spiritual path besides knowing spirituality also knows the world. Therefore the term 'paśyataḥ' has been used for them. The worldly people perceive only the night (they remain asleep in the dark), they don't perceive the day (Divinity), but a 'Yogī' perceives the day as well as the night (the worldly pleasures and prosperity as dark)—this is the difference between the two. For example a child has perceived only childhood, not youth, but an old man besides perceiving the old age has also perceived childhood and youth. A hoarder of wealth doesn't know renunciation while a renunciate who has renounced the mundane wealth knows the value of collection of wealth and also its renunciation. This is a rule that a man engrossed in worldly affairs cannot know the reality about the world. By keeping himself aloof from the world, he can know the reality about the world because in fact he is separate from the world. Similarly a person can realize God by identifying himself with God because he (the self) has his identity with God.

He who is established in 'Is' knows both 'Is' and 'not'; but he who is established in 'not' does not know (perceive) even 'not' in its reality as ever non-existent, then how will he know 'Is' (the real)? He can't know. He has no capacity to know them. He who knows 'Is' does not bear ill will with the person who assumes the existence of 'not', but the person who assumes the existence of 'not' bears ill will with the person who knows 'Is'.

Link:—The world is just like a dark night to the seer. Then how does he live in the world? The answer to these queries is provided in the verse that follows.

आपूर्यमाणमचलप्रतिष्ठं
समुद्रमापः प्रविशन्ति यद्वत्।
तद्वत्कामा यं प्रविशन्ति सर्वे
स शान्तिमाप्नोति न कामकामी॥७०॥

āpūryamāṇamacalapratiṣṭhaṁ
samudramāpaḥ praviśanti yadvat
tadvatkāmā yaṁ praviśanti sarve
sa śāntimāpnoti na kāmakāmī

Just as waters of different rivers enter the ocean, which though full, remains undisturbed; likewise the man in whom all enjoyments are merged and attains tranquillity, but not he, who hankers after such enjoyments. 70

Comment:—

'Āpūryamāṇamacalapratiṣṭhaṁ samudramāpaḥ praviśanti yadvat'—In the rainy season rivers expand and are flooded by heavy rain storms. All the rivers continue to pour themselves into an ocean, but its magnitude remains the same. In summer, when heat evaporates the water of rivers and these become narrow with shallow water, even then the expanse of an ocean remains the same. It is ever full and never seeks water from streams and rivers. It means, that it ever remains satiated, and always within limits.

'Tadvatkāmā* yaṁ praviśanti sarve sa śāntimāpnoti'— A

* Here the term 'Kāma' has not been used for desires but for the objects of pleasures which are desired.

self-controlled seer, is like an ocean. He also comes across worldly enjoyments, but these all merge in him without causing any perturbation or agitation in his body and mind. Thus, he attains supreme peace. This peace is not due to mundane objects, but it emanated from God-realization (Gītā 2/46).

In this illustration, the realized soul is compared to an ocean and the water of the river, is compared to mundane objects. Both the water of the ocean and that of the river, are of the same category. But the realized soul is quite different in nature. There is a world of difference between the two. The perfect soul is sentient eternal, real, limitless and endless, while the enjoyments are insentient, perishable, unreal, limited and have an end. Secondly, the waters of rivers enter the ocean and merge in it, but the mundane objects flowing towards the enlightened soul, do not reach the self, these merely reach his body and inner sense. Thus the illustration of a river and the ocean, though is not fully applicable here. It only describes the state of one's body and inner sense. This does not explain the state of his real self.

'Na kāmakāmī'—Worldly enjoyments and pleasures cannot satisfy a man, who hankers after them. He can never be satisfied. He can never be free from desires, anxieties and burning sensation. So how can he attain peace? The reason is, that the insentient cannot satisfy the sentient; the sentient can be satisfied only by sentient.

Appendix—It is because of one's desire that this world appears to be insentient (Matter) but actually it is none other than the Supreme Soul (Divinity) (God)—'Vāsudevaḥ sarvam' (Gītā 7/19), 'sadasaccāhamarjuna' (Gītā 9/19). When a person is freed from desires, all objects get pleased with him. How to know it? We know it because necessities automatically come to such a person without any effort. The things are eager to approach him for being fruitful through utilization by him. But availability or non-availability of objects does not arouse any morbid feelings in him, because he has no desire. From his view-point objects have no value (importance). On the other hand a person having desires, always remains perturbed (disquiet) whether he receives things or not.

Link:— Now, Lord Kṛṣṇa concludes the answer to the last question, "How does the man of steadfast wisdom, walk viz., what is his mode of conduct?"

विहाय कामान्यः सर्वान्पुमांश्चरति निःस्पृहः ।
निर्ममो निरहङ्कारः स शान्तिमधिगच्छति ॥ ७१ ॥

vihāya kāmānyaḥ sarvānpumāṁścarati niḥspṛhaḥ
nirmamo nirahaṅkāraḥ sa śāntimadhigacchati

He, who gives up all desires, and moves about without the sense of mine and egoism and shuns the thirst for necessities of life, attains tranquillity. 71

Comment:—

'Vihāya kāmānyaḥ sarvānpumaṁścarati niḥspṛhaḥ'—An earnest wish for something is, 'kāmanā' (desire) while an earnest wish for acquiring or preserving necessities of life is, 'spṛhā' (thirst). A man of steadfast wisdom lives devoid of longings and desires and has no thirst, for acquiring or preserving even the necessities of life, as he has attained the supreme bliss, for which the human body was bestowed upon him. So, he becomes free from all cares and does not mind even if his body lives or dies.

In this verse, as well as in the fifty-fifth verse of this chapter emphasis has been laid on renunciation of desires, because in the Discipline of Disinterested Action, without abandoning these no striver can possess steadfast wisdom. A striver has affinity for the world, only because of desires. If desires are given up, no affinity for the world remains.

'Nirmamaḥ'—A man of stable wisdom, has not the least-sense of mine, with men, things and even his body and senses, because he has received them from the world. Therefore, they belong to the world, not to him. It is a blunder to have a sense of possession over things acquired. On rectification of this blunder the sense of possession over persons, objects, body and sense-organs is totally wiped out.

'Nirahaṅkāraḥ'—'I am this body'—to have this notion is egoism. The realized soul is, free from the egoism. The body, sense-organs, mind and intellect are visible in some light. This ego is, also perceived in this light. From the view-point of this light, all these are objects of perception. An onlooker (seer) is, quite different from the seen—this is the rule. With this realization, a man of steady wisdom, becomes quite free from egoism.

'Sa śāntimadhigacchati'—A man of steadfast wisdom attains peace. It does not mean that he attains peace after being free from desire, thirst for enjoyment, attachment and egoism. The fact is that peace is inherent and spontaneous. But a man by having desires to enjoy worldly pleasures cannot realize that peace. But, as soon as he becomes free from desire, thirst for necessities, a sense of mine and egoism, he can realize that peace.

In the verse, out of the four—(desires, thirst for necessities, the sense of mine and egoism), egoism is more important than the other three, because a striver after becoming free from egoism, becomes free from the other three also. If there is no egoism, how will the sense of mine persist, who will desire and for whom will he desire?

Now the question arises, when the renunciation of desire

etc., is also included in the renunciation of egoism, why has Lord Kṛṣṇa described the renunciation of desire separately? The answer is, that out of these four, desire is gross while thirst for necessities is subtle; the sense of mine, subtler; and egoism the subtlest. So, by abandoning desire, it becomes easy to abandon the other three.

Nothing can be gained merely by desire, what is destined, we will get. Having such a faith, we should discard desires. 'spṛhā' is a subtle form of desire. In the absence of desire even it persists. It (spṛhā) is the desire to have bare necessities of life. In its fulfilment also we are not free. Whatever is to happen, will happen. Then why should we have 'spṛhā'? When we cease to be dependent on food, water and clothing, 'spṛhā' is destroyed. After renouncing desires and 'spṛhā' the sense of mind in the body remains. It is not a rule that this possessive spirit, preserves articles and these are ruined without this spirit. Therefore, the possessive spirit serves no purpose. With renunciation of all the three—desire, 'spṛhā' (subtle desire) and possessive spirit, renunciation of ego, becomes very easy, otherwise it is very difficult.

How to get rid of Egoism & a Sense of Mine

From the standpoint of the Discipline of Disinterested Action: (Karmayoga)—'Nothing is mine; because I have no independent claim on things, persons, circumstances, incidents and situations etc. When nothing is mine, it means that I need nothing as I need food, water and clothes for the body, only if it is mine; but if it is not mine, I need nothing for it. When there is clear understanding that nothing is mine and I need nothing, there is no question of egoism (feeling of 'I'), because egoism persists by accepting affinity for the body, things and circumstances etc. The fact is that the so-called body of mine has an affinity for the world, so it should be used to render service to the world, because I for myself need nothing. By having this sort of feeling, egoism perishes and a striver becomes free from egoism and a sense of mine.

From the standpoint of Discipline of Knowledge:—every man has the knowledge that 'I am'. In 'I am', I, is a fragment of nature and 'am' denotes 'reality' (Eternal Existence). This 'am' is used with 'I'—In the absence of 'I', 'am' will not stand, only 'Is' will remain.'

'I am', 'you are', 'this is' and 'that is'—all these four, are in respect of individuals, space and time. This is limited conception. If this limited conception is not maintained, then universal 'Is' remains. When a striver is established in this universal 'Is', he becomes completely free from the sense of 'I' and 'mine'.

From the standpoint of Discipline of Devotion (Bhaktiyoga)—What is called 'I' or 'mine' actually belongs to God, because had the persons, things, body been mine, I might have protected them from decay and possessed them forever. But it is not so. It means that the so-called body of mine, senses, mind, intellect etc., are His and I am also His. By having this sort of feeling, a striver becomes free from the sense of mine and from egoism.

Appendix—The Lord by the expression 'so'mṛtatvāya kalpate' (Gītā 2/15) explained attainment of perfection by Jñānayoga. Now by the expression 'sa śāntimadhigacchati' he mentions the perfection by Karmayoga. It means that by being established in Pure-consciousness (Self) immortality is attained and by renouncing Matter (ego), tranquillity (peace) is attained.

'Egoism' really does not exist, it is merely assumed in the self. If it had really existed, we could not have been free from egoism and the Lord would have also not told us to be free from egoism. But the Lord mentions 'nirahaṅkāraḥ', so it means that we can be free from egoism. This is also our experience that the self is free from egoism. In sound sleep egoism disappears while the self exists—this is clearly perceived when we arise from sleep. In sound sleep egoism merges in 'avidyā' (ignorance), but the self remains. Therefore after arising from sleep (remembering that) we say "I slept so comfortably that I knew nothing." This memory proves that he (the self), who slept comfortably and who knew nothing, was there. Otherwise who experienced comfort and who knew nothing? In 'I knew nothing' there is no egoism and he who had this knowledge is the self, free from egoism.

A woman's nose-ring fell into a well. A man got down into the well in order to search the nose-ring out. He searched it out and was very pleased. But at that time he could not utter any word because voice (an evolute of fire) and water are opposites. Therefore after coming out of water he could speak that he had found out the nose-ring. Similarly in sound sleep at the merger of egoism in ignorance, a man feels that he enjoyed a carefree sleep but he can't express it at that time because there is no means to utter words. After arising from the sound sleep he has the memory of that joy (comfort). Memory is born of experience—'anubhavajanyaṁ jñānaṁ smṛtiḥ'.

Thus in sound sleep everyone feels that egoism does not persist but no one feels that the self does not exist. Egoism can't persist without us but we (self) can live without egoism and do live. Our self is consciousness solidified. This eternal entity is not dependent on anyone but everyone is dependent upon it. If we had not been different from egoism, we would have been only in the form of egoism, then in sound sleep at the merger of egoism we would have also no existence. But we exist, it proves that we have our existence without egoism. In wakefulness and dream, egoism appears and in sound sleep egoism merges but we (the self) ever exist. What neither appears nor merges is our identity.

Having given up all the desires, for the maintenance of the body some requirement of things, persons is felt that is called 'spṛhā' (necessity). Not to talk of the necessities for the maintenance of the body, the man of steadfast wisdom does not even need the body because the necessity of the body makes a man dependent. Necessity is born only when a man accepts a thing as his own which is not his. A Karmayogī does not accept anything as his own and for him, but he regards it as the world's and for the world only. So he has no necessity.

'Kāmanā' (desire) and 'spṛhā' (necessity)—renunciation of both means that there should not be any desire for things and there should not be any necessity for the maintenance of the body. The reason is that the desire for the maintenance of the body is also enjoyment of pleasure. Not only this but even the win for peace, salvation and self-realization is 'Kāmanā' (desire). Therefore real disinterestedness consists in not having desire even for salvation.

In this verse there is prohibition (negation) of 'Aparā prakṛti' (lower or insentient nature). The 'Jīva' (the embodied soul) because of egoism has sustained 'Aparā prakṛti' (universe)—'yayedaṁ dhāryate jagat' (Gītā 7/5). Therefore by being free from egoism, the lower nature is negated (affinity is renounced) and the self (soul) becomes free from the bondage of birth and death. If everything is renounced, even then egoism remains (persists) but if egoism is renounced, everything is renounced.

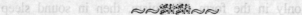

Link:—In the next verse, there is description of a person and his condition, as a result of being free from desire, thirst

for necessities of life, the sense of mine and egoism, and closes the subject.

एषा ब्राह्मी स्थितिः पार्थ नैनां प्राप्य विमुह्यति।
स्थित्वास्यामन्तकालेऽपि ब्रह्मनिर्वाणमृच्छति ॥७२॥

eṣā brāhmī sthitiḥ pārtha naināṁ prāpya vimuhyati
sthitvāsyāmantakāle'pi brahmanirvāṇamṛcchati

O Pārtha, such is the state of a God-realized soul. Having attained this state, he overcomes delusion. Being established in this state, even at the hour of death, he attains brahmic bliss (identification with the absolute state). 72

Comment:—

'Eṣā brāhmī sthitiḥ pārtha'—This is the Brāhmī state viz., the state of a God-realized soul. On being free from egoism, individuality is completely wiped out and then a striver is automatically established in God. Individuality persisted only due to affinity with the world. With renunciation of affinity individuality is completely gone. The term 'Eṣā' refers to 'very near'. It denotes the expressions 'vihāya kāmān' (giving up desires), 'niḥspṛhaḥ' (free from thirst for necessities), 'nirmamaḥ' (free from the sense of mine) and 'nirahaṅkāraḥ' (free from egoism), used in the preceding verse.

Having heard the Lord's declaration—"When your intellect transcends the mire of delusion and confusion, by hearing conflicting doctrines, you will realize union with God", Arjuna was inquisitive to know about that state of union with God. So Arjuna, raised four questions, in order to know the marks of a man of steadfast wisdom. Having answered those four questions, the Lord declares here that this is a state of Godhood (union with God). In this state of eternal union with God, no individuality remains, only the Divinity pervades. In order to point out this important fact the Lord addresses Arjuna as 'Pārtha' here.

'Naināṁ prāpya vimuhyati'—So long as, a man has egoism (the feeling of 'I') in the body, he is deluded. Lack of discrimination between the real and the unreal, is delusion. The man's self being real, if he identifies himself with the unreal; this identification is delusion. When a striver knows the unreal as unreal, his affinity to it ceases* and he realizes that he is already established in the real. With this realization he is never deluded (Gītā 4/35).

'Sthitvāsyāmantakāle'pi brahmanirvāṇamṛcchati'—The human body has been bestowed upon man, only for God-realization. So the Lord gives an opportunity, even to vilest sinner, to attain Him by establishing himself in Him, even at the time of death viz., by breaking off his affinity with matter. Lord Kṛṣna has also anounced it, in the thirtieth verse of the seventh chapter, "One who knows My integral being, comprising Adhibhūta (the field of matter), Adhidaiva (Brahma) and Adhiyajña (the unmanifest Divinity) even at the time of death, attains Me." Similarly, He has also announced in the fifth verse of the eighth chapter, "He who departs from this body, thinking of Me alone, even at the time of death, attains Me; there is no doubt about it."

By the above expression, the Lord declares the glory of this Brāhmī state (Godhood). By being established in this state, even at the time of death, one attains Brahma. As the Lord declared about equanimity that even a little practice of it protects one from great fear (of birth and death) (2/40), so He declares here that if one gets established in this Brāhmī state, even at the time of death by breaking off his affinity with matter, he attains Brahma. Attachment to matter (non-

* By knowing the unreal as unreal, a man becomes free from it, because in fact the unreal has no existence. The unreal seems to exist in the light of the real. If a person does not become free from the unreal even after knowing it as unreal, it proves that he has not actually known it.

self), is the only obstacle to the attainment of this state. If a person renounces the attachment, even at the time of death, he realizes his real axiomatic state of Godhood.

Now, a question arises, how a man who could not attain God throughout his life, attains Him at the time of death, when his body and intellect both grow weak. The answer is that man's union with Him is natural, only he has to realize this fact* and this can be realized, either by God's or saints' grace or by good influences of past actions.

The word 'api' (even) means, that during life if he attains a state of Godhood (Brāhmī state) he becomes a liberated soul. But, even at the time of death if he becomes free from a sense of mine and egoism, he attains Him immediately without any sort of practice, meditation and trance etc.

By using the terms 'Brahmanirvāṇam' (Oneness with Brahma), Lord Kṛṣṇa means to say, that the striver of the Discipline of Disinterested Action (Karmayoga), attains the same Brahma as striver of the Discipline of Knowledge (Jñānayoga) (Gītā 5/24—26). The same fact has been pointed out, in the fifth verse of the fifth chapter when he declares, "The supreme state which is attained by a Sāṅkhyayogī (the follower of the Discipline of Knowledge), is attained also by the Karmayogī (the follower of the Discipline of Disinterested Action).

Something Noteworthy

Man himself is sentient but he accepts his affinity for the insentient. Therefore, instead of attaining salvation or God-realization, he goes to ruin. By using his discrimination he aims to attain God, while out of delusion he wants to have affinity to the Matter.

Delusion is born of egoism, and a sense of mine or desire. To accept the body as 'I' or 'Mine' is, delusion born of egoism, a sense of mine, while the wish to acquire or preserve something, is the delusion born of desire. Arjuna like other worldly people, had delusion born of egoism and a sense of mine, as well as desire. In the sentence used in the first chapter—'We who are righteous persons clearly see the sin,' is an example of delusion, born of egoism; 'These kinsmen will be destroyed", is that of delusion born of the sense of mine and 'We should not fight otherwise, we shall incur sin and go to hell', is that born of desire.

To remove this delusion, Lord Kṛṣṇa has talked about two kinds of discrimination—discrimination between the real and the unreal (2/11—30) and discrimination between discharging one's duty and abandoning it (2/31—53).

While discriminating between the body and the soul, Lord Kṛṣṇa explained, that there was never a time when he or those kings were non-existent nor they would cease to exist in future. It is a fact that these bodies did not exist before, nor will they exist in future and in the interim also, they are changing every moment, as every born one passes through babyhood, youth and old age. He also explained, that as a man discarding worn-out clothes, takes new ones, likewise, the embodied soul, casting off worn-out bodies, enters into others, which are new. So he should not grieve.

While explaining discrimination between discharging one's duty and abandoning it, He said, "There is nothing more welcome for a man of the warrior class, than a righteous war, which is an open gateway to heaven; if you do not wage it, you will incur sin. But if you fight treating pleasure and pain, gain and loss, victory and defeat, alike, you will not incur sin. Your right is to perform your duty, but never to its fruit. Let not the fruit of action, be your object, nor let your attachment be, to inaction. Therefore, perform your duty being fixed in Yoga, because equanimity consists in remaining even-minded, in success and failure. A man who, endowed with equanimity performs his duty, becomes free from virtues and vices in his lifetime. When your intellect transcends the mire of delusion, and the confusion by hearing conflicting statements, it becomes poised and firmly fixed, in meditation (on God), you will attain union with God."

Appendix—The striver devoid of the sense of mine and egoism gets dissociated from the material world called as 'Asat division' and realizes his natural owner abidance in Brahma i.e., Sat division. This abidance is known as 'Brāhmī sthiti'. Having attained this state no owner of this body remains, in other words there is none who assumes this body as 'I' or 'mine' and individuality is wiped out. It means that our reality is not dependent on egoism. Even rid of egoism ever Reality stands which is called 'Brāhmī sthiti' or 'abidance in Brahma'. Once this 'Brāhmī sthiti' (eternal union) is realized, then a man never gets deluded (Gītā 4/35). If even at the time of death, being free from the sense of mine and egoism, he realizes this 'Brāhmī sthiti' (state of Godhood), he attains brahmic bliss (identification with the absolute state) immediately.

By being free from the sense of mine and egoism, Brahma (the Absolute) or enlightenment is attained. Then a man becomes free from the sense of mine, from desire and from doership. The reason is that the embodied soul has sustained the universe because of egoism—'ahaṅkāravimūḍhātmā kartāhamiti manyate' (Gītā 3/27), 'Jīvabhūtāṁ mahābāho yayedaṁ dhāryate jagat' (Gītā 7/5). If he renounces egoism, the universe will not exist any more. Having attained the Absolute (if he has the latencies or impressions of devotion), he will know God in entirety naturally because the universal soul is the support of Brahma.

Nothing is mine—by accepting this truth, a man becomes free from the sense of mine. I need nothing—by accepting this fact, a man becomes free from the interested motive. I have to do nothing for myself—by accepting it, a man becomes free from egoism.

ॐ तत्सदिति श्रीमद्भगवद्गीतासूपनिषत्सु ब्रह्मविद्यायां
योगशास्त्रे श्रीकृष्णार्जुनसंवादे साङ्ख्ययोगो
नाम द्वितीयोऽध्याय: ॥ २ ॥

oṁ tatsaditi śrīmadbhagavadgītāsūpaniṣatsu brahmavidyāyāṁ
yogaśāstre śrīkṛṣṇārjunasaṁvāde sāṅkhyayogo
nāma dvitīyo'dhyāyaḥ

Thus with the words Oṁ, Tat, Sat, the names of the Lord, in the Upaniṣad of the Bhagavadgītā, the knowledge of Brahma, the Supreme, the scripture on yoga and the dialogue between Śrī Kṛṣṇa and Arjuna the second chapter, entitled 'Sāṅkhyayoga', ends.

In the Discipline of Knowledge discrimination occupies an important place and Lord Kṛṣṇa started His gospel with this discipline. So this chapter is designated: Sāṅkhyayoga.

Words, letters and Uvāca (said) in the Second Chapter

(1) In this chapter in **'Atha dvitīyo'dhyāyaḥ'** there are three words, in **'Sañjaya Uvāca'**, **'Śrībhagavānuvāca'** etc., there are fourteen words, in verses there are nine hundred and fifty-seven words and there are thirteen concluding words. Thus the total number of the words, is nine hundred and eighty-seven.

(2) In this chapter in **'Atha dvitīyo'dhyāyaḥ'** there are seven letters, in **'Sañjaya Uvāca'**, **'Śrībhagavānuvāca'** etc., there are forty-five letters, in verses, there are two thousand, four hundred and three letters and there are forty-five concluding letters. Thus the total number of the letters is two thousand and five hundred. In this chapter, out of the seventy-two verses the fifth, seventh, eighth, twentieth, twenty-second and seventieth—in each there

are forty-four letters; in the sixth verse there are forty-six letters, in the twenty-ninth verse there are forty-five letters and in each of the remaining verses there are thirty-two letters.

(3) In this chapter **'Uvāca'** (said) has been used seven times, **'Sañjaya Uvāca'** twice, three times **'Śrībhagavānuvāca'**, **'Arjuna Uvāca'** twice.

Metre Used in the Second Chapter—

Out of the seventy-two verses of this chapter, the fifth, sixth, seventh, eighth, twentieth, twenty-second, twenty-ninth and seventieth—these eight verses are of **'Upajāti'** metre. In the first quarter of the fifty-second and sixty-seven verses, 'na-gaṇa' being used there is **'na-vipulā'** metre; in the first quarter of the twelfth, twenty-sixth and thirty-second verses and in the third quarter of the sixty-first and sixty-third verses, 'ra-gaṇa' being used there is **'ra-vipulā'** metre; in the first quarter of the thirty-sixth and fifty-sixth verses 'bha-gaṇa' being used there is **'bha-vipulā'** metre; in the first quarter of the seventy-first verse and in the third quarter of the thirty-first verse 'ma-gaṇa' being used there is **'ma-vipulā'** metre; in the first quarter of the forty-sixth verse 'sa-gaṇa' being used there is, **'sa-vipulā'** metre; in the first and third quarters of the thirty-fifth verse 'na-gaṇa' being used there is, **'jātipakṣa-vipulā'** metre; in the forty-seventh verse in the first quarter 'bha-gaṇa' and in the third quarter 'na-gaṇa' being used there is, **'saṁkīrṇa-vipulā'**, metre. The remaining forty-nine verses, have of the right **'pathyāvaktra'** Anuṣṭup metre.

|| Shri Hari ||

Third Chapter

INTRODUCTION

The teaching of Gītā is based on man's experience. While starting this gospel, (from 2/11), Lord Kṛṣṇa first of all clarifies that the body and the soul are totally different from each other. The body is transitory, unreal, limited and perishable, while the soul is eternal, real, omnipresent and imperishable. Therefore, one should neither feel sad at the destruction of the perishable nor should have a desire to maintain the imperishable—this is called discrimination. This discrimination is very essential in all the three disciplines of Action, Knowledge and Devotion. When a man discriminates the self from the body, the desire for salvation is aroused. Not to speak of salvation even the desire for heaven etc., is aroused, when a man regards his own self as different from the body. Therefore, the Lord starts His gospel with discrimination.

This topic of discrimination, begins with the eleventh verse of the second chapter and continues upto the thirtieth verse. The Lord, instead of using philosophical terminology, has used simple terms to enable people to understand the topic easily. It means, that every person deserves God-realization because the human body has been bestowed upon us, only to realize Him. So, every human being can realize God, by giving due importance, to discrimination.

For this topic, even the term 'intellect', has not been used by the Lord. In order to distinguish the real from the unreal, the imperishable from the perishable, the eternal from the transitory and the soul (spirit) from the body, there is, need only for discrimination rather than intellect. Discrimination is beyond intellect. As prakṛti (nature) and Puruṣa (spirit) both are without beginning (Gītā 13/19), so is discrimination, which distinguishes, the real from the unreal. This discrimination has been bestowed upon all creatures by God, and it is revealed in the intellect. Birds and beasts, also know what should or should not be eaten. Even trees and creepering plants feel hot and cold and experience favourable and unfavourable circumstances. Human beings, are specially endowed with this discrimination, which can release them from the bondage of birth and death and leads them, to eternal quietude and bliss.

When this discrimination is aroused i.e., when a man can distinguish between the spirit and the body, his affinity for the world, including senses, mind and intellect, is renounced and his intellect, becomes purified and equanimous.

In the Discipline of Action the resolute intellect is single (Gītā 2/41).* When a man firmly resolves that he has to attain salvation, favourable or unfavourable circumstances are no obstacle and thus he attains equanimity, without making any effort. When a man resolves to attain God-realization, his attachment and attraction for the world begins to disappear. Attachment to pleasure and prosperity, is the main obstacle to the attainment of a resolute intellect (Gītā 2/44).

Having laid emphasis on resolute intellect, in the Discipline of Action, the Lord asks Arjuna, specially to perform his duty with equanimity. He declares, "You have a right to action alone, but never at all to its fruit" (2/47); "Perform your duty being steadfast in Yoga" (2/48) viz., equanimity. The Lord also declares, "Far inferior to the Yoga of wisdom, is action" (2/49) i.e., action performed for its fruit, is far inferior to the Yoga of wisdom (equanimity). He further declares, "Seek thou refuge

* In the Discipline of Knowledge there is predominance of discrimination, in the Discipline of Devotion there is predominance of reverence and faith while in the Discipline of Action there is predominance of resolute intellect. But it does not mean that in the Discipline of Action there are no discrimination, reverence and faith. What it means is that resolute intellect predominates. Similarly in the Disciplines of Knowledge and Devotion also there is resolute intellect.

in equanimity." Then He declares, "Endowed with wisdom (evenness of mind), one casts off during this life both good and evil deeds; therefore devote thyself to Yoga; Yoga is skill in action" (2/50).

Arjuna had already made up his mind not to fight. So in the thirty-first verse of the first chapter, he said, "I do not foresee any good in slaying my kith and kin." Then in the forty-fifth verse, he says, "What a great sin have we decided to commit, by preparing ourselves to slay our own people!" In the fifth verse of the second chapter, Arjuna says, "It is better to live by begging, than to slay these honoured teachers (elders)." In the third verse of the second chapter, Lord Kṛṣṇa directs Arjuna to arise, shaking off his petty faint-heartedness, while Arjuna declared his determination not to fight in the ninth verse of the second chapter.

Listener cannot understand what a preacher preaches, if he is already full of prejudice. That is why, Arjuna could not have a thorough grasp of the topic explained to him, by Lord Kṛṣṇa.

He could not make out the real meaning of Lord Kṛṣṇa's words. These appeared to him to be ambiguous and confusing. So Arjuna puts questions to Lord Kṛṣṇa in the next two verses, in order to get his doubt cleared.

अर्जुन उवाच

ज्यायसी चेत्कर्मणस्ते मता बुद्धिर्जनार्दन।
तत्किं कर्मणि घोरे मां नियोजयसि केशव॥ १॥
व्यामिश्रेणेव वाक्येन बुद्धिं मोहयसीव मे।
तदेकं वद निश्चित्य येन श्रेयोऽहमाप्नुयाम्॥ २॥

arjuna uvāca

jyāyasī cetkarmaṇaste matā buddhirjanārdana
tatkiṁ karmaṇi ghore māṁ niyojayasi keśava
vyāmiśreṇeva vākyena buddhiṁ mohayasīva me
tadekaṁ vada niścitya yena śreyo'hamāpnuyām

Arjuna said:

If you think that knowledge is superior to action, O Janārdana (Kṛṣṇa), why then do You make me do a dreadful deed, O Keśava (Kṛṣṇa)? With your complex words You seem to bewilder my mind; therefore, tell me plainly the one principle, by which I may attain the highest good. 1-2

Comment:—

'Janārdana'—By this term Arjuna means to suggest, that as God fulfils desires of His devotees He will undoubtedly fulfil his desire also.

'Jyāyasī cetkarmaṇaste matā buddhirjanārdana tatkiṁ karmaṇi ghore māṁ niyojayasi keśava'—Its a common human weakness, that one puts queries to others with a view to getting a response, which would support his own views. It is cowardice, because valour consists in carrying out the instructions of the preacher whether these are, favourable or hostile. It is because of this weakness or cowardice, that he experiences difficulty in unfavourable circumstances. When he finds himself unable to face the unfavourable circumstances, he disguises himself as a good man i.e., the evil masquerades itself as a virtue. It is very difficult to renounce this sort of evil. In the case of Arjuna also, the evil of the renunciation of his duty has disguised itself as a virtue of non-violence. So, he regards knowledge as superior to action and asks Lord Kṛṣṇa, why he urges him to do a savage deed, of fighting.

The Lord, in the thirty-ninth verse of the second chapter, referred to equanimity (evenness of mind), but Arjuna took it to be, knowledge. Therefore, he tells the Lord, that He had already told him, "This, which has been taught to thee, is wisdom concerning Sāṅkhyayoga (Discipline of Knowledge); but now listen to wisdom concerning Karmayoga (Discipline of Action); endowed with which, thou shalt cast off the bondage of action." He had also told him, "Action is far inferior to the Discipline of

Wisdom (Knowledge)" (2/49). Thus, if according to the Lord, knowledge is superior to action, He should not urge him to be engaged, even in virtuous actions such as oblation, charity and penance etc., which are sanctioned by scripture. But still, He is urging him to do the savage deed of the slaughter of warriors, in the war. Why?

First, Arjuna, filled with enthusiasm, ordered Lord Kṛṣṇa to place his chariot between the two armies so that he could observe the warriors, eager for battle. But, when Lord Kṛṣṇa, having placed the chariot between the two armies, in front of Bhīṣma and Droṇa and other kings, asked Arjuna to behold those Kurus assembled there, his delusion, because of his attachment to his kinsmen, was aroused. So he thought, knowledge to be superior to action, as in the case of knowledge a man has not to perform such savage deeds as the slaughter of warriors in a war. So Arjuna asks Lord Kṛṣṇa, why he urges him to perform such a savage deed.

Here the term 'Buddhiḥ' has been taken in the sense of knowledge, otherwise he would not have put this question. If Arjuna had understood 'equanimity' by the term 'Buddhiḥ', then the Lord's statement would have not appeared as confusing. The reason is, that the Lord, in the forty-eighth verse of the second chapter, had already asked him to perform action being steadfast in equanimity. Using the term 'confusing words' will be purposeful only, when there might have been two contentions in the mind of Arjuna and only then this question might arise, "If you consider knowledge superior to action, then why do you urge Me to take savage action?" In the third chapter in response to Arjuna's question, Lord Kṛṣṇa declares, that in this world there are two disciplines—the Discipline of Knowledge and the Discipline of Action. It means, that Arjuna took the meaning of the term 'Buddhiḥ', to be knowledge.

A striver can receive the correct answer to his question,

only if he puts it with faith and reverence. Arjuna has full faith in Lord Kṛṣṇa and holds him in great reverence. Therefore, his question shows, that he is even prepared to perform the savage deed of fighting, in order to attain salvation.

'Vyāmiśreṇeva vākyena buddhiṁ mohayasīva me'—Arjuna says, that sometimes he asks him to perform his duty (2/48) while another time He asks him to seek refuge in knowledge (2/49). Thus, with an seemingly mixed words, He seems to bewilder his mind i.e., Arjuna is not able to understand whether he should perform his duty or take refuge in knowledge.

Here, the use of the term 'eva' (as it were) two times, shows Arjuna's reverence for Lord Kṛṣṇa. It is because of this reverence for the Lord, that he regards the utterance of the Lord as true, thinking that He is not confusing him. But because of his own lack of understanding, the Lord's utterance seems to him to be perplexing and it bewilders his mind. Had the Lord in fact bewildered his mind, then who would have removed his delusion?

'Tadekaṁ vada niścitya yena śreyo'hamāpnuyām'—Arjuna requests Lord Kṛṣṇa to tell him decisively, one principle either of action or of knowledge, by which he may attain the highest good or bliss. Arjuna is repeating the same request which he had already mentioned, "Tell me decisively what is good for me (2/7).

Appendix—So long as we accept (assume) the existence of the world, an action seems dreadful or pleasant. The reason is that by cognising the entity of the world, we have our eye on an action rather than on our duty. But when we mind our duty, the action does not seem dreadful or pleasant.

Link:—The Lord, in the next three (third, fourth and fifth) verses, answers the complex words said, in the first two verses.

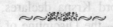

श्रीभगवानुवाच

लोकेऽस्मिन्द्विविधा निष्ठा पुरा प्रोक्ता मयानघ।
ज्ञानयोगेन सांख्यानां कर्मयोगेन योगिनाम्॥ ३॥

śrībhagavānuvāca

loke'smindvividhā niṣṭhā purā proktā mayānagha
jñānayogena sāṅkhyānāṁ karmayogena yoginām

The blessed Lord said:

O sinless Arjuna, in this world to achieve equanimity a twofold path has been enunciated by Me before, the path of Knowledge, for men of renunciation (Sāṅkhyayogī), and the path of Action, for men of action (Karmayogī). 3

Comment:—

[Arjuna did not want to fight. So he misunderstood the term 'Buddhi' (intellect), which stands for equanimity but he took it to mean knowledge. But the Lord had already used the terms 'Buddhi' and 'Buddhiyoga' for equanimity (2/39, 49 etc.) Therefore, here also Lord Kṛṣṇa is describing equanimity which can be acquired by both the Disciplines of Knowledge and Action.]

'Anagha'—The question put by Arjuna, how to attain on the highest good or bliss, shows his freedom from sin, because the keen desire to attain bliss, destroys all the sins of a striver.

'Loke'smindvividhā niṣṭhā purā proktā mayā'—Here, the term 'loke' denotes human body, because both the Disciplines of Knowledge and Action can be practised, only in human life.

The term 'Niṣṭhā' stands for equanimity, which can be attained either through the Discipline of Knowledge or the Discipline of Action. In order to distinguish the two, the Lord, in the thirty-ninth verse of the second chapter, declared, "This is equanimity concerning Sāṅkhya, which has been taught to you (from the eleventh to the thirtieth verses). Now listen about equanimity concerning Yoga (Discipline of Action) (from the thirty-ninth to the fifty-third verses)."

The term 'purā' also denotes "time immemorial", as well as, the immediate past. Here it has been used in the latter sense i.e., in the preceding chapter, when doubt arose in Arjuna's mind. In both the disciplines which have already been described in the preceding chapter, there is no mention of the renunciation of actions.

Something Remarkable

Here, Lord Kṛṣṇa has mentioned two disciplines—the Discipline of Sāṅkhya (Knowledge) and the Discipline of Yoga (Action). Corresponding to the two types of Disciplines there are two types of 'puruṣas', in this world (Gītā 15/16). These are, the perishable (mortal world) and the imperishable (immortal self). To remain equanimous in success and failure, gain and loss of the perishable is known as the Discipline of Action, while having a disinclination for the perishable and being established in the imperishable is the Discipline of Knowledge. But above these two there is the Supreme Person who is beyond the perishable, and is superior to the imperishable, as described in the scriptures, and the Veda (15/18). Thus a wholehearted surrender to the Lord, is called the Discipline of Devotion. Therefore, in the Discipline of Action there is predominance of the perishable, in the Discipline of Knowledge there is predominance of the imperishable, while in the Discipline of Devotion there is predominance of God (Supreme Person).*

The state of 'niṣṭhā' (equanimity), can be attained by strivers, either through knowledge or through Action, but identification

* In fact in both Karmayoga and Jñānayoga our relation with God remains established. God Himself has prescribed these disciplines (Yogas), for the salvation of man. The strivers following these two disciplines carry out the rules prescribed by God. The only thing is that the striver following these two disciplines does not totally depend upon God.

with the Lord, is not their own (niṣṭhā). In Sāṅkhya state strivers experience distinctly, the existence of their own selves, as well as, that of the world and try to cut asunder the affinity for the world. A Karmayogī offers to the world, everything (including even his body), that he has derived from it and removes affinity from the world. In this way, both of them get established in their true form—the Self. But in the state of wholehearted surrender to God, a striver in the beginning, does not feel the existence of God, but he believes that there exists something unique (God) which is above and apart from the Self, as well as, the world. Thus he accepts God with a firm belief and faith and dedicates himself to Him. Therefore, in Sāṅkhya and Yoga, there is predominance of 'knowing' whereas, 'accepting' (Faith) is of much import in Bhagavanniṣṭhā.

There is no difference between 'knowing' and 'accepting'. 'Accepting' is equally indubitable (firm) as 'knowing'. There is no scope for a debate for an accepted thing. A child takes its mother to be its own. No doubt ever crops up in its mind. Therefore, in Gītā, wherever the term 'knowing' has been used with reference to Bhaktiyoga, it should be taken as 'accepting'. Similarly, in connection with Jñānayoga and Karmayoga, the term 'accepting' should be taken to mean 'knowing'.

The state of equanimity depends on the disciplines of the Jñānayogī and Karmayogī, but in Bhagavanniṣṭhā the devotee depends entirely, on the grace of God.

The Discipline of Devotion has been described in the Gītā time and again. In this chapter also, the Lord having described the Disciplines of Knowledge and Action, explains, the Discipline of Devotion in the thirtieth verse, by declaring, "Surrender all actions to Me." Similarly, in the fifth chapter also, having described the two Disciplines, in the tenth verse, He declares, "The knower of Truth performs actions offering these to God," while, at the end of the chapter, He declares that He is the enjoyer of sacrifices and austerities and so on.

'Jñānayogena sāṅkhyānām'—These are modes of nature, (prakṛti), which act on the modes (Gītā 3/28) and so a striver, is not related to them. Thus, by thinking so, when a striver renounces the agency of doership in all actions it is known as, the Discipline of Knowledge (Jñānayoga).

At the beginning of the gospel of the Gītā while describing Sāṅkhyayoga (the Discipline of Knowledge), the Lord clarifies, the imperishable self from the perishable body, by terming these as 'sat' (real) and 'asat' (unreal) (Gītā 2/16).

'Karmayogena yoginām'—The Discipline of Action, consists in performing one's duty according to one's caste, stage of life, nature, circumstances, according to the ordinance of the scriptures, renouncing attachment to it and desire for its fruit, and remaining equanimous in success and failure.

The Lord has primarily described the Discipline of Action, in the forty-seventh and forty-eighth verses of the second chapter. In the forty-seventh verse, there is mention of the principle of the Discipline of Action, while in the forty-eighth verse, there is description of the method of performing action.

Appendix—Karmayoga and Jñānayoga—These two paths being in the world are worldly—'loke'smindvividhā niṣṭhā'. In Karmayoga there is predominance of 'Kṣara' (perishable) (world) while in Jñānayoga there is predominance of 'Akṣara' (embodied soul) (imperishable). The perishable and the imperishable also are there in the world only—'dvāvimau puruṣau loke kṣaraścākṣara eva ca' (Gītā 15/16). Therefore Karmayoga and Jñānayoga—both are worldly paths.

By attaching importance to the soul (Self) and the world—there are two paths. If without attaching importance to the soul and the world, importance is attached only to God, there are not two paths but there is only one unworldly path of 'Bhagavanniṣṭhā' (devotion).

In worldly paths (Karmayoga-Jñānayoga) a striver's endeavour is important. In practising the spiritual discipline a striver holds that his effort is predominant. But when a striver practises spiritual discipline by depending on God without considering his effort as dominant, then his path is unworldly (divine). The reason is that by being connected with God all becomes unworldly. Unless and until there is affinity for God, all is worldly.

Neither think others as evil doers, nor wish evil to others nor do evil to others—with this outlook 'Karmayoga' begins. Nothing is mine, I need nothing and I have to do nothing for myself—by accepting this truth 'Jñānayoga' begins.

न कर्मणामनारम्भान्नैष्कर्म्यं पुरुषोऽश्नुते।
न च सन्न्यसनादेव सिद्धिं समधिगच्छति॥ ४॥

na karmaṇāmanārambhānnaiṣkarmyaṁ puruṣo'śnute
na ca sannyasanādeva siddhiṁ samadhigacchati

Not by non-performance of actions, does a man attain freedom from the bondage of actions; nor by mere renunciation, does he attain perfection. 4

Comment:—

'Na karmaṇāmanārambhānnaiṣkarmyaṁ puruṣo'śnute'—In the Discipline of Action, performance of action is inevitable, because for a sage who wishes to attain success in Yoga, action is the means (6/3).*

A man has an impulse for action, which can be pacified by the performance of actions, without having any desire for fruits. If a striver performs actions having a desire for fruits, this impulse is not pacified, it is rather enhanced.

'Naiṣkarmyaṁ aśnute'—When a striver performs his duty,

* If he does not perform action, how will he come to know whether he remained equanimous in success and failure or not?

without any desire for fruit, he attains to the state of actionlessness i.e., he is released from the bondage of action. Such actions do not bear fruit, in the same way as a roasted or boiled seed loses its potence to sprout. Such actions lose their power of involving a man, in the bondage of birth and death.

A man can renounce desire, when he perform actions only for the welfare of others, as actions have affinity for the world, while the affinity of self is, for God. So long as he performs actions for himself, he cannot renounce desire and as long as he does not renounce desire, he cannot attain to the state of actionlessness.

'Na ca sannyasanādeva siddhiṁ samadhigacchati'— In the first half of this verse, the Lord has declared that a Karmayogī does not attain the state of actionlessness by non-performance of actions. In the second half, He declares that a Sāṅkhyayogī (a follower of the Discipline of Knowledge) does not attain perfection viz., a state of actionlessness by mere renunciation of action.

It is necessary for a striver to renounce the sense of doership, in order to attain perfection. So a Sāṅkhyayogī (follower of the Discipline of Knowledge) instead of renouncing the performance of action, must renounce egoism.

In Sāṅkhyayoga, actions can be performed and they can also be renounced to a certain extent, but in Karmayoga (Discipline of Action), action is necessary as, it is the means to attain success in Yoga viz., perfection (Gītā 6/3).

A Vital Fact

The Gītā, teaches a man, how to attain spiritual perfection by performing one's duty. It inspires him to perform actions, rather than to renounce them. So the Lord lays emphasis, on performing actions, in both the Disciplines of Action and Knowledge.

It is natural that when a striver aims at salvation, he gets tired of the worldly affairs and wants to renounce those affairs.

Similarly, Arjuna also being tired of actions, asks Lord Kṛṣṇa why He is urging him to be engaged in this terrible action of waging war, when both the Disciplines of Action and Knowledge lead to equanimity. B'ut the Lord, orders Arjuna to perform actions in both the Disciplines. By the Discipline of Action, He orders him to perform action by being even-minded (Gītā 2/48), while in the Discipline of Knowledge He orders him to fight (Gītā 2/18). Therefore, the Lord urges people to perform actions rather than to renounce these. But the Lord asks them to renounce desire and attachment which are like poison, in actions.

A striver instead of renouncing the performance of actions, should renounce his attachment to them. Yogīs (men of action), having abandoned attachment, perform actions only by the body, mind, intellect or merely by the senses, in order to render service to the world, without any selfish motive (Gītā 5/11). In the Discipline of Knowledge, there is predominance of discrimination, between the real and the unreal. Therefore, a Jñānayogī assumes that it is modes which are acting on the modes i.e., all the actions are performed by the body, senses, mind and intellect etc., while he does nothing at all (Gītā 3/28, 5/8-9).

All strivers experience that as soon as, a keen desire for salvation is aroused in them, they have disinclination for actions, things and persons (members of the family). But being attached to a body, they have a desire for rest, which is an obstacle to their progress. Generally, strivers believe, that they can progress in the spiritual field by renouncing actions, things and company of people. But the fact is, that renouncement of attachment to actions, things and people is an important factor. In the Discipline of Knowledge, it is difficult to renounce attachment, without keen dispassion. But in the Discipline of Action, attachment is easily renounced, by performing actions for others, even without keen dispassion.

In the Gītā, it is also mentioned that a striver may practise spiritual discipline in solitude. But in solitude, a sāttvika (virtuous) person devotes his time, in being busy with spiritual practice and adoration, a rājasa (passionate) person spends it in projections and distractions, while a tāmasa (ignorant) man, wastes it in sleep, indolence and heedlessness. Therefore, a striver should have an inclination to dwell in solitude, in order to devote his time and energy to spiritual activities, but he should perform his mundane duty also, very promptly without being attached to it. He should be attached, neither to people nor to inaction. Detachment leads a striver to salvation very quickly. In fact external solitude is not the real solitude, because the body is also a fragment of the world. Therefore, real solitude consists in renouncing affinity with the body and the world i.e., in renouncing egoism and attachment.

Appendix—The divinity which is ours, is in us and is now, is not realized by doing something because that is never unattained. We shall do some action, then that reality will be realized—this conception strengthens identification of the self with the body. Every action has a beginning and an end, therefore by action only the thing will be gained which does not really exist. But because of affinity for Prakṛti in every being, there is an inner urge for actions which does not enable him to be actionless. In order to pacify this urge, it is inevitable not to do what ought not to be done, and do without the sense of mine and with disinterest what ought to be done viz., not to do any action for oneself but do only for the welfare of others. By doing actions for oneself, the impetus for actions will never end because the self is eternal while actions are transitory. Therefore by performing actions selflessly for the welfare of others, the urge for actions calms down, affinity for Prakṛti gets renounced and God, Who pervades everywhere and every time will be revealed and realized.

न हि कश्चित्क्षणमपि जातु तिष्ठत्यकर्मकृत्।
कार्यते ह्यवशः कर्म सर्वः प्रकृतिजैर्गुणैः ॥५॥

na hi kaścitkṣaṇamapi jātu tiṣṭhatyakarmakṛt
kāryate hyavaśaḥ karma sarvaḥ prakṛtijairguṇaiḥ

For, no one under any circumstances can remain even for a moment, without undertaking action; everyone is compelled to act, by the modes born of nature (prakṛti). 5

Comment:—

'Na hi kaścitkṣaṇamapi jātu tiṣṭhatyakarmakṛt'—In the Disciplines of Action, Knowledge and Devotion, no striver can ever remain without performing actions. Hence the terms 'Kaścit' (anyone), 'kṣaṇam' (a moment) and 'jātu' (verily) are uncommon. Here, the term 'kaścit' denotes, that no one whether he is wise or ignorant, can remain without performing action. Though a wise man may have no relation with his so-called body, yet actions are constantly performed by it. The term 'kṣaṇam' denotes, that a man does not assume that he performs actions constantly, but he cannot remain without performing action, even for a moment, so long as he assumes his affinity for the body. The term 'jātu' means that a man cannot remain without performing action, in any state such as wakefulness, sleep, sound sleep and unconsciousness. The Lord explains the reason by the term 'avaśaḥ' (helplessly) in the second half of the verse, by declaring that he has to act helplessly by impulses born of nature. Nature is ever changeful. A striver has to do nothing for himself. He has to perform actions sanctioned by the scriptures, for the welfare of others. So far as forbidden actions are concerned, they cannot be performed by a striver, because his aim is God-realization.

Many people regard, only those actions as actions, which are performed by the gross body. But according to the Gītā, the activities undertaken by the body, speech or mind are also regarded as actions (Gītā 18/15). And those actions, whether physical or mental to which a man is attached, lead him to bondage.

Generally, people regard their professions, such as business, service or teaching and nursing of children etc., as actions, but they do not consider eating, drinking, sleeping, waking and thinking etc., as actions. So, when they renounce their profession, they think that they are not performing actions. But it is a serious error on their part. All the activities performed by the physical body, for the purpose of earning a living, actions performed by the subtle body like sleeping and thinking and in trance, performed by the causal body, are all regarded as actions. So long as, a man has ego and sense of mineness with the body, the activities performed by body are actions as the body is an evolute of nature and nature is never inactive. So, a person having egoism and attachment to the body, cannot remain without performing action, in either of the states, either of activity or inactivity.

'Kāryate hyavaśaḥ karma sarvaḥ prakṛtijairguṇaiḥ'— Everyone is made to act helplessly, by the modes of nature (prakṛti) because nature and its modes are ever active (Gītā 3/27, 13/29). Though, the soul is inactive, detached, imperishable, uniform and unconnected, yet so long as, it being attached to nature and its evolute—the gross, subtle and causal bodies wants to derive pleasure and remains helpless under the control of nature (Gītā 14/5). This helplessness of the self, under the control of nature, is due to affinity with nature. This has also been mentioned, in the eighth verse of the ninth chapter and the nineteenth verse of the eighth chapter.

Individual nature is moulded by tendencies and tendencies are born of modes and modes in their term evolve from prakṛti. Therefore, to be subjected to nature or modes or prakṛti is one and the same thing. As a matter of fact, subjection to the prakṛti and its evolutes, is the root-cause of all bondage. The same, on different occasions, has been defined as subjection to time, nature, action and prakṛti etc. So long as, the self (soul) does not become free from nature and its modes i.e., does not realize God, it remains helpless under the control of modes, time, nature, pleasures and even persons, property etc. But when it transcends the modes of nature and realizes the self or God, it does not remain helpless, it attains freedom which is axiomatic.

Something Noteworthy

There are two states of prakṛti—active (gross) and inactive (subtle). Performance of action, is the active state, while remaining idle in sleep etc., is the inactive state. But, even in the inactive state nature does not remain inactive, and activity goes on, in its subtle form. When a person is awakened by someone, he says that he was aroused, in half sleep. This proves, that the process of sleep continued even, in the inactive state. In the same way, activity continues in a trance, dissolution (pralaya) and final dissolution etc., in its subtle form.

In fact nature never remains inactive because it is ever-changing. In the self (spirit or soul) there is no doership, but having assumed Its affinity for bodies etc., the evolutes of nature, It becomes helpless, under the control of nature. It is because of helplessness, that though, being a non-doer, assumes Itself, as doer. All the actions of the universe, such as seeing, hearing, breathing, digestion of food etc., are performed by nature. So is the case with the states of childhood and youth. But the embodied soul, is bound by regarding itself as the doer of some actions.

Nature constantly undergoes changes, while in the purer self there is never any change. In fact, the worldly things have no existence of their own. The kaleidoscopic heap, seems to exist in the form of things. When a man assumes his affinity for things, he cannot remain without performing actions, even for a moment in any state. If a striver realizes that all the activities are confined to the things and he has not the least relation with them, then only can he get rid of his helplessness. A Karmayogī (follower of the Discipline of Action) gets rid of this helplessness by renouncing the desire and attachment to the ever-changing things.

Whatever has been said, by the Lord here in this verse, has also been said, in the eleventh verse of the eighteenth chapter when He declares, "It is indeed impossible for an embodied being, to abstain from actions altogether."

Appendix—All actions are performed only in Prakṛti. But a man by accepting his identity with nature (prakṛti) becomes dependent on the modes of nature—'avaśaḥ' and he gets contaminated by actions. Therefore no person who assumes his affinity with nature, under any circumstances, can remain even for a moment without undertaking action in any state as wakefulness, sleep, sound sleep, faint, trance, creation-new creation, dissolution and final dissolution etc.

How is an action performed in the states of sound sleep, faint and trance? When a man sleeps and any person awakes him in between, he says that he was awakened without having a full (complete) sleep. It proves that at the time of sleep, the action from incompletion to completion was going on. Similarly in faint and trance also an action goes on. In Pātañjala Yogadarśana this action has been called 'pariṇāma'.* Pariṇāma means current of variation viz., flow of change.† It means that from the beginning of trance to the state of relapse, an action goes on. If there is no action, there can't be relapse from the state of trance. At

* vyutthānanirodhasaṁskārayorabhibhavaprādurbhāvau nirodhakṣaṇacittānvayo nirodhapariṇāmaḥ

sarvārthataikāgratayoḥ kṣayodayau cittasya samādhipariṇāmaḥ

tataḥ punaḥ śāntoditau tulya pratyayau cittasyaikāgratāpariṇāmaḥ

(Vibhūtipāda 9, 11-12)

† Atha ko'yaṁ pariṇāmaḥ?—Avasthitasya dravyasya pūrva dharma nivṛttau dharmāntarotpattiḥ pariṇāmaḥ.

'What is 'pariṇāma'?—the change of the state from the original (existing) one to the other new one is 'pariṇāma'.

(Yogadarśana Vibhūti 13, Vyāsa Bhāṣya)

the time of trance there is 'pariṇāma' and at the end of trance there is relapse.

'Sahajāvasthā' or 'Sahaja Samādhi' (natural state of self-realization) transcends all states of Prakṛti. In it there is no action in the least, an action is not possible. Therefore in Sahajāvasthā there is neither 'pariṇāma' (current of change) nor vyutthāna (relapse). The reason is that activities take place only in Prakṛti and its evolutes, never in the self. 'Kāryate hyavaśaḥ karma'—We are helplessly driven to action, but we are quite free in having or not having attachment or aversion for them.

Link:— In the fifth verse, it has been mentioned that no one can remain without action for a moment, even, one may object to these that a person could regard himself as free from action, by forcibly suspending the functions of the senses. The answer comes in the next verse.

कर्मेन्द्रियाणि संयम्य य आस्ते मनसा स्मरन्।
इन्द्रियार्थान्विमूढात्मा मिथ्याचारः स उच्यते ॥ ६ ॥

karmendriyāṇi saṁyamya ya āste manasā smaran
indriyārthānvimūḍhātmā mithyācāraḥ sa ucyate

He who while, restraining the organs of action, thinks of sense-objects in his mind, he, of deluded understanding is a hypocrite. 6

Comment:—

'Karmendriyāṇi saṁyamya ya āste manasā smaran indriyārthān-vimūḍhātmā mithyācāraḥ sa ucyate'— Here the term 'Karmendriyāṇi' does not stand only for the five organs of action (speech, hand, foot, anus and generative organ) but also stands for the five sense-organs (ear, skin, eye, taste and nose) because actions cannot be performed by the organs of action alone without sense-organs. Besides this if only the organs of action such as hand and foot etc., are restrained but the sense-organs such as ear and eye are not restrained hypocrisy is not fully proved.

In the Gītā, sense-organs have also been included within the organs of action.Therefore, in the Gītā only the term 'Karmendriya' rather than 'Jñānendriya' has been used. In the eighth and ninth verses of the fifth chapter the actions of the sense-organs such as seeing, hearing and touching etc., have also been innumerated along with actions of the organs of action. It proves, that in the Gītā, the sense-organs are also included, in the organs of action. According to the Gītā, the activities performed with the mind, are also included in actions (Gītā 18/15). It means, that every evolute of nature is active, because nature is ever-active.

Though the term 'saṁyamya' means full control over senses, yet here it signifies, only their outward restraint. The reason is, that he who has completely controlled his senses, cannot be called a hypocrite.

A man of foolish understanding (who cannot distinguish the real, from the unreal) restrains the senses forcibly, from running after sense-objects but thinks of the objects of enjoyment, with his mind and assumes this state, as actionless. Such a person is called a hypocrite. The reason is, that outwardly he has restrained the organs and senses, but because of egoism, attachment and desire, he performs action by enjoying pleasure, while thinking of the objects of enjoyment.

Worldly pleasures can be enjoyed externally, as well as internally. As external pleasures leave their influence, so do the internal ones, which are enjoyed by thinking of the objects of enjoyment viz., by being attached to them. External pleasures can be renounced by applying discrimination, thinking of adverse consequences or to maintain social decorum. But, there is no such obstacle, in the enjoyment of internal pleasures. A person goes on enjoying these with his mind, and develops a false pride that he has renounced these pleasures. Thus, internal pleasures prove very fatal for him. Therefore, a striver should very carefully restrain his mind from thinking of the objects of enjoyment.

Arjuna also wants to renounce the performance of actions, and asks Lord Kṛṣṇa why He urges him to engage in the terrible deed. In response to his question the Lord replies, that a person who, having renounced the actions externally, has egoism, attachment and desire etc., but thinks that he is not performing any action, is a hypocrite. It means that striver instead of renouncing the performance of actions, should perform them promptly, renouncing desire and attachment.

Appendix—Worldly pleasures can be enjoyed externally as well as internally by mind. Enjoyment of pleasures physically and relishing them by thinking of sense-objects—there is no difference between the two.

The same impression is made by dwelling on sense-objects in the mind as it is made by physical enjoyment of pleasures. If one relishes the memory of pleasures, then several years may pass but that pleasure remains the same (fresh). Therefore the thought of pleasure gives birth to a new pleasure. Not only this but relish of pleasures, by thinking of them, causes greater harm. The reason is that a man can renounce external pleasures in order to escape adverse public opinion and to maintain social decorum, but in the enjoyment of pleasures with the mind there is no such external obstacle. Therefore a man gets a good chance to enjoy them with the mind. So relishing pleasures with the mind is very harmful for a striver. In fact renunciation of pleasures mentally is the real renunciation (Gītā 2/64).

Link:—In the fourth verse, the Lord laid emphasis on the performance of actions, in both the Disciplines of Action and Knowledge. In the fifth verse, He declared, "No one can remain even for a moment without performing action." In the sixth verse, He said, "He who, restraining the organs of actions forcibly regards himself as actionless, is a hypocrite." It means that renunciation of actions, is not true renunciation. Therefore, He in the next verse explains the marks of real renunciation.

यस्त्विन्द्रियाणि मनसा नियम्यारभतेऽर्जुन।
कर्मेन्द्रियैः कर्मयोगमसक्तः स विशिष्यते॥७॥

yastvindriyāṇi manasā niyamyārabhate'rjuna
karmendriyaiḥ karmayogamasaktaḥ sa viśiṣyate

But he who controls his senses through the mind. O Arjuna, and engages himself in the path of action, with the organs of action and sense, without being attached, is superior. 7

Comment:—

[The term 'tu' (but) has been used in order to declare that such a follower of the Discipline of Action, free from attachment, is superior, not only to a hypocrite, but also to a follower of the Discipline of Knowledge.]

'Arjuna'—The term 'Arjuna' means, pure in nature. The Lord addressing him as Arjuna, says that being pure in nature, he should have no doubt about the performance of his duty.

'Yastvindriyāṇi manasā niyamya'—Here the term 'Manasā, stands for all the inner senses—(mind, intellect, faculty of reflection and ego) and the term 'Indriyāṇi' denotes, all the ten organs of action and sense-organs. 'Controlling the senses by the mind' means that by applying discrimination a striver should realize that the self has no affinity for the senses and the mind. When the senses are controlled by the mind, these can be engaged in or deviated from, any activity as the striver wishes.

Senses are controlled, only when attachment to them is renounced totally. In the eleventh verse of the twelfth chapter also, there is mention of control over senses for a Karmayogī. It means that a striver can follow the path of action, only by controlling the senses.

In the preceding (sixth) verse Lord Kṛṣṇa talked, about a hypocrite who forcibly restrains his senses, while here in this verse He is talking of, preventing the senses from indulging in forbidden actions and engaging these in actions, which are sanctioned by scriptures. When actions are performed according to the scriptural injunctions, senses are automatically controlled.

'Asaktaḥ'—A man is attached to (i) actions, and (ii) their fruit. It is attachment, and not actions or their fruit, that is the root of all evils. Attachment is the main stumbling block to perfection. So a striver instead of renouncing actions, should renounce attachment. He can be free from attachment, when he, without regarding the body, senses, mind and intellect as his or for him, starts performing his duty promptly for the welfare of the world, by considering these of the world and for the world. By doing so, his attachment to the fruit of actions automatically perishes.

All actions, including thinking and trance, have nothing to do with the self (Gītā 5/11). Though the self is naturally unattached, yet by developing attachment, it gets attached to the world. The real merit of a Karmayogī consists in being free from attachment. Freedom from attachment means, having no desire for the fruit of actions.

A common man performs actions in order to fulfil his desire, while a striver performs actions having the aim of renouncing attachment. Such a striver is called here an 'Asaktaḥ' (unattached).

A striver following the path of action, can renounce attachment and desire for fruit, more easily than the striver, who follows the path of knowledge. A Karmayogī, only through disinterested actions without any other means, can be free from attachment and desire for fruit, while a Jñānayogī, in order to do away with his sense of egoism and attachment, has to follow the path of action i.e., he has to perform actions without, having any desire for fruit (5/6, 15/11). The reason is, that unless dispassion is developed and body consciousness is removed, Sāṅkhyayoga is difficult to practise, without having practised Karmayoga beforehand. Through the practice of Karmayoga a Sāṅkhyayogī gets completely detached, and then through the practice of Jñānayoga, he attains perfection. As soon as a Karmayogī renounces attachment, he attains equanimity.Therefore, the Lord declares, that actions need not be renounced but these should be performed, without attachment. It is attachment, which needs to be renounced. In Karmayoga (Discipline of Action), action is performed for the welfare of others, while 'Yoga' (union) is for one's own self. Arjuna considers action in relation to himself, therefore, he thinks that fighting is a terrible act. So the Lord clarifies, that it is attachment to action, rather than action, by itself, which is terrible.

'Karmendriyaiḥ karmayogaṁ ārabhate'—As the term 'Indriyāṇi' stands for all the ten senses, so does the term, 'Karmendriyaiḥ' denote the ten senses. If they are taken as the five organs of action alone, such as hand, foot and speech etc., how could actions be performed without seeing, hearing and thinking? Therefore, all the internal and external senses and organs, by which actions are performed, are included in 'Karmendriyaiḥ.'

When an action is performed, for the welfare of others without any selfish motive, it is called 'Karmayoga' or the Discipline (Path) of Action. When a person performs actions for himself, he is attached to the actions and their fruit. But, when he performs these for others, actions and their fruit are related to others, while he is related to God i.e., he realizes his real relation with God, the eternal. Thus, performance of one's duty according to one's caste and circumstances etc., selflessly, is the beginning of Karmayoga (Discipline of Action).

Strivers following the Discipline of Action are of two types:—(i) Those who are interested in performing actions, but their main aim is to attain salvation. Such strivers need not start new actions. They have to make proper use of the available circumstances. (ii) Those who are more interested in rendering service to others, in providing comfort to others and in improving the society, than in their attainment of salvation. Such strivers, can start performing new actions, with the aim of doing away with their attachment.

In the Gītā, Lord Kṛṣṇa asks Arjuna to make a proper use of available circumstances, because Arjuna had a keen desire to attain the highest good i.e., to attain bliss or salvation (Gītā 2/7; 3/2; 5/1).

'Sa viśiṣyate'—He, who performs actions for the welfare of others, having renounced his selfishness and fruit for action, is superior as his all actions are directed towards the service of the world, All his possessions and body are also, for the service of others. His selflessness is of such a degree that his ego (of the sense of rendering service), is completely annihilated. Thus he becomes totally detached and liberated.

When a striver resolves to attain salvation, he wants to renounce actions, by regarding these as stumbling blocks to salvation. But the fact is, that it is not the action but it is the selfish motive in the performance of actions, which is an obstacle. Therefore, the Lord declares that a person, who without attachment performs action for the welfare of others, is superior to those hypocrites, who restrain the organs of action but have the sense-objects in mind. Even a person who performs action in order to receive its reward, such as heaven etc., is superior to a hypocrite. Then, there is no doubt that a Karmayogī who performs actions for the welfare of others without having any selfish motive, is superior. At the beginning of the fifth chapter, Arjuna asks Lord Kṛṣṇa to tell him for certain which one of the two, Sannyāsa or Yoga (renunciation of actions or their unselfish performance) is better. Lord Kṛṣṇa replies that both lead to salvation, but unselfish performance of action is better, than its renunciation. Similarly, here also he declares a Karmayogī, who performs actions, for the welfare of others selflessly, to be superior.

Appendix—In a striver if there is eagerness for salvation, there is generosity in his nature and there is compassion in his heart viz., he gets happy (pleased) with the happiness of others and becomes sad (compassionate) with the sufferings of others—a striver having possessed these three traits becomes eligible for Karmayoga. Being fit for Karmayoga, Karmayoga is easily practised.

In Karmayoga there is one division of 'Karma' (duty) and one division is of 'Yoga'. Proper utilization of one's things, power, ability; and rendering service to people—this is duty. By discharging one's duty there is disunion (disconnection) from the assumed union with the world—this is yoga. Duty has its relation with the world and yoga has its relation with God.

Link:—In response to Arjuna's question, why the Lord was urging him to take such a dreadful action as, warfare, He replied, "No one can ever remain even, for a moment without performing action." "Then He explained that he who, restraining the organs of action, thinks of the sense-objects, is a hypocrite, while he who engages himself in action without expecting any reward, is superior. Now in the next verse, He orders Arjuna to perform his allotted duty.

नियतं कुरु कर्म त्वं कर्म ज्यायो ह्यकर्मणः।
शरीरयात्रापि च ते न प्रसिद्ध्येदकर्मणः॥ ८॥

niyataṁ kuru karma tvaṁ karma jyāyo hyakarmaṇaḥ
śarīrayātrāpi ca te na prasiddhyedakarmaṇaḥ

Do perform thy prescribed duty, for action is superior to inaction. Besides even the maintenance of the body would not be possible for thee, by inaction. 8

Comment:—

'Niyataṁ kuru karma tvam'— A man is permitted to perform two types of actions—those as laid down in the scriptures such as, fasts and worship etc., and the allotted duty according to one's caste, order of life, nature and circumstance, such as eating food, doing business, construction of a house and guiding a person who has lost his way and so on. A man cannot perform all actions as laid down in the scriptures, thoroughly. But he can very easily abandon the forbidden actions; non-performance of prescribed actions is not very harmful. Abandonment of forbidden actions, such as falsehood, theft and violence etc., is very beneficial. When he abandons forbidden actions, actions sanctioned by the scriptures, are automatically performed by him.

In the Discipline of Action, action according to one's caste and sanctioned by the scriptures, is one's allotted duty, whether it is terrible or mild. Here Lord Kṛṣṇa explains to Arjuna, that as a Kṣatriya (member of the warrior class) it is his duty to fight (Gītā 18/43). Though the action involves violence and bloodshed, yet it is his allotted duty. In the second chapter also, the Lord told him that having regard for his own duty he should not falter (Gītā (2/31). In fact 'svadharma' (One's own duty) and 'niyatakarma' (allotted duty), both are one and the same. For Duryodhana being a member of the warrior class, it was his duty to fight, yet it was not his allotted duty, as being unjust he wanted to usurp the Pāṇḍava's kingdom. For him, it was not a righteous and prescribed, duty.

'Karma jyāyo hyakarmaṇaḥ'—The Lord, in this verse is, answering the question put in the first verse, by using the same term 'jyāyaḥ' (superior). There, Arjuna put the question why He was urging him to perform the terrible action of waging the war, when according to Him knowledge was superior to action. In response to his question the Lord declared, a person following the path of action, to be superior to person, following the path of inaction. Thus, Arjuna wants to escape the battle, while the Lord exhorts him to fight, as it is his allotted duty. Therefore, the Lord in the eighteenth chapter declares, "One should not abandon the duty suited to one's nature, even though it may be easy" (18/48), because by abandoning it, one is exposed to sin and one continues to be attached to it. Therefore, performance of allotted duty, is superior to renunciation of actions. Performance of actions without attachment, is far superior to those performed with attachment, because by doing so, affinity for actions is totally renounced. Therefore, the Lord in the first half of this verse, orders Arjuna to perform his allotted duty without attachment, while in the second half He declares that maintenance of the body would not be possible by inaction either.

In the Discipline of Action the Lord's main principle is "Action is superior to inaction." The same fact has been pointed out by the Lord, when he declares, "Let not thy attachment be to inaction" (Gītā 2/47). The reason is, that he who shirks his duty wastes his time in heedlessness, laziness and sleep or performs forbidden actions, which mislead him to a downfall.

It is better to be detached from actions by performing them, rather than through their non-performance. A person is in bondage, due to desire, attachment, partiality etc., whether he performs actions or not. In the path of action, if a striver has the aim to renounce desire, it can be renounced very easily, through the performance of action for the good of others.

'Śarīrayātrāpi ca te na prasiddhyedakarmaṇaḥ'— Arjuna had a misconception in his mind, that his affinity for actions would be automatically renounced, if he did not perform action. Therefore, Lord Kṛṣṇa persuades him to perform actions by several pleas, one of these was, that even the maintenance of body would not be possible, by inaction.

As in the Discipline of Knowledge, affinity for the world is renounced by discrimination, in the Discipline of Action, affinity is renounced by performing one's duty sincerely and thoroughly. Therefore, the Discipline of Action, should in no way be regarded as inferior to the Discipline of Knowledge. A Karmayogī, regarding the body as belonging to the world, uses it in rendering service to the world i.e., he has no sense of 'mineness', with it. He identifies the physical, subtle and causal bodies respectively, with the gross, subtle and causal world, while a Jñānayogī identifies himself with Brahma, the Absolute. Thus a Karmayogī, identifies the insentient elements while a Jñānayogī, identifies the sentient ones.

A Vital Fact Pertaining to Spiritual Discipline

Generally strivers such as Arjuna, commit an error, that they insist on non-performance of actions. Secondly, while practising spiritual discipline they want favourable circumstances, so that they may attain their aim quickly. But such a desire, is a stumbling block to their spiritual progress.

A striver who wants to attain bliss easily and quickly, is a pleasure-seeker rather than a striver, because by doing so he has an eye, not on the spiritual discipline but on its fruit. The result is, that he gets tired of spiritual discipline and thus attains his aim late. A striver, who has a single-minded determination to attain bliss, is bent upon practising the spiritual discipline, whole-heartedly without thinking of the difficulties, duration, pleasure and pain. Not to talk of a striver, even a greedy merchant bears all hardships, without caring for hunger and thirst etc., as long as customers continue to come and there is a good sale. Similarly, a striver practises spiritual discipline with reverence and devotion, without caring for comfort and even the bare necessities of life. He has a keen desire to attain his object. He bemoans if he finds himself unable to overcome any obstacle in the path of spiritual discipline, while a striver, who derives pleasure out of the spiritual discipline, gets angry when he finds an obstacle, in his way. The curiosity or desire of a striver enhances every moment, while the latter thinks of relaxing, having attained the aim quickly. The former thinks that he has nothing to do, except practising the spiritual discipline under all circumstances. So he applies his full power and attains bliss. But the latter, when he does not succeed quickly, may get disappointed. Therefore, a striver should attach more importance to the means, rather than to the end, like Goddess Pārvatī who in the Rāmacaritamānasa declares, "I have a firm determination that I shall marry only Lord Śiva, otherwise I shall remain unmarried even though millions of births may pass. I shall not disobey the preaching of sage Nārada, even if Lord Śiva may ask me to do so, a hundred times" (1/81/5). Mother Pārvatī is not time-conscious, in her penance.

In this verse, Lord Kṛṣṇa through Arjuna urges all strivers to perform their allotted duties very promptly, by renouncing the desire for favourable circumstances and pleasures, which are the main stumbling blocks to spiritual progress.

Appendix—A Karmayogī, who performs actions in a disinterested way, is not only superior to those who do not perform action or to those who do actions in an interested manner but is also superior to a 'Jñānayogī'—'Tayostu karma sannyāsātkarmayogo viśiṣyate' (Gītā 5/2). Therefore the Lord here is laying special emphasis on the performance of actions in a disinterested way.

Link:—In the preceding verse, Lord Kṛṣṇa declared that without performing action we cannot keep body and soul together. It proves that performance of action is essential. But actions lead to attachment and bondage. So how can a man be free from this bondage? The Lord, answers the question in the next verse.

यज्ञार्थात्कर्मणोऽन्यत्र लोकोऽयं कर्मबन्धनः।
तदर्थं कर्म कौन्तेय मुक्तसङ्गः समाचर॥ ९॥

yajñārthātkarmaṇo'nyatra loko'yaṁ karmabandhanaḥ
tadarthaṁ karma kaunteya muktasaṅgaḥ samācara

The mankind is bound by actions other than those done for the sake of sacrifice. Therefore, O son of Kuntī (Arjuna), perform action for that (yajña) sake, and without attachment. 9

Comment:—

'Yajñārthātkarmaṇo'nyatra'—According to the Gītā, every duty is 'Yajña' (sacrifice). The term 'Yajña' includes sacrifice, charity, penance, oblation, pilgrimage, fast, study of the Vedas and all physical, mundane and spiritual actions. Professions such as business, service and teaching etc., sanctioned by the scriptures, are also included in 'Yajña'. Other actions, which are performed in order to comfort others and for the welfare of others, are also included in the term 'Yajña'. Attachment perishes very quickly by performing actions for the sake of sacrifice and all actions of a Karmayogī are dissolved (Gītā 4/23) i.e., they instead of leading the person to bondage, reduce the stock of his past actions also to nothing.

In fact, a man's inclination is judged by his aim, rather than by his actions. As a businessman's aim while having a transaction is to earn money, and he thinks of money, as soon as he shut his shop, similarly, a striver who performs action for the sake of sacrifice, has the aim of God-realization and as soon as the action is over, he is inclined towards God.

The people of different Varṇas (castes) have their allotted duties and actions. A Brāhmaṇa (a member of the priest class) can depend on charity which is a source of his living, while it is not allowed for a Kṣatriya (a member of the warrior class). Similarly, performance of actions without having any desire for fruit, is a man's own duty while performance of actions expecting their fruit is not his own duty. Similarly, forbidden actions are also not included in one's own duty, and so is the case, with actions which are performed in order to gain pleasure, honour, praise and comfort etc.* Therefore, a striver should take precaution lest the action should be performed with a selfish motive. In fact a striver is he, who is ever on the alert in this regard.

If a person receives a visitor with open arms, in order to create a good impression of his gentleness upon him, it means that the action has been performed, with a selfish motive. Therefore, such an action cannot be called a sacrifice. Similarly, if a person puts a question to an orator in a meeting or in a discourse in order to impress the orator and the audience, his action is not performed for the sake of sacrifice (Yajña). It means that a striver should perform action by renouncing his selfish motive and desire.

A striver should not take any action for pleasure and prosperity, or even for the maintenance of the body. If actions are performed for the maintenance of body, it means that there is a desire to live. Actions should be performed for the sake of sacrifice alone. Any action taken for personal welfare, leads to bondage. Indeed, the supreme striver is he who performs actions for the welfare of others, even without having a desire to attain salvation. The welfare of others also involves one's own welfare. Therefore, all the mundane and spiritual actions should be performed, for the welfare of others.

Action which is performed for one's own self, leads to bondage. Therefore, even actions such as remembrance, reflection, meditation and even a trance should be practised for the welfare of the world. Thus whatever a striver does with his physical, subtle and causal bodies, does only for others, not for himself. By doing so, his affinity for the world is renounced and he is

* When a man performs actions for himself, it means that he has a desire for the fruit of actions and where there is desire for the fruit of actions, there is the possibility of the performance of forbidden actions.

united with God. This is known as Karmayoga.

'Loko'yaṁ karmabandhanaḥ'— Only human beings are entitled to take action in the form of performing a duty (sacrifice), as has been described by the Lord relating to the topic, of the wheel of creation (3/14—16). He who performs actions with an interested motive is bound, while he, who performs actions, for the welfare of others, performs his duty and attains liberation from bondage. It is not action but attachment and selfishness, which bind him.

'Tadarthaṁ karma kaunteya muktasaṅgaḥ samācara'—Here the term 'muktasaṅgaḥ' (freedom from attachment) denotes, that actions should be performed without entertaining the feeling of 'mine', and attachment to actions, things, body, mind and intellect etc. If the feeling of 'mine' and attachment are renounced, actions are automatically performed for the welfare of others, and if a striver has no other actions to perform, he automatically gets established in the self. Consequently, only actions which are prescribed by the scriptures, are performed by him.

The renunciation of duty out of indolence and carelessness, is declared to be 'Tamas' (Gītā 18/7) which results in delusion i.e., such a person is born in the wombs of the deluded. He who abandons a duty, because it is painful, such relinquishment is Rajas (Gītā 18/8) the fruit is pain (Gītā 14/16). Therefore, here Lord Kṛṣṇa does not exhort Arjuna to renounce actions but He orders him to perform actions efficiently and enthusiastically renouncing selfishness, mineness, attachment, desire for fruit and partiality etc., according to the ordinance of the scriptures. Such relinquishment is regarded 'Sāttvika' (Gītā 18/9). The Lord Himself further declares that there is nothing in the three worlds that must be done by Him, yet He is engaged in action (3/22-23).

A person becomes slack in performing actions because of two factors—(1) It is in the nature of human beings that they perform action with a view to reaping the fruit. But when, according to the Discipline of Action, he realizes that actions are to be performed without the desire for fruit, he thinks why he should perform actions at all. (2) If having started action, he realizes that it will bear adverse fruit, he feels that he should not perform it.

A Karmayogī has neither any desire nor expectation of the perishable fruit of action, he performs actions, only in order to do good to the world. So there cannot be any slackness in the performance of duty.

A Vital Fact

Generally, a person does an act promptly and efficiently, only if it serves his selfish motive, but such an action binds him. In order to be free from the bondage, he should perform actions prescribed by the scriptures, disinterestedly.

In the Discipline of Action, all actions are performed for others. Who are others? Not only other beings and things, but the so-called our own bodies—gross, subtle, (senses, mind, intellect and life-breath) and causal (including 'ego') are also, included in the term 'others'*. The reason is, that the self (soul) is a fragment of sentient God, while these bodies and things are the fragments of insentient 'prakṛti' (matter). All actions are performed through the evolutes of nature such as body etc., and for the body and the world which are also evolutes of nature, while the sentient neither undergoes actions, nor are actions performed for the sentient. So actions can never be performed for the self. But

* Like the world the body, senses, mind and intellect are also different from us. Therefore, a Karmayogī without assuming them as his own, serves them. He does not let the body become sleepy, indolent, heedless, idle and pleasure-seeking. Thus he renders service to the body. He renders service to the senses by not allowing them to be engaged in worldly pleasures. He renders service to the mind by not allowing it to think of doing harm to others or thinking of sense-objects or futile things. He serves the intellect by not allowing it to think of the duties of others. He serves all of them by having neither the feeling of mineness nor attachment.

when the self assumes worldly insentient things, such as a body etc., as 'I', 'Mine' and 'for me', he performs actions for himself. By performing actions for others, attachment and the feeling of 'mine' perish easily.

Everybody can realize that the states of the body (childhood, youth etc.,) undergo change, but he remains the same. This unchanging self (soul) has its identity with God, while the changing body, senses, mind and intellect etc., have their identity, with the world. Whatever action is performed by us, is performed with body and senses etc., not by the self. This shows that we have nothing to do for ourselves, we have to do only for the world. When we perform actions for ourselves, we are bound by those actions—"The man is bound by actions, other than those performed for the sake of sacrifice (Yajña)."

The imperishable and unchanging self, has no affinity for the perishable and changing body, senses, mind and intellect etc. Therefore, there is nothing one's own and for one's own self. We can do nothing without the help of the body etc., therefore we have to do nothing for the self. The self can never lack anything. Without want there can arise no desire. Therefore, It needs nothing for Itself. In this way, when a man's affinity for actions and things is severed, if he is inclined towards knowledge, he realizes the self. On the other hand, if he is inclined towards devotion, he attains to the state of exclusive devotion.

Appendix—A man is not bound by performing actions but he is bound by 'anyatra karma' viz., actions which are done with a selfish motive (for himself) (Gītā 3/13). Therefore the expression 'yajñārthātkarmaṇo'nyatra loko'yaṁ karmabandhanaḥ' means—nothing is to be done for one's own self.

A man can be free from the bondage of actions only when he renders service to the world with the body, things, ability and strength (power) which he has received from the world and covets no fruit. The reason is that the world can't provide us the thing which we aim at. We want bliss, want immortality, want carefreedom, want fearlessness, want independence (self-dependence). But all this will not be available to us from the world but it will be available by snapping off our ties with the world. In order to get dissociated with the world, it is necessary that whatever we have received from the world, we surrender it to the world in its selfless service.

Link:—The Lord in the preceding verse declared, "The man is bound by actions, other than those performed for the sake of sacrifice." Therefore, in order to be free from bondage, actions instead of being renounced, should be performed, only in the spirit of performing a duty (yajña). The Lord confirms the same fact, by giving other reasons in the next three verses.

सहयज्ञाः प्रजाः सृष्ट्वा पुरोवाच प्रजापतिः।
अनेन प्रसविष्यध्वमेष वोऽस्त्विष्टकामधुक्॥ १०॥
देवान्भावयतानेन ते देवा भावयन्तु वः।
परस्परं भावयन्तः श्रेयः परमवाप्स्यथ॥ ११॥

sahayajñāḥ prajāḥ sṛṣṭvā purovāca prajāpatiḥ
anena prasaviṣyadhvameṣa vo'stviṣṭakāmadhuk
devānbhāvayatānena te devā bhāvayantu vaḥ
parasparaṁ bhāvayantaḥ śreyaḥ paramavāpsyatha

At the beginning, when the creator (Prajāpati) created living beings with sacrifice (Yajña) and said, "By this shall you propagate; let this fulfil all your requirements for the sacrifice (yajña)." By this gratify the gods and let the gods foster you, these caring for each other selflessly through your duties, you shall attain to the supreme good. 10-11

Comment:—

'Sahayajñāḥ prajāḥ sṛṣṭvā purovāca prajāpatiḥ'—One, who creates beings or things etc., it becomes his duty to preserve them. Brahmā is the creator and Lord of creation and so he always thinks of the preservation and salvation of creation. Thus, he is known as 'Prajāpati' (The Lord of creation).

At the beginning of creation Brahmā, the creator, created man by providing him with power for performing actions and also bestowed upon him discrimination.* The right use of desirable and undesirable circumstances, leads to salvation. Therefore, the creator bestowed upon mankind discrimination, in order to enable them to make the right use of the favourable and unfavourable circumstances.

Beasts, birds and trees etc., even without having the power of discrimination, naturally do good to others; but by God's grace, special power of discrimination has been bestowed upon mankind. So if a man does not perform forbidden actions, by attaching importance to his discrimination, naturally actions for the welfare of others are performed by him.

Though the term 'prajā' (creation) stands for gods, sages, manes, mankind and other beings (beasts, birds and trees etc.,) yet mankind is particularly, responsible to rear all beings. Therefore, here the term 'prajāḥ' stands for mankind.

The Discipline of Action (Karmayoga) has been functioning from time immemorial. In the third verse of the fourth chapter, also the Lord by the term 'purātanaḥ' declares that the same ancient Yoga has been taught to Arjuna by Him, which was lost to the world by a long lapse of time. The same fact has been pointed out here in this verse, in a different way by the term 'purā' (at the beginning) by declaring, "Not only I, but also Brahmā, at the beginning of creation, having created men ordered them to follow the Discipline of Action." It means that, this Discipline of Action has been going on from time immemorial. It is nothing new.

* Brahmā, the creator creates mankind under the instruction of God and with His power. So in fact God is the real creator of creation (Gītā 4/13;17/23).

In the fourth chapter (from the twenty-fourth to the thirtieth verses), all the sacrifices for God-realization through wealth, austerities, Yoga (spiritual exercise), vital force etc., have been described. Generally the term 'yajña' is taken as oblation, or sacrifice. But in the Gītā, the term stands for all the prescribed actions as laid down in the scriptures. All the duties performed according to one's caste, order of life, religion, nature, time and circumstances etc., are included in the term 'yajña'. Actions performed for the welfare of others, are also included in yajña (sacrifice). It is a man's responsibility, to perform such a sacrifice (duty).

'Anena prasaviṣyadhvameṣa vo'stviṣṭakāmadhuk'— Brahmā, the creator says to mankind, "By the performance of duty shall you propagate and by doing so you shall get all the requisites necessary for performing your duty."

Arjuna was not willing to perform his duty. Therefore, Lord Kṛṣṇa says to him that he should learn the lesson of performing his duty, from the creator's words. By performing his duty for the welfare of others, he would progress here, as well as hereafter.

Performance of actions in a disinterested way, leads to salvation, while performance with a selfish motive, leads to bondage. Here, is explained the topic of performance of duty, without having any desire for fruit. Therefore, the term 'iṣṭakāma' does not stand for the desired material, it stands for the required material for sacrifice (duty).*

* In the preceding verse Lord Kṛṣṇa declared, "The world is bound by actions other than those performed for the sake of sacrifice i.e., by actions performed with the desire for fruit." Further in the thirteenth verse He declares, "Those sinful ones who cook food for their own sake i.e., perform actions for fruit, verily eat sin." Thus in the preceding as well as the next verse there is mention of renunciation of the desire for fruit. So in the middle verses (tenth, eleventh and twelfth) also it should be interpreted as the renunciation of the desire for fruit. If the meaning of the term 'Iṣṭakāma' is taken as the desire for fruit, it does not fit this context, as such actions lead to bondage. So the term stands for the required material for sacrifice (performance of duty).

A Karmayogī (the follower of the Discipline of Action), is ever ready to render service or do good to others. Therefore, according to the ordinance of Brahmā, the creator, such a Karmayogī does not lack the required capacity and material for rendering service to others, and for the maintenance of his body. All this required material is easily available to him. According to the ordinance of Brahmā everybody has been offered this material, in order to enable him to perform his duty.

In fact, this human body has not been bestowed upon human beings to enjoy pleasures (Mānasa 7/44/1). Therefore, there is no mention in anyone of the scriptures, that man should enjoy worldly pleasures. Society also does not permit a person to enjoy pleasures freely. On the other hand the scriptures, as well as, society urge a man to bring comfort to others and to do good to them. It is mentioned in the scriptures, that a father should foster his son, but it is not mentioned that he is authorized to expect service from his son. Similar is the case with others, such as a son and a wife etc.

A Karmayogī always wants to give but not to receive, because the desire for fruit, besides being a stumbling block to salvation, is an obstacle to receiving worldly things. This is everybody's experience, that no one wants to offer anything to a person who hankers after it. Therefore, Brahmā says, that a man can attain the supreme good (salvation) by performing his duty in a disinterested manner, without having any desire for reward.

In the expression 'devānbhāvayatānena' the term 'deva' denotes all beings, such as men, gods, sages and manes etc., because the aim of the striver, following the path of action, is to nurture every being. So Brahmā, the creator orders men to offer sacrifice, in the form of the performance of duty, in order to foster and nurture other people for their advancement. Each man devoted to his own duty, attains perfection viz., salvation (Gītā 18/45). Men are free in the performance of their duty; so they should make proper use of this freedom.

'Te devā bhāvayantu vaḥ'— Trees and plants etc., naturally bear flowers and fruits, but their growth is luxuriant if these are tended properly. Similarly, a man should perform his duty by nurturing and fostering the gods by offering worship and service to them. By doing so, he is sustained by the gods with timely rain etc. But when he does not perform his duty properly, the gods do not properly protect and so he has to face calamities, such as a deluge and drought etc.

'Parasparaṁ bhāvayantaḥ'—This expression should not be interpreted to mean that we should serve others only, if they serve us. It should mean, that we should perform our duty by serving others, without bothering about of what others do. He, who cares for the duties of other people, deviates from his own duty, and has a downfall. Moreover, it is beyond our power to force anyone, to perform his duty. We have to perform our duty of fostering others and doing good to them, to the best of our resources, such as intellect, power, time and material etc. In that way, our affinity for the insentient (matter), will be totally renounced.

We have to serve all our relatives, such as parents, wife, sons, brothers, brother's wives etc., in a disinterested way by regarding service as our obligatory duty to them according to the scriptural injunctions. We are born, to repay our debt by serving, because we are indebted to them. It is an error on our part, if we expect any reward from them or lay claim to them. We have to serve all beings, but the first preference should be given to those kith and kin, who have a claim on our service.

It is an accepted fact that the body, senses, mind, intellect and possessions are neither ours nor for us. If we sincerely perform our respective duties, we will add immensely, to the welfare of the world.

A Vital Fact Pertaining to Duty and Right

In the Discipline of Action a striver by performing his duty, safeguards the rights of others. It is the duty of a son to serve his parents, and the parents have a right to such service.What is the right of others, is our duty. Therefore, every person should perform his duty, in order to safeguard the rights of others, without paying heed to whether they perform their duty or not. A man deviates from his duty by thinking of the duty of others and then has a downfall. Nowadays, in families and society at large, disquietude, conflict, friction and disorder etc., are rampant. The root cause is, that people demand their rights but they do not perform their duty. Therefore, Brahmā, the creator preaches to the gods and men, that it is their duty to do good to each other.

'Śreyaḥ paramavāpsyatha'—Generally people hold that the statement, that the gods and men by fostering each other, shall attain the supreme good, is an exaggeration. But in fact, it is not so. If anyone is doubtful about it, he himself can translate this principle into practice and see the same result. When the trust-money is returned to the owner by a person, he has not the least affinity for that money, similarly when we utilize worldly things in rendering service to the world, our affinity for the world and worldly things, is renounced. As soon as, this affinity is renounced, supreme good is attained. Therefore, it is an error to take Brahmā's word, as an exaggeration.

So long as, a person performs actions for himself, he is bound by them, and his actions do not come to an end. But when he does nothing for himself, nothing remains to be done by him and he does not commit sin, because desire is the root of sins (Gītā 3/37). Therefore, a striver in order to attain supreme good (salvation), should perform his duty by renouncing attachment and the desire for fruit, according to the ordinance of the scriptures. By doing so, attainment of salvation is axiomatic.

Renunciation of one's desire, leads to the welfare of the entire world. He, who enjoys pleasures, being attached to them in order to satisfy his desire, performs an act of violence (downfall), for himself as well as for those who lack those materials because they are sad due to the shortage of those materials. Thus a pleasure-seeking person cannot escape sins. On the other hand, one gets peace from those people who follow the spiritual path, as everyone can lay equal claim to spiritual assets. Thus according to Brahmā, the creator, if a man performs his duty renouncing desire and attachment, he can attain the supreme good viz., salvation, without any doubt.

Here, attainment of the supreme good has been specially mentioned for human beings, rather than gods. The aim of the gods is not to attain salvation. But they offer rewards to men, according to their actions, provide required matter to them for performing actions and enjoy the reward for their good actions performed in the past. They do not provide the required matter disinterestedly. But, when even the vilest sinner can attain salvation; the gods can also attain salvation if they have a desire to do so. However generally, their aim is to enjoy the heavenly pleasures, so they have no desire to attain salvation.

Appendix—Man alone is qualified for performing new actions, while eighty-four lac forms of lives, life of gods and life of beings residing in hells, are the lives to reap the fruit of their past actions. Men with interested motives go to heaven in order to enjoy heavenly pleasures. Therefore the gods follow their responsibility and discharge their duty not disinterestedly. Therefore eligibility for salvation is only for men.

Salvation is innate while bondage is caused one. Human life is only to attain salvation. Therefore the person who discharges his duty, naturally attains salvation—'parasparaṁ bhāvayantaḥ śreyaḥ paramavāpsyatha.' For salvation no new work needs to be done, but whatever work a man does, if he does it for the welfare of others, by renouncing selfishness, egoism and the desire for fruit, it will lead him to salvation. Without disinterested motive, if a man performs his duty, he goes to higher regions such as heaven etc. The heaven which is attained by performing grand religious sacrifice, can be attained by a Kṣatriya just by discharging his duty of fighting in a war.

As Brahmājī has told the gods and men to do good to each other in selfless spirit through their duties, similarly it should be interpreted that the people of the four Varṇas (castes) should do good to each other. If the people of the four Varṇas (social orders) discharge their duty for the welfare of each other, it will lead them to salvation.

The entire universe has been created in the manner that there is nothing (object or action) for one's ownself but everything is only for others—'idaṁ brahmaṇe na mama'. For example a chaste wife is only for her husband, not for herself. A woman's organs appeal to a man, not to a woman. Similarly a man's organs appeal to a woman, not to a man. A mother's milk is only for the child, not for her own self and the child's activities are to please the mother, rather than to itself. Parents are for the good of their offspring and the offspring are for the good of their parents. The audience is meant for the speaker and the speaker is meant for the audience. It means that one should not derive pleasure (comfort) himself but should provide it to others. The universe has not been created to enjoy pleasures but to attain salvation.

The gods also by renouncing their selfishness, can do good to others. Therefore among gods also there have been sages such as Nārada etc. Though the Lord's ordinance does not deprive anyone of God-realization (salvation) but a man is predominantly and naturally eligible (qualified) for it.

Here a question may arise that we do good to others but others instead of doing good to us, do evil to us, then how will 'parasparaṁ bhāvayantaḥ' be applicable? The answer is that if we do good to others, others will not be able to do evil to us. They will have no power to do evil to us. Even if they do evil to us, they will repent for it afterwards and will lament for it. If they do evil to us; there will be many others to do good to us and to sympathize with us. In fact there is no ordinance anywhere to do evil to anyone. A man because of aversion does evil to others. 'Parasparaṁ bhāvayantaḥ' (service to each other selflessly through one's duty)—this applies to mankind. Without following it people are suffering pain.

इष्टान्भोगान्हि वो देवा दास्यन्ते यज्ञभाविताः ।
तैर्दत्तानप्रदायैभ्यो यो भुङ्क्ते स्तेन एव सः ॥ १२ ॥

iṣṭānbhogānhi vo devā dāsyante yajñabhāvitāḥ
tairdattānapradāyaibhyo yo bhuṅkte stena eva saḥ

Fostered by the sacrifice (yajña), the gods, will bestow upon you all the requisite necessary for performing your duty. He who relishes these, without using these in the service of others, is verily a thief. 12

Comment:—

'Iṣṭānbhogānhi vo devā dāsyante yajñabhāvitāḥ'—Here the term 'Iṣṭabhoga' does not stand for the desired objects because in the preceding (eleventh) verse there is mention of attaining the highest good and this verse in related to that verse. Secondly, as long as a man has desire, he can't attain the highest good. So here this term means that the gods will supply him all the required material for the performance of sacrifice (duty).

Here the expression 'Yajñabhāvitāḥ devāḥ' means that the gods provide the required material to men by regarding it as their right (responsibility). Men are indebted to them. So they have to perform sacrifice (duty).

'Tairdattānapradāyaibhyo yo bhuṅkte'—Brahmā used the

expression, 'Te devāḥ' for the gods, because before him they were men, not gods. But here the term 'Ebhyaḥ' stands for nearness. For God, everyone is near Him (Gītā 7/26). It proves that the holy words from Divine lips, begin here.

Here, the term 'Bhuṅkte' does not stand only for eating, but for enjoyment of all the objects (food, clothes, house and money etc.,) required for the maintenance of a body.

We owe this body to our parents, and it is they, who have fostered it. For our knowledge, we are grateful to our preceptors and sages. The gods have provided us with the material necessary for the performance of duty. The manes guide us, how to provide ourselves with comforts. Beasts, birds, trees and creeping vines etc., sacrifice themselves, in order to provide comfort to others and do good to them (though they are not aware of it). Thus, whatever material, strength, ability, rank, authority, wealth and property we possess, we owe it all, to others. So whatever we possess, should be devoted to the service of others.

The body, senses, mind and intellect etc., are not ours, these came from the world. So, if we want to enjoy worldly pleasures by regarding these as our own, they lead us to bondage. But if we perform our duty by utilizing these in rendering service to the other people, from whom we have received them, without expecting any reward, we can get rid of the bondage.

Generally, strivers think that if they render service to the worldly people, they would be attached to them and would get entangled in the world. But the Lord's gospel proves, that it is not service but desire, which leads to bondage. So, it is every man's duty, like the gods, to serve others and do good to them, according to his resources. The Lord and gods do not expect more from him.

'Stena eva saḥ'—Here, in the expression 'Saḥ stena' (he is a thief) the purpose of using the singular number is to emphasise the fact that, he, who without performing his duty, of giving the required objects (food, water, clothes etc.,) to others, enjoys them all alone, is a thief.

The person who without repaying the rightful due of others and enjoys the objects himself, is a thief. Thus a thief is, he who performs actions with a selfish motive in order to gain honour and praise etc. Such a person can never gain purity and peace of mind.

This body is neither different nor can be different from the world, because it is a fragment of the world. Therefore, if a person assumes the body as his, without accepting the world as his, this assumption gives birth to pairs of opposites such as attachment and aversion and also evil propensities such as pride, individuality and unevenness of mind etc. A striver following the path of action, gets rid of the pairs of opposites such as attachment and aversion etc., easily, because whatever such a striver does, he does for the welfare of the world. He even practises the spiritual discipline, not for his own salvation, but for the salvation of the entire world. The reason is, that if he regards his salvation different from the salvation of others, it means that he has unevenness of mind, which is a stumbling block to his spiritual progress. He, who uses the body, senses, mind and intellect etc., which he has received from the world, for his selfish motive, is dishonest.

An Important Fact Pertaining to Duty

According to Indian culture, a man's only aim is to attain salvation. Therefore, Brahmā, the creator, at the beginning of creation, urged men to perform their duty while fostering one another, without any selfish motive (Gītā 3/10).

Members of a family commit an error, that they perform actions under the influence of desire, mineness, attachment and selfishness etc. So they have to suffer here, as well as hereafter. They fall a prey to quarrel, fight, envy and jealousy etc., while hereafter, they have to reap the adverse fruit of the actions performed by them. When a person serves others in the hope of reward, he is attached to persons and things. This attachment leads him to bondage. A selfish man is not liked or praised by anyone. In a family, objects get concealed from a passionate and pleasure-seeking person. On the other hand, if a person serves others with all his resources, he attains salvation and is also praised, honoured, comforted and supplied things, even though he is unwilling to receive them. A Karmayogī has no desire to win honour or praise etc., because desires and pleasures bind him.

Desire for pleasure diverts a man from the performance of duty, and is conducive to his downfall. So a striver, following the path of action, should always think of doing good to others including the members of his family, without having any pride of doership. As a mother's milk is meant only for a child, similarly, whatever material a man possesses, is only for others. Therefore, a man should not regard his possessions as his own and for him. The possessions will perish but bondage in the form of attachment and feeling of mineness will prevail. So the Lord declares, that he who enjoys the objects, regarding these as his own, is a thief.

A man is indebted to the gods, sages, manes, birds beasts, trees and creeping plants etc., because it is in their nature to serve him and do good to him. Therefore, five kinds of sacrifice (for sages, for gods, for creatures, for manes and for men) have been prescribed in the scriptures. By this fivefold sacrifice (duty), he can satisfy all of them. Therefore, having shouldered this responsibility by making use of his freedom, he can attain to the supreme good.

The gods etc., do their duty. If men do not perform their duty, there is a commotion not only among the gods but in the entire universe. Consequently there are natural calamities such as a deluge, drought, earthquake and famine etc. The Lord in the Gītā (3/23-24) declares, "If ever, I did not engage Myself in action, unwearied, men in everyway, would follow My path and I should be the creator to disordered life as well as, of destruction of beings" (Gītā 3/23-24). As a whole bullock cart faces a series of jerks, when even a small portion of a wheel is damaged, similarly even if a single person deviates from his duty, he leaves an adverse effect on the entire universe. On the contrary, as the recovery of a diseased limb makes the whole body healthy, similarly the person who performs his duty sincerely and efficiently, does good to the entire universe.

Brahmā, the Creator, ordered both gods and men to perform their duty. The gods follow a certain code of conduct, but men ignore it due to their folly. They start laying a claim to the matter, which has been bestowed upon them for the welfare of others. Moreover, they have been endowed with freedom, so that by making proper use of it, they may be free from the bondage of actions, in which they have been placed in, since infinity. But, by misusing that freedom they get attached to actions and their fruit. Consequently, they get entangled and head for suffering in numberless future births. Therefore, men should serve all beings such as God, gods, sages, manes and men etc., with all the resources and possessions which have been bestowed upon them.

Question:—How will a Karmayogī keep his body and soul together, if everything is to be utilized in the service of others?

Answer:—In fact this question arises only, when a man assumes the identity of the self, with the body. A Karmayogī does not accept his affinity for the body. He regards the body as the world's and, therefore, serve the world with it. He has his eyes on the imperishable self, rather than on the perishable body. Only the person who is mindful of his body, can ask such a question.

As long as a person is eager to enjoy worldly pleasures, he is keen to remain alive and fears death. A Karmayogī has no desire for pleasures, all his actions are performed in order to render service to others, so he does not care, even to live alive. The question how he will maintain his body, does not arise in his mind. In fact he who performs his duty, disinterestedly for the welfare of the world is an asset to the world which provides for his living. In the domain of God when there is provision for the maintenance of the bodies of ordinary creatures, such as beasts, birds, insects, germs, trees and plants etc., whose lives are for the good of others, how is it possible that there will be no provision for the maintenance of the body of the striver who serves all beings, with all his resources including his body?

The preserver Lord by His grace, has equally bestowed upon beings the material required for the maintenance of their bodies. A mother is a living example to prove this fact. The mothers' breasts, where there is blood in abundance are filled with sweet and nourishing milk as soon as a baby is born. Whether it is through the grace of God or through fate, a man gets the things necessary for his living. So there is no need to worry about it. In the domain of God when there is a provision for the maintenance of the body of even the vilest sinner or a confirmed atheist, will there not be any provision for maintaining the body of a Karmayogī ? Therefore, it is futile to raise such a question.

Appendix—The term 'yajña bhāvitāḥ' means fostered, worshipped, enriched by sacrifice. Being in the middle world the man can foster all living beings who are living in the upper as well as the lower region. The man has been settled in the middle region so that he may do good to all. Therefore the man is qualified (eligible) for attaining salvation.

Link:—In the ninth verse, the Lord having declared that mankind is not bound by actions, which are performed for the sake of sacrifice, ordered Arjuna to perform action for that sake. The same order of the Lord was confirmed by Brahmā's word. Now in the next verse, He explains what the fruit of the performance and non-performance of sacrifice (duty) is.

यज्ञशिष्टाशिनः सन्तो मुच्यन्ते सर्वकिल्बिषैः।
भुञ्जते ते त्वघं पापा ये पचन्त्यात्मकारणात्॥ १३॥

yajñaśiṣṭāśinaḥ santo mucyante sarvakilbiṣaiḥ
bhuñjate te tvaghaṁ pāpā ye pacantyātmakāraṇāt

The righteous who eat the remnants of the sacrifice are released from all sins; but those sinful ones who cook food for themselves verily devour sin. 13

Comment:—

'Yajñaśiṣṭāśinaḥ santaḥ'—When duties are performed according to the scriptural injunctions, without any hope of reward, equanimity (in the form of a remnant of the sacrifice) is achieved. The main factor in the Discipline of Action is, that an action is performed only with the material which is received from the world. Therefore; an action is called 'Yajña' only if by it selfless service is rendered to the world. After performing sacrifice (action) the residue 'Yoga' (Equanimity) is, for oneself. This 'Yoga' (Equanimity) is the essence which has been called 'nectar' in the fourth chapter (4/31).

'Mucyante sarvakilbiṣaiḥ'—Here the term 'kilbiṣaiḥ' means sins viz., bondage. The Lord has used the adjective, 'sarva' (all), which means that having realized equanimity, a man is released from all bondage. All his actions performed in the past, (as stored and ripe ones) as well as those performed ones at present, melt away i.e., are reduced to nothing (Gītā 4/23).* When his actions have been reduced to nothing, he attains to the eternal Absolute (Gītā 4/31).

* When he has no desire, his stored actions of the past disappear. So long as the body is alive, desirable and undesirable circumstances appear according to the fortune, but he remains unaffected by them. Thus actions in the form of fortune also disappear. As far as the actions of the present are concerned, they are turned into inaction i.e., they don't bear any fruit because they are performed without any desire for fruit.

In the ninth verse of this chapter, the Lord declared, "mankind is bound by actions, other than those, performed for the sake of sacrifice." While in the twenty-third verse of the fourth chapter He declared, "All the actions of the man who works for the sake of sacrifice, are dissolved." The same fact has been pointed out here, in this verse. It means, that people who realize equanimity, the remnant of sacrifice, are liberated from all bondage. Not only the sinful actions, but also the virtuous actions which are performed, with the hope of fruit, are conducive to bondage. He who has attained equanimity as remnant of sacrifice, casts away both good (virtues) and evil (sins) (Gītā 2/50).

Now think over the root of bondage. The desire, that this should happen and that should not happen, is the root of bondage. Desire is the cause of all sins (Gītā 3/37). So it must be renounced.

In fact, desire has no independent existence of its own. It is born of a feeling of want in the self, while in the self (soul) no paucity, is ever possible. So the self has no desire. But a man's self by identifying itself with the unreal body etc., feels the missing objects for the body, as shortage in him, and thus has a desire for the unreal. He should realize that he (self) ever remains the same, while the worldly objects and actions appear and disappear, these are born and perish. So, how can the perishable fulfil the desire of the imperishable? Therefore, it is a folly to hanker after those sense-objects. They cannot make up the deficiency. If a serious and proper thought, is given to this point, desires can be wiped out easily.

When a striver renders service with his body and things etc., without regarding these as his and for him, his affinity with the body and things etc., is renounced and he realizes the real self. Then, he feels no want. Such a man is liberated from the bondage of the world, while he is alive.

'Ye pacantyātmakāraṇāt'—All kind of desire, selfishness, attachment etc., are included in the expression 'ātmakāraṇāt' (for their own sake). The more selfish a man is, the greater a sinner he is.

Here the term 'pacanti' denotes, all the mundane actions such as eating, drinking, walking, sitting and so on. Whatever action a selfish man performs, either for himself or for others, performs only for himself. On the other hand, a striver who, having renounced selfish motives while performing his duty, works for others only, even when he appears to work for himself. He, who uses the objects which he has received from the world for his own enjoyment, actually cooks food for his own sake. It is a great sin to regard the body, a fragment of the world, as one's own and for one's own self. But he who without, regarding the body as his own, supplies necessities such as food, water and clothes etc., to it, and does not allow it to be lazy, heedless and pleasure-seeking, renders service to it and becomes free from the feeling of mineness and attachment to it.

Man himself, has to reap the fruit of actions performed by him. But his actions affect the entire world. He who performs actions for himself, deviates from his duty. That deviation results in calamities such as famines, epidemics and deaths etc., in a country. So, it is proper on the part of a man, that he should do nothing for himself, should regard nothing as his own and should desire nothing for himself.

He who expects the perishable fruit of actions, is also like those who cook food, for their own sake. So the Lord in the first verse of the sixth chapter, declares that a Karmayogī should perform his allotted duty without depending on the fruit of actions. When a man totally renounces dependence on the fruit of action, he does nothing for himself and thus gets estahlished in Yoga.

'Bhuñjate te tvaghaṁ pāpā'—The Lord condemns the sinful ones, who perform actions for themselves. Such persons store so many sins which are not exhausted even after suffering tortures in hells and eighty-four lac forms of lives, but their sinful actions remain as stored actions (sañcita karma). Human life is such a marvellous field in which, as we sow so shall we reap for many births to come*. Therefore, a man must resolve not to commit sins in future i.e., must not perform actions for himself. Such a resolution means a great power. The fact is, that all the sins of a man who resolves to follow the spiritual path, cease to be committed by him.

Appendix—The body, ability, rank (position), authority, knowledge and power etc., which a man possesses, have been obtained and will be lost. Therefore they are not ours and are not for us, but they are for rendering service to others. Our Indian culture is summed up in this principle. As all the organs of the body are for the welfare of the body, so all the people of the world are for the welfare of the world. A man may be of any country, guise, Varṇa (social order), āśrama (stage of life) etc., may easily attain salvation by rendering service to others through his actions.

Whatever characteristic we have, is for others, not for us. If all the people follow this idea, no one will remain bound but all will become liberated souls. If you use the things which you have received from the world is the service of others, what have you spent of your own? It leads you to salvation free of cost. Besides this, nothing needs to be done for salvation. We are responsible to spend only whatever we possess, we have no responsibility to spend more than that. A man can't do more than that. If we spend the things, ability and strength etc., completely in rendering service, we shall attain complete salvation.

In fact the body is useful only for the world, not for one's own self because the body is not for us at all. The body is

* In fact this human birth is the first as well as the last birth of all births. If a man realizes God, it is the last birth. But if he does not attain God-realization, it is the first one of the infinite births.

needed in order to do some action. If nothing is to be done, then what is the need of the body? Therefore to do any action for one's own self with this body, is a flaw. We can't do anything for the self with the thing which we have received, but with that we can serve the world. The body is a fragment of the world; therefore whatever will be done with it, will be only for the world. The body-senses-mind-intellect can't go beyond the world, they can't be separated from the world. Therefore performance of actions for one's own self, is not human nature but it is demoniac and devilish nature. In fact a man is only a human being in the real sense, who does actions for the welfare of others. He who performs actions for one's own pleasure, verily devours sin viz., ever remains sad, while those who work for the welfare of others, are released from all sins viz., become happy forever—'yajñaśiṣṭāmṛtabhujo yānti brahma sanātanam' (Gītā 4/31).

Link:— Arjuna puts the question to Lord Kṛṣṇa, "Why do You urge me to perform this savage deed?" In response to his question, the Lord having given several reasons, propounds the necessity of performing sacrifice (duty) in order to maintain the world order, in the next two verses.

अन्नाद्भवन्ति भूतानि पर्जन्यादन्नसम्भवः।
यज्ञाद्भवति पर्जन्यो यज्ञः कर्मसमुद्भवः॥ १४॥
कर्म ब्रह्मोद्भवं विद्धि ब्रह्माक्षरसमुद्भवम्।
तस्मात्सर्वगतं ब्रह्म नित्यं यज्ञे प्रतिष्ठितम्॥ १५॥

annādbhavanti bhūtāni parjanyādannasambhavaḥ
yajñādbhavati parjanyo yajñaḥ karmasamudbhavaḥ
karma brahmodbhavaṁ viddhi brahmākṣarasamudbhavam
tasmātsarvagataṁ brahma nityaṁ yajñe pratiṣṭhitam

From food, creatures come into being; from rain, food is produced; from sacrifice (yajña) comes rain and sacrifice is born

of action. Know that, action has its origin in Brahma (the Veda) and Brahma springs from the Imperishable. Therefore, the all-pervading Infinite (God) ever vests in sacrifice (yajña). 14-15

Comment:—

'Annādbhavanti bhūtāni'—'Anna' stands for the articles of food which are eaten to nourish the body. Food is the cause of birth, growth and nourishment of living beings. Soil is the food for insects which depend on it for its life. All beings such as men, birds, beasts, trees and plants etc., grow from food and nourished with it.

'Parjanyādannasambhavaḥ'—All the articles of food are brought about by rain. Foliage and corn are produced by rain (water). Soil is also created through water only. The necessities of life such as food, clothes and shelter etc., somehow or the other, have affinity with water and rain is the basis of water.

'Yajñādbhavati parjanyaḥ'— Generally the term 'yajña' stands for offering of oblations to sacred fire. But here according to the gospel of the Gītā and in the context of Karmayoga, it denotes performance of all duties such as oblation, charity and penance etc. In sacrifice, importance is attached to renunciation or relinquishment. In oblation one has to offer (renounce) food and purified butter etc., in penance he has to renounce pleasure and in performing his duty, he has to renounce selfishness and comfort etc.

In Bṛhadāraṇyaka Upaniṣad, there is an anecdote. The creator Brahmā having created the gods, men and demons, expounded on the letter 'D'. Men because of their mentality of hoarding, took it as, 'Dāna' (Charity), the gods because of their luxuriant pleasures took it as, 'Damana' (self-control) and demons because of their violent nature took it as 'Dayā' (Mercy). Thus the aim of his preaching was to inspire them, to do good to others. The thundering of cloud which makes a 'D D D' sound, reminds us of Brahmā's preaching (charity, self-control and mercy), as our duty (Bṛhadāraṇyaka 5/2/ 1—3).

How would it rain through the performance of duty?

Example is better than precept. 'Whatever a great man does, the same is done by others' (Gītā 3/21). If men perform their duty, the gods will also perform their duty by nurturing men through rain (Gītā 3/11). In this connection, there is an interesting anecdote. Four farmers, in the rainy season considering it their duty, started to plough their field even without rain. The peacocks saw them performing their duty. So to perform their duty they began to make their calls. Hearing their sound, the clouds performed their duty by thundering. Having heard the thunder, Indra, the lord of the gods, also thought of performing his duty, through a rainfall.

'Yajñaḥ karmasamudbhavaḥ'—All the actions performed disinterestedly as laid down in the scriptures, are included in the term 'Yajña'. To offer oblation to the sacred fire, is 'Yajña' (Duty) of a celibate. For women performance of domestic duties such as cooking and serving her husband and other members, is 'Yajña'. Prescription of medicines for a patient is 'Yajña', for a physician. Similarly, study by students, and business by the businessmen, without expecting any reward, done for the welfare of others, can be regarded as 'Yajña' performed by them. Thus actions performed according to one's caste, order of life and circumstances, in accordance with the ordinance of the scriptures, without expecting any fruit, are called 'Yajña'. Whatever type of Yajña it may be, it is performed through action only.

A physician having removed harmfulness of a poison prescribes it to his patients. This purified poison like nectar, cures deadly diseases. Similarly, when a striver performs actions by purifying them of the poison of desires, attachment, selfishness and pride etc., these like nectar cure him of the deadly disease of the cycle of birth and death. Such actions are also called 'Yajña'.

'Karma brahmodbhavaṁ viddhi'— The methods of performance of various kinds of sacrifices, are known from the Vedas (Gītā 4/32). So it has been said, that action has its origin in the Veda. Here the term 'Veda' stands for the four Vedas—Ṛk, Yajus, Sāma and Atharva, jurisprudence, Purāṇa (18 very old historical records) and epics such as the Rāmāyaṇa and the Mahābhārata etc., and also other scriptures.

'Brahmākṣarasamudbhavam'—Here the term 'Brahma' stands for the Veda. The Veda springs from the Imperishable God (Gītā 17/23). Thus God is the root of all.

The Veda springs from the Imperishable God. The Veda explains the methods of the performance of duty. Men carries out the duty methodically. Sacrifice is performed by the fulfilment of duty. Rain arises from sacrifice. Food is produced from rain. Creatures come into being from food. Out of those creatures men perform sacrifice by accomplishing their duty*. Thus the wheel of creation goes on.

'Tasmātsarvagataṁ brahma nityaṁ yajñe pratiṣṭhitam'—Here, the term 'Brahma', stands for the Imperishable God (Who is endowed with attributes and is formless). The all-pervading God, specially vests in sacrifice (duty). It means that God remains present in duty performed without any hope for reward. Therefore, strivers who seek God-realization can realize Him easily by performing their duty (Gītā 18/46).

Question:—How does the all-pervading God remain manifest only in sacrifice? Does He not remain present at other places?

Answer:—God always pervades equally, everywhere. He is not limited and impermanent. Therefore, He is called omnipresent. He is available in sacrifice, this means that He is manifest in sacrifice. As water exists everywhere under the earth, but it is

* Yajña (Sacrifice) (actions for the welfare of others) is naturally performed by all moving and unmoving beings except human being. But it is only man who can apply his mind in its performance because he has got ability and right to do so.

available in a well and as the water of the pipe is available only through the tap or the hole, similarly the all-pervading God specially manifests in sacrifice.

Performance of actions for one's own self and assumption of affinity for the insentient body etc., are the obstacles to God-realization. These obstacles are removed, when duty is performed without hoping for any reward, and for the welfare of others and then God, Who is ever attained, is naturally realized. Therefore, Lord Kṛṣṇa is urging Arjuna to perform his duty, by offering several reasons and examples.

Link:—In order to maintain the world order, it is man's responsibility to perform his duty. Therefore, the Lord in the next verse criticizes a man who does not perform his duty.

एवं प्रवर्तितं चक्रं नानुवर्तयतीह यः।
अघायुरिन्द्रियारामो मोघं पार्थ स जीवति॥ १६॥

evaṁ pravartitaṁ cakraṁ nānuvartayatīha yaḥ
aghāyurindriyārāmo moghaṁ pārtha sa jīvati

O Pārtha, he who does not, in this world, follow the cycle thus set in to motion, is sinful, and sensual desires, and lives in vain. 16

Comment:—

[Here the Lord, while concluding the topic started in the ninth verse, addresses Arjuna as 'Pārtha' to remind him that he is the son of Pṛthā (Kuntī) who performed her duty even by suffering troubles throughout her life. So he should also perform his duty. In fact the action which he was regarding as terrible, was not really terrible, it was a sacrifice (duty). He who performs his duty, follows the wheel of creation, while he who does not perform his duty, does not follow this cycle.]

'Evaṁ pravartitaṁ cakraṁ nānuvartayatīha yaḥ'—As a broken fragment of the wheel of a chariot, gives a series of jerks to the charioteer, as well as to the driver, similarly a man who does not follow the wheel of creation, creates an obstacle in the smooth running of that wheel.

As the limbs and body, have close affinity, so have man and the world. When a man performs his duty by renouncing desire, feeling of 'mine', attachment and egoism etc., he gratifies the entire creation.

'Indriyārāmaḥ'—Sensual is he, who enjoys the worldly objects through his senses, by having desire and being attached to the sense-objects. Such a person is inferior even to beasts, because beasts instead of performing sinful actions, are purified by receiving the fruit of their sins of the past. But a man committing new sins, has a downfall and by creating disturbance in the wheel of creation, hurts the entire creation.

'Aghāyuḥ'—The life of such a man is sinful, because he who wants to enjoy sensual pleasures, cannot escape sin. The person who hankers after selfishness, pride, pleasures and prosperity, causes suffering to others and thus he is of a sinful nature. Saint Tulasīdāsa in the Rāmacaritamānasa declares, "Those who are malicious, engrossed in adultery, slanderous and hanker after the riches of others, are vile and sinful devils in human forms" (7/39).

'Moghaṁ pārtha sa jīvati'—The Lord condemns such a person who does not perform his duty by saying, that such a person lives in vain i.e., it will be better if he were dead. If such a man dies, people will not have to suffer without him. During the exile of Lord Rāma, the wild tribes said, that if they did not steal anyone's clothes and utensils, it meant that they were rendering service to Him (Mānasa 2/251/2). Similarly, such persons who do not perform their duty, should not at least disturb the wheel of creation. By doing so they could render service to creation.

Such a person who does not follow the cycle of creation, has been said to be a thief (3/12), feeding on sin (3/13) and a sinful and sensual person, who lives in vain by this verse.

Gosvāmī Tulasīdāsa also in the Rāmacaritamānasa, declares about such a person—His envy is like fire, anger like that of the god of death, sins and evils are like the treasure of the god of wealth and he does evil to others like the comet. It is good if such a person like Kumbhakarṇa goes on sleeping for a long time (1/4/3).

Appendix—The description, which has been given from the ninth to this verse, means only to render selfless service to others.

Link:—The Lord has condemned the person who does not perform his duty, in order to renounce his affinity with the world, in the preceding verse. Now, in the next two verses, He talks about the enlightened soul, who having performed his duty, has renounced affinity for the world.

यस्त्वात्मरतिरेव स्यादात्मतृप्तश्च मानवः।
आत्मन्येव च सन्तुष्टस्तस्य कार्यं न विद्यते॥ १७॥

yastvātmaratireva syādātmatṛptaśca mānavaḥ
ātmanyeva ca santuṣṭastasya kāryaṁ na vidyate

But, for a person who takes delight only in the self, is satisfied with the self and content in the self alone, verily there is no further work to be done by him. 17

Comment:—

'Yastvātmaratireva syādātmatṛptaśca mānavaḥ ātmanyeva ca santuṣṭastasya'—Here the term 'tu' (but) has been used to differentiate, a person, who has become enlightened having performed his duty, from the person who does not perform his duty, as described in the preceding verse.

So long as a person assumes his affinity for the world, he rejoices in the sensual pleasures, wife, sons and family, remains satisfied with food and is content in riches. But they cannot provide him with perfect and lasting rejoicing, satisfaction and contentment, because the world is ever-changing, insentient and perishable while the self is uniform, sentient and imperishable. So how can the self be satisfied and be contented with the world, when there is not even the least affinity between the two?

A man cannot take delight in the world constantly. A newly married couple take delight in each other but that joy or attraction does not continue to exist after the birth of one or two babies. Sometimes, an old woman is heard saying, about her husband, "It is good, if the old man dies." The satisfaction provided by food and riches etc., is momentary and temporary, also.

In fact, the worldly objects cannot provide lasting delight, satisfaction and contentment to man. If these had provided real delight, satisfaction and contentment, man would have never felt their absence. In the self, delight, satisfaction and contentment naturally exist because the self is real and the real never ceases to be (Gītā 2/16). As the real always exists, there is no deficiency in it and without that no desire is born. So there is no desire in the self. But when the self by an error assumes its affinity with the world, it seeks delight, satisfaction and contentment in the world, and has a desire for the worldly objects. When one desire is satisfied and the second is not born, at that time, he remains free from any desire and that state of freedom provides him with delight. But, man by error thinks that he has received delight, satisfaction and contentment by the satisfaction of desire. Had he got that delight by the satisfaction of desire, that delight should have continued unabated and there would have been no more desire for that object again. In fact, it does not happen so. When one desire is satisfied, another new desire is born and the process continues. When one has desire, it means he feels a deficiency and when he receives the desired object, he becomes a slave to it. Thus a man with a desire ever remains sad.

Here, a point needs attention. A striver rightly thinks that lack of desire is the root of delight, while desire is the root of sorrows. But the people attached to the world think otherwise. They think that they get delight in having received objects or things and they are, sad without them. If they realize the reality like the strivers, they could also get rid of desires.

People, who perform actions with the expectation of fruit, deserve, to follow the Discipline of Action (Śrīmadbhāgavata 11/20/7). Such people derive joy, satisfaction and contentment out of the world. So the Lord, having described such persons who perform actions without the desire, for their fruit declares that such strivers, unlike the worldly people, are delighted, contented and satisfied in the self (Gītā 2/55).

In fact delight, satisfaction and contentment are not different from each other, yet they seem to be different, because of a person's affinity for the world. As soon as this affinity is renounced, an enlightened soul is delighted, satisfied and contented in the self, their difference which seemed to exist, disappears.

The Lord in this verse, has used the terms 'eva' (Only) and 'Ca' (And) twice, while further in the eighteenth verse, He has used these terms, once. That shows, that a Karmayogī (One who follows the Discipline of Action) does not suffer a shortage of delight, satisfaction and contentment and needs no greater bliss than this one (Gītā 6/22).

'Tasya kāryaṁ na vidyate'—The aim of the performance of actions for a man, is to attain salvation or God-realization. When this aim is achieved by anyone following the Disciplines of Actions, Knowledge or Devotion, nothing remains to be done, known and acquired by him and that is the supreme achievement of a human life.

In the self, there is no shortage. But so long as a man because of his affinity for the world, feels shortage in him (self) he performs actions for himself by regarding the body as 'I' and

'Mine'. In that case there remains some work which needs to be done by him. But when he, instead of performing the actions for himself, performs them for others, such as body, senses, mind, intellect, life-breath, parents, wife, sons, family, society, country and the world, his affinity for the world is renounced. When his affinity for the world is completely renounced, nothing remains to be done by him, because there is no activity then in the self. Whatever action is performed, that is performed because of the affinity for the world, by worldly things. Therefore, work is to be done by those, who have affinity for the world.

An action is performed, when there is desire to acquire something, and desire is born of want. The enlightened souls have no want, so they have to do nothing.

When through the Discipline of Action, an enlightened soul is delighted, satisfied and contented in the self, and nothing remains to be done, known and acquired by him, he transcends prescription and prohibition. Though such a God-realized soul, rises above the ordinance of the scriptures, yet his actions are in accordance with the scriptural injunctions, and these are examples for others.

The expression 'Tasya kāryam na vidyate', does not mean that no action is performed by that God-realized soul. But it means that though no work remains to be done by him, actions are performed by him, for the welfare of others. As the activities such as lowering and raising of eyelids, breathing and digestion etc., go on automatically, similarly, all exemplary activities prescribed by the scriptures are automatically performed, by the enlightened soul, (as he has no sense of doership).

Appendix—A Karmayogī performs all actions with a selfless motive to serve the world. As the Ganges is worshipped with Ganges-water; similarly by applying the body, senses, mind, intellect and ego, which he has received from the world, in rendering service to the world, the connection with the body and the world is snapped off and the Self or Divinity is revealed. Therefore he takes delight and is gratified and is contented in the Self alone.

The worldly injunction and prohibition—both are indeed prohibition (negation) because these two can't last (remain). A Karmayogī having renounced affinity for the world rises above all prescriptions and prohibitions. 'Tasya kāryaṁ na vidyate' (He has no duty to perform).

नैव तस्य कृतेनार्थो नाकृतेनेह कश्चन।
न चास्य सर्वभूतेषु कश्चिदर्थव्यपाश्रयः॥ १८॥

naiva tasya kṛtenārtho nākṛteneha kaścana
na cāsya sarvabhūteṣu kaścidarthavyapāśrayaḥ

For him in this world, there is no gain whatsoever, in the performance of an action or its non-performance, nor does he have any self-interest in other beings. 18

Comment:—

'Naiva tasya kṛtenārthaḥ'—Everyone has a tendency to do some work or the other, for himself. So long as a man has the tendency to acquire worldly things, some work remains to be done by him. He is bound by the desire of acquiring something or the other. Performance of duty is inevitable in order to get rid of that desire.

Actions are performed in two ways—either in order to satisfy desire or to get rid of desire. Common men work in order to satisfy their desires, while a Karmayogī performs actions, in order to get rid of desires. Therefore, an enlightened soul being free from desire, has not the least affinity for the performance of duty. Actions are performed by him, automatically without any selfish motive, for the welfare of the entire creation.

Such a God-realized soul realizes that all the worldly objects, body, senses, mind and intellect etc., are not his own, but these belong to the world.

So, these should be utilized for the world. This is, because no action can be performed without the help of the world. Apart from this, matter required for action, is also an offshoot of the world. It is in no way related to one's own self. Therefore, nothing is ours. The cosmos can never be meant for an individual. Here, lies the fault with man, that he tries to utilise the cosmic entity for his individual purposes. This generates unrest. If he utilises his body, senses, mind, intellect and matter etc., for universal use, he can get a state of quietude. This characteristic exists in an accomplished Karmayogī, that all his so-called body, senses, mind, intellect and matter etc., are utilised for the service of the entire world. Thus, he is totally unconcerned about his bodily activities. Even then, a great person instinctively performs excellent deeds, ideal for the generality of men. Thus, by utilizing these for the world, he attains great peace and his actions are exemplary.

'Nākṛteneha kaścana'—He, who assumes his affinity for the body, senses, mind and intellect etc., and remains inclined towards indolence and sloth, does not want to perform actions, because he wants to enjoy pleasure which arises from sleep, indolence and sloth, and which is declared to be of the nature of ignorance (Gītā 18/39). But, how can a great soul, who transcends even the Sāttvika happiness, be inclined towards pleasure, arising out of ignorance? When he has not even the least affinity for body etc., how can he be inclined towards indolence and heedlessness etc.?

A Vital Fact

Generally strivers attach importance to actionlessness. They want to place themselves in trance (Samādhi) and, being completely unattached with actions, so that no thoughts are left to act. This is an excellent and useful thing no doubt, but not as a principle (final truth). Though inaction is superior to action, yet it is not the goal.

Inclination and abstention, both are within the realm of nature. Upto the 'Nirvikalpa' trance, every stage is within the reign of prakṛti, because deviation is possible even at this stage. Every action takes place in prakṛti. Even a deviation from trance involves action and without action such deviation is impossible. Therefore like walking, speaking, laughing and hearing etc., sleeping, sitting, standing, keeping quiet, fainting and going into a trance, also are actions. The real essence (conscious self) is free from inclination and abstention both. The self, is an untainted illuminator of action and inaction both. When a person identifies the self with the body, actions are divided into two classes—performance and non-performance. But in fact, both of these belong to the same class. Till attachment to the body persists, non-performance of an action, is also an action. As 'go' is a verb so 'stand' is also a verb and both involve activity, though in the former the activity is clearly seen, while in the latter it is not apparent.

The question of performance or non-performance of actions, arises only when a man has affinity with a body. Unless such affinity is there, no action is possible.

An enlightened soul who renounces his total affinity for nature, and its evolutes, (the insentient matter), realizes the self, which transcends both activity and non-activity. Therefore, a striver should renounce his affinity for matter (egoism and attachment to the body). The self (tattva) ever remains the same, as always.

'Na cāsya sarvabhūteṣu kaścidarthavyapāśrayaḥ'—When a great soul has not the least selfish affinity for a body and the world, all his actions are automatically performed for the welfare of others. As limbs of a body are ever engaged in doing good for the body, the body (a fragment of the world) of that enlightened soul, ever remains engaged in doing good to the world. Moreover, he has not the least pride or desire for fruit or selfish motive, like a hand when it washes the face.

In the preceding verse, the Lord declared that there exists no work that needs to be done by a God-realized soul. In order to explain the reason, the Lord mentions three factors—(1) Such a soul has no interest in what is done. (2) He has no interest in what is not done. (3) He does not depend on anything or creature for any interest of his.

In fact, the self has no interest in what is done or what is not done and has no affinity with, either any being or thing because no action is performed by the self. All actions are performed, only when the self assumes its affinity for nature, and the things born of nature. Therefore, no action is to be performed for the self.

So long as a man has a desire to do, to acquire and to live, and he is afraid of death, he has got to perform actions. But when he renounces this desire and is not afraid of death, he has not to perform action, but action (duty) is automatically performed by him. One who is susceptible to deviation from duty needs advice.

An Important Fact

In the Gītā, Lord Kṛṣṇa explains the marks of a God-realized soul according to the Discipline, which they follow as strivers. The same description has been given here, in the seventeenth and the eighteenth verses.

The topic of the Discipline of Action, begins from the thirty-ninth verse of the second chapter, but the gist has been explained in the forty-seventh verse of the second chapter, when the Lord declares it in four stages:—

(1) Thy right is to work only.

(2) Have no desire for its fruit.

(3) Do not be the cause of the fruit of action.

(4) And let thy attachment be not towards inaction.

In this verse (3/18) is the description of a God-realized soul, who has attained perfection through Karmayoga, as described in the previous verse. Whatever, has been said there, (in 2/47) in the second and the third point for the striver, the same has been said, in the second half of this verse, for the God-realized soul, that he has no affinity for any creature or thing. Similarly, whatever has been stated in the first and the fourth point for the striver, the same has been said, in the first half of this verse for a God-realized soul, that he has no interest in what is done or what is not done. Thus, in the verses seventeenth and eighteenth, the description of the marks of a God-realized soul, who has realized Him, through the Discipline of Action, has been given.

According to the Discipline of Action, the eighteenth verse should have preceded the seventeenth verse, because when a God-realized soul, has no interest in what is done or what is not done, and when he does not depend on any creature for any interest of his, he gets joy, satisfaction and contentment in his own self. But, in the sixteenth verse the Lord declared, "He who does not perform his duty, lives in vain." Therefore, in the seventeenth verse by using the expression 'Yaḥ tu' (who but), the Lord explains that if a God-realized soul, does not perform his duty, he does not live in vain, but his life is very useful, as he has attained the aim of human life. Therefore, nothing remains to be done by him.

The state in which nothing remains to be done, can be attained even by a common man, by performing his duty, efficiently without expecting any reward, because everyone deserves to attain Him. The practice of Karmayoga, can be performed in all circumstances. The desire for sensual pleasure, is the main obstacle to the performance of one's duty. So, if a striver wipes out this desire for pleasure by serving others, without having any selfish motive, he can attain supreme peace by getting rid of all pains, and sorrows of life. As far as the supreme peace is concerned, everyone is equally deserving, to attain it, while it is not possible, for everyone to have worldly possessions in equal share.

Appendix—In the world 'performance of action' and 'non-performance of action' are related expressions. Therefore 'I have to do nothing'—this is also an action. But in Godhood 'inaction is natural and automatic. The reason is that the divine entity has nothing to do with action or inaction. Therefore a God-realized Karmayogī has neither any relation with a thing, nor with a person nor with an action—'yo'vatiṣṭhati neṅgate' (Gītā 14/23). From his view-point nothing exists except the divinity.

Link:—The Lord in the next verse explains, what a striver should do in order to attain the state of a God-realized soul, described in the preceding verse.

तस्मादसक्तः सततं कार्यं कर्म समाचर।
असक्तो ह्याचरन्कर्म परमाप्नोति पूरुषः॥ १९॥

tasmādasaktaḥ satataṁ kāryaṁ karma samācara
asakto hyācarankarma paramāpnoti pūruṣaḥ

Therefore, perform duty efficiently without attachment, for by actions without attachment, man attains the Supreme. 19

Comment:—

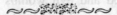

'Tasmādasaktaḥ satataṁ kāryaṁ karma samācara'—The term 'Tasmāt' (therefore) has been used to connect the preceding verse with this verse. In the preceding verse, the Lord declared that actions are performed by a God-realized soul, for the welfare of others though there is no need for him to perform these. Therefore, the Lord uses the term 'tasmāt', to make Arjuna to realize God, by performing his duty without expecting any reward. The reason is, that the self has no interest in what is done or what is not done. Actions are ever performed for others, not for the self. When a striver performs actions for others, his attachment to perform actions disappears, and he gets established in the self. He is attached to them, when he thinks "I am body", "The body is mine" and regards the perishable objects such as body etc., as significant.

It is attachment, not action, which leads to one's downfall. Being attached to the body, senses, mind, intellect and other mundane objects etc., a man performs actions, in order to derive pleasure out of them. This attachment for the materialistic objects etc., leads him to the cycle of birth and death. The Lord declares, "Attachment to the modes born of nature, is the cause of the birth of soul in good and evil wombs" (Gītā 13/21). When a striver performs actions without attachment, his affinity for the insentient (matter) is renounced.

All actions of a striver who performs them, being free from attachment, are automatically for the welfare of all creatures, while the person who is attached to mundane objects and actions etc., cannot do good to others.

So far, we have used mundane materials such as a body etc., for our own pleasure and prosperity. Therefore, we are indebted to the world. We can repay our debt by performing our duty for the welfare of the world. When we perform action for ourselves, instead of being free from debt, we run into debt, more and more. Therefore, we have to take birth in the world again and again, in order to free ourselves of debt. By performing actions for the welfare of others, we get out of the old debt and we cease to run into new debt, as we perform actions in a disinterested way. Thus, we are liberated from bondage.

An action cannot be performed constantly, but attachment remains constant. So the Lord by the expression "Satataṁ asaktaḥ" urges Arjuna, to be constantly free from attachment. A striver, should perform his duty, prescribed by the scriptures constantly without attachment. In fact attachment also does not remain constant. Even when the world itself is not constant, it is ever-changing how can its attachment remain constant? In spite of that, in the assumed ego, attachment seems to be there, constantly.

'Kāryam' viz., duty is that, which can be done and must be done. In other words, duty is action, which must be performed for the welfare of others, according to the ordinance of the scriptures and according to one's capacity, by renouncing one's selfish motive. In this way, duty is linked to the welfare of others.

Everyone has the freedom and capability to perform one's duty. It can be performed very easily. But it is because of heedlessness, indolence and desire for fruit, that its performance seems difficult. A man can perform his duty, independently under all circumstances. Attachment perishes through the performance of duty, while it enhances through the non-performance of duty. By performing duty for the welfare of others, we get rid of our present attachment and by not expecting any reward from them get rid of future attachment.

The term 'samācara' means, that the duty must be performed very carefully, enthusiastically, promptly and duly, so that the aim may be attained. If there is the least dereliction of duty, it creates a great hurdle in the path, of a Karmayogī. A man's duty according to his caste, order of life, nature and circumstances prescribed by the scriptures is 'sahaja karma' (innate duty). One should not give up one's innate duty, even though it may have flaws (Gītā 18/48), because by doing so, one does not incur sin (Gītā 18/47). So, the Lord seems to urge Arjuna, to perform his innate duty of waging war, because he is a Kṣatriya (a member of the warrior class), even though the act may seem terrible to him. An innate duty must be performed without attachment, as it leads to equanimity.

Something Noteworthy

When a being is born as a human being, he is provided

with all the matter, such as body, riches, property etc., and he has to leave behind all the materials here, when he departs. It proves that he has been granted this material in the same way, as a clerk is provided with the material in the office, so that he may work with it. But it does not mean, that it is his. As a clerk is paid for doing the office work, similarly a striver who performs actions for the world, his affinity for the world is renounced and he realizes his identity (unity) with God. This unity with God, is his reward.

This world is the field for practising spiritual discipline. Whatever material has been provided to us here, is only for practising spiritual practices, rather than for pleasure and prosperity. It is, neither ours nor for us. If and when, we gain our own objectives viz., the Supreme Bliss (God-realization), (Self-realization) nothing remains to be gained after that i.e., there remains no desire for anything else (Gītā 6/22). But we may acquire innumerable worldly things, the desire to acquire more, is never satisfied, it rather enhances.

When by error, a person accepts a thing as his own and for him he is attached to it. The Discipline of Action is an easy and good method, to wipe out this error. A Karmayogī, who without assuming a thing as his own and for him, uses it in order to render service to others, is easily liberated from the worldly bondage, as he performs actions for the world, by renouncing attachment, a feeling of 'mine' and desire etc., for the same. Thus the flow of his actions, is towards the world and he is liberated. On the other hand, a common person who performs actions with attachment, with feelings of 'mine' and desire etc., the flow of actions is towards him and so he is tied to these.

'Asakto hyācarankarma'—It is a man, who establishes a link with the world, and not the world with him. A striver should perform actions for the welfare of the world without attachment, having no desire for their fruit. His present affinity for the things and persons of the world is renounced, by rendering service to them, and with things and persons of the future by having no desire for these.

In a fair, volunteers render service to the public, without expecting any reward. So they sleep soundly without even remembering any person of the public. Similarly, a striver who serves others without expecting any return not ever honour and praise etc., does not remember them and is thus easily liberated from the worldly bondage.

In the Discipline of Action, actions are performed for the welfare of others, without any attachment. Attachment can be wiped out, only when actions are performed according to the scriptural injunctions (Mānasa 3/16/1). Attachment can never be wiped out by performing forbidden actions.

'Paramāpnoti pūruṣaḥ'—As in the thirty-fourth verse of the thirteenth chapter the Lord has mentioned attainment to the Supreme by the term 'param' (the supreme) for a Sāṅkhyayogī (follower of the Discipline of Knowledge), similarly, it has been mentioned here by the same term for a Karmayogī, (follower of the Discipline of Action). It means that a striver according to his taste, inclination and faith, attains God-realization, by anyone of the Disciplines of Action, Knowledge or Devotion (Gītā 5/4-5). God is, He Who pervades everywhere, everytime, Who is everyone's and is attainable to everyone, undoubtedly and automatically.

Question:—How can the pride of doership which is an obstacle to God-realization, be wiped out?

Answer:—Common people perform actions for themselves, thinking that they are the doers. But a Karmayogī thinks that whatever he has acquired from the world, is not his, but it is of the world. Therefore, with the body, senses, mind, intellect, money and material etc., which he has acquired from the world, he renders service to the world. Thus his pride of doership perishes.

A Karmayogī, does not perform actions, in order to enjoy their fruits. He regards, the body as a fragment of the world. Therefore, there is nothing special to be proud of, if the body renders service to the world, in the same way, as a hand is not proud of rendering a great service to the face, by washing it.

A man performs actions in order to achieve a goal. As soon as the action is over, he gets engrossed, in that goal. As a businessman starts business in order to earn money, but as soon as his transaction is over, he starts counting the money without even thinking of customers etc., who had come to buy articles from his shop. A worldly man, having a mundane aim, remains engrossed in the world but he cannot be identified with the world, in spite of doing so, because the world is kaleidoscopic and insentient, while the self is uniform and sentient. But the striver who performs actions having God-realization as his aim gets identified with God, (whether he realizes this fact or not), because both of these are uniform and sentient. In this state of identification, no question can arise regarding the pride of doership.

Actions have a beginning and an end. So a person who performs an action, also ceases to be a doer, as soon as the action ends. But being under an illusion, he regards himself as a doer, even when he does not perform any action. Thus by considering himself as a doer constantly, his pride of doership, instead of perishing, enhances. An orator, considers himself an orator even when he does not make a speech. He regards himself superior to the audience and wants the people to honour and serve him and to fulfil his necessities. But if he regards himself as an orator only, during the period of a speech and not afterwards, he will expect no reward from the audience, and thus his doership will merge in his aim.

As an eater regards himself as an eater, only when he eats food, a Karmayogī also regards himself as a doer, only when he performs actions and not at other times. Suppose a Karmayogī, delivers discourses and he has won high fame; in spite of that, if an occasion arises to hear a discourse, he can easily listen to it, without expecting any honour, respect and status, as now he considers himself a listener, not a speaker, without any superiority complex. He becomes a hearer or a speaker, according to the need of the moment. Thus his pride of doership does not remain constant. A thing which changes actually, does not exist. So how can a relationship with it remain constant? By thinking so, a striver comes to realize his egolessness.

An actor in a drama plays the role of Hariścandra, but while playings that role, he does not regard himself as a real Hariścandra. Similarly, a Karmayogī, while performing all actions according to the scriptural injunctions, does not regard himself, as a doer. He, like an actor, serves the world with the worldly things, without regarding these as his or for himself. Thus he has no pride of doership, in the least.

Similarly, he accepts his affinity for his kith and kin, while serving them, only in order to serve them. He performs his duty to the best of his capacity and resources, towards his wife, children and other members, even though they are ugly, hard-hearted and quarrelsome. Moreover, he thinks that his wife or children are not only his, but also of others. For example, his wife is her children's mother, her father's daughter, her brother's sister and so on. Thus, they have also a claim on her. Similar, is the case with other relatives such as father, sons and brothers etc. So a striver performs his duty efficiently, like an actor without thinking of the duty of others. By having the pride of doership, a man thinks of the duty of others and by thinking so, he deviates from a duty, while a Karmayogī does not accept his constant affinity for his caste, order of life, sect and circumstances etc., and so he performs his duty efficiently. A thing which is not constantly in existence, is for that matter, not in existence at all. Thus, the sense of doership of a Karmayogī automatically perishes.

A Vital Fact

A man has his identity with God, if he has no sense of doership unless he ignores the reality. As a swing while moving, stops still for a fraction of a second, at the rope end, in the same way, there is always the state of actionlessness (equanimity) after a swinging action ends and the second one begins. Secondly, if we perceive in the right perspective, we come to know that as the rope of the swing when it moves, remains straight, a man also remains in a state of equanimity, even while working. If he wants to realize this fact, he can do so, as soon as an action is over. In case a striver is ever careful, in this respect, he can realize equanimity or his identity with God, where there is no sense of doership.

In order to wipe out the pride of doership, a striver should distinguish the real which really exists, from the unreal (illusion) which seems to exist. The world which is changing always is illusory while the all-pervading Lord is real and He is automatically attainable to everyone—from Brahmā, the creator, to even an ant, equally.

The world which seems to exist, is every second getting destroyed. The senses, mind and intellect etc., with which the world is seen, reflect nothing but illusion. The all-pervading Lord Who ever exists, is always attainable to us. Therefore, in the Gītā it has been declared, "The unreal has no existence and the real never ceases to be" (2/16).

All the worldly objects and actions are nothing but an illusion. Actionlessness, exists at the beginning and the end, of every action. And this is a rule, that whatever is at the beginning and the end also remains in the middle. Therefore, actionlessness automatically exists, even when an action is going on. That actionless essence viz., the Sentient or God is the illuminator, of both actions and actionlessness and He, transcends the two.

It is because of our attachment (affinity) to the illusion (objects, actions and persons etc.,) that we cannot realize God. As soon as attachment is renounced, ever attainable God is realized. Therefore, when being free from attachment, we apply this illusion (body and objects etc.,) in the service of the illusory (world), the flow of this illusion (body and objects etc.,) is towards the world and God the divine essence that is ever attainable, remains.

Link:—Has there been any person who attained perfection (God-realization) through the performance of action, without attachment? The Lord answers the question in the next verse.

कर्मणैव हि संसिद्धिमास्थिता जनकादयः ।
लोकसङ्ग्रहमेवापि सम्पश्यन्कर्तुमर्हसि ॥ २० ॥

karmaṇaiva hi samsiddhimāsthitā janakādayaḥ
lokasaṅgrahamevāpi sampaśyankartumarhasi

It was by action alone, that Janaka and others attained perfection. Thou should perform selfless action, also for the good of the world. 20

Comment:—

'Karmaṇaiva hi saṁsiddhimāsthitā janakādayaḥ'—The term 'ādi' stands for, 'beginning' as well as, 'like'. Here the former meaning does not apply because before Janaka, there had been great souls like Vivasvān, Vaivasvata Manu and king Ikṣvāku, who had attained perfection through the performance of action (Gītā 4/1-2). Therefore, here it is used in the latter sense which means that some great souls like Janaka, before and after him, leading householder's life attained salvation by action.

This Discipline of Action is very old. By this discipline, Janaka and several other great souls have attained salvation or God-realization. Therefore, if anyone at present or in future, wants to realize God through the path of action, he without regarding the body and the objects as his own, should apply these in the service of the world by considering these as the world's. In fact, they belong to the world. By doing so one's affinity with the world is easily renounced and God is attained. Therefore, the Discipline of Action is an easy, good and independent means to realize God.

Here the expression, 'Karmaṇā eva' stands for the expression 'Asakto hyācarankarma' i.e., performance of action without attachment. By performing the actions thus, a man is liberated from their bondage otherwise he is enslaved (Mahā., Śānti. 241/7).

It is the characteristic of the style of the Gītā, that the Lord briefly repeats the main idea of the preceding verse in the next one also, which is of great help to a striver. Performance of action without attachment explained in the preceding verse, is explained in brief in this verse by the expression 'Karmaṇā eva'. Similarly, He will explain the main point, described in the sixth verse of the twelfth chapter, again in the seventh verse in brief, in the expression, "Whose mind is set on Me".

Here the Lord instead of the expresssion 'Karmaṇā eva', could have used the expression 'Yogena eva'. But here the topic is of the performance of action without attachment. Therefore, the Lord has used this expression, which suits the context.

In fact, the sentient Lord cannot be realized through insentient actions alone. The stumbling block to God-realization is removed through the performance of action, without attachment. Then the all-pervading God is realized.

A Vital Fact Pertaining to God-realization

Generally people think that they can attain God, by performing action or by making effort. They hold that, as they have to make a lot of effort in order to meet a high officer, they will have to make much more effort, (in the form of penance, fasts etc.,) in order to attain God, Who is the Lord of infinite universes. But that is an error on their part.

Human life has a great affinity for actions. So in the Gītā it is mentioned, "Meeting death when passion prevails, the embodied soul, is born among those attached to action" (14/15). Therefore, a man has an inclination for action and he wants to attain his aim through actions. He believes that as the worldly things can be acquired through actions, so God could also be realised by action. So he tries to attain Him through action. But the fact is, that the Imperishable Lord cannot be attained by actions. Only the perishable worldly things, can be acquired through actions, because all actions are performed with the help of a perishable (body, senses and mind etc.,) while God is realized by total renunciation of affinity for the perishable.

Every action has a beginning and an end, so its fruit is also perishable. A thing which is at some distance (unacquired), with the point of view of space or time can be acquired by action. Thus, only the worldly things which are perishable, changeful and confined, can be acquired through action. But the Lord Who pervades everywhere and Who is uniform and imperishable, cannot be attained through action. He is naturally attainable. Worldly things cannot be acquired by thinking alone but the Lord can be realised by thought, because He is close to us. The fact is, that the Lord is not attained by thinking alone, but when a striver thinks of the Lord, he stops thinking of the world. As soon as thinking about the world is renounced, the ever attainable Lord is realized.

Not only the all-pervading God, is never away from us but His being away from us, is impossible also. He is much nearer, these even the supposedly close 'I'ness, which is limited spatially and temporally, but God knows no limitation. In order to experience such a close and ever available God, it is deceiving one's self, to apply logic and arguments as if it were a worldly object.

Worldly things cannot be acquired only by having a keen desire, while God can be realized, only by having a keen desire.

Human life is meant to have a keen desire for God-realization, not for sense enjoyment. This desire is not aroused, because man has a desire for worldly pleasures and prosperity. If desire for pleasure and prosperity is renounced, a keen desire for God-realization may be aroused instantly and God may also be realized immediately.

It is necessary to clearly understand, the difference between the 'aim' and the desire, for fruit. God-realization is the aim of human life, while desire to acquire perishable things, is the desire for fruit of action. An aim is achieved, while desire for fruit of action is wiped out. Self-realization or God-realization is the aim, rather than the fruit. Action which is performed in order to attain an aim, cannot be called an action with 'desire for fruit'. Therefore, a Karmayogī performs all actions, with an objective rather than with a desire for fruit.

In Karmayoga (Discipline of Action), prescribed actions are performed with the aim of renouncing affinity for actions (matter). Such a striver performs actions for the welfare of others, by renouncing selfish desire for fruit, while a common man performs actions for himself, with the desire for fruit. In the case of the latter, the action is turned into fruit and so the fruit has its affinity for the action; while aim has no affinity for action. When a striver performs action for the welfare of others, without expecting any reward, his misconception that the Lord is far away from him, is removed.

'Lokasaṅgrahamevāpi sampaśyankartumarhasi'—The word 'loka' includes three aspects—(1) Human world (2) Creatures of the world (3) All the scriptures (except the Vedas). Performance of actions (of daily routine) for the human world and its creatures, according to the ordinance of the scriptures is 'Lokasaṅgraha' (maintenance of the world).

'Lokasaṅgraha' means to persuade the people to turn to the real, by dissuading them from the unreal. If a great soul, through his word and action, persuades people to turn towards the real, from the unreal, it leads them to salvation.

If he performs his duty merely as a show, it is not 'lokasaṅgraha'. He should perform his duty sincerely, according to his caste, order of life and sect etc.

No action is as such either superior or inferior. Whatever action is performed, according to one's caste, order of life, sect, time and circumstances, is regarded as superior. Actions are regarded as superior and inferior according to their form and fruit.* When desire for fruit is renounced, all actions lead to perfection or God-realization. As far as renunciation of affinity for the insentient (matter) is concerned, all actions—superior or inferior, are of equal importance.

No one can live without the help of others. A body is acquired from the parents; knowledge and education is received from preceptors. Food stuff, clothes, a house and other necessities of life, are prepared by others. Thus everyone has to depend on others for his necessities. Therefore, every person is indebted to others. In order to get out of this debt, he has to perform his duty for the welfare of others, without any selfish motive. When he does not regard the body and other worldly objects in the least as his own or for him, he is freed from the debt.

Appendix—Here the expression 'Karmaṇaiva hi saṁsiddhi-māsthitāḥ' proves that Karmayoga is an independent discipline for salvation. The kings such as Janaka etc., also attained perfection by performing actions because they ruled over their empire in order to serve others and to comfort them rather than for their selfish end.

'lokasaṅgrahamevāpi sampaśyankartumarhasi'—this expression means that you should set an example to the people that by practising Karmayoga supreme goal is attained.

---

* Oratory is regarded as superior to sweeping. Less charity seems to bear less fruit while more charity seems to bear more fruit.

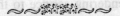

Link:—How action leads to the maintenance of the world, is discussed, in the next verse.

यद्यदाचरति श्रेष्ठस्तत्तदेवेतरो जनः।
स यत्प्रमाणं कुरुते लोकस्तदनुवर्तते॥२१॥

yadyadācarati śreṣṭhastattadevetaro janaḥ
sa yatpramāṇaṁ kurute lokastadanuvartate

Whatsoever an ideal person does, he is followed by others, as well. Whatever standard he sets, the world follows the same. 21

Comment:—

'Yadyadācarati śreṣṭhastattadevetaro janaḥ'—An ideal man, is he who knows the reality about the world (body etc.,) and the self. He realizes that the body, senses, mind, intellect, riches, property and family etc., are not his, but these belong really to the world. Not only this, but he does not regard renunciation, dispassion, devotion, knowledge and other virtues also as his own, because by doing so, his egoism is nourished which is an obstacle to self-realization. The feelings, "I am a renouncer," "I am dispassionate," "I am a devotee" and "I am a knower" nourish his egoism and thus these are stumbling blocks to Self-realization. There is no personal ego at all in a Self-realized person the prime ego remains only for common dealings and is engaged in rendering service to the world, as it belongs to the world (Gītā 7/4; 13/5).

The body, riches, family, position, ability and authority etc., which have been provided to us by the world, are neither meant for our pleasure nor for our possession, but these are for service of others. He who enjoys these himself, is verily a thief (Gītā 3/12). All of these belong to the world and so great men utilize these in rendering service to the world. They have a natural inclination, for the welfare of all beings.

The feeling of selflessness, causes unity and love, while a

feeling of selfishness, causes strife, the former, leads to salvation while the latter to degradation. By regarding the body as 'I', 'Mine' and 'For me' the feeling of selfishness, is caused. Great men who do not accept a feeling of affinity for the body, have no selfish motive. So all their actions, are for the welfare of others. The sight, touch, talk and thinking of such great men, automatically lead to the welfare of people. Even, the air which touches them does good to the people.

Such great men are of two kinds—(1) 'Avadhūta'—the hermit kind, who lead a holy and lonely life; such hermits are ideal only as hermits, not for common folk. (2) 'Ācārya'—Model for others—who are an example to others. Their actions are, according to the scriptural injunctions. They have neither egoism nor a sense of 'mine'. Their actions are automatically performed, for the welfare of the world. They leave their sweet smell by destroying bad smell, just like a blooming flower. Such great men have their identity with the Lord, because both of them work for the welfare of the entire world.

Different limbs of a body, constitute the body and remain ever prepared to help one another. When anyone is injured, and they consider its recovery as that of the entire body. Similarly, all the beings of the world, in spite of being different, are one and the same, and the performance of duty by one, is for the welfare of the entire world.

As far as actions and words of the great men, are concerned, they leave a gross impression which is restricted, because actions are limited. But, as far as their feelings are concerned, their influence is subtle and limitless, as the feelings are limitless. They set examples for other people, by performing duty, according to their caste, social order, sect etc., and make a strong impression on others.

Though a great man does not perform any action for himself, as he has no pride of doership, yet people feel that he performs actions. So the term 'ācarati' (Doer) has been used. Actions are automatically performed by him, for the welfare of others, without any selfish motive. Though he has nothing to do (Gītā 3/17), and has no egoism (Gītā 2/71), yet duty is naturally and efficiently performed by him, which is automatically for the welfare of the entire world.

An Important Fact

It is generally observed, that whatever actions are performed and whatever standards are set, by great men these are followed by common people.

Common people who attach importance to wealth and position, follow the examples set by millionaires and leaders, regarding them as great, though they may not be really so. The rich people and leaders, resort to evil practices such as falsehood, forgery, dishonesty, thefts and corruption, to gain riches, fame and status in society. The common people who consider them great, follow those evil practices. Thus, evils become rampant in the society, without any schooling or teaching.

How shocking and surprising it is, that at present a millionaire is regarded as great, but a devotee, who chants the name of the Lord a hundred thousand times a day, is not considered great. People do not think that when a millionaire dies, he will not take a single penny with him, while the whole wealth of chanting of the Lord's name, will ultimately go with the devotee.

Great and noble men, such as teachers, preachers, priests, leaders and rulers etc., who hold positions of honour in society, should perform their duties very carefully, so that they may leave a good impression upon other people, who may follow the standards set by noble men. They are just like drivers, who carry the passengers to their destinations or might cause accidents.

'Sa yatpramāṇaṁ kurute lokastadanuvartate'—A great man is free from such evils as desire, feeling of mine, attachment, selfishness and favouritism and he does not attach importance to perishable objects. His word automatically, influences people and they follow his preaching.

Here a doubt may arise, why the Lord has used, 'He sets a standard' and also 'Whatever a great man does' when either one of these might have been sufficient. The clarification is, that though the deed is important, yet a great man cannot perform acts of the people from different castes, orders of life etc. He sets a standard by his word, quoting scriptures and historical characters, so that people of other castes, orders of life and creed etc., by performing their duty, sincerely and promptly may attain perfection (Gītā 18/45). By following his advice, they start to perform their duty according to their castes, creeds and orders of life etc.

Though the scope of such deeds is limited while that of standard set (word) is wide, yet the Lord has used, five terms 'Yat', 'Yat', 'Tat', 'Tat' and (specially) 'Eva', for the deeds of a great man. He has used only two terms 'Yat' and 'Tat' for the standard set by him. It means that the deeds of a great man have five times the effect, while standard set (word) has only twice the effect. Therefore, the Lord in the twentieth verse of this chapter, has laid special emphasis, on the performance of duty, for the welfare of the world.

If a great man instead of performing his duty, according to his caste, creed and stage of life etc., preaches the gospel as a (standard) only, it will not influence people. They will think that these are merely precepts, which need not be translated into practice, because the man himself is only preaching, not practising. Therefore, a great man has to do good to the people by performing his duty, as well as by setting standards i.e., through word.

Only those people, who have faith in a great man follow his deeds and the set standard (word). But if a person does not regard a great man as really great, he will not follow the deeds and standard (word) set by him.

In modern times people do not have much inclination for spiritualism, in spite of a lot of preaching. The reason is, that preachers themselves, do not practise, what they preach. So it is a shot in the air. But on the other hand, there are preachers who believe in the maxim "Example is better than precept." Their shot hits the target and inspires men to practise spiritual discipline. Spiritual discourses leave some impression on almost everyone, but those who are devotees and have reverence, are immensely benefited.

Link:— Now, the Lord in the next three verses, lays emphasis on the performance of duty by citing His own example.

न मे पार्थास्ति कर्तव्यं त्रिषु लोकेषु किञ्चन।
नानवाप्तमवाप्तव्यं वर्त एव च कर्मणि॥ २२॥

na me pārthāsti kartavyaṁ triṣu lokeṣu kiñcana
nānavāptamavāptavyaṁ varta eva ca karmaṇi

There is nothing in the three worlds, O Arjuna, that is for me to do, nor is there anything unattained, that should be achieved; yet I engage Myself, in action. 22

Comment:—

'Na me pārthāsti kartavyaṁ triṣu lokeṣu kiñcana nānavāptam-avāptavyam'—The Lord is not confined to one world. So He is saying that there is nothing in the three worlds, that should be done by Him. All men, beasts and birds etc., perform actions, in order to attain something or the other. But the Lord mentions here, an uncommon fact, that He also performs action, though there is nothing which should be done or attained by Him.

Though God has nothing to do for Himself, yet He incarnates for the welfare of others and performs action for the protection of the good, for the destruction of the wicked and for the establishment of righteousness (Gītā 4/8). The Lord creates the universe, also for the salvation of creatures. He has created heavens, so that beings may reap the fruit of their virtuous actions. Eighty-four lac, forms of lives and hells, have been created, so that beings may reap the fruit of their evil actions, while human life has been created so that a human being, having transcended virtues and vices, may attain salvation viz., God-realization. This is possible, only when he does nothing for himself. All his activities—actions, with the gross body, thinking with the subtle body and trance with the causal body, should be applied to the welfare of the world. The reason is, that this threefold body, is not of one's own, but it belongs to the world. Therefore, a Karmayogī considers the body, senses, mind, intellect and all the matter etc., of the world, (which in fact belong to the world) and he utilizes them in rendering service to the world. If he uses these in order to enjoy pleasures, he commits a blunder. When a person accepts worldly things as his own he wants to reap the fruit and in order to reap the fruit, he has to perform action. Thus, so long as a man perform action in order to attain something, his duty remains to be performed by him.

If we give a serious thought to the subject, we realise that a man has to do nothing for himself, because God Who is to be attained is ever-attainable and the self is eternal while actions and their fruits are perishable. So, how can the perishable (actions and their fruits) have their affinity for the imperishable (self)? Actions have their affinity for the body and the world, rather than the self. Therefore, there is nothing to be done for the self. When there is nothing to be done for the self, how can there be anything to do for God?

While talking about an enlightened soul, who has attained perfection through the Discipline of Action, the Lord (in the seventeenth and eighteenth verses of this chapter) declared, "There exists no action to be done, by such an enlightened soul who is delighted, satisfied and contented, in the self. Such a soul has nothing to do with the performance or non-performance of actions, and he has not the least affinity for selfishness, with any being. Yet he performs actions for the welfare of the world." Similarly, the Lord declares, for Himself, there is nothing that should be done by Him, yet He is engaged in action for the welfare of the world. It means that an enlightened soul becomes identical with the Lord (Gītā 14/2) and as the Lord is a model in the three worlds (Gītā 3/23; 4/11), similarly an enlightened soul is a model in this world (Gītā 3/25).

'Varta eva ca karmaṇi'—Here, the Lord by the term 'eva' (only) means to say, that He performs actions enthusiastically, promptly, carefully and thoroughly.

As the compartments of a train attached to an engine, follow the engine, similarly the Lord and the saints (who have nothing to do and nothing more to attain), perform their duty and other people follow them. These latter people have a desire to act and to attain, something or the other. They get rid of this desire by performing their duty, without expecting any reward. If the Lord and the saints, did not perform their duty, the people would also follow their path, and they would become indolent and heedless and would perform forbidden actions. So they would not get rid of desires. Therefore, duty is automatically performed by the Lord and the saints, for the welfare of the whole humanity.

As the Lord always performs His duty, He never abandons it, similarly a striver should always perform his duty, so that he may attain God easily. If an aspirant does not perform his duty, he remains deprived of God-realization.

Appendix—In Mahābhārata the Lord has declared His duty in the three worlds to sage Uttaṅka—

dharmasaṁrakṣaṇārthāya dharmasaṁsthāpanāya ca
taistairveṣaiśca rūpaiśca triṣu lokeṣu bhārgava
(Āśva. 54/13-14)

'For the protection and establishment of righteousness, I manifesting Myself in several Form and guise, behave (act) accordingly.'

यदि ह्यहं न वर्तेयं जातु कर्मण्यतन्द्रितः।
मम वर्त्मानुवर्तन्ते मनुष्याः पार्थ सर्वशः॥ २३॥
उत्सीदेयुरिमे लोका न कुर्यां कर्म चेदहम्।
सङ्करस्य च कर्ता स्यामुपहन्यामिमाः प्रजाः॥ २४॥

yadi hyahaṁ na varteyaṁ jātu karmaṇyatandritaḥ
mama vartmānuvartante manuṣyāḥ pārtha sarvaśaḥ
utsīdeyurime lokā na kuryāṁ karma cedaham
saṅkarasya ca kartā syāmupahanyāmimāḥ prajāḥ

For, if I did not engage Myself in action without care, men would in everyway follow My path, O Arjuna. If I did not perform action, these worlds would perish and I would prove to be the creator of confusion and for the destruction of these people. 23-24

Comment:—

[In the twenty-second verse, the Lord by a positive inference, laid emphasis on the performance of duty. In this verse, He by the negative inference, mentions the harm that would be done if He did not perform duty.]

'Yadi hyahaṁ na varteyaṁ jātu karmaṇyatandritaḥ'—The term 'Hi' has been used here to support the expression "I engage Myself in action", used in the preceding verse.

The Lord declares that it is impossible for Him, not to perform action. But if it is so assumed that He does not perform action—in this sense the expression 'Yadi jātu' (If ever) has been used.

The term 'atandritaḥ' means, that actions should be performed, very carefully and promptly, renouncing indolence and heedlessness. By doing so, affinity for actions is renounced.

As a stiff twig is easily broken but an elastic one cannot be easily broken. Similarly, affinity for actions is renounced, if these are performed, carefully and promptly, but these are not renounced if performed, indolently and heedlessly. Therefore, the Lord (in the nineteenth verse) has used the term 'Samācara' (Perform well) and here the term 'atandritaḥ' (unwearied), has been used.

If there is recollection of an action, time and again, it means, that there has been some fault (desire, attachment, incompletion, indolence, heedlessness, indifference etc.,) in the performance of that action and so affinity for it, has not been renounced.

'Mama vartmānuvartante manuṣyāḥ pārtha sarvaśaḥ'—By this expression, the Lord seems to declare that those who follow His path really deserve to be called human beings, while those who while away time because of indolence and heedlessness, and demand their rights, do not deserve to be called human beings even though in human-garb.

In the twenty-first verse of this chapter, the Lord declared, "Whatever a great man does, the same is done by others as well; and whatever standard he sets, is followed by others," while here, He declares, "Men in everyway follow My path". It means that a great man is a model for the human world only, while the Lord is a model for the three worlds.

The Lord incarnates in the world, to set an example to other people. He who does not live for himself, and knows the art of living, in the world. The world is an educational institution, where we have to learn how to do good to others, by renouncing desire, attachment and selfishness etc. Through this lesson, we have to attain salvation. The only aim of human life, is to perform our duty by serving others and doing good to them, including members of the own family and try to lead one another, to salvation.

'Utsīdeyurime lokā na kuryāṁ karma cedaham'—The Lord (in the twenty-third verse) explained the harm if He performed action unweariedly and now (in the twenty-fourth verse) He explains the harm that could be done if he did not perform action.

'Though, it is not possible for the Lord not to perform action, yet if it is so assumed'—in this sense the Lord has used the term 'Cet' (If)—this expression means, that a man should not be attached to inaction (Gītā 2/47). Therefore, the Lord by citing His own example says, that He performs action even though there is nothing unattained, which remains to be attained by Him. And if He did not perform action (according to the caste and order of life in which He has incarnated), He would be the creator of confusion of castes and cause destruction of the people. It is so, because by renouncing their duty, men will also got steeped in the mode of ignorance (Gītā 14/18).

The Lord is a model for the three worlds and all beings follow Him. Therefore, if the Lord does not perform His duty, no one in the three worlds, will perform his duty and thus they will suffer a downfall.

'Saṅkarasya ca kartā syāmupahanyāmimāḥ prajāḥ'—If the Lord did not perform action (duty), these worlds would perish and He would be the root cause of their destruction, but this is not at all possible.

The term 'saṅkara' stands for the mixture of two castes. Arjuna (in the fortieth and the forty-first verses of the first chapter) said, "If I fight the family will be ruined. With the ruin of the family, the immemorial religious rites of the family will be destroyed. With the destruction of the religious rites, impiety will overcome the whole family. By the prevalence of impiety, the women of the family will become immoral. With the corruption of women, mixing of castes (intermingling of castes) will result." Thus, Arjuna meant to say, that war would lead to the mixing of castes.* But the Lord contradicts Arjuna's

* Even according to the argument of Arjuna, non-performance of duty (action) is the cause of confusion of castes. Confusion of castes arises only when

statement, by citing His own example when He declares that confusion of castes, would arise by the non-performance of duty. Therefore, here Lord Kṛṣṇa seems to urge Arjuna to wage the war, otherwise he would be the creator of mixed castes.

An Important Fact

The Lord, answers Arjuna's question, "Why do You urge me to engage in this terrible action?" In the twenty-second, the twenty-third and the twenty-fourth verses, by citing His own example that He engages Himself in action even though He has nothing to do personally with it and nothing to attain in the three worlds. Therefore, He urges him to be engaged in action.

The Lord gives Arjuna a hint, that He had agreed to be his chariot-driver and he as His chariot-warrior is performing His duty very carefully and efficiently, so that other people may follow His example as He stands as a model for them. So he should also perform his duty as a Kṣatriya (member of the warrior class) carefully and efficiently.

Link:— Having described the need for the performance of duty, by Him, the Lord in the next two verses, urges a man of knowledge to perform action, carefully.

सक्ताः कर्मण्यविद्वांसो यथा कुर्वन्ति भारत।
कुर्याद्विद्वांस्तथासक्तश्चिकीर्षुर्लोकसङ्ग्रहम्॥ २५॥
न बुद्धिभेदं जनयेदज्ञानां कर्मसङ्गिनाम्।
जोषयेत्सर्वकर्माणि विद्वान्युक्तः समाचरन्॥ २६॥

---

women are corrupted and they become so by non-performance of their duty. If women believe that they should perform their duty by remaining chaste, in the same way as their husbands performed their duty by sacrificing their lives, they cannot neglect their duty. Thus by performing their duty, they will maintain their chastity and there will be no mixing of castes.

saktāḥ karmaṇyavidvāṁso yathā kurvanti bhārata
kuryādvidvāṁstathāsaktaścikīrṣurlokasaṅgraham
na buddhibhedaṁ janayedajñānāṁ karmasaṅginām
joṣayetsarvakarmāṇi vidvānyuktaḥ samācaran

As ignorant men act with attachment to action, O, Bhārata (Arjuna), so should the wise act without attachment, thus wishing the welfare of the world. Let no knowing man, realising the self, unsettle the minds of ignorant people, act with attachment but he should make others to act, while himself performing his duties with devotion. 25-26

Comment:—

'Saktāḥ karmaṇyavidvāṁso yathā kurvanti bhārata'—The expression 'saktāḥ avidvāṁsaḥ' has been used, for those ignorant men attached to worldly pleasures, who have full faith in the scriptures, the ordinance of the scriptures and also the actions sanctioned by the scriptures, and who are neither enlightened nor vile but are attached to actions, pleasures and objects. They are called ignorant (unwise) because of their desire, though they have bookish knowledge of the scriptures. They are well-read but are not enlightened. They are called ignorant, because they perform actions for themselves.

Such ignorant people, perform their duty scrupulously according to the ordinance of the scriptures without heedlessness and indolence believing that it will not bear fruit, if duty is not performed scrupulously according to strict scriptural ordinance. The Lord urges wise people, to act in the same way, without attachment for the welfare of the world.

'Kuryādvidvāṁstathāsaktaścikīrṣurlokasaṅgraham'— 'asaktaḥ' and 'Vidvān'—unattached wise men, are enlightened souls* who are totally free from desire, a feeling, of 'mine', lust, favouritism,

* The supreme state (of God-realization) which is obtained by men of renunciation is also attained by men of action (Gītā 5/4-5), yet in that state also there is a little difference in their marks and natures according to the path each

selfishness etc., and who have not the least attachment, to body and other objects etc.

The expression 'Lokasaṅgrahaṁ cikīrṣuḥ' (wishing the welfare of the world) has been used for the expression 'Lokasaṅgrahaṁ evāpi saṁpaśyan' (with a view to the welfare of the masses) used in the twentieth verse of this chapter and explained, in the twenty-first verse.

All actions of wise men, are naturally performed for the welfare of the world. They have also no egoistic notion, that they are engaged in the welfare of others. As a licentious person, is attached to sensual pleasures, the greedy to riches and an infatuated one to the family, the wise are engrossed, in the welfare of all beings, naturally and without any egoistic feeling. Because of the total renunciation of affinity, for the materialistic world, their so-called bodies, senses, minds and intellects etc., are inclusive of the term 'loka' (world) used in the expression, 'lokasaṅgraha' (welfare of the world).

People think that such wise men have a desire to be engrossed in the welfare of the world, but in fact they have no desire at all. They regard the body, senses, mind, intellect, objects, position, riches, ability and all other resources, as of the world and for the world, which these really are. So all of them, automatically remain engaged in rendering service to the world, without any expectation of reward.

The terms, 'yathā' (as) and 'tathā' (so), have been used, to point out that as ignorant men scrupulously act for their selfish motive, so the wise should act, without attachment, aiming at the welfare of the world. When the wise perform actions thus for the welfare and salvation of all beings, good and sweet feelings, automatically propagate.

---

followed. The men of renunciation remain indifferent to actions while men of action perform actions very promptly. This difference is not hard and fast. It is found in some realized souls.

An ignorant person performs action scrupulously, in order to reap its fruit, while a wise man is neither attached to the fruit of action, nor has any duty to perform. So, it is possible for him to be indifferent to action. Therefore, the Lord directs him to act, without attachment.

In the twenty-first verse, a great (wise) man was called a model, but here he has been called a follower. It means that a wise man may either be a leader (model) or a follower, as automatically good to the world is done by him. For example, Lord Rāma preaches a gospel to His subjects and also goes into exile by obeying His father. In both cases, welfare of the world is done by Him because He has nothing to do either with the performance or non-performance of such actions.

A wise man who performs actions without attachment, having no desire for its fruit, automatically leaves an impression on the ignorant people, who are attached to action, whether it is clearly noted or not. Not only people, but beasts and birds are also influenced by such feelings and actions.

Something Noteworthy

So long as, a man does not perform prescribed actions without desire for fruit, his cycle of birth and death continues. As long as, he works for himself, he has to act, because the self is eternal, but an action and its fruit are perishable. Therefore, it is everyone's obligatory duty, to work for the welfare of others, without any selfish motive.

The Discipline of Action (performance of action without desire for fruit) seems difficult, because we attach importance to the worldly objects. If we resolve, that we have to perform all actions for the welfare of others without any desire, the path of action will become easy, and quick.

In fact, there is no importance as such of the object, rather it is of its use. That use is significant, only when one does not attach much value to the object. No worldly object is personal, it belongs to the world. But it has been given to us, so that we may make a proper use of it. When we regard it as our own, it becomes difficult for us to use it for the welfare of others. In fact, it is neither an object nor an action which leads to bondage but it is attachment to it which binds.

The wise, perform actions for the welfare of the world without any egoistic notion, because they hold that whatsoever possessions such as body, senses, mind, intellect, position etc., have been acquired from the world, and these belong to the world. So it is honest on our part, to use the worldly-materials, in the service of humanity; there is nothing creditable in returning trust money to its owner. In doing so, we are simply relieved of our responsibility—a debt has been repaid. In like manner, by using our possessions in the service of the world, we merely repay the debt we owe to the world, since it is only from the world, that we have received these possessions.

'Na buddhibhedaṁ janayedajñānāṁ karmasaṅginām joṣayetsarvakarmāṇi vidvānyuktaḥ samācaran'—A wise man without attachment, who has been described in the twenty-fifth verse by the expression 'Asaktaḥ vidvān,' has been called 'Yuktaḥ vidvān' here.

An enlightened soul, who remains, equanimous, is unmoved under all circumstances, whose senses are controlled and to whom a clod, a stone and a piece of gold, are same, is called 'Yuktaḥ Vidvān' (wise man established in the self) (Gītā 6/8).

Ignorant men attached to prescribed action, who have been described in the twenty-fifth verse by the expression 'Saktāḥ Avidvāṁsaḥ' have been called by the expression 'Karmasaṅginām Ajñānām' here. These people have been called 'Karmasaṅgī' (attached to action) and 'ajñānī' (Ignorant), because they perform action prescribed by the scriptures, for themselves, (in order to gain pleasure, honour and praise etc.)

Great men have greater responsibility, because common men follow them. Therefore, the Lord urges the wise man, that he should not perform any such action or make any such utterance, as may lead the ignorant to a downfall, which has been called here 'as buddhibhedam' (unsettlement in the minds). Therefore, a wise man should perform virtuous actions, according to his caste and order of life for the welfare of other people, so that they may be inspired to perform their duty, without any desire for fruit. This rule also applies to important persons of society and a family that they should perform their duties scrupulously, and they may set an example for other members of society and family.

Some of the examples, of unsettling the minds of ignorant people, are as follows:—

1. Knowledge is superior to action. Actions bind a man. This type of preaching undermines faith in action.

2. Everybody performs actions with a selfish motive. Desire for fruit is natural. Why should a man perform action, if he has, no desire for its fruit? Such thoughts unsettle the minds of ignorant people.

3. When a person performs actions, with the desire for their fruits, he has to take birth again and again, to reap the fruit of his actions. Thus common people cease to have faith in the fruit of action. Such statements unsettles the minds of ignorant people. Consequently, they renounce the performance of virtuous actions, even though they remain attached to their fruit.

The fact is, that it is not action, but attachment, which leads to bondage. Thus an enlightened soul instead of confusing the minds of ignorant people, should perform his obligatory duty, according to his caste and order of life and also get it performed by others, so that they, instead of having a downfall, may rise to a higher level. He should admire their virtuous actions, and make them aware of the evil actions, so that they may renounce these. Moreover, he should explain to them, that it is not proper to have a desire for the fruit of virtuous actions, such as sacrifice, charity and adoration etc., because this fruit is nominal. It is just like selling a precious jewel for the price of pebbles and so it is not a wise act. But if they act without desire for fruit, it will lead them to bliss.

Similarly, he should not confuse the minds of ignorant people, about adoration and spiritual practice. Generally, people say that it is futile to chant the Lord's name, without concentration. But an enlightened soul should preach, that chanting of the Lord's name never goes in vain. But if the name is chanted with concentration, it expedites spiritual progress. Everyone possesses some virtue or the other. Therefore, when an enlightened soul wants to preach a sermon to a common man, he instead of reproaching and insulting him, should praise his virtues and then should preach the sermon. Such a sermon makes a strong impression, upon the common man. The chief of a family or the society should also do the same.

The Lord through the terms 'samācaran' (duly performing) and 'joṣayet' (should get them to perform) directs a wise man (i) to perform his duty, scrupulously according to the scriptural injunctions, (ii) he should make the ignorant men, who are attached to action, perform their duty.

Ostentation in the performance of actions is hypocrisy, which is a mark of demoniac nature (Gītā 16/4). Therefore, the Lord orders people to perform actions, not for show, but for the welfare of the people. An enlightened soul should set other people, who are attached to action, to act by performing their duty scrupulously, without attachment and also by preaching a sermon. He should inspire them to discard selfishness, and also inspire them through his example and precepts, to perform prescribed actions and to refrain from forbidden actions.

Appendix—Enlightened exalted souls and God—both are free from egoistic notion. Therefore they perform their duty for the welfare of others, not for themselves. A striver should do nothing for himself because in the self there is no sense of doership. The act of deviating the people from the sinful (wrong) path and directing them towards the virtuous (right) path is welfare of others. The method of the welfare of others is—to act according to the ordinance of the scriptures; but a striver from within should have the feeling that he has to do nothing for himself. But he should not divulge the fact among people that he does nothing for himself.

Link:—Now, the Lord distinguishes the unwise from the wise, in the following verses.

प्रकृतेः क्रियमाणानि गुणैः कर्माणि सर्वशः ।
अहङ्कारविमूढात्मा कर्ताहमिति मन्यते ॥ २७ ॥

prakṛteḥ kriyamāṇāni guṇaiḥ karmāṇi sarvaśaḥ
ahaṅkāravimūḍhātmā kartāhamiti manyate

All actions are performed, in all cases, by the modes of nature (prakṛti). He whose mind is beguiled by egoism thinks, "I am the doer." 27

Comment:—

'Prakṛteḥ kriyamāṇāni guṇaiḥ karmāṇi sarvaśaḥ'—All the functions of the world, such as birth and growth of bodies and plants, flow of the Ganges and changes in worldly things etc., as well actions, such as seeing, hearing, eating and drinking etc., are carried out by the modes of nature. But, a man deluded by egoism divides all activities performed by cosmic energy, into two parts—To the first part, belong actions, which he thinks he does not perform but occur naturally—such as formation of the body and digestion of food etc. The second part, consists of those actions which he thinks he performs, such as seeing, speaking and eating etc. A man out of delusion regards himself as the doer of the latter class of actions. Intellect, ego, mind, five subtle elements, ten organs of perception and actions, and five objects of senses—these are also called the modes of nature, because they are the evolutes of the three modes of nature, (goodness, passion and ignorance). The Lord declares that all actions are performed by the modes of nature, not by the self.

'Ahaṅkāravimūḍhātmā'—'Egoism' is a state of mind, while he (the self) is the knower of that state. But by an error, he identifies the self with that state, and thus he is deluded by egoism.

As a body denoted by the term 'Idam', is different from the self, so is egoism. 'Idam' cannot be 'I'—this is the rule. But, when he regards egoism as self, he is known as 'ahaṅkāravimūḍhātmā' (one whose mind is deluded by egoism). This assumed egoism is not wiped out by efforts, as these involve the ego. But, it is wiped out by non-acceptance viz., non-assumption.

An Important Fact

Egoism is of two kinds:—

(i) Real* as 'I am' (relating to one's existence).

(ii) Unreal (assumed)—as 'I am body'.

'Real egoism' is natural and eternal, while unreal egoism', is unnatural and perishable. Real egoism, can be forgotten but cannot perish, while unreal egoism may appear, but cannot exist. A man commits an error, that he forgets real egoism (self) and assumes the unreal egoism (I am the body) to be true.

'Kartāhamiti manyate'—Though all actions are performed by modes of nature, yet a person whose mind is deluded by egoism,

* Real egoism in fact is not egoism. It is an aggregate of Truth, Knowledge and Bliss. It is called, 'real', because it never changes, while the unreal egoism, changes. Today a man is uneducated. Having received schooling he says he is educated. Thus the unreal egoism changes. But he (the self) remains the same. As soon as he ceases to identify himself with the unreal egoism, the real egoism, as the aggregate of Truth, Consciousness and Bliss, remains.

thinks that he is the doer, because he regards egoism, as the self. It is because of this egoism that he identifies the self with the body, senses, mind and thus regards the self as the doer. This egoism is self-made and so it can be eliminated by the self. The method, to throw it out is, through non-assumption. This false assumption, can be rooted out, if he realizes that he (the self) is different from the body, senses and mind etc.

Performance of actions and non-performance of actions—all are activities. Sleeping, waking, sitting, walking and trance etc., are included in activities, which take place in nature, while the self is free from performance and non-performance of actions. The self is the illuminator and knower of them. A man automatically remains established in the self, but the self assumes its affinity for actions. This assumed affinity, is called 'egoism'.

An Important Fact

As a wave is a part of an ocean, so the ocean and the wave belong to the same class. Similarly a body, a fragment of the world and the world, belong to the same class. The soul (self) is different from the world or the body. Man does not take the world, to be his own Self 'I' but he does take, even though wrongly, his body to be so.

Just as a wave without an ocean, has no independent existence of its own, similarly, without the world, there cannot be any separate existence of the body. But, when a man, whose mind is deluded by egoism, identifies the self with the body, several desires are born in him, as he has desire for family, riches, praise and pleasures etc. He does not realize, that by identifying the self with the body, he is already a captive and these desires will strengthen the bondage and will hurl him into the abyss of adversity.

Even though a striver during his disciplining period, may not feel that he is above and beyond the modes of prakṛti but when he accepts to be so with a strong faith, he starts feeling himself beyond prakṛti. Thus, just as a person, is bound due to his wrong assumptions, in the same way he is freed from his shackles through correct assumptions, because it is a principle that an assumed fact, ceases to be by unassuming it. The same fact, has been pointed out by the Lord, in the eighth verse of the fifth chapter by the term 'manyeta' (should believe) when He declares, "The man, who is united with the Divine and knows the truth, thinks that he does nothing at all". By such thinking, a striver realizes the truth.

When even the unreal assumptions such as 'I am the body', 'I am doer', become so steady, that it seems difficult to renounce these; why would the reality, 'I am not the body' and 'I am not a doer', not become steady? And once the reality is confirmed, how can it be abandoned?

Appendix—All actions take place in the material realm. In the sentient realm there is no action at all. He whose mind is beguiled by egoism thinks "I am the doer." 'The mind being beguiled by egoism' means to assume the self's identity with ego, a fragment of Aparā (lower or insentient) Prakṛti (nature) viz., to assume ego as the self (I am this). This is known identification.

He who regards himself as the doer is sentient but he regards the insentient 'ego' as the 'self'. It means that he who regards ego as the self, who assumes himself unipresent, is in fact a fragment of God. In that self no sense of doership is possible (Gītā 13/29). In fact the self can't be identified with the body—'śarīrastho'pi kaunteya na karoti na lipyate' (Gītā 13/31) but he assumes his identification with the body 'kartāhamitimanyate'. In fact there is no identification, it is merely an assumption. It means that the self does not become a doer but there is only assumption of doership due to lack of discrimination—'manyate'. As soon as he thinks himself to be the doer, scriptural sanction-prohibition applies to him and he has to become the enjoyer (experiencer) of the fruit of action.

In the self there is no action. An action takes place where there is some empty space. How can an action take place in the solid self? But when a person assumes himself to be a doer, the action of Prakṛti, with which he accepts his relationship, bears fruit for him, which he has to endure. The reason is that he, who is a doer, is an experiencer.

The self has no relationship at all with any 'Kāraka' (case). Therefore in the self there is not even an iota of doership. The realm of doership is different. By now the actions which have been performed in the species of gods, men, animals, birds, gnomes and devils etc., out of them no action could have an access to the self, nor the body could have an access to the self, because the division of action and object (body) is quite different, from the division of the self. But without attaching importance to this discrimination, a man gets bound by action and its fruit.

He who feels that something is to be done, has affinity with ego because without the sense of doership no action is possible. The sense of doership crops up as one thinks of doing something. With the sense of doership, there is performance of action and by performing an action, the sense of doership is strengthened. Therefore by practising the spiritual discipline being an agent a striver can't be free from egoism. An action done with the sense of egoism, can never lead to salvation, because egoism is the root of all misfortunes, of birth and death. If actions are not performed for one's own self, affinity for egoism does not persist viz., affinity for the entire nature (Prakṛti) is renounced. Therefore a striver instead of attaching importance to the performance of action, should attach importance to discrimination. By attaching importance to discrimination, discrimination is naturally revealed clearly and it guides a seeker. Afterwards this discrimination is transformed into Real-Knowledge.

तत्त्ववित्तु महाबाहो गुणकर्मविभागयोः ।
गुणा गुणेषु वर्तन्त इति मत्वा न सज्जते ॥ २८ ॥

tattvavittu mahābāho guṇakarmavibhāgayoḥ
guṇā guṇeṣu vartanta iti matvā na sajjate

Having true knowledge of the respective spheres of modes (guṇa) and actions, the knowing soul does not get attached with them, by realising that, it is an interplay of the modes. 28

Comment:—

'Tattvavittu mahābāho guṇakarmavibhāgayoḥ'—Here the term 'Tu' (but) has been used to distinguish the enlightened soul, from the person whose mind is deluded by egoism, as described in the preceding verse.

The three modes of goodness, of passion and of ignorance, are born of nature. The entire universe, including the body, senses, mind, intellect, creatures and objects etc., is constituted of the three modes. This is the sphere of the modes of nature. Actions performed with body etc., is a sphere of action.

The modes (objects) and actions, are ever-changing and transitory. The matter, has its origin and end; actions have a beginning and end. To know this fact properly is, having a true knowledge of modes and actions, along with their divisions. This is the truth, about the modes of nature and their actions. The soul, (self) never undergoes any action. It is ever unconnected and changeless i. e., it has no connection with things and actions. This is the truth about the soul.

The ignorant, when he assumes his relation, with the two spheres of modes and actions, gets himself bound. Philosophically, the main reason of this bondage is ignorance, but from the stand-point of a striver, the main cause is, 'attachment.' Attachment is, a lack of discrimination. It perishes when discrimination is aroused. This discrimination is particularly, found in human beings. What is needed is, simply to give it due importance and to arouse it. Therefore, a striver should wipe out attachment.

The striver, who does not assume his affinity for modes, (things) and actions, knows the reality of the modes of nature, and their actions. He may know the reality, either of the modes of nature and their action or the self, the result is the same i.e., he knows the reality of the two.

How to Know This Truth?

1. Though the Supreme self dwells in the body, yet it neither acts nor is tainted (Gītā 13/31). Evolutes of nature (body, senses, mind, intellect etc.,) are called 'this'. 'This' cannot be 'I'.When 'this' (body etc.,) is not 'I', how can actions performed by this (body etc.,) be 'mine'? It means, that the body, senses, mind and intellect etc., are the evolutes of Nature, while the self is totally unconnected with them. So how can 'the self' be the doer of actions? He who realizes this fact, is not in bondage. When he realizes, that he does nothing at all, (Gītā 5/8), it means, that he realizes that he (the self) is different from actions.

2. All the movements, such as seeing, hearing, eating and drinking etc., are actions, while food stuff and liquids etc., are objects. These actions and objects, are known by the sense-organs (eye, ear, tongue etc.). The sense-organs, are known by the mind, the mind is known by the intellect, and the intellect is known by egoism (I'ness). This egoism, is also illumined by the sentient light, which is the knower, the illuminator and base, of all of them.

How to know the self (sentient) which is beyond egoism?

In sound sleep, though intellect merges into ignorance, yet having awaken from sleep, a man says that he slept soundly. It means, that he existed even, during a sound sleep. Otherwise, he would not have known (experienced), that he slept soundly. Thus, everyone in every state, realizes 'I am'. These are called enlightened souls who, have renounced their affinity even for

'I' (egoism) and have realized the self.

We have a real affinity for changeless God, while our affinity for the changing nature, is merely assumed. If we renounce our affinity for Nature, through discrimination, it is known as 'Jñānayoga' (Discipline of Knowledge). If this affinity is renounced by performing duty, for the welfare of others, it is known as 'Karmayoga' (Discipline of Action). When we renounce our affinity for nature, we realize Yoga, (i.e.,) union with God. Otherwise, it is merely Jñāna (knowledge) and karma (action). Those who realize this real affinity for God, having renounced the affinity for nature, are, 'tattvavit' (enlightened souls).

'Guṇā guṇeṣu vartanta'—The body, senses, mind and intellect etc., are also called modes, as these are born of modes of nature, and all actions are performed by them. Out of ignorance, a man by assuming his affinity for these modes, becomes a doer of actions i.e., by regarding the actions and objects, as his own and he becomes a doer. But, when he realizes that the self is different and is an illuminator, he cannot think, that he is a doer.

A train, having received power from the engine, runs with the help of a driver. The engine supplies power but the train reaches its destination only when the driver drives it. The engine has no senses, mind and intellect. Therefore, it needs a driver (man) with senses, mind and intellect. But, a man has an engine in the form of body and has also senses, mind and intellect to drive it. But the senses, mind and intellect function having received inspiration from the source of light. First, light is reflected in the intellect, from the intellect it goes to the mind, from the mind it goes to the senses, and then the engine (body) functions. Intellect, mind, senses and the body—these are modes and their illuminator, is the self which is not connected with them. Therefore, the modes are acting on the modes.

Mostly, the people follow examples set by great men. Therefore, the Lord declares that as a great man, holds that it is the modes which are acting on the modes, and does not get attached to them, while he works for the welfare of the world; similarly a striver should also do the same.

A Vital Fact Pertaining to Nature And Spirit

There is always an attraction between senses and objects, if these belong to the same class. Ears have attraction for words, skin for touch, eyes for form, tongue for taste and nose for smell. Thus, all the five senses have attraction, for their sense-objects. Any sense cannot have an attraction, for the object of another sense. For example, the eye cannot have attraction, for melodious words. The self in fact, has no attraction for nature, as it is not of the same character. It is changeless, eternal, pure and uniform, while nature is, quite otherwise. But by identifying Itself with a body, a fragment of nature, it has attraction for nature. The attraction of the embodied soul, for the worldly objects, is really attraction of nature in nature. The senses of doership and enjoyership, are in nature, not in the pure self.

Lord Kṛṣṇa (in the thirty-first verse of the thirteenth chapter) declared of the self, "Though It dwells in the body, yet It neither acts not is tainted." The soul, is said to be the cause, in regard to the experience of pleasure and pain" (Gītā 13/20), when it (the soul) resides in nature (Gītā 13/21) i.e., it identifies Itself, with body etc. It means that it is because of Its identification with nature (body and senses etc.,) that It becomes happy or sad.

Because, prakṛti, inert as it is, is incapable of experiencing pleasure and pain, and the 'Self' (conscious), alone cannot become enjoyer, without association with Prakṛti.

The self is free from the kaleidoscopic, qualities of prakṛti, but it is certainly capable of assuming a relation with prakṛti. It is not, at all inert like a stone, on the contrary it is Knowledge incarnate. Had the soul not been competent to assume affinity, how could it establish relation with prakṛti? how could it assume the activities of prakṛti taking place in it (the soul); how could it assume doership or enjoyership in it? Assuming or not assuming relation, is a feeling and not an action.

The self, possesses competence to establish a relation or otherwise; but on its own it is incompetent to act. Only kaleidoscopic agents can have the capability of taking action. The Self is by nature, changeless whereas prakṛti, changes every moment. In other words, activeness is innate in prakṛti. Therefore, by establishing affinity, with prakṛti, the 'Self' supposes itself to be the doer (Gītā 3/27).

It is a merit, rather than a demerit, of the soul that It undergoes no change. It ever remains the same and is uniform. It cannot change, in the same way, as ice cannot be hot. But it is free and so it depends upon it, whether it accepts its affinity for nature or not, though really it has no affinity with nature.

When the soul identifies itself with the body, it has attraction for nature and then It performs actions and has to reap the fruit in the form of pleasure and pain. In fact, pleasure and pain have no separate existence. Therefore, the Lord urges men to renounce their assumed affinity for nature, by considering that it is the modes, which are acting on the modes, while the (soul or self) is, quite detached from them.

As a matter of fact, disassociation is already there and association is wrongly assumed. Therefore, it is necessary to give up this assumed relation and to realise the fact, that it is only modes that are reacting on modes.

'Iti matvā na sajjate'— Here, the term 'matvā' has been used for 'knowing'. An enlightened soul, distinguishes the soul from nature, and so he is not attached to the modes of nature.

By using the term 'matvā', the Lord seems to direct striver, not to be attached to the modes of nature, by regarding these, as different from the self.

An Important Fact

The methods followed by a Karmayogī, (man of Action) and a Jñānayogī (man of knowledge) are different. The former, tries to wipe out his assumed identity with the body etc. In the Bhāgavata, it is mentioned, "Persons with desires, deserve to follow the path of action" (11/20/7). Lord Kṛṣṇa in the Gītā, has also laid emphasis on the performance of duty, when He declares, "Not by non-performance of action does a man attain actionlessness" (Gītā 3/4). "For a sage, who wishes to attain to Yoga, action is said to be the means" (Gītā 6/3). A Karmayogī, performs action for others, not for himself; therefore, he does not become an enjoyer. When he does not become an enjoyer, his sense of doership, automatically perishes. He becomes doer, only in order to reap the fruit of action. He does not remain a doer, if he does not desire the fruit of action. Therefore, in fact a Karmayogī also does not become, a doer.

In Sāṅkhyayoga (Discipline of Knowledge) there is predominance of discrimination. Such a striver holds, 'It is the modes which are acting on the modes'. By thinking so he does not become a doer of actions. The same fact, has been pointed out by the Lord (in the twenty-ninth verse of the thirteenth chapter) when He declares, "He who sees, that all actions are performed by nature alone, and that the self is not the doer, he verily sees." When he does not remain a doer, there does not arise any question of his being, an enjoyer.

In this chapter, the Lord has laid great emphasis on the performance of action; as "It was by action alone that Janaka and others attained perfection" (3/20); "I engage Myself in action" (3/22); "A wise man also performs actions, for the welfare of the world without attachment, as an ignorant man acts from attachment" (3/25-26). It proves that performance of actions, is good in everyway.

Appendix—He, who is not deluded by egoism, is an enlightened soul. This enlightened soul has been mentioned 'tattvadarśī' (the seer of truth) in the sixteenth verse of the second chapter. An enlightened soul transcends the spheres of mode (guṇa) (objects) and actions totally.

So long as a striver has affinity for the world, he can't be an enlightened soul. The reason is that a man can't know the world so long as he is attached to it. The world can be known only when he disconnects himself from the world—this is the rule. Similarly a man cannot know God by assuming himself apart from God. He can know Him only by identifying himself with Him—this is the rule. The reason is that really we are different from the world and are identical with God. The body is identical with the world while we (self) are identical with God.

प्रकृतेर्गुणसम्मूढाः सज्जन्ते गुणकर्मसु।
तानकृत्स्नविदो मन्दान्कृत्स्नविन्न विचालयेत्॥ २९॥

prakṛterguṇasammūḍhāḥ sajjante guṇakarmasu
tānakṛtsnavido mandānkṛtsnavinna vicālayet

Those who are deluded by the modes of nature, remain attached to those modes and actions. Man of perfect knowledge, should not unsettle the minds of the ignorant, who know only little. 29

Comment:—

'Prakṛterguṇasammūḍhāḥ sajjante guṇakarmasu'—The three modes (goodness, passion and ignorance) of nature, bind a man. The mode of goodness (sattva), binds by attachment to happiness and knowledge; the mode of passion (rājasa) by attachment to action, and the mode of ignorance (tāmasa) by heedlessness, indolence and sleep (Gītā 14/6—8). In this verse, is a description of those ignorant people, who are deluded by the modes of nature i.e., who are bound by them, but who have faith in the scriptures, in prescribed virtuous actions and in the fruit of those actions. These people have been called 'the ignorant people attached to action' (in the twenty-fifth and twenty-sixth verses). They are attached to actions and objects, in order to enjoy worldly and heavenly pleasures. Therefore they cannot understand the advice as to how to rise, above them. So the Lord has called them ignorant.

'Tānakṛtsnavido mandān'—Ignorant people, perform virtuous actions with the expectation of perishable fruits. They remain attached to the acquired materials, such as wealth etc., and have a desire to acquire the unacquired ones also. It is because of their attachment and desire, that they do not know reality about modes (objects) and actions.

Ignorant people know what prescribed actions are, and how these should be performed well, but they do not know the reality, about modes and actions. So, it has been said that they know only little i.e., they are men of imperfect knowledge and they have been called ignorant, because they are interested in enjoying worldly pleasures and prosperity.

'Kṛtsnavinna vicālayet'—A man of perfect knowledge, who knows the reality about the sphere of the modes and actions should not confuse the minds of the ignorant ones, otherwise they would renounce virtuous actions and would have a downfall. Such a wise man, has been called 'unattached wise man' (in the twenty-fifth verse) and 'balanced (established in the self) wise man' (in the twenty-sixth verse of this chapter).

The Lord (in the twenty-fifth verse) directed a wise man to act by using the term 'Kuryāt' while in the twenty-sixth verse He ordered him to engage the ignorant men in action, by the term 'Joṣayet'. But the Lord, by the expression, 'Na vicālayet', instead of ordering him, makes a bit of relaxation, by declaring, that he should not at least unsettle the minds of the ignorant, with his hints or words or actions. The reason is, that the Lord does not enforce strict discipline on the liberated souls nor do the scriptures. Actions are automatically performed, by their, so-called, bodies for the welfare of the world.*

An enlightened soul, whether he is a Karmayogī or a Jñānayogī, has not the least attachment, either to actions or objects, because he knows the truth that there is no real affinity between him and actions or objects.

The ignorant, perform virtuous actions in order to gain the heaven. Therefore, the Lord has ordered the wise men, not to unsettle the minds of the ignorant people with their hints, words or actions, otherwise they would lose their faith and interest in virtuous actions, and would give these up; which would lead them to a downfall. Therefore, such people should be dissuaded from a desire for fruit, rather than from actions, prescribed by the scriptures. It is not only proper, but also indispensable, to dissuade them from desire for the fruit of action, in order to release them from the bondage of a cycle of birth and death.

Appendix—Arjuna's question was why the Lord urged him to perform such a dreadful deed. The Lord answers his question in several ways by which He means to declare, "My aim is not to engage you in a terrible deed but I want you to renounce your affinity for actions." Karmayoga aims at renouncing affinity for actions.

Link:—The Lord, in the next verse explains, what a striver should do to be free from attachment, to action and its fruit.

मयि सर्वाणि कर्माणि सन्न्यस्याध्यात्मचेतसा।
निराशीर्निर्ममो भूत्वा युध्यस्व विगतज्वरः॥ ३०॥

mayi sarvāṇi karmāṇi sannyasyādhyātmacetasā
nirāśīrnirmamo bhūtvā yudhyasva vigatajvaraḥ

* There is difference between 'Kriyā' and 'Karma'. When the person has

Surrendering all actions to Me, with the mind firmly fixed on the Highest and free from desire and the feeling of meum and disconcertedly doing your duty of waging the war. 30

Comment:—

'Mayi sarvāṇi karmāṇi sannyasyādhyātmacetasā'— Generally a striver believes that he has to perform obligatory actions, but these lead him to bondage. In order to clarify his misconception, the Lord urges him to surrender all actions to Him, with discriminative insight, without having the least affinity for these. In fact, all actions of the world, are performed by Lord's power. The body, senses, mind, objects and power etc., are, the Lord's and the Lord is his. By thinking so, when a striver performs actions, those actions instead of leading him to bondage, steer him to salvation.

Every person, knows that he cannot keep the body, senses, mind, intellect and material objects etc., under his control, according to his desire. These belong to nature while the self is, a fragment of the Lord (Gītā 15/7). So, real surrender consists in accepting these as of the Lord's, rather than his own. Therefore, 'surrender' means, the renunciation of assumed affinity, for objects and actions, by attaching importance, to discrimination.

By the expression 'adhyātmacetasā', the Lord means to say, that one should have a spiritual aim (of God) rather than a mundane one. The man who has fixed his aim, has a discriminative insight. In fact, a man's aim or necessity is, to attain the imperishable, (spiritual) while his desire is to gain the perishable. A striver should decide upon the aim of his life, instead of having a desire.

From either the philosophical or the scientific point of view,

---

the egoistic notion that he is the doer, his 'Kriyā' becomes a 'Karma' which bears threefold fruit—pleasant, unpleasant and mixed (Gītā 18/12). But when he has no notion of doership, his 'Kriyā' does not turn into 'Karma' i.e., does not bear fruit, it is performed just like an impulse (nature) (Gītā 3/33).

material objects such as, body etc., cannot be proved to be one's own. They have been bestowed upon him, so that he may make its right use. But, when he lays a claim on them, he is bound. Therefore, when a striver through discrimination, accepts the objects and actions as the Lord's, it means that he surrenders these to Him.

In the verse, the expression 'Adhyātmacetasā', has been used specially. It means. that it is out of ignorance that the perishable body or world, seems to be one's own. If discrimination is applied, the perishable body or world, cannot seem as one's own, only the Lord will appear as his own. Attachment to the world, leads to degradation, while detachment leads to progress (i.e., upliftment).

"The two lettered 'Mama' i.e., 'this is mine' is death and the three lettered 'Na Mama' i.e., 'this is not mine' is immortality" (Mahā. Śānti. 13/4), Āśvamedhika 51/29).

An Important Fact Pertaining to Surrender

The Lord urges a man to surrender all actions to Him because, he considers the body, senses, mind, intellect, life-breath, material and actions, his own and for himself. But in fact, these are neither his nor can be his. How can the perishable have affinity for the imperishable? Therefore, surrender all actions either to the world or to nature or to God, the result will be the same, as the world is an evolute of nature and God, is the Lord of nature.Thus, both the world and nature, belong to God. Therefore, a striver should think, that he is God's and his so-called possessions, are also God's i.e., he should renounce his feeling of mineness to these. In that case, he has to expect nothing, either from the world or from God. The Lord Himself looks after his wants (needs). When a striver, surrenders his body etc., to Him, these do not seem, to him to be his own. If these appear to him to be his own, it means that he has not surrendered them, to Him.

Therefore, the Lord exhorts a striver to surrender these to Him, with a discriminative insight. Thus, when a striver surrenders these to God, he comes to know the truth, that in fact these are the Lord's, not his.

The fact of surrender to God, is so unique, that even if we surrender out of feeling of surfeit, it brings us immense benefit. In fact, actions, objects, the body and the self, are not ones' own. Actions can be surrendered even after their accomplishment.But real surrender is achieved only when we renounce our affinity with objects and actions. This abandonment is possible, when we discern that instruments (body etc.,) objects, actions and the embodied self, are only God's. A striver commits an error, that he tries to surrender actions and objects to God, but he does not surrender his body etc., and the self to Him. Thus his surrender, remains incomplete. Therefore, a striver should think, that all the objects including his body, senses, mind, intellect and the Self, belong to God, which are really His.

A mere outward renunciation of actions and objects, is not real surrender. Real surrender, consists in regarding the objects and possessions as His. If a striver surrenders these to God by regarding these as his own, the Lord reciprocates by returning these manifold, in the same way, as seeds sown, turn into a rich harvest. But, still it is in a limited amount. However, when he surrenders these to Him regarding them as His, He offers Himself to him, and also feels indebted to him.

The Lord is very much pleased with such a surrender. Even when it does not help the Lord, in anyway. But its doing so striver is released from the bondage of actions. When a child hands over the key lying in a courtyard, to the father, the latter is very much pleased with the baby and wishes it a long life. Why? The reason is, that the child has good feelings, when it offers the key to the father ever though it belongs to him. Similarly, God is pleased with the striver, who offers all objects, the body and the self to Him, and is indebted to him.

An Important Fact Pertaining to Desire

The Lord has created the human body in a most unusual way, and the Lord by His grace has abundantly bestowed upon a human being, the materials for his existence and spiritual practice including discrimination. When man, disregarding his discrimination, uses the things for his selfish motive, and has a desire to acquire more things, he is enslaved and he has to follow the cycle of birth and death. Every man knows the reality, that family, circumstances, ability, power, body, senses, mind and intellect etc., have been acquired. These were neither his in the past, nor would remain his, in the future, because they never remain the same, and are ever-changing. If, having realized this fact, man ceases to depend on these, without attaching importance to them, he can attain salvation, without any doubt. Attachment to these, is the root cause of bondage. His attachment to these gives birth to several other desires, which lead him to sin, pain, sorrow and hell etc. All these things, are perishable while the self is imperishable. So he should perform his duty by renouncing desires.

Here, a doubt may arise, how would he be inclined to act, without desire. The clarification is, that a man is inclined to act for the satisfaction of desires, as well as, to get rid of these. Common men perform actions, in order to satisfy their desires, while strivers act for the purification of their souls, in order to get rid of desires (Gītā 5/11). In fact, actions are performed, in order to get rid of desires rather than to satisfy them.

The aim of human life is to attain God. When this aim is achieved, nothing more remains to be acquired. Only those people, who have forgotten the real aim of human life i.e., God-realization, remain inclined to act, in order to satisfy their desires. The Lord has called such people wretched or pitiful, as they seek the fruits (of their actions) (Gītā 2/49). On the other hand, those strivers, who perform actions by renouncing their fruits, in order to be free from desires, have been called wise (Gītā 2/51).

The feelings of rendering selfless service, Self-realization and God-realization, are aims, rather than desires, while the feeling to acquire perishable objects, is desire.Therefore, it is wrong to think, that a man is not inclined to act without desire. Actions are performed scrupulously, in order to attain one's aim.

Man (soul), is a fragment of God but his disinclination for God and inclination towards the world, gives birth to necessity, as well as, desires.When he totally renounces his assumed affinity for the world, his necessity is fulfilled, and he gets rid of desires.

'Nirāśīrnirmamo bhūtvā yudhyasva vigatajvaraḥ'—When all actions and objects are surrendered to God, even then a fragment of desire as the sense of mine and grief, can remain. For example, if we offer a book to someone, and we see him studying that book, we think that he is studying the book, given by us. In order to free us from this minor attachment, the Lord urges us not to have a desire to acquire anything, nor to be attached to the acquired things and not to be grieved for the things lost. The criterion for surrender is, that a striver has no fragment of desire, no feeling of mine and no grief.

When a striver surrenders all actions and objects to God, sometimes because of past impressions (influences), he feels that he has not got rid of desire, the sense of mineness and grief. Such a striver need not lose heart, because only he who perceives desire, the sense of mineness and grief, becomes free of them. Similar, is the case with egoism. Every human being fully deserves to get rid of desire, and a sense of mine and grief.

In the whole Gītā the term 'Jvara' (mental fever viz., grief) has only been used here. In a war, a warrior is grieved at the death of his kith and kin. Therefore, Lord Kṛṣṇa directs Arjuna to fight, delivered from grief, as his duty as a member of the warrior class. The Lord, means to say that a striver should perform his duty by surrendering it to God, and being free from desire, a sense of mineness and grief. Remaining equanimous in success and failure, pleasure and pain, a sense of mineness and aversion etc., is known as a state of 'Vigatajvaraḥ' (freedom from grief). In fact, all the mental defects, such as a sense of mineness, aversion, worry, agitation and turmoil etc., are included in, 'Jvara'.

An Important Fact

When a striver has God-realization as the only goal of his life, all his possessions and things, whether superior or inferior, are surrendered to God. Having surrendered his actions and objects, he surrenders his desire, the sense of mineness and grief, which appear in him, to God. Thus, he becomes a staunch devotee with exclusive devotion.

For a sage who wishes to attain Yoga, action is said to be the means (Gītā 6/3), because, while performing action he comes to know his defects, (desire, the sense of mineness etc.).* Therefore, (in the twelfth verse of the twelfth chapter) the renunciation of the fruit of action, has been considered to be better than meditation. The reason is, that in meditation a striver pays attention so that the mind is not volatile. When his mind is fixed, he regards it, as his success and does not pay heed to other defects, such as desire and sense of mineness etc. Therefore, the Lord in this verse orders Arjuna to perform his duty of fighting, so that he may come to know his defects also.

As the Lord (in the forty-eighth verse of the second chapter) instructs Arjuna to perform his duty while being equanimous in success and failure, here, He asks him to fight being free

* A volunteer offers his service being a member of a voluntary committee. But when he is honoured or praised, he relishes it i.e., derives pleasures out of it. This is wrong. Thus such defects become known only when actions are performed.

from desire, the sense of mineness and grief. When even such a savage deed as fighting, can be performed with equanimity, what other action is there which cannot be performed with equanimity? Equanimity can be attained by believing, "I am neither my body, nor the body is mine nor is it for me," which is also, a fact.

It is possible to do an act worth doing, only when a striver's aim is focussed on God, and not on the world. As the striver advances gradually, on the path of God-realization, his vices, like desire, myness and attachment etc., diminish automatically and he experiences his Self to be positioned in equanimity. As soon as the practice of equanimity gets perfect, the doership is vanished completely and identification with the aim is established. As a rule, the ego perishes when there remains no desire to do anything, for one's own good gain.

Arjuna wants to attain salvation, without performing his duty, of fighting. When Arjuna asks for a way to salvation, the Lord orders him to fight, as it is his duty. According to the Lord, salvation can be attained, through the path of action or knowledge or devotion.

Appendix—By now the Lord answered Arjuna's question (why do you urge me to perform such a dreadful deed?) in several ways. Now in this verse the Lord tells him the method to perform actions through the path of devotion to God.

'Surrender all actions to Me'—By this expression the Lord means to say, "Without regarding actions and objects as yours and for you, regard them as Mine and for Me." The reason is that God is entire (complete) and all actions and objects (Adhibhūta) (matter) are within the entire form of the Lord (Gītā 7/29-30). Here the term 'mayi' (Me) has been used for the entire form of the Lord.

In this verse by the expression, 'mayi sarvāṇi karmāṇi sannyasya' Bhaktiyoga (the path of devotion); by the expression, 'adhyātmacetasā' Jñānayoga (the path of knowledge); and by the expression, 'nirāśīrnirmamo bhūtvā yudhyasva vigatajvaraḥ' Karmayoga (the path of action) have been mentioned.

Link:—Having outlined His teaching (principle) in the preceding verse, in the next two verses, the Lord substantiates, the same.

ये मे मतमिदं नित्यमनुतिष्ठन्ति मानवाः।
श्रद्धावन्तोऽनसूयन्तो मुच्यन्ते तेऽपि कर्मभिः॥ ३१॥

ye me matamidaṁ nityamanutiṣṭhanti mānavāḥ
śraddhāvanto'nasūyanto mucyante te'pi karmabhiḥ

Persons who always follow this teaching of Mine, with faith and without question, are released from the bondage of all actions (Karma). 31

Comment:—

'Ye me matamidaṁ nityamanutiṣṭhanti mānavāḥ śraddhāvanto'nasūyanto'—A person belonging to any caste, creed, sect and order of life etc., who wants to be released from the bondage of actions, should practise this teaching. By realizing the fact, that the body, senses, mind, intellect, objects and actions etc., are not one's own, men are released from this bondage. 'Śraddhāvantaḥ', is he who has a firm faith in and devotion for the Lord and His teaching.

A man is released from bondage, when he regards the material objects, such as body etc., neither as his nor for him. Having faith in this truth, it becomes easy to renounce the assumed affinity for the insentient.

A striver having faith, only listens to the divine discourses and translates these into practice. This human body has been bestowed upon us, so that we may realize God. So we should try to arouse a yearning to realize Him. When this yearning is aroused, other virtues such as faith, promptness and self-control etc., are naturally inculcated in our mind.

The Lord has laid emphasis on faith and also freedom from petty objections, because even a man of faith can have a carping nature, to some extent. So the Lord urges strivers to be totally free from cavil. The Lord also lays emphasis on this very fact, while glorifying the study of the Gītā when He declares, "A man who hears this gospel with faith and uncritically is liberated (Gītā 18/71).

When a man holds that the teaching of the Lord is good, but it reveals His boastful and egoistic nature; or how could actions lead to salvation, when these are conducive to bondage—such opinions show a man's critical spirit. So, a striver should be free from this sort of attitude.

In fact, all objects belong to the Lord, but by an error, a man regards these as his own and so he is enslaved. It is because of his attachment and desire, that he has to suffer. Therefore, the Lord, out of His grace and affection, urges him to surrender all actions and things to Him, so that he may attain eternal bliss, though He lacks nothing, and is perfect.

The Lord's teaching is called, an universal doctrine. Here the Lord's teaching or discipline has been described by the term 'Matam'. The Lord, out of His natural simplicity and absence of vanity, has called the universal principle, as mere 'Mata.' His teachings ever remain the same, without undergoing any modifications. It depends, upon a man whether he has faith in it or not.

Here, the adjective 'nityam' (constant) does not qualify 'Matam' (teaching) but it modifies 'anutiṣṭhanti' (practise) (follow), because the Lord is eternal (constant) and so all objects pertaining to Him, are also eternal. His teaching is also eternal. So the Lord emphasizes that it should be practised constantly.

Question:—What is the doctrine of the Lord, and how should it be practised (followed)?

Answer:—All acquired things are not ours—this is the considered view of the Lord. Whatever materials—body, senses, mind, intellect, life-breath, riches, property, objects etc., there are, these are the evolutes of nature and the world is also an evolute of nature. So, all of these have identity with the world; while the self, being a fragment of God, has its identification with Him. Therefore, all of these are not our personal possessions, but have been bestowed upon us, so that we may utilize them properly. Besides, these, the virtues such as good conduct, renunciation, dispassion, kindness and forgiveness etc., are, also not personal; being divine traits they also belong to God. Had these been ours these would have also remained with us and no one could have acquired them, without our permission. But it is not so. When we accept these as ours, we are proud of these and pride is a root of demoniac endowment.

When we regard a thing, which really is not ours, as ours, it captures us. Materialistic things, such as body etc., are neither ours nor for us. Had they been ours, they might have provided us full satisfaction, when we acquired them. But these never satisfy us, and add fuel to desires. But if we realize God, we are fully satisfied, and we attain perfection and nothing further remains to be gained (acquired). As, a lost child is not pleased and satisfied with any other woman (though she is also a mother), except his own mother, similarly, we are not satisfied with any other state except God-realization. Therefore, so long as we have the desire to acquire something, it, means that we have not acquired our very own object viz., God.

We neither brought the worldly things with us, nor can we carry these with us and at present also, these are deserting us, constantly. While presently these are under our possession. It behaves that, we use these for the welfare of the world, rather than lay claim to them. The Lord is so generous and gracious, that He bestows these upon us in, such a way, that they appear to us to be ours. If we use them for our selfish motive, it means that we misuse His generosity and grace. Therefore, a striver in order to rectify his error, should surrender these to Him, with a discriminative insight.

If a striver whose only aim is God-realization, gives a serious thought to the topic, he will come to know the truth, that all the acquired things such as, the body, rank, right, education, knowledge, riches and property etc., belong to the world, and so they should be utilized, for the world. We may call them either of the world or of nature, or of God, but these are not ours. So how can they be for us.

A striver has, neither to regard a thing as his, nor has to perform any action for him. The actions, which are performed by him for himself, bind him because the Lord declares, "One is bound by actions, other than those performed, for the sake of sacrifice (Yajña)" (Gītā 3/9), "Actions including the stored ones of the person who performs them for the sake of sacrifice are dissolved entirely"(Gītā 4/23).

God is the almighty Lord of all the worlds (Gītā 5/29). When, a man regards himself as the lord of his objects and possessions, he forgets the real Lord, and thinks of those objects and possessions. Therefore, a striver should live like a servant to the Lord, Who is the only master of the entire universe. By becoming an instrument in His hands, he should perform his duty, with the body, senses, mind, intellect and material bestowed upon him by Him, without having any pride of ownership.

Having surrendered everything and action to God, he should not be swayed, by the pairs of opposites, such as profit and loss, honour and dishonour, pleasure and pain etc., because these are the gifts of God and so they are His. Performance of duty, joyfully, under the available circumstance means, the practice of His teaching.

'Mucyante te'pi karmabhiḥ'—The Lord, seems to say to Arjuna, that He was ordering him in clear terms to surrender actions to Him. By obeying Him, he will undoubtedly be released from bondage. Moreover, if other people also, whom He has not ordered this way practise His teaching, they will also be released from bondage even though they may not believe in Him.

Appendix—The Lord's opinion is the real and foremost principle, within which all views and doctrines are included. The Lord without pride with a simple and polite heart, calls His principle (Siddhānta) as opinion (Mata). It means that the Lord has not insisted upon his opinion or the opinion of anyone else but he has put forth his view being impartial.

An opinion is not universal but it is personal. Everyone can express his opinion but a principle is the basic and supreme truth of universal character which everyone has to follow. Therefore there can be difference of opinion between the teacher and the pupil but there can't be difference in principle. Sages, hermits and philosophers name their opinion as 'principle' but in the Gītā the Lord names His principle as 'Mata' (opinion). There are differences in the opinions of sages, hermits, philosophers and teachers etc., but the Lord's opinion viz., principle is universally accepted without any difference of opinion.

ये त्वेतदभ्यसूयन्तो नानुतिष्ठन्ति मे मतम्।
सर्वज्ञानविमूढांस्तान्विद्धि नष्टानचेतसः ॥ ३२ ॥

ye tvetadabhyasūyanto nānutiṣṭhanti me matam
sarvajñānavimūḍhāṁstānviddhi naṣṭānacetasaḥ

But those who demur at My teaching and do not follow it, deluded of all knowledge, and discrimination, know them to be doomed to destruction. 32

Comment:—

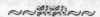

'Ye tvetadabhyasūyanto nānutiṣṭhanti me matam'—Having shown the advantage of practising His teaching (in the thirty-first verse) here the term 'tu' (but) has been used, to distinguish those who do not follow His teaching, from those who do follow.

Some people hold that as worldly, selfish people, want to acquire worldly objects and also want to get profit themselves, similarly, the Lord wants all actions to be surrendered to Him and also that He should be regarded, as the Lord. Those who think so, find fault with His teaching.

Similarly, 'those who think that in worldly affairs, desire is a must, and it is impossible to renounce attachment, aversion and a feeling of mine, also slight His teaching.

Those people who hanker after worldly pleasures and prosperity and regard the body, objects and actions etc., as theirs, and for them, do not follow His teaching.

'Sarvajñānavimūḍhān tān'—Those who do not follow the Lord's teaching are under delusion regarding worldly knowledge (sciences, arts etc.). They remain engrossed, in inventions and scientific discoveries, like motor cars, aeroplanes, radios, televisions etc. Similarly, they remain engaged in knowing about painting, architecture, arts, crafts, mystical formulas, incantations, implements, different scripts and languages, custom traditions and other developments. They are fully convinced, that there is nothing beyond these things (Gītā 16/11). Such people, are said to be under delusion regarding knowledge.

'Acetasaḥ'—They are devoid of discrimination, because they cannot distinguish the real from the unreal, righteous from unrighteous, salvation from bondage and so on. They remain ignorant, like animals. "Of vain hopes, of vain actions, of vain knowledge and senseless, they verily are" (Gītā 9/12).

'Viddhi naṣṭān'—Know those human beings who do not follow the Lord's teaching, to be doomed to destruction. It means, that they will be subjected to the cycle of birth and death.

A man can attain salvation, upto the time of death (Gītā 8/5). Therefore, those people, who do not follow the Lord's teaching in this life at present can follow it, at sometime in future because of good company etc., and can attain salvation. But if they do not follow His teachings even upto death, they should be known to be doomed, to destruction, because they are deprived of God-realization.

He, who does not follow the Lord's teaching, performs actions out of attachment and aversion, which are his foes (Gītā 3/34). Transient objects and actions perish, but a man while performing actions, comes under the sway of attachment and aversion, which lead him to lower births and hells. Therefore, the Lord declares, that such a man will be doomed to destruction.

In the thirty-first verse, the Lord declares that those who follow His teachings are released from the bondage of actions, while in this verse He declares, that those who do not, follow His teaching, are to be doomed to destruction. It means, that the Lord urges upon people to follow His teachings, even if they do not believe in Him. If they do not follow His teaching, they will be doomed to. But if a striver, believing in Him, follows His teaching, He offers Himself to him. If he, without believing in Him, follows His teaching, He leads him to salvation. It means, that he who believes in Him, attains His love while he who follows His teaching, attains salvation.

Link:—Why are those people, who do not follow the Lord's teaching, doomed to destruction? The Lord, answers the question in the next verse.

सदृशं चेष्टते स्वस्याः प्रकृतेर्ज्ञानवानपि।
प्रकृतिं यान्ति भूतानि निग्रहः किं करिष्यति॥ ३३॥

sadṛśaṁ ceṣṭate svasyāḥ prakṛterjñānavānapi
prakṛtiṁ yānti bhūtāni nigrahaḥ kiṁ kariṣyati

Even a wise man acts in accordance with his nature. All

beings follow their own nature. What them can restraint do? 33

Comment:—

'Prakṛtiṁ yānti bhūtāni'—All actions are performed, either according to one's own nature or according to the Lord's principles, (scriptural injunctions). One's nature can be of two kinds, either free from attachment and aversion, or having attachment and aversion. If a man, on his way, happens to see a notice board. His casting a glance at it, is, neither because of attachment nor aversion, nor from an angle of principle. It happens through his pure personal nature. We read a letter received from a friend, with some feeling of attachment, while that of an enemy with aversion. We study sacred texts such as the Gītā and the Rāmāyaṇa, according to the Lord's principle. The only aim of human life is God-realization. Therefore, actions which are performed, with the aim of God-realization, are performed, according to His principles i.e., according to the scriptural injunctions.

All actions, such as seeing, hearing, smelling, touching etc., are performed according to one's nature and according to His principle. Nature, free from attachment and aversion, is not faulty, while nature with attachment and aversion is. Actions, which are performed out of attachment and aversion, bind a man because they make his nature impure. On the other hand, actions which are performed according to God's principles, lead to salvation, because these purify one's nature. It is, because of impure personal nature, that the assumed affinity for the world, is not renounced. As soon as his nature is purified, the assumed affinity is easily, renounced.

Actions, are automatically performed, by the so-called body of a wise man, because he has no sense of doership. All actions of a striver, whose aim is God-realization, are performed, according to the scriptural injunctions. As a greedy, person is always careful, that he should not sustain any loss, a striver is always careful lest he should perform an activity with attachment or aversion.

By being careful, a striver's nature is purified and consequently, he is liberated from the bondage of his actions.

Although, all actions are performed by modes of nature, yet an ignorant man, whose mind is deluded by egoism, thinks that he is the doer (Gītā 3/27). Affinity for objects and actions, gives birth to attachment and aversion, which lead him on to the cycle of birth and death. But, he who has no affinity for nature (prakṛti), sees that the self is not the doer (Gītā 13/29).

It is attachment for material objects, which influences a person to perform, evil actions. For a striver, attachment is the main cause of bondage. Attachment dwells in assumed egoism, and appears in mind, intellect, senses and sense-objects.

Egoism is of two kinds—

1—When a self (soul), identifies the self with the insentient (matter) and,

2—The cosmic ego, a mode of nature—'Mahābhūtānya-haṅkāraḥ' (Gītā 13/5). The latter form egoism, is flawless, as it is an instrument, like the mind, intellect and senses etc., while the former kind, is defective. A wise man, does not identify the self with the body, and so all his actions are performed by the modes of nature i.e., by the latter kind. But an ignorant man, who regards the body, as 'I' and 'mine', and all actions as his and for him, is, because the assumption of actions as his, and for him, causes attachment.*

'Sadṛśaṁ ceṣṭate svasyāḥ prakṛterjñānavānapi'—A perfect soul, being free from attachment and aversion, acts in accordance with pure nature. He is not swayed by nature. As a learned man, speaks a language which he knows, similarly, the Lord also, behaves in

* As the body automatically develops and changes, similarly all the actions are naturally performed. But a common man remains engrossed in (practical) actions because of attachment and aversion while a wise man being free from attachment and aversion does not get engrossed in them.

accordance with His incarnation, as Rāma or Kṛṣṇa or a fish, a tortoise or a hog etc., but does not remain completely under sway of nature (prakṛti). Similarly, those enlightened souls who have renounced their affinity for matter (prakṛti) may vary in their nature, but are not swayed by it. So, their actions are nothing more than gestures of action, while common men, who have not renounced their affinity for matter, act according to individual natures (natural propensities) and remain completely under its sway.

Here the term 'Svasyāḥ' implies, that the nature of a wise man is flawless, and so he is not under the sway of nature, he rather controls nature. Actions, bear fruits only when a man performs these, with a sense of 'doership' and selfishness. A wise man, remains free from the vanity of doership and also from selfishness. So actions performed by him, are pure and even ideal, for other strivers.

Impression of the past, and the present births, influence of parents, society, company, education, environment, study, adoration, thoughts, actions and feelings, make up a man's nature. The nature, varies from person to person and everyone is free to make it pure. The nature of one enlightened soul, varies from that of the other, but it is pure (free from attachment and aversion). So they are not swayed by nature. On the other hand, the ignorant (having attachment and aversion) have to perform actions by force according to their own evil nature, which they themselves have acquired.

'Nigrahaḥ kiṁ kariṣyati'—The wise men perform virtuous actions enjoined by the scriptures according to their pure nature, while the ignorant perform evil actions under the sway of their bad nature.

When Arjuna wanted to abstain from fighting, the Lord says to him, "Thy nature will compel thee" (Gītā 18/59), "Thou shalt do even against thy will, fettered by thine, own acts, born of thy nature" (18/60).

As, a motor car cannot cross the limit of 100 miles per hour in its speed, a wise man cannot act, against his pure nature. One with an impure nature is like a damaged car. A damaged car can be repaired in two ways— (i) by the driver himself, (ii) by sending it to a workshop. Similarly, the impure nature can be purified in two ways— (i) through the performance of actions, without attachment and aversion (Gītā 3/34), (ii) through perfect surrender to the Lord (Gītā 18/62). If a motor car functions smoothly, it means that we are not under its control, but if it breaks down it means, that we are affected by it. Similarly, a wise man, because of his pure nature, is not under the sway of nature, while an ignorant man because of his impure nature, has to act under the influence of nature.

A man, who attaches importance to worldly pleasures and prosperity, is sure to have a downfall, even though he may be learned. On the other hand, he who does not attach importance to the insentient (matter) (prosperity and pleasure) and whose aim is God-realization, is surely, to have upliftment, even though he is not learned. The reason is, that feelings, thoughts and actions of a man, whose aim instead of enjoying worldly pleasures and prosperity, is God-realization, are conducive to his uplift (salvation). Therefore, a striver, first of all should decide upon the goal of his life—God-realization. Then, in order to attain that aim, he should perform his duty, being free from attachment and aversion. An easy method, of being free from attachment and aversion, is that we render service to others, with our acquired materials such as body etc., without regarding these as ours and for us, and without expectation of any reward.

If a striver does not want to come under the influence of nature, he should perform his duty, by fixing an ideal for himself. The ideal (model) can be of two kinds— (i) The Lord's teaching (ii) Wise men's actions. By following, the Lord's teaching or wise men's actions, a striver's nature is purified and he realizes

God, Who is ever attainable. On the other hand, the man, who without following the Lord's teaching or the wise men's actions, performs actions out of attachment and aversion, is doomed to destruction (Gītā 3/32).

As we cannot forcibly obstruct the course of a river, but can turn it to another direction, similarly, we can turn the flow of our actions, towards the welfare of others. When we perform acts for the welfare of others, then the direction is towards the world, and we, the strivers, are liberated from the bondage of actions.

Appendix—Even a wise man acts according to his nature. No one can act without being guided by the circumstantial causes. As a teacher teaches a pupil alphabet (a, b, c) in conformity with the standard of his pupil, similarly a wise man acts and behaves with a common man by putting himself in the latter's situation.

'Ceṣṭate'—This term means that he does not perform actions but activities are naturally performed by him according to his nature. The shaking of the leaves of a tree is not an action (sin or virtue) bearing fruit. Even so a man free from the sense of doership has no incentive to perpetrate sinful or virtuous acts, he can never commit a sin or virtue.

The wise men remain engrossed in the welfare of others because their nature as strivers has been to do good to others—'sarvabhūtahite ratāḥ' (Gītā 5/25, 12/4). Therefore though nothing remains to be done, to be known and to be attained by them, yet their nature is to do activities beneficent to all. It means that when by remaining engrossed in the welfare of others, their affinity for the world is totally renounced, they have not to work for the welfare of others but because of the natural inclination of the past, good is naturally done by them as a matter of habit.

Link:— Every man is born with his own nature. Therefore, he has to act according to his nature. Now, the Lord in the next verse, explains how to purify one's nature.

इन्द्रियस्येन्द्रियस्यार्थे रागद्वेषौ व्यवस्थितौ।
तयोर्न वशमागच्छेत्तौ ह्यस्य परिपन्थिनौ॥ ३४॥

indriyasyendriyasyārthe rāgadveṣau vyavasthitau
tayorna vaśamāgacchettau hyasya paripanthinau

Attachment and aversion of man abide in each and every sense-object through the feeling of agreeableness or disagreeableness towards its senses. Let no one come under their sway, for they are his waylayers and foes. 34

Comment:—

'Indriyasyendriyasyārthe rāgadveṣau vyavasthitau'—Each sense has attraction for a pleasant aspect (ear, eye, skin, tongue and nose for sound, sight, touch, taste and smell respectively), and aversion for an unpleasant one.

In fact, attachment and aversion do not abide, in the sense-objects. If they had abode in the sense-objects, the same objects might have been pleasant (desirable) or unpleasant (undesirable) equally, to everyone. But it does not happen. Rain is desirable for a farmer, but not so for a potter. Moreover, the same object is sometimes pleasant, while it is unpleasant at other time, to the same person. Cool air, is pleasant in summer but unpleasant in winter. Thus, we have attraction and aversion by regarding these as desirable and undesirable. Therefore, the Lord has declared, that attachment and aversion of man abide in the sense-objects.

In fact, attachment and aversion abide in assumed 'ego' ('I'ness).* The assumed affinity for the body is called 'ego'. So

* The term 'Asya' in the expression 'Rasavarjaṁ raso'pyasya (Gītā 2/59) used by Lord Kṛṣṇa also denotes that attachment and aversion abide in the assumed 'ego' (in a striver).

long as, there is assumed affinity for the body, attachment and aversion, exist in 'ego' and appear to be abiding in the intellect, mind, senses and objects of senses. These attachment and aversion in their gross forms have been called 'desire' and 'anger' (from the thirty-seventh to the forty-third verses of this chapter). In the fortieth verse, it has been said, that this desire exists in the senses, the mind and the intellect, because it appears to abide in them. As attachment and aversion appear to subsist in the sense-objects, similarly attachment and aversion appear to inhabit in senses, mind and intellect. In fact, the senses, the mind and the intellect are merely instruments. So, there is no question of the desire and anger or attachment and aversion existing in them. Besides this, the Lord declares in the fifty-ninth verse of the second chapter, "The objects of the senses turn away, from the man who abstains from feeding on them but the taste for them remains. Even the taste turns away when the Supreme is seen."

'Tayorna vaśamāgacchet'—The Lord assures strivers, that they should never be disappointed, in the means and ends, if attachment and aversion appear. The scriptures, rather than attachment and aversion, should be the authority for determining what should be done and what should not be done (Gītā 16/24). If a striver acts or abstains from action, with attachment and aversion, it means that he is affected by attachment and aversion. If a person performs actions, or abstains from actions with attachment and aversion, attachment and aversion, are strengthened. This strengthening, leads a man to a downfall.

When a striver starts worship, renouncing the worldly affairs, good and bad thoughts of the world come to his mind, and he gets perturbed. The Lord urges him not to be perturbed, because these are perishable, and appear and disappear. In fact, thoughts have no existence of their own, because as a rule what is born must die. In fact, these thoughts do not come to mind, these rather, slip away from the mind. Thoughts remain suppressed, when a man is busy with worldly affairs, but when he stops his work, the suppressed thoughts, have an outlet. Therefore, a striver, without having attachment or aversion, should remain indifferent to these. Similarly, he should have neither attachment nor aversion, for persons and things etc.

The Means of Overcoming Attachment and Aversion

When actions are performed, out of attachment and aversion, attachment and aversion are strengthened and these are transformed into impure nature. This impure nature, brings a man under its sway. Then the actions performed by him, bind him. So, during the performance or non-performance of actions, a striver should not come under their influence. This is the means, to obliterate attachment and aversion, which is explained here. Previous to this, the Lord also declared, another means. The Lord said, "Those who constantly follow this teaching of Mine, are released from bondage of actions" (Gītā 3/31). So a striver should follow His teachings, so that he may get rid of attachment and aversion. When a striver surrenders, his actions, body, senses, mind, intellect and himself to God, and performs his duty free from desire, egoism and grief, his attachment and aversion perish. So a person should follow His teachings, while he performs actions or abstains himself from actions.

The entire universe is an evolute of nature and a body is a fragment of the universe. So long as a man is attached to a body, he comes under the sway of attachment and aversion, while acquiring and abandoning things etc. When actions are performed or abandoned with attachment and aversion, the performance or non-performance of those strengthen attachment and aversion. But if these are either performed or abandoned according to the scriptural injunctions, attachment and aversion perish. If a person does not know the ordinance of the scriptures, he should keep in mind, the great sage Vedavyāsa's teaching—"O men, listen to the gist of righteousness and follow it. The gist is—We should not do to others, what we do not wish to be done to us (Padma Purāṇa, Sṛṣṭi. 19/355-56).

Liberated souls always follow the scriptural injunctions. That is why Bhīṣma Pitāmaha, offered food and water to the manes on kuśa grass, though his father's hand was clearly visible to him (Mahābhārata, Anuśāsana. 84/15—20). Therefore, a striver should perform, all actions according to the ordinance of the scriptures.

For a striver who wants to get rid of attachment and aversion, the scripture is the authority for determining what should be done. The heart of an enlightened soul, totally free from attachment and aversion, is so pure, that his thoughts, feelings and actions are nothing but, the ordinances of scriptures,* even if he may be illiterate. Thus his words and actions are exemplary (Gītā 3/21) and by following such teaching and actions, strivers get rid of attachment and aversion.

Some people believe that attachment and aversion, are natural tendencies (natural inclinations of the mind) which cannot be wiped out, but it is wrong, as these appear and disappear. When a striver practises spiritual discipline, they become bearer—it is every striver's experience; and whatever grows scarce, may perish altogether. The Lord has declared, that these come to mind (Gītā 2/55) but do not stay there permanently. Moreover, He has called these as modifications, (Gītā 13/6) which have a beginning and an end, rather than 'Dharmas'. Evenness of mind, in the desirable and the undesirable, has been called spiritual discipline (Gītā 13/9). Had attachment and aversion, been permanent features of the mind, it could not have attained, the state of evenness. This means that they come to the mind and can be wiped out.

* The heart of the person who never renounces righteousness also becomes pure. Great poet Kālidāsa while describing king Duṣyanta declares—"Where there is doubt, there the inclination of the heart of a virtuous person is the testimony" (Abhijñānaśākuntalam 1/21).

A man, through discrimination, knows that nature (matter) prakṛti and Soul (spirit) are different from each other. But, the soul identifies itself with the body (born of nature), and this identification is called 'ego' (I) in which attachment and aversion exist, and both these strengthen egoism. These—(attachment and aversion) seem to abide in the intellect, because of which one's own beliefs appear pleasant, while the beliefs of others unpleasant. These seem to abide in the mind, and what one thinks as desirable, while what others think, is undesirable. These seem to also in senses, due to which favourable objects seem pleasant, while unfavourable ones appear unpleasant. These may also appear, in the objects of senses (sound, touch, sight, taste, smell), as favourable and unfavourable. When egoism (identification of the self with the body) is rooted out, attachment and aversion, totally perish, because egoism is their base.

'I am a servant', 'I am an inquisitive learner', 'I am a devotee' etc., this is how one may feel. These me—a 'servant', 'learner' and 'devotee', reside in the same 'I' in which attachment and aversion, co-exist. Attachment and aversion, abide neither exclusively in inert nor in conscious state. These live, only in assumed, relation between the inert and conscious, yet these live mainly, in the inert. In the state of identification of soul with the matter, the material part is attracted towards matter alone, but it appears also in the conscious soul, due to this identification. Attraction for the insentient (matter) is attachment. When a striver identifies the self with the body, he feels difficulty, in renouncing attachment and aversion. But when he has an eye on the Self, he has no difficulty in renouncing attachment and aversion, because these have no existence of their own. These are born, only when one identifies the self with the body etc.

If a striver has attachment for good company, adoration and meditation etc., he has aversion for the world. But if he has 'love' (devotion) for God, he will have no aversion for the world, but he will be indifferent to the world.*

If a man has attachment for one object, he has aversion for an other, but when he has love (devotion) for God, he develops dispassion. Dispassion, leads to selfless service by wiping out desire for pleasure. Then the body, senses, mind, intellect and ego, are automatically engaged in the service of the world. Consequently, attachment and aversion, which abide in ego, totally perish when affinity to the self for the body etc., along with ego, is renounced.

All actions of a person, are performed according to his nature or according to scriptural injunctions. If something is done, with a view to spiritual progress only, it is done in obedience to the above rule. Nature, can be pure (free from attachment and aversion) and impure (with attachment and aversion). It cannot be totally renounced, but it can be purified i.e., made free from attachment and aversion. As the course of the Ganges cannot be forcibly obstructed, but its direction can be changed, similarly, action cannot be totally renounced, but their flow (course) can be changed i.e., can be made free from attachment and aversion. This is a vital teaching of the Gītā. It is, neither the performance nor non-performance of actions, but attachment and aversion, which are the stumbling blocks to a striver's spiritual progress. So, the Lord declares, that a wise man, is he who has neither attachment for agreeable actions nor aversion for disagreeable ones (Gītā 18/10). Generally, strivers

* Whether a striver has attachment or love (devotion) to holy company can be illustrated by the following example:—If anybody creates an obstacle to a striver's good company, adoration or meditation and he gets angry with him, it means that he has attachment. But if he feels sad, it means that he has love. The reason is that there are obstacles to the spiritual discipline when his determination is not firm. So he is sad because of his shortcoming. Similarly, if he is biased against any religion or sect, it means that he is attached to his own religion or sect.

In fact even attachment to the good company, adoration and meditation is not bad because this spiritual practice leads the mind to the thought of God (Śrīmadbhā. 7/1/31).

are not on their guard against attachment and aversion. Their activities come under the sway of these. Therefore, a striver should perform actions, according to scriptural ordinances in order to be free from attachment and aversion. By doing so his nature will automatically, be improved.

When desire mixed with attraction or aversion, is born, and we act according to its dictates, attraction and aversion, get strengthened and if we act according to the principles enunciated these get wiped out.

When good and evil thoughts come to the mind of a striver, he should neither have attachment nor aversion for these, he should neither support nor oppose these. He should remain indifferent by thinking that he (the self) is different and so the self has no affinity, for these.

If a striver finds himself helpless, in renouncing attachment and aversion, he should take refuge in the omnipotent Lord, Who is his most disinterested friend. By His grace, he overcomes attachment and aversion (Gītā 7/14) and attains supreme peace (Gītā 18/62). The assumption is that the body, senses, mind, intellect, ego and all the worldly objects belong to the Lord, take refuge in Him. So, a striver should serve Him, in order to please Him offer the materials provided by Him,without expecting any reward. Expectation of a reward leads to affinity for the insentient (matter).

'Service to others, without expecting any reward', is the means to wipe out attachment and aversion. All our possessions, including the physical, subtle and causal bodies, as well as ego, are to render service to the world, because these are essentially the same, as is the world. An assumption, that these are different from the world, leads to bondage. A striver, should not derive pleasure out of things and actions, with a physical body, out of thinking, with the subtle body and out of trance with the causal body. In fact, this human body is not for pleasures (Mānasa 7/44/1).

Secondly, the body, senses, mind, intellect and objects etc., with which service is rendered, are fragments of the world. How can fragments of the world be ours when the world is not ours? We cannot render service to others with these in a disinterested way, if we regard these as ours. Therefore, we should regard these as, of those whose service is rendered with these. A devotee surrenders these to God, by regarding these as His. Similarly, a Karmayogī surrenders these to the world, by regarding these as the world's.

A Vital Fact Pertaining to Service

He alone can render true service to others, who never requires anything for himself. The desire for money in lieu of service, is no doubt a desire, but an inclination to serve, is also a desire, because it results in a desire for riches. A striver, should not have a desire to acquire money, even for rendering service, to others. If he gets an opportunity, he should render service according to his resources, but he should have no desire to render service. He who derives pleasure by rendering service to others, or has the sentiment that people are benefited by him, or expects honour and praise, or gets pleased by receiving honour and praise, in reality enjoys pleasures, instead of rendering true service. If a striver derives pleasure out of this, it gives birth to attachment and desire. In fact, the objects with which he renders service to others, belong to them. So, there is no obligation if their trust property is returned to them. Does anyone want reward for having washed his face with his own hands?

Question:—How can service be rendered without objects and money etc? So, what is the harm if anyone desires money and objects, in order to render service to others?

Answer:—Service, with material objects is, a gross type of service. Real service is a sentiment or feeling, and not an action. Action leads to bondage, while service, releases from bondage.

A sense of service impels a man to use his possessions, in the service of others. Real service is rendered through feelings, rather than through actions. A man of generous feelings can render service even with limited resources, he has. He, who attaches importance to objects cannot render service, with these, because he has pride in doing so, and thus he derives pleasure out of his action, whether he knows it or not. A shopkeeper, gives articles to others, but he does not render service, because he has a desire to receive money in exchange. Similarly, money which is paid as tax to the king (state), cannot be called, charity. If a person offers charity or food or water to someone, in order to reap its fruit, his affinity for the object is not renounced. But, if he offers the articles, without expecting any reward, it means that he renders service and his affinity for those objects, is renounced.

Only he who lays claim to a thing i.e., is the real owner of a thing, can receive such a thing given by us. We, repay debt, by offering the thing back to him. He, who is in greater need of something actually, is a deserving hand to receive it. He takes it from us, only if it is his, otherwise not.

He, who renders service to others from his heart, arouses feelings of service in their hearts also. If, this feeling is not aroused in their hearts, it means that there has been a flaw (such as of reaping the fruit) in the service. A striver, should be on the alert, in this respect. While rendering service, he should never expect to be called, virtuous or good, because this feeling develops pride in him.

A striver, should live in the world, in order to render service to others by performing his duty. He should never cause any harm to anyone, in the least. He should share the joys and sorrows of others, because that gives them moral strength, that there is someone who is sharing their joys and sorrows. In this way, happy men will become happier and the sad will be consoled. He should console the sad, by quoting Lord Rāma, king Nala and king Hariścandra etc., who had to face adverse situations, though they were very noble and virtuous. Moreover, there are many others who are in a more pitiable condition. Thus one should try to console them, be prepared to help them and remain engaged in their welfare, by having good feelings. Those, who share the pleasures and pains of others, are saints (Mānasa 7/38/1).

Now a doubt may arise, that we shall never be free from sorrow, if we share the sorrow of other people, because the world is full of it. To share, the sorrow of others, means to have the feeling to alleviate their suffering and to make efforts for it. This will give us happiness, rather than make us sad. The explanation is, that other people will also share our sorrows i.e., they will try to help us, in doing away with our sorrow. So, we should try to share the sorrow of others from our heart, and according to our resources. When we share their sorrow, all our resources are automatically, utilized, to relieve them of their sorrow and suffering. It is beyond our power to make others happy, but it is upto us to use our resources, in order to help the sad in removing their sorrow. This renunciation of the means of happiness, will bring us peace of mind.

A striver should always have the feeling that no one should ever suffer in the least. Everyone is free, in having such generous feeling. This feeling is a service itself. Actions and objects are limited, while feeling of generosity, is unlimited. So a striver can attain the unlimited Lord, by unlimited feelings. How can He be attained by the limited resources such as actions and objects? Therefore, those whose possessions and resources are limited, can also render great service, by having generous feelings.

A striver, who does not regard the body, senses, mind and intellect etc., as his, can share the joys and sorrows of others. In fact, the body, senses, mind and intellect etc., are neither his nor for him. Similar, is the case with objects, resources and persons. These are also not his personal property. Everyone, whether he is rich or poor, educated or uneducated, can renounce this assumed affinity for these. As soon as, this assumed affinity is renounced, and one renders service to others, by those things regarding them as theirs, he gets rid of attachment and aversion, easily.

'Tau hyasya paripanthinau'—In the spiritual discipline, attachment and aversion, are the waylayers to rob a striver, of his spiritual property. But, a striver does not pay heed to this fact. Therefore, he does not progress in the spiritual field as much as he should have. Generally, strivers complain that they cannot concentrate their minds, on God. But this lack of concentration is not such a stumbling block, as are attachment and aversion. When attachment and aversions are renounced, the mind can easily concentrate.

Total renunciation of actions, pertaining to one's nature, is beyond a striver's power, but their performance without attachment and aversion, is within his power. So, the Lord urges strivers, not to come under their sway for these are his waylayers. In fact, attachment and aversion are naturally perishing. But, a striver by holding that they dwell in him, accepts their existence and then acts, by coming under their influence. So he does not get rid of them. If he holds that they do not dwell in him and so he does not act, being swayed by them, these will automatically perish.

Appendix—When we assume that others are instrumental in providing pleasure and pain to us, then attachment and aversion ensue viz., we get attached to the thing which we think provides pleasure to us and have aversion to the thing which provides pain to us. Therefore attachment and aversion are born by one's own error, there is no other reason. It is because of attachment and aversion that we fail to perceive the world as the manifestation of God but we view it as insentient (inert) and perishable. If attachment and aversion are rooted out, it is not insentient but all manifests as God—'vāsudevaḥ sarvam' (Gītā 7/19).

When evils such as attachment and aversion appear, one should not come under their sway viz., he should not perform forbidden actions being swayed by them. Being affected by them, if actions are performed, the evils (flaws) will be strengthened. But if actions are not done being swayed by them, the man will be filled with enthusiasm. For example, if anyone uttered bitter words to us but we didn't get angry, we would be filled with enthusiasm and joy that we could escape anger. But we should hold that it was not done by our own power; but by God's grace otherwise we would have been overpowered by it. If a striver perceives any defect, he should not be under its sway and should not assume it in him. If attachment and aversion had existed in the self, they would have remained as long as the self had existed. But this is everyone's experience that we ever exist but attachment and aversion don't stay forever, they are fleeting. Attachment and aversion can't have an access to the self because the self's category is quite different from that of attachment and aversion. He, who knows the fleeting nature of attachment and aversion, is different from them. Therefore attachment and aversion are different from us and they are also different from the mind and intellect etc., in which they make a visit—'manogatān' (Gītā 2/55). 'Indriyasyendriyasyārthe rāgadveṣau vyavasthitau'—this expression means that a man should not be attached to desirable or undesirable circumstances but should make proper use of them viz., in desirable circumstances he should serve others while in undesirable circumstances he should give up the desire for favourable circumstances. The expression 'tayorna vaśamāgacchet' means that he should not be happy and sad in favourable and unfavourable circumstances. To feel happy and sad means to be attached to the fruit of action and the person who is attached to the fruit of action gets tied down—'phale sakto nibadhyate' (Gītā 5/12).

Link:—When we rise above attachment and aversion, what should we do and what should we refrain from doing? The Lord, answers this question, in the verse that follows:—

श्रेयान्स्वधर्मो विगुणः परधर्मात्स्वनुष्ठितात्।
स्वधर्मे निधनं श्रेयः परधर्मो भयावहः ॥ ३५ ॥

śreyānsvadharmo viguṇaḥ paradharmātsvanuṣṭhitāt
svadharme nidhanaṁ śreyaḥ paradharmo bhayāvahaḥ

Better is one's own duty (dharma) though devoid of merit, than the duty of another well performed. Better is death in one's own duty, than of another, which is fraught with danger. 35

Comment:—

'Śreyān*svadharmo viguṇaḥ paradharmātsvanuṣṭhitāt'—The duty of another person according to his caste, order of life, etc., may outwardly seem full of merit, be easy to perform, be attractive, provide riches, comforts, honour and praise etc., and enable one to live with comfort throughout his life, yet as forbidden to him. These are fraught with fear (pain). On the other hand, one's own duty, according to one's caste and order of life, may be devoid of merit, be difficult to perform, not appealing and not providing riches, comforts, honour or praise etc., and may be painful, throughout life, yet these should be performed without expecting any reward, as these leads to salvation. Therefore, a person should always perform his duty, without expecting any reward, without a sense of 'mine' and without attachment.

Performance of duty, for a man is but natural and innate. A man is born, according to his actions, and actions are decided, by his birth (Gītā 18/41). Through the performance of his own duty, he attains perfection (Gītā 18/45). Therefore, one should not give up one's duty ordained by one's nature, even if it seems

* The term 'Jyāyasī' (Superior) (3/1) used in the question put by Arjuna and the term 'Śreyān' are synonymous. It means that the Lord has answered Arjuna's question in this verse with particular attention.

to be tainted with blemish (Gītā 18/48).

Arjuna thinks, it is better to live in this world by begging, than to fight (Gītā 2/5). So the Lord makes it clear to Arjuna, that begging being the duty of a beggar, is not his duty, because he is a Kṣatriya (a member of the warrior class), and not a beggar. In the first chapter, when Arjuna said that only sin would accrue to them by fighting (1/36), the Lord said, that having abandoned his own duty and forfeited his fame, he would incur sin (2/33). Further, the Lord declared, "Treating alike pleasure and pain, gain and loss, victory and defeat, engage thou in battle; thus, thou shall not incur sin" (2/38). In the eighteenth chapter also He declares, "Better is one's own duty though devoid of merit, than the duty of another well performed and he who performs his duty ordained by one's own nature, incurs no sin" (18/47). It means, that a man incurs sin only when duty is performed with attachment and aversion. When a striver performs his duty scrupulously, being free from attachment and aversion, he realizes equanimity, which leads him to freedom from sorrow and pain (Gītā 6/23). So the Lord urges Arjuna, time and again, to perform his duty of fighting without attachment and aversion. By performing his duty he would be detached from actions, develop dispassion, and attain the goal of life. Through the selfless performance of duty, actions flow towards nature (prakṛti) and so a striver has no affinity for these. Therefore, a striver should perform his duty, with the view to root out attachment, for actions.

Lord Kṛṣṇa is convincing Arjuna that having taken birth in the warrior class and fighting is his duty he had to treat alike victory and defeat, gain and loss, and pleasure and pain believing that he had no concern as such with war but he had to act in order only, to remove attachment with actions. The body, senses, mind, intellect and matter etc., are meant for performing duty alone.

One's duty done according to one's caste and order of life,

even though it may appear devoid of merit, leads to salvation. A Kṣatriya's duty of fighting, which involves violence may seem devoid of merits as compared with that of a Brāhmaṇa such as serenity, self-restraint, austerity, purity and forgiveness etc., yet a Kṣatriya (member of the warrior class) should fight, as it will lead him to salvation.

According to one's caste and order of life etc., outwardly actions (duties) may seem terrible or mild, but these are performed with the only aim of God-realization. When a person forgets the real aim of life i.e., God-realization and attaches importance to worldly objects, actions seem terrible or mild to him. Under no circumstances should one, discard his duty.

'Svadharme nidhanaṁ śreyaḥ'— If people ever gained, comfort, pleasure, property, riches, honour and praise etc., by performing their duty, there could be seen crowds of righteous people. But, duty is not performed, keeping in view pleasure or pain, but it is performed according to the teachings of the Lord or the scriptures, without expecting any reward. So, while performing his duty, if a striver suffers pain, that pain leads him to his spiritual progress. In fact, that pain is not pain, but is penance or austerity, which is conducive to progress, as penance is performed for ones own self, while duty is performed for others. Penance which is performed intentionally, does not prove so beneficial, as penance, in the form of pain, which comes uninvited.Those who die while performing their duty, become immortal. From the worldly point of view also, it is observed, that those who do not deviate from their duty in spite of suffering pain, are admired and honoured. Patriots who suffered tortures, went to jail and were hanged, in order to make the country independent, are praised and honoured even today. On the other hand, those who are sent to jail, because of their crimes are condemned and dishonoured. It means, that the person who performs his duty without expecting any reward, may suffer pain and even may meet with death, but that pain wins honour and praise here, and leads him to salvation hereafter, because he has an eye on righteousness.

Question:—How to know for certain, that death while performing one's own duty, leads only to salvation?

Answer:—The Gītā is a gospel of Lord Kṛṣṇa Himself. So, there should not arise any doubt, about His teaching. Secondly it is a matter of faith and belief, rather than reasoning, yet some aspects clarify the doubts:

(1)—Whatever, is not known to us should be decided by the scriptures.* It is mentioned in the scriptures, that he who protects righteousness, is protected by the righteous (Manusmṛti 8/15) i.e., righteousness leads him to salvation. Therefore, the responsibility of salvation of a person, who follows righteousness falls on the righteous and the preachers of righteousness, such as God, the Vedas, the scriptures and the sages and ascetics. It is their power which leads one to salvation. In the scriptures, it is mentioned that a chaste woman, attains salvation. She does not attain salvation, because of the virtues of her husband and his power, but because of the power of the Lord, the Vedas and the scriptures etc., who have made this law (ordinance). There is no doubt about it.

(2) History also reveals the fact, that he who performs his duty with righteousness attains salvation. King Hariścandra did not deviate from truth, in the face of adversity, insult and dishonour. Consequently, he along with his subjects attained the Supreme Abode (Mārkaṇḍeya Purāṇa, Devībhāgavata etc.).

(3)—Nowadays we come across many incidents of rebirth, which reveal that creatures take to higher or lower births according to their good or bad deeds†.

* The scripture which removes doubts and reveals secrets, gives us all the light of knowledge. Therefore, he who has no knowledge of the scriptures, is blind.

† Kalyāṇa monthly magazine—43rd year (1968) Paraloka Aura Punarjanmāṅka (Special Issue—pertaining to the Next-World and the Next-Birth).

(4) Not to speak of a believer, even a non-believer, by performing his duty scrupulously, without any selfish motive, gains peace or joy, which is a characteristic of the mode of goodness. This peace, is a signal for salvation or the supreme peace. Therefore, our own experience proves, that performance of one's duty while discarding forbidden actions, leads to salvation.

A Vital Fact

It is the real duty of a man (the self), being a fragment of the Lord, to attain salvation and to believe, that he is, only the Lord's and only the Lord is his. Even duty, according to one's caste, stage of life and body etc., are not real duties because these are assumed, and are not of the self. In all of these, a man has to depend on others, while in one's own real duty, he is totally independent and without the least dependence, on anyone. Therefore, a striver himself may be a lover, a seeker of knowledge or a devotee, as he has not to depend on anyone else. A lover, transmuted by love, becomes one with the Beloved; a seeker of knowledge, transmuted by knowledge, becomes one with Him Who is all Knowledge, and a servant changed by service, becomes one with the Master. Similarly a striver transformed by Sādhanā, (Spiritual discipline) becomes one with God.

A striver having the aim of God-realization, does not hanker after riches, honour, praise, comforts and luxuries. He is not at all worried about these, nor is he pleased having acquired them, because his aim is only God-realization, rather than acquisition of riches, honour and praise etc. So all the worldly actions, are performed scrupulously and solemnly, for the Lord's sake by him. As a businessman, takes a lot of trouble, to earn more and more money, and as a patient, undergoes an operation happily, in order to recover from a disease; a striver remains pleased and satisfied, even in defeat, loss and pain, in order to attain his aim of God-realization. For him, the desirable and the undesirable circumstances, are the means to practise spiritual discipline.

When a striver, having resolved to realize God, starts performing his duty scrupulously, he does not deviate from the performance of his duty, even in the face of adversity. He faces that adversity happily, taking it to be a penance.

When a striver, assumes the body as 'I' and 'mine', it submits to attachment and aversion. While coming under the sway of attachment and aversion, a man strays away from his duty. Had the body been 'I' (the self), it would have remained with the self, or the self would have been destroyed with the destruction of a body. But it is not so. Similarly, if the body had been mine, nothing would have remained to be acquired, after acquiring it. But, the desire to acquire more, continues. It means that the real thing has not yet been acquired, and the acquired things, such as the body etc., are not mine. How can the body be mine, when I have neither brought it with me, nor can carry it with me, nor can change it as I desire? Thus, every striver knows that a body is neither 'he' nor 'his'. But the strivers do not attach importance to this knowledge, so they cannot get rid of attachment and aversion. If a striver sometimes, happens to feel a body as 'I' and 'mine', he should instead of attaching importance to this feeling, give importance to his knowledge. By this, he realizes the self, and then he gets rid of attachment and aversion. Being free from attachment, the knowledge, of what ought to be done and what ought not to be done, is naturally revealed in his mind and accordingly actions are performed.

'Paradharmo bhayāvahaḥ'—Though the performance of duty of another, appears easy, yet it is fraught with fear i.e., its consequence is disastrous. Having discarded, selfish motive, if a man performs his duty for the good of others, there is no fear for him, from any quarters.

Question:—Having described the duties, of Brāhmaṇas (priest class), Kṣatriyas (warrior class), Vaiśyas (trader class) and Śūdras (labour class) in the forty-second, forty-third and forty-fourth verses respectively, the Lord, in the first half of the forty-seventh verse declared, "Better, is one's own duty destitute of merit, than the duty of another well performed." According to the present verse, the duty of another is said to be fraught with fear. Therefore, the duty of a Brāhmaṇa should be disastrous for others, such as the Kṣatriya etc. But scriptures advise all people to inculcate the inborn qualities of a Brāhmaṇa in their lives. Why ?

Answer:—Controlling of the mind and senses etc., (Gītā 13/7—11; 16/1—3) are common duties, which should be performed by everyone. These are natural duties for a Brāhmaṇa, so he can perform these easily, while members of other castes, may not perform these so easily. Common duties are also a part and parcel of natural duties. Besides the common duties, when a man performs duties born of his nature, he does not incur sin, though it may appear that he incurs sin. For example, if a Kṣatriya fights valiantly without selfishness and malice, by regarding it as his duty he incurs no sin. The Lord declares,"He who performs his duty ordained according to his nature, incurs no sin" (18/47). Besides common duty and one's own duty, the duty of another is fraught with fear, because it is prohibited by scripture. It will deprive other persons of their rightful means of livelihood, and it will lead him to hell. Therefore, the Lord asks Arjuna to perform his duty of fighting, which is better than begging. Begging, is prohibited for Arjuna, being a Kṣatriya it is not beneficial for him.

A Vital Fact Pertaining to One's Duty & the Duty of others

Nature (prakṛti) and its evolute (body and world), are different from God and the self (soul). Duty of the self is one's duty, while the duty of nature, the body and the world, is the duty of another. Absence of modification, flawlessness, imperishability, eternity, desirelessness and non-attachment, are duties of the self, while modifications, flaws, transitoriness, mortality and desires for pleasures, prosperity, honour and praise etc., are the duties, of the body and the world and therefore, are the duties of another. The duty of the self is imperishable, because the self is imperishable, while the duty of the body is perishable, as the body ever undergoes change.

Renunciation, (the Discipline of Action), knowledge (the Discipline of Knowledge) and love (the Discipline of Devotion), being axiomatic, are one's own duty. These need no practice, as practice is done by the body and whatever has affinity for the body, is the duty of another.

To be united with God, is one's own duty, while to be a pleasure seeker, is the duty of another; to remain detached is one's duty, while to be attached is the duty of another; to render service is one's own duty while to have desire is the duty of another; to be a lover is one's own duty while to be passionate is the duty of another. It means, that whatever is connected with the self is, one's own duty, while whatever is connected with nature (prakṛti), is the duty of another. One's own duty is sentient, while the duty of another is insentient.

The self is a fragment of God while the body is a fragment of nature (prakṛti). The desire for Self-realization and God-realization, is the duty of the self, because the self is a fragment of God, while the desire for pleasure and prosperity is the duty of another (paradharma). This desire for pleasure and prosperity, is aroused by accepting affinity for an unreal body. A desire for one's ultimate good, is one's duty because being a fragment of God, one's own desire is the desire of God Himself, and not that of the world.

A man is independent in performing his own duty of God-realization or Self-realization or salvation, because in this there is no need of body, senses, mind and intellect etc., but only the need to sever connection with them. In performing duty for another, a man is dependent because that needs the body, senses, mind, intellect, things and persons etc.

When a man practises spiritual discipline in order to realize God, without accepting his affinity for the body, his practice is his own duty. All the means followed, in order to attain Self-realization or God-realization, are included in one's own duty (svadharma) while all the actions done for the world, are included in the duty for another (paradharma). Thus, practising the three Disciplines (Action, Knowledge and Devotion) is a man's own duty, while hankering after worldly pleasures and prosperity, having accepted affinity for the body, is the duty of another.

All the virtuous actions such as a pilgrimage, fast, penance, meditation and trance etc., performed with physical, subtle and causal bodies, with the expectation of reward i.e., with a selfish motive, turn to be 'paradharma' (the duty of another). But if these are performed for the welfare of others, without expecting any reward, these become, 'svadharma' (one's own duty). The reason is, that the self is desireless, while desire is born by having affinity for nature (prakṛti). So, when a man having desire, performs his duty, it becomes the duty of another. One's own duty, leads to salvation, while the duty of another leads to bondage.

Every man having a disinclination for the duty of others, should perform his own duty of God-realization or Self-realization, for which this human body has been bestowed upon him. As far as, the performance of duty of another is concerned it can be performed in lower births as also heaven etc., where the only aim is the enjoyment of pleasures. A man is independent and capable of performing his own duty, while he is dependent and incapable of performing the duty of another. He is sad when he has a desire to acquire worldly objects, and depends on them having acquired them. This dependence is 'paradharma' (the duty of another). But, when there is no desire, there is no question of any want or dependence. That is 'svadharma' (one's own duty). While performing one's own duty, a man may have to undergo a lot of suffering adversity, and even may lose his life, but it will lead him to salvation (God-realization), while the duty of another, even though full of merit and easy to perform, is fraught with danger i.e., leads him to the cycle of birth and death.

All the pains, sorrows and worries etc., of the world, are born by the performance of the duty of another, while the performance of one's own duty leads him to the eternal bliss.

Appendix—According to his birth and actions whatever a striver assumes himself, his 'dharma' (duty) is 'svadharma' for him and whatever is forbidden for him, that is 'paradharma' (duty of another) for him; as a striver assumes himself to be of a particular 'Varṇa' (order of life) and 'Āśrama' (stage of life), for him the duty of the man of that 'Varṇa' and 'Āśrama' is 'svadharma'. If he thinks himself to be a pupil or a teacher, study or teaching is 'svadharma' for him. If he assumes himself to be a servant or inquisitive (Jijñāsu) or devotee, then service or inquisitiveness or devotion is 'svadharma' for him. Evils such as theft and violence etc., which involve ill and harm of others cannot be 'svadharma' for anyone but that is 'kudharma' or 'Adharma'.*

Performance of action in a disinterested way for the welfare of others (viz., Karmayoga) is 'svadharma'. In the Gītā 'svadharma' (one's own duty) has been mentioned 'sahajakarma', 'svakarma' and 'svabhāvajakarma'.

Performance of action against one's duty is 'akartavya' and 'not to discharge one's duty' is also 'akartavya' (neglecting of duty) (Gītā 2/33).

---

* In every dharma these three are there—'kudharma', 'adharma' and 'paradharma'. The feeling to harm others and diplomacy etc., are 'kudharma in dharma'. To kill an animal in a sacrifice is 'adharma in dharma'. The 'dharma' of the people of other 'Varṇa' and 'Āśrama' is 'paradharma in dharma'. Kudharma, adharma and paradharma—these three don't lead a person to salvation. The dharma (duty) which involves renunciation of selfishness & pride and welfare of others at present and in future leads to salvation.

Link:—Why does a man not perform his own duty, when he knows that one's own duty is better, even though devoid of merit than the duty of another, well discharged? For this Arjuna, puts a question, in the verse that follows—

अर्जुन उवाच

अथ केन प्रयुक्तोऽयं पापं चरति पूरुषः।
अनिच्छन्नपि वार्ष्णेय बलादिव नियोजितः॥ ३६॥

arjuna uvāca

atha kena prayukto'yaṁ pāpaṁ carati pūruṣaḥ
anicchannapi vārṣṇeya balādiva niyojitaḥ

Arjuna said:

But, why is a man impelled to commit sin, as if by force, even against his will, O Vārṣṇeya (Kṛṣṇa)? 36

Comment:—

'Atha kena prayukto'yaṁ pāpaṁ carati pūruṣaḥ anicchannapi vārṣṇeya balādiva niyojitaḥ'—Lord Kṛṣṇa has been addressed as 'Vārṣṇeya', because he belonged to the Vṛṣni clan. In the preceding verse, Lord Kṛṣṇa praised the performance of one's duty, and duty as performed, according to one's caste and clan. So Arjuna, addresses the Lord as Vārṣṇeya. A sensible man does not want to commit sin, by thinking of its bitter and sad fruit.

Here the term 'anicchan' does not mean, discarding desire for pleasure and prosperity. It rather, stands for the renunciation of desire, to commit sin. A sensible man does not want to commit sin, but it is the desire for pleasure and prosperity, which deviates him from the performance of his duty and forces him to perform sinful acts.

The expression 'balādiva niyojitaḥ' (as if driven by force) has been used, to point out the fact that a sensible man, by knowing the bitter fruit of a sinful act does not want to commit it, yet he is forcibly driven to it. From this, it appears that some force is there, to compel him to commit sins.

The root of this sin is desire, for worldly pleasures and prosperity. But a man does not give any heed to this desire, and so he is unable to know the root of evils (sins). He understands that he wants to abstain from committing sins, but some entity is forcibly engaging him, in sins. Duryodhana also declares:—

"I know what is righteousness, but I am not inclined to it; I also know what is unrighteousness, but I cannot get rid of it. There is some 'deva' (force) in my heart, which drives me to act" (Garga-Saṁhitā, Aśvamedha. 50/36).

The term 'deva' used by Duryodhana stands for desire, (for pleasure and prosperity) which forces him to commit sin, and not to follow righteousness.

The expression 'Kena prayukto'yaṁ pāpaṁ carati'—also shows that he is impelled to commit sin by some other force.

The Lord, in the thirty-fourth verse, said, "Attachment and aversion (which are subtle forms of desire and anger) are, the foes of a striver (i.e., these are the roots of sins)". As it was said in a general way, Arjuna could not understand this point. So he puts this question. Arjuna, means to ask whether it is lack of faith or carping spirit or villainous nature or clouded understanding or force of one's own nature or attachment and aversion, or disinclination for one's own duty and inclination to the duty of another (described from the thirty-first verse to the thirty-fifth verse), which drives a man to commit sin. Besides these, is it God or fortune or time or circumstance or action or bad company or society or custom or any government law etc., which is impelling him to commit sin?

Link:— The Lord answers the question, in the next verse.

श्रीभगवानुवाच

काम एष क्रोध एष रजोगुणसमुद्भवः।
महाशनो महापाप्मा विद्ध्येनमिह वैरिणम्॥ ३७॥

śrībhagavānuvāca

kāma eṣa krodha eṣa rajoguṇasamudbhavaḥ
mahāśano mahāpāpmā viddhyenamiha vairiṇam

The Blessed Lord said:

It is desire and it is anger, born of the mode of passion (rajas), most greedy and most sinful. Know this to be the enemy concerned. 37

Comment:—

'Rajoguṇasamudbhavaḥ'—The Lord, in the seventh verse of the fourteenth chapter, declares, "The mode of passion springs from desire and attachment", while here, He declares that desire is born of a mode of passion. It means, that desire is born of the mode of passion, while desire enhances passion (attachment). A person believes that worldly objects provide him pleasure, so he has a desire to acquire them in order to enjoy pleasure. This desire, gives birth to attachment. So long as this process continues, he cannot get rid of sinful acts.

'Kāma* eṣa krodha eṣa'—A man, has a desire for sensual pleasure and prosperity. Sometimes, sins are committed under the sway of desire, while other times, these are committed, under the sway of anger. Through desire and anger, different types of sins are committed. Therefore, these two terms have been used. This desire is the root of all sin†. When it is not

* 'I should get this, I should get this'—this is desire. Such a desire is known as 'Kāma'.

† Though disinclination for God and not attaching importance to discrimination are also the cause of sins, yet here desire has been said to be the root of sins because here in this chapter of the Discipline of Action, the aim of a striver is to get rid of desire.

satisfied, it gives birth to anger. The singular number, has been used for desire and anger in order to explain that only desire is the root of sins.

When a desire is satisfied, it gives birth to greed; but if it is not satisfied, it gives birth to anger. If the person, who is a stumbling block to the satisfaction of our desire, is more powerful than we, fear is born instead of anger. Therefore, in the Gītā, besides desire and wrath, fear has also been mentioned as 'delivered from desire, fear and anger' (4/10) and 'free from desire, fear and anger' (5/28).

An Important Fact Pertaining to Desire

Whatever we may desire, does not happen, and whatever we do not desire, happens—this is suffering. Desire is the root of all sins and sufferings. A man with a desire cannot get happiness, even in a dream (Mānasa 7/90/1). If desire is renounced, there is no question of any suffering.

Craving for perishable objects, is called desire, while the need for God-realization, which may appear to be like desire, is not really desire. The reason is, that desire is never satisfied, but it is strengthened by sense enjoyments, while the need of God-realization, is fulfilled having realized God. A man has desire for something, which is different from him (the self), while God is one with the self. Similarly, the need of rendering selfless service (the Discipline of Action), Self-realization (the Discipline of Knowledge) and devotion to God (the Discipline of Devotion) are not desires. In fact, the need of the self (soul) is to realize God but he (the self) has a desire to acquire the perishable objects etc., because his discrimination is veiled.

A doubt may arise here as to how the worldly affairs will go on, without desire. The clarification is, that worldly affairs relate with actions and commodities; rather than with desires. Actions are performed outwardly and so their fruit in the form of objects and circumstances etc., is also external, while desire is internal.

Nothing in the world, can be acquired by having desire. It is the fruit of effort. People have a desire to become rich, yet they remain poor. All the people, except the liberated souls, have a desire to remain alive, but they die. A man's actions bear fruits, according to his fate or fortune, not because of his desire. Whatever, is allotted cannot be blotted, whether you have desire for it or not. As, a man has to undergo unfavourable circumstances unwillingly, he would also face favourable circumstances. A man may bear pain, blame and dishonour etc., without any desire. Similarly, he may gain pleasure, praise and honour, without desire as a result of his fate.

A man may have a desire for immediate pleasures and prosperity, or for future fruits, for his actions. But a desire is the root of pain, here as well as hereafter, so a man should renounce, desire.

It is out of desire that a man performs actions. When there is an excess of this desire, it forces him to perform forbidden actions. It is because of desire that he is more attached, to the unreal. As soon as, he renounces desire, his affinity for the unreal is renounced.

When desire is satisfied, we attain the same state in which we were, before desire was aroused. When desire, say of receiving a hundred rupees, was not aroused in a striver's mind, he was desireless, and again after having received that amount, he becomes desireless. It is because of his attachment to the worldly pleasures, that new desires are born. Thus, desire are never satisfied.

Some people believe that desires cannot be totally renounced. But the fact is, that desires cannot be maintained. These appear and disappear, have a beginning and an end, and constantly decay. If we do not have new desire, the old desire, whether satisfied or not, disappears itself.

Everyone's desires, may not be satisfied forever but these can be renounced forever, because these are transitory. The difficulty in renouncing desire is, that we have a feeling of 'mine'. If we become free from this feeling of 'mine', we shall become, desireless. Desirelessness will lead to detachment. When we become free from the feeling of 'mine', desire and attachment, we attain uniformity, desirelessness and independence automatically.

We must pay attention to this vital fact. We think that it is difficult to renounce desires. But is it easy to satisfy these? It is impossible to satisfy all the desires. Even king Daśaratha, the father of Lord Rāma, could not satisfy his desire, of not sending his son into exile. Thus, if satisfaction of desires is impossible, and renunciation is difficult. Which one is easier—satisfaction or renunciation? The answer is clear, that desires can be renounced rather than satisfied. But we commit an error when we try to satisfy desires, but we do not make efforts to renounce them. Therefore, a striver should renounce desires.

Desires are of four kinds:—

1. Desires which satisfy necessities of life.*

2. Desire which is personal and just, but is beyond our power. Such a desire should be rooted out, by offering it to God†.

---

* There are four criteria for such a desire—

(i) It is born at present (as desire for food when one is hungry).

(ii) The material to satisfy it is available at present.

(iii) It is impossible to live without satisfying it.

(iv) It's satisfaction does evil neither to him nor to others.

Thus the necessity should be satisfied. When the necessities are satisfied, a man gets strength to renounce desires. But he should not derive pleasure out of the satisfaction of even necessities otherwise it will be conducive to the birth of new desires which can never be satisfied.

† 'There should not be injustice and exploitation in the world.' A striver having offered such a desire to God, becomes carefree. The Lord satisfies it if He thinks it proper.

3. Satisfy the just desire of others for their welfare and within our power to satisfy. Thus by satisfying the desires of others, we get strength to renounce our own.

4. Other desires, besides, the above-mentioned ones, which can be rooted out, by reflection.

'Mahāśano mahāpāpmā'—Desire is such an enemy, that is not satiated by, sense-enjoyments. Tulasīdāsa in Vinaya Patrikā declares, "This fire of desire is never extinguished by the churned-butter of sense-enjoyments" (198).

As desire for prosperity, is never satisfied, similarly, the desire for sense-enjoyments, is never satisfied, but rather strengthened. So, it has been called, all devouring, and most sinful, because it is the root of all sinful actions, such as theft, robbery and violence etc.

As soon as, desire is born, it induces man to have a disinclination for his duty, for the self and for God, and an inclination towards perishable world. Consequently, he commits sins, which lead to hell and birth, in lower bodies.

It is, because of the desire for sense-enjoyments, that the changing and perishable world, (body etc.,) seems real and one seeks pleasure out of it. At the time of enjoyment, he forgets the kaleidoscopic nature of objects and regards these and himself, as permanent. If he realized this fact, he, instead of getting entangled in the mirage of pleasures, will have his eye directed to God and the Self, Who are real. It shows, that a man enjoys the worldly sense-enjoyments, by having a disinclination for the real, God or Self; and by enjoying the sense-enjoyments, he develops a disinclination for God.

Such a depraved one can't avoid violence, for himself as well as, for others. When a rich man leads a luxurious life and enjoys worldly pleasures, the poor are sad, to see him, suffer. Moreover, he (the self) being a fragment of God is sentient, but when one attaches importance to riches or luxuries, the insentient, he becomes a slave to these and has a downfall. All the worldly materials are limited, so these should be shared by all the people. He, who enjoys the share of others, is a sinner. So a man, should have only the bare necessities of life. In the scriptures, it is mentioned that even bare necessities of life should be satisfied, only after offering these to parents, preceptors, children,women and old people etc.

A gratifier destroys worldly material, does violence to those who suffer shortage, and leads himself to a downfall, while a wise man (liberated soul) does not do so, because all actions, are performed by him, according to scriptural injunctions for the maintenance of a body, without expecting any fruit (Gītā 4/21; 18/17). All the possessions, including the body of such a wise man, are utilized automatically, for the welfare of all beings.

The need to maintain the body, is neither all-devouring nor most sinful, and it is satisfied, as hunger, after having a meal. But a desire is never fully satisfied, the more we satisfy it, the more intense it becomes.

'Viddhyenamiha vairiṇam'—In fact, a man attains peace, having renounced the desire for worldly objects. Yet out of ignorance he believes that he has attained peace by acquiring the worldly objects (i.e., by satisfying the desire). Thus, by considering desire to be a source of enjoyment, he regards it as a friend and well-wisher. So, the desire never perishes. Therefore, the Lord urges us to know the desire, to be an enemy, because it, having blurred our discrimination, leads us to sins.

Desire, is the root of all sins, sufferings and hell, here as well as hereafter. It results in no benefit.

An Important Fact

An important and easy means, to get rid of desire, is to render service to others with the body, senses, mind, intellect and life-breath etc., without any selfish motive.

In the, Discipline of Action, actions performed with the physical body, thinking with the subtle body and trance with the causal body, are done only for the world, not for one's own self, because the gross body, the subtle body and the causal body have their identity respectively, with the gross, subtle and causal world. By doing so, one should not derive any pleasure out of them.* It makes him free from attachment, to the fruit of action and thus he easily becomes free from attachment to action.

'I should be obeyed', 'this thing may serve my purpose', 'Whatever, I say should be honoured'—these are all desires. A desire is very disastrous. When a man satisfies the just desires of others, according to his resources, it enables him to renounce his own desires. If we cannot fulfil the desires of others, at least we should have the sentiment to do so.

Egoism, attachment and desire, bind a man to the world, through separation, defect and disquietude, respectively. Renunciation of desire, leads to detachment, while detachment leads to non-egoism. A striver, following the Discipline of Action, does not regard the body, senses, mind, intellect, egoism and objects etc., as his or for him, but he regards these as the world's and for the world, by realizing the reality about them.

When a striver resolves, not to give pain to others, he starts rendering service to them. If by chance, anyone suffers because of his action, he very humbly tenders a sincere apology. Even if the sufferer does not forgive him, he is automatically forgiven by God. While rendering service to others, a striver should never expect any reward in return. By doing so this enemy (desire) is easily overcome.

Appendix—The desire to derive pleasure from a thing, a

* The desire to derive pleasure out of either service or the thought of the welfare of others or trance and to maintain them, is an obstacle to God-realization (Gītā14/6). Therefore, a striver should be detached from the three modes—of goodness, of passion and of ignorance because the self is free from all attachment.

person or an action is named 'kāma'. This evil in the form of 'Kāma' involves endless flaws, endless defects and endless sins. Therefore so long as a man has desire, he can't be totally free from flaws, defects and sins. The desire to get pleasure causes evils. He who has no desire becomes free from evils.

The fruit of action is of three kinds—pleasant, unpleasant and mixed (Gītā 18/12). Out of the three the fruit of desire that accrues is only unpleasant.

Prārabdha does not compel a man to resort to sinful acts but it is the desire that directs a man to sinful acts. An urge for an activity may be there for enjoyment of fruits of past actions due to Prārabdha but there cannot be any sinful act as there is no need to commit such a sin for enjoyment of fruits of destiny.

Kāma (desire) is born of 'Rajoguṇa' (the mode of passion). Therefore the cause of sins is 'Rajoguṇa' and their effect (evolute) is 'Tamoguṇa' (the mode of ignorance). All sins are born of 'Rajoguṇa'.

Link:— 'It is a sin', even knowing this a man commits sin. What is the reason that this knowledge does not help? The Lord explains in the next two verses.

धूमेनाव्रियते वह्निर्यथादर्शो मलेन च।
यथोल्बेनावृतो गर्भस्तथा तेनेदमावृतम्॥ ३८॥

dhūmenāvriyate vahniryathādarśo malena ca
yatholbenāvṛto garbhastathā tenedamāvṛtam

As fire is covered by smoke, as a mirror by dust, and as an embryo by placenta, so is this (knowledge) concealed by desire. 38

Comment:—

'Dhūmenāvriyate vahniḥ'— As fire is covered by smoke, so is this knowledge, (discrimination) covered by desire.

Discrimination is revealed in the intellect. There are three divisions of intellect—of the nature of 'goodness' (Sāttvika), of 'passion' (Rajas) and of 'ignorance' (Tamas). The intellect by which one knows, what ought to be done and what ought not to be done, is of the nature of 'goodness'. The intellect, by which one wrongly understands, what ought to be done and what ought not to be done, is of the nature of 'passion', while the intellect by which one sees all things in a perverted way (contrary to the truth) is, of the nature of 'ignorance' (Gītā 18/30—32). When desire is born, even the intellect of goodness (Sāttvika) is covered by desire, as fire by smoke, then the intellect of the mode of passion (Rajas) and ignorance (tamas) will definitely be covered by it, of which there is no doubt.

As soon as, a desire is born, one's spiritual path is covered with its smoke. If it is given scope for enhancement, it makes the path totally dark. By thinking that the desired objects are deserting us constantly, we can destroy desires.

We have desire to acquire the worldly objects, because these appear to be beautiful and charming. The desire veils our discrimination, which is a privilege of human birth. Just as, fire can burn even when it is covered with smoke, so can discrimination work, if a man becomes cautious, as soon as desire is born. A man can get rid of desire at the outset, by thinking of the kaleidoscopic and transitory nature, of the worldly objects etc., which he wants to acquire.

'Yathādarśo malena ca'—When dirt accumulates on the surface of a mirror, it cannot reflect an object. Similarly, the dirt of desire, covers knowledge (discrimination), and a striver cannot decide what he ought to do and what he ought not to do. Because of desire, he hankers after worldly pleasures and prosperity, and he has a downfall. This is the second stage of desire.

A striver, should realize that it is not a thing, but its proper use, which is significant. So, instead of having a desire to acquire more and more, he should think to make a proper use of it. Moreover, he cannot acquire objects merely by desire.

The less importance, he will attach to the worldly objects, the more importance he will attach to God. When he stops attaching importance to the worldly objects altogether, he will realize God and desire will totally be eliminated.

'Yatholbenāvṛto garbhaḥ'—When, dirt accumulates on the surface of a mirror, even though it does not reflect a face, yet it can be known that it is a mirror. But when an embryo is covered by the placenta, it cannot be known, whether the child is male or female. Similarly, knowledge (discrimination) is, so much veiled at this third stage, that he totally forgets his duty and his desire is intensified.

If desire is not satisfied, it gives birth to anger. From anger arises delusion; from delusion there is destruction of discrimination; from destruction of descrimination one does not do, what ought to be done, but indulges in evil acts, such as falsehood, fraud, dishonesty, injustice, oppression and other sinful acts. The Lord does not want to call such people, human beings (men). Therefore, the Lord while describing such people, in the sixteenth chapter (from the eighth to the eighteenth verses), has not used any such word which stands for human beings. The Lord has called the people, who have heaven as their goal, 'Kāmātmānaḥ' (desire incarnate) (Gītā 2/43), because they are the embodiments of desires. Having identified themselves with desires, they hold that there is no higher aim than the gratification of desires (Gītā 16/11).

[When desires are strengthened, a man totally forgets, that the real aim of human life is God-realization. But if due to past influences or good company, or any other factor, he comes to know the real aim of human life, he can attain salvation or God-realization.]

'Tathā tenedamāvṛtam'—In this verse, the Lord has given three illustrations, pertaining to the covering of discrimination by desire. It means that discrimination is covered by desire, in three stages. But those who hold that desire is the cause of happiness, and so depend on it, cannot renounce it (desire), while strivers who practise spiritual discipline, know it in its reality and can root it out.

The Lord here, has described the three stages of desire, so that a striver may kill the enemy, in the form of desire, as directed by Him, in the forty-first and forty-third verses of this chapter. In fact, desire crosses the first two stages so quickly, that a man cannot perceive these phases. Then desire leads him, to all sorts of sins and sufferings. Therefore, a striver, through discrimination, should not allow a desire to arise. But if it is born, it should be renounced either in the first or the second stage, it should not be allowed to reach the third stage.

An Important Fact

As smoke, shows the presence of fire, and as a mirror and an embryo are identified even when these are covered respectively, with dust and placenta, so discrimination is possessed by every human being, even when it is covered by desire. But due to the force of desire, discrimination is not used.

According to the scriptures 'Mala' (sin) (Impurity), 'Vikṣepa' (distraction) and 'āvaraṇa' (veil), are said to be, the three stumbling blocks to God-realization. These defects, are born of the affinity of man, for the unreal world. This affinity for the world is, created because of desire. Thus the root of all the evils, is desire. When desire is renounced, affinity for the unreal world, is renounced. When affinity for the unreal, is renounced, all the evils perish and discrimination is revealed.

So long as, the worldly objects seem real, beautiful and charming, a man attaches importance to them. This attachment, is the main obstacle to God-realization, as it is conducive to the three defects—sin, confusion and veil. Out of these three, sin is regarded as the most deadly defect. Desire is the root of sin. When a striver resolves not to commit sin in future, the defects are rooted out and his sin, begins to decay. But when he renounces the desire, totally, all his sins perish.

In the Śrīmadbhāgavata, Lord Kṛṣṇa has pointed out that a man with desire can attain salvation, by following the Discipline of Action (Performance of action) without expecting fruit—'Karmayogastu kāminām' (11/20/7). So a person who is not free from desire, need not lose heart, because only he who has a desire, will get rid of it. Desires can be renounced easily, through the Discipline of Action. When a striver performs any act, whether it is mundane or spiritual, he should think, "Why do I perform it and how do I perform it?" By thinking so, he will constantly have an eye on the aim of his life. Consequently, he will perform only virtuous actions, being free from attachment and the desire for fruit. This performance of actions without attachment, and desire for reward, will lead him to salvation.

Appendix—Desire is the main obstacle to God-realization. As there is a jar full of water, in it we have to do two actions—the first is to empty the jar and the second is to fill it with ether. But in fact two actions are not to be performed but only one is to be performed—to empty the jar. Empty the jar and the ether will be filled itself. Similarly renunciation of desire and God-realization—these two are not be done. Renounce the desire and God will be automatically realized. It is because of desire that God seems to be unrealized.

आवृतं ज्ञानमेतेन ज्ञानिनो नित्यवैरिणा।
कामरूपेण कौन्तेय दुष्पूरेणानलेन च॥३९॥

āvṛtaṁ jñānametena jñānino nityavairiṇā
kāmarūpeṇa kaunteya duṣpūreṇānalena ca

O Arjuna, Knowledge (jñāna) is enveloped by this constant enemy of the wise, (a discerning soul) in the form of desire, which is insatiable like, fire. 39

Comment:—

'Etena'—This term has been used for desire, which has been declared by the Lord as most sinful, in the thirty-seventh verse of this chapter.

'Duṣpūreṇānalena ca'— As fire is never satiated, when clarified butter is added to it, it rather rages stronger, so is desire never satisfied, by enjoying the objects of desire, it is rather strengthened (Śrīmadbhāgavata 9/19/14; Manusmṛti 2/94). The fire of desire, devours everything which comes into its contact.

Sundaradāsa, has also expressed the same idea, when he says, "The richer a man grows, the more he hankers after worldly prosperity. A poor man, may desire to gain only a few rupees, but when he gains them, he has desire for a hundred and then a thousand, and after that a million and then a billion and trillion and then the ownership of the entire universe. Yet, this form of desire, will not be satiated. It is only, by contentment, that this desire can be subdued.

A poor man, is not so greedy, as is a rich man. When a man earns a hundred rupees, he desires to earn a thousand rupees. It means that he feels that he needs nine hundred more. When he earns a thousand rupees, he desires to have, ten thousand rupees. It means that he needs nine thousand more. When he gains ten thousand rupees he has desire to gain a lac of rupees. And he needs ninety thousand more. Thus the richer he grows, the more greedy he becomes. On the other hand, a contented man, being free from all desires, is the king of kings.

In fact it is not wealth, but desire for wealth, which is an obstacle to God-realization.This desire, deprives the rich and the poor equally, of God-realization, as it can never be satiated. A man can only get rid of it by renouncing it.

'Kāmarūpeṇa'—The desire to derive pleasure, out of the affinity for the insentient is called 'Kāma'. This desire manifests itself in different forms, such as lust (for gold, power and of the flesh), craving (for things), attachment (to loving and charming objects), hope (to acquire something) and greed (to acquire more and more). When a man's desire is intensified, it is followed by solicitation. These are, the different forms of desire.

'Jñānino nityavairiṇā'—Here, the term 'Jñāninaḥ' stands for the wise striver, who remains engaged in practising the spiritual discipline, because it is he, who recognizes this enemy in the form of desire, and slays it. The worldly people consider it as pleasant.

The Lord declares, that desire is the constant enemy of a wise striver. As, soon as desire is born, a thought comes to his mind, that it will lead him to suffering. Desires involve dependence on the world and create importance of the world, which are stumbling blocks to the spiritual path. It pricks him at the outset, that it will result in adversity.

The ignorant, who are engrossed in sensual pleasures, hold that desire is their friend, because they derive pleasure out of the objects. Without desire objects cannot provide pleasure. But the fact is, that desire and the pleasures, lead him to sorrow, suffering, imprisonment and hell etc. Thus, desire is a constant enemy of the ignorant also, but they are not aware of it, while wise strivers are aware of it.

'Āvṛtaṁ jñānam'—Every being is, endowed with

discrimination. In the case of man it can develop, but in birds, beasts and other births, it is confined to the maintenance of the body. In the case of men also, it is veiled by desire, which does not let them follow the spiritual (sentient) path of God-realization, but keeps them engaged in mundane pleasures.

Everyone, likes loving and true words, and hates harsh and false words. It means that every person has the knowledge (discrimination) of good and bad, virtue and vice, right and wrong. In spite of this knowledge, an ignorant person uses harsh language, tells a lie and does not perform his duty scrupulously, because his discrimination is concealed by desire.

A man thinks that he derives joy out of sense-objects, but in fact, he gets joy by renouncing them. Everyone knows that during wakefulness and sleep a man feels happy and sad, because of his affinity, for the sense-objects. But during sound sleep he does not remember, sense-objects at all. So, when he awakes he says that he had a very peaceful and sound sleep. Moreover, he gets tired during wakefulness, while he is refreshed after sound sleep. It means, that it is renunciation of the sense-objects, which provides joy or peace.

When a man desires money, his mind is attached to it. But when it is acquired, the mind renounces this attachment and so he feels happy. Had the money provided him joy, he would have never felt sad, so long as he had money. But he feels sad, even after possessing that money.

When a man desires anything, he becomes dependant on it. Suppose, a man has a desire to buy a watch he feels sad, without it; this is dependence upon it. He thinks that if he acquires money, he can buy a watch i.e., he feels independent if he has money, and dependent without money. But this is a wrong notion. If he acquires money and buys a watch he, instead of having dependence on the watch, has dependence on money, because money is also different from, the self. When a man's discrimination is hid by desire, he realizes his dependence on objects, but he does not realize his dependence, on money. He thinks that he has become independent, because of money. It is very difficult to renounce such a dependence, which disguises itself as independence.

The world is transitory. All the worldly objects such as the body, wealth, property etc., are decaying every moment, and are separating from us. But while enjoying these, we forget that they are temporary, we regard them as eternal and permanent. Not to talk of the common people, even a striver gets entangled in pleasures by considering these as eternal and permanent. It so happens, because his discrimination is enveloped by desire.

An Important Fact

The Lord declares, that desire is the constant enemy of the wise, so that a man may save himself from it and may attain bliss, desire being the root of all sins and sufferings. Once, a man was looking for his wife. People asked him, "What is the name of your wife?" He replied, "Disgrace." They again asked "What is your name?" He replied, "Wicked." People said, "Don't be agitated, she is a very chaste and faithful wife, she will come to you, because disgrace ever accompanies the wicked." Similarly suffering automatically accompany the man, who hankers after perishable pleasures.

A man wants to avoid suffering, but he does not renounce desire, which is the root cause of suffering. In the Rāmacaritamānasa it is declared, "A man can't attain bliss, even in a dream, so long as he does not renounce desire" (7/90/1). The Lord, by the terms 'analena' and 'duṣpūreṇa', wants to explain that desire for enjoyment of worldly objects, is never satiated.

The more he enjoys them, the more, the desire for these is strengthened. In order to satiate it, he is inclined to sinful acts. When he has desire for wealth, he wants to earn it, by fair means or foul. Then, at the second stage the desire engages him in theft and robberies, while in the third stage it leads him to commit violence and even murder. Thus the desire for pleasure, makes life miserable, here as well as hereafter.

Appendix—The main obstacle to the practice of spiritual discipline is the desire for pleasure which is born by the contact of senses with sense-objects. This obstacle lingers for a long time. Wherever a striver indulges in pleasure, there his spiritual progress is arrested. As much as even the pleasure (joy) from trance, hinders his progress.* Even the desire of 'Sāttvika' happiness and attachment to it arrest his spiritual progress—'sukhasaṅgena badhnāti' (Gītā 14/6)†. Therefore the Lord has declared that desire is the constant enemy of a wise (discriminating) striver—'na teṣu ramate budhaḥ' (Gītā 5/22) and 'duḥkhameva sarvaṁ vivekinaḥ' (Yogadarśana 2/15).

Link:—In order to kill an enemy, it is necessary to know where it resides. Therefore, the Lord, in the next verse, mentions the seat of desire, the constant enemy of the wise (discerning soul).

इन्द्रियाणि मनो बुद्धिरस्याधिष्ठानमुच्यते।
एतैर्विमोहयत्येष ज्ञानमावृत्य देहिनम्॥ ४०॥

indriyāṇi mano buddhirasyādhiṣṭhānamucyate
etairvimohayatyeṣa jñānamāvṛtya dehinam

*Worldly pleasures are born of union with sense-objects while the joy derived from trance is born of disunion with sense-objects. Worldly pleasures lead to ruin (fall) while the enjoyment of joy derived from trance arrests (hinders) a striver's progress.

† Attachment to Sāttvika joy is a hindrance in the path of God-realization and attachment to Rājasa-Tāmasa pleasures leads to ruin.

The senses, the mind and the intellect are said to be its abode. Veiling of wisdom by the senses, mind and intellect deludes, the embodied soul. 40

Comment:—

'Indriyāṇi mano buddhirasyādhiṣṭhānamucyate'—Desire, is said to have five abodes—(1) objects (Gītā 3/34), (2) senses, (3) mind, (4) intellect and (5) assumed ego ('I') viz., doer (Gītā 2/59). Though it seems to reside in five abodes, yet in fact, it resides in the 'assumed ego'. As it seems to abide in these five places, these are called its seats.

All actions are performed, with the body, senses, mind and intellect. If desire resides in these, it hinders the performance of spiritual actions. Therefore, a Karmayogī (man of action), having abandoned attachment and the fruit of actions, performs actions, only by the body, senses, mind and intellect, for the purification of the self (Gītā 5/11).

In fact, desire resides in the assumed ego (i.e., identification of the self with the body etc.). This ego or 'I'ness, is merely assumed that, 'I belong to a particular caste, creed or order of life"—this is a mere assumption. Sins perish, after bearing fruits, but desire which resides in the assumed ego, gives birth to new sins. Therefore, it is desire which binds the embodied soul.

In the Mahābhārata, it is mentioned, "In the world it is only desire which binds a man. He who is liberated from the bondage of desire, becomes eligible to attain the Eternal (Absolute)" (Śāntiparva 251/7).

'Etairvimohayatyeṣa jñānamāvṛtya dehinam'—It is because of desire, that a man does what he ought not do, and does not do what he ought to do. Thus the embodied soul is deluded, by desire.

In the second chapter, the Lord declared—'From desire

springs anger' (2/62) and 'From anger arises delusion' (2/63). It means, that if anyone becomes an obstacle to the satisfaction of a desire, anger arises. But if the desire is satisfied, it gives birth to greed, and from greed arises delusion. Desire is, an evolute of the mode of passion, while delusion, is an evolute of the mode of ignorance.The mode of passion and the mode of ignorance, are not far from each other.* Desire, deludes the embodied soul, through senses, mind and intellect. The desire, which is an evolute of the mode of passion, is transformed into delusion, which is an evolute of ignorance.

A man has a desire to enjoy sense-objects (sensual pleasures). Firstly, he does not get those desired sense-objects. However, if he gets them, they do not stay. In spite of it, he desires to get them somehow or the other, and thinks of so many devices to obtain them. Therefore, first desire attracts the senses, towards objects. Then the senses, attract the mind, while the senses and the mind attract, the intellect. Thus desire, veiling wisdom, through the senses, mind and intellect, deludes the embodied soul and drives it to ruin.

It is a rule that if a master terminates the service of a sincere servant, he is not likely to get such a sincere servant again. Similarly, if a servant does not carry out the order of a virtuous master and does not serve him, he will not get an opportunity to work under such good masters. In the same way, if a person by misusing the human body, instead of realizing God, wastes it in hankering after worldly pleasures, and prosperity, he will not get this human life again. It is, because of the impurity of mind, that a man rejects good things; and the mind is tainted by, desire. Therefore, first of all, a striver should renounce desire.

* Among the modes of ignorance, passion and goodness the ratio of the distance is 1:10:100. It means that modes of ignorance and passion are near each other, while the mode of goodness is far-away from them.

'Dehinam vimohayati'—It means that, desire deludes only the embodied soul i.e., the soul which has identified itself with the body, and has accepted the relationship of 'mine' with it. The Lord, at the beginning of His gospel, explained that the soul is different from the body (Gītā 2/11—30). This is also everyone's experience. The desire covering wisdom, deludes the embodied soul (the soul which accepts its affinity for the body), but not the pure soul. A man (the soul) assuming the body as 'I ', 'mine' and for 'me', attaches importance to the perishable objects and gets attached to them, which, creates affinity for them. This affinity gives birth to desire. Desire, having deluded the man (embodied soul), leads him to worldly bondage.

Link:—The Lord, in the next verse, tells Arjuna the device of eliminating this enemy i.e., desire, and directs him to kill it.

तस्मात्त्वमिन्द्रियाण्यादौ नियम्य भरतर्षभ।
पाप्मानं प्रजहि ह्येनं ज्ञानविज्ञाननाशनम्॥ ४१॥

tasmāttvamindriyāṇyādau niyamya bharatarṣabha
pāpmānaṁ prajahi hyenaṁ jñānavijñānanāśanam

Therefore, O best of Bharatas (Arjuna), first control the senses then, kill, this sinful destroyer, of wisdom and realization. 41

Comment:—

'Tasmāttvamindriyāṇyādau niyamya bharatarṣabha'— Senses, are said to be controlled, when they do not enjoy the sense-objects, but are used in order to maintain the body or to attain a spiritual goal. It means, that they should neither have an aversion to disagreeable action, nor an attachment for agreeable action (Gītā 18/10). Actions performed with attachment and aversion, strengthen attachment and aversion and these drive a man to ruin. Therefore, let the scriptures be the authority for determining what should be done and what should not be done (Gītā 16/24).Thus, by following scriptural injunction, pertaining to the performance of prescribed actions, and non-performance of forbidden actions senses are controlled.

So long as, a man is swayed by his senses, he cannot have an eye on the goal of life. Without having an eye on the goal of life i.e., without attaining it, desire cannot be totally killed. So, first the Lord urges to control the senses, in order to kill desire.

First, the senses get entangled in their objects, by which desire for those objects is born. When a man performs actions with desire, he comes under the full sway of senses and has a downfall. But, he who performs his duty, by controlling the senses, without expecting any fruit, quickly attains salvation.

'Enaṁ jñānavijñānanāśanam'—The term 'Jñāna' also stands for the knowledge of the scriptures (Gītā 18/42). But in this context the term, stands for discrimination (what should be done and what should not be done). The term, 'vijñāna' stands for Self-realization.

Discrimination and Self-realization—both are axiomatic. All the people have not realized the self, but discrimination has been bestowed upon them. The term 'Anicchannapi', used by Arjuna, in the thirty-sixth verse of this chapter, also proves that every human being possesses this faculty of discrimination. It is by discrimination that he knows, what is virtue and what is vice (sin). So, it is by discrimination that he does not want to commit a sin. But, when discrimination is veiled by desire, he commits sin without thinking of the consequences. When discrimination is aroused, he performs actions, having thought of the consequences.

Thus, desire veils discrimination, as well as Self-realization i.e., it does not let these reveal themselves. So it has been called, the sinful destroyer. In fact it does not destroy them, but it hides them. This 'Veiling' has been called destroying, here Discrimination and Self-realization, are never destroyed, while desire is destroyed. If clouds appear before the eyes, it is said that the sun has been covered by clouds. But in fact, the sun is not covered, it is the eyes which are covered. Similarly, when it is said that desire has veiled discrimination and Self-realization, it means that these are not veiled, but it is the intellect which is concealed.

'Pāpmānaṁ hi prajahi'—Desire, is the root of all sins. Having veiled discrimination, it makes a man blind. So he cannot recognize the distinction between virtues and sins, and thus indulges in sins, which lead him to ruin. So the Lord orders to slay desire by declaring it sinful.

A man wants to lead a lonely life of an ascetic, by renouncing household affairs but he does not renounce desire; he does not even think of renouncing it. If desires are renounced, everything will be set right automatically. When a man dies with unfulfilled desires, these lead him to the next birth. It means, that desires lead him to the bondage of birth and death. Thus, desires do nothing, except binding him.

When a man is attracted towards worldly objects, desire is born. This desire veils discrimination and he indulges in sense-pleasure. The pleasure of birds and beasts, is confined to the joy born of the contact of senses, with objects. But, a man desires objects and money and indulges in hoarding money. In order to hoard money, he adopts foul means such as falsehood, fraud, thefts and robberies etc. Moreover, he becomes proud of himself. This pride is a demoniac trait. Thus, he is totally damned, Therefore the Lord orders Arjuna, to slay sinful desire.

इन्द्रियाणि पराण्याहुरिन्द्रियेभ्यः परं मनः ।
मनसस्तु परा बुद्धिर्यो बुद्धेः परतस्तु सः ॥ ४२ ॥
एवं बुद्धेः परं बुद्ध्वा संस्तभ्यात्मानमात्मना ।
जहि शत्रुं महाबाहो कामरूपं दुरासदम् ॥ ४३ ॥

indriyāṇi parāṇyāhurindriyebhyaḥ paraṁ manaḥ
manasastu parā buddhiryo buddheḥ paratastu saḥ
evaṁ buddheḥ paraṁ buddhvā saṁstabhyātmānamātmanā
jahi śatruṁ mahābāho kāmarūpaṁ durāsadam

It is said that the senses are superior to the gross body, greater (higher, more powerful, illuminator, pervasive and subtle) than the senses is the mind; greater than the mind is the intellect, but greater than the intellect is desire. Thus, knowing that desire is beyond intellect, subduing the self by one's self, destroy this, O mighty-armed Arjuna, the tough enemy in the form of desire, which is hard to conquer. 42-43

Comment:—

'Indriyāṇi parāṇyāhuḥ'—Senses are superior to body or objects of senses. It means, that senses know the objects but objects do not know senses. Senses live without objects, but without senses, the existence of objects is not proved. Objects cannot illumine senses, but senses illumine objects. Senses remain the same while objects go on changing objects come within the range of senses, while senses do not come within the range of objects. Eyes (senses) can perceive the physical body and objects, but the body and objects cannot perceive the senses. So senses are greater, more powerful, more subtle and have a wider range of activity, than objects and the physical body.

'Indriyebhyaḥ paraṁ manaḥ'— Senses, do not know the mind, while the mind knows all the senses. Every sense, knows only its own objects, but does not know the objects of other senses. Ears can perceive only sound, but cannot perceive touch, form, taste and smell. Similarly, tongue can only taste, nose can only smell, eyes can only see, and skin can only touch. But the mind knows the five senses, and their objects. Therefore, the mind is superior, more powerful, more subtle, has a wider range of activity, than senses and is, their illuminator.

'Manasastu parā buddhiḥ'—The mind, does not know the intellect, but the intellect knows the mind and senses. The intellect, knows whether the mind is quiet or turbulent and whether senses function properly or not. It means, that the intellect knows the mind and its thoughts, as well as the senses and their objects. Therefore, the intellect is greater, more powerful, more subtle and has a wider range of activity, than the mind and is its illuminator.

'Yaḥ buddheḥ paratastu saḥ'—The master of intellect is ego; therefore, a person says 'My intellect'. Intellect is an instrument and 'ego' is the doer. The instrument depends, on the doer. Desire, resides in the insentient portion of ego. But, it is because of the identification of the self with the insentient body etc., that desire seems to reside, in the pure self (the sentient).

In fact, desire resides in 'ego' 'I', because ego has the desire to enjoy pleasures and so becomes the enjoyer. The enjoyer, enjoyment and the object to be enjoyed, belong to the same class, otherwise the enjoyer cannot be attracted towards the objects. But, there is no desire in the self, which is the illuminator of the enjoyer, enjoyment and the object to be enjoyed. All the insentient objects, such as the body, the mind, the senses, the intellect and the ego are fragments of nature (prakṛti). Beyond ego there is the self, a fragment of God. The self, is the base, the root, the cause, the inspirer of the body, senses, mind, intellect and ego, and is subtler, greater, stronger, wider than all of them, and is also their illuminator.

There is pleasure or pain in the insentient nature (prakṛti) of the embodied soul, while the sentient (soul) does not undergo any modifications, such as pleasure or pain etc. The self (soul) is the knower of any modification. But, when It identifies Itself with the insentient (body etc.,) it has to undergo pleasure and pain. The sentient, (soul) by identifying Itself with the insentient (body etc.,) becomes the enjoyer. In the inert only, there is no enjoyership. The enjoyership, remains in the ego (where there is identification of the soul with the body). The term 'asya', used in the fifty-ninth verse of the second chapter, denotes the enjoyer, while the term 'Parama' denotes, God, unattached Universal Soul. 'When a striver realizes, 'Parama' (God or Self) his taste or relish, also turns away (Gītā 2/59). A man, has desire in order to derive pleasure or joy, while the self is, naturally, a heap of joy. Therefore, on God-realization or Self-realization, desire (desire for sensual pleasure) totally perishes, forever.

A Vital Fact

The physical (gross) body, is the object of senses, senses are the external instruments, while mind and intellect, are the internal instruments. Senses are beyond, (superior, stronger, wider, subtler and illuminator) the physical body, while intellect is, body and senses. Ego which is the doer, is beyond intellect and desire resides, in the ego. The self is sentient, unaltered (uniform) and an embodiment of truth, consciousness, and bliss consolidated. But when It identifies Itself with the insentient body etc., ego is born and the self, becomes the doer or agent. Thus the doer (agent) has two aspects—the insentient one and the sentient one. A man (the embodied soul), because of the insentient aspect, is attracted towards the world i.e., the worldly desires are born, while because of the sentient aspect, he is attracted towards God or the spiritual discipline.* As the insentient aspect is perishable, so are the worldly desires, and as the sentient aspect, is eternal, so are the spiritual desires (needs). The mundane desires, are renounced, while the spiritual ones (of the renunciation of the world, of Self-realization, of devotion to God), are satisfied. The mundane desires can appear, but cannot exist, while the spiritual desires can be suppressed but cannot perish, because the former are unreal while the latter are real. Therefore, a striver should neither hope for the fulfilment of the mundane desires, nor lose heart by thinking of the non-fulfilment of spiritual desires.

In fact, the only desire of a man (the soul) is to realize God, Whose fragment he is. But by identifying himself with the body etc., he, by an error of judgment, forgets the real desire, and hankers after worldly pleasures and prosperity. But, the real never ceases to be. The desire for the real can never be destroyed. In a striver two sorts of desire remain—one for God-realization and the other, for worldly pleasures. So, there is a duel between the two. It is because of the duel, that when a striver practises spiritual discipline such as adoration, meditation and good company etc., his spiritual desires are aroused, but at

---

* The identification of the self with the body etc., can be explained by an illustration. A block of iron with four edges has no burning power but when by coming into contact with fire it identifies itself with fire, it develops the burning power and fire, in spite of having no edges, becomes of four edges. But a magnet attracts only iron, not fire because iron and magnet belong to the same class and the fire automatically calms down. In the same way when there is identification of the self with the body, the sentient portion is attracted towards God, while the insentient towards the world. When the sentient portion is attracted towards God the insentient is left because it is perishable. But when the insentient portion is attracted towards the world, the sentient one remains because it is eternal.

other times he hankers after worldly pleasures and prosperity. While having mundane desire, a striver cannot even resolve, that he has to practise spiritual discipline. He cannot progress in the spiritual path, so long as spiritual desire, is not aroused. When he resolves, that he has only to realize God, the duel ceases and only the keen spiritual desire remains, which enables him to realize God easily (Gītā 5/3). So, for a striver it is indispensable to root out this duel, between mundane desire and the spiritual one.

The self, has an automatic attraction or inclination, towards God whose fragment It is. This attraction is known, as devotion. When the Self accepts Its affinity for the world, that devotion, is suppressed and desire springs. So long as there is desire, devotion (love) is not aroused. Without devotion, desire is not killed. The insentient fragment, hankers after sensual pleasures, while the sentient one, is attracted towards God. Therefore, in fact, desire resides in the insentient fragment, but it is so because the two are identified. When the sentient (self) does not accept Its affinity for the insentient, desire perishes. It means, that as soon as, the sentient (Self), renounces Its affinity for the insentient (body etc.,) 'Ego' (the identification of the self with the insentient) perishes and consequently, desire perishes.

Desire abides, in the insentient fragment of ego. The reason is, that an enjoyer can be attracted towards objects of enjoyment of the world, (the world which is seen), the senses and intellect with which the world is seen, only if these belong to the same class, because attraction is possible for the objects of the same class only. As eyes are, attracted to the beautiful colour or form, so is the case with other senses. Intellect is attracted towards discrimination or thought, not to sound etc. If it is attracted, it is, because of its association with senses.

Similarly, the self has Its identity with God, and so It is attracted towards God. This identity, can be realized only when the Self totally renounces, Its affinity for the insentient (Matter). As soon as, this identity is realized, devotion (Love) is aroused, in which there is total lack of matter (the unreal).

The insentient fragment, 'causal body', is a very subtle fragment of the cosmic intelligence, which is an evolute of nature. Desire, resides in this causal body. It is because of the identification of the self with the causal body, that desire seems to reside in the self. When there is no identification, a man realizes the self which is pure and uniform. In that case, desire perishes totally.

'Evaṁ buddheḥ paraṁ buddhvā'—In the previous verses, it has been explained, "The senses are greater than the body, greater than the senses, is the mind and greater than the mind is the intellect." But now in this verse, when the Lord declares, that greater than intellect, is desire, He means to say, that desire resides in 'ego', not in the self. Had it resided in the self, it might have never perished. It is born, when the self accepts its affinity for the insentient body etc. In fact, it resides in the insentient fragment, (matter), but appears in the Self. Therefore, knowing this desire, which is beyond intellect, a striver should eliminate it.

'Saṁstabhyātmānamātmanā'— The method, to slay this desire, is to restrain, the self by the self viz., to accept the real affinity of the self, for the pure self or for God whose fragment It is. The same fact, has been pointed out by the Lord, in the fifth and the sixth verses of the sixth chapter when he declares, "One should raise oneself by one's self alone" and "The self has been conquered by the self."

The self is a fragment of God, while the body, senses, mind and intellect are fragments of the world. When the self having a disinclination for God, has an inclination to nature (the world), desires are born, Desires are born, when there is privation and a man (the self) feels it, because of his affinity for the world, because the world is unreal, has no existence (Gītā 2/16) but like a mirage, it seems to exist. As soon as, the affinity for the world is renounced, desires perish, because the self has no deficiency as the Lord declares, "The real never suffers any deficiency" (Gītā 2/16).

Even when, a man has disinclination for God, and assumes his affinity for the world, his real desire (need or hunger) remains to realize God, whose, fragment he (the self) is. He wants to remain alive forever, he wants to possess all knowledge and he wants to be happy forever—this is his desire to attain God, who is the Embodiment of Truth, Consciousness and Bliss. But, it is because of his affinity for the world, that by an error of judgment, he wants to satisfy this desire (need), by enjoying worldly pleasures. But this desire, can never be satisfied with worldly objects, so it will have to be discarded.

He, who has established his affinity, for the world, is also capable of renouncing it. So the Lord orders Arjuna, to slay this desire by dissociating himself from the world, through his own efforts.

This dissociation, needs no practice because practice is done with the help of the world (body, senses, mind and intellect). In fact, a man gets established in the self or realizes God, by renouncing affinity for the world.

A Vital Fact

When the self accepts Its affinity, for the world, it has a desire to enjoy worldly pleasures, as well as, to realize God. He (the self) by an error wants to satisfy the need for God-realization (who is Truth, Consciousness and Bliss) by worldly materials. Therefore, both his desires, remain unfulfilled.

A man can know the world, by dissociating himself from it, and the Lord, by identifying himself with Him, because he (the self) is different from the world, while he has identity with God. But he accepts his identity or affinity, for the world, in order to acquire worldly things, which is never possible. Similarly, he accepts that he is different from God which is also not a reality. Spiritual desire, is necessary, in order to root out worldly desires. When spiritual desires grow up mundane desires, automatically, perish. When mundane desires, are rooted out, spiritual desire is satisfied viz., God, Who is ever attainable, is attained.* God always pervades everywhere, but a man does not realize Him, because of his entanglement with worldly desires.

'Jahi śatruṁ mahābāho kāmarūpaṁ durāsadam'—The term 'Mahābāho' means, one possessed of long and mighty arms i.e., a brave warrior. By addressing Arjuna, as 'mahābāho', the Lord means that he is brave enough to slay the enemy, in the form of desire.

It is hard for a man to conquer this enemy, so long as he has affinity for the world. This desire, deviates even the wise from the performance of their duty, by covering their discrimination, and so they have a downfall. Therefore, the Lord has said, that it is hard to conquer. So, a striver, instead of losing heart, should be aware of this enemy.

Desires appear and disappear, whether these are fully

---

* When all the desires of a striver are rooted out, the mortal man becomes immortal and he very well realizes the Eternal" (Kaṭhopaniṣad 2/3/14; Bṛhadāraṇyaka 4/4/7).

"O Lotus-eyed! when a man renounces all his desires he attains God-realization" (Śrīmadbhāgavata 7/10/9).

satisfied or partly satisfied, or not satisfied at all, while the self ever remains uniform, and knows their appearance and disappearance. So he can easily renounce his affinity for them, which is merely assumed. Therefore, a striver should not be afraid of desire, if he is determined* to attain his aim, he can slay 'desire', very easily.

Everyone is independent, qualified, deserving and able to realize God, but it is not so with desire, because these can never be satiated. The Lord, has bestowed upon beings this human body, so that they may attain Him. So they can easily renounce desires, but it is because of their attachment to the worldly persons and objects etc., that it seems difficult to renounce desires.

The Lord, creates unfavourable circumstances, so that man may be warned, not to have desire for favourable circumstances, otherwise these will lead him to suffering. It is a rule that he who has a desire for worldly persons and objects, cannot escape pain. The Lord declares, "The pleasures that are born of contacts (with objects) are only sources, of pain (Gītā 5/22).

The soul possesses infinite strength. It is because of the power derived from the soul, that intellect, mind and senses, seem powerful. But It forgets Its strength because of Its affinity for the insentient, and regards itself as subordinate to the intellect, mind and senses etc. Therefore, it is necessary to know the Self, and recognize Its power, in order to kill the enemy in the form of desire.

---

*A man's only aim is to attain the imperishable Lord, not the perishable world. He has a desire to acquire the perishable objects. Aim remains the same constantly while desire change. Aim is realized while desires may or may not be satisfied but they disappear. A man wants to realize his aim (God) even though his body may be broken into pieces.

Desire, is born out of affinity of the self, for the insentient (Matter) and it resides in it, but seems to reside in the self. If one does not accept affinity for the insentient, desire has no existence. Therefore, when the Lord urges Arjuna, to slay desire, He means to say, that desire has no existence of its own. A desire appears and it automatically disappears. So, if one has no new desires, the old ones automatically disappear.

A man becomes aware of something wanting in himself, only when he regards the worldly objects, such as the body etc., as 'I', 'mine' and 'for me', but he wants to make up for the lack, by worldly materials. So, he has desire to acquire these. But it is impossible to make up that lack, by those materials because he (the self) is imperishable, while these are perishable. Thus, he by desiring transitory objects, gains nothing, but suffering. Therefore, by calling desire an enemy, the Lord urges Arjuna to slay it.

This desire can be easily eliminated through the Discipline of Action, because a striver following the Discipline of Action, performs every major or minor act, for the good of others, rather than to satiate his own desire. All his actions are performed, for the welfare of others without any selfish motive. All his resources, are not his own, but have been acquired and are likely to be lost. So, he uses, them, for the welfare of the world, by regarding these as the world's, without any selfish motive. Thus, he gets rid of desires easily, and consequently, attains his aim of God-realization. Then, nothing further remains to be done, to be known, and to be acquired for him.

Appendix—Here the Lord has mentioned senses, mind and intellect but He has not mentioned 'ego'. Ego is greater than intellect. In the fourth verse of the seventh chapter also the

Lord has mentioned ego after intellect—'bhūmirāpo'nalo vāyuḥ khaṁ mano buddhireva ca, ahaṅkāra itīyaṁ me .....'. Therefore here also the term 'saḥ' should be interpreted as 'desire' which abides in ego.

Unless and until the self is realized, desire abides in ego. After Self-realization desire does not persist in ego—'paraṁ dṛṣṭvā nivartate' (Gītā 2/59). Bliss abides in the self but a man by according reality and importance to non-self wants to derive pleasure from it. As long as there is affinity for the non-self, desire persists but when affinity for the non-self (inert matter) is renounced, then 'Prema' (real love) ensues.

The desire is in the self—'raso'pyasya' (Gītā 2/59). Being in the self it is an obstacle to Self-realization. If it is not in the self but is in senses-mind-intellect, how is it an obstacle to Self-realization by us? It is because of its abode in the self that the self feels happy and sad and becomes a doer and an enjoyer. In fact the desire does not abide in the self but it is merely an assumption and therefore it can be wiped out. Therefore desire is seated in the self only through assumption.

A man assumes a thing, which abides in ego, to be abiding in the self. Ego is identified with the self and desire abides in that ego. Therefore so long as ego persists, attraction viz., 'desire', which belongs to the same class to which ego belongs, persists and when ego perishes, then attraction viz., 'true love' belonging to the class of the 'self' ensues. In desire there is attraction for the world while in true love there is attraction for God.

All the three worlds and endless universes are 'sense-objects'. Sense-objects are in one region of senses, senses are in one region of the mind, the mind is in one region of the intellect, the intellect is in one region of the ego and the ego is in one region of the self. Therefore the self is very huge within which there are all the three worlds and endless universes. But a man (the self) by assuming his affinity for ego, a fragment of lower (insentient) nature, feels himself very small (unipresent).

ॐ तत्सदिति श्रीमद्भगवद्गीतासूपनिषत्सु ब्रह्मविद्यायां योगशास्त्रे
श्रीकृष्णार्जुनसंवादे कर्मयोगो नाम तृतीयोऽध्याय: ॥ ३ ॥

Oṁ tatsaditi śrīmadbhagavadgītāsūpaniṣatsu brahmavidyāyāṁ yogaśāstre śrīkṛṣṇārjunasaṁvāde karmayogo nāma tṛtīyo'dhyāyaḥ

Thus with the words Oṁ, Tat, Sat, the names to the Lord, in the Upaniṣad of the Bhagavadgītā, the knowledge of Brahma; the Supreme, the scripture of Yoga, the dialogue between Śrī Kṛṣṇa and Arjuna, ends the third discourse, designated 'Karmayoga or the Discipline of Action'.

This chapter is designated 'Karmayoga' (the Discipline of Action), because the Discipline of Action has not been described so clearly in any other chapter, as in this.

Words, letters and Uvāca (said) in the Third Chapter

(1) In this chapter in **'Atha tṛtīyo'dhyāyaḥ'** there are three words, in **'Arjuna Uvāca'** etc., there are eight words, in verses there are five hundred and forty-two words and there are thirteen concluding words. Thus the total number of words, is five hundred and sixty-six. (2) In this chapter in **'Atha tṛtīyo'dhyāyaḥ'** there are seven letters, in **'Arjuna Uvāca'** etc., there are twenty-six letters, in verses there are one thousand, three hundred and seventy-six letters and there are forty-five concluding letters. Thus, the total number of words, is one thousand, four hundred and fifty-four. In each of the verses of this chapter there are thirty-two letters.

(3) In this chapter there are four **'Uvāca'** (said) **'Arjuna Uvāca'** twice and **Śrībhagavānuvāca'** twice.

Metres Used in the Third Chapter—

In this chapter, 'ra-gaṇa' being used, in the first quarter of first and thirty-seventh verses, and in the third quarter of eleventh verse, there is **'ra-vipulā'**; 'na-gaṇa' being used in the first quarter of fifth verse there is **'na-vipulā**; 'bha-gaṇa' being used, in the first quarter of nineteenth, twenty-sixth and thirty-fifth and in the third quarter of eighth and twenty-first verses, there is **'bha-vipulā**; 'na-gaṇa' and 'ra-gaṇa' being respectively, in the first and third quarter of the seventh verse there is **'saṅkīrṇa-vipulā'** metre. The remaining, thirty-three verses, have the characteristics of **'pathyāvaktra'** anuṣṭup metre.

|| Shri Hari ||

Fourth Chapter

INTRODUCTION

The Lord, in the thirty-ninth verse of the second chapter, said to Arjuna, "This is the wisdom of Sāṅkhya given to thee, to attain equanimity, O Arjuna. Now listen; about equanimity to be acquired, through the Discipline of Action, in which a person by performing action for the welfare of others, without any selfish motive, attains equanimity." Thus according to the context, in response to Arjuna's question, Lord Kṛṣṇa having described the marks of a man of steady wisdom, completes this topic.

At the beginning of the third chapter, Arjuna asked Lord Kṛṣṇa, "If You think that knowledge is superior to action, why do You urge me, to do this savage deed (war)?" In response to his question, the Lord, from the fourth to the twenty-ninth verses, lays emphasis on the performance of actions, by which a man attains equanimity. In the thirtieth verse, He says that surrendering all actions to Him, with a discriminative insight, free from desire and egoism he should perform actions without mental agitation. In the thirty-first and thirty-second verses, He declares the sweet fruit of following His preaching (explained in the previous verse) and the harm in not following it. In the thirty-fifth verse, He declares, "Better is death in one's own duty." In the thirty-sixth verse Arjuna asks, "By what is a man impelled to commit sin?" The Lord replies, "It is desire, all devouring and most sinful, which is the enemy," and ordered Arjuna to slay this enemy.

Though, the Lord's teaching continues from the thirty-seventh verse, yet in the forty-third verse, when the answer to Arjuna's question is over, sage Veda Vyāsa concludes the third chapter, and begins the fourth chapter. It shows that the Lord having answered Arjuna's question, takes a pause and then starts again, the Discipline of Action, which was being described in the forty-seventh and forty-eighth verses of the second chapter, by the term 'Imam' (This) in the first verse of the fourth chapter. Therefore, the fourth chapter is regarded, as an appendix to the third chapter.

There are two important factors pertaining to the Discipline of Action—(1) Performance of actions and, (2) special knowledge about action. Arjuna wants to renounce the performance of action, so he says to Lord Kṛṣṇa, "Why do You ask me to be engaged in this savage deed?" Therefore, the Lord, lays special emphasis on the performance of duty, specially in the third chapter, while in the fourth chapter, He imparts knowledge about actions. He declares, "I shall teach thee such action, (the nature of action and inaction), after knowing which, thou shalt be liberated from evil (the wheel of birth and death) (4/16).

This Karmayoga, in spite of being without beginning, was lost to the world through, a long lapse of time, because of the absence of scholarly teachers (sages), who could impart it. The Lord, in the first three verses, describing how Karmayoga was handed down from ancient times, proves how it existed from times immemorial.

श्रीभगवानुवाच

इमं विवस्वते योगं प्रोक्तवानहमव्ययम्।
विवस्वान्मनवे प्राह मनुरिक्ष्वाकवेऽब्रवीत्॥ १॥

śrībhagavānuvāca

imaṁ vivasvate yogaṁ proktavānahamavyayam
vivasvānmanave prāha manurikṣvākave'bravīt

The Blessed Lord said:

I taught this imperishable Yoga to Vivasvān (the sun-god); who expounded it to Manu, and Manu proclaimed it to Ikṣvāku. 1

Comment:—

'Imaṁ vivasvate yogaṁ proktavānahamavyayam'—The kings, such as Sūrya, Manu and Ikṣvāku, who have been mentioned by the Lord, were householders and they attained perfection, through the Discipline of Action, leading a householder's life. Therefore, here the words 'Imam, avyayam yogam' (this imperishable Yoga) stand for 'Karmayoga', (the Discipline of Action).

Though Karmayoga has been described in the Purāṇas (historical records), and Upaniṣads (philosophical parts of the Vedas) also, yet it is not as thoroughly detailed, as in the Gītā.

The Lord is eternal, His fragment, the soul is also eternal and so is the affinity of soul for the Lord. Therefore, all the disciplines (of Action, Knowledge and Devotion) are also eternal.* Here, the term 'Avyayam' shows, that Karmayoga is eternal.

The affinity of the soul for God is eternal. Just as a chaste wife does not have to make effort to be dear to her husband, in the like manner, a striver does not have to put in any effort, in order to belong to God. But, when he accepts his affinity for perishable actions, objects and incidents etc., he does not realize his eternal affinity for God. Therefore, a Karmayogī, in order to, renounce his assumed affinity for the world, utilizes his body, senses, mind and intellect etc., for rendering service to the world, by regarding them as the world's. He thinks, that just as the smallest particle of dust, is a fragment of the huge earth, so is the body, a fragment of the vast universe. By accepting this belief, 'Karmas' (actions) will be performed, for the world, but 'Yoga' (Nityayoga or eternal union) will be for himself i.e., he will realize his eternal union with God.

By the terms 'Vivasvate proktavān', the Lord wants to explain to the strivers that as the sun in the solar system while performing its action by providing heat and light, remains

* Lord Kṛṣṇa declares in the eighth chapter of the Gītā that the bright and the dark paths of the world are verily thought to be eternal (Gītā 8/26).

unengrossed; similarly, all the strivers should perform actions without attachment according to available circumstances, (Gītā 3/19). They should, also impart this teaching of Karmayoga, to others for the public welfare by remaining unengrossed (without desire for fruit, without a sense of 'mine' and without attachment).

The sun-god, was king at the beginning of creation. Lord Kṛṣṇa taught this imperishable Yoga to the sun-god. It means, that Lord Kṛṣṇa was the first preceptor in the beginning, and so has Karmayoga come from times immemorial. It seems that the Lord, tells Arjuna, "Whatever teaching about 'Karmayoga' I am imparting to you, is not new but eternal."

Question:—Why did the Lord teach this Yoga to the sun-god, at the beginning of creation?

Answer:—(1) The Lord taught it to him, because He knew that he was a deserving candidate.

(2) Such teaching is imparted to the first born, as Brahmā, the creator, who created man and imparted teaching to them (Gītā 3/10), in order to, inspire them to perform their duty. In the universe also, the sun-god was the first born, and then the entire universe was born of him. The Lord, taught this Yoga, first of all to the sun-god.* He meant to get it imparted, through the sun-god to all his progeny, by way of transmission by succession.

(3) The sun, is the eye of entire creation. He imparts knowledge to all the people and when he rises, they wake up and are engaged in their work. He sets an example to them for the performance of their duty. He has been called, the soul of the entire world†. Therefore, teaching imparted to the sun-god

* In the scriptures the sun-god has been called 'Savitā' which means the creator. The western scholars also regard the Sun as the creator.

† In the Mahābhārata it has been said addressing the sun-god, "O sun-god, you are the eye of the entire world and the soul of all beings. You are the birth-place and the inspirer of the good conduct of the followers of the path of action."

"You are the abode which should be attained by the Sāṅkhyayogīs. You will also be communicated to all beings. Therefore, Lord Kṛṣṇa first of all, taught this imperishable Yoga to the sun-god.

In fact, this teaching imparted by Lord Kṛṣṇa (the manager of the world-theatre), to the sun-god, is a drama staged by Him, for the welfare of the world. As Lord Kṛṣṇa taught Arjuna, the incarnation of Nara, the wise sage, for the welfare of the world, so did He teach, this Yoga to the sun-god, the embodiment of knowledge, for the welfare of the entire world. This Yoga has done a lot of good to the world, is doing and will continue to do, in future also.

'Vivasvānmanave prāha manurikṣvākave'bravīt'— Karmayoga, is the main course of action for householders. Out of celibacy, household life, the retired and the renounced, orders—the four stages (orders) of life—household life is most important, because it is a householder that provides for the other stages of life. A householder, by performing his duty, can easily realize God. He need not change the order of life. Lord Kṛṣṇa in mentioning the names of the kings, such as the sun-god, Manu and Ikṣvāku, wants to say, that at the beginning of creation, they as householders, having slain desires, realized God. Lord Kṛṣṇa and Arjuna were also householders. Therefore, Lord Kṛṣṇa through Arjuna, teaches all householders that they can realize God, as householders, without leading a secluded life as ascetics by performing their duty.

In spite of being a householder, Arjuna thinks that it is better to live, in this world even by begging than to perform a savage deed, of slaying honoured teachers in war (Gītā 2/5) viz., he thinks that the renounced order of life is superior to the household life. Therefore, the Lord says to him that he is a

are the base of Karmayogīs. You are the free gateway to salvation and you are the refuge for the salvation-seekers. You hold the entire world. This world is illumined by you. You sanctify it and it is preserved by you without any selfish motive (Vanaparva 3/36—38).

noble householder of the royal family. So performance of actions will lead him to salvation, in the same way, as renunciation leads an ascetic to salvation. Karmayoga, consists in the utilization of available circumstances. So Karmayoga (the Discipline of Action), can be followed by people of every caste, creed, country and order of life.

The Lord, has mentioned the names of noble and influential kings of the past, so that people may draw inspiration from them, in order to perform their duty.

An Important Fact

Attachment (affinity) for actions and objects, is a stumbling block to Karmayoga. When a householder renounces pleasure, his zest also comes to an end. When a person starts enjoying pleasure, such as eating a sweet dish, he relishes it very much. But, as he goes on eating it, the taste diminishes and finally, it ceases. But, he commits an error, as he does not make that distaste permanent, by attaching importance to it. He regards this distaste as satisfaction, (reward). But the fact is, that is the state of deficiency in which he has no power of having pleasure.

The interest or desire which diminishes or perishes, cannot be the characteristic of the self and therefore, It (the self) has no real affinity for the objects etc., which he desires or wants. Our real affinity is, for God and therefore, devotion while following a spiritual path for God-realization, is ever enhanced. Even when, he realizes God, his devotion increases continuously, and it is transformed into love (devotion). The self, is also real, so no one has a desire in the least for one's own negation.

When actions, instruments (body, senses and mind etc.,) objects and materials, are perishable how can these bear imperishable fruit? How can pleasure and satisfaction, be derived from the fruit of perishable things to match the pleasure and satisfaction, achieved on God-realization? Therefore, a striver has to renounce his affinity for actions, instruments (such as body, senses and mind etc.,) and objects. He can renounce this affinity, only when he does nothing for himself, wants nothing for himself and regards nothing as his own. But he utilizes everything, by regarding it as of the world in rendering service, to the world.

A Karmayogī, performs actions scrupulously and lovingly, without desire, attachment and feeling of 'mine'. Desire, attachment and a sense of 'mine' pollute actions, while careful and loving nature, purifies these. When actions are performed with desire, attachment and a sense of mine, objects are destroyed, and man has a downfall. The thought of actions come to the mind, time and again i.e., affinity for those actions continues. But when actions are performed scrupulously, devotedly and lovingly, there is proper use of objects, and man is elevated and the thought of actions do not come to mind i.e., affinity for these is renounced. As soon as, this affinity for actions is totally renounced, a striver realizes the self or God, who is ever present and existent.

Everyone, can easily assume that whatever he possesses is not his own, but is acquired, just as he has acquired the body from parents, education and knowledge from preceptors and so on. It means that every man, even the richest one, has to depend on others, in one way or the other. So, it is his duty to render service to others, with all his possessions, because he has acquired them from others. This, is known as Karmayoga, no one is dependent and unable to follow it and for its practice.

In fact, duty is that which can be performed easily, which must be performed and by performing which a man certainly attains his aim. A man is not responsible for the performance of action, which he cannot perform. And, what is forbidden, must not be done. When a person does not perform forbidden actions, he either does nothing or he performs only prescribed actions.

Duty is always performed, for the welfare of others, without expecting any reward. Actions, with the expectation of reward, should not be performed, because these lead to bondage. But, it does not mean that actions are performed, without any aim. An act without any aim, cannot be performed by anyone, except by insane person. There is a vast difference, between fruit (reward) and aim. Reward, is perishable while aim is eternal. A man's aim is to attain God who is ever attainable, and for which this human life has been bestowed upon him. He cannot realize God, without performing his duty, in a disinterested manner. He cannot perform his duty, so long as he indulges, in reward for actions, heedlessness and indolence etc.

In fact, performance of duty needs no effort, it is performed automatically. But when a man performs action for himself with egoism, attachment, desire and a sense of 'mine', it involves effort. Therefore, the Lord declares, "Action which involves strain (effort), is said to be of the nature of passion" (Gītā 18/24).

As the Lord, is ever engaged in the welfare of all beings, so is His power. As a news broadcast by a particular radio station, is received on the same frequency by radio-sets, similarly, when a Karmayogī performs all his actions for the welfare of the world without any selfish motive, his power, is identified with the all-pervading, benevolent power of God and his actions become uncommon. Thus, because of Lord's power, his actions are conducive to the welfare of the world. Therefore, there is neither any obstacle in the way of performing his duty nor does it involve any strain.

A man, can perform his duty without depending on any person or circumstance. According to Karmayoga (the Discipline of Action), giving help to others according to their need, is service. When the engine of a car goes out of order and the driver is trying to push it forward, if someone helped him, it is service. But, he who looks for service, does not render real service, but he performs actions, only because by doing so, his aim is mundane rather than spiritual. Service is rendered according to available circumstances. Therefore, a Karmayogī neither changes circumstances nor does he seek these but utilizes these. The utilization of the available circumstances, is Karmayoga.

एवं परम्पराप्राप्तमिमं राजर्षयो विदुः।
स कालेनेह महता योगो नष्टः परन्तप॥ २॥

evaṁ paramparāprāptamimaṁ rājarṣayo viduḥ
sa kāleneha mahatā yogo naṣṭaḥ parantapa

This Yoga handed down thus, in regular succession, came to the royal sages. But through long lapse of time, it was lost to the world, O oppressor of the foes (Arjuna). 2

Comment:—

'Evaṁ paramparāprāptamimaṁ rājarṣayo viduḥ'— The kings, such as the sun-god, Manu and Ikṣvāku, learnt the Karmayoga, followed it and also, inspired their subjects to follow it. Thus, it was handed down in regular succession to the families of the royal sages. This Karmayoga is a special lare of the kings (the warrior class). Therefore, every member of the warrior class should know it. Similarly, the heads and leaders of a family, society, village and town etc., must also know it.

In ancient days, the kings who knew Karmayoga, administered the affairs of state smoothly, without being attached to royal pleasures. They had a natural inclination for the welfare of the subjects. The great Saṁskṛta poet Kālidāsa writes about the kings of solar dynasty:—

"Those kings levied a tax on their subjects in the same way, as the sun sucks water from the earth, in order to supply it to the earth in the form of rain, a thousand times more."

It means, that the tax realized from the subjects by kings, was all used for public welfare. In order to, provide for their household expenses, they followed occupations, like farming.

By practising Karmayoga, they were automatically endowed with, singular knowledge and devotion. Therefore, even great sages went to those kings, in order to learn wisdom. Śrī Vedavyāsa's son named Śukadeva, went to king Janaka, in order to gain wisdom from him. In the fifth chapter of the Chāndogyopaniṣad it is mentioned, that six sages together went to king Aśvapati, in order to learn knowledge of Brahma, the Supreme.* Having mentioned kings, such as Janaka and others in the twentieth verse of the third chapter, and the sun-god, Manu and Ikṣvāku etc., here, as Karmayogīs, Lord Kṛṣṇa wants to urge Arjuna that he should also perform actions accordingly (follow Karmayoga) as the ancestors did, in former times, as he was also a householder and a member of the warrior class (Gītā 4/15). Moreover, it was very easy for him to learn it, because he belonged to the warrior class.

'Sa kāleneha mahatā yogo naṣṭaḥ'— God is eternal and the means—Karmayoga, Jñānayoga and Bhaktiyoga (Disciplines of Action, Knowledge and Devotion) etc., are also eternal, as they have been laid down by God. Therefore, they never cease to be. The Lord declares, "The real, never ceases to be" (Gītā 2/16). The yogas are eternal, even if these are not practised. Therefore, here the term 'Naṣṭaḥ' means, passing out of sight, rather than out of existence.

In the first verse of this chapter, this Yoga has been called imperishable. Therefore, if this term 'Naṣṭaḥ' is taken as 'out of existence' there will be a contradiction between the two statements. Moreover, the Lord again in the third verse declares, that He is going to reveal the same ancient Yoga, to Arjuna. It means that the religious texts and the learned sages who possessed knowledge of this Yoga, and practised it, had more or less disappeared from the earth.

---

* King Aśvapati declares, "In my kingdom there is neither a thief, nor a miser, nor a drunkard, nor one who does not offer oblation to the consecrated fire, nor an ignorant person nor an adulterer; then how can there be a prostitute" (Chāndogyopaniṣad 5/11/5)?

The Lord declares, that it was through a long lapse of time, that it disappeared, because at the beginning of creation, the Lord taught it to the sun-god, then it was handed down in regular succession and the royal sages come to know it. But due to the absence of great spiritual souls, possessed of the knowledge of this Yoga, it could not be handed down. So, at present only a few people know and talk about it.

Though this doctrine was not practised, yet it did not cease to be, because without selflessness, which is the essence of Karmayoga even other disciplines (such as of knowledge and devotion) cannot be constantly practised. A Jñānayogī through discrimination, by regarding actions as 'Asat' (unreal), renounces his affinity for these, while a Bhaktiyogī renounces affinity for them by surrendering these to God. No affinity, howsoever, is to be maintained. This is the doctrine of 'Karmayoga'. Therefore, a Jñānayogī and a Bhaktiyogī will have to adopt the principles of 'Karmayoga', even though they may not practise it. It means, that at present, though it has been lost, yet as a doctrine it exists.

The fact is, that in Karmayoga, Karma (actions) have not disappeared but 'Yoga' (selflessness) has disappeared, because a man performs actions with a selfish motive. It means, that strivers have a firm belief that they will attain God, through actions in the same way as they acquire worldly things through actions. But they forget the reality, that God is, ever attained. Actions, are performed for the world while 'Yoga' (union with God) is, ever for one's own self. Yoga is not attained through actions, as is self-evident.* Therefore, the generality of the assumption that

* Yoga is attained by performing one's duty for the welfare of the world without any selfish motive. Action is performed in order to attain the state of actionlessness—'Action is said to be the means to attain to Yoga' (Gītā 6/3). When actions are performed with a selfish motive, the impetus for actions is enhanced. But when they are performed for the welfare of others the impetus for actions perishes. It means that nothing remains to be done by doing for others while actions are continuously performed when one does for himself. When nothing remains to be done, the striver realizes his union (which is self-evident) with God.

this Yoga can be attained through action, has practically caused the disappearance of yoga.

This human body, has been bestowed upon us, so that we may practise Karmayoga i.e., serve others without any selfish motive. But, we are so much absorbed in hankering after pleasures, prosperity and honour etc., that we do not pay heed to it. Thus, this knowledge has been lost, because we have forgotten it.

A man by rendering service can control not only birds, beasts and persons but also the gods, manes, sages, saints and even God. But having forgotten this practice, he has been overpowered by pleasures, which lead to hell and eighty-four lac forms of lives. This is called concealment of Karmayoga.

स एवायं मया तेऽद्य योगः प्रोक्तः पुरातनः।
भक्तोऽसि मे सखा चेति रहस्यं ह्येतदुत्तमम्॥ ३॥

sa evāyaṁ mayā te'dya yogaḥ proktaḥ purātanaḥ
bhakto'si me sakhā ceti rahasyaṁ hyetaduttamam

It is the same ancient Yoga, that has been declared to thee today by Me; for thou art My devotee and My friend; and this Yoga is the supreme secret. 3

Comment:—

'Bhakto'si me sakhā ceti'—Arjuna regarded Lord Kṛṣṇa, as his companion (comrade) (Gītā 11/41-42) but now he has become His pupil (Gītā 2/7) i.e., earlier he was a comrade-devotee, while now, he has become a disciple-devotee. An order can be given or a sermon can be preached, only to a disciple rather than to a friend. The Lord preached His sermon, only when Arjuna surrendered to Him i.e., took refuge in Him.

The secret, which is not disclosed even to a comrade, is revealed to a disciple, who surrenders himself to his preceptor.

Arjuna also says to Lord Kṛṣṇa, "I am Thy disciple, teach me, who have taken refuge in Thee." Therefore, the Lord reveals His secret to him.

It was because of Arjuna's reverence for Lord Kṛṣṇa, that he, instead of opting for a well-equipped army chose unarmed Lord Kṛṣṇa alone, (as his chariot-driver).*

Common people, regard the objects bestowed upon them by God as theirs (while in fact they are not theirs), but they do not regard the Lord, (Who is actually theirs), as theirs. They, instead of having an eye on the glorious Lord, look at His glory. Having attached importance to the glory, their intellect becomes so dull, that they do not even believe, in His existence i.e., they do not even look towards Him. Some people adore Him, in order to gain riches and glory etc. Though riches lie at the feet of devotees, yet true devotees do not adore Him for riches, but they adore Him to attain Him. Those who hanker after riches, are devotees (slaves) to riches, while those who want to attain God, are His real devotees. Arjuna, having abandoned riches or glory (well-armed Nārāyaṇī army), chose Lord Kṛṣṇa. Consequently, it was only he, to whom the gospel of the Gītā was preached on the battlefield, though there were other great souls such as Bhīṣma, Droṇa, Yudhiṣṭhira etc., near by. Finally Arjuna was able to regain the kingdom also.

'Sa evāyaṁ mayā te'dya yogaḥ proktaḥ purātanaḥ'—By these terms, the Lord does not mean to say, that He has given a full description of this Yoga, but it means that whatever has been declared by Him is complete in itself. Further, having answered Arjuna's question concerning His manifestation (incarnation), the Lord, again starts the topic of Karmayoga.

---

* "Having heard the words of Lord Kṛṣṇa Arjuna, the son of Kuntī , chose unarmed Lord Kṛṣṇa as his helper while he could have chosen the well-armed Nārāyaṇī army consisting of 1,09,350 foot soldiers, 65,610 horses, 21,870 chariots and 21,870 elephants" (Mahābhārata, Udyogaparva 7/21).

The Lord declares, that the same Karmayoga, which was taught to the sun-god at the beginning of the creation, has been taught to Arjuna. He declares that through long lapse of time, this Yoga was lost to the world and he also was not manifest. Now he has manifested Himself and has also revealed this Yoga again. Therefore, Karmayoga, which has liberated people from bondage of actions from time immemorial, will also liberate them today.

'Rahasyaṁ hyetaduttamam'—As the Lord teaches His supreme secret to Arjuna, in the sixty-sixth verse of the eighteenth chapter, by declaring, "Take refuge in Me alone; I shall then liberate thee from all sins." Here also, He discloses His supreme secret by declaring, "I taught this imperishable Yoga to the sun-god at the beginning of creation and I am preaching the same to you today."

The Lord seems to say to Arjuna that though He, while playing the role of his chariot-driver, is obeying him, yet He is preaching to him the same Yoga, which was taught to the sun-god at the beginning of creation. He is disclosing this secret to him, because He is his devotee and also a loving friend.

Not to talk of a common man, even a striver, pays attention to the preaching, but he does not pay attention to the preacher. Having listened to this sermon on Yoga and having studied it, a striver thinks over it, and he does not take the preacher as the omnipresent, Lord Kṛṣṇa Himself. So, the Lord, by using the term Rahasyam' (secret) introduces Himself and urges a striver to behold Him, ever.

When the Lord declares that He preached the gospel of Yoga to the sun-god and is preaching the same to him, He also means to say, that He is the preacher or the preceptor, of the entire humanity. As an actor, while playing his role does not disclose his identity to the audience, but reveals it to his bosom friend; the Lord also discloses to His devout devotee, His identity. This is His supreme secret.

Karmayoga, can also be regarded as a supreme secret. The supreme secret is, that actions which bind a man (the soul), may also liberate him from bondage. If actions are performed with a selfish motive, by regarding the objects as one's own, these lead him to bondage. But, if these are performed, without any selfish motive for the welfare of others, they lead him to liberation (salvation). This Karmayoga, can be practised independent of all the circumstances—favourable or unfavourable, riches or poverty, health or sickness etc.

While practising Karmayoga there are three important factors, which need attention—

(1) The self, is real (imperishable), while all the objects which are acquired, are unreal (perishable). So, how can the perishable be possessed by the imperishable? 'So nothing is mine.'

(2) 'I need nothing for myself', because the self lacks nothing. Moreover, how can the perishable objects be useful for the imperishable self?

(3) 'Nothing is to be done for the self'. The first reason is, that the self is a fragment of God, who is sentient, while actions are insentient. The self is eternal, while actions and their fruits, are transitory. Therefore, when anyone performs actions for the self, he (the self), is attached to those actions and their fruits. Actions and their fruits, disappear but attachment for these continues, which is the cause of his birth and death. The Lord declares, "Attachment of the soul to the modes of nature, is the cause of its births, in good and evil wombs" (Gītā 13/21).

The second reason is, that the responsibility for actions is his, who can perform these i.e., who possesses the resources to perform these, and who wants to acquire something or the other. The self, being actionless, uniform, unchanging and perfect, can do nothing, without accepting its affinity for the body. Therefore, the self has nothing to do for itself.

The third reason, is that the self is real and perfect. It

lacks nothing. The Lord, declares, "The real, never suffers any deficiency." (Gītā 2/16). When It lacks nothing, there is no question for It to have any desire, in order to acquire anything. Therefore, It has to do nothing for Itself.

In Karmayoga, Karmas (actions) are performed for the world, while 'Yoga' (union with God) is for the self. When actions are performed for one's own self, one cannot realize one's union with God. When the full flow of actions is towards the world, we realize God, because the body, senses, mind, intellect, objects, riches and property etc., whatever we possess, is not different from the world and is of the world. So, these are to be used for rendering service, to the world. Therefore, actions are to be performed for others, in order to renounce affinity for the world, in the form of objects and actions. This is known as Karmayoga. By this Karmayoga, the attachment for action, the desire to acquire and to live, and the fear of death, perish.

As, for actions performed, in the sunlight, the sun remains detached, similarly, all action performed in the light of the self, the self also remains detached, because the self is sentient and unchanging, while actions are insentient and changing. But when by an error, it accepts Its affinity even in the least, for objects and actions i.e., regards them as Its, and for it then those actions bind It.

As the sun performs its duty always very punctually and scrupulously, so does a Karmayogī perform his duty efficiently and promptly.

If Karmayoga is rightly followed, a Karmayogī, having the influence of Jñāna (Knowledge) attains knowledge, while with a disposition of devotion, attains devotion, automatically. By following Karmayoga, a striver does supreme good to the entire world, whether other people perceive it or not, realize it or not. He works as a fountain of inspiration for others, and thus renders service to them.

A Vital Fact

The Lord, while beginning the gospel of the Gītā, has described, from the eleventh verse to the thirtieth verse of the second chapter, that every being experiences or realizes, 'I am'. Even trees and mountains feel this, though these cannot express it. This can be clearly seen among beasts and birds, because they fight with each other, as they notice their own existence; otherwise why should they fight? "I am distinct from the body and the world"—this is a common experience of every human being. It is called discrimination. As far as a man is concerned, he has been specially endowed with discrimination by God. The pity is, that he does not respect it and use it appropriately.

Senses, mind and intellect, are the fragments of nature (prakṛti) and so whatever is known, through these, is knowledge born of nature. The knowledge of scriptures that is acquired through the senses, mind and intellect, is also born of nature. The knowledge of God, is far superior to this knowledge. Therefore, He can be known only by the knowledge of the self. When a man attaches importance to the knowledge of the self i.e., discrimination (wisdom), he develops the power to know 'Who I am', 'What is mine', 'What is sentient and what is insentient', 'What is God and what is nature (prakṛti)', and so on. The same discrimination, is applied for Karmayoga also—this is something vital.

In Karmayoga, two important factors predominate—(1) There is no doubt about one's own existence, 'I am'. (2) Whatever objects we possess are not ours, because these are acquired; these were neither ours in the past, nor will remain ours, in future. 'I' (the self) remains the same while these objects—body, senses, mind, intellect etc., are changeable and perishable. As actions appear and disappear, so does their fruit. So actions and objects, have their affinity for the world, not for the self. When this discrimination (wisdom) is aroused, desire perishes. When desire perishes, self-evident actionlessness, is revealed i.e., Karmayoga is accomplished.

Discrimination (wisdom) is enveloped by desire (Gītā 3/38-39). A man cannot discriminate between the right and the wrong, because he hankers after worldly prosperity and pleasures, in having a selfish motive. Thus, he cannot decide what ought to be done and what ought not to be done. He wants to find out a solution, to the riddles of life through the body, senses, mind and intellect or by changing the circumstances. But circumstances cannot be changed by him. So he gets more and more entangled, and cannot decide his duty. But, when his discrimination (wisdom) is aroused, he gets rid of the desire for pleasure, prosperity and selfishness; and then he clearly sees his duty, and then all entanglements perish.

Actions, bear fruit in the form of outward circumstances, such as riches and poverty, praise and blame, honour and dishonour, fame and defame, profit and loss, birth and death and health and sickness etc. He who becomes, either happy in favourable circumstances or sad in unfavourable circumstances, by accepting his affinity for them, is a fool. Why? The reason is, that he cannot change the circumstances, but he can rise above these i.e., can remain detached from them, by making proper use of them. In favourable circumstances he should render service to others, while under unfavourable conditions, he should neither feel sad nor should he desire favourable circumstance. Such a striver, easily gets liberated from worldly bondage.

Undesirable circumstances, are fruits of sinful actions. So, sinful actions which hurt others should not be performed, even in a dream. But in unfavourable circumstances, which are the fruits of sinful actions of the past, worry, sadness and fear etc., automatically come to his mind, even though he does not commit new sins. A striver, should not be attached to these. He should believe that these come to his mind in the same way, as a cow whom he has sold visits his house, because of old habit. As the cow stops, coming to his house and starts living in the new place, similarly, when a striver does not get attached to these feelings, these stop coming to his mind.

Even when, discrimination (wisdom) is not fully aroused, a Karmayogī has a determinate intellect, and he has to renounce affinity for the perishable, which is not his and he has to render service to the world without enjoying worldly pleasures. It is because of his determinate intellect, that he ceases attaching importance to worldly pleasures. Then, he cannot be entangled in the mirage of pleasures. Thus his determinate intellect, leads him to salvation. Good company and the study of the scriptures strengthen this intellect. Therefore, every striver should have a firm intellect, that he has to attain salvation. Everyone is independent in having this determination, without seeking the least help, from anyone else.

Link:—The Lord declared, that He had taught the imperishable Yoga to the sun-god etc., and He was teaching the same Yoga to him (Arjuna). Having heard His words, Arjuna had the curiosity to know, how Lord Kṛṣṇa Who was sitting before him, had taught this Yoga to the sun-god, at the beginning of creation. In order to get this point cleared, Arjuna puts a question, in the next verse.

अर्जुन उवाच

अपरं भवतो जन्म परं जन्म विवस्वतः।
कथमेतद्विजानीयां त्वमादौ प्रोक्तवानिति॥४॥

arjuna uvāca

aparaṁ bhavato janma paraṁ janma vivasvataḥ
kathametadvijānīyāṁ tvamādau proktavāniti

Arjuna said:

You are of recent origin, while the birth of Vivasvān dates back to remote past. How then am I to understand, that Thou did declare it to him, in the beginning? 4

Comment:—

'Aparaṁ bhavato janma paraṁ janma vivasvataḥ'— Arjuna asks Lord Kṛṣṇa, that He was born in the house of Vasudeva a few years ago, while Vivasvān (the sun-god) was born earlier at the beginning of creation. So how could he believe, that He had taught this Yoga to the sun-god.

This question of Arjuna expresses his curiosity, rather than argument or blame. He wants to hear from Lord Kṛṣṇa, the secret of His Divine descent, because only He was capable of revealing this secret, to him.

'Kathametadvijānīyāṁ tvamādau proktavāniti'— Arjuna asks Lord Kṛṣṇa, how he should understand that He had taught this Yoga at the beginning of creation; because He was born later while the sun-god had been born earlier at the beginning of creation. As the Lord had recounted about several generations of the sun-god, it proves that He had imparted this knowledge, much earlier.

Link:—In response to Arjuna's question, the Lord reveals His omniscience, to manifest His Divine descent.

श्रीभगवानुवाच

बहूनि मे व्यतीतानि जन्मानि तव चार्जुन।
तान्यहं वेद सर्वाणि न त्वं वेत्थ परन्तप॥ ५॥

śrībhagavānuvāca

bahūni me vyatītāni janmāni tava cārjuna
tānyahaṁ veda sarvāṇi na tvaṁ vettha parantapa

The Blessed Lord said:

Many births of Mine have passed as well as of thine, O Arjuna;

I know them all, but thou knowest not, O scorcher of foes. 5

Comment:—

[In the third verse, the Lord said to Arjuna, "You are My devotee and My friend." So Arjuna put to Him a question, quite frankly and without any hesitation. Arjuna was curious to know, the secret of His Divine descent. So the Lord reveals the secret. When a devotee has curiosity to know some secret, the saints also reveal it to him.* Saint Tulasīdāsa also declares in the Rāmacaritamānasa—"Sages do not conceal a secret, when they come across, a deserving hand" (1/110/1).]

'Bahūni me vyatītāni janmāni tava cārjuna'—Lord Kṛṣṇa, says to Arjuna that both of them have passed many births. But His manifestation (which will be described in the sixth verse) is different from his birth, (which will be described in the nineteenth verse of the eighth chapter and the twenty-first and the twenty-sixth verses of the thirteenth chapter).

In the twelfth verse of the second chapter, the Lord declared, "Never was there a time when I was not, or when you or these kings were not, nor will there ever be, a time hereafter, when we all shall cease to be." It means that God and His fraction, soul—both are without beginning and eternal.

'Tānyahaṁ veda sarvāṇi'—There are some Yogīs (ascetics), who by practising spiritual discipline possess an intuitional knowledge, and come to know of their previous births. Such Yogīs, are called 'Yuñjāna yogīs'. On the other hand, there are

* The saints remain concealed and don't reveal themselves. But they reveal themselves in the following three cases.

(i) When a devout devotee having great reverence for those saints, has curiosity to know them.

(ii) When a devout devotee's body is cast off.

(iii) When the saint goes to cast off his body.

In the second and the third cases the saints reveal themselves even to those devotees who have not so much of reverence for them, but they respect them from their heart and want to know them.

other Yogīs, who naturally know everything of the past births of all beings, without practising any spiritual discipline. The Lord is such a 'Yuktayogī' Who knows of the beings of the past, the present and the future (Gītā 7/26). Knowledge of God, knows no bounds of past, present and future and it is constantly present. The Lord in spite of pervading everywhere, everything, every person, and every circumstances etc., transcends, them all.

[The Lord's statement, "I know them all" should thrill strivers with delight, because the Lord knows them and has an eye on them, whatever they are.]

'Na tvaṁ vettha parantapa'—A man does not possess intuitional knowledge to know of previous births as he is attached to perishable objects and persons etc. Similar, was the case with Arjuna. He did not want to fight, because his kith and kin would be killed. He declared, in the thirty-third verse of the first chapter, "Those for whose sake we desire kingdom, enjoyments and pleasures, stand here in battle, renouncing their lives and riches." It shows, that Arjuna desired kingdom, enjoyment and pleasure and so he did not know about his previous births.

Accumulation of materials, such as riches etc., for enjoyment and pleasure, is called 'parigraha'. When a person, totally renounces this tendency for accumulation, he develops an intuition, which enables him to know of previous births (Pātañjala yogadarśana 2/39).

The world, actions and objects are changing and unreal. So it naturally suffers deficiency, while the self has no such shortage, at all. But when he assumes his affinity for the world, he feels shortcoming in him and wants to make these up, by having desires. In order to satisfy those desires, he remains absorbed in different activities day and night but desires are never to be satiated. Due to desires man acts as if he is unconscious. Not to speak of the knowledge of several births, he does not even know his duty, of the present i.e., what he should do and what he is doing.

Link:—The Lord, in the preceding verse, explained that He and Arjuna had passed through many births. Now, in the next verse, He explains the secret of his descent (incarnation).

अजोऽपि सन्नव्ययात्मा भूतानामीश्वरोऽपि सन्।
प्रकृतिं स्वामधिष्ठाय सम्भवाम्यात्ममायया॥ ६॥

ajo'pi sannavyayātmā bhūtānāmīśvaro'pi san
prakṛtiṁ svāmadhiṣṭhāya sambhavāmyātmamāyayā

Though I am unborn, of imperishable nature, the Lord of all beings, yet, subordinating My nature (prakṛti), I manifest Myself, through My Yogamāyā (divine potency). 6

Comment:—

[This is the sixth verse and in this verse, there is a description of six things—God is birthless, imperishable and the Lord of all being, these three things pertain to God*; prakṛti (Nature) and

* Lord Kṛṣṇa has described in the Gītā that some people know Him as birthless, imperishable and the Lord of all beings while others don't know. The description is as follows—

1. (a) He who knows Him as birthless.

"He who knows Me as unborn and beginningless, the great Lord of the worlds, he among mortals, is undeluded and freed from all sins" (10/3).

(b) Those who don't know Him as birthless.

"This deluded world does not know Me, the unborn and imperishable" (7/25).

2. (a) Those who know him as imperishable.

"The great souls worship Me with a single-mind, knowing Me as the imperishable source of beings" (9/13).

(b) Those who don't know Him as imperishable.

"The foolish don't know My higher, imperishable and supreme nature" (7/24).

3. (a) Those who know Him as the Lord of all beings.

"He who knows Me as the enjoyer of sacrifices and austerities, the great Lord of all the worlds, and the friend of all beings, attains peace" (5/29).

(b) Those who don't know Him the Lord.

"The deluded don't know My higher nature as the great Lord of all beings" (9/11).

Yogamāyā, (the divine potency), these two pertaining to His power, and the sixth one, is His manifestation.]

'Ajo'pi sannavyayātmā'—The Lord, by this expression, explains that, unlike common men, He is without birth and death. People take birth and die, but He in spite of being birthless, manifests Himself, and in spite of being imperishable, conceals Himself. Both manifestation and concealment, are his unearthly sport (pastimes).

All beings were unmanifest before birth, and will be unmanifest, after death, these are manifest only in the middle (Gītā 2/28) while the Lord, ever remains revealed like the sun. As the sun, before rising and after setting, remains the same, but it is not seen by all the beings all the time; so is the case with God Who ever remains revealed, but seems to be manifested and concealed.

Other beings, have to take birth under the subordination of nature (prakṛti), according to the actions of the past, while God manifests Himself of His own accord. Beings, take birth grow, become old and die, moreover, they have to undergo pleasure and pain. But, that is not so in the case of God. He does not undergo any change. He incarnates Himself, as Lord Rāma or Kṛṣṇa etc., displays His sports as a child, and an adolescent and then continues to be an adolescent with a healthy and handsome body, without undergoing any change for hundreds of years. Therefore, picture of God, are prepared without a beard and moustache, (if a modern artist shows them, that is something different). Thus, unlike other men, God is neither born, nor does He, undergo any modifications, nor does He die.

'Bhūtānāmīśvaro'pi san'—In spite of, being the only Lord (great Lord) of all beings, God becomes a child, when He incarnates Himself. But even then, He possesses His Lordly nature—as Lord Kṛṣṇa killed an ogress named Pūtanā, of a very huge and horrible body, when He was only six days old. He killed the demons—Śakaṭa, Tṛṇāvarta and Agha respectively, when He was three months old, one year old and five years old respectively. Thus, in His childhood, He killed several demons. He raised the Govardhana mountain, on the tip of His finger, when He was only seven years old.

In spite of being the Lord of all beings, when He manifests Himself, He does not hesitate even to perform, the most menial job. This is His divine superiority. He works, as a chariot-driver of Arjuna, and obeys him, yet His Lordliness, over Arjuna and other beings remains intact. That is why, in spite of being a charioteer, He preaches him, the gospel of the Gītā. Lord Rāma carries out the order of His father, Daśaratha and goes into exile for fourteen years, yet His Lordliness over Daśaratha and other beings, has not suffered, in the least.

'Prakṛtiṁ svāmadhiṣṭhāya'— The Lord's pure nature (prakṛti) is different, from the three modes of nature—of goodness, of passion and of ignorance. This pure nature, is His divine potency, transcendental power, or delighting power. It is the embodiment of truth, consciousness and bliss. It is, also called the sentient power or power of grace. The same divine or transcendental power is known as Śrī Rādhā* or Śrī Sītā. It is, also called 'devotion' or the supreme knowledge, by which God is attained.

Prakṛti (nature), is the Lord's power, which is neither different from God nor is one with Him. For example, fire has two kinds of power, of lighting and burning. The first, removes darkness as well as fear, while the latter, is used for cooking and heating purposes. But, both these powers are neither different from fire, as these are nothing but fire, nor are they one with fire, because they can be subdued by sacred formulas, and herbs etc.

As, the lighting and the burning powers of fire, remain innate

* The Lord manifests Himself with His pure nature (Prakṛti) i.e., His transcendental power which works for Him. Śrī Rādhā is His divine power and she has several female friends who are the embodiments of devotion and they bestow devotion upon His devotees. A person devoid of devotion can't know them. A devotee can know them only by the grace of Lord Kṛṣṇa and Śrī Rādhā.

in a match-box, so does God's power remain unexposed even though He pervades everywhere, all the time, in all things and persons etc. The Lord, manifests Himself by keeping His nature (prakṛti) under control. As fire is not seen, until it is revealed with its lighting and burning power, so is the Lord not beheld until He manifests Himself with His transcendental power, even though He pervades everywhere all the time.

Śrī Rādhā, Śrī Sītā and Śrī Rukmiṇī etc., are the Lord's own divine powers. He pervades everywhere universally, yet He does not perform, any activity. Whatever He does, He does with His divine power. The drama, that He stages with His divine power, is so wonderful and uncommon, that human beings having heard, sung and recollected it, are sanctified and they attain salvation.

The same divine power, in the case of devotees, who are the worshippers of the attributeless aspect of the Absolute, becomes the supreme knowledge of Brahma; while for devotees who worship the Lord endowed with attributes, that power becomes devotion. When a devotee has an exclusive devotion for God, His divine power is revealed in him, in the form of his devotion. This devotion is so singular, that it attracts God and He in spite of being formless, has to reveal Himself, endowed with that, form. This devotion, is also bestowed upon devotees by Him.

The divine power of God, in the form of devotion, is perceived in two ways—disunion and union. It is by God's grace, that there is disunion of a devotee from God, because in that state, he becomes so much restless to meet Him, that his attachment to the world is totally renounced and God manifests Himself. In the Discipline of Knowledge, the divine power of God is revealed in the form of keen desire to know. This keen curiosity to know, compels a striver to know the real Essence. Then, in the form of the supreme knowledge of Brahma, it roots out ignorance and illumines the real self. But the divine power of disunion, is more powerful even than this. 'Where is God?' 'What should I do to attain Him?' 'Where should I go?' When a devotee becomes restless, to attain Him, his restlessness roots out all his sins, and reveals Him to him. This restlessness, is a better means of God-realization, than knowledge (wisdom or discrimination).

A Special Fact

The Lord, manifests Himself by keeping His nature (prakṛti) under control, and stages, the drama of human life. As fire by itself, does nothing, its lighting power provides light and its burning power, burns things, so the Lord does nothing, but it is His divine power, which does everything. In the scripture Sītā declares, 'It is I, who killed Rāvaṇa and other demons, while Lord Rāma did nothing'.

Like man and his power, God and His power, are neither different from each other, nor are one. God cannot separate His power from Him; so it is not different from Him. A man remains the same, but his power changes so it is not identical with him. Therefore, philosophers have called it, neither different nor one. This power is indescribable. The devotees of Lord Kṛṣṇa call that power as Śrījī (Rādhājī).

As a male and a female are two distinct entities, that way Lord Kṛṣṇa and Rādhājī are not two. Lord Kṛṣṇa and His power, Rādhājī in the Discipline of Knowledge become one, while, in the Discipline of Devotion become two, Lord Kṛṣṇa and Rādhājī become two*, so that they may stage the drama of human life, in order to exchange love and thrill the devotees with delight. When they become two, it is difficult to judge, who is superior, and who the lover and who the beloved. Both of them, appear

*Lord Kṛṣṇa and Rādhā are the oceans of savour, they are one but they have become two in order to stage the drama of human life (Śrī Rādhātāpanīyopaniṣad).

uncommon and unique and they are attracted towards each other. They are pleased by seeing each other. Their pastime of love, for each other is enhanced. This is called 'Rāsa' (sport).

The Lord's powers are infinite and limitless. His powers can be classified into two groups, pertaining to glory and those pertaining to sweetness or love. By His majestic power, He does wonderful sports and feats, which none else can do. By this very power, we find in Him excellence, eminence, singularity and divinity which are neither heard nor seen anywhere else. While He exercises His sweet power, He Himself is overwhelmed, and forgets that He is Lord. When He manifests Himself in a sweet mood, He appears to be very sweet and loving. He plays, with cowherds like an ordinary cowherd. Similarly, He plays the role of a friend, a son and a husband and so on, in the drama of life. Thus He thrills His devotees with delight, with His sweetness and love, by not disclosing His glory and grandeur.

The Lord, reveals one of His powers at a time, either that of glory or that of sweetness. When any doubt arises in the sentiment of sweetness, His power or glory is revealed. Lord Kṛṣṇa as a cowherd, searches for calves. But, when doubt arises, about their whereabout, His power is revealed and He immediately comes to know, that the cows have been taken away by Brahmā, the creator.

The Lord is also the handsomest, so every being is naturally attracted towards Him. Seeing His beauty, the women of Mathurā say to each other—

"Lord Kṛṣṇa is the quintessence of handsomeness, no one can compete with Him in the entire universe, He is handsome, even without any outward make up, or ornamentation. No one is ever satisfied by seeing His countenance, because His charm ever remains fresh. All kinds of fame, beauty and glory, depend upon His handsome appearance. It is very rare to behold Him. What penances the cowherdesses must have performed so that they ever beheld His sweet countenance" (Śrīmadbhā. 10/44/14)?

Śrī Śukadevajī says:—"O Parīkṣit! All the citizens of Mathurā and other people of the country, who were sitting on the dais, having seen Lord Kṛṣṇa and Balarāma, were so much pleased that their eyes and faces were glowing and filled with curiosity. They were not satisfied by looking at their handsome faces through their eyes and it seemed as if they were imbibing them with their eyes, licking them (with their tongues), smelling them (with their noses) and embracing them to their chests" (Śrīmadbhā. 10/43/20-21).

Having seen the beauty of Lord Rāma, king Janaka was filled with joy and declared that his dispassionate mind, having seen the sweet and handsome face of Lord Rāma, was so much enamoured as a 'Cakora' (the Indian red-legged partridge) is, by the moon (Mānasa 1/216/2).

Even the wild tribes, such as Kola and Bhīla got enamoured of Lord Rāma's countenance. They salute Lord Rāma, offer their presents to Him, behold Him, with great affection. They are so much enamoured of Him that they remain standing there just like statues. Their bodies are thrilled and their eyes are flooded with tears of love (Mānasa 2/135/3).

Not to talk of the Lord's devotees, even demons, such as Khara-Dūṣaṇa who have enmity with Lord Rāma, are wonder-struck with His charm. So they say:—Out of all the snakes, demons, gods, men and ascetics, whom we have seen, conquered and killed throughout our life, we have never seen such beauty (Mānasa 3/19/2).

'Saṁbhavāmyātmamāyayā'—The Lord, does not reveal Himself, to those who have a disinclination for Him, and He appears to them, as a common man. 'He stages a drama of His human life, by keeping His divine potency concealed' (Śrīmadbhāgavata 10/29/1).

A devotee comes to know God, while a non-believer does not know Him. The more a devotee is inclined towards Him, the more He reveals Himself to him.

Deluded people cannot know Him, because of their delusion and because of the divine potency of the Lord (Gītā 7/25). They cannot understand the infinitude of God, even when He manifests Himself before them just as He manifested Himself in the form of Draupadī's unending saree. Yet because of their delusion Duḥśāsana, Duryodhana and Karṇa etc., could not know, His manifestation.

If a person gets rid of his delusion, he can realize the self or God, but cannot behold Him.*

One can have a vision of the Lord, only when He unveils Himself, by removing the veil of His divine potency. A man can get rid of this own delusion, but it is beyond his power to do away with God's divine potency. If a person takes refuge in Him, He removes his delusion and also helps him, to behold Him.

The different plays, that the Lord stages, are accomplished with the help of His divine potency. So people can see those plays and enjoy these. If staged without the help of divine potency, no one can, either see these, or relish these.

An Important Fact Pertaining to Incarnation

The term, 'avatāra' means descent, one who has descended. The all-pervading Lord Who is, Truth, Consciousness and Bliss, by His special grace, manifests Himself as a common being. His peculiarity lies in being small, in spite of being Supreme, while it is otherwise with common men. It is His peculiarity, that He in spite of being boundless, becomes very small. Though, He

* It is not a rule that having realized the self a devotee may behold God. But having beheld God, he realizes the self. So Lord Rāma in the Rāmacaritamānasa declares:—'The wonderful reward of My vision is that man easily realizes the Self' (3/36/5).

upholds, infinite universes yet He is known as 'Giradhārī,' because he lifted a mountain, 'Govardhana'. It is nothing surprising in His case as in each of Whose pores, infinite universes exist, to uphold a mountain. But, it is His peculiarity, in upholding it, as well as in manifesting Himself, as a common man.

He plays His part in the drama of human life, as a common innocent boy. While playing, He was defeated by other cowherds, consequently, He had to carry the victor on His back.

The wise, remain absorbed in the self, but His devotees relish His pastimes. Even Brahmā, the leader of the wise, was wonder-struck by beholding His pastimes, and so are the great saints and ascetics who cannot understand the secret of His play and remain dumb-founded. The Lord by His grace, enables those devotees, who are exclusively devoted to Him, to know the secret of His pastimes (Mānasa 2/127/2). Lord Kṛṣṇa while grazing cows, kills huge bodied demons, in no time. Despite being a boy, His Lordliness remains the same as usual.

As a learned teacher, utters the letters 'a' 'b' 'c' etc., while teaching the alphabet to a boy by descending to the boy's standard; so does the Lord of infinite universes, preach the gospel to us, by becoming one of us, His wonderful and unearthly pastimes, lead people to salvation, whether they listen to them, study or sing them.

Appendix—The Lord carries on His pastime with the help of Prakṛti. Therefore Sītājī declares, "I have performed all the deeds, Lord Rāma has done nothing (Adhyātma Rāmāyaṇa, Bālakā. 1/32—43). But like the man the Lord is not subordinated to Prakṛti—'prakṛtiṁ svāmadhiṣṭhāya'. The reason is that for the Lord Prakṛti is not different from Him but is identical with Him (Gītā 7/4-5). The Lord has to manifest Himself before the man who is seated in Prakṛti, therefore He reveals Himself by subordinating His Prakṛti (nature). Then only men can behold Him.

Link:—In the next verse, the Lord, reveals the occasion of His manifestation.

यदा यदा हि धर्मस्य ग्लानिर्भवति भारत।
अभ्युत्थानमधर्मस्य तदात्मानं सृजाम्यहम्॥ ७॥

yadā yadā hi dharmasya glānirbhavati bhārata
abhyutthānamadharmasya tadātmānaṁ sṛjāmyaham

Whenever, there is a decline in righteousness and an upsurge in unrighteousness, O Arjuna, I then manifest Myself. 7

Comment:—

'Yadā yadā hi dharmasya glānirbhavati bhārata abhyutthānam-adharmasya'—When righteous, innocent, weak, pious and spiritual people, are exploited by unrighteous, cruel, strong, wicked and mundane people, and when moral values are lost and immorality prevails—that state, is the state of a decline of righteousness, and upsurge of unrighteousness.

The terms 'Yadā yadā' (whenever) show, that God manifests Himself, whenever there is need for His manifestation. Example—when the seas were churned, God in the form of unconquered Lord Viṣṇu, churned the seas as a divine Tortoise, held Mandarācala (mountain), pressed it hard, as a being with a thousand arms, and as a bewitching woman distributed the nectar among the gods. Thus, God manifested Himself, in different forms, at the same time.

The root, of the decline of righteousness and the rise of unrighteousness, is its attraction towards the perishable. As the body of a child, is inherited from the parents' bodies, so, is the universe created, by nature (prakṛti) and God. Out of these, (nature and its evolute), the world ever-undergo modifications, while God and His fragment, the soul, ever remain uniform, without the least modification. When a man, has a desire to derive pleasure out of mundane objects, he starts having a fall.

The more he is attached to worldly pleasures and prosperity, the more increase there is, in unrighteousness. The more this unrighteousness rises, the more vices, such as sins, strifes and riots etc., prevail, in the society.

There is a decline of righteousness through the Satya age, to Tretā, Dvāpara and Kali ages, respectively. In the Satya age righteousness flourishes. In Tretā, the decline begins, in Dvāpara there is a rapid decline and in Kali age, unrighteousness prevails. Then, God manifests Himself, for the establishment of righteousness.

'Tadātmānaṁ sṛjāmyaham'—Whenever, there is a decline of righteousness and rise of unrighteousness, then the Lord manifests Himself for the destruction of unrighteousness and for the establishment of righteousness.

When there is a decline of righteousness and increase in unrighteousness, people are inclined to unrighteousness, which leads them to a downfall. The Lord, is the disinterested friend of all beings, so He manifests Himself, in order to check their fall.

When actions are performed with a selfish motive i.e., for reward, there is a decline of righteousness; and when a man, having deviated from his duty performs forbidden actions, there is rise of unrighteousness. It is desire, which is the root of all unrighteousness, sins and injustice etc., (Gītā 3/37). Therefore, God manifests Himself, in order to root out this desire and propagate the principle of the performance of actions, without expectation of any reward.

Here, a doubt may arise why at the present, in the wretched Kali age, God does not manifest Himself, when there is such a decline of righteousness and rise of unrighteousness. The clarification is, that the time is not yet ripe. During the Tretā age, the demons having killed many sages, piled up their bones. But, at present righteous persons are leading a pious and peaceful life, and nobody kills them. Secondly, when there is decline of righteousness and rise of unrighteousness, by God's direction saints come to earth or true strivers reveal themselves; these establish righteousness. Sometimes, the liberated souls living in divine abode also come to earth, to help the people to attain salvation, as representatives of God. Where, there are such strivers and saints, there is, neither so much decline of righteousness, nor so much increase in unrighteousness, as at other places where there are, neither strivers nor saints.

When people do not follow the teachings of strivers and saints, but start to kill them, and when there are left, only a few righteous persons to propagate righteousness, and there is a decline in righteousness, then God manifests Himself.

Link:—Having described the occasion of His manifestation, in the preceding verse, the Lord now reveals, the aim of His manifestation, in the next verse.

परित्राणाय साधूनां विनाशाय च दुष्कृताम्।
धर्मसंस्थापनार्थाय सम्भवामि युगे युगे॥८॥

paritrāṇāya sādhūnāṁ vināśāya ca duṣkṛtām
dharmasaṁsthāpanārthāya sambhavāmi yuge yuge

For the protection of the good as for the destruction of the wicked as for the establishment of righteousness, I manifest myself from age to age. 8

Comment:—

'Paritrāṇāya sādhūnām'—God manifests Himself, in order to protect the good, because they destroy unrighteousness and propagate righteousness.

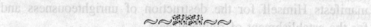

The term, 'sādhūnām' (of Sādhus) has been used for those good men, who naturally are inclined towards the good of others, who remember and chant the name, and think of form, qualities, glories and pastimes etc., of God, who propagate these among people and who depend on God.

He, whose only aim is God-realization, is a good person (sage) while one who hankers after worldly pleasures and prosperity, is not a good person.

When a man, attaches importance to the perishable world, desires are born. As desires increase, goodness disappears, but when desires are renounced, goodness appears. Because, desire is the root of evil. Goodness leads to salvation of one's self and to the welfare of others.

Good people, are even engrossed in the good of beasts, birds, trees, mountains, men, gods, manes and sages etc., through their thoughts and deeds. In the Rāmacaritamānasa the citizens of Ayodhyā say to Lord Rāma, "O foe of demons, in the world there are only two, who do good to others, without any selfish motive, they are, You and Your devotees" (7/47/3).

If people come to know the thoughts and feelings of these Sādhus, they will ever bow to them. But if they know the thoughts and feelings of the wicked, there would be quarrels and strifes.

Here, a doubt may arise, why are such people seen suffering, when God protects them. The clarification is, that the Lord protects their good feelings, rather than their bodies, riches, honour and fame etc. The reason is, that those good people do not attach importance to the mundane objects, because by doing so, they may turn bad. The Lord also, would not attach importance to them.

Devotees truly never desire, worldly objects. They are happy in unfavourable circumstances, because these lead them to spiritual upliftment. Devotion, develops in unfavourable circumstances, because their attachment, which causes their downfall, is renounced. Therefore, the Lord protects the good, by creating unfavourable circumstances for them.

'Vināśāya ca duṣkṛtām'—The wicked, propagate unrighteousness and destroy righteousness. So the Lord manifests Himself, for their destruction.

Those who, because of many desires, remain absorbed in vices, such as falsehood, fraud, deception and dishonesty etc. Those who exploit the virtuous and good persons; those who remain engaged in doing evil to others; those who do not know what ought to be done and what ought not to be done; and those, who always condemn God and the scriptures, such persons, of demoniac nature, have been called wicked. The Lord manifests Himself for the destruction of such wicked persons.

Question:—The Lord declares, that He is the same to all beings and there is none hateful, to Him (Gītā 9/29); then why does He destroy the wicked?

Answer:—As the Lord is a disinterested friend of all beings, no one is hateful to Him. But he who is an enemy of His devotees, is also His enemy. In the Rāmacaritamānasa, it is said, "He who offends a devotee of Lord Rāma, has to burn in the Lord's fire of anger" (2/218/2-3).

God is called, a devotee of His devotees (Śrīmadbhāgavata 10/86/59). So the wicked, who offend His devotees, are destroyed by Him. Devotees, destroy sins while God destroys sinners.

As His grace is revealed in protecting the good, so is His grace revealed in destroying the wicked as He does evil to none (2/183/3). Moreover, He purifies them by destroying them.

Saints also establish righteousness but they do not destroy the wicked. Destruction of the wicked is brought about by the Lord in the same way, as a simple injury may be dressed by a compounder but a major operation is performed only by a civil surgeon.

Both the parents are equally interested in the welfare of their son. When the son does not pay attention to his studies, and indulges in mischief, both of them want to set him right. The father beats him, so that he may give up his bad habit. The mother, checks the father from beating him. Being faithful, it is her duty to follow her husband's footsteps. So should she also start beating the boy, because she is faithful? No, it is her duty to protect the boy, otherwise he may receive a severe beating. The father, also does not want to give him a good beating, but he wants the son to get rid of his bad habit. Similarly, God is like a father, while saints are like a mother. First, the Lord and saints urge people to give up their wickedness, but when they do not mend their ways, God has to manifest Himself for their destruction. If they give up their wickedness, there is no need to destroy them.

The attributeless Absolute, is not antagonistic to nature, illusion and ignorance, it rather, gives existence inspires and nourishes these. God, whether He is attributeless or is endowed with attributes, fosters all beings, equally without any distinction. Even the earth, created by Him, provides room equally to everyone, whether he is virtuous or wicked. Similarly, all of them are equally provided with the necessities of life, such as food, water, air and sunlight. Thus the Lord is an ocean of generosity and equanimity, even to the vilest person. If a person just thinks of His generosity, he gets thrilled with delight and starts bowing to Him.

The Lord, is not opposed to wicked person, but He is opposed to their wicked actions as those actions are injurious, to the world, as well as to them. The Lord is a disinterested friend of all beings. Therefore, He destroys the wicked, in order to do good to the world, as well as to those wicked persons. How generous He is, that having killed those wicked persons He sends them to His own abode!

Now a question may arise, whether the Lord Himself will have to come to kill us, if we go on committing sins. If it is as so, we shall attain salvation easily, otherwise we shall have to control our senses, mind etc., and inculcate virtues and practise spiritual discipline. The answer is, that the Lord destroys only those wicked who cannot be destroyed by anyone, else. Secondly, performance of good actions will lead us to virtues, which would pave the way to our salvation. But if we are killed by anyone else, or die a natural death while performing sinful actions, what will be the consequences? How would our desire of being killed by the Lord, be fulfilled? Therefore, sinful actions, should not be performed at all.

'Dharmasaṁsthāpanārthāya'—Establishment of righteousness, consists in preaching and propagating the selfless performance of actions. Unrighteousness propagates, due to the performance of action with a selfish motive and due to the attachment to the unreal. Therefore, the Lord manifests Himself, in order to propagate the performance of selfless actions, through His deeds. When this feeling is propagated, righteousness, is naturally established.

The Lord is the abode of righteousness (Gītā 14/27). So He manifests Himself, in order to establish righteousness well. In fact, righteousness never perishes, it only declines. Whenever there is a decline of righteousness, the Lord re-establishes it (Gītā 4/1—3).

'Sambhavāmi yuge yuge'—The Lord, manifests Himself, from age to age. He also descends to the mortal world, several times in the same age, according to the need of the hour. He incarnates Himself as 'Kāraka Puruṣas', as well as saints. The incarnations of the Lord and His 'Kāraka Puruṣas' (representatives), are casual or occasional, while saints are regularly born.

Now, a doubt may arise, whether the omnipotent Lord cannot protect the good, destroy the wicked, and establish righteousness without manifesting Himself. The clarification is, that He can do wonders without His manifestation also and go on doing so, yet He manifests Himself in order to shower His special grace on beings, for their welfare.* During His incarnation, His vision,

* The Lord manifests Himself as a human being in order to shower His special grace on beings and He stages the drama of human life in such a manner that it conduces them to be devoted to Him (Mānasa 1/192).

touch, talk etc., and later on, the practice of hearing, thinking, chanting and following His sport, lead people to salvation.

The Lord, comes to the mortal world in different incarnations, according to the need of the times. He remains perfect, during all the incarnations.

Though there is, nothing that should be done by Him, nor is there anything unattained that should be attained (Gītā 3/22), yet He performs all actions by manifesting Himself, from time to time, only for the welfare of the world. Therefore, human beings, should also perform their duty, for the welfare of others.

In response to Arjuna's question which he put in the fourth verse, the Lord explains the three main differences between men's births and His births (manifestations):—

(1) Difference in knowledge:—Many births of men, as well as of the Lord, have taken place. Men do not know them all, only the Lord knows.

(2) Difference in birth:—Men have to take birth, under the subordination of nature, (prakṛti), in order to reap the fruits of their virtuous and evil actions, and then to realize God. God manifests Himself of His own accord, governing His nature (prakṛti) through His divine potency (4/6).

(3) Difference in actions:—Men perform actions, in order to satisfy their desires, though it is not the aim of human life, while the Lord acts, only in order to enable beings to attain salvation (4/7-8).

Link:—In response to the question put, in the fourth verse, by Arjuna, the Lord started describing the divine character of His birth. Now in the next verse He, of His own accord, explains the merit of knowing the divine character of His birth, as well as actions, in order to explain the performance of actions without expectation of fruit (Karmayoga).

जन्म कर्म च मे दिव्यमेवं यो वेत्ति तत्त्वतः।
त्यक्त्वा देहं पुनर्जन्म नैति मामेति सोऽर्जुन॥ ९॥

janma karma ca me divyamevaṁ yo vetti tattvataḥ
tyaktvā dehaṁ punarjanma naiti māmeti so'rjuna

He who thus knows in reality the true nature of My divine birth and action, (Karma) and he having abandoned the body, is not reborn; but he comes to Me, O Arjuna. 9

Comment:—

'Janma karma ca me divyam'— The Lord is beyond birth and death, He is birthless and imperishable. His manifestation in human body, is not like the birth of common men. He manifests Himself of His own accord* in order to stage the drama of human life, for the welfare of beings.

The form (body) of the Lord, unlike other beings, is not made of flesh and blood. The bodies of beings are full of virtues and vices. They are transitory, sick, mundane, changing, material and are born of ovum and semen, while the Form of the Lord, is free from virtues and vices. It is eternal, healthy, spiritual, unchanging, divine and is revealed. The bodies of gods, are also divine, but the Form of the Lord, is far superior to those of the gods and even the gods are ever eager to see this Form (Gītā 11/52).

When the Lord descended on the mortal world, as Lord Rāma and Lord Kṛṣṇa, mother Kausalyā and Devakī, did not give birth to Them. First, He revealed to them His four-armed divine Form, with conch, disc, mace and lotus, and then staged the drama of a child, then the mother, requested Him to conceal that divine Form. The description has been, very clearly, given, in the Rāmacaritamānasa 1/192, as well as Śrīmadbhāgavata 10/3/30 and 10/3/46.

---

* Uddhava tells Lord Kṛṣṇa, "You are the Supreme beyond Nature (Prakṛti) and You are Brahma, the very embodiment of knowledge; even then You have manifested Yourself as a human being of Your own accord" (Śrīmadbhā. 11/11/28).

When Lord Rāma returned to His Abode, He, unlike common men, disappeared from this mortal world along with His body (Form), His body was not left on the earth. It is said in the Rāmāyaṇa by Vālmīki, that having heard the words of Brahmā, the creator the very wise Lord Rāma, having decided, entered the splendour of Lord Viṣṇu, with His three brothers, in His Form. As far as Lord Kṛṣṇa is concerned, the same fact, is mentioned about Him in Śrīmadbhāgavata that He also went to His Abode, in His Form (11/31/6).

The same sort of description is available in Rāmacaritamānasa, when sage Vālmīki says to Lord Rāma, that His Form is divine and unaltered, only a deserving one knows the reality about Him, when He manifests Himself as a human being, for protecting saints and gods, and preach and act as a worldly king.

Once, sages Sanaka etc., were going to the Abode of Lord Viṣṇu. The gatekeeper would not let them go in and they cursed him. Knowing that His gatekeeper had insulted the sages, Lord Viṣṇu Himself came to the entrance. Having a vision of the Lord, and receiving the divine smell of basil leaves and shoots, while bowing to Him, their bodies and hearts were thrilled, and excited, though such wise sages, ever remain established in the imperishable Lord (Śrīmadbhā. 3/15/43). As the smell of the Lord's lotus feet, is divine, His clothes, ornaments and weapons etc., are also divine, sentient and very singular.

Having heard, studied and recollected the pastime of the Lord, people's hearts are purified and they get rid of ignorance—this is the divine nature of His actions. Lord Śaṅkara, Brahmā, the creator, sages, such as Sanaka etc., divine sage, Nārada etc., who are the embodiments of knowledge, having sung and heard of His divine pastime, get absorbed in them. A person who visits the places, where the Lord staged the drama of His human life, with reverence and faith and resides there, attains salvation. It means that the Lord manifests Himself and carries on His pastimes in order to enable the people to attain salvation. Therefore, people attain their aim by reading, hearing and thinking, of His divine pastimes.

In the fourth verse, Arjuna put the question to the Lord pertaining to His birth, but here, the Lord starts describing his action of his own accord. By doing so, it seems as if the Lord wants to emphasize the fact, that a man's actions can also be divine, though his birth cannot be divine as human life has been bestowed upon him only to perform, such actions. Actions are divine, when these are free from desire, for reward, attachment and a sense of 'mine.' Divine actions, lead to liberation from the bondage, of the present as well as past actions, and these naturally do good to others.

In fact, actions become impure, when a man accepts his affinity for perishable objects; and these lead him to bondage. This affinity, makes not only actions but also objects and mind, impure. As soon as, this affinity is renounced, all the three become pure. It is affinity for the perishable, which is the main obstacle to salvation.

'Evaṁ yo vetti tattvataḥ'—God in spite of, being without, birth imperishable and the Lord of all beings, manifests Himself, of His own accord, and by keeping His nature (prakṛti) under control, for the welfare of all beings. He who knows this fact, realises the divine nature, of the births of the Lord.

Though all actions are performed by Him, yet He is a non-doer i.e., He has no pride of doership (Gītā 4/13), nor does He desire, the fruit of actions (Gītā 4/14). He who knows fact, knows the divine nature of the Lord's actions.

As the Lord manifests Himself, for the welfare of the entire creation and as He remains detached from actions, similarly, those people, who live for the welfare of the world, and remain detached from actions, know the divine nature of His births (manifestations) and actions.

'Tyaktvā deham punarjanma naiti'—There is nothing in the three worlds, that is to be done by the Lord, nor is there anything unattained, that should be attained by Him (Gītā 3/22), yet He manifests Himself in this mortal world, by His grace to inspire beings to attain salvation. He carries on His wonderful pastime, also for the same purpose. When a person recites, hears, reads or thinks of his pastimes, he is linked with the Lord. When he is connected with the Lord his tie with the world is cut off. When this bond with the world is snapped, he is not reborn i.e., he is liberated, from the bondage of birth and death.

In fact, it is not action but desire, which binds a man and this desire is man-made. In order to satisfy his desire, he performs actions with a selfish motive, being attached to these, they bind him. As desire is enhanced, he is inclined towards sinful actions, which lead him to his birth, in evil bodies and to hell. But, when he performs actions without a selfish motive for the welfare of others, his actions become divine and uncommon, they do not lead him to bondage and he is not reborn.

'Māmeti so'rjuna'—When a man assumes his affinity for perishable actions, the ever-attainable Lord, seems unattained, to him. But, when actions are performed without expecting any reward, for the welfare of others, their direction is towards the world and the ever-attained Lord, is realized.

It is because of the Lord's divine nature, that He descends to this mortal world, in order to shower His grace upon beings. Those who know this fact, become His devotees and then remain absorbed only in His adoration or devotion (Mānasa 5/34/2). This devotion, leads to salvation. Similarly, when a man knows the divine nature of His actions then his actions also become divine viz., pure and then these lead him, as well as others, to God-realization (salvation) as he renounces his affinity for the world. It is the affinity, which is an obstacle to salvation or God-realization.

A Vital Fact

Actions are transitory and perishable, and so is their fruit, while the self (soul) is uniform and eternal. Therefore, in fact the self has no affinity for actions, the affinity is merely assumed. While performing actions, if a man realizes that he has no affinity for them, his actions become divine. This is the reality, about actions and this is Karmayoga.

When a man identifies himself, with active nature (prakṛti), it gives an impetus to action. He can never remain even for a moment, without performing action (Gītā 3/5). He thinks, that as worldly objects are acquired by performing actions, so can the Lord be realized through them. But, it is an error of judgement, because only perishable objects, rather than the imperishable, Lord, can be acquired through perishable actions. The imperishable Lord, can be attained by renouncing affinity for actions. This affinity for action can be renounced more easily, through the Discipline of Action, than through the Discipline of knowledge. It is so because when all action with gross, subtle and causal bodies is performed, for the welfare of the world without any selfish motive, their flow is towards the world, and so affinity for action is renounced.

The Lord, by using the terms 'Māmeti' wants to explain, that He whom, a man wants to attain through the performance of actions is ever attained. What efforts are required to attain Him who is ever attained and ever-existent? Whatever was not otherwise attained is attained, by effort?

Two aspects are noteworthy in this regard—origin and discovery. Originated, is that which has no independent, existence, and which was absent in the beginning and perishes in the end. Discovered, is that which has a separate existence forever. But God seems to get concealed, when importance is attached to mundane actions and objects. When one uses actions and objects in rendering service to others, his affinity for actions and objects is automatically renounced and ever attainable God is revealed. This is called discovery of the ever attained.

Carelessness and indolence, in the performance of actions and the desire for fruit of actions are the main stumbling blocks to God-realization. If actions are performed without the desire for fruit in rendering service to others, the affinity for actions is renounced and we realize our affinity for God which is naturally eternal.

Appendix—If actions are performed for the welfare of others in a disinterested way or they are performed for the Lord's sake, those actions become divine and lead to salvation. But the actions performed ridden with desire for one's own self become impure and lead to bondage.

Actions done without the sense of doership are of divine character. When actions are not performed for one's own self, the sense of doership is wiped out.

The Lord's most insignificant action as well as the most significant action is His 'pastime'. In His pastime the Lord while acting like common men remains untainted (Gītā 4/13). The Lord's drama of life is divine. This divine nature of His drama is singular and is different from the divine nature of gods. The divine nature of gods in comparison with men is relatively divine and is limited while the Lord's divinity is absolute and infinite. Though the actions of liberated, enlightened and God-loving exalted souls are also divine but they are not like the Lord's pastimes. Even the common pastime of the Lord is very uncommon (unworldly). As the Lord's 'Rāsalīlā' seems worldly yet by reading it and by listening to it, a striver's lust (sex) is wiped out (Śrīmadbhā. tenth canto, thirty-third chapter, fortieth verse).

This world is the beginningless incarnation of God—'ādyo'vatāraḥ puruṣaḥ parasya' (Śrīmadbhā. 2/6/41). It means that God has manifested Himself in the form of the world.

But the embodied soul, because of his attachment to pleasures without recognising it as the manifestation of God, has sustained it as the world—'jīvabhūtāṁ mahābāho yayedaṁ dhāryate jagat' (Gītā 7/5). In order to wipe out this notion, a striver should firmly believe that whatever is perceived (seen) is the manifestation of God and whatever is happening is the pastime of the Lord. By assuming (accepting) this, the world will not remain as the world and 'there is nothing except God'—this truth will be realized. In other words the world will disappear and only God will remain. The reason is that by thinking (accepting) everything and person as the manifestation of God and every action as the Lord's pastime, attraction for pleasure and also attachment—aversion will not persist. When attachment to pleasure is wiped out the actions which seemed worldly, will appear divine as the pastime of the Lord and the attachment to pleasure will be transformed into love (devotion) for God.

The Lord carries on this pastime according to the Form in which He manifests Himself.* When He takes the form of an

---

* Lord Kṛṣṇa says to the sage Uttaṅka—

dharmasaṁrakṣaṇārthāya dharmasaṁsthāpanāya ca
taistairveṣaiśca rūpaiśca triṣu lokeṣu bhārgava

(Mahābhārata, āśva. 54/13-14)

"For the protection and establishment of righteousness I manifest Myself in many species and act according to those Forms and Guises."

yadā tvahaṁ devayonau vartāmi bhṛgunandana
tadāhaṁ devavat sarvamācarāmi na saṁśayaḥ
yadā gandharvayonau vā vartāmi bhṛgunandana
tadā gandharvavat sarvamācarāmi na saṁśayaḥ
nāgayonau yadā caiva tadā vartāmi nāgavat
yakṣarākṣasayonyostu yathāvad vicarāmyaham

(Mahābhārata, āśva. 54/17—19)

'O Bhṛgunandana! when I manifest Myself as a deity, then I behave and act like deities, there is no doubt about it. When I incarnate as a 'Gandharva' (celestial singers & musicians), I behave and act as a Gandharva, there is no doubt about it. When I manifest Myself as a 'nāga' then I behave like 'nāgas. I by manifesting Myself as a gnome or as a devil, I behave and act just like them.'

idol, he like a picture carries on the drama (pastime) of being motionless. If He doesn't remain immovable, how will His manifestation as an idol be proved? The Lord descended to this world as Rāma and Kṛṣṇa etc., and also as a fish and a tortoise etc. He carried on His pastime according to His Form. As in 'varāhāvatāra' (incarnation as a boar) he played the drama as a boar and in 'Vāmanāvatāra' (incarnation as a dwarf) he carried on the pastime as a celibate. Therefore a striver should hold that whatever is happening now is only the Lord's pastime.

Link:—The Lord, in the next verse, describes the traits of those devotees, who know the divine nature of His birth and action.

वीतरागभयक्रोधा मन्मया मामुपाश्रिताः।
बहवो ज्ञानतपसा पूता मद्भावमागताः॥ १०॥

vītarāgabhayakrodhā manmayā māmupāśritāḥ
bahavo jñānatapasā pūtā madbhāvamāgatāḥ

Freed from attachment, fear and anger, absorbed in Me and taking refuge in Me, purified by the penance of knowledge, many have attained union with My Being. 10

Comment:—

'Vītarāgabhayakrodhāḥ'—When a man, has disinclination for God, he gets attached to the perishable objects. It is, because of his attachment, that he has the sense of 'mine,' for the objects acquired and a desire for those unacquired. He has greed for the acquired objects and gets angry with those who are obstacles to the acquisition of those objects. If persons, who are obstacles, are stronger than him, it causes fear. Thus, attachment to perishable objects gives birth to fear, anger, greed, desire and feeling of 'mine,' and such other vices. If attachment is renounced, all these vices perish. If instead of regarding the objects as ours and for us, we regard these as of others and for others, and render service to others with these, attachment perishes because in fact, we have no affinity for such objects and actions.

The Lord, without any selfish motive descends to the mortal world, in order to inspire beings to attain salvation, as He is a disinterested friend, of all beings. When a man has a firm belief that He is the disinterested friend of all beings, he is attracted towards God. The attraction for Him wipes out attraction, (attachment) for the world. For example, in childhood children play the game of marbles and have attraction for the same. They ever quarrel for their possessions. But, when they grow old, instead of having attraction for marbles or toys they have attraction for money. But, when they are inclined towards God, they have no attraction for mundane objects and riches etc. Their attachment for them, is renounced. As soon as it is renounced, fear and anger are rooted out, because both of these depend on attachment.

'Manmayā'—When, a man knows the truth about the divine nature of the Lord's birth and actions, He becomes, dear to him. So he takes refuge in Him, and gets absorbed in Him.

Those, who have attraction for mundane pleasures get absorbed in the desire for pleasure (Gītā 2/43), while those, who have attraction for God ever remain absorbed in Him (Nārada-Bhaktisūtra 70). They lose their individuality, because of their exclusive devotion to Him, and identify themselves with Him.*

'Māmupāśritāḥ'—The expression, 'Vītarāgabhayakrodhāḥ' denotes, total severance of connection with the world, while it also indicates that a striver taking refuge in Him, gets absorbed in Him.

* Cowherdesses became just like their loving Lord Kṛṣṇa in gait and manners, laughter and merriment, glance, speech, inclination and facial expression etc. They having forgotten themselves totally became the embodiment of Lord Kṛṣṇa and copying His pastime began to utter,"I am no one else but Lord Kṛṣṇa (Śrīmadbhā. 10/30/3).

A man has to depend upon something or the other in this world. He (the soul) in spite of being a fragment of God, having no inclination for Him, relies on perishable objects, such as riches etc., which lead to his downfall. Not only this, but even if he depends, on intellect, in order to perform virtuous actions, on the practice of spiritual discipline or on renunciation of pleasure and prosperity, he cannot realize God, quickly. So long as, he (the self) does not depend on God, his dependence on world does not end, and he has to suffer pain.

A man, is attracted towards loving persons and objects, such as his wife and son etc., while he, depends on his superiors, such as parents and elders etc. But a devotee of the Lord, has attraction for Him and also depends on Him, because for him, He is most loving and superior to all.

'Bahavo jñānatapasā pūtā madbhāvamāgatāḥ'—Though a man, is purified through the Discipline of Knowledge also, yet the term 'Jñāna' (knowledge), has been used, for knowing the reality about the divine nature of the Lord's birth and action. This knowledge, purifies the man, because the Lord is the purest of the pure. The soul being a fragment of God, is naturally pure. In the Mānasa it is declared, "The soul is sentient, pure and naturally, a heap of joy" (7/117/1). By attaching importance to the perishable and by having the feeling of 'mine' with them, he (the soul) becomes impure. When a man knows reality about the divine birth and divine actions of God, his attraction for the perishable and his feeling of 'mine' for them, totally perish and then all impurity comes to an end, and he emerges very pure.

This is Karmayoga. So the term, 'Jñāna' can stand for knowledge of Karmayoga, in which all acquired things, such as the body, senses, mind, intellect, rank, ability, authority, riches and property etc., are not one's own or for one's own self, but are of the world and for the world. Why? The reason is, that he (the self) is eternal; so how can perishable things stay with the imperishable soul, and be useful for It? Perishable things, such as the body etc., were neither with us before, nor will remain with us after death, and at present also, they are being destroyed every moment. We have a right, to make proper use of acquired objects, rather than to lay claim to them. These things (objects), belong to the world and so they should be used in rendering service to the world; this is their proper use. But if anyone regards these as his, or for him, it is a bondage or impurity for him.

When a person, does not regard perishable things, as his or for him, it means that he performs the penance of knowledge, which purifies him. The penance of knowledge, is superior to all other austerities. Through this, the assumed affinity for the insentient (matter), is renounced totally. So long as, a man assumes his affinity for the insentient, he is not so easily purified by any other penance, as he is purified by that knowledge, through which, his affinity for matter is renounced. Being purified, by the penance of knowledge, a man attains to His Being, which is Truth, Consciousness and Bliss. It means, that as the Lord is eternal, he also resides in Him constantly; as the Lord is untainted and unaffected he also remains untainted and unaffected. As nothing remains to be done by God, nothing further remains to be done by him. A man, through the Discipline of Knowledge, also attains to His Being (Gītā 14/19).

Many devotees, having been purified by the penance of knowledge, have attained Him. So strivers at present, also being purified by the penance of knowledge, should attain Him. Everyone, is independent in attaining Him, because this human body has been bestowed upon them, only to attain God.

Link:—The devotees attain Him. Now the question arises, how they attain Him. The Lord answers the question, in the next verse.

ये यथा मां प्रपद्यन्ते तांस्तथैव भजाम्यहम्।
मम वर्त्मानुवर्तन्ते मनुष्याः पार्थ सर्वशः॥ ११॥

ye yathā māṁ prapadyante tāṁstathaiva bhajāmyaham
mama vartmānuvartante manuṣyāḥ pārtha sarvaśaḥ

O Pārtha! However, the way devotees worship Me, so do I approach them; for all men ultimately follow My path. 11

Comment:—

'Ye yathā māṁ prapadyante tāṁstathaiva bhajāmyaham'— Howsoever, devotees seek God, so does He meet them, and grant them their hearts' desires. He reveals Himself, to a devotee, in the same form in which he thinks of Him. If a devotee thinks of Him, as his preceptor, He becomes an excellent preceptor. Similarly, God becomes a worthy father or mother, son, brother, friend or even, an obedient servant, according to the desire of the devotee. If a devotee, feels restless without God, He also becomes restless without, His devotee.

Arjuna regarded Lord Kṛṣṇa, as his friend and wanted to make Him his chariot-driver. Therefore, He became his chariot-driver. Sage Viśvāmitra, treated Him as a disciple; so He became his disciple. Therefore, with whatever sentiment devotees seek Him, He correlates, by the same sentiment. The Lord of infinite worlds, reciprocates to the sentiments of His own created common beings. How generous affectionate and merciful He is!

This topic reveals, that the Lord manifests Himself for the sake of His devotees. He descends to the earth, according to the sentiment of His devotees. It is mentioned in the Upaniṣad, 'The Lord felt lonely' (Bṛhadāraṇyaka 1/4/3). So He manifested Himself in different forms and started His sport. Similarly, when devotees have a desire to take part in divine sport in the company of the Lord, He manifests Himself, in order to take part. When a devotee, cannot suffer his separation from God, God also cannot bear it from him.

Though the words 'Yathā' (in whatever way) and 'Tathā' (so) explains, that in whatever way a devotee seeks Him, He reciprocates his sentiments, yet there is a great difference in their manner. If a devotee takes one step towards God, God may take hundreds of strides to meet him. The Lord is omnipresent, omnipotent and omniscient. Moreover, He is His devotee's supreme and unselfish friend and true to His resolve. A devotee should use his full power to attain Him, then the Lord is attained, through His limitless power.

A striver himself, creates obstacle in God-realization, because he does not apply his intellect, resources, time and power etc., to the full extent, in order to attain Him. If he, without regarding these as his own, utilizes them fully for God-realization, he may realize Him soon. Actually, they are the Lord's, because they have been bestowed upon by Him. A feeling of 'mine', is the main obstacle to God-realization. Man himself, is also a fragment of God, but he considers himself separate from God, while the Lord does not think so.

In fact, a striver cannot develop devotion to God, through the performance of actions. Devotion, is automatically bestowed upon a devotee, who takes refuge in Him. The refuge (surrender), is the best sentiment out of all the other feeling such as of service, of friendship, of affection and of sweet love etc. The Lord seems to declare, that if a devotee dedicates his possessions to Him, God would offer His possessions to the devotee; and if he offers himself to Him, God reciprocates. What an easy and economic transaction, God-realization is!

When a devotee, surrenders himself at His feet, He does not even remember his sins, of the past. He only thinks of his present emotions, hundreds of times (Mānasa 1/29/3).

In this (eleventh) verse, there is no description of scriptural subjects, such as dualism or non-dualism, the Lord endowed with attributes or attributeless, or different kinds of salvation etc. But, here is a description of the feeling of 'mine', with God. 'Only God is mine and I am only God's—this feeling of 'mine' for God, enables a striver to attain Him, quickly and easily. Therefore, a striver should accept his affinity for God, even if he does not understand it. By doing so, he will realize his affinity for Him which is real.

Question:—The Lord, reciprocates the same sentiment with which a devotee seeks Him. If a devotees approaches Him with the sentiment of hatred or enmity etc., will the Lord, reciprocate the same?

Answer:—This is a topic of surrender (refuge) to Him, rather than of hatred or enmity. So, no such question, should arise. Even then, if we think over the question seriously, we come to realise that the purpose of the Lord in reciprocating the same sentiment to the person concerned, is to inspire him for salvation.* The Lord is a disinterested friend of all beings (Gītā 5/29). Therefore, he thinks of their welfare and acts, accordingly. He does the same, even for those who may have feelings of hatred and enmity, for Him. When Lord Rāma sents Aṅgada as a messenger to the court of Rāvaṇa, He urges him to convey his message in such a way that His purpose may be served and it may contribute to his (Rāvaṇa's) welfare (Mānasa 6/17/4).

Not only the Lord, but His devotees, are also disinterested friends of all beings (Śrīmadbhāgavata 3/25/21). When, even a devotee cannot harm anyone, how can the Lord, Who is the most merciful and disinterested friend of all beings, harm anyone? A person, may have affinity for Him with any sentiment yet He inspires him for salvation only. As a bath in the Ganges, both in winter and summer is rewarding, yet while bathing in winter a man feels cold and during summer, he feels refreshed. Similarly,

* Many persons out of desire, hatred, fear and love having concentrated their minds on God, being purged of their sins, have attained God in the same way as devotees attain Him through devotion (Śrīmadbhāgavata 7/1/29).

those devotees who worship Him with devotion attain eternal bliss, but that bliss is not attained by those who have negative feelings of hatred or enmity for Him.

'Mama vartmānuvartante manuṣyāḥ pārtha sarvaśaḥ'— Whatsoever, a great man does, the same is done by others, as well (Gītā 3/21). God is the supreme Being. He is superior to all the great men. So all people follow Him. The same fact, has been pointed out, in the second half of the twenty-third verse of the third chapter.

The Lord, ever remains prepared to reciprocate the sentiment of His devotee. King Daśaratha treats Him, as his son. So He becomes an obedient son and cannot disobey His father.* The Lord, wants to reveal the secret that a devotee should accept the same relationship with Him, which he has with a persons who is most loving to him, whether he is his son, father or whether she is his mother. By doing so, the Lord will become most loving to him and thus the person will be able to attain Him easily.

Secondly, the Lord wants to urge the people, that by following His footsteps they should also become worthy sons or parents or brothers, husbands, wives or sisters etc. Moreover, they should render service to other members of a family, without expecting any reward from them and without being proud of their action. Those who have affinity with parents and other relatives, only for rendering selfless service to them, follow the Lord's path in the real sense. By doing so, for the good of others they will be free from the feeling of 'mine', and they will develop devotion for God and attain Him.

An Important Fact

Egoistic notions and selfishness, are the stumbling blocks to

* Lord Rāma declares, "I can enter fire, can eat deadly poison and can jump into the sea in order to carry out the order of My father (Vālmīki Rāmāyaṇa, Ayodhyā. 18/28-29).

devotion for God. When a man loves anyone, without egoism and selfishness, that love automatically flows towards the Lord. It is because of egoism and selfishness, that his love is confined to narrow limits. But, when such evil propensities are renounced, his love becomes widespread. In that case, the assumed affinity for the world perishes, and instinctively the real affinity for God is revealed.

The man (soul) is a fragment of God (Gītā 15/7) and so his affinity for God, is natural. But when he (the soul) having forgotten this real affinity, assumes the affinity for the world, he has to follow, the cycle (bondage) of birth and death. This bondage is twofold. One is due to his not realizing his real affinity with God. Another, is due to his assumed affinity with the world. But when he realizes his real affinity for God i.e., takes refuge in Him, he becomes free from worry, fear, sorrow, and doubt. Then, he is said to follow, the Lord's path.

Appendix—Though this universe is clearly the manifestation of God, yet the Lord reveals Himself before us in the same Form in which we perceive (see) Him. We regarding the self as body need things and desire them, then God manifests Himself in the form of those things. If being established in the 'Asat' (unreal), we perceive (see) the unreal, the Lord is also perceived in the unreal form. As a child wants a toy, its father brings it a toy even by spending money, similarly whatever we want, the most merciful God ever being eternal Ṛeality appears before us in the same form. If we don't desire pleasures, why should the Lord appear before us in the form of pleasures? Why need He assume the artificial Form?

Though the terms 'yathā' and 'tathā' ('as' and 'so') have been used for the Lord's nature, yet the Lord ever showers His great grace upon beings because an insignificant being can't be compared with the supreme Lord. What is the strength of its own in a being except the sense of pride? Even then if a person is attracted towards God, God is also attracted towards the person. As Vidurānījī was oblivious of herself after beholding Lord Kṛṣṇa, Lord Kṛṣṇa also was not in Himself and he ate the skin of banana offered by Vidurānījī and relished it.

In the Lord's nature 'yathā-tathā' are applicable in actions rather than in feelings. The Lord also showers His love and grace on an atheist ever in the same way as He showers it on a theist (believer). Therefore in the Lord's 'yathā-tathā' there is no selfish motive but it is the Lord's glory (greatness) otherwise how can a common being be compared with the greatest Lord? Even then he makes friends with an ordinary being and elevates him equal to His rank. The Lord does not regard Himself as great—this is His greatness.

Link:—In the preceding verse, the Lord declared, "As men approach Me, so do I accept them." It means, that it is very easy to realize God. Then why do people not worship God? The Lord answers the question, in the next verse.

काङ्क्षन्तः कर्मणां सिद्धिं यजन्त इह देवताः।
क्षिप्रं हि मानुषे लोके सिद्धिर्भवति कर्मजा॥ १२॥

kāṅkṣantaḥ karmaṇāṁ siddhiṁ yajanta iha devatāḥ
kṣipraṁ hi mānuṣe loke siddhirbhavati karmajā

Those who desire the fruit of their actions, worship the gods; because success is quickly attained, by men through action. 12

Comment:—

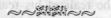

'Kāṅkṣantaḥ karmaṇāṁ siddhiṁ yajanta iha devatāḥ'—A man, is eligible to perform new actions, and it is seen that success is attained through action. So, he firmly believes that God is also realized, through action (penance, meditation and trance etc.,) just as, worldly objects are acquired through actions. He, does not pay attention to the fact, that worldly things are acquired through actions, as they are limited, they are not ever attained, they are separate from us, and they are changeful, while the Lord cannot be acquired, through action, as He is not a product of action. He pervades everywhere, is ever attained, is not separate from us (the self) and is unchanging. So, He can be attained, as soon as a keen desire to realize Him, is aroused. Keen desire for God-realization, is not aroused, because of the preference, for worldly pleasures and prosperity.

The Lord, is like a father, while the gods are like shopkeepers. We can take a thing from a shopkeeper, only by paying the money but we can take it from the father, free of cost. Similarly, we have to perform rituals according to scriptural methods for gods, in order to obtain fruits from them, while God bestows upon us our necessities, free of cost. Moreover, as a shopkeeper gives even hazardous things, such as, a match box or a knife etc., to a boy on payment, but if the boy wants such things from his father, the latter will not only refuse but take away, the money also. A father gives only beneficial things to a boy. The gods, also bestow upon their devotees, harmful gifts without thinking of their welfare, at the due completion of a ritual. But the Lord, like a father, bestows only those gifts, which are for the welfare of devotees. In spite of this fact, the ignorant or dull-witted people, because of their attachment, sense of mine and desire for the perishable materials, worship other gods, as they do not realise the glory, the benevolence and selflessness, friendliness of the Lord (Gītā 7/20—23; 9/23-24).

'Kṣipraṁ hi mānuṣe loke siddhirbhavati karmajā'— This human world, is the field for actions. Besides this, other worlds, such as heaven and hell etc., are for reaping fruits of past actions. The Lord also declares, 'Below in the world of men stretch forth the roots (of the universe as a tree) entangling man, in the bondage of actions (Gītā 15/2). But the other worlds (heaven and hell etc.,) exist, so that human beings may reap desirable or undesirable fruits respectively of their virtuous and evil actions.

Only human beings, are eligible to perform new actions, which bear fruit here, as well as hereafter. Beasts and birds etc., cannot perform new actions.

In this human world those people, who are attached to action, live (Gītā 14/15). It is because of their attachment to actions, that they are charmed by success, which is attained through action. This success is attained quickly, but it is shortlived. When actions are transitory, how could success attained through actions, be permanent? Therefore, the fruit of perishable actions, is also perishable. Those who perform actions with a desire for fruit, think of the fruit only, they do not think of the perishable nature, of that fruit. They take refuge in the gods and worship them, only because they bestow upon them success quickly, when rituals are duly completed. But because of their desire for fruit of action, they never get liberated, from the bondage of action. Consequently, they have to follow the cycle of birth and death.

The real success of human life is God-realization and that cannot be attained, through action. A striver cannot even follow, the Disciplines of Action, Knowledge and Devotion, which are the means of God-realization, through action. He can attain Yoga, not through action but through the, renouncement of actions.

Question:—Action is, said to be, the means to attain Yoga (Gītā 6/3). Then, how is it, that a man cannot attain Yoga through action?

Answer:—In Karmayoga, actions are performed, in order to renounce affinity for actions, and the material for actions. Yoga (union with God) is natural. So Yoga or God-realization cannot be attained through actions. In fact, actions are unreal, but when these are performed for the sake of the Supreme, they are called 'Sat' viz., real (Gītā 17/27).

When a person, performs action with a selfish motive, he does not realize Yoga (i.e., eternal union with God). In Karmayoga, actions are performed for others, not for one's own self i.e., not for their fruit (Gītā 2/47). Actions, which are performed with a selfish motive, bind a man (Gītā 3/9) while actions, which are performed for others, liberate him, from the bondage of actions (Gītā 4/23). When actions are performed for others, affinity for actions and their fruit is renounced, and that renouncement is conducive to the realization of Yoga i.e., union with God.

While performing actions, a man has to depend on the changing objects, such as the body, senses, mind, intellect, person etc., which are different from the self (soul). The self, ever remains uniform without undergoing any modification, at all. Therefore, in Self-realization there is no need, in the least for the objects, such as the body etc., which are different from the self. A man, naturally realizes the self, as soon as he renounces his assumed affinity for worldly objects etc., which are different from him (the self).

Link:—Having described the object of His manifestation, in the eighth verse, the Lord explains the merit of knowing the divine character of his actions, in the ninth verse. There He explained, that actions lose their divine character i.e., become impure, when these are performed with a desire for fruit. In the next two verses, the Lord specially, explains how, they gain their divine character (purity).

चातुर्वर्ण्यं मया सृष्टं गुणकर्मविभागशः।
तस्य कर्तारमपि मां विद्ध्यकर्तारमव्ययम्॥ १३॥
न मां कर्माणि लिम्पन्ति न मे कर्मफले स्पृहा।
इति मां योऽभिजानाति कर्मभिर्न स बध्यते॥ १४॥

cāturvarṇyaṁ mayā sṛṣṭaṁ guṇakarmavibhāgaśaḥ
tasya kartāramapi māṁ viddhyakartāramavyayam
na māṁ karmāṇi limpanti na me karmaphale spṛhā
iti māṁ yo'bhijānāti karmabhirna sa badhyate

The fourfold order was created by Me according to the modes of their nature and action (Karma). Though, I am the creator, know Me, the immortal Lord, to be a non-doer. Since I have no craving for the fruit of actions, these do not taint Me. He who knows Me thus, (in reality) is not affected by actions. 13-14

Comment:—

'Cāturvarṇyaṁ mayā sṛṣṭaṁ guṇakarmavibhāgaśaḥ'—The Lord, created the four castes (order)—Brāhmaṇa, Kṣatriya, Vaiśya and Śūdra, according to the modes of nature, and actions of previous birth.* Besides human beings, the Lord created the gods, manes and other forms of life also, according to the modes of their nature and action, without showing the least partiality.

The fourfold caste (order), does not apply only to human beings, but also to birds, beasts and trees etc. Among birds, pigeons are regarded as Brāhmaṇa; hawks, kites and crows are regarded respectively as Kṣatriya, Vaiśya and Śūdra. Similarly Pīpala, Nīma, Tamarind and Acacia, are regarded respectively as Brāhmaṇa, Kṣatriya, Vaiśya and Śūdra. But, here the term 'Cāturvarṇyaṁ' stands only for human beings, because they can understand this distinction and can perform their duty, accordingly.

When the Lord declares, that the fourfold caste was created by Him, He means to say that all of these are his fragments and He is their disinterested friend. Therefore, He always thinks of their welfare. On the other hand, they are neither fragments of the gods nor are the gods their disinterested friends. So they should worship Him, only though the performance of their own duty (Gītā 18/46).

---

* The four castes (orders of society) (Brāhmaṇa, Kṣatriya, Vaiśya and Śūdra) are classified according to the mode of nature. In Brāhmaṇa the mode of goodness predominates; in Kṣatriya the mode of passion predominates, while the modes of goodness is secondary; in Vaiśya the mode of passion predominates, while the mode of ignorance is secondary (subordinate); while in Śūdra the mode of ignorance predominates. Thus the castes were determined on the basis of the mode of nature.

'Tasya kartāramapi māṁ viddhyakartāramavyayam'—Though, the Lord creates, preserves and destroys the entire universe yet He remains unconnected, (untainted) as He has no feeling of doership. He is called 'Avyayam' (unspent) only He is the material, as well as, the efficient cause of creation. For example, in a pot of clay, clay is material cause and the potter is the efficient cause, because while creating the world He remains uniform; neither His energy is spent to create it, like the potter who spends his energy to make a pot, nor is the material consumed, when the pot is made.

The soul, being a fragment of God is also imperishable. But, a man does not realize this fact, because he regards the acquired body, senses, mind, intellect, wealth and property etc., as his own, and for himself. As soon as, he regards these as the world's and for the world, he will realize his immortality.

By using the term 'Viddhi', the Lord urges strivers, to understand the divine nature of His actions. When actions are performed without having any affinity for those or, the material and the fruit of actions, then these become divine.

'Na māṁ karmāṇi limpanti na me karmaphale spṛhā'—When the Lord, creates the universe, He has not the least affinity for his actions, nor is there any flaw or partiality etc., in His actions, nor any attachment or feeling of 'mine', or desire for the fruit of actions. So those actions do not taint Him.

All perishable objects, are fruits of actions. The Lord urges strivers, that they, like Him should have no craving for the fruit of actions. If they perform actions, without having any craving for the fruit of actions, the actions will not bind them.

In the thirteenth verse, the Lord explained that He is a non-doer i.e., He has no sense of doership, in spite of performing all actions, such as the creation of the universe etc. In this verse, He explains that He has no craving for the fruit of actions. Therefore, a striver should also perform actions, without a sense of doership and without having any desire for the fruit of actions. By doing so, he is automatically liberated from the bondage of actions.

'Iti māṁ yo'bhijānāti'—Desires are born, when a man has an eye on the perishable mundane objects and then he cannot know the reality about God, Who is immortal. As soon as, desires are renounced, the inner sense is purified and then naturally one reflects on God. By having an eye on Him, he comes to know that, He is a disinterested friend of all beings, and all actions performed by Him, aim at the welfare, of all beings. The Lord, bestows this human body upon us, in order to enable us to be liberated from the bondage of actions. But, a man without knowing this fact, assumes his affinity for actions, and is thus held captive. Therefore the Lord in spite of having, neither a sense of doership, nor, desire for fruit, creates the universe by His grace, so as to inspire human beings, to attain salvation, by becoming free from the bondage of actions. When a man knows Him thus (in reality), he is attracted to Him. So Lord Śiva in the Rāmacaritamānasa says to Umā, "He who knows the nature of Lord Rāma, ever remains engrossed in His adoration" (5/34/2).

'Karmabhirna sa badhyate'—The Lord's actions are ever divine. The actions of saints and sages also become divine. Not only saints and sages, but also men can make their actions divine, by doing away with desire, attachment and a sense of 'mine', which are impurities in actions. When actions are purged of impurities, these become divine and they do not bind men. These lead them, as well as others, (who follow them), to salvation.

An easy means, to make actions divine is to use the objects etc., acquired from the world, to render service to the world, without regarding these as one's own, and for one's own self.

We should give a serious thought to the fact, that we neither brought the objects, such as the body etc., with us, when we came, nor can we carry these with us when we go, or change these of our own accord, nor maintain them. Similarly, the subtle and the causal bodies, being the evolutes of nature (prakṛti), also undergo modifications and therefore, we have no affinity for these. Moreover, those objects are not for us, because had they been for us, or having acquired them, there would have been no further desire, to acquire anything else. So it is a blunder to accept these as ours, and for us. They seem to us to be ours, so that we use them in rendering service to others rather than to lay a claim on them.

We should have no desire to acquire anything from the world nor even, to gain any favour from God. We should rather surrender ourselves to Him. The Lord Himself, has provided all the necessities of life to us, because He is very gracious and merciful. He knows our needs more than we know ours as we are dull-witted while, He is very sharp. So, without desiring anything, we should use the things that we possess, for the welfare of others without any selfish motive. By doing so our affinity for actions and objects etc., is renounced and God, Who is an embodiment of Bliss is realized.

Appendix—Though the author of worldly creation, the non-doership of God remains unaffected, similarly the non-doership of the self also remains unaffected—'śarīrastho'pi kaunteya na karoti na lipyate' (Gītā 13/31). But being deluded, he thinks that he is the doer—'ahaṅkāravimūḍhātmā kartāhamiti manyate' (Gītā 3/27).

'Karma', 'Kriyā' and 'Līlā'—the three may appear to be the same but really they are totally different. The 'Kriyā' which is done with the sense of egoism and bears desirable and undesirable fruit, is called 'Karma' (action). The 'kriyā' (activity) which is done without the sense of doership and which does not bear fruit, is called 'kriyā' as breathing, opening and closing the eyes, movement of the pulse, beating of the heart etc. The 'Kriyā' which is free from the sense of doership and from the desire for fruit, and also divine, and for the welfare of the world, is called 'Līlā'. Actions done by worldly people are karma and by liberated people are kriyā* and by God they are mere sports or say 'Līlā'—'lokavattu līlākaivalyam' (Brahmasūtra 2/1/33) viz., as the world without real existence appears to be existing, similarly the Lord's activity such as the creation of the universe etc., is merely His pastime. It means that the Lord in spite of being the non-doer seems to be a doer because of His pastime.

'Cāturvarṇyaṁ mayā sṛṣṭaṁ guṇakarmavibhāgaśaḥ'—this expression proves that according to the Gītā a person's caste is determined by his birth. A person's caste or Varṇa (order of life) is determined by the caste of his parents. The word 'jāti' is made from the root 'janī prādurbhāve' which proves that the caste is determined by birth. By 'Karma' there is the word 'kṛti' which is made from the root 'ḍukṛñ karaṇe'. But the caste is fully preserved by only discharging the duty prescribed for one's own caste.

Link:—Describing the divine character of His actions, in the preceding verse, and citing examples of ancient seekers of liberation, in the next verse, the Lord advices Arjuna to perform his duty disinterestedly.

एवं ज्ञात्वा कृतं कर्म पूर्वैरपि मुमुक्षुभिः।
कुरु कर्मैव तस्मात्त्वं पूर्वैः पूर्वतरं कृतम्॥ १५॥

evaṁ jñātvā kṛtaṁ karma pūrvairapi mumukṣubhiḥ
kuru karmaiva tasmāttvaṁ pūrvaiḥ pūrvataraṁ kṛtam

Having known this, the ancient seekers of salvation also

* The Lord has also called it 'Ceṣṭā' in the Gītā—Sadṛśaṁ ceṣṭate' (3/33)

performed action (Karma); therefore, do thou also perform action, as the ancients did, in former times. 15

Comment:—

[The Lord here, concludes the topic of the divine character of actions, which He began in the ninth verse.]

'Evaṁ jñātvā kṛtaṁ karma pūrvairapi mumukṣubhiḥ'—Arjuna was a seeker of liberation (salvation), but he did not think that the performance of his duty (of fighting) would lead him to salvation. So he wanted to renounce the duty, as to him it was horrible (Gītā 3/1). Therefore, Lord Kṛṣṇa urges Arjuna to attain salvation, through performing his duty, and cited the example of ancient seekers of liberation, who attained salvation by performing their duty.

The Lord, is emphasizing the same fact here, which He mentioned, in the twentieth verse of the third chapter, by citing the example of Janaka and others, and, in the first and second verses of this chapter, by citing examples of Vivasvān, Manu and Ikṣvāku etc.

It is mentioned in the scriptures, that when desire for liberation is aroused in a striver, he should abandon actions, because in that case, he becomes eligible to attain knowledge (wisdom), rather than to perform actions.* But here, He urges Arjuna, a seeker of liberation, to perform his duty in a disinterested manner, and cites the example of other ancient seekers of liberation.

Karmayoga (Discipline of Action) consists, in remaining established in Yoga (union with God) while performing duty, and in performing duty while remaining firm in Yoga. Actions are performed for the world, while Yoga (union with God) is for one's own self. Performance of actions and non-performance of actions, are two states. A Yogī, transcends the two, without

* Actions should be performed so long as a striver does not develop dispassion or has no reverence to listen to My (God's) life-history (Śrīmadbhāgavata 11/20/9).

being attached to either of the two. This Yoga is detachment incarnate. This is not a state. It is God-realization.

The Lord, in the fourteenth verse, declared, "Actions do not taint (bind) Me, since I have no craving for the fruit of actions." A person, who having known this skill (Karmayoga) performs actions, by renouncing the desire for fruit, is not bound by actions, as the Lord declares, "He who is attached to the fruit of action, is bound" (Gītā 5/12). Actions, which a man performs, in order to gain pleasures or wealth or honour and praise or paradise etc., bind him (Gītā 3/9). But, if he performs actions, for the well being of others, without any selfish motive, to renounce his affinity for the world, the actions do not bind him (Gītā 4/23). The reason is, that when actions are performed for others, the flow is towards the world and thus attachment for them perishes. No new affinity for them is born, because there is no desire for the fruit.

'Kuru karmaiva tasmāttvaṁ pūrvaiḥ pūrvataraṁ kṛtam'— The Lord orders Arjuna to perform actions, for the welfare of the world, like other seekers of liberation, because he is also a seeker of liberation.

All the mundane materials, such as, the body, senses, mind and intellect etc., required for the performance of actions, have their identity with the world, while they are different from the self. They have been acquired from the world, so that service to the world may be rendered, with them. If they are used by a person in performing actions for himself, he gets attached to those actions, but if all actions are performed for the welfare of others, he is not attached to them. As soon as, this attachment is renounced, he realizes his Yoga i.e., union with God, which is eternal.

Appendix—In the thirteenth and fourteenth verses the Lord declared, "I perform actions such as the creation of the universe etc., but those actions don't bind Me because I am free from the sense of doership and the desire of fruit." Here the Lord declares that the seekers of salvation have also performed actions by renouncing the sense of doership and the desire for fruit. The reason is that actions performed with the sense of doership and with the desire for fruit alone lead to bondage. Therefore the Lord asks Arjuna to perform actions in the same way as the seekers of salvation have performed.

In Jñānayoga first there is renunciation of the sense of doership and then the desire for fruit automatically disappears. In Karmayoga first there is renunciation of the desire for fruit and then the sense of doership easily get extinct.

Link:—In the preceding verse, the Lord explained that having known the divine character of actions, the ancient seekers of liberation performed actions. Now, the Lord in the next verse, starts the topic of, knowing the truth about action.

किं कर्म किमकर्मेति कवयोऽप्यत्र मोहिताः ।
तत्ते कर्म प्रवक्ष्यामि यज्ज्ञात्वा मोक्ष्यसेऽशुभात् ॥ १६ ॥

kiṁ karma kimakarmeti kavayo'pyatra mohitāḥ
tatte karma pravakṣyāmi yajjñātvā mokṣyase'śubhāt

What is action? What is inaction? As to this, even the wise are confused. Therefore, I will explain to you what action is, by knowing which, you shall be liberated, from its evil effect (i.e.,) worldly bondage. 16

Comment:—

'Kiṁ karma'— Common men believe that activities done with the body and senses are mere actions, while non-performance of an act, is inaction. But, the Lord declares that activities performed with body, speech and mind, are actions (Gītā 18/15).

An action, is determined by the motive by which, it is performed. An action, such as adoration of a goddess, is of the mode of goodness, but if it is undertaken with the motive of fulfilling mundane desires, it becomes a mode of passion. If it is undertaken with the motive of someone's ruin, the same action is, of the mode of ignorance. In the same way, actions which are performed without attachment, a sense of mine and desire for fruits, are classed as inaction, and these do not bind a man, to the fruit of action. It means, that truth about action cannot be determined by outward activity only. In this connection, even wise men, possessing knowledge of the scriptures get confused, i.e., they are, at a loss to understand the truth. An action is classed, as an action or inaction, or is forbidden, according to the motive with which it is performed. Therefore, the Lord declares, that He will explain to Arjuna, what action is, why and how it binds a man, and how he can be liberated from it and by knowing the truth about it.

If a man, has a sense of mine, attachment and desire for fruits, it means that action is being performed by him i.e., he is tainted by that action, even though he does not perform an outward action. On the other hand, if he has neither a sense of mine, nor attachment nor desire for fruit, it means that actions are not being performed by him i.e., he is not tainted by such actions, even though he performs actions. Thus performance or non-performance of actions is inaction, if he has no attachment, while performance or non-performance of actions is classed as action, if he has any attachment.

'Kimakarmeti'—The Lord, divided action into two groups—actions and inaction. Actions, bind a man, while inactions (which are undertaken for others) liberate him.

In reality, physical abjuring of actions, is not inaction. The Lord, has declared that the renunciation of actions, through delusion is stated to be, of the nature of 'ignorance' (Gītā 18/7). The exclusion of action, from fear of physical suffering, is called 'passionate' (Gītā 18/8). In the renunciation of the nature of 'ignorance' and 'passion', the affinity for actions is not renounced, though the performance of actions is. Renunciation, in which attachment and desire for reward, are abandoned, is regarded as one of 'goodness' (Gītā 18/9). In fact, this is called 'inaction', because affinity for actions is renounced in such a exclusion. Therefore, inaction, consists in the performance of actions, by remaining untainted by them.

Even the wise are confused, about the truth of what, an inaction is. The reality about an action or an inaction is, that it should not bind a man. Arjuna holds that he will attain salvation if he does not indulge himself in the cruel deed of fighting. So the Lord declares, that a man does not attain to perfection, by mere renunciation of action (Gītā 3/4) but he can attain it, even by engaging himself in battle (Gītā 2/38).

Thus inaction, consists either in the performance of actions by remaining untainted or in remaining untainted, while performing actions.

'Kavayo'pyatra mohitāḥ'—How can common men understand the truth about action and inaction, when even the learned who are well-versed in the scriptures, are at a loss to grasp this topic? It means, that only the liberated souls or the Lord knows, the truth about action and inaction.

'Tatte karma pravakṣyāmī'—A man, (the soul) is bound by actions, so he would also be liberated, by action. The Lord promises here that, He will declare the reality about actions, so that they may not lead him to bondage and he may be liberated from the bondage of the cycle of birth and death.

In fact, it is neither action nor inaction,which binds a man, but it is the desire, the sense of mine and attachment, which bind him. If he renounces desire and feelings of possession and attachment, he is liberated, while performing action, and not by performing it. One, who understands this fact, knows the reality about actions.

In the fiftieth verse of the second chapter, the Lord declared, "Yoga is skill in action." It means that Yoga viz., equanimity (evenness of mind) is the means to be liberated from the binding nature of actions. Arjuna could not understand this point; therefore, the Lord promises to explain this point again.

An Important Fact

'Karmayoga' is not an action. It is selfless service. In it non-attachment predominates. Service and non-attachment—both are not actions. Discrimination, plays an important role in both of these.

As the body, senses, mind and intellect etc., are acquired these are transitory. They should be used, only in rendering service to the world, because these have been acquired from the world. Moreover, these will have to be renounced. But, the Self or God Who is ours, can never be renounced. Only that which is really not ours, but we have assumed as ours, is renounced. In fact, this is not renunciation, it is discrimination.

All materials, (the body, senses, mind and intellect etc.,) are neither of the self, nor for the self, but are of the world and for the world. The self ever remains unaffected and uniform, while the materials are changing. Therefore whatever action is performed, with these materials is for the good of others, not for the self. In this there is a vital fact, that no action can be performed, without materials. Even the greatest writer cannot write, without ink, pen and paper, which are of the world. Therefore, when a person, uses the articles of the world for the world, he in fact, does not render any service to the world, he gives the things of the world to the world. Thus he merely uses his discrimination. Thus, it is discrimination which leads to renunciation and service.

Discrimination has been bestowed upon beings from time immemorial. Had it been the fruit of virtuous action, how could virtuous actions have been performed, without discrimination? It is discrimination by which one can resolve, to perform virtuous actions, by renouncing evil actions. As discrimination is self-evident, so is Karmayoga (Discipline of Action) which involves no labour. Similarly, in the Discipline of Knowledge, the self (Which is detached) is self-evident, while in the Discipline of Devotion, the affinity for God is self-evident.

'Yajjñātvā mokṣyase'śubhāt'—The self, is good and virtuous, while the ever-changing world, is bad or evil. The self, in spite of being an eternal fragment of God, and developing a disinclination for God, has got entangled in the perishable world. The Lord declares, that He will describe reality about action, by knowing, which he (Arjuna) will be liberated from its evil effect i.e., worldly bondage of the cycle of birth and death.

[The topic of knowledge of action, which begins in this verse, will be concluded in the thirty-second verse with the declaration, "Thus knowing, thou shalt be liberated".]

A Vital Fact

In the term, 'Karmayoga' Karma (actions) are performed for the world, while Yoga (union with God), is for the self. Action and non-action—these are the two states of action, which involve egoism. So long as, a man has egoistic notions he has, affinity for the world; and so long as he has affinity for the world, he continues to have egoistic notions. But 'Yoga' transcends the two states. In order to realize that Yoga it is essential to be free from egoism. The method of being free from egoism, is performance or non-performance of actions, by being equanimous and remaining equanimous during performance or non-performance, of actions. It means, that he should have equanimity (evenness of mind) during the performance and non-performance of actions (Gītā 2/48), i.e., he should remain untainted.

Those, who believe that a man is inclined towards the world by performance of actions, and is inclined towards God through non-performance of actions, and having a disinclination for the world, meditate on God and experience a trance, also perform actions. The feeling, that God (perfection) will be attained through meditation and trance, is also a subtle form of action, because one expects God-realization through performance of actions, in the form of meditation and trance, while God is beyond action, as well as inaction.

The Lord declares, that He will explain the reality about action by which one will attain God, immediately. God pervades everywhere, all the time, through things, persons, bodies, senses, minds, intellects and life-breaths etc., equally. He remains united with us, when we perform actions and when we do not perform actions. But, we are unable to realize Him, because of our affinity for actions and objects, born of nature (prakṛti).

A man has an egoistic notion, equally during the performance of actions, as well as during the non-performance of actions, but his egoism merges in the world, when he instead of performing actions for himself, performs these, for the welfare of the world.

Link:—In the next verse Lord Kṛṣṇa inspires Arjuna to know the reality of action and inaction.

कर्मणो ह्यपि बोद्धव्यं बोद्धव्यं च विकर्मणः।
अकर्मणश्च बोद्धव्यं गहना कर्मणो गतिः ॥ १७ ॥

karmaṇo hyapi boddhavyaṁ boddhavyaṁ ca vikarmaṇaḥ
akarmaṇaśca boddhavyaṁ gahanā karmaṇo gatiḥ

The reality about actions must be known, as well about forbidden actions, even so the reality about inaction, must be understood; for mysterious, is the nature of action. 17

Comment:—

'Karmaṇo hyapi boddhavyam'— He, who remains untainted while performing actions, knows the truth about actions, described in the eighteenth verse, by the expression, "He who sees inaction in action."

Actions can be divided, into three groups, according to the motive by which these are performed (i.e.,) action, inaction and forbidden action. An activity undertaken, according to spiritual injunctions with a desire for fruit, is called, action. Action which is performed, being free from the desire for fruit, sense of mine and attachment, for the welfare of others, is classed, as inaction. Even prescribed action, performed with the motive of doing evil to others, or giving pain to them, is classed as, forbidden action.

'Akarmaṇaśca boddhavyam'— He, who performs actions, while remaining untainted, knows the reality about inaction, described in the eighteenth verse, by the expression 'action in inaction.'

'Boddhavyaṁ ca vikarmaṇaḥ'—When a man has desire, actions are performed. But when desire is enhanced, then forbidden actions (sinful) are done.

The Lord, in the thirty-eighth verse of second chapter, declared, "Treating alike, pleasure and pain, gain and loss, victory and defeat, get ready for battle, the horrible deed involving violence; thus thou shalt not incur sin." It means, that if actions are performed with equanimity, the seemingly forbidden actions are also transformed, into inaction.

Forbidden actions, are called 'Vikarma'. Desire is the cause of forbidden actions (Gītā 3/36-37).* Therefore, in order to give up forbidden actions, one should renounce desire. The essence of 'Vikarma' (sin), is desire and to know the essence of 'Vikarma', is to abandon all forbidden actions physically and so leave no trace of desire which is the cause of 'Vikarma'.

* In the sixteenth chapter where the demoniac nature has been described there from the eighth verse to the twenty-third verse the term 'Kāma' (desire) has been used nine times. It shows that desire is the cause of demoniac nature (forbidden actions).

'Gahanā karmaṇo gatiḥ'—It is difficult to understand, which actions bind a man and which liberate him. Even learned men, knowing the scriptures cannot decide, 'What is action?' 'What is inaction?' and 'What is forbidden action?' Arjuna also, finds himself in a dilemma and so he thinks, that the performance of his duty of fighting is a cruel deed. Therefore, the Lord states, that mysterious is the nature of action.

Question:—In this verse, the Lord declares, that truth about forbidden actions must be known, while He does not make mention of the forbidden actions, in the topic from the nineteenth verse to the twenty-third verse. Why?

Answer:—In the topic (from the nineteenth verse to the twenty-third verse), the Lord, has prominently mentioned inaction in action so that all actions may turn to inaction i.e., actions may not lead to bondage. A desire is the root of every action. As the desire intensifies, it results in forbidden actions. Therefore it is said that Vikarma is quite near to karma. Therefore, the Lord has referred to forbidden actions, as wretched, so that men may renounce these, as well as the desire which is their main root.

First, desire leads a man to action, and then its enhancement, leads one to perform forbidden actions. But, when desire is renounced, all actions turn to, inaction. The significance of the topic, discussed in these verses, is to know the essence of inaction and what leads to annihilation of desires. When desire is renounced forbidden actions are not performed. So the Lord, does not consider it necessary to include 'Vikarma', in the topic, from the nineteenth to the twenty-third verses. Secondly, the Lord does not want to dwell upon forbidden actions in detail, because these must be renounced as they lead to sins and hells. But, in this topic there is an emphasis on, the renunciation of desire—in 4/19 by the expression 'devoid of desires and thoughts of the world', in 4/20 by, the expression 'having abandoned attachment to the fruit of action', in 4/21 by the expression 'having no desire', in 4/22 by 'even-minded in success and failure', and in 4/23 by 'One who is devoid of attachment and works for sacrifice.'

Thus, the Lord has said, that truth about forbidden actions must be known, so that a man, having known it, may renounce desire, which is the root of forbidden actions.

Appendix—It is very difficult to gaze what fruit an action bears at present and in future for others. While performing an action a man thinks that it is of benefit to him but actually it causes harm to him. He may work for profit but it may end in loss. He acts for pleasure whereas his act results in pain. The reason is that due to the sense of doership and the desire for fruit (attachment to pleasure), man cannot determine the true nature of actions.

Link:—In the next verse, the Lord eulogizes a person who knows the truth, about actions.

कर्मण्यकर्म यः पश्येदकर्मणि च कर्म यः।
स बुद्धिमान्मनुष्येषु स युक्तः कृत्स्नकर्मकृत्॥ १८॥

karmaṇyakarma yaḥ paśyedakarmaṇi ca karma yaḥ
sa buddhimānmanuṣyeṣu sa yuktaḥ kṛtsnakarmakṛt

He, who sees inaction in action and action in inaction, is wise among men, he is a Yogī and performs all his duties. 18

Comment:—

'Karmaṇyakarma yaḥ paśyet'—'Seeing inaction in action' means, to remain untainted during performance or non-performance of actions. It means also that performance or non-performance of actions, is not for the self. When a man thinks that he is the doer and so he should reap the fruit of action, he is bound by such actions. As actions are perishable, so is their fruit. The self, is eternal and has no affinity for the changing actions, and their fruits. Yet, It is bound, because of the desire, for fruit. Therefore, the Lord in the fourteenth verse declared, "Actions don't bind

Me, because I have no desire, for the fruit of actions." It is the desire for fruit, which binds one. The Lord declares, "He who is attached to the fruit of action, is bound" (Gītā 5/12).

If a striver, has no desire for fruit, new attachment does not arise; and old attachment perishes, when actions are performed for the welfare of others. Thus, he becomes, totally dispassionate. This dispassionate nature, turns all actions into inaction.

A man, has to take birth either to be free of obligations or receive these from others, for all previous births. This exchange has been going on for several births. He cannot get rid of the cycle of birth and death, so long as, he does not repay his debt. The way to close his account is, that he should pay to others what he owes to them and should not expect them to repay to him, their debts. Thus, the account will be closed and, he will be liberated, from the cycle of birth and death (Gītā 4/23).

If a person does nothing for himself, and has no desire, he gets detached from all actions and objects etc., because all objects and materials etc., such as the body, senses, mind, intellect and life-breaths are of the world, not one's own as these have been acquired from the world, so that service may be rendered to the world with these. Therefore, when a striver performs all actions (service, adoration, chant, meditation entrances also) for the welfare of the world, the flow of action is towards the world and the striver, remains detached and untainted. This is 'seeing inaction in action.'

So long as, a striver has affinity for the body and the world, the performance or non-performance of actions, will be included in action. So, a Karmayogī should remain untainted (detached), while he performs actions, as also while he does not. When a man performs actions, without having any desire for fruit, profit, honour, praise and pleasure, here or hereafter, it means, that he is detached (untainted) during the performance of actions. Similarly, when he does not perform any action, he should not desire, in the least, to gain honour, praise, pleasures and bodily rest etc., by non-performance of actions.

He, who abandons action, because it is painful or out of fear from physical suffering or practises relinquishment of passion, (Rājasa Tyāga)while he who renounces his obligatory duty out of delusion, indolence and heedlessness, practises Tāmasa Tyāga. Both kinds of relinquishment, must be totally abandoned. Similarly, if a man does not perform action, so that he may enjoy the state of meditation or trance or liberation, he does not get detached from nature (prakṛti). When he renounces his full affinity for nature, he remains untainted while performing actions or not performing these.

'Akarmaṇi ca karma yaḥ'— 'Seeing action in inaction' means, performing action or not performing it, by being detached (untainted).

Worldly people want to gain, something or the other, through performance and non-performance of actions, while a Karmayogī's only aim through the two, is the welfare of the world, by remaining detached. The Lord declares, "For him there is no interest, in what is done or what is not done" (Gītā 3/18). If he has any self-interest, he is not a Karmayogī, but is rather a doer of actions.

So long as, a striver assume his affinity for nature, he holds that he progresses in the mundane sphere through the performance of actions, while in the spiritual sphere, through their non-performance. But, in fact, it is not so. As walking and eating etc., are actions of the physical body, so are reflection and meditation, the actions of the subtle body and trance, the action, of the causal body. Therefore, he who performs his duty (action) for the welfare of the world, by remaining detached (untainted), sees inaction in action. The same, has been pointed out, in the forty-eighth verse of the second chapter, by the Lord, when He declares, "Perform action, being steadfast in Yoga (equanimity)."

Activity or non-activity with some motive in the world, are both actions. To remain quite detached, while doing actions or refraining from them throughout, and being detached, while there is performance or non-performance of actions,—this total detachment under all circumstances, is called 'Yoga', and is 'Karmayoga.'

A striver should remain equanimous, during the performance or non-performance of actions, called Karmayoga.

Question:—Why has the Lord mentioned 'inaction in action' and 'action in inaction', while in both cases, inaction or detachment, is the predominating factor?

Answer:— When a man sees inaction in action, there remains the dominance of detachment. But, when he sees action in inaction, there is predominance of performance or non-performance of action. It means, that detachment has its affinity for the self, while performance or non-performance of actions, has its affinity for the world, including the body. Therefore, detachment is one's own duty, while performance or non-performance of action, is the duty of another. In order to differentiate the two, the Lord has mentioned 'seeing inaction in action' and 'action in inaction'.

In the Discipline of Action, there is performance or non-performance of action, for the welfare of the world without attachment, because, while performing actions, one should remain detached and while remaining detached, one should perform actions—these two aspects are the principles of the Gītā.

'Pravṛtti' (activity) and 'Nivṛtti' (non-activity)—both are in domain of nature. Nature is ever-changing and So is performance or non-performance of actions, while the Self Which is the illuminator and base of the two, ever remains uniform without undergoing any modification. In order to explain this fact, the Lord has declared, that he who sees inaction in action, and action in inaction both is wise. It means, that a striver while remaining established in the self, should perform actions for the welfare of the world viz., as a sacrifice (Yajña).

'Sa buddhimānmanuṣyeṣu'—The striver, who sees inaction in action and action in inaction i.e., remains detached (untainted), and knows the truth about action. Unless he is detached i.e., regards objects and actions as his, and for him, it means that he has not known the reality about actions.

In order to, know the truth about God, a striver has to identify the self with Him, while in order to know the reality about the world, he has to separate the self from the world (actions and objects), for he (the self) has identity with God, while he is different from the world. All actions, are transitory while the self is eternal.

As a common man cannot remain unsoiled, in a coal cellar, only a wise man could do so, similarly, only a wise man can remain detached from actions, while performing these. Therefore, here as well as in the tenth verse of the eighteenth chapter, the Lord calls such a man wise among men. He wants to say that for such a wise man, nothing further remains to be known.

'Sa yuktaḥ'—A Karmayogī, remains equanimous in success and failure, because he totally renounces the desire, for the fruit of actions. Here the term ' Yoga', stands for equanimity. One is a Yogī, because he remains established, in equanimity.

Every being has a natural union with God, but he forgets it, because he assumes his affinity for the world. When he performs actions for the welfare of the world, by renouncing desire for fruit, a sense of possession and attachment, his assumed affinity for the world is renounced and he realizes his union with God, which is natural and eternal. For such a Yogī nothing remains to be attained, for he has achieved Divinity.

'Kṛtsnakarmakṛt'—So long as, a man has to attain something or the other, he has to perform actions viz., his attachment for actions, does not wither.

Perishable actions bear perishable fruits. So long as, one

has desire for the perishable, he will have to undertake actions. But, on having renounced all affinity for the perishable, he attains to the Imperishable Lord and nothing further remains to be done. Then, a Karmayogī has nothing to do, with the performance or non-performance of actions, i.e., he becomes a performer of all actions.

When nothing remains to be done, to be known and to be attained by such a Karmayogī, he is liberated from the evil, bondage of the wheel of birth and death in the world (Gītā 4/16, 32).

Appendix—There are two spheres—one of action and the other of inaction. Out of these two, inaction is the essence. Therefore he who sees inaction in action viz., while performing an action remains untainted and he who sees action in inaction viz., while remaining untainted performs action, for him nothing remains to be done, to be known and to be gained. As at the beginning of an action 'Gaṇeśajī' is worshipped but during the performance of the action 'Gaṇeśajī' is not worshipped all the time. But it is not the case here of remaining untainted in actions at the beginning only. Therefore the Lord has mentioned inaction in action and action in inaction. It means that one should never be tainted (desire for fruit and the sense of doership) viz., he should ever remain untainted.

In the eighth verse of the third chapter the Lord declares that the performance of an action is superior to inaction—'karma jyāyo hyakarmaṇaḥ' while here He declares that it is better to see inaction (non-doership) than the performance of action; and for the person who is thus untainted, nothing remains to be done, to be known and to be gained. It proves that a man should be free from the desire for fruit and from the sense of doership because these two severally bind a man.

Link:—Now, the Lord in the next two verses, describes the

enlightened soul (sage) who sees inaction in action and action in inaction, i.e., who knows the truth about action.

यस्य सर्वे समारम्भाः कामसंकल्पवर्जिताः ।
ज्ञानाग्निदग्धकर्माणं तमाहुः पण्डितं बुधाः ॥ १९ ॥

yasya sarve samārambhāḥ kāmasaṅkalpavarjitāḥ
jñānāgnidagdhakarmāṇaṁ tamāhuḥ paṇḍitaṁ budhāḥ

He, all whose undertakings are free from Saṅkalpa and desire and whose actions are burnt up in the fire of wisdom, him the seers, call wise (Paṇḍita). 19

Comment:—

'Yasya sarve samārambhāḥ kāmasaṅkalpavarjitāḥ'—Thinking of sense-objects and remembering these time and again, and thinking that some of these are good, useful and pleasurable, is a mental resolve (Saṅkalpa) and 'Vikalpa (uncertainty) is antithesis of Saṅkalpa, "these are not good and are injurious." This type of thinking, the Vikalpa-intellect is the abiding place of positive and negative projections. When negative projections, give way to positive ones, at that time a desire to obtain those objects arises. This is known as "Kāma'. In an accomplished Karmayogī, projection and desire, both are absent e.g., there remains neither 'Saṅkalpa, which is the origin of desire nor desire which is its product. Therefore, all actions of a 'Karmayogī' are free from resolve and desire.

'Saṅkalpa' and desire, are the two seeds of action. If they are no longer there, action becomes inaction, that is to say, actions lose their binding potentiality. In a liberated soul, these two are absent, so actions performed by that are not binding. Even though, he does everything, in order to maintain social order and protect the chain of social obligations, yet he is quite untainted with his actions, whatsoever.

The Lord, has prescribed on occasions the renunciation of desires (6/4), of mental projections (2/55), and of both these (6/24-25). Therefore, wherever in Gītā renunciation of 'Saṅkalpa' is prescribed, it must always be together with desire as well. In a nutshell, a striver should give up projections and desires both.

There are four states of a motor car.

1. When a motor car stands still, in the garage, its engine does not function and the wheels don't move forward.

2. The engine starts functioning, but the wheels do not, move forward (it's all loss and no gain).

3. The engine functions and the wheels move and cover some distance.

4. On a downward slope, the engine is stopped, while the wheels move and cover a distance (it's all gain and no cost).

Similarly, a man may have four states—

1. Neither desire, nor action.

2. Desire but no action (it's all loss and no gain).

3. Desire as well as action.

4. Action, but no desire (it's all gain and no cost).

The best state of a motor car is the fourth one, when the car runs, but no petrol is consumed. Similar, is the case with man. The best state is when he performs action, without having any desire. Even the wise, call such a man a sage.

'Samārambhāḥ'—Here, this term stands for, the undertaking of a Karmayogī, which are free from attachment and aversion. It does not stand for the word 'ārambha' (undertaking), used in the twelfth verse of the fourteenth chapter, because there 'pravṛtti' (activity) and 'ārambha'—two terms have been used. There, the term 'pravṛtti' stands for the performance of duty, while the term 'ārambha', stands for the undertaking of actions for pleasures and prosperity. A sage or an enlightened soul, performs action scrupulously according to the ordinance of the scriptures, for the welfare of all beings.

The terms 'sarve', expresses the meaning, that all his

undertakings are free from the thought of the world and desire. From morning till night, whatever he does, for the maintenance of his body, such as washing, eating, walking etc., and for spiritual upliftment, such as chant, adoration, reflection, meditation and trance, is free, from the thought of the world and desire.

'Jñānāgnidagdhakarmāṇam'—Wisdom, consists in knowing the truth that actions have their affinity for the body and the world, not for the self, because, actions have a beginning and an end, while the self remains stable. All actions, are burnt in the fire of this wisdom i.e., actions cannot bear fruit in the form of bondage (Gītā 4/16,32).

In fact, the body and actions, have their identity with the world, while the self is different from these. But, by an error, he (the self) assumes his affinity for these. Great souls have no affinity for their so-called, bodies. As actions are performed by the entire world, so are actions performed by their so-called, bodies. Thus, when they are detached from actions, not only their present actions, but also the stock of past actions are burnt, in the fire of wisdom. As far as, their fate (prārabdha karma) is concerned, it creates favourable and unfavourable circumstances, but being detached from the fruit of actions they neither feel happy nor sad. The 'prārabdha karmas', get effaced by creating transitory circumstances.

'Tamāhuḥ paṇḍitaṁ budhāḥ'—It is easy to know the reality about an ascetic, who having renounced actions externally ever remains absorbed in the adoration of God, but it is very difficult to know the truth about a man living a householder's life who performs his duty scrupulously without being attached to actions, in the least. The sages also declare, "Those who have renounced the world, enlighten others, and everyone knows them. But a householder saint, is rarely known."

As a lotus leaf in spite of being born in water and living constantly in touch with it, is not tainted by water, so does a Karmayogī, in spite of being born in a life-of-action (human life) and in spite of living, in this world of actions, while performing actions, does not get attached to these.* Detachment from actions, is not an easy task. Therefore, the Lord, in the eighteenth verse, has called him wise among men, while here He declares, that the wise call him a sage. It means, that such a Karmayogī, is the wisest among the wise.

त्यक्त्वा कर्मफलासङ्गं नित्यतृप्तो निराश्रयः ।
कर्मण्यभिप्रवृत्तोऽपि नैव किञ्चित्करोति सः ॥ २० ॥

tyaktvā karmaphalāsaṅgaṁ nityatṛpto nirāśrayaḥ
karmaṇyabhipravṛtto'pi naiva kiñcitkaroti saḥ

One having abandoned attachment to actions and their fruit, ever content, without any kind of dependence, he does nothing even though fully engaged in action. 20

Comment:—

'Tyaktvā karmaphalāsaṅgam'—If a man thinks, that he is the doer while performing action, regards the body and the senses etc., as his, considers the action as his and for him and expects its fruit, then, he becomes the cause of fruit of action. But an enlightened soul, totally renounces his affinity for the mundane materials and so he is not, in the least, attached to materials for action, to action and to the fruits of action. Thus, he does not become the cause of the fruit of action.

As, an army fighting under the guidance of a king, with material supplied by him gains victory over an enemy, but the credit for the victory goes to the king; similarly, a soul attached to the body, senses, mind and intellect etc., is held responsible, for the fruit of actions performed by these.

*** Even Renunciation of actions of a deluded person is conducive to action while even performance of actions of a wise man leads to actionlessness (Aṣṭāvakra Gītā 18/61).**

A great soul, having not the least attachment for actions, and material for actions, is not attached to the fruit of actions.

In fact, the self has no attachment for actions and their fruits, because It is sentient, imperishable and unaltered, while actions and their fruits are insentient, perishable and undergo modifications. But when It assumes Its affinity, by an error, for them, it is bound. If It renounces this assumed affinity, It will realize its detachmemt from actions, and their fruits.

'Nirāśryaḥ'—Even, a king or an emperor, has to depend on circumstances, time, objects and persons etc. But an enlightened soul, does not depend on these, because having realized the self or God, he remains satisfied in the self, whether he acquires anything or not.

'Nityatṛptaḥ'—The soul, being a fragment of God is real, and the real never ceases to be (Gītā 2/16), but when it assumes its affinity for the unreal, it feels a deficiency. In order to compensate for the shortage, it has a desire for worldly objects. It is satisfied by acquiring the objects but that satisfaction is temporary as the objects are perishable. How could the unreal, satisfy the real? Therefore, so long as, the soul assumes Its affinity for the perishable actions and objects, and depends on these, It does not realize, the satisfaction automatic, which is eternal. The same eternal satisfaction has been referred in the seventeenth verse of the third chapter, by the expression 'ātmatṛptaḥ' (satisfied with the self).

'Karmaṇyabhipravṛtto'pi naiva kiñcitkaroti saḥ'—The term, 'abhipravṛttaḥ' means, that all actions are scrupulously performed by emancipated soul, because he is not at all attached to actions and their fruits. All his actions, are performed for the welfare of the world.

He who is attached to the fruit of action, cannot perform actions, scrupulously, because a lot of his energy is wasted, by thinking of the fruit.

The term 'api' (even or though) means, that such an enlightened soul does not perform an action at all, though he is fully engaged, in action. It is because of his detachment, that all his actions change into inaction.

When he does nothing, how could he be bound by the fruit of actions? Therefore, the Lord, in the twelfth verse of the eighteenth chapter, declares that a Karmayogī, who has renounced the fruit of action, does not reap the fruit of action i.e., becomes free from the bondage of action.

Prakṛti (nature) is ever-active. Therefore, so long as, a man has affinity for the modes of nature (actions and objects), he gets attached to them, even without performing action. If he has no affinity (attachment) for the modes of nature, he does nothing, even though, he is ever-engaged in action, as all his actions are performed, for the welfare of the world.

Appendix—So long as a man has the sense of doership, during the performance of action or non-performance of action, he remains a doer. But when the sense of doership is wiped out, he does nothing at all or his action or inaction never comes under the category of action at all.

Link:—Having described the detachment of an enlightened soul, in the nineteenth and the twentieth verses, now the Lord, in the twenty-first verse, describes the detachment of a striver who does not perform duties enjoined by the scriptures, while, in the twenty-second verse, He describes the detachment of a striver, who performs his duties.

निराशीर्यतचित्तात्मा त्यक्तसर्वपरिग्रहः।
शारीरं केवलं कर्म कुर्वन्नाप्नोति किल्बिषम्॥ २१॥

nirāśīryatacittātmā tyaktasarvaparigrahaḥ
śārīraṁ kevalaṁ karma kurvannāpnoti kilbiṣam

Having no desires, with his mind and body fully subdued, giving up all attachments and possessions, even though performing action necessary for the maintenance of the body, a Karmayogī, incurs no sin. 21

Comment:—

'Yatacittātmā'—A man, cannot keep his body, senses, mind and the self, under control, because of hope or desire. When he has no hope or desire, his body, senses and mind etc., automatically remain under his control, and then no futile action is performed by him.

'Tyaktasarvaparigrahaḥ'— If a Karmayogī is a recluse, he renounces all worldly possessions. But, if he is a householder, he does not accumulate any worldly object, to derive pleasure out of it. He, by regarding it as the world's, uses it in rendering service to the world. It is inevitable for every striver not to hanker after, mundane pleasure.

[This is the only verse in the whole of Gītā, where there is description of renunciation, of all worldly possessions. In the tenth verse of the sixth chapter, there is an explanation of the renunciation of possessions, for a Yogī who practises meditation, while in the fifty-third verse of the eighteenth chapter, there is an account of the renunciation of possession, for a Yogī, who has attained the supreme state of knowledge. But here, in this verse, renunciation is superior to those renouncements, because only here, the adjective 'sarva' (all) has been used with 'parigrahaḥ' (possessions). The term, 'aniketaḥ' (homeless or having no fixed abode) has been used, for freedom from attachment to the abode, in the nineteenth verse of the twelfth chapter, for a Bhaktiyogī.]

'Nirāśīḥ'—A Karmayogī, has no hope, no desire and no lust. He does not hanker after worldly pleasure and prosperity. Even if, he is not able to renounce his hope or desire totally, he aims at their renunciation.

'Śārīraṁ kevalaṁ karma kurvan'—The actions expressed in

this term may be of two kinds— (i) actions which are undertaken by the body and, (ii) actions which are performed, for the maintenance of the body. The former, have been described, in the eleventh verse of the fifth chapter, when the Lord declares, "Men of action having abandoned attachment, perform actions only with the body, mind, intellect or even with the senses, for the purification of the self." But, this verse is pertaining to detachment of the striver, who does not even perform duties, enjoined by the scriptures. Therefore, here it is used in the latter sense i.e., actions (as eating, drinking, bathing, washing etc.,) which are necessary, for the bare maintenance of the body, are performed, by a man of action, who has abandoned attachment.

'Nāpnoti kilbiṣam'—He, who is attached to the performance or non-performance of action, in the least, incurs sin i.e., follows the cycle of birth and death. But, the man of action, being free from hope or desire, is not attached to the performance or non-performance of action, so he incurs no sin, all his actions change into inactions.

Such a Karmayogī (man of action), does not indulge in indolence and heedlessness. These two are, also enjoyments. Lying idly in a lonely place is an enjoyment and indulgence in useless and forbidden actions, is also an enjoyment. Through such indulgences, a man enjoys himself. Thus he incurs sins. But a Karmayogī, who is given to performing some action, does not indulge in indolence and heedlessness. His mind, senses and body, are under his control. Moreover, he is free from hope, desire and a sense of possession etc. So, forbidden actions cannot be performed by him, and thus he incurs no sin. Had he indulged in indolence and heedlessness in the least, it could not be said of him, that he incurs no sin.

Now a doubt arises, why it has been said that he incurs no sin, when forbidden actions cannot be performed by him. The clarification is, that all undertakings are enveloped by defects (sins). The Lord declares, "All undertakings are clouded by defects, as fire by smoke" (Gītā 18/48). The root of sins, is desire or a sense of mine or attachment. A Karmayogī (man of action), is free from desire, sense of 'mine' and attachment, or he has such an aim, so he has nothing to do, with the performance or non-performance of action. Therefore, he does not incur incidental sin, during the performance of his duty, nor does he incur sin, by the renunciation of his duty, enjoined by the scriptures.

A second doubt may arise here, that the Lord has directed even a wise man (who has attained perfection), to perform action for the welfare of the world (3/25-26). The Lord has also declared, "There is nothing in the three worlds, that should be done by Me, nor is there anything unattained, that should be attained, yet I engage Myself in action" (Gītā 3/22—24). Therefore, will a Karmayogī, who does not engage himself in action for the welfare of the world, not incur sin? The clarification is, that he will incur no sin, because he is free from desire, attachment etc., and a sense of mine. Though the Lord and wise men (enlightened souls), are totally free from desire and attachment etc., yet out of compassion (grace), they perform actions for the welfare of the world, even when it is not obligatory for them (Gītā 3/18). Such ascetic-Karmayogīs, as described in the verse, are also ideal for ascetic strivers of Karmayoga and are automatically, a source of inspiration for strivers and common folk.

The third doubt that arises, is that the Lord, in the thirteenth verse of the third chapter declared, "Those wicked people who prepare food for their own sake, verily eat sin", while here, He declares that he who performs action for the mere maintenance of body incurs no sin. Thus there seems to be a contradiction. The clarification is, that so long as there is desire for pleasure as well as attachment to actions, and materials, he incurs sins, whether he performs actions or does not perform these, but when he becomes free from desire and attachment, he incurs no sin.

Question:—Can this verse not be included in the verses

pertaining to the Discipline of Knowledge, as these reflect the marks of a man of knowledge?

Answer:—The first point is, that here the context is of Karmayoga. Secondly, a Jñānī (liberated soul), holds that he does nothing at all (Gītā 5/8) i.e., he sees inaction in action. So it cannot be said about him, that he incurs no sin while performing action, because he does not think he is a doer or he performs any action at all.

Though in the striver, who follows the path of action, discrimination is not clearly revealed, yet he has a determinate intellect, about three facts, that nothing is his, nothing is required for him, and nothing is to be done for him. Having resolved this, he remains detached, from actions in spite of performing these.

Generally, people believe that a Karmayogī leads the life of a householder, while a Jñānayogī follows the renounced order. But, in fact it is not so. A Jñānayogī (man of knowledge) is he, who can discriminate between self and body, whether he leads the life of a householder or of a renounced order. But, he who cannot discriminate self from the body, despite a determinate intellect about above-mentioned three facts, is only a Karmayogī, whether he is a householder or is of a renounced order.

यदृच्छालाभसन्तुष्टो द्वन्द्वातीतो विमत्सरः।
समः सिद्धावसिद्धौ च कृत्वापि न निबध्यते॥ २२॥

yadṛcchālābhasantuṣṭo dvandvātīto vimatsaraḥ
samaḥ siddhāvasiddhau ca kṛtvāpi na nibadhyate

Content with what comes to him without desire for fruit, free from antithetic influence and envy, even-minded in success and failure, even though performing action, he (Karmayogī) is not bound by these. 22

Comment:—

'Yadṛcchālābhasantuṣṭaḥ'—A Karmayogī, performs action

scrupulously without expecting any fruit. As he has no desire for fruit of action, he remains even-minded in success and failure, profit and loss, honour and dishonour and praise and blame etc. He remains equanimous, in all favourable and unfavourable circumstances, without feeling happy or sad. He has knowledge of profit and loss, and accordingly, he makes wise efforts also. But, in effect he feels neither happy nor sad. Even if evenness of mind is lost, a striver, should not lose heart, because the disturbance of mind is short-lived and disappears quickly.

The term 'lābha' denotes, profit as well as loss, agreeable as well as disagreeable, whatsoever is obtained.

'Vimatsaraḥ'—A Karmayogī, identifies himself with all beings. He realizes his self as the self, in all beings (Gītā 5/7). So he is not at all envious of any being. A Karmayogī, is very cautious lest he should be envious of any being, because all his actions are performed for the welfare of the world. If he is envious of anyone in the least, his undertakings cannot be for the welfare of the world.

Envy is a subtle evil. Even neighbouring businessmen, friends and members of a family, are seen getting envious of each other, because of each other's good fortune. Where, there are antagonistic feelings, this evil is found in abundance. Therefore, a striver, should be on his guard against this evil.

'Dvandvātītaḥ'—A Karmayogī, transcends the pairs of opposites, such as profit and loss, honour and dishonour, praise and blame, pleasure and pain, and desirable and undesirable circumstances. So, he has a balanced state of mind, free from attachment and aversion etc.

Similarly, there can be the influence of the opposites in beliefs, one may believe in the Lord, Who is endowed with form and attributes, while the other may believe in the Lord Who is formless and without attribute; one may believe in the dualistic principle, while the other in the non-dualistic principle.

Whether mind is absorbed in God or not, whether seclusion is procured or not, whether peace is attained or not, and, whether success is achieved or not, a striver, is free from all such pairs of opposites, like a balance which remains steady, when there is equal weight on either side. A Karmayogī, free from the pairs of opposites, is easily released from the bondage of the world (Gītā 5/3).

'Samaḥ siddhāvasiddhau ca'—He remains even-minded in accomplishment or non-accomplishment of the work and for getting or not getting its fruit in success and failure, pleasure and pain, without having attachment or aversion for them. The same evenness of mind by the expression has been pointed out here as well as in the forty-eighth verse of the second chapter.

When a striver realizes, the three facts, that nothing is his, nor is for him and nothing is to be done for him, he attains a state of total evenness of mind.

'Kṛtvāpi na nibadhyate'—When a Karmayogī is not bound, even while acting, there is no question of his being bound without acting. He remains free, from attachment in these two states.

As a Karmayogī who performs action merely for the maintenance of the body, is not bound, so is a Karmayogī, who performs actions, sanctioned by the scriptures, not bound.

In fact, it is neither performance nor non-performance of actions, which binds a man but it is attachment to these which binds him. Similarly, it is detachment, which liberates him from bondage. A Karmayogī, like an actor, plays his part according to his caste and order of life and being detached from them. He is not at all attached to the changing nature (Prakṛti), he remains established in the eternal self.Therefore, he automatically remains even-minded, and thus is not bound, by actions even while performing these.

If a serious thought is given, it becomes clear, that equanimity is natural. Everyone, knows that he remains the same in both favourable and the unfavourable circumstances. It means, that circumstances change, but he (the self) remains the same. However we commit an error, that we keep an eye on circumstances, but we do not watch the Self. Consequently, we feel happy or sad.

Link:—The Lord, in the first half of the ninth verse of the third chapter, by a negative inference, declared, "The mankind is bound by actions other than those performed for the sake of sacrifice." He describes the same fact, by a positive inference, in the next verse.

गतसङ्गस्य मुक्तस्य ज्ञानावस्थितचेतसः।
यज्ञायाचरतः कर्म समग्रं प्रविलीयते॥ २३॥

gatasaṅgasya muktasya jñānāvasthitacetasaḥ
yajñāyācarataḥ karma samagraṁ pravilīyate

All actions of a man, who is devoid of attachment, who is liberated, whose mind is established in knowledge of the self, who works for the sake of sacrifice (yajña) are destroyed. 23

Comment:—

[This verse, is an important one about the Discipline of Action, because only here, it is mentioned that all actions of a Karmayogī, are destroyed. Similarly, the thirty-sixth verse of the fourth chapter, is an important verse on the Discipline of Knowledge, while the sixty-sixth verse of the eighteenth chapter is an important verse, on the Discipline of Devotion.]

'Gatasaṅgasya'—Attachment, to actions, objects, incidents, circumstances and persons, leads to bondage i.e., the cause of birth of the soul in good and evil bodies (Gītā 13/21). When a man performs actions for the welfare of the world, without any selfish motive, he becomes free from attachment, for actions and objects.

In fact, a man (the self) is inherently detached,

(Bṛhadāraṇyaka 4/3/15). But in spite of being detached, he gets attached to the body, senses, mind, intellect, objects, circumstances, and men etc., by regarding these as his own, and is thus bound by desire for pleasure. So long as, he wants to satiate his desire, his attachment is enhanced. In fact, whatever is to happen, will happen and whatever is not to happen will not happen, whether one desires it or not. Therefore, he who has any desire, gets entangled in vain, and has to suffer pain.

A Karmayogī, considering the acquired things of the world, neither of his own nor for himself, utilizes these, in rendering service to the world. Thus the flow of things and actions, is towards the world and the self remains the same, as it is, non-attached.

He has no egoistic notion of rendering service to others because he thinks that he has discharged his debt by returning thing to the one to whom it belonged. If egoistic notion subsists, it binds a Karmayogī. It subsists only when he considers, the materials for service, as his own. When the subtle egoistic notion, is rooted, then only pure service remains. Moreover, he does not expect any reward, in the form of money, honour, praise, position and authority etc., because he does not lay claim to these. He wants, neither to be called a generous man, nor gets pleased if praised by calling him, generous, or derives pleasure out of his act of service. By doing selfless service, he gets placidity of mind. If that placidity is not enjoyed, he automatically realizes, axiomatic detachment.

'Muktasya'—A man (the soul), in spite of being different, from actions and objects, such as the body etc., assumes these as his own, because of desire, attachment and a sense of mine, and is thus bound. By following the Discipline of Action, when the assumed affinity is renounced, the Karmayogī becomes detached. This detachment leads him to liberation.

'Jñānāvasthitacetasaḥ'—He, who ever remains conscious of the self, has his mind ever established in its knowledge. When he becomes conscious of the self, he gets established in the self. In fact, he had already been established in the self, but he only now realizes the fact.

In fact, knowledge is gained of the world, rather than of the self, because the self is an embodiment of knowledge. The world, consists of actions and objects. The self, being sentient, is different from insentient actions and objects. The self is their illuminator. As soon as, a striver realizes this fact, his affinity for actions and objects, is renounced and he realizes, that he is, naturally, established in the detached self.

'Yajñāyācarataḥ karma samagraṁ pravilīyate'—One form of, 'Seeing inaction in action', is to work for the sake of sacrifice (yajña). Performance of actions for the welfare of others, without a selfish motive, is called 'Yajña', (sacrifice). He, who works for the sake of sacrifice, gets liberated, while he, who performs actions other than those, that are performed for the sake of sacrifice, is bound (Gītā 3/9).

Actions and objects, are the evolutes of nature (prakṛti). Both of them have a beginning and an end, i.e., they are perishable. They neither existed, before they were seen, nor will exist, when they have gone. It means, that in the middle, they merely seem to exist, but actually they do not exist, as it is a rule, that whatever does not exist, at the beginning and at the end, also does not exist in the middle (at present). But the self, the illuminator of objects and action, is sentient and remains stable. Though, It has no affinity for objects and actions, when It assumes its affinity, for them, it is bound. The method by which to be liberated from this bondage, is to work for the welfare of others, without having any selfish desire for fruit.

In the world, there are innumerable objects and undertakings, which one assumes as his own, by having attachment, desire and a sense of mine for these he gets bound when having renounced attachment, desire and a sense of mine, he renders, service with them regarding them as of others', all his actions (of past as well as present) are dissolved, and he realizes, his natural detachment.

An Important Fact

(1) An agent, an instrument and action, are the threefold basis, of action (Gītā 18/18). Out of the three, the real basis is the agent, because the instrument and the action, depend on the agent.

If we give a serious thought to the topic, we come to realize, that a desire to act, arises, only when we have a desire to acquire something, or the other. The desire to act, makes us an agent, or a doer. This sense of doership, binds a man. When a man, performs an action with the desire to acquire anything, his sense of doership, is strengthened. But, when a Karmayogī, without having any desire to acquire anything, works for the sake of sacrifice i.e., for the welfare of others, his doership, is utilized for the welfare of others and he realizes, that he is detached from actions and objects etc. His actions are not accumulated as in the absence of doership, all his actions are neutralized.

In the Discipline of Action, renunciation of a sense of mine, is important, while in the Discipline of Knowledge, renunciation of 'egoism', is important. If a striver, renounces one of these, the other is automatically renounced. In the Discipline of Action, first there is renunciation of a sense of mine and then renunciation of egoism, naturally follows; while in the Discipline of Knowledge, the order is reversed. In absence of 'I'ness and 'mineness', the doership and enjoyership, both melt away.

When, a man of action, has neither a sense of doership, nor has any desire, he has not to reap the fruit of action, in the same way as a criminal has not to suffer torture or punishment, if he dies. When a person, does not want to reap the fruit of his actions, all his actions are dissolved.

(2) In the ninth verse of this chapter, the Lord declared, "He who thus knows, in their true nature, My divine birth and action, comes to Me." The birth, can be divine only of the Lord, but actions of men, can also be divine. In the fourteenth verse of this chapter, the Lord declares, that his actions are divine, as he has no desire for the fruit of actions and thus, he is not bound by them i.e., his actions, change into inaction. In this way, if a striver, also performs actions, without expecting the fruit of actions, his actions also, change into inaction. Then, in the fifteenth verse, He declares, "Having known this, men who sought liberation, also performed actions." In the sixteenth verse, He resolves to teach the reality about action, while in the seventeenth verse, He declares that one should understand the true nature of action, of forbidden action and of inaction. In, the eighteenth verse, He declares, that he who see inaction in action and action in inaction, is wise among men.

Desire is the known root of actions. When desire is, enhanced, forbidden actions are performed, but when desire is renounced, actions are changed into inaction. The main purpose of the Lord, is to describe inaction, (from the sixteenth to the thirty-second verse). Therefore, He has described renunciation of desire, which is the root of actions and forbidden actions in each of the verses from the nineteenth to the twenty-third, along with inaction* and the topic has been concluded in the thirty-second verse.

---

* Examples of the renunciation of desires— 'Devoid of desires' (4/19); "Having abandoned attachment to the fruit of action" (4/20); "Having no hope or desire" (4/21); "Satisfied with what comes to him by chance" (4/22) and "Devoid of attachment" (4/23).

Examples of inaction—

"Actions have been burnt by the fire of knowledge" (4/19); " He does nothing thought engaged in action" (4/20); "While performing actions he incurs no sin" (4/21); "Though acting he is not bound" (4/22); " The whole action is dissolved" (4/23).

Appendix—One is 'Kriyā', one is 'Karma' and one is 'Karmayoga'. The body passes from babyhood to youth and from youth to old age—this is 'kriyā'. By this 'Kriyā' a man neither incurs sin nor virtue, it neither leads him to salvation nor to bondage. Similarly the flow of the river Ganges is mere a 'kriyā'. If a man gets drowned in its current or it may prove helpful in farming etc., the Ganges does not incur any sin or virtue. When a man by assuming affinity with 'kriyā' becomes a doer viz., he does 'kriyā' for himself, then this 'kriyā' bears fruit and it becomes 'Karma' (action). Karma leads to bondage—'yajñārthātkarmaṇo'nyatra loko'yaṁ karmabandhanaḥ' (Gītā 3/9). In order to be free from the bondage of actions, when a man does nothing for himself but works for the welfare of others in a disinterested way, it is 'Karmayoga'. By Karmayoga bondage for actions is destroyed—'yajñāyācarataḥ karma samagraṁ pravilīyate'. With the annihilation of bondage 'yoga' is attained viz., eternal union with God is realized.

This twenty-third verse is the main verse of Karmayoga. As the Lord by the expression 'jñānāgniḥ sarvakarmāṇi bhasmasāt kurute' (Gītā 4/37) has declared that the fire of knowledge reduces all actions to ashes and by the expression 'ahaṁ tvā sarvapāpebhyo mokṣayiṣyāmi mā śucaḥ' (18/66) He has declared He will liberate a devotee from all sins, similarly in this verse He has declared by the expression 'yajñāyācarataḥ karma samagraṁ pravilīyate' that all the actions including past ones of a karmayogī melt away.

Link:—In the preceding verse, the Lord declared, "All actions of a man, who works for the sake of sacrifice, are dissolved." The term 'sacrifice', in this context, stands for duty, according to a person's caste and order of life etc. Therefore, the Lord, in the next seven verses, explains several forms of sacrifice as duties, for the strivers, according to their inclination, faith and qualification.

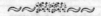

ब्रह्मार्पणं ब्रह्म हविर्ब्रह्माग्नौ ब्रह्मणा हुतम्।
ब्रह्मैव तेन गन्तव्यं ब्रह्मकर्मसमाधिना॥ २४॥

brahmārpaṇaṁ brahma havirbrahmāgnau brahmaṇā hutam
brahmaiva tena gantavyaṁ brahmakarmasamādhinā

For him, the ladle with which yajña offering is made is Brahmaṇa, the fire and the act of offering oblation, is also God. By God, as offeror of sacrifice, is the oblation poured into the fire of God. God shall be attained by him who is absorbed in God, in the act of such sacrifice (yajña). 24

Comment:—

[Oblation, is important in sacrifice. The oblation becomes one with fire, when it is poured into fire, it has no separate existence of its own. Similarly, when all the means of God-realization, have no existence apart from God, these become sacrifice.

To perceive, God in all sacrifices, is to see reality, as it is not a conception. Actually objects are not real, and to visualize these as real, is an error.

All, the sacrifices described, from the twenty-fourth verse to the thirtieth verse, are included in 'Karmayoga', because the Lord at the beginning of this context, declared, "I shall teach thee, what action is (the nature of action and inaction), knowing which, thou shalt be delivered from evil" (4/16). At the end, He declared, "Know all sacrifices as born of action, and thus knowing, thou shalt be liberated" (4/32). In the middle, also He declared, "To one who works for the sake of sacrifice, the whole action is dissolved" (4/23). The important factor, is that all actions of a person, who performs them for the sake of sacrifice, are changed into inaction. Therefore, in all these sacrifices, there is a description of, inaction in action.]

'Brahmārpaṇaṁ brahma haviḥ'—The ladle, with which an oblation is poured into the fire, has been called 'arpaṇam'—that is God.

Sesame seed, barley and ghee, which are poured as oblation into fire, are also God.

'Brahmāgnau brahmaṇā hutam'—He, who performs the sacrifice, is God (Gītā 13/2), the fire into which the oblation is poured, is God and the act of pouring oblation, is also God.

'Brahmakarmasamādhinā—Just as person while offering sacrifice, looks at the ladle, the sacrificial oblation, and fire etc., as Brahma, similarly in every action, he who regards the doer, the action, the instrument and matter as Brahma, for him all actions are Brahma and thus he is merged in Brahma.

'Brahmaiva tena gantavyam'—When he views everything, as no other than God, he attains Him.

Cultured people, recite this verse while having meals, so that this activity may be changed into a sacrifice (yajña). When a striver has his meal, he beholds God, in the following way:—

(i) The hand, with which the food is put into the mouth, is God. "With hands and feet everywhere, He exists" (Gītā 13/3).

(ii) The food is God. "I am the melted butter" (Gītā 9/16).

(iii) He who eats the food, is also God. "The soul is a fragment of Mine" (Gītā 15/7).

(iv) The fire, that abides in the stomach, and by which food is digested, is also God. "I am the fire, lodged in the body of all creatures" (Gītā 15/14).

(v) The action of offering food, to the fire, which abides in the stomach, is also God. "I am the offering" (Gītā 9/16).

(vi) The fruit of eating, the remnants, (residual food) of the sacrifice, is also God. "Those who eat the sacred food that remains, after a sacrifice, attain to the eternal Absolute" (4/31).

A Vital Fact

The world, which is an evolute of nature (prakṛti), is in fact, seen in the form of objects and actions. The world, in the form of objects and actions is ever-changing and ever undergoes modifications. But, due to attachment, we do not perceive the changing nature, of objects; we perceive these chiefly, as objects. All objects and activities are going to naught. Therefore, the world is practically, a naught. There is existence, only of the transcendental Absolute. In fact the world does not exist, but it seems to exist, in the light of the eternal Absolute. The non-existence of the world is explained below—

The world appears in three states—birth, life and death. But, actually there is no life. What seems life, is nothing but the process from birth to death.

A man (or an object), starts to die the day, he is born, though it is said that he is born, he lives and he dies. If a man, has to live alive say for fifty years and he is twenty years old, it means that he has to be alive only for thirty years i.e., he has died forty percent, and his life remains, only sixty percent. In fact, he is dying every moment the seen is changing into the unseen. But the world seems to exist, in the light of the Absolute Who is eternal. Lord Kṛṣṇa declares, "All is God" (Gītā 7/19) (Chāndogya. 3/14/1).

दैवमेवापरे यज्ञं योगिनः पर्युपासते।
ब्रह्माग्नावपरे यज्ञं यज्ञेनैवोपजुह्वति॥ २५॥

daivamevāpare yajñaṁ yoginaḥ paryupāsate
brahmāgnāvapare yajñaṁ yajñenaivopajuhvati

Some Yogīs offer sacrifice to God alone; while others offer the self as sacrifice by the sacrifice of discrimination in the fire of the Supreme. 25

Comment:—

'Daivamevāpare yajñaṁ yoginaḥ paryupāsate'—In the preceding verse, the Lord described, a striver who beholds God, in all objects and actions. Here, by using the term 'apare' He describes strivers, who perform sacrifice, but who are different from those mentioned, in the preceding verse.

Here the term 'Yoginaḥ', stands for those strivers, who perform actions, without expecting any reward.

Those who instead of regarding actions and objects as theirs and for them, regard these as the Lord's and for Him, perform sacrifice to God, as He is the Lord, even of the gods. Therefore, those persons who, without having the least attachment, a sense of mine and desire for objects and actions, hold that they are only of the Lord, perform sacrifice to Him.

'Brahmāgnāvapare yajñaṁ yajñenaivopajuhvati'—The term 'apare', has been used, to bring out the distinction between sacrifice mentioned in the first half of this verse, and the second half.

When, the soul identifies Itself with matter, It becomes an embodied soul. But when a person (the soul), by discrimination, having a total disinclination for matter, merges in God i.e., has not the least separate existence, apart from God, it is called sacrifice.

Appendix—The expression 'brahmāgnāvapare yajñaṁ yajñenaivopajuhvati' may also mean other Yogīs in order to serve Brahma—the embodied world perform duty sacrifice for the sacrifice in the form of welfare of others viz., they perform all actions for the welfare of others (Gītā 3/9, 4/23).

श्रोत्रादीनीन्द्रियाण्यन्ये संयमाग्निषु जुह्वति।
शब्दादीन्विषयानन्य इन्द्रियाग्निषु जुह्वति॥ २६॥

śrotrādīnīndriyāṇyanye saṁyamāgniṣu juhvati
śabdādīnviṣayānanya indriyāgniṣu juhvati

Some offer hearing and other senses, as sacrifice into the fire of restraint; others offer sound and other objects of senses into the fire of senses. 26

Comment:—

Śrotrādīnindriyāṇyanye saṁyamāgniṣu juhvati'—Here, the offer of senses, into the fires of restraint has been called, sacrifice. It means that some do not allow the senses—ear, eye, skin, tongue, and nose, to incline towards the sensual objects of sound, sight, touch, taste and smell. They constantly restrain their senses.

The senses, the mind, the intellect and the ego, are said to be under complete restraint, when these are totally free, from attachment (Gītā 2/58-59, 68).

'Śabdādīnviṣayānanya indriyāgniṣu juhvati'—Sound, sight, touch, taste and smell, are the five sensual objects. The discipline in which these objects of sense, are offered in the fire of sense, becomes a sacrifice. It means, that even when the objects of senses, come in contact with senses, the senses remain free from attraction and repulsion, or attachment and aversion (Gītā 2/64-65).

In both the sacrifices, mentioned in this verse, perfection or God-realization, is attained, when there is total absence of attachment. This process, of two kinds as sacrifice, has been described, in order to root out attachment.

In the first one, a striver controls his senses in solitude, through discrimination, chant and meditation etc. When there is full restraint, he becomes, free from attachment and then he remains equable, both in loneliness, as well as in practical life.

In the second case, a striver in his practical life, moves about among sense-objects with the mind, intellect and ego and the senses, free from attraction and repulsion i.e., attachment and aversion. When he becomes free from attachment, he remains the same, both in loneliness and practical life.

सर्वाणीन्द्रियकर्माणि प्राणकर्माणि चापरे।
आत्मसंयमयोगाग्नौ जुह्वति ज्ञानदीपिते ॥ २७ ॥

sarvāṇīndriyakarmāṇi prāṇakarmāṇi cāpare
ātmasaṁyamayogāgnau juhvati jñānadīpite

Some others again, offer sacrifice with the functions of the senses and those of the breath (vital energy), into the fire of Yoga of self restraint, kindled by knowledge. 27

Comment:—

'Sarvāṇīndriyakarmāṇi prāṇakarmāṇi cāpare'—In this verse, a trance (concentration of the mind on God or the self), has been called a form of sacrifice. It means, that in the state of trance, when the Yogī concentrates his mind on God, his senses (sense-organs and organs of action), cease to function, these become calm.

When a Yogī concentrates his mind on God, the function of the breath, is offered (sacrificed) i.e., the breath also ceases to function. In the state of trance, breath ceases to function, in two ways—the first, is by breath-control, in which breath is suspended. By practice, it can be suspended for hours and then for days, together. By this process of restraining breath, the duration of life is lengthened, in the same way, as the age of a frog is lengthened. When it rains, sand also flows with water. A frog is embedded by that sand. When the sand dries, the frog remains there and its breath ceases to function. But when it rains again next year, in the rainy season, it comes back to life.

In the second way, the mind is concentrated on God or the self, and when the mind is totally concentrated, breathing automatically stops.

'Jñānadīpite'—Both, the trance and sleep, have their affinity for the causal body. Therefore, both of these appear to be of the same state. Here, by the expression 'jñānadīpite (kindled by knowledge), the Lord explains, that there is a vast difference between the two. In the state of trance, the knowledge that God pervades everywhere, remains kindled, while during slumber all his inclinations merge in ignorance. During trance, breath ceases to function while during slumber, breath functions. In slumber, no trance is possible.

'Ātmasaṁyamayogāgnau juhvati'—The Yogīs, who concentrate their mind, sacrifice all the functions of senses and those of the breath, into the fire of the Yoga of self-restraint i.e., having suspended the function, of all the senses, breath, mind and intellect, they get fixed in trance. In that state, all senses and breath cease to function and the consciousness of God who is All Truth-Knowledge-Bliss, remains fully awakened.

द्रव्ययज्ञास्तपोयज्ञा योगयज्ञास्तथापरे।
स्वाध्यायज्ञानयज्ञाश्च यतयः संशितव्रताः ॥ २८ ॥

dravyayajñāstapoyajñā yogayajñāstathāpare
svādhyāyajñānayajñāśca yatayaḥ saṁśitavratāḥ

Others again, offer as sacrifice (yajña) their wealth or their austerities or their Yoga, while others with self restraint and rigid vows, offer study of the scriptures and knowledge, as sacrifice (yajña). 28

Comment:—

'Yatayaḥ saṁśitavratāḥ'—Non-violence, truth, non-stealing, celibacy and to refrain from hoarding—these five are yama, the five great vows. These five vows, have been very much eulogized, in the scriptures. The aim of these vows is, to enable a man to have disinclination for the world. The expression 'Saṁśitavratāḥ' (persons of rigid vows), has been used for the strivers, who fulfil these vows. Besides them, other strivers who perform the vows of the four other kinds of sacrifice, mentioned in the verse, are also persons of rigid vows. They have been called 'Yatayaḥ' (persons of self-restraint), because they having self-restraint, make efforts, in performing the sacrifice of their own choice and taste.

The term 'Yajñāḥ' (sacrifice), has not been used with the expression 'Saṁśitavratāḥ', as it has been used with the other four terms. 'Saṁśitavratāḥ' (person of rigid vows) has not been considered, a separate sacrifice.

'Dravyayajñāḥ'—The sacrifice of wealth, includes the construction of wells, tanks, temples and inns, as well as, offering of charity in the form of food, water, clothes, medicines and books etc. Those, who utilize their wealth and material possessions, for the welfare of others, without any selfish motive, by regarding these as of others only, offer their wealth, as sacrifice. To perform sacrifice, a man does not need to use anything more, than what he actually possesses. As a person, expects a child to perform, only the action which he is capable of performing, so does the omniscient Lord, and the world expect us to perform sacrifice, which we are capable of performing.

'Tapoyajñāḥ'—'Tapoyajñāḥ' (austerity as sacrifice), consists in facing difficult and unfavourable circumstances, happily. Observing fast and keeping mum, etc., are also austerities, as sacrifice. But, the best sacrifice, consists in the performance of one's duty happily, even in the most unfavourable circumstances,without the least deviation from it. Such austerity, proves fruitful quickly.

Rubbish may be harmful for health, but it works as a manure in farming. Similarly, unfavourable circumstances, work as austerity, if the striver faces these happily. A man feels happy in favourable circumstances and feels unhappy in unfavorable circumstances, because of his attachment to pleasure. If he is not attached to pleasure, he can understand, the merit of unfavourable circumstances.

'Yogayajñāstathāpare'—Here, the term 'Yoga', stands for equanimity. Evenness of mind in success and failure, praise and blame, honour and dishonour and pleasure and pain, is called 'Yogayajñā' (Yoga as sacrifice). In this sacrifice, a striver has neither attachment for favourable circumstances, nor aversion for unfavourable circumstances.

'Svādhyāyajñānayajñāḥ'—Study of the scriptures, such as the Gītā, the Rāmāyaṇa, the Bhāgavata, the Vedas and the Upaniṣad etc., as well as, the study of one's own self and inclinations—all constitute, the holy sacrifice of knowledge.

The Lord, while explaining the merit of the study of Gītā declares, "He who studies this sacred dialogue (the Gītā) of ours, by him, I would be worshipped through the sacrifice of knowledge" (Gītā 18/70). It means, that the study of Gītā is a sacrifice of knowledge. He, who is lost in reflection, of the gospel of the Gītā and makes efforts to understand it, performs the sacrifice of knowledge.

अपाने जुह्वति प्राणं प्राणेऽपानं तथापरे।
प्राणापानगती रुद्ध्वा प्राणायामपरायणाः ॥ २९ ॥
अपरे नियताहाराः प्राणान्प्राणेषु जुह्वति।
सर्वेऽप्येते यज्ञविदो यज्ञक्षपितकल्मषाः ॥ ३० ॥

apāne juhvati prāṇaṁ prāṇe'pānaṁ tathāpare
prāṇāpānagatī ruddhvā prāṇāyāmaparāyaṇāḥ
apare niyatāhārāḥ prāṇānprāṇeṣu juhvati
sarve'pyete yajñavido yajñakṣapitakalmaṣāḥ

Others offer as sacrifice (yajña), the outgoing breath in the incoming, and the others in reverses restraining the course of the outgoing and incoming breaths, solely absorbed in control of their breaths (prāṇāyāma). Others who regulate their diet, could offer the breath of life to the vital air (prāṇa). All these are knowers of yajña and by that have their sins destroyed. 29-30

Comment:—

'Apāne juhvati prāṇaṁ prāṇe'pānaṁ tathāpare prāṇāpānagatī ruddhvā prāṇāyāmaparāyaṇāḥ'*—Heart is the abode of outgoing

* In this verse is one subject, 'others' and one verb, 'sacrifice' therefore, here restraint of birth includes inhalation, retention and exhalation of breath.

breath, while the seat of incoming breath, is anus. The Yogīs, practise inhalation through the left nostril. That air having taken the life-air which abides in the heart with it, passing through the navel merges with the incoming breath. This is called 'Pūraka' (Inhalation). When the outgoing and the incoming breaths, are restrained, it is called 'Kumbhaka' (retention of breath). After that, the air from inside is exhaled through the right nostril. That air, having taken the outgoing and the incoming breaths, is exhaled. This is, sacrifice of the outgoing breath, in the incoming breath. It is called 'recaka' (exhalation). Inhalation is practised by uttering the name of the Lord four times, while retention, of breath is practised by uttering the same name, sixteen times, and exhalation, is practised by uttering the same name eight times.

Thus Yogīs, through the left nostril, practise inhalation, retention of breath and exhalation and then, through the right nostril practise inhalation, retention of breath and exhalation. Repetition of this process, is known as the sacrifice of restraint of the breath. When restraint of breath is practised, in order to attain God, without expecting any other reward, all sins perish.

'Apare niyatāhārāḥ prāṇānprāṇeṣu juhvati'—Only those strivers, who regulate their diet can offer as sacrifice their life-breaths (prāṇa) for life-breaths. He who eats too much or abstains too much from eating, cannot practise this restraint, of breath (Gītā 6/16-17).

The sacrifice of life-breaths (prāṇa) by life-breaths means, sacrifice of the incoming breath into the incoming breath and of the outgoing breath, into the outgoing breath, i.e., the acts of inhalation and exhalation, both are suspended. This is called 'Stambhavṛtti prāṇāyāma' (absolute restraint of the breath). Through this restraint of the breath, passions are naturally controlled and sins are destroyed. When this sacrifice is practised, with the aim of God-realization, it leads to the purification of the mind and then to God-realization.

'Sarve'pyete yajñavido yajñakṣapitakalmaṣāḥ'—The expression 'sarve'pyete' (all these), has been used for those strivers, who perform sacrifice (duties), as described from the twenty-fourth verse to the first half of the thirtieth verse. Performance of these sacrifices, destroys their sins, and leads them to god-realization.

In fact all sacrifices aim at the renunciation of affinity, for actions. Those, who know this fact, are the real knowers of sacrifice. When affinity for actions, is totally renounced, God is realized. Those who perform sacrifice, instead, for God-realization, for acquiring pleasure here as well as hereafter, do not know, the reality about sacrifice. It is desire for the perishable pleasures, which leads to bondage. The Lord declares, "Those who seek worldly enjoyment repeatedly go and return" (Gītā 9/21). Therefore, those who perform, even great sacrifices with worldly desires, have to follow the bondage, of birth and death.

An Important Fact

During sacrifice, oblation is offered into fire. The oblation has different shapes, It loses its identity and becomes one with the fire. Similarly, when all the means of God-realization, which have been described here as sacrifice, are offered to God, these lose their identity, and become one with God. If these retain their separate existence, it means, that they have not been offered, as sacrifice.

The Lord, started this topic of the reality of actions, (seeing inaction in action), from the sixteenth verse. The reality about actions is, that he who performs actions as sacrifice i.e., for the welfare of others, is not bound by them. As everything put into fire is burnt to ashes, so are actions, which are performed for the sake of sacrifice, dissolved entirely i.e., are reduced to nothing (Gītā 4/23).

Day to day actions, performed for the welfare of others, without any selfish motive, lead to God-realization. But, even virtuous actions, performed with a selfish motive (with the expectation of their fruits) cannot lead to God-realization, because it is a desire for the perishable, which binds a man. So long as, he assumes his affinity for the world, in the form of its materials and actions, he has attachment to acquire something and to do something. This attachment, is called a desire to acquire and an 'urge to act'.

In fact, the real desire (need) of a man is, to attain God whose fragment, he is. But, he wants to satisfy this need by acquiring worldly objects because of his inclination for the world and disinclination for God. How can, the perishable objects satisfy the imperishable fragment (the self) of the Lord? So long as, he has an inclination for the world, he has a desire to acquire something or the other. In order to, acquire it, he has to act. Thus, so long as, he has a desire to acquire and an urge to act viz., he has affinity with materials and actions, he has to follow, the cycle of birth and death. How to get liberated from this cycle? One can be liberated from, this cycle of birth and death, when one performs actions for the welfare of others, without having any desire. This is called sacrifice or an ideal for others, or actions for the welfare of others.

When actions, are performed for the welfare of others, the affinity for the world is renounced, and a man gets detached from these. If actions are performed for the sake of the Lord, a striver's affinity, for the world is renounced, he gets detached from actions, and he attains devotion to God which is an uncommon trait, of a striver.

Appendix—Performance of actions without any selfish motive, only for the welfare of others is called 'yajña' (sacrifice). By sacrifice all actions are transformed into inaction viz., they don't lead to bondage. There is mention of twelve kinds of sacrifice from the twenty-fourth verse to the thirtieth verse and they are as follows—

(i) Brahmayajña—Realizing the doer, the action, the instrument and object etc., in every action as Brahma.

(ii) Bhagavadarpaṇarūpa yajña—Assuming all actions and objects only God's and only for Him.

(iii) Abhinnatārūpa yajña—Having total disinclination for the unreal, merger in God viz., having no independent existence of one's own apart from God.

[Kartavya-karmarūpa yajña—performance of all actions for the welfare of others.]

(iv) Saṁyamarūpa yajña—In loneliness not to allow the senses to incline mentally towards the sensual objects.

(v) Viṣaya-havanarūpa yajña—In day to day life to keep the senses free from attachment and aversion even when the senses come in contact with sense-objects (Gītā 2/64-65).

(vi) Samādhirūpa yajña—By restraining all the functions of the senses and breath to get established in trance kindled by knowledge.

(vii) Dravya yajña—Utilization of all materials for the service of others in a selfless spirit.

(viii) Tapoyajña—Facing difficulties happily while discharging one's duty.

(ix) Yogayajña—To remain equanimous in success and failure, in favourable and unfavourable circumstances.

(x) Svādhyāyarūpa jñānayajña—Study of the sacred scriptures and chanting the Lord's holy names etc., for the good of others.

(xi) Prāṇāyāmarūpa yajña—Control of breaths by 'pūraka' (inhalation), 'Kumbhaka' (retention) and 'recaka' (exhalation).

(xii) Stambhavṛtti (fourth) prāṇāyāmarūpa yajña—By regulating the diet, suspension of the acts of inhalation and exhalation.

All these mean that all our actions should be performed

in the form of sacrifice and then our life will be successful. It means that we have to do nothing for ourselves. We have no affinity for actions and objects. We have relationship with God Who is devoid of actions and objects.

Link:—The Lord, from the twenty-fourth verse to the first half of the thirtieth verse, described twelve kinds of sacrifice, while in the second half of the thirtieth verse, He eulogized strivers who perform sacrifices. Now, He in the next verse, explains what is gained, through their performance and what is lost through their non-performance.

यज्ञशिष्टामृतभुजो यान्ति ब्रह्म सनातनम्।
नायं लोकोऽस्त्ययज्ञस्य कुतोऽन्यः कुरुसत्तम॥ ३१॥

yajñaśiṣṭāmṛtabhujo yānti brahma sanātanam
nāyaṁ loko'styayajñasya kuto'nyaḥ kurusattama

Those who partake sacred remnants after a sacrifice (yajña), attain to the eternal Absolute; even this world is not pleasant for him who performs no sacrifice; how then can he have happiness in any other world, O Best of the Kurus (Arjuna)? 31

Comment:—

'Yajñaśiṣṭāmṛtabhujo yānti brahma sanātanam'—Those, who realize equanimity, having performed sacrifice i.e., having performed duty without any selfish motive, are said to have taken the remnants of the sacrifice. Such people, are released from all sins, and attain to the eternal Absolute (Gītā 3/13).

A man (the self), is eternal. It is because of his attachment to the perishable, that he believes that he dies. When he, having utilized his so-called possessions, for the welfare of the world, gets detached from them, he realizes the fact, that he is eternal.

When action is performed as duty i.e., for the welfare of others without any selfish motive, it becomes a sacrifice (yajña).

Action performed, with a selfish motive leads to bondage. In a sacrifice all possessions offered to others; for his own-self, he performs only action, which is inevitable for the bare maintenance of body (Gītā 4/21). Such an action, is also included in sacrifice. This human body has been bestowed upon us, so that we may perform sacrifice. If we use it, in order to gain honour, praise, comforts and luxuries etc., it leads us to bondage. But, if with it, actions are performed only for the sake of sacrifice, it leads to liberation and one attains to the Eternal Absolute.

'Nāyaṁ loko'styayajñasya kuto'nyaḥ kurusattama'—In the eighth verse of the third chapter, the Lord declared, "Even the maintenance of the body would not be possible by inaction." Similarly, here He declares, "This world is not felicitous for him who performs no sacrifice, how then can he have happiness in, any other world?" He, who performs actions, with a selfish motive disturbs peace, causes disorder and strife, and does not attain salvation.

A selfish member, who does not perform his duty, is not liked even by members of one's family. Non-performance of duty, causes quarrels, strifes and annoyance in the family. He who wants to lead a peaceful life in the family, should perform his duty by rendering service to other members of the family. By doing so, he becomes a source of inspiration for others and thus unity and peace prevail, in the family and in the world, here as well as hereafter. On the other hand, he who does not perform his duty scrupulously, does not lead a happy life, here as well as hereafter.

Link:—In the sixteenth verse of this chapter the Lord promised to explain the truth about actions. Having described it in detail now He concludes the topic.

एवं बहुविधा यज्ञा वितता ब्रह्मणो मुखे।
कर्मजान्विद्धि तान्सर्वानेवं ज्ञात्वा विमोक्ष्यसे ॥ ३२ ॥

evaṁ bahuvidhā yajñā vitatā brahmaṇo mukhe
karmajānviddhi tānsarvānevaṁ jñātvā vimokṣyase

Thus, many forms of sacrifice have been described in detail in the Vedas. Know them all as born of action and having known these as such thou shalt be liberated from the bondage of action. 32

Comment:—

'Evaṁ bahuvidhā yajñā vitatā brahmaṇo mukhe'—Besides, the twelve forms of sacrifice, which have been described, from the twenty-fourth verse to the thirtieth verse, there are many other forms of sacrifice, which have been explained in detail, in the Vedas. The reason is, that according to their inclination, nature and faith, strivers, follow different spiritual disciplines.

In the Vedas, there is description of self-centred rituals which people perform, in order to reap their perishable fruit. So, they go to heaven and enjoy divine pleasures of the gods, there. But, having enjoyed them, when fruits of their virtuous deeds are exhausted, they return to the world of mortals, and these follow, the cycle of birth and death (Gītā 9/21). Self-centred rituals, are not enunciated here. But, here is an outline of selfless sacrifice, by performing which a striver attains to the Eternal Absolute (Gītā 4/31).

In the Vedas, there is not only the description of the means of enjoying heavenly pleasures, but there is also reference to spiritual practice, such as hearing of Vedic texts, cognition (reflection on what is heard), constant musing (constant and profound meditation), restraint of breath and trance (super conscious state), as the means of God-realization. These have been mentioned here, in this verse.

In the fourteenth and the fifteenth verses of the third chapter, the Lord declares, "Sacrifice is born of the Veda, and the omnipresent God, ever abides in sacrifice we should resort to such sacrifice, only for God-realization."

'Karmajānviddhi tānsarvān'—The expression, 'tānsarvān' (the all) has been used, for all the twelve sacrifices, described from the twenty-fourth to the thirtieth verse here, as well as, different forms of sacrifice described in the Vedas.

The expression 'Karmajānviddhi' (born of action) means, that all forms of sacrifice are born of actions. Activities undertaken with the body, words uttered with the mouth and thoughts of the mind, are all included, in actions. The Lord declares, "Whatever action a man performs, that is undertaken by the body, speech or mind" (Gītā 18/15).

Arjuna, wants to attain salvation, but he wants to renounce his duty of fighting, by regarding it, as a sin. Therefore, the Lord by using the expression 'Karmajānviddhi', explains to him, that whatever spiritual practice he will do by renouncing war, will also be, the performance of action. The Lord declares, that it is not action, but total renunciation of affinity for actions, which leads to salvation. Therefore, he should perform his duty of fighting, remaining detached from actions, in order to attain salvation, because it is not actions but it is attachment to them, which binds him (Gītā 6/4). It is also easy for him to perform the duty of fighting, because it is his natural or innate duty (specific duty).

'Evaṁ jñātvā vimokṣyase'—The Lord, in the fourteenth verse of this chapter, declared, "I have no desire for the fruit of actions. So actions do not bind me. He who knows Me thus, is not bound by actions." It means, that he who has learnt the art of remaining detached from actions, while performing these and translates it into practice, gets liberated from the bondage of actions. The same fact, has been pointed out by the Lord, in the fifteenth verse, when He declares, "Having known thus, the actions were performed by those ancient men, who sought liberation." In the sixteenth verse, He promised to explain the true nature of action and inaction, by knowing which, he would be liberated from the cycle of birth and death. In the present verse, He concludes the topic, by declaring that, having known thus, he will be liberated. It means, that when a person performs his duty, only for the welfare of the world without expecting any fruit, he is liberated from the bondage of actions.

In the world, innumerable actions are performed, but a man is bound only by those with which he establishes his affinity. By having this affinity, he gets pleased or displeased, and thus he is bound by those actions. But when he renounces his affinity, for the body and actions, he is liberated, from the bondage of actions.

Link:—Having heard the description of sacrifice, a striver has a curiosity to know which one of the sacrifices is superior to the others. The Lord, answers the question, in the next verse.

श्रेयान्द्रव्यमयाद्यज्ञाज्ज्ञानयज्ञः परन्तप।
सर्वं कर्माखिलं पार्थ ज्ञाने परिसमाप्यते॥ ३३॥

śreyāndravyamayādyajñājjñānayajñaḥ parantapa
sarvaṁ karmākhilaṁ pārtha jñāne parisamāpyate

Knowledge, as a sacrifice (yajña) is superior to any material sacrifice, O harasser of the foes (Arjuna). All actions and objects in their entirety, culminate in knowledge (jñāna). 33

Comment:—

'Śreyāndravyamayādyajñājjñānayajñaḥ parantapa'— Sacrifices, which require material objects and actions, are called 'Dravyamaya'. The suffix 'Maya' with the term 'Dravya', denotes large quantity. As with the preponderance of earth the earthenpot is called मृन्मय so with the preponderance of material the sacrifice is called material sacrifice. Knowledge as a sacrifice, is superior to any material sacrifice, because in knowledge-sacrifice, there is no need for material objects and actions.

The Lord, declares that all sacrifices are born of

action (4/32). But here He declares, that all actions culminate in knowledge i.e., knowledge as a sacrifice, is not born of actions but is born of discrimination. Therefore, knowledge, as a sacrifice, mentioned here, does not stand for knowledge, as sacrifice (described in 4/28). It stands for the process of acquiring knowledge from teachers, who are well-versed in the scriptures, as will be described in the thirty-fourth verse. Material sacrifice, described here, stands for the twelve forms of sacrifice already described. Having performed material sacrifice, the knowledge-sacrifice, is offered. If we consider minutely, we come to know that knowledge-sacrifice is also born of actions, but in knowledge-sacrifice, there is predominance of discrimination.

'Sarvaṁ karmākhilaṁ pārtha jñāne parisamāpyate'—The terms 'sarvam' and 'akhilam', both are synonyms. Therefore, the expression 'Sarvaṁ karma' should mean, all actions, while the word 'akhilam' would stand for, all material objects.

So long as, a man performs actions for himself, he has affinity for them, and consequently his mind remains impure. But, when he does not perform them for himself, his mind is purified.

The mind is tainted by three kinds of defects—sins, volatility of mind, and ignorance. When a striver performs actions, for the welfare of others without any selfish motive, his first two defects i.e., sins and volatility of mind, come to an end. In order to get rid of the third defect, having renounced actions, he goes to his preceptor, so that he may impart knowledge, to him. At that time, he does not aim at actions and material objects, but his aim is God-realization. This is known, as culmination of all actions and material objects, in knowledge i.e., God-realization through the attainment of true knowledge.

A Common Method to Attain Knowledge

In the scriptures, there are eight inward spiritual means to attain knowledge. These are —(1) Discrimination. (2) Dispassion.

(3) Six traits (Quietism, self-control, piety, indifference, endurance and composure). (4) Desire to attain salvation. (5) Listening to Vedantic texts. (6) Cognition. (7) Constant and deep meditation. (8) Self-realization.

Discrimination (viveka), consists in distinguishing, the real from the unreal. Renunciation of the unreal or having a disinclination for the world is called dispassion (vairāgya). Deviation of the mind from the sense object is quietism (śama). Control over the senses is 'dama'. Reverence for God and the scriptures is called 'piety' (Śraddhā). Total resignation from the world, is 'Uparati'. Forbearance in the pairs of opposites such as heat and cold, is endurance (Titikṣā). Freedom from doubt is composure (Samādhāna). The desire for salvation, is called 'Mumukṣutā.

When desire for salvation, is aroused, a striver having renounced material objects and actions, goes to a learned God-realized preceptor. He hears the Vedantic texts, which remove his doubts, which is known as hearing (śravaṇa). Then, he thinks of the reality, about God which is known cognition (Manana). If he holds that the world is real and God does not exist— this is an opposite conception. Removal of this contrary conception, is called constant and profound meditation (Nididhyāsana). When, having renounced affinity for all material objects, one gets established in the self, it is called self-realization (tattvaṁ padārtha saṁśodhana).*

In fact, all these spiritual disciplines are practised, in order to renounce the affinity for the unreal. That which is renounced, is not for one's own self, but the result of renunciation (God-realization), is for one's own self.

Appendix—In 'Dravyamaya yajña' (material sacrifice), there is predominance of material objects and actions; therefore

* Those who hanker after worldly pleasures and prosperity hear the Vedantic texts, think over the sense-objects, have a constant and profound meditation on riches and attain pains and sorrows.

it is 'Karaṇa sāpekṣa' (dependent on sense & other organs). In Jñānayajña (Knowledge-sacrifice) there is predominance of discrimination. Therefore it is 'Karaṇa nirapekṣa (independent of sense and other organs). Therefore knowledge as sacrifice is superior to material sacrifice. In Jñānayajña, affinity for all actions and objects is renounced viz., after God-realization nothing remains to be done, to be known and to be attained because no other existence remains except God.

Link:—Arjuna wants to attain Self-realization. Therefore, the Lord, having described different methods as sacrifice for Self-realization, now explains, how to attain Self-realization, through the knowledge as sacrifice.

तद्विद्धि प्रणिपातेन परिप्रश्नेन सेवया।
उपदेक्ष्यन्ति ते ज्ञानं ज्ञानिनस्तत्त्वदर्शिनः॥ ३४॥

tadviddhi praṇipātena paripraśnena sevayā
upadekṣyanti te jñānaṁ jñāninastattvadarśinaḥ

Learn that by your obeisance humble reverence, by questioning and by your service; the wise who have realized the truth, will instruct thee, in (that) knowledge (jñāna). 34

Comment:—

'Tadviddhi'—Arjuna, in the beginning declared, "I don't foresee any good by slaying my own people, in the fight" (Gītā 1/31) and "Only sin will accrue to us, if we kill these malignants" (Gītā 1/36). He also declared, "It is better to live in this world, even by begging, than to slay these honoured teachers" (Gītā 2/5). Thus, according to Arjuna, it is better to renounce fighting, which is his duty, rather than to fight. But, according to Lord Kṛṣṇa, it is not necessary to renounce actions in order to gain knowledge (wisdom) (Gītā 3/20; 4/15). Therefore, it seems that the Lord, warns Arjuna that if he, because of his lack of faith in Him, does not believe in what He preaches, he should go to a wise preceptor, who has realized the truth and he would impart him the knowledge of self-realization, through the traditional practice of knowledge.*

The Lord further, in the thirty-eighth verse, declares, "Through the constant practice of the Discipline of Action, a striver without any other spiritual practice, attains the knowledge of the self. He needs no help from others.

'Praṇipātena'—He should go to a teacher, with profound humility and perfect devotion, and through prostration surrender himself, his body and possessions etc., to him. He should be very submissive and very cautious, that in no way disrespect is meted out to a preceptor. He should keep his inquisitiveness always, awake.

'Sevayā'—He should render service to his preceptor, with his body and objects and try to please him, by carrying out his orders and acting, according to his wish.

A striver, renders the greatest service to the saints (great souls) by translating their principles into practice, because their principles are more dear to them, than even their bodies. They remain prepared to sacrifice their life, in order to protect their principles.

'Pariprasnena'—A striver, should ask questions of his preceptor, with inquisitiveness, simplicity and humility, in order to know the reality about God, rather than to display his own learning or to put his preceptor on test. He should put such

* First of all having performed his duty according to his caste and order of life scrupulously, a man having purified his mind should renounce the performance of actions. After that having possessed the traits such as quietism and self-control etc., he should go to the God-realized preceptor in order to attain the knowledge of Self-realization.

In order to gain that knowledge the inquisitive striver, having taken the fuel used in a sacrifice, with profound humility, should go to the God-realized preceptor who is well-versed in the scriptures.

questions, "Who am I?" What is the world? What is the cause of bondage? What is salvation? How can I realize God? What are the obstacles to my spiritual practice? How to do away, with these obstacles? Why am I unable to understand this topic of God-realization?" Thus, he should satisfy his curiosity and gain knowledge from his preceptor.

'Jñāninastattvadarśinaḥ'—The expression 'Tattvadarśinaḥ', stands for the seers of truth, who have realized God, while the term, 'Jñāninaḥ' stands for the wise, who are well-versed in the Vedas and the scriptures. A striver, should go to such a wise seer, and acquire knowledge from him.

In regard to, the purification of mind, there are three kinds of strivers, who are qualified to gain that knowledge—the superior, the mediocre and the inferior. The superior ones, are those who attain knowledge of the self, merely by listening to Vedantic texts.* The mediocre ones, attain this knowledge by hearing, cognition, constant and deep meditation. The inferior ones, have several doubts. In order to, clarify those doubts it is necessary, to possess knowledge of the Vedas and the scriptures. Without possessing knowledge, even such a preceptor who has realized the truth, cannot clarify the doubts of his disciples. Similarly, even a learned preceptor, who has not realized the truth, cannot lead his disciple, to Self-realization. Therefore, a preceptor should be, one who is wise and who has realized, the truth.

'Upadekṣyanti te jñānam'—By obeisance, by service and by asking questions with profound humility, a striver will be able to gain knowledge from the preceptor, as the latter is specially inspired, to impart true knowledge in view of the disciple's profound humility and perfect devotion. It does not mean, that a high-souled man, expects these, but without humility and devotion, the striver will not be able to gain that knowledge.

---

* The superior ones are those who have a burning desire to realize the Truth at once.

Here, the term 'Jñānam' stands for Truth-realization, or Self-realization. In fact a striver, does not gain knowledge about the self, but he gains it about the world. When a striver, comes to know the truth about the unreal world, his affinity for the world is renounced and he realizes the self, which is self-evident.

The term 'Upadekṣyanti' (instruct) means, that the great souls instruct a striver, but it is not necessary that he should attain self-realization. The reason is, that faith is a trait of the heart. A man may prostrate, question and serve, hypocritically. Further, in the thirty-ninth verse, He declares, "The man who has faith, gains knowledge (wisdom)'. Therefore, here it is mentioned, that the wise will instruct him, in that knowledge, while in the thirty-ninth verse, it is mentioned that a man, who has faith, gains knowledge.

Link:—Having explained how to attain Self-realization through knowledge, as sacrifice the Lord, in the next three (thirty-fifth, thirty-sixth and thirty-seventh) verses, explains the real merit or glory of Self-realization.

यज्ज्ञात्वा न पुनर्मोहमेवं यास्यसि पाण्डव।
येन भूतान्यशेषेण द्रक्ष्यस्यात्मन्यथो मयि॥ ३५॥

yajjñātvā na punarmohamevaṁ yāsyasi pāṇḍava
yena bhūtānyaśeṣeṇa drakṣyasyātmanyatho mayi

Having known it, thou shalt not, O Arjuna, again get beguiled like this; and by that knowledge thou shalt see all beings, without exception in yourself and then in Me. 35

Comment:—

'Yajjñātvā na punarmohamevaṁ yāsyasi pāṇḍava'—The Lord, in the preceding verse, said, 'The wise will instruct thee in (that) knowledge." But, merely by listening, a man does not realize, the self. The Lord declares, "Even after hearing, no one understands, the self" (Gītā 2/29) because, the self, is beyond the access of mind and speech etc. The self, can be realized by the self, when a striver attaches importance, to discrimination. When he attaches importance, to discrimination, ignorance totally perishes and discrimination changes, into self-realization. And affinity is totally renounced, for the insentient. Then one never gets deluded.

In the first chapter of the Gītā, Arjuna gets deluded, when he believes that it his kinsmen are killed in the battle, no one will remain alive to offer them water and rice offering. So, they would go to hell. Moreover, it would be difficult for living women and children, to earn their living, in order to maintain their bodies. Having realized the self, a striver does not get deluded like this, because his affinity for the world, is totally renounced.

'Yena bhūtānyaśeṣeṇa drakṣyasyātmani'— When he realizes the self, he sees all beings (infinite universes), in the self. As a person, having awaken from sleep sees the entire creation of his dream, in him, so does a striver, having realized the self, see all beings, in the self. The same fact, has been pointed out by the Lord, in the twenty-ninth verse of the sixth chapter, when He declares, "A Yogī sees all beings as assumed in the self."

'Atho mayi'—A striver, having gained knowledge of the self, by hearing, cognition constant and deep meditation etc., or from the preceptor, sees all beings in the self—this is the realization of 'Tvam' (self-realization). Then he sees all beings and the self in God—this is realization of 'Tat' (God-realization). Thus, he realizes the identity of the self with God, and, then nothing remains for him, except God. The trio, of the seer, the sight, and the seen, gets extinct. When this trio gets lost, there remains, no perceiver. Therefore, the expression, 'he perceives', refers to the feeling prevailing in the inner sense of that perfect soul.

The sea and its waves, may seem different but both of these

are, one and the same—both of these are nothing but water. The sea and the waves, are limited while the element, water, is unlimited. Therefore, he who sees water in both the sea and the waves, sees reality. As are the sea and its waves, so are the world and the body. As waves appear and disappear in the sea, so are bodies born and these perish, in the world. But, both of these have no independent existence of their own, only God has independent existence. In God, there is, neither world nor body. These seem to exist because of the existence of God. Both the body and the world because of their affinity for nature, are limited, while God is limitless. He who, instead of seeing the world and bodies, perceives the Supreme Lord existing equally in all beings, notices reality (Gītā 13/27).

Appendix—Self-realization or destruction of ignorance takes place only once and forever. It means that there is no repetition of Self-realization. The self once realized is realized forever. The reason is that when ignorance has no independent existence, then how will ignorance prevail? We are freed from ignorance because we are ever free from it and the self is realized because it is ever realized.

The self is existence and knowledge itself. By disregarding Knowledge itself we have accepted the unreal and by accepting the unreal, indiscrimination overwhelms. It means that turning away from knowledge itself we accept the existence of the unreal and by accepting the existence of the unreal, discrimination is neglected. In fact knowledge itself has not been disrespected, but its disregard has been from time immemorial. If we assume that we have disrespected knowledge, it shows that first we had knowledge. Therefore if we respect it now, again it may be neglected. But the knowledge is attained only once and forever.

After self-realization one is never deluded because in fact delusion has no existence. Only the non-existent perishes and only the ever existent is attained.

The universe is within the sphere of the embodied self and the embodied self is within the sphere of the Supreme Soul, therefore a striver sees the universe in himself 'drakṣyasyātmani' and then he sees the self in God—'atho mayi'. In 'drakṣyasyātmani' there is Self-realization (Jñāna viz., knowledge) and in 'atho mayi' there is God-realization (Vijñāna). In Self-realization there is bliss of the self while in God-realization there is supreme bliss. By 'laukika niṣṭhā' (Karmayoga and Jñānayoga) the self is realized and by 'alaukika niṣṭhā' (Bhaktiyoga) God is realized.

"All is God"—Thus the knowledge of God in its entirety is God-realization. In Self-realization (salvation) there remains an iota of subtle ego because of which there is difference of opinion among philosophers and in their philosophical thoughts. If there is no iota of subtle ego, then how can there be difference in philosophical opinions? But by God-realization even an iota (trace) of subtle ego does not remain and all the philosophical differences come to an end. It means that as long as there is 'ātmani', there are philosophical differences. But when 'Vāsudevaḥ sarvam' (all is God) is realized, all differences come to an end, 'atho mayi' expresses this God-realization. In such realization no existence apart from God is intuited.

अपि चेदसि पापेभ्यः सर्वेभ्यः पापकृत्तमः ।
सर्वं ज्ञानप्लवेनैव वृजिनं सन्तरिष्यसि ॥ ३६ ॥

api cedasi pāpebhyaḥ sarvebhyaḥ pāpakṛttamaḥ
sarvaṁ jñānaplavenaiva vṛjinaṁ santariṣyasi

Even if you are the most sinful of all sinners, you shall undoubtedly, cross all sins by the boat of knowledge (wisdom), alone. 36

Comment:—

'Api cedasi pāpebhyaḥ sarvebhyaḥ pāpakṛttamaḥ'—There

are, three categories of sinful persons—(1) The sinful. (2) The more sinful. (3) The most sinful. The Lord uses the superlative degree, to emphasize the fact, that even the most sinful of all sinners can cross the ocean of sin, by the boat of knowledge, of the self.

The Lord assures strivers that, not only the strivers who are engaged in spiritual practice, having renounced sins, even those, who have committed innumerable sins, need not lose heart, as far as attainment of salvation (God-realization) is concerned. Even the most sinful person, can attain salvation in this life, even immediately if he resolves, never to commit sin, but only to attain salvation or self-realization. The sins, of such a person of firm resolve, perish in no time.

As darkness of hundreds of years disappears, as soon as a lamp is lit, it does not take time, so do sins disappear, as soon as knowledge of the self is gained.

The Lord uses the term 'Cet' (if) to clarify the point, that generally sinners are not engaged in spiritual practice, but it does not mean that they cannot be engaged in it. If by coming into contact, with a great soul or by being influenced by an incident or circumstance or environment etc., they resolve, that they have to gain knowledge of the self, or God, they cross the ocean of sins, by the boat of knowledge, of the self.

The Lord, in the thirtieth and the thirty-first verses of the ninth chapter, declares, "Even if, a man of most vile conduct worships Me with exclusive devotion, he must be regarded as righteous, for he has rightly resolved and he attains to eternal peace very quickly."

'Sarvaṁ jñānaplavenaiva vṛjinaṁ saṁtariṣyasi'—All the sins, are incurred when a man assumes his affinity for nature and its evolute, the body and the world. When he gains knowledge of all the self, his affinity for them is totally renounced, and he gets rid of sins.

When he gains knowledge of the self, it means that he acquired the boat of knowledge. Even the most sinful of all sinners crosses the ocean of sins, by the boat of knowledge of the self. This boat, is such as can neither be broken nor can a hole be made into it, nor be sunk. Through it, one can cross the ocean of sins.

This boat of knowledge of the self, can be gained through knowledge-sacrifice (4/33). Discrimination, occupies an important place, from the very beginning in the knowledge-sacrifice and attains perfection in the knowledge of the self. When this perfection is attained, sins perish totally.

Appendix—Here the Lord by the expression 'pāpebhyaḥ sarvebhyaḥ pāpakṛttamaḥ' has mentioned the extreme limit of a sinner. Though the term 'pāpebhyaḥ' being used in plural number denotes all sinners, yet the Lord has used the term 'sarvebhyaḥ' with it. The term 'sarvebhyaḥ' also stands for 'all'. Even by using these two terms the Lord has used the term 'pāpakṛttamaḥ' in the superlative degree which stands for the most sinful of all sinners. The term 'pāpakṛt' is in the positive degree, then 'pāpakṛttara' is in the comparative degree and 'pāpakṛttama' is in the superlative degree. It means that even the most sinful of all sinners can gain knowledge (wisdom). The reason is that the number of sins may be large but they are unreal, while knowledge (wisdom) is real. How can the unreal face the real? Sin is impure while knowledge is the purest among the pure (Gītā 4/38). How can an impure thing suppress the pure thing? Therefore sins have no power to suppress knowledge. The main obstacle to the attainment of wisdom is attachment to the perishable pleaṣure (Gītā 3/37—41). It is because of attachment to pleasure that a man has no relish for spirituality and without the taste for spirituality, it seems very difficult to gain knowledge.

यथैधांसि समिद्धोऽग्निर्भस्मसात्कुरुतेऽर्जुन।
ज्ञानाग्निः सर्वकर्माणि भस्मसात्कुरुते तथा ॥ ३७ ॥

yathaidhāṁsi samiddho'gnirbhasmasātkurute'rjuna
jñānāgniḥ sarvakarmāṇi bhasmasātkurute tathā

As blazing fires burn fuel to ashes, O Arjuna, so, does the fire of knowledge, reduce all actions to ashes. 37

Comment:—

'Yathaidhāṁsi samiddho'gnirbhasmasātkurute'rjuna'— In the preceding verse, the Lord declared, "You can cross the ocean of sins, by the boat of the knowledge of the self." Now, the question arises, what will happen to the ocean of sins which still exists. The Lord clarifies the point, by giving another illustration. He declares, that the blazing fire reduces fuel to ashes, so does the fire of knowledge, reduce all actions (sins) to ashes, i.e., all sins perish.

'Jñānāgniḥ sarvakarmāṇi bhasmasātkurute tathā'— As blazing fire reduces fuel to ashes, so does the fire of knowledge, reduce the three kinds of actions (i.e.,)—prārabdha (in the form of fate), śañcita (accumulated actions) and Kriyamāṇa (the present actions), to ashes. It means, that when a man gains knowledge of the self, his affinity for the actions or the world is totally renounced. Consequently, the world loses its independent existence and there remains, only God.

In fact, all actions are performed by the modes of nature (Gītā 13/29). But a man is bound by these, when he thinks that he is a doer. An actions, such as circulation of blood, growth of the body, breathing and digestion etc., are performed by the modes of nature, so are eating, drinking, walking, sitting, seeing and speaking etc., undertaken. But when one holds, that he is the doer of those actions, these bind him. A sense of doership, changes activities into action, otherwise they are mere activities.

By knowledge of the self, the stock of accumulated actions,

is totally destroyed, because, all accumulated actions depend on ignorance. All present actions are destroyed i.e., change into inaction, because one has no sense of doership as they do not bear any fruit. As far as Prārabdha actions (Fate) are concerned, these produce favourable and unfavourable circumstances, but a man of knowledge, is not in the least affected by them. He remains equanimous, without feeling sad or happy. Thus, when he has no affinity for actions, in the least, all his actions are reduced to ashes i.e., and are changed into inaction.

Link:—The Lord, in the first half of the next verse, reveals the glory of knowledge, while in the second half, He glorifies Karmayoga (the Discipline of Action).

न हि ज्ञानेन सदृशं पवित्रमिह विद्यते।
तत्स्वयं योगसंसिद्धः कालेनात्मनि विन्दति॥ ३८॥

na hi jñānena sadṛśaṁ pavitramiha vidyate
tatsvayaṁ yogasaṁsiddhaḥ kālenātmani vindati

Verily, nothing purifies in this world, like knowledge (jñāna). He who has been perfected in Yoga fully finds it automatically and positively in the self. 38

Comment:—

'Na hi jñānena sadṛśaṁ pavitramiha vidyate'— Here the term, 'Iha' stands for the human world, because only human beings, are qualified to gain purity. Such opportunities are not available, in other species. All rights, in other species are acquired through a human body only.

The belief in the independent existence of the world, and the desire to derive pleasure out of it, give birth to all sins (Gītā 3/37). By the knowledge of the self, when the world ceases to have its independent existence, all sins are totally destroyed and a man becomes completely pure. Therefore, in the world, there is no other means as capable of sanctifying as knowledge.

The means, such as performance of sacrifice, charity, penance, adoration, vows, fasts, chanting the Lord's name, meditation, breath-restraint, bath in sacred rivers, such as the Ganges, the Yamunā and the Godāvarī, destroy sins of a man and purify him. But none of these is as purifying as is knowledge of the self, because all of them are means, while knowledge, is the end.

God, is the purest among the pure (Viṣṇusahasra. 10). The knowledge of self, being conducive to the realization of God, Who is the purest (most sacred), is very pure.

'Yogasaṁsiddhaḥ'—'Yogasaṁsiddhaḥ' (perfected in Yoga) stands, for the great soul who has attained perfection, in Karmayoga. Such a great soul, in the fourth verse of the sixth chapter, has been called 'Yogārūḍha' (one who is enthroned or established in Yoga). This state is, the last stage of Karmayoga. When a striver attains this state, he realizes the self and his affinity for the world, is totally renounced.

In Karmayoga (the Discipline of Action), all actions are performed for the welfare of the world without any selfish motive and without a sense of doership. By doing so, a striver's affinity for the body and the world, which are evolutes of nature, is totally renounced. It means, that in that case, the world has no independent existence, only actions, are performed. This is known as perfection in Yoga.

When a man is attached to action, and its fruit, he does not realize 'Yoga' i.e., union with God. In fact, a man has no affinity for actions and material objects, because he (the self) is eternal, while these are transitory (perishable). What can the eternal (Imperishable) self, gain from perishable actions? The self can gain nothing by actions—this is called 'Karmavijñāna' (science of action). Having realized this science of action, a man has no desire to reap the fruit of actions, in the form of pleasure etc., and then he realizes his natural and eternal, union with God, which is called 'Yogavijñāna' (Science of Yoga). This is called perfection in Yoga.

'Tatsvayaṁ kālenātmani vindati'—The knowledge of the self, which reduces all actions to ashes, and like which, there is no purifier in this world, is found in the self immediately, when a Karmayogī becomes, perfect in Yoga.

In the thirty-fourth verse, the Lord said, that a striver should go to a wise preceptor, who would instruct him in (that) knowledge. But by doing so, it is not necessary that he would gain knowledge, of the self. But here, He declares that a Karmayogī having become perfected in Yoga, gains this knowledge, assuredly.

The term 'Kālena', used in this verse, needs special attention. The Lord, has used the third inflexion, which means that through the discipline of action, one certainly gains knowledge of the self or realizes God.*

The term 'Svayam', shows that a Karmayogī gains the knowledge of the self, while performing his duty, without the guidance of a preceptor, or the scriptures or any other means.

The expression 'Ātmani vindati' means, that a Karmayogī, in order to gain knowledge of the self, need not go anywhere else. When he becomes perfected in Yoga, he finds this knowledge, in the self.

As the Lord pervades everywhere, He also pervades the self. But, a person does not realize this fact, because of his inclination towards the world and disinclination for God.When he performs his duty scrupulously, for the welfare of others without any selfish motive, his affinity for the world is renounced i.e., his identity with the body, sense of meum and desire, for the world perish, and he finds this knowledge in the self easily. The Lord

* In the term 'Kālena' instead of the second inflexion Kālam, third inflexion has been used which shows that the fruit will be surely reaped i.e., through Karmayoga the striver will certainly find this knowledge in the self.

declares, "He who is free from dualities (the pairs of opposites), is released, easily from bondage" (Gītā 5/3).

This knowledge of the self, cannot be gained by the senses, mind, intellect and other means (instruments). One will find the knowledge of the self, in himself. The reason is, that the sentient self can't be known by the insentient senses, mind and intellect etc. The means such as, listening to Vedantic texts, cognition and constant and deep meditations etc., may help, in removing the obstacles such as notion of impossibility of gaining knowledge and contrary sentiments etc., but they cannot induce a man, to gain the knowledge of self. He can gain that knowledge, by renouncing his affinity for the insentient. As the world can be seen with an eye but an eye cannot be seen by itself, but it can be said, that the organ with which any object is seen, is the eye. So it can be said, that He who is the Knower of all persons and objects etc., and by Whom all objects etc., are known, is the self or God, Who is not known by any means (Bṛhadāraṇyaka. 2/4/4).

An Important Fact

Having studied, the verses from the thirty-third to the thirty-seventh, it seems that the Lord has glorified the Discipline of Knowledge (Jñānayoga). But if we give a serious thought to this, we come to know, that the Lord says, that knowledge of the self, which is so glorious and pure and for gaining which He is advising to go to preceptors, who are well-versed in the scriptures, and can be easily and certainly, gained through the Discipline of Action (Karmayoga). The Lord declares, "He who is perfected in Yoga, finds this knowledge of the self automatically, in himself" (Gītā 4/38). Thus, He has actually glorified, the Discipline of Action. He means to say, that the knowledge of the self, which we can gain from wise preceptors through obeisance, questioning and service and by carrying out their directions, practising cognition, and constant and deep meditation, can be gained also by performing one's duty of fighting. It is not certain, whether he will gain, the knowledge of the Self from the preceptors, because they may themselves not have, realized the Truth. Besides, he may not have reverence for them. In this process, first he will see all beings in his self, and then in the Lord (Gītā 4/35). Thus, in this process of gaining knowledge, there is possibility of doubt and delay. Therefore, the Lord exhorts Arjuna, to follow the Discipline of Action (performance of duty) by which he will gain knowledge of the Self, certainly and immediately. So, He does not want to preach him the common method (of eight, inward spiritual means), to gain knowledge.

Lord Kṛṣṇa Himself, is the Lord of all the great souls. So, how can He order Arjuna to go to the wise, who have realized the Truth and learn knowledge from them? Further, in the forty-first verse of this chapter, the Lord eulogizes the Discipline of Action (Karmayoga), and clearly orders Arjuna, in the forty-second verse, to fight by being, fixed in equanimity.

Appendix—'Pavitramiha'—affinity for the world causes impurity; on Self-realization, when the universe totally ceases to be, then there is no question of the persistence of impurity. Therefore in the knowledge (of the self) there is neither impurity nor inertness nor modifications.

The term 'iha' stands for 'this world'. It means that Self-realization is worldly while God-realization is unworldly.

Link:— The Lord, in the next verse, explains, who is eligible to attain that knowledge.

श्रद्धावाँल्लभते ज्ञानं तत्परः संयतेन्द्रियः।
ज्ञानं लब्ध्वा परां शान्तिमचिरेणाधिगच्छति॥ ३९॥

śraddhāvāँllabhate jñānaṁ tatparaḥ saṁyatendriyaḥ
jñānaṁ labdhvā parāṁ śāntimacireṇādhigacchati

He who has faith and is devoted to it (i.e., knowledge) and who

controls his senses, gains knowledge (wisdom) and having gained knowledge he achieves the Supreme peace in no time. 39

Comment:—

'Tatparaḥ saṁyatendriyaḥ'—In this verse, it is mentioned that a man who is full of faith, gains knowledge. A man lacking faith, may think that he has faith. So the Lord, has used two adjectives 'saṁyatendriyaḥ' (who has subdued the senses) and 'tatparaḥ' (devoted), as the criteria of faith. The striver, who has subdued his senses, can be called, devoted to knowledge. If senses have not been subdued, and these hanker after sensual pleasures, it means, that the striver is not, fully devoted, to the knowledge of the Self.

'Śraddhāvāँllabhate jñānam'—The esteemed belief in God, saints, righteousness and scriptures, is called 'Śraddhā' (faith).

So long as, a striver does not realize God, he should have as much faith in Him, as he has when he has seen something himself. God pervades everywhere, but He is not realized, because he believes that He is far away from him. When he thinks that He is in him, and his only aim is to realize Him, he gains knowledge of the Self or God.

The world being ever-changing has no existence of its own, but it seems to exist because of the existence of God. When a striver has this faith, he gains knowledge of the self immediately. It is only because of his lack of faith, that he does not gain this knowledge immediately.

So long as, senses are not subdued and a striver is not keen in his efforts, his faith may be regarded, as imperfect. If the senses are attracted towards their objects, there cannot be any concentration of effort. That results, in the dominance of something other than practice. Unless, there is exclusive devotion to practice, faith cannot mature. Because of immature faith, only realization of the truth (Self), is delayed, otherwise there is not at all, any cause for delay, in realizing, the Self that is ever available and ever present.

A person through obeisance questioning and service, should gain knowledge from wise preceptors, as mentioned in the thirty-fourth verse. But, it is not certain, that he will acquire it because, he can prostrate, question and serve the preceptor, hypocritically, not from the heart. But, here in this verse, it is mentioned that he gains knowledge, certainly because he has faith, which is a trait of the heart (Gītā 17/3).

When a striver, has faith that he must gain knowledge of the self immediately, this is called 'Śraddhā'. God is ever-existent and 'I am also existent and I want to realize God.' Why then delay? Fully developed faith, immediately leads to God-realization.

An Important Fact

How surprising it is, that the changeful world attracts us, while the eternal Lord, does not attract us! The reason is, that we regard the transitory world, as permanent, and want to derive permanent joy out of it, which is impossible.

In fact, all the worldly objects, including the body, senses, mind etc., are perishing (decaying), while the Self is eternal. Had the self not been eternal, who might have seen the changes? If a man (the self) had identity with the body, he (the self) would have also died, with the death of a body. But it is not so. Thus, it is by error that he identifies the self with the body otherwise, the self is eternal, while the world, body, senses, mind etc., are transitory.

Secondly, in this verse, the term 'labhate', has been used. It means, the attainment of something, which is eternal or whichever exists. A thing, which has no pre-existence or which is created and compounded, its acquisition cannot be called 'labhate'. The reason is, that the thing which did not exist in the past, and will not exist in future, only appears in the interim, is not but acquired. To regard acquisition of such a thing appearing in the interim, is a disrespect to discrimination. The self existed before the world was created, and It will exist after the destruction of the world. Actually, the world does not exist, it seems to exist. The unreal has no existence and the real never ceases to be. As soon as, we realize this fact, it means that we have faith which will inspire us, to gain knowledge of the self.

'Jñānaṁ labdhvā parāṁ śāntimacireṇādhigacchati'—The Lord, in the third verse of the ninth chapter, declared, in the negative, "Those have no faith in this Dharma (knowledge of the Self), return to the world of death, without attaining Me." The same fact, has been mentioned here, in a positive form, when the Lord declares, "He who has faith, attains to the supreme peace" i.e., is liberated, from the cycle of birth and death. Why does a man not attain, the supreme peace? The answer is, that a man seeks the supreme peace in the perishable world—persons and objects etc., by having a disinclination, for God. The supreme peace, abides in all beings naturally, but because a person seeks it in the perishable world, he cannot attain it. When he gains knowledge of the self, his affinity for the world, which is an abode of sorrow, is totally renounced and he attains the supreme peace, which is axiomatic (natural).

Appendix—'Śraddhāvāllabhate jñānam'—esteemed belief, faith and discrimination are necessary for all the strivers. Yes, in Karmayoga and Jñānayoga there is predominance of discrimination and in Bhaktiyoga there is predominance of belief-faith. At first the Self-realization is attainable—this faith a striver must have, then only he will strive for it.

Link:—In the next verse, the Lord speaks ill of the person, who lacks discrimination, who has no faith and who is of a doubtful disposition.

अज्ञश्चाश्रद्दधानश्च संशयात्मा विनश्यति।
नायं लोकोऽस्ति न परो न सुखं संशयात्मनः ॥४०॥

ajñaścāśraddadhānaśca saṁśayātmā vinaśyati
nāyaṁ loko'sti na paro na sukhaṁ saṁśayātmanaḥ

One who is devoid of discriminative insight, and has no faith, who is of a sceptical nature, perishes. For the sceptic, there is neither this world nor the world beyond, nor any happiness anywhere. 40

Comment:—

'Ajñaścāśraddadhānaśca saṁśayātmā vinaśyati'—The man, whose discrimination is not aroused, or the man whose discrimination is aroused but he does not attach importance to it, and who lacks faith, such a man of doubting nature, perishes i.e., is deprived of the spiritual path. Such a person of doubting nature, uses neither his own discrimination, nor listens to the teachings of others. So, how could his doubts be removed and how can he progress spiritually?

It is natural, for a striver who follows the spiritual path to be confronted with doubts, because his knowledge is imperfect, this is known as ignorance.* Therefore, the appearance of doubt is natural, and it is not very harmful. But it proves harmful, when a person does not make effort to remove it, and he rather wants, to maintain it. In such cases, the doubt becomes a principle for the person, and he holds that spiritual practice, is nothing but hypocrisy. So, he ceases to believe in God and the scriptures etc., and becomes an atheist. Consequently, it leads to his downfall. Therefore, a striver should try to remove his doubt. By doing so, he will gain knowledge. It is characteristic of a striver to investigate and discover.

---

*Ajñāna' (ignorance) does not mean total absence of knowledge but it means imperfect knowledge. A man (the self) being a fragment of God can't lack knowledge (discrimination) totally. But he attaches importance to the unreal by regarding as real. Moreover he has no disinclination for the unreal, even when he regards it as unreal. This is ignorance. If he makes the right use of his knowledge (discrimination), his ignorance will perish and discrimination will be revealed because ignorance has no independent existence.

A striver, should go on proceeding further to attain his aim. He should not be satisfied with, what he has known. He should have a burning desire to remove his doubts, and acquire knowledge. By adopting such an attitude, his doubts are removed by saints or scriptures or by other means. If there is, no one to remove his doubts, it is removed by God's grace.

An Important Fact

The soul, is a fragment of God (Gītā 15/7). Therefore, when It has a desire to attain God, and feels sad and uneasy without attaining Him, He cannot tolerate his sadness, and He satisfies his desire. Similarly, when a striver, gets uneasy or sad, in order to remove his doubts, the Lord Himself, removes his doubts and frees him from sadness, he has not to pray to Him even. An intense feeling of a person to have his doubt removed does reach God automatically.

The Lord, is a disinterested friend of all beings (Gītā 5/29). So, He ever remains prepared to do away with restlessness, sadness and doubts of a man, somehow or the other. One commits an error, that having known a little he feels that, he has attained perfect knowledge. This pride leads to his downfall.

'Nāyaṁ loko'sti na paro na sukhaṁ saṁśayātmanaḥ'—In this verse, there is description of such a man of suspicious nature, who is ignorant i.e., who lacks discrimination and who is faithless i.e., does not follow the preaching of others. Such a man, of sceptical nature, perishes. For him, there is neither this world, nor the world beyond, nor any happiness.

In practical life, a man of doubting nature, behaves badly towards others, because he suspects their integrity and actions etc. He also cannot attain salvation, because it requires a determinate intellect, or firm resolve and a man of doubting nature, cannot resolve, whether he should chant the Lord's name, study the scriptures, perform mundane actions or attain God-realization and so on. Because of his doubting nature, he cannot attain happiness or peace. Therefore, a striver through discrimination and faith, must get rid of a doubt.

When a striver, comes across two contradictory statements, it leads to scepticism. Such scepticism can be removed, either by discrimination or through a reverential study of scriptures, or by following the advice of saints and holy men. Thus, if a sceptic is lacking in knowledge, he should acquire knowledge and wisdom. If he is wanting in faith, he should endeavour to gain faith. It is, because without especially enhancing either of these two, his scepticism cannot be removed.

Appendix—If a man has knowledge, his doubt is destroyed—'Jñānasañchinnasaṁśayam' (Gītā 4/41) or if he has faith, then also his doubt can be wiped out—'śraddhāvāllabhate jñānam' (Gītā 4/40). If there is lack of both knowledge and faith, then doubt cannot be slashed. Therefore the sceptic who is devoid of knowledge (discrimination) and has no faith (belief) viz., he who neither knows himself nor follows the instructions of others (the wise), has a downfall or is ruined.

Link:— The Lord, having started the topic of the Discipline of Knowledge in the thirty-third verse, discussed the method of attaining knowledge and revealed its glory. Then, He declared, ''Knowledge which can be gained through prostration and service etc., from the teacher, can be automatically gained by a man, who has attained perfection in Karmayoga.'' After that He described the person who is eligible to attain this knowledge as also the person, who is ineligible for it. Thus, he concluded the topic.

Now the question arises, what should a Karmayogī do, in order to attain perfection in Yoga. The Lord, answers the question, in the next verse.

योगसन्न्यस्तकर्माणं ज्ञानसञ्छिन्नसंशयम्।
आत्मवन्तं न कर्माणि निबध्नन्ति धनञ्जय॥ ४१॥

yogasannyastakarmāṇaṁ jñānasañchinnasaṁśayam
ātmavantaṁ na karmāṇi nibadhnanti dhanañjaya

He, who has renounced all actions by Yoga, whose doubts have been destroyed by knowledge and who takes shelter in 'yoga', him, actions do not bind, O winner of wealth (Arjuna). 41

Comment:—

'Yogasannyastakarmāṇam'—All objects, such as body,senses, mind and the intellect etc., which seem ours, have been bestowed upon us, so that we may render service to others, with them, rather, than to lay a claim on these. Therefore, if these are utilized, in rendering service to others, by considering them as theirs, the flow of actions and objects is towards the world, and we realize equanimity, which is axiomatic. Thus, such a Karmayogī, who through equanimity has renounced his affinity for actions, is called 'Yogasannyastakarmā', (one who has renounced actions by Yoga).

When a Karmayogī sees, inaction in action, and action in inaction i.e., ever remains detached, during performance or non-performance of actions, he is really 'Yogasannyastakarmā'.

'Jñānasañchinnasaṁśayam'—Generally, a man has doubts how he will be able to renounce his affinity for actions, while performing them, how he will attain salvation, if he does not work for himself, and so on. But when he knows the reality about actions, all his doubts are dispelled.* He comes to know very well, that actions and their fruits are transitory, while the self, ever remains uniform. Therefore, actions have their affinity for the world, rather than for the self. In this way when actions are performed with a selfish motive, a man is attached to these i.e., develops affinity for them. But, when they are performed for others, without any selfish motive, affinity for them is renounced.

---

*The reality about actions has been described from the sixteenth to the thirty-second verses of this chapter. Out of them the eighteenth verse is an important one.

It proves, that performance of action for others, not for one's own self, leads to salvation.

'Ātmavantam'—A Karmayogī, aims at Self-realization. So, he ever remains self-possessed. All his actions, including eating, drinking, sleeping and sitting etc., are performed for others (the world), because actions have an affinity for the world, not for the self.

'Na karmāṇi nibadhnanti'—When, a Karmayogī does not perform any action for himself, his affinity for actions is renounced and he gets liberated, from the worldly bondage forever (Gītā 4/23).

In fact, it is not actions which lead to bondage, but it is desire for fruit, sense of mine, attachment and the sense of doership for actions, which lead one to bondage.

Link:—In the preceding verse, the Lord declared, "Doubts are destroyed by knowledge, and affinity for actions, is renounced by equanimity." Now in the next verse, He orders Arjuna to resort to Yoga, having cut asunder his doubt.

तस्मादज्ञानसम्भूतं हृत्स्थं ज्ञानासिनात्मनः।
छित्त्वैनं संशयं योगमातिष्ठोत्तिष्ठ भारत॥ ४२॥

tasmādajñānasambhūtaṁ hṛtsthaṁ jñānāsinātmanaḥ
chittvainaṁ saṁśayaṁ yogamātiṣṭhottiṣṭha bhārata

Therefore, having cut asunder, with the sword of knowledge (jñāna), any doubt in thy heart, that is born of ignorance, while taking shelter in Yoga and then stand up (for the fight), O Bhārata (Arjuna). 42

Comment:—

'Tasmādajñānasambhūtaṁ hṛtsthaṁ jñānāsinātmanaḥ chittvainaṁ saṁśayam'—In the preceding verse, the Lord declared, "He who has renounced affinity for all actions by Yoga (equanimity), whose doubts have been dispelled by knowledge, and who is self-possessed— actions do not bind him i.e., he is liberated from the bondage of birth and death. Therefore, He by using the term 'Tasmāt' (therefore), inspires Arjuna to perform his duty. Arjuna had a doubt how the cruel deed of fighting, would lead him to salvation. Moreover, he was in a dilemma, whether he should follow the Discipline of Action or that of Knowledge. So the Lord advises him, to remove his doubt, so that he may perform his duty scrupulously. A doubting soul, can, never perform his duty efficiently.

The expression 'ajñānasaṁbhūtam' (born of ignorance), means that all doubts are born out of ignorance i.e., when a man does not understand the true nature of actions and Yoga. Ignorance, consists in regarding actions and objects, as one's own and for one's own self. So long as, there is ignorance, doubt resides in the heart, because actions and objects are perishable, while the self is imperishable.

In the third chapter, emphasis has been laid on the performance (discharge) of duty, while in the fourth chapter, there is an emphasis on knowing the truth, about Karmayoga. The reason is, that action can be performed scrupulously, only when reality is known about it. Moreover, if the truth about actions is known, such actions, which bind a man, can liberate him from bondage (Gītā 4/16,32). Therefore, in this chapter, the Lord has laid special emphasis on, knowing the truth about actions.

In the preceding verse, also the Lord pointed out this fact, by the expression 'Jñānasañchinnasaṁśayam' (whose doubts have been destroyed by knowledge). All the doubts of a man, who comes to know the skill of performance of actions, (duties) are destroyed. This art of action, consists in doing nothing, for one's own self.

'Yogamātiṣṭhottiṣṭha bhārata'—Arjuna had sunk into the seat of his chariot, casting away his bow and arrow (Gītā 1/47). He gave the Lord, a flat denial by declaring that he would not fight (Gītā 2/9). Here, the Lord directs Arjuna to stand up, for a fight having resorted to Yoga. The same order was given to Arjuna, in the forty-eighth verse of the second chapter, when He said, "Perform action, being steadfast in Yoga." The term 'Yoga', stands for equanimity (evenness of mind). The Lord declares, "Evenness of mind is called, Yoga" (Gītā 2/48).

Arjuna thought, that sin would accrue to him by fighting (Gītā 1/36, 45). Therefore, Lord Kṛṣṇa orders him to fight by having evenness of mind; thus he would not incur sin (Gītā 2/38). In this way, we see that performance of duty by being equanimous, is a means to be liberated from, the bondage of actions.

In the world, innumerable actions are performed, but we remain free from their bondage, because we have neither attachment nor aversion for them. It is because of attachment or aversion, that we are linked with actions. When we become free, from attachment and aversion i.e., get established in equanimity, we are not connected with actions and thus become free, from the bondage of actions.

The self, ever remains equanimous and uniform, while actions and their fruits, always undergo changes. When actions are performed for others and objects are regarded as others' and for them, affinity for actions and objects, is totally renounced and equanimity, which is axiomatic, is automatically realized.

ॐ तत्सदिति श्रीमद्भगवद्गीतासूपनिषत्सु ब्रह्मविद्यायां योगशास्त्रे
श्रीकृष्णार्जुनसंवादे ज्ञानकर्मसन्यासयोगो नाम चतुर्थोऽध्याय: ॥ ४ ॥

oṁ tatsaditi śrīmadbhagavadgītāsūpaniṣatsu brahmavidyāyām
yogaśāstre śrīkṛṣṇārjunasaṁvāde jñānakarmasannyāsayogo
nāma caturtho'dhyāyaḥ

Starting with Oṁ, Tat, Sat, the names of the Lord, in the Upaniṣad of Bhagavadgītā, the knowledge of Brahma, the supreme, the scripture of Yoga and the dialogue between Śrī Kṛṣṇa and Arjuna, this is the fourth discourse so designated:

"The Yoga of Knowledge as well as the Discipline of Action and Knowledge."

This fourth chapter, is designated as 'Jñānakarmasannyāsa-yoga', because in this chapter there is the description of 'Karmayoga' (the Discipline of Action) and 'Sāṅkhyayoga' (the Discipline of Knowledge), in order to attain the Supreme Knowledge i.e., God-realization.

Words, letters and Uvāca in the Fourth Chapter

(1) In this chapter in **'Atha caturtho'dhyāyaḥ'** there are three words, in **'Arjuna Uvāca'** etc., there are six words, in verses there are five hundred and eleven words, and there are thirteen, concluding words. Thus the total number of the words, is five hundred and thirty-three.

(2) In this chapter in **'Atha caturtho'dhyāyaḥ'** there are seven letters, in **'Arjuna Uvāca'** etc., there are twenty letters, in verses, there are one thousand three hundred and forty-four letters, and there are fifty concluding letters. Thus the total number of the letters, is one thousand four hundred and twenty-one. Each of the verses of this chapter consists of thirty-two letters.

(3) In this chapter **'Uvāca'** (said) has been used three times—**Śrībhagavānuvāca'** twice and **'Arjuna Uvāca'** once.

Metres Used in the Fourth Chapter—

Out of the forty-two verses of this Chapter, in the first quarter of the thirty-first and thirty-eighth verses, and in the third quarter of the second, tenth, thirteenth and fortieth verses, 'na-gaṇa being used there is **'na-vipulā'** metre; in the first quarter of the sixth verse, 'ra-gaṇa' being used there, is **'ra-vipulā** metre; in the first quarter of the twenty-fourth verse and in the third quarter of the thirtieth verse, 'bha-gaṇa' being used there, is **'bha-vipulā'** metre. The remaining thirty-three verses, possess the characteristics of right, **'pathyāvaktra'**, anuṣṭup metre.

|| Shri Hari ||

Fifth Chapter

INTRODUCTION

Lord Kṛṣṇa, in the fourth chapter, from the thirty-third to the thirty-seventh verse, praised the tradition of going to teachers, who have realized the Truth, having renounced actions and sense-objects and directed Arjuna to gain knowledge from them (Gītā 4/34). In this process of Self-realization, it is indispensable to meditate upon God in solitude by renouncing action. Arjuna did not want to fight, because he thought that he would incur sin, by fighting. He wanted to attain salvation. So Arjuna thought, that the Lord was asking him to gain knowledge, by renouncing actions.

Then the Lord, in the thirty-eighth verse of the fourth chapter, declared, "He who is perfect in Yoga, gains it (knowledge) in the Self." It means that a striver following the Discipline of a action, need not go to the great persons, who have realized truth nor has he to practise any other spiritual discipline, in order to gain knowledge. Thus Karmayoga (the Discipline of Action) as the means of Self-realization has been commended here.

Arjuna, in the thirty-third verse of the fourth chapter, heard the glory of the customary method of gaining knowledge and in the thirty-fourth verse by the term 'viddhi', he held it as the Lord's order for him to gain knowledge by that method. He heard the praise of Karmayoga (the discipline of action), in the thirty-eighth verse and the forty-first verse. In the forty-second verse, He ordered him to perform his duty of fighting. Thus, having heard the glory of 'Jñānayoga' and 'Karmayoga' both, and also His order to gain knowledge and to perform one's duty, Arjuna, could not decide which one of the two disciplines, was better. Therefore, in order to get his doubt cleared by Lord Kṛṣṇa, Arjuna puts a question.

अर्जुन उवाच

सन्न्यासं कर्मणां कृष्ण पुनर्योगं च शंससि।
यच्छ्रेय एतयोरेकं तन्मे ब्रूहि सुनिश्चितम्॥ १॥

arjuna uvāca

sannyāsaṁ karmaṇāṁ kṛṣṇa punaryogaṁ ca śaṁsasi
yacchreya etayorekaṁ tanme brūhi suniścitam

Arjuna said:

O Kṛṣṇa thou praisest, the renunciation of actions externally (Sāṅkhyayoga) as well as their unselfish performance (Karmayoga), tell me, for certain, which one of the two is decidedly conducive to my good. 1

Comment:—

'Sannyāsaṁ karmaṇāṁ kṛṣṇa'—Arjuna, did not want to fight, because he did not want to kill his kinsmen. In order to support his stand, Arjuna put forward several arguments, as in the first chapter. He said, that fighting would incur sin (Gītā 1/45). According to him, it was better to live in the world even by begging than to fight (2/5) and he bluntly said to Kṛṣṇa, that he would not fight (2/9).

Generally, a listener interprets a preacher's word, according to his own views. Having seen his kith and kin, Arjuna, out of delușion, thought it proper, to abandon his duty of fighting. So, he interpreted the Lord's word, according to his view, that He was praising the attainment of Self-realization, by renouncing actions.

'Punaryogaṁ ca śaṁsasi'—The Lord, in the thirty-eighth verse of the fourth chapter, declared, "He who is perfected in Yoga, finds this knowledge (wisdom) of the Self, certainly without the aid of any other spiritual discipline." Keeping this fact in mind, Arjuna says to the Lord, that sometimes He praises the Discipline of Knowledge (4/33), while at other time He commands the Discipline of Action (4/41).

'Yacchreya etayorekaṁ tanme brūhi suniścitam'—This question, was put by Arjuna, in the seventh verse of the second chapter also. In response, the Lord, having explained Karmayoga, ordered Arjuna to perform action, being established in Yoga, (even-mindedness), in the forty-seventh and forty-eighth verses of the second chapter. Again, in the second verse of the third chapter, Arjuna asked the Lord, "Tell me decisively, the one way by which I may attain to the highest good, (bliss or salvation)." In response, the Lord, in the thirtieth verse of the third chapter, ordered him to fight, being free from desire, feeling of mineness and mental woe (grief) while, in the thirty-fifth verse He declared, "Better is one's own duty, though devoid of merit than the duty of another well discharged."

In this chapter also, the Lord clearly declares, "The unselfish performance of action, is better than the renunciation of action" (5/2); "a Karmayogī is easily set free, from bondage" (5/3); "renunciation is difficult to attain, without Yoga (Karmayoga) but a Karmayogī attains, quickly, the Absolute" (5/6). Thus, the Lord explains to Arjuna, that he should follow the Discipline of Action, by which he can attain to the Absolute, very quickly and easily.

Arjuna was, especially interested in attaining salvation. So, time and again, he asked Lord Kṛṣṇa, the way to attain salvation (2/7; 3/2; 5/1). A keen desire, plays an important role, in attaining salvation. Even without dispassion, a striver having a keen desire for salvation, can follow the Discipline of Action, in order to attain his aim of salvation. Arjuna was not totally dispassionate, but he had a keen desire to attain salvation, and so he was a deserving candidate.

The thirty-second verse of the first chapter and the eighth verse of the second chapter, reveal that, not to speak of the kingdom on earth, Arjuna does not even desire to attain, an unrivalled sovereignty, over the gods. But it does not mean that Arjuna had no desire to gain a kingdom and pleasures, because he said that he longed neither for victory nor kingdom nor pleasures, by slaying his kinsmen. It means, that he was prepared to gain victory or kingdom, without slaying his kinsmen. Again, in the sixth verse of the second chapter, he said, "We don't know whether we shall conquer them, or they will conquer us, and we do not want to live by slaying them." It means, that if it was certain, that they would conquer the enemy and if they could get the kingdom without slaying them, they were prepared to gain it. Further, in the thirty-seventh verse of the second chapter, the Lord said to Arjuna, that he would be benefited in either case. If he was killed, he would go to heaven, and if he became victorious, he would enjoy the earth. Had Arjuna, no desire, in the least, to go to heaven and to enjoy the worldly pleasures, the Lord, perhaps, would not utter such words. It means, that Arjuna could not cultivate real dispassion, but he had a desire to attain salvation, which is also clear in this verse.

Link:—Now, the Lord answers Arjuna's question.

श्रीभगवानुवाच

सन्न्यासः कर्मयोगश्च निःश्रेयसकरावुभौ।
तयोस्तु कर्मसन्न्यासात्कर्मयोगो विशिष्यते॥ २॥

śrībhagavānuvāca

sannyāsaḥ karmayogaśca niḥśreyasakarāvubhau
tayostu karmasannyāsātkarmayogo viśiṣyate

The Blessed Lord said:

'Sannyāsa' (discipline of knowledge) and 'Karmayoga' (discipline of action) both lead to salvation. But of the two 'Karmayoga' is superior to 'Sāṅkhyayoga'. 2

Comment:—

[According to the principle of the Lord every person can

follow the Disciplines of Action and Knowledge, (Renunciation of Actions) of whatever caste, order of life and sect etc., he may be because His precept is not for the people of any particular caste, order of life or sect etc. In the first verse of this chapter Arjuna called the customary method of gaining knowledge by approaching enlightened soul having renounced actions as 'Karmasannyāsa' (Renunciation of Actions). But according to the Lord's precept a person can gain knowledge by following the Discipline of knowledge even without renouncing actions. Therefore, the Lord, supporting the customary principle of Arjuna, answers the question according to His own tenet.]

'Sannyāsaḥ'—Here, this term, 'Sannyāsaḥ' stands for 'Sāṅkhyayoga' (Discipline of Knowledge), rather than renunciation of actions. While answering Arjuna's question, the Lord discusses the path of 'Sāṅkhyayoga', in order to gain knowledge. Through that Sāṅkhyayoga, every man, while performing his duty, according to his caste, order of life and sect etc., in every circumstance, can gain knowledge, of the self i.e., attain salvation.

In the 'Sāṅkhya' discipline, there is prominence given to discrimination. This discipline cannot be successful, without keen dispassion and discrimination. While following this discipline, a striver keeps his eye only on God, without accepting the independent existence of the world. So, the Lord declares, "The goal of the Unmanifested, is hard to reach by the embodied being" (Gītā 12/5). In the sixth verse of this chapter, also the Lord declares, that Sannyāsa is difficult to attain without Karmayoga, and Karmayoga is an easy means, to get detached from the world.

'Karmayogaśca'—Every human being, has been attached to the performance of actions, from time immemorial. In order to, do away with this attachment, performance of action, is indispensable (Gītā 6/3). Karmayoga, is the art of performing actions, in order to, get rid of this attachment. In Karmayoga, (Discipline of Action), every action, whether trivial or otherwise, is not to be taken note of; but it has to be performed, for the welfare of others without any selfish motive, in order to get detached from it. So long as, actions are performed with a desire for their reward, one remains attached to these.

'Niḥśreyasakarāvubhau'—In response to Arjuna's question, which he put in the first verse, the Lord says, that both Sāṅkhyayoga and Karmayoga, lead to salvation, because the same equanimity is attained, through both of these. The same fact, has been clarified, in the fourth and the fifth verses of this chapter. It has also been pointed out by the Lord, in the twenty-fourth verse of the thirteenth chapter, when He declares, "Some attain knowledge, of the self by the path of knowledge, while others attain it by the path of action." Thus, both the paths of knowledge and action, are independent paths, to attain God (Gītā 3/3).

'Tayostu karmasannyāsāt'—Sāṅkhyayoga, is of two kinds—one has been described, in the thirty-fourth verse of the fourth chapter, in which there is physical renunciation of actions, while the other has been described, from the eleventh to the thirtieth verses of the second chapter, in which there is no renunciation of actions. Here the expression 'Karmasannyāsāt' stands, for the two kinds of Sāṅkhyayoga.

'Karmayogo viśiṣyate'—The Lord, in the third verse, explains that a Karmayogī should be regarded as a perpetual Sannyāsī, (with the spirit of renunciation), because he is easily released from worldly bondage. Again, in the sixth verse, He declares that renunciation is difficult to attain, without Karmayoga and a Karmayogī quickly attains to the Absolute. It means, that in Sāṅkhyayoga (Discipline of Knowledge), there is need of Karmayoga, while in Karmayoga, there is none for Sāṅkhyayoga. Thus, out of the two, which lead to salvation, the path of action, has been declared to be superior, by the Lord.

A Karmayogī, performs actions for the welfare of the world and also to set an example to the masses (Gītā 3/20), without any selfish motive. This sort of action is called a sacrifice in Gītā. He, who performs actions for himself is bound (Gītā 3/9, 13). But a Karmayogī, who works only for the welfare of the world without any selfish motive, is liberated from the bondage of all actions (Gītā 4/23). Therefore, Karmayoga is better of the two.

The path of action, can be followed by all the people, of all castes, creeds and order of life etc., under all circumstances. But the Karmasannyāsa (renunciation), Arjuna talks about, can be followed, only under special circumstances (Gītā 4/34), because all the people cannot come across such great men, who have realized the truth. Moreover, they cannot have full faith, in those great souls and have an opportunity to live, in their company. Thus Karmayoga, is better of the two.

Karmayoga, consists in making proper use of available circumstances, even savage deeds of fighting. No one is incapable, and dependent on following this path of action, because in it, there is no desire to acquire anything. It is the desire, which makes a man incapable and dependent.

A sense of doership, and the desire to reap the fruit of actions, lead to bondage. A Sāṅkhyayogī and a Karmayogī both, have to renounce their affinity, for the world. A Sāṅkhyayogī, roots out a sense of doership through dispassion and discrimination, while a Karmayogī, discards it by performing actions, for the welfare of others, without any desire for the fruit of actions. Thus, the former is liberated by renouncing a sense of doership, while the latter is liberated, by renouncing desire to reap the fruit of action. If a striver, renounces the sense of doership, his desire for the fruit of action, is also renounced; and if he renounces the desire for the fruit of action, his sense of doership is renounced. A man, has a sense of doership, only when he has a desire, to acquire something or the other. When actions are performed without desire for fruit, these change, into inaction. Thus a Karmayogī is like as instrument, has no sense of doership.

A striver, tries to renounce his attachment to the worldly beings, objects and circumstances etc., because it leads him to bondage. In order to renounce it, he does not consider any being or object etc., as his own nor does he do and desire anything, for himself. All his actions are performed for the welfare of others, without any selfish motive. The desire for fruit of action causes a sense of doership and a sense of 'mine'. If he has no desire for the fruit of action, his sense of doership, comes to an end. It is not actions, but attachment to them and the desire for fruit, which lead to bondage. When one does not derive pleasure out of actions, nor does he desire fruit, how can a sense of doership remain? When he has no desire for the fruit of action, his sense of doership merges, in the aim (God) for which action is performed and then only God remains.

The 'egoism' of a Karmayogī, perishes quickly and easily, because he works for others. So his egoism is, also absorbed in rendering service to others. But the egoism of a Jñānayogī, (he who follows the path of knowledge) continues to exist, as he holds that he is a 'Mumukṣu' (seeker of salvation) and he works for his salvation. A Karmayogī, performs all activities for the good of others. Thus his ego subsides. On the other hand, a Jñānayogī practises discipline, for his well-being. His ego subsists, as he practises discipline, for himself.

A prominent feature of 'the Discipline of Knowledge', is the lack of independent existence of the world; while an important feature of 'the Discipline of Action', is lack of attachment. A striver, following the Discipline of Knowledge, through discrimination, wants to hold that there is no independent existence of the world but due to his attachment to the worldly objects, it is very difficult for him to hold this opinion, in his practical life. But a striver, following the Discipline of Action, gets rid of his attachment automatically, as his aim, is to render service to others, without any selfish motive. Moreover, it is easy for a Karmayogī, to renounce objects, as these will be utilized by others; while it is difficult for a Jñānayogī to renounce them, by regarding these, as transitory and illusive, unless his dispassion, is very keen. Secondly, a Jñānayogī easily abandons objects of inferior quality, but these of superior quality which he considers useful for him, cannot be easily, abandoned. But a Karmayogī, may offer objects which are useful for him to others, easily, because he believes that these will be used by others. If there is, an extra slice of bread in a plate, we try to put away the one which is stale, spoiled and dry; but if we want to give a slice to anyone, we will give a good one, so that it may be used by him. So, the Discipline of Knowledge, is very difficult to practise, without renouncing attachment. It is because of attachment that a Jñānayogī, being entangled in worldly pleasures, may have a fall.

A man, cannot renounce attachment, merely by knowing the unreal, as unreal.* Though objects seen on a screen, in the cinema are unreal, yet a cinema-goer gets attached to the cinema and wastes his time, money, eyesight and character. It is attachment, rather than the object which bind a man. Thus, an object which may be either real or unreal, or it may transcend the two, but it binds a man if he is attached to it. So a striver, should try to root out this attachment.

Appendix—Though without 'Yoga' both 'Karma' and 'Jñāna' lead to bondage yet performance of actions does not lead to as much ruin as the bookish knowledge does. Mere bookish knowledge can lead to hells—

'ajñasyārdhaprabuddhasya sarvaṁ brahmeti yo vadet
mahānirayajāleṣu sa tena viniyojitaḥ
(Yogavāsiṣṭha sthiti 39)

---

* A man can renounce the unreal by regarding it as unreal by being established in the self. This establishment in the self does not depend on instruments such as the mind and intellect etc., because they themselves are unreal. How can we get rid of the unreal while our affinity of the unreal subsists and we depend upon it for realising the Real?

'He, who preaches the gospel 'all is Brahma' to an ignorant man, condemns that man to the snare of fightful hells."

Therefore the man who perform actions is superior to the man possessing bookish knowledge. Then what can be said about the superiority of the person who follows the Discipline of Action! A Jñānayogī is useful only for himself but a Karmayogī is useful for the entire universe. He, who is useful for the universe, is also useful for himself—this is the rule. Therefore a Karmayogī is superior to a Jñānayogī.

The Discipline of Action can be practised without the Discipline of Knowledge but the Discipline of Knowledge is difficult to attain without the Discipline of Action (Gītā 5/6). Therefore Karmayoga is superior to Sāṅkhyayoga, Discipline of Devotion is superior to Discipline of Action. Therefore in the Gītā there is description first of Sāṅkhyayoga, then of Karmayoga and afterwards of Bhaktiyoga.* In this order the Yogas have been discussed.

Karmayoga and Jñānayoga—both bear the same fruit (Gītā 5/4-5). In their practices 'Karmayoga' and 'Bhaktiyoga' are one—'maitraḥ karuṇa eva ca' (Gītā 12/13); because Karmayoga and Bhaktiyoga—in both, feeling of providing happiness to others reigns. In the performance of actions 'Karmī' (One who perform actions) and 'Karmayogī' (who without attachment acts for the welfare of others) are one (Gītā 3/25) and in the performance of actions, an enlightened soul and God are similar (one) (Gītā 3/22—26). In this way a Karmayogī becomes one with a Karmī,

---

* The same order has been followed in the Bhāgavata—

yogāstrayo mayā proktā nṛṇāṁ śreyovidhitsayā
jñānaṁ karma ca bhaktiśca nopāyo'nyo'sti kutracit
(Śrīmadbhā. 11/20/6)

"I have mentioned three yogas for the men who want to attain salvation—Jñānayoga, Karmayoga and Bhaktiyoga. Besides these three there is no other way for salvation."

a Jñānayogī, a Bhaktiyogī and God, all the four—this is the special characteristic of Karmayoga.

In 'Sāṅkhyayoga' a subtle trace of ego may persist but in 'Karmayoga' because of the total detachment from actions and objects, no subtle trace of ego subsists. In Karmayoga, 'Akarma' remains (Gītā 4/18) while in Sāṅkhyayoga the soul (self) remains (Gītā 6/29).

Link:—Now, the Lord in the next verse, explains why Karmayoga is better of the two.

ज्ञेयः स नित्यसन्न्यासी यो न द्वेष्टि न काङ्क्षति।
निर्द्वन्द्वो हि महाबाहो सुखं बन्धात्प्रमुच्यते॥ ३॥

jñeyaḥ sa nityasannyāsī yo na dveṣṭi na kāṅkṣati
nirdvandvo hi mahābāho sukhaṁ bandhātpramucyate

He who neither hates nor desires anything should be known as a Nitya Sannyāsī (ever a renouncer); for, free from dualities (pairs of opposites) he is liberated easily from bondage, O mighty-armed (Arjuna). 3

Comment:—

'Mahābāho'—The term 'Mahābāho', stands for one who is mighty-armed i.e., brave, and also for one, whose brothers and friends, are great men. Arjuna's friend, was Lord Kṛṣṇa, the disinterested friend of all beings, and his brother was Yudhiṣṭhira, the most righteous person, who had no enemy. By addressing Arjuna as 'Mahābāho', the Lord means to say, that he possesses the might to follow the path of action easily.

'Yo na dveṣṭi'—A Karmayogī, does not hate any being, object, circumstance or principle etc., but he renders selfless service to everyone. If he has the least, hatred for anyone, he cannot follow, the Discipline of Action, scrupulously. He should give priority, in rendering service, to a person for whom he bears, even a little malice. The Lord, by using the expression 'Na dveṣṭi', first of all, wants to impress, that he who deems someone, as bad and wants to harm him, cannot grasp the secret of 'Karmayoga'.

A Vital Fact

For a Karmayogī, it is more significant to renounce evil, rather than to do good, for the welfare of others. Actions and objects are limited and, therefore, only limited service, can be rendered with such resources. But, when a man renounces evil, his unlimited inward feeling, is prominent. Secondly, by doing good to others, a person cultivates notion of pride, which is the root of all demoniac traits. Where there is imperfection, there is pride. On the contrary, where there is perfection, pride is out of the question.

If a serious thought is given, it becomes clear that no good can be done, without the help of perishable objects. In fact, those perishable objects are not ours, but they are of those, whose service is rendered with them. Then, if a man is proud of doing good, it is attachment to the perishable. So long as, a man is attached to the perishable, he cannot attain Yoga. The pride of doing good, is more disastrous, than other evils, because it settles, in the sense of 'I'ness. Actions and their fruits disappear, but pride settled in the sense of 'I'ness, never disappears. Secondly, an evil as an evil, can be easily renounced. But when an evil disguises itself as a virtue, it is difficult to renounce it. In the same way, we can easily discard iron hand cuffs, but we find it difficult to discard gold ones, because they look like ornaments. When evil is renounced, by a man, good to the entire world, is automatically done by him. A person, free from evil, does good to the entire universe, even while, leading a secluded life, in a Himalayan cave.

'Na kāṅkṣati'—Renunciation of desire, is very important, in Karmayoga. A Karmayogī does not desire, any being or object or circumstance. Renunciation of desire, is very much connected with the welfare of others. By rendering service to others, we get the required strength to give up desire.

In Karmayoga, it is a doer who is desireless, not action. Being inert, actions are not desireless or otherwise. All actions, are dependent on the doer. A doer being desireless, his actions are called desireless. Those actions, without expectation of fruit, are called 'Karmayoga'. 'Karmayoga' and 'Niṣkāma-karma'—both are synonyms. 'Karmayoga' is never 'Sakāma' (with a selfish motive). The desireless doer, remains detached from the fruit of action.

When actions are performed without any selfish motive, it is called Karmayoga. When actions are performed in this way, the doer becomes detached, from the fruit of actions. But, when he performs actions by being attached to fruit of actions, he is bound (Gītā 5/12). When all actions are performed for the welfare of others, without any selfish motive, a striver is easily set free, from bondage. Therefore a doer should ever remain desireless. The more, selfless he is, the more efficient, the practice of the discipline. On being totally desireless, the Karmayogī reaches, consummation.

'Jñeyaḥ sa nityasannyāsī'—Arjuna thought it better to live in the world even by begging, than to fight (Gītā 2/5). So in response to his statement, the Lord seems to clarify, that such renunciation apprehending the death of teachers is external (outwardly); but real renunciation consists, in being free from attachment and aversion, while performing action.

Further, in the first verse of the sixth chapter also, the Lord declares, "He who does not light the sacred fire, is not a Sannyāsī." It means, that a person who renounces all actions, such as sacrificial fire etc., is not a Sannyāsī. Sannyāsa (renunciation), is an inward attitude, by which a Karmayogī renounces his dependence, on the world. Such a Karmayogī is a real Sannyāsī (renouncer).

Sannyāsa (renunciation), consists in the performance of actions without being attached to them, in anyway. A striver, who has no affinity for actions, has never to reap its fruit (Gītā 18/12). Therefore, a Karmayogī, while performing actions sanctioned by the scriptures, is ever a Sannyāsī (renouncer).

It is difficult to follow, the Discipline of Knowledge, without following the Discipline of Action. Therefore, a striver who follows the Discipline of Knowledge, is first a Karmayogī and then a Sannyāsī (Sāṅkhyayogī). But, for a Karmayogī it is not necessary to follow the Discipline of Knowledge. So, a Karmayogī is a Sannyāsī (renouncer), from the very beginning.

He, who has renounced attachment and aversion, need not go to the renounced order. When a striver resolves, that any person, object, senses, mind and intellect, are neither his nor for him; and he has neither attachment nor aversion for them, he is, ever a renouncer. A Karmayogī, while performing either mundane or spiritual actions, ever remains detached. This detachment is real renunciation. Therefore, he should be known, as one who has ever the spirit of renunciation.

'Nirdvandvo hi......sukhaṁ bandhātpramucyate'*—At the beginning of the spiritual discipline, a striver has opposite experiences in the form of attachment and aversion. He, through good company, study of scriptures and discrimination, decides on God-realization as his aim, but his so-called mind and senses, etc., are naturally, inclined towards pleasure and prosperity. Thus, sometimes he wants to attain God, while at other times, he hankers after worldly pleasures and prosperity. His inclination changes

* There is description of this sort of release from bondage in the Gītā in the following expressions:—'Shall cast off bondage of action' (2/39); 'protects one from great fear' (2/40); 'one casts off in this life both good and evil deeds' (2/50); 'shall be liberated from the evil' (4/16, 9/1); 'shall cross all sins (4/36); 'having attained Me these great souls don't take birth here which is the place of pain and which is non-eternal' (9/28); and 'I straightway deliver from the ocean of death-bound existence' (12/7) and so on.

according to the company he keeps. But he cannot enjoy, the worldly pleasures undisturbed, because the latent impressions of good company etc., cause dispassion (disinclination for pleasures) in his mind. Thus, there is a duel between pleasure and spiritual practice. Egoism, hinges on this duel. When a striver, has a determinate intellect, only to realize God, rather than to hanker after worldly pleasures and prosperity, this duel comes to an end and his egoism, merges in God.

There is a struggle between, the pairs of opposites, so long as a man, derives pleasures out of the persons and objects etc. This inclination for pleasure does not let the determination for God-realization, become firm. So there is a struggle. When a striver has a determinate intellect, that he has to work for the welfare of others without hankering after worldly pleasures, he becomes free from the pairs of opposites.

By the expression 'Na dveṣṭi na kāṅkṣati', the Lord, advises strivers, that they should be free from antithetical feelings. Hate (aversion) and desire (attachment), are stumbling blocks to God-realization. A man, has to reap the fruit of his past actions, in the form of desirable and undesirable circumstances, whether he desires them or not. But, it is an error, that he is attached to desirable circumstances and has aversion for the undesirable ones. As soon as, this error is rectified through discrimination, he becomes free, from attachment and aversion.

Secondly, the self always exists independently, without the help of objects, persons and actions etc. A man, (the self) (the soul), has its existence, during sound sleep, also when he is oblivious of the entire world. In the wakeful and dreamy states, he can exist, even without any being and object. So, why should he have attachment or aversion for them? By thinking so, attachment and aversion, come to an end.

Attachment and aversion, are perishable, but a person being attached to persons and objects etc., wants to maintain these. As far as desire for God-realization is concerned, it ever remains uniform, because the self is a fragment of God. But the desire seems to increase and decrease, because of his less and more attachment for the world, respectively. His desire to live, to know and to be happy, is in fact, the desire to attain the Truth, Knowledge and Bliss i.e., God. This desire, constantly prevails in a human being. When attachment to the world, is renounced and there is only one desire for God-realization, he becomes free, from the pair of opposites.

A striver, following anyone of the three paths—of action, of knowledge or of devotion, must be free from the pairs of opposites. So long as, there is delusion of the pairs of opposites, a man is not liberated from bondage (Gītā 7/27). Attachment and aversion, are enemies which are the stumbling blocks to God-realization (Gītā 3/34). When a striver, becomes free from dualities, (pairs of opposites), attachment and aversion perish, and then he attains, God easily.

It is because of attachment and aversion, that a man gets entangled in the worldly snare. All spiritual disciplines, are practised in order to, wipe out attachment and aversion.* When attachment and aversion are wiped out, the ever-present Lord is naturally attained without effort. The reason is, that He is not realized through unreal, but is realized, by renouncing the unreal. The unreal world seems to exist, because of attachment and aversion. It automatically goes, into extinction. So, if a striver is neither attached to nor has an aversion, for the perishable world, he will naturally attain salvation i.e., will be released, from bondage.

Appendix—Equanimity in favourable and unfavourable circumstances and freedom from the feeling of pleasure and pain is to be 'nirdvandva' viz., free from dualities (pairs of opposites).

---

* The only desired aim of all spiritual practices of Yogīs is to get rid of attachment to the entire world (Śrīmadbhāgavata 3/32/27).

In identification (of the self with the non-self), if there is predominance of the sentient, there is eagerness (curiosity) and if there is predominance of the insentient, there is desire. A man has the real hunger for the imperishable Divinity but he has the relish for the perishable because he wants to satisfy the hunger of the imperishable by the perishable. This duality between hunger and relish strengthens a man's worldly bondage. When his attachment and aversion to the world are wiped out, then his thirst for Self-realization is fulfilled and his desire is wiped out and he becomes free from dualities (pairs of opposites).

Link:—In the first half of the second verse of this chapter, the Lord declared, "Disciplines of Knowledge and Action—both lead to salvation." The Lord, explains the same point, in the next two verses.

साङ्ख्ययोगौ पृथग्बालाः प्रवदन्ति न पण्डिताः ।
एकमप्यास्थितः सम्यगुभयोर्विन्दते फलम् ॥ ४ ॥

sāṅkhyayogau pṛthagbālāḥ pravadanti na paṇḍitāḥ
ekamapyāsthitaḥ samyagubhayorvindate phalam

The ignorant, not the wise, speak of the Discipline of Knowledge (Sāṅkhyayoga) and Discipline of Action (Karmayoga), as different. He, who is well established in one, gets the fruit of both. 4

Comment:—

'Sāṅkhyayogau pṛthagbālāḥ pravadanti na paṇḍitāḥ'—Arjuna, in the first verse of this chapter, called the method of gaining knowledge from the wise who have realized the Truth, having renounced actions, as Karmasannyāsa. In the second verse, the Lord, attaching importance to His principle, called it Sannyāsa and Karmasannyāsa. Now, the Lord calls it 'Sāṅkhya'. By Sāṅkhya, He means establishment in the self by discriminating, the self from the body. According to Him, 'Sannyāsa' and

'Sāṅkhya', are synonyms, in which there is no need of renouncing actions physically.

What Arjuna calls 'Karmasannyāsa' is undoubtedly, a kind of 'Sāṅkhya' mentioned by the Lord, because after receiving instruction from a preceptor a striver, comes to know reality, about the body and the soul.

The Lord, by the term 'Bālāḥ', means to convey that those, who say that Sāṅkhya (Discipline of Knowledge) and Karmayoga (Discipline of Action), produce different results, are children viz., and ignorant, even though, they may be aged and intellectual. But the wise, say that both of these produce the same result, though they may be different, as means. The Lord Himself, in the third verse of the third chapter, declared the twofold path—the path of knowledge and that of action—different as means, but the goal is one.

'Ekamapyāsthitaḥ samyagubhayorvindate phalam'—In the Gītā, time and again, it has been pointed out, that the result of the practice of Sāṅkhyayoga, (Discipline of Knowledge) and that of Karmayoga (Discipline of Action), is the same. In the twenty-fourth verse of the thirteenth chapter, the Lord declares that the self or God can be perceived, both through the path of knowledge and that of action. In the nineteenth verse of the third chapter, it has been mentioned, that a man reaches the Supreme, through the Discipline of Action, while in the fourth verse of the twelfth chapter and the thirty-fourth verse of the thirteenth chapter, it has been mentioned, that strivers reach the Supreme by following the Discipline of Knowledge. Thus according to the Lord, both of the paths lead to the same destination.

Appendix—He who knows the scriptural topics but does not know the reality about 'Sāṅkhyayoga' and 'Karmayoga' deeply, is indeed a child viz., is ignorant.

In whole of the Gītā the term 'phala' (fruit) for the imperishable reality has been used only in this verse. The term 'phala' means 'result'. Karmayoga and Jñānayoga—the Lord's purpose in calling the reality attained by these two disciplines as 'phala' is that in these two disciplines, a man's effort is important. In Jñānayoga effort in the form of discrimination is important and in Karmayoga effort in the form of action for the welfare of others, is important. A striver's own effort (labour) proves fruitful, so it has been called 'phala' (fruit). This fruit is not perishable. Karmayoga and Jñānayoga—both of them bear fruit in the form of Self-realization or attainment of the Absolute.

'Performance of duty' is Karmayoga and 'Inclination to do nothing' is Jñānayoga. The reality which is attained by doing nothing, is attained by discharging one's duty. 'Performance' (to do) and 'non-performance' (not to do) are the means (spiritual disciplines) and the reality which is attained by these means is the end (goal).

~~~

यत्साङ्ख्यैः प्राप्यते स्थानं तद्योगैरपि गम्यते।
एकं साङ्ख्यं च योगं च यः पश्यति स पश्यति॥५॥

yatsāṅkhyaiḥ prāpyate sthānaṁ tadyogairapi gamyate
ekaṁ sāṅkhyam ca yogaṁ ca yaḥ paśyati sa paśyati

The supreme state, which is attained by the Sāṅkhyayogī is also reached by the Karmayogī. He, who sees that the ways (as result) of Sāṅkhyayoga and Karmayoga are one, perceives the reality. 5

Comment:—

'Yatsāṅkhyaiḥ prāpyate sthānaṁ tadyogairapi gamyate'—In the second half of the preceding verse, the Lord declared, "He who is well established in Sāṅkhyayoga or Karmayoga (performance of action), gets the fruit of both i.e., attains God-realization." The same fact, is being pointed out by the Lord here, in this verse by declaring, that the state which is attained by a Sāṅkhyayogī, is also attained by a Karmayogī.

The Lord, uses the term 'api' (also), here to remove the
~~~

doubt of those people, who think that God can be realized only by the Discipline of Knowledge, rather than by the Discipline of Action.

A striver, through both the disciplines, has to renounce his affinity for actions i.e., for active prakṛti (nature). A Karmayogī, in order to, distinguish the sentient from the insentient, has to use the discrimination of a Jñānayogī, even during spiritual practice. Similarly, a Jñānayogī (Sāṅkhyayogī), has to adopt the method of Karmayoga, of not performing action for himself. A Sāṅkhyayogī's discrimination, is to be utilized to distinguish the soul, from the body (world); and the actions of a Karmayogī are performed, in order to, render service to the world. When two strivers—one following the path of Sāṅkhyayoga and the other of Karmayoga—attain perfection, both of them reach the same destination i.e., have liberation (Gītā 3/3).

The world is uneven. The closest, worldly relationship is not free from this unevenness, while the Lord is even and uniform. So, He can be realized by renouncing affinity, for the world. There are two paths—of knowledge and of action, available to renounce, this affinity. Jñānayoga (the Discipline of Knowledge), consists in thinking that the real self lacks nothing, and so there is no question of any desire or attachment in the real self. By thinking so, a striver gets detached. In Karmayoga, a striver renders service to others, with those objects he is attached to and to those persons he is attached to, without any selfish motive. Thus in the Discipline of Knowledge, through discrimination, while in the Discipline of Action through service, affinity for the world is renounced.

'Ekaṁ sāṅkhyaṁ ca yogaṁ ca yaḥ paśyati sa paśyati'—In the first half of the preceding verse, the Lord declared by negative inference, "The ignorant, not the wise, speak of the Sāṅkhyayoga and the Karmayoga, as different." The same fact, is being pointed out here, by positive inference when the Lord declares, "He who sees that the ways (as result) of Sāṅkhyayoga and Karmayoga, are one, he sees (truly)."

Thus the gist, of the fourth and the fifth verses, is that the Lord regards both the Disciplines of Knowledge and Action, as independent spiritual disciplines and the fruit of both is God-realization. Those who do not know this reality, are called ignorant, while those who know this reality, are designated wise, by the Lord.

An Important Fact

When a striver, attains perfection in anyone of the spiritual disciplines, he has neither a desire to live, nor fear of death, nor a desire to acquire anything, or do anything.

A perishable body, need not be afraid of death, because it is decaying all the time, while the self, need not have a desire to live, because it is eternal. Then, who is afraid of death and who has a desire to live? The answer is, that when the self identifies Itself with the body, it is afraid of death and it has a desire, to live. Both of these, (the desire to live and the fear of death) can be wiped out, by the Discipline of Knowledge (discrimination).

The self, lacks nothing; therefore, it has no desire to acquire anything, and so no desire to do any work. But when it identifies itself with a body, It feels the lack. Then, It has a desire to acquire, something or the other; and in order to acquire that, It has to act. The desire to acquire and to act, perishes through Karmayoga.

When either the Discipline of Knowledge or the Discipline of Action, attains perfection, the desires to live, to acquire and to act, and the fear of death, totally perish.

Appendix—Sāṅkhyayoga and Karmayoga—both disciplines being worldly are one and the same. In Sāṅkhyayoga a striver gets established in the self and being established in the self, matter (non-self) is renounced. In Karmayoga a striver renounces matter and having renounced matter (non-self), he gets established in the self. In this way the result of both—Sāṅkhyayoga and Karmayoga is attainment of divinity (pure-consciousness) viz., Self-realization.

To apply the body in the service of the world is Karmayoga and to detach the self from the body is Jñānayoga. Either apply the body in the service of the world or get the self detached from the body—both will bear the same fruit viz., by both these disciplines, having renounced affinity for the world, one will get established in the self.

Here in the fourth and fifth verses the first half of the fourth verse has connection with the second half of the fifth verse and the first half of the fifth verse has connection with the second half of the fourth verse.

Karmayoga, Jñānayoga and Bhaktiyoga—out of these three disciplines, Jñānayoga and Bhaktiyoga are more popular but there is less popularity of Karmayoga. The Lord in the Gītā also declares, "This Karmayoga through long lapse of time is lost to the world" (Gītā 4/2). Therefore about Karmayoga, there is a general belief that this is not an independent means of God-realization and so a striver following the Discipline of Action afterwards either follows Jñānayoga or Bhaktiyoga as—

tāvat karmāṇi kurvīta na nirvidyeta yāvatā
matkathāśravaṇādau vā śraddhā yāvanna jāyate

(Śrīmadbhā. 11/20/9)

A person should perform actions by the time till he develops dispassion for pleasures (he becomes eligible for Jñānayoga) or he develops faith in listening to My pastime and life story (he becomes qualified for Bhaktiyoga).

But here the Lord declares that just like Jñānayoga, Karmayoga is also an independent discipline for God-realization. Besides these fourth and fifth verses in several other verses also the Lord has mentioned that Karmayoga is an independent means to attain Self-realization or the Supreme peace or salvation or God-realization as—'tatsvayaṁ yogasaṁsiddhaḥ kālenātmani vindati' (4/38), 'yogayukto munirbrahma nacireṇādhigacchati' (5/6), 'yajñāyācarataḥ karma samagraṁ pravilīyate' (4/23), 'jñānāgnidagdhakarmāṇaṁ tamāhuḥ paṇḍitaṁ budhāḥ' (4/19); 'yuktaḥ karmaphalaṁ tyaktvā śāntimāpnoti naiṣṭhikīm' (5/12).

In Śrīmadbhāgavata also Karmayoga has been mentioned as an independent means for God-realization—

svadharmastho yajan yajñairanāśīḥ kāma uddhava
na yāti svarganarakau yadyanyanna samācaret
(11/20/10)

'He, who being situated in his own 'dharma' (duty) and renouncing the desire for pleasure, worships God by the performance of his duty and does not do any action with an interested motive, has not to go to heaven or hell viz., he is freed from the bondage of actions.

asmiṁlloke vartamānaḥ svadharmastho'naghaḥ śuciḥ
jñānaṁ viśuddhamāpnoti madbhaktiṁ vā yadṛcchayā
(11/20/11)

The Karmayogī being situated in his own dharma (duty) in spite of discharging all his duties in this world, being free from the fruit of sinful and virtuous actions, attains Self-realization or Supreme devotion (Parābhakti).

It means that Karmayoga (the Discipline of Action) makes a striver qualified for Jñānayoga (the Discipline of Knowledge) or Bhaktiyoga (the Discipline of Devotion) and also independently leads him to salvation. In other words it can be said that Karmayoga is a means for Jñānayoga or Bhaktiyoga and is also an end viz., it can lead to Self-realization or Supreme devotion.

Link:—In the second verse of this chapter, the Lord declared, the Discipline of Action to be better, than the Discipline of

Knowledge. The Lord emphasizes the same fact, in another way, in the next verse.

सन्न्यासस्तु महाबाहो दुःखमाप्तुमयोगतः।
योगयुक्तो मुनिर्ब्रह्म नचिरेणाधिगच्छति॥ ६॥

sannyāsastu mahābāho duḥkhamāptumayogataḥ
yogayukto munirbrahma nacireṇādhigacchati

But the discipline of knowledge, O mighty-armed (Arjuna), is difficult to attain without the discipline of action; the sage who is adept in Karmayoga (the discipline of action), quickly attains to the Absolute. 6

Comment:—

'Sannyāsastu mahābāho duḥkhamāptumayogataḥ'—The term 'tu' (but), has been used to explain, that the Discipline of Action (Yoga), is necessary for the success of Sāṅkhyayoga (the Discipline of Knowledge), because the latter is difficult to attain without the former, while the former can be practised, without the latter.

A Sāṅkhyayogī's aim, is to realize God. But, so long as he has attachment, not to talk, of God-realization, he cannot even understand, the Discipline of Knowledge.

An easy way to wipe out attachment, is to follow the Discipline of Action. In this discipline, all actions are performed for the welfare of others. By doing so attachment, is naturally wiped out. So having wiped out attachment, through this discipline, the practice of Discipline of Knowledge, becomes easy. Therefore, the success of the Discipline of Knowledge, is difficult without resorting to the Discipline of Action.

'Yogayukto munirbrahma nacireṇādhigacchati'—A Karmayogī, who is cautious to remain unattached, and thinks of the welfare of others, has been called a 'Muniḥ' (sage).

A Karmayogī, during the performance of every action, whether significant or trifling, keeps in mind that he has to perform it, without any selfish motive, only for the welfare of others. By thinking so, his attachment is easily renounced.

Thus the Lord explains, that a Karmayogī, quickly attains to the Absolute. Attachment to the world, is an obstacle to God-realization. When a striver, following the path of action, works for the welfare of others, his attachment is totally renounced, and with the total renunciation of attachment, God Who is ever-attainable, is naturally, realized. The same fact, has been pointed out, in the thirty-eighth verse of the fourth chapter, when He declares, "He, who has attained perfection by Yoga (Discipline of Action), finds the knowledge of the self i.e., God-realization, certainly and naturally." In this path, there is neither any difficulty, nor delay nor any need for any other means.

The second reason is, that an embodied being, cannot abandon, actions entirely; but he who relinquishes the rewards of actions, is verily called a man of renunciation (18/11). It denotes, that an embodied being cannot renounce action, but at least, he can renounce desire, for the fruit of actions. Therefore, the Discipline of Action (Karmayoga) is easy to practise.

While revealing the glory of the Discipline of Action, the Lord declares, "Peace immediately follows the renunciation of fruit of action" (Gītā 12/12); and "Such a Karmayogī is easily set free, from bondage" (Gītā 5/3). Thus, the Discipline of Action is easy, quick and an independent means of God-realization.

Link:—Now in the next verse the Lord describes the marks of a Karmayogī.

योगयुक्तो विशुद्धात्मा विजितात्मा जितेन्द्रियः ।
सर्वभूतात्मभूतात्मा कुर्वन्नपि न लिप्यते ॥ ७ ॥

yogayukto viśuddhātmā vijitātmā jitendriyaḥ
sarvabhūtātmabhūtātmā kurvannapi na lipyate

The Karmayogī, whose mind is pure, has controlled his body and has subdued his senses and whose self is one with the self of all beings, is not tainted by actions even though he acts. 7

Comment:—

'Jitendriyaḥ'—Senses, are said to be subdued, when they are free from attachment and aversion. When senses become free from attachment and aversion, they cannot deflect the mind.* A striver can engage them, in any activity as he wishes.

It is necessary for a striver, who follows the Discipline of Action, to subdue his senses. Therefore, Lord Kṛṣṇa lays special emphasis on the control of the senses, in the Discipline of Action as He declares—"Controlling the senses by the mind" (3/7); and "Control thy senses from the beginning" (3/41). A Karmayogī, has ever to perform actions, therefore, he can deviate from the right path, if his senses are not under control. He can render selfless service to others, for their welfare, only when, his senses are under control.

'Viśuddhātmā'—When a person, attaches importance to worldly objects, his mind, becomes impure, because he has desire to acquire worldly objects. When he has, the only aim of God-realization, his mind is purified more quickly, than it is by any other method. Therefore, fixing of an aim, plays an important role, in the Discipline of Action.

'Vijitātmā'—While following, the Discipline of Action, a striver must renounce bodily comfort. If he engages himself in indolence and carelessness, he will not be able to follow this discipline. So he should control, his body.

'Sarvabhūtātmabhūtātmā'—A Karmayogī, identifies himself

* The person, who after hearing, touching, seeing, eating and smelling, gets neither pleased nor displeased; should be known as one who has subdued his senses (Manusmṛti 2/98).

with all beings.* As all other limbs, are engaged in serving an injured limb, automatically without any sense of pride or doership or desire for fruit etc., so does a Karmayogī, render service to others, by identifying himself with them, without any pride or sense of doership, or desire for fruit etc.

As a person, in spite of having different dealings with different limbs, loves them equally, so does a Karmayogī treating beings differently, according to scriptural and social decorum, love them equally. To efface attachment, it is very necessary for him, to identify himself, with all beings.

It is in the nature of a Karmayogī, to be generous. Generosity is generated, when a Karmayogī identifies himself, with the soul of others.

An Important Fact

Actions and objects, are transitory and ever-changing, while we (the self), is permanent and uniform. So actions and objects, are continually abandoning us. If we abandon these, we can attain salvation or supreme peace, because the two belong to two different classes. The objects and actions, are to be utilized in rendering service to others, without having any pride, because in fact, they are theirs. This service, involves no effort.

We can serve others by objects and actions, only on developing generosity in us. Here, one point needs attention, that we ourselves are generosity personified. Therefore, generosity involves, neither expenditure, nor effort. We should be pleased by seeing a man happy, and take pity and feel sad, by seeing a man, sad. Seeing a happy man, we should wish every being to be happy, and seeing one sad, we should wish, no one to be sad.

According to the Lord,* pleasure and prosperity, are two

* Either get detached from one's own body or identify the body with those of others both will bear the same fruit. A Jñānayogī gets detached from his body while a Karmayogī identifies his body with those of others. This identification makes him generous.

stumbling blocks to spiritual progress (Gītā 2/44). When we feel happy, after seeing a man happy, our desire for pleasure perishes, because we have become happy without enjoying pleasure. Similarly, our desire for prosperity perishes, because we spend money (prosperity) and material, naturally according to our best capability to remove the suffering of a sad person, by being sad with him, as we identify ourselves with him. In such happiness or pity, there is an uncommon relish, which conduces a man to renounce affinity, for actions and objects, and then he (the self) realizes his identity with God.

'Yogayuktaḥ'—The Karmayogī, whose mind is pure, who has controlled the body, who has subdued his senses and whose self is the Self of all beings, is called 'Yogayuktaḥ' (devoted to the path of action).

A striver, is not naturally inclined towards spiritual discipline, because his aim and his inclination, are different. So long as, there is importance of the world in the mind, there is struggle between the aim and inclination. Generally, a striver's aim is to realize God, Who is imperishable while his inclination is towards perishable, worldly beings, objects and circumstances. When his aim and inclination, are identified, spiritual discipline is automatically practised, speedily. Here the term 'Yogayuktaḥ' (devoted to the path of action), has been used for such a Karmayogī, whose aim and inclination, have become one i.e., God-realization.

In Karmayoga, there is no desire in the least, for fruit of actions, but there is certainly an aim, to be achieved. The fruit and the aim, are different. An aim is one, which can be ever achieved by everyone. Thus, one's aim is God-realization and He can be realized, without any action and practice. The fruit is perishable, while God is eternal. A Karmayogī, does not desire the perishable, because this desire is an obstacle to God-realization. When a Karmayogī's, only aim is God-realization, he is called 'Yogayukta' (devoted to the path of action).

He, who has been called 'Yogayuktaḥ' here, has been called 'Yogārūḍhaḥ' (one who has attained to Yoga), in the fourth verse of the sixth chapter.

'Kurvannapi na lipyate'—A Karmayogī, in spite of performing actions is not bound by actions. A sense of mine, for actions, desire for the fruit of actions, and for pleasure, and a sense of doership* bind a man, to actions. The gist is, that desire to acquire something or the other, leads, a man to bondage. As a Karmayogī, has no desire to acquire anything, he is not tainted (bound) i.e., his actions change into inaction.

A Sāṅkhyayogī, is not bound by actions, because he thinks that it is the modes which are acting on the modes (Gītā 3/28); while a Karmayogī is not bound, as he performs actions, for the welfare of others, without any selfish motive.

The term 'api' (even), shows that a Karmayogī remains untainted, not only during the performance of action but also during their non-performance (Gītā 4/18). He has no interest, in the performance or non-performance of actions (Gītā 3/18). He always remains, untainted.

It means that, a Sāṅkhyayogī having renounced his affinity for the insentient, identifies himself with the sentient, while a Karmayogī identifies his so-called body, mind, senses, objects and actions etc., with the world i.e., instead of regarding them as of his and for himself, he regards them as the world and for the world. With this attitude of mind, he cannot have any egoistic feeling, in providing comfort to others, doing good to them and performing righteous acts, for them. Therefore, while performing action, he has no sense of doership i.e., is not tainted by action.

---

* The Lord while describing Karmayoga, in the forty-seventh verse of the second chapter by the expression 'Mā karmaphalaheturbhūḥ' means to say that a striver should renounce the sense of mine, the desire for pleasure and the sense of doership while by the expression 'Mā phaleṣu kadācana' He exhorts him to renounce the desire for the fruit of action.

Appendix—When a Karmayogī having renounced affinity for the body, senses and mind (inner sense) realizes his identity with all beings, then in spite of performing actions, the egoistic notion does not persist in him. Being free from egoism, the actions performed by him don't lead to bondage (Gītā 18/17).

Link:—Having described the marks of a Karmayogī, the Lord in the next two verses, describes the attitude of a Sāṅkhyayogī, while undertaking activities, with the senses.

नैव किञ्चित्करोमीति युक्तो मन्येत तत्त्ववित्।
पश्यञ्शृण्वन्स्पृशञ्जिघ्रन्नश्नन्गच्छन्स्वपञ्श्वसन् ॥ ८ ॥
प्रलपन्विसृजन्गृह्णन्नुन्मिषन्निमिषन्नपि ।
इन्द्रियाणीन्द्रियार्थेषु वर्तन्त इति धारयन्॥ ९ ॥

naiva kiñcitkaromīti yukto manyeta tattvavit
paśyañśṛṇvanspṛśañjighrannaśnangacchansvapañśvasan
pralapanvisṛjangṛhṇannunmiṣannimiṣannapi
indriyāṇīndriyārtheṣu vartanta iti dhārayan

The Sāṅkhyayogī, who knows the truth, believes, even though seeing, hearing, touching, smelling, eating, walking, sleeping, breathing, speaking, emitting, grasping, opening and closing the eyes, that he does nothing; he holds that the senses move among the sense-objects. 8-9

Comment:—

'Tattvavit yuktaḥ'—Here, this expression, stands for the wise striver following the Discipline of Knowledge, who has realized the truth, that all actions are performed by prakṛti (nature) and he has no affinity for them, he is merely a witness, of the activities of senses.

A 'Tattvavit' (knower of the truth), is he who thinks, that he (the self) is not the doer; is different from the body, senses, mind, intellect and life-breath, which perform the activities.

In fact, a man (the self) is a non-doer, but by an error he regards the self, as a doer (Gītā 3/27). Actually all the cosmic, as well as individual actions are performed by Nature. But a man, by identifying himself with the body, regards its action as his action. So long as, he has in the least a sense of doership, he is called a striver. But when he realizes, that the Self is not at all the doer, he is called a great soul, who knows the truth. As a person, having awakened from sleep, has nothing to do with a dream, so has a great soul, having known the truth, no affinity for actions performed by the body and the senses etc.

Such a great soul, knows the truth that the self is different from the modes of nature by which actions, are performed. The self, is the base and illuminator of all the objects and actions etc., It pervades everywhere, and does not undergo any change, while objects and actions, undergo. The same fact, of distinction between the nature (Kṣetra) and soul (Kṣetrajña), has been pointed out by the Lord, in the sixteenth verse of the second chapter, in the fourth and the fifth verses of the seventh chapter and in the second, the nineteenth, the twenty-third and the thirty-fourth verses, of the thirteenth chapter.

'Paśyañśṛṇvanspṛśañ......unmiṣannimiṣannapi'—Here, the five actions—seeing, hearing, touching, smelling and eating, pertain to five senses (eye, ear, skin, nose and tongue), while walking, grasping, speaking and emitting, these four actions relate to the five organs of actions*—feet, hands, tongue, genital organ and anus. Sleeping, is an activity of the mind, breathing of life-breath, opening and closing the eyes, of the sub-life-breath named Kūrma.

Thus, by mentioning the above thirteen actions, the Lord has

* Here the description of the five organs of action has been included in four actions, i.e., within 'emitting' the actions of both the genital organ and the anus have been included.

described all possible actions performed by sense-organs, organs of action, mind, life-breath and sub-life-breath. It means that all actions are performed by the body, senses, mind, intellect and life-breath etc., the evolutes of nature, rather than by the self. Secondly, it also denotes that a Sāṅkhyayogī can also perform other acts, such as eating or drinking, business, preaching, writing, reading, hearing and thinking etc., and also other acts for maintaining the body according to caste, order of life, nature and circumstances etc.

A man, considers himself a doer of those acts, which he performs intentionally i.e., by applying his mind and intellect etc., such as reading, writing, thinking, seeing and eating etc. But there are several other activities, such as breathing, opening and closing the eyes, which are performed unintentionally. Then, why has the Lord mentioned, in this verse, that a man should not regard himself as a doer of these acts? The answer is, that breathing is a natural activity, yet in breath-restraint (prāṇāyāma) etc., breathing becomes an intentional activity. Similarly, eyes can also be opened and shut intentionally. So the Lord, has mentioned that a man should not hold, that he is a doer. Secondly, the Lord by mentioning, breathing, opening and closing the eyes, wants to convey, that as a man during these activities thinks that he does nothing, so should he consider himself a non-doer, while other activities are performed.

All the above-mentioned activities, cannot be performed, without a base and an illuminator. The Lord, mentions these activities, in order to draw the attention of the strivers, to the self, which in spite of being the base, and illuminator of all these activities, does nothing.

'Indriyāṇīndriyārtheṣu vartanta iti dhārayan'—The question arises, how are actions performed, when there is no doership in the self. The Lord, answers the question, by declaring that actions are performed, when senses move among the sense-objects i.e., the self remains the non-doer (untainted).

The term 'Indriyāṇi' (senses) includes the sense-organs, the organs of action, mind, life-breath and sub-life-breath etc. There are five objects of senses—sound, touch, sight, taste and smell. The senses move among these objects. All the senses and objects of senses, are the evolutes of nature. So all the actions are performed, by nature. The Lord declares:—

"All kinds of actions are done, by the modes of nature" (Gītā 3/27).

"All actions are performed by nature, alone" (Gītā 13/29).

The senses, and the sense-objects, being the evolutes of modes of nature, are called modes. So it is said, "It is the modes, which are acting on the modes" (Gītā 3/28). "There is no agent, other than the modes" (Gītā 14/19). It means, that when it is said that actions are performed by prakṛti (nature), or by modes of nature or by the senses—these three amount to one and the same.

Nature, always undergoes modifications, while the self never undergoes any, It ever remains free from a sense of doership. Nature can never be inactive, while in the self, no action is possible. The self is the illuminator of actions, while actions are subject to illumination.

'Naiva kiñcitkaromīti manyeta'—It means, that the self, was neither a doer in the past, nor is at present, or will be in future. Nature is ever active and all actions are performed by Nature, while the self, does nothing. But when the self identifies Itself with the evolute of Nature, and regards the activities of nature as Its activities, It becomes, a doer (Gītā 3/27).

As a man, sitting in the compartment of a moving train, does not move himself but he cannot remain without covering the distance covered by the train, while he is seated in a compartment. Similarly, when a man, assumes his affinity for the physical (gross), subtle or causal body, which are the evolutes of active Nature, he becomes a doer of actions performed by these.

A Sāṅkhyayogī, never assumes his affinity for the body, senses and mind etc., so he never regards himself, as a doer (Gītā 5/13). As actions, such as the growth of a boy from childhood to youth, changing of black hair into grey and white, digestion of food and weakening or strengthening of a body automatically take place, so does a Sāṅkhyayogī think, that all other activities are undertaken naturally and he is not their doer.

In the Gītā, a person who regards himself as a doer of actions, has been spoken of adversely. The Lord declares, "He whose mind is deluded by egoism, thinks that he is the doer" (3/27). "He who looks upon himself as the doer (agent), he of perverted mind and untrained understanding, does not see (truly)" (18/16). But the Lord praises a person, who sees the self as actionless, by declaring, "He who sees that all actions are performed by nature (prakṛti) alone, and likewise that the self is not the doer, he verily sees (13/29).

The Lord, uses the term 'eva' (even), in order to convey that a striver should never think, that he is a doer. By doing so, his sense of doership comes to an end and his actions change into inaction. The same idea, has been conveyed by the Lord, in the thirty-third verse of the third chapter, by the term 'Ceṣṭate', which means that his actions are nothing more than mere gestures, of actions.

The second interpretation of the term 'Eva', is that even when a man identifies himself with the body and considers himself the doer, he cannot be the doer. It is merely an assumption, which can never come true. The Lord, in the thirty-first verse of the thirteenth chapter, declares, "The imperishable supreme self, though dwelling in the body, neither acts nor is tainted." "The soul, residing in Nature experiences pleasure and pain" (Gītā 13/21). In spite of experiencing the modes born of nature, the man (self), ever remains the same. But he gets tainted, because he does not see, the self.

The Self, is sentient while the world, including the body, is insentient. So the self experiences pleasure and pain. Why? The reason is, that it identifies itself with the body (world) and experiences pleasure and pain. But if It knows, its true nature that It is imperishable, uniform and untainted, while nature in the form of the world, the body and pleasures and pains, is perishable, then it cannot be an experiencer, of pleasures and pains etc.

An Important Fact

The Lord, in the twenty-seventh verse of the third chapter, declared, "He whose mind is deluded by egoism, thinks that he is the doer." Here, in this verse also, the same fact has been pointed out by the Lord through a negative inference, when He declares, "The Sāṅkhyayogī who knows the truth realizes that he does nothing. Here the term, 'Manyeta' (think) does not mean, 'to assume' but 'to realize'. The self, remains a non-doer during the performance and non-performance of actions, equally. So, the great soul who has known the truth, realizes that the self ever remains the same, as a non-doer, either during the performance or non-performance of actions. The self, as the base and illuminator, never undergoes the least modification.

The self, never lacks anything, but when It identifies Itself with nature, It feels a deficiency in It, and so It desires objects, in order to make up. In order to fulfil that desire, It becomes a doer.

No action, can be performed without nature, because the instruments, such as the senses and the body etc., with which actions are performed, belong to nature. So a doer, has to depend on them. As a goldsmith howsoever an expert he may be, cannot prepare ornaments, without instruments, such as an anvil and a hammer etc. In the same way, a doer cannot perform action without instruments. Thus qualifications, ability and instruments—all the three belong to nature (prakṛti), but these appear to be in the self, because of affinity for Nature. The instruments, undergo modifications while the self ever remains the same. Therefore, they have no affinity for the self.

A man (the self) thinks, that he is a doer by assuming his affinity for Nature, otherwise there is no doership, in him. As a Brāhmaṇa ever remains convinced that he is a Brāhmaṇa, so does a great soul, who knows the truth, believe that he is not a doer.

Appendix—A discriminating Jñānayogī by performing actions with senses of perception, organs of actions, mind (internal instrument) and life-breath first assumes 'I myself do nothing' and afterwards he realizes it. In fact in the Divine Existence neither an action is performed nor any activity happens. All actions performed in the gross, subtle and causal bodies actually take place in Prakṛti, not in the self. Therefore the self has no connection at all with any action.

Through ignorance a man by identifying 'ego' with the self, is deluded—'ahaṅkāra vimūḍhātmā' (Gītā 3/27); the same man by the use of discrimination by detaching the self from ego, becomes 'tattvavit' (an enlightened soul) viz., he has no sense of doership. He ever remains established in the divine self.

The self, being deluded by egoism by an error, thinks itself a doer and is thus bound by actions and their fruit and paves the way to eighty-four lac forms of lives. Now if a man regards himself as detached from egoism and does not consider himself a doer viz., realizes the self as it is, there is no surprise about his being an enlightened soul (liberated soul). It means that by assuming the unreal as real, unreal appears to be real, then what is the surprise, if by accepting the real as real, it is seen real?

In fact when a man assumes the self as a doer and an enjoyer, at that time also he is neither a doer nor an enjoyer—'śarīra-stho'pi kaunteya na karoti na lipyate' (Gītā 13/31). The reason is that the self is merely an Ever-Existent Reality. In that Reality there is no ego and ego has no existence. Therefore 'I am a doer'—however firm this assumption may be but it is certainly an error. An error is wiped out as soon as it is realized that it is an error—this is the rule. A cave may have been dark for hundreds of years, but darkness disappears immediately as soon as there is light, it doesn't need years and months to disappear. Therefore a striver should firmly hold 'I am not a doer'. Then this assumption will no longer remain an assumption but it will be transformed into realization.

"In 'I' this is identification of both sentient and insentient." 'I' is used for matter (identified ego) and also for the sentient (self). For example—'I am a doer'—in it there is perception of insentient and 'I am not a doer'—in it (being negation of matter) the self is perceived. He, who has an eye on matter viz., regards ego as the self, is deluded—ahaṁkāra vimūḍhātmā' and who has an eye on the sentient (the self free from ego) is an enlightened soul.

When a striver at present 'I myself do nothing'—thus endeavours to realize the self as a non-doer, he faces a serious problem. When he remembers virtuous actions done in the past, he gets pleased that he had done very good actions. When he remembers the forbidden actions done in the past, he becomes sad that he had done such a sinful act and he had committed such a blunder. Thus the impression of the past actions make him happy and sad. In this connection there is a vital point which needs attention. The self is never a doer—neither at present nor in the past nor in the future. Therefore a striver should perceive that as the self is a non-doer at present, so was it in the past. The reason is that the present has become the past. The self is merely an Ever Existent Entity in which no performance of action is possible. Actions are performed only by an ignorant man whose mind is deluded by egoism (Gītā 3/27). A striver feels happy and sad and is worried by remembering the past actions, that is also really because of egoism. At present being deluded by egoism viz., by having affinity for egoism, a striver feels happy and sad. If we perceive from the cursory (gross) point of view, as the past has no existence now, so are the actions of the past clearly non-existent. If we perceive from the subtle point of view, we perceive that as in the past, the present was non-existent, so was the past also non-existent. Similarly as the past is non-existent now, so is the present non-existent now. But the entity (the self) ever exists. It means that the self is totally free from the limits of past, present and future time. The self transcends the limits of time. Therefore the self is never a doer. In that entity, which transcends time and state (condition), imposition of doership and enjoyership by connecting it with a particular time or situation, is ignorance. Therefore the memory of the actions performed in the past, is the memory of the person whose mind is deluded by egoism rather than of an enlightened soul.

'Naiva kiñcitkaromi' means that actions have no existence but the entity exists. Therefore a striver should have an eye on that entity. That entity being divine is 'Knowledge personified' and being immutable is 'bliss personified'. This bliss is integral, quiet and immutable (uniform).

Because of the identification of the self with the body, in every action a man thinks that he himself is the doer as 'I see, I hear etc.' An action takes place in the body but a man assumes it in the self. In the self there is no action, the self is free from the performance or non-performance of actions (Gītā 3/18). Therefore even when the actions are performed by the body, a man should have an eye on the self and hold, "I do nothing at all."

Link:—Having described, in the seventh verse, how a Karmayogī remains untainted by actions, and in the eighth and the ninth verses, how a Sāṅkhyayogī remains untainted, the Lord, in the next verse, describes how a Bhaktiyogī, remains untainted by actions.

ब्रह्मण्याधाय कर्माणि सङ्गं त्यक्त्वा करोति यः ।
लिप्यते न स पापेन पद्मपत्रमिवाम्भसा ॥ १० ॥

brahmaṇyādhāya karmāṇi saṅgaṁ tyaktvā karoti yaḥ
lipyate na sa pāpena padmapatramivāmbhasā

He who performs actions, dedicated to God and abandoning all attachment, is not tainted by sin, just as a lotus-leaf is not moistened by water. 10

Comment:—

'Brahmaṇyādhāya karmāṇi'—A body, senses, mind, intellect and the life-breath bestowed by God, belong to Him. Therefore, how can a devotee, following the path of devotion, regard actions which are performed by body and senses etc., as his? He holds, that all actions are being performed by the Lord for Him; he is merely an instrument, in His hands.

The Lord, wants to convey that it is He, Who performs all actions with His senses. A striver, realizing this fact, should think that He is the doer, of all actions.

The worldly objects, such as the body etc., are not a person's own, these have been acquired, and these abandon him. So these should be utilized, in rendering service to others, as offerings to God. A person, cannot keep these as he wishes, neither can he change these, nor carry these with him, when he leaves his body. So, it is not honesty on his part, to regard these as his own. They are the Lord's, and so these should be, accepted as His.

A Karmayogī, offers all actions and objects, to the world, a Jñānayogī to nature, and a Bhaktiyogī, to God. God, is the master of both nature and the world, and so it is better to offer these to Him.

'Saṅgaṁ tyaktvā karoti yaḥ'—A man, is said to have abandoned attachment, when he has not, the least, attachment or attraction for beings, objects, senses, mind, intellect, life-breath and actions, and has no sense of mine, or desire for them.

Besides ignorance, which has been called the cause of life and death, in the scriptures from the stand point of the spiritual discipline attachment to the modes, is the chief cause of an embodied soul's birth, in good and evil bodies (Gītā 13/21). Ignorance, is based on attachment, therefore, when attachment is renounced, ignorance also perishes. Desire springs, from attachment (Gītā 2/62), and is the root of all sins (Gītā 3/37). Thus here in this verse, it is mentioned, that attachment which is the root of sins, should be abandoned otherwise a man will go on committing sins. In its absence, he incurs no sin.

A man's, affinity for action, is not renounced, so long as, he derives pleasure by performing it, and remains attached to its fruit, it is rather enhanced. Attachment of a person does not consist in merely desire for fruit of action, but also in being called good by others. So, action should be performed, without the least desire for pleasure, comfort or honour etc. If there is desire for getting pleasure, anyhow in the least, then that action is for one's self.

'Lipyate na sa pāpena padmapatramivāmbhasā'—A devotee, following the Discipline of Devotion, while living in the world and performing actions, in order to offer these to God, is not tainted, (bound) in the same way, as a lotus-leaf living in water is not soiled by water.

Desire for the world, and having a disinclination for God, is the root of all sins. Desire, springs from attachment. Where, there is no attachment, there is no desire and so sins cannot be committed, without attachment.

All undertakings are covered by defects (evils), as fire by smoke (Gītā 18/48). But, he who has renounced, hope, desire and attachment, becomes free from all defects. When actions are performed, in order to be offered to God, having abandoned attachment, a striver becomes free, from the accumulation of all sins (Gītā 9/27-28). Therefore, a Bhaktiyogī, totally becomes, free from sins.

Here, the term 'pāpena' (sin), stands for the fruit of past actions, in the form of virtue or vice, which cause the soul to be born in good and evil bodies. A Bhaktiyogī, is never tainted (bound) by that fruit, in the form of virtue and vice. The same fact, has been pointed out by the Lord, in the twenty-eighth verse of the ninth chapter, when He declares, "Thus, shalt thou be freed, from the bonds of actions, yielding good and evil fruits."

Appendix—Here God endowed with attributes has been called 'Brahma' (the Absolute). It means that God is all—He is endowed with attributes and is also attributeless; He is endowed with form and is also formless. In His entirety all characteristics are included (Gītā 7/29-30). In Śrīmadbhāgavata also Brahma (attributeless-formless), Paramātmā (with attributes and formless) and Bhagavān (endowed with attributes and form)—all the three have been mentioned as one.* It means that within 'Saguṇa' (God endowed with attributes) Brahma, Paramātmā and Bhagavān—all the three are included, but within 'Nirguṇa' (attributeless) only Brahma is included because in 'Nirguṇa' there is negation of attributes. Therefore 'Nirguṇa' is limited while 'Saguṇa' is entire.

'Vaiṣṇavas' (the devotees of Lord Viṣṇu) call the function of the Lord endowed with attributes and form 'Brahmotsava' (function of the Absolute). Arjuna has also addressed Lord Kṛṣṇa as 'Brahma'—'paraṁ brahma paraṁ dhāma pavitraṁ paramaṁ bhavān' (Gītā 10/12). In the Gītā Brahma has been mentioned by three names—'Oṁ, 'tat' and 'sat' (17/23). Because of the relationship between the name and the 'nāmī' (person having the name) He is proved to be 'saguṇa' (endowed with attributes).

Link:—In the next verse, the Lord explains, how Karmayogīs perform actions.

* vadanti tattattvavidastattvaṁ yajjñānamadvayam
brahmeti paramātmeti bhagavāniti śabdyate (1/2/11)

कायेन मनसा बुद्ध्या केवलैरिन्द्रियैरपि।
योगिनः कर्म कुर्वन्ति सङ्गं त्यक्त्वात्मशुद्धये॥ ११॥

kāyena manasā buddhyā kevalairindriyairapi
yoginaḥ karma kurvanti saṅgaṁ tyaktvātmaśuddhaye

The Yogīs, having discarded attachment, perform actions, merely with the body, mind, intellect and senses, for the purification of the self. 11

Comment:—

'Yoginaḥ'—Here the term 'Yoginaḥ', stands for Karmayogīs. The Yogīs, who perform actions, offering these to God, are called Bhaktiyogīs, while those, who perform these in order to render service to the world, without any selfish motive, are called, 'Karmayogīs'. A Karmayogī, while performing actions, regards his so-called body, senses and mind etc., as the worlds', and not his own, as they have their identity, with the world.

'Kāyena manasā buddhyā kevalairindriyairapi'—In fact, the body, senses, mind and intellect etc., which a common man regards as his own, are not his, because these have been acquired from the world and they will abandon him. So, it is an error on his part to assume, that these are his. All of these have their identity, with the world.

If we give a serious thought to it, we come to realise that the body etc., are not ours, in anyway. They belong either to God or to nature (prakṛti); or to the world. Thus, it is an error to regard these as ours, and to have a sense of mineness with them. The term 'Kevalaiḥ' (merely), has been used here to root out this sense of mineness with them.

Here, the term 'Kevalaiḥ', being plural, is an adjective, for senses. But, it does not mean that sense of mineness for mere senses, is to be renounced, it means that sense of mineness for the body, mind, intellect and the entire world, is to be abandoned, for which a person, has attachment. When a girl, is married into a family, her relationship with her in-laws, is automatically established. In the same way, when a man is attached to any worldly object, he gets attached to the entire world. So the term 'Kevalaiḥ', should be taken as abandonment of sense of mineness for the body, senses, mind and intellect.

In fact, a doer (agent) himself, should become detached. By doing so, his attachment for body, senses, mind and intellect etc., is totally abandoned. The reason is, that the body, senses and mind etc., are, quite different from the self. A sense of mineness with these is merely assumed, it is not natural.

In the Discipline of Action, renunciation of the desire for fruit is important, (Gītā 5/12). Common people, perform actions in order to reap their fruit, but a Karmayogī performs these to root out attachment to the fruit. But a person, who regards the body, senses, mind, intellect and life-breath etc., as his own, cannot renounce, the desire for fruit,* as he assumes, that when the body etc., are his, he should also reap the fruit of actions, performed by him. Therefore, if a striver wants to wipe out the desire for fruit, it is indispensable for him, that he should, not regard the body etc., as his own.

When it rains, it is useful for crops and people etc., but, rain is not aware of the fact, that it is falling and doing good, to the world. Similarly, senses should not have a feeling of doership, when they render service to others. But, if some service is rendered by the senses, body, mind or intellect, and gives us a sensation of elation, it means that the service has not been performed with a feeling of detachment. On the contrary it is a sign of attachment and possession.

'Saṅgaṁ tyaktvātmaśuddhaye'—[Vide the explanation in the tenth verse, for the expression 'Saṅgaṁ tyaktvā.]

* If a person has no desire for the fruit but regards the body etc., as his own, the fruit of action becomes his motive which has been forbidden by the Lord by the declaration, "Let not the fruit of action be thy motive" (Gītā 2/47).

Generally, it is thought that a heart is purified when sins (accumulated sin), volatility of mind and ignorance, are removed. But, in fact, purification of the heart, consists in total renunciation of attachment, (or a sense of mine), with the body, senses, mind and intellect. The body, etc., never regards us as theirs but, we assume these, as ours. This assumption of mineness, is impurity. Saint Tulasīdāsa in the Rāmacaritamānasa declares, "Let the filth of the sense of mine, be burnt" (7/117 A). So, heart gets purified when there is total renunciation of affinity, of an egoistic notion and sense of mine etc.

The term 'Kevalaiḥ', denotes the aim of renunciation of the sense of 'mine', with the body, senses, mind and intellect, while the expression 'Ātmaśuddhaye', denotes total renunciation of a sense of 'mine'. When a striver's aim, is to renounce the sense of mine, yet this sense prevails, in its subtle form. When, this sense of mine in its subtle form, also perishes totally, it is known as a state of purification of the inner sense.

The sense of mine, also resides in egoism. When this sense of mine, is totally renounced, egoism also becomes free from this sense of mine, and the self (heart) is, totally purified.

'Karma kurvanti'—A Karmayogī, performs actions to totally renounce, a sense of mine, in its subtle form, from the body, senses, mind and intellect etc.

So long as, a person has a desire for the fruit of action, and so long as, he assumes that the body, senses and mind etc., are his own, he cannot be liberated from, the bondage of actions. Therefore, a Karmayogī performs actions for the welfare of others, without having a desire for the fruit of actions, and without regarding the objects of action (body, senses, mind and intellect etc.,) as his own. For a sage, who wishes to attain to Yoga, action (for the welfare of others), is said to be, the means (Gītā 6/3). The more, he continues working for the welfare of others, the more his attachment and sense of mine, are renounced and thus his self (heart) is purified.

Appendix—The heart is not purified by trying to purify it because it is not purified so long as we regard it as ours, since the assumption of mineness with it is the main impurity. Therefore in the Rāmacaritamānasa it has been declared, 'Let the filth of mineness be burnt!' (Mānasa, Uttara. 117 A). The Lord here also by using the term 'kevalaiḥ' has mentioned not to have the sense of mineness with the inner sense. Purification of the inner sense consists in total renunciation of the sense of mineness with the body, senses, mind and intellect. Therefore Karmayogīs act in a detached manner in order to wipe out the sense of mineness totally from the inner sense. They don't perform any action for their own Self. The reason is that so long as the sense of mine persists, mere actions are performed, but Karmayoga is not practised. When actions are not performed for one's own self, then Karmayoga proceeds towards Self-realization.

A Karmayogī first acts aiming at freedom from the sense of mineness, then his aim is achieved.

Link:—The Lord, in the next verse, explains the merit or glory of Karmayoga by positive, as well as negative inference.

युक्तः कर्मफलं त्यक्त्वा शान्तिमाप्नोति नैष्ठिकीम्।
अयुक्तः कामकारेण फले सक्तो निबध्यते॥ १२॥

yuktaḥ karmaphalaṁ tyaktvā śāntimāpnoti naiṣṭhikīm
ayuktaḥ kāmakāreṇa phale sakto nibadhyate

The Karmayogī attains everlasting peace (God-realization), by abandoning attachment to the fruit of action; whereas he who acts with a selfish motive, being attached to the fruit of actions through desire acquires bondage. 12

Comment:—

'Yuktaḥ'—The meaning of this term, is taken according to the context. In the eighth verse of this chapter, the term 'Yuktaḥ' has been used for the 'Sāṅkhyayogī', who does not regard himself, as a doer of actions, while here it has been used for the Karmayogī, who has renounced the fruit of action.

All strivers, whose aim is to attain equanimity, are 'Yuktaḥ' or 'Yogī. In the present verse, it has been used for a Karmayogī, who having a determinate intellect, has renounced worldly desires.

'Karmaphalaṁ tyaktvā'—This expression, means the renunciation of desire for fruit and also, renunciation of attachment, because in fact it is not the fruit of actions which is renounced, it is desire for the fruit of actions, which is renounced. That fruit may be reaped, either immediately or in the future. When a striver, regards nothing as his, does nothing for him, desires nothing for him, it means that he has renounced, the desire for the fruit of actions.

A man's prārabdha (fate), is determined by the hoard of his past actions, and according to that he is born in good and evil wombs. In human life, actions which are performed, produce impressions that are added to the stock. But, when he renounces attachment to the fruit of actions, such actions cannot bear fruit, like roasted seed and these change, into inaction (Gītā 4/20). Because of the effect of actions, which are performed without desire for the fruit of actions, the latent impressions of the old actions, (accumulated of past actions), are reduced to nothing (Gītā 4/23). Thus, the cause of his rebirth, melts away.

Fruit of actions, is of four kinds:—

(1) Visible—The fruit of present actions, which is visible immediately, as satisfying one's hunger after having a meal, is a visible fruit.

(2) Unforeseen—Fruit, which will be reaped in future, in the form of favourable or unfavourable circumstances etc., here or hereafter. This fruit is unforeseen. At present the action goes to the accumulated stock of actions.

(3) Received as fruit of past actions:—The body (with its caste, order of life) wealth, property and favourable or unfavourable circumstances, which have been bestowed upon us, as a result of past deeds.

(4) Unreceived, fruits yet to be reaped in future:—Favourable and unfavourable circumstances, which we have to receive in future as ordained by destiny (prārabdha karma).

Out of the four kinds, of fruit of action, the visible and the unforeseen, depend on present actions, while the received and unreceived ones, depend on prārabdha karma. When a striver, does not desire the visible fruit, nor does he feel displeased or pleased, having received it; and does not expect the unforeseen one; nor is he attached to the received, fruit nor feels happy or sad having received it, and does not desire, the unreceived one, then, it is said that he has renounced, the fruit of action.

Common people, perform actions with a desire for the fruit of actions, and during performance, they go on thinking of that desire. As a businessman makes transactions for profit and goes on thinking about profit and feels happy with profit, and sad with loss; similarly, all people perform actions, having desire for favourable gains, such as wife, son, riches, honour and praise etc. But, a Karmayogī performs actions, by renouncing desire, for fruit.

Now a question arises, why should a man perform actions, if he has no desire? The answer is, that none can ever remain still for even a moment, without performing action (Gītā 3/5). Even if, it is accepted that a man can abandon actions, to a great degree, even then, so long as, he is attached to the world, he will think of sense-objects and that is also, an action. The thought, of sense-objects, finally leads him to ruin (Gītā 2/62-63). Therefore, so long as, a striver does not renounce attachment totally, he cannot be liberated, from the bondage of action. The old attachment, is wiped out by performance of action, while, the new one does not arise, when actions are performed for the welfare of others, and without any selfish motive.

In fact, it is ignorance if actions are performed with desire for fruit, because firstly actions and their fruits are perishable, and secondly, these will bear fruit, according to fate whether desired or not. A man cannot have, increase or decrease in fruit, by mere desire.

When actions are performed for the welfare of others, without desire for fruit, affinity for these, is renounced. A Karmayogī, does not perform actions without an aim, like an insane man, but he performs these having a high aim of God-realization. To realize his aim, he works for the welfare of others. As he is not attached to the body, he performs actions, promptly and scrupulously, without such evils, as indolence and heedlessness.

A Vital Fact

If actions, which are performed, to acquire the worldly materials, are performed, for the welfare of the world, with the aim of God-realization, and without any selfish motive, these actions can lead a man to God-realization. In the, twentieth verse of the third chapter, it has been declared, "Janaka and others attained perfection, verily by action only," while in the third verse of the sixth chapter, it has been stated, "Action is said, to be the means with a sage, who wishes to attain to Yoga." These facts, reveal that God can be realized by actions. Pārvatī and Manu-Śatarūpā etc., also realized God, through performance of actions, in the form of penance. It is also mentioned in the scriptures, that He can be realized through chanting, meditation, good company, study of scriptures and cognition etc. On the contrary, it is also mentioned, that He cannot be realized, through actions, such as penance etc., (Gītā 11/53). How to reconcile the two?

The answer is, that in fact God is not attained through any action. He is also, not a fruit of action. God pervades everywhere, everything, incident, circumstance and person etc., all the time. He is ever-attainable to everyone, and everyone abides in Him, only. No one can ever be separate, from Him. But, a man being attached to perishable body, senses, mind, intellect and objects etc., which are evolutes of insentient nature, has a disinclination for God, Who is his. Spiritual discipline, is to be practised, in order to wipe out this attachment or affinity.

Through the performance of penance etc., when this affinity for the insentient, is renounced, God, Who is ever-attainable, is attained. This affinity can be very easily renounced, when actions are performed for the welfare of the world, without any selfish motive.

The sentient and eternal Lord, cannot be bought, for all the wealth of the world. All the worldly objects, stand nowhere, when all of them are compared to the imperishable Lord. Moreover, a thing which is bought for a particular amount, is cheaper than that amount. Thus if God is realized by performing actions, it means, that He is cheaper than actions.

Here is a vital point, which calls for attention. Generally, strivers during spiritual practice depend on and have affinity for the body, senses, mind, intellect etc., with which, they perform that spiritual activity. So long as, they have affinity for these i.e., the insentient, they cannot realize God. As soon as, this affinity is renounced, God is realized. God-realization is not possible, through matter, rather it is by snapping our connection with it.

The body, senses, mind and intellect etc., belong to the same class, to which the world belongs. So these should be utilized, in rendering service to the world (this is Karmayoga). A striver, should not accept his affinity for these, nor should be depend on them, as he cannot get rid of the unreal, by having affinity for the unreal. Actions are performed, without any selfish motive, in order to renounce affinity, for the unreal. When this affinity is totally renounced, disinclination for God perishes, and ever-attained God, is realized.

'Śāntimāpnoti naiṣṭhikīm'—It has stood the test of experience, that when a person has neither desire, for the worldly objects, nor is attached to them, he attains peace. Even, during sound sleep when the world is forgotten, a man experiences peace. Similarly, one attains peace, when he completes any assignment or task, such as the marriage of his daughter. If he renounces his affinity, (desire and attachment) during wakefulness, he will attain peace. But if he enjoys this peace, he cannot attain everlasting peace or the supreme peace,* because this peace is not an end, but a means to attain the supreme peace, called Yoga (Gītā 6/3).

So long as, a striver remains attached to peace, which he attains by renouncing his affinity for the world, he is bound (Gītā 14/6) and he cannot attain, the supreme, uniform and eternal peace.

'Ayuktaḥ kāmakāreṇa phale sakto nibadhyate'—The term 'Ayuktaḥ', has been used for a person, who works with a selfish motive. Such a person, because of his several desires, being attached to fruit of actions, has to follow, the cycle of birth and death. A person cannot acquire things etc., merely by having a desire. Secondly he cannot possess these forever, even if he has acquired them. So, it is futile to have a desire for acquiring objects etc., saint Tulasīdāsa in the Vinaya-Patrikā declares, "All worldly objects will abandon you, in the end; it is better, if you abandon, them right now" (198).

It does not mean, that their physical abandonment (renouncement) leads to salvation, or God-realization. Had it been so, all persons who left their bodies, (at the time of death) would have attained salvation. But, it is not so. In fact it is desire, a sense of mine and attachment to these which are to be renounced, because these lead to bondage i.e., end to the cycle

*This everlasting (supreme) peace is God-realization. It has been called 'eternal peace' (9/31), 'the supreme peace' (4/39; 18/62) and 'peace' (5/29, 2/70-71) in the Gītā.

of birth and death. When actions are performed, for the welfare of others, their flow is towards others, and any assumed affinity for them, is easily renounced.

Appendix—In fact practice of the spiritual discipline in order to attain salvation or God-realization is also attachment to the fruit of action. A man has formed the habit to do a piece of work with the desire for its fruit; therefore it is said that one should practise spiritual discipline for salvation or God-realization.

In fact spiritual practice is needed in order to wipe out attachment to the world; otherwise salvation is axiomatic. The Lord is ever attained. God-realization is not the fruit of an action. Therefore the yearning for the performance of action in order to attain God is also the desire for fruit.

A striver should not think that this spiritual practice will bear this fruit. Desiring the fruit is an attachment to the fruit which does not allow the spiritual discipline to be followed scrupulously. Therefore instead of thinking of the fruit, a striver should practise spiritual discipline promptly which will naturally lead him to divine perfection. If a striver goes on thinking for the fruit, he will not attain divine perfection.

We shall attain the transcendental state or the desireless state and then we shall be happy—in this way the desire to derive happiness or pleasure is also the desire for fruit which hinders a striver from becoming transcendental and desireless.

Link:—Having dwelt upon Karmayoga, the Lord now comments at length, upon Sāṅkhyayoga.

सर्वकर्माणि मनसा सन्न्यस्यास्ते सुखं वशी।
नवद्वारे पुरे देही नैव कुर्वन्न कारयन्॥ १३॥

sarvakarmāṇi manasā sannyasyāste sukhaṁ vaśī
navadvāre pure dehī naiva kurvanna kārayan

The embodied (soul) having controlled the senses, and having renounced the performance of all actions by discrimination, in the abode of nine gates, neither acting nor causing others to act, he rests happily in the self. 13

Comment:—

'Vaśī dehī'—When a man is attached, to the senses, mind and intellect etc., these control him, but when he renounces attachment to them, they remain under his control. A Sāṅkhyayogī being so, is called 'Vaśī'.

So long as, a man has the least attachment for the evolutes of nature, (body, senses etc.,) he has to remain under the control of nature (Gītā 3/5). Prakṛti (nature), ever remains active. Therefore, a man cannot refrain himself, from performing actions, so long as he is, attached to Nature. But a Sāṅkhyayogī, who is not at all attached to the gross, subtle and causal bodies, the evolutes of Nature, do not become the performer of actions. Though such a Sāṅkhyayogī, has not the least attachment for the body, yet, he is called the embodied one, as he seems so, to the common people.

'Navadvāre pure'—Two ears, two eyes, two nostrils, a mouth—these seven, located in the upper part of the body, while the genital organ and the anus located in the lower part of the trunk, these nine openings, have been called, the nine gates. This body has been called the city of nine gates, in order to clarify the point, that as the abode and those who inhabit the abode, are different, so are a body and the soul. As a person, living in the city does not regard activities undertaken in the city, as his own, so does a Sāṅkhyayogī not regard activities of the body, as his own.

'Sarvakarmāṇi manasā sannyasya'—Here, the expression 'Sarvakarmāṇi', stands for the thirteen types of actions performed, with the body, senses, mind, intellect and life-breath, as described in the eighth and ninth verses, of this chapter.

Here the expression 'Manasā sannyasya' means 'renouncing

the doership in actions through discrimination'. If the meaning of the expression is taken as 'renouncing mental actions' only, it will not be proper, because according to the Gītā, 'renouncing mental action' mentally, is also an activity of the mind (Gītā 18/15). So, there is doership of this mental activity. Therefore the renouncement of actions mentally, means renouncing the affinity of doership through discrimination. A Sāṅkhyayogī does not regard himself, as the doer, he leaves the doership in the body.

'Naiva kurvanna kārayan'—A Sāṅkhyayogī becomes, neither a doer himself, nor does he make others, doers. As he is, not in the least attached to the body, senses, mind and intellect etc., he cannot regard actions performed by them, as his. In the eighth verse of this chapter also the Lord has pointed out the same fact, when He declares, "The man who knows the truth, thinks that he does nothing at all." In the thirty-first verse of the thirteenth chapter, also He declares, "The Supreme Self dwelling in the body, does not act."

Here a doubt arises, that it is true that the self does not perform actions, but it can inspire others to perform actions. The clarification is, that as with the rise of the sun, people are engaged in different activities, such as farming, study and business etc., even though the sun does not cause them to perform, either prescribed or prohibited actions. Had the sun, itself caused them to act, then it would have been responsible for their virtues and sins. Similarly, 'prakṛti', derives its existence and power, from God, but He never causes it, to act. This fact, has been described by the Lord by the expression 'Na kāryan', so does nature, having received power from God or Self, function, but the self does not inspire anyone to act.

'Āste sukham'—All human beings, dwell naturally, in the self. But they believe that they rest, in the body, senses, mind, intellect and life-breath. So they cannot realize the reality, that they rest in the Self. But a Sāṅkhyayogī, realizes that he rests in the self, which is perfect and uniform, and this belief involves no labour. So, here the word 'Āste' (rests) has been used, while in the twenty-fourth verse of the fourteenth chapter, the term 'Svasthaḥ' (dwells or rests in the self) has been, used.

The self, is the origin of all origins and it needs, no base. This state of 'resting in the self', has also been conveyed, in the twentieth verse, by the expression, "Such a knower of God, rests in God."

Appendix—'Naiva kurvanna kārayan'—The idea to do an action is an obstacle to Self-realization. The feeling of performing an action causes the sense of doership and the sense of doership leads to individuality. Performance of action is in Prakṛti, in the self there is actionlessness. Therefore performance of action connects us with Prakṛti and by non-performance of action we get established in the self. 'I have to do nothing'—this notion is also within the area of the performance of action. Therefore a striver should have nothing to do with the performance of an action or its non-performance—'naiva tasya kṛtenārtho nākṛteneha kaścana' (Gītā 3/18). The self is free from performance of an action or its non-performance viz., it is a transcendental entity.

'Vaśī'—By attachment to the modes of Prakṛti a man becomes 'avaśa' viz., helpless (Gītā 3/5). This helplessness is wiped out by Jñānayoga and the man becomes 'vaśī' viz., his life becomes independent and transcendental.

Link:—In the preceding verse, the Lord declared, "The embodied (soul) neither acts, nor does it cause others to act." Now, the question arises, whether God causes others to act? The Lord, answers the question, in the next verse.

न कर्तृत्वं न कर्माणि लोकस्य सृजति प्रभुः ।
न कर्मफलसंयोगं स्वभावस्तु प्रवर्तते ॥ १४ ॥

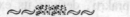

na kartṛtvaṁ na karmāṇi lokasya sṛjati prabhuḥ
na karmaphalasaṁyogaṁ svabhāvastu pravartate

Neither the sense of doership nor the nature of actions does the Lord determine for the mankind, nor does He link actions with their fruits. But it is the personal nature alone, that impacts. 14

Comment:—

'Na kartṛtvaṁ na karmāṇi lokasya sṛjati prabhuḥ'—The term 'Prabhuḥ', has been used here, because the universe is created by the Lord, Who is endowed with attributes. He is omnipotent and He controls, the entire universe. Though, He conducts the activities of the entire universe, yet He remains, a non-doer (Gītā 4/13).

All actions, are performed by the modes of nature, but out of ignorance, a man identifies himself with nature and becomes a doer of actions, which are done by nature in fact (Gītā 3/27). God has not made man the doer. If He had made him the doer, the Lord, in the eighth verse of this chapter, would not have said—The man, who is united with the Divine, and knows the truth thinks, "I do nothing at all." It means, that this sense of doership is self-made, and so it can be renounced by the man, who has inculcated it.

The Lord, does not decree whether a person, will have to perform a particular virtuous or evil deed. Had it been so decreed by Him, the prescribed and prohibited actions mentioned by scriptures, preceptors etc., would have been of no avail, and a man would not have had to bear, the fruit of his actions. The expression 'Na karmāṇi', proves that a man is independent, in the performance of actions.

'Na karmaphalasaṁyogam'—A man, has to reap the fruit of actions, which he performs. Actions, being insentient cannot decide upon their result. So, it is ordained by God (Gītā 7/22). The Lord, awards the fruit of actions, but He does not bring about union with fruit of actions. It is the man, who brings about this union. He, out of ignorance, having become a doer and having been attached to fruit of actions, has to feel happy, and sad. If he himself, does not get attached to fruit of actions, he can be free, from it. The term "Sannyāsinām' (renouncers), in the twelfth verse of the eighteenth chapter, has been used, for such persons who are not attached to the fruit of actions. They have not to reap the fruits of their actions, here or hereafter. If God had connected actions with their fruit, a man would have, never been liberated, from the fruit of actions.

In the, forty-seventh verse of the second chapter, the Lord declares, "Let the fruit of action, not be thy motive." It means, that it depends upon a man, whether he feels happy or sad and whether the fruit of action is his motive or not? If the Lord had ordained the fruit of action then a man would have never become even-minded in pleasure and pain, and he would have never performed actions having abandoned attachment, or the fruit of actions, which has been emphasized by the Lord, time and again in the Gītā (vide 4/20, 5/12, 14/24 etc.).

Question:—In the scriptures, it is mentioned that the Lord causes those, whom He wants to send to the higher worlds, to perform virtuous actions, while He causes those whom He wants to send to the lower worlds, to perform, evil actions. Thus the declaration, "Neither agency nor actions does the Lord create nor does, He connect actions, with their fruits," seems contrary to the ordinance of the scriptures.

Answer:—In fact, the scriptures do not mean, that the Lord sends them to the higher or lower worlds, by causing them to perform virtuous or evil actions, but these mean, that the Lord purifies them by enabling them to reap the fruit of their past actions by creating circumstances* so that, they may attain God or His love.

* Being overpowered by desire a man performs good (virtuous) and bad (evil), actions (Gītā 3/37) which lead him to the higher worlds (heaven etc.,)

If the scriptures are interpreted, in the way, that the Lord causes people to perform virtuous or evil actions, so that they may go to higher or lower worlds, then man, will become dependent, in performing actions. Prescription and prohibition by the scriptures and saints, and instruction of the preceptors, will prove to be futile. So this interpretation, does not seem to be justified.

'Svabhāvastu pravartate'—It is, because of his nature, that man becomes a doer, performs actions and connects actions, with their fruit. Man himself, is responsible, to form this nature. So long as, there are attachment and aversion in nature, it is not purified; and as long as nature, is not purified, a man is overpowered, by nature.

The Lord, mentions here the same fact, which he has already stated in the thirty-third verse of the third chapter, when He declared, "Beings follow their nature."

So long as, a man acts according to his nature, he will become a doer, will perform actions and will link actions, with their fruit. Thus, he will remain dependent, and this dependence is self-created. If man renounces doership, actions and association of actions, with fruit which he has made himself, he can realize that he is ever untainted (uncontaminated).

Appendix—The sense of doership, action and attachment to the fruit of action—it is not God's creation, but it is the man's (embodied soul's) own creation. Therefore the man is responsible for its renunciation also.

'Svabhāvastu pravartate'—In fact renunciation of affinity for the world is natural; but because of the perception of naturalness in unnaturalness, affinity for the world is seen natural. This individual nature is not natural and untainted but it is one's own creation.

---

and lower worlds (hells etc.). A man has desires by making a misuse of the freedom which has been bestowed upon him so that he may attain salvation.

Link:—When the Lord, neither creates agency (doership), nor does he force anyone to perform action, or bring about union of the actions and their fruit, how can He reap the fruit of action? The Lord, answers the question, in the next verse.

नादत्ते कस्यचित्पापं न चैव सुकृतं विभुः।
अज्ञानेनावृतं ज्ञानं तेन मुह्यन्ति जन्तवः॥१५॥

nādatte kasyacitpāpaṁ na caiva sukṛtaṁ vibhuḥ
ajñānenāvṛtaṁ jñānaṁ tena muhyanti jantavaḥ

The All-pervading Lord, acquires neither sin nor the virtue of any; as knowledge, is enveloped by ignorance; therefore, beings get deluded. 15

Comment:—

'Nādatte kasyacitpāpaṁ na caiva sukṛtaṁ vibhuḥ'—The Lord, Who has been termed 'Prabhuḥ', in the preceding verse, has been called 'Vibhuḥ', here.

A man, can reap the fruit of action in two ways, by performing actions himself, or by causing others to perform actions. But, the Lord neither performs actions, nor does He cause others to perform these. So, He has not to reap their fruit.

The sun, provides light to the entire universe and men commit sins and also perform virtuous actions, but the sun has nothing to do, with those sinful or virtuous actions. Similarly, nature and the entire universe, receive power from God and with that power people perform virtuous and sinful actions. But, those actions performed by the people, have not the least connection, with God. The Lord, has given freedom to man, whether he connects actions with their fruits, or offers actions and their fruit, to God. He who, by misusing the freedom given by the Lord, becomes a doer and reaps the fruits of actions, is bound. The Lord, does not accept these actions and their fruit as His. But he, who by making right use of freedom, offers his actions and their fruit to God, is liberated, and the Lord accepts such actions, and their fruits.

As, in the twenty-fifth verse of the seventh chapter, by the term 'sarvasya' (all), and, in the twenty-sixth verse of the same chapter, by the term 'Kaścana' (anyone), the Lord has talked about common people, so has He described by the term 'Kasyacit' common people, who regard themselves, as doers and enjoyers of fruits, rather than about devotees. As far as, devotees are concerned, the Lord accepts a leaf, a flower, a fruit or a little water, which is offered to Him, with devotion (Gītā 9/26-27).

'Ajñānenāvṛtaṁ jñānam'—The knowledge of the self, is self-evident to all the people, but this knowledge is enveloped in ignorance. It is because of this ignorance that beings are deluded. He, who thinks 'I am the doer', is deluded (Gītā 3/27). A man, can wipe out this delusion by discrimination, which has been bestowed upon him by God. Therefore, in the eighth verse of this chapter, it has been said, that a Sāṅkhyayogī should ever think, "I do nothing at all", while, in the thirteenth verse it has been said, that he should mentally renounce, all actions by discrimination.

All objects, such as a body etc., are constantly undergoing change, while the self, never experiences any change. When a man identifies the self, with kaleidoscopic objects, it means, that he is swayed by ignorance. But, when he realizes that the self is different, from the kaleidoscopic worldly materials, his ignorance is wiped out and the knowledge of the self, is illumined automatically. The reason is, that knowledge of the self is veiled, when one assumes affinity with the evolutes of Nature.

The term 'Ajñāna', does not mean total absence of knowledge, but it means imperfect knowledge, as there cannot be, total absence of knowledge. Knowledge of the senses and intellect, is also imperfect. When a person, attaches importance to this imperfect knowledge, and is influenced by it, he does not keep an eye on real knowledge—this is known as 'enveloping of the knowledge, by ignorance'.

The knowledge of intellect, is more extensive, than that of senses, or that of the mind. The knowledge of intellect, illumines, the knowledge of the mind and senses, but it cannot illumine nature, whose evolute it is. When it cannot even illumine Nature, how can it illumine the sentient, which transcends Nature? Thus, the knowledge of intellect, is imperfect.

'Tena muhyanti jantavaḥ.'—The Lord, by using the term 'Jantavaḥ', has condemned human beings, by saying that those persons, who do not attach importance to discrimination, are in fact, animals, because without discrimination there is no difference, between the two.* A human being, is a human being not merely by virtue of human form, but because of his sense of discrimination. As far as sensual pleasures are concerned, even animals enjoy these. But, the aim of human life, is not to hanker after them instead, it is to realize, the self or God, Who is free from pleasure or pain. Those who know, what ought to be done and what ought not to be done, deserve to be called strivers.

He, who believes that he is a doer, and who having the motive of fruit of action, feels happy or sad—such a man, is said to be, deluded out of ignorance. We are forced to do virtuous and evil actions. How can we get rid of them? To be happy and to be sad, is the fruit of our actions. How can we rise above these? To have such conviction, is delusion.

Man, (self) is a non-doer, and is also, free from pleasures and pain. It is out of ignorance, that he becomes a doer and feels happy or sad, by bringing about union with fruit of actions. The term 'tena', stands for this delusion (ignorance). The ignorant, out of delusion feel happy and sad. The same fact, has been

* Food, sleep, fear and sex are common between men and animals. Men are superior to animals because of their sense of discrimination. Without discrimination they are just like animals (Cāṇakyanīti 17/17).

pointed out, by the expression 'tena muhyanti jantavaḥ' (by that, beings are deluded).

Appendix—As the dark has no power to cover the sun, so has ignorance no power to cover knowledge. The unnatural has been assumed as natural—this is ignorance by which a man is deluded. Therefore this is merely a notion, not a fact that knowledge is covered by ignorance. If a man so desires, then by attaching importance to his discrimination, he can destroy this delusion (ignorance) (Gītā 5/16).

In fact knowledge is not covered but intellect is covered. But to a man, knowledge appears to be covered; therefore here the term 'āvṛta' has been used. The same fact has been mentioned in the thirty-ninth verse of the third chapter by the expression 'āvṛtaṁ jñānametena' (Gītā 3/39). Ignorance is non-existent or a negation. It has no existence. A non-existent thing cannot veil the knowledge. Therefore opposite knowledge viz., perception of naturalness in unnaturalness is ignorance*. If the vision of unnaturalness is discarded, naturalness automatically reveals itself, then a man will realize his identity with omnipresent God. It is because of individuality that sins and virtues attach to us; therefore having realized identity with the omnipresent God viz., by the destruction of individuality, sins and virtues no more attach to us.

Because of ignorance viz., opposite knowledge (natural intellect in the unnatural) a man becomes 'jantu' (animal)—'tena muhyanti jantavah.' Similarly the embodied soul because of its affinity for matter (non-self) becomes 'Jagat' (world) (matter) (Gītā 7/13).

We have regarded the Lord Who is ever identified with us (the self) as separate and we have assumed the body which is different from us as identified with us—this is ignorance.

---

* Anityāśuciduḥkhānātmasu nityaśucisukhātmakhyātiravidyā (Yogadarśana 2/5)

Link:—In the preceding verse, the Lord declared, "Beings are deluded because knowledge is enveloped by ignorance." The Lord explains the glory of knowledge, in the next verse which is illumined, when ignorance is destroyed, through discrimination.

ज्ञानेन तु तदज्ञानं येषां नाशितमात्मनः।
तेषामादित्यवज्ज्ञानं प्रकाशयति तत्परम्॥ १६॥

jñānena tu tadajñānaṁ yeṣāṁ nāśitamātmanaḥ
teṣāmādityavajjñānaṁ prakāśayati tatparam

But, to those whose ignorance is destroyed by knowledge (discrimination), such knowledge lights up the supreme self, like the sun. 16

Comment:—

'Jñānena tu tadajñānaṁ yeṣāṁ nāśitamātmanaḥ'—The term 'Tu' (but), has been used to show that, in this verse there is description of something different, from the preceding verse.

Whatever, was called 'Ajñānena' in the preceding verse, has been called here 'tat ajñānam' (that ignorance).

Ignorance, consists in identifying the self with the body, while knowledge comprises in regarding these as two separate entities.

If we have an egoistic notion and a sense of mine with the body and the world—this is ignorance. The self, ever remains the same, while a sense of 'I' and the sense of 'mine', change. In the past, we were children and toys were very dear to us, but now we are young or old and regard, our wives, sons and riches etc., as ours. Thus, we see that the sense of 'I', and of 'mine', are undergoing change while the self, ever remains the same. That is knowledge, or discrimination.

The perception of the eternal in the transitory, of the pure in the impure, of pleasure in pain and of the self in the non-self is ignorance.

Thus a striver should realize this reality through discrimination, and renounce the sense of 'I' and that of 'mine'. This is called destruction of ignorance, by knowledge. A person, identifies the uniform self, with the kaleidoscopic world etc., because, he does not attach importance to discrimination. A striver, who having aroused this discrimination, renounces the sense of 'I' and that of 'mine' with the perishable world, his discrimination lights up the supreme self, i.e., he realizes God, who is Truth-Consciousness-Bliss consolidated.

'Teṣāmādityavajjñānaṁ prakāśayati tatparam'—When discrimination is fully aroused, a striver has no affinity, at all for the kaleidoscopic world. Then he realizes the self, and then the Supreme-Self is illumined i.e., the Self realizes Its identity with the Supreme-Self.

The word 'param', here as well as, in the fifty-ninth verse of the second chapter and the thirty-fourth verse of the thirteenth chapter, has been used for the Supreme (Supreme-Self or God).

The term 'prakāśayati', signifies that, as in the dark, objects are not seen, but these are noticed when the sun rises, so is the Supreme-Self, Who is ever-attained is not realized because of ignorance. As soon as ignorance is destroyed, the Supreme-Self, is realized.

Appendix—Ignorance is destroyed only by discrimination, not by effort—'yatanto'pyakṛtātmāno nainaṁ paśyantyacetasaḥ' (Gītā 15/11). The reason is that destruction of ignorance is not possible by the performance of action and by doing labour. By doing labour, affinity for the body persists because without having connection with the body, no labour is done. Secondly by making effort to wipe out ignorance, ignorance is strengthened, because an effort is made to wipe it out only when we accept its existence.

The opposite notion (ignorance) of naturalness in unnaturalness is self-made. By attaching importance to discrimination that ignorance is removed.

Link:—The Lord in the next verse explains how to reach the state from which there is no return.

तद्बुद्धयस्तदात्मानस्तन्निष्ठास्तत्परायणाः ।
गच्छन्त्यपुनरावृत्तिं ज्ञाननिर्धूतकल्मषाः ॥ १७ ॥

tadbuddhayastadātmānastanniṣṭhāstatparāyaṇāḥ
gacchantyapunarāvṛttiṁ jñānanirdhūtakalmaṣāḥ

Those, whose mind and intellect are wholly absorbed in God, who remain constantly identified with Him, and having finally become one with Him, their sins having been wiped out by wisdom, they reach a state, from which there is no return. 17

Comment:—

[God can be realized by two means—first, He (the reality) can be realized by renouncing the unreal through discrimination, and secondly, by thirst for the real. The unreal can be attained through actions, rather than through thirst. How God can be realized through thirst, is explained in this verse.]

'Tadbuddhayaḥ'—A striver, through intellect should have a conviction, that the Lord pervades everywhere. He existed before the world was created, exists now and will also exist if the world is being destroyed. This is known as absorbing of the intellect in Him.

'Tadātmānaḥ'—Here the term 'Ātmā', stands, for the mind. When a striver resolves, that only the Lord pervades everywhere, his mind automatically thinks of Him only.

'Tanniṣṭhāḥ'—When the mind and the intellect of a striver, are absorbed in God, he realizes that he is naturally established in Him. But, so long as, the mind and the intellect do not get absorbed in God i.e., a striver, does not think and resolve, of His all-pervasive nature, he cannot realize, that he is naturally established, in Him.

'Tatparāyaṇāḥ'—Such strivers, instead of having a separate entity, become one with God. Their identity is merged in God, and thus they become an embodiment of God.

Unless the striver, and the spiritual practice become one, the discipline is not continuous. But, when the striver loses his egoistic notions, his means merges in the end, because both of these are identical.

'Jñānanirdhūtakalmaṣāḥ'—Through discrimination (wisdom or knowledge), between the real and the unreal, a striver gets rid of the unreal. It is because of his affinity for the unreal, that he commits sins, and is bound. When his affinity for the unreal is totally renounced, his sins and virtues, are totally wiped out.

'Gacchantyapunarāvṛttim'—Attachment to the unreal, is the cause of rebirth. The Lord declares, "Attachment to the modes, is the cause of soul's birth, in good and evil wombs" (Gītā 13/21). When our attachment for the unreal is wiped out, there is no question of our return, to the mortal world.

A thing, which is finite, moves from one place to another, but one, which is all-pervasive, wherefrom is it to come and whither is it to go. God pervades all space, time, objects, circumstances, equally. He never moves, and so is the case with great souls, as they have identified themselves with Him. They also do not move. The scriptures declare— A God-realized soul, here and now, merges in God. His vital force, does not migrate (Bṛhadāraṇyaka 4/4/6).

Regarding his so-called body, it is said that he is not reborn. In fact, the term 'Gacchanti' (go) stands for acquiring the knowledge of the self, which immediately leads to realization of God who is ever-realized.

Appendix—When the notion of naturalness in unnaturalness is wiped out, then no other independent existence besides God persists and a striver becomes the embodiment of God which is really axiomatic. Therefore there is no question of his return to the mortal world (worldly bondage)—'sarge'pi nopajāyante pralaye na vyathanti ca' (Gītā 14/2).

Link:—The Lord in the next verse describes the attitude (vision) of God-realized souls.

विद्याविनयसम्पन्ने ब्राह्मणे गवि हस्तिनि।
शुनि चैव श्वपाके च पण्डिताः समदर्शिनः॥ १८॥

vidyāvinayasampanne brāhmaṇe gavi hastini
śuni caiva śvapāke ca paṇḍitāḥ samadarśinaḥ

Sages equate a learned and humble brāhmaṇa, a cow, an elephant or even a dog, or a lowly (outcaste), as these have a vision of God, in all of them. 18

Comment:—

'Vidyāvinayasampanne brāhmaṇe gavi hastini śuni caiva śvapāke ca paṇḍitāḥ samadarśinaḥ'—Here, two adjectives 'learned' and 'humble', have been used for Brāhmaṇa, in order to show his perfection, as generally a learned person is not humble, and he becomes proud of his learning.

Dealings of a sage with a learned brāhmaṇa, a pariah, a cow, an elephant and a dog would be different. Equal dealings are neither proper nor possible. The scriptures also support this view. A learned and humble ḅrāhmaṇa, rather than a pariah is adored, milk is drunk of a cow, rather than of a bitch, while an elephant rather than a dog can be used for riding. When the Lord says, that sages see them with an equal eye, He means to say, that they behold the Lord, pervading everywhere. Therefore, they do not see with an unequal eye.

Here, a doubt may arise, how can their dealings be different, if they have an equal eye? The explanation is, that we see all the parts of our body (forehead, feet, hands and anus etc.,) with an equal eye and think of their welfare, yet our dealings with these are different. When anyone is touched with our feet we feel sorry and beg his pardon, but we do not do so if he is touched with our arm. We show reverence for others, by bowing our head and folding hands, rather than feet. A hand has to be washed, if it touches anus, but it is not washed, if it touches a hand. Showing the forefinger and the thumb to someone, have different meanings, which are well-known to all. In this way, a man has different dealings with different parts of the body, but he loves them equally. He, is not indifferent to any afflicted limb. He, through the likeness of the self, sees equality everywhere, be it pleasure or pain (Gītā 6/32). In this way, the wise also have different dealings with different beings according to the difference in their food, qualities, conduct and caste etc., and it is proper also. They behold the Lord, pervading everywhere and so they love all beings and think of their welfare equally, without having any evil propensities, such as attachment, aversion, pride and partiality etc. They have an automatic inclination, to remove the sufferings of other beings and to console and comfort them, in the same way as a person tries to remove the pain of any limb of his body. So, it is said that they see everyone, with an equal eye. The Lord, has mentioned of this equality of vision or even-mindedness, several times in the Gītā as "He, who is equal-minded, excels" (6/9); "He sees the same, everywhere" (6/29); "He, through the likeness of the self, sees equality everywhere" (6/32); "Even-minded everywhere" (12/4); "He, who sees the supreme Lord abiding equally in all beings, never perishing when they perish, verily sees" (13/27); and "He sees the same Lord equally dwelling everywhere" (13/28).

Śrī Śaṅkarācārya declares:—

A man should be non-dual in feelings, rather than in dealings (Tattvopadeśa).

An Important Fact Pertaining to Equanimity

Now-a-days, people talk a lot, about equanimity. But it must be understood in the right perspective.

Equanimity, is not child's play but an embodiment of God. The Lord declares, "Those, whose minds get rooted in equanimity, overcome the world (birth and death) and realize the Absolute (God)" (Gītā 5/19). This state of equanimity, is attained when others' pleasure and pain, become a striver's own pleasure and pain. The Lord declares, "O Arjuna, he who through the likeness of the self, sees equality (equanimity) everywhere, be it pleasure or pain, is considered a perfect Yogī" (Gītā 6/32).

A striver, attains equanimity when he is engaged in removing the suffering of others, in the same way, as he gets engaged promptly in removing his own suffering. Explaining the marks of a saint, Tulasīdāsa declares—

'Saints feel happy and sad in the happiness and sadness, of others' (Mānasa 7/38/1).

So long as, a man desires pleasure, he cannot attain equanimity, in spite of his best efforts. But, when he has a keen desire to provide comfort to others, to do good to them, and he thinks of their salvation, he becomes equanimous. A striver, should begin such activity, with his family. He should try his best to remove the suffering of his parents, wife, sons and other near and dear ones, even if he has himself to suffer. By doing so, he will attain peace. Similarly, he should try to remove the suffering of others. By doing so he will be thrilled with joy. We should serve, those to whom we are not attached or we should renounce our attachment for those, whom we serve—the result will be the same.

Saint Tulasīdāsa in the Mānasa declares, "Lakṣmaṇa serves Lord Rāma and Sītā with the same zeal, as that with which, an ignorant man serves his body" (2/142/1).

It is not wise to serve one's own body, because even an animal does so. A mother-monkey, loves its youngone so much, that it does not leave the youngone, even when the latter dies.

But, when someone gives it any eatable, it eats itself, without giving it to its youngone. Even if the youngone tries to eat, the mother scares the youngone away, as long as attachment is there, equanimity is out of the question.

We should serve others, in a disinterested manner. If anyone goes astray, we should guide him in a pleasant way to follow the right path. By doing so, we shall feel peace and happiness. If we do not guide him, we cannot experience peace. Let any one try this and see. Similarly, if we invite a thirsty person to have a drink of cold water, it gives us satisfaction, and peace of mind. This kind of happiness or peace leads us, to salvation while the desire to seek pleasure, leads us to degradation. In the same way, when religious discourses are arranged, we should politely request people to take comfortable seats, so that they may listen to the discourse properly, instead of commanding them, in an authoritative tone. By doing so, we shall derive satisfaction and peace. But, if we command them in an authoritative tone, it will reveal our pride which will prick others and we shall not be able to attain peace. By such behaviour, we can never attain equanimity.

Those, who are engrossed in the welfare of all beings attain the Lord (Gītā 12/4) because He is a disinterested friend, of all beings (Gītā 5/29). It is He, Who rears all beings, whether they are believers or non-believers. Water quenches the thirst, of both the staunch believer and non-believer, the sun, provides light to both, air helps everyone to breathe, and the earth provides room to everyone, without any distinction, whether they believe in God or not. Thus, everybody has an equal share in the things, created by God.

Equanimity or equality, does not mean that food should be eaten and marriages should be arranged without taking into consideration caste, creed or colour etc. Equality, in such dealings leads to degradation. It is, the god of death who has equal dealings with all, because all the beings whether they are saints or householders, animals or gods, have to die.

Animals also have equality of dealings. A dog enters a brāhmaṇa's kitchen with unclean feet, in the same way as it enters the kitchen of a sweeper, because it does not distinguish between a brāhmaṇa and a sweeper. But the same behaviour on the part of a man cannot be ignored. Equanimity, consists in removing the suffering of others and in doing good to them. This equanimity, purifies him and his heart. But if one does not observe purity in food etc., his heart gets impure which leads to disquietude. Superficial equality, is against the ordinance of the scriptures and the decorum of society, and it causes conflict in society.

The scriptures do not support the view that the brāhmaṇas (priest class) are high by caste, while the śūdras (labour class) are low. The brāhmaṇas through preaching, the kṣatriyas (the warrior class) through protection (heroism), the vaiśyas (the trading class) through trade, and the śūdras (the labour class) through physical labour, should serve the members of all castes. But, it does not mean, that members of other castes should not do physical labour, while performing their duty. All of them should labour equally during the performance of their duty. Everyone should render service to others and co-operate with them with all the resources he possesses.

In the past, people followed the varṇa (caste) system and āśrama (order of life) system and led a happy and peaceful life. But today the Varṇāśrama system is being replaced by factions and groups. In villages people cannot even get water because the owners of the wells do not allow those people, who support the candidates of the rival parties, to draw water from their wells. Among the members of the same family also, there are feuds because they support different parties. How miserable is the condition!

If we want to attain equanimity, we should try to remove the sufferings of others whether they belong to our caste, order of life, religion or sect etc., or not, and should also do good to them. They may be, the devotees of Lord Rāma or Lord Kṛṣṇa or Lord Śiva or they may be muslims or christians etc., we should equally think of their welfare. We should never be partial to the people of our own caste or creed or group etc., nor should we feel happy and sad, when our own group or creed gain victory or suffer defeat over a rival group or creed etc. We should help them and satisfy their needs, to the best of our capacity and resources, without having feelings of envy, jealousy, hatred and pride etc., as upliftment is possible through righteous feelings, virtues and good conduct. Moreover, we should have the feelings that all beings should be happy, and free from disease and none should ever suffer, in the least. Having such feelings, we should do good to others—that is equanimity.

Appendix—A Brāhmaṇa, a pariah, a cow, an elephant and a dog—(the bodies of) all these are changing every moment and are going into non-existence but the reality ever abiding in them never changes, it ever remains the same. The wise perceive that reality only. As an ant extracts grains of sugar mixed with sand, in the same way the discerning eye of the wise perceives the real entity pervading the unreal world. It means that whether there is a Brāhmaṇa or a pariah, a cow or a dog, an elephant or an ant; in all these heterogeneous beings, the wise have an equal eye. In spite of inequality in their dealings, they have never an inequal eye.

Link:—In the next verse the Lord explains the glory of equanimity.

इहैव तैर्जितः सर्गो येषां साम्ये स्थितं मनः ।
निर्दोषं हि समं ब्रह्म तस्माद्ब्रह्मणि ते स्थिताः ॥ १९ ॥

ihaiva tairjitaḥ sargo yeṣāṁ sāmye sthitaṁ manaḥ
nirdoṣaṁ hi samaṁ brahma tasmādbrahmaṇi te sthitāḥ

Even here, the whole world is conquered by those whose minds are vested in equanimity. As God is flawless and equal, therefore, they become merged in God (Brahman). 19

Comment:—

'Yeṣāṁ sāmye sthitaṁ manaḥ'—When a person realizes, that he is established in God or Self, and when he renounces attachment, aversion, desire and unevenness of mind etc., his mind and intellect, naturally get established in equanimity. Though outwardly there is no obvious difference between the dealings of a great soul and a common man, yet inwardly there is a lot of difference. The mind of a great soul remains equanimous, flawless and quiet, while that of a common man, uneven, defective and disquiet.

In the morning, when the sun rises, it is not seen in the east if it is hidden behind high mountains, in that direction, but its light can be seen, on the top of a high mountain in the west. It shows, that the sun has risen, even if it is not visible, in the east. Similarly, those, whose minds and intellects remain untainted by honour and dishonour, praise and blame, pleasure and pain, etc., and are free from attachment, aversion, joy and sorrow, are naturally established, in the self. The reason is, that for a person without being established in the self, it is impossible to maintain evenness of mind and intellect.

'Ihaiva tairjitaḥ sargaḥ'—Here the plural has been used in the term 'taih', (by those) by the Lord, to explain that all men can realize God and can conquer the entire world.

The expression 'Iha eva', means that even here, during a lifetime, in this world, they can conquer the world i.e., can be liberated from this world.

The body, senses, mind, intellect, beings, objects, incidents and circumstances etc., are all different from the self. He, who depends on them, is dependent. He, who attaches importance to them, and desires them, remains dependent i.e., is defeated. But when he renounces attachment to them, and sincerely gives up desire for them, it means that he has overcome, them. Till, slavery to desire persists, he is a vanquished, one.

Only, a defeated person wants to win over and subdue others. In fact no one can defeat others, without subduing himself. For example, if a king or a scholar, wants to defeat others, he will have to resort to his army, capability, learning, wisdom etc.

A man, becomes dependent as soon as his desire is born. This dependence remains, whether desire is satisfied or not. When the desire is not satisfied, a person remains dependent for want of the object of his desire. But, when that desire is satisfied, he depends upon the object, he has acquired, though he does not realize, this dependence because his intellect is veiled by ignorance. He, feels himself to be independent.

A wise man, becomes totally independent, because he has no desire at all, and such a man is victorious, though he has no desire to overcome, others. He needs nothing, in the world, while the world needs him.

Such an equanimous great soul, who has overcome the world, is not tempted by much mundane pleasure and is not shaken, even by the heaviest sorrow (Gītā 6/22). He has not the least desire for any beings, objects and circumstances etc. Though he knows of desirable and undesirable circumstances, and makes effort to be free from the undesirable ones, yet they have no effect on his mind.

'Nirdoṣaṁ hi samaṁ brahma'—All flaws and heterogeneity, are found in a man, because, of his affinity for nature. But, God is flawless, equanimous and unattached because, He has no affinity for nature.

'Tasmādbrahmaṇi te sthitāḥ'—God, is flawless and equanimous. Therefore, great souls, whose minds are flawless and equanimous, are established in God.

When a man is attached, to the kaleidoscopic and unreal world, all flaws and heterogeneity are born. As great souls, do not attach any importance to the unreal, they remain flawless and equal and so they remain established in God. As, where there is smoke there must be a fire, because without fire, smoke is not possible; so are those, whose minds are established in equality, established in God, because without being established in God, full equanimity (equality) is not possible.

When a man himself gets established in God, his mind is also established in equanimity. It is only when, they have attained the state of equanimity, that great souls are said to have attained, God-realization or equanimity. This equanimity, has been called Yoga in the Gītā (2/48). According to the Gītā, this attainment of equanimity, is regarded as perfection of human life.

The topic of Jñānayoga (the Discipline of Knowledge), was started in the thirteenth verse. The term 'Jantavaḥ' (beings or animals), used in the plural number in the fifteenth verse, continued upto this nineteenth verse. The Lord, by using the plural number, means to explain that all those people who are deluded, can attain God-realization. But, in the present verse the term, 'Brahmaṇi' has been used in the singular, which indicates that all people attain the same God. Every person, whether he is a brāhmaṇa (member of the priest class) or a pariah, attains the same Lord, Who was attained by great sages such as Sanaka etc.

Appendix—Here the term 'mana' should be interpreted as intellect because it is not the mind which gets established in equanimity but it is intellect which gets established. Mind is concentrated in meditation. This is the topic of steadfast intellect. Steadfastness of the mind persists only in meditation, not while engaged in dealings but steadfastness of intellect persists constantly. It is not the steadfastness of mind but the steadfastness of intellect which leads to salvation. Steadfastness of mind brings about 'Siddhis' (mysterious accomplishments). Therefore steadfastness of the mind is not of so much value as is the steadfastness of intellect. The Lord in the second chapter also has glorified a man of steadfast wisdom (intellect). In the next verse also the Lord has mentioned that an undeluded person with a firm intellect becomes one with Brahma (God)—'sthirabuddhirasammūḍho brahmavid brahmaṇi sthitaḥ'.

By error a striver may not think himself to be an enlightened soul, therefore this mark has been mentioned that if there is no equanimity in intellect, one should understand that he has not attained Self-realization, this is merely his misconception. The mark of equanimity in intellect is—freedom from attachment and aversion, pleasure and pain etc. Having realized the self, equanimity ever persists in intellect. Intellect never deviates or stirs from this equanimity.

Those, whose intellect is established in equanimity, become free from attachment and aversion. Their equanimous intellect naturally remains firm in the fact that all is God. When there is no other entity besides God then who should have aversion and towards whom? When only that one ever-existent entity is realized, then no desire persists, and no disquietude remains.

Link:—The Lord, in the next verse, explains how to get established in God (the Absolute), and what are the marks of such a sage, who gets established in Him.

न प्रहृष्येत्प्रियं प्राप्य नोद्विजेत्प्राप्य चाप्रियम्।
स्थिरबुद्धिरसम्मूढो ब्रह्मविद् ब्रह्मणि स्थितः॥ २०॥

na prahṛṣyetpriyaṁ prāpya nodvijetprāpya cāpriyam
sthirabuddhirasammūḍho brahmavid brahmaṇi sthitaḥ

He, who neither rejoices on obtaining what is pleasant, nor grieves on receiving what is unpleasant and who, is of firm understanding and unbewildered, such a knower of God vests in God. 20

Comment:—

'Na prahṛṣyetpriyaṁ prāpya nodvijetprāpya cāpriyam'—To get agreeable beings, objects, incidents and circumstances, appealing to the body, senses, mind, principles, caste, creed and scriptures, is called acquisition of 'priya' (agreeable) and what is contrary to it is 'apriya' (disagreeable). When, a striver obtains pleasant (desirable) beings, objects, and circumstances etc., according to his desire, he should not feel happy. Similarly, when he meets with unpleasant ones, he should not be sad. He knows the desirable and the undesirable ones, but he is neither attached to the desirable nor has an aversion for, the undesirable. Mere knowledge of the agreeable and disagreeable, is not a flaw, if one remains free from joy or grief.

The mind, knows the desirable (pleasant) and the undesirable (unpleasant), while the doer becomes happy and sad. Though all actions, are performed by the modes of nature, yet he whose mind is deluded, by egoism thinks, "I am the doer," feels happy and sad. But, he who knows the true character of the self (soul) and the modes of nature, understands, that it is the modes, which are acting on the modes (Gītā 3/28). So he knows, that he is not the doer and thus there is no question for him (the self) to be happy or sad.

'Sthirabuddhiḥ'—The self, can be known by the self, without the help of the instruments, such as the body, senses, mind and intellect etc. The knowledge, which is acquired with mind and intellect etc., is imperfect, as it is neither permanent nor certain (doubtless). But, the knowledge of the self by the self is permanent, uniform and certain. A great soul, who has realized this knowledge of the self, by the self has such a balanced and firm mind, that there remains, neither any doubt nor option nor contrary feelings in it. So, he is called 'sthira-buddhiḥ' (one with firm intellect or understanding).

'Asammūḍhaḥ'—Commonly, deluded people, do not behold

the omnipresent Lord, ever-pervading everywhere, they believe that the world (which is really transitory and unreal), is real. But, the undeluded, are those who are completely free from such belief.

'Brahmavit'—God, cannot be realized by a person, who does not identify himself with Him. But, when he identifies himself with Him, without having any separate entity, he realizes Him. In God-realization, the liberated soul, the means and God, all the three, become one. There remains no trio, only realization is left. In fact, who has realized God—this cannot be explained. The reason is, that such a liberated soul, becomes one with God (Brahma), and he has not the least pride of his achievement, that he has realized God.

'Brahmaṇi sthitaḥ'—In fact, all beings are essentially and constantly established in Brahma (God), but by an error they assume that they are established in body, senses, mind and intellect etc. So they cannot realize the truth, that they are established in Him. But a great soul, in all circumstances, realizes that he is established in Him, naturally and constantly.

An object may be established in another object, but establishment in God, is distinct from it. When a great soul identifies himself with God, only God remains, he completely loses his separate entity. So long as, he thinks that he is established in Him, it means that he has not fully identified himself with Him, and he still has finiteness.

Appendix—In sound sleep and in a swoon a man's affinity for the body is renounced involuntarily viz., due to ignorance the mind merges in ignorance. Therefore in these states a man does not feel pleasant and unpleasant and also bodily pain etc. But a liberated exalted soul renounces his affinity for the body discriminately. Therefore he knows the pleasant and the unpleasant and also bodily pain etc., but he does not feel rejoiced and agitated, happy and sad in them. His dependence on the body, senses, mind and intellect is wiped out.

Knowing Brahma and getting established in Him—both are one and the same.

Link:—A person is naturally established in God. The Lord, in the next verse, describes the means of attaining that state.

बाह्यस्पर्शेष्वसक्तात्मा विन्दत्यात्मनि यत्सुखम्।
स ब्रह्मयोगयुक्तात्मा सुखमक्षयमश्नुते॥ २१॥

bāhyasparśeṣvasaktātmā vindatyātmani yatsukham
sa brahmayogayuktātmā sukhamakṣayamaśnute

When a person is no longer attached to external sense-objects, he finds happiness in the self. Having completely merged himself with Brahma (God), he enjoys eternal bliss. 21

Comment:—

'**Bāhyasparśeṣvasaktātmā**—He, who, instead of being attached to the body, senses, mind, intellect, life-breath etc., as well as, to objects of senses, such as sound and touch etc., is attached, only to God, is known as, unattached to external contacts. A striver whose attachment has not been totally wiped out, but whose aim has been to wipe it out, should also be included among those strivers, who have renounced attachment, as they quickly get rid of it because of their firm resolve.

This detachment is necessary, in order to attain the state mentioned in the preceding verse, in which a striver neither rejoices on obtaining, what is pleasant, nor grieves on getting what is unpleasant.

So long as, a man is attached to sense-objects etc., internally or externally, he cannot realize the self. All these objects are transitory and constantly undergo change, but because of attachment to them a man has not an eye on their kaleidoscopic nature and derives pleasure out of them. But in fact they cannot provide pleasure; it is renunciation of affinity for them, which provides pleasures. Therefore, a man feels pleasure in sound sleep when he forgets his affinity for sense-objects.

A man, has a wrong notion that he cannot live without external contacts, but in fact, he cannot live with constant external contacts. To forget, all external contacts he sleeps. Thus he regains freshness, vitality and health, which he can never get, in the wakeful state. Therefore, he considers sleep very essential. Energy, is gained through dissociation, with objects.

When a man goes to bed, he means to renounce his affinity for external objects, as also, to work after waking from sleep. As he attaches more importance to work, he does not pay attention to the renunciation of his affinity, for objects. He sleeps and awakes having affinity for objects.

It is very surprising that if a person who was our relative dies, our affinity, for him continues. The reason is, that the assumed affinity can be wiped out only, when the person who has assumed it, renounces it. As soon as, he renounces it, he attains salvation, which is natural.

The affinity with external objects is unreal, while our affinity with God is real. A man, assumes his affinity with external objects, in order to derive pleasure out of them. But it results in sufferings (Gītā 5/22). By realizing this fact, attachment to external objects is destroyed.

'Vindatyātmani yatsukham'—When attachment to the external objects is wiped out, a striver finds Sāttvika happiness. Happiness derived out of the affinity, for the external objects, is Rajas (of the mode of passion). A person goes on enjoying this rājasa (of the mode of passion) happiness, so long as he does not gain sāttvika (of the mode of goodness), happiness. When he ceases attachment to the rājasa happiness he gains sāttvika happiness.

'Sa brahmayogayuktātmā'—As soon as attachment for the world is lost, a striver identifies himself, with Brahma (God). As with the disappearance of darkness, light is revealed, so when attachment to the world is erased, the striver is identified with Brahma. Both, happen simultaneously. Yet disappearance of darkness, is prior to illumination of light—it is deemed so. Similar, is the case with effacement of attachment and establishment in God. In the first verse of the thirteenth chapter, it is described, that the knower of the field (the self), is different from the field (body), while in the second verse it is said, that the self has Its identity with the Supreme Self. Similarly, in this verse by the expression 'bāhyasparśeṣvasaktātmā' (with the self unattached to external contact), it is explained that the self is different from the body and the world, this expression 'Brahmayogayuktātmā, elucidates the identity of the self with God.

Having become detached from pleasure and having found sāttvika happiness, a striver may have a subtle egoistic notion, by thinking 'I am happy', 'I am wise', 'I am flawless', 'I have no duty to perform' and so on. In order to get rid of this subtle egoistic notion, it is necessary that a striver, should identify himself with God totally, otherwise he cannot remain totally free, from the sense of individuality.

'Sukhamakṣayamaśnute'—So long as, a striver goes on enjoying sāttvika pleasure, he has egoism (attachment), in subtle form. But, when he ceases to enjoy this sāttvika happiness, his egoism perishes totally and he realizes God, Who is sentient, uniform and imperishable. This is known, as eternal bliss. This is also called infinite bliss (6/21; 6/28), absolute bliss (14/27) and so on. Having attained this eternal bliss, there is natural attraction for God, and this attraction is known as supreme devotion (Gītā 18/54). This devotion ever-increases i.e., the Lord, seems to be revealed in new forms, to such a devotee. In this connection, there is a point which needs attention. If a striver, thinks that his devotion was imperfect in the past, but now it has attained perfection, it means that the striver has not attained perfection, as he is an aspirant still. But, if in spite of perceiving novelty in the Lord, he feels that his devotion was supreme in the past also, it means that he has attained perfection.

Link:—In the preceding verse, the Lord declared, "When a person is not attached to external contacts, he attains eternal bliss." In the next verse, He explains how to renounce attachment for sense-objects.

ये हि संस्पर्शजा भोगा दुःखयोनय एव ते।
आद्यन्तवन्तः कौन्तेय न तेषु रमते बुधः॥ २२॥

ye hi saṁsparśajā bhogā duḥkhayonaya eva te
ādyantavantaḥ kaunteya na teṣu ramate budhaḥ

The pleasures that are born of attachment (with objects), are only sources of pain, these have a beginning and an end, O son of Kuntī (Arjuna), no wise man finds happiness in them. 22

Comment:—

'Ye hi saṁsparśajā bhogāḥ'—Pleasure is derived from the contact of senses, with their objects—sound, touch, colour, taste and smell. A man, also derives pleasure out of honour, praise, beings, objects, circumstances etc. Man is not free in acquiring sense-objects. If somebody, eulogizes the doctrines we respect, we feel happy—that is also a sort of enjoyment. It means, to derive pleasure through beings, objects, circumstances and states by body, senses and mind is known, as 'bhoga' (enjoyment).

Not only the forbidden pleasure, but also those which are sanctioned by the scriptures, must also be renounced, because these are obstacles, to God-realization. Pleasure can be derived, only by having affinity for insentient (matter), while it is a must to renounce affinity, for the insentient (matter), to attain God-realization.

'Ādyantavantaḥ'—All the pleasures have a beginning and

an end, these are impermanent, kaleidoscopic (Gītā 2/14) and insentient, while the self is permanent, unchanging and sentient. The sense-objects never identify with the self, therefore, the self cannot gain happiness from pleasure. The self, is a fragment of God (Gītā 15/7), therefore, it can attain eternal bliss from God (Gītā 5/21) alone.

As soon as, a person realizes, that these pleasures have a beginning and an end, are transitory, and fleeting, the effect of pleasure and pain, is lessened for him. Therefore, the expression 'ādyantavantaḥ', is a panacea, to root out the effect of pleasure.

'Duḥkhayonaya eva te'—All the pleasures born of contacts, are only sources of pain. Pleasure is born of pain and ends in pain. A man feels happy having acquired a thing, in the same proportion as its lacking was causing pain to him, and again feels sad having lost it.

A libertine cannot escape pains or sorrows, because sensual pleasures can be enjoyed by having affinity for the insentient (matter); and this affinity, for the insentient is the cause of great suffering, in the form of birth and death.

In the 'Pātañjalayogadarśana', it is stated, "A wise man does not indulge in pleasures, because these result in three kinds of pains. These pains are called 'pariṇāmaduḥkha' (pain as a result), 'tāpaduḥkha (affliction) and 'saṁskāraduḥkha'. Moreover, contradictions in the modes of nature, also result in pain.

Sensual pleasures, which appear like nectar at first, are like poison in the end (Gītā 18/38), because in enjoying these, energy and objects are lost. So the result is pain. This is 'pariṇāmaduḥkha.'

When a person, beholds others enjoying those pleasures which he cannot enjoy, because he does not possess those objects, or when he is afraid to lose them or when he is incapable of enjoying these in spite of his attachment for them, he is filled with grief, in spite of the fact, that the objects are available to him. This is 'tāpaduḥkha'. He remembers the lost pleasures—this is pain, in the form of latent impressions. This is called 'saṁskāraduḥkha'.

A person, wants to enjoy pleasure because of his inclination to them, but his discrimination checks him from enjoying them. Similarly, while listening to divine discourses, because of the mode of ignorance, he feels sleepy he wants to derive pleasure, from sleep. But because of the mode of goodness, he thinks that he should avail himself of such golden opportunities, which are very rare. Thus there is a contradiction or say tussel in the modes of nature and this internal fight is very painful for strivers.

In the enjoyment of pleasure, a person is dependent because these can be enjoyed according to one's fate, while he is independent in God-realization, as this human body has been bestowed upon him, only to attain Him. Pleasure cannot be enjoyed equally, even by two persons, while God can be realized by everyone, even in this Kali-age, as He was realized in the Satya-age, by great sages. Pleasures cannot be enjoyed forever, by all persons, while God can be realized forever, by everybody. It means, that there is a difference in acquiring pleasure i.e., all people cannot acquire these. But, there is no difference, as for as renunciation of pleasures is concerned, all can renounce pleasure.

The word 'eva' means that pleasure is, doubtlessly and certainly, a source of pain. There seems to be happiness, in them but in reality, there is none in the least.

'Na teṣu ramate budhaḥ'—A wise man, unlike a common man does not delight in pleasure, because he regards these as sources of pain. He, does not become a slave to them.

A wise man, knows that all the sorrow, suffering, sin and hell etc., depend, on a desire for pleasure. Therefore, he who attaches importance, to this knowledge, is wise. He, who knows that pleasures are sources of pain, yet, desire them and delight in them, does not deserve to be called, wise as a wise man, neither desire nor takes delight in them.

Appendix—The pleasure derived from contact with objects, persons and actions, is the root of sorrows. He, who enjoys pleasures, has to suffer pain—it is the rule. In fact the hope, the desire for pleasures and taking enjoyments, don't provide happiness but they provide sadness. The union of pleasures is transient and their disunion is eternal. A man by attaching importance to the transient feels sad. He should think whether the desire for pleasure will provide pleasure and end his sufferings. The desire for pleasure neither provides pleasure nor ends sufferings. The desire for pleasure in order to wipe out pain, is the root of pain.

One is—'suffering pain' and one is—'effect of the pain'. When a man suffers pain, then he has a desire for pleasure; and when he has the effect of pain, then the desire for pleasure is wiped out and he has a distaste for pleasure. By suffering pain, a man feels sad and by the effect of pain, he rises above pain. Because of the effect of pain, instead of being engrossed in pain, he thinks of its reason why he has to suffer pain. By reflecting upon it, he comes to know that except attachment to pleasure, there neither is, nor was, nor will be, nor can be any other reason. Any circumstances are also not the reason because the circumstances do not stay even for a moment. No person can cause us pain because he destroys our old sins and enables us to progress further. The world is also not the cause of pain because whatever change takes place, is not to provide us pain but it is to enable us to progress. If there is no change, how will development take place? Without change how will a seed grow into a tree? How will Ovum-Semen make a body? How will a baby become a youth? How will a fool become learned? How will a patient become healthy? It means that natural change leads to development. In the world, change is the quintessence of progress. Without change, the world would have become static and motionless like picture. Therefore change is not to be blamed but the desire to derive pleasure from this change is to be blamed. God is also not the cause of pain because He is the abode of bliss, in Him there is not even an iota (trace) of pain.

'Na teṣu ramate budhaḥ'—A wise (discriminating) man does not delight in pleasures because the desire for pleasure is the constant enemy of the wise 'jñānino nityavairiṇā' (Gītā 3/39). An ignorant person likes pleasures because vices appear as virtues because of indiscrimination. All pleasures are born of evils. If there is no blemish in the inner sense, there cannot be any pleasure taking. Only a wise person can perceive his flaws. Therefore he does not take delight in pleasures viz., does not enjoy pleasures.

A wise (discriminating) man has no desire for the thing which does not stay with him forever. By using his discrimination he accepts the truth, "Anything, person, ability and power which acquired, are neither mine nor for me. Not only this but in infinite universes, there is not anything which is mine and which is for me. Even the most loving thing is not mine forever and will not stay with me forever." Therefore a wise man determines that he can live happily forever without the objects and persons that are not likely to stay with him forever.

Link:—In the preceding verse, the Lord declared, "pleasures born of contacts, are only sources of pain." Then the question arises, who is happy? The Lord, answers the question, in the next verse.

शक्नोतीहैव यः सोढुं प्राक्शरीरविमोक्षणात्।
कामक्रोधोद्भवं वेगं स युक्तः स सुखी नरः॥ २३॥

śaknotīhaiva yaḥ soḍhuṁ prākśarīravimokṣaṇāt
kāmakrodhodbhavaṁ vegaṁ sa yuktaḥ sa sukhī naraḥ

He, who is able to resist the impulses born out of desire and anger, and overcomes these before he gives up his body, is a Yogī (liberated person) and he is indeed a happy man. 23

Comment:—

'Śaknotīhaiva yaḥ soḍhuṁ prākśarīravimokṣaṇāt kāmakrodhodbhavaṁ vegam'—Every being, possesses unusual discrimination but it remains latent in birds and beasts etc., who know only how to maintain their body. In the life of gods etc., this discrimination remains concealed because these bodies are for the enjoyment of pleasures. In human life also, the discrimination of those, who hanker after pleasure and prosperity, remains veiled, but time and again, their sense of discrimination, makes them realise that pleasure and prosperity, result in pain and sin. A person, remains entangled in them, because he does not attach importance to discrimination. Therefore, a person by attaching importance to discrimination, should make it a permanent feature; and he has no restriction in doing so. By that he can be free from evil propensities, such as attachment, aversion, desire, anger etc. Therefore, by using the term 'Iha' (here) in this world the Lord exhorts human beings to resist the impulses of desire and anger, so that they may be happy forever, by controlling them.

This human body, has been bestowed upon us, so that having controlled the impulse of desire and anger, we may attain salvation. Every human being, without any distinction of caste, colour or creed etc., is qualified and deserving in controlling these impulses.

A man could die at any moment. So he should be ever cautious, not to be swayed by desire and anger, and he should control these, here in this life, before giving up the body. Secondly, it can also be interpreted that before the body starts functioning under their sway, these should be controlled.

As soon as, the thought of hankering after pleasure comes to the mind, a striver, should become alert, that he is a striver and so it is not proper for him to get entangled in pleasure. He should immediately renounce such thoughts.

It is because of attachment to objects—believing that these

are beautiful and give pleasure, that—such thoughts crop up. Such thoughts, give rise to desire to acquire them and we get angry with persons, who create obstacles, in their acquisition.

As soon as thoughts of desire and anger come to mind, these should be renounced otherwise, later it becomes very difficult to control these urges. As soon as, a thought arises, there is disquietude, excitement and struggle etc., in the mind. So such a man cannot be happy. But when he resists these impulses, he becomes happy. Sometimes, a person can control these impulses out of fear, in the presence of another man who may be more powerful, than he. Similarly, he can control these out of greed, in business etc., in order to earn money. But, this control cannot make him happy, because in such cases, instead of getting entangled in desire and anger, he gets caught in fear and greed. Moreover, a person, who resists impulses of desire and anger, has been called a Yogī. But, no one becomes a Yogī, who has not renounced thoughts (Gītā 6/2). Therefore, for a striver it is better to renounce thought, as soon as, it comes to the mind, rather than to resist the impulses of desire and anger.

A striver, can control desire and anger by realizing the fact that these are not inherent in him, as the self is permanent, while they are transitory. Secondly, how can these be in him, when he knows that he is different from them? Thirdly, a person can be free from desire and anger (Gītā 5/26; 16/22) it means that only he who is in reality free from them, can be free. Fourthly, the Lord has called desire and anger (the gross forms of attachment and aversion), the modification of nature (Gītā 13/6). So they remain in nature (prakṛti), not in the self, as the self does not undergo any modification. Thus, desire and anger do not abide in the self. He who considers them abiding in the self, invites them to overcome him.

'Sa yuktaḥ naraḥ'—The Lord, in the fifteenth verse of this chapter, has called such persons, 'Jantavaḥ' (animals), whose knowledge is veiled by ignorance. Here, He has called a person, who controls the impulses of desire and anger, 'naraḥ' (a man). It means, that only he who has controlled these urges, deserves to be called, a man, otherwise, he is just like an animal.

He, who remains established in equanimity, is called a Yogī. He, who by attaching importance to discrimination is not swayed by desire and anger, is established in equanimity (even-mindedness).

'Sa sukhī'—Not to talk of men, even birds and beasts cannot lead a happy and peaceful life, if they are swayed by desire and anger. So, only a man, who has controlled these impulses is happy, otherwise evils such as disquietude, volatility and struggles are born and a man cannot be happy. A person, who depends on perishable persons and objects etc., and who, wants to derives pleasure, out of them by having affinity for them, can never be happy—this is a rule.

Appendix—In the mind first 'sphuraṇā' an idea (a thought which flashes on the mind) flashes. If a thought is accompanied with the feeling of reality for it, attachment to it and insistence on it, it is linked to us and it is transformed into a Saṅkalpa. This Saṅkalpa gives birth to contemplation which in its turn gives an impetus to evil propensities such as desire and anger etc., (Gītā 2/62-63). The topmost priority of a striver should be not to let the impetus (impulse) be born viz., he should not allow it to develop into a Saṅkalpa. Secondly if the impetus however is born, he should not act according to it.

Link:—Having described the sad plight of a person, who is swayed by desire and anger, the Lord, in the next verse, explains the glory of a person, who is happy within himself.

योऽन्तःसुखोऽन्तरारामस्तथान्तर्ज्योतिरेव यः।
स योगी ब्रह्मनिर्वाणं ब्रह्मभूतोऽधिगच्छति॥ २४॥

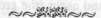

yo'ntaḥsukho'ntarārāmastathāntarjyotireva yaḥ
sa yogī brahmanirvāṇaṁ brahmabhūto'dhigacchati

One who is happy in God, rejoices in God and is illumined in God, that Yogī (Sāṅkhyayogī) identified with Brahma, attains to the beatitude of God (Brahma nirvāṇa). 24

Comment:—

'Yo'ntaḥsukho'ntarārāmastathāntarjyotireva yaḥ'—'Antaḥ sukhaḥ' (one who is happy within himself), is he, who instead of being happy in possessing the worldly objects, is happy only in God. Besides God, none is his object of happiness. He constantly enjoys God.

He, constantly remains happy within himself and so he needs no outward (external) objects etc. He remains happy within himself, because the self cannot inflict pain upon the self, and the self, cannot have disinclination, for the self.

The outwardly or external objects etc., cannot be acquired, by everyone forever, while the internal self can be attained by everyone forever.

'Antarārāmaḥ'—(One who rejoices within himself), is he who instead of rejoicing in external pleasure, rejoices in the self or in God, during spiritual practice, as well as in practical life.

The Lord, is the illuminator and base of all the mundane knowledge of senses and intellect etc., 'antarjyotiḥ' is a striver who ever remains illumined.

Mundane knowledge, has a beginning and an end, while the knowledge of God constantly, remains the same without undergoing any change at all. A Sāṅkhyayogī, naturally possesses knowledge, that only God pervades everywhere.

'Sa yogī brahmanirvāṇaṁ brahmabhūto'dhigacchati'—A striver, following the path of Sāṅkhya (knowledge), realizes that he is established in Brahma (God), which shows his egoistic thinking as he believes 'I am liberated', 'I am established in Brahma (God).' So long as this egoistic notion prevails, it means, that he is not a God-realized soul i.e., he has not attained perfection. So, such a striver should not be satisfied, with this state.

The expression 'Brahmanirvāṇam', means the attainment of Eternal Peace, without the least disquietude.

When a Sāṅkhyayogī, identifies himself with God, only God remains, he does not retain his separate entity, in the least, he attains perfection, or God-realization. In 'Brahma bhūta' state, a striver realizes that he is identified with Brahma. But, when his egoistic notion (individuality) perishes, none remains to realize this identification. He himself becoming Brahma (God), attains to Brahma (God).

Appendix—Here the term 'antaḥ' should mean God rather than 'antaḥ karaṇa' (internal organ). The reason is that he who is happy within the internal organ, who rejoices within the internal organ and who is tranquilly illumined within the internal organ, can't attain Brahma (God). Brahma is attained having renounced affinity for the internal organ.

Link:—In the preceding verse, the Lord explained the glory of a Sāṅkhyayogī who remains happy within himself. In the next verse, He explains the state of the Sāṅkhyayogīs, who are actively engaged in the welfare of all beings.

लभन्ते ब्रह्मनिर्वाणमृषयः क्षीणकल्मषाः ।
छिन्नद्वैधा यतात्मानः सर्वभूतहिते रताः ॥ २५ ॥

labhante brahmanirvāṇamṛṣayaḥ kṣīṇakalmaṣāḥ
chinnadvaidhā yatātmānaḥ sarvabhūtahite ratāḥ

Those holy men whose sins are destroyed, whose doubts (dualities) are annihilated, whose minds are disciplined and who are devoted to the welfare of all beings, attain the beatitude of God. 25

Comment:—

'Yatātmānaḥ'—The strivers, whose aim is God-realization, have not to control their minds, bodies, senses and intellects, but they are instinctively and easily controlled. When, they are controlled, strivers become free from evils, such as attachment and aversion, and all their activities are for the welfare of others.

So long as, a striver regards the body, senses, mind and intellect as his, and for him, these are not controlled by him; and they have such evils as attachment, aversion, desire and anger etc. So a striver is controlled by them. Therefore, a striver should not regard these as his, and for him. By doing so, they come under his control. Here the expression 'Yatātmānaḥ', has been used, for those cautious and alert strivers, who do not regard the body, senses, mind and intellect as theirs, and who consider these as different from the self.

'Sarvabhūtahite ratāḥ'—Egoistic ideas are the main stumbling block for a striver following Sāṅkhyayoga, in the way of God-realization. By effacing egoism, in order to realize the automatic identity with God, it is necessary to have sentiments of the welfare, of all beings. Those, who rejoice in the welfare of all beings, can easily wipe out their egoistic thoughts.

He, who wants to identify himself with the all-pervading Lord, must remain careful about the welfare of all beings. As a person, is careful about the welfare of all the parts of his body, which have different shapes, names and functions, so does a striver, think and work for the welfare of all beings, without any distinction of caste, creed, colour, order of life and spiritual practice etc. He beholds the Lord, pervading every being, equally. Therefore, when a person gets engrossed in the welfare of all beings, his selfishness easily comes to an end, and he realizes his identity with God.

'Chinnadvaidhā'—So long as, a striver does not have a firm resolve to realize God, he has duality, in his mind. But when he has a firm resolve, his doubt or duality disappears, and he is promptly engaged in spiritual practice.

'Kṣīnakalmaṣāḥ'—Affinity for nature (prakṛti) is the root, of all sins and evils. When a striver realizes, that he (the self) is different from nature and its evolutes, such as body, senses, mind and intellect etc., he accordingly becomes free from all sins and evils.

'Ṛṣayaḥ'—The term 'Ṛṣ', means knowledge. He who attaches importance to knowledge (discrimination), is a 'Ṛṣi' (sage or holy man). In the olden days, sages attained God-realization, by leading a householder's life. In this verse also, there is a description of those strivers, who practise spiritual discipline with discrimination, in order to realize God while performing mundane duties. Therefore, strivers who attach importance to their discrimination, are also sages (holy men).

'Labhante brahmanirvāṇam'—In fact, Brahma (God) is attainable by all human beings. But having identified himself with the kaleidoscopic body etc., a person has a disinclination for God. When his affinity for the perishable objects, such as the body etc., is renounced, all sins, evils and doubts are destroyed, and he attains Brahma (God), Who pervades everywhere.

The Lord, explains by the word 'Labhante' (attains), that a Sāṅkhyayogī merges in Brahma (God), in the same way as waves merge in sea. As waves, are not different from the sea, as both of them are one and the same, in the same way, the soul and the supreme soul, are one and the same.

Appendix—From the view-point of the people a Jñānayogī is seen to be devoted to the welfare of others (sarvabhūtahite ratāḥ) but in fact he does not do good to others but good (welfare) to others is naturally done by him.

Link:—In the twenty-fourth and twenty-fifth verses, the

Lord explained, how a striver following the path of Sāṅkhya (knowledge), can attain God. The Lord, in the next verse, explains the excellence of such God-realized souls.

कामक्रोधवियुक्तानां यतीनां यतचेतसाम्।
अभितो ब्रह्मनिर्वाणं वर्तते विदितात्मनाम्॥ २६॥

kāmakrodhaviyuktānāṁ yatīnāṁ yatacetasām
abhito brahmanirvāṇaṁ vartate viditātmanām

To those wise, who are freed from desire and anger, who have subdued their minds and who have realized the self for them the beatitude of God (Brahmic bliss) pervades on all sides. 26

Comment:—

'Kāmakrodhaviyuktānāṁ yatīnām'—The Lord declares, that in the God-realized souls, there remains no trace of evil propensities, such as desire and anger etc. Those evil propensities are born, when man has affinity for the unreal perishable objects (body, senses, mind and intellect etc.). But when he realizes his identity with God, he has no attraction at all for the entire world, including his body and mind etc. So, there is no question of the birth of evils, such as desire and anger, in him. If a striver has desire and anger even in subtle forms, he should not consider himself, a liberated soul.

Desire for perishable objects, is 'Kāma'. A man, has a desire only when he lacks something. In Asat (unreal) always there is deficiency or lacking, while the real self is not wanting in anything. But, when he (the self) identifies himself with the unreal, he feels something lacking in him. This want, gives birth to desire. If desire is not satisfied, anger is born. Thus, there is no desire in the self, but when It identifies Itself with the unreal, It seems to have a desire. So how can those, who have no identity with the unreal and who have realized the self, experience privation?

Strivers, feel that they are not swayed so much by desire

and anger now, because of their spiritual practice as they were influenced in the past, without spiritual practice. It shows, that these feelings have lessened through spiritual practice. It means, that they can be wiped out also, by spiritual practices.

Strivers realize (i) desire and anger are not so frequent as they were in the past, (ii) they are not so strong as they were, in the past, (iii) their duration is not so long as, it was in the past. But, sometimes a striver feels otherwise i.e., he feels that they are more forceful now, than they were in the past. The reasons for that are (i) through spiritual practice, attachment for pleasures is perishing, but perfection is not attained, (ii) because of the purity of heart and mind, a little desire or anger, seems too much to a striver, (iii) a striver, feels bad, if anything goes against his wish but he does not care about it. But this feeling accumulates. At last, the accumulated feelings blow up, even at the slightest provocation. Other people, are also surprised why he lost his temper, so easily.

Sometimes, a striver judges himself by his inclinations, and holds that he has attained perfection. But, in fact so long as, he realizes that he has attained perfection, it means that still he has some trace of egoism left (individuality) and he has not attained perfection.

'Yatacetasām'—The mind, is not subdued, so long as, a man is attached to the unreal. But when great souls renounce this attachment to the unreal, their minds are subdued.

'Abhito brahmanirvāṇaṁ vartate viditātmanām'—Those great souls, who have realized the self, which is the aim of human life, are called 'Viditātmanām'.

Such great souls, here as well as hereafter, remain established, in Brahma (God), the abode of eternal peace. As a common man, while performing different activities, remains established in his body constantly, so does a great soul remain established in Brahma constantly, while undertaking different activities, because he has nothing to do with that non-Self (Asat).

*Link:—The Lord, in the next two verses, explains that God, Who can be realized through the paths of Action and Knowledge, can also be realized through the path of meditation.**

स्पर्शान्कृत्वा बहिर्बाह्यांश्चक्षुश्चैवान्तरे भ्रुवोः ।
प्राणापानौ समौ कृत्वा नासाभ्यन्तरचारिणौ ॥ २७ ॥
यतेन्द्रियमनोबुद्धिर्मुनिर्मोक्षपरायणः ।
विगतेच्छाभयक्रोधो यः सदा मुक्त एव सः ॥ २८ ॥

sparśānkṛtvā bahirbāhyāṁścakṣuścaivāntare bhruvoḥ
prāṇāpānau samau kṛtvā nāsābhyantaracāriṇau
yatendriyamanobuddhirmunirmokṣaparāyaṇaḥ
vigatecchābhayakrodho yaḥ sadā mukta eva saḥ

Shutting out all external objects, fixing the vision between the eyebrows, making the inward and the outward breaths move within the nostrils evenly the sage, who has controlled the senses, mind and intellect, who is bent on liberation, who has cast away desire, fear and anger, is ever liberated. 27-28

Comment:—

'Sparśānkṛtvā bahirbāhyān'—All objects, except God are external. 'Shutting out external object' means, that external objects should not be thought of.

The affinity for the external objects, is renounced in the path of Action, through service, while in the path of knowledge through discrimination. Here, the Lord declares that this affinity can be renounced, through meditation. In meditation, when a striver meditates only on God, he has a disinclination for external

* The path of meditation is an independent means for a striver to realize God and it can also be used by the strivers following the paths of Action, Knowledge and Devotion. Chanting the Lord's names, meditation, good company and study of the scriptures are useful and necessary for every striver.

objects. It is not the external objects, but his assumed affinity (attachment) for them, which is an obstacle to God-realization.

'Cakṣuścaivāntare bhruvoḥ'—Here the expression 'Bhruvoḥ antare', may stand for, fixing vision between the eyebrows as well as, for fixing it at the tip of the nose (Gītā 6/13).

During meditation, if the eyes are completely shut, a striver may feel sleepy and if these are completely open, the scene and objects which are before his eyes, may draw his attention and create an obstacle. In order to, remove these distractions, it has been said that with half-closed eyes, the gaze should be fixed, between one's eyebrows.

'Prāṇāpānau samau kṛtvā nāsābhyantaracāriṇau'—The breath exhaled, is 'prāṇa' while the breath inhaled is 'apāna'. The speed of 'prāṇa breath' is fast, while the speed of 'Apāna breath' is slow. In order to, regulate the process of exhalation and inhalation, so that both of these may take equal time, first, the apāna breath is inhaled, through the left nostril, and then the prāṇa breath is exhaled, through the right nostril. Then, the apāna breath is inhaled through the right nostril and the prāṇa breath is exhaled, through the left nostril. This process of exhalation and inhalation, should take equal time. Through constant practice the flow of the prāṇa and the apāna breath, becomes even, gentle and subtle (thin). When, there is no sensation of air inside or outside the nostril and in the throat etc., it should be understood, that the flow of the prāṇa breath and apāna breath, has become even. When this flow bcomes even, (because of the aim of God-realization), the mind starts meditating on God. This control of the breathing process, has been described here, because it plays an important role, in the path of meditation.

'Yatendriyamanobuddhiḥ'—There are two sources of knowledge—senses and intellect. In between the two, the mind has its place. A man, is to be cautious, whether his mind is under the influence of senses or intellect or both senses and intellect. Senses, tempt the mind towards sense-objects, while intellect guides it to think of the consequences. Those people, whose minds are swayed by senses, indulge in worldly sensual pleasures, while those, whose minds are guided by intellect, do not rejoice in pleasures born of contact (Gītā 5/22).

Generally, strivers' minds are controlled, both by senses and intellect. A sort of struggle goes on, in their minds. They, neither attach full importance to their discrimination, nor do they enjoy, worldly pleasures. This dualism (struggle) is an obstacle to meditation. Therefore, the Lord means to say, that the mind should be controlled by intellect (discrimination), rather than by senses.

'Munirmokṣaparāyaṇaḥ'—A striver, whose aim is God-realization, has been called here, 'Mokṣaparāyaṇaḥ'. As the Lord, pervades everywhere all the time, He is attainable to all. But He is not quickly attained, by people, because they have not a firm resolve. As soon as they have a firm resolve, He will be realized. In fact, the aim (resolve) is pre-determined, because this human body has been bestowed upon human beings, so that they may attain God. But, they forget this aim. So they have to realize this aim. When they realize this aim, they will have a desire for God-realization. This desire, wipes out all the worldly desires and leads strivers, to God-realization. The Lord, has used this expression 'Mokṣaparāyaṇaḥ', so that a striver may realize, that his aim is God-realization.

In all the spiritual disciplines—of Action, of Meditation, of Devotion and of Knowledge etc., a firm resolve, (aim) plays a very important role. How can a striver attain perfection or God-realization, if he has not a firm resolve (aim) to attain Him? So emphasis has been laid here on a firm resolve by the expression, 'Mokṣaparāyaṇaḥ', in the path of meditation.

'Vigatecchābhayakrodho yaḥ'—We are angry with a man, who is a stumbling block to the satisfaction of our desires, if he is weaker than us. But we are afraid, if he is stronger than us. Similarly, we are afraid of death, if we have a desire to live and are angry with those, who do not let us fulfil our desires. Therefore, desire is the root of fear and anger. If a man has only the aim of God-realization, he can be free from fear, anger and desires. As soon as, he is free from desires, he attains liberation (salvation), as it is the desire to acquire objects and to be alive, which leads him, to the bondage of birth and death. A striver should think seriously, whether he can acquire objects and be alive, by escaping death merely by having desires. If it is not so, he should have a firm resolve that he has to realize God only. By doing so, he can be immediately liberated. But, if he has a desire to acquire objects and to live, the desire will never be fulfilled and he cannot be free, from the fear of death as also from anger. Therefore, it is necessary to be desireless, in order to be liberated.

Things are not acquired by mere desires. To get a thing or not to get a thing, does not depend upon mere desire, but it is God's dispensation. Then, what is the difficulty in discarding desires when they cannot procure us objects? No one, can escape death and acquire things by desiring. But if desires are renounced, life can be blissful. If a person has no desire to live, even death will provide him joy. Life becomes sad, when he has desires and these are not satisfied; and death appears horrifying, when he has a desire to live. Therefore, he who has renounced the desire to acquire things, as well as to live is liberated, even during this life and he becomes immortal.

'Sadā mukta eva saḥ'—The assumption of affinity for the perishable objects, is bondage while renunciation of this assumed affinity, is liberation. He, who is liberated is not at all influenced, by any incident, circumstance, praise, blame, favour, disfavour, life and death etc.

The expression 'Sadā mukta eva', shows that in fact, a striver (the self) is ever liberated, but he cannot realize the reality, because of his assumed affinity (attachment) for the perishable world. As soon as, this assumed affinity is renounced, he realizes his natural state of liberation or salvation.

Appendix—'Shutting out external objects' means to detach the self from the body "I am not the body; the body is not mine and the body is not for me." Every striver will have to accept these three facts whichever spiritual discipline he may follow. If we don't accept our affinity for the body, salvation is axiomatic.

In the twenty-fourth verse the term 'antaḥ' was used, therefore here the term 'bāhya' (external) has been used. In fact there is nothing external but it is merely an inclination. The term 'bāhya' is used when we assume that there is another entity but in fact there is only one entity. Therefore the expression 'sparśānkṛtvā bahirbāhyān' means there should not be the assumption at all of any other existence besides the Divinity.

Link:—Having described the paths of Action and of Knowledge, the Lord explained the path of meditation, which is useful for both the paths. Now, in the next verse, He describes the path of devotion, which easily leads to salvation (peace).

भोक्तारं यज्ञतपसां सर्वलोकमहेश्वरम्।
सुहृदं सर्वभूतानां ज्ञात्वा मां शान्तिमृच्छति॥ २९॥

bhoktāraṁ yajñatapasāṁ sarvalokamaheśvaram
suhṛdaṁ sarvabhūtānāṁ jñātvā māṁ śāntimṛcchati

Having realised Me, as the enjoyer of all sacrifices (yajña) and austerities (tap), the Great Lord of all the worlds and the unselfish friend of all creation, he attains peace. 29

Comment:—

'Bhoktāraṁ yajñatapasām'—When a person, performs any good action, he regards the body, senses, mind, intellect and objects etc., with which he performs actions, as his own; and he regards the person, for whom good action is performed, as the enjoyer. If he worships a god, he considers, the god as enjoyer, and if one renders service to a hungry man by offering him food, he considers that hungry man, as the enjoyer of food. In order to dispel this misunderstanding, the Lord declares that only God is the enjoyer of all good actions, because He is seated in the hearts of all.* Therefore, the Lord should be considered the enjoyer of all virtuous actions, such as adoration and offering food and water etc., to anyone. A striver, should aim at the Lord, rather than at beings.

In the twenty-fourth verse of the ninth chapter, also the Lord declares, "I alone am the enjoyer of all sacrifices (yajñas)."

Secondly, the body, senses, mind, intellect and objects etc., with which virtuous actions are performed, are not a person's own, these belong to God. By an error, he regards them as his own; and by regarding them as his own, and performing actions for himself with them, he becomes an enjoyer of those actions. Therefore, the Lord exhorts him, to perform all actions only for Him. By doing so, those actions will not bear fruit for him, and his affinity for actions will be renounced.

It is desire, which influences a man to perform evil actions. When he, having renounced desire, performs all actions only for God, he cannot perform evil actions; and his affinity for virtuous actions, is also renounced, by performing actions only for Him. Thus, having renounced affinity for all actions totally, he attains the Supreme Peace.

'Sarvalokamaheśvaram'—There may be different lords, in different worlds, but all of them are governed by God. So He is the Supreme Lord of the lords, of all the worlds. It means that only God is the Lord of the entire creation. So, how can an

* "He is seated in the hearts of all" (Gītā 13/17); "I am seated in the hearts of all" (Gītā 15/15); "The Lord abides in the hearts of all beings" (Gītā 18/61).

honest man regard anything of the world, as his own?

Generally, people regard, the bodies, senses, minds, intellects, life-breaths, families, riches and property etc., as their own, but they say that God is the Lord of the entire universe. Now the question arises, whether it is wise to say so. No, when people regard, themselves as an owner of every person and object etc., what remains there is whose lord He is? Therefore, only he who regards nothing as his, can call, God as the Lord of the entire universe.

A man is free to make the right use of objects, such as body etc., but he is not free to regard these as his own. If he, instead of regarding these as his own, offers them to God, by regarding them as His, he attains Supreme Peace.

'Suhṛdaṁ sarvabhūtānāṁ jñātvā māṁ śāntimṛcchati'—Those, who know* that God, Who is the Lord of the lords of all the worlds, is a disinterested friend of all beings; and no one else does them so much good as He, and no one preserves them and loves them so much as He, they attain Supreme Peace. Why should we be full of fear, worry, disturbance and disquietude etc., when the omnipotent Lord is the disinterested friend, of all of us?

Only God and his devotees, are interested in the welfare of living creatures, in a selfless manner. There is nothing unattained that should be attained (Gītā 3/22) by Him; therefore, He is naturally a disinterested friend of all. A devotee, also thinks of the welfare of all beings and does good to them (Śrīmadbhāgavata 3/25/21). The disinterested nature of devotees, has descended upon them, only from God.

God is the Enjoyer of all sacrifice and austerities. He is the great Lord of all the worlds, and He is the most disinterested friend, of all beings. Out of these three facts if strivers accept just

* Here 'knowing' stands for assumption. Firm assumption is in no way less than knowledge.

one, they attain Supreme Peace in the form of God-realization. If they accept all the three, God, is realized instantaneously.

'Desire', 'a sense of mine for worldly objects' and 'disinclination for God', are the three stumbling blocks to God-realization. The Lord, by the expression 'Bhoktāraṁ yajñatapasām', means to say, that a striver should have no desire and should do nothing for himself. By the expression 'Sarvalokamaheśvaram' He means to say, that he should regard nothing as his i.e., he should renounce the desire for pleasure, and should not lay claim to objects and persons. By the expression 'Suhṛdaṁ sarvabhūtānām', He says that he should regard only God as his. If he accepts one of these facts the remaining two are automatically translated into practice by him, and he realizes God.

A man, can renounce desire for pleasure, only if he does not regard any being or object as his. If he has a sense of possession over them, he will expect some reward or the other, from them. When a striver renounces the desire for pleasure, his sense of mine, is renounced; and if he renounces the sense of mine, his desire for pleasure is renounced. When he renounces his senses of mine for all objects and persons, only God remains his, and he realizes his real affinity, for Him. As soon as, the desire for pleasures is renounced, or the sense of 'mine' is renounced, or the striver realizes his real affinity for God, he attains Supreme Peace, because if he translates anyone of these into practice, the remaining two, are automatically translated into practice.

A man, should perform action and also know the art of their performance. He cannot perform actions properly and scrupulously, without either of the two. Therefore, in the third chapter, the Lord has laid special emphasis on the performance of actions, but has also said, that a striver should know what action is; in the fourth chapter He has laid special emphasis on the knowledge of the true nature of action, and also mentioned the necessity of performing action. In the fifth chapter, the Lord has described both the paths of Knowledge (Sāṅkhyayoga) and of Action (Karmayoga), as means of God-realization, yet He has declared, that the path of Action is superior, to that of Knowledge. In this chapter, the Lord having systematically described the paths of Action and Knowledge, in answer to Arjuna's question has dealt with the path of meditation, in brief and of his own accord described the path of Devotion, in the last thereby expressing his aim that every striver should follow this path which is the best of all.

ॐ तत्सदिति श्रीमद्भगवद्गीतासूपनिषत्सु ब्रह्मविद्यायां योगशास्त्रे
श्रीकृष्णार्जुनसंवादे कर्मसन्न्यासयोगो नाम पञ्चमोऽध्यायः॥ ५॥

oṁ tatsaditi śrīmadbhagavadgītāsūpaniṣatsu brahmavidyāyāṁ
yogaśāstre śrīkṛṣṇārjunasaṁvāde karmasannyāsayogo
nāma pañcamo'dhyāyaḥ

Thus, with the words Oṁ, Tat, Sat, the names of the Lord, in the Upaniṣad of the Bhagavadgītā, the knowledge of Brahma, the Supreme, the scripture of Yoga and the dialogue between Śrī Kṛṣṇa and Arjuna, this is the fifth designated discourse: "The Yoga of Action and Knowledge."

This fifth chapter is designated, as 'Karmasannyāsayoga' (The Yoga of Action and Knowledge), because in it there is description, of both the paths of action and of knowledge.

Words, letters and Uvāca (said) in the Fifth Chapter

(1) In this chapter in **'Atha pañcamo'dhyāyaḥ'** there are three words, in **'Arjuna Uvāca'** etc., there are four words, in verses there are three hundred and fifty-two words, and there are thirteen, concluding words. Thus the total number of the words, is three hundred and seventy-two.

(2) In this chapter in **'Atha pañcamo'dhyāyaḥ'**, there are seven letters, in **'Arjuna Uvāca'** etc., there are thirteen letters, in verses, there are nine hundred and twenty-eight letters, and

there are forty-eight concluding letters. Thus, the total number of letters is nine hundred and ninety-six. Each of the verses of this chapter, consists of thirty-two letters.

(3) In this chapter **Uvāca** (said) has been used twice, **'Arjuna Uvāca'** once and **'Śrībhagavānuvāca'** once.

Metres Used in the Fifth Chapter—

Out of the twenty-nine verses, of this chapter in the first quarter of the thirteenth and twenty-ninth verses na-gaṇa' being used there is **'na-vipulā'** metre; in the third quarter of the twenty-second verse 'ma-gaṇa' being used there, is **'ma-vipulā'** metre. The remaining twenty-six verses, are possessed of the characteristics of right **'pathyāvaktra'** Anuṣṭup metre.

|| Shri Hari ||

Sixth Chapter

INTRODUCTION

In the beginning of the fifth chapter, Arjuna asked Lord Kṛṣṇa, which of the two, the Discipline of Knowledge or the Discipline of Disinterested Action, is better. Lord Kṛṣṇa replied, "Both of them lead to supreme bliss, but Yoga of action is superior to the Yoga of knowledge (5/2)."

Lord Kṛṣṇa described, upto the twenty-sixth verse of the fifth chapter, how these lead to supreme bliss. Then, He described in brief the Discipline of Meditation, in two verses, which is helpful in the Discipline of Knowledge as well as Action and it leads to supreme bliss, independently. Then, He concluded the fifth chapter, by explaining the glory of devotion towards Him out of His own will.

Lord Kṛṣṇa in the sixth chapter further explains, the superiority of the Discipline of Disinterested Action.

श्रीभगवानुवाच

अनाश्रितः कर्मफलं कार्यं कर्म करोति यः।
स सन्यासी च योगी च न निरग्निर्न चाक्रियः॥ १॥

śrībhagavānuvāca

anāśritaḥ karmaphalaṁ kāryaṁ karma karoti yaḥ
sa sannyāsī ca yogī ca na niragnirna cākriyaḥ

The Blessed Lord said:

He who undertakes action without desiring its fruit, is both a Sannyāsī (Sāṅkhyayogī) and a Yogī (Karmayogī). He is not a Sannyāsī (renouncer), one who has merely renounced the sacred fire (ritual) and is not a Karmayogī, who has merely stopped all actions. (1)

Comment:—

'Anāśritaḥ karmaphalam'—Lord Kṛṣṇa, appears to say, that a man should not depend on men, things, incidents, circumstances and actions etc., because they are all perishable and kaleidoscopic, and he himself, being a fragment of God, is imperishable and constant. So, how can the perishable, satisfy the imperishable? Man thus feels a void. Moreover, he gets attached to them and that attachment is the cause of his birth in good and evil bodies (Gītā 13/21). If he renounces this attachment, he may realize emancipation which is axiomatic. In fact, he is naturally emancipated. But, it is because of attachment that he cannot realize this emancipation. Therefore the Lord declares, that a person should discharge his duty for duty's sake, without having any attachment to the fruit of action. Abandoning the fruit of action, a Yogī attains peace in the form of God-realization; whereas, he who works with a selfish motive, being attached to the fruit of action, is bound (Gītā 5/12).

A man, without depending on anyone of the three bodies—physical, subtle and causal, which are the fruits of actions, should use them in the welfare of all beings. He should, render selfless service to others, with the physical body, think of the welfare and salvation of others with the subtle-body, and offer stability (trance) acquired through the causal body, for the welfare of the world. These bodies belong to the world, not to us and so, they are for the service of the world, not for us. They have their identity with the world, while they are distinct from the self. Not to depend on these bodies means, 'not to expect the fruit of action', and to work for the welfare of the world means, 'to discharge one's duty'. One who, discharges one's duty for duty's sake, without expecting its fruit viz., serves the world, with worldly things. Being a Karmayogī, is extolled as a Sannyāsī in this verse, and one who renounces mineness from the worldly things, is a Tyāgī i.e., Yogī.

The result, of discharging duty without expecting its fruit, will be that he will not develop new attachment, as he does not perform actions for himself; and old attachment will perish, by doing good to others. By performing actions, his impulse for actions will also disappear. Thus renunciation of attachment, will spontaneously lead to salvation. The desire, to get hold of the perishable is bondage, and to renounce this desire is, emancipation. The method to attain emancipation, is that one should not depend on the perishable viz., should not have any affinity for it.

'Kāryaṁ karma karoti yaḥ'—'Kāryam' and 'duty' are synonyms. What can be easily performed, is a must, and what can never and be forsaken, is called a duty. Discharge of duty is not impossible, not even hard. What ought not to be done, is not duty, it is 'Akartavya' (that should not be done). Activities, which ought not to be done are of two types. (1) Those that are beyond our capacity. (2) Those which are forbidden by scriptures and traditions. Such activities, are never to be done. The gist is, that we should resort to prescribed duties without expecting any return, with a detached spirit, for the welfare of others. One should, discharge one's duty, in accordance with the ordinance of scriptures, for the welfare of others and without expecting its fruit, in order to do away with attachment for action, as well as its fruit.

Actions, are performed, with two attitudes of mind—for obtaining worldly things and for wiping out attachment for actions and their fruits. The inspiration to perform actions, with the latter attitude, is given here.

'Sa sannyāsī ca yogī ca'—He who, discharges his duty in the above mentioned way, is a Sannyāsī and a Yogī. He is a Sannyāsī, because he discharges his duty without attachment for action and its fruit and is a Yogī, because he remains equanimous in pleasure and pain, while discharging his duty.

His sense, of doership and enjoyership, is destroyed by doing actions without expecting any reward. Thus all his links with actions, and the fruits are, totally cut asunder. Therefore, that Karmayogī has been called a 'Sannyāsī.'

Arjuna thought it better to renounce the physical performance of actions and thus be a Sannyāsī. So, in 2/5, Arjuna said, that it was better to live on alms, than to wage war. So Lord Kṛṣṇa, says to Arjuna, "O Arjuna, the conception you have about a Sannyāsī is not right. He, who discharges his duty for duty's sake, without being attached to the fruit of action, is a real Sannyāsī."

'Na niragniḥ'—By forgoing household fire viz., 'Havana' and sense-objects etc., a person, is not a Sannyāsī in the real sense. Till he has importance and attraction for material objects, he cannot be a real Sannyāsī.

'Na akriyaḥ'—Generally, people think that a Yogī, is he who abandons all things and actions, and leads a secluded life in a state of trance. But, Lord Kṛṣṇa wants to say, that a Yogī, is he who discharges his duty, by ceasing to depend on the perishable viz., without expecting any fruit from action. A secluded life, with senses under control, may inspire man to attain some accomplishments (Siddhi), but it cannot lead him to God-realization. By merely discarding actions physically, he cannot be called, a Karmayogī. A Yogī, in the real sense, is he who performs his duty and having no dependence at all, on perishable objects.

A man, has an instinct for action. So sometimes, it is observed that good strivers who attempted to devote themselves to adoration and meditation in solitude, had to engage themselves in performing actions, for the welfare of others, by giving up their secluded life. The momentum of the impulse for action, is pacified, only when actions are performed selflessly solely for the welfare of others. In that case, equanimity is attained and that equanimity leads to God-realization.

An Exceptional Fact

The feelings, of egoism (I'ness) and attachment or Mineness, are man-made. First, a man accepts that he is a householder, but when he becomes a Sādhu, he says that he is a Sādhu. Thus his egoism changes. Similarly, he has attachment for a thing which he possesses. But, when he gives it to someone, permanently, he has no attachment left for it. It proves, that feelings of egoism and attachment, are not real but are only assumed. Had they been real, these might not have ceased to be, because 'The real, never ceases to be' and if it ceases to be, it means that it is not real, but is unreal, as 'The unreal has no existence' (Gītā 2/16).

The Self (soul), which is the base of egoism and attachment, is a fragment of God and is ever-existent and has identity with God, Who pervades everywhere. In the self, there is neither egoism nor attachment, but man by identifying himself with the body and the worldly things, accepts these as in him. Actually, he is free and capable of identifying himself with them. But, it is upto him, whether he accepts this identification or does not. It is not so, that he is not free or capable to breaking off, this identification. It is, he himself who has accepted this affinity with the body and the world, and not otherwise. Therefore, he who can assume this connection, can also snap it. Every human being, is free to accept that he is a householder or a Sādhu. Similarly he can accept things as his own or not his. He accepts, that he is a baby, a boy, a youth and an old man at different stages of life. Similarly, he accepts toys as his own in babyhood or boyhood while in youth and old age he accepts money and property etc., as his own. Thus, he can accept an affinity or renounce it. This affinity, can be renounced easily, because it is based on mere assumption.

The Self is eternal while the body and the world, are transient. Therefore, affinity between the eternal and the transient cannot be everlasting. When the self accepts this affinity, it seems that egoism and attachment are part and parcel of the self and it is difficult to renounce them. But it is wrong. This affinity is not real, it is only an assumed one. Because the self is the illuminator and the onlooker, while the body is an object to be illumined and looked on; the Self is beyond space, while a body is confined to space. The self is sentient, while the body is insentient; the self is the knower, while the body is to be known. The Self is the knower, till relation with the body is there. In the absence of this relation, the Self is Knowledge-incarnate. In that knowledge, there is neither 'I', nor 'mine'. There is total negation of egoism and mineness. Thus, they are poles apart. The self, actually is none else, but the Absolute, Who neither has, nor had, nor will have egoism and attachment, or mineness in the least.

Appendix—The entire universe from an ant upto the abode of Brahmā, is the fruit of action. The world is formed of objects, persons and actions. Everything is acquired and is lost, there is union and disunion of every person, and every action begins and ends. The man, who having renounced dependence on the three—things, persons and actions, discharges his duty, is a true Sannyāsī and a Yogī. He who, without renouncing the desire for the fruit of action, renounces mere sacred fire, is not a true sannyāsī and he, who renounces performance of actions, is not a true Yogī. The reason is that a man gets bound by desire for the fruit of actions, not by fire or actions.

In the third verse of the third chapter the Lord mentioned the two fold path—the path of knowledge and the path of action. Then in the fourth and the fifth verses of the fifth chapter the Lord mentioned that both Sāṅkhyayoga and Karmayoga bear the same fruit. Now the Lord with the same notion declares that he who has renounced the desire for the fruit of action, is a real Sāṅkhyayogī and a real Karmayogī. It means that by mere cessation of the functions of the mind a man does not become a Yogī. He becomes a Yogī only when he renounces the desire for the fruit of actions. The reason is that so long as the the desire for the fruit of actions persists, by cessation of the functions of mind 'Siddhis' (occult powers or accomplishments) can be achieved, but salvation can not be attained.

Link:—In the preceding verse, it is mentioned that he, who is a Sannyāsī is a Yogī. So, in the next verse, Lord Kṛṣṇa explains the relationship between Karma Sannyāsa (Discipline of Knowledge) and Karmayoga (Discipline of Action).

यं सन्न्यासमिति प्राहुर्योगं तं विद्धि पाण्डव।
न ह्यसन्न्यस्तसङ्कल्पो योगी भवति कश्चन॥ २॥

yaṁ sannyāsamiti prāhuryogaṁ taṁ viddhi pāṇḍava
na hyasannyastasaṅkalpo yogī bhavati kaścana

O Pāṇḍava, what they speak of as Sannyāsa, know that to be the same as Karma Yoga; for none becomes a Yogī without renouncing thought of the world. 2

Comment:—

'Yaṁ sannyāsamiti prāhuryogaṁ taṁ viddhi pāṇḍava'—In the beginning of the fifth chapter, Lord Kṛṣṇa explained, that the Yoga of Knowledge and the Yoga of Action, both lead to Supreme Bliss (5/2), and the supreme state, is attained equally by both the means (5/5) viz., both of them are the same. Similarly, here He points out, that as a Sannyāsī is a renouncer, a Karmayogī, is also a renouncer.

In the ninth verse of the eighteenth chapter also, Lord Kṛṣṇa says, "An action which is performed as a duty, giving up attachment and fruit, is regarded as 'Sāttvika' form of renunciation." By this renunciation, a man becomes a renouncer, or a Yogī, as he totally gets detached, from objects and actions. Similarly, a Sannyāsī renounces doership, and is thus a renouncer. It means, that there is no difference between a Yogī and a Sannyāsī viz., both are the same. Therefore, Lord Kṛṣṇa, in the third verse of the fifth chapter, said, "The Karmayogī should ever be considered a Sannyāsī (renouncer), for he has transcended the pairs of opposites, such as attachment and aversion."

'Na hyasannyastasaṅkalpo yogī bhavati kaścana'—Different thoughts come into the mind. The thought for which there is attachment or aversion of the mind, becomes a 'saṅkalpa' (pursuit of the mind). Without renouncing that pursuit, no one can become a Yogī (Sāṅkhyayogī or Karmayogī), but he is a voluptuary, because union (affinity) for God is 'Yoga', and one who has a desire for pleasure, is a voluptuary, not a 'Yogī', because instead of attachment for God, he is attached to pleasure. But, when he renounces, the desire for the unreal, he becomes a renouncer and realizes his eternal union, with God. As men are sensual, so are birds and animals, because they have also, not renounced pursuits of the mind.

It means, that so long as there is the least affinity for the unreal, a man cannot become a 'Yogī', in spite of a lot of practice, trance and a secluded life, according to the gospel of the Gītā.

Though the process of Discipline of Sannyāsa, and that of Yoga, are different, yet as far as renunciation of the pursuits of the mind is concerned, both are, one and the same.

Link:—In the next verse, Lord Kṛṣṇa explains how to attain that 'Yoga', which has been praised, in the previous verse.

आरुरुक्षोर्मुनेर्योगं कर्म कारणमुच्यते।
योगारूढस्य तस्यैव शमः कारणमुच्यते॥ ३॥

ārurukṣormuneryogaṁ karma kāraṇamucyate
yogārūḍhasya tasyaiva śamaḥ kāraṇamucyate

To the contemplative soul (muni) who desires to attain to the height of Karmayoga (in the form of equanimity), action without motive, is said to be the means. For the same person when he masters Yoga, serenity (tranquillity of mind) is said to be the means, to God-realization. 3

Comment:—

'Āruruksormuneryogaṁ karma kāraṇamucyate'—He, who desires to rise to the heights of Yoga (equanimity), action without motive, is spoken of as the means. Every human being, who is born, nourished and is living his life has been dependent on others. All his possessions, body, senses, mind, intellect and ego all are evolutes of nature. Therefore, till he through these does not render service to others, he will not rise to the height of Karmayoga, or in other words, he will not attain equanimity. It means, that a man should discharge his duty, by rendering service to others with all his means, because whatever means (including his body, senses, mind, intellect and ego) he possesses, belong to society; and all the things have identity with the world, not with the self. By rendering service to others, the flow of actions, will be directed towards the world, and man himself will attain equanimity. The same fact, has been explained, by Lord Kṛṣṇa (in Gītā 4/23), "He, who performs actions, for the welfare of others, his actions melt away viz., do not lead him to bondage." And, in Gītā 3/9 He declares, "Man is bound by actions, other than those performed for the sake of sacrifice viz., he is bound, when he performs these with a selfish motive."

How is action without motive, the means to rise to the heights of Karmayoga (equanimity)? The answer is, that our equanimity will be judged, only when we perform actions. While performing actions if we aim to remain equanimous, in pleasure and pain, it means that our action, is the means to rise to the height of Yoga, otherwise not.

'Yogārūḍhasya tasyaiva śamaḥ kāraṇamucyate'—Affinity for the unreal, causes disquietude, because the Self is eternal and permanent, while all the worldly objects such as bodies etc., are transient and kaleidoscopic. But when the Self accepts his affinity with them and foresees their destruction or they actually perish, he becomes disquiet. But, if he utilizes them in rendering service to others, his affinity breaks off, he rises to heights of Yoga and attains, tranquillity. If he enjoys that tranquillity, it will delay his progress. But, if he does not get attached to it, and does not enjoy it, that tranquillity becomes the means of his God-realization.

Appendix—The striver who desires to attain to the height of Karmayoga (equanimity), action without motive is said to be the means; and the serenity thus attained, is the means to God-realization. It means that an action is not the means to attain God but serenity attained by renouncing affinity for actions, is the reason. This serenity is a means rather than an end.

When actions are performed discriminately, attachment (impetus) to actions is wiped out, because actions have no power to wipe out attachment but through discrimination it is possible. He, who desires to attain to the height of Karmayoga, performs all actions discriminately. When discrimination develops, then a striver realizes helplessness in the fulfilment of his desire and feels a lack (shortage) in its unfulfilment. No one wants dependence and shortage but a man does not get rid of these two by having a desire.

Having attained to the height of Karmayoga, a striver should not be pleased because this pleasure will arrest his progress and so God-realization will be delayed (Gītā 14/6). As a boy takes interest in games and sports, but when he grows up, he starts taking interest in earning money, then his taste for play is naturally wiped out. Similarly until God is realized, a striver relishes serenity. But if he does not relish that serenity and becomes indifferent to it, his relish is naturally wiped out and very soon he realizes God.

To attain to the height of yoga, action is the means viz., while performing actions for the welfare of others without any selfish motive, a striver gets detached from all actions etc., then he attains to the height of yoga. Actions come to an end but yoga (equanimity) ever persists.

A Karmī (Bhogī) performs actions and a Karmayogī also performs actions but there is a vast difference in their aims. The former performs actions to satisfy his desire, while the latter performs actions in order to renounce attachment. A 'Bhogī' (pleasure-seeker) works for himself while a Karmayogī works for others. Therefore though both are equal as far as performance of actions with attachment is concerned, yet the striver who works for others in order to renounce attachment, attains to the height of yoga. A yogī's equanimity will be judged only when he performs actions without attachment 'vṛddhā nārī pativratā' (an old woman is chaste).

What has been called 'Śama' (serenity)) here, the same has been called 'prasāda' (placidity or purity of mind) (Gītā 2/64). If a striver does not take delight in this serenity, he attains everlasting peace (Supreme Bliss) (Gītā 6/15). Renunciation of the fruit of action leads to supreme peace (Gītā 12/12). If a striver does not take delight in peace (serenity), he attains uninterrupted relish (Self-realization) and if he is not satisfied with 'akhaṇḍa rasa' (unbroken relish), he attains infinite Bliss (supreme love).

Link:—What are the marks of a Yogī who has risen to the heights of Karmayoga? The explanation, comes in the next verse.

यदा हि नेन्द्रियार्थेषु न कर्मस्वनुषज्जते।
सर्वसङ्कल्पसन्न्यासी योगारूढस्तदोच्यते॥ ४॥

yadā hi nendriyārtheṣu na karmasvanuṣajjate
sarvasaṅkalpasannyāsī yogārūḍhastadocyate

When a man ceases to have any attachment, either for the objects of senses or for actions (Karma) and has renounced all thoughts of the world, he is said to have attained Yoga and is called Yogārūḍha. 4

Comment:—

'Yadā hi nendriyārtheṣu na karmasvanuṣajjate'—Firstly, a striver should not be attached to objects of five senses—sound, touch, colour, taste, smell; to favourable circumstances, incidents, men, comfort, respect and praise etc. He should not enjoy them, and should not be pleased with them. He should remain detached, by thinking that all of these are transient and perishable.

The means to get detached from the objects of senses, is not to derive pleasure out of fulfilment of desires. One should not be pleased with desirable objects, circumstances, incidents and persons etc. If he derives pleasure out of sense-objects, these enhance attachment. Therefore, a striver should, neither desire favourable circumstances, nor derive pleasure out of them. In this way, his senses will not get attached, to sense-objects.

Secondly, a man feels absence of favourable objects etc., without acquiring these and having acquired them, he becomes a slave to them. Actually, he is a slave in both the cases. First, he was a slave because he wanted to acquire them, and then he became a slave, lest they should slip away. But in the second case, he does not realize his servility. He rather feels, that with their acquisition he is free. This is mere deception. Similarly, deriving pleasure out of favourable circumstances, is a deception, as such pleasure, spoils his nature and gives birth to desire, to enjoy pleasure, again and again. This desire for pleasure, misleads him to the shackles of birth and death. To desire, and to expect favourable circumstances, and then to feel happy on their acquisition is the root of all miseries and sins. If this desire is discarded, a man attains equanimity.

Thirdly, whatever extra money and objects, besides our necessities, we possess are not ours, they are of the poor and the needy. So, we should hand these over to the poor and the needy people, and should think that by doing so, we are free from debt. Thus, we shall not get attached, to objects and riches etc.

'Na karmasvanuṣajjate'*—As a striver, should not be attached to objects of sense, he should also not be attached, to actions and their fruits. If action is performed well, it gives pleasure, but if it is not, it gives pain. This pleasure or pain, is attachment by action. So a striver, should perform actions carefully and efficiently without being attached to them, because they are transient, while his self, is eternal. So how can they have any effect on him? He is affected only, when he is attached to them, and that attachment misleads him to the cycle of birth and death. So, he should not be attached either to objects of senses or to actions. By doing so, he becomes completely detached from nature, which consists of only actions and objects. Thus he attains Yoga.

Here a point needs attention that generally there is attachment to actions for their fruits and the fruits are the pleasures. So, if this attachment for pleasure perishes, attachment to actions will also perish. Then, why has Lord Kṛṣṇa mentioned cessation of attachment to actions? The reason is, that there is an independent attachment for actions also. Even without a desire for fruit, there is a momentum of impulse for actions; so a man wants to perform an action. A man, ceases to have that attachment by performing actions, either for others or for God. So, Lord Kṛṣṇa, in the twelfth chapter, first exhorted Arjuna to seek to attain Him, through Yoga (Discipline) of practice. But, if he was unable to practice, Lord Kṛṣṇa asked him, to be intent on performing actions for Him (12/10). It means, that a striver who cannot concentrate his mind, on God and if there is an inner urge for actions, he should perform actions, only for God. Thus, the attachment of a striver, who follows the Discipline of Devotion,

* Here the term 'Karmasu' has been used in the plural number which shows that the man who is attached to actions has a desire to perform several actions and reap their fruits. But in the forty-fifth verse of the eighteenth chapter the term 'Karmaṇi' has been used in the singular number in order to show that a man free from attachment performs several actions with one intellect that he has to perform his duty.

will be blotted out. Similar, will be the result, in case of a striver who follows the Discipline of Action, if he performs actions, for the welfare of others.

As there is, attachment for action, there is also attachment, for inaction. A striver, should have no attachment for inaction also, because inaction causes idleness and laziness, which are 'Tāmasika' traits; while attachment to action, misleads to futile pursuits with 'Rājasika' traits.

How long will a striver take, to rise to the height of Yoga? To answer this question, Lord Kṛṣṇa has used the terms 'Yadā' and 'Tadā' viz., 'when' and 'then'. It means, that as soon as, he ceases to have any attachment for the objects of senses, and for actions, he attainsYoga.

Man himself, being a fragment of God, is eternal and free but he gets attached to the perishable worldly bodies and objects, the evolutes of nature and this attachment leads him to bondage. If he has a firm determination, not to enjoy worldly objects and actions today, he will at once attain Yoga, because Yoga (equanimity) is axiomatic. We do not realize it (the real), because we are attached to the unreal.

'Sarvasaṅkalpasannyāsī'—Out of all 'sphuraṇās', the 'sphuraṇā', which is pleasing and to which we are attached, becomes a 'saṅkalpa'.

This 'saṅkalpa' proves to be pleasant or unpleasant, because of favourable or unfavourable circumstances. A man, has attachment to favourable circumstances, while he has aversion for the unfavourable ones. Thus, this 'saṅkalpa' being always harmful leads to nothing but bondage. It is conducive, neither to Self-realization, nor to selfless service or to devotion to God or for good relations, with the family. Thus, a striver should renounce, this 'Saṅkalpa', by thinking that it involves neither one's own welfare nor of the world, it is conducive neither to the service of the family nor to God-realization (Self-realization). So, a striver should be free, from all 'saṅkalpas' (thoughts of the world).

If a striver, does not get attached to the thought, it is a 'sphuraṇā'. If a 'sphuraṇā' does not assume the shape of a 'saṅkalpa', it vanishes naturally. This 'sphuraṇā', should also be renounced, because it wastes time though it does not cause much harm and a downfall. But a striver must renounce 'saṅkalpas', because without renouncing them, he does not attain Yoga; and without attaining Yoga he does not realize God. Something remains to be done by him and his human life is not successful. He does not develop devotion to God and he does not, become totally free from sufferings.

In the second verse of this chapter, the Lord declares, by a negative inference, that none becomes a Yogī without renouncing thoughts of the world, while in this verse He declares more positively that a man attains Yoga, by renouncing thoughts of the world. It means, that a striver should have no thought of the world in the least.

Methods to Renounce, All Thoughts of the World

(i) God has bestowed this human birth, the last of all births upon us, by His grace for our salvation. So, we have not to waste this valuable time of human life, in futile thought of the world. By thinking so, the pursuit of mind, can be renounced.

(ii) A striver, following the Discipline of Action, has to discharge his duty, without attachment (Gītā 3/19) at present, while the thoughts that come to his mind, are either of the past or the future. So a striver, should not be entangled in them.

(iii) A striver, following the Discipline of Devotion, should think that God is existent here and now, He is his and is in him, while the thoughts that come to the mind, are either of the past or the future. So, it is a blunder to think of the pursuits, which do not exist now, but not to think of God, Who has His existence now. By thinking so, a striver should renounce all thoughts of the world.

'Yogārūḍhastadocyate'—Equanimity, in success and failure, is called Yoga (Gītā 2/48). Attainment of equanimity is attainment of Yoga. Equanimity leads to God-realization. In the second verse of this chapter, Lord Kṛṣṇa declared, that none becomes a Yogī without renouncing the thoughts of the world, and here, He has declared that by renouncing all thoughts of the world, a man is said to have attained Yoga. It proves, that all the Disciplines as that of Knowledge, or that of Action, lead to attainment of Yoga (Gītā 5/5) as both disciplines culminate in the renunciation of all thoughts of the world.

Appendix—What is the mark of the yogī who has attained to the height of Karmayoga? For this the Lord has mentioned three factors—not to be attached to objects (things and persons), not to get attached to actions; and to renounce all thoughts of the world viz., to renounce one's own will. It means that he should not be attached to sensual pleasures and actions and should not insist from within that it should occur and it should not occur. He, who is neither attached to objects nor to the lack of objects; is neither attached to actions nor to the lack of actions and who has no 'Saṅkalpa' (projection of the mind), is said to attain to the height of Karmayoga. It means that he should not insist on availability or non-availability of objects, union or disunion of persons and performance or non-performance of actions (Gītā 3/18).

A striver should reflect upon whether there is anything which will ever stay with us and with which we shall ever stay. Is there any person who will ever live with us and with whom we shall ever live? Is there any action which we shall ever go on performing and which will ever be performed by us? Neither a thing nor a person nor an action will ever stay with us. One day we shall be devoid of a thing, a person and an action. If we accept their disunion at present and get detached from them, then freedom from the bondage of worldly life is axiomatic. It means that the union with things, persons and actions is transient but their disunion is eternal. By accepting the eternal fact, the eternal divinity is attained and no lack remains.

Detachment from sense-objects and actions means—freedom from desire and from the sense of doership. If a striver is not attached to pleasures and objects, he becomes free from desires; and if he is not attached to actions, he becomes free from the sense of doership. Being free from desire and from the sense of doership, he naturally gets established in the self. In fact he does not get established but he is already established but he does not realize it because of his desire and the sense of doership. If there is absence of desire and the sense of doership, the striver realizes his self-evident abode in the self.

As while writing, we use a pen and we put the pen in its original position as soon as the writing is over, similarly a striver should use the body, while working and put (leave) it in its original position as soon as the work is over viz., should get detached from it; then after every action he will be established in yoga (equanimity). If he is totally detached from actions, he will attain to the height of yoga.

Attachment to Kriyā (pleasure) and objects (prosperity) leads to ruin (downfall) (Gītā 2/44), therefore a striver should neither be attached to actions nor to the fruit of actions (Gītā 2/47, 5/12). He should not enjoy pleasure born of his resolve viz., he should not derive pleasure from the fulfilment of his resolve. He should not resolve even for his salvation because the resolve for salvation strengthens (the existence of) bondage. Therefore renouncing all worldly thoughts he should remain quite indifferent.

Link:—In the previous verse, Lord Kṛṣṇa explained the marks of a Yogī and by giving the terms 'Yadā' (When) and 'Tadā', (Then) explained, that man is free in attaining Yoga viz., in attaining Self-realization. So, Lord Kṛṣṇa inspires every human being to uplift himself by his own self.

उद्धरेदात्मनात्मानं नात्मानमवसादयेत्।
आत्मैव ह्यात्मनो बन्धुरात्मैव रिपुरात्मनः॥५॥

uddharedātmanātmānaṁ nātmānamavasādayet
ātmaiva hyātmano bandhurātmaiva ripurātmanaḥ

Let a man emancipate himself by his own self; and not degrade himself; for he himself is his friend as well as his enemy. 5

Comment:—

'Uddharedātmanātmānam'—A man should lift himself by his own self. It means, that he should lift himself, above the body, senses, mind, intellect and life-breath, because all of these belong to matter (nature) and have identity with matter, while his self, is a fragment of God and has identity with Him. It also means, that he should lift himself from the limited 'I', to the unlimited 'Self''. So, for God-realization, there is no need to depend, on the insentient, the unreal, because attachment for the unreal, or dependence on the unreal, is the main obstacle to God-realization. There is no need of the body, senses, mind and intellect, to attain God Who is one's own. He, is in him, exists now and here, because the real cannot be attained by the unreal, the real, can be attained by renouncing connection with the unreal.

Secondly, as it was explained in the previous verse, a man should cease to have any attachment for objects, actions and thoughts, and raise himself above them. It is everyone's experience, that objects, actions and thoughts, have a beginning and an end. They are born and decay; are united and disunited, but his self remains the same, without the least modification. Therefore; detachment from these means, lifting himself by his own self.

Man possesses discrimination, by utilizing which, a striver

can lift himself and can realize God. A striver, by following the Discipline of Knowledge, can discriminate between the real and the unreal, and thus get established in his own self. A striver, following the Discipline of Devotion, accepts that he is God's and God is his, and this feeling leads him to God-realization. A striver, following the Discipline of Action, by using discrimination, utilizes the so-called body, senses, mind and intellect in rendering service to others and thus by breaking off his affinity with them, gets established, in his own self. Thus, his discrimination leads him to God-realization, whatever discipline, he may follow.

An Exceptional Fact About God-realization

Think of—'I am not body', because the body changes, while I remain the same; 'This body is not mine', because I cannot keep this body healthy, and in my possession, as long as I wish; 'This body is not for me', because if it had been for me, I might have not had any other desire. Secondly, this body is changeful, while I am eternal. How can this kaleidoscopic body, be of any use to the eternal 'Self'? Thirdly, if it had been for me, it would have lived with me forever, but it does not live. Therefore, if a man thinks seriously, and sticks to the thought, 'I am not body', 'The body is not mine' and 'The body is not for me', he will realize God spontaneously.

Now, a question arises, why Lord Kṛṣṇa has said, that a man should lift himself by his own self, when God, preceptors, saints and scriptures, also lead a man to God-realization. The answer is, that all of them will lead us to God-realization, only if we have faith in them; and it depends upon us, whether we have faith or we do not. It is, because of the lack of faith and desire, that several incarnations of the Lord, and many saints and liberated souls, could not enable us to realize God. But, those who had faith in them, realized Him. Therefore, a striver by having faith in them and by obeying them should realize God. It is an unique opportunity for us, that this human body has been bestowed upon us in this Kali-Age, so that we may realize God, not only once, but several times during this life. But, we can realize Him, only when we ourselves want to do so.

Secondly, man has degraded himself, as he has accepted his affinity for the world, the world has not accepted that affinity, which breaks off, every moment. If one does not accept any new affinity, he may realize God.

'Nātmānamavasādayet'—He, should not degrade himself. It means that he himself being uniform and sentient, should not enslave himself, by having dependence on the transient and insentient worldly objects, such as riches, ranks etc. By virtue of his riches and ranks, he assumes himself to be elevated. This elevation, is of his virtues rather than his own. This dependence amounts to his degradation. But, how shocking and surprising it is, that he regards this degradation as promotion, and dependence as independence!

'Ātmaiva hyātmano bandhuḥ'—A man, himself is his friend, when he accepts that there is no need for mundane things, such as body, senses, mind, intellect etc., in God-realization. Secondly, he should have faith in his guide, in God, saints and scriptures. They will lead him to God-realization. By having this faith, he himself is his friend.

'Ātmaiva ripurātmanaḥ'—He himself, is his enemy, when he accepts his affinity with the worldly body, senses and mind etc.

In the second line of the verse, the term 'Eva' (only), has been used twice, to emphasize the fact, that he and only he himself, is his friend and foe; anyone else, neither is, nor can be his friend and foe. By accepting his affinity with the world, he is his enemy and by accepting no affinity in the least, with the world, he is his friend.

Appendix—A man himself, rather than anybody else, is

responsible for his salvation (God-realization) or for his downfall. God has bestowed upon us this human body and he has also gifted us with all the requisites. Therefore for salvation no other person is needed, similarly no one else is responsible for our fall. The person himself by becoming attached to the modes, takes repeated birth and death (Gītā 13/21).

Preceptor (spiritual guides), saints and God lead a man to salvation when a man himself has faith and belief in them, accepts them, has an inclination towards them, takes refuge in them and carries out their orders. If he does not accept them as their own, how will they lead him to salvation? They can't. If he does not became a disciple, what will the 'guru' (spiritual guide) do? As other persons will provide food to a (hungry) man but the hunger should be his own. If he has no hunger of his own, what is the use of the food provided to him by others? Similarly if a striver is not sincerely devoted to his aim, what is the utility of the gospel preached by the spiritual guide, saints and exalted souls?

There is never lack of spiritual guides, saints and God. There have been many great saints, preceptors and incarnations, but we have not attained salvation. It proves that we have not accepted them. Therefore we ourselves are responsible for our salvation and ruin. He, who thinks others responsible for his salvation and fall, can never attain salvation.

In fact God is present, the preceptor is present, the supreme truth is present and ability and strength in a striver are also present. The only obstacle to their revelation, is the attachment to the perishable pleasures. The responsibility to wipe out this attachment to pleasures, goes to the striver because he himself has been attached to them.

Initiation (initiating or being initiated) is not the principle of the Gītā. A man is his own preceptor, therefore he has to preach the gospel to his own self. When all is God (Vāsudevaḥ sarvam), then who except God is a preceptor and who will preach the gospel and to whom will he preach it? Therefore the expression 'uddharedātmanātmānaṁ' means that instead of perceiving defects in others, a man should perceive defects in his own self and try to get rid of them and preach the gospel to himself. He himself should become his preceptor, he himself should become his leader and he himself should become his ruler.

Link:—In the preceding verse, Lord Kṛṣṇa declared that a man himself is his friend and he himself is his enemy. How is he himself, his friend or enemy? The Lord, provides an answer, in the verse that follows.

बन्धुरात्मात्मनस्तस्य येनात्मैवात्मना जितः।
अनात्मनस्तु शत्रुत्वे वर्तेतात्मैव शत्रुवत्॥ ६॥

bandhurātmātmanastasya yenātmaivātmanā jitaḥ
anātmanastu śatrutve vartetātmaiva śatruvat

To him, who has conquered his self by himself, his own self is a friend; but to him who has not conquered the self, his own self acts as his foe. 6

Comment:—

'Bandhurātmātmanastasya yenātmaivātmanā jitaḥ'—Nothing resides, in a man except, the pure self. He does not at all depend, on the lower self viz., body, senses, mind and intellect etc. He renounces his dependence on these altogether, and gets established in his own self. He is the one, who has conquered himself.

How to know, that a man is established in his own self? When his mind is set well in equanimity, it means that he is established in his own self, because the Absolute is, free from blemish and is equanimous (Gītā 5/19). It means that by being established in the Absolute he has conquered himself by his own self. Actually he was already established in the Absolute, but he could not realize it, as he had assumed his body, mind and intellect etc., as his.

In this world, a man cannot defeat anyone without the help of others, and this help of others, means his own defeat. How? For example, if you want to defeat others, either with arms or with arguments, you have to depend on arms or arguments, then only, you can defeat others. It means that you are first defeated, by arms or arguments. Thus one cannot conquer others, without his own defeat. But, one who has no need of others, in the least, conquers himself by his own self, and he himself, is his friend.

'Anātmanastu śatrutve vartetātmaiva śatruvat'—He, who thinks, that the body, senses, mind, intellect, riches and prosperity etc., are necessary, for him and who depends on them, is his own foe. He thinks, that by accepting these as his own, he has controlled them and conquered them. But, the fact is, that he has been defeated by them. When he takes his defeat as victory, it means that his own self, is his foe.

The term 'Śatrutve', means that a man by depending on worldly things, and by accepting his affinity with them, works as a foe for himself, as he himself, is sentient, but he attaches importance to the insentient and depends on them. The more claim, he lays on material objects, the more he becomes, a slave to them. Further, he harbours desire for respect, honour and fame, that lead to his fall. He concedes, that he is elevating himself but actually it is the reverse. This proves, that he himself, is his own enemy, in disguise.

How surprising it is, that a man by attaching importance to matter, by forgetting God-realization, as the real aim of human life, wants to maintain the memory of his so-called body, and name by his photos and statues, during the lifetime, as well as after death! Thus, he in spite of being sentient (self), gets entangled in the slavery of matter, (non-self) and acts as his foe.

By using the term 'Śatruvat', Lord Kṛṣṇa means to explain,

that a man by accepting his affinity with the body, senses, mind and intellect etc., thinks that he has become their master but actually he is their slave. Though, he does not think of harm to himself, yet the consequences are harmful and ruinous, and so Lord Kṛṣṇa has declared, that his own self acts as his foe, because, dependence on the mundane, finally misleads a man, to the cycle of birth and death.

Appendix—If a man has not the sense of 'I' and 'mine' in respect of his body, he himself is his friend and if he has the sense of 'I' and 'mine' in the body, he himself is like an enemy to himself viz., by giving existence to the non-self, he acts like an enemy to himself. 'Śatruvat'—Whatever loss an enemy causes, the same loss he himself incurs. In fact as much loss a voluptuary does to himself, so much loss can't be done even by an enemy. If we perceive in the right perspective, we come to know that an enemy does only good to us. He cannot do evil to us. The reason is that he can have an access only to objects, he can't reach the self. Therefore what more can he do than to destroy the perishable? The destruction of the perishable will do us good only. In fact we sustain loss only, if we nurse ill-feelings.

Link:—What happens to the man, who has conquered the self by the self, has been described, in the next three verses.

जितात्मनः प्रशान्तस्य परमात्मा समाहितः।
शीतोष्णसुखदुःखेषु तथा मानापमानयोः॥ ७॥

jitātmanaḥ praśāntasya paramātmā samāhitaḥ
śītoṣṇasukhaduḥkheṣu tathā mānāpamānayoḥ

The self-conquered one whose mind is perfectly calm, in the midst of antithetical pairs, such as cold and heat, favourable and unfavourable, joy and sorrow, honour and dishonour, is in constant communion with, the Supreme-Spirit. 7

Comment:—

[In the sixth verse, the term 'Anātmanaḥ' (of unconquered self), and the term 'Jitātmanaḥ' (of the self-controlled), have been used. It means that man who accepts his affinity of 'I'ness and 'Mineness', with the body etc., his own self, acts as the foe. But a self-controlled person, who does not accept his affinity, with mundane objects, such as body etc., as his own self is his friend. In this way, the man of unconquered self, ruins himself, while a self-controlled man, remains in communion with the Supreme-Spirit.]

'Jitātmanaḥ'—One, who has not the least, affinity with the mundane, such as body, senses, mind and intellect etc., is self-disciplined or self-controlled. Such a self-controlled man, does good to himself, as well as to the world.

'Śītoṣṇasukhaduḥkheṣu praśāntasya'—Here, 'Śīta' and 'Uṣṇa' do not denote only cold and heat, 'Śīta' and 'Uṣṇa' are merely, objects of touch. A self-controlled person, is really he who controls all senses, from sense-objects. Therefore, 'Śīta' and 'Uṣṇa', cannot be taken in a limited sense. They denote, favourable and unfavourable circumstances. It means, that one should not be pleased with favourable circumstances and incidents etc., or displeased with unfavourable circumstances and incidents etc., but remain perfectly calm, in the midst of the two.

In favourable circumstances, a man feels a sort of, coolness, while in unfavourable circumstances he feels a kind of warmth. A striver, should be cautious that his permanent peace is not disturbed, by this seemingly cold and heat. He should not be happy and sad, with favourable and unfavourable circumstances.

Now let us try to understand what 'Joy', and 'Sorrow', imply:

(i) Generally, people think that a person who lives in luxury is joyful, but one who cannot enjoy luxuries, is sorrowful.

(ii) A man, does not possess even the bare necessities of

life, but is satisfied with what he possesses, and is joyful, while the man who leads a life of luxury is worried at heart, lest the luxuries should be lost and is sad or sorrowful.

In the Gītā, 'sukha' and 'duḥkha', have been described, in two ways. The favourable circumstances and pleasure derived out of these is called 'sukha'. Similarly, unfavourable circumstances and sorrow derived from these is called 'duḥkha'. Where in the Gītā it is said, 'samaduḥkhasukhaḥ' (12/13; 14/24), 'śītoṣṇasukhaduḥkheṣu samaḥ' (12/18), it means, that he remains evenminded in 'sukha', and 'duḥkha'. But where the Gītā says, 'Dvandvairvimuktāḥ sukhaduḥkhasañjñaiḥ', there, it refers to the void of 'sukha' (pleasure) and 'duḥkha (pain). In the former case, 'sukha' and 'duḥkha', have their entities but one remains equanimous, without being affected by them. In the latter case, there is no entity of either 'sukha' or 'duḥkha'. In sum total, both lead to the same goal.

Now, a question rises, why Lord Kṛṣṇa, has used two pairs of opposites 'Śīta and Uṣṇa' (cold and heat) and 'Sukhaduḥkha' (joy and sorrow), when 'cold' and 'heat' also stand for favourable and unfavourable circumstances. The explanation, is that past-actions result in favourable and unfavourable circumstances, while actions of the present, result in success and failure, (joy and sorrow). But a self-controlled man, remains perfectly calm and serene, in both states.

This explanation, seems to fit the context, because the expression 'Nendriyārtheṣu anuṣajjate', used in the fourth verse of this chapter, has been referred to here, by the expression 'Śīta-Uṣṇa', while the expression 'Na karmasu anuṣajjate' used there has been specified by the expression 'Sukha-Duḥkha'. It means, that where it is mentioned that he remains detached in favourable and unfavourable circumstances as a result of the fruit of past actions, while in success and failure, as the fruit of present actions. Here, it is mentioned that he remains calm, in both cases.

'Tathā mānāpamānayoḥ'—He is perfectly calm in honour and dishonour also. Now, a question arises, that honour or dishonour, is also a result of actions of the past, and therefore, is included in favourable and unfavourable circumstances. The explanation, is that in favourable and unfavourable circumstances, no one else, becomes an instrument, while in honour and dishonour (including praise and censure), someone else, becomes the instrument. But, the self-controlled man remains calm, whether he is honoured or dishonoured, by others.

How to Remain Calm in Honour and Dishonour?

In honour, a striver should not think that it is the result of his virtuous or good actions, but he should consider it, a virtue of the person who has shown honour to him. While, he should think of dishonour, as a result of his past actions, and feel obliged to the other person, who has purged him of his sins, by becoming an instrument of dishonour. Thus a striver, will become calm in honour and dishonour.

'Paramātmā samāhitaḥ'—Equanimity, in cold and heat, joy and sorrow, honour and dishonour, proves that he has attained God-realization, because without internal bliss, a man cannot remain calm, in both favourable and the unfavourable circumstances, success and failure or honour and dishonour. Therefore, Lord Kṛṣṇa, in the Gītā has declared in 5/19, "Men whose mind is established in equanimity, have conquered, the mortal plane"; and in 6/22, He declares, "Getting into the infinite beatitude of the Self, he does not reckon any other gain greater than that, and wherein established he is not moved, even by the heaviest affliction" and so on.

Appendix—He, whose own self is like a friend viz., who has not the sense of 'I' and 'mine' in the body, remains equanimous and unaffected in favourable and unfavourable circumstances, pleasure and pain, honour and dishonour. Such a man is an enlightened Karmayogī viz., he has realized God—this should be recognised. The reason is that favourable and unfavourable circumstances, pleasure and pain, honour and dishonour are fleeting but God ever remains the same.

ज्ञानविज्ञानतृप्तात्मा कूटस्थो विजितेन्द्रियः।
युक्त इत्युच्यते योगी समलोष्टाश्मकाञ्चनः॥८॥

jñānavijñānatṛptātmā kūṭastho vijitendriyaḥ
yukta ityucyate yogī samaloṣṭāśmakāñcanaḥ

The Yogī whose mind is satiated with 'Jñāna' (knowledge) and 'Vijñāna' (equanimity), who remains unshaken ever, whose senses are compliant, to whom a clod, a stone and a piece of gold, are the same, is spoken of, as one who has attained God-realisation. 8

Comment:—

'Jñānavijñānatṛptātmā'—It is in the context of the, Discipline of Action. So here, the knowledge how to perform an action is 'Jñāna', and equanimity in success and failure is, 'Vijñāna'.

Action, thought and trance, performed respectively with the physical, subtle and causal body, for one's own self, is not knowledge (Jñāna), because it and its fruits have a beginning and an end. But himself being a fragment of God, is eternal. So, how can the transient and insentient, satisfy the eternal and sentient? This knowledge, that actions and their fruits cannot satisfy his own self, is knowledge (Jñāna). By having this knowledge, when a person remains equanimous in success and failure, that is called 'Vijñāna'. He himself gets satisfied with 'Jñāna' and 'Vijñāna'. Thus for him nothing remains to be done, to be known and to be achieved.

'Kūṭasthaḥ'—'Kūṭa', is a block of iron on which things made of iron, silver and gold etc., are hammered into different shapes, by smiths, but it remains the same. Similarly, the self-disciplined man, remains unshaken, in all circumstances.

'Vijitendriyaḥ'—A striver, following the Discipline of Action, has to conquer the senses, because while performing actions, he may have attachment and aversion. Therefore, Lord Kṛṣṇa in 12/11 has said, 'Subduing your mind, senses etc., relinquish the fruit of all actions.' It means, that in abandoning the fruit of action, senses have to be subdued. Thus a striver who, while following the spiritual discipline remains careful in subduing his senses, his senses, are finally conquered when he realizes God.

'Samaloṣṭāśmakāñcanaḥ'—To a Yogī, a clod, a stone and a piece of gold, are the same. In dealings, he knows the value of each one of them. So, he keeps gold in the shelf, while lets a clod and a stone, lie outside. But he remains equanimous, in gain and loss. He views all the things of the world, with an equal eye, because he knows that all of these, are transient. He remains established in God, Who pervades everywhere equally, and His axiomatic equanimity, abides in him.

'Yukta ityucyate yogī'—Such a Karmayogī, satisfied with 'Jñāna' (knowledge), and 'Vijñāna' (equanimity), unshaken in all circumstances, with senses subdued, and equanimous, is spoken of as a Yogī viz., one who has attained Yoga or equanimity.

सुहृन्मित्रार्युदासीनमध्यस्थद्वेष्यबन्धुषु ।
साधुष्वपि च पापेषु समबुद्धिर्विशिष्यते ॥ ९ ॥

suhṛnmitrāryudāsīnamadhyasthadveṣyabandhuṣu
sādhuṣvapi ca pāpeṣu samabuddhirviśiṣyate

He, who regards well-wishers, friends, foes, neutrals, mediators, the hateful, the relatives, saints and sinners, all alike, stands out supreme. 9

Comment:—

[In the eighth verse, there is description of equanimity in

objects, while here there is description of equanimity, in persons. The objects, cannot perform any action, while persons perform actions for themselves as also, for others. So, it is difficult for them to have equanimity in them. Therefore, the person who has a benevolent and impartial, attitude to all and regards them alike, even after noticing differences, in their conduct stands out supreme.]

'Suhṛnmitrāryudāsīnamadhyasthadveṣyabandhuṣu'—One, who is engrossed in the welfare of others, like a mother, without any selfish motive, is called 'Suhṛd' (disinterested friend), while one who returns good for good, is a friend.

The foe, is he who does evil to others without any cause, but the hateful is one, who does evil to others, having some selfish motive or any other cause.

The neutral, is he who remains indifferent, to two groups or men, if they are fighting and the mediator, is one who desires compromise, for the welfare of both.

He has a benevolent and impartial attitude, towards his relatives, as well as those hostile, to him.

'Sādhuṣvapi ca pāpeṣu samabuddhirviśiṣyate'—His dealing, with saints and sinners, is different but he thinks about the welfare of both of them, and also does good to them equally, because according to him all persons, are different manifestations of the same Divinity. As the Lord, is a disinterested friend, of all beings (Gītā 5/29), the Yogī is also a disinterested friend, of all beings, (Śrīmadbhāgavata 3/25/21).

Here, Lord Kṛṣṇa, by using the phrase 'Sādhuṣvapi ca pāpeṣu', means that if he regards saints and sinners alike, he will regard all people alike, because men are judged by their actions. The Lord, also lays emphasis on conduct (actions), by declaring, "Whatever a great man does, the same is done by others" (Gītā 3/21). If he regards men who perform virtuous actions, and also those who perform evil actions alike, it means, that he stands supreme, because it is difficult to have a benign and equanimous attitude for the sinners.

In the world, people generally have a tendency to observe actions of others. By doing so, they cannot observe their real self, that remains the same, while actions always undergo changes. Secondly, they specially observe, evil actions of others which mislead observers to degradation, because, by doing so, they attach much importance, to those evil actions. Therefore, Lord Kṛṣṇa in this verse, has explained that a Yogī regards saints and sinners alike, because he believes that God alone, creates the phenomenon and so, all that is God. Thus, the Yogī stands supreme.

An Exceptional Fact

According to the gospel of Gītā, 'Equanimity is called Yoga' (2/48). One who attains equanimity does not need any other virtue, for God-realization. He becomes wholly virtuous spontaneously, and he conquers the mortal plane (5/19). In Viṣṇu Purāṇa, Prahlāda has said, that equanimity is God's adoration (1/17/90). We can attain, such a significant equanimity, by being free from evil. The means to be free from evils, are (i) Do not regard anyone as evil. (ii) Do not do any harm to anyone. (iii) Do not think ill of anyone. (iv) Do not perceive evils in others. (v) Do not hear evil of others. (vi) Do not speak ill, of others. By following these six rules, we shall be free from evil. As soon as, we are free from evil, we shall become virtuous, because virtue is our real nature.

We make efforts, and follow the spiritual discipline, in order to, become virtuous. But, we do not become virtuous, because we do not renounce evil, altogether and even a fragment of an evil, arouses pride of having virtue, which leads us to several other evils. But when evil are rooted out, we become virtuous, spontaneously. When we become virtuous, we automatically, do good to others. By doing so, all the world provides us the necessities of life, without our asking and without working hard. Thus, we cease our dependence, on the world. This freedom from dependence, on the world, enables us to attain equanimity, which is axiomatic and then we have nothing to do, we become liberated souls.

Appendix—The sphere of evenness (equanimity) is different from that of unequality. God is equanimous (equal) and the world is uneven. An enlightened Karmayogī remains equanimous, even having different dealings with different persons. He regards a clod, a stone, a piece of gold, a well-wisher, a friend, an enemy, a neutral, a mediator, the hateful, a saint and a sinner alike, though dealings with them can neither be the same, nor should be the same and cannot be done the same. The reason is that he has realized, 'there is nothing else besides God'.

If there is an idol of Lord Viṣṇu made of gold and there is toy-dog made of gold, both having the same weight will also cost the same. Lord Viṣṇu is the best and most venerable Deity while the dog is a mean and untouchable animal, in outward dealings there is a vast difference between the two but as far as the metal, gold is concerned, there is no difference between the two. Similarly in the world there is outward diversity among people as a friend, a foe, an exalted soul, a wicked person; good, bad, gentle, vile, virtuous, sinful, righteous, immoral, learned and foolish etc., but in essence all of them are only the manifestation of God. Only God has revealed Himself in different forms. He who knows this fact recognizes Him, others don't recognize Him.

While bathing, when soap is applied to the body, if the body is seen in a mirror, it looks bad and clumsy. At certain parts, marks like blisters appear, somewhere lines appear. But the person does not feel sad that he is suffering from a disease.

The reason is that he knows that these marks will be rubbed off when the body is washed in water. Similarly all beings are the manifestations of God but outwardly they appear different because of difference in bodies and their nature. In fact in spite of their different appearance, they are the manifestations of God but it is because of our attachment and aversion that they appear different.

The fact which was mentioned in the second verse of the fifth chapter by the expression 'Karmayoga Viśiṣyate' (Karmayoga is superior to Sāṅkhyayoga), the same fact has been mentioned here by the expression 'samabuddhirviśiṣyate'. An equanimous person remains untainted. Untaintedness leads to yoga while taintedness leads to 'bhoga'. There is equanimity in the three yogas but it is specially important in Karmayoga, because Karmayoga being the worldly spiritual discipline, a Karmayogī faces more oddities in life than other yogīs.

Link:—Equanimity (evenness of mind), which is attained by the Discipline of Action, is also attained by the Discipline of Meditation. So Lord Kṛṣṇa, while starting the subject of meditation, gives inspiration for meditation.

योगी युञ्जीत सततमात्मानं रहसि स्थितः।
एकाकी यतचित्तात्मा निराशीरपरिग्रहः॥ १०॥

yogī yuñjīta satatamātmānaṁ rahasi sthitaḥ
ekākī yatacittātmā nirāśīraparigrahaḥ

A Dhyānayogī, should constantly engage in meditation, living alone in seclusion, having subdued his mind and body, and having got rid of bonds of desires and possessions for enjoyment. 10

Comment:—

[Here Lord Kṛṣṇa is describing in detail, the Discipline of Meditation, which was referred to in brief, in the twenty-seventh and twenty-eighth verses of the fifth chapter. Here, the word 'Yoga', which has been derived, from the root 'Yuj samādhau' means, controlling the activities of the mind.]

'Aparigrahaḥ'—Meditation, is practised by disinclination for the world, and inclination for God. For its practice, the first means to be adopted, is 'Aparigrahaḥ'. 'Aparigrahaḥ' means freedom from accumulation of possessions. Nothing, should be accumulated for one's pleasures, because mind is attracted towards possessions and pleasures, and so it cannot be engaged in meditation.

'Nirāśīḥ'—It means, that a striver should not be free from outward prosperity and pleasures only, but also should get rid of desires and hopes for prosperity and pleasures, because these are all obstacles to God-realization. Therefore, a striver should always be aware of these desires and hopes.

'Yatacittātmā'—Even, by renouncing pleasures and prosperity, and also desire for them, there is possibility of attachment. Therefore, a striver should keep his body and mind under control. By controlling them, new attachment will not be aroused. The means to control them, is that no action should be performed being attached to it, because attachment leads a body to laziness and idleness, and senses, to pleasures, and mind, to the thought of pleasures and futile thinking.

'Yogī'—A Yogī, is one who is devoted to meditation, whose aim is only God-realization, rather than enjoyment and accomplishment.

'Ekākī'—A striver, should live alone, without any assistant, because in company he is likely to be engaged in conversation. In the absence of company because of attachment to him he is likely to be haunted by that. Thus he will not be able to meditate on God.

'Rahasi sthitaḥ'—A striver, should live in seclusion, on the banks of a river, or in a forest, or a temple, or a lonely room, meant for adoration and meditation only. The atmosphere, should be such, that there is no hindrance in meditation.

'Ātmānaṁ satataṁ yuñjīta'—Thus a striver, living alone in seclusion, as mentioned above, should concentrate his mind on God, with a firm determination to be engaged only, in meditation without having the least thought, of worldly affairs, whatsoever might happen. He, should be on the alert, because alertness is spiritual discipline.

A striver, should think of God, not only at the time of meditation, but also while performing other actions, without any attachment to these, because the thought of God, helps in meditation, while the thought of God in meditation, helps a striver in thinking of Him, during his mundane affairs. It means, that a striver should always remember that he is a striver viz., he should always remember God, and think of Him, even when he performs worldly actions. He should harbour, no thought of any worldly transaction, otherwise it will be a hindrance, in his meditation. Therefore, while sitting for meditation, he should have a firm resolve, that he has to meditate only on God, whatever may happen. By this resolve, it will be easy for him to meditate on God.

A striver has a complaint, that he cannot concentrate his mind, on God. The reason, is that he wants to concentrate his mind on God, without breaking off his affinity, for the world. Therefore, a striver should break off his affinity, for the world as it is this affinity or attachment, or a sense of mine, which influences the mind. Therefore, a striver can concentrate his mind and engage in meditation, by only having the aim of God-realization and being detached from all persons and things etc. If such detachment is not there, these will haunt his memory.

An Exceptional Fact

Initially, Arjuna was prepared to wage the war and he also got prepared at last. But, in between he thought that to wage war was a sin. Thus, it was a question, of performing an action or not to perform it. So, it arose in the context of the Discipline of Action. But how other disciplines, such as of Knowledge, Devotion and Meditation were explained, in Gītā.

Arjuna retreats from the war, because he thinks that sin, would accrue to him, by killing his kinsmen. So he requests Lord Kṛṣṇa, to tell him what was good for him (2/7; 3/2; 5/1). Therefore, Lord Kṛṣṇa explains to him, the different means including gifts, rituals, penances, study of the Vedas and different kinds of disciplines leading to God-realisation. But, in all the means, Lord Kṛṣṇa has emphasized the fact that the aim to attain perishable things, is the main obstacle, to God-realization. If a striver, has only the aim of God-realization, and performs actions with equanimity those actions, would lead him to salvation or God-realization.

Appendix—Karmayoga,* Jñānayoga and Bhaktiyoga are the Karaṇanirapekṣa disciplines (independent of sense and other organs) but Dhyānayoga (the Discipline of Meditation) is a Karaṇasāpekṣa discipline (dependent on sense and other organs). Now the Lord starts the description of Dhyānayoga.

Link:—In the previous verse, Lord Kṛṣṇa offered inspiration for meditation. Now, in the next three verses, He explains what sort of setting, one should have and what process he should undergo.

शुचौ देशे प्रतिष्ठाप्य स्थिरमासनमात्मनः।
नात्युच्छ्रितं नातिनीचं चैलाजिनकुशोत्तरम्॥ ११॥

śucau deśe pratiṣṭhāpya sthiramāsanamātmanaḥ
nātyucchritaṁ nātinīcaṁ cailājinakuśottaram

* In Karmayoga (Path of Action) 'Karma' (action) is Karaṇasāpekṣa (dependent on instruments) but 'Yoga' (equanimity) is Karaṇanirapekṣa (independent of instruments).

Having well arranged his seat (āsana) in a clean and unpolluted place covered by Kuśa-grass, a deer-skin and a cloth, one over the other, neither too high, nor too low. 11

Comment:—

'Śucau deśe'—The place, is pure in two ways—(i) A naturally pure place such as the bank of the Ganges, a forest and the place near a holy basil, myrobalan (Āṁvalā), Pīpala tree etc. (ii) Place cleaned with cow-dung and by sprinkling water, or by removing two inches of soil from the surface. A clean place of natural beauty, invigorates and elevates the mind.

'Cailājinakuśottaram'—According to the text a Kuśa-grassmat, a deer-skin, and a cloth, should be spread one over the other* yet there should be spread a Kuśa mat below, a deer-skin in the middle and a cloth at the top. The deer-skin should be of a deer, which is not killed, but which is dead, in the natural way, as the skin of deer, which is killed is regarded, as impure. If a deer-skin, is not available, a rug can be spread. Over the rug, soft cotton cloth should be spread. Kuśa-grass, is supposed to be made from the hair of, boar-incarnation of the Lord and thus is considered holy. Deer-skin is spread over a Kuśa-grass mat, so that Kuśa-grass may not prick the skin and an electric current of a body, may not pass through the Kuśa-grass, to the earth, as a deer-skin is a bad conductor, of electric current. A soft cotton cloth is spread over the deer-skin, so that the bristles of deer-skin, may not stick into the body and the striver feels comfortable.

'Nātyucchritaṁ nātinīcam'—The seat of the plank-bed, should neither be too high, nor too low, because if it is too high, a striver while meditating may doze off, fall down and be injured; but if it is too low, creeping insects, may disturb him in his meditation.

* The order of the text does not seem reasonable and proper because Kuśa-grass pricks the body. Therefore, it should be interpreted as a Kuśa-grassmat below, a deer-skin in the middle and a cloth at the top, because the order of the meaning is more forceful than the order of the text.

'Pratiṣṭhāpya sthiramāsanamātmanaḥ'—The platform or the plank-bed, should be fixed firmly. Moreover it should belong to him and be used by him only, because there may be bacilli in it, of others, if it is used by them. Similarly, a striver should have his own rosary, a bag for the rosary, and a spoon, used in religious ceremonies etc. Not only this, but according to the ordinance of scriptures, a striver should not use the seat, shoes and shirts etc., of others, otherwise he has to be a sharer in their virtues and sins. One should not sit, on the seat of saints and ascetics because, it is a dishonour to them. If one touches their seats and clothes etc., with feet, then it is also, a sin.

तत्रैकाग्रं मनः कृत्वा यतचित्तेन्द्रियक्रियः।
उपविश्यासने युञ्ज्याद्योगमात्मविशुद्धये॥ १२॥

tatraikāgraṁ manaḥ kṛtvā yatacittendriyakriyaḥ
upaviśyāsane yuñjyādyogamātmaviśuddhaye

While seated on his seat, concentrating the mind and controlling the thinking faculty (citta) and the senses, he should practise Yoga, for self-purification. 12

Comment:—

[After explaining the kind of a seat, now Lord Kṛṣṇa, in the twelfth and thirteenth verses, explains the process, how one should practise meditation.]

'Tatra āsane'—This phrase, has been used for the seat with a Kuśa-grassmat, a deer-skin and a cloth, described in the previous verse.

'Upaviśya'—He should sit still on the seat, in a comfortable posture, as 'Siddhāsana', 'Padmāsana' or 'Sukhāsana', etc., without moving the body. It is said, about the posture that a striver should be able to sit in that posture continuously for three hours, without moving the body. By doing so, the mind and life-breath naturally become calm, and free from volatility. Volatility of mind, does not allow the body to remain motionless. The motion of the body and urge for action do not allow the mind, to remain steady and calm. Therefore, it is very essential that the body should remain motionless.

'Yatacittendriyakriyaḥ'—While seated, the mind and the senses should be kept under control. A striver should control his body, senses and mind, even in practical life, otherwise they cannot be controlled easily, while he meditates. It means, that he should lead a regulated and disciplined life, as has also been pointed out, in the sixteenth and seventeenth verses of this chapter.

'Ekāgraṁ manaḥ kṛtvā'—While meditating, he should make a firm resolve, that he has to engage himself only in meditation. If however, worldly thoughts crop up, he should think, that it is time only for meditation and not for worldly thoughts. If time passes in worldly thoughts, no useful purpose will be served, and he will be a loser, both ways. Thus, he should concentrate his mind, on God, without having any thought of mundane affairs. Even then, if a worldly thought comes to the mind, he should neither support it nor oppose it. By doing so, the thought will disappear as it is transitory. The thought, affects him, only if he accepts his affinity with it, but if he remains indifferent to it will automatically perish, because it is perishable and transient. In the world, there are good and bad actions. If we do not have any affinity with them, they would not affect us. Similarly during meditation, if we do not have any affinity, with thoughts, our mind will not get tainted. It will remain calm and composed.

'Yuñjyādyogamātmaviśuddhaye'—One should practise the Yoga of meditation for self-purification. Desire for worldly things, pleasures, honour, praise, name and fame etc., is impurity of the self, and by renouncing all the desires, to have the only aim of God-realization, is self-purification.

Yoga, is a power which can be used either for accomplishing

worldly pleasures, or for God-realization. If it is used for worldly accomplishments, it cannot be helpful in self-purification or God-realization. But if it is used for God-realization, it will be conducive to God-realization.

समं कायशिरोग्रीवं धारयन्नचलं स्थिरः।
सम्प्रेक्ष्य नासिकाग्रं स्वं दिशश्चानवलोकयन्॥ १३॥

samaṁ kāyaśirogrīvaṁ dhārayannacalaṁ sthiraḥ
samprekṣya nāsikāgraṁ svaṁ diśaścānavalokayan

Let him hold the trunk, head and neck straight and steady, gazing at the tip of his nose, without looking around. 13

Comment:—

'Samaṁ kāyaśirogrīvaṁ dhārayannacalam'—The portion of the body from the neck to waist, is called 'Kāya' (trunk), while the portion from neck to top is called, head. All postures are useful, from meditation and health point of view. Out of those postures, Lord Kṛṣṇa has taken the essential feature, necessary for meditation, i.e., to keep neck, back and head in a straight position. While meditating, the trunk, head and neck should be held straight, so that the spinal cord may remain vertical. In this posture, the mind becomes calm and concentrated quickly. If one bends forward, he feels drowsy, if he bends backward, there is stupor and if he bends sideways, he becomes capricious. If he feels drowsy, he should walk a little, and then again with a firm determination, should repractise meditation by holding the trunk, head and neck straight.

'Diśaścānavalokayan'—He should not look in any direction, because by looking here and there, the neck will bend, which will disturb his meditation. So the neck should be held straight.

'Samprekṣya nāsikāgraṁ svam'—He should look at the tip of his nose, with his half-closed eyes. If he closes his eyes, he may feel sleepy. But if the eyes are open, he is likely to look at the other objects within sight and so there may be distraction in meditation. Thus, Lord Kṛṣṇa means to say, that he should keep his eyes half-closed, because by doing so, the eye-balls assume steadiness and seem as if they are looking at the tip of the nose.

'Sthiraḥ'—He should sit steady, without any activity of the body or senses, just like a statue continuously for three hours. Moreover, there should not be any activity of the mind also. By doing so, he will overcome the strain of the posture and will become 'Jitāsana' (conqueror of the posture).

Appendix—Here gazing at the tip of the nose is not important but concentration of the mind is important.

Link:—Blissful meditation (Yoga) on God, (endowed with attributes and form) and the good flowing out of it, have been explained, in the next two verses.

प्रशान्तात्मा विगतभीर्ब्रह्मचारिव्रते स्थितः ।
मनः संयम्य मच्चित्तो युक्त आसीत मत्परः ॥ १४ ॥

praśāntātmā vigatabhīrbrahmacārivrate sthitaḥ
manaḥ saṁyamya maccitto yukta āsīta matparaḥ

Serene and fearless, firm in the vow of celibacy, with mind controlled, the vigilant Yogī should sit meditating on Me and having Me alone, as the Supreme Goal. 14

Comment:—

'Praśāntātmā'—Serene-minded, is he who is free from attachment and aversion. Attachment and aversion of the striver, whose aim is only God-realization, without having any worldly desire, (by becoming languid) perish, and with the disappearance of attachment and aversion, a striver attains peace, which is spontaneous. It means, that attachment and aversion, born of the affinity for the world, disturb serenity or peace. One, who attains this peace, is serene-minded.

'Vigatabhīḥ'—Fear of disease, censure, dishonour and death arise, only because man accepts the affinity of 'I'ness and Mineness, with the body. But when he abandons this affinity, he becomes free from all fears, because he thinks that even if the body perishes, it will make no difference as his mind dedicated to God, he will attain salvation, the ultimate goal of life.

'Brahmacārivrate sthitaḥ'—Here, it does not mean only vow of continence, but also includes that a celibate should lead a disciplined and controlled life, according to the order of his preceptor, free from sensual pleasures, honour, praise and comforts etc. He should not in the least, enjoy worldly things in any state, under any circumstance, either during meditation, or in practical life, but use them only as necessities of life.

'Manaḥ saṁyamya maccittaḥ'—Having controlled the mind of all worldly affairs, he should think of God's form, play, virtues, glory and excellence etc. It means, that by shutting out all worldly thoughts, he should devote his mind to God only. The thoughts that come to mind, are either of the past or the present. So he should neglect them, by thinking that these have no existence at present. Moreover, the world actually does not exist, it merely seems to exist, while God existed in the past, exists now and will also exist, in future. So, he should think of Him, instead of thinking about the world.

'Yuktaḥ'—He should remain vigilant, in diverting his mind from worldly affairs and concentrate it on God, even while engaged in worldly affairs, because vigilance during engagement in worldly affairs, will help him in meditation, and that awareness during meditation will be helpful to him, in his practical life.

'Āsīta matparaḥ'—While sitting, he should have the only aim of God-realization, without having any other desire, or lust or attachment or mineness, in the least, as has also been pointed out, in the tenth verse of this chapter.

Appendix—To consider any special trait as one's own is to invite demoniac nature in oneself. Therefore the Lord by the term 'matparaḥ' mentions that the striver following the path of meditation should depend on Him. By depending on God, evils (flaws) are quickly removed and the striver is not proud of his speciality. This is the special trait of devotion.

In this verse 'mana' and 'citta'—these are two terms which are synonyms have been used. With 'mana' anything is reflected upon time and again and with 'citta' only one thing is thought of. Therefore here the expression 'manaḥ saṁyamya maccitaḥ' means that the world should not be reflected upon viz., detach 'mana' from the world and with 'citta' he should think of God viz., concentrate 'citta' on God.

युञ्जन्नेवं सदात्मानं योगी नियतमानसः ।
शान्तिं निर्वाणपरमां मत्संस्थामधिगच्छति ॥ १५ ॥

yuñjannevaṁ sadātmānaṁ yogī niyatamānasaḥ
śāntiṁ nirvāṇaparamāṁ matsaṁsthāmadhigacchati

Thus, constantly meditating on Me, the Yogī of controlled mind attains everlasting peace, (Supreme Bliss) abiding in Me (Nirvāṇa). 15

Comment:—

'Yogī niyatamānasaḥ'—One, who has controlled his mind is called 'Niyatamānasaḥ'. A Yogī's mind, can be subdued, only if his exclusive aim is God-realization, without having any affinity for the world. Affinity for the world, does not allow the mind to be subdued.

A striver commits an error, if he thinks that he is a householder, having some caste, creed and colour etc. Thus he cannot meditate. A striver, should think that he is a striver, whose only aim is to meditate on God. His aim is not to attain, mystic power. Thus, by changing his 'I'ness, he will be able to concentrate his mind, on God. With the change of 'I' sense, the inner sense would automatically change.

'Yuñjannevaṁ sadātmānam'—The word 'Evam' (thus), has been used for meditation and concentration of mind, described from the tenth to the fourteenth verses.

'Yuñjan ātmānam' means, that a striver should concentrate his mind on God, diverting it from the world. 'Sadā' means that he should practise meditation regularly, in seclusion and daily life, always having the aim of God-realization. Such practice, leads to an early success.

'Śāntiṁ nirvāṇaparamāṁ matsaṁsthāmadhigacchati'—This is a state, when established, nothing further remains to be attained. This state, is called Supreme-Peace or Supreme-Bliss or emancipation or salvation. A striver, attains peace by breaking off affinity with the world, while he attains Supreme-Peace, by attaining God-realization. The process of meditation, culminates in 'Nirvikalpa sthiti', (state of mind where there is absence of all thoughts). But, this is also a state, as it does not remain constant, as there is deviation from it, at times. This is not God-realization. Further to it, there is 'Nirvikalpa bodha', which is Self-realization (God-realization). This is called Supreme-Peace. The same Supreme-Peace (in 5/12) has been called, 'Naiṣṭhikīm Śāntim' (final peace) and (in 9/31) 'Śaśvacchānti' (Eternal Peace).

Link:—In the next two verses, there is the description of the regulations, that a Yogī has to observe, in his earthly life.

नात्यश्नतस्तु योगोऽस्ति न चैकान्तमनश्नतः।
न चाति स्वप्नशीलस्य जाग्रतो नैव चार्जुन॥ १६॥

nātyaśnatastu yogo'sti na caikāntamanaśnataḥ
na cāti svapnaśīlasya jāgrato naiva cārjuna

Yoga is not successful for him who eats too much, nor for one, who does not eat at all; or for him who sleeps too much, nor too little. 16

Comment:—

'Nātyaśnatastu yogo'sti'—Yoga is not possible, for him who eats too much.* Too much eating, causes thirst for water. So he has to drink much water. Too much water, makes the stomach heavy and the body too. If he overeats, he becomes dull and lazy, and may suffer from indigestion, which causes disease in the body. So he cannot concentrate his mind, in adoration and spiritual practice etc. So how can Yoga be possible for him?

'Na caikāntamanaśnataḥ'—Yoga, is also not possible, for him who eats too little. If he is underfed, he will feel hungry, think of food again and again, and become weak. His body, will languish and life will become hard to live. He will be inclined to keep lying down. It will be hard, to sit for meditation. Thus he cannot concentrate his mind, on God. So how is Yoga possible for him?

'Na cāti svapnaśīlasya'—Oversleep, makes a striver idle, lazy and inert. In oversleep, the striver cannot sleep soundly, and so different thoughts come to the mind. Thus, oversleep is a hindrance to the practice of meditation.

'Jāgrato naiva cārjuna'—This Yoga is not possible for him, who sleeps too little. By keeping aware he feels drowsy, and cannot practise meditation.

Men, of sāttvika disposition, while having spiritual discussions, narrating and listening to lives of saints, devotees and incarnations of God, have so much joy and get so much engrossed in them, that they do not feel drowsy, at all even by remaining awake,

* If a person's food is less than that of others but is more than his appetite, it is known as too much.

throughout a night. This wakefulness helps them reach a state, which transcends the three modes of Nature (prakṛti).

Similarly, devotees in adoration, loud chanting and constant remembrance of God, are so much engrossed, that they do not feel hungry. This cannot be said as 'not eating' (अनश्नतः) because all doings by men while devoted to God, become 'Sat'.

युक्ताहारविहारस्य युक्तचेष्टस्य कर्मसु।
युक्तस्वप्नावबोधस्य योगो भवति दुःखहा॥ १७॥

yuktāhāravihārasya yuktaceṣṭasya karmasu
yuktasvapnāvabodhasya yogo bhavati duḥkhahā

Yoga which brings out the cessation of the travails of the world is accomplished only by him, who is moderate in diet and recreation, temperate in action and regulated in sleep, and wakefulness. 17

Comment:—

'Yuktāhāravihārasya'—Food (livelihood) should be earned, by honest means, it should be pure, easily digestible, light, a bit less than necessary and items of food must be in accordance with, the ordinance of scriptures and Āyurveda. Recreation, such as physical exercise and walking etc., should be resorted to, moderately.

'Yuktaceṣṭasya karmasu'—All actions, should be performed, according to one's caste, creed, country, condition and capacity, following the ordinance of the scriptures, and happily for the welfare of others.

'Yuktasvapnāvabodhasya'—One, should be moderate in sleep. He should remain awake in the day, go to bed early at night, and rise early in the morning. Here, the term 'Avabodhasya', (wakefulness) has a special meaning, that a striver should be spiritually aroused, as this human life has been bestowed upon him, to attain salvation. The term 'Yukta' (moderate), means, that similar rules do not apply to all the persons for diet, recreations, actions, sleep and wakefulness. But, everyone should be moderate in them, according to circumstances he is in.

'Yogo bhavati duḥkhahā'—Thus, the Yoga of a Yogī, who is moderate in diet, recreation etc., brings about a cessation of the toil and troubles of the world.

There is an exceptional difference between, yoga (meditation) and bhoga (pleasure). In 'yoga' there is abnegation of 'bhoga'. In 'bhoga' there is not total negation of 'yoga'. In 'bhoga', what happiness a man derives, is a result of disconnection of the contact with the unreal. But, man does not pay attention to this fact, and thinks that there is pleasure in contact, with worldly things. So, he gets attached to sense-objects. He cannot experience yoga, which brings about the cessation of miseries, of the world. In this Yoga, there is total negation, of worldly enjoyment.

An Exceptional Fact

This verse on meditation, is useful for all strivers. By following it, they may attain salvation. There are, four factors described in it—(1) moderate in diet and recreation, (2) moderate in action, (3) moderate in sleep and (4) moderate in wakefulness.

We have twenty-four hours, at our disposal. If twenty-four hours are divided say into four parts, we get six hours for each of the above activities (i) six hours for eating, recreation and physical exercise etc., (ii) six hours for actions for earning livelihood viz., farming, business and service etc., (iii) six hours for sleep and (iv) six hours for wakefulness viz., meditation, adoration, constant remembrance and loud chanting etc., for God-realization.

These can also be divided into two parts (i) Income and (ii) Expenditure. Actions and wakefulness, are the means of income, while eating, recreation and sleep involve expenditure. For income and expenditure, we have two kinds of capital—(i) worldly riches (capital) and (ii) age.

Man's Capital

- worldly riches
  - expenditure → eating, recreation
  - income → action for earning livelihood
- age
  - expenditure → sleep
  - income → wakefulness (spiritual discipline)

Let us first think about worldly capital (worldly riches). If a person earns more, it is alright, but if his expenses are more than income, it will not be good, it will ruin him. If a person, devotes only four hours to eating and recreation etc., he may devote eight hours to his profession, earning his livelihood.

Now, let us think about age. If he gets refreshed by four hours' sleep, he should devote eight hours to worship, meditation and spiritual discipline. This spiritual discipline, should be enhanced everyday because we have come to be born for God-realization, not for accumulation of mundane wealth etc.

Secondly, we should remember God, while earning our livelihood and also, while we go to bed. At bed time, a striver should think that he has to devote time to devotion and adoration, while lying in the bed. While lying down if he sleeps, it is alright but he should not aim at sleeping. Again, when he wakes after sleep, he should be engaged in adoration, meditation, devotion and study of scriptures etc. While discharging his duty, or performing actions, he should always remember, God. Thus each and every activity of his life would become part and parcel of one's worship.

Appendix—The verses sixteen and seventeen are certainly useful for the strivers following the path of meditation but they are also very useful for strivers following other paths.

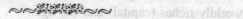

Link:—In the preceding two verses, regulations that a Yogī has to observe, in his earthly life, have been described. Now, in the next verse, Lord Kṛṣṇa explains, when a striver, is said to be established in Yoga.

यदा विनियतं चित्तमात्मन्येवावतिष्ठते।
निःस्पृहः सर्वकामेभ्यो युक्त इत्युच्यते तदा ॥ १८ ॥

yadā viniyataṁ cittamātmanyevāvatiṣṭhate
niḥspṛhaḥ sarvakāmebhyo yukta ityucyate tadā

When the perfectly controlled mind is fixed on the self (ātman) alone, free from desires for enjoyments, then the person is said to be, an achiever of Yoga. 18

Comment:—

[In this chapter, from the tenth to the thirteenth verses, there is description of the seat and posture suited to meditation. In fourteenth and fifteenth verses, there is description of meditation on God (with attributes and form), with its fruit. In, sixteenth and seventeenth verses, there is mention of regulations for all strivers of meditation. In the verses, from the eighteenth to the twenty-third, there is description of meditation of the self with its result.]

'Yadā viniyataṁ cittamātmanyevāvatiṣṭhate'—'When a well disciplined mind,* free from the thought of the world, gets established in the self, whichever remains the same, without any modification.' In the self, there is enjoyment or bliss which does not, let the mind deviate from it and thus the mind by having this relish, gets engrossed in it.

*The five stages of the mind are—'Mūḍha', 'Kṣipta', 'Vikṣipta' (confused), 'Ekāgra' (concentrated) and 'Niruddha' (tied up). In the first two stages a striver is not entitled for Yoga. The person with a Vikṣipta (confused) mind is entitled for Yoga, his mind sometimes rests but sometimes does not rest in the self. When the mind is concentrated, that is called 'Savikalpa samādhi'. But the next stage is when the mind is completely settled then that is called 'Nirvikalpa samādhi' or Yoga. Here in 'Viniyataṁ cittam' as well as in the fifteenth verse of this chapter, there is the hint of 'Savikalpa samādhi'.

'Niḥspṛhaḥ sarvakāmebhyo yukta ityucyate tadā'—When one is completely free, from desires for all objects and pleasures, here, as well as hereafter, he is called a Yogī.

The terms 'yadā' (when) and 'tadā' (then), denote that as soon as, a person with disciplined mind, rests in the self alone, free from desires for enjoyments, he becomes a Yogī.

An Exceptional Fact

In this verse, there are two important aspects—one is, that the mind should rest in the self, and the other is, that it should be free from desires, for all objects etc. It means, that when the mind gets focussed in self, it does not think of any objects, persons or circumstances etc., as it gets engrossed in the self. Similarly, if mind rests in the self, the Yogī, becomes completely free from all desires, lust and aspiration, etc. Not only this but he has no desire, even to have the bare necessities of life, and then he is a yogī, in the true sense of the term.

The same state, has been hinted at, in the fourth verse of this chapter, for a Karmayogī, when the Lord declares, "When a man ceases, to have attachment for sense-objects, or for actions and renounces all thoughts of the world, he is said to have attained, Yoga (6/4). The difference is, that a Karmayogī performs actions, for others only. So, he gets totally detached, from actions and objects. Then, he attains Yoga. A Dhyānayogī concentrates his mind on the self, and when the mind gets established in the self, he has no desire for actions and objects, not even, for the bare necessities of life. It means, that a Karmayogī's desires, are first wiped out and then he attains Yoga, while a Dhyānayogī's mind, first gets established in the self, and then his desires are wiped out. Thus, a Karmayogī applies his mind to the service of the world and gets established in the self, while along with the mind Dhyānayogī himself gets established in the self.

यथा दीपो निवातस्थो नेङ्गते सोपमा स्मृता।
योगिनो यतचित्तस्य युञ्जतो योगमात्मनः॥ १९॥

yathā dīpo nivātastho neṅgate sopamā smṛtā
yogino yatacittasya yuñjato yogamātmanaḥ

'As a lamp in a windless place, does not flicker', this is the simile used to describe the disciplined mind of a Yogī, practising meditation, on the Self. 19

Comment:—

'Yathā dīpo nivātastho neṅgate sopamā smṛtā, yogino yatacittasya yuñjato yogamātmanaḥ'—As a flame of a lamp, in a place perfectly sheltered against wind, does not flicker, but remains steady, in the same way when the mind of a striver, rests in the Self alone, it becomes free, from all desires.

The Yogī, who has subdued his mind, is called 'Yatacittasya'. In the preceding verse, such controlled mind has been described as 'Viniyata'.

There is no place without wind, which exists everywhere. Somewhere, it is in its active form, while at other places, it is inactive. Here, the term 'Nivātasthaḥ', does not refer to total lack of wind, it rather refers, to the absence of its active state.

Now, a question may arise, why the mind has been compared, to the flame of a lamp which may flicker, and not to a mountain which neither flickers nor shakes. The answer is, that unlike a mountain, the mind does flicker like a flame. It is very difficult, to keep a flickering item steady. So, it has been compared to a flame. Secondly, as there is light in a flame, there is awareness of God, in the mind. Though, in sound sleep and a trance, there is an equal forgetfulness, of the world, yet, in sound sleep mind merges in ignorance, and so there is no awareness, of the self. In a trance the mind remains conscious of the Self. Due to these reasons, an illustration of the flame has been given, here. This fact, has also been pointed out, in the twenty-seventh verse of the fourth chapter, by 'jñānadīpite'.

Link:—The state, in which perfection is attained, is described in the next verse.

यत्रोपरमते चित्तं निरुद्धं योगसेवया।
यत्र चैवात्मनात्मानं पश्यन्नात्मनि तुष्यति॥ २०॥

yatroparamate cittaṁ niruddhaṁ yogasevayā
yatra caivātmanātmānaṁ paśyannātmani tuṣyati

When the mind, disciplined by the practice of Yoga becomes tranquil and when the Yogī beholding the Self (Ātman) by his Self, he is contented in the self. 20

Comment:—

'Yatroparamate cittaṁ niruddhaṁ yogasevayā, yatra caivātmanātmānaṁ paśyannātmani tuṣyati'—The determination to practise meditation on the self is 'Dhāraṇā', while the continuous flow of the mind, towards the self, disregarding other thoughts, is called 'Dhyāna' (meditation). Meditation, has three aspects, the meditative, (one who meditates), the act of meditation and the aim to be achieved viz., self. So long as, there is knowledge about the three, it is meditation. But, when the mind gets so much engrossed, in the aim, that nothing remains except the aim, that state is called 'Samādhi' (trance). This is called 'Saṁprajñāta samādhi'. After practising it for a long time, it changes into 'Asaṁprajñāta samādhi'. The distinction between the two, is that in the former, consciousness of the trio, regarding by way of the object and its name and the relation between the name and the object of meditation, persists. But in the latter, only the object of meditation remains, by becoming oblivious of the two. The former, is also called 'ekāgra' (concentration of mind), while the latter 'niruddha' (tied up state).

The 'samādhi' (trance), of 'niruddha' state, (tied up state) is also of two types—'sabīja' (with seed) and 'nirbīja' (without seed). In the former, because of subtle desire 'Siddhiyān', (accomplishments) appear. These accomplishments, are in the form of worldly riches, which are obstacles to God-realization or Self-realization. Therefore, regarding these as meaningless, a Yogī, becomes quite indifferent to them, and then he rises to the height of 'Nirbīja samādhi' (trance without seed), which in this verse has been referred to as 'Niruddham' (tied up state of trance).

In meditation, while having disinclination for the mundane, a striver gets joy or peace, which is far superior, to mundane pleasures. This joy, enhances as a striver rises to the higher states of trance, by practising meditation. While progressing he reaches the stage of 'Nirbīja samādhi' (trance without seed). If he does not enjoy ever that state of joy, then he is satisfied in the self by the self.

'Uparamate' (attains quietness) means, that mind, being insentient cannot catch the self, which is sentient. So, it becomes quiet and at that moment, a Yogī ceases all affinity for the mind.

'Tuṣyati' means, that he is not satisfied with anything, else, except the self.

The gist, of this verse is, that a Yogī realizes the self in him, by his own self, as the Self ever remains, the same. Our affinity, with the world, is the only obstacle to realize it. When by meditation the mind becomes tranquil a Yogī's affinity with the mind, and the world, is renounced and he realizes, the Self in his own self.

An Exceptional Fact

The aim of human life, can be achieved by, both the Discipline of Meditation, as well as the Discipline of Action. But, there is a little difference between the two. In meditation, when the mind of a striver becomes peaceful, and does not enjoy the state of trance, he is satisfied, in the self by the self. In the Discipline of Action, when a striver abandons all desires of the mind, he is satisfied in the self by the self (Gītā 2/55).

In the Discipline of Meditation, when the mind is absorbed in the Self, a Yogī experiences, trance. When he does not enjoy that state, his affinity with the mind is broken off, and he is satisfied in the self.

In the Discipline of Action, when there is tendency of all the actions, senses, mind, intellect and body etc., for the welfare of others, all desires, are abandoned. As soon as, desires are abandoned, the Yogī's affinity, with the mind is broken off, and he is satisfied in the self.

Appendix—The mind is not concentrated on the self, it can't reach the self but it becomes indifferent. The reason is that the mind belongs to a different class from that of the self. The mind is lower (insentient) nature and the self is higher (sentient) nature. Therefore the self rests in the self—'ātmanātmānaṁ paśyannātmani tuṣyati'.

'Beholding the self by the self' means that the self cannot be perceived by senses but it can be perceived only by the self. Whatever is thought of with the mind, that is only of sense-objects (the non-self), rather than of God. Whatever is determined with the intellect, is of the objects of the intellect, not of God. Whatever is described with the tongue, is of the objects of the tongue, not of God. It means that with the mind, intellect and tongue there is reflection, determination and description which are the evolutes of Prakṛti (non-self). But God is realized by having dissociation with the mind, intellect and tongue viz., by renouncing affinity with them.*

* If there is the only aim of God-realization, then reflection, determination and description with the mind, intellect and tongue are not improper, but they became the means to the end. But if a striver gets satisfied in them and thinks that he has attained perfection, then that satiation becomes obstacle to his aim.

Here the Self-realization which is attained by the Discipline of meditation, the same is attained by Karmayoga (path of action) (Gītā 2/55). The difference is that 'Dhyānayoga' (Discipline of Meditation) is dependent on instruments (Karaṇasāpekṣa) while Karmayoga is a 'Karaṇanirapekṣa' (independent of instruments) discipline. In 'Karaṇasāpekṣa' discipline, renunciation of affinity for Matter (non-self) is delayed and there is possibility of a striver's deviation or downfall from Yoga.

Link:—What happens, after the Yogī is satisfied in the self by the self, is described in the next verse.

सुखमात्यन्तिकं यत्तद्बुद्धिग्राह्यमतीन्द्रियम्।
वेत्ति यत्र न चैवायं स्थितश्चलति तत्त्वतः ॥२१॥

sukhamātyantikaṁ yattadbuddhigrāhyamatīndriyam
vetti yatra na caivāyaṁ sthitaścalati tattvataḥ

When he feels that supreme and transcendental bliss while his discrimination remains fully awakened, and wherein established, the said Yogī, never moves away from reality (tattva). 21

Comment:—

'Sukhamātyantikaṁ yat'—The bliss which a Yogī feels, is infinite and there cannot be any bliss greater than this because it transcends the three attributes (modes) and is axiomatic. This bliss, has been called an imperishable bliss (5/21), infinite bliss (6/28) and absolute bliss (14/27).

This bliss, has been called infinite here, because, it is superior to Sāttvika joy, which is born of placidity of mind by meditation, on God. This infinite bliss, is not born, but it is unborn and axiomatic.

'Atīndriyam'—This supreme bliss, transcends sensual pleasures. It means, that it is superior to rājasika joy, which is derived from the contact of senses with their objects. It is beyond our power, to obtain rājasika joy because it is beyond our power to obtain individual's desired sense-objects. So, we are dependent to obtain these, while there is no such dependence in attaining infinite bliss. That can be felt in the self by one's own self. In attaining it you don't require any individual, any sense-object and even your mind and senses. You are quite free in having it by your own self.

'Buddhigrāhyam'—It means, that it is superior to the tāmasika joy, which arises from sleep, indolence and carelessness. A man derives joy from sound sleep, but in sound sleep, his mind is merged. Joy is also derived from indolence and heedlessness but at that time mind is not awake and discrimination is lost. But in infinite bliss, the mind is not merged, nor is discrimination lost. It is beyond the access of intellect, being an evolute of matter, while bliss, is the characteristic of the Self, which is beyond matter.

Thus in this verse, it has been explained that the supreme bliss, is far superior to the sāttvika, rājasika and tāmasika joy, and it transcends all the three modes.

'Vetti yatra na caivāyaṁ sthitaścalati tattvataḥ'—A Yogī feels bliss in his own self, and established there, he does not move from reality viz., this bliss continues endlessly and spontaneously. When, the muslims imprisoned Śivājī's son, Saṁbhājī, made him blind and removed his skin off, to force him to embrace their religion, but he did not do so and thus he did not go astray and discard his religion. It means, that nothing can force a person to move away from his beliefs. When no force, makes a person to change his beliefs, how can anyone force a Yogī to deviate from supreme bliss, or how can he himself abandon that supreme bliss? He cannot.

It means, that a man never moves from Supreme Bliss, because it is a characteristic of the Self (Soul). He changes only, when there is the least affinity with matter. Thus, by affinity for matter, a man may have a fall, even from a trance. So long as, he has affinity for matter, his self cannot merge, in the Cosmic Self, because matter is always active.

Appendix—Having realized the self, a Dhyānayogī feels imperishable and integral bliss which is ātyantika (infinite) (supreme) viz., it is superior to Sāttvika joy; 'atīndriyam' viz., it is superior to Rājasika joy and 'buddhigrāhya' viz., it is superior to Tāmasika joy.

When the Lord declares the imperishable bliss as 'buddhigrāhya' He does not mean that it can be intuited (attained) by intellect. The reason is that intellect is the evolute of Prakṛti, then how can it have an access to the bliss which transcends Prakṛti? Therefore the purpose in declaring it as 'buddhigrāhya' is that it is superior to Tāmasa joy. The joy, which is derived from sleep, indolence and carelessness, is Tāmasa (Gītā 18/39). In sound sleep intellect merges in ignorance; and in indolence and heedlessness, intellect does not remain fully awake. But in self-evident imperishable bliss, intellect does not merge in ignorance but remains fully awake—jñānadīpite' (Gītā 4/27). Therefore it has been called 'buddhigrāhya' because intellect remains awake but intellect has no access to it.

As in a mirror there is reflection of the sun, the sun is not there, similarly in the intellect there is reflection of that bliss, the bliss is not there; therefore it is called 'buddhigrāhya'.

It means that the integral bliss is far superior to Sāttvika, Rājasa and Tāmasa joy, it transcends them. In spite of being called as 'buddhigrāhya', it totally transcends intellect.

The self associated with the intellect (Prakṛti) is 'buddhigrāhya', not the pure Self. In fact the self cannot be attached to Prakṛti but he (self) assumes his attachment to Prakṛti—'yayedaṁ dhāryate jagat' (Gītā 7/5).

Link:—Why a Yogī, does not move from Reality, is described in the next verse.

यं लब्ध्वा चापरं लाभं मन्यते नाधिकं ततः ।
यस्मिन्स्थितो न दुःखेन गुरुणापि विचाल्यते ॥ २२ ॥

yaṁ labdhvā cāparaṁ lābhaṁ manyate nādhikaṁ tataḥ
yasminsthito na duḥkhena guruṇāpi vicālyate

And, having gained which state he does not reckon any other gain greater than that, and wherein established, he is not shaken even by the greatest affliction. 22

Comment:—

'Yaṁ labdhvā cāparaṁ lābhaṁ manyate nādhikaṁ tataḥ'— When a person, expects more happiness in something else, than what he possesses, there is every possibility of his reverting to that. A man, wants to attain Supreme Bliss, or infinite bliss, and he runs after sleep, indolence and heedlessness, the tāmasika joys. But he abandons these, because he feels that the joy derived from the contact of the senses with their objects is more pleasant than this one. He abandons it, also when he feels that Sāttvika joy which is born by placidity of mind, by meditation on God, is superior to it. He abandons it too, when he feels, the Supreme Bliss. There is no greater bliss than this. By gaining this, he has nothing else to seek, because there is no gain, greater than this.

'Yasminsthito na duḥkhena guruṇāpi vicālyate'—A man, may also abandon something, if it results in affliction in spite of its gain. A man, may abandon an attempt to achieve a goal, if he feels that there is some danger. But here Lord Kṛṣṇa, says that a Yogī having been established in the Supreme Bliss, cannot be shaken even by the greatest suffering. If he is hanged or his limbs are broken to pieces, or his body, is ground to powder between mill-stones or his skin is stripped off his body, or, his body is put into boiling oil, yet he is not shaken.

Why is he not shaken even by the greatest punishment? The reason, is that a Yogī established in the Supreme Bliss, has no body consciousness. So the harm inflicted on the body, does not affect him. He feels pain or affliction, only if he identifies himself with matter (Gītā 13/21). But, when he by breaking off his affinity, with matter, is established in the Supreme Bliss, of the self, afflictions or sufferings cannot have any access to him, and so he is not shaken even by the heaviest suffering.

Appendix—This verse is the touchstone for all disciplines. A striver following any discipline—Karmayoga, Jñānayoga, Dhyānayoga and Bhaktiyoga etc., should test himself on this touchstone. In order to know his state this verse is very useful for a striver. Every being has an aim to wipe out sufferings and to attain bliss. Therefore every striver should attain the state described in this verse. If this state has not been attained, it means that his spiritual discipline has not attained perfection. A striver may not discontinue his practice or he may regard his imperfection as perfection, so this verse should be the criterion.

A man can attain such a rare state—in which there is endless gain and there is not an iota of suffering but by indulging in accumulation and enjoyments he causes limitless harm to himself.

Link:—Now in the next verse Lord Kṛṣṇa gives inspiration to gain that Supreme Bliss.

तं विद्याद्दुःखसंयोगवियोगं योगसञ्ज्ञितम्।
स निश्चयेन योक्तव्यो योगोऽनिर्विण्णचेतसा ॥ २३ ॥

taṁ vidyādduḥkhasaṁyogaviyogaṁ yogasañjñitam
sa niścayena yoktavyo yogo'nirviṇṇacetasā

This separation from the assumed union with pain, (travails of worldly life) is called Yoga. This Yoga, (which aims at union with

God or at equanimity), should be practised with determination and without a tired and inattentive mind. 23

Comment:—

'Tam̐ vidyādduḥkhasam̐yogaviyogam̐ yogasañjñitam'— Our union with pain and birth is the result of accepting our affinity with the world, and this affinity is merely assumed not real. We can be delinked from this union, because it is merely assumed, and is not natural. However, strong, our assumption may be, and it may be for a long time, we can cut it asunder, as it is impermanent. As soon as, we are disconnected from this union, with pain (body and world) we attain Yoga i.e., we feel our union with the Self, which is constant, eternal and spontaneous. But we forget this latter union, because of our accepting affinity, with the world. By breaking off this affinity, our memory is revived. Therefore, Arjuna in the seventy-third verse of the eighteenth chapter, says that he has regained his memory. It means, that Arjuna has not gained anything new, but he has regained his memory, that he has a constant union with God (Self).

Here in this verse, Lord Kṛṣṇa has defined Yoga, as disconnection of union with pain, while in 2/48, he has defined it as equanimity in pleasure and pain. In fact, both, the definitions are one and the same, because equanimity in pleasure and pain, turns into a state of separation from union, with pain.

Patañjali has defined Yoga, as the control of mind (Yogadarśana 1/2) and when the mind is controlled, one rests in the Self (1/3). But in the Gītā, Lord Kṛṣṇa has defined Yoga, as in this verse, one's union with the self, which is axiomatic.

The term 'tam' (that), has been used for a state of a Yogī of disciplined mind. This state has been hinted at, by the term 'Yatra' (where), in the first half of the twentieth verse of this chapter, where it has been mentioned that the mind attains quietude. In the second half of the twentieth verse, where it is mentioned that a Yogī gets established in the self. In the first line of the twenty-first verse, He explained the importance of supreme bliss, by using the term 'yat' (which), while in the second line, by using the term 'Yatra' (where), He explained the state of a Yogī. In the twenty-second verse, He explained gain by the term 'Yam' (which), and 'yasmin' (in which). Thus, Lord Kṛṣṇa by using the term 'Yat'*, six times from the twentieth verse to the twenty-second verse, has explained the singular state of a Yogī. The same state, has been glorified here, by the term 'tam' (that).

'Sa niścayena yoktavyo yogo'nirviṇṇacetasā'—This Yoga of meditation, should be practised by a striver, by having the aim of attaining Yoga (equanimity) with determination and with an undistracted mind, as has been described from the eighteenth verse to the twentieth verse of this chapter. In order to, realize this state of equanimity, a striver should have a fixed mind, that he has to attain Yoga (equanimity), even in the face of all temptations and afflictions.

'Anirviṇṇacetasā' means, that a striver should not feel despondent and distracted in attaining that Yoga, in spite of obstacles and afflictions. He should think, that he has to realize God, perfection or equanimity even if, he has to spend years and births together, and even if he has to face most serious afflictions. He should think, that he has wasted innumerable births and suffered tortures in hell, but has not attained his aim of God-realization, though his past sins have been destroyed. So, he should devote his full time (span of his present life), power and resources to, realize Him.

Appendix—The division of worldly union viz., Saṁyoga is different from that of Yoga. There is 'Saṁyoga' with that object (or person) or action with which we can't stay forever and which can't stay with us forever. There is 'Yoga' with that with whom we can stay forever and who can stay with us forever. Therefore in the world there is 'Saṁyoga' with one another and with God

* 'Yatra', 'Yam' and 'Yasmin' are the words formed from the word 'Yat'.

there is yoga. In fact there is no union with the world and no disunion from God viz., whatever we gain in the world is not permanent hence it is no gain at all and God is never separate from us. The assumption of the union with the world and disunion from God is ignorance and it is the greatest blunder of a man. Certainly there is disunion from the worldly union but there is no disconnection at all from the union with God.

A man wants union (with worldly things) but he has to face disunion, therefore the world is said to be the abode of sorrows—duḥkhālayamaśāśvatam' (Gītā 8/15). A desire leads to the union with pain (sufferings). If a striver is free from desires, there is no union with sufferings and there is union with God.

The union of an embodied being with God is eternal. This axiomatic eternal union is called 'Yoga'. This eternal union prevails in all places, all the time, in all actions, in all things, in all persons, in all states, in all circumstances and in all incidents. It means that there has neither been, nor is, nor will be nor can be any disunion from this eternal union. But by assuming connection with the unreal (body) the eternal union is not realized. As soon as there is separation (renunciation of connection) from the assumed union with the unreal in the form of pain, the eternal union is realized. This is the chief Yoga of the Gītā and in order to realize this yoga there is description of Karmayoga, Jñānayoga, Dhyānayoga and Bhaktiyoga etc. But these disciplines (paths) will be called 'Yoga' only when there is total renunciation of affinity with the unreal and there is realization of eternal union with God.

The Lord has defined Yoga in two ways—

(i) Equanimity is called Yoga—'samatvaṁ yoga ucyate' (Gītā 2/48).

(ii) Termination of union with pain in the shape of the worldly transmigration (travails of worldly life)—'taṁ vidyād-duḥkhasaṁyogaviyogaṁ yogasañjñitam' (Gītā 6/23).

Either call it equanimity or call it disconnection of union with pain in the form of the world—both are one and the same. It means that by getting established in equanimity, there will be disunion from the union with the world, and by the disunion of the union with the world, a striver will get established in equanimity. By anyone of these two, the eternal union with God will be realized. If we see from the subtle point of view that 'taṁ vidyādduḥkhasaṁyogaviyogaṁ yogasañjñitam' is the first stage and 'samatvaṁ yoga ucyate' is the later stage in which there is attainment of 'naiṣṭhikiśānti' (everlasting peace), 'paramaśānti' (supreme peace) or 'ātyantika sukha' (eternal bliss).

Equanimity is being attained naturally and sufferings are also disappearing naturally. Only that is attained who is ever attained and only that is renounced which is ever renounced. The attainment of the ever attained is called Yoga and renunciation of the ever renounced is also called yoga. The pleasures that are derived from the contact with sense-objects, persons and actions are only sources of pain viz., they cause sufferings (Gītā 5/22). Therefore union with the world rather than disunion causes sufferings. There is no disunion of the joy (bliss) which is attained by disunion (renunciation of affinity) from the world because it is eternal. When there is disunion in both union and also disunion, it means that disunion is eternal. This eternal disunion is called 'Yoga' in the Gītā.

God being ever-existent is called 'Is' and the world being never really existent is called 'Not'. A vital fact is that while we try to perceive 'Is' then pure 'Is' is not perceived but if we observe 'Not' as negation, pure 'Is' to intuited. The reason is that while we perceive 'Is' we make such perception through the mind, intellect and other such 'Vṛttis' then 'Is' to be perceived. 'Is' associated with such 'Vṛttis', but while we perceive 'Not' then our 'Vṛttis' themselves being 'Not' will be also shunned and pure 'Is' will be intuited. As while removing rubbish, the broom is also discarded after removing rubbish as it is also rubbish and the (clean) house remains. It means that 'God pervades everywhere'—by reflecting upon it with the mind and by determining it with intellect, our connection with 'Vṛtti' will persist. But 'the world is separating from us every moment'—thus by perceiving the world as non-existent, our affinity with the world and the 'Vṛtti' will be renounced and pure Supreme Reality (God) will remain.

Link:—In the next verse, Lord Kṛṣṇa explains the topic of meditation on God, Who is without attribute and formless, in order to attain Yoga (equanimity).

सङ्कल्पप्रभवान्कामांस्त्यक्त्वा सर्वानशेषतः ।
मनसैवेन्द्रियग्रामं विनियम्य समन्ततः ॥ २४ ॥

saṅkalpaprabhavānkāmāṁstyaktvā sarvānaśeṣataḥ
manasaivendriyagrāmaṁ viniyamya samantataḥ

Completely giving up all desires arising from thoughts of the world, and restraining the senses, from all sides, by the mind. 24

Comment:—

[The state, which is attained by disinterested action (6/1—9), is attained by meditation on God with attributes and form (6/14-15), as by meditation on the self (6/18—23), is also attained by meditation on the Absolute, Who is formless and attributeless, which is described here.]

'Saṅkalpaprabhavānkāmāṁstyaktvā sarvānaśeṣataḥ'—Thoughts of worldly things, persons and incidents etc., come to the mind, when the man is either attached to or hateful for these and, it becomes a 'Saṅkalpa' (pursuit of the mind). This seed of pursuit, sprouts and grows into a plant of desire. It should happen and it should not happen—this is desire. Thus desire born of thought, should be completely abandoned.

The term 'Kāmān' (desires), which is itself plural, yet to emphasize that all the desires of different kinds, should be abandoned another term 'Sarvān' has also been given here.

'Aśeṣataḥ' means, that the seed of desires should be completely destroyed, otherwise it may sprout and grow into a forest of desires stretching for miles and miles.

'Manasaivendriyagrāmaṁ viniyamya samantataḥ'—Objects of five senses—sound, touch, colour, taste and smell, should be fully restrained by the mind. 'Samantataḥ' means, that the mind also should not think of sensual pleasures, and in the mind there should not be any temptation for worldly praise, honour and comfort etc., in the least. One, who practises meditation should resolve, to renounce affinity for all material objects.

Appendix—First there is 'Sphuraṇā' (mere flash of thought) and then it is changed into 'Saṅkalpa' (pursuit of the mind). When we take 'Sphuraṇā' as existent and get attached to it and further we insist on its implementation then it changes into a 'Saṅkalpa'. 'Sphuraṇā' is like the glass of a mirror in which no photograph of a man is taken but 'Saṅkalpa' is like the film of a camera which immediately catches the impression.

Link:—In the next verse, Lord Kṛṣṇa explains what should be done, to give up all desires and to restrain the senses.

शनैः शनैरुपरमेद्बुद्ध्या धृतिगृहीतया।
आत्मसंस्थं मनः कृत्वा न किंचिदपि चिन्तयेत्॥ २५॥

śanaiḥ śanairuparamedbuddhyā dhṛtigṛhītayā
ātmasaṁsthaṁ manaḥ kṛtvā na kiñcidapi cintayet

One's intellect (mind) fixed firmly, he should gradually attain tranquillity; with the mind centred on God, and he should not think of anything else. 25

Comment:—

'Buddhyā dhṛtigṛhītayā'—A striver, should not feel dejected and disappointed, that he has not been successful, in meditation on God, after practising for a long time. He should have patience and determination, that he has to attain God, whatever may happen,* because there is no gain better than this. Thus, he should control his intellect, without caring for worldly pleasures, praise, honour and comfort etc.

'Śanaiḥ śanairuparamed'—In being indifferent, to worldly pleasures, he should not make hasre, but he should become indifferent gradually, and finally achieve quietude. He should have neither attachment nor aversion, for pursuits of the mind. If we abandon a thing there is a possibility of a feeling of aversion persisting for it but there should not remain even a trace of the feeling of aversion for any object of the world. It is said that we should become indifferent to it. Here, attainment of an attitude of indifference has also been mentioned, because God, the sentient is beyond the access of mind, being as evolute of matter; which is insentient. As a lamp, which receives light from the sun cannot illumine the sun, so mind, which receives energy from God, cannot have access to Him but can be indifferent to the world. Secondly, in the world, there is nothing but affliction, therefore, it is futile to think of the world. So, one should become quiet, tranquil and indifferent.

'Ātmasaṁsthaṁ manaḥ kṛtvā'—God pervades everywhere, even in thoughts, so thoughts are nothing, except God, who is their base and illuminator. Secondly, God is eternal and always the same, without any modification, while persons, things and circumstances etc., are born and they decay viz., and have no existence. So fixing the mind on God, and having a firm

* He should have an iron determination that he will not leave his seat without realizing God even though his body may get parched and even his skin, flesh and bones may decay.

determination of the existence of God, alone he should not think at all.

'Na kiñcidapi cintayet'—It has already been said, that he should not think of the world. God is all-pervasive, he should also not think so. By that, his affinity with the mind, will persist. A meditator, and the mind, will have their existence, so having resolved, that God pervades everywhere, he should not think of anything else. Thus by becoming tranquil, he will realize the ever-existent self which has already been described in the twenty-second verse.

An Exceptional Fact in Connection with Meditation

The most important fact, is that God (manifest or unmanifest), pervades everywhere—in all persons, things, incidents, circumstances and actions and there is never any modification in Him, while matter always undergoes modifications. As a diver dives, into an ocean and perceives water all-around, similarly, a striver, should feel God all-around and also, in him. The only aim of mankind, is to realize God, Who is ever realizable, but He is not felt, because we divert our attention towards perishable things.

If we had an exclusive devotion to attain Him, our mind would be automatically concentrated, on Him. Ether is around us and so is God, but we do not pay attention to it. Therefore, a striver abandoning all thoughts of the world, should be indifferent and quiet. He, while concentrating his mind on God, commits an error, that he opposes a thought that comes to the mind, and then has affinity for it. Similarly, he has affinity for a thought, if he is attached to it. Therefore, a striver should neither oppose any thought nor support it, he should only remain indifferent and attain tranquillity or quietude.

All projections and distractions of the mind, are transient, so if these are born, they would decay, certainly. We should not accept our affinity for them. We should accept our affinity for God, who pervades everywhere. When, we confine ourselves to a body, our separate entity, comes into existence that, 'I am'. This individuality is also encompassed by God, who is limitless, even, tranquil and also truth, knowledge and bliss as well as, the illuminator of all things and actions. All objects and actions are illumined by one light. This light, has a relation either with all objects, actions and persons, or with none. This light, remains as it is. Similarly, God as light, has no relation with objects and actions etc., these objects and actions are transitory, while the Lord is without origin. Being established in Him, one should not think of anything.

One, 'Cintana' (thinking), is done, while the other is automatic. We should not resort to it (thinking). If some thought crops us, we should remain neutral and indifferent. An ice-cube (block of ice), dropped into water is water, and is also surrounded by water. Similarly, all projections and distractions are within God, and God is in them.

Moreover, when a striver meditates upon, the memory past incidents etc., comes to mind, which have no current existence. But, a striver by accepting their existence, strengthens them. So, he should remain indifferent to them, without having attachment or aversion for them. They will perish, in the same way as, they are born. We have a constant affinity, with God, we are His, and He is ours. So, a striver by accepting the fact, that he is always established in Him, should sit quietly without thinking of anything else. He should not accept his affinity with a thought, that comes to his mind itself. By doing so, the thought will perish, and he will be fixed in God, because he always remains fixed on Him.

Waves rise in a sea, but in water there is neither, sea nor waves. Similarly in God, there is neither world nor thoughts. Only He pervades, equally everywhere. Clouds appear and disappear in the sky, but the sky remains, the same. Similarly, while meditating, thoughts come to mind and slip away while God who is everywhere, remains the same. God is all-around, inside as well as, outside. Everything, sentient or insentient, animate or inanimate, is God Himself. He is both at hand and far away. He is incomprehensible, because of His subtlety (Gītā 13/15). He is All Truth, All Knowledge and All Bliss. Everywhere, there is bliss, bliss and only bliss.

While, discharging duties and performing actions, we should accept that God is all-pervading and undivided. It will help us in meditating, on God, while meditation on God will be helpful to us in our practical life, viz., in remembering Him, when we perform our duties. Therefore, a striver while meditating in seclusion or performing actions in society, should always accept that God pervades everywhere, in all, the time, persons, things, incidents and actions etc. So, we should always remain established in Him, without thinking of anything else.

Appendix—The Discipline of Meditation is of two types—(i) to concentrate the mind (ii) to renounce affinity for the mind by discrimination. Renunciation of affinity by using discrimination immediately leads to salvation. In the world so many virtuous and sinful actions are done but we have no connection with them, similarly we have no connection with the body, senses, mind and intellect. This is known as 'uparati' (indifference). We should have no connection with the 'Vṛtti'. In 'Śrīmadbhāgavata' is mentioned—

sarvaṁ brahmātmakaṁ tasya vidyayā'tmamanīṣayā
paripaśyannuparamet sarvato muktasaṁśayaḥ

(11/29/18)

The devotee who follows the above-mentioned discipline (worship of God with all actions of mind, tongue (speech) and body) has the determination, "All is God". Then by this spiritual knowledge, being free from all kinds of doubts, perceiving God pervading everywhere, he should become 'uparāma' (indifferent) viz., 'All is God'—even this should not be thought of but God should be seen face to face.

God as in the form of eternal-existence pervades all places, time, actions, objects, states, circumstances, incidents etc., equally. Places and time etc., have no existence but God ever exists. So first a striver should have the determination with the mind and intellect 'God exists'. Then he should give up this determination also and be quiet viz., he should think of nothing. He should think neither of the self nor of non-self, nor of God, nor of the world, nor of union, nor of disunion. If he thinks of anything, the matter (inert) will be thought of. The reason is that if he thinks of anything, 'Citta' (mind) will accompany him. If an instrument (Citta) accompanies him, the world will not be renounced because an instrument is also a part of the world. Therefore in 'na kiñcidapi cintayet' there is disconnection from 'Citta' (the instrument) because when an instrument is not with him, then there will be real meditation. Even in the most subtle reflection, 'Vṛtti' persists. But when there is no reflection, the 'Vritti' disappears. Therefore a striver should be indifferent to reflection even. As the soil mixed with water slowly settles down naturally when the water is still, similarly all evils (flaws) by keeping quiet slowly calm down naturally, ego melts and the real self (the Reality) (free from egoism) is realized.

Here the terms 'śanaiḥ śanaiḥ' have been used for giving up 'Vṛtti'. By using the words 'śanaiḥ śanaiḥ' the Lord means to say that the striver in order to be indifferent, should not apply force, should not make haste because the impression gathered through life after life, are not wiped out hastily. Haste makes volatility firm and permanent but 'śanaiḥ śanaiḥ' (gradual effort) destroys volatility.

Without connection with Prakṛti, there can't be any 'cintana', 'manana' (reflection) etc. If a striver thinks of the Supreme Reality, the mind will be used; if he determines, intellect will be used; if he sees, the eyes will be used; if he hears, the ears will be used and if he says anything, the tongue will be used. Similarly if he assumes 'Is', then assumption and he who assumes will persist, and if he negates 'not', he who negates will remain. If he renounces the sense of doership, "I am not a doer' this subtle ego will persist viz., by renunciation, the thing renounced and he who renounces will remain. Therefore a striver should become 'uparāma' (indifferent) viz., he should neither assume nor negate nor receive nor renounce but should accept the self evident and natural Divinity and become quiet from within and from without. 'I have to keep quiet'—this insistence (pursuit of the mind) should also not be maintained, otherwise he will have the sense of doership. 'Quietude' is self-evident or automatic (it requires no initiative).

A striver should give up these four—'I', 'thou (you)', 'this' and 'that', and then only 'Is' (Reality) remains. He should accept that self-evident 'Is' and should not think of anything. If a thought comes to the mind, he should have neither attachment nor aversion to it, he should neither be pleased nor displeased with it, he should consider it neither good nor bad nor he should accept it in him. He should not think of anything but if a thought crops up, that is not harmful. Air blows, sometimes it is hot, sometimes cold, it rains—we are not to be blamed for these occurrences because we have no connection with them. We are blamed if we are connected with matter. Therefore if any thought crops up, be indifferent to it, don't get mixed with it viz., we should not hold, "I think or 'thinking' is done in me." But we should hold, "Thoughts come to the mind and I (self) have no connection with the mind."

In the expression 'ātmasaṁsthaṁ manaḥ kṛtvā' the term 'manaḥ' stands for intellect because volatility is the trait of mind and steadfastness is the trait of intellect. Therefore the term 'ātmasaṁstham' means that instead of volatility, there should be steadfastness. As 'This is a particular village'—when this assumption becomes firm, we have not to think of it again and again, similarly 'God exists'—if this assumption is firmly rooted, then we'll have not to think of His existence repeatedly. Therefore whatever is self-evident, what is the need to think of it? So by thinking of the self, the self is not realized because by thinking of the self, the thinker remains and existence of the non-self persists. When we assume the existence of the non-self, then we'll renounce the none-self and think of the self.

'Na kiñcidapi cintayet'—this is also known as 'Cupa Sādhana', 'mūka satsaṅga', and 'acintya kā dhyāna'. In it there is neither 'an action' through the physical body nor there is 'thinking' through the subtle body nor 'constancy' (trance) through the causal body. In it senses are inactive, mind is also composed, intellect is also silent viz., there is no activity of the body, senses, mind and intellect. All are silent, no one speaks. Whatever was to be seen, has been seen; whatever was to be heard, has been heard, whatever was to be spoken, has been spoken; and whatever had to be done, has been done; now there is no interest (taste) in seeing, hearing, speaking and doing etc.,—in such a state 'Cupa Sādhana' (silent discipline) is practised. This discipline is superior even to trance because in it affinity for intellect and ego is renounced. In 'samādhi' (trance), 'laya', 'vikṣepa', 'kaṣāya' and 'rasāsvāda'—these four flaws (obstacles) persist but 'Cupa Sādhana' is free from these flaws. 'Cupa Sādhana' (silent discipline) is devoid of Vṛtti.

Link:—What course a striver should adopt, if he is unable to attain tranquillity; is explained, in the next verse.

यतो यतो निश्चरति मनश्चञ्चलमस्थिरम्।
ततस्ततो नियम्यैतदात्मन्येव वशं नयेत्॥ २६॥

yato yato niścarati manaścañcalamasthiram
tatastato niyamyaitadātmanyeva vaśaṁ nayet

By whatever cause, the restless and unsteady mind wanders away, he should restrain it and continually concentrate it, on God.* 26

Comment:—

'Yato yato niścarati manaścañcalamasthiram tatastato niyamyaitadātmanyeva vaśaṁ nayet'—Mind does not remain steady, in the aim fixed by a striver. So it is called unsteady. It thinks of worldly pleasures, and objects so it is called, restless. It means, that it neither is fixed on God, nor renounces the world. Therefore, a striver should restrain the mind from worldly objects and thoughts, with discrimination, and place safely it at the feet of the Lord. He should be cautious in subduing the fickle and unsteady mind. He should, not be lax in it. It means, that a striver should understand, that the base and illuminator of those objects and thoughts, is only God. This is concentration on God.

Means to Concentrate the Mind on God

(i) A striver, should restrain the mind when it is diverted to persons, things and circumstances etc., and concentrate it, again and again, on God.

(ii) All the beings and things, in this universe are manifestations of God. So he should understand, that whatever thought comes to his mind, is nothing but God. Thus, he should concentrate his mind, on God.

(iii) Mental rubbish stored inside the mind begins to come out at the time of meditation, because when one was busy with other activities, it could not find an outlet. By thinking thus, a striver should not be perturbed. He should, rather continue his efforts to concentrate, his mind.

* In the whole of Gītā emphasis on practice has been laid only in this verse.

(iv) A striver cannot meditate on God, because he meditates on Him, by accepting himself as of the world, while really he is God's. Therefore, he should accept the reality, "I am only God's, and only God is mine. I am not of the body and the world, and the body and the world, are not mine." By accepting affinity for God, which is a reality the mind will automatically be concentrated on Him.

(v) A striver, should not leave any part of work, pending. He should, either do the work first, or remove its thought from his mind, and then start meditation on God, with a calm mind.

(vi) He should do away with all pursuits and distractions of the mind, by offering these as an oblation to the fire-god.

(vii) He should, wink his eyes several times and then shut these. By winking, as the outward scene is cut off, so are the pursuits and distractions of the mind, eliminated.

(viii) He should exhale air forcibly from his lungs two or three times, and then hold his breath as long as he can. Then, he should start breathing slowly and come to a natural state of breathing. By doing so, pursuits and distractions of the mind, disappear.

Appendix—If according to the preceding verse, a striver may not practise silent discipline, then he should restrain the mind from worldly objects and thoughts, and concentrate it on God. An excellent means to fix the mind on God is that wherever the mind wanders, there he should perceive (see) God and whatever thoughts come to the mind, they should be regarded as the manifestation of God.

There is a vital point that so long as a striver assumes any other entity besides God, his mind cannot be totally restrained. The reason is that so long as we recognize any other entity, attachment can't be totally wiped out and without total destruction of attachment, mind can't be totally controlled. If attachment persists, mind can be restrained to a certain extent by which worldly 'siddhis'—accomplishments are achieved but Divinity is not attained. If any other entity is assumed, then the mind is controlled for sometime and then there is deviation viz., there are two states—trance and relapse. The reason is that without assuming the other entity, two states are not possible. Therefore the mind can be totally restrained by assuming that there is no any other entity besides God.

Link:—The result of concentration of mind on God, is explained, in the next two verses.

प्रशान्तमनसं ह्येनं योगिनं सुखमुत्तमम्।
उपैति शान्तरजसं ब्रह्मभूतमकल्मषम्॥ २७॥

praśāntamanasaṁ hyenaṁ yoginaṁ sukhamuttamam
upaiti śāntarajasaṁ brahmabhūtamakalmaṣam

Great sāttvika happiness, truly comes to the Yogī, whose mind is calm, whose passions are subdued, and who is without sin. 27

Comment:—

'Praśāntamanasaṁ hyenaṁ yoginaṁ sukhamuttamam, upaiti śāntarajasaṁ brahmabhūtamakalmaṣam'—'Akalmaṣam' (sinless), is he, who is free from tamas disposition, such as obtuseness, inactivity, heedlessness and delusion (14/13).

'Śāntarajasam' (whose passions are subdued), is he, whose rajas propensities, of greed, activity, undertaking of actions with a selfish motive, restlessness and a thirst for enjoyment, are subdued.

'Praśāntamanasam' (one of peaceful mind), is he, whose mind, becomes calm because he renounces all tāmasika and rājasika passions, and is free from mundane pursuits and distractions. Here, the term 'Praśānta' means, that a Yogī, does not accept the mind as his own and so his mind, becomes free from attachment and aversion. Thus, his mind becomes calm, naturally.

'Enam' (this), has been used for the Yogī who attains

tranquillity, as explained in the twenty-fifth verse. Such a Yogī, attains sāttvika happiness.

In the second half of the twenty-third verse, the Lord offers an inspiration to practise the Yoga of meditation, with determination. He, who practises this Yoga, verily attains sāttvika happiness. The term 'hi' used here denotes this certainty.

'Sukhamupaiti'—It means, that a Yogī has not to make effort to attain that Supreme Bliss, but it verily comes to him.

युञ्जन्नेवं सदात्मानं योगी विगतकल्मषः।
सुखेन ब्रह्मसंस्पर्शमत्यन्तं सुखमश्नुते ॥ २८ ॥

yuñjannevaṁ sadātmānaṁ yogī vigatakalmaṣaḥ
sukhena brahmasaṁsparśamatyantaṁ sukhamaśnute

The sinless Yogī thus, submerging his self always in God, easily enjoys, the infinite bliss of oneness with the Brahma (the Absolute). 28

Comment:—

'Yuñjannevaṁ sadātmānaṁ yogī vigatakalmaṣaḥ'—Here the term 'Yuñjan' does not mean, to fix the mind on God through practice. It significies one's identity, with God. This identification is not through mental pursuits. A Yogī constantly unites his self with God, and thus becomes free from the feelings of egoism, and mineness. This freedom from mineness and egoism, means freedom from sins, as affinity of egoism and mineness, with the world is the root of sins.

The phrase 'Yuñjannevam', in the fifteenth verse, has been used for the Lord with attributes, while here it has been used for the Absolute viz., the Lord without attributes. Similarly, in the fifteenth verse, emphasis has been laid to fix the mind on God, through practice, by the term 'Niyatamānasaḥ', while here by the expression 'Vigatakalmaṣaḥ', emphasis has been laid on renouncement of affinity, with, non-self. There, the mind by meditating on God, is absorbed in Him and thus the world is renounced, while here by renouncing affinity with the world, the Yogī gets established in God. Thus, the result of both, is the same.

'Sukhena brahmasaṁsparśamatyantaṁ sukhamaśnute'—In unity with God, the feeling of 'I' does not exist, nor does there remain its least impression. Infinite bliss is the state, in which a Yogī is immersed in God, and loses his identity. A Yogī attains this bliss, which has been named 'Imperishable Bliss' (5/21) and 'Supreme Bliss' (6/21), all these names denote the same, Divine Bliss.

Link:—Now, in the next verse, Lord Kṛṣṇa explains the change of vision, that takes place in the Yogī.

सर्वभूतस्थमात्मानं सर्वभूतानि चात्मनि।
ईक्षते योगयुक्तात्मा सर्वत्र समदर्शनः॥ २९॥

sarvabhūtasthamātmānaṁ sarvabhūtāni cātmani
īkṣate yogayuktātmā sarvatra samadarśanaḥ

The Yogī, whose mind is steeped in Yoga, looks on all with an equal eye, sees his self present, in all beings and all beings mere as appearance within his self. 29

Comment:—

'Īkṣate yogayuktātmā sarvatra samadarśanaḥ'—The Yogī sees the same divinity in all. As toys made of sugar in the shape of various birds, animals and men are of the same stuff, sugar; various arms and weapons of iron; various toys made of clay and various ornaments of gold, likewise it is the self, that has assumed various forms in the universe. So, a Yogī sees the self, in all objects and beings.

'Yogayuktātmā'—It means, that the mind of the Yogī, by constant practice of meditation is absorbed in the self, and then his affinity, with the mind breaks off, which has been indicated by the expression, "Sarvabhūtasthamātmānaṁ sarvabhūtāni cātmani."

'Sarvabhūtasthamātmānam'—As a worldly person, sees himself in all his limbs, a Yogī, sees his self, in all the creatures. As in a dream, different persons, animals and objects are a man's own creation, and they all disappear when he awakes, similarly a Yogī, sees his own Self, in all beings because there is no such existence of the world, as in a dream, it is transient and kaleidoscopic. It means, that whatever he sees, is his Self.

'Sarvabhūtāni cātmani'—He sees all beings, as assumed in the self. As different colours, are born of light and are seen only in light, and as different objects born of the sun, are seen only in the light of the sun; so does a Yogī, see that all beings are born of the self, merge in the self and are perceived, as assumed ones, in the self. It means, that one sees the entire creation, as a manifestation of the self, only.

In this verse, it is mentioned that a Yogī sees the Self present in all beings, but it is not said that he sees all beings, present in the Self. The reason is, that the Self exists in all the creatures, but the creatures do not have their existence, in the Self, because they are born and decay, while the Self ever remains the same.

His dealings may differ, with different creatures, but he sees all, with an equal eye, as he sees the same divinity, in all.

Link:—Lord Kṛṣṇa, in the next verse, explains how a devotee (Dhyānayogī), described in the fourteenth and fifteenth verses, sees God, everywhere.

यो मां पश्यति सर्वत्र सर्वं च मयि पश्यति।
तस्याहं न प्रणश्यामि स च मे न प्रणश्यति ॥ ३० ॥

yo māṁ paśyati sarvatra sarvaṁ ca mayi paśyati
tasyāhaṁ na praṇaśyāmi sa ca me na praṇaśyati

He, who sees Me (the universal Self) present in all creatures, and sees all beings existing in Me, I am never out of sight for him, nor is he ever out of My sight. 30

Comment:—

'Yo māṁ paśyati sarvatra'—A devotee, sees Me in all persons, animals, birds, gods, demons, things, incidents and circumstances. When Brahmājī, stole cowherds and calves, Lord Kṛṣṇa Himself assumed the form of cowherds and calves with their flutes, clothes and ornaments etc.* This drama of His manifestation, continued for one year, but nobody could know it. One day, Balarāma, the elder brother of Kṛṣṇa, saw cows, leaving their young calves who were left at home, run towards the big calves. Then, by intuition he realized, that Lord Kṛṣṇa had manifested Himself, as those calves. Thus, a devotee sees God, pervading, everywhere.

'Sarvaṁ ca mayi paśyati'—He sees, all beings existing in Me. As Lord Kṛṣṇa shows Arjuna His divine form, He asks him to behold the entire creation, both animate and inanimate in His one limb (11/7). Arjuna also says, "O Lord, I behold in Your body all gods and multitude of different beings" (11/15). Sañjaya also says, "Arjuna then saw the whole universe, with its many divisions within His body" (11/13). Thus, a devotee sees the whole creation existing, in Him.

'Tasyāhaṁ na praṇaśyāmi'—When a devotee sees everywhere Me in each and every object, how can I be out of sight for him? I always, remain within his sight.

---

* Lord Kṛṣṇa assumed the forms of cowherds and cows, the same, in number, bodies, limbs, sticks, horns, flutes, leaves, nets made of strings and the ornaments. Their age, habits, nature, names, behaviour and states were all the same, as those of original ones. At that time, the voice of the Vedas, that the whole is the form of Lord Viṣṇu, embodied itself (Śrīmadbhā. 10/13/19).

'Sa ca me na praṇaśyati'—When a devotee sees God everywhere, God also sees him everywhere, because Lord Kṛṣṇa declares, "However, men approach Me, so do I seek them (viz., carry out their desires)" (Gītā 4/11). It means, that when a devotee identifies himself with God, God in His Universal Self, sees him everywhere. Thus, he is never out of His sight.

Now, a question arises, why Lord Kṛṣṇa says, that the devotee only is never out of His sight when He declares, that none is out of my sight, "I know the beings of the past, the present and the future" (7/26). The answer is, that though none is out of sight of the Lord, the Lord, sees him everywhere, who sees the Lord everywhere. But, for those who have a disinclination for God, and are attached to the world, He is not manifest (Gītā 7/25). Because of his disinclination for Him, he also remains out of His sight, Lord Kṛṣṇa declares, in the twenty-ninth verse of the ninth chapter, "I am equally present in all beings; there is none hateful or dear to Me. But they who worship Me with devotion, are in Me and I also am, in them."

Appendix—In the preceding verse the Lord mentioned the soul (self) but now he mentions the Supreme Soul (God). A striver following the discipline of meditation because of the past impression of knowledge, has predominance of discrimination; while the other striver, having the impression of devotion, has predominance of faith and belief. Therefore the 'Dhyānayogī' with the latent impression of knowledge discriminately sees the self present in all beings 'sarvabhūtasthamātmānaṁ sarvabhūtāni cātmani' (Gītā 6/29). While the 'Dhyānayogī' having the latent impression of devotion with faith and belief sees God everywhere—'yo māṁ paśyati sarvatra sarvaṁ ca mayi paśyati'.

The expression 'yo māṁ paśyati sarvatra' means that he sees Me in others and also in himself. The expression 'sarvaṁ ca mayi paśyati' means that he sees others in Me and also sees himself in Me.

As snow is lying everywhere, then how will it hide? If snow is put behind that snow, then also snow will be seen. Similarly when God manifests Himself in all forms, then how can He hide, where can He hide and behind whom can He hide? The reason is that there is no other entity except God. In the supreme soul (God) there is no division of the body and the self, the real and the unreal, the insentient and the sentient, God and the world, 'saguṇa' (with attributes) and 'nirguṇa' (without attributes), 'sākāra' (with form) and 'nirākāra' (without form) etc. In Him only, there are several divisions and in several divisions only He prevails. He is not an object to be known by discrimination but He can be known by faith and belief. Therefore "All is God"—a striver should assume it, he should accept it with faith and belief. If he accepts this truth firmly, he will realize the same truth.

A striver first sees God far away, then he sees Him nearby, after it he sees Him in himself and finally he sees only God. A Karmayogī sees God nearby, a Jñānayogī sees Him in himself and a Bhaktiyogī sees God pervading everywhere.

Link:—The relationship between a devotee and the Lord, is further elucidated.

सर्वभूतस्थितं यो मां भजत्येकत्वमास्थितः ।
सर्वथा वर्तमानोऽपि स योगी मयि वर्तते ॥ ३१ ॥

sarvabhūtasthitaṁ yo māṁ bhajatyekatvamāsthitaḥ
sarvathā vartamāno'pi sa yogī mayi vartate

He, who established in union with Me, worships Me as abiding in all beings, though engaged in all forms of activities, dwells in Me. 31

Comment:—

'Ekatvamāsthitaḥ'—In the previous verse, Lord Kṛṣṇa explained that He is never out of sight of a devotee, nor is he ever out of sight of Him. Why? Because a devotee identifies himself with God, who abides in all beings viz., he develops intense love, for Him.

In accordance with non-dualistic principle, a devotee has no identity of his own, his identity is merged in the Lord, while, in dualistic tenets the Lord and the devotee assume separate entities outwardly, though inwardly they are one and the same* just as a husband and a wife possessing two different bodies regard, themselves as one, and so two friends, who deem themselves as one. Due to intense love, duality does not exist. A devotee, who worships God, with wholehearted devotion, gets established in communion with Him. This oneness and the sameness of a devotee and God, is called 'Ekatvamāsthitah'.

'Sarvabhūtasthitaṁ yo māṁ bhajati'—God pervades everywhere in all persons, things, incidents and circumstances etc., viz., all is God, He puts on the appearance of the entire phenomenon, (7/19)—this is his worship, to God.

'Sarvabhūtasthitam'—By this phrase, it seems as if God abides only in beings, but actually it is not so, He abides, in each and every particle of the universe. In ornaments made of gold there is nothing, but gold. When ornaments were not made, there was gold, even now gold exists in them and there will remain gold even when the ornaments are broken or spoiled. But, it does not mean that there is gold only in those ornaments, not anywhere else. Similarly, God existed, before the creation of the world, He exists now, and He will exist at the end of the creation. But, to explain the fact that all beings are just like ornaments, and God is like gold, it is said that only God abides, in all beings and He also abides, at all places.

---

* In the Discipline of Knowledge the devotee identifies himself with God and loses his identity, while in the Discipline of Devotion to exchange and enhance true (spiritual) love, the Lord and the devotee like Śrī Kṛṣṇa and Rādhājī, being one and the same become two.

'Sarvathā vartamāno'pi sa yogī mayi vartate'—He, while discharging his duties, according to the ordinance of the scriptures abides in Me, because in his view there is no independent entity, except Me.

In the thirteenth chapter, in the context of the Discipline of Knowledge, Lord Kṛṣṇa announced, "Even though engaged in all sorts of activities, he is not born again" (13/23); while here, He says, "Though engaged in all sorts of activities, he dwells in Me." 'He is not born again,' means that he is emancipated, 'He dwells in Me' means, that the devotee, by becoming one with God, has a unique relish of spiritual love, which is infinite and which ever enhances.

Here, Lord Kṛṣṇa says, that that devotee dwells in Him. Here a question arises, whether other creatures don't dwell in Him. The answer is, that all creatures dwell in Him, but by attaching importance to the world, they neither know, nor accept that they dwell in Him. They, because of egoism and mineness, uphold this universe (Gītā 7/5). They don't regard the world, as manifestation of God, but regard it as a separate entity and attach importance to it by declaring, 'We are worldly people,' while a devotee realizes, that it is God Who manifests Himself, as multitudinous beings viz., so all is God, and so a devotee always dwells in Him.

Appendix—A devotee sees the entire universe as the manifestation of God. From his view-point besides God no other entity exists. For him the seer (onlooker), the seen and 'that act of seeing'—all the three are only the manifestation of God—'Vāsudevaḥ sarvam' (Gītā 7/19). As the Ganges is worshipped with the water of the Ganges, similarly a devotee's all dealings are focussed on God. As a person who has identified himself with the body, while performing all actions, dwells in the body, similarly such a devotee while discharging his duties, abides in God.

In the thirteenth chapter the Lord declares—'sarvathā vartamāno'pi na sa bhūyo'bhijāyate' (13/23)—a Jñānayogī performing duties in everyway is not born again and here he declares for a devotee 'sarvathā vartamāno'pi sa yogī mayi vartate' viz., 'a devotee engaged in all forms of activities, dwells in Me'. It means that by the path of knowledge a striver is freed from the cycle of birth and death and he attains salvation; but by the path of devotion, he is freed from the cycle of birth and death, attains oneness with God and develops intimate kinship with Him. The same idea has been expressed in the Gītā in the following ways—'tasyāhaṁ na praṇaśyāmi sa ca me na praṇaśyati' (6/30), 'priyo hi jñānino'tyarthamahaṁ sa ca mama priyaḥ' (7/17), 'jñāni tvātmaiva me matam' (7/18), 'ye bhajanti tu māṁ bhaktyā mayi te teṣu cāpyaham' (9/29). In the Discipline of knowledge because of the presence of an iota (trace) of subtle ego there can be philosophical differences but in the Discipline of Devotion because of oneness with God, not even an iota of subtle ego and the philosophical differences caused by that ego remain. In 'na sa bhūyo'bhijāyate' a striver having realized the self gets established in the self, the self remains, while in 'sa yogī mayi vartate' only God remains, the Yogī does not remain as a Yogī but he becomes an embodiment of God.

Link:—Now Lord Kṛṣṇa explains, the merit of an enlightened Yogī (who believes in God, Who is without form and attributes).

आत्मौपम्येन सर्वत्र समं पश्यति योऽर्जुन।
सुखं वा यदि वा दुःखं स योगी परमो मतः ॥ ३२ ॥

ātmaupamyena sarvatra samaṁ paśyati yo'rjuna
sukhaṁ vā yadi vā duḥkhaṁ sa yogī paramo mataḥ

That Yogī, O Arjuna, is regarded as supreme, who looks on

all as one, like his own body and who sees the pleasure and pain of all, with a similar eye. 32

Comment:—

[What has been mentioned, as 'Identified with Brahma (the Absolute)' or 'Attainment of Infinite Bliss', in the twenty-seventh and twenty-eighth verses respectively, in this verse, Lord Kṛṣṇa explains the behaviour of such an enlightened Yogī towards others. "Such a Yogī is devoted to the welfare of all beings" (5/25, 12/4).]

'Ātmaupamyena sarvatra samaṁ paśyati yo'rjuna'—An ordinary person, regards the injury of any of his limbs as his own, because according to him he and his limbs are one and the same. But a Yogī regards others as his own Self and thinks of their harm as his own harm. If any afflicted person comes before him then that Yogī tries to alleviate the suffering of that man in the same way as he attempts to alleviate the suffering of any limb of his own body. Meaning thereby that as an ordinary man is engaged in providing comfort to his body. So too the Yogī is automatically engaged in making others happy.

'Sarvatra' (everywhere), means that he is engaged in promoting the welfare, of all beings without any distinction of caste, creed and colour and does good, even to animals, birds, trees and plants etc. By him, efforts are automatically made to alleviate, their suffering.

He knows, that limbs have different shapes and functions, yet he makes efforts to soothe the afflicted limbs, equally. Hands cannot be used, as feet. If by chance, a hand is touched by another hand, we do not wash it. But, if it touches a foot, it is to be washed. When an organ of excretion is cleaned by a hand, we wash the hand, with clay. Thus, one observes, touchability and untouchability with others, also in accordance with the ordinance of scriptures. But, it does not mean, that he hates them. He loves all of them and does good to them, as he does to his own limbs.

'Sukhaṁ vā yadi vā duḥkham'—To feel happy and sad, on the analogy of his body does not mean, that if a person is injured, this enlightened soul, feels that injury in his body. If it were taken as such, the affliction of the enlightened soul, would be enormous, because the world is full of afflicted persons. It means, that as an ordinary and ignorant person attached to his body, makes efforts to relieve bodily pain promptly, an enlightened soul does the same, to others; and as an ignorant man is not proud of such actions performed for his body, an enlightened one is also not proud of performing these for others. He is naturally engrossed in the welfare of others. Moreover, an enlightened soul, can bear his bodily pain and remain indifferent to it, but he cannot bear the pain of others, and so always remains prepared to relieve their suffering. So he thinks that he has the power to bear the pain, as he knows that he himself is different from his body, while the ignorant people have no power to bear the pain, as they identify themselves with their bodies. Indra, the king of the gods, beheaded sage Dadhīci—though the latter had caused no offence to the former. Dadhīci was brought to life, by Aśvinīkumāras, the twin sons of the sun who are supposed to be the physicians of the gods. But, when Indra demanded bones of Dadhīci, to make a thunderbolt, Dadhīci offered him his bones, by abandoning his body.

Here a question arises, that an enlightened soul, is prepared to remove the pain of others, while he shows indifference to his own bodily pain, and suggests it, that he lacks equanimity. The answer is, that this attitude is superior to equanimity, because it becomes his nature, without having the least unevenness of mind.

'Sa yogī paramo mataḥ'—That Yogī, is regarded as supreme, because he sees nothing but God pervading everywhere, all the time and remains established in union with Him.

An Exceptional Fact

(i) For a Yogī of meditation, it has been said, "He looks

on all as one, on the analogy of his own self." For a Yogī of Discipline of Action, it has been said, "He identifies his self, with the self of all beings" (5/7). For a Yogī of the Discipline of Knowledge, it has been said, "He is devoted to the welfare of all" (5/25, 12/4). But in the Discipline of Devotion, a devotee sees the Lord (the universal self) present, in all beings (6/30) and he worships Him through the performance of his own duty (18/46). It means, that a striver, following the Discipline of Action as well as Knowledge, should see his own self in all beings, while a striver following the Discipline of Devotion, should see the Lord, his beloved Deity, present in all beings.

(ii) A feeling of brotherhood is an excellent one. But, when self, interest comes in, as in the case of the Kauravas and Pāṇḍavas, this feeling of brotherhood changes into enmity. But he who looks on all alike, on the analogy of his own body, cannot have feelings of enmity, for anyone. For example, no one gets angry with the teeth or pulls them out, if they accidently happen to bite the tongue or lips. Similarly, an enlightened Yogī, has no enmity for anyone, he takes joys and sorrows of others, as his own. Superior to this feeling, is one that God is present in all beings. Thus a devotee sees his favourite Lord, everywhere. So, Lord Kṛṣṇa declares him to be superior to others. He says, "He is considered by Me to be, the best Yogī" (6/47), "I consider them to be the best Yogīs" (12/2), "Those devotees are extremely dear, to Me" (12/20) and so on.

Appendix—A common man sees the self in the body. He does not want pain in any organ, does not have aversion to any organ but regards all the organs as his own equally. Similarly a devotee beholds God in all beings and tries to alleviate their sufferings and to comfort them equally. He regards the objects, ability and power etc., not as his own but as God's. As the Ganges is worshipped with the water of the Ganges and the sun is worshipped with an earthen lamp, similarly a devotee offers the Lord's things in rendering service to Him—'tvadīyaṁ vastu govinda tubhyameva samarpaye'.

As having proper dealings with different organs of the body, a common man regards them as the self and tries to alleviate their pain and to comfort them equally. Similarly according to the saying 'as a deity, so the worship', dealings with a Brāhmaṇa and a pariah, with a sage and a butcher, with a cow and a dog will be different according to the ordinance of the scriptures but the devotee beholds God in all of them and so he tries to alleviate their sufferings and to comfort them equally without any distinction.

As a devotee assumes the identity of God with the soul of all beings (Gītā 6/31), similarly he assumes the identity of all bodies with his own body. Therefore he feels happy with the happiness of others and sad with the sadness of others—'para dukha dukha, sukha sukha dekhe para' (Mānasa, Uttara. 38/1). He like the joys and sorrows of his own body, takes the joys and sorrows of others as his own. 'To feel sad with the sadness of others' means to make efforts to alleviate the sorrows of others, rather than to become sad seeing them sad, similarly in order to be happy himself, he has not to alleviate the sorrows of others, but being compassionate he has to make efforts to make others happy. It means that he has not to enjoy happiness himself but he has to feel happy by seeing that the other person has got rid of sorrows and has become happy.

There is so much difference between the eyes and the feet that we see with eyes and we walk with feet, the eye is the sense of perception while the foot is the organ of action. In spite of so much difference, there is so much identity that a thorn runs into the foot and the eyes are filled with tears; dust falls into the eyes and the feet totter. It means that we can't separate the body from the world and can't separate the world from the body. Therefore if we take care of own body, similarly we should take care of the world; and if we are indifferent to the world, we should be indifferent to our body. Accept anyone of these two—this is honesty.

Link:—Lord Kṛṣṇa explained the Discipline of Meditation, as a means to attain equanimity, from the tenth verse to the thirty-second verse. A doubt arises in Arjuna's mind, and he puts it before Lord Kṛṣṇa, in the next two verses.

अर्जुन उवाच

योऽयं योगस्त्वया प्रोक्तः साम्येन मधुसूदन।
एतस्याहं न पश्यामि चञ्चलत्वात्स्थितिं स्थिराम्॥ ३३॥

arjuna uvāca

yo'yaṁ yogastvayā proktaḥ sāmyena madhusūdana
etasyāhaṁ na paśyāmi cañcalatvātsthitiṁ sthirām

Arjuna said:

O Kṛṣṇa, this Yoga of equanimity has been preached by You but I do not perceive its stability, due to restlessness of mind. 33

Comment:—

[Lord Kṛṣṇa, in the gospel of Gītā, has laid great emphasis on equanimity, in success and failure etc. This equanimity, leads a man to salvation. Arjuna was afraid of sins by waging war. So Lord Kṛṣṇa, exhorted him, "Treating alike pleasure and pain, gain and loss, victory and defeat, engage yourself in the battle. Thus you will incur no sin" (2/38). In this world, people incur so many sins, but we are not held responsible for these, because we are equanimous. Similarly, while performing actions and discharging our duty, if we remain equanimous, those actions do not lead us to bondage. Therefore, Lord Kṛṣṇa in the beginning of this chapter said, "He who discharges his duty, without expecting the fruit of actions, is a Sannyāsī and a Yogī." The result of renouncing the fruit of actions is equanimity. Lord Kṛṣṇa described, the Discipline of Meditation, as a means of attaining equanimity, from the tenth to the thirty-second verses. Keeping this equanimity in mind Arjuna puts forth his doubt before Lord Kṛṣṇa.]

'Yo'yaṁ yogastvayā proktaḥ sāmyena madhusūdana'—Here the doubt which Arjuna conveys to, Lord Krṣṇa, is not about the thirty-second verse, but about meditation, because in the thirty-second verse there is reference to an enlightened soul who is always equanimous. Therefore, here the word 'Yaḥ' (which) denotes, Yoga (equanimity) and 'Ayam' (this) denotes meditation, detailed from the tenth verse to the twenty-eighth verse.

'Etasyāhaṁ na paśyāmi cañcalatvātsthitiṁ sthirām'—Here, Arjuna seems to mean, that equanimity can be easily attained, by the Discipline of Action, but it is difficult by the Discipline of Meditation, owing to restlessness of mind.

It means, that a striver cannot concentrate his mind on God, so long as the mind is restless, and without concentration of mind, equanimity cannot be attained.

Link:—In the next verse, Arjuna describes the restless nature of mind, with the help of an illustration.

चञ्चलं हि मनः कृष्ण प्रमाथि बलवद्दृढम्।
तस्याहं निग्रहं मन्ये वायोरिव सुदुष्करम्॥ ३४॥

cañcalaṁ hi manaḥ krṣna pramāthi balavaddṛḍham
tasyāhaṁ nigrahaṁ manye vāyoriva suduṣkaram

The mind, verily is, O Kṛṣṇa, restless, turbulent, obstinate powerful therefore, I consider it as difficult to control, as the wind. 34

Comment:—

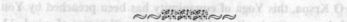

'Cañcalaṁ hi manaḥ kṛṣna pramāthi balavaddṛḍham'—Arjuna addresses the Lord as Kṛṣṇa, because He has the power of attraction. So, He should attract his mind and concentrate it on Him, because it is very difficult for him to control it, as it is unsteady and restless. Besides being restless, it is turbulent, it distracts a striver from the right course. Moreover, it is obstinate and strong.

According to Lord Kṛṣṇa, "Desire has five locals:—the senses, mind, intellect, sense-objects and self" (Gītā 3/40, 3/34, 2/59). Actually desire (Kāma) vests, in the embodied Self, but it seems to reside, in senses, mind and intellect etc. Unless it is removed from the self, it appears in the senses and mind etc., from time to time. But, when it is destroyed from the self, it does not appear anywhere. This proves, that so long as desire subsists in the self, the mind torments a striver. Therefore, the mind has been called turbulent. Similarly, the senses torment the mind, of a striver. So, the mind has been called turbulent, in the sixtieth verse of the second chapter. It means that when desire appears in the mind and senses, it torments the striver and does not allow him to remain established, in the self.

Because of the desire inhering in the self the mind is attracted intensely towards objects etc., and does not abandon them, in anyway. So it is called obstinate. This obstinacy of the mind is very strong, and so the mind is called strong. It forcibly distracts a striver, from his course and leads him to sensual pleasures. So it has been mentioned in scriptures, "Mind leads a man to emancipation, and bondage." But the mind, remains turbulent, obstinate and strong, so long as desire rests, in the self. When a striver himself, becomes free from desires, objects and senses do not affect him at all, and turbulence, obstinacy and strength of the mind, perish.

Restlessness of the mind, is an obstacle so long as, desire resides in the self. But when desire is rooted out, it is not an obstacle in the least. It is mentioned in the scriptures—

"When the feeling of egoism ('I'ness with matter) is rooted

out, and one realizes God, one's mind perceives God, everywhere viz., one attains by constant trance (natural trance)."

'Tasyā'haṁ nigrahaṁ manye vāyoriva suduṣkaram'—It is difficult to control, this restless, turbulent, strong and obstinate mind. As one cannot catch hold of wind, in the same way, mind cannot be controlled easily, it is very difficult to control it.

Appendix—The Lord in the twenty-ninth verse mentioned the experience of the striver who meditates on the self, while from the thirtieth to the thirty-second verses he mentioned the experience of the striver who meditates on God endowed with attributes and form. In these verses the Lord means that the final result of the discipline of meditation is to see the self or to see God in all. The Dhyānayogī, having the impression (latency) of knowledge, sees the self in all; while the Dhyānayogī, having the impression of devotion, sees God in all. To see the self in all is 'ātmajñāna' (Self-realization) and to see God in all is 'God-realization'. In Self-realization there is predominance of discrimination, in God-realization there is predominance of belief and faith, not the predominance of the steadiness of mind. But in Arjuna's mind the impression of the discipline of meditation mentioned from the tenth to the twenty-eighth verses was lingering. Therefore he regarded fickleness of the mind as an obstacle to Self-realization or to God-realization. He did'nt pay attention towards the impression of knowledge or devotion but he thought of the volatility of mind. Therefore he thought that volatility of mind was the obstacle to Self-realization or God-realization.

Link:—In the next verse, Lord Kṛṣṇa by supporting Arjuna's statement, explains the way of controlling the mind.

श्रीभगवानुवाच

असंशयं महाबाहो मनो दुर्निग्रहं चलम्।
अभ्यासेन तु कौन्तेय वैराग्येण च गृह्यते॥ ३५॥

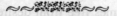

śrībhagavānuvāca

asaṁśayaṁ mahābāho mano durnigrahaṁ calam
abhyāsena tu kaunteya vairāgyeṇa ca gṛhyate

The Blessed Lord said:

Doubtless, O mighty-armed, the mind is restless and hard to control; but by practice and by dispassion O son of Kuntī, it can be done. 35

Comment:—

'Asaṁśayaṁ mahābāho mano durnigrahaṁ calam'—Lord Kṛṣṇa addresses him as 'Mahābāho' viz., mighty-armed, to tell him that he is brave, so he should maintain patience and courage and not lose heart. Moreover, He supports his statement, that undoubtedly mind, is restless and hard to control.

'Abhyāsena tu kaunteya vairāgyeṇa ca gṛhyate'—Arjuna's mother, Kuntī possessed discrimination and dispassion. She had demanded a boon of adversity, from Lord Kṛṣṇa.* Such cases are rare in history. So Lord Kṛṣṇa, wants to remind Arjuna, that he is the son of such a dispassionate mother. Being dispassionate, he should concentrate his mind, on God.

An earnest, regular and persistent attempt, to concentrate the mind on God, is called practice. This practice should be done with respect and adoration, for God by attaching importance to Him. This practice is of two kinds:—

(i) A striver should concentrate his mind on the target and being indifferent to thoughts, that come to mind.

(ii) A striver, should concentrate on his deity, wherever the mind wanders.

There are some other ways also, of concentrating the mind on God.

* O preceptor of the world, grant us adversity so that we may have your rare vision which may enable us not to be reborn.

(Śrīmadbhā. 1/8/25)

(1) A striver should exhale air two or three times, and then think that he has discarded the world of his mind, and so whatever thoughts will come to mind, will be a manifestation of God only—this is 'Vāsudevaḥ sarvam'.

(2) Recite the name of the Lord, and listen to it. There should not be any time-lag between the recitation of one name, and the next.

(3) Recite Gods name and count the number through the mind, without using fingers or a rosary of beads, to count.

(4) Recite, one, name of the Lord, as 'Rāma' (with the voice) and remember another name, as 'Kṛṣṇa' (within the mind).

(5) Chant the name within the mind.

(6) Think of a form of the Lord, from top to toe and from toe to top.

(7) Think that the Lord is standing before you. Think of His form. Write mentally, on His toes, five names, on the lower part of the leg, three names, a little above it, two names, a little above it three names, below and above the knee, one name each, on the thigh, three names, on the righthand side of the waist, two names, on the rib, three names, on the shoulder, two names, on the upper part of the arm, three names, above and below the elbow, two names in the form of a ring, on the five fingers five names, round the throat, four names as half of a garland, in the ear, two names as an earring, on the righthand side of the crown, six names, by making three rings.

Thus, by writing fifty-four names, on the righthand side and fifty-four names on the lefthand side, we think of all the limbs of the Lord and count the hundred and eight beads of a rosary. We can do this once or twice a day.

Thus, there are different methods of concentrating ones mind on God. A striver can also think of other means himself.

This practice of concentration, needs dispassion because the more dispassionate a man is, the easier it will be for him to concentrate his mind, on God. If he has no attachment for the world, he will not think of the world. If a thought, because of past influences, comes to his mind, he should become indifferent to it, without having any attachment or aversion. By doing so, the thought perishes. Thus by practice and dispassion, a mind can be controlled.

The Methods to Develop Dispassion

1. The world is kaleidoscopic, while the self never changes, in the least. We cannot live with the world and the world cannot live with us. Our babyhood, boyhood and youth, have passed. Similar, is the case with circumstances. By thinking of reality, we can become dispassionate.

2. We should satisfy, the just desires of our family and relations, according to our power, ability and resources, without hope of reward. Thus, old attachment is wiped out, and new attachment is not born.

3. We should think that all sins, crimes and pains, are the fruits of attachment, while peace and bliss, are the fruits of dispassion. By thinking so, we can develop dispassion.

Link:—In the next verse, Lord Kṛṣṇa explains, for whom this Yoga of meditation is possible, and for whom it is not possible.

असंयतात्मना योगो दुष्प्राप इति मे मतिः ।
वश्यात्मना तु यतता शक्योऽवाप्तुमुपायतः ॥ ३६ ॥

asaṁyatātmanā yogo duṣprāpa iti me matiḥ
vaśyātmanā tu yatatā śakyo'vāptumupāyataḥ

Yoga is hard to realise by one whose mind is not completely subdued but it can easily be achieved by him, who has controlled

his mind and who strives ceaselessly; such is My conviction. 36

Comment:—

'Asaṁyatātmanā yogo duṣprāpa'—It is my opinion, that Yoga is hard to attain, for one whose mind is not subdued, because restlessness of mind is not such a great obstacle, to attain Yoga as is the uncontrolled mind. As a chaste wife controls her mind but she does not concentrate. So too, a striver should control his mind. By controlling the mind, a striver, can concentrate on God.

Generally, strivers have a tendency to be engaged in spiritual discipline with faith, but they do not make persistent efforts, with the result, that their mind and senses, are not controlled and thus Yoga is difficult to attain. That is why even ever and everywhere present God is not easily attained.

Strivers have no disinclination for pleasures, as they have for the forbidden food, such as meat etc. Eating forbidden food, causes degradation. But enjoyment of sense-objects with attachment, causes much more degradation. In eating meat, strivers have a notion, that this is a prohibited item, but while enjoying sense-objects, they do not have this thought. Worldly pleasures leave their influence, which continues for ages and which induces them to incur sins. Due to this inclination for pleasures, they are unable to control their mind and senses, and so they find it difficult to attain Yoga.

'Vaśyātmanā tu yatatā śakyo'vāptumupāyataḥ'—Yoga can be attained, by him who has controlled his mind and who strives ceaselessly viz., one who is regulated in diet and recreation, sleep and wakefulness—such is My conviction.

A striver, who wants to control his mind, should understand that he is a devotee and a striver, not sensual, he is God's and so, he should take refuge in Him; he is a seeker after knowledge, and so he should obtain it; he is a servant and so he has to serve others, without having any desire. Thus, if a striver changes his ego, ('I'ness), the mind can easily be and quickly, controlled.

When mind is purified, it is controlled spontaneously. Attachment of mind for the perishable, is its impurity. When the striver has an exclusive aim, of God-realization, his attachment is renounced, and his mind becomes pure.

A striver should always be careful, he should never have, a claim on others' things etc., because by laying such a claim his mind becomes impure. In business, service or other transactions, he should never adopt foul means, he should never try to take the share of others, but he should give a part of his own share, to them. By doing so, his mind is purified.

A Vital Fact

In the Discipline of Meditation, Arjuna said, "Mind is restless, therefore, I consider it as difficult to control, as the wind." In response to this problem Lord Kṛṣṇa, offered a solution, by saying, "It can be controlled by practice and dispassion." Out of these two, for meditation, practice is more significant (Gītā 6/26), while in the Discipline of Knowledge, dispassion is more important. Though dispassion is helpful, in the Discipline of Meditation, yet in this discipline, mind can be controlled, even when attachment persists. According to the philosophy of Patañjali, one's mind can be controlled by practice. If dispassion is the cause of concentration, how can one gain accomplishments, or worldly fruits, by the concentration of mind? How concentration of mind could result in getting occult powers or worldly fruits unless one had a desire for them. If these were obtained as a result of concentration of mind, it proves that concentration can be had with desires subsisting in the mind. But when the aim is to realize God, concentration of the mind and a trance, are helpful in God-realization.

The next stage, after concentration of the mind, is trance. There is a minor deviation from the state of trance also. It means, that in that state there lingers affinity for matter. When this affinity breaks off, a striver realizes the Self, from where there is no deviation. Lord Kṛṣṇa, in the gospel of Gītā, did not talk much, about the concentration of the mind, because it was not His aim. Concentration of mind according to Him, is only a means to achieve an end, either mundane or spiritual, while attachment for the world, is the main obstacle to God-realization. Therefore, a striver should renounce his affinity for matter. First, a striver may have attraction for a trance, but when he attains a state of trance, he has no attraction for it, he becomes indifferent, to it. As soon as, he becomes indifferent to it, he gets established in the self, which is called the attainment of Yoga. This Yoga, (unity), is constant and eternal.

Appendix—In fact in order to attain perfection by the discipline of meditation, restraint of the mind is not so necessary as is its purification. 'Purification of the mind' means not to be attached to the sense-objects. He who has purified his mind, attains perfection by the discipline of meditation by making efforts.

Whatever the Lord said in the thirty-first verse by the expression 'sarvabhūtasthitaṁ yo māṁ bhajatyekatvamāsthitaḥ' in that the main obstacle is not to behold God in all beings and everywhere; and whatever the Lord declared in the thirty-second verse by the expression 'ātmaupamyena sarvatra samaṁ paśyati yo'rjuna'—the main obstacle is attachment and aversion. But Arjuna by an error thought the volatility of mind as an obstacle. In fact volatility of mind is 'not an obstacle but not to behold God in all beings and everywhere' and 'attachment-aversion' are obstacles. So long as attachment and aversion persist, a striver can't behold God in all beings and everywhere and as long as he does not behold God in all beings and everywhere viz., he has the assumption of any other entity besides God, the mind can't be totally restrained.

When a 'Vṛtti' is restrained, it means that there is existence of the 'Vṛtti'. Because we accept its existence that is why we think restraining it. In the self there is no 'Vṛtti'. Therefore if we restrain the 'Vṛtti' the mind will be restrained for sometime and again there will be relapse (deviation). If we don't assume any other entity besides God, then there is no question of relapse. The reason is that if there is no other entity, there is no question at all of the existence of mind even.

Link:—In the preceding verse, Lord Kṛṣṇa said, that Yoga is hard to attain for one whose mind is not completely subdued and who does not strive ceaselessly. So Arjuna, in the next two verses, puts question, about the fate of such an imperfect Yogī.

अर्जुन उवाच

अयतिः श्रद्धयोपेतो योगाच्चलितमानसः।
अप्राप्य योगसंसिद्धिं कां गतिं कृष्ण गच्छति॥ ३७॥

arjuna uvāca

ayatiḥ śraddhayopeto yogāccalitamānasaḥ
aprāpya yogasaṁsiddhiṁ kāṁ gatiṁ kṛṣṇa gacchati

Arjuna said:

O Kṛṣṇa, he who, though of faith, is lax in his striving and whose mind deviates from Yoga, having failed to attain perfection in it, what end does he meet? 37

Comment:—

'Ayatiḥ śraddhayopeto yogāccalitamānasaḥ'—One is imbued with the faith, that Yoga leads to perfection. So he performs adoration and meditation, with devotion and faith. But he does not strive ceaselessly, because he has not subdued his passions and controlled his mind. He, thinking of the sensual pleasures due to attachment for them, has not been able to attain, the goal of Yoga. What happens to such a striver, at the time of death?

'Aprāpya yogasaṁsiddhiṁ kāṁ gatiṁ kṛṣṇa gacchati'—What fate will the striver meet, whose mind has deviated from Yoga, and who has not realized God?

It means, that he did not incur sin, so he cannot go to hell. He cannot go to heaven either, because he has no desire for heaven. He cannot be reborn, because he performed worship and meditation, with interest and faith. But at the time of death other thought comes to his mind, and so he cannot think of God. What will happen to him?

By addressing the Lord as Kṛṣṇa, Arjuna means to say, that He who attracts all creatures is the controller of their destiny. Therefore, he asks Him in which direction, he will attract him and what fate he will meet with.

Appendix—In 'karaṇasāpekṣa' discipline (discipline dependent on instruments), a striver with mind, gets established in the self—'yadā viniyataṁ cittamātmanye vāvatiṣṭhate' (Gītā 6/18). Therefore by having connection with the mind, his mind deviates and so there is possibility of his falling from yoga. When a striver regards 'karaṇa' (instruments) as his own, then he practises 'karaṇasāpekṣa' discipline (discipline dependent on instruments). A Dhyānayogī by regarding the mind (karaṇa) as his own concentrates it on God. By fixing the mind, he falls from Yoga. Therefore the reason for his falling (deviating) from Yoga is dependence on instruments. This 'karaṇasāpekṣatā' (dependence on instruments) is not required in the three disciplines—Karmayoga, Jñānayoga and Bhaktiyoga.

A Dhyānayogī is reborn because of the deviation of the mind viz., by falling from His discipline; but a Karmayogī or a Jñānayogī is reborn because of the worldly attachment.

In Bhaktiyoga there is dependence on God, so He provides special protection to his devotee—'yogakṣemaṁ vahāmyaham' (Gītā 9/22), 'maccittaḥ sarvadurgāṇi matprasādāttariṣyasi' (Gītā 18/58).

कच्चिन्नोभयविभ्रष्टश्छिन्नाभ्रमिव नश्यति।
अप्रतिष्ठो महाबाहो विमूढो ब्रह्मणः पथि॥ ३८॥

kaccinnobhayavibhraṣṭaśchinnābhramiva naśyati
apratiṣṭho mahābāho vimūḍho brahmaṇaḥ pathi

O mighty-armed, the deluded and fallen in the path of God, without any hold, upon the world does he not perish like a broken cloud, deprived of both God-realization and worldly enjoyment? 38

Comment:—

[Arjuna seeks clarification, about the fate of a striver who has failed to attain perfection in Yoga.]

'Apratiṣṭho mahābāho vimūḍho brahmaṇaḥ pathi'—He renounces the desire, for worldly pleasures, honour and praise etc., and follows a spiritual discipline. But, he is not able to realize God, and at the time of death deviates, from Yoga viz., does not think of God.

'Kaccinnobhayavibhraṣṭaśchinnābhramiva naśyati'—Does he not perish like a broken cloud, deprived of both God-realization and worldly enjoyments? A split cloud does not descend on earth as rain, is separated from the main body and cannot join the other parts. Thus it is shattered. In similar the fate of a striver who renounces his dependence on the world, but at the same time fails to realize God? Does he meet with damnation?

Here, the illustration of a cloud is not quite apt, because a part of a cloud and the main body of clouds and the part to which it was going to rejoin—all the three belong to the same class, they are matter. But in the case of a striver, the world is matter (insentient), while he himself and God, are sentient. Thus they do not belong, to the same category.

In this verse, Arjuna means to say, that the soul being a fragment of God, is imperishable. If it has the aim to attain heaven, it might have gone to heaven or hell or the other lower births of beasts and birds, but still would have remained in the world. What is the fate of a striver, who has renounced dependence on the world with the aim of attaining God, but could not realize the same and at the time of death, could not think of God?

An Exceptional Fact

Here failing in both does not mean that he has fallen from Yoga as well as God-realization. A striver cannot have a downfall, if he has attained God-realization. Here the illustration of a cloud, with a part separated from the main body and not joining the other clouds and is scattered in between the two, is not very apt, as a striver, who has not yet realized. God cannot be said, to have fallen from God-realization. Moreover, once God-realization is attained, there is no question of being detached from it. Thus, if a person fails to think of God at the last moment, he may be said to have failed in attaining God, but he cannot be said to have failed in both i.e., Yoga and God-realization. Therefore fallen from both here means that he is deprived of both God-realization and worldly enjoyments. Arjuna has also dwelt upon the same point, in the thirty-seventh verse. Thus a striver can deviate from Yoga, only if he has not realized God. After God-realization, there is no question of deviation or downfall from Yoga.

Link:—In the next verse, Arjuna prays to Lord Kṛṣṇa to dispel his doubt, expressed in the previous verse.

एतन्मे संशयं कृष्ण छेत्तुमर्हस्यशेषतः।
त्वदन्यः संशयस्यास्य छेत्ता न ह्युपपद्यते॥ ३९॥

etanme saṁśayaṁ kṛṣṇa chettumarhasyaśeṣataḥ
tvadanyaḥ saṁśayasyāsya chettā na hyupapadyate

O Kṛṣṇa, please dispel this doubt of mine completely; for who other than Yourself, can do so? 39

Comment:—

'Etanme saṁśayaṁ kṛṣṇa chettumarhasyaśeṣataḥ'—A striver having the aim of God-realization, becomes free from sins, and so cannot go to hell. He cannot go to heaven, because he has no such aim. He cannot be reborn as a man, because this is also not the aim of his life. He deviates from the path of God-realization. Does such a striver not perish like a broken cloud?

'Tvadanyaḥ saṁśayasyāsya chettā na hyupapadyate'—No one can dispel this doubt completely. This puzzle of the scriptures, can be solved by scholars, possessing knowledge. A Yogī, who has attained this state by practice, can know the solution to a certain extent. But You are omniscient, You know the fate and end of all creatures.* So You can dispel this doubt of mine, completely says Arjuna.

Appendix—Arjuna believed that Śrī Kṛṣṇa was an incarnation of God, so here he puts the question to Him about the Dhyānayogī, what fate he meets if his mind deviates from Yoga and also tells him that no one else can dispel this doubt besides Him. It is because of his belief that Śrī Kṛṣṇa was God that he shunning the Lord's Nārāyaṇī army well-equipped with arms and ammunition consisting of 109350 foot soldiers, 65610 horses, 21870 chariots and 21870 elephants welcomed unarmed Lord Kṛṣṇa on his side.

Link:—In the next verse, Lord Kṛṣṇa clears the doubt, raised by Arjuna.

श्रीभगवानुवाच

पार्थ नैवेह नामुत्र विनाशस्तस्य विद्यते।
न हि कल्याणकृत्कश्चिद्दुर्गतिं तात गच्छति॥४०॥

* Bhagavān (God) is He Who knows about birth and death, good-fate and ill-fate, knowledge and ignorance of all creatures.

(*Viṣṇu Purāṇa* 6/5/78; *Nārada Purāṇa, Pūrva.* 46/21)

śrībhagavānuvāca

pārtha naiveha nāmutra vināśastasya vidyate
na hi kalyāṇakṛtkaściddurgatiṁ tāta gacchati

The Blessed Lord said:

O Pārtha, there is no fall for him, either here or hereafter; for none who works for self-redemption, meets with an evil end. 40

Comment:—

[Arjuna is much anxious, to know the end of a striver, who has failed to attain perfection, in Yoga. Lord Kṛṣṇa knows Arjuna's anxiety and so He removes it.]

'Pārtha naiveha nāmutra vināśastasya vidyate'—O son of Pṛthā, a striver who deviates from Yoga, never falls (Gītā 6/41—45). It means that he does not go to a state, inferior to what he has already attained. His spiritual practice, and aim go with him, to his next birth and he will not take birth, again and again.

Sage Bharata, by renouncing his kingdom observed penance, in seclusion. There, out of pity, he was attached to a young deer, with the result that he had to get birth, as a deer. But he did not fall to a state inferior to what he had already attained, even in the life of a deer. In that life also, it remembered its past (Śrīmadbhāgavata Section V, Chapter VII, VIII). Similarly, one who practises Yoga, but fails to attain perfection, may get birth even as an animal, but does not fall to a state inferior to what he has already attained, as he retains the spiritual propensities, stored up in the previous birth. This draws him towards God. I myself have observed a dog sitting with devotees, listening to religious discourses and moving about, with a group of devotees, who were chanting, the Lord's name loudly.

'Na hi kalyāṇakṛtkaściddurgatiṁ tāta gacchati'—Here 'tāta', a word of endearment, has been used. In the whole Gītā, this word has been used only once. It shows Lord Kṛṣṇa's great affection and grace, for Arjuna. The pronouncement of the Lord, is a great assurance for all strivers, "The doer of good never comes to grief", or 'One who works for self-redemption, never meets with an evil fate'. It means, that a striver who, without being attached to pleasure and prosperity, and engaged, in spiritual discipline to attain God-realization, has no fall, because He is his saviour.

One, who is engrossed in the welfare of all creatures, and thinks of God-realization, is the most loving to Him, because he is His fragment. So he has a real affinity for Him. How can he meet with ill fate? Sometimes, it may seem, that he had fallen to a state inferior to what he had already attained. But it so happens, because of his pride. The Lord, gives him a warning, so that he may be aware of his state and turn towards Him again with zeal. Lord Kṛṣṇa disappeared during His drama (pastime) of human life, from the midst of the Gopīs. At that time, they were very much perturbed and were at their wits end. Then He reappeared again and said to them, that He had disappeared adoring them (Śrīmadbhā. 10/32/21). Their welfare and memory were lingering, in Him. When a person is inclined towards Him, he is most loving to Him because He thinks that after having lost his way for long however he has started following the right way. God, like a mother, always promotes the welfare of a devotee.

It means that feelings of spirituality once germinated, cannot be wiped out, because whatever is done for God, becomes real (Gītā 17/27) viz., the real never ceases to be (Gītā 2/16). Therefore, Lord Kṛṣṇa says, that one who works for self-redemption never meets with an evil destiny, because the impressions of the past, always inspire him towards spirituality. Even, if one goes to lower births, his nature will be superior, to that of other members of his class.*

Though Arjuna puts the question, "What end, does a striver

* One whose nature has been good cannot take birth as a harmful poisonous creature such as a snake or a scorpion etc.

meet, at the time of death?" Yet Lord Kṛṣṇa answers, that there is no fall for him, here or hereafter. Now a question arises, why Ajāmila and Bilvamaṅgala, were overpowered by prostitutes, and why there was a fall for them. The answer is, that people thought that they had a fall, but actually it was not so. After leaving the body, Ajāmila was escorted by courtiers of the Lord; and Bilvamaṅgala, became a devotee of God. A devotee, following spiritual discipline, may seem to have been degraded sometimes, because of his carelessness. But, he never falls to a state inferior to what he has already attained. If he happens to have association, with the good or misfortune befalls him, he again starts following the spiritual path, speedily.* But delay in God-realization is indeed, a kind of downfall for him. Bad company etc., are decidedly obstacles for a striver, to spiritual progress. So he should always beware of bad company, and should never be overpowered by sensual pleasures and lust etc.

Link:—In the previous verse, Lord Kṛṣṇa assured Arjuna, that there is no fall for a striver, either here or hereafter, and he never meets with an evil destiny. Now, Lord Kṛṣṇa in the next verse, answers the question put by Arjuna, in the thirty-seventh verse, about a striver who has failed to attain perfection, in Yoga.

प्राप्य पुण्यकृतां लोकानुषित्वा शाश्वतीः समाः।
शुचीनां श्रीमतां गेहे योगभ्रष्टोऽभिजायते॥ ४१॥

prāpya puṇyakṛtāṁ lokānuṣitvā śāśvatīḥ samāḥ
śucīnāṁ śrīmatāṁ gehe yogabhraṣṭo'bhijāyate

The fallen Yogī having attained to the world of the righteous

* If such a person by accident falls into bad company, he does not abandon his virtues as a snake does not abandon the jewel which exists in its head (Mānasa 1/3/5).

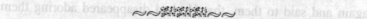

and having lived there for countless years, is reborn in the house of the pious and prosperous. 41

Comment:—

'Prāpya puṇyakṛtāṁ lokān'—Those people, who make offerings etc., in accordance with the ordinance of scriptures, attain the worlds of the righteous viz., heaven. It means, that the righteous not the sinners, attain heaven. But strivers who have no desire to reap the fruit of their virtuous actions, attain heaven without much effort, while people who perform oblation, attain heaven by making efforts. Moreover, in heaven also, their subtle passion lingers, because their aim is to enjoy pleasure. Those, who at the time of death, deviate from Yoga, attain heaven, but they become indifferent to pleasures, as their aim is not to enjoy pleasure. They have to go to heaven, because of their subtle desire, which is an obstacle to God-realization.

'Uṣitvā śāśvatīḥ samāḥ'—Heaven, is attained, both by those who perform penances and actions with some interested motive, as also, by those whose aim is to realize God, but deviate from Yoga. However there is a vast difference, between the two. The former, having enjoyed heavenly pleasures, return to this world of mortals on the exhaustion of their merit, and thus they can stay there for a limited period only, while the latter, can stay for an unlimited period, because their aim has been God-realization. Because of having a latent desire they go to heaven, but they cannot be entangled in pleasure there. And their spiritual development is not affected. The reason is, when even a seeker of the Yoga, transcends the fruit of actions (6/44), how can one, who has deviated from Yoga, get entangled?

'Śucīnāṁ śrīmatāṁ gehe yogabhraṣṭo'bhijāyate'—The devotee, who has deviated from Yoga after enjoying celestial pleasures, ceases to have any taste in them and is reborn in the house of the pure and prosperous, as a result of his sacred and spiritual pursuits. There he, though subject to senses, feels drawn towards

God, by force of his prenatal habit (6/44).

The pious and prosperous, are those who earn their livelihood by honest means, who never have a claim on other's things, whose conduct and feelings are pure, who do not attach importance, to worldly pleasures and who regard all the resources, as means to attain God; while those who regard themselves, as master of riches and lay claim to them, are not indeed pious and prosperous, but are their slaves.

Link:—In the next verse, Lord Kṛṣṇa of His own accord, describes the destiny of other strivers, who fall from Yoga.

अथवा योगिनामेव कुले भवति धीमताम्।
एतद्धि दुर्लभतरं लोके जन्म यदीदृशम्॥ ४२॥

athavā yogināmeva kule bhavati dhīmatām
etaddhi durlabhataraṁ loke janma yadīdṛśam

Or (if he has developed dispassion) he is born in a family of enlightened Yogīs; but this kind of birth is very difficult to have in this world. 42

Comment:—

[There are two kinds of strivers—with having subtle desires, and without such desires. The striver, whose aim is to realize God and is interested in spirituality, but his desires have not been wiped out completely, after living for countless years in heaven, is reborn in the house of the pious and prosperous. This type of striver, has already been described in the previous verse. In this verse, there is a description of the striver, who is free from desire, has developed dispassion, has only, the aim of God-realization and practises Yoga, but has not attained perfection and deviated from Yoga. Such a striver, instead of going to heaven, directly takes birth in a family of enlightened Yogīs.]

'Athavā'—I have answered your question, about a striver who deviates from Yoga, at the time of death. Now I want to tell you about a dispassionate striver, who has disinclination for the world, and is interested in spiritual perfection, but at the time of death however if he deviates from Yoga.

'Yogināmeva kule bhavati dhīmatām'—The dispassionate striver, is born in the family of the enlightened Yogīs, who have realized God and whose intellects are fixed in Him. It is mentioned in the scriptures that the beings born in the family of the enlightened Yogīs must get enlightenment (Muṇḍaka. 3/2/9).

'Etaddhi durlabhataraṁ loke janma yadīdṛśam'—Such a birth, is very difficult to obtain in this world. In the family of enlightened Yogīs strivers get a favourable environment, which draws out the latent Yoga element in them, and leads them rapidly towards their goal.

An Exceptional Fact

In the verse 'Etat' refers to a striver born in the family of the enlightened Yogīs, while 'Īdṛśam' means that he has got a chance to have company of the enlightened Yogīs. In the world, there are two kinds of people 'Binduja' and 'Nādaja'. Those who are born of ovum and sperm of parents are called 'Binduja', while those who start following the spiritual path by the preaching of great souls, are 'Nādaja'. Here, he who is born in a family of enlightened Yogīs after falling from Yoga, is 'Binduja' while the striver who gets an opportunity to have the company of liberated souls, is 'Nādaja'.

In the scriptures, it is mentioned that it is difficult to obtain human life, but it is even more difficult to have company of great souls. Nāradajī, has also written in his book 'Bhaktisūtra' that the company of great souls, is very difficult, inaccessible and infallible. The reason is, that great souls are very rare, and if by God's grace one gets their company,* it is difficult to recognise them. But the company of great souls, never goes in vain.

Link:—In the above verse, Lord Kṛṣṇa stated that a dispassionate striver, takes birth in the family of enlightened Yogīs. In the next verse, He explains what happens to him after his birth, there.

तत्र तं बुद्धिसंयोगं लभते पौर्वदेहिकम्।
यतते च ततो भूयः संसिद्धौ कुरुनन्दन॥४३॥

tatra taṁ buddhisaṁyogaṁ labhate paurvadehikam
yatate ca tato bhūyaḥ saṁsiddhau kurunandana

There he regains knowledge of the previous birth and he strives more than ever before for perfection, O joy of the Kurus. 43

Comment:—

'Tatra taṁ buddhisaṁyogaṁ labhate paurvadehikam'—The term 'Tatra' (there) has been used to describe the condition of the dispassionate striver after his birth in the family of the enlightened souls.

'Paurvadehikam'—(Acquired in the former body) and 'Buddhisaṁyogam' (spiritual discernment) phrases mean, that the dispassionate striver, does not go to heaven, but is born in a family of enlightened Yogīs, where he regains knowledge of the previous birth, and is naturally drawn towards God, because of the impressions and latencies of the previous birth and continues to practise Yoga. A traveller, while travelling on foot feels tired, and sleeps on one side of a footpath. But, when he awakes, he has not to cover the distance, which he has already covered. Similarly a striver, regains the knowledge of the previous birth. He is like a student, who goes through old lessons and grasps these immediately. Thus, favourable impressions of the previous birth, are aroused in him.

'Yatate ca tato bhūyaḥ saṁsiddhau'—In favourable surroundings, a striver tries harder, than before, for perfection.

If we interpret, that both kinds of strivers, who deviate from Yoga, go to heaven, and out of them, the one who has desire for pleasure is born, in the house of pious and prosperous, while the other who has no lust is born in a family of enlightened Yogīs, will it make any difference? Yes, it will. We cannot call the striver, 'Paurvadehika' (of the former body) if he is reborn after going to heaven, because the duration of his stay in heaven, will come in between the two births. Moreover, in heaven he cannot have union with knowledge, because there is abundance of pleasure, in heaven.

There is one more point, which needs attention. A striver, having lust goes to heaven. But why should a striver who is free from passion and lust, go to heaven? It is a kind of punishment to send, such a striver to heaven, which is fully unjustified.

Appendix—The spiritual progress pertains to the self and the mundane progress pertains to the non-self. Therefore the worldly wealth gets destroyed but the spiritual wealth is not destroyed even by falling (deviating) from Yoga. The spiritual progress can be veiled but cannot be destroyed and is revealed at times.

The impressions of the spiritual practice of the previous life that are settled (left) in a striver's intellect, have been called here 'buddhisaṁyoga'.

Link:—In the previous verse, Lord Kṛṣṇa explained that a striver who is born in a family of enlightened Yogīs regains, knowledge of the previous birth and strives more than before, for perfection. Now he describes the striver who deviates from Yoga, and is born in the house of the pious and prosperous.

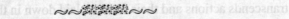

पूर्वाभ्यासेन तेनैव ह्रियते ह्यवशोऽपि सः।
जिज्ञासुरपि योगस्य शब्दब्रह्मातिवर्तते ॥ ४४ ॥

pūrvābhyāsena tenaiva hriyate hyavaśo'pi saḥ
jijñāsurapi yogasya śabdabrahmātivartate

One who takes birth in the house of the prosperous, though subject to the senses, is drawn towards God because of the former practice; as even seeker of the Yoga of equanimity also transcends the fruit of Vedic rituals performed with some motive. 44

Comment:—

'Pūrvābhyāsena tenaiva hriyate hyavaśo'pi saḥ'—A striver, who is born in the house of the pious and prosperous, does not get such a favourable environment and company, as the one who is born in the house of enlightened Yogīs, yet because of sacred and spiritual propensity stored up in the previous birth, he is drawn towards God, in spite of his attachment to pleasures.

'Avaśo'pi' means, that though he has lived in heaven for countless years and enjoyed pleasure there, and in the house of the prosperous also, there are pleasures in abundance, he is overpowered by his senses. In spite of all this, he is drawn towards God, by force of the practice of the previous births. The reason is, that the passion for pleasure is unreal, while the influence of the spiritual life, is real. So the real influence draws the striver, who deviates from Yoga, towards God.

'Jijñāsurapi yogasya śabdabrahmātivartate'—In this verse, Lord Kṛṣṇa explains the importance of a seeker of Yoga, in order to describe the importance of the Yogī. When the seeker of Yoga, transcends actions and their fruits as laid down in the Vedas, how can he having a firm determination for God-realization, have a fall? He will surely, attain salvation or God-realization.

The seeker of Yoga is he who attaches more importance to Yoga than pleasures and prosperity but his desire for pleasures and prosperity has not been wiped out. He has not attained perfection (to Yoga) and is a seeker of Yoga. Even such a seeker transcends the actions and their fruits. Then the striver who has deviated from Yoga is far superior to the seeker. The same fact has been explained by Lord Kṛṣṇa in the fortieth verse of the second chapter when He declares, "In this path of Yoga (equanimity) there is no loss of effort and even a little practice of this discipline protects one from great fear (of birth and death) viz., leads him to salvation." Thus the one who practises Yoga cannot have a fall, he will undoubtedly attain perfection or salvation.

An Exceptional Fact

(i) Such strivers who practise Yoga but deviate from it are very rare. Among thousands of people scarcely one strives for perfection (Gītā 7/3) and it is he who deviates from Yoga. There is great glory of such strivers. Even the seeker of the Yoga transcends the fruits of actions viz., he develops disinclination even for the highest level of celestial existence, the Brahmaloka (the abode of Brahmā), because all the worlds including that of Brahmā involve return and rebirth while he does not want rebirth. When there is so much glory of the seeker of Yoga, how far superior should the striver who practises Yoga, be? The reason is that his aim has been to attain Yoga (equanimity) though at the time of death he has deviated from Yoga.

Therefore, if a striver has an exclusive aim to attain God-realization, he will transcend the fruits of actions, performed with some motive as laid down in the Vedas.

(ii) Even if a striver fails to attain equanimity, he should have it as his aim. As Tulasīdāsajī has said in the Rāmacaritamānasa about himself that he is a man of the meaner sort but his ambition is very high, he wants to get nectar though even butter milk is not available to him (1/8/4). It means that the striver should have a lofty aim and he should have a keen desire to achieve that aim. It is God's nature that He does not mind the error of action of the striver but He notices what he wants, feels, aims and remembers hundreds of times what he has in his heart and is pleased with it (1/29/2-3).

A blind saint went to a temple to behold the Lord. One day a person asked him why he had gone to the temple when he was unable to see the Lord. The saint replied, "It is true that I am unable to see Him. But is He also unable to see me? My purpose is served when He beholds me."

Similarly, we may not attain equanimity but we should have an aim to attain it. By doing so our purpose will be served because God is omniscient and He knows what a striver has in his heart.

Appendix—The worldly virtues (such as feeding poor etc., with desire for fruit) are virtues contrary to sins but the divine virtues inculcated through association with God are extraordinary. Therefore the worldly virtues do not draw a man towards God; but the virtues pertaining to God, draw man towards God. These virtues are not dissipated by bearing fruit (Gītā 2/40). Renunciation of worldly desires and inclination towards God—these two are virtues pertaining to God.

'Pūrvābhyāsena tenaiva'—This expression means that though in the present life the striver does not get an opportunity of good company and good discussion pertaining to God, yet because of the past latencies he is drawn towards God. In this past practice there is no action (pravṛtti) but there is (automatic progress) 'gati'.* In 'jijñāsurapi yogasya śabdabrahmātivartate' also there is no practice of action but there is progress as 'gati'. It means that in this practice there is no effort and there is no doership

* In order to know the distinction between 'Pravṛtti' and 'Gati' vide appendix to the sixth verse of the fifteenth chapter (6/45).

but there is 'gati' (automatic elevation). In 'gati' there is the power of attracting a striver towards God. An endeavour for spiritual gain is an action while 'gati' automatically goes on (due to past latencies).

Link:—Now Lord Kṛṣṇa in the next verse describes the condition of the striver who having deviated from Yoga and taken birth in the house of the pious and prosperous, is drawn towards God.

प्रयत्नाद्यतमानस्तु योगी संशुद्धकिल्बिषः ।
अनेकजन्मसंसिद्धस्ततो याति परां गतिम् ॥ ४५ ॥

prayatnādyatamānastu yogī saṁśuddhakilbiṣaḥ
anekajanmasaṁsiddhastato yāti parāṁ gatim

A Yogī who strives painstakingly, and purified from sins and perfected through more than one birth, reaches the Supreme state. 45

Comment:—

[A dispassionate striver who deviates from Yoga by taking birth in the family of enlightened Yogīs and striving more than before attains perfection or God-realization. But how the striver taking birth in the house of the pious and prosperous realizes God, is elucidated in this verse.]

'Tu'—It means when the seeker of the Yoga of equanimity transcends the fruit of actions performed with some motive as laid down in the Vedas, why the Yogī who strives with assiduity should not transcend the fruit of actions and attain perfection. He will attain the Supreme Goal without doubt.

'Yogī'—Yogī is he who wants to attain equanimity or God-realization and who does not get entangled in the pairs of opposites such as attachment and aversion, pleasures and pain etc.

'Prayatnādyatamānaḥ'—It means that he very assiduously and promptly strives for perfection and his spirituality progresses steadily. He remains constantly conscious that he has to follow this path.

The striver deviating from Yoga takes birth in the house of the pious and prosperous and is drawn on one side towards God by force of the former practice, while on the other side towards the world because of the worldly temptation. If he by diligent efforts and manly behaviour renounces worldly pleasures, he will realize God. The reason is that when even a seeker of Yoga transcends the fruit of action, why will a Yogī who strives with assiduity not realize God? As a person engaged in forbidden action after getting a shock, deviates from it and strives more for God-realization, a striver by taking birth in the house of the pious and prosperous strives hard for God-realization.

'Saṁśuddhakilbiṣaḥ'—By striving for God-realization, he is purged of all sins viz., his desire for pleasures, prosperity, praise and honour etc., is completely wiped out. His diligent efforts reveal that he is purged of all sins.

'Anekajanmasaṁsiddhaḥ'*—Spirituality has enhanced in him through successive births. He has been purified from sins in the human birth by practising Yoga, in the second birth in heaven by having disinclination for pleasures, and in the third birth in the house of the pious and prosperous by striving assiduously for God-realization. Thus he is purified from sins through many births.† Here many births denote these three births.

* 'Anekajanma' (many births) means more than one birth.

† Similarly, a dispassionate striver who has deviated from Yoga is purged of sins first by being dispassionate and secondly by striving promptly for God-realization by getting birth in the family of the Yogī. Thus these two births are many births for him.

'Tato yāti parāṁ gatim'—Therefore, he reaches the supreme state. It means that he attains the Supreme Bliss, by gaining which he does not reckon any other gain greater than that, and wherein established he is not moved even by the heaviest affliction (Gītā 6/22).

A Vital Fact

In fact every human being has passed through many births already. Therefore he has been called 'Aneka-janma-saṁsiddha'. In heaven he enjoyed the fruit of his virtuous actions and thus was purged of virtues. In hells by suffering tortures he was purged of sins. Similarly, in the eighty-four lac forms of lives by getting the fruit of his sinful actions he was purged of sins.* Thus by being purified from virtues and sins he has perfected himself.

Secondly, a human being by striving assiduously can attain the Supreme State or Supreme Goal because the Lord by His grace has bestowed upon him this human birth, the very last of all births so that he may attain the Supreme Bliss. Therefore, every person should strive assiduously to attain perfection or the Supreme Bliss.

Link:—In the next verse Lord Kṛṣṇa describes glory of Yoga.

तपस्विभ्योऽधिको योगी ज्ञानिभ्योऽपि मतोऽधिकः।
कर्मिभ्यश्चाधिको योगी तस्माद्योगी भवार्जुन॥ ४६॥

tapasvibhyo'dhiko yogī jñānibhyo'pi mato'dhikaḥ
karmibhyaścādhiko yogī tasmādyogī bhavārjuna

The Yogī is superior to ascetics (not devoid of desires), superior

* A man becomes impure by misusing this human life meant for salvation by doing sins and injustice. In heaven, hell and other births he is only purified.

to men of learning (Śāstras); and also superior to the ritualists. Therefore, Arjuna, do be a Yogī. 46

Comment:—

'Tapasvibhyo'dhiko yogī'—An ascetic, is one who bears hardships voluntarily, in order to obtain power and enjoyment, here and hereafter. A Yogī, is deemed superior to such ascetics, because he through desirelessness, attains the Supreme Goal.

'Jñānibhyo'pi mato'dhikaḥ'—'Jñānī' (men of learning), in this context are those, who possess knowledge of scriptures, such as the knowledge of the Disciplines of Knowledge, Action and Devotion etc., and deliver discourses, but whose aim, is to enjoy pleasure and prosperity. A Yogī, is superior to such men of learning.

'Karmibhyaścādhiko yogī'—A Yogī, is superior to those ritualists, who perform elaborate rituals, such as sacrifice, charity, and pilgrimage etc., in order to, obtain pleasure and prosperity etc., here and hereafter, because the Yogī's aim is to realize God, while the ritualists has a desire, for worldly enjoyments etc.

Thus a Yogī, is superior to ascetics, also men of learning and ritualists, because his aim is to attain God-realization, while others' aim, is to enjoy worldly pleasure and prosperity etc. Ascetics, men of learning and ritualists—all the three, are engaged in activities. Forbearance in ascetics, learning in Jñānīs, and rituals, in ritualists are special characteristics of the three. All the three, having selfish interests, are not Yogīs but Bhogīs (sensuous). If they had been selfless Yogīs, God would have neither compared them with a Yogī, nor would He have declared, a Yogī superior to them.

'Tasmādyogī bhavārjuna'—Therefore, Arjuna, be a Yogī free from attachment and aversion viz., remain detached just like a lotus leaf which though constantly in touch with water, does not permit being wetted with it. The same fact, has been explained by Lord Kṛṣṇa when He declares, "Be established in Yoga, O Arjuna" (Gītā 8/27).

In the beginning of the fifth chapter, Arjuna asked Lord Kṛṣṇa, "Which of the two renunciation of action (Sāṅkhyayoga), or performance of action (Karmayoga), is better?" In response to his question Lord Kṛṣṇa explained Sāṅkhyayoga (the Discipline of Knowledge), Karmayoga (the Discipline of Action) and Dhyānayoga (the Discipline of Meditation). But He, before this verse, did not advise him to be a Yogī. It is only here that He directs him to be a Yogī, because it is decidedly good for him.

Appendix—There are two different spheres—one for 'Bhogīs' (voluptuary) and the other for 'Yogīs'. A 'Bhogī' is not a 'Yogī' and a 'Yogī' is not a 'Bhogī'. Those who work with an interested motive are 'Bhogīs'; while those who work in a disinterested manner are 'Yogīs'. Therefore a Yogī, who has no desire for fruit, is superior to ascetics, men of learning and ritualists who have selfish motives.

Link:—In the previous verse, Lord Kṛṣṇa praised a Yogī and, ordered Arjuna to be a Yogī. But Lord Kṛṣṇa, did not explain which Yogī—of Action or Knowledge or Meditation or Devotion, he should be. Therefore, Lord Kṛṣṇa, in the next verse orders him to be a Yogī of Devotion.

योगिनामपि सर्वेषां मद्गतेनान्तरात्मना।
श्रद्धावान्भजते यो मां स मे युक्ततमो मतः ॥ ४७ ॥

yogināmapi sarveṣāṁ madgatenāntarātmanā
śraddhāvānbhajate yo māṁ sa me yuktatamo mataḥ

Of all Yogīs, he who devoutly worships Me, with his mind focussed on Me, is considered by Me to be the most superior Yogī

or the most devout one. 47

Comment:—

'Yogināmapi sarveṣām'—Those Yogīs, who want to break off their affinity for Matter and practise the Disciplines of Action, Knowledge and Meditation etc., are superior to ascetics, and ritualists etc. But he who devoutly worships Me, is the best of all.

'Yaḥ śraddhāvān'—He, who has faith only in Me, and My glory, and existence, worships Me, with his mind focussed on Me.

'Madgatenāntarātmanā māṁ bhajate'—When a striver, accepts the affinity that he is God's and God is his, his mind gets engrossed, in God automatically. As the mind of a girl after her marriage is absorbed in the affairs of the house, of her father-in-law, a devotee's mind gets absorbed in God, without making any effort. His mind, while he performs several duties of his routine, clings to God, automatically.

All activities, whether spiritual such as meditation, worship etc., or secular, such as eating, sleeping or pertaining to livelihood, such as farming, business or service etc., of a devotee, who becomes only God's, without having any attachment for the world, are included in adoration.

Lord Kṛṣṇa in the fifty-fifth verse of the eleventh chapter, explains the traits of a devotee having exclusive devotion to God, who works for the Lord's sake, depends on Him, is devoted to Him, is free from attachment and is without hatred, for any being.

'Sa me yuktatamo mataḥ'—All strivers, who having disinclination for the world, are inclined towards spirituality, and want to realize God, are devout. Those, who seek refuge in the Lord, who is endowed with attributes, but is formless viz., all-pervading Lord, are more devout. However, those who take refuge in the Lord, Who is endowed with attributes, are the most devout.

A devotee, who is most devout, will get mastery over all kinds of disciplines, (Yogas) such as of Action, Knowledge and Devotion etc., because God is the great Lord of all the Yogas (disciplines), and when a devotee takes refuge in Him, he becomes the most devout.

The most devout, devotee never falls from Yoga, because his mind never abandons the Lord, and therefore, the Lord also does not abandon him. At the time of death, because of unconsciousness or much pain, if he is unable to think of God, God thinks of him.* So how can he fall from Yoga?

It means, that a devotee who wholeheartedly depends on God without depending on anyone else, or even on his efforts does not fall from Yoga. God does not let him down. But, he who attaches value to worldly things and relies on his efforts, for him there is possibility to fall from Yoga. His fall, may be due to his mind's diversion towards the world. A devotee, does not fall because at the time of death, he calls the Lord due to his sole dependence on Him. Even if he is unable to think of the Lord, the Lord thinks of him, because of his exclusive devotion and thus he instead of falling, from Yoga, attains Him.

The Lord declares, such a Yogī is the most devout Yogī. It does not mean, that other Yogīs do not attain Yoga. It means, that though all the Yogīs by breaking off their affinity for the world, become completely free from bondage and sins, and attain the Supreme Bliss, yet, spiritual love manifests itself in him, who becomes God's and that love accelerates every moment without any decay, extinction and satiation. It is because of

* The Lord declares—"I myself think of the wood-like and stone-like devotee at the time of his death and bestow upon him the Supreme State. If a devotee at the time of death because of phlegm and wind etc., can't think of Me, I Myself think of him. If I don't do so, no one else can be more ungrateful than I."

this manifestation, that the Lord regards, such a devotee, as the most devout.

In the beginning of the fifth chapter, Arjuna asked Lord Kṛṣṇa, "Which of the two, the Yoga of Knowledge or the Yoga of Action, is better?" Lord Kṛṣṇa replied, "The Yoga (discipline) of Action, is superior to the Discipline of Knowledge." But He did not tell him which discipline, was good for him. After describing these in the fifth chapter, in the beginning of the sixth chapter, He laid emphasis on the glory of, the Discipline of Action. Then He described that equanimity, which is attained by the Discipline of Action, is also attained by the Discipline of Meditation, and He explained the Discipline of Meditation. Then Arjuna said, that unsteadiness of mind is an obstacle to meditation. So Lord Kṛṣṇa clarified the doubt. After that Arjuna asked, "What fate does a striver, whose mind is diverted from Yoga at the time of death, meet with?" Lord Kṛṣṇa, answered the question and, in the forty-sixth verse while describing the glory of Yoga, ordered him to be a Yogī. But, Lord Kṛṣṇa did not clearly mention, which Yoga in his opinion, is superior to others. So, in the forty-seventh verse, He himself declares, "He who devoutly worships Me, is the best Yogī". But, Arjuna is not able to understand His view-point, and so he again puts the question, at the beginning of the twelfth chapter, "Who is the better of the two—the devotees, who with their minds constantly fixed in You, adore You, possessed of form and attributes, or those who adore only the Imperishable Formless Brahma?" In response to this question Lord Kṛṣṇa says, "I consider them to be the best Yogīs who, endowed with supreme faith, and ever-united through love, with Me, worship Me, with mind centred on Me."

An Exceptional Fact

The Lord, declares that a devotee following the Discipline

of Devotion, is the best Yogī of all the other Yogīs, because the man (soul) is a fragment of God, and by accepting his affinity for the world and the body, he is bound. When he breaks off this assumed affinity, he becomes free and happy. Though in this freedom, there is no dependence, on things, men and actions etc., yet if he enjoys this freedom by thinking, "I am free from pain and desire," he has subtle affinity, for the world. This is finiteness (limitedness), in assumed freedom. This state is called, state of having become one, with the eternal (Gītā 18/54).

This subtle egoism is also wiped out by being established in that state of identity with the eternal, because by having no affinity for matter and its evolutes, egoism which is a fragment of Matter, comes to an end. It means, that Yogīs of Action and Knowledge, become free from egoism, with the passage of time. But, the egoism of a Yogī of Devotion perishes in the very beginning, as he becomes God's. A Yogī of Devotion, possesses the traits of friendliness, compassion etc., for all beings (Gītā 12/13), which are rarely found, in the Yogīs of Action and Knowledge. It means that a devotee, following the Discipline of Devotion, regards himself as insignificant from the very beginning* and he develops the virtues of politeness, friendliness, compassion and self-satisfaction etc., during the period when he strives, and these virtues attain maturity during the state of perfection. Therefore, subtle egoism, of a devotee perishes. So the Lord has called such a devotee, the best.

The uniqueness of devotion, is that it accelerates in the new form, it does neither attenuate, nor perish, nor get satiated. The Lord also longs for such devotion, or love. This desire of the

---

* A devotee regarding himself inferior to a blade of grass, being more tolerant than a tree, showing respect to others without expecting respect from them, always should chant the name of the Lord.

Lord, is fulfilled by His devotee. So the Lord, has called him superior to others.

There is one more point, which needs attention. In the, Disciplines of Action and Knowledge, a striver has his own faith or belief, and he makes efforts accordingly, while a devotee without having any independent faith or belief of his own, depends completely on God, he identifies his desire with His desire. He does not worry, even to attain salvation or God-realization. The Lord Himself, provides him with the means, for his bodily maintenance and protects, what has already been provided, to him.

Appendix—A man is said to be established in that thing or person where his mind and intellect get fixed (Gītā 12/8). Here the expression 'madgatenāntarātmanā' denotes that his mind is focussed on God, and the term 'Śraddhāvān' denotes that his intellect is fixed on God. Therefore such a devotee because of his intimate kinship with God is established in Him.

Out of all the Yogīs such as Karmayogī, Jñānayogī, Dhyānayogī, Haṭhayogī, Layayogī and Rājayogī etc., the devotee of God is the best of all. The same fact about His devotee has also been mentioned in several other references as 'te me yuktatamā matāḥ' (12/2), 'bhaktāste'tīva me priyāḥ' (12/20) and 'sa yogī paramo mataḥ' (6/32).

Devotion is the most important of all the disciplines for God-realization. Not only this but all the disciplines end in devotion. Karmayoga and Jñānayoga etc., are means but Supreme Love is an end. Devotion is so extensive that it is at the beginning of every discipline and is also at the end. Devotion at the beginning of every discipline consists in the form of attraction towards God because without attraction no one can engage himself in spiritual practice. At the end of a discipline, devotion is transformed into the form of Supreme Love which enhances every moment—'madbhaktiṁ labhate parām' (Gītā 18/54). Therefore in 'Brahmasūtra' the 'Dharma' in the shape of the devotion for God has been declared as superior to other 'Dharmas'—'atastvirajyāyo liṅgācca' (3/4/39).

This verse proves that Lord Kṛṣṇa is the entire Being and His devotion is unworldly. In attainment of the Supreme Love only lies the fulfilment of human life.

ॐ तत्सदिति श्रीमद्भगवद्गीतासूपनिषत्सु ब्रह्मविद्यायां योगशास्त्रे
श्रीकृष्णार्जुनसंवादे आत्मसंयमयोगो नाम षष्ठोऽध्यायः ॥६॥

oṁ tatsaditi śrīmadbhagavadgītāsūpaniṣatsu brahmavidyāyāṁ yogaśāstre śrīkṛṣṇārjunasaṁvāde ātmasaṁyamayogo nāma ṣaṣṭho'dhyāyaḥ

Thus with the words Oṁ, Tat, Sat the names of the Lord, in the Upaniṣad of the Bhagavadgītā, the knowledge of Brahma, the Supreme, the science of self-control Yoga and the dialogue, between Śrī Kṛṣṇa and Arjuna, this is the sixth designated discourse.

By self-control viz., control of the mind, the Yogī of Meditatio attains Yoga (equanimity). So this chapter is designated 'Ātmasaṁyamayoga' (Yoga of self-control or Yoga of the control of mind).

Words, letters and Uvāca (said) in the Sixth Chapter—

(1) In this chapter in **'Atha ṣaṣṭho'dhyāyaḥ'** there are three words, in **'Arjuna Uvāca'** etc., there are ten words, in verses there are five hundred and seventy-three words and there are thirteen concluding words. Thus the total number of words is five hundred and ninety-nine.

(2) In this chapter in **'Atha ṣaṣṭho'dhyāyaḥ'** there are six letters, in **'Arjuna Uvāca'** etc., there are thirty-three letters, in verses there are one thousand five hundred and four letters and

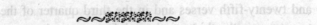

there are forty-seven concluding letters. Thus the total number of the letters is one thousand five hundred and ninety.

(3) In this chapter **'Uvāca'** (said) has been used five times—**'Śrībhagavānuvāca'** thrice and **'Arjuna Uvāca'** twice.

Metres Used in the Sixth Chapter

Out of the forty-seven verses, of this chapter, in the first quarter of the first and twenty-sixth verses, 'bha-gaṇa' being used there is **'bha-vipulā'** metre; in the first quarter of the tenth, fourteenth and twenty-fifth verses and in the third quarter of the fifteenth, twenty-seventh, thirty-sixth and forty-second verses, 'na-gaṇa' being used there is **'na-vipulā'** metre; and in the third quarter of the eleventh verse, 'ra-gaṇa' being used, there is **'ra-vipulā'** metre. The remaining thirty-seven verses, are possessed of the characteristics of right **'pathyāvaktra'** Anuṣṭup metre.

॥ Shri Hari ॥

Seventh Chapter

INTRODUCTION

Lord Krsna, in the forty-sixth verse of the sixth chapter, described the glory of a Yogī and in the forty-seventh verse, He declared, "Of all Yogīs, he, who devoutly worships Me, with his mind focussed on Me, is considered by Me, to be the most devout Yogī." When a devotee thinks of God, he gets absorbed in Him. Similarly when something concerning His devotee is discussed, God also becomes enraptured in it. In the same state of mind, also Lord Kṛṣṇa, full of grace and affection for Arjuna, starts the seventh chapter on his own.

श्रीभगवानुवाच

मय्यासक्तमनाः पार्थ योगं युञ्जन्मदाश्रयः।
असंशयं समग्रं मां यथा ज्ञास्यसि तच्छृणु॥ १॥

śrībhagavānuvāca

mayyāsaktamanāḥ pārtha yogaṁ yuñjanmadāśrayaḥ
asaṁśayaṁ samagraṁ māṁ yathā jñāsyasi tacchṛṇu

The Blessed Lord said:

Listen, O Pārtha (Arjuna), how, with your mind attached to Me, and taking refuge in Me and practising Yoga, you will, without any doubt, know Me fully. 1

Comment:—

'Mayyāsaktamanāḥ'—He, whose mind is attached to Me alone, has not to think of Me, but his mind always remains absorbed in Me. He is not, in the least, attached to the sensual pleasures of this world or the next world, and remains indifferent to comfort, name, fame and other, earthly or heavenly acquisitions.

There are two means, by which mind may be attached to Him.

(i) A striver, who from his heart depending only on God, adores Him, his mind, by His grace is attached to Him. As a servant, in his master's house, even without doing any work as the master did not allot any work for him on a day gets payment, a devotee with the only aim to attach his mind to Him by depending upon Him, gets success in attaching his mind to Him, by His grace.

(ii) God pervades everywhere, at all times and in all things, men and creatures etc., and He belongs to all. So a devotee thinks, that He is here, He is present at the time, He is in him, and belongs to him also. By believing so, if he chants His name, his mind gets attached to Him very easily, during spiritual practice.

'Madāśrayaḥ'—He takes refuge in Me alone viz., and depends on Me, alone.

It is in the nature of man, that he depends on someone, or the other. Being a fragment of God, he actually seeks God. But he, without knowing his true affinity for God, accepts his affinity for the body and the world. All the worldly things, including body, are perishable and so they cannot satisfy him, while God, is eternal, gracious and omnipotent, so he, by accepting his affinity for Him, should depend on Him only, and be subject to His will, because He creates even unfavourable circumstances, for his welfare.

Mind in God, gets absorbed through love. Love develops through affinity. Dependence is sought, upon the greatest and the most powerful, God is omnipotent. Therefore, a striver should rely on Him only, and remain happy in His dispensation. He needs nothing, such as, an individual, an object or any circumstance. Dependence on God, in this way is 'Madāśrayaḥ'.

'Yogaṁ yuñjan'—A striver by accepting his true affinity for God, remaining equanimous in success and failure, adores Him. His performance of different activities either spiritual or mundane, is practice of Yoga. It means that he, depending on God with his mind attached to Him, accepts his union with Him, while discharging his duty. All his activities, are according to His will. He does not act in such a way, that he may suffer disunion from Him.

'Asaṁśayaṁ samagraṁ mām'—He, whose mind is attached to the Lord, who depends on Him and who has accepted his true affinity for Him, knows Him in full, without any doubt viz., he knows that the Lord, manifests Himself in the form of Lord Śiva, Gaṇeśa, Sūrya (the Sun) and Viṣṇu. He is known both with form and attributes; and without any form and attribute. He is also in the form of incarnations.

A Jñānayogī, can know Him and realize Him. But a devotee, can know Him in full, and have His vision in the form of his favourite deity. The Lord does not stop thinking of the devotion of His devotees.

'Yathā jñāsyasi tacchrṇu'—By the term 'Yathā'*, Lord Kṛṣṇa says, that He will tell him how to know Him; and by the word 'tat'†, He means, that He will tell him that, which he wants to know. In these words, Lord Kṛṣṇa by using the second person for Arjuna, asks him to listen to Him, how he will know Him, in full.

In the forty-seventh verse of the sixth chapter, in the expression 'He who worships Me endowed with faith, is deemed by Me, to be the most devout', the Lord by using 'he' the third person, makes a general statement, while here in the expression 'Hear how you shall know Me' He uses the second person pointedly

* The term 'Yathā' has been used to describe how to know him from the gross to the subtle (As water is subtler than earth, fire is subtler than water and air is subtler than fire etc.). It has been described from the fourth to the seventh verses of this chapter.

†'Tat' means that God is the seed of the world. It has been described from the eighth to the twelfth verses of this chapter.

to address Arjuna, how he will know Him fully.

In the first six chapters, the word 'Samagraṁ' (in full), has not been used for the Lord. So, this term signifies, different forms of the Lord, as well as, His glory and other divine traits, while this term, in the twenty-third verse of the fourth chapter, in the expression 'He who works for the sake of sacrifice, the whole action, is dissolved' the term, 'whole' has been used for totality of actions.

An Exceptional Fact

(i) Lord Kṛṣṇa means that a devotee will know Him in full, if he, instead of having attachment for pleasures, is attached to Him. If he instead of depending on body, family and prosperity, depends on Him, and if he has no desire of his own.

(ii) Real affinity for God, is called 'Yogaṁ' and assumption (acceptance) of that affinity incessantly, is called 'Yuñjan'. It means, that a striver instead of assuming his affinity for body, mind and senses etc., should realize his real affinity, for God.

In fact practice of Yoga is not so important, as renunciation of attachment, for and dependence, on the world. By doing so, meditation upon God will be practised automatically, and all actions will be performed, without any desire for their fruit. In such a case, he will not have to practise Yoga. It means, that he who attaches importance to the perishable worldly things and persons etc., cannot know, the all-pervading God. If a man has links with a great man of the society, he feels exalted. Similarly, when our intimacy is aroused with God, who is our disinterested friend and well-wisher and Whose fragment we are, how much more exalted we must feel! In that case, unique and supreme love, is aroused and the striver's mind gets attached, to Him and he depends on Him, quite spontaneously.

Synonyms of Śaraṇāgati (Surrender)

'Āśraya', 'Avalambana', 'Adhīnatā', 'Prapatti' and 'Sahārā', are synonyms of the term 'surrender' (refuge), yet they have different meanings.

(1) **Āśraya:**—We cannot live, without the support of earth. In the same way, we cannot live, without the support of God. This is called 'Āśraya'.

(2) **Avalambana:**—If a man's arm is broken, it is dressed and slung from the neck, with a band. Thus the arm, is supported with a sling, while hanging from the neck. In like manner, a helpless person seeks refuge in God. This support is called 'Avalambana'.

(3) **Adhīnatā:**—It is of two kinds: (a) Someone may force us to depend upon him. (b) We ourselves may willingly, depend on some other. Similarly, a devotee with exclusive devotion and without any selfish motive, becomes an attendant upon God, by regarding Him, as his master. This service with exclusive devotion, is called 'Adhīnatā'.

(4) **Prapatti:**—When a devotee, like a helpless person, offers obeisance before a great man, prostrates before God, it is called 'Prapatti'.

(5) **Sahārā:**—When a devotee, in order to be liberated, from the cycle of birth and death, takes refuge in God, like a drowning man who catches at a straw, it is called 'Sahārā'.

A devotee, is said to take refuge in God, when he is attached only to God and depends only on Him i.e., when he fixes his mind and intellect only, on God. When a man himself takes refuge in God, with his mind and intellect, he possesses all the virtues, of a surrendered devotee.

When a striver resolves, that his so-called mind and intellect, are God's, his mind is naturally attached to Him, and he depends only on Him i.e., he becomes 'Mayyāsaktamanāḥ' and 'Madāśrayaḥ'.

In fact, all the worldly things are in the process of decay every moment, and we being eternal, have no real affinity with them. So, if we renounce this assumed affinity, and only aim at salvation, we shall take refuge in Him automatically, because we are God's, despite ever having developed disinclination for Him, due to our inclination, for the world. As soon as, this assumed affinity or inclination are renounced, our affinity or inclination for God, will manifest itself, and that is axiomatic.

Appendix—The devotee, whose mind has been naturally attracted towards God, who has taken refuge in God and who has accepted his axiomatic eternal union (intimate relationship) with God, knows God in full. All is God this is the integral (entire) form of God.

In the term 'mayyāsaktamanāḥ' there is predominance of love (devotion) and in 'madāśrayaḥ' there is predominance of faith (belief).

'Samagraṁ mām'— In this expression the term 'samagraṁ' is adjective and the term 'māṁ' (God) is the noun qualified. A devotee's affinity instead of being with adjective is with the noun-qualified i.e., with God.

In the expression 'śraddhāvān bhajate yo mām' used at the end of the sixth chapter, what is the form of 'mām'? The Lord answers the questions here—'mām' is My entire form.

'Yathā jñāsyasi tacchṛṇu'—I shall describe My full form in such a manner, using such a device, in such a style that you will easily know My real form.

Arjuna in the preceding chapter expressed his doubt—'etanme saṁśayaṁ kṛṣṇa' (6/39). Therefore the Lord here declares that He will unfold to him the fact by which he will have no doubt.

Link:—In the first verse, Lord Kṛṣṇa asked Arjuna, to listen to how he would know Him in full. Now in the next verse, He promises to tell him about it.

ज्ञानं तेऽहं सविज्ञानमिदं वक्ष्याम्यशेषतः ।
यज्ज्ञात्वा नेह भूयोऽन्यज्ज्ञातव्यमवशिष्यते ॥ २ ॥

jñānaṁ te'haṁ savijñānamidaṁ vakṣyāmyaśeṣataḥ
yajjñātvā neha bhūyo'nyajjñātavyamavaśiṣyate

I shall unfold to you, in full, this knowledge (Jñāna) along with secrets of manifest Divinity, having known which nothing more remains to be known. 2

Comment:—

'Jñānaṁ te'haṁ savijñānamidaṁ vakṣyāmyaśeṣataḥ'—Lord Kṛṣṇa declares:—O Arjuna, I Myself shall teach you in full, this 'Jñāna' (knowledge) and 'Vijñāna' (real knowledge of manifest Divinity).* No one else, can describe Me in full, because their knowledge about Me, is limited, so they cannot know Myself, in full†, as My knowledge is limitless and imperishable, being ever omniscient. After knowing it, nothing else remains to be known.

In the sixteenth verse of the tenth chapter, Arjuna says to Lord Kṛṣṇa, "You alone can describe in full, Your divine glories" (10/16). So Lord Krsna in response to his curiosity, says, "I shall tell you of My important divine glories, because there is no end to My manifestations" (10/19). At the end of this chapter again, He declares, "There is no end of My divine glories" (10/40). Here (in 7/2) He declares, "I shall unfold to you the true essence of real knowledge (realization) and having

* Here the adjective 'Vijñāna' qualifies the noun 'Jñāna' and so is superior to 'Jñāna'. Here the belief that the world is born of the Lord and again merges in Him is knowledge (wisdom) (Jñāna) while the realization, that in the world there is nothing else except the manifestation of God, is the real knowledge (Vijñāna).

† A man cannot describe his own experience in full because the thoughts and feelings cannot be clearly expressed in words. When a man cannot express his own experience in words, how can he teach and unfold the knowledge (wisdom) along with real knowledge like the Lord?

known which, nothing else remains to be known." It means, that God's glories, manifestations and powers etc., are endless. In the Rāmacaritamānasa also, it has been declared, "The form of the Lord without attribute, is easy to know, while the form endowed with attributes, is too difficult to understand. His manifestations, are so varied, that even ascetics find themselves, at their wits end.

It means that there is no end to the glories of the Lord, endowed with attributes. So, how could a man know Him, by using his mind? But a man can know the Divine essence, which is all-pervading. As in different ornaments, made of gold, there is nothing but gold, similarly, in the whole universe, there is nothing else, except Divine manifestation. A man, can know of gold without knowing about different ornaments. Similarly, a striver, can know that God pervades everywhere, in all creatures and things etc., even though, he may not know the names of different creatures and things etc., which form parts of His divine glories. By knowing the reality about God, nothing else remains to be known, in the same way, as thirst is quenched, after drinking water.

In the second verse of the tenth chapter, the Lord declared, "Neither gods nor great sages, know the secret of My birth." In the third verse, He declares, "He who knows Me, as unborn and without beginning, among men, is undeluded and purged of all sins." Now, a question arises, how a man can know Him, when even gods and great sages, do not know Him. The answer is, that if a striver, accepts Him as unborn and without beginning, with a firm faith, it means that he knows Him, because it is within the power of man, only to accept Him as unborn and without beginning. As a child, cannot see a marriage procession of its parents, so to gods, sages, liberated souls etc., cannot know of incarnations, godly sports and divine glories, of the Lord, because He is limitless and unfathomable. But a devotee can know Him in essence.

In order to know the Lord in reality, in the Discipline of Knowledge, there is pre-eminence of knowledge, while in the Discipline of Devotion, there is pre-eminence of assumption, or acceptance. If reality is accepted firmly, it cannot be given up, because it is real. When no one, can force a man to renounce, even a false assumption, how can an assumption of real affinity for God, be renounced? This assumption, is in no way, less significant than knowledge; it is as effective as knowledge.

In the Discipline of Devotion, there is pre-eminence of acceptance. In the first verse of the tenth chapter, Lord Kṛṣṇa says to Arjuna, "O mighty-armed, listen to My supreme word, which I speak to you, out of a desire to do you good." Here, 'listen' means 'accept'. Importance is attached to acceptance, because it is, the context of devotion. In the Discipline of Knowledge, importance is attached to knowledge. In the first verse of the fourteenth chapter, Lord Kṛṣṇa declares, "I impart to you, the supreme knowledge, the best of all forms of knowledge, acquiring which, all sages have attained the highest perfection." In the Discipline of Devotion, a striver knows Him by accepting His Existence, while in the Discipline of Knowledge, a man accepts Him, by knowing Him. In perfection, both of them, are identified.

An Exceptional Fact Pertaining to Knowledge (Wisdom) and Real Knowledge of Manifest Divinity

The world, is born of the Lord and it merges into Him. Therefore, He is the root of the world—this belief (acceptance) is knowledge. There is nothing in the world, except God viz., the world is nothing except manifest Divinity—this realization, is real knowledge (Vijñāna).

Lord Kṛṣṇa (in 7/4—6) declares, "My nature, is of two kinds—lower and higher and I am the origin of the whole universe." By this declaration, Lord Kṛṣṇa referred to knowledge (Jñāna). "There is nothing else, besides Me. Like clusters, of yarn-beads, formed by knots on a thread, all this is threaded on Me" (7/7). By this declaration Lord Kṛṣṇa explains what real knowledge (Vijñāna) is?

"I am the sapidity in water, the light in the moon and the sun, the eternal seed, of all beings. Whatever other entities there are, born of sattva (the mode of goodness), of rājasa (the principle of activity), (the mode of passion) and of tāmasa (the principle of inertia), (the mode of ignorance), know these all, as evolved from Me, alone" (7/8—12). By this declaration, He explains the essence of knowledge. "In reality neither I exist in them nor they in Me viz., I manifest Myself in all forms, because none have their free existence" (7/12). By this declaration, He explains realization (Vijñāna).

"The whole of this creation, is deluded by objects, evolved from the three modes of nature (prakṛti). But those who are not deluded, by the modes of nature and accept that these are born of Me and are absorbed in Me—by accepting so, they take refuge in Me alone, and cross the divine illusion of Mine. Such devotees, are of four types—a seeker of worldly objects, a sufferer, the seeker of knowledge, and a man of wisdom. All these, are noble but the man of wisdom is extremely dear, to Me and he is My own Self" (7/13—18). By this declaration, He explains of knowledge, "The man of realization, who realizes, that all is God, is very rare (7/19)." By this declaration He explains realization, (Vijñāna).

"Those who, being motivated by desires worship gods, gain perishable fruit, while those who are My devotees, attain Me. I am not manifest to those, who do not know Me, as the unborn and imperishable Supreme Spirit. I know the beings of the past, the present and the future, but no one knows Me. Those, who are subject to illusion, by the delusion of pairs of opposites, follow a cycle of birth and death. But, the sins of those who worship Me with a firm resolve, come to an end, and they become free from the pairs of opposites" (7/20—28). By this declaration also, He explains knowledge (Jñāna), "Those who take refuge in Me, know Brahma (the Infinite), Adhyātma (Embodied souls), Karma (Action), Adhibhūta (Matter), Adhidaiva (Brahma) and Adhiyajña (the unmanifest Divinity), viz., they realize that I manifest Myself, in all the movable, as well as the immovable (7/29-30). By this declaration He explains realization (Vijñāna).

'Yajjñātvā neha bhūyo'nyajjñātavyamavaśiṣyate'—After knowing this wisdom, and with realization, nothing remains to be known. It means that there is nothing else besides Me (Gītā 7/7), and that all, is God (7/19). After knowing this reality, nothing else remains to be known. On the other hand, if a striver possesses all knowledge about the world, without knowing Me, all his efforts are in vain, they bear no fruit.

Whatever, a striver knows with his senses, mind and intellect, is not true knowledge about God, because these all belong to matter and matter cannot know reality, which is beyond matter. When one takes refuge in Him, he knows Him naturally, without making any effort, because He can be known by the self, rather than, with mind and intellect etc.

Appendix—The Parā Prakṛti (higher nature) and the Aparā Prakṛti (lower nature) have no independent existence—this is 'jñāna' (knowledge) and the higher and the lower nature—all is God—this is 'Vijñāna'. Therefore all including 'ego' is only God—this is Jñāna with Vijñāna.

'Jñātavyam'—which must be known and which can be known is called 'Jñātavya'.

Having known 'Jñāna' with 'Vijñāna' viz., the entire form of God, nothing remains to be known viz., he who wants to know the Pure-Reality, nothing remains to be known to him. The reason is that when there is nothing else besides God (seventh verse of this chapter), then what more will remain to be known?

Someone may raise a question that the Lord declares that

he will tell 'Jñāna' with 'Vijñāna', it means that the primary importance goes to 'Jñāna' while 'Vijñāna' is of secondary importance. But actually it is not so, only 'Jñāna' can lead to salvation but 'endless bliss of love' is attained only when it is accompanied by 'Vijñāna'. 'Jñāna' is like money and 'Vijñāna' is the feeling of attraction. Money does not provide the pleasure which attraction for money provides. Similarly the bliss that is attained by 'Vijñāna' (devotion) is not attained by 'Jñāna' (knowledge). In 'Jñāna' there is constant relish but in 'Vijñāna' there is such a relish which goes on increasing every moment. Therefore while declaring 'Jñāna' with 'Vijñāna', the Lord specially aims at 'Vijñāna' and he wants to explain that it is superior to 'Jñāna' because 'Vijñāna' stands for the Lord's entire form.

Link:—In the second verse, Lord Kṛṣna said, "I shall unfold to you this knowledge with Realization, having known which nothing remains to be known." How is it that men do not know the reality, about God, when nothing else remains to be known? In the next verse, Lord Kṛṣṇa answers the question.

मनुष्याणां सहस्रेषु कश्चिद्यतति सिद्धये।
यततामपि सिद्धानां कश्चिन्मां वेत्ति तत्त्वतः ॥ ३ ॥

manuṣyāṇāṁ sahasreṣu kaścidyatati siddhaye
yatatāmapi siddhānāṁ kaścinmāṁ vetti tattvataḥ

Among thousands of men, hardly one, strives for perfection and of those who do, scarcely one, knows Me in essence. 3

Comment:—

'Manuṣyāṇāṁ sahasreṣu kaścidyatati siddhaye'*—Among

* If a word is used as an adjective of number, its number is singular. But in the sixth inflexion it has not only the singular number but all the three numbers. Here in the word 'Manuṣyāṇāṁ' there is sixth inflexion in connection with the thousand

thousands of men, scarcely one strives for perfection. It means, that only those persons who do not indulge in the sensuous pleasures like eating, drinking and enjoying themselves like animals, are human beings, in the true sense of the term. Out of those, men who follow virtues and righteousness, are only in thousands. Out of those thousands, hardly one strives for Divine perfection or Divine bliss,* having gained which, one thinks that there is no greater gain beyond it, and there is not the least sorrow.

Persons, who have no desire to go to heaven, and to enjoy worldly pleasures, respect and praise etc., even when they get an opportunity and have an inclination to them, but because of past impressions who do not deviate from their principles and aims, and want to attain, Divine perfection, are rare.

Pleasure and prosperity, are obstacles to spiritual progress. Worldly pleasures, seem pleasant only in the beginning. If strivers, think over the result of pleasure and prosperity, that these are gateways to hells and eighty-four lac forms of lives, they will start taking to spiritual practice. Most of the people, hanker after worldly pleasure and prosperity. Some people, who transcend worldly pleasures, run after heavenly pleasures. But, there are only a few aspirants, who strive for Divine perfection or God-realization. If we turnover the pages of history, such aspirants are very rare. Most of them, are those who have performed actions and penances etc., in order to, reap fruits.

---

number and there is seventh inflexion in the plural number in the word 'Sahasrāṇi'. Therefore, the expression 'Manuṣyāṇāṁ sahasreṣu kaścidyatati siddhaye' means 'Manuṣyāṇāṁ sahasrāṇi bhagavati rucim kurvanti sahasreṣu kaścit siddhaye yatati ca' i.e., 'thousands of men have an inclination to God but one of those thousands of men strives to attain perfection.

* Divine perfection does not mean worldly and heavenly enjoyments and accomplishment such as 'Aṇimā, Mahimā' and 'Garimā' etc., because they lead to a downfall and to the cycle of birth and death (9/21). Therefore, here perfection means God-realization.

In fact, it is not difficult to attain, God-realization but there are only a few aspirants who strive, sincerely from their heart, to realize Him. Now, a question arises, why do not strivers strive for God-realization? The answer is, that there are two stumbling blocks—attraction of sensual pleasures and hope to realize Him, in future.*

'Yatatāmapi siddhānām'†—Here, 'Siddha' (the successful one), is the striver whose mind has been purified, and whose only aim, is to realize God. Though (in 7/19) the man of realization who realizes that all is God, is called a great soul, yet in this context, great souls are those strivers, who possess divine nature, worship the Lord constantly, with exclusive devotion (Gītā 9/13), and strive to realize Him.

Here, 'Yatatām' means, that strivers want to realize God, from their heart and so strive for Divine perfection, and naturally think of Him, with reverence.

'Kaścinmāṁ vetti tattvataḥ'—'Scarcely one knows Me in reality.' Here it does not mean, that the strivers who strive to know Him, cannot know Him. But, at present, anyone striver out of the assiduous strivers, knows Him in reality; out of those who know Him, scarcely anyone can speak of Him, and explain to others. Other learned persons, may be there who may have

* God always pervades everywhere, all persons, things, incidents, circumstances and actions etc. Therefore, God-realization need not be left for the future. He is now, here, in everyone and everyone's. Moreover, He is superior to all the persons etc. By having this belief, mind will be attracted towards Him automatically and a burning desire to realize Him immediately will be aroused.

† Here the striver has been called 'Siddha' (successful one) according to 'Śāṭī-sūtra-nyāya' because he will attain perfection in the same way as a saree will be prepared of the Sūtra (thread). If a striver depending on God, having exclusive devotion for Him adores Him in order to realize Him, he will attain perfection, there is no doubt about it. As far as a saree is concerned it may be prepared out of the thread or even any other cloth may be prepared out of the thread or the thread may be destroyed. But the devotee who adores God with exclusive devotion will certainly attain perfection.

knowledge, but they cannot explain to others. Thc Lord declares, "One looks upon Him, as a marvel; another, likewise speaks of Him, as a marvel" (Gītā 2/29).

Generally, people give illustrations about this verse, in order to explain, that it is very difficult to attain, Divine perfection. But actually, it is not so. In order to attain Divine perfection, it is difficult to have keen desire and for the fulfilment of that desire, it is not easy to have the company of liberated souls. Here, Lord Kṛṣṇa says to Arjuna, "I shall unfold (teach) to you in full, this knowledge, combined with realization and you will know it." Such an omniscient speaker, as Lord Kṛṣṇa Himself, and such an inquisitive striver as Arjuna, are very rare. The fact is, that it is difficult to have keen desire. By having keen desire, a striver has no responsibility of his own, the responsibility is shouldered by the Lord.

By using 'tattvataḥ' (In truth), Lord Kṛṣṇa means that a striver comes to know the truth (reality), about Him, that He manifests Himself in the form of Lord Śiva, Gaṇeśa, Sūrya (the sun), Viṣṇu, by incarnations and He is possessed of form and attributes and He is also, without form and attributes i.e., he knows that there is no existence, in the least, besides the Lord.

Appendix—Out of all the God-realized souls who have attained perfection after striving, following the disciplines of Karma, Jñāna and Dhyāna etc., the devotees, who know the entire form of God in reality, in the shape of 'all is God' are very rare, indeed (7/19).

'Yatatāmapi siddhānām'—those liberated souls, are dissatisfied with their state of liberation and from within they have a yearning, a hunger to have supreme devotion (infinite bliss). Therefore it is mentioned in the Brahmasūtra—'muktopasṛpyavyapadeśāt' (1/3/2)—'that God Who is an embodiment of love (devotion) is realizable (attainable) even by the liberated souls'. The reason is that by attaining salvation, the desire for the perishable relish is wiped out but the hunger for endless relish is not satisfied. That hunger is aroused by God's grace. It means that those, who practise spiritual discipline by having faith and belief in God, who have the latent impression of devotion, God does not let them be satisfied with knowledge, does not let them stay there, and makes the relish of salvation insipid for them.

A Karmayogī, a Jñānayogī, a Dhyānayogī, etc.,—all can attain perfection (salvation) but all of them don't know God in His entire form. Therefore the expression 'yatatāmapi siddhānām' means that by striving, they have attained perfection with their own method but they don't know My entire (full) form. The reason is that My entire form can be known by supreme devotion—'bhaktyā māmabhijānāti yāvānyaścāsmi tattvataḥ' (Gītā 18/55).

'Kaścinmāṁ vetti tattvataḥ'—Here the term 'mām' stands for God in his entire form. The entire form of God can be known by God's grace, not by thought (Gītā 10/11). Arjuna also after hearing the gospel of the Gītā said to Lord Kṛṣṇa, "By Your grace my delusion is destroyed and memory is gained"—'naṣato mohaḥ smṛtirlabdhā tvatprasādānmayācyuta' (Gītā 18/73). As while feeding the cow licks her calf with fondness, it provides so much nourishment which the calf can't get only by drinking milk. Similarly the knowledge which is gained by God's grace, can't be gained by thought because while thinking, the entity of the self persists.

He who knows only attributeless God, does not know Him in reality but he who knows both God endowed with attributes and also attributeless God (entire) knows God in reality.

By Karmayoga 'quiet bliss' (peace) (quietude) is attained because attachment to the world causes disquietude. By Karmayoga renunciation of attachment to the world causes peace—'tyāgācchāntiranantaram' (Gītā 12/12). By Jñānayoga 'unbroken bliss' is attained. This unbroken bliss is also called 'self-bliss' because it is the bliss of the self. In self-bliss the self merges into Brahma (Absolute) viz., as Brahma is truth, consciousness and bliss solidified, similarly the self becomes truth, consciousness and bliss solidified—'mama sādharmyamāgatāḥ' (Gītā 14/2). Though having attained the self-bliss (Self-realization) a striver lacks nothing, yet the striver, who has the latent impression of devotion and depends on God's grace, is not satisfied with that self-bliss.* Within him there is hunger for endless bliss. Therefore by Bhaktiyoga, endless bliss is attained. Self-bliss is the bliss of the fragment (soul) but endless bliss is the bliss of the whole (God) (supreme soul). This is the principle that the pleasure which is caused by the attraction of an object, is not caused by the knowledge of that object. As the pleasure which is derived from the greed for money, is not derived from the mere knowledge of money. By knowing the money we shall know how to make use of it, but there will not be special attraction. 'Gain more and more money'—this attraction will persist by being greedy for money. In fact there is no pleasure in gaining money but it seems because of the evil of greed, but God's bliss is because of pure love and this bliss really exists. The reason is that being a fragment of God, the embodied self has an automatic attraction towards Him. This is the principle that a fragment is naturally attracted towards the whole; as a stone being a fragment of the earth when thrown upward naturally is attracted towards the earth, fire is naturally attracted towards the sun (upward)† and rivers naturally flow towards the sea and so on.

---

*He who attains salvation is naturally satisfied, but he who has the impressions of devotion is not satisfied. The reason is that God showers his special grace on such a devotee and does not let him stay there. (7/3)

†Here a doubt may crop up that the sun does not shine at night, then why does fire rise upward at night? The clarification is that whether it is day or night, the sun may shine anywhere but he is always above the earth. Therefore as the people in India see the sun above the earth, so do the people of America (which is almost in the opposite direction of India) also see the sun above the earth.

Why do we need God? If we reflect upon it, we come to know that there is such a necessity which can't be satisfied either by our own self or by the world. In order to alleviate sufferings and to attain supreme peace, there is no necessity for God. The reason is that if desires are totally renounced, our sufferings will end and Supreme Peace will be attained—'tyāgācchāntira-nantaram' viz., we shall attain salvation, we have necessity for God in order to attain Supreme Love because we are fragments only of God.

The man who wants to be liberated from worldly sufferings, who wants to be independent, being free from dependence, attains salvation. But the man, who being tired of the worldly sufferings thinks, "If there had been anyone my own who would have given me refuge in himself, who would have embraced me and who would have removed my grief, sin, lack, fear and monotony etc., attains devotion." It means that God is not needed to attain salvation but he is needed to attain devotion. When a man comes to know that in such a vast world, in endless universes, there is nothing mine but only He is mine, in Whose one fragment endless universes are situated, then he feels the necessity for God from within. The reason is that only the thing, which ever stays with us and with which we may ever stay, can be ours. Only God can be the entity Who may not be separated from us and from Whom we may not be separated.

Now the question arises when a man needs God, why is He not attained? The answer is that a man lives comfortably without attaining Him, he forgets his necessity. He remains satisfied with objects, ability and power etc., which are available to him. If he realizes the need for God and can be ill at ease, there is no delay in God-realization. The reason is what should be the delay in attaining Him Who is ever attained? God is not a tree that the seed is sown today and it will bear fruit after years. He is present at all places, all the time, in all things, in all states and in all circumstances the same as He is. We have turned away from Him, he has not turned away from us.

Link:—In the second verse, Lord Kṛṣṇa promised Arjuna to unfold to him knowledge combined with realization. In keeping with His promise, Lord Kṛṣṇa proceeds, in the next verse, to explain knowledge with realization.

भूमिरापोऽनलो वायुः खं मनो बुद्धिरेव च।
अहङ्कार इतीयं मे भिन्ना प्रकृतिरष्टधा॥४॥*
अपरेयमितस्त्वन्यां प्रकृतिं विद्धि मे पराम्।
जीवभूतां महाबाहो ययेदं धार्यते जगत्॥५॥

bhūmirāpo'nalo vāyuḥ khaṁ mano buddhireva ca
ahaṅkāra itīyaṁ me bhinnā prakṛtiraṣṭadhā
apareyamitastvanyāṁ prakṛtiṁ viddhi me parām
jīvabhūtāṁ mahābāho yayedaṁ dhāryate jagat

Earth, water, fire, air, ether, mind, intellect, ego—these constitute My nature (prakṛti) eightfold divided. This is My lower (insentient) nature; but different from it, O mighty-armed, is My higher (sentient) nature—the life-element (Jīva), by which this universe is sustained. 4-5

Comment:—

'Bhūmirāpo'nalo vāyuḥ khaṁ mano buddhireva ca ahaṅkāra itīyaṁ me bhinnā prakṛtiraṣṭadhā apareyamitastvanyāṁ prakṛtiṁ viddhi me parām'—God is the origin of the whole creation. Wielding His own nature, He brings forth the whole creation. This nature is called the lower Nature (aparā prakṛti), while the embodied soul, which is a fragment of God, is called higher

* The entity which is kaleidoscopic and never remains the same has been mentioned as perishable (in 15/16), lower (insentient) Nature (in 7/4) and of twenty-four categories—five subtle elements (ether, air, fire, water and earth), ego, intellect, Primordial Matter, ten organs, mind and five objects of senses (sound, touch, colour, taste, smell) (in 13/5).

nature (parā prakṛti). The lower nature, is inferior, insentient and changeful, while higher nature is superior, sentient and changeless.

Every man's nature, is different. As a man's nature, cannot be proved to have its own separate entity, independent of that man, similar is the case with that of God's nature. This nature is God's own disposition, therefore, it is called as His nature. Similarly, the embodied soul, being a portion of God, cannot be proved to have its own separate existence, independent of God, as it is God itself. Though God itself, but it is named nature, because of its affinity with lower nature. As it accepts the activities of the Lower Nature as its own, or in other words attributes the doership to himself, therefore, it is called, superior Nature, or embodied soul, otherwise, it is nothing else but God. When it becomes free, from the bondage of being a doer, and an enjoyer (Gītā 18/17) it is no more higher nature, or embodied soul.

Here the Lower Nature, includes earth, water, fire, air, ether, mind, intellect and ego. If out of these eight, five gross elements are supposed to represent the gross creation and the three, (mind, intellect and ego) are to represent the whole subtle creation, then this description of nature, remains incomplete, as it leaves out the causal creation. To prove that in this description of nature, all parts of nature, have been included, the venerable commentators, have interpreted these in the following way. According to them the five gross elements stand for gross as well as their causes, five subtle tanmātrās, mind stands for its origin ego; intellect stands for cosmic intelligence and 'ego' stands for the causal nature. Thus, this interpretation includes full description, of cosmic nature, as it includes all the three gross, subtle and causal creation.

In scriptures, this cosmic nature has been described as prakṛti and vikṛti. Here, a point needs attention, that Lord Kṛṣṇa has not described lower and higher nature from the view-point, of prakṛti and vikṛti or Nature-cum its evolutes. Had the Lord defined so, He would not have called the individual soul, as higher nature, because the soul is neither prakṛti—the cause of any evolute nor vikṛti—the evolute itself. The soul is immutable and changeless. It proves, that the Lord, has described matter, as lower nature, and the individual soul, as higher nature, just in order to distinguish, the insentient from the sentient.

According to this author, this eightfold division of Nature, includes the gross and subtle, creation only. The five gross elements enumerated here, include the gross creation. These five elements, also represent subtle creation, as these are evolutes of five subtle tanmātrās. Mind, intellect and ego, described here, are also part of the subtle creation.

The ego has two aspects. The ego is matter, in its nature, and it is a modification, or a trait of the inner sense (अन्तःकरण). It is a sort of an instrument. This is called, in the fourth verse, as ego a part of lower nature. The second aspect of ego, is one's own personality and it represents itself as a 'doer'. This is described, in the fifth verse of this chapter, by the name of higher nature. This 'ego', is the result of the soul's identification, with causal body.

This identification, has two aspects—insentient and sentient. The insentient factor, is the causal body and one who cultivates egoistic notion, is sentient factor, until Self-realization, this ego persists assuming itself always, as 'doer'. During deep sleep, it lies dormant or is not manifest. After waking up "I slept soundly and am awake", a man making this statement, represents the ego, the higher nature. After waking up he thinks, "where and how he is", this is wakefulness of mind, and when he knows, that he is at a particular place and time, it is the wakefulness, of the intellect. Thus, one who experiences his entity, is the ego, representing higher nature, and through the ego, with which he experiences, is a trait of the inner sense, it is lower nature.

When soul, the sustainer and illuminator of this lower nature—identifies itself, with this nature, it is then called higher nature, or the embodied soul. This fact, has been described in Gītā by the term 'ययेदं धार्यते जगत्'—by whom this insentient Nature, is sustained.

If this sentient nature (soul or spirit), without having any inclination for the insentient nature, has an inclination for God i.e., accepts Him as Its own, it realizes the Self and then its (soul's or man's) attachment, for the world, turns into love for God.*

This Divine love, is limitless, it is in the form of bliss, and it increases every moment. After attaining it, nothing else remains to be attained; and after realizing the Self, nothing remains to be known and after applying all the objects etc., of the lower nature for the service of the world, and having disinclination, for them, nothing remains, to be done. This is the state of perfection, of human life.

'Prakṛtiraṣṭadhā apareyam'—It seems, that this eightfold lower nature is individual, lower nature, because a man is bound because of his affinity for his body. If a man (soul) does not accept his affinity for it, there is no question of any bondage. Man himself (soul or spirit), sustains this universe viz., accepts his relationship with the universe, and that relationship leads him, to bondage.

An individual body, has no separate entity, different from the universe. When a man (the self), assumes his affinity for the body, he is bound. If he does not assume this affinity, there is no question of bondage.

In the seventh verse of the fifteenth chapter, Lord Kṛṣṇa

* The striver following the Discipline of Knowledge will have revelation of love for God in the form of Self-realization while a devotee following the Discipline of Devotion will have that revelation in the form of Divine love. Thus from this point of view the striver following the Discipline of Knowledge and that following the Discipline of Devotion—both become one.

declares, "The soul in the body, is an eternal fragment of Myself." But it attracts the mind and the senses, that rest in Matter viz., it accepts the mind and the senses as its own. In the same way in the fifth verse of the thirteenth chapter, Lord Kṛṣṇa describes the universe as Kṣetra (field) and, in the sixth verse, describes its evolutes (modifications). But actually these evolutes are found, not in the universe, but in the body. Thus, affinity for the body, is the main obstacle to emancipation. This body, being a fragment of the universe, cannot be separated from it.

The fact is, that primordial Matter, is neither a means nor an obstacle to emancipation. When a striver does not accept his affinity for it, it proves helpful. But, when he accepts his affinity for it, it proves an obstacle, because this affinity for prakṛti (matter), gives birth to egoism ('I'ness). This egoism, is the cause of bondage. By the phrase 'Itīyaṁ me', Lord Kṛṣṇa, warns us that this Primordial Matter or lower nature, is His. So a striver should not accept it as his own, otherwise this affinity will lead him, to the cycle of birth and death.

In egoism ('I'ness), there are two desires—desire for pleasure, as well as desire for knowledge. The desire for pleasure, can be wiped out by the Discipline of Action, while the desire for knowledge can be satisfied by the Discipline of Knowledge. Thus, a striver who is firmly established in either of the two, gets the fruit of both (Gītā 5/4-5) i.e., when the desire for pleasure is wiped out, the desire for knowledge is satisfied. When the desire for knowledge is satisfied, the desire for pleasures, is wiped out. When the desire for pleasures is wiped out, or the desire for knowledge is satisfied, there develops detachment, automatically. If a striver does not enjoy that detachment i.e., he is not pleased with that state, he attains Self-realization and his human life, proves fruitful.

'Jīvabhūtām'—Actually, the soul is a fragment of God, but by accepting its affinity for physical, subtle and causal bodies, it has become an embodied soul. It accepts its affinity, in order to, enjoy mundane pleasures, which lead It to great affliction, in the form of birth and death.

'Mahābāho'—O Arjuna, being mighty-armed, you are very brave and powerful and you can understand the difference between the lower nature (matter) and the higher nature (Soul). Therefore, understand it.

'Yayedaṁ dhāryate jagat'*—In fact, this universe is a manifestation of God i.e., all the universe is God (7/19) and He is being and non-being both (9/19). The man (soul), has sustained this universe i.e., the man (soul), by accepting the free existence of this universe, has started using it for his own pleasure, and thus it has led him to bondage. If he takes this universe, as a manifestation or revelation of God, he will be free, from the shackles of birth and death.

The world, is transitory and kaleidoscopic, but man thinks it permanent and pleasing, because of his temptation and attachment for pleasure and things, by having feelings of 'I' and 'mine'. It is because of his attachment for pleasure and prosperity, that he cannot behold this world, as a manifestation of God. As a debouch cannot behold a woman, as mother, so can a person having attachment for the worldly pleasure and prosperity, not perceive that the Lord Himself, has manifested Himself, in the form of the world. This attachment for pleasure sustains the universe, i.e., is the cause of sustaining, the universe.

Secondly, all human beings, are born of sperm and ovum, which themselves are filthy and impure. But a voluptuary thinks, the body as charming and beautiful, because of his attachment for pleasure. This thought makes the world.

Once a gentleman said to a saint, who was standing on the bank of a river, "Sir, the water of this river and the men, on the

* In the Gītā the term 'Jagat' (universe) denotes higher Nature (in 7/13), lower Nature (in 7/5) and higher and lower Nature both (in 7/6).

bridge are flowing." The saint said, "O brother, it is not only the water of the river, or the men that are moving, but the river and the bridge themselves, are also moving." It means, that all of these are moving towards, destruction. One day they will come to an end. Actually the whole world is perishing every moment. In fact, the soul is neither born nor does It decay. But, by identifying Itself with the body, It accepts the body's birth and death as Its own, birth and death. If It does not identify itself with the body nor does It accept its affinity for it, this world will have no existence at all.

The term 'Idam', means that as both body and the world are one, and the same, their difference is not real, it is merely assumed. Therefore, Lord Kṛṣṇa, in the thirteenth chapter, says that this body is spoken of as a field (kṣetra) (13/1); but where there is a description of this field, it is a description of the world (13/5), while the evolutes such as desire, aversion, pleasure and pain etc., have been described part of the individual body (13/6). It means, that the world and the body are essentially the same. If we accept the body as 'I', it gives birth to egoism ('I'ness), and if we accept the body as 'mine', it gives birth to 'mineness', and both of these lead to bondage. If we realize, that the body and the world belong to one and the same class, and the man himself (soul) and God belong to one class, which is quite different from that of the body and the world, egoism ('I'ness) and 'mineness' perish' automatically. These can be wiped out, by the three Disciplines of Action (2/71), Knowledge (18/53) and Devotion (12/13). It means, that the assumed affinity for matter, should be broken off and it can be, by accepting reality through discrimination.

An Exceptional Fact

A teacher and a pupil have their own separate entity or existence. But by having love and regard for each other, there is a further affinity between the two.* Similarly, the soul which is a fragment of the Lord, has accepted its affinity, with a body and the world. It is because of this affinity, that there appears to be a third entity, which is called 'I'ness. This affinity of 'I'ness, is merely assumed, not real. But the soul, by accepting it as real, gets into bondage. A teacher and a pupil, have a separate existence, and both of them accept their affinity for each other. But, out of the soul (sentient) and the world (insentient or matter), only the soul has Its own existence. By an error it accepts Its relationship with the world, which is changing and perishing, every moment. This assumed relationship, is also decaying every moment. But it seems real to those, who want to seek pleasure in the world. It is because of their attachment for worldly pleasures, that a world, which is never attained, seems to be attained; while God, Who is ever attainable seems unattained to them. As soon as, they are free from this assumed affinity for the world, they will realize the reality of their affinity—that they have their affinity for God; and only He, not the world, can be attained.

To wipe out this feeling of 'I'ness, a striver should have a firm belief, that he is different from matter, he should not expect anything from the world, but perform actions for the service of the world, because, whatever strength, intelligence and resources he possesses, he has received from the world. By following, this Discipline of Action, the direction of actions and objects, is towards the world and the self, remains, so he attains self-realization. By following, the Discipline of Knowledge, also by using discrimination a striver, by breaking off his affinity for things and actions, of the world, attains self-realization. Thus, by breaking off his affinity for matter, he becomes free from his assumed, 'I'ness. Devotion to God, is aroused in the Discipline of Devotion, by accepting 'I am only God's, and only God is

* In teacher-taught relationship the duty of the teacher is to do good to the pupil and the duty of the pupil is to serve the teacher. In the same way every relationship of the world is to do good to others or serve others without any selfish motive.

mine, I am not of the body, and the world, and the body and the world, are not mine'. Then a striver having disinclination for the world, depends only on God and thus he becomes free from the affinity of the world, and egoism ('I'ness).

Thus, by following, the Discipline of Action, the Discipline of Knowledge, or the Discipline of Devotion, in the right perspective, a striver, becomes free from the affinity of matter and realizes, God.

Appendix—When the self gets identified with the lower nature viz., is identified with 'ego' and assumes itself 'I am', then by becoming an embodied soul, it is called higher nature. On one side of the 'ego' (I), there is the world (lower nature) and on the other side there is God. But the embodied soul instead of accepting God, accepts His lower nature and sustains it in the form of the world which leads him to the bondage of birth and death.

'apareyamitastvanyām'—Different from 'aparā' (lower) is 'parā' (higher) and different from 'parā' is 'aparā'. 'Aparā' is different viz., belongs to another class. By catching (sustaining) the alien this 'parā' has become 'jīva' (embodied soul)—'jīvabhūtām'.

Aparā (kaleidoscopic) and parā (unchangeable)—both are God's nature viz., power. Being powers of God, both are identified with God because without the powerful, the power has no independent existence. As nail and hair, in spite of being lifeless, are not different from the living body, similarly the lower nature, in spite of being insentient, is not different from God—Who is sentient—'sadasaccāhamarjuna' (Gītā 9/19). In this way when 'aparā' and 'parā'—both prakṛtis are the embodiments of God, then what remains besides God? Nothing remains—'Vāsudevaḥ sarvam' (Gītā 7/19).

God's integral form consists of both parā and aparā nature meaning that Parā, Aparā; Sat, Asat; sentient and insentient all are God.

'Yayedaṁ dhāryate jagat' means that this world has no existence in the eye of God as well as in the eye of an exalted soul. It exists only in the eye of the individual soul. In the eye of God 'Sat' and 'Asat' all is He Himself सदसच्चाहमर्जुन (Gītā 9/19) and in the eye of the exalted soul "All is God" वासुदेवः सर्वम् (Gītā 7/19).

A man (the embodied soul) because of attachment and aversion has sustained the world in his intellect. The same fact has been pointed out in the seventh verse of the fifteenth chapter by the expression 'manaḥ ṣaṣṭhānīndriyāṇi prakṛtisthāni karṣati'. By cognising the existence of the world, attachment and aversion arise.

The embodied self assumed the existence of the world and attached importance to it. By attaching importance, the desire for pleasure sprang up which in its turn led it to the cycle of birth and death. It means that by assuming any other entity besides God, the being has been snared in the worldly bondage. Therefore it is the being's responsibility not to assume any other entity besides God. If it does not assume the entity of the world, where is the world?

The Lord declares that earth, water, fire, air, ether, mind, intellect, ego—these eight constitute 'aparā' (insentient) prakṛti.* As the earth is insentient and is to be known, so is ego insentient and is to be known. It means that earth, water etc.,—all the eight belong to the same 'jāti' viz., class (category)†. Therefore

* If there is one thing common in several things, that is called 'jāti'. Earth, water, fire, air, ether, mind, intellect and ego—in these eight there is oneness of 'jāti' (class) but there is not oneness of form viz., in spite of one class, their forms are different. Therefore it has been called 'aṣṭadhā' (eightfold). Being the evolutes of 'aparā prakṛti' (lower nature), here earth, water etc., have been called 'aparā prakṛti'.

† Earth is gross. Water is more subtle than earth. Fire is more subtle than water. Air is more subtle than fire. Ether is more subtle than air. Mind is more subtle than ether. Intellect is more subtle than mind. Ego is more subtle than intellect.

the class to which the earth belongs, ego also belongs to the same class viz., ego like a clod is insentient and is objective in nature. Therefore the Lord has mentioned 'ego' as 'this'—'etad yo vetti' (Gītā 13/1). 'Etat' (this) is never 'aham' (I). Therefore the Lord by saying 'ego' as 'this' means that 'ego' is not 'the self'. When the sentient (self) identifies itself with 'ego', then it gets bound—'ahaṁkāra vimūḍhātmā kartāhamiti manyate' (Gītā 3/27). This is called 'cijjaḍagranthi'.

'Ahaṅkāra itīyaṁ me'—the pure ego is matter (insentient) in its nature and belongs to the 'aparā prakṛti' (lower nature) but 'I am'—this identified ego is not only of 'aparā prakṛti' but it is conjoined with 'parā prakṛti' (sentient). On Self-realization the latter ego, which leads to birth and death, does not persist but the former (ego of aparā prakṛti) remains.

Actions and objects are neither in 'parā prakṛti' nor in God but they are in 'aparā prakṛti'. 'Aparā prakṛti' is in the form of actions and objects. The Lord with the help of 'Prakṛti' brings into being the whole creation. 'Parā prakṛti' viz., the embodied soul, by being attached to actions and objects (Aparā prakṛti) and depending on them, gets bound. Attachment to the 'Aparā prakṛti' and dependence on it means 'to sustain the world'. Therefore the Lord at the very beginning of the seventh chapter has mentioned—to be attached to Him and to take refuge in Him by the expression—'mayyāsaktamanāḥ pārtha yogaṁ yuñjanmadāśrayaḥ'. If a striver (the embodied soul) is not attached to 'Aparā prakṛti' and does not take refuge in it; he will attain salvation. If he is attached to (loves) God and takes refuge in him, he will become a 'Bhakta' (devotee).

The world has no independent existence. The soul has cognised the existence of the world which leads it to bondage. The soul sustains the world which causes pleasure, pain, bondage

In aparā prakṛti ego is the most subtle. Thus the Lord has described aparā prakṛti from the gross to the subtle in due order.

and leads it to the eighty-four lac forms of life, to the life of ghosts, evil spirits, devils and deities etc., and also paves the way to hells. Sattva, Raja and Tama—the three modes don't cause any obstacle but attachment to the modes carries it to the higher regions or middle regions or lower regions—'kāraṇaṁ guṇasaṅgo'sya sadasadyonijanmasu' (Gītā 13/21). The soul itself gets attached to the modes. Aparā prakṛti does not get attached to anyone. Neither Prakṛti nor modes, nor senses; nor mind nor intellect gets attached. But the embodied soul itself gets attached and thus it feels pleasure and pain and follows the cycle of birth and death. The soul is independent because it is 'parā' viz., the higher nature. The poor aparā prakṛti does nothing because it is insentient and is free from desire. The being getting attached to it and making proper use or misuse of it, goes to high (good) and low (evil) wombs and goes astray. It means that the being in spite of being unchangeable, being attached to the changeable world, becomes the kaleidoscopic world (embodied soul)* (Gītā 7/13). It has an eye on the body only, it does not even think of its divine nature.

The self identifies itself with the world viz., with the body, senses, mind, intellect, ego which is altogether different from it—this is sustenance of the world. In fact the world is not ours, because if we had attained the thing which is ours, our desires would have ended forever and we would have been free from mineness, fear, worries and desires. But the world can't afford us such a thing which is ours viz., of which there is never any disunion. The entity which is ours, can't be attained by the world but can be attained by renouncing attachment to the world. Our thing (entity) is God. We are the fragments of that God—'mamaivāṁśo jīvaloke' (Gītā 15/7). The method to attain Him (from the view-point of Karmayoga) is that the objects (body etc.,) received from the world, should be used to

* Here the term 'Jagat' stands for the 'changeable'—'gacchatīti jagat'.

render service to the world without desiring any fruit. A striver should not be attached to any action or object. It is better not to harm anyone than to serve them. If we don't harm anyone and do not do evil to others, service will be naturally rendered to them, we shall have not to render it.* We are not proud of the action which takes place itself and there is no desire for its fruit. Having renounced pride and the desire for fruit we attain the thing which is really ours.

In fact 'aparā prakṛti' has no separate existence at all besides God—'nāsato vidyate bhāvaḥ'. The individual self has cognised its (aparā prakṛti's) special existence. As money has no importance of its own but we attach importance to it because of our greed for it. We are attracted towards the object to which we attach importance. We attach importance, when we accept evil i.e., some faults†. It is due to the evil of lust for sex, there is attraction for woman; because of the evil of greed there is attraction for money; because of the evil of delusion, there is attraction for family and so on. But when we identify ourselves with those evils, we don't perceive those evils as evils and we don't know that we, by assuming their (aparā prakṛti's) existence, are attaching importance to them. When this identification is wiped out, evils stay no more in us and

* If we don't do evil to others, there will be two things—either we shall do nothing, or if we do, only service will be rendered. By doing nothing and by serving others—by these two things, attachment to the world is renounced. The reason is that by doing nothing, no evil is done and by the service which is rendered itself to others all evils are wiped out. As while eating food a man holds 'I eat'—thus the pride which is attached is not attached in the digestion of food because food is digested itself. Similarly when service is rendered itself, the pride of doership and attachment to the fruit of action, are naturally renounced.

† All the worldly pleasures are born of evils. When we accept evils, they seem to provide pleasure. Because of the lust for sex a man can't live without woman. Because of greed a man can't live without wealth. Because of delusion a man can't live without family. It is because of evils that a man can't perceive the value of renunciation.

virtues are not apparent (viz., they don't come to light).

In endless universes, three worlds, fourteen spheres, insentient-sentient, unmoving-moving, land creatures-aquatic creatures-sky creatures, placental-born from egg-born of perspiration-sprouting from ground, Sāttvika-Rājasa-Tāmasa, men, deities, manes, celestial-musicians, animals, birds, insects, moths, ghosts-spirits-devils-brahmarākṣasa (demons) etc., whatever beings are seen, heard, studied and imagined, in all of them there is nothing besides the two natures (Prakṛti)—'parā' (higher) and 'aparā' (lower). Whatever is seen, heard, studied and imagined; and the body-senses-mind-intellect-ego by which the actions of seeing, hearing, studying and imagining are performed, are all 'aparā'. But he who sees, hears, studies, thinks, knows, assumes is 'parā'. 'Parā' and 'aparā'—both being the powers of God, are inseparable from God viz., they are the manifestations of God. Therefore in the inside and outside of endless universes and in the form of infinite universes, there is nothing else besides God—'vāsudevaḥ sarvam' (7/19), 'sadasaccāhamarjuna' (9/19). All the philosophies and diverse opinions of the world have been propounded by their heads (ācāryas) but 'Vāsudevaḥ sarvam' is not the philosophy or opinion of a particular 'ācārya' (head) but it is the irreversible principle of Lord Kṛṣṇa within which all philosophies and diverse opinions are included.

The individual self has assumed the independent existence of the 'aparā' (world)—'yayedaṁ dhāryate jagat'. 'Aparā' is God's but this self is bound because it has assumed 'aparā' viz., body-senses-mind-intellect-ego its own and for itself. Therefore if a striver perceives (sees) the world, it is his personal view. The personal view is not a principle. Whatever is seen is limited while the 'Reality' is limitless. As the sun appears like a metallic dish, but actually it is not of the size of a metallic dish but it is several times bigger than the earth.

If the world is in cognizance of a striver, he should serve

it in a disinterested manner. The assumption that the world is his and for him and also the tendency to derive pleasure out of it, is anti spiritual discipline and is the cause of bondage. The reason is that the body-senses-mind-intellect etc., whatever we have, is of the world and for the world. Therefore if the things received from the world, are used in rendering service to the world, the world will not appear as the world but it will be seen as the manifestation of God, which really it is. It means whether a striver assumes the world as true or the self as true or God as true, by anyone of the assumptions, he can practise spiritual discipline and can attain the final reality 'Vāsudevaḥ sarvam'.

Link:—In the previous verse, Lord Kṛṣṇa said, "The higher (sentient) nature, has sustained the lower (insentient) nature." He clarifies it, in the next verse.

एतद्योनीनि भूतानि सर्वाणीत्युपधारय।
अहं कृत्स्नस्य जगतः प्रभवः प्रलयस्तथा॥ ६॥

etadyonīni bhūtāni sarvāṇītyupadhāraya
ahaṁ kṛtsnasya jagataḥ prabhavaḥ pralayastathā

Know, that all beings have evolved from this twofold prakṛti (the insentient and the sentient nature). I am the origin (prabhava) of the entire creation and then, it dissolves in Me (pralaya). 6

Comment:—

'Etadyonīni bhūtāni'—All the beings—gods, men, animals, birds etc., which move and also trees, creepers and grass etc., which do not move, have their origin, in the union of My insentient and sentient Nature.

In the twenty-sixth verse of the thirteenth chapter also, the Lord declares, "Whatever being, moving or unmoving is born; know that, as emanated from the union of Kṣetra (matter) and

Kṣetrajña (spirit)." The same fact has been pointed out, in the fourth verse of the fourteenth chapter, when He declares, "My prakṛti (nature) (primordial matter), is the womb of the bodies of creatures and the soul (seed), which resides in those bodies, is My fragment." The same seed or soul, has been called His higher (sentient) Nature (7/5), and His eternal portion (15/7).

'Sarvāṇītyupadhāraya'—In the universe all the moving and unmoving creatures, are born of the union of the sentient and the insentient nature (matter). It means, that soul has accepted matter, as its own, and keeps its company, and so beings are born—So think of this fact i.e., understand it in the right perspective, or accept it.

'Ahaṁ kṛtsnasya jagataḥ prabhavaḥ pralayastathā'—All objects emanate from God, and again dissolve in Him. So the Lord declares, "I am the origin of the entire creation, and again it dissolves in Me."

The Lord, is the source of entire creation because, creation comes into existence, by His will* (Chāndogya. 6/2/3). As a potter, makes earthenwares and a goldsmith makes ornaments of gold, so does the Lord create this world. Thus, like a potter and a goldsmith, He is an efficient cause, of this world.

The universe, again dissolves in Him. As an earthen vessel is of clay, it was clay in the past, before it was moulded into this shape and will remain clay, when the vessel is broken into pieces. Similarly, the creation is born of the Lord, resides in Him and merges (dissolves) in Him. Thus, he is the material cause of this creation. This is knowledge. The realization, that in the world there is nothing besides the manifestation of the Lord, is Vijñāna (real knowledge of Manifest Divinity).

---

*There is a fact which needs attention that only Kṣetrajña (spirit), not Kṣetra (Matter) has accepted this affinity. If it does not accept this affinity, it can't be reborn because, "Attachment to these Guṇas (modes) is the cause of his birth in good and evil wombs" (13/21).

In the expression 'Kṛtsnasya jagataḥ', Lord Kṛṣṇa declares Himself to be the origin of entire creation, and also its dissolution. Here it is appropriate for Him, to talk of Himself as the origin and dissolution of Matter (insentient Nature). But how is the origin of soul (sentient or higher nature) and its dissolution, possible? The soul is eternal, omnipresent, immovable, constant and everlasting (Gītā 2/24), while the world is ever-changing. But, here the word 'creation' denotes, both the lower nature (matter) and higher nature (Soul). The reason is, though the soul is eternal, changeless and constant, yet It identifies Itself with perishable matter and thus accepts its (insentient's) creation and dissolution as Its (sentient's) own creation and dissolution. So, the soul is said to be born and decayed. Therefore, Lord Kṛṣṇa, has declared Himself to be the origin of the entire creation and also its end. Thus, within creation, (i.e.,) all the moving, unmoving; sentient, insentient beings, will be included. Moreover, Lord Kṛṣṇa, in the thirteenth verse of this chapter, declares, "The whole of this creation, being deluded by objects evolved from the three modes of nature, does not know Me." Only the sentient can know Him. Therefore the term "Jagat" (universe), includes both matter (the insentient), as well as soul (the sentient).

In the eighth verse of the sixteenth chapter, according to men of demoniacal traits, the universe includes both insentient and sentient beings, because they accept all beings, not only insentient ones, as unreal. If the term 'Jagat' (universe), is interpreted as only matter, the followers of non-dualistic principles, who accept the universe as unreal, untrue and baseless, will be included, among men of demoniacal traits, which is totally improper and unjustified. Similarly, in the twenty-sixth verse of the eighth chapter, there is description of the two paths, the bright and the darkness of the world. But the paths, can be followed by the sentient only. The sentient, by identifying with matter, is called 'Jagat' (world or universe).

Thus, we conclude that soul by identifying Itself with Matter, is called embodied soul (world or universe). But, when having disinclination for Matter, it realizes its identity, with pure consciousness (God), this individual soul becomes, the Cosmic Soul. Such a person is called a Yogī.

Appendix—The 'Aparā prakṛti' is that which may know neither (to) itself nor others. The 'Parā Prakṛti' is that which may know itself and also others. All beings moving and unmoving are born by the union of the two—aparā and parā (Gītā 13/26).

The main defect is one which appears in different forms with the difference in places and that is—attachment to the 'aparā'. If this evil is born, it will give birth to all other evils and if this evil is wiped out, all evils will be wiped out. Similarly the basic virtue is also one which reveals all virtues and that is—attachment to God.

We may assume 'aparā' eternal or transient but our relationship with it is transient—this is a unanimous fact. This attachment to this aparā is the cause of birth and death—'kāraṇaṁ guṇasaṅgo'sya sadasadyonijanmasu' (Gītā 13/21). This is the seed cause of the world.

"I am the origin of the entire creation and again it dissolves in Me—It means that I create this moving-unmoving world and only I am created; I destroy the world and only I am destroyed because besides Me there is no other cause or effect of this world (Gītā 7/7) viz., I am its instrumental cause and I am its material cause. Therefore I have manifested Myself in the form of the world." In the nineteenth verse of the ninth chapter also the Lord declares—'amṛtaṁ caiva mṛtyuśca sadasaccāhamarjuna' viz., 'I am immortality as well as death; I am also being and non-being both'. In Śrīmadbhāgavata the Lord declares—

ātmaiva tadidaṁ viśvaṁ sṛjyate sṛjati prabhuḥ
trāyate trāti viśvātmā hriyate haratīśvaraḥ

(11/28/6)

"Whatever thing there is manifest or unmanifest that is only omnipotent God. The entire creation which is appearing, He is its efficient cause and He is also its material cause viz., he creates the universe and He Himself is created as the universe. He is the protector and he is the protected. The same Soul-Universal, God destroys the universe and He Himself is the universe which is destroyed."

In Taittiriyopaniṣad it is mentioned, "I am food and I am also the eater of the food"—'ahamanna-mahamannamahamannam, ahamannādo'hamannādo'hamannādaḥ (3/10/6).

It means that aparā and parā prakṛti and all beings that are born by their union—all of them are only God. The cause is also God and the effect is also God.

Link:—In the preceding verse, Lord Kṛṣṇa declared Himself to be the origin of the whole universe (world). In the next verse, He declares that besides Him there is nothing else, in the universe.

मत्तः परतरं नान्यत्किञ्चिदस्ति धनञ्जय।
मयि सर्वमिदं प्रोतं सूत्रे मणिगणा इव॥७॥

mattaḥ parataraṁ nānyatkiñcidasti dhanañjaya
mayi sarvamidaṁ protaṁ sūtre maṇigaṇā iva

O Arjuna, of this world there is no other cause higher than Me. As yarn beads are strung on the thread, so all the worlds are permeated by Me. 7

Comment:—

'Mattaḥ parataraṁ nānyatkiñcidasti dhanañjaya'—There is nothing else besides Me, the origin of the universe. As air is born of ether, resides in ether and merges in ether without having any independent existence of its own, so is the universe born of the Lord, remains established in Him and merges in Him i.e., the universe has no independent existence of its own, besides the Lord.

Here the term 'Parataraṁ', means that the Lord is the root cause of all things, persons, incidents, circumstances and time etc., of the world. He, is the cause of all causes. There is no cause of Him. It means, that they all seem to exist, in His true light, only He pervades, all of them.

Lord Kṛṣṇa, in the second verse of this chapter, announced that He would unfold in full, the knowledge (wisdom) along with real knowledge of the manifest Divinity (Vijñāna), having known which, nothing else would remain to be known. But, here He declares, that there is no other origin of the universe, besides Him. In both the verses, by using, the expression 'Na anyat' (No anything), He means that, when there is nothing besides Him, how can anything else remain, to be known after knowing Him? Therefore, Lord Kṛṣṇa says, "All this is threaded (strung) on Me" and further, He declares 'All is God' (7/19) and 'I am being and non-being both' (9/19). The effect, has no independent entity, except its cause. The cause, only is manifest in its effect. When the cause, is realized (known), the effect, merges in the cause. It means that the effect has no separate identity from the cause. Similarly, it can be realized, that God is the cause and the world, is the effect. Hence, the world has no separate entity from God. This is God-realization. Actually, it is He who manifests Himself in different forms i.e., this universe is nothing besides, Divine manifestation. Thus a striver, will come to know that the entire universe, is His manifestation.

'Mayi sarvamidaṁ protaṁ sūtre maṇigaṇā iva'—"The whole universe, like clusters of yarn-beads formed by knots on a string, is threaded on Me." As in the cluster of yarn-beads and in the thread, there is nothing besides the thread; in the world, there is nothing else, besides the Lord. As the beads and thread, though being one and the same, seem different, all the beings having different shapes and names, seem to be different, but actually, it is all Divine manifestation. Lord Kṛṣṇa, in the second verse of the thirteenth chapter, declares, "Know Myself, to be the 'Kṣetrajña' (soul) in all the Kṣetras (fields or matter)." It means, that His lower nature in the form of beads, is His own self and His higher nature in the form of thread, is also His own self. He pervades both the two. So long as, a striver attaches importance to the world, he cannot realize God, Who pervades everywhere, in this universe. But, when one comes to know the reality, he realizes that He and only He pervades, everywhere, and there is nothing else, besides Him. To stress the fact, that all things are pervaded only by God, the Lord has described Himself, as the cause of all manifestations.

Appendix—As the clusters of yarn-beads formed by knots on a string are threaded, in them there is nothing besides the thread, similarly in the world there is nothing else besides God. It means that aparā prakṛti in the form of yarn-beads and parā prakṛti in the form of the thread—in both only God pervades. In the formation of yarn-beads there is predominance of aparā prakṛti and in the formation of thread there is predominance of parā prakṛti. The term 'Maṇigaṇāḥ' has been given in plural number which means that the aparā prakṛti consisting of unmoving-moving, aquatic creatures-land creatures-sky creatures, fourteen spheres and eighty-four lac forms of life etc., is divided into infinite forms and infinite groups.

The distinction between Aparā and Parā is because of the Aparā prakṛti, as the soul by assuming the existence of the Aparā, by valuing it and by establishing relationship with it, has become the embodied soul (fifth verse of this chapter). Therefore Aparā prakṛti is there in the world as well in the embodied soul. But in God there is neither Aparā, nor Parā; nor the world nor the embodied soul. It means that there is neither thread nor beads but only cotton is there. Similarly there is neither aparā nor parā but there is only God. The same fact has been described by the Lord ahead upto the twelfth verse. From the term 'mattaḥ' used in this verse upto the expression 'matta eva' used in the twelfth verse, the Lord has mentioned this fact that there is nothing else besides Him. Here the term 'mattaḥ' denotes entire God (God in full) Who is the owner of both prakṛtis—Parā and Aparā.

The cause changes into effect; as cotton is changed into thread and the seed grows into a plant. Therefore God being the Supreme cause of all, only He manifests Himself in all forms—'Vāsudevaḥ sarvam'. Therefore it is a misperception to see any other entity besides God.

'Mattaḥ parataraṁ nānyatkiñcidasti'—He who is better (superior) of the two is called 'paratara'. God is unique (unparalleled), besides Him there is nothing else, then how can He be 'paratara' (superior to anyone)? The term 'paratara' does not apply to Him. Here the term 'paratara' has been used in order to mention the uniqueness of God. It means that there is nothing else besides God and therefore there is no question of anyone being superior to Him. In the Upaniṣad it is mentioned—

puruṣānna paraṁ kiñcitsā kāṣṭhā sā parā gatiḥ

(Kaṭha. 1/3/11)

"There is nothing else besides that Puruṣa. He is the Highest limit and the Supreme destination of all." Arjuna while addressing Lord Kṛṣṇa also says—

'Na tvatsamo'styabhyadhikaḥ kuto'nyolokatraye'pyapratima-prabhāva'—"In all the three worlds, there is none equal to You; who could then possibly excel You (Gītā 11/43)?"

Link:—Now Lord Kṛṣṇa, in the verses eighth to twelfth, declares that He Himself becomes all the manifestations.

रसोऽहमप्सु कौन्तेय प्रभास्मि शशिसूर्ययोः।
प्रणवः सर्ववेदेषु शब्दः खे पौरुषं नृषु॥८॥

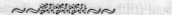

raso'hamapsu kaunteya prabhāsmi śaśisūryayoḥ
praṇavaḥ sarvavedeṣu śabdaḥ khe pauruṣaṁ nṛṣu

O son of Kuntī! I am the taste in water, radiance in the moon and the sun; I am the sacred syllable Oṁ, in the Vedas, sound in ether, and manliness, in men. 8

Comment:—

[Generally people attach a lot of importance to money. So, greedy people have a natural inclination to earn money and accumulate it. Similarly, by accepting the fact that the Lord is the source of the entire creation (7/6), there is no existence of the creation besides the Lord. By accepting this fact, a striver has his natural inclination, towards Him without making any effort. The same fact, has been pointed out by the Lord, in the eighth verse of the tenth chapter, when He declares, "I am the source of the creation, all things evolve from Me. Knowing this, the wise adore Me, with all their heart." In the forty-sixth verse of the eighteenth chapter, He declares, "He from whom the evolution of all beings is, by whom all this is pervaded, worshipping Him through the performance of his own duty, man attains perfection." Here the same principle is explained further.]

'Raso'hamapsu kaunteya'—'O son of Kuntī! I am sapidity in water'. Water emanates, from a subtle form of sapidity, (rasa tanmātrā)* it remains in it and it merges in it. If the taste is removed from water, water cannot remain water.

'Prabhāsmi śaśisūryayoḥ'—"I am radiance† (light), in the

* The causes of the five gross elements—earth, water, fire, air and ether are respectively smell, taste, form, touch and sound which are called five Tanmātrā (seeds). These five seeds can't be known by senses and mind but they are only assumed by hearing the scriptures. The evolutes of these five seeds are also smell, taste, form, touch and sound which can be known by senses and mind.

†In subtle element fire there are two powers—radiance (brilliance) and combustion (burning). Radiance is called 'Prabhā' and combustion is known as 'Teja'. The power of radiance can function without the power of combustion as in gems and the moon, but the power of combustion can't function without radiance. Here in this verse there is predominance of radiance while in the ninth verse of

moon and the sun." Without radiance the moon and the sun, will lose their essence.

'Praṇavaḥ sarvavedeṣu'—"I am the syllable Oṁ, in all the Vedas." First of all, there was revelation of the syllable Oṁ. It was from this sacred syllable Oṁ, that Gāyatrī was revealed and it was from Gāyatrī, that the Vedas were revealed. Therefore, the gist of the Vedas, is the sacred syllable Oṁ.

'Śabdaḥ khe'—Ether, emanates from the subtle element, sound, it remains in it and merges in it. Therefore, sound manifests itself as ether. Without sound, ether is meaningless.

'Pauruṣaṁ nṛṣu'—"I am manliness in men." It is not enough for a man to possess the human body, in order to gain worldly riches, knowledge, name and fame etc., but all these are perishable. The real man, is he who has attained God-realization, the ultimate aim of human life. God existed in the past, exists now and will also exist, in future, because He is eternal. Therefore, a man's 'Puruṣārtha' exertion consists in making efforts with promptness and zeal, to realize God. Without attaining Him, human life is, in vain.

Appendix—In the sixth and seventh verses the Lord has mentioned that He is the cause of the entire creation. Therefore now the Lord describes His divine glories in the form of 'cause' from the eighth verse to the twelfth verse. Though the effect has special characteristic which is not found in the cause, yet the cause has its independent existence viz., without cause the effect has no independent existence. As earth (clay) is the cause and jar is its effect. Water can be filled in a jar but this characteristic is not found in the earth. But without earth (clay) a jar has no independent existence. It means that the cause is changed

---

this chapter there is predominance of the power of combustion. So there the term 'Teja' has been used.

The sun and fire possess both of these powers while in the moon there is only radiance, and instead of combustion there is mildness.

into effect. In making a jar, the doer, the material (cause) and the effect—the three are not one viz., the cause (clay) and the effect (jar) are of one class but the doer (potter) has his different (independent) existence. But in creating the universe the doer, the material and the effect—these three are only God. Therefore sapidity is also God and water is also God. Radiance is also God and the moon and the sun are also God. 'Oṁ' is also God and the Veda is also God. Sound is also God and ether is also God. Manliness is also God and man is also God.

[The earth is changed into the form of a jar but God does not change into the form of the world. The reason is that the thing which is changed is mutable while God is immutable. As in the dark a string (rope) appears in the form of a snake or the snake appears in the form of a coil, similarly God appears in the form of the world. It means that in God there is no distinction of effect and cause because there is nothing besides Him. There is a distinction between the cause and the effect from the man's point of view. Therefore in order to explain it to men, by assuming the existence of some other thing or the other, God is described, discussed, considered and reflected upon and there are questions and answers etc., on Him—'nodyaṁ vā parihāro vā kriyatāṁ dvaitabhāṣyā.]

पुण्यो गन्धः पृथिव्यां च तेजश्चास्मि विभावसौ ।
जीवनं सर्वभूतेषु तपश्चास्मि तपस्विषु ॥ ९ ॥

puṇyo gandhaḥ pṛthivyāṁ ca tejaścāsmi vibhāvasau
jīvanaṁ sarvabhūteṣu tapaścāsmi tapasviṣu

I am pure fragrance of the earth, the lustre in fire; I am the life-force in all beings, and austerity in ascetics. 9

Comment:—

'Puṇyo gandhaḥ pṛthivyām'—The earth is born of subtle

element, smell, stays with it, and merges in it. The earth, is of no importance without pure fragrance, fragrance is a characteristic of earth. So, the Lord declares, "I am pure fragrance in earth." The Lord, uses the objective 'puṇya' (pure) in order to explain that naturally there is pure fragrance in the earth. But bad smell is produced, because it becomes polluted.

'Tejaścāsmi vibhāvasau'—Combustion is born of subtle element, fire, is inherent in it, and at the end, merges in it. Therefore, in fire combustion is the essence. In fire, if there is no combustion it is useless. So the Lord is that combustion.

'Jīvanaṁ sarvabhūteṣu'—Lord Kṛṣṇa declares, "I am life, in all beings." All beings possess life-power, by which they are alive. It is because of that power, that man even in sound sleep, remains different from a dead man.

'Tapaścāsmi tapasviṣu'—Endurance, in the pairs of opposites, is called austerity (tapa). But real austerity, is that in which a striver remains uniform (unchanged), unaffected in difficulties, which he has to face, in realizing God. This austerity, is an invaluable possession, of ascetics. Without austerity, they cannot be called ascetics. So Lord Kṛṣṇa declares, "I am, austerity in ascetics."

Appendix—In the creation of the universe God is the agent (doer), God is the cause and God is the effect. Therefore smell and earth, lustre (combustion) and fire, life-power and beings, austerity and ascetic—all of them (cause and effect) are only God. The reason is that Parā and Aparā—both being the power of God are inseparable from Him. Therefore the entire universe which is born by the union of Parā and Aparā is only the manifestation of God.

'Puṇyo gandhaḥ'—'Gandha-tanmātrā' (smell-subtle element) is the cause and earth is its effect. By calling the smell pure the Lord means to say that the cause (tanmātrā) is ever pure. Impurity is caused by alteration (modification) in the effect. Therefore as fragrance tanmātrā is pure, similarly sound, touch, colour and taste—tanmātrās should also be considered pure.

बीजं मां सर्वभूतानां विद्धि पार्थ सनातनम्।
बुद्धिर्बुद्धिमतामस्मि तेजस्तेजस्विनामहम्॥ १०॥

bījaṁ māṁ sarvabhūtānāṁ viddhi pārtha sanātanam
buddhirbuddhimatāmasmi tejastejasvināmaham

O Pārtha, know Me as the eternal, (Sanātana) seed of all beings; I am the intelligence of the intelligent, the glory (splendour), of the glorious. 10

Comment:—

'Bījaṁ māṁ sarvabhūtānāṁ viddhi* pārtha sanātanam'— O Pārtha, I am the eternal seed (source), of all beings. All of them, are born of Me, Who am their seed, they live in Me and in the end, merge in Me. They without Me have no existence of their own.

A seed, grows out of a tree and it perishes, after creating a tree. But the seed, described in this verse, is eternal without its origin and end. In the eighteenth verse of the ninth chapter, it has been called an 'Imperishable seed'. Remaining imperishable and unaltered, this eternal seed, is the source, producer, resort and illuminator, of the entire universe.

In the Gītā, the word 'seed', has been used, both for God and the embodied soul. In this verse, 'Seed' denotes God, because here, the divine glories have been described. In the thirty-ninth verse of the tenth chapter also, the word 'seed' denotes, God because there, Lord Kṛṣṇa declares, "I am the seed of all beings." In the eighteenth verse of the ninth chapter also, this word has

* In the sixth verse of this chapter Lord Kṛṣṇa used the term 'Upadhāraya' (know) and here he uses the term 'Viddhi' (know). It means that he wants to say that the striver should understand, know and accept the fact that the universe is nothing besides the Divine manifestation.

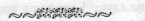

been used for God, because, in the nineteenth verse of that chapter, Lord Kṛṣṇa says, "I am being and non-being both." In the fourth verse of the fourteenth chapter, the term 'seed', stands for embodied soul. The seed, signifies the embodied soul, only when, it has accepted Its affinity for matter (nature), otherwise it is a super-soul (God).

'Buddhirbuddhimatāmasmi'—"I am the intelligence, of the intelligent." People are called intelligent, only because of their intelligence, otherwise they would be called, dull.

'Tejastejasvināmaham'—The Lord, is the glory of the glorious. This glory is a divine trait. Liberated souls, possess a special aura, which enables even dissolute and immoral persons, to become virtuous.

An Exceptional Fact

God, is the origin of the whole universe. He always pervades, everywhere. He exists, even when the entire universe perishes. In the universe, there is nothing besides God. Therefore, in the Upaniṣads (parts of different branches of Vedas), there are illustrations of gold, clay and iron. As in ornaments, made of gold, there is nothing besides gold, in the pots made of clay there is nothing besides clay and in the arms and weapons made of iron, there is nothing besides iron. Similarly, in the entire universe which is born of God, there is nothing besides, God. In the Gītā Lord Kṛṣṇa, has given the illustration of a seed. A seed, is born of a tree and after giving birth to a tree, it perishes. But, God is not an ordinary seed, He is an eternal seed (7/10) and an imperishable one (9/18). It means, that unlike an ordinary seed which after creating another tree, perishes, He does not perish, He remains the same.

Gold, clay and iron, are seen with physical eyes, in ornaments, earthenwares and arms respectively, but God is not seen in the world. So the seed too is not seen in a tree. When a tree sprouts the seed in the form of fruit, then we come to know that the tree is born of that particular seed, though the tree grows out of a seed and ends in a seed. Similarly, God, is the seed of the entire universe. This universe is born of Him, and merges in Him. In the end only God remains (Śrīmadbhāgavata 10/3/25). Those, who see only the tree and the world instead of the seed and God, do not observe in the right perspective. It is only, He Who reveals Himself, in various forms (Chāndogya. 6/2/3).

The universe, including a body, is made of five subtle elements—earth, water, fire, air and ether, but it so appears only if we think over it deeply otherwise not. If we say that these physical bodies, are made of earth because there is predominance of earth-element, people without a deep thought, do not believe, because they say that bodies are different from earth (clay) with which they wash hands. But if the entire universe is burnt to ashes, nothing will remain, besides earth (clay).

If we think deeply, we come to know that a body, is born of the parents' sperm and ovum, which arise from corn (grain), grown out of earth. Thus a body is said to be born of earth. In the end, it merges in earth. After death a body is either buried, or burnt or eaten by animals and birds. In either case it returns, into earth. Thus, the origin and end of a body, is earth. It means, that its middle, is also earth, though it is not seen with physical eyes but it can be conceived by thought. Similarly, by thinking seriously, the world can be perceived, as a manifestation of the Lord. In the entire universe, there is nothing else besides the Lord. Having created the universe (the bodies), He has also entered it (Taittirīyopaniṣad 2/6). He, as the self (soul) also abides in these bodies. Thus the entire universe is His manifestation.

Appendix—The Lord's purpose in calling Himself the seed of all beings is that all beings are His manifestation. There are infinite universes and in those universes—there are endless beings. But the seed of those endless beings is only God. In spite of the creation of endless universes, there is no diminution in that seed, because that seed is not subject to diminution (Gītā 9/18). With that one seed several kinds of universes are born (Gītā 10/39). We may scan the seed with a keen sight (subtle sight) yet the fruit, flowers and leaves will not be visible in it because they are latent in that seed in their causative form. Even the two leaves born of the same tree, are not similar—Even this diversity is present in that seed.

There are several kinds of a thing in the universe. In different countries there are several castes (classes) of human beings. In their bodies there is so much difference that even the lines of the thumbs of two men are not similar. Their shapes, natures, interests, temperaments, assumptions and feelings etc., are also different. There are several kinds of cows, buffaloes, sheeps, goats, horses, camels and dogs etc., and in each kind (class) there are several sub-classes. Among trees also each kind of tree has several classes. Similarly there are endless differences in each kind of knowledge (art). There are three main colours and by their mixture several colours are formed. Out of them in each colour there are so many differences that two men don't perceive a colour similarly. Thus in the universe any two things, which appear similar, are not really similar. In spite of so much diversity, the seed of the universe is only one. It means that God alone manifests Himself in numberless forms and in spite of manifesting Himself in different forms He remains one.*

God is endless from all viewpoints such as place and time

* In spite of diversity among beings, there should be the unity of love among them. As a thorn pricks the foot but the eyes are filled with tears, the same feeling for the welfare of others should prevail among all beings—'sarvabhūtahite ratāḥ' (Gītā 5/25, 12/4). Only love is the feeling which knows no distinction. There can't be any distinction in love. All become one in love. In knowledge there is no difference in reality but differences in opinions persist. In love there is no difference in opinions. Therefore there is nothing beyond love. By love even the Lord of the three worlds becomes submissive to the will of the lover.

etc. When even the universe created by God is endless (limitless), how can a limit be set to God? Upto this day whatever has been thought of, whatever has been said, whatever has been written, whatever has been assumed about God, even if all this is combined, it remains incomplete about Him. Not only this even God Himself can't describe the full details about Himself, if He is able to describe it, how will He remain endless?

बलं बलवतां चाहं कामरागविवर्जितम्।
धर्माविरुद्धो भूतेषु कामोऽस्मि भरतर्षभ॥ ११॥

balaṁ balavatāṁ cāhaṁ kāmarāgavivarjitam
dharmāviruddho bhūteṣu kāmo'smi bharatarṣabha

O Arjuna, I am the strength of the strong without their desire and passion; in beings, I am desire that is not in conflict, with virtue or scriptural injunction. 11

Comment:—

'Balaṁ balavatāṁ cāhaṁ kāmarāgavivarjitam'—The strength, free from desire and attachment, utilized on noble and holy cause and sanctioned by scripture and saints, gets sanctified and therefore the Lord declares, "I am the strength of the strong, free from desire and attachment." This strength is acceptable.

Lord Kṛṣṇa Himself, has explained that the strength possessed of attachment and desire, should be abandoned (17/5) because it is a demoniacal trait. Similar, is the case with strength used in 16/14, 16/18 and 18/53. In 6/34, it has been used as an adjective for mind, and it is a demoniacal trait, because it also possesses, attachment and desire. Thus, such strength (power), is to be abandoned. But, strength free from desire and attachment, as explained in 7/11 as well as in 17/8, is sanctified strength, which is acceptable.

'Dharmāviruddho bhūteṣu kāmo'smi bharatarṣabha'—"I am

righteous passion approved by the scriptures." Desire, free from attachment and pleasure* is laudable, because it helps in producing offsprings and it remains under control of man. But sexual desire, possessed of attachment and pleasure, misguides a man, enables him to perform actions, against dictates of scriptures and leads him to afflictions, sins and degradation.

People who, by using birth-control methods, indulge in sexual intercourse for sensual pleasure, pave their way to hell. Men and women, in the true sense of the terms, are those who have the capacity to produce children, otherwise they are impotent. An eunuch, is not authorized to perform religious rites, such as religious sacrifice and offer water and food etc., to manes. A woman, is called a mother, because she gives birth to children, who call her mother. If the potentiality of generating children is destroyed, she no more deserves to be addressed as 'Mother'—a very venerable vocative. Therefore, strivers should have sexual desire to produce children, according to ordinance of the scripture, in order to lead a pious family life, or they should observe celibacy.

Appendix—The entire moving universe is born of passion. Therefore a man's passion not conflicting with righteousness and which is approved by the scriptures, is the manifestation of God. The Lord has already declared—"mattaḥ parataraṁ nānyatkiñcidasti" (7/7) (there is nothing else besides Me) and further He will declare—"ye caiva sāttvikā bhāvā" (7/12) (all entities born of sattva, rājasa and tāmasa are evolved from Me) and 'Vāsudevaḥ sarvam' (7/19) (all is God). Therefore just as righteous desire is the manifestation of God, similarly unrighteous passion is also not different from God. Those who act being guided by unrighteous desires, pave the way to hells in the forms

* Here the desire stands for the desire of the householders sanctioned by the scriptures rather than the desire which has been mentioned as the most sinful in the thirty-seventh verse of the third chapter.

of God because hells are also God only. But the aim of the Gītā is not to lead a man to hell or to the cycle of birth and death but is to lead him to the attainment of salvation. The aim is ever for salvation or bliss, not for sufferings. No one wants pain (suffering). Arjuna has also entreated Lord Kṛṣṇa to tell him the highest good for him.* For example, words are good and also bad, but in grammar only the good words are reflected upon, because grammar etc., also aim at a man's salvation.

ये चैव सात्त्विका भावा राजसास्तामसाश्च ये।
मत्त एवेति तान्विद्धि न त्वहं तेषु ते मयि॥१२॥

ye caiva sāttvikā bhāvā rājasāstāmasāśca ye
matta eveti tānviddhi na tvahaṁ teṣu te mayi

Whatever entities are born of sattva (mode of goodness or purity), of rajas (mode of activity or passion) and tamas (the mode of inertia or ignorance), know them all, as evolved from Me; yet still neither I am in them, nor are they, in Me. 12

Comment:—

'Ye caiva sāttvikā bhāvā rājasāstāmasāśca ye'—It means, that in the entire universe, all the Guṇas (attributes of things and actions) evolve from God. He is the root, support, base and illuminator of all of these. Whatever, singularity is seen in the entire universe, that is the Lord's. So, a man should have inclination towards Him, rather than, towards the mode of goodness etc. This inclination towards God, will lead him to emancipation, while inclination towards the mode of goodness etc., will lead him to bondage.

Actually all the objects, attributes (modes) and actions, are

* 'yacchreyaḥ syānniścitaṁ brūhi tanme' (Gītā 2/7)
'tadekaṁ vada niścitya yena śreyo'hamāpnuyām' (Gītā 3/2)
'yacchreya etayorekaṁ tanme brūhi suniścitam' (Gītā 5/1)

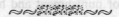

nothing else, besides the manifestation of the Lord. Now a question arises, when every action is a manifestation of the Lord, why is there, sanction or prohibition for these? The answer is, that actions which are sanctioned by scriptures, result in favourable and happy circumstances, while actions which are prohibited (forbidden), result in unfavourable and sad circumstances. So, if a person performs forbidden actions, regarding these as manifestation of the Lord, the Lord as a result of those actions will manifest Himself, in the form of punishment and hell.

As far as actions are concerned, a striver should perform only those actions, which are sanctioned by the scriptures. As far as, acceptance (assumption) and knowledge, are concerned, one should accept that God exists and he should know the self or the world. By assuming the existence of God, he should develop a keen desire to attain Him. He should try to please Him, by obeying Him and by following His principles. He should also know that bodies and the universe, are kaleidoscopic and perishable, and these are neither his nor meant for him. By knowing this fact, he should cease attachment for them. By doing so, he will realize the reality. But, even after knowing the fact that they are perishable, if a striver, attaches importance to them, he will not be able to attain emancipation.

'Matta eveti tānviddhi'—All are evolved from the Lord viz., He is all in all; the cause and the effect, which seems distinct. But, the effect has no separate and independent existence, from the cause. Therefore, the effect is a manifestation of the cause, only. As in ornaments made of gold, there is nothing else, besides gold, similarly the universe evolved from God is nothing else, besides God.

By using the phrase 'Matta eva' Lord Kṛṣṇa, means that His lower nature and higher nature, are not different from Him. As an appendix to the seventh chapter in the ninth chapter, Lord Kṛṣṇa declares, "Through My nature, I bring forth again and again, all this multitude of beings" (9/8) and further, He declares, "With Me as the supervisor, nature brings forth, the whole creation" (9/10). Actually, both of the declarations, are one and the same. In both the cases, there is predominance of God. The same fact, has been pointed out here in 7/6. "I am the source and the end of the entire universe." While concluding it, He declares, "Whatever entities there are born of sattva, rajas and tamas, know them all, as evolved from Me."

The Lord, having promised to discuss knowledge and realization, started the topic by mentioning that among thousands, one scarcely knows Him, in truth. Then having explained His higher and lower natures, He mentioned these as the source of all beings. Then, He explained that He, is the source of the universe (7/7). The same fact, has been pointed out here, while concluding the topic of His divine glories, when He declares "Know that the sattva (mode of goodness), the rajas (mode of passion) and the tamas (mode of ignorance), are evolved from Me."

'Na tvahaṁ teṣu te mayi'—"I am not in them, and they are not in Me." It means, that those attributes have no independent existence of their own, besides the Lord. All actions, objects, are born and then they decay. If the Lord, had been in them, with their decay He would have also decayed. But, He never decays. It means, that He is not in them. If they had been in Him, they should have also been imperishable, like Him. But it is not so, they perish, while He is eternal. It means, that they are not in Him. As a seed, takes the shape of a tree with its branches, leaves, flowers etc., but these cannot be perceived in it, similarly, nature, constituted of the three categories (modes)—sattva, rajas and tamas has origin in Him, but He is not perceived, in them. Actually, there is nothing else, besides Him.

As clouds evolve from ether, reside in ether and dissolve in ether, yet ether, remains the same, without any modification. All the divine glories, described from the eighth verse upto this verse, evolve from the Lord, reside in Him and dissolve in Him. But He is not in them and they are not in Him i.e., they are nothing else, besides Him. The Lord by pointing out this fact, wants to warn people, that they should not be entangled in worldly pleasures and prosperity, because there is nothing else, besides Him. So they should attach importance, only to Him.

An Important Fact

All the entities born of sattva, rajas and tamas, are born of God's nature and as God and His Nature, are one and the same. It means, that they are born of God and they dissolve in Him. But, the higher nature (embodied soul), has accepted its affinity with Nature (Matter). It has accepted it as its own, and for its own—this is sustaining the world by an embodied soul and so it is born and it decays. In order to, free man from this bondage of birth and death, Lord Kṛṣṇa declares, that all entities born of sattva, rajas and tamas are born of Him. Similarly, He declares, in the tenth chapter, "These diverse feelings of creatures, emanate from Me alone" (10/5) and "I am the source of all creation and everything in the world, moves because of Me" (10/8). In the fifteenth chapter also He declares: "Memory, wisdom and ratiocinative faculty emanate from Me" (15/15). When everything emanates from God, it means that man actually has no affinity for the attributes (modes). Therefore, if one does not accept his affinity for them, they cannot lead him to bondage i.e., to the cycle of birth and death.

In the Gītā, in the context of devotion also, Lord Kṛṣṇa declares, that He is all—"I am being and non-being both" (9/19) and Arjuna also says, to Lord Kṛṣṇa, "You are being (existent) and non-being (non-existent) both, and also beyond, both of them" (11/37). Lord Kṛṣṇa also, declares about a devotee having exclusive devotion "Such a devotee realizes, that all this is God" (7/19). A devotee having exclusive devotion, like a chaste wife who perceives only her husband, and thinks of no other man even in dream, beholds nothing else besides, God.

In the Discipline of Knowledge, the Lord declares, the real and unreal, as separate entities. "The unreal has no existence, and the real never ceases to be" (2/16). Similarly, matter (nature) spirit, and Kṣetra (field)—Kṣetrajña (knower of the field) are described in the Gītā, time and again, as "Know matter and spirit to be both, without beginning" (13/19); "The knowledge of Kṣetra (field or matter) and kṣetrajña (spirit), is true knowledge" (13/2); "Whatever being, is born, the unmoving or the moving know it, as emanated from the union of Kṣetra (Matter) and Kṣetrajña (spirit) (13/26); 'Kṣetrajña (the Lord of the Kṣetra viz., spirit), illumines the whole Kṣetra (field or matter) (13/33); "Those who perceive with an eye of wisdom, this distinction between the Kṣetra and Kṣetrajña, reach the Supreme" (13/34). Thus, by distinguishing the two, a striver realizes, that self is unconnected with Matter, and is totally untainted.

A striver, should possess both devotion and knowledge. In, the Discipline of Devotion, there is predominance of devotion, while knowledge is secondary. In the Discipline of Knowledge, there is predominance of knowledge while devotion occupies a secondary place. In, the Discipline of Devotion, it is believed that all the entities (beings) born of sattva, rajas and tamas, evolve from Him (7/12) while, in the Discipline of Knowledge, it is thought, that qualities (modes) of sattva (goodness), rajas (passion) and tamas (ignorance), are born of prakṛti (nature) (14/5). Both types of strivers, accept that they are free from those qualities (modes), and both of them realize, the same reality which cannot be called, either dual or non-dual, neither, real nor unreal.

The strivers, following the Discipline of Devotion, having exclusive devotion identify themselves with God and thus become free from Matter, while devotees following the Discipline of Knowledge, by discriminating between matter and the spirit, realize the self, and thus become free from matter.

Appendix—While explaining in details the notion of the expression 'mattaḥ parataraṁ nānyat kiñcidasti' (there is nothing else besides Me) (7/7), whatever the Lord told in the preceding four verses and whatever He has not told—all that has been concluded in this verse. The Lord declares, "All the Sāttvika, Rājasa and Tāmasa modes evolve from Me and I provide them existence and agility; yet neither I am in them nor are they in Me viz., only I am all. Therefore the striver who wants to attain Me, instead of getting entangled in these modes, should be inclined to Me. If he gets entangled in these modes, he can never attain salvation or devotion."

The modes that are seen, heard and understood and that are not seen, heard and understood—all of them should be included within the term 'ye' (whatever).

The Sāttvika, Rājasa and Tāmasa modes have been called 'bhāva' because they evolve from God. It means that God is in the form of 'bhāva' (ever-existent)*, therefore only the existent 'bhāva' will evolve from Him, how will 'abhāva' (Non-existent) evolve? As all these 'bhāvas' (modes) evolve from Him, so all of them are the manifestations of God—'bhavanti bhāvā bhūtānāṁ matta eva pṛthagvidhāḥ' (Gītā 10/5). It means that with the body-senses-mind-intellect whatever Sāttvika, Rājasa and Tāmasa feelings, actions, objects etc., are perceived, they are all only God†. Even the 'sphuraṇā' (mere fleeting thought) that comes to the mind whether good or bad, is only God. In the world whatever good or bad, pure or impure, friend or enemy,

---

* nāsato vidyate bhavo nābhāvo vidyate sataḥ (Gītā 2/16);

'madbhāvaṁ so'dhigacchati' (Gītā 14/19)', 'sarvabhūteṣu yenaikaṁ bhāvamavyayamīkṣate' (Gītā 18/20).

† manasā vacasā dṛṣṭyā gṛhyate'nyairapīndriyaiḥ
ahameva na matto'nyaditi budhyadhvamañjasā
(Śrīmadbhā. 11/13/24)

wicked or noble, virtuous or sinful etc., is seen, heard, thought of and understood etc.,—all is only God. Besides God there is nothing else anywhere.

If there is any selfish motive and we have a desire to take anything from others, then Sāttvika, Rājasa and Tāmasa—these three different kinds appear. But if there is no selfish motive and we have an eye on the welfare of others, then these are nothing but the manifestation of God. If we regard them for us and derive pleasure from them, they pave the way to ruin (Gītā 3/37).

'The three modes are evolved from Me'—by saying this the Lord means that a striver instead of having an eye on these modes, should have his eye on Him Who transcends these modes viz., he having assumed the existence and greatness of the Lord, should establish relation with Him so that he may attain Him, and being free from the sufferings forever, may attain the Supreme bliss. 'I am not in them and they are not in Me'—by saying this, the Lord means, "If anyone instead of attaching importance to Me as reality and my greatness, attaches importance and value to Sāttvika, Rājasa and Tāmasa modes, objects and actions and is attached to them, he instead of attaining Me, will follow the cycle of birth and death—'kāraṇaṁ guṇasaṅgo'sya sadasadyonijanmasu' (Gītā 13/21).

The Lord uses the expression 'matta eva' as if He wants to say, "The three modes are evolved from Me, then instead of having an inclination to Me, why do you get entangled in the modes? Those who get entangled in these modes, can't worship Me (Gītā 7/13). But those devotees, who don't get entangled in these modes, worship Me (Gītā 7/16, 10/8). These modes are not lasting because the cause stays, the effect does not stay. As gold stays, ornaments don't stay; earth stays (persists), the jar does not remain; God remains, modes don't stay (remain). The modes are kaleidoscopic and perishable but God ever remains the same, He is neither kaleidoscopic nor perishable. Therefore

God is not attained by modes, but He is attained by renouncing attachment to the modes. Therefore by overpowering Tamoguṇa by Rajoguṇa and Rajoguṇa by Sattvaguṇa, the striver has to transcend all the three guṇas (modes).

Here a point needs special attention that God endowed with attributes and form is in fact only attributeless because He is free from the modes of Sattva, Raja and Tama but He possesses virtues such as glory, sweetness, beauty and generosity etc. Therefore the devotion to God Who is endowed with attributes and form, is also called 'Nirguṇa' (free from the modes of goodness etc.,) as 'manniṣṭhaṁ nirguṇaṁ smṛtam', 'manniketaṁ tu nirguṇam', 'nirguṇo madapāśrayaḥ', 'matsevāyāṁ tu nirguṇā' (Śrīmadbhā. 11/25/24—27).

Question—When all is God, why are Sāttvika-Rājasa-Tāmasa 'bhāvas' (modes) to be renounced?

Answer—As in the earth there is water everywhere but that is available in the well, similarly God exists everywhere but the place where He attained is 'Yajña' (performance of duty selflessly)—'tasmātsarvagataṁ brahma nityaṁ yajñe pratiṣṭhitam' (Gītā 3/15). But Sāttvika-Rājasa-Tāmasa bhāvas (entities) are not places where God is available viz., by them God is not attained (Gītā 7/13). Therefore they are not useful for a striver. So the Lord has declared—'Neither I am in those modes nor are they in Me.'

As in the field of millet, only millet is substantial, stalks and leaves are not substantial. The aim of the farmer is only to get millet. In order to get millet, he waters the field and manures it for nourishing the soil (field) so that he may get the millet of a good quality. Similarly a striver should aim at attaining God, not the world. In order to attain God, a striver should serve the world without any selfish motive. There is value of millet rather than of stalks and leaves, because at the beginning there is millet and in the end also millet remains. After taking out millet whatever stalks and leaves are left, they are not useful for men, but they are feeds for animals. Similarly Sāttvika, Rājasa and Tāmasa modes are for the deluded (unwise). These three modes bind a man (Gītā 14/5). Therefore these modes in spite of being the manifestations of God are not for the self but their use with discrimination is for worldly dealings. As poison is also the manifestation of God but that is not to be taken.

As leaves and stalks also emanate from the seed of millet but there is no millet in them and in the millet there are no stalks and leaves, similarly though the Sāttvika-Rājasa-Tāmasa modes evolve from God, yet God is not in them and they are not in God.

Link:—Lord Kṛṣṇa, in the twelfth verse, said that entities born of Sattva, Rajas and Tamas, are born of Him, still neither He is in them, nor are they in Him. It means, that God is free from Matter (Nature), and its evolutes. Similarly, soul being an eternal portion of God, is also free. But how is it bound? The answer follows:—

त्रिभिर्गुणमयैर्भावैरेभिः सर्वमिदं जगत्।
मोहितं नाभिजानाति मामेभ्यः परमव्ययम्॥ १३॥

tribhirguṇamayairbhāvairebhiḥ sarvamidaṁ jagat
mohitaṁ nābhijānāti māmebhyaḥ paramavyayam

Beguiled by these threefold dispositions (guṇas) of Nature (prakṛti) this world (embodied soul) does not know Me, who is beyond these and imperishable as well. 13

Comment:—

'Tribhirguṇamayairbhavairebhiḥ...paramavyayam'—The three disposition (modes) of Nature—sattva, rajas and tamas, evolve and dissolve. A man, by identifying himself with these modes, thinks himself as sāttvika, rājasika or tāmasika. Being deluded by them, he cannot deem that he is an eternal fragment of God. Losing sight of this eternal affinity with God, he accepts his affinity with transitory mental tendencies—this is his delusion.

The term 'Jagat' (world), here denotes 'embodied soul.' The spirit (soul), because of its identity with the kaleidoscopic body is called 'Jagat' (world). It accepts, the body's birth, death, health and sickness etc., as its own. So long as, it continues to accept its identity with the body, it will remain the world i.e., it will go on following the cycle of birth and death, without living permanently anywhere.

Men are deluded, because they accept as separate entities the three modes of nature, besides God. If they accept these as Divine manifestation, they cannot be deluded.

Delusion arises, out of either of the assumptions, regard the body as yours, or accept yourself as the body. Acceptance of the body as yours, is 'mineness' while acceptance that the self, is body is egoism. This Egoism and 'mineness', is called, delusion. It is because of delusion, that a man cannot know, the reality about God. It is a rule, that a man can know the world by isolating himself from it, and he can know God by identifying himself with Him, because, he is totally different from the body, and one with God.

Our affinity with God, is natural because we are His eternal fragment, but our affinity with body and the world, is man-made and artificial. If we accept this artificial affinity as real, that is our delusion, and it obstructs in realizing real affinity.

Now, there is a question, whether first man turned away from God, or got deluded by the three modes of nature. Philosophers are of the opinion, that both of them have been there from times immemorial, they are without beginning. Therefore it cannot be said which of these is former and which is latter. Man should make the right use of freedom given to him, by God. By doing so, he can transcend the three modes of Nature, and be free from the cycle of birth and death. This proves, that by misusing his freedom, and being entangled in sensual and ephemeral pleasures, he cannot realize God.

By the term 'Paramavyayam', Lord Kṛṣṇa says, that He is above the threefold modes of nature i.e., He is unconnected with and free from them, there is no modification in Him. Moreover, He is imperishable. But the man, deluded by modes of nature cannot know His real self.

Appendix—The man, who instead of seeing God, perceives (sees) Sāttvika, Rājasa and Tāmasa dispositions (modes), enjoys them and derives pleasure from them, he is deluded by those dispositions viz., is bound by God's Divine illusion, and the result is that he follows the cycle of birth and death. It means that Sāttvika, Rājasa and Tāmasa dispositions (actions, objects, time, nature and modes etc.,) are transient while God is eternal. Those who enjoy the transient, get bound; but those who having renounced the transient, take refuge in God, get liberated (Gītā 7/14).

In this verse the term 'Jagata' has been used for the embodied soul. It means that the being by according reality, by valuing and by being attached to the entity which really does not exist, becomes 'Jagata'. The sentient (by flouting Viveka) becomes insentient. The higher nature (prakṛti) becomes lower nature. The soul assumes the origin and destruction of the world as its origin and destruction, and the profit and loss of the world as its own profit and loss. As a man, by becoming, obsessed with desire, becomes 'kāmātmānaḥ' viz., gets practically identified with desire (Gītā 2/43); and by intimate kinship with God 'manmayāḥ' viz., gets absorbed in God (Gītā 4/10); similarly the embodied soul (self) being deeply attached to the world becomes the world (Jagata). The only difference is that a striver's (the self) identity with God is eternal but identity with desire or 'Jagata' (world) is transient.

A man (the self) has assumed the existence of other entity besides God, by assuming its existence he regarded it as valuable, by valuing it he got attached to it and by being attached to it, he lost his independent existence and became 'Jagata'. He who regards the existence of the world only, forgets one's own reality and becomes 'Jagata' which is unreal; and who assumes the existence of God, being oblivious of the independent existence of his own, becomes God—'mama sādharmyamāgatāḥ' (Gītā 14/2) Who is real.

The Lord calls the embodied soul 'Jagat' because of not cognising the fact that "I am sentient", man started assuming the insentient body as 'I' (his own self) and as 'mine'. The self though attributeless and imperishable yet because of being 'Jagata' gets bound by Sāttvika-Rājasa-Tāmasa modes—'nibadhnanti mahābāho dehe dehinamavyayam' (Gītā 14/5). In fact the self being a fragment of the divine God is divine only (Gītā 13/31) but being attached to the mundane 'Jagata' he becomes mundane (worldly). From ego (the elements) downward to the earth—all is 'Aparā Prakṛti'—lower nature (Gītā 7/4). Therefore as the earth is insentient (matter), so is ego also matter. When the self being identified with ego becomes 'ahaṅkāravimūḍhātmā' viz., assumes ego as the self, then having a gradual downfall it (he) becomes the insentient world viz., its divinity (sentience) is lost (forgotten) and it does not realize its divinity.

Those who don't get attached to the modes, the matter vanishes for them but they see only God everywhere—'Vāsudevaḥ sarvam' (all is God) (Gītā 7/19). But those who are attached to modes, can't see God but see the world only, therefore they perceive God also as worldly. They perceive even the transcendental Lord, bound by modes and see immortal (imperishable) God as mortal (perishable) (Gītā 7/24). A devotee sees nothing else besides God but the worldly people, attached to the modes, see only the world, nothing else. Therefore a devotee attains only bliss while a worldly person suffers only sorrow—'duḥkhālayam' (Gītā 8/15).

Link:—Now, in the next verse, Lord Kṛṣṇa explains, why a man does not know Him, and how he can know Him.

दैवी ह्येषा गुणमयी मम माया दुरत्यया।
मामेव ये प्रपद्यन्ते मायामेतां तरन्ति ते॥ १४॥

daivī hyeṣā guṇamayī mama māyā duratyayā
māmeva ye prapadyante māyāmetāṁ taranti te

This Divine illusion of Mine, consisting of the three guṇas (modes of Nature), is difficult to overcome; however; those who perpetually worship Me alone could penetrate it. 14

Comment:—

'Daivī hyeṣā guṇamayī* mama māyā duratyayā'—The Divine illusion of the Lord, consisting of the three modes of nature—Sattva, Raja and Tama is extremely difficult to surmount. People because of the desire of pleasures and prosperity, cannot be free from this illusion. Because of their attachment for the world, including the body and its pleasure and pain etc., they get entangled in them. This Divine illusion, is hard to surmount, when they accept the independent existence of the modes of Nature. If they do not accept their separate entity, besides God, they will overcome this Divine illusion.

'Māmeva ye prapadyante māyāmetāṁ taranti te'—Those, who take refuge in Me, alone cross this illusion, because instead of beholding the three modes of Nature they behold Me only. As has already been described, these three modes of nature are neither

---

* Lord Kṛṣṇa in the twelfth verse has declared that the three modes of goodness, of passion and of ignorance proceed from Him. The same fact has been pointed out here when the Lord declares that His illusion consisting of the three modes is divine. The term 'Eṣā' stands for the threefold modes of nature by which the world is deluded as has been described in the thirteenth verse.

The Divine illusion has been called to be consisting of the three modes because this illusion in the form of the modes of Nature is the evolute of Nature. These are the modes rather than Nature (Prakṛti) which bind the man (soul).

in Me nor am I, in them. I perform all actions without having the least attachment. Thus, those who know this reality, do not get entangled, in the three modes and pierce this illusion. They do not depend on mind and intellect etc., because they know that mind and intellect etc., also belong to nature (matter), which perish every moment. So they have a disinclination towards matter, and an inclination towards Me, because they know that soul is an eternal fragment, of Mine.

Lord Kṛṣṇa, by using the terms 'Māmeva', means to say that they take refuge only in Him, because they do not accept any other existence, besides Him. Thus, those who without depending on money, material and men etc., take refuge in Him only i.e., depend on Him only, cross this illusion.

The senses, body, mind, intellect and worldly possessions, belong to the Lord and therefore, these are to be used in the service of the Lord, without any selfish motive. If we do not do so, we are dishonest and we do not perform our duty. But, if we use it in His service, He gets pleased and by His grace, we penetrate the veil of illusion.

Actually, all things have been given to us by God, but we feel proud of them, by thinking these as our own. This is an error. God is so gracious and generous that He gives the things, in such an unique way, that He does not show that they have been given by Him. So we accept these as our own. Only devotees, can realize His grace and generosity. But, those who have disinclination for Him, cannot realize that all the things have been bestowed upon them, by God, by His grace and they cannot possess them forever. So they cannot have an exclusive devotion, for God.

This verse means, that those who take refuge in Him i.e., those who possess divine traits, cross His Divine illusion, and those who take refuge in gods i.e., those who possess, demoniacal traits—attaching importance to body and pleasures etc., cannot cross His Divine illusion. Such persons, possessing demoniacal traits have to return to life even though they might have gained, the world of Brahmā, but they have to follow, the cycle of birth and death.

Appendix—When a man turning away his face from the world, takes refuge in God, then he crosses (overcomes) the 'Māyā' (the evolute of the lower nature) viz., his ego is totally destroyed. 'Refuge in God' means to identify the self with God viz., to accept the entity of God only. He should assume neither the independent entity of the self nor of the 'Māyā'. He should depend neither on ego nor on 'Māyā' (modes). It needs no exertion, no effort.

The man himself has assumed the existence of 'Māyā'—'yayedaṁ dhāryate jagat' (Gītā 7/5), 'manaḥ ṣaṣṭhānīndriyāṇi prakṛtisthāni karṣati' (Gītā 15/7). If he, not recognising the existence of 'Māyā', had taken refuge in God, he would have crossed the 'Māyā' viz., for him the 'Māyā' would have had no existence.

A man, by depending on the insentient (matter) viz., by assuming it as his and for him, himself becomes insentient (matter) and is called 'Jagata' (Gītā 7/13). But by depending on God, he attains divinity and becomes a devotee. By becoming a devotee, the world is lost to him viz., for him the world does not remain the world but it becomes the manifestation of God which it really is.

By the term 'māmeva' the Lord means to say, "The soul is a fragment of only Mine (My own) (mama eva)—'mamaivāṁśo jīvaloke' (Gītā 15/7). Therefore if a striver takes refuge only in Me (mām eva), he crosses the 'Māyā'. So the devotees, who take refuge in Me, have no relationship with anyone else besides Me, their relation with anyone else is impossible because they hold that there is no other entity at all, besides Me. They don't see anyone else and anyone else is not seen to them. From their view-point there is neither existence nor value of the lower nature and they don't regard it as theirs. They regard it as My manifestation as really it is."

The devotees who follow the guidance of 'Viveka', having renounced dependence on ego viz., by renouncing the world, depend on God. But those who cannot follow the dictates of their Viveka, but have the predominance of faith and belief, such simple hearted and straightforward devotees with their ego (as they are, so) take refuge in God. The Lord Himself destroys the ego of such devotees (Gītā 10/11).

Link:— In the previous verse, Lord Kṛṣṇa said, "Those who take refuge in me alone, cross the Divine illusion of Mine." Then why do all creatures not take refuge in Him? The answer follows:—

न मां दुष्कृतिनो मूढाः प्रपद्यन्ते नराधमाः।
माययापहृतज्ञाना आसुरं भावमाश्रिताः॥ १५॥

na māṁ duṣkṛtino mūḍhāḥ prapadyante narādhamāḥ
māyayāpahṛtajñānā āsuraṁ bhāvamāśritāḥ

The evil-doers, the deluded, the lowest of men, deprived of discrimination (wisdom) by illusion (māyā) having succumbed to demoniacal nature, do not take refuge in Me. 15

Comment:—

'Na māṁ duṣkṛtino mūḍhāḥ prapadyante narādhamāḥ'— Those, who are evil-doers and deluded, do not take refuge in Him. Evil-doers are those, who have attachment, for the acquired worldly kaleidoscopic things, and who have desire to get unacquired ones. Fulfilment of desires, leads to greed and obstacles to fulfilment of desires, lead to anger. Thus, those who because of their desire, enjoy sensual pleasures against the ordinance of scriptures, because of greed, commit sins, such as falsehood, fraud, betrayal and dishonesty etc., and because of anger, have feelings of envy, jealousy and enmity and commit violence, are all evil-doers.

Desire, evolves when a man attaches importance to any worldly entity. This desire, leads a man to delusion and he thinks that he should, enjoy worldly pleasures and should live. Thus he instead of seeking refuge in God, seeks refuge in perishable things and objects etc., owing to pre-ponderance of the mode of their ignorance.

Men are deluded, because they cannot discriminate, between the real and the unreal, the imperishable and the perishable, the improper and the proper etc., and they are disinclined, towards God. Such evil-doers and deluded ones, cannot have a resolve, for spirituality, then how can they take refuge in Him?

Those evil-doers and deluded ones, are the lowest of men. They are lower than, even animals, because animals follow rules of nature, while they do not. Moreover, animals, while suffering the fruit of their previous actions, move higher towards human life, whereas, human beings by having this body (bestowed upon them for God-realization) by doing sins and injustice, follow the path, which leads them to hell and animal-life. Lord Kṛṣṇa, has declared about such people (Gītā 16/19-20)—"I repeatedly, throw those evil, cruel, haters, and vilest among men, into demoniacal wombs. Thus cast, they sink into, still lower depths."

'Māyayāpahṛtajñānā āsuraṁ bhāvamāśritāḥ'— Deluded by, the wonderful illusion of the Lord, consisting of the three modes of nature (7/14) possessing demoniacal traits viz., busy with bringing up senses, body and mind etc., such people have total disinclination for Him, and thus cannot seek refuge in Him. Secondly, such people, are so much deprived of discrimination, that they cannot perceive the perishable nature of the worldly things, and so they hanker after prosperity, pleasure, praise etc. They consider it to be their chivalry and success, and think that there is no aim of life, besides them. So they cannot perceive reality about the world that it is perishable and they have no lasting connection with it.

The term 'asu', stands for, vital force (prāṇa). In spite of, perceiving them as active and perishable, they are ever-engaged in nourishing them. They attach importance only, to mundane objects, which are necessary for the maintenance of their life. They attach more importance to money, than to necessities of life. Money is not usable by itself. It is useful through commodities. They attach importance, not only to money, but to its quantum. The quantum enhances pride, which is a demoniac trait, and leads to all afflictions and sins.*

An Important Fact

Here Lord Kṛṣṇa has declared, that evil-doers do not seek refuge in Him, while in the thirtieth verse of the ninth chapter, He declares that even if the vilest sinner worships Him with exclusive devotion, he should be considered a saint, and he secures lasting peace. How? The answer is, that the vilest sinner has no natural inclination to God, but if his unfavourable circumstances or grace of saints or any virtuous action of the past, inspires him to take refuge in Him, he becomes a saint because God is equanimous to all, without having any hatred or liking (Gītā 9/29). He, equally showers His blessings, upon all creatures, whether they are vile or virtuous.

In fact, a vile person is more deserving, as far as God's grace is concerned, because he thinks that he has no virtue. As a mother, loves all her sons equally, the Lord's heart is naturally gracious to all beings. The Lord, the mother of all ages, loves all creatures equally. Therefore, if a man seeks refuge in Him, the Lords' heart, melts with a great compassion and He instead

* Pride is the root of the world which is in the form of birth and death and it causes innumerable kinds of afflictions and miseries (Mānasa 7/74/30).

of thinking of his past errors, thinks of what he has in his heart now (Mānasa 1/29/3).

It has been declared by Him, in the Rāmacaritamānasa that even a man having envy with all beings but finding himself helpless, in the world, however takes refuge in God, He by His grace, without paying any heed to his pride, delusion, fraud and deception etc., keeping his good sentiment in view makes him a saint very quickly (5/48/1-2).

A righteous man, depends on his righteousness and so does not depend on God exclusively, while a vile person, without having any support, depends on the Lord exclusively. Therefore the Lord's heart melts, and thus the vile person, becomes a saint. Moreover, the nature of evil-doers does not allow them to take refuge, in God. But, if anyone somehow or the other, takes refuge in Him, He is ever-prepared to embrace him. Therefore, in the two contexts, there is no contradiction, but God's grace, is revealed in both of these.

The virtuous and vile, are not those who perform virtuous and vile actions. But, virtuous are those, who have inclination for God, while vile are those, who have disinclination for Him. Though performance of actions, such as oblation, charity, penance, pilgrimage, fast is good, but when these are performed for their fruit, they are not so valuable, as is the inclination for God, because God's grace enables a man to become pious very quickly. Being pious is far superior to piety gained, through virtuous actions. Therefore, when a man being helpless and disappointed from all quarters, invokes Almighty, His heart melts and enables him, to become a loving devotee to Him.

Feelings of the heart, are more important, than actions performed, with the body, while exclusive devotion of one's own self, is far superior to such feelings. No evil can stand, where there is exclusive devotion. It is this, which enables a man to become pious very quickly, because the soul being an eternal portion of the Lord, is pious. It is because of sins and ill-feelings, that he has become impious.

Appendix—Those people who don't take refuge in God, depend on the fiendish, demoniacal and delusive nature (Gītā 9/12). They have an eye on the world only (objects and actions). They don't believe in the existence of God, then there is no question of their taking refuge in God. Their final aim is to hoard riches and to enjoy pleasures—'kāmopabhogaparamā etāvaditiniścitāḥ' (Gītā 16/11). Their wisdom being carried away by 'Māyā'., they come under the sway of 'Māyā. Being under the sway of 'Māyā', they can't cross it.

'Māyayāpahṛtajñānāh'—This expression means that 'Māyā' has overwhelmed their 'Viveka'. They remain engrossed in 'Māyā' viz., they indulge in enjoying pleasures, in accumulation of wealth, in decoration of the body and the house etc. They make new inventions which provide pleasure and comfort to the body and they attach special importance to them. How can such people, who know only the transitory and ephemeral objects, know the unchangeable reality? They don't even cast a glance and can't cast a glance at the Supreme truth.

Link:—In the previous verse, Lord Kṛṣṇa declared "The evil-doers having embraced the demoniac nature, do not take refuge in Me." Then who take refuge in Him? It is delineated, in the next verse.

चतुर्विधा भजन्ते मां जनाः सुकृतिनोऽर्जुन।
आर्तो जिज्ञासुरर्थार्थी ज्ञानी च भरतर्षभ॥ १६ ॥

caturvidhā bhajante māṁ janāḥ sukṛtino'rjuna
ārto jijñāsurarthārthī jñānī ca bharatarṣabha

Four kinds of virtuous men worship Me, O Arjuna; the seeker, of wealth, the afflicted, those who quest for knowledge, and the wise (Jñānī). 16

Comment:—

'Caturvidhā bhajante māṁ janāḥ sukṛtino'rjuna'—There are, four types of virtuous men (devotees), who worship God viz., seek refuge in Him. In the preceding verse, the Lord talked of the evil-doers, while here He talks of the virtuous. These virtuous men, don't perform actions, for their fruit, but for God, by having affinity for Him. They are of two types. First, are those who perform oblation, charity and penance etc., and other actions, according to their caste and creed etc., in accordance with the ordinance of scriptures for God. The second ones are those, who have constant remembrance of God, loud chanting of His name and are engaged in narrating or listening to stories of the drama of Lord's human life.

Those, who are inclined towards God, are fortunate and virtuous, and deserve to be called, human beings. Their inclination might have evolved, either from virtuous actions of the past, their frustration in life, their thoughtfulness, good company or study of the sacred books etc. Inclination towards Him, is prosperity and disinclination for Him, is adversity (Mānasa 5/32/2).

God has bestowed upon man, this human body so that he may realize God. Man is independent, in realizing Him. Therefore, if a man, by making proper use of this body, by giving up actions, which are not sanctioned by scriptures, is engaged in God-realization, he can attain Him, easily. But if he does not make proper use of his freedom, and does the contrary, he paves the way to hell and eighty-four lac forms of life. Thus, only persons who are engaged in adoration of the Lord, are virtuous and they deserve to be called men.

'Ārto jijñāsurarthārthī jñānī ca bharatarṣabha'—The distressed (sufferer), the seeker of knowledge, the seeker of wealth and a man of wisdom—all the four types of virtuous men, worship God viz., seek refuge in Him.

(1) A seeker of wealth—Devotees, who seek, wealth only

from God, are seekers of wealth. They worship God to gain wealth. Their conviction is, that none else besides God, can fulfil their desire for wealth. Holding this view, they recite and chant God's name and adore Him, scrupulously for getting riches.

One who resorts to worldly means, for fulfilling his desire for wealth, but sometimes invokes God for it, is not a devotee to God, he is a devotee to riches.

But, devotees of God seek wealth only from Him. Such devotees gradually develop inclination, for God, and their desire for wealth, slow by diminishes and finally it disappears. Dhruva was such a devotee.

One day, Dhruva wanted to sit in the lap of his father, but his step-mother did not allow him to do so. She said, "You have not worshipped God. You are unlucky, because you are the son of your unlucky mother. So you do not deserve, to sit in the lap, of your father." Dhruva narrated the incident to his mother. His mother said, "My darling, she is right. Both of us have not worshipped God." Dhruva said, "Mother, now I am going to adore God." Saying these words Dhruva made for the forest, for adoration. On the way, he met sage Nārada, who said to him, "O innocent boy, where are you going, all alone? In the jungle, there are wild animals which will devour you. Come with me to the king. He, on my request will make arrangement for your mother, as well as for you." Having listened to Nārada, his faith in God was intensified and he said, "Sire, I want to be engaged in adoration (tapa)." Having learnt of his determination, sage Nārada imparted to him the sacred Mantra of twelve letters, (Oṁ namo bhagavate vāsudevāya), and advised him, to meditate upon the four-armed Lord Viṣṇu and then directed him to go to Madhuvana, for adoration.

Dhruva worshipped the Lord, with such a firm belief, that the Lord revealed Himself to Dhruva, within six months. The Lord granted him the boon that he would become an heir to the throne, but Dhruva was not pleased with this boon. His mind was purified by adoration, and so he felt ashamed that he committed a mistake in having a desire to gain a kingdom. It means that Dhruva wanted to gain kingdom but not by any other means, besides devotion and adoration. By means of adoration, he gained a kingdom and his desire, perished. Thus, a seeker of wealth devotee seeks wealth only from God.

Now-a-days people, who want to earn money by foul means, sometimes pray to God to grant them money. Such people are seekers of wealth, but they are not devotees of God, because instead of believing Him, they believe in falsehood, fraud and other foul means, while devotees, depend on God only, and by having affinity for Him adore Him only. Such devotees, because of any factor, such as past-influence etc., sometimes, desire for favourable circumstances. They are devotees, no doubt, but due to this desire, they are called, seekers of wealth.

(2) Distressed (sufferer) devotees—Such type of devotees, pray to God in adversity. They pray only to God, to do away with their miseries and misfortunes. Such a distressed devotee, was Uttarā*, because she did not seek refuge in anyone else, except the Lord, to get rid of her troubles.†

Those, who having affinity with God, depend on Him only and do not desire, for favourable circumstances, but sometimes,

---

* The examples of Draupadī and Gajendra (the elephant) are not befitting because they adopted other means to be free from suffering. Draupadī sought help from others and also used her power to do away with her suffering. Similarly, the elephant also sought the help of other male and female elephants and also used his power. Thus both of them went on suffering. But as soon as both of them sought refuge only in God, they were relieved of their sufferings.

† O Lord of the gods, Master of the world, the great Yogī, protect me from the burning iron-arrow which is moving quickly towards me. O Omnipotent, there is none besides You in the world who can protect me because all the people are killing each other. O Lord, it will not make much difference if this red-hot arrow burns me but it should not destroy the fruit of my womb.

the desire itself evolves in them, to be free from suffering. Such devotees are also distressed ones.

(3) Devotees, as seekers of knowledge—The devotees, who want to know the self, and reality, depend only on God, having exclusive devotion for Him. Uddhava, can be named among such devotees. Lord Kṛṣṇa, imparted to him divine knowledge which is known as 'Uddhava Gītā' (Śrīmadbhāgavata 11/7—30).

Those, who having affinity for God, are engrossed in His adoration but sometimes, because of company or past influences want to know the self or divinity, are also called, seekers of knowledge.

(4) Men of wisdom—The term 'Ca', has been used, to show the superiority of the men of wisdom, to other three types of virtuous men. Devotees, who neither have a desire for favourable circumstances, nor are worried about the unfavourable ones, nor have a desire to know the self, but by depending on God, are engrossed in divine devotion, are called men of wisdom. They perceive, the desirable and undesirable circumstances, as sport of God. They ever remain engrossed, in His devotion without having a desire, in the least. The Gopīs, whose desire was nothing besides Lord Kṛṣṇa's happiness, can be named, among such devotees.

Here, a fact needs attention that the seekers of wealth, the distressed, and the seekers of knowledge, who adore the Lord, devotion for God is aroused in them, and they are called, devotees. But those who seek knowledge, wealth and freedom from suffering, by anyother means, have no affinity for God, and so devotion is not aroused in them, so they cannot be called devotees.

Saint's utterances, affirm that it is God alone, who loves His devotees, whereas devotees merely surrender, themselves to God. It is so, because he alone is qualified to be a true lover, who does not expect anything from others. A devotee, has only affinity for God. God actually surrenders Himself, to all His creatures. When a devotee surrenders himself to God without having a desire, in the least, he is called a man of wisdom viz., a devout devotee. In that case, he has no separate entity, he becomes one with God, viz., there is only God's entity.

An Exceptional Fact

(1) Four boys were playing. Just then, their father, came with four mangoes. At the sight of the mangoes, one of the sons, asked for a mango, the second cried for a mango. Both of them, were given a mango each. The third one, only looked at the mangoes and the fourth one went on playing, without even having a look at the mangoes. The father, gave one mango to each of the other, two boys also. Here the boy who asked for the mango is a seeker of wealth, the one who wept is distressed, the one, who looked at the mango, is a seeker of knowledge, and the fourth one, is a man of wisdom. The seeker of wealth seeks favourable (desirable) circumstances, the sufferer seeks to do away with suffering, the seeker of knowledge, wants to know God, while the wise (devout devotee), seeks nothing.

All the above-mentioned men, are virtuous, because they depend on God predominantly. So they are different from men, who have fallen from Yoga (Gītā 6/41-42). Similarly the seekers of wealth and distressed devotees, are different from, those selfish persons who perform actions for their fruit, because their wisdom has been lost by various desires (Gītā 7/20), so they are included among men, of demoniacal traits. Among the devotees, such as seekers of wealth etc., the degree of superiority or inferiority in their devotion, is due to desire. In spite of desire, they are not 'Hṛtajñānāḥ' viz., their wisdom has not been carried away. Rather, the Lord has called them noble (7/18), and virtuous, and thus has praised them.

Those, who seek refuge in the Lord may have hidden

desires but there is predominance of devotion for God, in them. So the more intimacy they develop for the Lord, their desires diminish and then they become unique. So the Lord has called them noble and declared the man of wisdom verily His own self (7/18).

(2) Acceptance of affinity with God, is the best means to attain Him. This affinity, wipes out all evil and defects. Moreover, the Lord does not look at defects, but He perceives affinity. All the creatures are His, but it is an error on their part, that by forgetting real affinity, they have accepted their affinity, with the world. As soon as, this error is rectified, they attain to Him. In having this affinity, a devotee need not resort to mind and intellect etc., while, in other means, he has to take their help.

Even the vilest creatures, are His. So He, as mentioned, in the sixteenth chapter of the Gītā, throws them into demoniacal wombs, so that they may be purified. The Lord, like a mother who does not consult a child while bathing him, does not consult the creatures, because He wants to purify them.

A devotee, has real affinity for God, but sometimes, he has a desire. In that case, there is predominance of affinity, while desire occupies a secondary place. Such devotees hold a higher position.

The second type of devotees, are those who want their desires to be satisfied, by other worldly people. But when they are not satisfied, they pray to God. Because, of the lack of exclusive devotion, they hold the second position.

The third type, is those who have affinity with God, so that their desires may be fulfilled. In this case, there is predominance of desire, while affinity with God occupies a subsidiary place.

A Vital Fact

Desire is of two types—spiritual and mundane.

(i) Spiritual desire—It is of two kinds, for salvation and for exclusive devotion.

In the desire for salvation, there is desire to know the self or reality. So, it is not desire, it is need or want. A need is, that which is positively satiated, and with its satiation no other need is born.* Need, means lack of something necessary, and this need is for God-realization.

The second kind of desire, is for exclusive devotion, in which a devotee surrenders himself to God, because he himself is His fragment†.

Thus desires mentioned above, are not really desires.

(ii) Mundane desire—It is also of two kinds—the desire to get pleasure and the desire to get rid of pains. Desire for comfort, luxuries, name, fame and pleasures etc., here and hereafter, are such that they lead a man, to bondage and degradation. These are demoniacal traits, which should be renounced.

The second type of desire, is to do away with pain. Pain can be caused by fate, such as flood, drought etc., which is known as 'ādhidaivika', or by creatures, such as lions, snakes and thieves etc., which is known as 'ādhibhautika, or it can be pertaining to mind and body etc., such as worry, fear, lunacy and diseases etc., which is called ādhyātmika.'‡

---

* A desire is never satisfied. One desire gives birth to other desires. As a man has desire for a certain amount of money. When he gains it, he desires more and thus his desire for money is never satisfied. Similar is the case with other perishable worldly things such as pleasures, praise, health and family etc. Thus desires should be renounced because they are never satisfied. Moreover these desires for the perishable have an access to the body and the name, not to the self. So they are not yours.

† The desire for exclusive devotion for God is superior to the desire for salvation; because in salvation he has a desire to get something, he wants to attain salvation but in exclusive devotion he wants to surrender himself to God, he gives himself to God. In salvation there remains ego in its subtle form while in devotion there is no ego.

‡ The 'Ādhyātmika' pain is of two kinds— 'Ādhi' and 'Vyādhi'. Worry is known as 'Ādhi' and physical disease is known as 'Vyādhi'. Ādhi is of two kinds—(i) Lunacy (ii) Worry, sadness, fear and agitation etc. Lunacy is the result of the

Actually the mundane desires, are never satisfied, because if one is satisfied, another spring up, and the process continues.

Appendix—In the fourteenth verse the Lord declared, "The devotees, who take refuge in Me, cross the 'Māyā' consisting of the three modes." Who are those devotees who take refuge in God?—this fact is related in this verse.

In the preceding verse the Lord described the evil-doers; now in this verse He describes the virtuous persons. The most deadly evil or sin is to assume the world, which is different from us (the self), to be our own, while the most virtuous act is to regard the Lord who is inseparable from us as our own. Therefore those who regard the world as theirs are evil-doers while those who regard the Lord as theirs, are virtuous.

A sensual man does not worship God, therefore a seeker of wealth can be the devotee of God but the seeker of pleasures cannot be the devotee of God. The reason is that the seeker of pleasure is more engrossed in the world, while a seeker of wealth is less engrossed in the world and he is more inclined towards God. Because of the assumption of any other entity to some extent besides God, a devotee is either the seeker of wealth or the afflicted or the seeker of knowledge. If there is no such assumption at all of any other entity besides God, then he becomes the wise (devotee). It means that because of the assumption of any other entity besides God, there are four kinds of virtuous men. In fact besides the existence of God no other entity is possible.

He who wants to know 'Jñāna' (knowledge) with 'Vijñāna' in other words he wants to know God fully (in full) is a 'Jijñāsu' (seeker of knowledge). A 'Jijñāsu' wants to know the glory, influence and power of God, therefore he has special relish in

actions of the past while worry and sadness are the results of ignorance. When a man possesses knowledge his worry and sadness are wiped out but he may suffer from lunacy as the fruit of his past actions.

the Lord's sportive display and stories. The Lord instead of using the word 'mumukṣu' (seeker of salvation) has used the term 'Jijñāsu' (seeker of knowledge) because a 'mumukṣu' is one who wants to realize the self, while a 'Jijñāsu' may want to realize the self or may want devotion. In a 'mumukṣu' there is predominance of attaining salvation, while in a 'Jijñāsu' devotee, there is predominance of surrendering himself to God. A 'mumukṣu' has knowledge of the Supreme (the Absolute) and a 'Jijñāsu' devotee has knowledge of 'Vāsudevaḥ sarvam' (all is God). A self-realized (enlightened) soul has knowledge of the Supreme but a devotee has the knowledge of God in its entirety (Gītā 7/29-30).

In the seekers of wealth, in the afflicted and in the seekers of knowledge, gradually attachment to the world decreases and attachment (devotion) to God increases. So long as a striver sustains the world, he remains the seeker of wealth or the sufferer or the seeker of knowledge. When he does not sustain the world, then he remains only a 'Jñānī' (the wise) (a devotee).

The devotee who has knowledge of God in full viz., 'all is God', has been called 'Jñānī'. The same 'Jñānī' devotee has been called 'Jñānavān' (the man of wisdom) in the nineteenth verse of this chapter.

An 'arthārthī' without being satisfied with the circumstances—available wants wealth. An 'ārta' is satisfied with the circumstances, he is placed in, but while he suffers pain, he can't tolerate it. In an 'arthārthī' craving for wealth is not predominant, eagerness for God is predominant. He has the desire for wealth but he wants this desire to be satisfied only by God. The reason is that God lacks nothing. The lower nature is only of God. The 'ārta' wants his sufferings to be removed only by God. The 'Jijñāsu' wants knowledge to be imparted by only God. But when a devotee has such a keen yearning to love God alone, then he no longer remains a seeker of wealth, a sufferer and a seeker of knowledge but he becomes a 'Jñānī' viz., a devotee having exclusive devotion to God.

An 'arthārthī' has constant attachment to wealth because he hankers after wealth every time. But an 'ārta' has no continuous relation with suffering because suffering does not persist all the time. A 'Jijñāsu' does not care for pleasure or pain, therefore he has neither a desire to get pleasure nor a desire to get rid of sufferings. The seeker of wealth and the sufferer—both by becoming seekers of knowledge become 'Jñānī' viz., devotees.

The devotee who is seeker of wealth when is gifted with wealth by God, repents of his mistake; as Dhruva repented of his desire for kingdom when he got the kingdom. But a sufferer-devotee does not feel so much sorry, but he has the notion that God frees sufferers from sufferings; as Draupadi and Gajendra (king of elephants) after being protected, didn't feel sorry, but they had an inclination towards God. A sufferer-devotee can't tolerate suffering—this is his weakness.

A Jijñāsu devotee does not know God in full. He is not satisfied by attaining salvation or enlightenment but he has hunger for love (devotion). But for a Jñānī-devotee besides God there is no other entity in the least at all, then how can he feel the lack of anything? Therefore the Lord has called a Jñānī (the man of wisdom) (the devotee with exclusive devotion) His own self (manifestation)—'jñānī tvātmaiva me matam' (Gītā 7/18).

Link:—Among the four kinds of virtuous men, the man of wisdom is the best, who is described, in the next verse.

तेषां ज्ञानी नित्ययुक्त एकभक्तिर्विशिष्यते।
प्रियो हि ज्ञानिनोऽत्यर्थमहं स च मम प्रियः ॥ १७ ॥

teṣāṁ jñānī nityayukta ekabhaktirviśiṣyate
priyo hi jñānino'tyarthamahaṁ sa ca mama priyaḥ

Of these, the best is the man of wisdom (Jñānī) steadfastly and exclusively devoted to Me; for most dear am I to the wise, and who is most dear to Me. 17

Comment:—

'Teṣāṁ jñānī nityayukta'—Among the four kinds of virtuous men, a man of wisdom is the best, because he is steadfast viz., he is constantly established in God. He thinks of nothing, besides God. As the cowherdesses while milking cows, churning curd and discharging other domestic duties, thought only of God* a man of wisdom while performing all the mundane and spiritual actions, is attached to God alone.

'Ekabhaktirviśiṣyate'—The man of wisdom, without having any desire of his own, has an exclusive devotion for God. So he is the best one.

Though all the four kinds, of virtuous men are engaged in God's devotion, yet the first three, have no exclusive devotion, because they have some desire or the other of their own. The seeker of wealth, seeks favourable circumstances, a sufferer seeks to do away with unfavourable circumstances, a seeker of knowledge, has a desire to know his self or Divinity. But, the man of wisdom (devout devotee) has exclusive devotion for God, without having any desire of his own.

'Priyo hi jñānino'tyarthamahaṁ sa ca mama priyaḥ'—I am extremely dear to the wise, because he has exclusive devotion for Me, without having any desire of his own. Therefore, he is extremely dear to Me.

Though all creatures, being fragments of God, are naturally

* The Gopīs of Vraja who, while milking cows, separating rice from paddy, churning curd, smearing the courtyard with cow-dung, rocking babies in cradles, lulling a baby to sleep, watering the basil and sweeping the house, sang the divine songs of Lord Kṛṣṇa's life-story with full devotion in an ecstasy of delight with their minds constantly attached to Him are virtuous and deserve congratulations.

dear to Him, and He brings up all of them, without any partiality, yet, those who have an inclination for Him, become especially dear, to Him.

When a devotee, becomes free from desires, axiomatic devotion (love) is aroused, in Him. This love, neither ends nor lessens, but increases every moment, and is limitless, endless and knows no satiety.

Appendix—The Lord has called His devotee who is exclusively devoted to him 'Jñānī' (wise) because "All is God"—this is the real and final knowledge (wisdom), there is nothing beyond it. Therefore the devoted (devout) devotee, who has realized this knowledge, is a real Jñānī (Gītā 7/19). The reason is that such a devotee holds that there is no other entity besides God, while a man who applies his Viveka, holds that there are two entities—the real and the unreal. It means that here the term 'Jñānī' has not been used for the liberated self-realized soul but it has been used for the 'Jñānī' viz., the devoted (devout) devotee who has realized 'All is God". In the Gītā, the Lord principally has called a devotee 'Jñānī' (7/16—18) because he is the highest and real 'Jñānī'. He loves God alone, therefore he is the best—'ekabhaktirviśiṣyate'.

The Lord's devotee who is the seeker of wealth is 'anityayukta' (not constantly established in God). The sufferers is less 'anityayukta' than the seeker of wealth. The seeker of knowledge is less 'anityayukta' than the sufferer. But a 'Jñānī' is totally 'nityayukta' (constantly established in God).

'Priyo hi jñānino'tyarthamahaṁ sa ca mama priya'—this expression means that when a devotee has realized 'Vāsudevaḥ sarvam', then between that devotee and God there is relationship of true love alone, nothing else. In the scriptures, this has been called every moment—increasing love and infinite bliss.

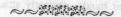

Link:—In the previous verse, Lord Kṛṣṇa declared the man of wisdom to be the best of all the four. The other three, are also not undervalued by Him. So He says in the next verse.

उदाराः सर्व एवैते ज्ञानी त्वात्मैव मे मतम्।
आस्थितः स हि युक्तात्मा मामेवानुत्तमां गतिम्॥ १८॥

udārāḥ sarva evaite jñānī tvātmaiva me matam
āsthitaḥ sa hi yuktātmā māmevānuttamāṁ gatim

All these are noble, but the man of wisdom (jñānī) is verily My own self; this is my view. For, such a devotee steadfast in Me and established in Me alone who am supreme goal. 18

Comment:—

'Udārāḥ sarva evaite'—All these are noble. The term 'Udārāḥ' (noble), has several interpretations—

(1) In the eleventh verse of the fourth chapter Lord Kṛṣṇa declares, "Howsoever men approach Me, even so do I seek them." A devotee, likes God and so does God like a devotee. But, a devotee is noble, because he accepts his affinity and surrenders himself first to God. He does not bother, whether God calls him His own or not.

(2) Devotees of the gods (deva) perform oblation, charity, penance etc., following the rules for fruits. The gods, grant them boons, as desired by devotees, without thinking of the welfare of devotees. But, God grants only boons, which are for their welfare and which enhance their devotion. He does not grant boons, by which their devotion is not enhanced and they may be entangled in the world, because He is the supreme father and the greatest well-wisher. So, the devotees of God, worship Him, not caring whether their desires are satisfied, or not. Thus, they are noble.

(3) Worldly pleasure and prosperity, obviously seem pleasant, while adoration does not seem to bear immediate

fruit, yet devotees adore the Lord without caring for pleasure and prosperity. So they are noble.

(4) One, who wants anything from God is called noble. It is so, because God Himself is very much noble and He regards one who wants anything from Him, as noble.

(5) Devotees with an exclusive devotion, want their mundane as well as spiritual desires, to be satisfied only by God. Because, of their exclusive devotion, they are noble.

'Jñānī tvātmaiva me matam'—The other three devotees, are noble, but a man of wisdom, is the Lord's own manifestation, and so is naturally, loving to Him. The self, is naturally loving to everyone. It knows no motive or cause. So, the term 'Tu' (but), denotes singularity, of the man of wisdom.

In divine love, the lover surrenders himself to his Beloved and identifies himself with Him. Similarly, the Beloved also surrenders Himself to His lover. So they identify themselves, with each other. This union in the Discipline of Knowledge, remains calm and constant. But, in the Discipline of Devotion (love), it increases every moment, and in it the lover and the Beloved even having separate entities, are one and in spite of, being identified with each other, are two. This love cannot be expressed, in words. In this divine love affair, even in seeming separation, there is constant union, while in natural union there is also union.

When a river flows into the sea, both of them, become one. But, sometimes a river flows towards the sea and sometimes the sea flows, towards the river. Similar is the case in divine love, of the lover and Beloved. This drama of divine love, between a lover and the Beloved, continues for infinite years, in infinite forms. There develops such an intense love, between the two, that it becomes difficult to know, who is the lover and who the Beloved. Both of them are Beloved, and both of them are lovers.

'Āsthitaḥ sa hi yuktātmā māmevānuttamāṁ gatim'—A man of wisdom by being steadfast in mind, remains established in God, who is supreme and above whom, there is none. Such a devotee remaining unaffected by favourable or unfavourable circumstances, is always absorbed in Him. He has a firm belief, that only God is his, and that affinity is enhanced in both desirable and undesirable circumstances. Thus, he remains firmly established in Him.

Appendix—The worldly seeker of wealth instead of yearning for God, wants only wealth, therefore he is a devotee of falsehood, fraud and dishonesty etc. From his heart he attaches much importance to wealth, therefore he is not generous (noble) but he is very miserly. Therefore the term 'generous' is not applicable to him. But the seeker of wealth, who is a devotee of God, from his heart does not attach importance to wealth but attaches importance to God. So he is not miserly but he is generous (noble). Therefore the Lord has called him noble. Here generous (noble) means renunciation. The seeker of wealth, the sufferer and the seeker of knowledge—all these devotees having renounced the world (pleasure and prosperity) have started worshipping God—this is their renunciation. Therefore all of them are noble—'udārāḥ sarve evaite'. Because of the predominance of their relationship with only God, the seeker of wealth, the sufferer and the seeker of knowledge also afterwards naturally become 'Jñānī' (devotees).

There is a vital point that atheism is more defective than a desire. Those who, instead of worshipping God, worship other deities, if they are desire-ridden, they follow the cycle of birth and death—'gatāgataṁ kāma kāmā labhante' (Gītā 9/21). But those who worship only God, if any desire remains in them, then by God's grace and by the influence of their worship, they attain God. The reason is that if a man is connected with

God in anyway, he attains only God* because basically he is a fragment of God.

The seeker of wealth, the sufferer and the seeker of knowledge—all the three have been called 'noble' by God. But those who don't worship God but worship other deities, the Lord instead of calling them noble, have called them men of meagre intellect (Gītā 7/23) and their worship has been called as the worship in a mistaken manner (Gītā 9/23). Their worship is in a mistaken manner because they regard gods as different from God viz., they don't regard gods as the manifestation of God and moreover they are desire-ridden. It means that 'not to behold God in all' is more harmful than 'to work with an interested motive' because in the former there is no relation with the sentient (divinity) (God).

An enlightened (self-realized) soul has his 'tāttvika ektā' (unity in essence) viz., 'Sadharmatā' (merger into God's Being) with the Supreme but a devotee has his 'ātmīya ektā' viz., he becomes the Lord's own self—'Jñānī tvātmaiva me matam'. In 'tāttvika unity' (Sadharmatā), there is 'abheda' between the self and Brahma viz., as Brahma is truth, consciousness and bliss solidified, similarly he also becomes truth, consciousness and bliss solidified and nothing else remains besides the Supreme Reality. But in a devotee's 'ātmīya' unity the self and God become 'abhinna' (inseparable). In this 'abhinnatā' the devotee and the Lord in spite of being one, become two in order to exchange love with each other. In this state both are lovers and both are beloved (Sometimes God is the lover and the devotee is the beloved and vice versa). Therefore in spite of

* kāmād dveṣād bhayāt snehād yathā bhaktyeśvare manaḥ
āveśya tadaghaṁ hitvā bahavastadgatiṁ gatāḥ

(Śrīmadbhā. 7/1/29)

"Not one, many men out of desire, malice, fear and love by concentrating (focussing) their mind on God and washing away all their sins, have attained God in the same way as a devotee attains Him by devotion."

being two, they remain only one.

A man (the self) is a fragment of God. The more disinclination he has for God, the more his ego is inflated; and the more inclination he has to God, the more his ego is wiped out. Even after being established in the self, he can have an iota (trace) of subtle ego. But in devotion living in developed oneness with God through devotion, a devotee's attachment to the lower nature (aparā prakṛti) is totally renounced and his ego is totally wiped out because ego is the evolute of aparā prakṛti. Therefore the Lord declares—'jñānī tvātmaiva me matam' (a Jñānī viz., devout devotee is verily My own self).

A seeker of wealth, a sufferer and a seeker of knowledge, gradually lose their independent entity (ego), while a Jñānī (devotee) has no independent entity. Therefore the expression 'tvātmaiva' means that a lover (devotee with exclusive devotion) has no independent entity besides God and only God remains viz., the lover becomes the manifestation of God—tasminstajjane bhedābhāvāt (Nārada. 41). This 'ātmīyatā' (intimacy) with God is dualism for devotion which a devotee accepts himself in order to enhance devotion and it is far superior to the non-dualism of Jñānayoga—'bhaktyarthaṁ kalpitaṁ (svīkṛtaṁ) dvaitamadvaitādapi sundaram'* (Bodhasāra, Bhakti. 42).

'Māmevānuttamāṁ gatim'—There is no other Supreme goal besides God. The term 'gati' has three meanings—knowledge, speed (act of going) and attainment. Here the term 'gati' has been used for attainment. Being the final attainable Reality, God is the Supreme goal to be attained.

'Asṭhitaḥ'—One steadiness is gained by practice and the other steadiness is natural. As every being feels 'I am'—this is natural steadiness in one's own self, similarly a wise devotee

* The non-dualism of devotion is not an imagination but it is an acceptance. The imaginative non-dualism is untrue and it is devoid of love.

(who has exclusive devotion) naturally remains established steadily in God.

Link:— In the next verse, Lord Kṛṣṇa describes, the man of wisdom, as mentioned in the previous verse, and indicates the kind of devotion he has.

बहूनां जन्मनामन्ते ज्ञानवान्मां प्रपद्यते।
वासुदेवः सर्वमिति स महात्मा सुदुर्लभः॥ १९॥

bahūnāṁ janmanāmante jñānavānmāṁ prapadyate
vāsudevaḥ sarvamiti sa mahātmā sudurlabhaḥ

In the very last of all births viz., in this human form, when a man of wisdom (jñānī) takes refuge in Me, realizing that everything is God, such a great soul (mahātmā) is very rare, indeed. 19

Comment:—

'Bahūnāṁ janmanāmante'—This human birth, is the last of all births. The Lord, has given man full right to be free, from the cycle of birth and death. But man, because of his attachment, for the world, failing to attain Him, returns to the path of the mortal world (Gītā 9/3). So Lord Kṛṣṇa, while describing men possessing demoniacal traits, declares that such fools, instead of attaining Him, sink into still lower and baser, depths (Gītā 16/20).

It is mentioned in the scriptures and in the utterances of saints, that the only aim of human life, is to attain salvation, it is not for enjoying the pleasures of the world, and heaven. Therefore, in the Gītā, such people who look upon heaven as a supreme goal are called unwise, (2/42) and of meagre intelligence (7/23).

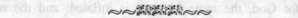

This human life, is the very first and the very last, of all births. It is the first, because the actions performed during this human life lead him to, eighty-four lac forms of lives and hell and in these forms of lives and hells he has to suffer pains and tortures, because of the vices he committed in the course of a human life. It is the very last, because a man can attain salvation or God-realization and be free, from the cycle of birth and death.

Lord Kṛṣṇa, in the sixth verse of the eighth chapter, declares, "Whatever being a man thinks of, when he leaves his body at the time of death, that alone does he attain." Therefore, the Lord has given him independence to think of the Lord, and attain salvation. Thus the Gītā, declares openly, "Even the vilest sinner and those who are of inferior birth, because of their sins of the previous birth, by taking refuge in Me, attain the Supreme Goal" (9/30—33). The Lord, has used the terms 'Pāpa yonayaḥ' (born of the sinful womb). It means that creatures of the inferior birth, such as pariah, animals, birds, insects, trees and creepers etc., all can be included. But, the difference between man and creatures of inferior births, is that man because of his discrimination, can follow the spiritual path, while other creatures cannot. But being fragments of God, all of them have got the right, to attain Him. Yet, many of the creatures because of God's and saints' grace, as well as, the influence of a place of pilgrimage etc., attain salvation. The gods, hanker after pleasures, in heaven. So they do not think of their salvation. But if they also think of God-realization due to any circumstances, they can realize, Him. It is mentioned in the scriptures, that Indra, the king of the gods, had true knowledge. The Lord, has bestowed this human life, the very last of all births upon us, so that we may attain salvation. So, if we just become instrument in his hand and be subservient to His will, we can attain salvation, undoubtedly.

A man should not misuse the independence given to him by God, by working against the ordinance of scriptures and against his own discrimination. In that state, of the right use of independence, either he will do nothing, or act according to ordinance of scriptures. If he has no interest for doing anything for himself, he will cease his affinity with senses, mind and intellect etc. The reason is, that when he has desire to do something, a sense of doership is born and he has affinity for senses and mind. He has affinity for the fruit of action, when he acts for himself. When he does nothing, there will neither be a sense of doership, nor desire for fruit and thus he will be established in the self. If he works according to ordinance of scriptures, without expecting a fruit for actions, the momentum for actions perishes, and his affinity with actions and things, breaks off and then new desires do not evolve, and old attachment perishes. Thus he automatically realizes the truth in the self (Gītā 4/38).

Lord Kṛṣṇa in the Gītā, declares—One who works without having any desire for the fruit of actions, all his actions melt away (4/23). One will be saved from all sins, by means of knowledge (4/36). The Lord, liberates His devotees, from all sins (18/66). He, who knows God as unborn and beginningless, is purged, of all sins (10/3). In this way, a devotee is purged of all sins, through all the three Disciplines of Action, Knowledge and Devotion. It means, that the aim of human birth, the very last of all births, is nothing besides, salvation.

If we have got good company, sacred books such as the Gītā, and realized the importance of the name of the Lord, it means that God by His special grace, has given us an opportunity, to attain salvation. But, it does not mean that we should stop adoration etc. We should devote, our time and energy, to attain Him by becoming an instrument, in His hands. If He had not decided to liberate us, from the cycle of birth and death, He by His grace, would not have bestowed this human birth, upon us (whose only aim is to attain God-realization). So, with a firm faith, that we'll attain salvation, we should follow a spiritual path, by becoming an instrument, in His hands.

A question may arise, that this human birth may be a fruit of virtuous actions of his previous birth. If we accept this assumption, we come to know that even animals, birds and insects etc., also get the fruit of their previous actions. If it were so, there would be no difference, between men and other creatures. In that case, it would not be correct to say, that human life has been bestowed upon us, by the kind grace of God. Then how can we regard human life, unique and glorious? The glory of human life, lies in surrendering ourselves to God and attaining salvation.*

'Vāsudevaḥ sarvam'—In the beginning of the universe, God Himself assumes different forms and at the time of its dissolution, only God remains. Thus, when at the beginning and the end, there is none besides God, how can someone else, be besides God, in the middle? This creation, has evolved out of Himself only. There was no other material, with Him besides Him. Therefore, the whole universe is nothing, besides His manifestation.

As in the case of ornaments, made of gold, there is nothing besides gold, as in the earthenware vessels there is nothing besides clay, and in toys made of sugar, there is nothing besides sugar, so in the universe, there is nothing besides God. So long as, a man is preoccupied with the beauty and forms of ornaments, he does not pay attention to the purity of gold. Similarly, so long as a man attaches importance to the world, he does not discern God, he does not perceive that "All is God."

A Yogī, identified with Brahma, attains the Beatitude of Brahma (5/24); the Yogī who has become one with Brahma,

---

* (1) After several births, in this human body, which one gets after a great industry and which in spite of being transient is very difficult to get, the wise man should try his best to attain salvation as quickly as possible before he dies. The sensual pleasures can be enjoyed in all births, so a man should not spoil this precious life in them (Śrīmadbhāgavata 11/9/29).

(2) This human body is the root of all good fruits and has been bestowed upon men by divine grace, in spite of being rare. This is a strong boat to cross the ocean of the world sailed by the preceptor-sailor and I (God) work as favourable wind to row it. In spite of so many facilities, if a man does not cross this ocean, he is the murderer of his own self (Śrīmadbhāgavata 11/20/17).

gains Supreme Bliss (6/27); and knowing the Lord, in essence, he enters into Him (18/54-55). According to the Gītā, the above-mentioned, are three states which change. But 'All is God' is not a state, this is reality, in which there is never any change. Whatever appears, as the world, is nothing besides God. The Lord Himself declares—

"Whatever is perceived with mind, tongue, eyes and other sense-organs, is nothing besides Me. There is no entity besides Me. Understand, this fact carefully" (Śrīmadbhā. 11/13/24). Thus, according to His declaration a man of wisdom (viz., the follower of divine love), sees the Lord everywhere "He sees Me, present in all beings and all beings existing in Me" (6/30). "He (the Yogī), though engaged in all forms of activities, dwells in Me" (6/31).

If a person, gets the thing desired, he feels very happy. Thus, we may very well imagine, how happy a devotee would feel, who beholds, God in everything. Overwhelmed with joy, the devotee of God, while describing the name, qualities, influence and sport of the Lord, and remembering these time and again, laughs, weeps, dances, sings aloud and becomes calm and quiet, and thus sanctifies, the entire universe. Thus, he becomes, full to the brim with divine bliss, and then for him, nothing further remains to be done, to be known and to be achieved.

For such a devotee, following the Discipline of Devotion, the so-called world, becomes divine. Being absorbed in God the body of a devotee also becomes unearthly or divine, as Mīrābāī's body merged into God's idol. In devotion, towards the Lord first there are three different entities—service, servant (devotee) and master (God). But when there is complete devotion, the devotee in the form of service merges into the master, and only the master (God) remains. Such devotees, who are ever engrossed in devotion to God, leave an indelible impression upon creatures, by their presence, touch and talk etc.

As long as, men have a desire to enjoy sensual pleasures, they cannot realize reality, about the world. But, when this desire is renounced, they perceive the world, as a manifestation of the Lord.

A Vital Fact

'Vāsudevaḥ Sarvam'—Divinity can be understood, in two ways—(1) The world has no existence, only God exists, (2) All is God viz., this world is the manifestation of God.

Strivers can follow, either of the two ways. Those, who are attached to the world should follow the first path, while those who are totally detached from the world and are engaged in meditation and adoration etc., should follow the second path. Though both, are one and the same, yet there seems to be a difference in them in the same way as, there seems to be difference in different kinds of ornaments of gold and the gold itself. In the former, there is predominance of discrimination, while in the latter there is predominance of devotion (faith). Devotees who worship attributeless God attach importance, to discrimination, while those who worship the Lord, with attributes attach importance, to devotion.

But in fact, both of these are the same. Therefore, Lord Kṛṣṇa, in the Discipline of Knowledge, has used acceptance in the sense of knowledge (3/28) while in the Discipline of Devotion, He has used knowledge in the sense of acceptance (5/29; 9/13; 10/3, 7, 24, 27, 41). There is one point which needs attention—To know God or to accept Him both is knowledge, while to know the world, as having its own separate existence, or to accept it as real both is ignorance.

By knowing, the reality about the world, the world loses its existence, and by knowing reality about God, one realizes, Him. Similarly, by accepting firmly, that the world is a manifestation of the Lord, the world, is seen as divine manifestation. Thus, by realizing divinity, knowledge and faith, become one.

'Iti jñānavānmāṁ prapadyate'—Those, who accept the existence of the kaleidoscopic world, are ignorant and foolish, while those who understand that the Lord pervades everywhere, in different forms, are learned and wise. Only the Lord is, at all places, in all beings and in all forms—this is realization of, a wise devotee. Therefore, in the nineteenth verse of the fifteenth chapter, he has been called 'Sarvavit' viz., he has known all, what was to be known.

The surrender of a man of wisdom, is different from that of a sufferer, the seeker of knowledge, and a seeker of wealth. So, the Lord has called him His own self (7/18) because according to him, there is none other entity, besides the Lord. The Lord Himself declares, 'Like clusters of yarn-beads formed by knots on a thread, all this is threaded on Me' (7/7). As in a rosary made of yarn-beads, there is nothing besides yarn, so in the world, there is nothing, besides God. One who realizes this fact, is said to take refuge, in Him. This realization is, real surrender to Him.

'Sa mahātmā sudurlabhaḥ'—Some of the people, never think of God-realization. A few think of it, but they have no exclusive devotion, for Him. A few make efforts, but soon lose heart, because of their ignorance in realizing Him. They miss this excellent opportunity, and thus, are deprived of the highest gain.

The Lord Himself, in the third verse of this chapter, declared, "Among thousands of men, scarcely one strives to realize Me, and of those who strive, scarcely one, knows Me in truth." The truth is "All is God." Such a great soul, is rare indeed. It does not mean that God cannot be realized, without facing several hurdles. But, it means that such devotees, who want to realize God from the core of their hearts, are rare. If a devotee wants to realize Him, he can realize Him, because the human birth's purpose, is nothing else, besides realizing Him.

All the people cannot enjoy worldly prosperity and pleasure, equally but all of them can realize God, as was realized by Lord Śaṅkara, Nārada, Vasiṣṭha, Sanaka-Sanandana and other sages, and ascetics etc. So, a man should never miss such a golden opportunity.

The Lord, possesses an unparalleled trait that He reveals Himself as food for the hungry, water for the thirsty, pleasure for the seekers of pleasure and also, as person, senses, mind, intellect and thoughts etc. In the form of pain, He warns us, that pain is the result of enjoyment of pleasure. So, if one enjoys sensual pleasure, he will have to suffer. So, he should not enjoy pleasure because, these are nothing besides the Lord and the Lord has to reveal Himself as pleasure for him. But how gracious the Lord is, that He reveals Himself as a creature desires! Such a great soul who realizes that, all is God, is very rare.

There was an ascetic, who worshipped God Gaṇeśa. He had an idol of Gaṇeśa, and another one of a rat, both made of gold. Both of these weighed equally. Once the ascetic decided to go on a pilgrimage. He went to a goldsmith to sell them. The goldsmith weighed them and told the ascetic, that the value of each of the two was the same. At this the ascetic grew angry with the goldsmith and asked him how a vehicle could be equal, in value to the Lord. The goldsmith replied, "Sir, I am not buying either God Gaṇeśa, or his vehicle, the rat. I buy gold. So I shall pay you according to their weight." Thus, as a goldsmith does not notice Lord Gaṇeśa or his vehicle, he sees only gold. So does a great soul behold God, he does not, see the world.

There was a saint who was walking along a road. He sat down to make water, in the field, of a farmer. The farmer, thought that he was stealing a water-melon from his field. So, he struck him a blow, with a stick. But afterwards he realized his mistake, and said, "Sir, forgive me for my mistake; I mistook you for a thief." The saint said, "There is no need to excuse you because you gave the blow to a thief, not to me." The farmer, felt very sorry and admitted the saint, into a hospital for necessary treatment. Then a man, came to offer him milk. The saint said, "O, you are very clever, first you injured me with a stick, now you are offering me milk. You play different parts, in the drama of life." The man, was a bit afraid, lest the saint should get him entangled and said, "Sir, I did not hit you." The saint said, "I very well know, that first you beat me and now you are offering milk. Who else, can be here besides you?" The saint, saw everyone as the revelation of the Lord. He who gave the blow, he who gave treatment and he who offered milk—all were manifestations of God, for the saint. So he talked accordingly.

Greatness of the Great Souls

It has been said, about great saints—

(1) The liberated great souls, continuously remain established in the self or in God. Their life, their company, their thoughts and the air touching their bodies, lead human beings to salvation.

(2) There are some people who do not know, the greatness of those great men. So, saints come down to the level of common people, and say that saints have done this. Their actions and words, constitute the scriptures.

(3) When they come down to a still lower level, they say, that saints should be obeyed.

(4) Strivers who do not obey the saints, are instructed to follow, the principles prescribed by them.

(5) When they go down still lower, they order them to do one thing or the other.

[Those who carry out the behest of saints, in them doctrines of saints, take practical shape. When a saint orders a striver to follow a principle, the striver by the saint's grace, gains a special power, by which his conduct changes without much effort, and that leads him to salvation. Even those, who follow the principles without receiving their orders, attain salvation.]

(6) Sometimes they curse or give boon to strivers, who refuse to obey them.

These, above-mentioned are six categories of saints, from the first rank to the sixth rank. The lower the level, to which they stoop, the more merciful they are. When they grant boons to a striver, or put him under a curse or scold him, they stoop to the lowest level, yet it is renunciation, because they have accepted the lowest level, for the welfare of humanity.

Similarly, God also remains established continuously, in His own Self. This is something of the first rank. But the same Lord, because of His excessive merciful nature, incarnates to lead creatures to salvation. The drama of His life, enables men to attain salvation. Sometimes, lowering Himself He preaches and by still lowering Himself, He govern people, and He orders and guides them. Finally, still lowering Himself further, He grants, a striver a boon, or lays him under a curse or separates him from his body, for his welfare and the welfare of the world.

Appendix—In the sixteenth verse the Lord mentioned that four kinds of devotees worship Him—the seeker of wealth, the afflicted, the seeker of knowledge and the wise—'caturvidhā bhajante māṁ'. In this verse He mentions the characteristics of the worship of a 'Jñānī'—"All is God"—this realization is the worship of a 'Jñānī', it is surrender to God. Real surrender (refuge) is that in which there remains no individuality of the devotee who takes refuge in God but only God, in Whom refuge is taken, remains.

'All is God'—this is real knowledge. Such an exalted souled devotee, possessing real knowledge, takes refuge in

God viz., he by losing his existence (I'ness), merges in God. Then I'ness does not persist viz., the lover does not remain but only God, the embodiment of love remains in Whom I—you (thou)—this—that—all these four do not remain. This is the real nature of surrender (refuge).

The term 'mahātmā' means—great (exalted) soul, the soul,* totally free from egoism, indiyiduality and unipresence. He, who has egoism, individuality and unipresence is 'alpātmā' (low soul).

Here the term 'Vāsudevaḥ' has been used in masculine gender; therefore here the expression 'Vāsudevaḥ sarvaḥ' should have been used. But here instead of the term 'Sarvaḥ' the term 'Sarvam' has been used, which is in neuter gender†. In the neuter gender all the three—masculine, feminine and neuter are included. In the Gītā for these three—the world, the soul and God, the words of three genders have been used‡. It means that 'Jagat', 'Jīva' and 'Paramātmā'—these three are included in the word 'Sarvam'. Therefore all the things, persons and circumstances etc., mentioned in the three genders are only the manifestations of God.

'Vāsudevaḥ Sarvam'—In it 'Sarvam' (all) is unreal while

---

*In the Gītā the Lord has used the term 'mahātmā' only for a devotee. The strivers, who follow the path of devotion, have been also called 'mahātmā'—'mahātmānastu māṁ pārtha daivīṁ prakṛtimāśritāḥ' (9/13), those who have attained oneness with God are also called mahātmā—'Vāsudevaḥ sarvamiti sa mahātmā sudurlabhaḥ' (7/19); those who have reached the state of highest perfection (Supreme love) have been called mahātmā—'nāpnuvanti mahātmānaḥ saṁsiddhiṁ paramāṁ gatāḥ' (8/15). Similarly in the Gītā the Lord has used the terms 'Sukṛtinaḥ' (7/16), 'Udārāḥ' (7/18), 'Sudurlabhaḥ' (7/19), 'yuktatamaḥ' (6/47, 12/2), 'adveṣṭā', 'maitraḥ', 'karuṇa' (12/13), 'atīva me priyāḥ' (12/20) etc., also only for the devotee.

†In a Compound word if the words of all the three genders are included, then the compound word ends in neuter genders.

‡Vide 'Gītā-Darpaṇa' article no. 99—'Gītā meṁ Īśvara jīvātmā aura prakṛti kī aliṅgatā'.

'Vāsudevaḥ' (God) is real. The unreal has no existence and the real never ceases to be—'nāsato vidyate bhāvo nābhāvo vidyate sataḥ' (Gītā 2/16). It means that only the real exists, the unreal has no existence at all. There is only God (Vāsudeva), all (Sarvam) is not there. But the strivers, who speak, who hear and who study, hold that there is existence of 'Sarvam' (world), therefore the Lord in order to wipe out this wrong notion of 'sarvam' (world) utters 'Vāsudevaḥ sarvam'.

In the scriptures different types of yogīs have been described such as Jñānayogī, Dhyānayogī, Layayogī, Haṭhayogī, Rājayogī, Mantrayogī and Anāsaktayogī etc., but the Lord does not declare that they are very rare. But He declares that the exalted soul who realizes 'All is God' is very rare indeed.

God is the seed of the entire world—'yaccāpi sarvabhūtānāṁ bījaṁ tadahamarjuna' (Gītā 10/39), 'bījaṁ māṁ sarvabhūtānāṁ viddhi pārtha sanātanam' (Gītā 7/10). Whatever products are produced from a kind of seed, they are the different forms of that seed only. The crop produced from wheat is the wheat-crop only. The farmers say that there is a good crop of wheat, the field is full of wheat (it appears to be merely grass and there is not even a single grain of wheat in it). But a businessman of a city will not accept that this is wheat. He will say that he has bought and sold so many bags of wheat and if he does not know what the wheat is; it is grass, in it there are stalks and leaves, it is not wheat. But a farmer, who cultivates the field, will say, "This is not grass which animals eat, but it is wheat." If a cow grazes plants of the wheat, the farmer says, "Your cow has grazed our wheat", while she has not eaten even a single grain of wheat. In the field even a single grain of wheat may not be seen, but the crop is wheat—in it there is no doubt. The reason is that first the seed of wheat was sown and when the crop is ripe, wheat will be taken out, and so in the mid state also it is only wheat. Now it appears to be green grass but when the crop is ripe, the wheat will be taken out of it. In this way God existed before the origin of the world—'sadeva somyedamagra āsīdekamevādvitīyam' (Chāndogya. 6/2/1), and in the end also God will remain—'Śiṣyate śeṣasaṁjñaḥ' (Śrīmadbhā. 10/3/25). Therefore in the mid state also all is only God—'Vāsudevaḥ Sarvam'.

So long as a striver has the egoistic notion, he is a 'bhogī' (voluptuary). I am a yogī—this is the enjoyment of yoga; I am wise—this is enjoyment of wisdom; I am a lover—this is the enjoyment of love. So long as he enjoys pleasures, there is possibility of his downfall. He who enjoys yoga, can also enjoy objects of senses; he who enjoys knowledge, can also enjoy ignorance and he who enjoys love, can also enjoy attachment. The reason is that he is possessed of such disposition, the habit for pleasure. When he no longer remains 'bhogī' (voluptuous), then only Yoga persists. With the persistence of yoga, a man attains salvation. But even after having attained salvation, the exalted soul has the latent impression (a subtle iota of ego) (Saṁskāra) of the spiritual discipline by which he attained salvation. This latent impression of ego does not let him be one with other philosophers. This is also because of the latent impression that there are differences among philosophers and their philosophical thoughts. The latent impression of a particular sect does not let the philosopher of that sect respect the sects of other philosophers. But when the love, which increases every moment, is attained, then the latent impression of his sect does not persist, he becomes one with other philosophers, all differences come to an end and 'Vāsudevaḥ sarvam' is realized. In fact then the exalted soul, who realizes, 'all is God' who knows it and who mentions it loses his identity and only God remains Who is the same from the time immemorial. By beholding God in all, all sects are equally respected because it is not possible to oppose one's own favourite God—'nija prabhumaya dekhahiṁ jagata kehi sana karahiṁ birodha' (Mānasa, Uttara. 112b).

There are two types of description about God and the soul—(i) God is the ocean and the soul is its wave viz., the wave belongs to the ocean and, (ii) the soul (self) is the ocean and God is its wave viz., the ocean belongs to the wave. Out of these two the wave belongs to the sea—this assumption seems to be proper. The ocean belongs to the wave—this assumption does not seem proper because the ocean is comparatively enduring while the wave is transient. Therefore the wave belongs to the sea, the sea does not belong to the wave. If a striver regards himself as the sea and God as the wave, it will be very improper because by this assumption the sense of ego will be inculcated and ego will remain eternal while God will become transient. The reason is that the self has maintained the sense of ego (individuality) from time immemorial. Therefore if we call the self as 'I' (ego), it is the same ego which we have maintained since time immemorial. Salvation is attained when this ego is wiped out. Besides the above-mentioned two assumptions, there is the third remarkable fact that in water-element there is neither the sea nor the wave viz., there is no distinction of the sea and the wave. This is the truth. The sea and the wave are relative terms but the water-element is independent (having nothing to do with the sea or the wave).

As in water-element, the sea, the river, rain, dew, fog, steam and cloud etc., all having lost their identity (individuality) become one, similarly in 'Vāsudevaḥ sarvam' (all is God), all spiritual disciplines having lost their identity become one as God. As in water-element there is no difference of forms, similarly in 'Vāsudevaḥ sarvam' there is no difference of opinions. Differences in opinions (sects) cause dissatisfaction but in 'Vāsudevaḥ sarvam', as there are no differences of opinions, so all are totally satisfied. In 'Vāsudevaḥ sarvam' there is neither a Yogī, nor a Jñānī nor a Premī—so the exalted soul, who has realized it, is very rare indeed.

Water is changed into different forms such as snow, fog,

cloud, hail, rain, river, pond and sea etc. If snow is put in a deep frying pan and the frying pan is put on fire, the snow melts into water. Then water is evaporated and then the steam by becoming atoms becomes shapeless. Water assumes the form of fog, it assumes the form of a cloud, the same becomes shapeless, the same assumes the form of snow, the same assumes the shape of hail, the same in the form of rain falls on the earth, the same assumes the form of a river and the same water assumes the form of the sea. In spite of assuming so many forms, the water as an element remains the same. Similarly God assumes numberless forms. As water being very cold turns into snow or ice and becoming liquid by heat turns into steam (vapour) and then is changed into the form of atoms; similarly God by getting cold in the form of ignorance, appears in the form of inert world, and by the heat in the form of knowledge appears in the form of subtle and sentient God. Water may appear in the form of snow or vapour or cloud etc., but essentially it is only water. It is nothing else besides water. Similarly God may appear in the form of the world and in other forms but He is only God. There is none else besides God.

A striver commits an error that keeping himself aloof (separate) he wants to behold the world as the manifestation of God viz., he perceives 'all is God' with his intellect. In fact not only the world, which is beheld as the manifestation of God but he who sees it is also the manifestation of God—'sakalamidamahaṁ ca vāsudevaḥ' (Viṣṇu purāṇa 3/7/32). Therefore a striver should assume that all including his body is only God viz., the body is the manifestation of God, senses are also His manifestation, the mind is also His manifestation, intellect is also His manifestation, the life-breath is also His manifestation and ego (I'ness) is also the Lord's manifestation. All is God—in order to accept this reality a striver should not apply his intellect but naturally without making any effort, should accept the truth as it is. Therefore in Śrīmadbhāgavata it is mentioned—

sarvaṁ brahmātmakaṁ tasya vidyayā'tmamanīṣayā
paripaśyannuparamet sarvato muktasaṁśayaḥ
(11/29/18)

When 'all is God'—it is determined then a striver by this spiritual science being free from all kinds of doubts, by beholding God everywhere, should become tranquil viz., 'all is God'—he should not think of it but God should be clearly seen to him.

It means that 'all is God'—he (the self) should remain indifferent to this notion also viz., there should remain neither the seer (one who sees), nor the seen (which is seen) nor the seeing (the action of seeing), but only God should remain.

'Vāsudevaḥ sarvam'—can be realized in different ways—

(i) Actions, objects and persons have a beginning and an end but the self ever remains the same. Therefore a man realizes that actions, objects and persons are perishing but the self never perishes. This realization from the discrimination point of view is the realization of 'Vāsudevaḥ sarvam' (all is God).

(ii) Before the creation of the universe only God existed and in the end also God will exist, then how can there be anyone else besides God in the mid-state? This is from the reasoning point of view 'Vāsudevaḥ sarvam'.

(iii) Only God is mine, besides God none is mine and if there is anyone else, let him be, what have we to do with him? This is from a simple, straightforward, believer-devotee's point of view 'Vāsudevaḥ sarvam'. As in Vraja a sage was talking to some one near the well, "Brahma (the Supreme) is so and so and the soul is so etc." A cowherds woman came there to draw water from the well, she heard the conversation and asked the other cowherds woman, "What are these Brahma and the soul?" The other woman said, "They should be our beloved's kith and kin, therefore these sages are talking about them, otherwise what have they to do with anyone else besides our beloved Lālā (Kṛṣṇa)?

(iv) The striver who is restless at heart in order to know

the Supreme Truth and so does not feel hungry in the day and whose sleep vanishes at night, he having listened to the discourse of a saint or having studied a book, firmly assumes that all is God. What is God? He does not know it but there is nothing else besides God—this is 'Vāsudevaḥ sarvam' from the view point of the belief in a saint's utterances. Having a firmer belief (faith) in saint's utterances than his own perception, he realizes that all is God.

If we reflect upon it from the philosophical point of view we come to know that there can be only one entity rather than two. From the faith-belief (devotion) point of view also all is God, there is no one else besides God. A devotee can't behold anyone else besides God and no one else besides God comes in his view.

Link:—In the verses, sixteen to nineteen, Lord Kṛṣṇa described four types of devotees, who seek refuge in Him. In the three verses that follow, the Lord describes those persons, who seek refuge in the gods.

कामैस्तैस्तैर्हृतज्ञानाः प्रपद्यन्तेऽन्यदेवताः ।
तं तं नियममास्थाय प्रकृत्या नियताः स्वया ॥ २० ॥

kāmaistaistairhṛtajñānāḥ prapadyante'nyadevatāḥ
taṁ taṁ niyamamāsthāya prakṛtyā niyatāḥ svayā

Those, whose discrimination (jñāna) has been subverted by various desires, influenced by their own nature, worship other gods and follow precepts relating to them*. 20

* In the fifteenth verse of this chapter it has been mentioned that the men are deprived of discrimination by delusion. But here they are deprived of discrimination by desires. There people depend on Matter to satisfy their desires while here they take refuge in the gods to satisfy their desires. There evils lead them to hells while here desires lead them to birth and death again and again.

Comment:—

'Kāmaistaistairhṛtajñānāḥ'—Their discrimination, has been led astray by desires, of this world, as well as of the next one. It means, that instead of applying their discrimination for God-realization, they remain engaged in, satisfying their desires. They have desire for worldly pleasure and prosperity, and hereafter they want to enjoy, heavenly pleasure.

They have desire for prosperity, greatness and pleasure, arising from pride. Similarly, they have a twofold desire, in performing virtuous deeds—to be considered pious, in this world and to enjoy pleasure, in the next world. Thus discrimination, is led astray by desires, and so they cannot distinguish the real from the unreal, the eternal from the transient, and emancipation from bondage.

'Prakṛtyā niyatāḥ svayā'—They are constrained by their own nature, because their discrimination is led astray by desires. Though a man cannot give up his nature, yet he can purify it, by removing evil. He is quite free, to make his nature pure and stainless. But, so long as, he aims at fulfilling his desires, he cannot purify his nature, and to him, it appears that his nature is powerful, while he is weak. When a striver, fixes his aim to be free from desires, he can purify and improve his nature, and is not constrained by it.

'Taṁ taṁ niyamamāsthāya'—A man, constrained by his own nature, undertakes several vows, and follows several methods, such as oblation, penance, charity, incantations etc., to satisfy his desire.

'Prapadyante'nyadevatāḥ'—Undertaking several vows, and following several methods, to satisfy desire, they instead of taking refuge in God, take refuge in the gods. They, instead of accepting the gods, as Divine manifestations, accept them as separate entities. So, the fruit reaped by them, is perishable (Gītā 7/23). If they accept the gods as Divine manifestations, they will gain immortal fruit.

They take refuge in the gods, because of desire and because of constraint, of their nature.

Appendix—The desires, that the Lord's devotees, who are seekers of wealth and also the afflicted have, are also possessed by the persons mentioned in this verse. But the difference between the two is that the seekers of wealth and the afflicted devotees have not predominance of desire but there is predominance of God in them, therefore they are not 'hṛtajñānāḥ' (discrimination has been led astray). But the persons described here have the predominance of desires; so they are 'hṛtajñānāḥ'.

The seekers of wealth and the afflicted devotees take refuge in only God but these persons leaving God aside, take refuge in other deities. Desires, deities, men and precepts—all these are various. If in spite of having several desires, only God is to be worshipped, then He will lead the devotee (worshipper) to salvation. But if desires are numerous and the deities worshipped are also numerous, then who will lead such a person to salvation?

There is no other entity besides God—this knowledge is veiled because of the desire for pleasure. The desire has been caused neither by prakṛti nor by God but it has been caused (made) by a man himself. Therefore it is his responsibility to wipe it out. The Lord by the term 'hṛtajñānāḥ' means to say that the discrimination has not been destroyed but because of desire it has been carried away. The same fact has been mentioned in the Gītā by the expressions, 'māyayāpahṛtajñānāḥ' (7/15), 'ajñānenāvṛtaṁ jñānam' (5/15) etc.

In the fifteenth verse of this chapter, in the expression 'māyayāpahṛtajñānāḥ' there is predominance of the mode of ignorance while the mode of passion is secondary, but in the expression 'kāmaistaistairhṛtajñānāḥ' used here, there is predominance of the mode of passion and the mode of ignorance is secondary. In the expression 'māyayāpahṛtajñānāḥ' there is predominance of the desire for wealth and in 'kāmaistaistairhṛtajñānāḥ' there is predominance of the desire for pleasure. The difference between the two is that the men deluded, deprived of discrimination by Māyā, don't worship gods but the men whose discrimination has been led astray by desires can worship gods. The reason is that there is no distaste for wealth—'jimi pratilābha lobha adhikāī' but there is certainly distaste for pleasures. In 'māyayāpahṛtajñānāḥ' a man depends on demoniac traits such as falsehood, fraud and dishonesty etc., but in 'kāmaistaistairhṛtajñānāḥ' there is dependence on God. Therefore in 'māyayāpahṛtajñānāḥ' there is special inertness (insentience) but in 'kāmaistaistairhṛtajñānāḥ' there is comparatively more consciousness (sentience).*

यो यो यां यां† तनुं भक्तः श्रद्धयार्चितुमिच्छति ।
तस्य तस्याचलां श्रद्धां तामेव विदधाम्यहम् ॥ २१ ॥

yo yo yāṁ yāṁ tanuṁ bhaktaḥ śraddhayārcitumicchati
tasya tasyācalāṁ śraddhāṁ tāmeva vidadhāmyaham

Whatever celestial form a devotee seeks to worship, with faith, I steady the faith of such a devotee, in that form. 21

Comment:—

'Yo yo yāṁ yāṁ tanuṁ bhaktaḥ.....tāmeva vidadhāmyaham'— The Lord, makes the faith of devotees steady in the gods, whom they seek to worship. The Lord, does not force them to have faith only, in Him. Faith in other gods, does not lead to salvation, because they adore them to satisfy their desire. But, He makes the faith of a devotee firm in Him, if he has faith in Him and

* 'Cetana' (sentient) is that which knows itself and also others, while Matter (insentient) is that which knows neither itself nor others.

† As here is the repetition of the words 'Yo' (who) and 'Yām' (which), in the sixth verse of the eighth chapter also there is repetition of the word 'Yām' (which). By this use the Lord means to say that as a man is free in the adoration of either God or the gods, he is free at his last moment to think of Him or of anyone else.

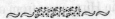

he wants to attain salvation, because He is a disinterested friend, of all beings (Gītā 5/29).

Now, a question arises, why the Lord does not make the faith of all persons firm only in Him? The Lord seems to answer the question, by saying that if He stabilizes their faith, only in Him, they lose their independence and He is proved, selfish. So, He sets an example for human beings, that they should be impartial, and should not motivate other people to have faith in them, and adore them only.

The second question that arises, that the Lord by stabilizing their faith in other gods, does not think of their welfare, because that faith does not lead them to salvation. The answer is, that if He stabilizes their faith in Him, apart from others, that will cease their reverence and faith, in Him. But, if they are given freedom, being intelligent and wise, they may be attracted towards Him, and that attraction will lead them to salvation. This, is the best way, to their salvation.

The third question was does the Lord, instead of uplifting them, degrade them by stabilizing their faith, in other gods? The answer is, that He stabilizes their faith not only in gods, but in anyone, whom they wish (desire) to adore and they are free to change their wish, because they have discrimination which is a divine gift to every human being. Had they been weak, incapable and helpless, in changing their inclinations (desire), then where is the glory in this human birth? By using this discrimination, they can kill the enemy in the form of desire (3/43).

Appendix—Generally a man wants to attract other people towards him, he wants them to become his disciple or servant, he wants them to follow his sect, he wants them to have reverence for him and to offer him regard, respect and worship and to obey him. But God in spite of being superior to all, does not make anyone dependent but He makes the faith of a devotee steady in the deity, whom he seeks to worship—this shows a great generosity and impartiality of God.

From God's point of view, all is His manifestation only—'mattaḥ parataraṁ nānyatkiñcidasti'. Therefore God is not partial to anyone in the least. But this impartial nature of God is not easily understood but it is clear only when it is deeply reflected upon. If a man understands (knows) this nature of the Lord, he becomes a devotee to Him.

umā rāma subhāu jehiṁ jānā
tāhi bhajanu taji bhāva na ānā

(Mānasa, Sundara. 34/2)

sa sarvavidbhajati māṁ sarvabhāvena bhārata

(Gītā 15/19)

The man who lacks something, tends to make the other person his servant (Dāsa). God lacks nothing, therefore how can He make anyone His servant (dependent)? But if a man wants to become a servant of God, He does not refuse and accepts him as a servant by showering His grace. This is His special generosity. As a man by seeing a lovely child gets pleased, it does not mean that the man has any selfish motive. Similarly when anyone becomes a servant of God, He is delighted with his simple heartedness—'moreṁ adhika dāsa para prītī' (Mānasa, Uttara. 16/4). In the eighteenth chapter of the Gītā when the Lord asks Arjuna to do as he wishes—'yathecchasi tathā kuru' and Arjuna is very much perturbed, then the Lord out of His grace says to Arjuna in order to console him, 'Take refuge in Me alone'—'māmekaṁ śaraṇaṁ vraja' (18/66). But before this utterance, the Lord says to Arjuna that this is the Supreme secret (18/64) and afterwards He forbids Arjuna to unfold the Supreme secret to everyone (18/67). It proves that though the Lord has no intention of making anyone His servant, yet if a man, without getting any other support, is perturbed and wants to become His servant, He out of His grace, accepts him. It means that if a man has faith in a deity, God makes his faith firm in that deity; and he who has faith in Him, the Lord makes his faith steady in Him—there is no doubt about it. The reason is that God minds the welfare of His devotee without any selfish motive of His own.

स तया श्रद्धया युक्तस्तस्याराधनमीहते।
लभते च ततः कामान्मयैव विहितान्हि तान्॥ २२॥

sa tayā śraddhayā yuktastasyārādhanamīhate
labhate ca tataḥ kāmānmayaiva vihitānhi tān

Endowed with faith, he worships that god, and obtains his desired fruition, as arranged by Me. 22

Comment:—

'Sa tayā śraddhayā yuktaḥ'—A devotee, whose faith has been made firm by Me, worships the god and obtains his desired enjoyment. Actually, his desire is satisfied by Me, but he feels that his desire has been satisfied, by the gods. The fact is, that the gods' power is nothing, besides My power, and they satisfy desires, as ordained by Me.

The gods, are just like government officers, in different departments. So, their power is limited. The gods at the most, can carry their devotees, to their worlds. But, after reaping the fruit of their virtuous deeds, they have to come back to this world (Gītā 8/16).

By using the phrase 'Mayaiva', Lord Kṛṣṇa means that the whole universe is managed by Him, and so whatever one obtains, is ordained only by Him. If a man, understands this mystery, he cannot help being attracted, towards Him.

Appendix—God has provided all the deities with different and limited rights. But God has limitless rights. This is the special feature of God that He does not rule over anyone, does not make anyone His slave, does not make anyone His disciple, but makes everyone His friend and He elevates him equal to Himself. As Niṣādarāja was a devotee who had attained perfection, Vibhīṣaṇa was a striver and Sugrīva was passionate, but Lord Rāma accepted all the three as His friends. The deities etc., don't possess this special virtue of making a devotee their friend. Therefore in the Vedas the soul has been declared as the friend of God—

dvā suparṇā sayujā sakhāyā samānaṁ vṛkṣaṁ pariṣasvajāte
(Muṇḍaka 3/1/1, Śvetā. 4/6)

In the Gītā Lord Kṛṣṇa has said to Arjuna—'bhakto'si me sakhā ceti' (4/3)—'thou art My devotee and My friend'. Here the Lord has called Arjuna a 'devotee' from Arjuna's point of view,* but from His point of view, He has called him 'friend'. 'Mamaivāṁśo jīvaloke' (15/7)—in this expression also the Lord by the term 'eva' has mentioned that the soul is His manifestation. 'The soul is My fragment only'—this expression means that in the soul there is no fragment of Prakṛti at all.

Link:—Now Lord Kṛṣṇa, describes the fruit according to worship.

अन्तवत्तु फलं तेषां तद्भवत्यल्पमेधसाम्।
देवान्देवयजो यान्ति मद्भक्ता यान्ति मामपि॥ २३॥

antavattu phalaṁ teṣāṁ tadbhavatyalpamedhasām
devāndevayajo yānti madbhaktā yānti māmapi

But, the fruit gained by these people of meagre intellect, is perishable. The worshippers of the gods reach the gods; whereas, My devotees attain Me, alone. 23

Comment:—

'Antavattu phalaṁ teṣāṁ tadbhavatyalpamedhasām'—The

* The Lord called Arjuna His devotee because Arjuna had taken refuge in Him—'Śādhi māṁ tvāṁ prapannam' (Gītā 2/7).

worshippers of the gods, gain finite and perishable fruit. Here, a question arises, that should the fruit ordained by God be imperishable? Then, why do they gain perishable fruit? The answer is, that they have desire for perishable fruit, moreover, they accept gods' entities, separate from God. But, if they worship the gods, without a desire for fruit or worship, them as Divine manifestations, having no separate entity, they can gain imperishable fruit (i.e.,) can realize God.

By using the term 'Tat', Lord Krsna means to say, that the fruit is ordained, only by Him, but because of desire, it becomes perishable.

By using the phrase 'Alpamedhasām', (meagre intellect), Lord Kṛṣṇa says, that such devotees are of meagre intellect, because they have to undertake several vows, and follow several methods, but the fruit is finite and perishable. So, in the worship of the Lord, a devotee without undertaking vows and without following various methods, gains infinite and imperishable fruit. Worshippers of the gods, follow the cycle of birth and death, while the worshippers of the Lord, being free from the shackles of birth and death, attain salvation.

'Devāndevayajo yānti madbhaktā yānti māmapi'—Worshippers of the gods attain at the maximum the gods, whereas devotees of the Lord, attain Him. As they are votaries of gods, they are not devoted to the Lord, so their intellect is meagre and mediocre. The devotees of God, whether they worship Him with a desire or without a desire, attain Him. But, it is not necessary that their desires, may be satisfied. God satisfies their desires only, if these are for their welfare. But if they are harmful, for the devotees, the Lord does not satisfy these.

Our affinity for God is eternal, but we are reminded of it through adoration. Having attained Him, there is no return to this world (Gītā 15/6). But our affinity with the gods, is not eternal and therefore, having attained to them, we have to return to this world of mortals (Gītā 9/21).

"My devotees attain Me alone." Having this feeling, the Lord has referred to four types of devotees—seekers of worldly objects, the sufferers, the seekers of knowledge and men of wisdom, virtuous and noble (7/16—18).

'Madbhaktā yānti māmapi'—It means, that even a vilest sinner, being His fragment may attain Him, if he abandons his affinity, for the world which is an assumed one.

An Exceptional Fact

The whole universe, is nothing besides, the manifestation of God. But, we are unable to realize this fact, because, first we accept the world as a separate entity from God, and secondly, we have desires. If we accept the universe as Divine manifestation, our desires, will be rooted out, or if we root out desires, the universe, will be seen as a Divine manifestation. Then, all our actions will be performed, as a service to God. If both are done together, we will be immensely and instantly benefited.

Appendix—The worshippers of the gods at the most can reach the abode of gods from where they have to return to the mortal world, but the worshippers of God attain Him only. If a striver regards the deity as the manifestation of God or worships him in a disinterested manner, he will attain salvation viz., will attain God. But if he does not regard the deity as the manifestation of God or if he does not worship Him in a disinterested manner, he will not attain salvation.

The defect in the worship of deities is that the fruit of their worship is perishable because their rights are also limited. Therefore those, who instead of God, worship other deities, they are men of meagre intellect. If they had not been the men of poor intellect, why would have they worshipped the deities, the fruit of whose worship is perishable? They would have worshipped God or would have regarded the deities as the manifestation of

God. The worship of God is very easy as it needs no technique, no rules, no labour; in it there is only predominance of devotion. But in the worship of deities, there is predominance of actions, prescriptions and objects.

A man may have the knowledge of several worldly sciences, arts and crafts etc., yet he is a man of meagre intellect. In fact that knowledge strengthens ignorance. But he who has known God, he may not have knowledge of the worldly science, art and craft etc., yet he is 'sarvavit' (knower of all) (Gītā 15/19).

Link:—Worshippers of the gods, gain the fruit which is finite and perishable. Then, why do men get entangled in it? Why do not they worship, God? An explanation comes in the next verse.

अव्यक्तं व्यक्तिमापन्नं मन्यन्ते मामबुद्धयः ।
परं भावमजानन्तो ममाव्ययमनुत्तमम् ॥ २४ ॥

avyaktaṁ vyaktimāpannaṁ manyante māmabuddhayaḥ
paraṁ bhāvamajānanto mamāvyayamanuttamam

Men who lack understanding think of Me, the unmanifest as a perceptible ordinary human being, not knowing My supreme state as immutable and unexcelled. 24

Comment:—

'Avyaktaṁ vyaktimāpannaṁ manyante māmabuddhayaḥ paraṁ bhāvamajānanto mamāvyayamanuttamam'—Men of poor understanding, think of Me as having been born, and dead, just like ordinary men. They think, that I am also manifested, in the mid-state only, like other beings (Gītā 2/28). They do not know Me, as imperishable, uniform, immaculate, all-pervading, untainted, beyond time, space and causation, and as an incarnation of God. So they, instead of worshipping Me, worship the gods.

There is not a total negation of discrimination in them. But, their understanding is poor, because they do not admit the perishable world, as perishable. Secondly, they know that if desires cannot be satisfied, they will have to be abandoned, but they do not abandon them.

They do not know My supreme state, immutable and unsurpassed. So, they for satisfaction of their desires, are attracted towards, the gods. Had they known Me, as unsurpassed, they would have worshipped Me, only.

(i) Men of understanding, are those who, accepting the Lord as unsurpassed, take refuge in Him. (ii) Men of poor understanding, are those who regarding the gods, as superior to them to take refuge in them. They are, somewhat polite and simple. (iii) Men without understanding, are those who regard God, as an ordinary human being, and think that they are supreme (Gītā 16/14). God, in spite of being imperishable, the Lord of the whole universe, manifests Himself, through His own divine potency, keeping His nature (prakṛti), under control. But men of poor understanding, do not know, that, He is beyond perishable matter and is superior to the imperishable soul.

An Exceptional Fact

Some people, interpret this verse to mean that those who think of the Lord, the unmanifest, as having manifestation, are of poor understanding, because they do not know Him, as unmanifest and formless. Others, interpret that those who regard Lord Kṛṣṇa, the incarnation of God, Who works as Arjuna's charioteer, as formless, are of poor understanding.

But, both views are not correct. The reason is, that the former will censure the Lord endowed with form, and His devotees, while the latter will censure formless God, and the devotees who worship a formless God. When, even the elements such as earth, water and fire etc., can be with form and without form, why can the Lord, not be with form and without form, with attributes and without attributes?

The Gītā, accepts both His aspects, the unmanifest, as well as, the manifest. In the sixth verse of the fourth chapter, Lord Kṛṣṇa declares that He, in spite of being unborn manifests Himself, in spite of being immortal, disappears and despite his being the Lord of the whole universe, becomes an obedient son or pupil, while in the fourth verse of the ninth chapter, He declares that all this is permeated by Him, in His unmanifest aspect. Thus, He can be both—manifest and unmanifest.

Appendix—God is manifest and also unmanifest; He is worldly as well as unworldly—'Vāsudevaḥ sarvam' (Gītā 7/19), 'sadasaccāhamarjuna' (Gītā 9/19). But men, who lack understanding, think of God as manifested from the unmanifest like other beings viz., regard Him as worldly (who is born and dead) for whom the Lord has said—

avyaktādīni bhūtāni vyaktamadhyāni bhārata
avyaktanidhanānyeva tatra kā paridevanā (Gītā 2/28)

'O Bhārata (Arjuna), all beings were imperceptible before they were born and will become so again when they are dead; they are perceptible only in the intermediate stage. Therefore why to lament?'

God like comman human beings is not manifest from the unmanifest, but at the same time being unmanifest, He manifests Himself and being manifest, He remains unmanifest.

'Param'—God endows the worshippers of deities with faith and also rewards them for their worship—this is God's supreme viz., impartial attitude.

'Avyayam'—Deities are relatively imperishable (immortal), they are not totally imperishable. But God is absolutely imperishable. Anyone else neither is nor can be imperishable like Him.

'Anuttamam'—God wants the welfare of all beings—this is the unexcelled feeling of the Lord. No other feeling can be superior to it.

Link:—Why do people think of the Lord as an ordinary man? The explanation comes next.

नाहं प्रकाशः सर्वस्य योगमायासमावृतः।
मूढोऽयं नाभिजानाति लोको मामजमव्ययम्॥ २५॥

nāhaṁ prakāśaḥ sarvasya yogamāyāsamāvṛtaḥ
mūḍho'yaṁ nābhijānāti loko māmajamavyayam

Veiled, by My divine potency (Yoga Māyā), I am not manifest to all. Hence ignorant folk do not recognize Me, as one unborn and imperishable Supreme. 25

Comment:—

'Mūḍho'yaṁ nābhijānāti loko māmajamavyayam'—I am unborn and imperishable (i.e.,) free from birth and death. But, I stage a play of My revelation, and disappearance. In spite of being unborn, I incarnate and in spite of, being imperishable, I disappear, in the same way as the sun rises and sets. Thus, those who know Me without birth and death, are undeluded (Gītā 10/3, 15/19). But those, who regard Me, as the Lord of creation, yet an ordinary mortal, subject to birth and death, are fools (Gītā 9/11).

The reason, why a man does not regard the Lord, as unborn and imperishable, is that he by forgetting his real affinity with Him, by error he has accepted his affinity with this body, "I am this body and this body is mine." It is because, of this veil, that he regards the Lord, as born and dead.

Men do not regard Him, as unborn and imperishable, because of two factors—One, is that He is concealed by His divine potency, and the second is due to their own folly. It can be explained, by an illustration. A man, remains confined to his house which is shut. He is free to go out of his house. But, he is unable to cross the walls round the city, when the gate of the walls, is shut. But, a king can open the gate of the city, and also force the sentry to open the gate of his house. Similarly, a man can get rid of his folly. But he can realize God only, by God's grace. Only, he whom God enables to realize Him, can know Him. If a man surrenders himself to Him, He removes his ignorance, as well as, His deluding potency.

'Nāhaṁ prakāśaḥ sarvasya yogamāyāsamāvṛtaḥ'—I, am not manifest, to a group of ignorant people, because they instead of recognizing Me, as unborn and imperishable Supreme-Spirit, neglect Me considering Me, as an ordinary man. It means, that I hide myself in My divine potency, to those, who regard Me as mortal, and I am not manifest to them. But, I am manifest to those, who having faith in Me, regard Me as unborn, imperishable and the Lord, of the whole creation.

The Lord's divine potency, is strange and uncommon. Men see God, who is hidden by His divine potency, according to their own sentiments.*

Here, the Lord has declared, that those who do not recognize Him as unborn and imperishable, are ignorant, while in the second verse of the tenth chapter, He declares, that neither gods nor great sages, know the secret of His birth. So, a doubt arises why the Lord has declared, those who do not recognize Him as unborn and imperishable, as ignorant, while He has not declared those gods and sages ignorant, who do not know, the secret of His birth. The clarification is, that the Lord Himself, has declared, that He is the origin of all the gods and great sages, and as a child cannot see the birth of his father, the gods and sages, cannot know the secret of His birth; but men can accept Him, as unborn and imperishable. If they do not do so, they are called, ignorant.

* When Lord Kṛṣṇa along with Balarāma came to the arena, he seemed diamond-hard to wrestlers, a virtuous person to common men, Cupid, the god of love to women, a kinsman to cowherds, a strict ruler to the cunning kings, a child to elderly people, death to Kaṁsa, gigantic to the ignorant, cosmic soul to the ascetics and favourite God to the devotees of the Vṛṣṇi clan. (Śrīmadbhā. 10/43/17)

Appendix—The fools who don't believe the existence of God, the Lord during the period of His incarnation being manifest to all others, is not manifest to them—ye yathā māṁ prapadyante tāṁstathaiva bhajāmyaham' (Gītā 4/11). In fact God does not want to remain unrevealed, but those who do not believe Him, how can He reveal Himself to them?

During the period of His incarnation, though He appears as a common human being of this world, yet He ever remains unworldly. But because of their attachment and aversion, the Lord appears to be an ordinary man to the ignorant people viz., He does not appear as an incarnation of God to them.

Link:—The Lord, is veiled by His divine potency, to those who do not recognize Him, as unborn and imperishable. But none can remain covered, with a veil before Him—This fact is mentioned, in the verse that follows.

वेदाहं समतीतानि वर्तमानानि चार्जुन।
भविष्याणि च भूतानि मां तु वेद न कश्चन॥ २६॥

vedāhaṁ samatītāni vartamānāni cārjuna
bhaviṣyāṇi ca bhūtāni māṁ tu veda na kaścana

I Know, O Arjuna, the created beings of the past, the present and the future, but the ignorant one, does not know Me. 26

Comment:—

'Vedāhaṁ samatītāni vartamānāni cārjuna bhaviṣyāṇi ca bhūtāni māṁ tu veda na kaścana'—Here, the Lord has used three adjectives, to express the past, the present and the future for the beings, but for Himself, He has used only the present. It means that in God's eye, the past, the future and the present are simply present. So, He knows all the beings of the past, the future and the present. As in a movie, the incidents, for persons seeing a movie seem to occur in the past, the future and the present, while in the film they are all in the present. Similarly, from the view-point of beings, there is distinction between the past, the future and the present, but in reality, there is only the present, because the beings are within a limit of time, while the Lord is beyond the limit of time. Time, things, men, incidents and circumstances etc., change, while God ever remains the same. Knowledge of the beings, who are bound by time, is limited, while knowledge of God, is limitless. The beings, by practising Yoga, enhance their knowledge, but that knowledge, is limited. Such Yogīs, are called 'Yuñjāna Yogī' (the ascetics who are practising austerities, but have not attained final beatitude). The Lord, is 'Yukta Yogī' i.e., He knows all beings and the whole world, all the time, without practising Yoga. All beings of the past, the future and the present, constantly abide in God; they can never be separated from Him. It is beyond His power, to separate Himself, from them. So, they can never escape, His observation.

'Māṁ tu veda na kaścana'—It means, that the ignorant folk, who do not recognize Me, as unborn and imperishable, but regard Me as an ordinary man, do not know Me, but I know, all of them. As a man from inside, can see the outerside through a curtain made from split bamboo sticks, hung on the door, but a man from outside the door, cannot see inside through it, the ignorant people, veiled by the curtain of divine potency, cannot see the Lord, while He can see all of them.

Now, a doubt arises, that as the Lord knows the future of all beings, it means that man's emancipation and bondage, are also predestined. Then, how can a man attain emancipation, or salvation, by making efforts?

The clarification is, that God has bestowed upon man, this last life. Now, it is upto him whether he attains salvation or he has a downfall (Gītā 7/27; 8/6), it is not decided by God.

The Lord Himself, in the nineteenth verse of this chapter,

declares, "In the very last of all births viz., in this human birth, man of wisdom, takes refuge in Me, realizing that, all this is God. Such, a great soul is rare indeed." It means, that men are free to attain salvation, or God-realization. If a man's rebirth in a particular womb, is predecided by God, it means that man is not free, in attaining salvation and there is no recourse for sanction and prohibition, preached by God, saints and preceptors, and in scriptures. Moreover, the Lord's declarations, "Whatever form any devotee with faith wishes to worship, that faith of his, I make steady" (7/21) and "Thinking of whatever being he at the end, gives up his body, to that being, does he attain" (8/6) will prove futile and man's worship and the freedom bestowed upon him, of the last thought, which determines his next birth, will also go, in vain.

The Lord by His grace bestows this human body, so that a man may attain salvation. In the thirty-third verse of the eleventh chapter, Lord Kṛṣṇa says to Arjuna, "These warriors have already been slain by Me. You, be merely an instrument." Similarly, the Lord, has bestowed upon men all the resources, for attaining salvation by His grace. He should merely become an instrument in his hand. The Lord also declares, "By receiving this boat, in the form of a human body and favourable wind, in the form of My grace, one, who does not attain salvation, commits, suicide" (Śrīmadbhā. 11/20/17). In the Gītā, it is also declared, "Seeing the same Lord dwelling equally in all, he does not kill his self, by the self and thereby reaches, the supreme state" (Gītā 13/28). It proves that the Lord has bestowed upon human beings, the right, resources and understanding, so that they can attain salvation. If they do not attain salvation, by receiving this priceless opportunity, they commit suicide and follow the cycle of birth and death. If on receiving this human body, a man makes proper use of the resources, without working against the ordinance of scriptures and God, his salvation is axiomatic, and there is no obstacle to it.

Thus, a man should have a firm determination, to make the best possible use of his resources, in accordance with the scriptures. But, if they are misused by an error, he should have a burning sensation, and pray to God, "O God, I regret for my error. Give me power, so that I may not deviate from your ordinances and principles." In such cases, God's help is certain.

Man's inability can be of two kinds—First, a man is not able to do a piece of work, because he has not got enough power, just as a servant, cannot lift a house and carry it, if desired by his master. Secondly, that he has the power and can do the work, but because of indolence, he does not do it. A striver, suffers from the latter sort of inability. In order, to do away with this inability, a striver should pray to God.

God can never wish that a human being may have to take, so many births, because He has given him freedom, to attain salvation. Not only this, the Lord would not wish countless animate and inanimate beings, to take births. God, does not force a man to follow the cycle of birth and death. Other beings, besides men, follow this cycle of birth and death according to the fruit of their actions. But, if anyone of those beings, either in human birth or even in any other birth, takes refuge in the Lord, He liberates him, from sins of infinite births (Mānasa 5/44/1).

Appendix—Here a doubt may arise that when the Lord knows all beings, it means that a man's bondage and salvation are predestined because the Lord's knowledge is eternal. This doubt arises because we assume the existence of the world and we value the world (it is our point of view). From the view-point of God and exalted souls, the world has no existence, only God exists—'Vāsudevaḥ sarvam'. Because of ego we have assumed the existence of the world and have valued it. Therefore the Lord talks about the past, the present and the future in our language. If He does not speak in our language, how shall we understand? As, if a teacher of English language who wants to teach us English, uses only English, we shall not be able to learn English.

The knowledge of God is eternal. All is within the knowledge of God. There is nothing else besides Him—'mattaḥ parataraṁ nānyatkiñcidasti' (Gītā 7/7). The embodied soul because of ego (ignorance) has sustained the world. Therefore bondage and salvation are man (the self)-made. In Pure-Reality there is neither bondage nor salvation but there is only God.* The purpose of the use of the term 'ca' two times is that no time is permanent. Neither the past nor the present nor the future ever stays but God ever exists. As the past and the future don't persist now, so is the case with the present also. The conjunction of the past and the future is called present. There is a formula of Pāṇini-grammar—'vartamānasāmīpye vartamānavadvā' (3/3/131) viz., near-present is also like the present. As the action which was performed in the past, is said in the present 'I have come now' and the action of the future is also said in the present 'I am going now'—this is near-present which is called present. Had there been present really, it would have never changed into past. In fact time is not present but only God is present. Therefore the Lord has used the verb in the present tense 'Vedāham' (I know). God is ever present in the past, at present and in future also, but in God there is neither past nor future nor present. God's present existence does not depend on time because God transcends all limits of time. Time has no existence either from the view-point of God or from the view-point of an exalted soul.

---

* na nirodho na cotpattirna baddho na ca sādhakaḥ
na mumukṣurna vai mukta ityeṣā paramārthatā (Ātmopaniṣad 31)

"There is no end (dissolution) and no origin; no one is bound and no one a striver; no one a seeker of emancipation and no one emancipated—this is Pure-Reality."

Link:—In the previous verse, Lord Kṛṣṇa declared, that no one knows Him. Why do people not know Him? The answer is provided, in the next verse.

इच्छाद्वेषसमुत्थेन द्वन्द्वमोहेन भारत।
सर्वभूतानि सम्मोहं सर्गे यान्ति परन्तप॥ २७॥

icchādveṣasamutthena dvandvamohena bhārata
sarvabhūtāni sammohaṁ sarge yānti parantapa

By the delusion of antithetic opposites, arising from desire and aversion, all beings (O scorcher of the foes in Bharata family), are subject to delusion viz., birth and death. 27

Comment:—

'Icchādveṣasamutthena dvandvamohena bhārata sarvabhūtāni sammohaṁ sarge yānti parantapa'—Delusion, arises from desire and aversion, and it is because of this that beings, having disinclination for God, follow the cycle of birth and death.

Man, by having disinclination for the world, should be engaged, in adoration of God. The main obstacle to this engagement, is that a man, without attaching importance to discrimination, performs actions being guided by attachment and aversion, and thus, he degrades himself. A man, has two contrary mental dispositions— inclination and disinclination. He, has to be inclined towards God, and to be disinclined, from the world i.e., he has to be devoted to God, and dispassionate, to the world. But, when he applies both these dispositions to the world, his devotion and dispassion, are respectively changed into attachment and aversion, which cause him to be entangled in the world and he has a total disinclination for God. Thus, because of his attachment and aversion, to the pairs of opposites such as pleasure and pain, etc., he cannot move towards spirituality, even though sometimes he may attend religious discourses, study the scriptures and think over them. But, because of his attachment to the world, he has a mind, that he has to make efforts to cause favourable circumstances, and to do away with, unfavourable ones, as he cannot maintain his body, without these.

Out of these pairs of opposites, if he is particularly attached to one, viz., God or has even aversion to Him, or may also lead him, to salvation. For example, Bilvamaṅgala was attached only to a prostitute, named Cintāmaṇi. He was scolded by her, that if he had worshipped the Lord, with the devotion with which he loved her mortal body, he would have attained salvation. As a result, of her scolding, his attention was diverted to God, and he attained salvation. Similarly, the attachment of Gopīs for Lord Kṛṣṇa, led them to salvation. Śiśupāla's aversion to Lord Kṛṣṇa got him salvation, while, Kaṁsa's fear of God gave him salvation. Though Śiśupāla and Kaṁsa also, attained salvation, yet they could not enjoy, the bliss of devotion. It means, that attachment or aversion, to God leads to salvation, while attachment or aversion to the world, leads to degradation.

By the pairs of opposites, attachment for the world becomes firm, because of desire for one, and aversion for the other. Therefore, Lord Kṛṣṇa, in the second chapter, orders Arjuna "Rise above the pairs of opposites" (2/45). He also declares, "He, who has transcended the pairs of opposites, is easily freed, from bondage" (5/3). "The undeluded devotee, freed from the pairs of opposites, attain an imperishable supreme state" (15/5). In the thirty-fourth verse of the third chapter also, the Lord has declared these, as man's main enemies (3/34). He also declares, "The men of virtuous deeds, being freed from delusion, in the shape of pairs of opposites, worship Me, with a firm resolve, in everyway" (7/28). Therefore, Lord Kṛṣṇa, has laid great emphasis on being free, from the pairs of opposites.

Why do beings follow a cycle of birth and death? According to scriptures, ignorance is the root of life and death. But according to saints, it is the misuse of the circumstances, arising from attachment. Performance of actions, with a desire for fruits, and misuse of circumstances i.e., performance of actions, against the ordinance of scriptures, leads a man to his birth in good and evil wombs through eighty-four lac forms of lives and hell.

Right use of the available circumstances, does away with delusion i.e., roots out the cycle of birth and death. How to make right use of circumstances? We should have a firm determination, not to misuse these i.e., not to act, against the ordinance of scriptures and decorums. By having this determination, circumstances will be used properly and rightly. By doing so, we shall not be proud of our virtuous actions, because we are determined, not to misuse the circumstances. Thus, we shall be free, from pride of doership. By doing so, we shall not have desire for the fruit of actions, because how can we have desire for fruit, when we are not the doer? Thus being free from doership, and fruit of action, emancipation is axiomatic.

Generally, strivers divide adoration and worldly affairs, in watertight compartments. They attach importance to adoration and meditation etc., but they do not pay attention to attachment-aversion, desire-anger etc., in their practical life. They are of an opinion that while performing action, attachment and aversion, are natural, they cannot be wiped out. Because of this assumption, of attachment and aversion, which are obstacles to their spiritual progress, continue. So a striver, does not make quick spiritual progress. He, while performing, either mundane or the spiritual affairs, should be free from, attachment and aversion.

A striver, should always keep the fact, in mind, "I am a striver and I have to realize God." Thus, by having only the aim of God-realization, both kinds of actions, mundane as well as spiritual, will become, parts of his spiritual discipline.

Appendix—Though the root cause of worldly bondage is ignorance, yet a man gets entangled in the world more by the pairs of opposites—attachment and aversion, than by ignorance. When a man regards any place, time, thing, person, circumstance etc., the cause of his pleasure and pain, then attachment and aversion evolve. A man gets attached to the thing or person whom he thinks to be the cause of his pleasure and he has an aversion to the thing or person whom he regards as the cause of his pain. When attachment and aversion are wiped out, a man is easily liberated from the worldly bondage—'nirdvando hi mahābāho sukhaṁ bandhātpramucyate' (Gītā 5/3).

The Lord in the thirteenth verse of this chapter has also declared, "Deluded by these threefold modes (guṇas) of Nature, a being does not know Me." Such deluded beings know neither the world nor God. Being engrossed in the world, a man can't know the world, and by keeping distance from the Lord, a man can't know the Lord. In fact a man knows the world by getting detached (separate) from the world and he knows God by identifying himself with Him. The world has no existence—this is the knowledge about the world. In fact the world which does not exist, which does not persist, what is the knowledge about it? The world exists—this assumption is ignorance.

Link:—In the previous verse, Lord Kṛṣṇa talked about beings, who are under delusion of the pairs of opposites. In the next verse, He talks about those, who have got over, the pairs of opposites.

येषां त्वन्तगतं पापं जनानां पुण्यकर्मणाम्।
ते द्वन्द्वमोहनिर्मुक्ता भजन्ते मां दृढव्रताः॥ २८॥

yeṣāṁ tvantagataṁ pāpaṁ janānāṁ puṇyakarmaṇām
te dvandvamohanirmuktā bhajante māṁ dṛḍhavratāḥ

But those men of virtuous deeds whose sins have been destroyed, being freed from the delusion of opposites, worship Me, with a firm resolve, in everyway. 28

Comment:—

'Yeṣāṁ tvantagataṁ pāpaṁ janānāṁ puṇyakarmaṇāṁ te

dvandvamohanirmuktā bhajante māṁ dṛḍhavratāḥ'—The term 'Tu' (but), has been used to show the singularity of those who, being free from delusion, worship the Lord. Men of virtuous deeds, are those who have realized, that the only aim of human life, is God-realization. They have a firm determination to realize Him, during this human life, which has been bestowed upon them for God-realization, and not for sensual pleasures. It means, that determination is a better means, than oblation, charity and penance etc., for purification, because this determination is of one's own self, while actions such as oblation, charity etc., are bodily acts.

'Antagataṁ pāpam' means, that when a man has a firm determination, that he has to realize God, all his sins are rooted out, because disinclination for God, is the root of sins. The saints, have said that, there are one and a half sins, and one and a half virtues. Disinclination for God is one sin, and to be engaged in evil and immoral actions, is half. Similarly, inclination for God is one virtue, and engagement in good and moral actions, is half. When a man surrenders himself to God, all his sins perish.

Secondly, those people whose sole aim is God-realization, are virtuous because by having this aim, all their sins come to an end. Even if, because of past influences, any sin, is committed, God, Who dwells in their hearts, destroys that sin.

Thirdly, if a man determines sincerely, never to commit a sin, in future, his sins, perish.

'Te dvandvamohanirmuktā bhajante māṁ dṛḍhavratāḥ'—Men of virtuous deeds, being free from delusion of the pairs of opposites, worship God, with a firm resolve. This duality (pairs of opposites), can be of several kinds.

1. Whether they should be engaged in divine adoration for salvation, or in worldly affairs for welfare of this world.

2. Whether they should worship Lord Viṣṇu, the preserver, Lord Śiva, the destroyer, Goddess Durgā, God Gaṇeśa or the

Sun. Out of these five sects, which one should they follow?

3. Which of the following principles—dualistic, non-dualistic, special-non-dualistic, pure-non-dualistic etc., should they follow?

4. Which of the Disciplines—of devotion, knowledge, action and meditation etc., should they follow?

5. There are pairs of opposites like—favourable and unfavourable circumstances, pleasure and pain, attachment and aversion etc.

A man of virtuous deeds, being free from all spiritual and mundane dualistic delusions, worships God with a firm resolve.

If a man has only the aim of God-realization, all pairs of opposites, come to an end, if he follows any spiritual discipline, principle, sect or method. A striver, should follow any path, with exclusive devotion and without criticizing other paths. He should respect the followers of other paths, without regarding them as inferior to him, and without considering their sect inferior to his. So long as, a striver disregards, others' principles, religions and sects etc., he cannot realize God. Therefore, a striver on paying due regard to all sects, principles and methods, should follow his own path, with full faith and undivided devotion. By doing so, his dualism comes to an end.

It is human nature, that when a man lives in spiritual environment, he thinks that salvation, is a great achievement of life. But, when he lives in mundane environment, he attaches greater importance to worldly affairs, and secondary importance to, adoration for God, because he thinks that he has to perform action in order to get the necessities of life, and there is not much use for adoration.

Those whose only aim is salvation, without caring for worldly pleasure and pain, profit and loss, fame and defame, regard and disregard etc., are free from delusion, of the pairs of opposites.

'Dṛḍhavratāḥ' means, that the striver has a firm resolve to worship God, whether he is dualistic or non-dualistic, endowed with form or formless, two-armed or four-armed. He is not much concerned, about different forms etc.*

When a striver, follows spiritual discipline he is confronted with three questions: What is God like? What is the nature of soul? What is the nature of the world? The answer, is, 'God exists'. He is not much concerned, about where He lives and what He does etc. Similarly, about the soul it is enough for him, 'I am', and about the world it is enough, to know that it is to be renounced. It means, that a striver, by depending on God and having disinclination for the world, which is to be renounced, has a firm resolve to attain Him. By having a firm resolve, he becomes free from the delusion, of the pairs of opposites. The gist of all the philosophies, is to have an inclination for God, by having disinclination for the world.

Secondly, a striver has no knowledge about God, Who is attributeless and neither has he beheld God endowed with attributes. But he knows, that the world is perishing every moment, and assumes, that in the world, there is nothing besides God. By having this knowledge and assumption, he worships God with a firm resolve. Just like a chaste wife who is faithful to her husband, a man of virtuous deeds, by depending on God, worships Him.

An Exceptional Fact

It is mentioned in the scriptures, including the Gītā, and also in the utterances of saints, the sinners, have no inclination for God. This is a general rule. But sins cannot force a man to have disinclination for God, because he is a fragment of

* He, who protects the one who being afraid of the very strong fast running death-snake, takes refuge in Him, and being afraid of Whom even death is running, I take refuge in Him (Śrīmadbhā. 8/2/33).

God. Therefore, his purity may be veiled by sins, but cannot be destroyed. Therefore, even the vilest sinner, who worships Him with exclusive devotion, becomes virtuous (Gītā 9/31).* Therefore, a man should never think, that his sins are obstacles to his adoration. Sins produce, unfavourable circumstances and then perish. If sins, had been obstacles to adoration, Lord Kṛṣṇa, would not have declared, "Even the vilest sinner, worships Me with exclusive devotion (Gītā 9/30). It means, that sins, are not obstacles to worship, the Lord. The sins of those who worship the Lord, with a firm resolve, surrendering themselves to Him, come to an end. So circumstances cannot be obstacles to adoration.

Men, having a desire for fruit of their virtuous actions, go to heaven, while the evil actions lead men to hell. But, God by His special grace, bestows the human body in between i.e., without forcing them to acquire the fruit of their actions. We have got this human life, for God-realization, so we should never be disappointed, as far as God-realization, is concerned.

This human life, is not meant for sensual pleasures. It is generally called a life for action. But, according to the principles and utterances of the saints, the only aim of this human life, is God-realization. Both the favourable and the unfavourable circumstances, are the means for God-realization. A striver, in favourable circumstances, should serve others, and in unfavourable circumstances, he should give up desire for favourable circumstances. By doing so, both types of circumstances, will become means for spiritual progress. In favourable circumstances, old virtues perish and there are also chances to be entangled, in sensual pleasures. But in unfavourable circumstances, old sins

* In other lives besides the human life this is not a rule that the nature may be purified. By reaping the fruit of sinful actions in eighty-four lac forms of lives and in hells, sins are wiped out but nature does not improve. But in human life in spite of having sins a striver's nature can be purified. Sins result in unfavourable circumstances such as disease etc., while good company, spirituality and change of doership change a striver's nature.

perish, and a man becomes more alert, and careful in spiritual discipline. Therefore, saints value unfavourable circumstances, more than favourable ones.

Appendix—The greatest virtue is to turn one's face towards God because this is the root of all virtues.* But to turn away one's face from God is the most deadly sin, because this is the root of all sins. But the men whose sins have been destroyed viz., who having a disinclination for the world, have inclined to God, they being free from the duality of attachment and aversion, pleasure and pain, joys and sorrows etc., worship God. This types of the devotees, who worship God, have been described in the sixteenth verse of this chapter by the expression 'caturvidhā bhajante mām'.

Attachment and aversion go on attracting a man towards the world. So long as a man is attached to one thing, he has an aversion to the other thing, because if a man is inclined to a thing, he will certainly have a disinclination for the other thing. As long as a man has attachment and aversion, he can't be totally inclined to God, because he remains connected with the world. The extent to which he is attached to the world, to the same extent he remains detached from God viz., he has a disinclination for God.

'Dṛḍhavratāḥ'—A man of lax nature can't renounce the unreal quickly. He has an idea and gives it up; then again he has another idea and also relinquishes it—thus by having different ideas and by giving them up, he inculcates this sort of bad habit. Because of this bad habit he has the bookish knowledge (rot learning) of renunciation of the unreal, but he finds himself helpless in renouncing it. Even if he renounces the unreal once; because of

* sanamukha hoi jīva mohi jabahīṁ, janma koṭi agha nāsahiṁ tabahīṁ.
(Mānasa, Sundara. 44/1)

his lax nature he again assumes the existence of the unreal. This lax nature of a striver is self-made. Therefore it is inevitable for a striver to have a firm resolve. Whatever plan is formed in the mind, he should stick to it. If he has a firm resolve even in petty matters, by the formation of this type of nature, he will acquire strength to renounce the unreal and to have disinclination for the world.

Link:—In the beginning of the seventh chapter Lord Kṛṣṇa declared that a striver with his mind attached to Him, taking refuge in Him and practising Yoga, would without any doubt, know, Him in full. Now, He concludes these three facts, in the next two verses.

जरामरणमोक्षाय मामाश्रित्य यतन्ति ये।
ते ब्रह्म तद्विदुः कृत्स्नमध्यात्मं कर्म चाखिलम्॥ २९॥*

jarāmaraṇamokṣāya māmāśritya yatanti ye
te brahma tadviduḥ kṛtsnamadhyātmaṁ karma cākhilam

Those who having taken shelter in Me, striving for deliverance from old age and death, know Brahma (the Infinite), the individual self and the entire field of action. 29

Comment:—

'Jarāmaraṇamokṣāya māmāśritya yatanti ye'—Here, deliverance from old age and death, does not mean that after knowing Brahma, the individual self and entire field of action, man will not suffer from old age and will not die. But it means, that old age and death will not be able to make him, sad. As in the thirty-fourth

* In the twenty-ninth and thirtieth verses in the phrase 'Māmāśritya' (having taken refuge in), 'Madāśrayaḥ'; in the term 'Yatanti' (strive), 'Yogaṁ yuñjan' (practising Yoga); and in 'Yuktacetasaḥ' (steadfast in mind), 'Mayyāsaktamanāḥ' (with mind clinging) have been concluded. Similarly the term 'Samagram' has been used for Brahma, Adhyātma, Karma, Adhibhūta, Adhidaiva and Adhiyajña.

verse of the thirteenth chapter, in 'Bhūta prakṛti mokṣam' the Lord says, that a striver realizes, that he is different from nature and its evolutes while here He means that a striver realizes, that he is different from the body and thus old age and death, have no effect on him.

A young man, is free from old age and death, only at present, but it does not mean that he has deliverance from these forever, while liberated souls are always free from these, because they have separated themselves from their bodies, which suffer from old age and death. When a man identifies himself with the body, he accepts the body's, old age and death, as his own. This is so, because he has assumed "I am the body and the body is mine." So in the eighth verse of the thirteenth chapter, Lord Kṛṣṇa exhorts Arjuna to perceive, pain and evil in birth, death, old age and disease. It means, that a striver should not accept his affinity of 'I'ness and 'mineness', with this body. When the affinity is renounced, he is delivered from old age and death, because his attachment for the body, is the cause of his birth, in good and evil bodies (Gītā 13/21). In fact, he is separate from the body, because the body decays and dies, while he lives ever.

In the phrase 'Māmāśritya yatanti ye', there are two aspects—to take refuge in Him, and to strive. If a man strives, he may feel proud of his achievement, as a result of striving. But, if he takes refuge in Him, he may become idle and lazy, and be engaged, in prosperity and pleasure. Therefore, a striver, should strive promptly, according to the ordinance of scriptures and give credit, for success to God.

So long as, a man attaches importance to the body, and the world, regarding these as permanent, he, in spite of striving, does not, realize God. Therefore, he should not attach importance to them. He should strive to remove, these two stumbling blocks (i.e.,) attaching importance to the body and the world, and accepting their independent existence. But, those who taking refuge in God, strive, are superior, because they feel that they are engaged in spiritual discipline, only by God's grace. Thus, by taking refuge in Him and having no pride, they realize the full form, of the Lord.

Those who strive, without taking refuge in Him for salvation, also know Him but they do not know, His entire form. As a man practises 'Prāṇāyāma' (the process of restraining breath), he achieves accomplishments (Siddhi), and if he rises above these, he knows formless God or gets established in his own self. Similarly, the Bauddhas and Jains, who do not believe in God, by following spiritual discipline according to their religion and by renouncing their affinity for the world, attain salvation. But, those who, having disinclination for the world, taking refuge in God, strive by knowing the Lord, in His entire form, receive divine love. To express this singularity, Lord Kṛṣṇa has used the expression 'Māmāśritya yatanti ye'.

'Te brahma tat (viduḥ)'—Thus by striving, they attain Brahma (the Infinite) who is formless, without attributes and who cannot be perceived, by mind, intellect and senses.

God exists, in all beings, because He pervades everywhere, every time, in all the things and men. But, He is not perceived, because we have attached importance to the transitory and kaleidoscopic body, and world, and have accepted their independent existence. So ever-attained God, seems to be unattained.

'Kṛtsnamadhyātmaṁ (viduḥ)'—The strivers know the entire individual self. In the tenth verse of the fifteenth chapter, Lord Kṛṣṇa says, "The ignorant do not perceive the soul, departing from one body and dwelling in the other, but those who possess eyes of wisdom, perceive." This perception, does not include knowledge of the number of beings, their activities and their fate. But, they do know that the self, (soul) is different from the body. Those who take refuge in Him, realize this reality.

By taking refuge in God, when a striver breaks up his affinity for actions and things, he realizes, that his self, as well as, the self of all the beings, is pure and detached from prakṛti. He comes to know, that he can never be identified, with actions and bodies, and he can never be separated, from his self. This knowledge constitutes the fullest spiritual essence of the self.

'Karma cākhilaṁ viduḥ'—The strivers know the entire field of action i.e., why and how, the universe is created. God has created, the bodies of the people according to a class (caste) they belong to. But because of detachment, the Lord remains a non-doer and has no craving, for the fruit of action (Gītā 4/13-14). Similarly, if a man performs his duty and actions, without feelings of doership, and without desire for the fruit of actions, he is nòt bound, by actions. Thus knowledge about the entire field of action, is that a man has no affinity for action, he is completely detached, from these.

The striver, who takes refuge in Him, with exclusive devotion, does not depend on things and actions. He, very well realizes that all things and actions, are kaleidoscopic and perishable. No action or thing, even in Brahmaloka (the abode of Brahmā), is eternal, these are subject to, appearance and disappearance. So he has, not the least affinity for actions. This is knowledge, about the entire field of action.

It means, that a striver by taking refuge in God knows Brahma (the Infinite), the individual self and the entire field of action i.e., he realizes, "In the world there is nothing else, besides God" (7/7) and "All this is God" (7/19). Thus, he comes to know that Brahma, the individual self, and entire field of action, are nothing else, besides God.

साधिभूताधिदैवं मां साधियज्ञं च ये विदुः ।
प्रयाणकालेऽपि च मां ते विदुर्युक्तचेतसः ॥ ३० ॥

sādhibhūtādhidaivaṁ māṁ sādhiyajñaṁ ca ye viduḥ
prayāṇakāle'pi ca māṁ te viduryuktacetasaḥ

Those, who realize Me in the Adhibhūta (the field of matter), in Adhidaiva (Brahmā) and in Adhiyajña (the unmanifest Divinity), and having a steadfast mind, realize Me, even at the hour of death. 30

Comment:—

'Sādhibhūtādhidaivaṁ māṁ sādhiyajñaṁ ca ye viduḥ'—[Having described attributeless and formless God, in the preceding verse, He describes God, Who is endowed with attributes and form in this verse.]

Here 'Adhibhūta', stands for matter, which has predominance of Tamas (the mode of ignorance). This matter has no independent existence, of its own. It is transitory and kaleidoscopic. But, it seems real, pleasant and attractive, because of God, Who is real, pleasant and attractive. As ice has no existence without water, matter is nothing, but manifestation of God. This is knowledge about God and matter.

'Adhidaiva', is Brahmā, the creator of the world. He has predominance of 'rajoguṇa' (the mode of passion). The Lord, manifests Himself as Brahmā also. This is true knowledge about Adhidaiva and God.

'Adhiyajña' is Lord Viṣṇu, who pervades everywhere, in the form of unmanifest Divinity. In Him, there is predominance of the mode of goodness. This is true knowledge, about Adhiyajña and God.

Knowledge about God, with Adhibhūta, Adhidaiva and Adhiyajña is, that He stands holding the entire creation in one limb, (Gītā 10/42; 11/7) and in His supreme divine form, there are Adhibhūta (Infinite universes), Adhidaiva (Brahmā) and Adhiyajña (Viṣṇu) etc. Arjuna also says, "O God, I behold in Your body, all the gods and multitudes of different beings, Brahmā, the Lord perched on a lotus, Lord Śiva and all the sages and celestial serpents" (Gītā 11/15). Thus, in reality, Lord Kṛṣṇa is Adhibhūta, Adhidaiva and Adhiyajña.

'Prayāṇakāle'pi ca māṁ te viduryuktacetasaḥ'—Steadfast in mind, are those, who remain equanimous in gain and loss, in prosperity and pleasures, and in becoming indifferent to the world, and are engrossed in worship of God. Such people, realize Him, at the time of death i.e., remain established in Him, even in the pangs of death, they do not lose heart in the least, in spite of great turmoil, in their physical and subtle bodies.

An Exceptional Fact About God's Entire Form

(1) All evils, are born, by accepting our affinity for matter and its evolutes—actions and things etc., and then those actions and things seem, to have their independent existence. But, if we by breaking up our affinity, for them get established in God, their assumed independent existence, merges into God.

In the world, we assume a thing or a person, as good or bad, but actually that thing or person, is nothing besides the manifestation of God. As far as decorum of caste, and Āśrama, (religious orders of different periods, of life), is concerned, we have to observe these in accordance with the ordinance of scriptures and great souls, because these are guides for attaining salvation.

There was existence of God, before this creation, and He

will exist after its dissolution. When a striver realizes this reality, about God, the universe merges into Him. It does not mean, that the creation perishes, but it means, that the striver does not attach importance to the world, which is an obstacle to salvation. As, in ornaments made of gold, there is nothing besides gold, a striver of steadfast mind realizes, that in the world there is nothing besides God. This fact has been explained, in the twenty-ninth and thirtieth verses.

(2) For the worship of God He is described in two ways—one with attributes and the second attributeless. The Lord, endowed with attributes is of two types—one endowed with attributes with form and the other endowed with attributes but formless. The attributeless Lord, is not of two types, He is only without attribute and formless. The formless Lord, is again of two kinds—one endowed with attributes, but formless and the other, attributeless and formless.

Devotees are of two types—one who worship God with attributes, and the other who worship God, without attributes. But both of them start their worship of the Lord, Who is endowed with attributes, but is formless. He assumes, that there is God, Who is the Supreme Lord and He is the most merciful, and the best one. Thus, though a devotee thinks of God, Who is attributeless and formless, yet with his intellect, he thinks of God, Who is endowed with attributes, and is formless.* The reason, is that intellect being the evolute of prakṛti (with attributes), cannot have access, to attributeless God.

* Adoration (Devotion) starts with God Who is endowed with attributes and is formless. So He has been described in that way in the twenty-eighth verse. Then in the twenty-ninth verse there is description of the Lord Who is attributeless and formless and in the thirtieth verse of One who is endowed with form and attributes. Thus each of them has been described in one verse. But in the eighth chapter each of the three types has been described in three verses eighth to tenth, eleventh to thirteenth and fourteenth to sixteenth respectively.

Worshippers, first worship God, Who is endowed with attributes and form. But so long as, His form is not fixed in their minds, they assume, "God exists and He is ours." The firmer His form gets fixed, the higher their adoration. In the end, when they are able to behold Him, talk to Him, touch Him and receive blessing from Him, their worship attains perfection.

Worshippers of attributeless God, think of Him, as One who pervades, everywhere. The subtler their disposition grows, the higher their worship, is. In the end when their attachment and egoism etc., are completely renounced, and no feeling of 'I'ness or 'You'ness, is left and only pure consciousness remains, their worship attains, perfection.

Thus, both the devotees after attaining perfection, become one i.e., both of them attain the same Lord. The worshippers of the Lord, endowed with attributes and form by His grace, also realize the Lord, who is without attributes and form. If a striver, adoring attributeless and formless God, has some devotional influence, and wants to behold Him, he can do so. If the Lord wants to make him an instrument, for His mission, He reveals Himself to him, as He revealed Himself to Madhusūdanācārya.*

(3) The Lord, is endowed with attributes and He is also attributeless, according to the feelings of devotees. Similarly, He is endowed with form and is also formless. Not only this, He is also beyond the two. But this reality is known only, when a devotee realizes Him.

The Lord, Who pervades everywhere with His divine traits, such as beauty, love, glory, grace, etc., is called, God endowed with attributes. He is of two kinds—

---

* One shrewd fellow who is adored by the followers of non-dualistic discipline, who is authorized to sit on the throne of paradise and who runs after cowherdesses forcefully had made me a slave of his feet.

(i) Endowed with attributes and formless—Just like the sky of which attribute, is sound, but is formless, the Lord pervading the entire universe, is endowed with attributes and is formless.

(ii) Endowed with attributes and form—When the Lord, Who is with attributes and is formless, manifests Himself through His own divine potency, keeping His nature (prakṛti) under control, and is perceived by senses is called, the Lord endowed, with attributes and form.

When a striver assumes, that God does not possess divine traits, He is called the Lord, without attributes and form.

Attributes are also of two kinds (i) Uncommon divine traits, such as beauty, love, glory and grace etc., (ii) Three modes of nature—sattva (mode of goodness), raja (mode of passion) and tama (mode of ignorance). God may, either be endowed with attributes and be formless, or He may be endowed with attributes and form, He, is beyond the three modes of nature. He, by controlling His nature, plays the role of the Lord of creation, preservation and destruction of the universe, and yet remains totally free from the modes of nature (Gītā 7/13).

The Lord, Who is never bound by attributes, and has full command over them, is called, the Lord without attributes. Therefore, such a Lord, can be called endowed with attributes, as well as attributeless, as also endowed, with form and also formless. He has been described, in His entire form, in the twenty-ninth and thirtieth verses.

A special note on the chapter

In this chapter, Lord Kṛṣṇa first explained His changeable lower (insentient) nature, by 'aparā' and unchangeable higher (sentient) nature by 'parā' (7/4-5). Then He explained, that He is the origin and end of the whole universe. But, in the beginning and in the end, only He exists (7/6-7). Then He explained, His comprehensiveness, by mentioning His seventeen divine manifestations, in the form of cause (7/8—12). Afterwards, He explained, that he, who is under delusion of three modes of nature i.e., who has accepted his affinity for the changing matter, cannot know Him, Who is beyond the modes of nature (7/13). In the fourteenth verse, He explained that His wonderful illusion, is extremely difficult to surmount. In the fifteenth verse, He explained, that evil doers do not seek refuge, in Him. In the sixteenth verse, He explained four types of virtuous men, who worship Him or take refuge in Him. Now a question arises, why Lord Kṛṣṇa has inserted the fifteenth verse, which seems to be out of context. The answer is, that had He not included the fifteenth verse, it would have remained to be said, "Evil-doers do not seek refuge, in Me."

There are two types of people, who take refuge in Him—first, those who regarding Him as God, take refuge in Him (7/16—19) and the second, those who regard Him as a common man worship, (take refuge in) other gods, in order to satisfy their desires (7/20—23). People worship, the gods for two reasons for their increased desires, and their failure to realize the greatness of God. Both of these, have been explained respectively, in (7/20—23) and (7/24). In the twenty-fifth verse, He has explained, that He is not manifest to those, who regard Him as an ordinary person. The twenty-fifth verse, seems to express that He is also veiled by divine potency. So, He has declared, in the twenty-sixth verse, that His knowledge is not veiled. People do not know Him, because of their attachment and aversion (7/27). But those, who are freed from delusion in the shape of pairs of opposites, worship Him with a firm resolve (7/28). Those who, taking refuge in Him, strive to know Him, in His entire form, at last attain Him (7/29-30).

If we delve deep into this chapter, we come to know, that there is description of inclination and disinclination for God. Those who have disinclination for God, and inclination for matter, follow the cycle of birth and death. But if they have inclination for God, they know the Lord who is endowed with attributes and is formless, who is attributeless and formless as also, who is endowed with attributes in entirety and attain Him.

Appendix—At the beginning of this chapter Lord Kṛṣṇa said to Arjuna, "I shall unfold to you this Jñāna with Vijñāna by which you will know Me fully, having known which nothing will remain to be known." Then the Lord in the nineteenth verse having said 'vāsudevaḥ sarvam' described His full form in brief. Now at the end of the chapter the Lord gives the details of His full form.

A striver has taken birth, and a disease (suffering) is not inevitable. Therefore here the expression 'jarāmaraṇamokṣāya' means that the devotees, who take refuge in God, are delivered from old age and death viz., they are not sad by thinking of their old age and they are not sad by thinking of the end, they will meet after death. They, having taken shelter in God, strive; therefore they know God in full with parā prakṛti and aparā prakṛti viz., know Jñāna with Vijñāna.

Though a Karmayogī and a Jñānayogī are also liberated from birth and death but a devotee besides being liberated from birth and death, knows God in His entire form. The reason is that a Karmayogī and a Jñānayogī attain equanimity by practising the discipline of action and the discipline of knowledge respectively from the beginning, but a devotee depends on God from the beginning. As he depends on God, the Lord by showering His grace, enables him to know Him in full.

In the third verse of this chapter the Lord declared, "One

who knows Me fully is rare—'kaścinmāṁ vetti tattvataḥ'. Here He explains, 'He who takes refuge in Me, knows Me in My entire form.' Therefore the main spiritual practice to know God in full (Jñāna with Vijñāna) is—surrender in God (māmāśritya). The reason is that God in full is not known by reflection but He is known by His grace, when a devotee with faith and belief takes shelter in Him. Therefore the Lord at the beginning used the term 'madāśrayaḥ' and in the end concludes this chapter by using the term, 'māmāśritya'.

'Brahma' (attributeless- formless), 'kṛtsna adhyātma' (endless souls of endless births) and 'akhila karma'(all the actions of origin-midstate-end etc.,)—this is the sphere of knowledge. In this sphere there is predominance of nirguṇa (attributeless) Brahma. 'Adhibhūta' (the entire universe consisting of five subtle elements including the body), 'adhidaiva' (all the deities such as Brahmā etc., with the presiding deities of mind-senses) and adhiyajña (immanent Lord Viṣṇu and all His forms)— this is the sphere of 'vijñāna'. In this division there is predominance of Saguṇa (endowed with attributes) God.

God with 'adhibhūta', 'adhidaiva' and 'adhiyajña' means that the 'Sat', 'Asat', 'parā-aparā'—all is God. There is nothing else besides God. If the real and the unreal are distinguished, it is the path of knowledge—'nāsato vidyate bhāvo, nābhāvo vidyate sataḥ. ubhayorapi....' (Gītā 2/16) and if they are unified, it is the path of devotion—'Śadasaccāhamarjuna' (Gītā 9/19).

There is description of 'Brahma' from the thirteenth verse to the twenty-sixth verse of the fifth chapter. 'Kṛtsna adhyātma' has been mentioned in the twenty-ninth verse of the sixth chapter by the expression 'Sarvabhūtasthamātmānam'. 'Akhila Karma' has been described in the eighteenth, twenty-third and thirty-third verses of the fourth chapter by the expression 'kṛtsna karmakṛt', 'karma samagram' and 'sarvaṁ karmākhilaṁ' respectively.

An action ends but the self and Brahma are never non-existent. In jurisprudence it is mentioned that the sense which perceives the existence of a thing, the same sense perceives the non-existence and also the class of that thing. Therefore the knowledge which enables a man to know actions (karma cākhilam), with the same knowledge, he knows the nothingness of actions viz., inaction—'karmaṇyakarma yaḥ paśyet (Gītā 4/18). Brahma (the Absolute), ātmā (the soul) and akarma (inaction)—the three are only one; this knowledge is the meaning of the expression—'te brahma tadviduḥ kṛtsnamadhyātmaṁ karma cākhilaṁ.'

An 'action' is limited, 'adhyātma' (self) is more extensive than 'action', 'Brahma' is more extensive than 'adhyātma'. But 'mām' (God in full) is superior even to Brahma because within 'Brahma' 'the entire form of God' is not included but within 'the entire form of God' Brahma is included.

The purpose of using the term 'kṛtsna' with adhyātma' is the aggregate of individual self, seen in different forms whom the Lord has called His 'parā prakṛti'. The Lord by giving the word 'akhila' with 'karma' means—all the virtuous and sinful actions, whose fruit leads the self to numerous wombs and numerous worlds; but the term 'kṛtsna' or 'akhila' has not been used with 'Brahma', it means that 'Brahma' is not numerous but is only one.

In the Gītā the Lord has mentioned two-fold path to achieve equanimity—Karmayoga and jñānayoga. The two paths are worldly—'loke'smindvividhā niṣṭhā' (Gītā 3/3); but Bhaktiyoga is 'alaukika niṣṭhā' (unworldly path). The reason is that in Karmayoga there is predominance of 'kṣara' (world) and in Jñānayoga there is predominance of 'akṣara' (soul). Kṣara and akṣara—both are in the world—'dvāvimau puruṣau loke kṣaraścākṣara eva ca' (Gītā 15/16), therefore Karmayoga and

Jñānayoga—both are worldly paths. But in Bhaktiyoga there in predominance of God Who transcends the perishable (Kṣara) and is superior to the imperishable (akṣara) (Gītā 15/17-18). Therefore Bhaktiyoga is the unworldly path. In the entire form of God, there is mention of Brahma, adhyātma and Karma—in them there is mention of the worldly path (Karmayoga and Jñānayoga)* and in 'adhibhūta, adhidaiva and adhiyajña there is mention of the unworldly path (Bhaktiyoga). 'Jñāna (knowledge) is worldly—'na hi jñānena sadṛśaṁ pavitramiha† vidyate' (Gītā 4/38) and Vijñāna is unworldly. The worldly and the unworldly—both are the manifestations of 'Samagra' (full form of) God—'Vāsudevah Sarvam'.

In the term 'loka' both insentient and sentient are included. The term 'loka' cannot denote either only insentient or only sentient. Therefore in 'laukika' both insentient and sentient are included but in 'alaukika' only sentient is included because 'alaukika' is ever divine. But in 'the entire form' (Samagra), 'laukika' (worldly) and 'alaukika' (unworldly)—both are included.

Here a point needs special attention that 'Brahma' Who is attributeless and formless is within the entire form of God. Generally people believe that within attributeless and formless Brahma, there is God endowed with attributes. They hold that Brahma is free from māyā and God is not free from Māyā. In fact this assumption is neither in accordance with the ordinance

* The term 'adhyātma' should mean 'Jñānayoga; and 'Karma' should mean 'Karmayoga'. Brahma is attained by both Jñānayoga and Karmayoga (Gītā 5/4-5).

Being the context of devotion, the Lord here has not described Jñānayoga and Karmayoga in detail. They have already been described in detail from the second to the sixth Chapter.

† Here the term 'iha' used within 'pavitramiha' stands for 'loka' (world).

of the scriptures nor is reasonable because when, in Brahma, there is no illusion (māyā) then how can God with 'māyā' be within Brahma? How is there 'māyā' in Brahma? But in the Gītā the Lord declares, "In a fragment of My entire form there is Brahma because I am the support of Brahma 'brahmaṇo hi pratiṣṭhāham' (Gītā 14/27) and this universe is pervaded by Me in My unmanifest form 'mayā tatamidaṁ sarvaṁ jagadavyaktamūrtinā' (9/4)." By these utterances the Lord means to say, "I am not a fragment of Brahma but Brahma is My fragment." Therefore if we reflect upon it in an impartial manner, it is evident that in the Gītā there is not predominance of Brahma but there is predominance of God. The entire form of God is complete within which God with attributes as well as attributeless; God with form and also formless are included.

In fact the entire form can be of God endowed with attributes only because within the word 'saguṇa' (God endowed with attributes), 'nirguna' (attributeless) (the Absolute) can be included, but within the word 'nirguṇa', 'saguṇa' cannot be included. The reason is that in 'saguṇa' there is no negation of 'nirguṇa' but in 'nirguṇa' there is negation of 'guṇas' (attributes). Therefore in 'nirguṇa the word 'samagra' (full or entire) cannot be used. So here with 'adhyātma' and Karma' the words 'kṛtsna' and 'akhila' have been used respectively but no such word has been used with Brahma. Therefore there is entirety (fullness) in God endowed with attributes rather than in attributeless Brahma.

Question—How are Brahma, adhyātma and Karma all the three 'laukika (worldly)?

Answer—The Lord has called Brahma 'akṣara' (imperishable)—'akṣaraṁ brahma paramam' (Gītā 8/3) and He has also called the soul 'akṣara'—'dvāvimau puruṣau loke kṣaraścākṣara eva ca' (Gītā 15/16). The soul and Brahma—both are one—'ayamātmā brahma' (Māṇḍūkya 1). The soul which by having connection with Prakṛti (body) is called 'jīva' (adhyātma) (embodied soul),* the same by having no connection with Prakṛti is Brahma'. Therefore according to the Gītā as 'jīva' is in the world, so is 'Brahma' in the world viz., Brahma is attained by the worldly paths (Karmayoga and Jñānayoga).

'Adhyātma viz., the soul has sustained the world 'yayedaṁ dhāryate jagat' (Gītā 7/5). The soul has no independent existence of its own. Therefore the soul by being attached to the world has become 'jagat' (worldly) (Gītā 7/13). Being in the world the soul is also 'laukika' (worldly)—'mamaivāṁśo jīvaloke' (Gītā 15/7), 'dvāvimau puruṣau loke ksaraścākṣara eva ca' (Gītā 15/16).

Actions are performed in two ways with an interested motive and in a disinterested manner. These two types of actions being in the world are laukika†.

Question:—How are 'adhibhūta', 'adhidaiva' and 'adhiyajña'—these three unworldly?

Answer:—'adhibhūta' viz., the entire world consisting of the five subtle elements, being the manifestation of God is unworldly—'amṛtaṁ caiva mṛtyuśca sadasaccāhamarjuna' (Gītā 9/19) "I am immortality as well as death; I am also being

---

* bādhyo biṣaya saneha te, tāte kahiyai jīva
alakha ajoṇī āpa hai, hariyā nyārau thīva

† In the world, actions performed with an interested motive—

'yajñārthātkarmaṇo'nyatra loko'yaṁ karmabandhanaḥ' (Gītā 3/9); 'kṣipraṁ hi mānuṣe loke siddhirbhavati karmajā'. (Gītā 4/12); 'Karmānubandhīni manuṣyaloke' (Gītā 15/2). In the world actions performed in a disinterested manner 'loke' smin-dvividhā.....yoginām' (Gītā 3/3).

In fact actions are neither 'Sakāma' nor 'Niṣkāma' but the doer is 'Sakāma' or 'Niṣkāma.' Therefore 'sakāma (interested motive) and 'niṣkāma' (disinterested manner) persist in the doer.

and non-being, both*. The cosmic form which Lord Kṛṣṇa revealed to Arjuna was also divine or unworldly†.

The Lord revealed His divine cosmic form in a part of His divine body‡. Therefore the world consisting of five subtle elements, being the cosmic form of God, is also unworldly§. The Lord has also called His 'vibhūtis' (divine glories) as divine viz., unworldly—'divyā hyātmavibhūtayaḥ'

---

* manasā vacasā dṛṣṭyā gṛhyate'nyairapīndriyaiḥ
ahameva na matto'nyaditi budhyadhva mañjasā
(Śrīmadbhā. 11/13/24)

Whatever is perceived (received) with the mind, with tongue, with eyes and with other senses, all that is only 'I'. Therefore there is nothing else besides Me—understand and accept this principle quickly after reflecting upon it.

† 'nānāvidhāni divyāni (Gītā 11/5), 'anekadivyābharaṇaṁ divyānekodyatāyudham' (11/10), 'divyamālyāmbaradharaṁ divyagandhānulepanam' (11/11); 'paśyāmi devāṁstava deva dehe.....sarvānuragāṁsca divyān. (11/15)

‡ The Lord declares—'ihaikasthaṁ jagatkṛtsnaṁ....mama dehe'(11/7).

Sañjaya utters—'tatraikasthaṁ jagatkṛtsnaṁ........apaśyaddevadevasya śarīre' (11/13).

Arjuna makes an utterance—'paśyāmi devāṁstava deva dehe' (11/15).

§ khaṁ vāyumagniṁ salilaṁ mahīṁ ca
jyotīṁṣi sattvāni diśo drumādīn.
saritsamudrāṁśca hareḥ śarīraṁ
yat kiñca bhūtaṁ praṇamedananyaḥ,
(Śrīmadbhā. 11/2/41)

Ether, air, fire, water, earth, planet, constellation, beings, animals, directions, trees, rivers, oceans—all are the bodies of God, by assuming this, a devotee bows to all with exclusive devotion.

bhūdvīpavarṣasaridadrinabhaḥ samudrapātāladiṅnarakabhāgaṇalokasansthā
gītā mayā tava nṛpādbhutamiśvarasya sthūlaṁ vapuḥ sakalajīva nikāya dhāma
(Śrīmadbhā. 5/26/40)

'O Parīkṣit! I have described to you the earth and within it—islands, varṣa (tracts), rivers, mountains, sky, oceans, netherworld, directions, hells, constellation and the situation of different worlds—this is God's very wonderful gross form which is the refuge of all the groups of beings.

(Gītā 10/19), 'mama divyānāṁ vibhūtīnām' (10/40)* But a person (embodied soul) out of ignorance with his intellect (because of attachment-aversion) perceives this 'jagata' (world) as 'laukika' (mundane) (matter). Therefore when ignorance is wiped out, inertness (matter) does not persist, only divinity remains.

'adhidaiva' viz., Brahmā etc., all the deities are unworldly, 'adhiyajña' viz., indwelling God in spite of lodging in the hearts of all, because of remaining untainted, is unworldly†.

In the expression 'Sādhibhūtādhidaivaṁ māṁ Sādhiyajñaṁ' the Lord mentions, "He who knows Me with adhibhūta, adhidaiva and adhiyajña," it proves that as these three are with God so they are unworldly, otherwise they are worldly. So long as there is no connection with God, all is worldly; when there is connection with God, all becomes unworldly. Therefore Karmayoga and Jñānayoga are 'worldly paths' as in them a striver's effort is important while 'Bhaktiyoga' is the unworldly path as in it there is predominance of refuge in God.

In fact there is no entity which is worldly. The real entity is only unworldly. But from the view-point of a striver the discrimination between the worldly and the unworldly has been mentioned. It means that this distinction between the worldly and the unworldly persists out of ignorance because of attachment and aversion. If attachment and aversion are

---

* Arjuna has also called 'vibhūtis' (glories) as divine—'vaktumarhasyaśeṣeṇa divyā hyātmavibhūtayaḥ' (10/16).

† dvā suparṇā sayujā sakhāyā samānaṁ vṛkṣaṁ pariṣasvajāte
tayoranyaḥ pippalaṁ svādvattyanaśnannanyo abhicākaśīti

(Muṇḍaka 3/1/1; Śvetāśvatara. 4/6)

Two birds—soul and God who keep company with each other and are friendly with each other, live by taking refuge in the same tree—body. One of them the soul (embodied soul) tasting the fruit of actions of that tree relishes (enjoys) them but the other (God) without relishing them only illumines them.

renounced, all is unworldly, spiritual and divine—'vāsudevaḥ sarvam'. The reason is that the mundane has no independent existence. It is because of attachment and aversion that the mundane seems to exist and is valued. It is because of attachment and aversion that a man (the self) has made the world, which is the manifestation of God, mundane and he himself has also become mundane.

The purpose of describing knowledge with 'Vijñāna' viz., the entire form of God is that non-self-self, the real-unreal, parā-aparā (higher and lower nature), kṣetra (it is constituted of 24 elements)—kṣetrajña (soul)—whatever persists is only God's manifestation. Therefore the Lord here at the beginning and at the end of the description of His entire form has used the term 'mām' (Me) which denotes His entire form—'māmāśritya' (7/29) and 'mām te viduḥ' (7/30).

The Lord has declared that the nature of actions is mysterious—'gahanā karmaṇo gatiḥ' (Gītā 4/17), but a devotee knows it also. Inaction in action and action in inaction (4/18)—a devotee knows these two also. It means that he knows actions and also the Discipline of Action (Karmayoga). A Karmayogī knows only Karmayoga; a Jñānayogī knows only Jñānayoga; but a devotee by God's grace knows both—Karmayoga and Jñānayoga.

The idea expressed in the first verse of this chapter by the expression 'yogaṁ yuñjanmadāśrayaḥ' has been expressed here by the expression 'māmāśritya yatanti ye'; and the idea expressed by the expression 'mayyāsaktamanāḥ' has been expressed here by the expression 'yuktacetasaḥ'. It means, "The devotee who takes shelter in Me attains the aim which is attained by Karmayoga and Jñānayoga viz., they know Brahma Who is the fruit (aim) of these two disciplines—'te brahma tadviduḥ' and they also know God in full—'māṁ te viduḥ'.

In the expression 'prayāṇakāle'pi' the term 'api' means that those devotees know God before the hour of death and also at the hour of death viz., their knowledge never disappears. Such devotees become 'yuktacetā (steadfast in mind) viz., their mind has no independent existence, it gets identified with God, only God remains. Being one (having eternal union) with God, they are neither separated from God nor is God separated from them. Such devotees at the time of death, even if some thought comes to their mind, they don't meet the fate of 'yogabhraṣṭa' (he who deviates from yoga) but attain God—'prayāṇakāle'pi ca māṁ te viduryuktacetasaḥ'. The reason is that from the view-point of those devotees, there is nothing else besides God, then where will their mind wander besides God? Why will it wander? How will it wander? If he thinks of anything, he will think of God only, then how will his mind deviate and without deviation of the mind, how will he fall from yoga? The reason is that in the discipline dependant on instruments (Karaṇa sāpekṣa), when the mind deviates from Yoga, then there is fall from Yoga—'yogāccalitamānasaḥ' (Gītā 6/37) but he, who beholds God everywhere, has his eternal union with God.

Some devotees want only emancipation (Salvation)—'jarāmaraṇamokṣāya' and some devotees want love (devotion)—'māṁ te viduryuktacetasaḥ'. The devotees who want salvation, they know Karmayoga and Jñānayoga (brahma, adhyātma and Karma) but the devotees who want love, they themselves, know God in full—'māṁ viduḥ'. God confers his devout devotees with Karmayoga (buddhiyoga) and Jñānayoga—both (Gītā 10/10-11). Bondage in the form of old age and death; and also salvation—both are worldly but love (devotion) is unworldly. Though devotion as spiritual-discipline is worldly but the aim being unworldly, that devotion is included in unworldly 'Sādhya bhakti' (devotion as an end)—'bhaktyā sañjātayā bhaktyā' (Śrīmadbhā. 11/3/31).

ॐ तत्सदिति श्रीमद्भगवद्गीतासूपनिषत्सु ब्रह्मविद्यायां योगशास्त्रे श्रीकृष्णार्जुनसंवादे ज्ञानविज्ञानयोगो नाम सप्तमोऽध्यायः॥७॥

oṁ tatsaditi śrīmadbhagavadgītāsūpaniṣatsu brahmavidyāyāṁ yogaśāstre śrīkṛṣṇārjunasaṁvāde jñānavijñānayogo nāma saptamo'dhyāyaḥ.

Thus starting with Oṁ, Tat, Sat, the names of the Lord, in the Upaniṣad of the Bhagavadgītā, the Yoga and the dialogue between Śrī Kṛṣṇa and Arjuna, this is the seventh designated discourse: "The Yoga of Knowledge and Realization."

In this chapter, there is description of knowledge and realization. The belief, that the Lord, is the root of the entire universe is knowledge, while realization is, that in the entire universe there is nothing besides, the Lord. By knowledge and realization, a devotee comes to know his real and eternal affinity for God i.e., "I am God's and God is mine." Therefore, this chapter is designated: "The Yoga of Knowledge and Realization."

Words, letters and Uvāca (said) in the Seventh Chapter—

1. In this chapter in **'Atha saptamo'dhyāyaḥ'** there are three words, in **'Śrībhagavānuvāca'** there are two words, in verses there are four hundred and six words and there are thirteen concluding words. Thus the total number of the words is four hundred and twenty-four.

2. In **'Atha saptamo'dhyāyaḥ'** there are seven letters, in **'Śrībhagavānuvāca'** there are seven letters, in verses there are nine hundred and sixty letters and there are forty-eight concluding letters. Thus the total number of the letters is one thousand and

twenty-two. Each of the verses is of thirty-two letters.

3. In this chapter there is one **Uvāca** (said) **'Śrībhagavānuvāca'**.

Metres Used in the Seventh Chapter

Out of the thirty verses, of this chapter in the third quarter of the sixth verse, and first quarter of the fourteenth verse, 'na-gaṇa' being used, there is **'na-vipulā'** metre; in the third quarter of the eleventh verse, and first quarter of the twenty-fifth verse, 'ma-gaṇa' is used there is **'ma-vipulā'** metre; in the first quarter of the seventeenth verse, 'ra-gaṇa' being used there is **'ra-vipulā'** metre, and in the third quarter of the nineteenth and twentieth verses 'bha-gaṇa' being used there, is **'bha-vipulā'** metre. The remaining twenty-three verses, have the characteristics of right **'pathyāvaktra'** Anuṣṭup metre.

|| Shri Hari ||

Eighth Chapter

INTRODUCTION

Lord Kṛṣṇa, at the end of the seventh chapter, while describing Him in entirety used the six words Brahma, Adhyātma, Karma, Adhibhūta, Adhidaiva and Adhiyajña, and explained that Yogīs who know Him, in entirety attain Him. For, getting clarification of these six words, Arjuna at the beginning of the eighth chapter, puts seven questions, to Him.

अर्जुन उवाच

किं तद्ब्रह्म किमध्यात्मं किं कर्म पुरुषोत्तम।
अधिभूतं च किं प्रोक्तमधिदैवं किमुच्यते ॥ १ ॥
अधियज्ञः कथं कोऽत्र देहेऽस्मिन्मधुसूदन।
प्रयाणकाले च कथं ज्ञेयोऽसि नियतात्मभिः ॥ २ ॥

arjuna uvāca

kiṁ tadbrahma kimadhyātmaṁ kiṁ karma puruṣottama
adhibhūtaṁ ca kiṁ proktamadhidaivaṁ kimucyate
adhiyajñaḥ kathaṁ ko'tra dehe'sminmadhusūdana
prayāṇakāle ca kathaṁ jñeyo'si niyatātmabhiḥ

Arjuna said:

What is that Brahma? What is Adhyātma? What is Karma (Action)? O Best among men! What is said to be Adhibhūta and what is called Adhidaiva? Who and how is Adhiyajña, here in this body, O Kṛṣṇa? And how can You be realized, at the time of death, by persons of steadfast mind? 1-2

Comment:—

'Puruṣottama kiṁ tadbrahma'—O Best among men! What do You mean, by the term 'Brahma'?

'Kimadhyātmam'—What is meant, by 'Adhyātma'?

'Kiṁ karma'—What do You mean, by 'Karma'?

'Adhibhūtaṁ ca kiṁ proktam'—What does the term, 'Adhibhūta' mean?

'Adhidaivaṁ kimucyate'—What is 'Adhidaiva'?

'Adhiyajñaḥ kathaṁ ko'tra dehe'smin'—What is 'Adhiyajña', and how is it in this body?

'Madhusūdana prayāṇakāle ca kathaṁ jñeyo'si niyatātmabhiḥ'—O Destroyer of the demon, named Madhu, how are You to be realized at the time of death, by those of steadfast mind i.e., by those, who having a disinclination for the world, worship You with exclusive devotion? Which of Your forms, do they know and how?

Link:—Lord Kṛṣṇa, in the next two verses answers the six questions, one by one.

श्रीभगवानुवाच

अक्षरं ब्रह्म परमं स्वभावोऽध्यात्ममुच्यते।
भूतभावोद्भवकरो विसर्गः कर्मसञ्ज्ञितः॥ ३॥

śrībhagavānuvāca

akṣaraṁ brahma paramaṁ svabhāvo'dhyātmamucyate
bhūtabhāvodbhavakaro visargaḥ karmasañjñitaḥ

The Blessed Lord said:

The Supreme Imperishable (Akṣara) is Brahma; one's own self (Jīvātmā) is called Adhyātma, the activity of the Lord which brings about the creation, is called, Karma (action). 3

Comment:—

'Akṣaraṁ brahma paramam'—The Supreme Imperishable is called 'Brahma'. Though in the Gītā, the term 'Brahma' has been used for 'Praṇava' (the holy monosyllable 'Oṁ'), Veda (sacred scriptures of the Hindus) and prakṛti (matter) etc., yet, here it has been used for the Supreme, Imperishable, attributeless-formless, Lord.

'Svabhāvo'dhyātmamucyate'—One's own self, is called 'adhyātma'. The path of spirituality is also called 'Adhyātma', and the science of the soul viz., metaphysics, is also called 'Adhyātma' (Gītā 10/32). But, here it has been used, for one's self.

'Bhūtabhāvodbhavakaro visargaḥ karmasamjñitaḥ'—The pursuit of mind, of the Lord (viz., the renunciation), that is the immediate cause of man, having come into existence, is called 'Karma'.

At the time of final annihilation, prakṛti (primordial matter or nature), is supposed to be inactive, while at the time of creation, prakṛti is supposed to be active. The cause of this activity, is the Lord's pursuit of mind to become manifold, from one. This pursuit of mind, is the cause of the creation. At the time, of final annihilation, beings with egoism and collected actions, merge into nature and then nature, including beings, merges into God. To activate, the merged nature, from the Lord's pursuit of mind, there is discharge or renunciation, which is the cause of man, having come into existence, and with it the chain of actions begins.

Lord Kṛṣṇa, in the fourteenth chapter, declares, "My prakṛti (nature) is the womb of all creatures; in which, I place the seed (germ) (14/3-4). Here, 'placing the seed' means, that the Lord links the souls with the bodies, according to fruit of actions, of their previous births. The bodies, are born of nature and in the bodies, the soul is a fragment of God (Gītā 15/7). Thus, all beings are born, by the union of nature and God.

In the twenty-sixth verse of the thirteenth chapter, the Lord declares, "Whatever being animate or inanimate, is born, know that, as emanated from the union of 'Kṣetra' (Matter) and 'Kṣetrajña' (Spirit or Soul)". The Lord's pursuit of mind, is the cause of this union. In that pursuit, there is no pride, of the Lord.

He has pursuit of mind, when past influences of actions of the previous births of beings at the time of final annihilation, get matured to bear fruit.* In this way, the actions of beings inspire the Lord, to have a pursuit of mind to change Himself, into manifold forms, from one. All actions performed by persons of different 'Varṇas' (castes), are called 'Karma'. It means, that an important act, is the Lord's pursuit of mind, and then the chain of actions begins.

Appendix—'Svabhāvo'dhyātmamucyate'—'parā prakṛti' is God's nature—'prakṛtiṁ viddhi me parām' (Gītā 7/5). Either call it 'prakṛti' or call it 'Svabhāva' (nature)—both are the same. This 'parā prakṛti' viz., 'the embodied soul' has been mentioned as 'adhyātma'. The Lord has called it His fragment—'mamaivāṁśo jīvaloke' (Gītā 15/7).

'Svabhāvo'dhyātmamucyate'— The second meaning of this expression is that in boyhood, youth and old age; in wakefulness, sleep and sound sleep; in eighty-four lac forms of life; in creation and dissolution; in new creation and final dissolution, the soul never ceases to be—'nābhāvo vidyate sataḥ' (Gītā 2/16) viz., the existence of the soul ever persists.

The action of the creation of the universe has been called 'tyāga' (renunciation), it means that in it there is renunciation of the constancy of divinity. The reason is that divinity is fixed and constant and renunciation of that constancy is Karma.'

The Lord's action of the creation of the universe is the earliest action* from which the tradition of actions followed. Therefore

* Beings while working continuously get tired and sleep in spite of having their pride of doership, attachment for the fruit of actions and collected actions. After sleep their tiredness is removed and their bodies, senses, minds and intellects are refreshed and they regain energy to work. Similarly, beings with the pride of doership, attachment for the fruit of actions and collected actions merge into Nature. The accumulated actions of those beings with the passage of time by becoming mature bear fruit. There the Lord has His pursuit of mind to give them birth according to their actions. His pursuit is called 'Action'.

within the term 'karma' (action), three types of actions are included (i) Creation of the universe, (ii) mere 'kriyā' which does not bear any fruit, (iii) virtuous and sinful actions which bear fruit.

The Lord's action of the creation of the universe is indeed 'akarma' (inaction). The Lord has also declared "tasya kartāramapi māṁ viddhyakartāramavyayam" (Gītā 4/13)—'though I am the creator of the universe, yet know Me, the immortal Lord, to be a non-doer.'

अधिभूतं क्षरो भावः पुरुषश्चाधिदैवतम्।
अधियज्ञोऽहमेवात्र देहे देहभृतां वर॥४॥

adhibhūtaṁ kṣaro bhāvaḥ puruṣaścādhidaivatam
adhiyajño'hamevātra dehe dehabhṛtāṁ vara

O best of the embodied, all perishable objects are Adhibhūta, Brahmā is Adhidaiva and I, dwelling as the Lord of Yajñas (witness) in this body, am Adhiyajña. 4

Comment:—

'Adhibhūtaṁ kṣaro bhāvaḥ'—The kaleidoscopic and perishable universe, consisting of the five subtle elements—earth, water, fire, air and ether, is called 'Adhibhūta'.

'Puruṣaścādhidaivatam'—The term 'Adhidaiva', has been used for Brahmā. At the beginning of the creation by God's pursuit of mind, there is revelation of Brahmā, the creator of the world, and then he creates the universe.

'Adhiyajño'hamevātra dehe dehabhṛtāṁ vara'—O best of the embodied, Arjuna! In this body I am Adhiyajña, i.e., I dwell as the inner witness, in this body.† Lord Kṛṣṇa, has declared the

* 'cāturvarṇyaṁ mayā sṛṣṭam'(Gītā 4/13); 'kalpādau visṛjāmyaham' (9/7); 'visṛjāmi punaḥ punaḥ' (9/8); 'ahaṁ bījapradaḥ pitā' (14/4)

† He dwells in the body. It means that the human body has discrimination and is capable of realizing God while other beings' discrimination is not aroused

same again, "I am specially seated, in the hearts of all" (13/17), "I am installed, in the hearts of all" (15/15), "The Lord dwells, in the hearts of all beings" (18/61).

'Ahameva atra* dehe' means, that in other bodies, beings reap the fruit of their previous actions and are not free to perform new actions; while in a human body new actions are performed, due to Lord's inspiration.† The actions which are performed by the Lord's inspiration, being free from attachment and aversion, are pure and they do not lead a man to bondage, while actions performed with attachment and aversion, lead to bondage, because these are not performed due to Lord's inspiration. The reason is, that attachment and aversion, are verily man's enemies (Gītā 3/34). It means, that forbidden actions can never be performed, with God's inspiration. The scriptures and jurisprudence, contain the inspiration (Command) of the Lord. Forbidden actions, are performed under the sway of desire (Gītā 3/37). If a man is not a victim of desire, he will perform actions, which are sanctioned by scriptures and which, have been called, actions ordained by one's own nature or innate actions, in the eighteenth chapter.

By using 'Dehabhṛtāṁ vara', for Arjuna, Lord Kṛṣṇa, wants to convey that the man who knows that the Lord is installed in the body, is the best. Even if he does not know, he should assume that in each atom of physical, subtle and causal bodies, the Lord pervades and the aim of human life is, to realize Him.

---

and they can't attain God-realization, though the Lord also dwells in their bodies. So a human being by utilizing this life should realize God in this very birth.

* In the second verse the term 'Atra' (Here) has been used for the context and the term 'Asmin' (This) for the body but here the term 'Atra' has been used for the body, because while putting the question. Arjuna has given a hint of the context, therefore there is no need for using the term 'Atra' in the answer.

† The Lord gives inspiration to human beings according to their nature. A man is free to be or not to be under the sway of attachment and aversion. He by depending on the scriptures, saints and the Lord can change his nature.

To attain that aim, he should carry out the command of the Lord, by performing action.

The terms 'Brahma', 'Adhyātma', 'Karma', 'Adhibhūta', 'Adhidaiva' and 'Adhiyajña', can be explained, by giving an illustration of water. When the sky is clear, we feel that there is nothing between us and the sun, yet there are atoms (molecules) of water. Water is transformed into clouds, by evaporation. Clouds turn to drops of rain. Those drops, at a low temperature, are frozen into snow. Similarly, the attributeless and formless Brahma (the Absolute), is like molecules of water, Adhiyajña (All-pervading Lord Viṣṇu) is water, as vapour, Adhidaiva (Brahmā) is, water as cloud, Adhyātma (Infinite embodied soul), is water as drops of rain, Karma (creation of the universe), is the activity of rain and Adhibhūta (perishable world), is water as snow.

It means, that as water takes different forms, the Lord also transforms Himself, into different forms. This knowledge about Him is complete (7/1) and so a man of aspiration realizes that, all this is God (7/19).

Though in essence, there is nothing besides the Lord, yet by discrimination, we see its two separate parts, a body and the soul. A devotee, perceives the Lord, (the Adored), the devotee (soul), and matter (the world). These three parts have been divided into six.

The Lord—Brahma (attributeless), and Adhiyajña (endowed with attributes).

The soul of two kinds—adhyātma (embodied soul which is bound) and Adhidaiva (Kāraka Puruṣa, a liberated soul).

The world has two separate forms—actions (heaps of change) and Adhibhūta (matter).

1. Brahma	→	←	6. Adhiyajña
2. Adhyātma	→	←	5. Adhidaiva
3. Karma (Action)	→	←	4. Adhibhūta

An Important Fact

(1) In the Gītā, Lord Kṛṣṇa has declared His existence in different ways, "All this is permeated by Me" (9/4); "By whom all this is pervaded" (18/46); "There is nothing else, besides Me" (7/7); "All this is God" (7/19); "I am the enjoyer and the Lord of all sacrifices" (9/24); "I am the enjoyer of sacrifices and austerities, the Supreme Lord of all the worlds" (5/29). Now let us think how to bring these into harmony.

All the strivers* in the world, want to attain God, by being free from the bondage of the world, because they want to attain a state of eternal peace and bliss. The worldly people, having affinity for the world, always suffer from disquietude and sorrow. The Lord, is the abode of infinite bliss, this is mentioned in scriptures and discourses of the saints who have also realized it.

Now, a question arises, that the world is clearly visible, while a striver has to assume the existence of God, Who is invisible. The striver starts adoration, by believing in the scriptures and the saints, as they declare, "The Lord pervades the entire universe." So long as, he attaches primary importance to the world, the Lord gets, a secondary place. But, by and by, when by constant devotion, his belief gets a firm footing, about the existence of God, a striver visualizes, that the world is perishing continuously. Finally, he perceives, that the world merely seems to appear, but has ever been non-existent, and the Lord existed in the past, exists now, and will exist in future, because He is eternal and in the world there is nothing besides Him. When a striver realizes "All is God", he becomes a 'Siddha' (perfect soul).

---

* Strivers are those who want to attain the state of perfect peace and infinite bliss, totally free from turmoil and sorrows. But the worldly people are those who hanker after worldly prosperity and pleasures and thus follow the cycle of birth and death.

(2) The Lord, is being and non-being, both (9/19); He is said to be, neither being nor non-being (13/12); He is being and the non-being, and also beyond the two (11/37). How to harmonize the different statements?

In fact, the Lord is very uncommon and unique. He cannot be perceived by senses, mind and intellect, which can merge into Him. The striver himself, can also merge into Him and attain Him, but cannot control Him.

There are two kinds of strivers—those having predominance of discrimination (mind), and those having predominance of faith, (devotion) (heart). But, it does not mean, that the former has no faith at all, and the latter, no discrimination at all. In the former, there is predominance of discrimination, while faith is secondary. In the latter, there is predominance of faith, while discrimination is secondary. In other words, it can be said, that the former first knows and then assumes, while the latter, first assumes and then knows.

A striver, whether he follows the path of discrimination or that of faith, can attain his aim quickly if he has taste for faith on (belief) and capability of his discipline. Because of interest, the mind is naturally motivated; because of faith (belief), intellect is naturally motivated, and because of capability, truth is understood. Strivers having predominance of discrimination, adore the Lord, Who is attributeless and formless, while the latter ones, adore the Lord, endowed with attributes and form. The former, says that He is neither being nor non-being, while the latter believes that He is the being, the non-being and also, beyond the two.

Thus we conclude that the Lord (Pure-consciousness) always remains the same, while the perishable world, changes continuously. When a man attaches importance to the perishable world, by having affinity for it, he has to follow, the cycle of birth and death. But, when he breaks up his affinity for the world, he realizes God. A striver having predominance of discrimination, breaks off affinity for the world (matter), by applying his discrimination and then Pure-Consciousness remains, while a devotee having faith in Him, by having disinclination for the world, attains Him through devotion. The former, by being established in the Absolute, Who is All-Truth, All-Consciousness and All-Bliss, attains indestructible and infinite bliss, while the latter by becoming one with Him, attains infinite and ever-enhancing bliss of love.

Thus, both the strivers by renouncing their affinity for the world, attain pure-consciousness, and realize that the Lord, is being and non-being both.

Appendix—All actions and objects which are kaleidoscopic and perishable are—'kṣara bhāva' which is the Lord's aparā prakṛti.

In knowledge there is union of the self with Brahma and in love there is intimate union (abhinnatā) of a devotee with the indwelling Lord. The Lord has declared here 'the indwelling' (adhiyajña) as His own Self. Therefore 'Brahma' is adjective and 'antaryāmī' (indwelling) is the noun qualified—'brahmaṇo hi pratiṣṭhāham' (Gītā 14/27). It means that the creator and controller of all beings Who has been mentioned as 'Samagra' (entire) in the Gītā, is the indwelling Lord Himself. The same 'indwelling' has been mentioned by the term 'aham' in the third and fourth verses of the fourteenth chapter in the expression—'mama yonirmahadbrahma tasmingarbhaṁ dadhāmyaham' and 'ahaṁ bījapradaḥ pitā'. In the Gītā it is mentioned for Brahma 'na Sattannāsaducyate'(13/12) and for entire God it is mentioned—'sadasaccāham' (9/19), 'sadasattatparaṁ yat' (11/37).

Link:—In the second verse, Arjuna's seventh question was, "How is one to realize You at the time of death?" Lord Kṛṣṇa, answers this question, in the next verse.

अन्तकाले च मामेव स्मरन्मुक्त्वा कलेवरम्।
यः प्रयाति स मद्भावं याति नास्त्यत्र संशयः॥५॥

antakāle ca māmeva smaranmuktvā kalevaram
yaḥ prayāti sa madbhāvaṁ yāti nāstyatra saṁśayaḥ

He, who departing from the body thinks of (remembering) Me alone even at the time of death, attains Me, there is no doubt about it. 5

Comment:—

'Antakāle ca māmeva smaranmuktvā kalevaram yaḥ prayāti sa madbhāvaṁ yāti nāstyatra saṁśayaḥ'—It means, that the Lord by bestowing this human body upon man, gave him an opportunity to attain salvation, through adoration. But, he did not avail himself of the opportunity. Now, being helpless, the only way open to him is to realize Him, by remembering Him at least while breathing his last.

'Māmeva smaran' means, that whatever a striver hears, sees, understands and assumes, is nothing besides the Lord. By assuming so, whatever a striver thinks, at the time of death is nothing else, besides the Lord. Thus if a striver thinks of Him, at the time of death, he will attain Him.

'Madbhāvam' means, that the striver attains the state of Godhood whether he is a dualist or a non-dualist—this is in accordance with the remembrance, at the last moment. That God may be endowed with attributes or attributeless, endowed with form or formless, two-armed or four-armed etc., according to one's worship.

Worshippers of the Lord, attain Him by thinking of Him, at the time of death. But even to the minds of those who do not worship Him, if somehow or the other, His thought comes, they also attain Him. As a person, remains established in a mode of nature (14/18), and as he dies during the predominance of Nature-born qualities, (Modes) of sattva (goodness) or raja (passion) or tama, (ignorance), he gains the same kind of world (Gītā 14/14-15), a devotee who at the time of death, remembers God, attains Him. At the end, devotees following different disciplines of worship become one, i.e., attain the same Lord, while persons having predominance of anyone of the three Nature-born modes, gain worlds according to the mode they possess viz., and follow a cycle of birth and death.

It is a special favour granted by the Lord, that a man at the time of death, by remembering Him, will attain Him, even though his conduct and life had been vicious, as the only aim of this human life, is God-realization. Otherwise, it is not befitting to the Lord Who has bestowed this human life and also to a person who has received it. Therefore, it is a warning to every person, that he should be careful to remember Him, all the time, because anytime, can be the time of death, as it keeps no calendar. In Ethics, it is mentioned that if a man wants to follow righteousness, and attain salvation, he should always remember that, he is in the grip of death.

A man, should utilize the special concession, granted to him, by God. If there is a person on the death-bed, he should be shown a picture of his favourite Deity, the name of his Deity should be chanted, and he should be reminded of his Deity's form. A spiritual atmosphere should be created, so that messengers of the god of death, may not approach him. Ajāmila, recited the name of the Lord 'Nārāyaṇa', and so messengers of God approached while the messengers of death, fled away. Then the god of death said to his messengers, "Where there is constant remembrance, loud chanting or narration of the stories of the Lord, never go there, because that place is out of our domain." By saying so, the god of death in thinking of God, tendered an apology to Him in these words, "O Lord, pardon my messengers for the offence, they have committed" (Śrīmadbhā. 6/3/30).

'He thinks of Him, at the time of death'. It means, that he may remember anyone of His forms, as that of Rāma, Kṛṣṇa, Viṣṇu, Śiva, Durgā, Gaṇeśa or His name, place, qualities or sport. By thinking of Him, a person attains Him, because by remembering God he forgets "I am, the body and the body, is mine."

A doubt arises here, as to how a man, who has not worshipped the Lord, throughout his life, can remember Him, at the time of his death. The answer is, that either by God's special grace, or by seeing a saint or by listening to the name, play, stories of the Lord or scriptures, he may think of God and thus may attain Him. If he is interested in the Gītā, and he is on a death-bed, the eighth chapter should be recited to him, so that he may think of God at that time, as there is a special description, of the glory about thinking of Him, at the time of death. The reason, is that being a fragment of the Lord, his affinity for Him is natural. Similarly, if he dies at a place of pilgrimage, such as Ayodhyā, Mathurā, Haridvāra, Kāśī etc., he will remember the Lord, because of the spiritual influence of that place of pilgrimage. He can also think of God, at the last moment, at a place, where a spiritual atmosphere of constant remembrance, loud chanting and stories of the Lord, prevails and where spiritual discourses are held. Some terrifying situation, could also remind, the man of God. If at the time of death, he somehow or the other, takes refuge in Him, he attains Him. If, all of a sudden he thinks of his salvation, he may attain salvation. Similarly, if a striver recites the name of the Lord, to someone at the time of his death, he may attain salvation. In the scriptures, it is mentioned, that if a saint, beholds either a man on a death-bed, or his dead body, the smoke of his burning pyre, or the ash of his pyre, he attains salvation.*

*** Once a religious minded gentleman was offering a little holy water of the Ganges to the people. One of the persons said that he would not be purified of his numberless sins with such a small quantity of holy water. He demanded a jug of that holy water. When he was offered it he drank it and said that he would be purged of his sins. At the time of death his**

An Important Fact

In the third and fourth verses of this chapter, the six terms, such as Brahma and Adhyātma etc., reveal the Lord, in His all comprehensive forms, indicating that, all is God. Thus, a great soul who has realized, that in this world there is nothing else besides, the Lord, has not to remember Him at the time of death, as he is all the time in a wakeful state, dream, sound sleep, instinctively conscious of His eternal presence, in the same way, as a common man always remembers, "I am."

He may live at anyplace, holy or unholy, at anytime, day or night, in anystate, wakefulness, sleep, sound sleep, unconsciousness, sickness, health etc., and in any circumstances, he will certainly attain, salvation.

Besides, the above-mentioned great souls, strivers, who worship the Lord, in His different forms and names by remembering anyone of His names or forms or plays or places, will, attain Him.

Besides them, other believers who somehow or the other, think of God at the time of death, though they are not engaged continuously in His worship, also attain Him.

Thus, the remedy of remembering the Lord at the time of death, is not applicable to liberated souls, but only to strivers and common people.

Appendix—The person, who could not attain salvation during his lifetime, if he even at the time of death, remembering God, departs from this body, he attains God—there is no doubt about it. Then he who ever remembers God, if he thinking of God at the time of death, attains God, what is the wonder in it? The Lord has endowed the man with great freedom so that however he may attain salvation. This is God's

---

life-breath passed through the tenth door and he attained salvation. (This anecdote was narrated by a striver.)

special grace showered on a man.

Link:—He, who thinks of the Lord, at the time of death attains Him. What becomes of those, who do not think of the Lord, but think of someone else? The answer follows, in the next verse.

यं यं वापि स्मरन्भावं त्यजत्यन्ते कलेवरम्।
तं तमेवैति कौन्तेय सदा तद्भावभावितः ॥ ६ ॥

yaṁ yaṁ vāpi smaranbhāvaṁ tyajatyante kalevaram
taṁ tamevaiti kaunteya sadā tadbhāvabhāvitaḥ

Whatever object or being a man thinks of at the time of his death or departure from the body, that alone does he attain, O Kaunteya (Arjuna) as having been always in these thoughts. 6

Comment:—

'Yaṁ yaṁ vāpi smaranbhāvaṁ tyajatyante kalevaraṁ taṁ tamevaiti kaunteya sadā tadbhāvabhāvitaḥ'—In this ordinance of the Lord, there is reflected His unique grace, that a man may attain Him, merely by thinking of Him, at the time of death. If he thinks of a dog, he gets birth as a dog, but if he thinks of the Lord, he attains Him. How, easily attainable the Lord is!

'Sadā tadbhāvabhāvitaḥ'—Whatever being, a man thinks of at the time of death, he obtains the same body, because before obtaining the other body he has no opportunity, no power, no freedom, to change the thought, which he has at the time of death. So, he remains engrossed, in the same thought. Then he, with air, water or food etc., enters the body of a man for whose actions, he has even the least affinity. Then, from the body of the man, he enters the body of a woman and takes birth. If a man thinks of a dog, at the time of death, he takes birth as a dog. But it does not mean, that by thinking of a house or wealth, he is born as a house or wealth. It means, that if he dies while thinking of a house, he may be born as a rat or a lizard in that house, and if he thinks of wealth, at the time of death, he is born as a snake. It means, that a person by thinking of a non-living object, at the time of death, is born as a living being, having a connection, with that non-living object.

Other creatures, such as birds and animals etc., remember objects or beings according to their actions, at the time of death and are reborn accordingly. But, the singularity of human body is, that his thinking at the last moment, does not depend on his actions, but on his own self. He is free, in having an affinity for anyone. If he has his affinity, for the Lord, and remembers Him at the time of death, all his artificial and assumed affinity, for worldly beings and objects, breaks up and he attains Him, because his affinity for Him is axiomatic.

An Important Fact

(1) A being is reborn in the body, he thinks of, at the time of death. As a man, rearing a domestic dog thinks of it at the time of death, he is born as a dog. As the programme broadcast from a particular radio station, is received at a particular wave-length and then spreads in the form of sound, the thought of a dog with which he has been connected in anyway, is caught by him. Then the soul with subtle and causal bodies, enters the body of the dog via water, air (breath) or food etc. Then, it enters the body of a bitch, and takes birth as a dog, at the right time.

This can be explained, with the help of an illustration. A person goes to a photographer and requests him, to take his photograph. The photographer advises him to keep a smiling face, without any movement. But when the photographer asks him to be ready, a fly sits on his nose and so he moves his face muscles, in order to remove that fly. The result is, that he gets the photograph with a distorted face. In the same way, a man is reborn, according to his thoughts at the time of death.

As far as, the time to take a photograph, is concerned, we know it, before hand, but we do not know, the time of death. So, by purifying our nature and thoughts, we should ever be alert, and think of Him, at all times (Gītā 8/5,7).

(2) In this directive of the Lord, seen is His justice, as well as grace. Generally, justice and grace, seem incompatible, because if there is justice, there cannot be grace (mercy). But, this rule is applicable to human beings, not to the Lord, as He is the most gracious one, and is a disinterested friend of all beings, (Gītā 5/29). So, all His ordinances and rules, are full of justice and mercy.

Whatever being, a man thinks of at the time of death, he gets the same form at rebirth. If he dies thinking of a dog, he is reborn, as a dog. This is God's justice. But He has given freedom to man, to think either of a dog or of a man, or of God, and this is His, mercy. A man can attain God, just by thinking of Him, as he can obtain the body of a dog, by thinking of it. If a man starts thinking of His justice and grace, he will be attracted towards Him, alone.

Appendix—In the twenty-first verse of the seventh chapter the Lord declared that a man is free in his worship by the expression 'yo yo yāṁ yāṁ tanuṁ bhaktaḥ', now in this verse He mentions the freedom of a man about the fate, he meets after death. It means that a man is free* in his worship and also in creating his fate after death, because of His most gracious nature, the Lord instead of creating an obstacle, rather helps him. By misusing this freedom, a gift of God, he meets an evil doom.

This is the special characteristic of the human life that a man may attain whatever he wants. There is no rare state which a man may not attain. A man can attain the state, in which

---

*nara tana sama nahiṁ kavaniu dehī, jīva carācara jācata tehī.
naraka svarga apaberga nisenī, jñāna birāga bhagati subha denī.

(Mānasa, Uttara. 121/5)

there is infinite bliss and there is not even an iota of affliction (Gītā 6/22). But by hankering after mundane pleasures and prosperity, he paves the way to eighty-four lac forms of life and hells. Therefore the Lord declares with shock—'aprāpya māṁ nivartante mṛtyusaṁsāravartmani' (instead of attaining Me, a man revolves in the path of the mortal world (9/3), 'māmaprāpyaiva kaunteya tato yāntyadhamāṁ gatim' (instead of attaining Me he sinks down to lower planes)' (16/20).

Whatever a man thinks of at the time of death, the same end he meets. In this connection there is a verse—

vāsanā yasya yatra syāt sa taṁ svapneṣu paśyati
svapnavanmaraṇe jñeyaṁ vāsanā tu vapurnṛṇām

'Whatever longing a man has, according to that longing he dreams. He meets his end (death) according to the dream viz., at the time of death he thinks of the object according to his longing and he meets his end according to that thought."

It means that at the time of death we cannot think of whatever we wish, but we shall think according to our latent tendency; and accordingly we shall meet our end. The thing to which we give existence and value; with which we accept our relationship and out of which we derive pleasure, we have latent desire for the same thing. If we hold that the world can't provide us with pleasure, we shall have no such desire for the world. If there is no such desire, then at the time of death, if any thought comes to the mind, it will be only of God because in principle—all is God—'Vāsudevaḥ sarvam'. 'Taṁ tamevaiti'—as the thread follows the needle, similarly whatever being, a man thinks of at the time of death, that alone does he attain.

Link:—When a man gains a body according to his thought at the time of death, what should he do to remember God? The way, is indicated, in the next verse.

तस्मात्सर्वेषु कालेषु मामनुस्मर युध्य च।
मय्यर्पितमनोबुद्धिर्मामेवैष्यस्यसंशयम् ॥७॥

tasmātsarveṣu kāleṣu māmanusmara yudhya ca
mayyarpitamanobuddhirmāmevaiṣyasyasaṁśayam

Therefore, think of Me at all times, and fight the war. With your mind and intellect dedicated to Me, you will surely come to Me. 7

Comment:—

'Tasmātsarveṣu kāleṣu māmanusmara yudhya ca'—Here, the terms 'Sarveṣu kāleṣu', have been used for thinking, not for a fight, because any action cannot be performed at all times, as every action has a beginning and an end, and it is everyone's experience. But, being always conscious of the aim of God-realization, He, is thought of, at all times.

When Lord Kṛṣṇa exhorts Arjuna to think of Him, at all times, He says, that as there is a limitation of time for other activities, such as having meals, taking sleep and earning livelihood etc., there is no such limitation of time, in thinking of the Lord. He should be thought of, at all times.

The expression 'Yudhya ca' (and fight), has been used to tell Arjuna, that he has obtained such an unsolicited opportunity for war (Gītā 2/32). So, he should perform this duty, by thinking of God. But the thought of God, is primary, while performance of the duty, is secondary.

'Anusmara' means, constant remembrance, of God. The second interpretation is, that God does not forget any being as He has declared, in the seventh chapter, "I know all beings" (7/26). When He knows all beings, it is natural for Him, to think of them. Therefore, if this being, thinks of Him, he attains salvation. In order to, be able to remember God, one must have a feeling of intense love for Him. The more intense, this feeling of love is, the oftener will, His remembrance come to one's mind.

'Mayyarpitamanobuddhiḥ'—Generally, it means, that a striver should surrender his mind and intellect, to Him viz., he should think of God, with his mind and have a determination with his intellect, to realize Him. But, it really means, that a striver should never think, the mind, intellect, senses and body as his own, even by an error, as all the worldly things, belong to God. So long as, a striver goes on thinking, that they are his own, they cannot be purified. The thought of accepting these, as one's own, is the main impurity which gives birth, to other impurities.

In fact, a man has his affinity only, for God, because he is His eternal fraction. So, how can he have any affinity for nature (matter)? A striver, by thinking of the mind and intellect, as God's, should surrender these to Him. Then, naturally he will realize God, because, he had a disinclination for Him, as he had an affinity for Nature (Matter) and its evolutes (i.e.,) the body, mind, intellect etc., and, affinity for these was a stumbling block.

Some of the philosophers, regard the worldly things, as God's, while others regard these as prakṛti's (nature's), but all of them agree, that they are not of men. Therefore, a striver by thinking these of God, should surrender them, to Him. By doing so, his eternal affinity for God, will be aroused.

'Māmevaiṣyasyasaṁśayam'—By surrendering your mind and intellect, to Me, you will attain Me, without any doubt, because I am ever attained to you. But, you are unable to realize this fact, because you have accepted your affinity, for the body and the world. So if you surrender the mind, intellect and yourself to Me, your eternal affinity for Me, will be revealed; there is no doubt about it.

Some Important Facts About Remembrance

Remembrance, is of three kinds—born of knowledge, born of affinity, and born of action. Remembrance, born of knowledge never ends. Remembrance born of affinity continues, so long as affinity continues, but remembrance born of action, is not constant. These are referred to in detail, is as follows:

(i) Remembrance born of knowledge—We have not to remember 'I am'. But, we commit an error by identifying ourselves, with the body. By knowledge, this error is wiped out and knowledge of 'I am', remains. In the Gītā, Lord Kṛṣṇa declares, "There was never a time, when I or you and these kings, were non-existent; nor is it that we shall cease to be in future" (Gītā 2/12). "This multitude of beings, born again and again, is dissolved at the commencement of Brahmā's night and rises again, at the commencement of his day" (8/19). In it, this multitude of beings is a portion of God, and what is dissolved and born, is body. If we renounce our assumed affinity for this perishable body, our remembrance, born of knowledge, remains constant.

(ii) Remembrance born of affinity—Actually, we have our real affinity for God, not for the body and the world, because we are His eternal portion. But, by accepting our affinity for the body and the world, we do not, realize our real affinity, for God. As soon as, we deny the assumed affinity, our real eternal affinity for the Lord, is automatically aroused and then there is constant remembrance, of the Lord.

(iii) Remembrance born of action or practice—It depends on practice. Ladies in villages, carrying a pitcher full of water, talk and walk, but are careful about the pitcher. An acrobat, while dancing and speaking, remains careful of a rope. A motor driver, while driving, changing the gear, handling the steering and talking to the conductor etc., remains careful about the road. All this, depends on practice. Thus remembrance of God, while performing different actions, is remembrance born of practice. This remembrance (born of practice) is, also of three kinds—(a) Remembrance of God, while performing mundane actions. In this primary importance, is attached to actions, and secondary to, remembrance of God. (b) Performing actions, while remembering

God. In it, primary importance is attached to the remembrance of God, and secondary to actions. Here, a person, remains careful that he should not forget God, even though worldly action, is not performed properly. (c) Performing actions, thinking them as God's. While performing actions, a striver thinks that he is fortunate enough that he is rendering service to God, through actions, because such actions are His. So, he has sweet remembrance of God, just like a father, who while performing different actions for his daughter's marriage remembers his daughter.

Spiritual pursuits are of two kinds—(i) Utterance of His name, loud chanting, listening to his sport, thinking of Him, and reading scriptures. (ii) Performance of actions, thinking them as God's, in order to please Him, without any selfish motive and in accordance with, the ordinance of scriptures. Such actions, are also included, in spiritual pursuits.

[At the end of the seventh chapter, Lord Kṛṣṇa, while describing His entire form referred to seven facts. On those seven facts, Arjuna put seven questions, at the beginning of the eighth chapter, and this topic is also over, in seven verses.]

Appendix—The Lord in the thirtieth verse of the seventh chapter said, 'prayāṇakāle'pi ca māṁ te vidur'yuktacetasaḥ' (they having a steadfast mind realize Me, even at the hour of death). Arjuna in the second verse of the eighth chapter put the question, "How can you be realised, at the hour of death, by persons of steadfast mind?" In response to this question the Lord said, "He who departing from the body thinks of Me alone, at the time of death, attains Me." He further said, "This rule is not applicable only to those who want to attain Me. But this is a common rule that whatever object or being a man thinks of at the time of death, that alone does he attain." (8/5-6). Death may visit at any time. There is no year, no month, no day, no hour, no minute, no moment, in which a being is free from the clutches of death. Therefore Lord Kṛṣṇa exhorts Arjuna to think of Him, at all times—'tasmātsarveṣu kāleṣu māmanusmara.' "Those who perpetually think of Me, I am easily attainable to them (8/14); because he may depart from the body any time, he will depart thinking of Me only, and thus will attain Me only." 'mayyarpita-manobuddhiḥ'—By thinking of God all the time, a striver's mind and intellect are dedicated to God. When a striver holds that the mind and intellect are not his and he has no connection with them—thus by renouncing the sense of mine in mind and intellect, they are naturally dedicated to God because they are the Lord's 'aparā prakṛti'. Though 'parā' and 'aparā'—both prakṛtis are of the Lord, yet parā prakṛti has no relation with aparā but it has its relation only with God because it is a fragment of God—'mamaivāṁśo jīvaloke' (15/7). Therefore a striver can be 'mayyarpitamanobuddhi' only when he does not accept his affinity with aparā but dedicates it (aparā) to God Who is its master viz., never assumes aparā as his and for him.

Here within 'mana'—'citta' and within 'buddhi'—'ahaṅkāra' should also be included. When mind and intellect are dedicated, the devotee is freed from the sense of mine and egoism.

In fact a devotee surrenders himself to God. When he surrenders himself, his all, including his so-called mind and intellect etc., are naturally surrendered to God. When all is surrendered to God, then 'all' does not persist but only God remains—'Vāsudevaḥ sarvam.'

Link:—Remembrance (thinking), born of practice, mentioned in the previous verse, is described, in the next verse.

अभ्यासयोगयुक्तेन चेतसा नान्यगामिना।
परमं पुरुषं दिव्यं याति पार्थानुचिन्तयन्॥ ८॥

abhyāsayogayuktena cetasā nānyagāminā
paramaṁ puruṣaṁ divyaṁ yāti pārthānucintayan

O Pārtha (Arjuna) he, who with his mind fixed in Yoga through meditation, and without wavering thinking of nothing else, and is at the time of death constantly engaged in contemplation of the Supreme Puruṣa (God), attains Him. 8

Comment:—

[In the twenty-eighth verse of the seventh chapter, the Lord endowed with attributes and formless, Who was described briefly has been detailed in the eighth, ninth and tenth verses, here.]

'Abhyāsayogayuktena'—In this expression, there are two words 'Abhyāsa', (practice) and yoga (equanimity). Practice, means, repeated concentration of mind on God, by diverting it from the world, while Yoga means equanimity—"Equanimity is called Yoga" (Gītā 2/48). Concentration of mind, results in joy, while its diversion leads to sadness. This is called practice, rather than, the Yoga of practice. It is called Yoga of practice, only when there is equanimity, in joy and sorrow. A striver, instead of attaching importance, to joy and sadness, should attach importance to his goal. That is establishment of mind, in Yoga.

'Cetasā nānyagāminā'—He should think of nothing else, viz., he should have no aim other than, God-realization.

'Paramaṁ puruṣaṁ divyaṁ yāti pārthānucintayan'—At the time of death with such a mind, constantly engaged in contemplation, of the Supreme Puruṣa viz., God endowed with attributes and formless, a striver attains Him.

Appendix—Arjuna put the question—'prayāṇakāle ca kathaṁ jñeyo'si niyatātmabhiḥ' (8/2) (How can You be realized, at the time of death, by persons of steadfast mind?) Having answered that question, the Lord now in the eighth, ninth and tenth verses describes the type of those who think of God at the time of death.

Link:—Now for concentration, the Lord describes, God Who is formless and is endowed with attributes.

कविं पुराणमनुशासितार-
मणोरणीयांसमनुस्मरेद्यः ।
सर्वस्य धातारमचिन्त्यरूप-
मादित्यवर्णं तमसः परस्तात् ॥ ९ ॥

kaviṁ purāṇamanuśāsitāra-
maṇoraṇīyāṁsamanusmaredyaḥ
sarvasya dhātāramacintyarūpa-
mādityavarṇaṁ tamasaḥ parastāt

He, who contemplates on the Omniscient, the ancient, the ruler, the minutest of the minute, sustainer of all, of form inconceivable, shining like the sun and beyond all darkness, (of ignorance). 9

Comment:—

'Kavim'—The Lord, is Omniscient, because He knows all the beings, and their good and evil actions.

'Purāṇam'—He is most ancient, because He is the origin of everything, sentient and insentient.

'Anuśāsitāram'—He, is the Ruler and Illuminator of all the senses, mind, intellect and ego. Secondly, He through scriptures, preceptors and saints, guide men to perform their duties, and by creating favourable and unfavourable circumstances, according to their virtuous and evil actions, purifies them. He is called a Ruler, as He makes ordinance for prescription and prohibition, and also, destroys old actions, in the form of virtues and sins, by enabling them to reap their fruits.

'Aṇoraṇīyāṁsam'—The Lord, is subtler, than even an atom. He is the subtlest of the subtle. He is, beyond the reach of mind and intellect. Even nature cannot be perceived, by them, because they are the evolutes of Nature. So, how can they have, an access to the subtlest Lord?

'Sarvasya dhātāram'—He, is the supporter and sustainer of infinite universes. So He is called, the sustainer of all.

'Tamasaḥ parastāt'—He is, supremely above and beyond, the darkness of ignorance. He is also the illuminator of ignorance.

'Ādityavarṇam'—His colour, is like the sun i.e., just like the shining sun, the Lord is the illuminator of minds and intellects, of all beings. All beings, receive light from Him.

'Acintyarūpam'—His form, is inconceivable, to the mind and intellect.

'Anusmaret'—It means, that one should contemplate, on God. God knows all the beings and so He remembers them. Therefore, they should also remember Him.

Now, a doubt arises, as to how, to think of Him, when He is inconceivable. The clarification is, that a firm belief, that He is inconceivable, is in fact, the thought of Him.

Appendix—God has been called 'kavim' (omniscient) because there is nothing beyond His knowledge. He has been called 'purāṇam' because He is beginningless, He transcends the limits of time viz., is the illuminator of time. He has been called 'anuśāsitāram' because all are naturally governed by Him. He is the ruler of both—the individual soul and the world—

kṣaraṁ pradhānamamṛtākṣaraṁ haraḥ kṣarātmānāvīśate deva ekaḥ

(śvetāśvatara. 1/10)

'Prakṛti is perishable and the soul, which enjoys it, is immortal and imperishable. God governs over these two—the perishable and the imperishable.'

The term—dhātāram' means that God sustains all beings (Gītā 15/17). The term 'ādityavarṇam' means that as there is naturally light in the sun always, similarly in God naturally there is always knowledge and enlightenment. God is an embodiment of knowledge and illumines the entire universe (Gītā 13/33). 'tamasaḥ parastāt'—this expression means that God transcends ignorance or aparā (the lower nature)—'yasmātkṣaramatīto'ham' (Gītā 15/18).

Link:—In the next verse, Lord Kṛṣṇa explains, how a devotee according to the thought, which he has at the time of death, reaches Him.

प्रयाणकाले मनसाचलेन
भक्त्या युक्तो योगबलेन चैव।
भ्रुवोर्मध्ये प्राणमावेश्य सम्यक्
स तं परं पुरुषमुपैति दिव्यम्॥१०॥

prayāṇakāle manasācalena
bhaktyā yukto yogabalena caiva
bhruvormadhye prāṇamāveśya samyak
sa taṁ paraṁ puruṣamupaiti divyam

By Yogic power, firmly holding the life-breath between the two eyebrows, at the time of death, concentrating on God, with a steadfast mind and full of devotion, he reaches the Supreme Puruṣa (God). 10

Comment:—

'Prayāṇakāle manasācalena bhaktyā yukto yogabalena caiva bhruvormadhye prāṇamāveśya samyak sa taṁ paraṁ puruṣamupaiti divyam'—Here, devotion stands for attraction for the Lord, and that attraction, is one's own, and is not of mind and intellect, etc. The Yogī contemplates on God, Who is formless and is endowed, with attributes.

By Yogic power, he holding the life-breath, in the space between the two eyebrows, in the principal nerve called 'Suṣumnā' which is situated in the circle with two leaves (Dvidala cakra) (leaving the body through the tenth door, situated in the skull), reaches the Supreme Puruṣa.

'Taṁ paraṁ puruṣamupaiti divyam'—He attains, the Supreme Divine Lord, Who is formless and is endowed with attributes, as described in the ninth verse.

Whatever, was said in brief, in the eighth verse, has been

explained in detail in the ninth and tenth verses, and thus the topic has been concluded.

In this context, there is a description of the worship of the Lord, Who is formless and is endowed with attributes. There is need for practice, in this worship. This practice, is not meant, for attaining accomplishments (siddhi), but for God-realization. This concentration of mind, on God, at the time of death, is a difficult task, which can be carried out, only by one who has a full command, over his life-breath, and mind.

A striver, should first have a determination that beyond ignorance, there is an unaffected and transcendental divinity—One, Who is the illuminator, base and inspirer, of all the beings. Then, he should love Him from his heart. By doing so, his mind will be concentrated, on Him naturally.

Appendix—The expression 'bhaktyā yuktaḥ' means that when a striver's attachment to the world is wiped out, he has attraction only for God, attraction for anyone else does not remain in him. The worldly people have attraction for 'aparā' (lower nature) but he, who having renounced attraction for 'aparā', is attracted towards God, becomes a devotee. The worldly people being attached to the body and the world become 'vibhakta' viz., separate from God but a striver who remains engrossed in the devotion of God, does not remain 'vibhakta' but becomes a 'bhakta' (devotee) viz., becomes one with God.

The term 'yogabalena' means that because of the past practice of yoga, the state of weakness usually visiting at the time of death cannot cause an obstacle to him, cannot cause any change in him. The strength (power) gained by regulating breath etc., is 'Yogabala'.

Link:—In the next verse, Lord Kṛṣṇa explains how to attain the Lord, Who is formless and attributeless.

यदक्षरं वेदविदो वदन्ति
विशन्ति यद्यतयो वीतरागाः।
यदिच्छन्तो ब्रह्मचर्यं चरन्ति
तत्ते पदं सङ्ग्रहेण प्रवक्ष्ये॥११॥

yadakṣaraṁ vedavido vadanti
viśanti yadyatayo vītarāgāḥ
yadicchanto brahmacaryaṁ caranti
tatte padaṁ saṅgraheṇa pravakṣye

I shall explain to you, in brief, the goal, which knowers of the Vedas term, as the Imperishable Oṁ, and into which enter, keen recluses, self-controlled, free from attachment and desiring persons, who strive for and practise celibacy. 11

Comment:—

[The attributeless and formless Lord, who was touched upon in brief, in the twenty-ninth verse of the seventh chapter, is described in detail in the eleventh, twelfth and thirteenth verses.]

'Yadakṣaraṁ vedavido vadanti'—That which, the knowers of Vedas, term as the Imperishable—attributeless-formless, and that ever remains uniform and has been called, the Supreme Imperishable Brahma, in the third verse of this chapter, is described here.

'Viśanti yadyatayo vītarāgāḥ'—Those striving recluses, who are totally free from attachment, who have become pure, and who have a yearning to attain Him, reach Him.

'Yadicchanto brahmacaryaṁ caranti'—Those, whose aim is only to realize God, and to realize Him, they practise celibacy, by controlling their senses, and passions.

'Tatte padaṁ saṅgraheṇa pravakṣye'—I shall speak to you, well in brief, of that essence, which has been described in the scriptures, as the Supreme, the Unique, the Absolute and, which is attained by worshippers. 'Speaking well', means speaking in such a way that adorers of the Absolute, will attain Him.

Appendix—In this verse secondarily the description of the four 'āśramas' (stages of life may be taken—as in 'yadakṣaraṁ vedavido vadanti' expression, there is a hint for household life because study of the Vedas is the main duty of a Brāhmaṇa (priest class). In the expression 'viśanti yadyatayo vītarāgāḥ—there is a hint for the retired order and the renounced order. In the expression 'yadicchanṭo brahmacaryaṁ caranti' there is a hint for the stage of celibacy.

A man can attain salvation in all the orders (varṇas) and stages of life (āśramas). Therefore the Lord has not described the stages of life clearly and He has described the Varṇas clearly in order to explain the people of the four Varṇas (castes) their different duties ordained by the scriptures. Arjuna was a Kṣatriya (a member of the warrior class) and he wanted to give up his duty of fighting in the war. Therefore the Lord described the duties of the four orders of life in order to remind Arjuna of his duty. To wage a war is 'varṇadharma', rather than 'āśramadharma'.

Link:—Lord Kṛṣṇa, in the next two verses, explains the means to attain the attributeless-formless Lord, at the time of death.

सर्वद्वाराणि संयम्य मनो हृदि निरुध्य च।
मूर्ध्न्याधायात्मनः प्राणमास्थितो योगधारणाम्॥ १२॥
ओमित्येकाक्षरं ब्रह्म व्याहरन्मामनुस्मरन्।
यः प्रयाति त्यजन्देहं स याति परमां गतिम्॥ १३॥

sarvadvārāṇi saṁyamya mano hṛdi nirudhya ca
mūrdhnyādhāyātmanaḥ prāṇamāsthito yogadhāraṇām
omityekākṣaraṁ brahma vyāharanmāmanusmaran
yaḥ prayāti tyajandehaṁ sa yāti paramāṁ gatim

Having restrained all the means of perception while fixing

the mind on the heart and the life-breath, in the head, remaining steadfast in yogic concentration, and chanting the one syllabled Brahma, 'Oṁ' thinking of Me, one who leaves the body thus attains the Supreme State. 12-13

Comment:—

'Sarvadvārāṇi saṁyamya'—(At the time of death), one should restrain all the media of perception (should close all the gates of the body), i.e., he should restrain his ears, skin, eyes, tongue and nose from the five senses of sound, touch, colour (form), taste and smell; and five organs of action—tongue, hands, feet, anus and generative organ, from acting, speaking, taking, going, passing stools and urine. Thus, the senses will be restrained.

'Mano hṛdi nirudhya ca'—The mind should be fixed in the heart, so that it may not hanker after sensual pleasures.

'Mūrdhnyādhāyātmanaḥ prāṇam'—He, should fix his life-breath, in the head i.e., by controlling his life-breath, he should fix it in 'Brahmarandhra', the suture on the top of the head.

'Āsthito yogadhāraṇām'—He should become steadfast, in Yogic concentration i.e., he should neither use his sense-organs, in performing actions, nor think with his mind, and have a full command, over his life-breath.

'Omityekākṣaraṁ brahma vyāharanmāmanusmaran'—After it, he should chant the one syllabled Brahma 'Oṁ', with his mind and think of the Supreme Imperishable Brahma, Who is attributeless-formless (Who has been described in the third verse of this chapter). The thought about Him, is that He pervades everywhere, all the things, persons, incidents and circumstances etc., end at all times.

'Yaḥ prayāti tyajandehaṁ sa yāti paramāṁ gatim'—He, who thinking of the attributeless and formless Lord, departs leaving the body (i.e., his life-breath passes through the tenth exit), attains the Supreme Goal viz., the attributeless and formless Lord.

Appendix—In the verses there is the description of the non-dualistic Yogī who practises yoga. The term 'Vyāharan' should mean mental pronunciation (utterance), because when the mind is fixed in the heart and the life-breath is fixed in the head, an articulate utterance is impossible.

Link:—The above-mentioned method, of attaining the attributeless and formless Lord, which is subject to practice, for a long time, is difficult to practise, for a common man. Therefore, Lord Kṛṣṇa, in the next verse, explains an easy method, to attain the Lord, endowed with attributes and form.

अनन्यचेताः सततं यो मां स्मरति नित्यशः ।
तस्याहं सुलभः पार्थ नित्ययुक्तस्य योगिनः ॥ १४ ॥

ananyacetāḥ satataṁ yo māṁ smarati nityaśaḥ
tasyāhaṁ sulabhaḥ pārtha nityayuktasya yoginaḥ

O Pārtha (Arjuna), the Yogī who perpetually thinks of Me and undividedly remains absorbed in Me, to him I am easily attainable. 14

Comment:—

[The Lord, endowed with attributes and form, referred to in the thirtieth verse of the seventh chapter, is discussed in detail here, in the fourteenth, fifteenth and sixteenth verses.]

'Ananyacetāḥ'—A striver, whose mind is not attracted in the least, towards prosperity and pleasures, and remains absorbed in God, and does not depend on anyone besides the Lord, is of undivided mind. He depends only on God, like a chaste wife, who totally depends on her husband, and thinks of him only, and like an obedient disciple or son, who depends on his preceptor or parents only.

Such a striver, worships the Lord endowed with attributes, such as Rāma, Kṛṣṇa, Śiva, Durgā, Gaṇeśa, Sūrya (Sun-God). He, without thinking of the other forms, of the Lord, as different from his own, worships his favourite Deity, with exclusive devotion. He has a firm belief, that he is only God's and only God is his; he is of none else, and none else is his.

'Satataṁ yo māṁ smarati nityaśaḥ'—'Satatam' means 'Constantly', from the time he is awake, to the time he goes to sleep. 'Nityaśaḥ' means, always i.e., he thinks of Him, from the day he knew Him, to the day he dies.

'Tasyāhaṁ sulabhaḥ pārtha nityayuktasya yoginaḥ'—I am easily attainable to such a devotee, who is absorbed in Me. 'Absorbed in Me' does not mean, that his mind, constantly dwells on Me. But it means, that he is devoted to Me, in a dedicated spirit, with full faith and love. For instance, a Brāhmaṇa by caste, always remembers that he is a Brāhmaṇa, not a Kṣatriya or a Vaiśya. He remains a Brāhmaṇa, whether he thinks of it or not. Similarly, a devotee has a firm belief, that he is only Mine and only I am his. He, who maintains this affinity, is called 'absorbed in Me.' His senses, body, mind, intellect etc., are not his. If he accepts his body and mind etc., as his own, I cannot be easily attainable to him.

The fact is, that we have identity with the Lord, not with the world. Our identity with the world, is impossible. But, by an error, we identify ourselves with bodies, and think that the Lord, is separate from us. The result is, that we have to follow the cycle of birth and death. But, if we realize the reality, the Lord, can be easily attainable to us.

From the eighth verse to the thirteenth verse, the Lord explained, that a striver should think of the Lord, Who is formless and endowed with attributes, as well as attributeless-formless. He can be attained by restraining the life-breath. But, at the time of death the process of restraining the breath is difficult, and it is easier to think of Him. The man, is an eternal fraction of the Lord and he has had his natural affinity for Him, from time immemorial. This affinity, is not subject to practice and action.

So, by realizing this real and natural affinity for the Lord, he with his body, senses, mind and intellect, should surrender himself to Him. By doing so, he need not worry in the least, about his salvation or attaining the Supreme Goal, in the same way as there is no worry in case of damage or destruction, of an article if it is insured. There is no difficulty in it. Therefore, the Lord, has declared that He is easily attainable, to such a striver.

Appendix—Ananyacetāḥ—when a devotee holds that there is no other entity besides God, then how will his mind wander? Why will it wander? where will it wander? Therefore he naturally becomes 'ananyacetāḥ' viz., he whose mind is undivided and who depends only on God—'satatarṁ yo māṁ smarati nityaśaḥ'—One is 'to do' and the other is 'to take place'. Whatever is done is an action and whatever takes place is remembrance (memory). As at the end of the Gītā, Arjuna said, 'smṛtirlabdhā' (18/73), the memory is not an action but it is remembrance (memory) of one's eternal relationship (intimacy) with God. The 'sense of mine' with God is the main factor for His memory. God is mine and He is for me—by this mineness, love (devotion) for God naturally develops and when we love, He is naturally and constantly remembered by us. Therefore at the beginning of the seventh chapter by the expression 'mayyāsaktamanāḥ' the Lord has mentioned to get attached to Him viz., to love Him. It means that when a striver regards only God as his and for him, He becomes loving (lovable) to him. When this lovingness (lovability) is developed, God is naturally remembered. 'nityayuktasya'—when a devotee is perpetually attached to God, he is called 'nityayukta'. In the seventeenth verse of the seventh chapter, the same fact has been pointed out by the expression 'teṣāṁ jñānī nityayuktaḥ.' In the term nityayukta' all the points mentioned in the first half of the verse, are also included.

'Tasyāhaṁ sulabhaḥ pārtha'—The Lord has declared a great soul to be rare—'sa mahātmā sudurlabhaḥ' (Gītā 7/19) but here the Lord declares that He is easily attainable. It means that in the world God is not rare but the devotees, who having known reality about Him, take refuge in Him, are rare. The reason is that if a striver seeks God, being omnipresent He will be available everywhere, but the loving devotee of God will be available only rarely.

hari duralabha nahiṁ jagatameṁ, harijana duralabha hoya
hari heryāṁ saba jaga milai, harijana kahiṁ eka hoya

God by His grace bestows upon a man this human body, with this body he can also pave the way to numerous wombs and even hells. But a devotee (saint) by showering his grace leads the man to God-realization.

hari se tū jani heta kara, kara harijana se heta
hari rījhai jaga deta haiṁ, harijana hari hī deta

In fact He who is ever attained, about Him no question arises whether He is attained easily or rarely. In order to renounce this misconception, the Lord has declared that He is easily attainable. The unreal (the body and the world) has no existence, but we recognise its existence, value it and are attached to it; therefore ever attained God has become rare. If we don't accept the existence of the unreal and don't value it, God's attainment is self-evident (natural), 'The unreal exists, it is ours and is for us'—this assumption means to give existence to the unreal, to value it and to be attached to it.

Link:—In the next two verses, Lord Kṛṣṇa explains the merit of His realization.

मामुपेत्य पुनर्जन्म दुःखालयमशाश्वतम्।
नाप्नुवन्ति महात्मानः संसिद्धिं परमां गताः॥ १५॥

māmupetya punarjanma duḥkhālayamaśāśvatam
nāpnuvanti mahātmānaḥ saṁsiddhiṁ paramāṁ gatāḥ

Having attained Me, the great souls (Mahātmā) are no more subject to rebirth—a transitory state and the abode of sorrow; for they have reached the state of highest perfection. 15

Comment:—

'Māmupetya punarjanma duḥkhālayamaśāśvatam nāpnuvanti mahātmānaḥ saṁsiddhiṁ paramāṁ gatāḥ'—If a great soul, has vision of the Lord or knows the reality about Him, or enters into Him, he, is not subject to rebirth. To take birth as a man or an animal or a bird etc., is painful. Therefore, rebirth is said to be an abode of pain.

When a man is reborn, he has to suffer so much of pain, as a man whose skin is stripped off. But, at that time, he is unable to express his pain. He simply cries. When he grows, he feels very sad, as his desires, are not satisfied. When he fails in an examination, he is so much dejected, that he thinks even of committing suicide. In youth, he feels afflicted, on not being married, according to his wish. On being married, he feels sad, not finding the spouse of his choice. When, girls attain puberty, parents suffer from anxiety, for not being able to arrange their marriage. Similarly, one feels much perturbed, during his married life, when he finds himself unable to bring up the members of his family, with limited resources. In old age, besides suffering from disease, he may bear insults. He develops cough and cannot sleep properly. At the time of death also, he has to suffer a lot of pain. Thus, there is no end of pains and sorrow for him.

Just like men, animals and birds etc., have also to suffer, a lot of pain in cold, hot and rainy seasons. The bigger animals kill, the young ones of the smaller animals. Thus, they are very sad. In this way, creatures have to suffer in hell and go through eighty-four lac forms of lives. Therefore, rebirth has been called, the abode of pain.

Rebirth is called transitory, because in the bodies, there is a continuous change. Nobody is permanent, and dies. So, rebirth is called, a path of the world of death (Gītā 9/3).

Lord Kṛṣṇa, might have only said, "Having come to Me, the great souls, are no more subject to rebirth." Why has He used the two adjectives 'Transitory' and 'Abode of pain'? By these adjectives, He says that, as the Lord incarnates for the protection of the virtuous, for the destruction of evil-doers and for the establishment of Dharma (Righteousness), similarly, liberated souls as saints are born on this earth, for the protection of the good, for the service of the evil-doers, and for enabling the people to follow righteousness. When the Lord incarnates, with Him they take birth as His courtiers or companions, (like the Gvālās) on the earth. But, their birth is not transitory and an abode of pain, because their birth is not the fruit of their actions, as is by the sweet will of the Lord.

The Lord, has called strivers as great souls, who possess divine nature (9/13), as men of realization (7/19) and as those who have attained the highest perfection (8/15). It means, that men, are petty souls by having their affinity for the unreal body and the world because, they depend on the body and the world. They are mere souls, when they are established in the self, because in that case there is possibility of their having 'egoism', in its subtle form. But, when they identify themselves with the Lord, by total surrender to Him, without having any independent existence of their own, they are great souls.

Lord Kṛṣṇa, in the Gītā, in the Discipline of Action and Knowledge, has not used the term 'Mahātmā' (great soul). He has used it in the Discipline of Devotion, only. It means that He regards devotion, as supreme.

The great souls, are no more subject to rebirth, because they have reached the highest perfection. As a greedy person desires to get more and more money, a devotee by recognizing the Lord, whose fraction he is, aspires to get more and more love and then he attains fathomless and limitless love, enhancing every moment.

This love, is the perfection of devotion, and there is no perfection beyond it.

An Exceptional Fact

By studying the Gītā, it is evident that Lord Kṛṣṇa, has attached the greatest importance to devotion. The Lord has declared, "He, who devoutly worships Me, is considered by Me to be the best Yogī" (Gītā 6/47). "I am easily attainable, to that Yogī who constantly thinks of Me, with undivided mind, always absorbed in Me" (Gītā 8/14). But a striver, by following anyone of the Disciplines of Action, Knowledge or Devotion, attains the same Supreme Goal. But a point needs attention here, that in the philosophy, in which the Lord is not regarded as Supreme, the followers by breaking off their affinity for the world, attain salvation but do not attain the Supreme Love, and thus do not get ever enhancing bliss or love. That ever enhancing bliss, or love has been called, the highest perfection here.

Appendix—In the seventh chapter the Lord declared that this world is the manifestation of God—'Vāsudevaḥ sarvam' (7/19) but here He declares that the world is the abode of sorrows—'duḥkhālayam'. It means that the person who derives pleasure from the worldly objects, persons and actions, for him this world is the abode of sorrows; but he who renders service to other persons with his objects and actions, for him the world is the manifestation of God. The expectation, the desire and the enjoyment of pleasures are the roots of severe sufferings. This is the irrefutable rule that he who enjoys pleasures, can't escape pain. Therefore a striver should have a firm determination not to enjoy pleasures. The moment he renounces the desire for pleasure, Supreme Peace (God-realization) immediately follows such renunciation—'tyāgācchāntiranantaram' (Gītā 12/12).

A man (the self) is a fragment of that entire God in Whose each pore, there are millions of universes. But he has got entangled in the body, an insignificant fragment of the lower nature. Because of this entanglement he, instead of attaining only bliss and bliss, is suffering only miseries and sorrows. As in the teats of a cow where there is only milk, there a cattle-louse drinks only blood. Goswāmī Tulasīdāsajī Mahārāja says—

ānǎ̄da-sindhu-madhya tava bāsā, binu jāne kasa marasi piyāsā
(Vinayapatrikā 136/2)

(A man's residence is in the ocean of bliss but he is dying of thirst without knowing this fact.)

आब्रह्मभुवनाल्लोकाः पुनरावर्तिनोऽर्जुन ।
मामुपेत्य तु कौन्तेय पुनर्जन्म न विद्यते ॥ १६ ॥

ābrahmabhuvanāllokāḥ punarāvartino'rjuna
māmupetya tu kaunteya punarjanma na vidyate

All worlds, from the abode of Brahmā downwards, are by nature subject to birth; But O Arjuna, O son of Kuntī, on attaining Me there is no rebirth. 16

Comment:—

'Ābrahmabhuvanāllokāḥ punarāvartino'rjuna'—O Arjuna! All the worlds from the abode of Brahmā downwards, are subject to return i.e., after living there, at the end of the enjoyment of the fruit of their virtuous actions, men have to return.

The highest plane of existence, is said to be the abode of Brahmā. In this mortal world of ours, the king, who possesses a prosperous kingdom, a young healthy body, no enemy, an obedient and sincere family, and servants, is regarded as completely happy. The mortal gods, who as a fruit of their virtuous actions, obtain the abode of gods after enjoying that fruit, again come back to the mortal world (Gītā 9/21). They, are a hundred times happier, than the kings. The permanent gods (Ājāna devatā), who at the beginning of universe, were gods and continue to be gods, till the end of the universe, are a hundred times happier, than mortal gods. Indra, the ruler of the gods, is regarded as a hundred times happier than permanent gods. The abode of Brahmā, is supposed to possess, a hundred times more happiness, than that of Indra and the bliss of a liberated soul, is regarded as a hundred times more happy than the abode of Brahmā. It means, that from the highest region of Brahmā, to the mortal world of the earth, happiness is limited, changing and perishable. But, the bliss of God-realization is limitless, fathomless, and permanent.

'Punarāvartinaḥ' also means, that a man being a fraction of God, is eternal. But, so long as, he is unable to realize God, he even after attaining the highest plane of existence, of the abode of Brahmā, has to come back.

Here a doubt arises, that even by beholding devotees, saints, liberated souls and representatives of the Lord, a man attains salvation, why do people not attain salvation by beholding Brahmā, in the abode of Brahmā? Why do they return? The clarification is, that the concession of salvation, by beholding, is applicable to men of this mortal world, only because this human body has been bestowed only for God-realization. This concession, has not been granted, for the other worlds. But in those worlds also, if anyone has a keen desire for salvation, he can attain it. Even amongst animals and birds, there have been devotees. But, such cases are, exceptions. Had this concession been granted in the other worlds, all those, going to the hell must have attained salvation, because all of them beheld 'Yamarāja', the god of death, a representative of the Lord. But, there is no mention in the scriptures, that they attained salvation. It proves, that in other worlds, a man even by beholding the liberated souls etc., does not attain salvation.

An Important Fact

This embodied soul is an eternal fraction of God. Divine

abode is that whence there is no return. As a man after finishing his journey returns to his home so this embodied being, having a fraction of divinity should also return to the supreme abode of his Lord whence there is no return. Question arises as to why after death does it return?

As a man, goes to a divine discourse, he returns to his house, after listening to it. But, if he forgets anything there, he has to go back again, to take it. Similarly if the soul, gets attached to wealth, property and family etc., it has to come back. The body dies, so it has to occupy place in any other body, of a man or an animal or a bird etc. The Lord, declares in the Gītā, "Attachment to the three types (modes), born of Nature, is the cause of his birth, in good and evil wombs" (13/21). It means, that he, who has desire and attachment, for the world, will have to come back.

'Māmupetya tu kaunteya punarjanma na vidyate'—'All the worlds, from the abode of Brahmā downwards, are subject to rebirth. But on attaining Me there is no rebirth.' Here 'Māmupetya' (having attained Me) means "See Me in reality, know Me in essence, and enter into Me" (Gītā 11/54).

The soul, has not to come back, because being a fraction of the Lord it reaches Him, and the Supreme Abode of the Lord, is its real home. Its real home, is not the abode of Brahmā etc., and so it has to come back from there. As a man, can board a bus or a train only upto the station, for which he has got the ticket, and then he has to get off. Similarly, a man has to come back, after enjoying the fruit of his virtuous actions, in the worlds of the gods. But if he is in his own house, he has not to leave it. A man cannot attain salvation, even after reaching the highest plane of existence. So a striver, should never aspire to enjoy the pleasure of the higher worlds.

All the worlds, including that of Brahmā, lead a man to bondage. Those persons who reach abode of Brahmā and return possess demoniac properties. This demoniac disposition leads one to bondage. If the man takes refuge in God, he is liberated from the bondage, because he possesses divine virtues (Gītā 16/5).

An Exceptional Fact

There are two kinds of persons, who go to the abode of Brahmā—those who perform virtuous deeds in order to enjoy the pleasures of the abode of Brahmā, and those whose aim is to attain God, but at the time of death, because of having a desire for pleasure, deviate from spiritual discipline and so they have to go to the world of Brahmā. The latter, at the time of final annihilation, are liberated with Brahmā, after enjoying pleasure there. This liberation is called 'Krama-Mukti', (gradual liberation or gradual salvation), when Brahmā after his span of life vacates the place for the succeeding Brahmā. But strivers, who realize the Lord here, their salvation is called 'Sadyo-Mukti' (instant Salvation).

In the second verse of this chapter, Arjuna asked Lord Kṛṣṇa, "How are You to be realized, at the time of death?" Lord Kṛṣṇa, answered this question, in the fifth verse. In the sixth verse, He explained the general rule that the predominating thought of the last moment, determines one's future destiny. In the seventh verse, He asks Arjuna, to think of Him, at all times. This seventh verse, is connected with the fourteenth verse. In between (from the eighth to the thirteenth verse) there is, context of the Lord, Who is endowed with attributes and is formless, and also attributeless-formless Lord.

The verses, eighth to sixteenth, prove that Lord Kṛṣṇa is the Supreme Lord, Who is endowed with attributes and is formless as well as the Lord, Who is attributeless and formless. So the supreme aim of a man's life is to attain ever-enhancing love for Him.

Appendix—Here a man may raise a doubt that when all worlds, from the abode of Brahmā downwards, are manifestations of God—'Vāsudevaḥ sarvam', then why are the people who go to those worlds, being reborn? The clarification is that the people, who go to those worlds, don't consider the worlds the manifestation of God but regard them as material for pleasure (Gītā 9/21). They go to the abode of Brahmā to enjoy pleasures. As the fruit of their virtuous deeds, they attain the worlds upto the abode of Brahmā and (when they exhaust their merit), they are reborn in the world of mortals.

Attachment to pleasure is the root of rebirth. Here the Lord by the expression 'ābrahmabhuvanāllokāḥ' means that a man has to return to the mortal world even after reaching the abode of Brahmā, the last limit of the mundane pleasures. All the pleasures of infinite universes cannot make a man happy and cannot free him from the pangs of birth and death, therefore he who hopes to derive pleasure from the world, is under illusion.

Two types of people go to the abode of Brahmā—those who go to the abode of Brahmā in order to enjoy pleasures and then return to this mortal world; and the others are those who along the bright path go to the abode of Brahmā and then with Brahmā they are liberated (Gītā 8/24). They don't return to this mortal world, this is because of the glory of their aim, it is not the glory of Brahmaloka (abode of Brahmā). One has certainly to return from the abode of Brahmā because neither an enjoyer nor a Yogī can live there forever. All upto the abode of Brahmā is the fruit of action. When every action has a beginning and an end, then how can its fruit be imperishable?

The term 'mām' in 'māmupetya' denotes entire-God (God in full), Who is the master of both parā and aparā. Having attained Him, there is no birth in this sorrowful world. But such God-realized souls also by God's will, can descend to this mortal world either as the representatives of God (Kāraka puruṣa) or as His incarnation. But such a birth does not depend on the performance of actions but it depends on God's will.

Link:—Persons even reaching abode of Brahmā return back—in the next verse, Lord Kṛṣṇa tells the reason for it.

सहस्रयुगपर्यन्तमहर्यद्ब्रह्मणो विदुः ।
रात्रिं युगसहस्रान्तां तेऽहोरात्रविदो जनाः ॥ १७ ॥

sahasrayugaparyantamaharyadbrahmaṇo viduḥ
rātriṁ yugasahasrāntāṁ te'horātravido janāḥ

Those who know, that a day of Brahmā lasts a thousand fourfold Yugas (Ages) and that his night, lasts a thousand fourfold Yugas, they know the reality, about Brahmā's day and night. 17

Comment:—

'Sahasrayugaparyantamaharyadbrahmaṇo viduḥ rātriṁ yugasahasrāntāṁ te'horātravido janāḥ'—In this mortal world, the combination of the four ages—satya, tretā, dvāpara and kali is called, a fourfold age. A day of Brahmā, lasts such a thousand fourfold age and so does his night.* With this standard of time, Brahmā's age is of a hundred years. Then Brahmā, after his span of time, merges into God, his world merges into nature and nature merges, into God. All those, who are born, are subject to death. The greatest pleasures, which are born of sense-contacts, are verily sources of pain (Gītā 5/22), and have a beginning and an end, while only God is beyond time. Thus, knowing this fact, the great souls do not attach the least importance to the heavenly

* A day of the gods lasts men's six months and so does a night. Thus a year of the gods lasts three hundred and sixty years of men. Similarly the duration of the four ages—Satya, Tretā, Dvāpara and Kali is equal to a divine age of the gods. It means that a divine age of the gods is equal to—Satya age of seventeen lac and twenty-eight thousand years, Tretā age of twelve lac and ninety-six thousand years, Dvāpara age of eight lac and sixty-four thousand years and Kali age of four lac and thirty-two thousand years—total forty-three lac and twenty thousand years. It is also called 'Mahāyuga' or 'Caturyugī'. Brahmā's one day lasts a thousand divine ages of the gods (men's four thousand, three hundred and twenty million years) and so does his night. This day of Brahmā is called 'Kalpa' or 'Sarga' (Creation) and the night is called 'Pralaya' (Dissolution).

pleasures, of even the world of Brahmā.

Link:—In the next verse, there is description of creation and dissolution, of the universe as per the day and night of Brahmā.

अव्यक्ताद्व्यक्तयः सर्वाः प्रभवन्त्यहरागमे।
रात्र्यागमे प्रलीयन्ते तत्रैवाव्यक्तसञ्ज्ञके॥ १८॥

avyaktādvyaktayaḥ sarvāḥ prabhavantyaharāgame
rātryāgame pralīyante tatraivāvyaktasañjñake

All manifest beings emanate, from the Unmanifest (Brahmā's subtle body) at the commencement of Brahmā's day; and at the beginning of his night, they merge in the unmanifested form. 18

Comment:—

'Avyaktādvyaktayaḥ sarvāḥ prabhavantyaharāgame rātryāgame pralīyante tatraivāvyaktasañjñake'—The bodies of beings, here have been called 'manifest', and, in the fourth verse of the fourteenth chapter, they have been called 'forms'. As an embodied one, has his self-made creation of 'I' and 'mine', when he wakes up from sleep and that creation merges in him, when he is asleep. Similarly, a multitude of beings, is dragged into the manifest state, from Brahmā's subtle body viz., prakṛti, when Brahmā wakes up and they merge in his subtle body then he retires to sleep. It means, that when Brahmā wakes up, there is creation and when he retires to sleep, there is dissolution. But, when his life-span of a hundred years is over, there is final annihilation, in which Brahmā merges into the Lord. The span of final annihilation, is equal to the age of Brahmā. At the end of the span of final annihilation, Brahmā emanates from the Lord and then there is a new creation of the universe (Gītā 9/7-8).

Appendix—In the sixteenth verse the Lord declared that all worlds, from the abode of Brahmā downwards, are subject to return. Why are they subject to return? The Lord answers the question in the seventeenth and eighteenth verses that the highest plane of existence, the abode of Brahmā, is within the limits of time. Describing that period the Lord mentions that however long that period may look but that is within the limits of time. But God is beyond the limits of time.

As when we are asleep at night, we forget the world and when we awake in the morning, the world is again thought of, similarly the entire creation merges when Brahmājī retires to sleep and in Brahmā's day the creation is manifest again. This is the last limit of night and day.

Brahmā's day and night are not determined by the sun but they are determined by Prakṛti.

भूतग्रामः स एवायं भूत्वा भूत्वा प्रलीयते।
रात्र्यागमेऽवशः पार्थ प्रभवत्यहरागमे॥ १९॥

bhūtagrāmaḥ sa evāyaṁ bhūtvā bhūtvā pralīyate
rātryāgame'vaśaḥ pārtha prabhavatyaharāgame

This multitude of beings, born again and again, under compulsion from prakṛti, merges at the commencement of Brahmā's night and rises again at the start of his day. 19

Comment:—

'Bhūtagrāmaḥ sa evāyaṁ'—This multitude of beings, which is subject to birth and death, from time immemorial, being a fraction of the Lord, is eternal and imperishable. It remains the same, at the time of creation and dissolution, as also on new creation and final dissolution. But by an error, beings assume their affinity with nature and its evolutes—body and worldly objects etc., which are kaleidoscopic and perishable. They do not want to leave, the bodies but these get discarded. Thus man (soul) has to be born and then, decay again and again. The wheel of birth will continue, as long as, he continues his affinity with the body and the world, which he assumed himself. He is free and capable of snapping this tie. Actually, he cannot keep this association permanently, because objects are ephemeral and perishable.

The Lord, created the multitude of beings, for His recreation, with a lot of material for sport. It is a rule of a game, (sport), that its materials, are only for the game's sake, not for laying personal claim on them. The beings, instead of taking part in the sport, attach themselves to the material, accepting it as their own, and thus getting entangled in it. So they have a disinclination, for God.

'Bhūtvā bhūtvā pralīyate'—Bodies are born and they die again. There is a constant change, in them. But the changeless soul, by having its affinity with the bodies, accepts their change, their birth and death, as its own. To be born and to die is 'Paradharma', and to realize God is, 'Svadharma'.

'Rātryāgame'vaśaḥ pārtha prabhavatyaharāgame'—Man by assuming the things, as his own, thinks that he is their master, but actually he becomes a slave to them. The more things, he possesses, the more dependent he becomes. He can never be liberated, from this dependence, unless he attains, God. So long as, he continues his affinity with nature, he will have to follow, the wheel of birth and death. By performing actions, and reaping their fruits, even at the time when Brahmā wakes up (creation), and when he retires to sleep (dissolution) (8/18), at the time when Brahmā manifests himself (new creation), and when he merges in the Lord (final dissolution) (9/7-8) and when he is made to act helplessly, by the modes of nature (3/5). It means, that he cannot be free from the painful cycle of birth and death, unless he realizes the self or God, and unless he renounces his affinity with nature. But when he is not swayed by Nature and objects born of Nature viz., he realizes the pure self, by totally renouncing affinity with nature, he is not reborn, even at the time of new creation and is not tormented at the time of final dissolution (Gītā 14/2).

He is subject to birth and death, only because he attaches importance to material objects. The helplessness of his birth and death is known as such, because of time, nature, action or modes. This helplessness continues, so long as, he derives pleasure which are born of sense-contacts. He, does not want to renounce this desire, and so he remains helpless. He thinks, that he is unable to be liberated from it, but actually this desire is self-made, and so it is his responsibility to renounce it. He can renounce it, if and when, he has a firm determination.

Appendix—There are two divisions—one division is of the kaleidoscopic world, the other division is of the unchanging divine entity. The multitude of beings, which is subject to birth and death from time immemorial, is born and merges again and again. The being, during the day and night of Brahmā, is born and dies again and again, It means that the unreal, which is born and merges is the world and that (the real), which remains the same (which was at the time of creation) is the self viz., the divine entity which is a fragment of God. Brahmājī's numberless nights and days may pass, but the self ever remains the same.

In the divine entity viz., in the self there is power to be attached to someone or something or to remain detached. By misusing the power viz., by being attached to matter, he is born and he dies—'kāraṇaṁ guṇasaṅgo'sya sadasadyonijanmasu' (Gītā 13/21). If he does not misuse this power, he cannot pave the way to birth and death. Therefore the main valour or objective of a man is not to be attached to matter but it is to be established in the self or take refuge in God, Whose fragment he (the self) is. In matter viz., in space, time, thing, person, action, state, circumstance, a change occurs, while in the self a change never occurs—this is every man's experience. But in spite of this experience a man remains bound by matter because of his attachment to pleasure and so he does not realize the self but remains forgetful of the self just like beasts and birds.

'Avaśaḥ'—By being attached to the lower nature, a man (the self) becomes helpless—'bhūtagrāmamimaṁ kṛtsnamavaśaṁ prakṛtervaśāt' (Gītā 9/8).* Therefore when the assumed attachment to Prakṛti is renounced, he is liberated.

Our existence does not depend on the lower nature viz., on objects, persons and actions. Everything is born and perishes, every man is born (union) and dies (disunion) and every action begins and ends. But entity (self) which knows these three (objects, persons and actions) does not undergo any origin and destruction, birth and death (union and disunion), beginning and end. That existence (entity) ever remains the same—'bhūtagrāmaḥ sa evāyam'.* This entity never ceases to be—'nābhāvo vidyate sataḥ' (Gītā 2/16). The realization of the natural establishment in this entity (self) is liberation or salvation (independence).

A man cherishes a false notion that having acquired a particular object, having met a particular person and having done a particular action, he will be free (liberated). But there is no such object or person or action which may lead him to liberation. The objects, persons and actions of Prakṛti make a man a slave. By becoming totally detached from them, a man can become free. Therefore a striver should form the habit of realizing that he is alone having no connection to objects, persons and actions, he should attach importance to this realization and remain established in it as much as he can. This is every one's experience that in sound sleep we live without objects, persons and actions but objects, persons and actions don't live without

---

*Here in (8/19) and in (9/8)—in both the verses 'bhūtagrāma' and 'avaśa' words have been used. The difference is that here is the description of creation and dissolution and in 9/8 there is description of new creation and final dissolution.

us. When we form the habit of living without them even in the state of wakefulness then we shall become independent (liberated). The assumption of our affinity with objects, persons and actions does not let us be independent and makes us dependent, though we don't wish so.

In God there are endless powers which are divine. In 'Māyā' (prakṛti) also there are endless powers but they are inert and kaleidoscopic—'mayādhyakṣeṇa prakṛtiḥ sūyate sacarācaram' (9/10). In devotion (love) for God, there is the most unique power. But that love is not revealed, as a striver gets satisfied in salvation (independence). There is dependence only by having affinity with matter; and when salvation is attained, that dependence totally perishes and the striver (self) becomes independent. But love (devotion) is more unique than this salvation. In salvation there is 'akhaṇḍa' (constant) bliss but in love there is 'ananta' (infinite) bliss.

A Jñānayogī attains salvation and a devotee attains love. In Bhaktiyoga a devotee is not dependent on God because God is not alien but He is a devotee's own. Submission to one's own is a special type of independence.

God is the most independent. A man (the self) becomes dependent on matter. If he destroys this dependence, he becomes independent. But if he takes refuge in God, he becomes supremely independent. Submission to God is the supreme independence in which even God becomes submissive to the devotee—'ahaṁ bhakta parādhīnaḥ (Śrīmadbhā. 9/4/63).

Link:—After describing the perishable world, the Lord in the next verse, describes the unmanifested Eternal Existence.

परस्तस्मात्तु भावोऽन्योऽव्यक्तोऽव्यक्तात्सनातनः ।
यः स सर्वेषु भूतेषु नश्यत्सु न विनश्यति ॥ २० ॥

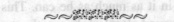

parastasmāttu bhāvo'nyo'vyakto'vyaktātsanātanaḥ
yaḥ sa sarveṣu bhūteṣu naśyatsu na vinaśyati

Beyond this unmanifest (Brahmā's subtle body), there is yet another unmanifested Eternal Existence, which does not perish, even though all beings perish. 20

Comment:—

'Parastasmāttu bhāvo'nyo'vyakto'vyaktātsanātanaḥ'—From the sixteenth to the nineteenth verse, it has been said that all the worlds, from the abode of Brahmā downwards, are subject to rebirth. But the Eternal Existence, is different from them—so the term 'Tu' (but), is used.

The word 'Avyaktāt', stands for the subtle body of Brahmā, because in the eighteenth and nineteenth verses, it has been mentioned that all manifest beings, emanate from Brahmā's subtle body, and again they merge in the same. The term 'Tasmāt', also stands for Brahmā's subtle body. The unmanifest Eternal Existence, is beyond Brahmā's subtle body, as well as, his causal body (primordial matter).

Beyond Brahmā's subtle body, there are two existences—primordial matter and God. This context, pertains to God. So unmanifested Eternal Existence, has been used for God, Who does not perish even when all beings, perish.

In the Gītā, all beings have been called unmanifest (2/28); Brahmā's subtle body has also been called unmanifest (8/18); Matter or nature, has also been called unmanifest (13/5). Beyond, all of them, the form of the Lord, whether manifest or unmanifest, is ever-existent. He was neither absent nor will be. He, can never be missing as He is eternal. He is Supreme. None can, ever be superior to Him.

'Yaḥ sa sarveṣu bhūteṣu naśyatsu na vinaśyati'—The unmanifested Existence, never perishes, even though, all beings perish. In that Absolute Existence, there is not the least modification, while in the entire universe, there are so many modifications.

Appendix—One is unchanging (permanent) entity—parā and the other is kaleidoscopic (temporary) entity—aparā. Parā never undergoes any change and Aparā is ever kaleidoscopic. Aparā never persists without change, cannot persist at all. It undergoes change in Brahmā's day and Brahmā's night and even in new creation and final dissolution.

If parā and aparā—both entities are unchanging, the wheel of birth and death may end, and if both are kaleidoscopic, then also the wheel of birth and death may end. But the parā in spite of being immutable, has assumed its affinity with changeful aparā and so it is ensnared in the wheel of birth and death. The soul by having affinity with jagat (world) has become jagat (Gītā 7/13). As a man by boarding a moving train, moves himself, similarly a man (the self) by seizing the kaleidoscopic world has become mutable (kaleidoscopic) and has started going astray in numerous wombs.

The purpose of calling God as 'parā' viz., the supreme is that the primordial matter (causal body) is superior to the subtle body of Brahmā and God is even superior to the primordial matter.

Link:—In the next verse, Lord Kṛṣṇa explains that perishable beings, after attaining Imperishable do not return.

अव्यक्तोऽक्षर इत्युक्तस्तमाहुः परमां गतिम्।
यं प्राप्य न निवर्तन्ते तद्धाम परमं मम॥ २१॥

avyakto'kṣara ityuktastamāhuḥ paramāṁ gatim
yaṁ prāpya na nivartante taddhāma paramaṁ mama

This Unmanifest, spoken of as the Imperishable, is said to be the Supreme Goal; that is My Supreme Abode on attaining which, there is no return. 21

Comment:—

'Avyakto'kṣara ityuktastamāhuḥ paramāṁ gatim yaṁ prāpya

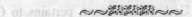

na nivartante taddhāma paramaṁ mama'—The Lord Who has been called 'Mām' (Me), in the twenty-eighth, twenty-ninth and thirtieth verses of the seventh chapter, 'Imperishable Brahma', in the third verse of the eighth chapter, 'Adhiyajña' (God); in the fourth verse 'Mām' (Me), in the fifth and seventh verses, 'Supreme Divine Puruṣa' (God), in the eighth verse, 'the Omniscient, the Ancient, the Ruler' etc., in the ninth verse, 'Mām' (Me) in the thirteenth, fourteenth, fifteenth and sixteenth verses, 'Unmanifest' and 'Eternal', in the twentieth verse, has been called here 'Unmanifest', 'Imperishable', 'the Supreme Goal' and 'the Supreme Abode', attaining Which, beings do not return. Similarly, in the twenty-seventh verse of the fourteenth chapter, He has declared, "I am the Abode of Brahma, the Immortal and the Immutable, the eternal Dharma (virtue), and Absolute Bliss." Thus, the Lord has explained here that He, Who has been described in different verses by different names, is One and the same.

Some people, think that the fruit of adoration of the Lord, Who is endowed with attributes, and He, Who is attributeless, is different. To remove this misconception, Lord Kṛṣṇa, in this verse, has made it clear that the Lord is one, and the same, and devotees according to their tastes and beliefs worshipping Him, in different ways and His different forms, attain the same Lord.

The other worlds, including that of Brahmā are subject to return i.e., beings after going there, have to return and thus they have to follow the wheel of birth and death, because they all, are within the domain of nature (matter) and are perishable, while the Abode of the Lord, is beyond Nature and is Imperishable. The beings, after going there, have no return, no birth. But, just like the Lord, Who incarnates by His own will, to enable the people to attain salvation the liberated souls by the Lord's will, can come to this earth as representatives of the Lord, in order to enable the people of this mortal world, to attain salvation.

Appendix—The terms unmanifest and imperishable etc., have no access to the Supreme, Who is to be attained. The reason is that the supreme is the independent entity which is free from unmanifest and manifest, imperishable and perishable, motion and rest. Having attained Him there is no return to this mortal world because He transcends all limits (of time etc.).

Link:—In the next verse, He explains that the Imperishable, can be attained by exclusive devotion.

पुरुषः स परः पार्थ भक्त्या लभ्यस्त्वनन्यया।
यस्यान्तःस्थानि भूतानि येन सर्वमिदं ततम्॥ २२॥

puruṣaḥ sa paraḥ pārtha bhaktyā labhyastvananyayā
yasyāntaḥsthāni bhūtāni yena sarvamidaṁ tatam

That Supreme Puruṣa, O Pārtha, in Whom all beings vest and by Whom all this is pervaded, is attainable only by His exclusive devotion. 22

Comment:—

'Yasyāntaḥsthāni bhūtāni yena sarvamidaṁ tatam'—Lord Kṛṣṇa, in the twelfth verse of the seventh chapter, said in the negative, "Whatever, entities there are born of sattva (quality of goodness), of rajas (principle of activity) (mode of passion), of tamas (principle of inertia) (mode of ignorance), know them all as evolved from Me alone. In reality, however, neither I exist in them, nor do they exist in Me." Here, He says in the affirmative, "All beings reside in Me and I pervade the whole world." This fact has been explained, both in the affirmative and in the negative, in the fourth, fifth and sixth verses of the ninth chapter. It means, that beings have no existence, apart from the Lord. They emanate from Him, reside in Him and merge into Him.

The Supreme Lord, pervades everywhere, every time, in

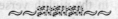

all things, actions and beings etc. Though ornaments made of gold, have nothing besides gold, yet people do not pay attention to gold, because they attach importance to the shapes, names, weights and prices etc., of different ornaments. Similarly, we being entangled in favourable and unfavourable circumstances of the perishable world, do not pay attention to the Lord, Who existed before the creation, exists now, and will continue to exist after the dissolution of the creation.

'Puruṣaḥ sa paraḥ pārtha bhaktyā labhyastvananyayā'—In the previous verse, the Lord Who has been called the Unmanifest, the Imperishable, the Supreme Goal etc., has been called here that Supreme Puruṣa, Who can be attained, by exclusive devotion only.

Devotees, who attach importance to the evolutes of Nature, which are called 'others', by accepting their independent existence, have no exclusive devotion, to the Lord, so they cannot attain the Lord quickly. If they accept every being, thing and action, as His manifestation, and then perform actions, in order to, please Him only, their devotion is exclusive, and so they attain the Supreme Lord. As water, exists as snow, hail, cloud, fog, dew, vapour, river, pond and sea etc., the gross, subtle and causal universe, which seems, is nothing besides the Lord. Therefore, all his actions such as eating, drinking, sitting, walking, speaking, sleeping etc., are nothing, but adoration of the Lord (Gītā 18/46).

An Exceptional Fact

Arjuna's question, "How are you to be known, at the time of death?" (8/2) seems to be full of emotion, because in spite of beholding, the Lord before him, he became curious to know His singularity. In response to his question, the Lord explains the general rule of thinking of Him, at the time of death, direct him to think of Him, at all times. Then, from the eighth verse to the sixteenth verse, He explained how to attain the Lord 'Endowed with attributes and formless', 'Attributeless and formless', and 'Endowed with attributes, and form', each in three verses. Out of the three, He explained, that attaining the Lord 'Endowed with attributes and formless' and 'Attributeless and formless', is difficult, because all the media of perception have to be restrained, while He, endowed with attributes and form, can be attained easily, depending on Him, and constantly by thinking of Him.

After the sixteenth verse, Lord Kṛṣṇa, in the next six verses, explained the special importance of the Lord, Who is endowed with attributes and form. In the first three verses, He explained the duration of Brahmā, and his world, while in the next three verses, He explained the superiority of His Own, and His Abode. It means, that He is exceptional than the subtle body of Brahmā. All forms of worship, are within His form. He can be realized, through supreme devotion. On His realization, strivers are not inclined towards other gods, nor is there any need for them. Then, He explained, that He can be attained, by exclusive devotion.

Thus, His abode is superior to Brahmā's, and His form is superior, to that of Brahmā. It means, that He is the ultimate goal of all beings, and they are all within Him.

Appendix—The devotion has been called exclusive (ananya)—it means that in devotion, there should neither be the smallest fragment of matter nor any latent impression of ego, nor any impression of one's own opinion viz., there should not be the least attraction anywhere. All is God—this realization is 'ananyabhakti' (exclusive devotion).

Craving for pleasures is only one but the material for pleasures of increasing degrees is available in numerous worlds. When a striver is not attracted even by the pleasures available in the abode of Brahmā and is not even satisfied with salvation, then he attains devotion.

In the seventh chapter the Lord declared "mattaḥ parataraṁ nānyat kiñcidasti' (7/7), the same fact has been mentioned here by the expression 'yasyāntaḥ sthāni bhūtāni yena sarvamidaṁ tatam.' The same fact will be mentioned in detail in the fourth and fifth verses of the ninth chapter. All this means that there is nothing else besides God viz., all is God.

Link:—In the sixteenth verse, Lord Kṛṣṇa explained, that all the worlds from the abode of Brahmā downwards, are subject to return, but on attaining Him, there is no rebirth. But, He has not explained the time (path) whence they do not return and also the time (path), for departing, whence they return. So He starts the topic—

यत्र काले त्वनावृत्तिमावृत्तिं चैव योगिनः।
प्रयाता यान्ति तं कालं वक्ष्यामि भरतर्षभ॥ २३॥

yatra kāle tvanāvṛttimāvṛttiṁ caiva yoginaḥ
prayātā yānti taṁ kālaṁ vakṣyāmi bharatarṣabha

Now, I shall advise you, O best of the Bharatas, the time (path) when the Yogīs leave their bodies never to return and also (path) when they depart, to return. 23

Comment:—

[Liberation from bondage in the mortal world, is called 'Sadyo Mukti' (instant Salvation) i.e., those who attain God by exclusive devotion, attain the highest perfection. Those who have subtle desire, at the time of death, go to the abode of Brahmā, and then are liberated with him. This salvation, is called 'Krama Mukti' (gradual Salvation). Those who go to the abode of Brahmā, to enjoy pleasure, are subject to return. 'Sadyo Mukti' (Salvation in this mortal world) has been described, in the fifteenth verse. Lord Kṛṣṇa, starts the topic to explain the other two.]

'Yatra kāle tvanāvṛttimāvṛttiṁ caiva yoginaḥ prayātā yānti taṁ kālaṁ vakṣyāmi bharatarṣabha'—The term 'Tu' (Verily), has been used to point out the topic which was left untouched. The word 'Kāla', stands for the path, which has been named as 'Gati' and 'Sṛti', in verses twenty-sixth and twenty-seventh respectively, in this chapter.

'Anāvṛttimāvṛttim'—Devotees, who possess discrimination i.e., who have a disinclination for worldly things and pleasures, and an inclination for God, depart never to return. Because of disinterestedness in their path, there is predominance of light (discrimination). But those, who have a disinclination for God, and are entangled in attachment and pleasure, depart to return, because their discrimination is covered. Their path is dark viz., there is predominance of ignorance. The term 'Caiva' (and even), is used for those, whose aim has been to realize God but at the time of death they have deviated from the path due to some desires lurking in them and so they after enjoying the heavenly pleasure, come back. Here, the word 'Yoginaḥ', has been used, both for those, who do not desire, the fruit of their actions, as also, for those who have a desire, for the fruit of their actions.

Appendix—He, who has affinity for the kaleidoscopic prakṛti (nature) has to return to this mortal world. But he, who is not attached to the kaleidoscopic prakṛti, has not to return.

Link:—In the next verse, Lord Kṛṣṇa describes, the path of the Yogīs (ascetics), who depart, never to return.

अग्निर्ज्योतिरहः शुक्लः षण्मासा उत्तरायणम् ।
तत्र प्रयाता गच्छन्ति ब्रह्म ब्रह्मविदो जनाः ॥ २४ ॥

agnirjyotirahaḥ śuklaḥ ṣaṇmāsā uttarāyaṇam
tatra prayātā gacchanti brahma brahmavido janāḥ

In the path, in which deities preside over effulgent fire, the day-light, the bright fortnight and the six months of the northern solstice, then departing after death, the knowers of Brahma (having attained Brahmaloka), finally reach Brahma. 24

Comment:—

'Agnirjyotirahaḥ śuklaḥ ṣaṇmāsā uttarāyaṇam'—In the bright path, first of all, there is the right of fire-god. Fire gives light at night, and that light works, for a short distance and for a short time, while the day-light, works for a longer distance and a longer time. A bright fortnight, is the night of manes. The light of this bright fortnight, remains for a very long distance and for many days in the sky. The northern path of the sun, is of six months, and is equal to a day of the gods. The light in the northern path, remains for a very long distance and time.

'Tatra prayātā gacchanti brahma brahmavido janāḥ'—Those, who pass along the bright path, first go to the territory, of the fire-god. Then the fire-god, hands them over, to the god of day, after they have crossed fire-god's territory. Similarly, the god of day, hands them over to the god of bright fortnight, and he hands them over to the god of the northward course of the sun, and he hands them over to the god, of the abode of Brahmā. Then with Brahmā, they are liberated and attain God.

Here, the term 'Brahmavidaḥ', has been used for those who know Brahma, and not for those, who have realized Him. If they had realized Him, they would have been liberated souls, they would not have gone, to the abode of Brahmā.

Appendix—The yogīs (ascetics), who during their spiritual practice had a craving to go to the abode of Brahmā or had an insistence on their opinion, they in an order first go to the abode of Brahmā and then are liberated along with Brahmā, when there is final dissolution.

brahmaṇā saha te sarve samprāpte pratisañcare
parasyānte kṛtātmānaḥ praviśanti paraṁ padam

(Kūrmapurāṇa pūrva. 11/284)

At the completion of the age of Brahmā, when there is final dissolution, then all pure hearted persons attain the Supreme Goal with Brahmā.

In salvation by stages the abode of Brahmā is just like a station on the way, where only the persons craving for pleasures, alight. But those, who have no craving for pleasures, don't alight there; as if we have no purpose on the way, there may be a station or a jungle, what difference does it make for us?

In Upaniṣads the order of the bright fortnight path has been described in different ways; as—

According to Chāndogyopaniṣad—the deity of 'arci', the deity of daylight, the deity of bright fortnight, the deity of the northern solstice, Saṁvatsara, āditya, moon, vidyut, and then to carry to the abode of Brahmā by an inhuman being (4/15/5; 5/10/1-2).

According to bṛhadāraṇyakopaniṣad—the deity of light, the deity of day, the deity of bright fortnight, the deity of the northern solstice, abode of deities, āditya, vidyut (vaidyuta deity) and then attaining 'Brahmaloka' by mānasa puruṣa (6/2/15).

According to Kauṣītakibrāhmaṇopaniṣad—the abode of fire, the abode of air, the abode of sun, the abode of Varuṇa, the abode of Indra, the abode of Prajāpati and then the abode of Brahmā (1/3).

In Brahmasūtra (4/3/2-3) also this topic has been discussed.

In Upaniṣads the bright fortnight path has been named 'devayāna', 'arcimārga', 'Uttaramārga', 'devapatha' and 'brahmapatha' also.

Link:—In the next verse, Lord Kṛṣṇa, describes the path of those, who depart to return.

धूमो रात्रिस्तथा कृष्णः षण्मासा दक्षिणायनम्।
तत्र चान्द्रमसं ज्योतिर्योगी प्राप्य निवर्तते॥ २५॥

dhūmo rātristathā kṛṣṇaḥ ṣaṇmāsā dakṣiṇāyanam
tatra cāndramasaṁ jyotiryogī prāpya nivartate

In the path, in which gods preside over smoke, the night, the dark fortnight and the six months, of the southern solstice, then traversing through, the Yogī (devoted to action with a motive) after death, catches the lunar light and he returns to the mortal world. 25

Comment:—

'Dhūmo rātristathā kṛṣṇaḥ ṣaṇmāsā dakṣiṇāyanam tatra cāndramasaṁ jyotiryogī prāpya nivartate'—In the dark path, the god of smoke, hands over those, who pass along that path to the god of night, when they have crossed his territory. Similarly, the god of night, hands them over to the god of dark fortnight, who hands them over to the god of the southern solstice. He hands them over to the god of lunar light, and they attain the divine worlds, such as heaven etc. Then after enjoying pleasure as fruit of their merit and virtue, they have to return.

Here, a point needs attention, that the lunar sphere which is seen, is not the lunar world, mentioned here, because the lunar sphere is near the earth, while the lunar world, is farther than even the sun. The nectar (energy), to the lunar sphere, comes from the lunar world, and that energy nourishes, all herbs and plants.

Here, the dark path stands, for the path which leads to the higher worlds. It has been called dark, because it is darker than the bright path. Ordinary men, are born in the mortal world after death, sinners go to the demoniac wombs, while vile sinners, to hell. Thus those, who pass along the dark path, are far superior to those who take demoniac births or go to hell, because this path is better and brighter, than other paths which lead, to the cycle of birth and death.

While returning from the dark path, the soul first comes to the sky, then to the clouds through air; and through rain, it enters the grain. Then, it enters men, when they eat food according to the fruit of actions, of the previous birth. From man it goes to woman, and takes birth. Thus, it follows the wheel of birth and death.

Now a question arises, as to why the Lord has called the people who perform actions, for their fruit, Yogīs (ascetics). There can be several reasons—

(i) The Lord in the Gītā declares, that those who are established in sattva (the quality of goodness), go to higher regions, while others go to middle or lower regions (Gītā 14/18). Here, there is a description of those, who go to the higher regions. Thus being superior to those, who go to the middle or lower regions, they have been called Yogīs.

(ii) They go to higher worlds, for enjoying heavenly pleasures, after having renounced mundane pleasures by self-control. They have been called Yogīs, because they become equanimous to some degree, whether they receive mundane pleasures or not in this world.

(iii) Their aim has been to realize God. But, at the time of death, they deviate from Yoga, because of their subtle desire for pleasure, so they go to higher worlds, such as the abode of Brahmā etc. After living there for a long time, they are born, in the houses of pious and wealthy men. Devotees, who deviate from

Yoga, go along this dark path. As persons, having an interested motive also pass through this path of yoga. Therefore they have been called Yogīs.

In the twenty-fourth verse, Lord Kṛṣṇa has used the expression 'Brahmavido janāḥ' (Brahma knowing people), in plural number, while in this verse He has used the term 'Yogī', in singular. It shows, that all men deserve God-realization and it is easy to attain Him, because He is naturally attained to all. So, the Lord, has used a plural number. But it is difficult to attain heaven, etc., because so many efforts have to be made and so many rituals to be observed, by a person. Moreover, from heaven he has to return to this mortal world. So, here a singular number has been used.

An Exceptional Fact

(1) Those, whose aim is to realize God, but their desire for pleasure is not rooted out, go to the abode of Brahmā. Thereafter, enjoying pleasure, their desire is wiped out and they are liberated from the bondage of birth and death, as described in the twenty-fourth verse.

Those, whose aim is to realize God, and have no desire for pleasure here or hereafter, but at the time of death deviate from meditation on the attributeless Lord, are directly born, in the family of enlightened Yogīs. There, by striving with greater vigour than before, for perfection, they attain salvation (Gītā 6/42-43).

Those, whose aim is to enjoy heavenly pleasures, ascend heaven, by virtue of their meritorious deeds, and return to the earth, when their fruit has been enjoyed (Gītā 7/20—23; 8/25; 9/20-21).

Those, whose aim is to realize God, and deviate from Yoga, because they could not root out the desire for worldly pleasures, at the time of death. So they obtain higher worlds, such as heaven etc., enjoy pleasures there, and then, take birth in the house of pious and wealthy men. There, by their former practice, they are drawn towards God and reach the Supreme Goal (Gītā 6/41, 44-45). Such strivers, are far superior to those, whose aim is to enjoy heavenly pleasures.

(2) Generally, people think that those who die, in day time, in a bright fortnight, and in the six months of the northward course of the sun, attain salvation, but those who die in nighttime, in a dark fortnight and in the six months of the southern passage of the sun, do not attain salvation. But, actually it is not so. This description has been given, only for those who go to higher regions. It does not apply to those, who go to hell or take birth in evil species. The fact, is that beings go to higher or lower regions, according to their actions, whether they die, in the daytime or nighttime, bright fortnight or dark fortnight, or northern or southern solstice.

Devotees who take refuge in the Lord, attain Him, whether they die in the daytime or nighttime, bright fortnight or dark fortnight, or northward course of the sun, or the southward course of the sun.

Now a doubt arises why Bhīṣma, a liberated soul, waited for the northward course of the sun, in leaving his mortal body. The clarification is, that Bhīṣma had not to go to the Abode of God. He being a god named Vasu, had to go to the world of the gods. There the doors remain closed, at the time of the southward course of the sun. So, if he went at that time, he would wait outside, to enter his world. He had the power to die, anytime, as he willed. So he thought it better to die and wait, as he could behold Lord Kṛṣṇa, and have good company, which would be useful for the welfare of everyone. So, he left the body, at the time of the northward course of the sun.

Appendix—Selflessness is Light and selfishness is Dark.

In Upaniṣads the order of the dark fortnight has been given in different ways—

According to Chāndogyopaniṣad—the god of smoke, the god of night, the god of the dark fortnight, the god of the southern solstice, the abode of manes, the sky, the moon and then return to the mortal world (5/10/3-4)

According to bṛhadāraṇyakopaniṣad—the deity of smoke, the deity of night, the deity of the dark fortnight, the deity of the southern solstice, the abode of manes, moon and then return to the mortal world (6/2/16).

In Upaniṣads the dark fortnight has been named—'pitṛyāna', dhūmamārga' and 'dakṣiṇamārga' also.

Link:—The next verse, is the concluding verse, on the topic of the two paths.

शुक्लकृष्णे गती ह्येते जगतः शाश्वते मते।
एकया यात्यनावृत्तिमन्ययावर्तते पुनः ॥ २६ ॥

śuklakṛṣṇe gatī hyete jagataḥ śāśvate mate
ekayā yātyanāvṛttimanyayāvartate punaḥ

These two paths—the bright and the dark, are considered to be the world's eternal paths. Proceeding by one, a man has not to return, while taking the other, he returns. 26

Comment:—

'Śuklakṛṣṇe gatī hyete jagataḥ śāśvate mate'—All creatures, according to their actions, or by God's grace, sometime or other, receive this human life, and then according to the actions of this human life, go to higher, middle or lower regions. Now, it depends upon them, whether they pass along the bright path or the dark path, because they are all linked to the two paths.

So long as, men attach importance to perishable objects of the world, and have a desire for them, they can go to lower regions, even after reaching higher ones. Similarly, being fraction of the Lord, they can go, to the higher regions. So, a striver should ever be alert and cautious. He should, never attach importance to perishable things of the world and should never hate a person, because that person being a fraction of the Lord, may be inclined towards Him any time.

As the Lord, has declared Yoga as imperishable, the two paths, bright and dark, are also imperishable and eternal.

'Ekayā yātyanāvṛttimanyayāvartate punaḥ'—Strivers proceeding by the bright path, have not to return; they go to the abode of Brahmā, and attain emancipation, with Brahmā. But persons proceeding by the dark path, return i.e., follow the cycle of birth and death.

Link:—Lord Kṛṣṇa, in the next verse, gives the merit of knowing, the two paths.

नैते सृती पार्थ जानन्योगी मुह्यति कश्चन।
तस्मात्सर्वेषु कालेषु योगयुक्तो भवार्जुन॥ २७॥

naite sṛtī pārtha jānanyogī muhyati kaścana
tasmātsarveṣu kāleṣu yogayukto bhavārjuna

Knowing these two paths in essence, O Pārtha, no Yogī is deluded. Therefore, O Arjuna, be saturated with Yoga, at all times. 27

Comment:—

'Naite sṛtī pārtha jānanyogī muhyati kaścana'—Strivers, who do not attach importance to perishable objects, are followers of bright path. But those persons, who are engrossed in the world and whose aim is to hanker after prosperity and pleasures, are in complete darkness. People who by controlling their senses, from the worldly pleasures, perform actions, such as oblation, penance and charity etc., in order to enjoy the heavenly pleasures, are also in the dark, because they have to return from the higher regions, and have to follow the wheel of birth and death.

Thus, a striver by knowing the secret of the two paths, becomes a Yogī i.e., he performs actions without having any desire for the fruit of actions, because he transcends the pleasures of this world, as well as, of the next one. Thus, he is not deluded.

A Yogī, is he whose aim, is to remain equanimous, in acquisition and non-acquisition, of worldly pleasure.

'Tasmātsarveṣu kāleṣu yogayukto bhavārjuna'—One who is determined, that he has to realize God, remains equanimous, in favourable and unfavourable circumstances, and incidents etc. Therefore Lord Kṛṣṇa directs Arjuna to be established in Yoga, in the form of equanimity i.e., without being affected, by favourable and the unfavourable circumstances, he should make their right use. In favourable circumstances he should, serve the world, and in unfavourable circumstances he should renounce, desire for favourable circumstances.

Appendix—Only the man ridden with desire gets deluded viz., paves the way to birth and death. The man, who knows the bright and the dark paths, being selfless, does not pave the way to birth and death viz., he does not pass by the dark path.

In the seventh verse of this chapter the Lord declared—'tasmātsarveṣu kāleṣu māmanusmara yudhya ca' and here He declares—'tasmātsarveṣu kāleṣu yogayukto bhavārjuna'—it means that thinking (remembrance) of God viz., to worship God is 'Yoga' and to be established in equanimity viz., to be detached from the world, is also Yoga. Both have the same result.

Link:—Lord Kṛṣṇa, now gives the merit of becoming a Yogī.

वेदेषु यज्ञेषु तपःसु चैव
दानेषु यत्पुण्यफलं प्रदिष्टम्।
अत्येति तत्सर्वमिदं विदित्वा
योगी परं स्थानमुपैति चाद्यम्॥ २८॥

vedeṣu yajñeṣu tapaḥsu caiva
dāneṣu yatpuṇyaphalaṁ pradiṣṭam
atyeti tatsarvamidaṁ viditvā
yogī paraṁ sthānamupaiti cādyam

The Yogī, who knows this secret, transcends the fruits of meritorious deeds, attached to study of the Vedas, performance of sacrifices, austerities and charities, and he attains the supreme primeval abode. 28

Comment:—

'Vedeṣu yajñeṣu tapaḥsu caiva dāneṣu yatpuṇyaphalaṁ pradiṣṭaṁ atyeti tatsarvamidaṁ viditvā yogī paraṁ sthānamupaiti cādyam'—The fruit of performing meritorious acts, such as austerities, sacrifices, penances, charities and pilgrimages etc., is perishable, because all those acts have a beginning and an end; so how could their fruit, be imperishable? The man (soul), because of ignorance gets entangled in perishable things and persons etc., though, he is an eternal fraction of the Lord. Thus a striver, who knows the secret of the bright and the dark paths, described from the twenty-third verse to the twenty-sixth verse, transcends, the fruits of meritorious deeds, of the performance of sacrifices, austerities and charities etc., because he comes to know that all the worlds of pleasures from the abode of Brahmā downwards are subject to return. But on attaining, the Lord, there is no rebirth (Gītā 8/16). He, also knows, that he is a fraction of the Lord, and so without getting entangled in perishable and kaleidoscopic things and pleasures, he can take refuge, in Him. Thus, he can attain, the primeval Abode viz., God* Who has been called in the twenty-first verse, of this chapter 'Supreme Goal', and 'Supreme Abode'.

The man, who is engrossed in pleasure and prosperity, cannot know, the Supreme primeval Abode viz., God. He himself, is responsible for this ignorance, because of his disinclination for God. He can wipe out this ignorance and error. If he renounces, the desire for sensual pleasure, he can know the supreme primeval Abode viz., the Lord. So a striver should make the best possible efforts, to attain the goal of human life, by renouncing desire, for perishable pleasure.

At the end of the sixth chapter, Lord Kṛṣṇa first, recited the merits of a Yogī, and then called upon Arjuna, to be a Yogī (6/46), but here, He first asked him to be a Yogī, and then explained, the merits of a Yogī. The reason, is that in the sixth chapter, the context is of the aspirant, who falls short of perfection in Yoga. Arjuna, then puts the question, "He whose mind deviates from Yoga, does not perish?" In response to his question, Lord Kṛṣṇa answers, "There is no fall for him, either here or hereafter. Not only this, even a seeker of Yoga, transcends the fruit of actions." Therefore, Lord Kṛṣṇa, first tells the merit of a Yogī and then orders Arjuna to be a Yogī. Here, Arjuna puts the question, "How are You to be known, at the time of death, by the self-controlled?" So, Lord Kṛṣṇa answers, "I am attainable by exclusive devotion." It means, that when a devotee, having total disinclination for worldly objects, takes refuge only in Him, He is attained, by that Yogī easily. So Lord Kṛṣṇa, first orders him to be a Yogī, and then explains the merit of a Yogī.

---

* "I am the prime cause in all respects of gods as well as of other seers" (Gītā 10/2); "I take refuge in that Primal Person (Gītā 15/4)."

ॐ तत्सदिति श्रीमद्भगवद्गीतासूपनिषत्सु ब्रह्मविद्यायां योगशास्त्रे
श्रीकृष्णार्जुनसंवादे अक्षरब्रह्मयोगो नामाष्टमोऽध्यायः॥८॥

oṁ tatsaditi śrīmadbhagavadgītāsūpaniṣatsu brahmavidyāyāṁ yogaśāstre śrīkṛṣṇārjunasaṁvāde akṣarabrahmayogo nāmāṣṭamo'dhyāyaḥ

Thus with the words—Oṁ, Tat, Sat, the names of the Lord, in the Upaniṣad of the Bhagavadgītā, the knowledge of Brahma, the Supreme, the scripture of Yoga and the dialogue between Śrī Kṛṣṇa and Arjuna, this is eighth designated discourse: "The Yoga of the Imperishable Brahma."

The terms 'Akṣara' (Imperishable), and 'Brahma', stand for God Who is attributeless-formless; with attributes-formless; and endowed with, attributes and form. The thought of anyone of the three kinds, leads a striver to, union with God. Therefore this chapter is designated:"The Yoga of the Imperishable Brahma."

Words, letters and Uvāca (said) in the Eighth Chapter

1. In this chapter in **'Athāṣṭamo'dhyāyaḥ'** there are three words, in **'Arjuna Uvāca'** etc., there are four words, in verses three hundred and seventy-seven words and there are thirteen words of colophon. Thus, the total number of words is three hundred and ninety-seven.

2. In **'Athāṣṭamo'dhyāyaḥ'** there are six letters, in **'Arjuna Uvāca'** etc., there are thirteen letters, in verses there are nine hundred and forty-five letters, and there are forty-seven letters of colophon. Thus the total number of letters, is one thousand and eleven. Out of the twenty-eight verses of this chapter, each of the ninth, eleventh and twenty-eighth verses, is of forty-four letters, the tenth verse is of forty-five letters, and each of the remaining twenty-four verses, is of thirty-two letters.

3. In this chapter **'Uvāca'** (said), has been used twice—**'Arjuna Uvāca'** once, and **'Śrībhagavānuvāca'**, once.

Metres Used in the Eighth Chapter

Out of the twenty-eight verses, of this chapter, in the ninth, tenth and eleventh verses, there is **'upajāti'** metre; in the twenty-eighth verse there is **'indravajrā',** metre. Out of the remaining twenty-four verses, in the third quarter of the second verse, and first quarter of the fourteenth verse, 'bha-gaṇa' being used there, is **'bha-vipulā'** metre; in the third quarter of the twenty-fourth verse, 'ma-gaṇa' being used there, is **'ma-vipulā'** metre; in the first quarter of the twenty-seventh verse 'ra-gaṇa' being used there is, **'ra-vipulā'** metre; and in the first quarter and the third quarter of the third verse 'na-gaṇa' being used there, is **'jātipakṣa-vipulā'** metre. The remaining nineteen verses are possessed of the characteristics of right, **'pathyāvaktra'** Anuṣṭup metre.